An Integrated Approach to Constitutional Law

THIRD EDITION

Aaron H. Caplan

Professor of Law

LMU Loyola Law School,

Los Angeles

860 Blue Gentian Road, Suite 350
Eagan, MN 55121
1-877-888-1330

Printed in the United States of America

ISBN: 978-1-68561-239-9

To the clients, colleagues, and students
who taught me constitutional law.

Third Edition Acknowledgments

The years between the second and third editions (2018–2023) were a time of constitutional ferment, with extreme political divisions stressing a system that did not envision them. Much deserves to be said about governance amidst polarization: to take one example, a Congress mostly paralyzed by close division effectively cedes power to the executive and the judiciary. But much of that falls outside the scope of this book, which is designed to teach aspiring lawyers the skills to navigate those aspects of the constitutional order most likely to affect their working lives (with an unavoidable focus on courts and legal doctrine).

In preparing this edition during tense constitutional times, I took comfort in the basic structure of the book, where a chronological survey precedes the topic-by-topic treatment of specific doctrines. It reminds us that change is a constant—and that we have lived in times of constitutional ferment more often than we like to realize.

Some work on this revised edition occurred while I was a visitor at the University of Iowa College of Law, whose hospitality I greatly appreciated.

I am indebted to the many student readers who spotted errors in the Second Edition, including: Rachel Ellis, Danielle Farahi, Emily Grubman, Lucy Humphreys, Nareg Kourouyan, Charles Lam, Michael Lozano, Ashleigh McLachlan, Amir Navab, Alice Newman, Mary Park, Giuliana Regina, Leticia Rodriguez, Claire Sears, Jennifer Smith, Elaine Sun, Samantha Tanski, Nicole Wentworth, Adam Witkin, Jordan Yallen, and Olivia Young. I sought to correct in this Third Edition the gaffes they identified, but with the furtive knowledge that I will be adding new ones.

This edition benefitted from the suggestions of those who teach with it, including Amanda Harmon Cooley, Jessica Levinson, Jesse Merriam, Eric Muller, and Chad Oldfather.

Special thanks to Matthew Babb (research assistance) and Leah Lee (conscience).

—Aaron H. Caplan
May 2023

Second Edition Acknowledgments

The Second Edition of *An Integrated Approach to Constitutional Law* reflects the experiences and ideas of students who used the First Edition. I am grateful for their questions, comments, and suggestions.

Many eagle-eyed student readers identified typos, grammatical errors, and other embarrassing lapses in the First Edition. These include Ethan Bearman, Kathleen Becket, Jeffrey Bloeser, Corrie Buck, Cory Burleson, Jennifer Carreras, Tyler Davis, Kimiko Elguea, Lauren Ellis, Avroham Feinstein, Amelia Finch, Stacy Griner, Melineh Kasbarian, Travis Kaya, Lauren Landers, Brendan Le, Amy Levitt, Christopher Levy, Jocelyn Lopez, Christopher Lynch, Clarisse Magtoto, Justin Maroldi, Cristina Medina, Allison Murray, Kevin Nguyen, Jose Ortiz, Caitlin Oswald, Karo Petrosyan, Elizabeth Quach, Ashley Rodriguez, Daniel Rowe, Kassandra Velasquez, Rachael Weatherly, Dawn Woollen, Anzhelika Zaborskikh, and Nicole Zerunyan.

I had outstanding support from research assistants Norvik Azarian, Alisa Lalana, and Weston Rowland. Professors Chad Oldfather and Justin Levitt provided valuable ideas and input. And everyone deserves a reference librarian as good as Tiffani Willis.

—Aaron H. Caplan
January 2018

First Edition Acknowledgments

This book would not have been written if the faculty at Loyola Law School, Los Angeles, had not taken the risk of inviting me to join their ranks. Their instruction and example taught me how to teach law, for which I am very grateful. Let me begin the thanks with my constitutional law colleagues: Evan Gerstmann, Allan Ides, Justin Levitt, Karl Manheim, Christopher May, Marcy Strauss, and Kimberly West-Faulcon. Thanks are also due to colleagues who teach and write in other areas: Sande Buhai, Brietta Clark, David Glazier, Paul Hayden, Justin Hughes, Kathleen Kim, Laurie Levenson, Jessica Levinson, Daniel Martin, Alexandra Natapoff, John Nockleby, Cesare Romano, Jennifer Rothman, Sean Scott, Ted Seto, Georgene Vairo, Michael Waterstone, and Gary Williams. I'll even thank a dean or two: David Burcham and Victor Gold. On this and many other projects, librarian Joshua Phillips has never failed me. Mell Banez, Pam Buckles, and Shawn Tracy provided valuable clerical assistance. Finally, no discussion of Loyola would be complete without its students. I thank them all, but especially those in my Constitutional Law Survey in the Spring and Fall semesters of 2013, who had little idea they were acting as beta testers for the material that now forms this book.

The book was completed while I was a scholar in residence at Seattle University School of Law. Thanks to Dean Annette Clark and Associate Dean Paul Holland for facilitating my visit and for first getting me started on the academic path as an adjunct professor years ago. At SU, I received valuable ideas and assistance on this project from Lorraine Bannai, Bob Chang, Maggie Chon, Brooke Coleman, Charlotte Garden, Christian Halliburton, Anna Roberts, Andrew Siegel, David Skover, and Ron Slye.

Many people outside these two law schools have helped with this book, either directly (through advice or assistance) or indirectly (by improving my thinking about, and teaching of, constitutional law). Hats off to Bill Araiza, Louise Franklin, and David Gartner, who went above and beyond the call of duty. Thanks also to Joseph Blocher, Anne Bloom, Daniel Caplan, Ellen Caplan, Richard Caplan, Erwin Chemerinsky, Joel Cohn, Ronald Collins, John Drimmer, David Eber, Riyaz Kanji, Linda Kerber, Ronald Krotoszynski, Leah Lee, Greg Magarian, Rick Mixter, Doug NeJaime, Roberta O'Meara, Gil Rodman, Robert Daniel Rubin, Sam Viviano, Eugene Volokh, and Nancy Weiss.

This book would be poorer if not for my colleagues in constitutional litigation during my years at Perkins Coie and the American Civil Liberties Union. Thanks to Pat Arthur, Venkat Balasubramani, Dave Burman, Cindy Cohn, Matt Coles, Sarah Dunne, Peter Eliasberg, James Esseks, David Fathi, Nick Gellert, Gail Gove, Kevin Hamilton, Julya Hampton, Doug Honig, Doug Klunder, Jim Lobsenz, David Loy, Dan Mach, Amy Miller, Margaret McKeown, Eric Nygren, Katie

Schwartzmann, Steve Shapiro, Rose Spidell, Art Spitzer, Nancy Talner, Kathleen Taylor, and Vic Walczak.

Ryan Pfeiffer and Carol Logie at Foundation Press deserve a round of applause for shepherding the project to completion and for enormous contributions to the book's visual and pedagogical appeal.

—Aaron H. Caplan
January 2015

Photo Acknowledgments

- Iwo Jima—© AP Photo/Joe Rosenthal
- Roscoe Filburn—Courtesy of Sue Ann Kern
- Railway Express Agency—Photo donated by Alvin A. Kahn, former president of Wearever Fountain Pen and Pencil Co.
- Milnut—Courtesy of Josh Blackman
- Gordon Hirabayashi—University of Washington Libraries, Special Collections SOC8109
- G.W. McLaurin—© Bettmann via Getty Images
- Elizabeth Eckford—© AP Photo/Will Counts
- Church in Boerne, TX—Jon Mallard (Creative Commons License)
- Lucky Dogs—Eugene Lazutkin (Creative Commons License)
- Ruth Bader Ginsburg—© AP Photo/Doug Mills
- Sharron Frontiero—© Bettmann via Getty Images
- Curtis Craig et al.—Courtesy of Curtis Craig
- Estelle Griswold—© Bettmann via Getty Images
- The Shelley Home—Courtesy of Josh Blackman, The Harlan Institute
- The Driskill Hotel, Photo by Kenneth Zirkel, 2011 (Creative Commons License)
- John Lawrence & Tyron Garner—© AP Photo/Michael Stravato
- Margaret Witt—Courtesy of ACLU of Washington
- Thea Spyer & Edith Windsor—Courtesy of Virginia Moraweck
- James Obergefell and John Arthur—Courtesy of James Obergefell

Table of Biographies

Summary Table of Contents

Detailed Table of Contents

PART I: THE BIG PICTURE 37

PART III: INDIVIDUAL RIGHTS 639

Chapter 18 Equality Rights 647

TABLE OF CASES

The principal cases are bold type. Cases cited or discussed in the text are roman type. References are to pages.

An Integrated Approach to Constitutional Law

THIRD EDITION

CHAPTER 1

How to Use This Book

A. An Integrated Approach for Integrated Cases

Almost every important constitutional law decision involves more than one legal doctrine. For example, litigation over individual rights like same-sex marriage and abortion may involve legal theories relating to equality, freedom, state-federal relationships, and the proper role of the judiciary. The Supreme Court opinion upholding the constitutionality of the Affordable Care Act discusses the federal government's powers (including the powers to regulate commerce, to impose taxes, to spend money, and to make laws necessary and proper to effectuate these and other powers), state-federal relationships, and the proper role of the judiciary.

In cases like these, lawyers and judges use many different constitutional tools to examine a single set of facts—but these tools are all part of an integrated toolkit, with each legal doctrine affecting the others. This book proposes that the best way for future lawyers to learn this toolkit is to begin using the tools in combination with each other from the very beginning of the course.

An illustration may help. It is possible to teach constitutional law one doctrine at a time, fleshing out the details of each topic before moving to the next. This approach is similar to downloading a computerized image pixel by pixel, as seen on the next page. By the end of the process, the entire picture is displayed at full resolution, but in the early phases of the download the final shape remains a mystery to the viewer. This method emphasizes the parts, leaving the whole for last.

Another way to download images begins by showing the general shape of the full picture at low resolution. The first glimpse may be blurry, but it indicates the relationships among the parts of the whole. The rest of the download adds successive layers of detail at increasingly higher resolution until the picture comes into final focus.

It is hard to comprehend a forest presented one tree at a time. Sketching the big picture first—even if it starts out looking a bit fuzzy—makes the details easier to comprehend when they are introduced later. This method also emphasizes how the interactions among constitutional ideas can be as important as each idea in itself.

B. The Big Picture: Powers and Their Limits

The picture of US constitutional law that will be presented in this book is based on the figure-ground illusion known as the Rubin Vase. Depending on one's choice of focus, the diagram might look like a vase or like two faces in profile.

A Rubin Vase

Translated to the realm of constitutional law, the dark area in the diagram (the vase) represents constitutionally acceptable government action, while the light areas (the two faces) represent constitutionally unacceptable government action. Phrased another way, the vase represents the government's power, while the faces represent limits on that power. For example, individual rights are a limit on government power; if a person has a constitutional right to do something, then the government's law-making power in that area is limited.

To decide if a law is constitutional, lawyers typically consider both the source of the government's power and any limits on it. Imagine that the US Congress is considering a bill to make it a crime to gamble on sports. To decide if the law is constitutional, one relevant question would involve the vase: does the federal government possess a power that allows it to criminalize gambling on sports? Another relevant question would look at the faces: do individuals have a constitutional right to gamble on sports? The answers to these questions often have a reciprocal relationship: saying yes to a power may mean saying no to a right, or vice versa.

The different areas in the diagram combine to create a roadmap for approaching every constitutional law question covered in this book:

> For government action to be constitutional, there must be a **source of power** authorizing that type of action, and the power must not be exercised in a way that violates **limits** based on constitutional *structure* or individual *rights.*

The book presents these concepts in three parts.

Part I sketches the big picture—the relationship of affirmative powers and negative limits. Government power is symbolized by the vase, limits arising from the structure of government are symbolized by the left face, and limits arising from individual rights are symbolized by the right face. Part I sketches this picture by presenting a set of historically important cases in roughly chronological order, the way the nation experienced them. Not every boundary within this picture will be in perfect focus by the end of Part I, but it will give you working knowledge of the structure of the US Constitution, the most significant events in the nation's constitutional history, and the most important topics of recurring constitutional dispute. The big picture outlined in Part I will be the framework for understanding the more detailed constitutional topics presented in Parts II and III.

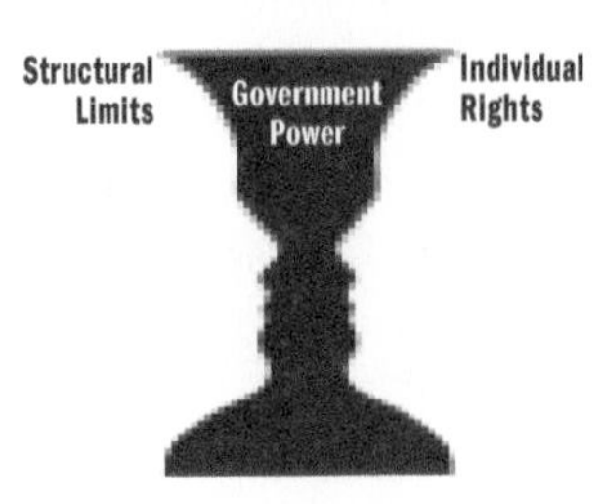

Part II sharpens the focus on the left-hand boundary: structural limits. A structural limit prevents one part of the government from exercising a power reserved for another part. The structural limit of supremacy means that states cannot exercise powers reserved for the federal government. The structural limit of federalism means that the federal government cannot exercise powers reserved for the states. And the structural limit of separation of powers means that branches within the federal government (legislative, executive, and judicial) may not take actions reserved to other branches.

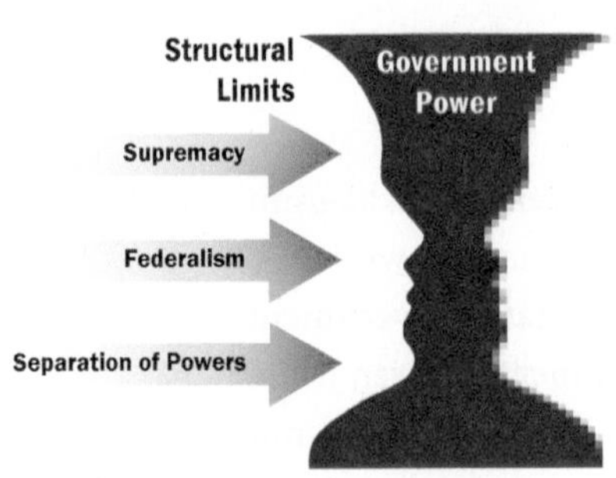

Finally, **Part III** sharpens the focus on the right-hand boundary: individual rights. Constitutional rights tend to serve three national values that sometimes overlap: equality (treating people similarly to each other), fairness (following proper procedures), and freedom (allowing people to do what they want). As examples of these three types of rights, Part III focuses on rights enshrined in the Fourteenth Amendment. Equality is exemplified by the Equal Protection Clause, fairness by the procedural due process doctrine, and freedom by the substantive due process doctrine.

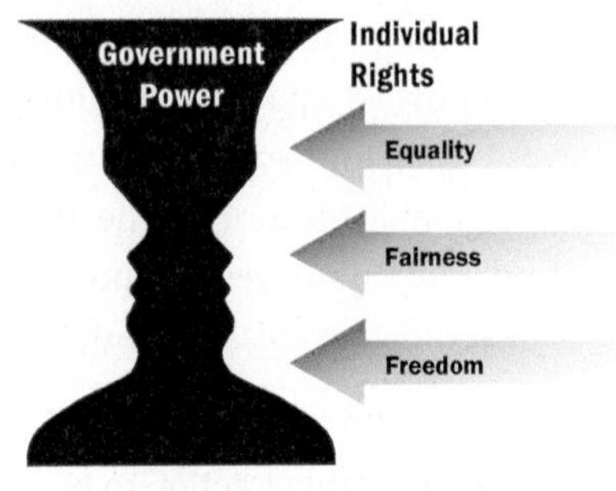

Each Part of the book concludes with a "Master Class"—a case or set of cases on a related topic providing an opportunity to review and reconsider the material in each Part. The Master Class for Part I (the big picture) studies the Civil Rights Act of the 1964; the Master Class for Part II (structural limits) studies the Affordable Care Act; and the Master Class for Part III (individual rights) studies gay rights.

The book's structure inevitably involves some repetition. As computer programmers would say, this is not a bug—it's a feature. Psychological research about learning has shown that a person's comprehension and long-term memory are better when material is presented in smaller doses spread over time, instead of in a single concentrated blast revisited only at exam time. The book's intentional repetitions also reflect historical reality. You will visit and revisit central constitutional questions just as the country has, continuing eternal debates as they resurface in new social and political contexts.

C. Features of the Book

Because Supreme Court opinions on constitutional topics can be complex, the book includes features to help you more easily understand and organize the material.

1. Kickstarters

kickstarter

To help you navigate between the chronological presentation of Part I and the topic-by-topic presentation of Parts II and III, the book contains a series of "Kickstarters"—modules that can be the starting point for your own outlines and notes.

By design, the Kickstarters are not sufficiently detailed to be a substitute for the assigned reading. However, the Kickstarters can help you get up to speed on the basics more quickly, so that you can spend more of your study time and class time delving into issues at greater depth. The book contains two types of Kickstarters.

The **Master Kickstarter** (found in Appendix C) suggests a structure for an outline of the course as a whole. Especially in Part I, the book presents cases in a different order than seen in the Master Kickstarter, but familiarity with it will help you situate your daily reading assignments within the big picture.

The **Topical Kickstarters** (found throughout Parts II and III) suggest methods for thinking about specific legal topics, such as the Spending Clause or the Equal Protection Clause. The topical Kickstarters should not be confused with a list of elements. No case law requires judges to write their opinions (or lawyers to write their briefs) in Kickstarter order. They are intended to provide a framework broad enough to encompass the questions that most commonly arise in each area. Familiarity with the topics in the Kickstarter should help you understand the cases that follow, prepare for class discussions, and draft your own more detailed outlines.

2. Flash-Forwards and Flashbacks

Eternal constitutional debates can arise in cases decided centuries apart from each other. The book contains two features designed to connect older and newer cases that grapple with similar problems. **Flash-Forwards** (found mostly in Part I) point forward in time, indicating factual and legal developments that arose after the opinion was issued. **Flashbacks** (found mostly in Parts II and III) point back in time, reminding you of precedents studied in earlier chapters.

3. Case Background

Even though some constitutional opinions are written in abstract terms, the facts of the cases matter just as much in constitutional law as any other area of law. To emphasize the importance of the facts—and to fill factual gaps the opinions might omit or downplay—the book provides longer-than-usual introductions to many cases. The case introductions make it easier to understand the opinions that follow. The goal is to give readers any necessary background information before the cases (not after, when it may be too late to avoid confusion). Occasional **sidebars** help explain passages that may not be self-explanatory for people studying constitutional law for the first time.

■ TERMINOLOGY

SIDEBARS: This is an example of a sidebar. The book's sidebars fall into four categories: TERMINOLOGY, HISTORY, BIOGRAPHY, OBSERVATION, and WEBSITE.

4. Study Questions

Questions appear before—not after—the major cases, to give you a sense of what to read for. By considering these questions in advance of class (by yourself individually, or even better with a group), you will find the class discussion more engaging. Indeed, your professors might ask some of these questions in class. Of course, they will also ask many questions not found in the book—but if you are able to answer the book's questions, you will likely have a strong enough understanding of the case to participate meaningfully in class discussion.

5. Case Editing

There's no avoiding it: Some constitutional law opinions are very long. In keeping with the book's philosophy of considering cases as an integrated whole, most opinions appear at close to their original length. Rest assured, the cases have been edited for length when appropriate—but not at the cost of eliminating their complexity. Keeping the cases largely intact avoids the confusion that can arise when cases are edited so heavily that important facts or connecting ideas are missing.

Stylistically, the book edits opinions with an eye towards ease of reading. Almost all internal punctuation and citations are omitted, with exceptions for citations to cases studied elsewhere in the book. Some paragraph breaks have been added or subtracted to improve the flow. To avoid the distracting use of [sic], the book substitutes modern spelling, capitalization, punctuation, and sometimes grammar if older versions would pose obstacles to modern readers. Deletions original to this book are marked with ellipses (. . .) and original additions are [within brackets]. Particularly for older cases, subheadings are occasionally added to aid comprehension.

6. Chapter Recaps

Chapter Recap

Each chapter ends with a short recap of that chapter's high points. The recaps are too brief to be a substitute for the assigned reading, but they can be a useful reminder of how the chapter's material relates to the big picture.

CHAPTER 2

Introduction to Constitutional Law

A. What Is Constitutional Law?

The Oxford English Dictionary defines a *constitution* as "the system or body of fundamental principles according to which a nation, state, or body politic is constituted and governed." It can be helpful to define *constitutional law*—at least as it is practiced in the United States—in three ways.

1. The Law That Governs the Government

A constitution controls how the government is constituted (its parts and their relationship to each other) and what it may do (its powers). In constitutional litigation, a government has taken some action—and a court is asked whether that action is permitted by the relevant constitution.

Because constitutional law governs the government, it generally does not govern the behavior of private persons or organizations. For example, the Fourth Amendment to **the US Constitution** does not allow the government to make an unreasonable search of your bedroom. If your neighbors make an unreasonable search of your bedroom, they have not violated the Fourth Amendment—although they might have violated other laws related to invasion of privacy or trespass.

Several terms convey the idea that a constitution governs the government but not private parties. *Public law* is a shorthand for laws that involve the government. Constitutional law is the most conspicuous form of public law, although other types of public law exist (including municipal law, administrative law, and tax law). Public law is distinguished from *private*

■ TERMINOLOGY

THE US CONSTITUTION: In this book, "constitution" (with a lower-case c) refers to the constitution of any state or nation. "Constitution" (with a capital C) refers to the Constitution of the United States of America.

law, which regulates the interactions among individuals. Many of the standard topics covered in the first year of law school (including property, contracts, and torts) are examples of private law.

2. The Law for Making Laws

The government has power to create *laws* (legally binding rules). Indeed, the most important functions of any government are making laws and then enforcing them. Should there be a minimum wage? Should there be a tariff on imported steel? Should there be a speed limit on two-lane roads? Instead of directly answering such questions, most constitutions establish procedures for answering them. In other words, constitutions provide the law for making laws.

This pyramid represents sources of law that tend to appear in modern constitutional systems.

Hierarchy of Laws in a Hypothetical Government

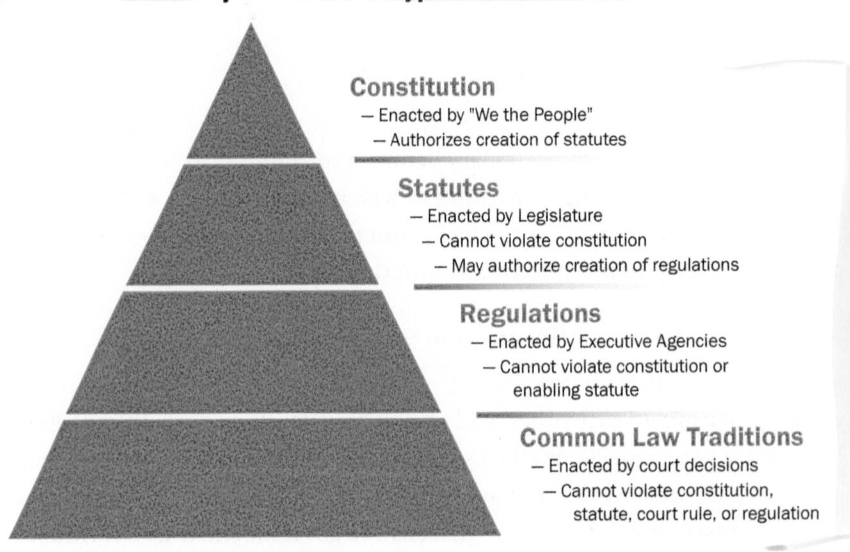
Constitution
– Enacted by "We the People"
– Authorizes creation of statutes
Statutes
– Enacted by Legislature
– Cannot violate constitution
– May authorize creation of regulations
Regulations
– Enacted by Executive Agencies
– Cannot violate constitution or enabling statute
Common Law Traditions
– Enacted by court decisions
– Cannot violate constitution, statute, court rule, or regulation

Constitution. The constitution sits at the top of the pyramid. It is the supreme law for the jurisdiction; laws created elsewhere in the pyramid will be unconstitutional to the extent they contradict portions of the constitution. In most modern nations and states, the theory behind the constitution is that it represents the will of the people, who are the ultimate sovereigns. See Ch. 3.A.1.

Statutes. Most laws are found in statutes enacted by a legislature. The legislature has leeway to enact whatever statutes it wishes, so long as it follows the constitution's laws for law-making. A constitution may include both procedural and substantive rules for the legislative process.

- A constitution will include a set of *procedures* for making laws. For example, the US Constitution requires that any law be approved by both the House of Representatives and the Senate. Art. I, § 7, cl. 2. The Nebraska constitution, by contrast, calls for a unicameral legislature (having a single house), unlike the bicameral (two-house) federal legislature.
- A constitution may also limit the *substance* of legislation by specifying the types of laws the government may (or may not) enact and enforce. The US Congress might follow entirely proper legislative procedures to enact a law making it a crime to criticize the President, but the substance of that law would violate the Free Speech Clause of the First Amendment to the US Constitution.

The procedures for lawmaking found in the US Constitution have generated relatively little controversy. As a result, most of the material studied in this book involves constitutional limits on the substance of legislation.

Regulations. Modern legislatures often delegate some law-making to administrative agencies. For example, the US Congress could create a Department of Education to oversee federal funding of schools. The statute creating the Department (usually known as an "enabling act" or sometimes an "organic act") might empower it to enact regulations having the force of law with regard to the use of those funds. If so, the enabling act could contain language establishing the agency's rules for making regulations (both procedural and substantive). An agency may not enact regulations that violate either its enabling act or the Constitution. Thus, if the Department of Education required recipients of federal funds to expel students who criticized the President, the regulation might violate the agency's enabling act as well as the Free Speech Clause of the US Constitution.

Common Law Traditions. Decisions by judges (collectively known as the common law) are an ancient source of legally binding rules. Since Roman times, it has been possible to sue a person in court for breaching a contract or committing a tort, even if no written constitutional provision, statute, or regulation says so. In common law countries like the US, common law traditions remain legally binding, unless (a) they are abrogated or overridden by duly enacted statutes or regulations, or (b) they are themselves unconstitutional. Thus, if a court decides, as part of its ever-evolving common law, to allow the President to sue students for their political criticism, the new tort could violate applicable statutes or regulations dealing with education law (if they exist) and would also violate the Free Speech Clause.

The rule from *Erie Railroad Co. v. Tompkins*, 304 U.S. 64 (1938)—usually studied in Civil Procedure classes—prevents federal courts from creating federal common law traditions that would displace state law counterparts. As a result, common law traditions for most subjects are created by the state courts.

Under Art. VI, § 2 of the US Constitution (the Supremacy Clause), the Constitution and laws of the United States are "the supreme law of the land," so states are required to abide by federal law notwithstanding any state law to the contrary. As a result, any action by a state or local government would be invalid if it violates federal law. In the diagram below, a law created at any level of a state pyramid would be invalid if it violated law created at a higher level within the state or federal pyramids.

State and Federal Legal Hierarchies

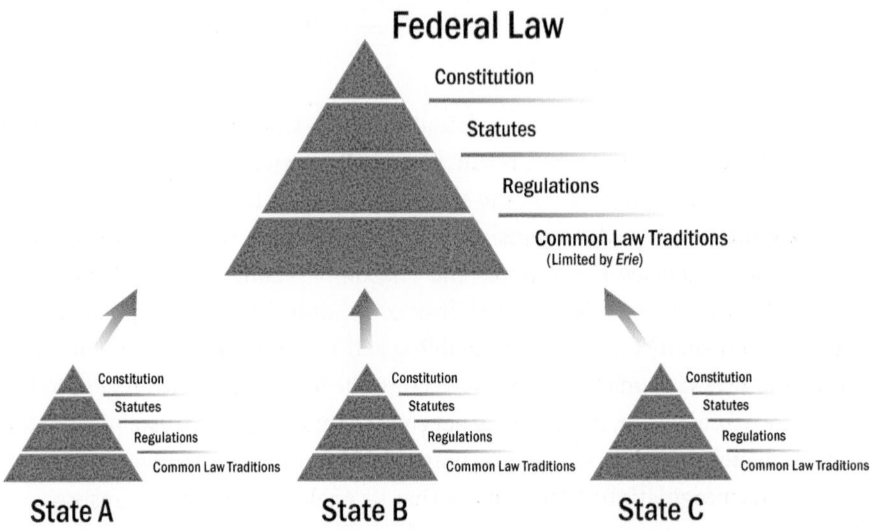

Federal Law
Constitution
Statutes
Regulations
Common Law Traditions
(Limited by *Erie*)

State A: Constitution, Statutes, Regulations, Common Law Traditions

State B: Constitution, Statutes, Regulations, Common Law Traditions

State C: Constitution, Statutes, Regulations, Common Law Traditions

Of all the potential conflicts between the various levels of legal authority, this book focuses on conflicts involving the top level of the federal pyramid: namely, whether an action of federal, state, or local government violates the US Constitution.

3. The Plan for Deciding Who Decides

Virtually any constitutional dispute could be phrased in terms of its results ("may the government do this?") or in terms of decision-making power ("who gets to decide what the government will do?"). Deciding who decides has huge ramifications, both for the present dispute and for similar disputes in the future.

The constitution of a hypothetical absolute monarchy would have a very short and simple plan for deciding who decides: The monarch decides everything. The US Constitution is far more complex, allocating decision-making authority among many different bodies. The Constitution "split the atom of sovereignty," *U.S. Term Limits, Inc. v. Thornton*, 514 U.S. 779 (1995) (Kennedy, J., concurring), releasing creative energy that might never find voice in an absolute monarchy.

Three "who decides" questions tend to arise most often in litigation involving the US Constitution.

Federalism: Levels of Government. The division of power between the levels of government is known as *federalism*. Some topics are decided exclusively at the national level by the federal government, such as immigration and naturalization. Others are decided exclusively at the state or local level, such as the traffic laws for local roads. Some involve concurrent decision-making, where the federal government may set minimum national standards that states may then supplement with additional laws. For example, a federal environmental law may make it illegal to discharge more than ten gallons of a toxic substance into a navigable waterway, and state law may forbid discharge of more than five gallons.

The text of the US Constitution expressly answers some questions involving the federal/state balance. For example, the federal government is allowed to coin money, Art. I, § 8, cl. 5, while the states are not, Art. I, § 10. But most federalism questions are open for interpretation. Whether a particular legal or social problem should be resolved by the federal government, the state governments, or both, is an eternal constitutional debate.

Separation of Powers: Branches of Government. Within a single level of government (national or state), the relevant constitution may assign specific decisions to different branches. For example, under the US Constitution, Congress may declare war, Art. I, § 8, cl. 11, but as the commander in chief of the armed forces, the President is responsible for tactical military decisions, Art. II, § 2. The President may be removed from office for treason, bribery, or other high crimes and misdemeanors, Art. II, § 4, but the decision is not for the Supreme Court to make: the removal will occur only if the House of Representatives votes to impeach (formally accuse) the President, Art. I, § 2, cl. 5, and the Senate thereafter finds that the President committed the accused wrongs, Art. I, § 3, cl. 6.

In addition to these expressly assigned roles, the US Constitution envisions a more general separation of powers, where "all legislative powers herein granted" are given to Congress, Art. I, § 1, "the executive power" to the President, Art. II, § 1, and "the judicial power" to the courts, Art. III, § 1. These terms are not expressly defined in the text, but as a general matter "legislative power" is the power to establish governmental policies, "executive power" is the power to execute (put into effect) those policies, and "judicial power" is the power to resolve disputes, including disputes arising from the policies or their execution. For example, the legislature could decide, by statute, that selling cocaine is a crime, but it could not decide that specified persons are guilty of selling cocaine and directly impose punishment on them. The executive—in the person of the prosecutor—investigates individual violations and files charges, and no punishment may be imposed until the judiciary resolves the dispute between the prosecutor and the defendant over the question of guilt. In the same way, the executive and the judiciary could not decide to punish people for selling cocaine in the absence of a statute defining the crime.

Separation of executive power from legislative power is primarily an American tradition. Most other modern democracies use a parliamentary system, where the executive is not independent of the legislature. In those governments, the prime minister or similar chief executive is selected by, and answers directly to, the parliament. The US Constitution allows state governments to adopt parliamentary systems, but as it happens all US states follow the federal government's three-branch system for separation of powers (although their chief executives are called "governors" instead of "presidents" and their legislatures are called "legislatures" or "assemblies" instead of "congresses"). The precise details of separation of powers may differ from one state constitution to another, but the basic concept remains consistent across American jurisdictions.

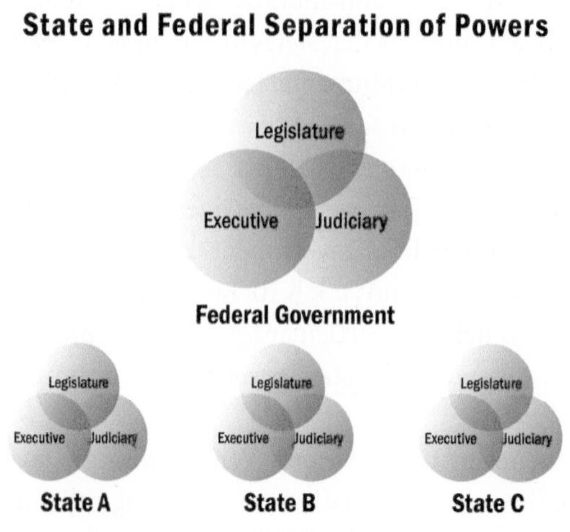

Individual Rights. Much of the Constitution outlines the relationships among governmental actors, but some portions control the relationship between the government and individuals, assigning *rights* to individuals that the government may not abridge. Some rights can be viewed in terms of decision-making authority. The First Amendment to the US Constitution, for example, prevents the government from deciding for individuals which religion to practice, which books to read, and which candidates to support. These decisions are beyond the reach of the government altogether, which means they may be made by individuals for themselves.

Disputes over individual rights may also implicate federalism and separation of powers, because they suggest yet another question: who gets to decide who gets to decide? Imagine a state legislature makes it illegal to speak any language other than English in one's home. The legislature evidently believes that it gets to decide that question, but affected individuals may believe that the US Constitution gives that decision to them. Under the American tradition known as *judicial review*, see Ch. 4, the federal judiciary has the last word on how the US Constitution allocates the power to decide which languages may be spoken at home. Giving the last word to a federal entity, rather than to the state legislature, has implications for federalism. And giving the decision to the judiciary, rather than to another branch of the federal government, has implications for separation of powers. For these reasons, how a judge feels about federal power in general, and judicial power in general, may affect how the judge feels about protecting individual rights.

B. Why Study Constitutional Law?

In most US law schools, Constitutional Law is a required course. It is important to study for at least two different reasons, one relating to the content of the material and another to the development of legal skills.

Content. All lawyers need at least a basic familiarity with constitutional law, no matter what their area of practice. Some lawyers have governmental entities as clients; those clients need to know how to work within the Constitution. All of the other lawyers will have clients who interact with the government; those clients need to know whether the government has violated the Constitution in its interactions with them. Even if your day-to-day practice does not involve regular work with constitutional law, full service to your private clients requires the ability to identify the most common constitutional problems when they arise.

In addition, knowledge of constitutional law is an important facet of informed citizenship. As a result, most Americans have a healthy interest in their Constitution.

Skills. Beyond its content, constitutional law is important for all law students because it emphasizes legal skills that may be different from the ones emphasized in other required courses.

How Precise Should a Constitution Be?

NON SEQUITUR © 1999 Wiley Ink, Inc. Dist. By UNIVERSAL UCLICK. Reprinted with permission. All rights reserved.

The first set of skills involve the interpretation of legal texts that might be called broadly worded, open-textured, or even vague. Is death by lethal injection "cruel and unusual punishment?" Does a court provide "due process of law" if the judge hearing the case has benefitted from millions of dollars of favorable campaign advertisements financed by one of the parties? Is a criminal defendant's right to "assistance of counsel" violated if the attorney fails to inform the defendant of the immigration consequences of a guilty plea or conviction? To answer these and similar questions, a court must do more than read the constitutional language in isolation.

The amount of specificity in a written law is sometimes described as the difference between comparatively specific *rules* and comparatively general *standards*. Consider two different approaches to writing a traffic code. A rule-based approach would develop a list of prohibitions whose meaning is unlikely to provoke much disagreement, such as "Do not drive faster than 50 miles per hour," "Keep your vehicle on the right side of the center line," "Turn on headlights after sunset," and "Do not pass a stopped school bus." The major benefit of precise rules is that they can be applied easily and reliably. So long as enough evidence is available, it is fairly simple to determine whether the driver was moving faster than 50 miles per hour. However, a full list of all the legal rules necessary to ensure traffic safety can become long, technical, and hard to remember. And no matter how detailed it is, it will run the risk of being incomplete. A rule-based traffic code written before the invention of mobile phones would not include a provision that said "Do not text while driving." The absence of a rule directly on point might mean that dangerous conduct is left unregulated.

A different approach to a traffic code might set forth a general standard, such as "Do not drive recklessly." The standard communicates the goal of the law in a few words that can be readily grasped and remembered. It also adapts to unforeseen circumstances without amendments. In a jurisdiction with a legally-binding standard against reckless driving, the government could take action against persons whose recklessness takes the previously unknown form of texting while driving. The texting driver could be charged with reckless driving, and it would be up to a jury to decide if the defendant's actions violated that standard. The adaptability of a standard comes at a cost, of course: it is flexible enough to reach novel situations, but it can be hard to predict how it will be interpreted by arresting officers, prosecutors, judges, and juries. Interpreting a broad standard as a method to decide a concrete legal dispute requires a type of reasoning that is different from the reasoning used to apply a precise rule.

Because both rules and standards have their uses, any complex legal system will include some of each. This means that any lawyer, even ones who do not regularly practice constitutional law, must learn how to work with standards. Transactional attorneys may need to interpret vague terms in a contract, deed, will, or trust. Attorneys in any field might need to interpret a vague statute or agency regulation. Constitutional law is an excellent subject for gaining experience with standards. The US Constitution includes some straightforward rules, but many of the great constitutional cases struggle with what *West Virginia State Board of Education v. Barnette*, 319 U.S. 624, 639 (1943), called "majestic generalities." These include terms like "equal protection of the laws" or "commerce among the several states" that express ideas through broad and evocative terms.

Broad language is inevitable in a constitution that is dedicated, at least in part, to announcing general principles. As Chief Justice John Marshall stated in *McCulloch v. Maryland*, 17 U.S. 316 (1819), "we must never forget that it is a *constitution* we are expounding." By this, he meant a set of standards rather than a detailed code of rules. In theory, the Framers could have written more rules into the Constitution, and this might have resolved some issues that perplex us today. But that approach might have led to no constitution at all, if the Framers became deadlocked over matters that did not require immediate solutions. Setting aside tasks for another day is an important part of statesmanship, but it means that those of us who live in what the Framers considered the distant future must make interpretive decisions about how to apply constitutional standards.

Rules and Standards in the US Constitution

Rules	Standards
• Each state has two Senators • President's term ends on January 20 • Treason conviction requires testimony of two witnesses to the same overt act, or a confession in open court	• No deprivation of life, liberty, or property without due process of law • No abridgement of freedom of speech • No unreasonable search and seizure

The second set of legal skills that are well-developed in a Constitutional Law class involve responding to change. The US Constitution is, in the grand scheme of things, a fairly new area of law when compared to truly ancient types of law like contracts, property, or torts. As a result, cases of first impression regularly arise with little precedent directly on point. Changes in constitutional interpretation are also likely to occur because legal decision-making based on standards is subject to disagreement; because eternal debates continue to resurface in novel settings; because the people deciding the cases change over time; and because the cases arise in contexts with ever-changing social, political, technological, and economic circumstances. The result is frequent change. Minimum wage laws were declared unconstitutional in 1923 but constitutional in 1937. Racial segregation was declared constitutional in 1896 but unconstitutional in 1954.

Any serious study of Constitutional Law requires learning about some decisions that have been overruled or abandoned. The story of why and how change occurred helps you understand today's law. And the ability to deal with future legal change is a skill that all lawyers need. No one studying law today can expect to have an entire legal career without experiencing any changes in law. Studying the shifts of the past helps prepare you for the shifts that are certain to arise in the future.

All this means that you may struggle dutifully to understand cases taught at one point in the course, and then you will need to struggle dutifully at a later point in the course to understand the cases overruling them. Once again: This is not a bug, it's a feature.

C. Methods of Constitutional Reasoning

Deciding specific cases consistently with a broadly-worded standard is rarely a mechanical enterprise; it requires careful reasoning and good judgment. For the most part, the US Constitution does not declare that any particular methods of judicial reasoning are required, preferred, or forbidden. (The Constitution's only mention of interpretation appears in the Ninth Amendment: "The enumeration in this Constitution, of certain rights, shall not be *construed* to deny or disparage others retained by the people.") In an influential lecture, Prof. Philip Bobbitt identified six general approaches that courts often use when applying the Constitution's intentionally broad language. Philip Bobbitt, *Constitutional Fate*, 58 Tex. L. Rev. 695 (1980). He noted that the methods are not mutually exclusive, and often overlap:

> I would emphasize that no sane judge or law professor can be committed solely to one approach. Because there are many facets to a single constitutional problem and . . . many functions performed by a single opinion, the jurist or commentator uses different approaches as a carpenter uses different tools, and often many tools, in a single project. . . . [W]e expect the creative judge to employ all the tools that are appropriate, often in combination, to achieve a satisfying result. Furthermore, in a multi-membered panel whose members may prefer different constitutional approaches, the negotiated document that wins a majority may, naturally, reflect many hues, rather than the single bright splash one observes in dissents.

■ TERMINOLOGY
METHODS OF REASONING: The first letters of the six methods of reasoning described here (text, precedent, structure, history, consequences, and values) can be combined into a mnemonic device: "The Perfect Sundae Has Chocolate and Vanilla."

Mastering various **methods of reasoning** will help you be more persuasive as a lawyer in any setting where you need to flesh out the meaning of an ambiguous document, whether it is a constitution, a statute, a will, or a contract.

1. Text

The textual approach seeks to resolve a controversy by reference to the words found in the text of the written constitution.

Not all constitutions are written. For centuries, the British have taken great pride in what they call their "constitution," but this term does not refer to a single authoritative document. The British constitution is primarily a tradition, not a text. This tradition deals with the usual topics for constitutions, such as the methods for lawmaking (a parliament consisting of two houses), allocation of decision-making power (assigning areas of responsibility between parliament and the crown), and a set of individual rights.

The US Constitution was one of the first world constitutions to take fully written form. A written constitution has the advantage of avoiding debates about what the constitution says. It does not eliminate debate about what those words mean, but the words cannot be ignored. Where the text allows for only one correct answer (senators must be "thirty" years old), we expect judges to enforce that answer. If the text does not seem to direct a single outcome (governmental takings of private property for public use require "just" compensation), we expect judges to reach results that are at least consistent with the text, even if not unambiguously commanded by it.

Careful textual arguments begin with the Constitution's choice of words. For example, the Eighth Amendment forbids excessive "fines." A lawsuit claiming that high tax rates violate the Eighth Amendment is in trouble from the start, because the text speaks about "fines," not "taxes." The context in which the chosen words appear will also be important. The ban on excessive fines appears in a sentence that also deals with the setting of bail and the infliction of punishment, suggesting a concern with the criminal process and not with raising governmental revenues. It may also be illuminating to consider how other portions of the Constitution use the same or different words. The word "fine" appears only in the Eighth Amendment, but the word "tax" appears in Art I, §§ 8–9, and in the Fourteenth, Sixteenth, and Twenty-Fourth Amendments. This contrast suggests that the Constitution envisions different meanings for "fines" and "taxes." The use of the word "tax" in multiple provisions might also mean that it has the same, or at least similar, meaning in each of them.

2. Precedent

The precedential approach considers how earlier courts resolved analogous cases.

Courts may issue rulings about the meaning of the Constitution only when necessary to resolve a "case" or "controversy" presented in the course of litigation. Art. III, § 2. Our common law litigation process, inherited from Britain, calls for courts to follow precedent. When a binding decision interprets the Constitution, later cases are expected to adhere to that interpretation.

The approach to precedent in constitutional cases is analogous to that found in legal areas dominated by judge-made common law traditions, such as contract, property, and torts. A court must synthesize a rule from earlier cases, separating holdings from dicta. It must then determine whether the earlier cases are on point or distinguishable. And it may consider whether the rule of those cases is so flawed that it should be limited or overruled, keeping in mind the societal benefits of legal stability.

Beyond these general similarities, however, an argument exists that a court should be more willing to overrule a mistaken constitutional interpretation than it would be to overrule a mistaken interpretation of a statute. The difference involves the relative difficulty of fixing a judicial mistake. If the Supreme Court misinterprets a statute, Congress can correct the problem through a majority vote changing the statute's language. But if the Supreme Court misinterprets the Constitution, changing the relevant language would require a constitutional amendment—a politically arduous process requiring two-thirds approval by both houses of Congress followed by ratification by three-fourths of the States. Art. V. Given the difficulty of amending the Constitution, this argument goes, it is preferable for the Supreme Court to fix its own mistakes when a later case presents the opportunity. (The argument in this paragraph is an example of reasoning from constitutional structure; see below.)

Whether courts are motivated by this structural reason, or from a more general impulse to get important questions right, the US Supreme Court has often overruled previous constitutional decisions. A full understanding of constitutional precedents includes both a "canon" of prominent cases to be followed and an "anti-canon" of prominent cases that are viewed as mistakes to be avoided. Even though some overruled cases are no longer good law, they are still discussed in court opinions and briefs, as a reminder of what the current law is not—or what it should not be.

3. Structure

The structural approach considers the structure of the government created by the Constitution.

The Constitution envisions a structure of interacting governmental institutions—state and federal, legislative, executive, and judicial. Even if the text of the Constitution does not explicitly resolve a particular question, the governmental structure created by the Constitution may suggest an answer to a dispute, especially disputes that seem to center on "who decides." If one result seems more consistent with the Constitution's structure for the government, this is a reason to favor that result. (Of course, questions about constitutional structure are not completely separated from questions about constitutional text, because the text tells us what the structure is.)

Structural arguments are most common in cases involving federalism (conflict between levels of government) and separation of powers (conflict among branches of government). A federalism example might involve a state law banning trucks over a certain length on its highways, even though longer trucks are allowed in neighboring states. This law will affect the flow of goods between states. The Constitution authorizes Congress to "regulate commerce among the several states," Art. I, § 8, cl. 3, and says nothing about the states' ability to regulate commerce. Yet state laws that change or reduce the flow of goods across state lines could interfere with Congress's decision-making power over interstate commerce. The Supreme Court has determined that the overall structure of the Constitution requires some limit on states' ability to pass such laws, because otherwise the states could impede Congress's enumerated power to decide how interstate commerce unfolds.

Few people consider the textual, precedential, or structural methods of reasoning to be inherently improper. Unfortunately, they are not guaranteed to lead to unanimously agreed-upon results. When text, precedent, and structure do not resolve cases on their own, other methods of reasoning can provide helpful insight. But depending on when, how, and why they are used, the following methods can be controversial.

4. History

The historical approach considers past events—other than court decisions—to help resolve a contested constitutional question. Court decisions are excluded from this discussion because reasoning from precedent is so prominent in law that it is usually treated as its own category.

As Oliver Wendell Holmes wrote, in some instances "a page of history is worth a volume of logic." *New York Trust Co. v. Eisner*, 256 U.S. 345 (1921). When applying a legal text, events before, during, and after its enactment may all shed light on its proper interpretation.

(a) *Before.* Most legal texts are drafted as a response to events occurring in the world. Knowing the circumstances that motivated the drafters can help reveal the text's purpose. In addition, drafters will have at least some awareness of prevailing legal practices, and those background assumptions may have influenced what they wrote (and what they left out).

(b) *During.* This is commonly known as "legislative history"—what was said and done during the process of creating and voting on the text.

(c) *After.* The laws made pursuant to a constitution after its enactment may show how its users understood it over time, separate and apart from any court precedents.

An example of historical argument appears in *Marsh v. Chambers*, 463 U.S. 783 (1983). The plaintiff argued that the Establishment Clause of the First Amendment did not allow a state legislature to start its sessions with a prayer from a chaplain. A majority of the Supreme Court disagreed, relying almost exclusively on history. Sessions of the Continental Congress that ultimately signed the Declaration of Independence began with invocations by chaplains. So did sessions of the First Congress in 1789, the very same Congress that drafted and approved the Establishment Clause. Sessions of Congress have opened with prayers by chaplains ever since, as have sessions of many state legislatures. This old and ongoing history convinced the majority in *Marsh* that the meaning of the Establishment Clause could not include a ban on legislative prayers.

Nearly everyone agrees that historical information can be useful when interpreting the Constitution, but there are major variations in emphasis beyond that general notion. Believers in "originalism" argue that today's judges should interpret the Constitution as it would have been understood at the time of its ratification—even if this means overruling post-ratification precedents, disregarding post-ratification societal changes, or creating unpleasant consequences. Opponents of originalism, sometimes described as supporters of the "living constitution" approach, argue that past practices are simply one source among many for constitutional interpretation, and that history is not dispositive. Most (but not all) modern-day originalists are self-identified legal and political conservatives. However, originalist-style arguments have been used at different times by people with varying political beliefs. And even people who are eager to draw lessons from history may disagree about what history tells us. *See, e.g., District of Columbia v. Heller*, 554 U.S. 570 (2008) (majority and dissent disagree as to the original understanding of the Second Amendment).

5. Consequences

The consequentialist approach asks which interpretation of the Constitution will produce the best consequences.

Any interpretation of the Constitution will have consequences (for the current litigants and any future ones). All else being equal, most people would prefer an interpretation leading to good consequences than to bad ones. Arguments about the likely future impacts of a decision are sometimes called "consequentialist," "utilitarian," "pragmatic," or "prudential" arguments, or arguments based on "public policy." A less complimentary term would be "result-oriented."

Some people argue that consequentialism is inconsistent with the rule of law, because courts are supposed to decide cases according to pre-announced principles, regardless of the outcome. There are also problems in applying consequentialist arguments. We cannot always know what the consequences of a decision will be, and even when we can, we must decide what constitutes a good or bad result, and for whom. These value judgments raise questions about whether judges, as opposed to other actors, should be the ones to decide which consequences society must live with.

On the other hand, pre-announced principles are sometimes not precise enough to resolve a particular case. Since a judicial decision in either direction will create consequences, it may be reckless not to consider them. Tort law and criminal law tend to penalize people who fail to consider the consequences of their actions, so why should we direct judges to do what we forbid for others?

Finally, even if we frown on consequentialist arguments, it is virtually impossible to prevent judges, who are only human, from considering them.

6. Values

The values-based approach to constitutional interpretation asks what basic social values the Constitution reflects as national priorities, and then seeks to decide modern cases consistently with those values.

Harper v. Virginia State Board of Elections, 383 U.S. 663 (1966), invoked values to answer a question not explicitly resolved by the Constitution's text. The Twenty-Fourth Amendment prohibits poll taxes as a condition of voting in federal elections, but says nothing about state and local elections. Plaintiffs challenged Virginia's state poll tax as a violation of the Equal Protection Clause, which also says nothing specific about state-level poll taxes. The majority opinion in *Harper* touched upon many values in deciding that it was unconstitutional for a state to require payment of poll taxes as a condition for voting in state elections. These include our values relating to democracy, to expanding suffrage to formerly disenfranchised groups, to economic opportunity, and to dislike of wealth-based social stratification. These themes were woven subtly into the opinion, without being separately identified as explicit bases for interpreting the Constitution. But the recourse to shared values goes a long way to explaining the result.

Applying the Constitution in light of our national values has some of the same pitfalls as consequentialism. Can values ever override the message from text, structure, or precedent? Whose values matter? Who gets to decide what our values are? And if a case involves competing values, how do we choose among them? Originalists may argue that only history provides a reliable guide to national values. Judicial conservatives may argue that judges should consider only those values expressed in legislation. Legal realists may argue that it is unrealistic and misleading to pretend that judges are not influenced by their values, so that the public is better served by opinions that transparently reveal and discuss the role of values than by opinions that purport to avoid value judgments while actually making them. And still others may argue that neither society at large, the legal system, nor the Constitution is well served by judges who are blind to our values.

D. Constitutional Reasoning in Action: *Ingraham v. Wright*

Ingraham v. Wright, 430 U.S. 651 (1977), considered whether corporal punishment of public school students can constitute "cruel and unusual punishment" under the Eighth Amendment. Many different methods of reasoning are on display in the majority and dissenting opinions. When reading the case, focus on the types of arguments the Justices use in support of their respective conclusions.

ITEMS TO CONSIDER WHILE READING *INGRAHAM v. WRIGHT*:

A. *Constitutional decisions are the product of litigation arising from concrete disputes between parties and decided within a procedural posture. Here, what happened in the world that gave rise to a dispute between parties? Who sued whom? In what court? Who won below, and at what stage? Which issues were presented for appeal, and how were they resolved by the opinion you read?*

B. *Identify the methods of reasoning found in the opinions. It will be useful to make a chart mapping the arguments in each category.*

	MAJORITY	DISSENT
Text		
Precedent		
Structure		
History		
Consequences		
Values		

C. *Do the methods of reasoning point in the same direction? If not, how is the conflict resolved?*

Ingraham v. Wright,

430 U.S. 651 (1977)

Justice Powell delivered the opinion of the Court [joined by Chief Justice Burger and Justices Stewart, Blackmun, and Rehnquist].

This case presents questions concerning the use of corporal punishment in public schools: First, whether the paddling of students as a means of maintaining school discipline constitutes cruel and unusual punishment in violation of the Eighth Amendment; and, second, to the extent that paddling is constitutionally permissible, whether the Due Process Clause of the Fourteenth Amendment requires prior notice and an opportunity to be heard.

Ingraham v. Wright

I

Petitioners James Ingraham and Roosevelt Andrews filed the complaint in this case on January 7, 1971, in the United States District Court for the Southern District of Florida. At the time both were enrolled in the Charles R. Drew Junior High School in Dade County, Florida, Ingraham in the eighth grade and Andrews in the ninth. . . . Named as defendants in all counts were respondents Willie J. Wright (principal at Drew Junior High School), Lemmie Deliford (an assistant principal), Solomon Barnes (an assistant to the principal), and Edward L. Whigham (superintendent of the Dade County School System).

Petitioners presented their evidence at a week-long trial before the District Court. At the close of petitioners' case, the District Court granted [the defendants' motion for a directed verdict], and dismissed the complaint without hearing evidence on behalf of the school authorities.

Petitioners' evidence may be summarized briefly. In the 1970–1971 school year many of the 237 schools in Dade County used corporal punishment as a means of maintaining discipline pursuant to Florida legislation and a local School Board regulation. . . . The authorized punishment consisted of paddling the recalcitrant student on the buttocks with a flat wooden paddle measuring less than two feet long, three to four inches wide, and about one-half inch thick. The normal punishment was limited to one to five "licks" or blows with the paddle and resulted in no apparent physical injury to the student. School authorities viewed corporal punishment as a less drastic means of discipline than suspension or expulsion. . . .

Petitioners focused on Drew Junior High School, the school in which both Ingraham and Andrews were enrolled in the fall of 1970. . . . The evidence, consisting mainly of the testimony of 16 students, suggests that the regime at Drew was exceptionally harsh. The testimony of Ingraham and Andrews, in support of their individual claims for damages, is illustrative. Because he was slow to respond to his teacher's instructions, Ingraham was subjected to more than 20 licks with a paddle while being held over a table in the principal's office. The paddling was so severe that he suffered a hematoma requiring medical attention and keeping him out of school for several days. Andrews was paddled several times for minor infractions. On two occasions he was struck on his arms, once depriving him of the full use of his arm for a week.

The District Court made no findings on the credibility of the students' testimony. Rather, assuming their testimony to be credible, the court found no constitutional basis for relief.

[Sitting en banc, the Court of Appeals] affirmed the judgment of the District Court. The Eighth Amendment, in the court's view, was simply inapplicable to corporal punishment in public schools. Stressing the likelihood of civil and criminal liability in state law, if petitioners' evidence were believed, the court held that "the administration of corporal punishment in public schools, whether or not excessively administered, does not come within the scope of Eighth Amendment protection." . . . The court refused to examine instances of punishment individually: "We think it a misuse of our judicial power to determine, for example, whether a teacher has acted arbitrarily in paddling a particular child for certain behavior or whether in a particular instance of misconduct five licks would have been a more appropriate punishment than ten licks."

We granted certiorari, limited to the questions of cruel and unusual punishment and procedural due process.

II

In addressing the scope of the Eighth Amendment's prohibition on cruel and unusual punishment, this Court has found it useful to refer to traditional common-law concepts and to the attitudes which our society has traditionally taken. So, too, in defining the requirements of procedural due process under the Fifth and Fourteenth Amendments, the Court has been attuned to what has always been the law of the land, and to traditional ideas of fair procedure. We therefore begin by examining the way in which our traditions and our laws have responded to the use of corporal punishment in public schools.

BIOGRAPHY

SIR WILLIAM BLACKSTONE (1723–1780) was an English judge and legal scholar who published an influential treatise titled *Commentaries on the Law of England.* American lawyers in the Framers' generation considered Blackstone to be a reliable encyclopedia of the common law concepts that were the starting point for the new states' own evolving bodies of common law.

The use of corporal punishment in this country as a means of disciplining schoolchildren dates back to the colonial period. It has survived the transformation of primary and secondary education from the colonials' reliance on optional private arrangements to our present system of compulsory education and dependence on public schools. Despite the general abandonment of corporal punishment as a means of punishing criminal offenders, the practice continues to play a role in the public education of schoolchildren in most parts of the country. Professional and public opinion is sharply divided on the practice, and has been for more than a century. Yet we can discern no trend toward its elimination.

At common law a single principle has governed the use of corporal punishment since before the American Revolution: Teachers may impose reasonable but not excessive force to discipline a child. **Blackstone** catalogued among the "absolute

Ingraham v. Wright

rights of individuals" the right "to security from the corporal insults of menaces, assaults, beating, and wounding," but he did not regard it a "corporal insult" for a teacher to inflict "moderate correction" on a child in his care. To the extent that force was "necessary to answer the purposes for which the teacher is employed," Blackstone viewed it as "justifiable or lawful." The basic doctrine has not changed. The prevalent rule in this country today privileges such force as a teacher or administrator reasonably believes to be necessary for the child's proper control, training, or education. Restatement (Second) of Torts § 147(2). To the extent that the force is excessive or unreasonable, the educator in virtually all States is subject to possible civil and criminal liability.

Although the early cases viewed the authority of the teacher as deriving from the parents, the concept of parental delegation has been replaced by the view—more consonant with compulsory education laws—that the State itself may impose such corporal punishment as is reasonably necessary for the proper education of the child and for the maintenance of group discipline. All of the circumstances are to be taken into account in determining whether the punishment is reasonable in a particular case. Among the most important considerations are the seriousness of the offense, the attitude and past behavior of the child, the nature and severity of the punishment, the age and strength of the child, and the availability of less severe but equally effective means of discipline.

Of the 23 States that have addressed the problem through legislation, 21 have authorized the moderate use of corporal punishment in public schools. Of these States only a few have elaborated on the common-law test of reasonableness, typically providing for approval or notification of the child's parents, or for infliction of punishment only by the principal or in the presence of an adult witness. Only two States, Massachusetts and New Jersey, have prohibited all corporal punishment in their public schools. Where the legislatures have not acted, the state courts have uniformly preserved the common-law rule permitting teachers to use reasonable force in disciplining children in their charge.

Against this background of historical and contemporary approval of reasonable corporal punishment, we turn to the constitutional questions before us.

III

The Eighth Amendment provides: "Excessive bail shall not be required, nor excessive fines imposed, nor cruel and unusual punishments inflicted." Bail, fines, and punishment traditionally have been associated with the criminal process, and by subjecting the three to parallel limitations the text of the Amendment suggests an intention to limit the power of those entrusted with the criminal-law function of government. An examination of the history of the Amendment and the decisions of this Court construing the proscription against cruel and unusual punishment confirms that it was designed to protect those convicted of crimes. We adhere to this long-standing limitation and hold that the Eighth Amendment does not apply to the paddling of children as a means of maintaining discipline in public schools.

A

The history of the Eighth Amendment is well known. The text was taken, almost verbatim, from a provision of the Virginia Declaration of Rights of 1776, which in turn derived from **the English Bill of Rights** of 1689. The English version, adopted after the accession of William and Mary, was intended to curb the excesses of English judges under the reign of James II. Historians have viewed the English provision as a reaction either to the "Bloody Assize," the treason trials conducted by Chief Justice Jeffreys in 1685 after the abortive rebellion of the Duke of Monmouth, or to the perjury prosecution of Titus Oates in the same year. In either case, the exclusive concern of the English version was the conduct of judges in enforcing the criminal law. The original draft introduced in the House of Commons provided: "The requiring excessive bail of persons committed in criminal cases and imposing excessive fines, and illegal punishments, to be prevented."

■ HISTORY

THE ENGLISH BILL OF RIGHTS: In the so-called Glorious Revolution of 1688, Parliament deposed the unpopular King James II in a bloodless coup. Parliament then offered the throne to William and Mary of Orange, so long as they agreed to respect "the rights of Englishmen." Many of these were then codified by Parliament as the Bill of Rights of 1689.

Although the reference to "criminal cases" was eliminated from the final draft, the preservation of a similar reference in the preamble indicates that the deletion was without substantive significance. Thus, Blackstone treated each of the provision's three prohibitions as bearing only on criminal proceedings and judgments.

The Americans who adopted the language of this part of the English Bill of Rights in framing their own State and Federal Constitutions 100 years later feared the imposition of torture and other cruel punishments not only by judges acting beyond their lawful authority, but also by legislatures engaged in making the laws by which judicial authority would be measured. Indeed, the principal concern of the American Framers appears to have been with the legislative definition of crimes and punishments. But if the American provision was intended to restrain government more broadly than its English model, the subject to which it was intended to apply—the criminal process—was the same.

At the time of its ratification, the original Constitution was criticized in the Massachusetts and Virginia Conventions for its failure to provide any protection for persons convicted of crimes. This criticism provided the impetus for inclusion of the Eighth Amendment in the Bill of Rights. When the Eighth Amendment was debated in the First Congress, it was met by the objection that the Cruel and Unusual Punishments Clause might have the effect of outlawing what were then the common criminal punishments of hanging, whipping, and earcropping. The objection was not

Ingraham v. Wright

heeded, precisely because the legislature would otherwise have had the unfettered power to prescribe punishments for crimes.

B

In light of this history, it is not surprising to find that every decision of this Court considering whether a punishment is "cruel and unusual" within the meaning of the Eighth and Fourteenth Amendments has dealt with a criminal punishment. See *Estelle v. Gamble*, 429 U.S. 97 (1976) (incarceration without medical care); *Gregg v. Georgia*, 428 U.S. 153 (1976) (execution for murder); *Furman v. Georgia*, 408 U.S. 238 (1972) (execution for murder); *Powell v. Texas*, 392 U.S. 514 (1968) (plurality opinion) ($20 fine for public drunkenness); *Robinson v. California*, 370 U.S. 660 (1962) (incarceration as a criminal for addiction to narcotics); *Trop v. Dulles*, 356 U.S. 86 (1958) (expatriation for desertion); *Louisiana ex rel. Francis v. Resweber*, 329 U.S. 459 (1947) (execution by electrocution after a failed first attempt); *Weems v. United States*, 217 U.S. 349 (1910) (15 years' imprisonment and other penalties for falsifying an official document); *Howard v. Fleming*, 191 U.S. 126 (1903) (10 years' imprisonment for conspiracy to defraud); *In re Kemmler*, 136 U.S. 436 (1890) (execution by electrocution); *Wilkerson v. Utah*, 99 U.S. 130 (1879) (execution by firing squad); *Pervear v. Commonwealth*, 72 U.S. 475 (1867) (fine and imprisonment at hard labor for bootlegging).

These decisions recognize that the Cruel and Unusual Punishments Clause circumscribes the criminal process in three ways: First, it limits the kinds of punishment that can be imposed on those convicted of crimes; second, it proscribes punishment grossly disproportionate to the severity of the crime; and third, it imposes substantive limits on what can be made criminal and punished as such. We have recognized the last limitation as one to be applied sparingly. The primary purpose of the Cruel and Unusual Punishments Clause has always been considered, and properly so, to be directed at the method or kind of punishment imposed for the violation of criminal statutes.

In the few cases where the Court has had occasion to confront claims that impositions outside the criminal process constituted cruel and unusual punishment, it has had no difficulty finding the Eighth Amendment inapplicable. Thus, in *Fong Yue Ting v. United States*, 149 U.S. 698 (1893), the Court held the Eighth Amendment inapplicable to the deportation of aliens on the ground that deportation is not a punishment for crime. And in *Uphaus v. Wyman*, 360 U.S. 72 (1959), the Court sustained a judgment of civil contempt, resulting in incarceration pending compliance with a subpoena, against a claim that the judgment imposed cruel and unusual punishment. It was emphasized that the case involved essentially a civil remedy[.]

C

Petitioners acknowledge that the original design of the Cruel and Unusual Punishments Clause was to limit criminal punishments, but urge nonetheless that the prohibition should be extended to ban the paddling of schoolchildren. Observing that the Framers of the Eighth Amendment could not have envisioned our present system of public and compulsory education, with its opportunities for noncriminal punishments, petitioners contend that extension of the prohibition against cruel punishments is necessary lest we afford greater protection to criminals than to schoolchildren. It would be anomalous, they say, if schoolchildren could be beaten without constitutional redress, while hardened criminals suffering the same beatings at the hands of their jailers might have a valid claim under the Eighth Amendment. Whatever force this logic may have in other settings, we find it an inadequate basis for wrenching the Eighth Amendment from its historical context and extending it to traditional disciplinary practices in the public schools.

The prisoner and the schoolchild stand in wholly different circumstances, separated by the harsh facts of criminal conviction and incarceration. The prisoner's conviction entitles the State to classify him as a "criminal," and his incarceration deprives him of the freedom to be with family and friends and to form the other enduring attachments of normal life. Prison brutality, as the Court of Appeals observed in this case, is part of the total punishment to which the individual is being subjected for his crime and, as such, is a proper subject for Eighth Amendment scrutiny. Even so, the protection afforded by the Eighth Amendment is limited. After incarceration, only the unnecessary and wanton infliction of pain, constitutes cruel and unusual punishment forbidden by the Eighth Amendment.

The schoolchild has little need for the protection of the Eighth Amendment. Though attendance may not always be voluntary, the public school remains an open institution. Except perhaps when very young, the child is not physically restrained from leaving school during school hours; and at the end of the school day, the child is invariably free to return home. Even while at school, the child brings with him the support of family and friends and is rarely apart from teachers and other pupils who may witness and protest any instances of mistreatment.

The openness of the public school and its supervision by the community afford significant safeguards against the kinds of abuses from which the Eighth Amendment protects the prisoner. In virtually every community where corporal punishment is permitted in the schools, these safeguards are reinforced by the legal constraints of the common law. Public school teachers and administrators are privileged at common law to inflict only such corporal punishment as is reasonably necessary for the proper education and discipline of the child; any punishment going beyond the privilege may result in both civil and criminal liability. As long as the schools are open to public scrutiny, there is no reason to believe that the common-law constraints will not effectively remedy and deter excesses such as those alleged in this case.

We conclude that when public school teachers or administrators impose disciplinary corporal punishment, the Eighth Amendment is inapplicable. . . .

IV

[The methods used by Florida schools when imposing corporal punishment do not violate procedural due process.]

V

Petitioners cannot prevail on either of the theories before us in this case. The Eighth Amendment's prohibition against cruel and unusual punishment is inapplicable to school paddlings, and the Fourteenth Amendment's requirement of procedural due process is satisfied[.] We therefore agree with the Court of Appeals that petitioners' evidence affords no basis for injunctive relief, and that petitioners cannot recover damages on the basis of any Eighth Amendment or procedural due process violation.

Justice White, with whom Justices Brennan, Marshall, and Stevens join, dissenting.

Today the Court holds that corporal punishment in public schools, no matter how severe, can never be the subject of the protections afforded by the Eighth Amendment. It also holds that students in the public school systems are not constitutionally entitled to a hearing of any sort before beatings can be inflicted on them. Because I believe that these holdings are inconsistent with the prior decisions of this Court and are contrary to a reasoned analysis of the constitutional provisions involved, I respectfully dissent.

I

A

The Eighth Amendment places a flat prohibition against the infliction of "cruel and unusual punishments." This reflects a societal judgment that there are some punishments that are so barbaric and inhumane that we will not permit them to be imposed on anyone, no matter how opprobrious the offense. If there are some punishments that are so barbaric that they may not be imposed for the commission of crimes, designated by our social system as the most thoroughly reprehensible acts an individual can commit, then, *a fortiori*, similar punishments may not be imposed on persons for less culpable acts, such as breaches of school discipline. Thus, if it is constitutionally impermissible to cut off someone's ear for the commission of murder, it must be unconstitutional to cut off a child's ear for being late to class. Although there were no ears cut off in this case, the record reveals beatings so severe that if they were inflicted on a hardened criminal for the commission of a serious crime, they might not pass constitutional muster.

Nevertheless, the majority holds that the Eighth Amendment "was designed to protect [only] those convicted of crimes," relying on a vague and inconclusive recitation of the history of the Amendment. Yet the constitutional prohibition is against cruel and unusual punishments; nowhere is that prohibition limited or modified by the language of the Constitution. Certainly, the fact that the Framers did not choose to insert the word "criminal" into the language of the Eighth Amendment is strong evidence that the Amendment was designed to prohibit all inhumane or barbaric punishments, no matter what the nature of the offense for which the punishment is imposed.

No one can deny that spanking of schoolchildren is "punishment" under any reasonable reading of the word, for the similarities between spanking in public schools and other forms of punishment are too obvious to ignore. Like other forms of punishment, spanking of schoolchildren involves an institutionalized response to the violation of some official rule or regulation proscribing certain conduct and is imposed for the purpose of rehabilitating the offender, deterring the offender and others like him from committing the violation in the future, and inflicting some measure of social retribution for the harm that has been done.

B

We are fortunate that in our society punishments that are severe enough to raise a doubt as to their constitutional validity are ordinarily not imposed without first affording the accused the full panoply of procedural safeguards provided by the criminal process. The effect has been that "every decision of this Court considering whether a punishment is 'cruel and unusual' within the meaning of the Eighth and Fourteenth Amendments has dealt with a criminal punishment." The Court would have us believe from this fact that there is a recognized distinction between criminal and noncriminal punishment for purposes of the Eighth Amendment. This is plainly wrong. Even a clear legislative classification of a statute as "non-penal" would not alter the fundamental nature of a plainly penal statute. The relevant inquiry is not whether the offense for which a punishment is inflicted has been labeled as criminal, but whether the purpose of the deprivation is among those ordinarily associated with punishment, such as retribution, rehabilitation, or deterrence.

If this purposive approach were followed in the present case, it would be clear that spanking in the Florida public schools is punishment within the meaning of the Eighth Amendment. The District Court found that corporal punishment is one of a variety of measures employed in the school system for the correction of pupil behavior and the preservation of order. Behavior correction and preservation of order are purposes ordinarily associated with punishment.

Without even mentioning the purposive analysis applied in the prior decisions of this Court, the majority adopts a rule that turns on the label given to the offense for which the punishment is inflicted. Thus, the record in this case reveals that one student at Drew Junior High School received 50 licks with a paddle for allegedly making an obscene telephone call. The majority holds that the Eighth Amendment does not prohibit such punishment since it was only inflicted for a breach of school discipline. However, that same conduct is punishable as a misdemeanor under Florida law, and there can be little doubt that if that same "punishment" had been inflicted by an officer of the state courts for violation of [the obscene phone call statute], it would have had to satisfy the requirements of the Eighth Amendment.

Ingraham v. Wright

C

In fact, as the Court recognizes, the Eighth Amendment has never been confined to criminal punishments.[FN4] Nevertheless, the majority adheres to its view that any protections afforded by the Eighth Amendment must have something to do with criminals, and it would therefore confine any exceptions to its general rule that only criminal punishments are covered by the Eighth Amendment to abuses inflicted on prisoners. Thus, if a prisoner is beaten mercilessly for a breach of discipline, he is entitled to the protection of the Eighth Amendment, while a schoolchild who commits the same breach of discipline and is similarly beaten is simply not covered.

FN4 In *Estelle v. Gamble*, 429 U.S. 97 (1976), a case decided this Term, the Court held that "deliberate indifference to the medical needs of prisoners" by prison officials constitutes cruel and unusual punishment prohibited by the Eighth Amendment. Such deliberate indifference to a prisoner's medical needs clearly is not punishment inflicted for the commission of a crime; it is merely misconduct by a prison official. . . .

The purported explanation of this anomaly is the assertion that schoolchildren have no need for the Eighth Amendment. We are told that schools are open institutions, subject to constant public scrutiny; that schoolchildren have adequate remedies under state law; and that prisoners suffer the social stigma of being labeled as criminals. How any of these policy considerations got into the Constitution is difficult to discern, for the Court has never considered any of these factors in determining the scope of the Eighth Amendment.

The essence of the majority's argument is that schoolchildren do not need Eighth Amendment protection because corporal punishment is less subject to abuse in the public schools than it is in the prison system. However, it cannot be reasonably suggested that just because cruel and unusual punishments may occur less frequently under public scrutiny, they will not occur at all. The mere fact that a public flogging or a public execution would be available for all to see would not render the punishment constitutional if it were otherwise impermissible. Similarly, the majority would not suggest that a prisoner who is placed in a minimum-security prison and permitted to go home to his family on the weekends should be any less entitled to Eighth Amendment protections than his counterpart in a maximum-security prison. In short, if a punishment is so barbaric and inhumane that it goes beyond the tolerance of a civilized society, its openness to public scrutiny should have nothing to do with its constitutional validity.

Nor is it an adequate answer that schoolchildren may have other state and constitutional remedies available to them. Even assuming that the remedies available to public school students are adequate under Florida law, the availability of state remedies has never been determinative of the coverage or of the protections afforded by the Eighth Amendment. The reason is obvious. The fact that a person may have a state-law cause of action against a public official who tortures him with a thumbscrew for the commission of an antisocial act has nothing to do with the fact that such official conduct is cruel and unusual punishment prohibited by the Eighth Amendment. Indeed, the majority's view was implicitly rejected this Term in *Estelle v. Gamble*, when the Court held that failure to provide for the medical needs of prisoners could constitute cruel and unusual punishment even though a medical malpractice remedy in tort was available to prisoners under state law.

D

By holding that the Eighth Amendment protects only criminals, the majority adopts the view that one is entitled to the protections afforded by the Eighth Amendment only if he is punished for acts that are sufficiently opprobrious for society to make them "criminal." This is a curious holding in view of the fact that the more culpable the offender the more likely it is that the punishment will not be disproportionate to the offense, and consequently, the less likely it is that the punishment will be cruel and unusual. Conversely, a public school student who is spanked for a mere breach of discipline may sometimes have a strong argument that the punishment does not fit the offense, depending upon the severity of the beating, and therefore that it is cruel and unusual. Yet the majority would afford the student no protection no matter how inhumane and barbaric the punishment inflicted on him might be.

The issue presented in this phase of the case is limited to whether corporal punishment in public schools can ever be prohibited by the Eighth Amendment. I am therefore not suggesting that spanking in the public schools is in every instance prohibited by the Eighth Amendment. My own view is that it is not. I only take issue with the extreme view of the majority that corporal punishment in public schools, no matter how barbaric, inhumane, or severe, is never limited by the Eighth Amendment. Where corporal punishment becomes so severe as to be unacceptable in a civilized society, I can see no reason that it should become any more acceptable just because it is inflicted on children in the public schools.

II

Ingraham v. Wright

[The dissenters disagreed with the majority's holding regarding procedural due process. Justice Stevens filed a separate dissent with additional discussion of that issue.]

Chapter Recap

A. Constitutional law is:

- The law that governs the government
- The law for making laws
- The plan for deciding who decides

B. Constitutional law deserves study both for its substance and because it teaches the lawyering skills of interpreting broadly-phrased legal standards and responding to legal change.

C. Lawyers use many methods to interpret open-textured terms in the Constitution, including:

- Text
- Precedent
- Structure
- History
- Consequences
- Values

Part I: The Big Picture

The Big Picture

Part One sketches the big picture of our constitutional system by presenting historically important precedents in roughly chronological order. As explained in Chapter 1 and reiterated here, that picture symbolizes the relationships between governmental powers (represented by the dark areas in the diagram) and the limits on those powers (represented by the light areas). The precise boundaries between these shapes may feel fuzzy, especially near the beginning of the course when the concepts are new to you. This is normal. The boundaries probably felt fuzzy for the nation as a whole when the concepts were new to everyone. The edges became sharper as more cases were decided.

A. The Parts of the Picture

The parts of the diagram combine to create a roadmap for approaching every constitutional law question covered in this book:

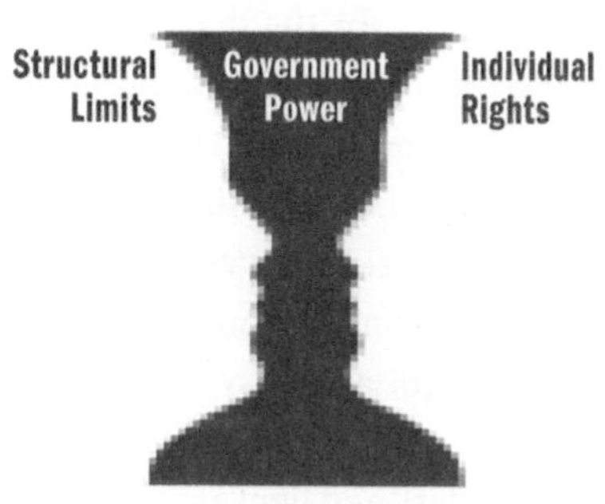

> For government action to be constitutional, there must be a ***source of power*** authorizing that type of action, and the power must not be exercised in a way that violates ***limits*** based on constitutional *structure* or individual *rights*.

The Master Kickstarter (Appendix C) presents these parts in outline form, where sources of power are listed under Roman Numeral I; structural limits under Roman Numeral II, and individual rights under Roman Numeral III.

Source of Powers. Governments may not act without a source of power. For US states, their open-ended sovereign authority is a source of power to make laws on any subject matter. By contrast, the federal government may exercise only the powers enumerated in the US Constitution. The federal powers studied in Part I of the book include the power to regulate commerce, the power to tax, the power to enact anti-discrimination laws, and the power to enact laws that are "necessary and proper" to execute other powers. Part I of the book also considers whether the federal government may exercise powers that are implied but not directly expressed in the text of the Constitution.

Structural Limits. Structural limits prevent one part of the government from exercising powers reserved for another part. These include limits arising from the allocation of powers between the national and state levels (federalism) and among branches at one level of government (separation of powers). From the nation's earliest days, battles have been fought over these boundaries, because the powers of each level of government have some overlap with the other. For example, some powers have been deemed exclusively federal or exclusively state, but it is more common for there to be concurrent authority where both levels may act. Structural limits introduced in Part I include federal supremacy over conflicting state laws, the role of the judiciary within the separation of powers, and the possibility of implied structural limitations.

Individual Rights. Individual rights limit how governments may exercise their powers over people. Individual rights studied in Part I include the now-abrogated right to enslave people and the now-enforceable right not to be enslaved; the right to equal protection of the laws; and the right not to have life, liberty, or property deprived without due process of law. Part I also introduces the ongoing dispute over the Constitution's protection of implied or unenumerated rights.

B. Interaction of the Parts

In the diagrams used in this book, a government action (represented by a star) will be constitutional if it falls within the dark area (symbolizing government power), but unconstitutional if it falls within the light areas (symbolizing limits on government power). Notice how the dark and light areas have a reciprocal relationship, where the shape of the vase determines the shape of the faces—and vice versa. This means constitutional cases can in theory

Constitutional and Unconstitutional Government Actions

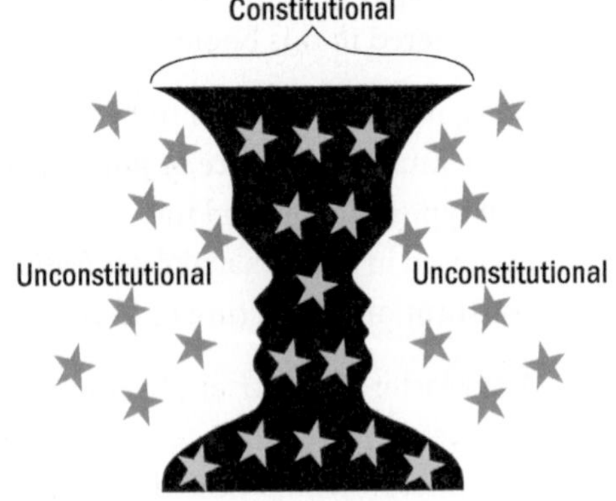

be approached from different angles: one could focus on the government's power (the vase), or on the limits to that power (the faces).

A few examples show how constitutional lawyers must become adept with the relationships between power questions and limits questions. A major constitutional battle in the early 20th century involved the ability of the US Congress to pass laws regulating labor standards. This was argued as a question of governmental power. In *Hammer v. Dagenhart*, 247 U.S. 251 (1918), the Supreme Court ruled that Congress did not have an enumerated power that would allow federal laws against industrial child labor. In *US v. Darby*, 312 U.S. 100 (1941), the Supreme Court overruled *Dagenhart*, finding that the Commerce Clause in fact did confer a power to regulate the conditions of industrial labor. In the diagrams for these two cases, note how the court's changing view about the scope of power meant that a law previously beyond the government's power later fell within it. Also note how even though *Dagenhart* and *Darby* were decided with reference to the scope of government power, they had an effect on the scope of individual rights (the right face). Under *Dagenhart*, where the government has no power to regulate labor conditions, an employer effectively has a right to hire child laborers. But under *Darby*, where the government has power to regulate, then the employer has no such right.

Changing Interpretations of Government Power

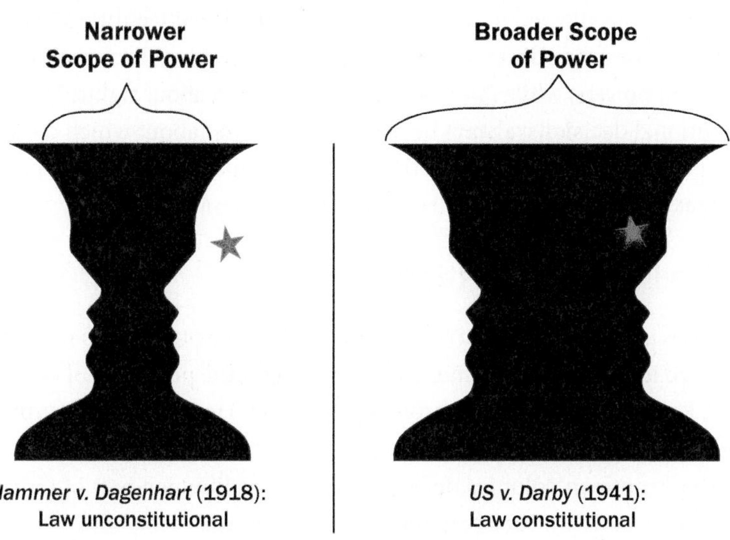

In other settings, a case may be argued in terms of limits, rather than powers. *Adkins v. Children's Hospital*, 261 U.S. 525 (1923), held that a minimum wage law violated the Due Process Clause, which at that time was interpreted to protect the (unenumerated) right to enter into the contracts of one's choosing—including contracts to work for low wages. This was reversed in *West Coast Hotel v. Parrish*, 300 U.S. 379 (1937), which held that the Due Process Clause did not protect that particular right. By ruling that the scope of rights under the Due Process Clause was less than previously thought, *Parrish* also had the effect of increasing the areas in which the government had the power to act.

Changing Interpretations of Individual Rights

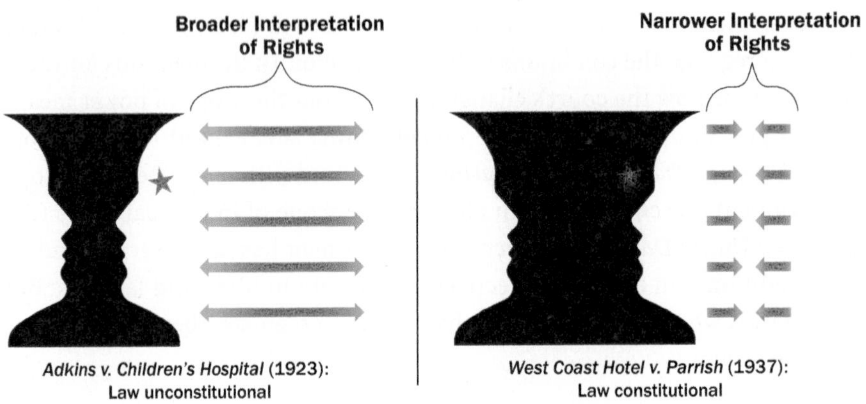

In both *Darby* and *Parrish,* the Supreme Court's decisions altered what the government was allowed to do and what individuals were entitled to do. But the decisions arose from different conversations. *Darby* was a conversation about government powers, while *Parrish* was a conversation about rights. While reading constitutional decisions, always be clear in your mind about which conversations are happening where. Distinguish the (parts of) opinions that discuss *powers* from those that discuss structural or rights-based *limits* on power.

C. The Historical Setting

Cases like *Darby* and *Parrish* show how the Constitution has not always been interpreted identically over time. To help highlight the processes of constitutional change, Part I is structured in chronological order. Here is a brief summary of the historical settings in which the changes occurred.

The American colonies declared themselves independent of Great Britain in 1776. State constitutions began to be drafted at that time, and the current US Constitution was drafted in 1787. **Chapter 3** (A Tour of the Constitution) describes how and why the Constitution was written as it was, and why it was quickly amended to include a Bill of Rights in 1791.

One of the first features of the new Constitution to take shape was the power of judicial review—the ability of federal courts to declare actions by states or by the federal government to be unconstitutional. Courts have the last word on the meaning of the US Constitution, which explains why so much American constitutional law must be learned through court decisions. **Chapter 4** (Judicial Review) explores the justifications for the power of judicial review.

Some of the first major constitutional controversies involved the balance of federal and state powers. Chief Justice John Marshall (who served 1801–1835) was an influential proponent of a strong federal government. **Chapter 5** (Early Federal-State Relationships) considers several crucial early decisions written by Justice Marshall that tended to favor federal power.

In contrast to Marshall, Chief Justice Roger Taney (1835–1864) was known in his time for his decisions limiting the power of the federal government and increasing power for the states. Today, the Taney Court is best remembered for its rulings in favor of slavery. **Chapter 6** (Slavery) considers how the Constitution functioned in an era that recognized an individual right to own slaves, supported by both national and local laws.

The political crisis that culminated in the Civil War (1861–1865) revealed the shortcomings of the Constitution's original decision to leave almost all questions about individual rights—including slavery—to the states. The era of Reconstruction following the Civil War saw major amendments to the Constitution, most conspicuously the Thirteenth Amendment (ratified 1865) eliminating slavery and the Fourteenth Amendment (ratified 1868) requiring the states to respect certain individual rights. The Supreme Court under Chief Justices Salmon P. Chase (1864–1873), Morrison Waite (1874–1888), and Melville Fuller (1888–1910) tended to deny that these amendments represented any radical change in the structure of American government. **Chapter 7** (The Reconstruction Amendments) explores how hostile the Court often was to anti-discrimination arguments, and how supportive it was of laws that discriminated on the basis of race, sex, and nationality.

Between approximately 1885 to 1937, a majority of the Supreme Court was devoted to restricting the ability of government to regulate the economy. This period, under Chief Justices Melville Fuller (1888–1910), Edward Douglass White (1910–1921), and William Howard Taft (1921–1930), is often known as "The *Lochner* Era," in honor of *Lochner v. New York* (1905), a decision that relied on a freedom of contract theory to strike down a state law establishing maximum hours of work for bakery employees. During these years, the Court also ruled that the Commerce Clause did not give the federal government much power to regulate in-state business activities. **Chapter 8** (The *Lochner* Era) explores how the Supreme Court's vision of limited government power over business expressed itself through a variety of legal doctrines.

One of the most dramatic shifts in American constitutional law was the Supreme Court's repudiation of the *Lochner* Era. After the onset of the Great Depression in 1929 and the election of Franklin D. Roosevelt as president in 1932, the federal government enacted statutes known as "The New Deal" to intervene in the economy, but the Supreme Court found many of them unconstitutional. A sense of constitutional crisis was brewing, with many believing that the will of the people ought not be thwarted by the Supreme Court. In 1937, the Supreme Court under Chief Justice Charles Evans Hughes (1930–1941) reversed the main pillars of the *Lochner* Era, allowing both state and federal governments to pursue economic regulations. **Chapter 9** (The New Deal Revolution) explores this dramatic turnaround.

After this reversal, the Court under Chief Justices Harlan Stone (1941–1946) and Fred Vinson (1946–1953) struggled to determine how far-reaching this latest constitutional change should be. If the Supreme Court should not intervene against economic regulations, which, if any, regulations should be found unconstitutional? **Chapter 10** (Levels of Scrutiny) considers the two-tiered solution that emerged, where some laws were scrutinized more stringently than others.

Under Chief Justice Earl Warren (1953–1969), the Supreme Court became known for its willingness to enforce the Bill of Rights, to the point where Warren Court decisions are sometimes referred to as a "rights revolution." Many of these developments are traditionally studied in other law school courses, especially Criminal Procedure, First Amendment, and Election Law. This book focuses on the Warren Court's decisions involving race discrimination. **Chapter 11** (The Civil Rights Movement and the Warren Court) shows how a number of separate constitutional doctrines were used to attack discrimination and segregation, just as earlier Supreme Courts had used a number of constitutional doctrines to uphold them. Continuing that theme, **Chapter 12** (The Civil Rights Act of 1964) is structured as a "Master Class"—a set of cases on a related topic that will allow you to pull together many of the concepts presented thus far.

Part I concludes in the late 1960s. Since then, American constitutional law has been dominated by responses to, and refinements of, the principles established up to that time. Legal developments under Chief Justices Warren Burger (1969–1986), William Rehnquist (1986–2005), and John Roberts (2005–present) are the subject of Parts II and III.

CHAPTER 3

A Tour of the Constitution

This chapter explores how the US Constitution was written and how it is structured. The Constitution's full text is reproduced in Appendix A, along with annotations showing the effects of later amendments. Appendix B identifies proposed amendments that were approved by Congress but not ratified by the States.

A. Political Background

1. States and Sovereignty

To understand the Constitution of the United States of America, one must first understand the concept of a state, which in turn rests upon the concept of sovereignty. As Sir William Blackstone explained it in 1765, under all forms of government "there is and must be in all of them a supreme, irresistible, absolute, uncontrolled authority, in which the rights of sovereignty reside." A sovereign government may make laws of any sort on any subject, using any method of law-making it chooses. Because the sovereign answers to no one, it cannot be sued or subjected to court orders without its consent—a concept known as *sovereign immunity*.

Who is in charge of the extraordinary power that comes with sovereignty? Blackstone believed that sovereign authority ought to be placed where "the qualities requisite for supremacy, wisdom, goodness, and power are the most likely to be found." In theory, a government could vest its sovereignty in a single person, an absolute monarch. In practice, Britain had a lengthy tradition of divided sovereignty, going back at least as far as the Magna Carta (great charter) of 1215, in which King John—politically weak and desperate for funds—agreed to share his powers in exchange for political and financial support from the aristocracy.

By the Framers' time, it was well accepted that Britain's sovereignty was divided between King and Parliament, with Parliament having the greater share. In addition to being shared, British sovereignty was limited in scope. The unwritten British constitution imposed both procedural and substantive limits on how King and Parliament could exercise their shared sovereign power.

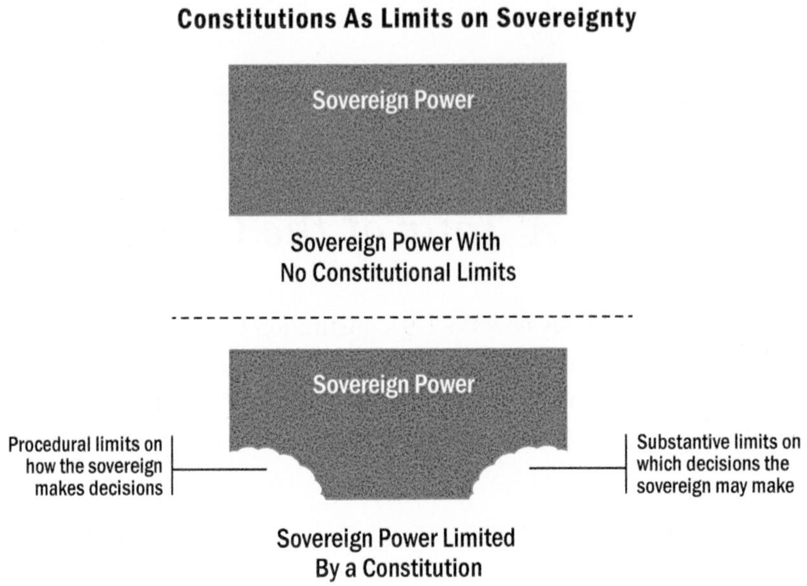

Constitutions As Limits on Sovereignty

Sovereign Power

Sovereign Power With
No Constitutional Limits

Sovereign Power

Procedural limits on how the sovereign makes decisions

Substantive limits on which decisions the sovereign may make

Sovereign Power Limited
By a Constitution

By the 1770s, the people of Britain's North American colonies became dissatisfied with British rule and their lack of representation in Parliament. Many colonists began to believe that sovereignty, properly understood, was not held by a King and an aristocratic Parliament, but by the people themselves. By the time of the Declaration of Independence in 1776, its authors could claim that this theory (known as *popular sovereignty*) was a "self-evident" truth: "Governments are instituted among men, deriving their just powers from the consent of the governed." Because the British government had exercised its sovereignty in a manner unacceptable to the people of the colonies, "it is the right of the people to alter or to abolish it, and to institute new government."

Upon independence, the colonists had to decide which government should be entrusted with the people's sovereignty. A few voices argued that sovereignty should be vested in a single national government representing all of the people of the former colonies. However, the consensus in the 1770s was that the colonies formed separate political communities who delegated their popular sovereignty to separate governments. These new sovereign governments were known as "states"—a word that roughly corresponded to what we would today call "nations." They were separate countries with only voluntary obligations to each other.

As the war for independence was fought from 1776 through 1783, the new states began drafting written constitutions for themselves that incorporated the best-liked features of the unwritten British constitution, such as division of the legislature into upper and lower houses, an independent judiciary, and statements of individual rights. Some of the more influential models included the constitutions of Massachusetts (drafted by John Adams) and Virginia (with a widely admired Bill of Rights drafted by George Mason). Whatever their differences, these early state constitutions all presumed that the state was a sovereign entity—which meant that the state government could enact any laws it wished, subject only to limitations found in the state constitution.

2. Confederation

Some colonial leaders had believed as early as the 1750s that independence would only be achievable through joint action by the colonies. Overall, a sense of unity among the colonies developed fairly slowly over the following decades. **Continental Congresses** convened in the 1770s to debate grievances against Britain and, where possible, to agree to collective action. But there was little sense that these Congresses were in charge of an independent government. As historian Gordon Wood explained, under the prevailing understanding "a state with more than one independent sovereign power within its boundaries was a violation of the unity of nature; it would be like a monster with more than one head, continually at war with itself, an absurd chaotic condition that could result only in the dissolution of the state."

The ad hoc Congresses of the late 1770s achieved a new measure of permanence under the Articles of Confederation and Perpetual Union, ratified in 1781. The Articles created a confederation of states whose joint business would be managed by a regularly-meeting entity known as a Congress. Unlike the sovereign states, who could do anything not prohibited by their constitutions, the Congress could do nothing unless authorized by the Articles. As explained in Article 2: "Each State retains its sovereignty, freedom and independence, and every power, jurisdiction, and right, which is not by this confederation expressly delegated to the United States, in Congress assembled."

■ TERMINOLOGY

CONTINENTAL CONGRESSES: For the Revolutionary generation, a "Congress" was a convention of delegates from independent governments. Today it might be called a summit meeting. The temporary nature of the Continental Congress can be seen in the closing paragraphs of the Declaration of Independence, which explained that the document was signed by "the Representatives of the united States of America, in General Congress, Assembled." Note how the word "united" was not capitalized. Not until The Articles of Confederation did the phrase "United States of America" become the official name of the nation.

In keeping with this vision of a confederation, the Articles gave the entity known as the "United States of America" little independent power. The Articles created no executive offices; instead, Congress appointed individuals to undertake specific tasks on its behalf, such as commanding the armed forces or negotiating treaties with foreign governments. Congress had no power to tax. To raise funds, it could politely request money from the states, which sometimes complied and sometimes did not. Each state had one vote in Congress. Ordinary actions could be taken if approved by a majority of voting states, but the most important actions (prosecuting the war effort and printing or borrowing money) required a supermajority of nine states, and any amendment to the Articles had to be unanimous. The unanimity requirement for amendments became a notorious stumbling block. In 1782, a proposal to amend the Articles to allow Congress to impose a 5% import tax failed because Rhode Island vetoed it. That state changed its mind when the proposal was floated again in 1786, but at that point New York single-handedly killed the proposal.

Comparison of Articles and State Constitutions

Articles of Confederation: What Congress May Do

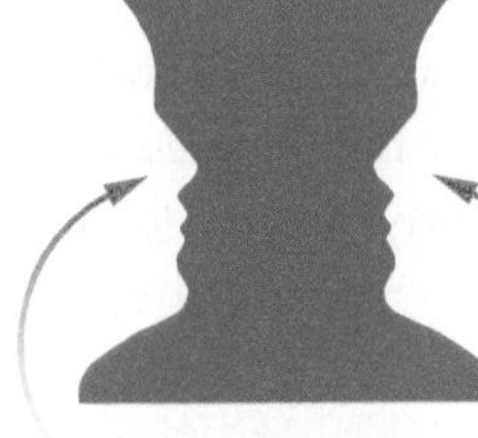

State Constitutions: What States May NOT Do

3. Reasons to Change the System

A chronic complaint under the Articles was that Congress accomplished little. Indeed, Congress frequently had to adjourn for lack of a quorum. Some prominent voices began to complain that America needed a more "energetic" government than the Articles could provide. The existing system seemed unable to respond to a number of worrisome problems.

Economic Problems. Generally speaking, the American economy was terrible in the 1780s. Part of the problem involved the money supply. Congress printed a national currency, but many people refused to accept it as payment. States began issuing their own paper currency, sometimes profligately. With a variety of competing currencies, some of them subject to sudden inflation, there was little certainty about the value of money. Another economic problem involved the national debt. Congress had borrowed heavily from Europe to finance the revolution, but Congress's lack of taxing power placed it in constant danger of a default, endangering the nation's credit for future loans. A third economic problem involved the lack of a coordinated trade policy, either internationally or among the states. Some states imposed tariffs on manufactured goods from Europe, while others kept their borders open—a combination that led to smuggling. States also engaged in protectionism against each other, erecting various trade barriers designed to benefit their internal industries at the expense of those in other states.

Political Problems. Most of the states were internally divided between camps that historians have labelled "conservatives" and "radicals." For conservatives, the war against Britain could best be termed the War of Independence. They wanted freedom from European control, but their vision for American society looked a lot like Britain, with political power concentrated among the wealthy. For radicals, the better term is Revolutionary War. The radicals saw independence from Britain as part of a larger project of broadening political freedoms for a wider swath of society.

As radicals and conservatives battled for political control of state houses during the 1780s, concern rose in many quarters that state governments were misbehaving. Where legislatures were controlled by conservatives, radicals believed that the state government was being structured for the sole benefit of the moneyed classes. Where legislatures were controlled by radicals, conservatives lamented that state government was favoring the debtor classes by enacting laws to forgive debts, confiscate property, and print too much money. In addition, state legislators generally had short terms in office, often for a single year. This meant that statutes—and even state constitutions—changed frequently, to the point where it became difficult to predict what the law would be from one year to the next.

Many people began to wonder if these problems reflected an excess of democracy. Legislatures that were too responsive to the popular passions of the majority could enact laws the minority considered tyrannical. The sharpest critics of state legislatures (who tended to be conservatives) fretted that states would descend into mob rule—or even that the experiment with representative democracy had failed.

Military Threats. The lack of effective national coordination placed the United States at military risk. England and France were drifting towards another of their periodic wars. If North America became one of the battlefronts (as it had during the French and Indian War of the 1750s and 1760s), the newly independent states might once again become colonies of the great powers of Europe. In addition, many states were at threat of armed conflict with Indians on their western frontiers, and Georgia shared a worrisome border with Spanish Florida. Despite all these foreign threats, the nation had no army. Washington's Continental Army that had won the war for independence had been disbanded, and the only operating military were local militias not under Congressional control.

Shays' Rebellion. The economic, political, and military dangers seemed to combine in Shays' Rebellion, an uprising in western Massachusetts that terrified leaders nationwide. Reacting to pressure from creditors in Boston who had been demanding repayment of loans to the state government, a series of conservative legislatures chose to raise revenue through new taxes and court fees. The taxes—especially land taxes—fell hardest on the rural poor as the economy worsened.

The state began to sell off farms and personal goods at sheriff's sales to recover unpaid taxes.

In late 1786, rebellions broke out in three western counties. Although they were not particularly well coordinated, the one led by Captain Daniel Shays had the highest profile. The rebels focused their attacks on courthouses to prevent them from carrying out foreclosures, but they also unsuccessfully attacked a federal arsenal in hopes of obtaining more weapons. The state was ill-equipped to deal with Shays' Rebellion. The governor called out the local county militias to combat it, but many of their members had already joined with Shays. Congress had no funds or troops to aid Massachusetts. Ultimately the rebellion was put down in February 1787 by an army privately funded by Boston merchants.

Shays' Rebellion was relatively small (around 4,000 people later acknowledged participation), unfocused, and would not likely have overturned the duly elected government of Massachusetts. Nonetheless, as a symbol of military vulnerability, economic weakness and political disarray, it caused nationwide fright. George Washington's military colleague Henry Lee fretted in a letter that the "malcontents" in Massachusetts had as their goals "the abolition of debts, the division of property, and re-union with Great Britain. . . . In one word my dear General, we are all in dire apprehension that a beginning of anarchy with all its calamities has approached."

B. The Constitutional Convention of 1787

Responding to the fears that the system faced collapse at the state and national levels, Congress in February 1787 called for a convention "for the sole and express purpose of revising the Articles of Confederation, and reporting to Congress and the several legislatures such alterations and provisions therein as shall . . . render the federal Constitution adequate to the exigencies of government and the preservation of the Union." The war hero **George Washington** agreed to preside over the convention, giving it instant credibility. The convention was held in Philadelphia that summer, in the same room where the Declaration of Independence had been debated.

The delegates included a concentration of national heroes, including the elder statesman Benjamin Franklin, who had been advocating independence since the 1750s. All were prosperous, literate, free White males. Many were lawyers, and most were well-versed in history and political philosophy. They included men who had served their states as governors, supreme court justices, and attorneys general. Others had served Congress as representatives, diplomats, or military leaders. Although they were capable of sophisticated discourse, they were no mere debating society. First and foremost, they were skilled politicians who advocated the positions they thought most favorable for themselves and their states. As a result, the US Constitution should not be viewed as holy writ, but as the product of hard-fought political compromise.

The convention met in strict secrecy. Confidentiality was important, because the delegates, inspired by a proposal masterminded by **James Madison**, had decided to deviate from the assignment given by Congress. Their recommendation would not be to revise the Articles of Confederation, but to scrap them in favor of a new system. If the delegates' task was to follow the instructions of Congress, they were unfaithful servants. But most delegates felt that they were convening not as agents of Congress, but as agents of the people of their states. The Declaration of Independence said that the people had the right to alter or abolish a dysfunctional government, so that is what the convention proposed.

1. Areas of Consensus

The delegates were able to reach rapid agreement on several basic principles.

a) Energetic National Government

On May 30, the third day of the convention, the delegates approved a resolution "that a national government ought to be established consisting of a supreme Legislative, Executive, and Judiciary." This resolution differed significantly from the theory behind the Articles of Confederation. There should be a "national government" (not a federation); it should be "supreme" (a core attribute of sovereignty); and it should have its own executive and judicial branches.

Consensus in favor of an energetic central government was easier to reach because almost none of the many people opposed to the idea were in the room. Some well-known patriots

BIOGRAPHY

As a Southerner commanding a mostly Northern army during the revolution, **GEORGE WASHINGTON** (1732–1799) earned nationwide respect. The founding generation admired him so much that many believed Washington could have been appointed King if he were not so committed to representative democracy. As President of the constitutional convention, Washington spoke little, but his mere presence contributed enormously to the convention's success. If the universally beloved General Washington thought a new constitution was a good idea, the proposal would be taken seriously.

JAMES MADISON (1751–1836) joined the independence movement as a young adult, but never saw combat because he stood only five-foot-four and weighed barely 100 pounds. After independence, Madison became active in Virginia politics, serving in the state legislature and later as part of Virginia's delegation to the Articles Congress. His impressive intellect, his ability to build coalitions, and his willingness to work harder than anyone else made him the most influential person at the convention of 1787. From this, he earned the nickname "The Father of the Constitution."

who opposed a central government (such as Patrick Henry) announced in advance that they would not attend. Of the two states that had notoriously prevented amendments to the Articles of Confederation, Rhode Island never sent a delegation to the constitutional convention, and New York's delegation often lacked a quorum, preventing it from voting. In the end, only a handful of people who were opposed to the central concept stayed with the convention to the bitter end.

b) State Sovereignty

There was no serious argument against the continued existence of states. Despite the suspicions that some delegates harbored against the existing state governments, they were by this time too politically entrenched to tamper with. This can be seen in the story of Alexander Hamilton's role in the convention. On June 18, he delivered a lengthy speech advocating that sovereignty be placed in a single national government, with states existing only as administrative subdivisions, much like British counties. Hamilton's proposal was so poorly received that he left the convention that week, returning only to sign the finished document in September.

By creating a national government that was "supreme" but comprised of states that retained their sovereignty, the delegates had designed an untried form of government. Madison later explained to the public that the new government was "part national" and "part **federal**." The national or central government would be supreme, but only within its areas of enumerated power. In all other areas, states could exercise their sovereignty to make whatever laws they wished. The most important power that states had but Congress lacked was known as *police power,* i.e., the power to enact laws for the health, safety, welfare, and morals of the community. The lack of federal police power remains a crucial difference between the two levels of government.

■ TERMINOLOGY

FEDERAL: The meaning of the word "federal" has shifted over time. As Madison used the term, a "federal" government was a (con)federation of independent states, the opposite of a "national" government. Today, the term "federal" most often refers to the national government created by the US Constitution. In some settings, the word "federal" refers to any system where multiple levels of government share sovereignty over the same territory.

c) Republicanism

There were two forms of government the delegates knew they did not want: hereditary monarchy and democracy. A monarchy—even a constitutional monarchy with significant powers placed in a parliament—was too prone to tyranny. Democracy—direct rule by the people—had the potential to be fickle, unstable, and equally tyrannical. An unjust law was unjust even if imposed by a majority, and if the majority consisted of selfish or uneducated people, the likelihood of unjust lawmaking would be even worse.

The preferred alternative was a republic—a representative democracy. In a republic, governmental decisions would be made by representatives selected by and accountable to the people. Once selected, these public servants were expected to exercise their best independent judgment, and not be obliged to enact a tyrannical proposal merely because a majority of the people was enamored of it. (The framers assumed there would be no organized political parties, a development that greatly affected the independence of representatives.) There would be two tricks to a successful republic: (a) mechanisms that would lead to selection of the most wise and virtuous public servants, and (b) incentives for those public servants to govern wisely, which would require an ideal combination of independence (freedom to pursue the public interest) and accountability to the people (to ensure that rulers did not become self-interested).

d) Separation of Powers

Although the legislature would be the most important ingredient of a successful republic, the delegates also wanted to place at least some powers outside the control of the legislature altogether. The philosophical preference for separation of powers was derived in significant part from the French Enlightenment philosopher Montesquieu, whose writings were widely respected in the colonies, especially among conservatives who feared the more radical state legislatures.

Putting judicial power beyond the reach of the legislature had been standard practice for centuries. The legislature should make the laws, but independent judges should decide whether laws had been broken in particular instances. A separately elected and **independent chief executive** was also considered an important check on legislative overreach. As with the legislature itself, the judicial and executive branches would require a good selection mechanism and the optimal balance of independence and accountability.

> ■ OBSERVATION
>
> **INDEPENDENT CHIEF EXECUTIVE:**
>
> Not all modern nations follow the American *presidential system* that separates the executive from the legislative branch. More popular is a *parliamentary system*, where the day-to-day administration of government is handled by a Prime Minister chosen by, and answerable to, the legislature. By avoiding the conflict or deadlock that can arise when a legislature and an independent President disagree over priorities, a parliamentary system makes it easier to enact and enforce laws that are preferred by the majority. Reasonable people have differed over whether that is a good or a bad thing.

2. Areas of Division and Compromise

In any negotiation, the devil is in the details. At the constitutional convention, three main topics proved to be especially contentious. The compromises reached on these topics have had lasting ramifications to the present day.

a) Representation in Congress

Madison and many others believed that a republic would be intrinsically illegitimate (and also likely to lose the respect of the populace) unless the legislature were apportioned according to population. Proportional representation was consistent with the view that the people of the United States formed a single political community for purposes of popular sovereignty. The alternative would continue the method of the Continental Congresses and the Articles, where each state had the same amount of representation. That approach was consistent with the view that each state was its own sovereign political community. But it also meant that a voter in a small state would have greater influence over the national legislature than a similarly situated voter in a large state.

The formula for representation was debated for weeks. At times it seemed likely to derail the effort altogether, with some of the more vociferous smaller states threatening to leave the convention. Some delegates argued that the small states' fear (that they would be the victims of legislation uniquely harmful to them) was more theoretical than real. According to Madison, "the States were divided into different interests not by their difference of size, but by other circumstances; the most material of which resulted partly from climate, but principally from their having or not having slaves. The great division of interests in the United States did not lie between the large and small States: it lay between the Northern and Southern." This reasoning did not satisfy the small states, who genuinely feared harm from a lack of influence.

The final resolution to this hard-fought debate was the "Connecticut Compromise," named after its proponent Roger Sherman of Connecticut. One house of the legislature would be apportioned by population, and the other by state. The small states were so insistent upon their equal representation in the Senate that Art. V of the Constitution forbids any future amendment that would reduce a state's equal suffrage in the Senate without its consent. Given the political reality that no small state would ever forfeit its **influence in the Senate**, the only way to create a national legislature with proportional representation in both houses would be to scrap the US Constitution in favor of an entirely new one.

OBSERVATION

INFLUENCE IN THE SENATE: According to the 2010 census, small states representing approximately 17% of the US population have enough votes in the Senate to defeat any bill.

For the Framers, apportioning the House of Representatives by population did not necessarily imply that the entire population would have the right to vote. No state had universal suffrage. Most followed some variation of the British tradition which gave the vote only to those who owned some minimum amount of property. Property qualifications for voting were justified in many ways, chief among them the widespread belief that the wealthy had better character than the poor. Other arguments were that landowners were more permanent and hence had a greater stake in the community; that they had a greater claim to representation since they were subject to more taxation; and that tenants could be easily manipulated into voting in their landlords' interests. Property qualifications were under challenge in some of the states, but at the time of the convention there was no uniformity among states in this regard. Since the convention was unlikely to agree on a national standard for voting qualifications, it was decided not to impose one. People could vote for the US House of Representatives if they could vote for the equivalent house of the state legislature. Art. I, § 2, cl. 1.

Aside from property qualifications, the states tended to have similar voter eligibility laws that reliably denied the right to vote to most of the population.

Women. Although women were understood to be citizens, the bundle of legal rules known as *coverture* dictated that a married woman's legal personhood was covered by that of her husband. A husband was analogous to a sovereign of the household, supreme over all others. It would violate the husband's domestic sovereignty for a wife to own property, enter into contracts, commence litigation, or decide where the family would live. All of this meant that a wife could not vote. To begin with, she owned no property. More to the point, women were assumed to be not intellectually capable of the task. Because it was assumed that wives would vote as their husbands dictated, allowing them to vote would effectively give married men more votes than single men. Besides, the theory went, the husband would give proper weight to the interests of the wife when casting his own vote.

With that said, the original US Constitution was predominantly gender neutral. Other than using the pronoun "he" to refer to office holders such as the President, it said nothing specific about sex, and no constitutional rights were expressly limited to men. As for voting, the US Constitution refers to voters as "electors," who could in theory be of any sex if state law allowed it. In the early republic only New Jersey allowed (unmarried, property-owning) women to vote, but it disenfranchised them in an 1807 statute that limited the vote to "free, white, male citizens."

People with Mental Disabilities. As a practical result of the property qualification, or by specific statute, those considered to be "idiots" or "insane" were not allowed to vote.

Minors. Then as now, only adults had the vote. Most states considered 21 to be the minimum voting age, although some adult rights—such as the right to marry—could be exercised by younger people.

Non-Citizens. Then as now, states tended not to allow resident aliens to vote in state elections.

Indigenous People. Europeans had been able to settle North America so rapidly largely because the communicable diseases they brought with them wiped out vast numbers of Native Americans. By the 1780s, most of the surviving Indians lived west of the areas of European settlement; they were considered aliens without voting rights. Those Indians who had assimilated into the European communities were treated as citizens. For purposes of apportioning the House of Representatives, the US Constitution excluded from the census all "**Indians not taxed**"—that is, those not assimilated into White communities. See Art. I, § 2, cl. 3 & Fourteenth Amendment, § 2.

HISTORY

INDIANS NOT TAXED: After Congress in 1924 made all Indians citizens of the United States, there are no longer any "Indians not taxed." *Squire v. Capoeman*, 351 U.S. 1 (1956).

Felons. The colonies followed British law, where for centuries serious crimes not punishable by death were subject to the sentence of "civil death" or outlawry. Civil death entailed the loss of almost all legal rights, including all political rights. The wise outlaw would simply leave the country in hopes of starting fresh somewhere else. Beginning in the 1790s, states began to write explicit limitations against voting by felons into their state constitutions. In some states, voting rights could be restored after release, but in most the disqualification was permanent.

Indentured Servants. Although the practice died out in the early 19th century, many young European males came to North America as indentured servants, who owed a term of labor (typically seven years) to their masters. Indentured servants were not considered free until their terms of labor expired, and hence they were not allowed to vote in any state. Nonetheless, the US Constitution included them in the census for purposes of calculating representation in the House. Art. I, § 2, cl. 3 (in the representation formula, "free persons" would include "those bound to service for a term of years").

Slaves. No state allowed slaves to vote. States varied as to whether they gave the vote to free Black people. New Hampshire, Massachusetts, New York, New Jersey, and North Carolina allowed them to vote, while other states did not.

b) Slavery

Almost 20% of the total population of the colonies were slaves of African descent. At independence, **slavery existed in all of the states**, but it was far more prevalent in the South. Although some delegates to the constitutional convention disliked slavery, no widespread abolitionist movement existed at the time, and there was never any serious consideration of forbidding slavery at a national level. The choice to continue or abolish slavery was a matter for state law. Nonetheless, the delegates were keenly aware that slavery represented the largest difference between North and South. The Southern delegates were extremely hard bargainers when it came to any proposal that might hinder their states' ability to maintain slavery, frequently threatening to walk out over the issue.

■ HISTORY

SLAVERY EXISTED IN ALL OF THE STATES: Pennsylvania was the first state to pass abolition legislation in 1780, in the form of a gradual emancipation law.
In 1783, Massachusetts became the first state to abolish slavery altogether, as a result of a court opinion holding that slavery violated the state constitution's statement that "all men are created free and equal."
The remaining Northern states adopted either gradual or immediate emancipation by 1804.

As written, the US Constitution did not contain the words "slave" or "slavery." Several provisions, however, make sense only in the context of slavery.

The Three Fifths Clause. Since the House was to have proportional representation, the convention needed to decide whether its seats would be allocated according to a state's total population or its voting population. A formula based on total population would give the voters in slave states a comparatively greater voice in the House, because fewer voters would have the power to elect the same number of representatives. For Southern delegates, this result seemed entirely just. In the aggregate, the Southern states had a smaller voting population than the North, so they wanted extra representation to ensure that their interests would not be routinely outvoted in the House. In addition, all states had some nonvoters (women, children, felons, etc.), and there was no reason for different treatment of the nonvoters who happened to be slaves. For the Northern delegates, the slave states were unjustly seeking greater representation simply because they happened to own a certain type of property. If a slave owner gets extra representation for his property, Elbridge Gerry of Massachusetts asked sarcastically, then why not give a Northern farmer extra representation for his horses and oxen?

Competing Formulas for Representation in the House

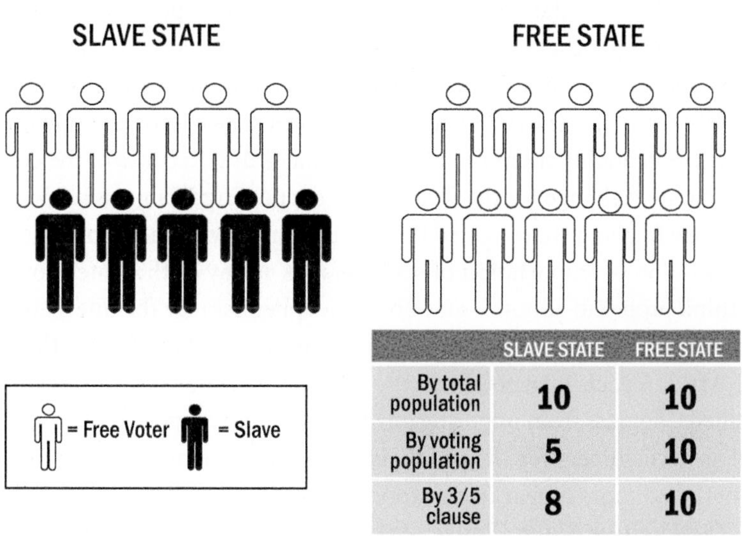

	SLAVE STATE	FREE STATE
By total population	10	10
By voting population	5	10
By 3/5 clause	8	10

The final resolution of this debate was the infamous Three Fifths Clause, which allocated seats in the House on a formula that counted "the whole number of free persons" (plus indentured servants but minus Indians not taxed) plus "three fifths of all other persons"—where the "other persons" were slaves. Art. I, § 2, cl. 3. The Three Fifths Clause did not mean that the Framers viewed slaves as three fifths of a person. For purposes of voting, they were zero fifths of a person. Or perhaps less, since they gave a representational bonus of three fifths of a person to their masters. As historian Richard Beeman noted:

> In reviewing the controversy over the three-fifths clause, one comes away with a depressing sense of the near-total absence of anything resembling a moral dimension to the debate. The three-fifths compromise was, fundamentally,

> about states' individual interests, not the morality of slavery. Those few Northerners . . . who voiced unhappiness with the idea of counting the slave population in apportioning representation did so either out of a fear that Northern interests were being sacrificed to those of the South or . . . the "disgust" that their white constituents may have felt about being considered even in the same category as slaves. . . . That uneasiness was generated at least as much by a deeply seated racism as by any humanitarian concern about the plight of enslaved Africans.

Protection for the International Slave Trade. The slave states with the strongest demand for imported slaves worried that Congress could use its power over international commerce to ban the slave trade, or use its taxing power to heavily tax imported slaves. (Although there was no significant abolitionist movement at the time of the convention, moral objections to the international slave trade were in the air. Less nobly, some states with large slave populations opposed the international slave trade in hopes they could profit from selling slaves domestically.) Protections for the international slave trade ultimately entered the Constitution as the result of an elaborate horse trade. In general, Northern states desired national power to regulate the economy more than Southern states did. Records of the convention reveal that in exchange for the Deep South supporting Congressional commerce power, New England states agreed that the national government could not prohibit "the migration or importation of such persons as any of the states now existing shall think proper to admit"—an elaborate euphemism for the international slave trade—before 1808, or at any time impose an import tax of more than $10 per slave. Art. I, § 9, cl. 1. (Another part of this bargain was Art. I, § 9, cl. 5, which prevented Congress from imposing any taxes on goods exported from states. Since the biggest customers for the products of Southern plantations were in Europe, the South had more to fear from export taxes.)

The Fugitive Slave Clause. Art. IV, § 2, cl. 2 obliged states to extradite fugitives from justice back to the states from which they had escaped. Late in the convention, with little discussion, the delegates added a parallel provision for the return of fugitive slaves—who were described as "person[s] held to service or labor in one state, under the laws thereof." Art. IV, § 2, cl. 3.

Proportionality of Direct Taxes. Southern states worried that a future abolition-minded Congress might impose an economically crushing tax on the ownership of slaves. To protect against this, the Constitution forbids any federal "**capitation** or other direct tax" unless it is "in proportion to the census." Art. I, § 9, cl. 4. A similar formula appears in Art. I, § 2, cl. 3, in the same sentence that contains the Three Fifths Clause. As a result, if the federal government imposed a nationwide tax of $1

■ TERMINOLOGY

CAPITATION: A capitation is a flat tax per person. It is also known as a "head tax," reflecting its origins in the Latin word *caput* (head), which also gives us the phrase *per capita*.

per person nationwide, it could tax no more than $0.60 per slave—and it could not tax slaves at all unless it was willing to tax all free persons. Artfully, the tax proportionality provisions protected slavery without including any euphemisms for slaves at all. Nonetheless, the text of the Constitution provides a subtle clue that this limitation on the tax power served slaveholders' interests: Art. V states that neither the tax proportionality requirement nor the protection of the international slave trade could be amended before 1808. The Framers considered these two concepts closely linked.

c) Choosing the President

Devising a method to choose the President proved to be one of the more frustrating tasks at the convention. Everyone knew that the universally respected George Washington would be the unanimous choice for the first president, but how should his successors be chosen? There was a general consensus against a nationwide popular election, since it might give the office to a demagogue who could skillfully manipulate mass opinion. The search for an alternative brought out rivalries between the big and small states, and the Northern and Southern states. The convention eventually considered and rejected dozens of motions on the subject of Presidential selection before finally settling on the Electoral College. Under that system, each state would choose "electors"—wise people whose job it would be to select the President. Art. II, § 1, cl. 2. After choosing the President, the Electoral College would disband, ensuring Presidential independence.

The tussles over representation in Congress repeated themselves with regard to representation in the Electoral College. The ultimate decision was that each state would have a number of electors equal to the sum of their senators plus their representatives. Art. II, § 1, cl. 2. This meant the Electoral College would not have proportional representation, creating the risk that its results would **not match the national vote**. The divergence between the Electoral College and the popular vote follows predictable patterns. Small-population states have extra influence, as they do in the Senate. While the Three Fifths Clause existed, voters in slave states would have extra influence, as they did in the House. As a result, between the founding and the Civil War, eight out of twelve Presidents—who held office for forty-nine of the nation's first sixty-one years—were slaveholders.

■ HISTORY

NOT MATCH THE NATIONAL VOTE: On five occasions, the presidential candidate receiving the most popular votes did not receive the most votes in the Electoral College: in 1824 (Andrew Jackson over John Quincy Adams); 1876 (Rutherford B. Hayes over Samuel Tilden); 1888 (Benjamin Harrison over Grover Cleveland); 2000 (George W. Bush over Al Gore); and 2016 (Donald Trump over Hillary Clinton).

C. A Tour of the 1787 Constitution

There is no substitute for reading the Constitution for yourself. This section is intended to help you work through the document, focusing on the parts that have proven (in hindsight) to be the more important features of the system.

Preamble

The Preamble explains why the Constitution was established: "to form a more perfect union, establish justice, insure domestic tranquility, provide for the common defense, promote the general welfare, and secure the blessings of liberty to ourselves and our posterity." It also says who established it: "We the people of the United States." In these famous opening words, the Preamble reflects the notion of popular sovereignty previously expressed in the Declaration of Independence.

The Preamble was written by Gouverneur Morris, as part of the Committee of Style that convened after the hardest negotiations had finished. Courts have never viewed the Preamble as a source of power for the federal government (i.e., it does not enumerate a power to "promote the general welfare"). At most, the Preamble has been used as a reference point when interpreting the operative language of the Constitution.

BIOGRAPHY

A child prodigy born to an influential New York family, **GOUVERNEUR MORRIS** (1752–1816) graduated from college at age 16 and became a lawyer at age 19. Although politically conservative, he ardently supported the independence movement. He was a signer of the Articles of Confederation, and during the war he helped preserve badly needed funding for George Washington's army. In 1787, Morris was the most frequent speaker at the Constitutional Convention, typically arguing in favor of stronger national powers (such as James Madison's never-adopted proposal for Congressional veto power over state laws). He was the only delegate to speak openly against slavery during the Convention, once calling it a "nefarious" institution "in defiance of the most sacred laws of humanity" and "the curse of heaven on the states where it prevailed."

Article I: The Legislature

Substance of Legislation. Congress is given "all legislative powers herein granted." Art. I, § 1. The term "herein granted" signals that Congress does not have "all" legislative powers the way an absolute sovereign would.

Most of the enumerated powers are found in Art. I, § 8, which deserves careful study. It begins with the phrase "The Congress shall have power. . ." A few other passages in the Constitution also state that Congress "shall have power" to do certain things, or that it "may" or "shall" do certain things. See Art. III, § 3, cl. 2; Art. IV, §§ 1, 3–4; and Art. V. Many of the amendments from the Thirteenth onward also contain enumerated powers. Notice the absence of "police power" (the power to enact laws for the health, safety, welfare, and morals of the community) or any generalized power to enact laws that seem like a good idea.

Art. I, § 9 is the flipside of § 8, because it identifies categories of laws that Congress cannot pass. Many of the clauses within Art. I, § 9 describe economic regulations that are off limits, such as export taxes or preferences for the ports of a single state. Others involve individual rights, such as the writ of habeas corpus (freeing a person from custody if they have not been duly tried and convicted); the ban on *ex post facto* laws (laws punishing conduct that was lawful when it occurred); the ban on bills of attainder (laws declaring persons guilty of crimes and imposing punishment without trial); and the ban on titles of nobility.

Art. I, § 10 identifies various laws that the states cannot pass. Many of these involve areas that are better handled at the national level, such as establishing a national monetary system and pursuing international diplomacy and warfare. Others are laws violating individual rights that irresponsible state legislatures had enacted under the Articles of Confederation, such as *ex post facto* laws, bills of attainder, and laws "impairing the obligation of contracts" (i.e., laws that had erased debts or made them more difficult to collect). Note how some of the enumerated powers of Congress in Art. I, § 8 are paired with prohibitions on similar state powers in Art. I, § 10, making doubly clear that certain powers are reserved to the federal government. For example, Congress may coin money, but States may not. Congress may create a system of bankruptcy, but states may not impair the obligation of contracts. Congress may raise and maintain an army and navy, but states may not "keep troops, or ships of war in times of peace."

Procedure for Legislation. The Congress is bicameral, with a House of Representatives chosen through election, Art. I, § 2, cl. 1, and a Senate appointed by state legislatures, Art. I, § 3, cl. 1. Not until the 17th Amendment (ratified 1913) were Senators directly elected. To become a law, a bill must pass both houses of Congress and be signed by the President, although if the President refuses to sign, it will become law if two-thirds majorities of both houses vote to override the veto. Art. I, § 7, cl. 2. The Framers saw divided legislative power as a protection against bad laws. It would be difficult for an oppressive or tyrannical law to overcome a series of gatekeepers, each of whom is responsible to a different constituency. To be enforced, a law must (a) gain majority support in a House where every member represents a different district; (b) gain majority support in a Senate where every member is selected by a state legislature; (c) be signed by a President who is accountable to the entire nation, and (d) be upheld as constitutional by federal judges who serve for life and will only be removed through death, retirement, or impeachment.

Article II: The Executive Branch

The President controls "the executive power." Art. II, § 1, cl. 1. Sections 2 and 3 of Art. II describe some attributes of the executive power more precisely, such as command of the military; appointment of judges, ambassadors, and other federal officers; negotiation of treaties; and granting of reprieves and pardons to federal prisoners. As a general matter, the President "shall take care that the laws be faithfully executed." Art. II, § 3. Beyond this, the Constitution provides little detail about the President's powers or duties.

Presidents and other officers of the United States, including federal judges, may be removed from office for "treason, bribery, or other high crimes and misdemeanors." Art. II, § 4. Removal occurs only if the official is impeached (charged) by the House of Representatives, Art. I, § 2, cl. 5, and convicted by two thirds of the Senate, Art. I, § 3, cl. 5. Impeachment was considered a humane improvement over the methods historically used in Britain to remove the King's highest officers, which involved bills of attainder, high-profile treason trials of questionable fairness, and death sentences.

Article III: The Judicial Branch

"The judicial power" is vested in one Supreme Court and "in such inferior courts as the Congress may from time to time ordain and establish." Art. III, § 1. (Congress has a corresponding enumerated power "to constitute tribunals inferior to the Supreme Court." Art. I, § 8, cl. 9.) The convention did not reach agreement on the need for federal trial courts; the competing option was for all federal laws to be enforced in state courts, subject to review by the US Supreme Court. Article III allows Congress to make that choice; ever since the first Congress in 1789 it has chosen to operate federal trial courts.

Just as Congress has enumerated powers, federal courts have enumerated subject matter jurisdiction. Art. III, § 2, cl. 1. The scope of federal subject matter jurisdiction tends to be studied in Civil Procedure, Jurisdiction, and Federal Courts.

The Constitution gives federal judges an extraordinary amount of independence. Unlike members of Congress and the President who face periodic elections, judges "shall hold their offices during good behaviour," Art. III, § 1, which has been interpreted to mean that they may be removed only through the impeachment process from Art. II, § 4. In addition, judicial salaries "shall not be diminished during the continuance in office," Art. III, § 1, to ensure that the legislature cannot control judicial rulings by tampering with judges' paychecks.

Finally, Art. III requires some protections for criminal defendants accused of violating federal law. These include a right to a local jury trial, Art. III, § 2, cl. 3, and significant limits on treason prosecutions, Art. III, § 3.

Article IV: Interactions Among States

Art. IV deals with the relationships among states, with an eye towards combining them into a working whole. States are to give "full faith and credit" to official records of other states. Art. IV, § 1. In its most common application, this means that a creditor who obtains a judgment on a debt from a court in one state may collect on that judgment in another state where the debtor holds assets.

States are not to discriminate against citizens of other states. Instead, out-of-state citizens are "entitled to all privileges and immunities of citizens [of that state]." Art. IV, § 2, cl. 1. This means, among other things, that citizens of one state may own property, operate businesses, or commence litigation in other states.

States are obliged to extradite fugitive criminals to the states where they face charges. Art. IV, § 2, cl. 2. Before slavery was abolished, states also had obligations to return fugitive slaves to the states from which they had fled. Art. IV, § 2, cl. 3.

Finally, Art. IV, § 3 gives Congress control over territories not yet organized as states, removing a probable source of contention and jealousy between states. Congress is also to contribute to the justice and domestic tranquility of the states by guaranteeing to them "a republican form of government," protecting them against invasion, and (if requested by the states) protecting them against "domestic violence." Art. IV, § 4.

Article V: Amendments

The US Constitution was designed to be easier to amend than the Articles of Confederation, although a high degree of consensus is still required for any changes. Amendments require two-thirds approval of both houses of Congress, followed by ratification by three-fourths of the states. Although not as extreme as the single-state veto that was possible under the Articles, the Art. V formula gives **states with small populations** a disproportionate ability to block amendments, since they have equal representation in the Senate notwithstanding population, and an equal voice in the state ratification process.

> ■ OBSERVATION
>
> **STATES WITH SMALL POPULATIONS:** With 50 states in today's Union, it takes 38 states to ratify a constitutional amendment. This means 13 states voting not to ratify will defeat an amendment—and according to the 2010 census, the smallest 13 states contain 4.4% of the total US population.

Article VI: Miscellaneous Provisions

Art. VI gathers provisions that do not fit neatly elsewhere. The most important of these declares that the US Constitution, laws enacted by the US Congress, and treaties negotiated by the President and ratified by the Senate "shall be the supreme law of the land." Art. VI, § 2. Federal law would control in both federal and state courts, "any thing in the constitution or laws of any state to the contrary notwithstanding." *Id.*

Showing the Framer's concern over the nation's creditworthiness, the new government would honor the debts accrued by Congress under the Articles. Art. VI, § 1. Also, people of any religion could hold office in the federal government, contrary to the practices in some of the states. Art. VI, § 3.

Article VII: Ratification Procedure

The Framers predicted that if unanimous approval of the states were required, the new Constitution would never take effect. There were many possible holdouts, most likely Rhode Island, which had sent no delegates to the constitutional convention. Ratification by a supermajority of nine out of thirteen states was deemed sufficient.

Moreover, ratification would not be channeled through the state legislatures (many of which were not trusted by the Framers). Under the theory of popular sovereignty, the people, not their public servants, had authority to alter or abolish governments. Each state was to convene a ratifying convention as the means to ascertain the will of the people in each state. Each state could choose its own method for staffing the convention, although in practice all of the ratifying conventions consisted of propertied free White males.

D. Ratification Conventions and the Bill of Rights

Ratification Conventions Begin. After the Framers signed the proposed Constitution on September 17, 1787, George Washington prepared a cover letter to the Articles Congress, explaining what the convention had done. His transmittal letter emphasized two things. First, the nation required a stronger central government, even if that meant the states would have less power than before. Second, Washington warned Congress not to tinker with the many compromises that had been hammered out during the convention.

The Articles Congress took Washington's hints, and relayed the proposed Constitution to the states without comment. By early January 1788, five ratification conventions had been held. Delaware, New Jersey, and Georgia ratified unanimously, Pennsylvania by a two-to-one margin, and Connecticut by a three-to-one margin. But the Massachusetts convention in February ratified by a narrow vote of 187 to 168. Opponents of the Constitution were becoming better organized, and ratification by nine states was not assured. Moreover, it was widely understood that Virginia and New York (the largest and most prosperous states) would need to ratify for the new government to have any chance for success.

The chief argument against the Constitution was simply that it would vest too much power in a central government. Depending on where you sat, that government ran the risk of being dominated by the wrong states. Besides, large powerful governments tended to be tyrannical, from the Roman Empire to the

British. The colonists had gone to war to be free of domination by a distant central government that was disdainful of local concerns; why should citizens of newly independent states seek to reconstruct a similar relationship? In **The Federalist** #10, James Madison made a clever counterargument. A properly structured large government would actually be *less* oppressive, he argued, because it would be harder for self-interested factions to dominate a diverse national legislature, as compared to a smaller and more localized legislature.

■ HISTORY

THE FEDERALIST: To build public support for the Constitution in New York, Madison—along with Alexander Hamilton and John Jay—published a series of pro-ratification articles under the pseudonym "Publius" in early 1788. They titled these papers *The Federalist,* even though their opponents believed that the proposed Constitution was too national and not federal enough. The name stuck. Those favoring the new Constitution became known as federalists, and its opponents anti-federalists. Although they were not the only publication circulated at the time, *The Federalist Papers* have since come to be regarded as a leading explanation of the philosophy and methods of the US Constitution. Meanwhile, articles published under pseudonyms including "Brutus," "Centinel" and "A Federal Farmer" opposed ratification. Historians later collected these writings into a set of *Anti-Federalist Papers*.

The Debate over A Bill of Rights. As the debates continued in the spring and summer of 1788, the most politically powerful argument against the proposed Constitution was its lack of a bill of rights. For example, most state constitutions protected citizens' freedom of speech, while the proposed Constitution explicitly protected only the speech and debate of members of Congress. Art. I, § 6, cl. 1. Congress would be able to engage in censorship one way or another, given its powers to tax, to regulate commerce, and to enact laws that were "necessary and proper" for carrying the other powers into effect.

Federal Government Under The Constitution (1787) and The Bill of Rights (1791)

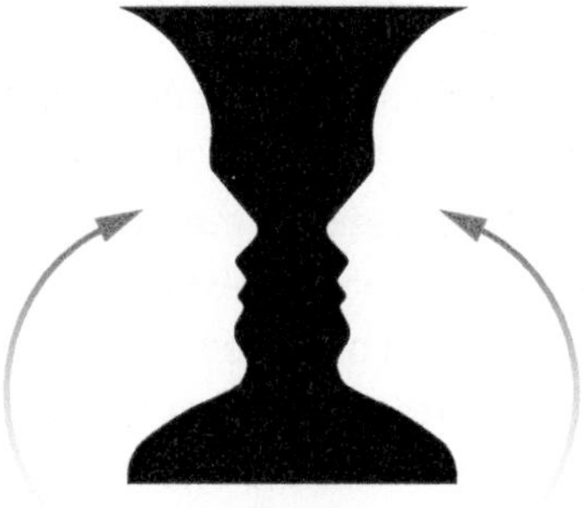

Limits
What Federal Government May NOT Do

Defenders of the Constitution argued that enumerated rights were simply not necessary. Oppressive national laws would not be passed, because they were not within the federal government's enumerated powers, and because the lawmaking process was divided among gatekeepers who could squelch oppressive proposals. Moreover, no list of rights could ever be complete. If a constitution expressly protected some list of enumerated rights, this would imply that all other rights were not protected. The Federalist arguments against a bill of rights had some logical coherence, but they could not explain why the Constitution *already* included some protections for individual rights, as found in Art. I, §§ 9–10, in Art. III, § 3, and Art. VI, § 3.

As the spring of 1788 wore on, Federalists realized that the absence of a federal bill of rights was a political liability. In response, they promised that once the Constitution was adopted, the first order of business would be to amend it to add a bill of rights. This proved to be a winning approach.

Ratification and Amendment. With ratification by Maryland, South Carolina, and New Hampshire by June 1788, the requisite nine states had approved the Constitution. Virginia and New York ratified during the summer, although the votes were close: 89 to 79 in Virginia, and 30 to 27 in New York. With eleven states on board, the new government was formed. The first Congressional elections were held in late 1788, and the first Congress convened in April 1789. As predicted, George Washington was unanimously elected President by the first Electoral College. The remaining states finally ratified after the new government was up and running: North Carolina in November 1789 and Rhode Island in May 1790. Wary to the end, the Rhode Island convention ratified by a narrow vote of 34 to 32.

The first Congress began the promised amendment process in 1789, culminating in ten amendments ratified in 1791. James Madison, now a representative from Virginia, was in charge of drafting. To deal with the problem that any list of rights would inevitably be incomplete, he proposed the text that became the Ninth Amendment: "The enumeration in this Constitution, of certain rights, shall not be construed to deny or disparage others retained by the people." Responding to requests for a clearer statement that states remained sovereign in areas not controlled by the supreme federal government, Madison included what became **the Tenth Amendment**: "The powers not delegated to the United States by the Constitution, nor prohibited by it to the States, are reserved to the States respectively, or to the people."

When presenting the proposed Bill of Rights to Congress, Madison observed a potential problem: it could be ignored by any majority with enough political power. For Madison, this was a serious problem that could ultimately be prevented only by genuine popular commitment to individual rights.

> It may be thought all paper barriers against the power of the community are too weak to be worthy of attention. I am sensible they are not so strong as to satisfy gentlemen of every description who have seen and examined thoroughly the texture of such a defense; yet, as [written descriptions of protected rights] have a tendency to impress some degree of respect for them, to establish the public opinion in their favor, and rouse the attention of the whole community, it may be one means to control the majority from those acts to which they might be otherwise inclined.

■ HISTORY

THE TENTH AMENDMENT: Madison told Congress that the Tenth Amendment "may be deemed unnecessary; but there can be no harm in making such a declaration" since the enumeration of federal powers in the original Constitution meant the same thing. Unlike the Articles of Confederation, which said Congress had only those powers "expressly delegated to the United States," the Tenth Amendment omits the word "expressly."

Madison's statement echoed a line attributed to Benjamin Franklin at the close of the constitutional convention. Franklin was asked by the Philadelphian Elizabeth Powel what sort of government the convention had designed. "A republic," replied Franklin, "if you can keep it."

Cartoon (c) 2005 Ruben Bolling; tomthedancingbug.com

E. Is the Written Constitution Complete? *Calder v. Bull*

The United States now had a written constitution. But as seen in the public debate over the need for a national Bill of Rights, questions remained over how complete any written constitution could ever be. Perhaps it omitted important rights or beneficial powers. When unforeseen circumstances arise (as they always do), could a government actually function if it is limited to the contents of a short document written by committee in a single summer?

The question is often framed as a conflict between *positive law* and *natural law.* Positive law refers to rules created by governing officials, nowadays in the form of written codes, statutes, or regulations. Natural law refers to rules that are understood to be beyond the control of mere officeholders: elemental principles that were unwritten but that nonetheless could be relied upon to justify political actions or judicial decisions. Those who adhere to natural law consider it to be superior to positive law.

Debates over the proper role for natural law have recurred in one form or another throughout American constitutional history. An early example is *Calder v. Bull*, 3 U.S. 386 (1798), a dispute over a Connecticut statute that retroactively expanded the time available to challenge a probate court ruling. The legal question was whether the statute was an *ex post facto* law forbidden by Art. I, § 10. The US Supreme Court concluded that it was not. In the process of deciding that question, an illuminating difference of opinion arose in dicta.

The lead opinion of Justice Samuel Chase suggested that state *ex post facto* laws were forbidden not only because of Art. I, § 10, but because of "the very nature of our free Republican governments."

> I cannot subscribe to the omnipotence of a State legislature, or that it is absolute and without control; although its authority should not be expressly restrained by the Constitution, or fundamental law, of the State. The people of the United States erected their Constitutions, or forms of government, to establish justice, to promote the general welfare, to secure the blessings of liberty; and to protect their persons and property from violence. . . There are acts which the federal, or State, legislature cannot do, without exceeding their authority. There are certain vital principles in our free republican governments, which will determine and overrule an apparent and flagrant abuse of legislative power; as to authorize manifest injustice by positive law; or to take away that security for personal liberty, or private property, for the protection whereof of the government was established.

■ OBSERVATION

A FEW INSTANCES: Several of the examples offered by Justice Chase had been used for centuries in British law as examples of legislation that would violate "the law of the land" (the term used in the Magna Carta of 1215) or that are undertaken "without due process of law" (a term in use since the 1300s). See Ch. 19.A.

> An act of the Legislature (for I cannot call it a law) contrary to the great first principles of the social compact cannot be considered a rightful exercise of legislative authority. The obligation of a law, in governments established on express compact and on republican principles, must be determined by the nature of the power on which it is founded. **A few instances** will suffice to explain what I mean: a law that punished a citizen for an innocent action, or, in other words, for an act which, when done, was in violation, of no existing law; a law that destroys, or impairs, the lawful private contracts of citizens; a law that makes a man a judge in his own cause; or a law that takes property from A and gives it to B. It is against all reason and justice, for a people to entrust a Legislature with such powers; and, therefore, it cannot be presumed that they have done it.

> The genius, the nature, and the spirit, of our State governments, amount to a prohibition of such acts of legislation; and the general principles of law and reason forbid them. The legislature may enjoin, permit, forbid, and punish; they may declare new crimes; and establish rules of conduct for all its citizens in future cases; they may command what is right, and prohibit what is wrong; but they cannot change innocence into guilt; or punish innocence as a crime; or violate the right of an antecedent lawful private contract; or the right of private property. To maintain that our federal, or State, legislature possesses such powers if they had not been expressly restrained would, in my opinion, be a political heresy, altogether inadmissible in our free republican governments.

In contrast, Justice Iredell's concurrence asserted that limits on government arose solely from constitutional text.

> [If] a government, composed of legislative, executive and judicial departments, were established by a constitution which imposed no limits on the legislative power, the consequence would inevitably be that whatever the legislative power chose to enact would be lawfully enacted, and the judicial power could never interpose to pronounce it void. It is true, that some speculative jurists have held that a legislative act against natural justice must, in itself, be void; but I cannot think that, under such a government, any court of justice would possess a power to declare it so. Sir William Blackstone, having put the strong case of an act of Parliament which should authorise a man to try his own cause, explicitly adds, that even in that case, "there is no Court that has power to defeat the intent of the Legislature, when couched in such evident and express words, as leave no doubt whether it was the intent of the Legislature, or no."
>
> In order, therefore, to guard against so great an evil, it has been the policy of all the American states, which have individually framed their state constitutions since the revolution, and of the people of the United States, when they framed the federal Constitution, to define with precision the objects of the legislative power and to restrain its exercise within marked and settled boundaries. If any act of Congress, or of the legislature of a state, violates those constitutional provisions, it is unquestionably void; though, I admit, that as the authority to declare it void is of a delicate and awful nature, the Court will never resort to that authority but in a clear and urgent case. If, on the other hand, the legislature of the Union, or the legislature of any member of the Union, shall pass a law within the general scope of their constitutional power, the Court cannot pronounce it to be void merely because it is, in their judgment, contrary to the principles of natural justice. The ideas of natural justice are regulated by no fixed standard: the ablest and the purest men have differed upon the subject; and all that the Court could properly say, in such an event, would be that the Legislature (possessed of an equal right of opinion) had passed an act which, in the opinion of the judges, was inconsistent with the abstract principles of natural justice.

flashforward

The Future of Natural Law. Justice Chase's approach—a direct appeal to a natural law more powerful than any written constitution—is obsolete. The Supremacy Clause of Art. VI, § 2 declares that the Constitution "shall be the supreme law of the land," not subordinate to anything else, including natural law. The legal realists of the early 20th century, led by Justice Oliver Wendell Holmes, argued in essence that all law is positive law: created, implemented, and changeable by living people. If law is what people say it is, then there is no natural law.

Nonetheless, the rhetoric of natural law still echoes in modern debates about judicial protection for unenumerated rights. Modern-day judges are unlikely to rely on what they consider to be "natural law," but they often note that the text of the Constitution itself indicates that there is to be protection for some unwritten rights. Most prominently, the government is forbidden to deprive people of "liberty" without due process of law. Since "liberty" is not defined, it may be necessary to consider sources outside the text of the Constitution to decide which freedoms count as protected "liberties." Similarly, the Ninth Amendment declares that the enumeration of some rights in the text should not be construed to disparage other (unnamed) rights "retained by the people." See Ch. 19.

Chapter Recap

A. The Constitution was the result of political compromise and intense negotiation.

B. The Constitution was written to create a national government that would be more "energetic" than a mere confederation of sovereign states, and be supreme over them. The new government would take the form of a republic with separation of powers.

C. The states would nonetheless continue to exist as sovereign entities, with power to enact any laws not forbidden by state or federal constitutions. By contrast, the federal government would have power to act only in those areas authorized by the US Constitution. The federal government's enumerated powers did not include a general police power.

D. The Constitution was quickly amended to add a Bill of Rights, enumerating a set of individual rights against abridgment by the federal government.

E. Debate continues over whether the Constitution requires the government to respect unenumerated rights.

CHAPTER 4

Judicial Review

Art. VI, § 3 requires legislators, executive officers, and judges (at both the state and federal levels) to be bound by oath or affirmation to support the US Constitution. Even if we assume utmost good faith from all of them, differences of opinion may arise about what the Constitution allows. How are these disagreements resolved?

In the context of enacting federal statutes, the Constitution provides a method of political resolution. If a majority of either house of Congress thinks a bill is unconstitutional, it will be voted down—regardless of the opinions of the other chamber, the President, or the Supreme Court. In effect, the system gives the last word on constitutionality to the house of Congress with the greatest objections. If the President thinks a bill that passed both houses of Congress is unconstitutional, it will be vetoed—regardless of the opinions of Congress or the Supreme Court. In this context, the system gives the last word on constitutionality to the President (subject to override). However, if a bill makes it through the political branches and then becomes a subject for litigation, our current system gives the last word to the judiciary. This is often phrased as the power of *judicial review*: the power of judges to review statutes and executive actions to decide if they are constitutional.

In theory, at least, once the Supreme Court announces its reasons for invalidating a statute or executive action, the other branches are expected to act accordingly in the future, regardless of their prior opinions about what the Constitution allows. The Court has not merely decided a single case; it has declared the Constitution's meaning for all.

A. The Counter-Majoritarian Power of Judicial Review

In a republic, decisions are to be made by a majority vote of the people's elected representatives. By contrast, federal judges are not elected, and are insulated from public opinion through life tenure and guaranteed salary. Art. III, § 1. This gives rise to what Prof. Alexander Bickel called the "counter-majoritarian difficulty" of judicial review in a republic. In a nation dedicated to majority rule, why should the Constitution's meaning be controlled by a tiny minority—a handful of judges who are not anyone's representatives?

It is possible for a civilized government with an independent judiciary to operate without such strong judicial review. In Britain and New Zealand, a court's opinion that a law is unconstitutional is purely advisory; Parliament may respond as it sees fit. In Canada, court rulings invalidating statutes are subject to override by Parliament. In North Dakota, a law will be struck down as a violation of the state constitution only if four out of five justices on the state supreme court concur. And in theory, one could construct a system with no judicial review at all. Judges would be obligated to enforce statutes as written, and legislators would be in charge of policing their constitutional limits, at risk of being voted out of office if their constituents form a different view of the constitution's meaning.

An anti-Federalist writing in 1788 under the pen name "Brutus" summed up his opposition to a system where life-tenured judges would have the power to invalidate acts of elected officials:

> There is no power above them, to control any of their decisions. There is no authority that can remove them, and they cannot be controlled by the laws of the legislature. In short, they are independent of the people, of the legislature, and of every power under heaven. Men placed in this situation will generally soon feel themselves independent of heaven itself.

Today's US Constitutional culture does not share Brutus's concerns. The only live question is not *whether* courts should have the power to declare laws unconstitutional (and to declare the meaning of the Constitution in the process), but *when* and *how* they should do so. Counter-majoritarian judicial review may pose a theoretical difficulty, but this is not viewed as a fatal flaw. A number of explanations have been offered in support of the American dedication to judicial review.

The Judge's Duty. On one level, judicial review is a simple matter of judges fulfilling their own oaths to support the Constitution. Judges have a duty not to use their positions in unconstitutional ways, which means they must not enter judgments that are premised on unconstitutional statutes or unconstitutional executive actions. Viewed this way, it would be more accurate to say that courts declare laws to be unenforceable in court, rather than to say that courts "strike down" laws. With that said, a rational Congress will not bother enacting laws that it knows will not be judicially enforced.

Protecting Minority Rights. The Framers feared tyranny of the majority, which they believed would be the inevitable result of majority rule with no mechanism to guarantee minority rights. Constitutional protection for minority rights, as seen in the Bill of Rights, is itself counter-majoritarian. It is not an anomaly for a system that contains counter-majoritarian limits on government power to include a counter-majoritarian institution to enforce them. As Alexander Hamilton wrote in The Federalist #78, the Constitution's individual rights provisions "can be preserved in practice no other way than through the medium of courts of justice, whose duty it must be to declare all acts contrary to the manifest tenor of the Constitution void. Without this, all the reservations of particular rights or privileges would amount to nothing."

Popular Sovereignty. For Hamilton in The Federalist #78, it was significant that the Constitution represented the desires of the people acting in their sovereign capacity. In any contest between what the people said in the Constitution and what the legislature (the people's servants) have said in statute, the Constitution must prevail. As a result, the power of judicial review does not "by any means suppose a superiority of the judicial to the legislative power. It only supposes that the power of the people is superior to both."

Policing the Political Process. In his influential book *Democracy and Distrust: A Theory of Judicial Review* (1981), Prof. John Hart Ely argued that the best use of judicial review is to ensure the effective functioning of the political process. As a general matter, Ely wrote, citizens and judges should accept the laws enacted by Congress—even the ones they don't like—because the lawmaking process is basically fair and representative. But some laws may make the political process operate unreliably (such as laws that reduce the fairness of elections) or carry tell-tale signs that the political process operated unreliably (such as invidious discrimination). By striking down laws like these, judicial review can be used to ensure that the political branches operate at their democratic best.

An Outside Referee. As mentioned in *Calder v. Bull* (1798), it had long been considered fundamentally unfair for a person to be a judge in his own case. This insight can be applied to separation of powers: The legislature has a built-in conflict of interest when it comes to assessing the constitutionality of its preferred laws. As Hamilton wrote in The Federalist #81, "From a body which had even a partial agency in passing bad laws," it cannot "be expected that men who had infringed the Constitution in the character of legislators, would be disposed to repair the breach in the character of judges." The conflict of interest can best be avoided by giving responsibility for constitutional interpretation to a referee outside of the lawmaking process.

The Least Dangerous Branch. As useful as an independent referee can be, a power-mad referee can control the whole game. In an often-quoted passage from The Federalist #78, *Hamilton argued that the judiciary would be the least likely branch to abuse its power.*

> Whoever attentively considers the different departments of power must perceive, that, in a government in which they are separated from each other, the judiciary, from the nature of its functions, will always be the least dangerous to the political rights of the Constitution; because it will be least in a capacity to annoy or injure them. The executive not only dispenses the honors, but holds the sword of the community. The legislature not only commands the purse, but prescribes the rules by which the duties and rights of every citizen are to be regulated. The judiciary, on the contrary, has no influence over either the sword or the purse; no direction either of the strength or of the wealth of the society; and can take no active resolution whatever. It may truly be said to have neither FORCE nor WILL, but merely judgment; and must ultimately depend upon the aid of the executive arm even for the efficacy of its judgments.

"Though individual oppression may now and then proceed from the courts of justice," Hamilton wrote, "the general liberty of the people can never be endangered from that quarter; I mean so long as the judiciary remains truly distinct from both the legislature and the executive."

Stability. The Framers envisioned that Congress—and especially the House of Representatives—would frequently change membership in response to elections. If the last word on constitutional meaning is placed with an ever-changing Congress, then the Constitution has the potential to be ever-changing as well, resulting in social and economic instability. Judges who have life tenure and whose method of work relies on adherence to precedent are more likely to give a stable interpretation to the Constitution across time.

Institutional Competence. In The Federalist #81, Hamilton argued that the judiciary would likely do a better job at the essentially lawyerly task of interpreting the Constitution. Judges will be "selected for their knowledge of the laws." Those who run for political office "cannot but be deficient in that knowledge" because "the members of the legislature will rarely be chosen with a view to those qualifications which fit men for the stations of judges."

Comparative Counter-Majoritarianism. The judicial branch can only be said to be counter-majoritarian when compared to other institutions. The political branches have their own counter-majoritarian features. Under the original Constitution of 1787, neither the President nor the Senate were directly elected. Meanwhile, the judiciary is not wholly beyond political control, since appointments are made by the President and the Senate, and judges can be removed through impeachment. The number of judgeships and the scope of federal court jurisdiction are under Congressional control. The insulation of the federal judiciary from the voters may be a difference of degree, not of kind.

Original Understandings. After independence, state courts interpreting the first wave of written state constitutions indicated that they had a power of judicial review over legislation. The notion was widely accepted in the Framer's time, as reflected in *The Federalist* and other writings. As a result, it was no surprise when the Supreme Court began to exercise judicial review over the actions of the federal government.

B. Judicial Review of Federal Government Action: *Marbury v. Madison*

The Supreme Court's first major statement on the power of judicial review was *Marbury v. Madison* (1803), an opinion asserting judicial authority to override unlawful actions of the executive and legislative branches. The facts leading to the litigation are intricate, but they reveal much about the complexities—and possibilities—of the American system of separated powers.

The Election of 1800. The Framers assumed that voters would select candidates for their individual wisdom and virtue, not for their affiliation with a faction that would seek to control government policies by force of numbers. These predictions quickly proved wrong, as two strong political parties established themselves while George Washington was still president. The Federalists (the party of Washington, John Adams, and Alexander Hamilton) favored a stronger federal government and tended to be supported by urban and commercial interests, while the **Republicans** (the party of Thomas Jefferson, James Madison, and Aaron Burr) favored a stronger role for the state governments and tended to be supported by agrarian interests. Under Art. II, § 1, cl. 3—written without political parties in mind—the candidate receiving the most votes from the Electoral College would be President, with the runner-up being Vice President. After political parties were added to the mix, the result of the presidential election of 1796 was a President Adams (71 electoral votes) and a Vice President Jefferson (68 electoral votes) from different and bitterly opposed parties.

TERMINOLOGY

REPUBLICANS: The party of Jefferson and Madison, founded in 1792 as a counterweight to the Federalist Party, originally called themselves Republicans. By the early 1800s, they began to be known as Democratic Republicans. Historians sometimes call them Jeffersonian Republicans. The party split in the 1820s into one now-defunct wing known as Whigs and another wing (headed by Andrew Jackson) known as Democrats—the precursor to today's Democratic Party. Today's Republican Party began as an anti-slavery party in the 1850s, and does not trace its lineage to the Jeffersonian Republicans.

Competition between the parties grew vicious during the John Adams presidency. Republicans accused Federalists of betraying the revolution by favoring an aristocratic central government controlled by moneyed interests with an unhealthy affinity for England. Federalists portrayed Republicans as nihilistic radicals with an unhealthy affinity for France, whose revolution had plunged Europe

■ HISTORY

THE SEDITION ACT: The Sedition Act was never appealed to the Supreme Court, because it expired by its own terms in early 1801 and President Jefferson pardoned all those convicted under it. Many years later, the Supreme Court stated: "Although the Sedition Act was never tested in this Court, the attack upon its validity has carried the day in the court of history." *New York Times Co. v. Sullivan*, 376 U.S. 254, 276 (1964).

into turmoil. In 1798, the federalist-controlled Congress passed **the Sedition Act**, which authorized criminal prosecution of those who spoke against Congress or the President (but not against the Vice President). A number of Republicans, including a sitting member of Congress, were prosecuted for their anti-Federalist speech.

The presidential election of 1800 took place amidst this contentious atmosphere. In the Congressional elections, Republicans took control of both houses of Congress. The Presidential race was excruciatingly close. In **the Electoral College**, Adams came in third with 65 votes. Two Republican candidates—Jefferson and Burr—were tied for the lead in with 73 votes each, throwing the election into the House of Representatives. Art. II, § 2, cl. 3. On February 17, 1801, just a few weeks before inauguration day, the House gave the Presidency to Jefferson and the Vice Presidency to Burr. Despite the messiness, the end result of the election was a remarkable achievement: the ruling party voluntarily relinquished office, and a new party took power without bloodshed. In light of European history, where political succession often triggered open warfare, a peaceful transition was no small achievement.

■ HISTORY

THE ELECTORAL COLLEGE: The difficulties surrounding the presidential elections of 1796 and 1800 prompted the 12th Amendment (ratified 1804). Under the revised system, a team of running mates would be elected President and Vice President, reducing the risk that the offices would be split between political rivals.

The Federalists Pack the Judiciary. The new Republican Congress and President would take office at noon on March 4, 1801. The Federalists, recognizing that they would soon lose control of two branches of government, took steps to maximize their control over the judicial branch.

On January 20, 1801, Adams nominated Secretary of State John Marshall to be Chief Justice, following the retirement of Chief Justice Oliver Ellsworth for health reasons. The Senate confirmed Marshall to the position on January 27. He agreed to finish his term as Secretary of State until the upcoming transfer of power on March 4.

On February 13, the lame duck Federalist Congress passed, and President Adams signed, the Judiciary Act of 1801. This statute created sixteen new federal trial court judgeships. While the nation needed more federal judges, Federalists used the timing of the Act to their political advantage. Adams nominated a full slate of sixteen new judges—all loyal Federalists—who were rapidly confirmed by the Senate. To add insult to injury, the Act also reduced the number of Supreme Court justices from six to five, so that Jefferson would not have an opportunity to name a replacement when the next sitting justice retired.

On February 27, 1801 Congress passed, and the President signed, the Organic Act for the District of Columbia, which used the enumerated power in Art. I, § 8, cl. 17 to provide for governance of the nation's new capitol city. (Philadelphia was the temporary seat of the federal government from 1790 until 1800.) Among other things, the Organic Act created 42 positions for Justices of the Peace. During a five-year term, a Justice of the Peace performed duties that today would be divided among a municipal judge, county clerk, city council member, and sheriff. Adams quickly nominated loyal Federalists for all 42 positions, and the Senate confirmed them on Tuesday March 3, 1801—the day before the new government was to take office.

The Republicans Respond. The Republicans were furious over what they called "the midnight judges." Jefferson complained that The Federalists "have retired into the judiciary as a stronghold, and from that battery all the works of Republicanism are to be beaten down and erased." Over the next few years, Republicans used various tools at their disposal to strike back.

To unseat the sixteen new federal circuit judges, the new Congress repealed the Judiciary Act of 1801, eliminating the newly created judgeships. The repeal posed a set of serious constitutional problems. Was it constitutional for Congress to effectively remove the judges from office without impeachment by eliminating their offices instead of acting against them individually? In a move that would effectively prevent the Supreme Court from ruling swiftly on the repeal, Congress postponed the Court's next term to early 1803. At that time, the Court upheld Congress's power to abolish lower court positions that it had the constitutional power to create. *Stuart v. Laird*, 5 U.S. 299 (1803) (announced a week after the decision in *Marbury v. Madison*).

For the D.C. Justices of the Peace, the haste with which they were appointed gave Jefferson an immediate opening when he took office on March 4, 1801. Under existing law, a person could not take public office without possession of a commission (a signed and sealed government document identifying that person as the duly appointed office holder). By around 9:00 pm on March 3, Adams had signed the Justice of the Peace commissions and sent them to the Secretary of State to receive the Great Seal of the United States. However, in the last-minute hubbub on March 4, many of the commissions were not delivered to their intended recipients. Upon discovering the sheaf of undelivered commissions, Jefferson instructed the new Secretary of State not to deliver them.

William Marbury (1762–1835)

Marbury's Lawsuit. William Marbury was a Federalist who expected but did not receive a commission to be a DC Justice of the Peace. On December 16, 1801, Marbury (along with the similarly situated

Dennis Ramsay, Robert Townsend Hooe, and William Harper) filed suit against Secretary of State James Madison, seeking a writ of mandamus ordering Madison to deliver the commission.

A writ of mandamus is a judicial order directing a government official to perform a legal duty. If mandamus was easily available, it would essentially put judges in charge of the entire government. To avoid this extraordinary concentration of power, a writ may issue only if the official's failure to act was unquestionably unlawful, and where no other legal remedy is available. If the official has legal discretion to decide whether or how to act, mandamus is improper. As a result, one of the legal questions in *Marbury v. Madison* was the scope of the judiciary's mandamus power against the executive branch.

Another legal question involved subject matter jurisdiction. Marbury needed to locate a court with original jurisdiction over the action, i.e., a court where the lawsuit could properly originate. In the American system, trial courts almost always have original jurisdiction, but original jurisdiction is occasionally proper in a court of appeals or even the Supreme Court. Art. III, § 2, cl. 2 of the US Constitution has this to say about original jurisdiction in the federal court system:

> In all cases affecting ambassadors, other public ministers and consuls, and those in which a State shall be party, the Supreme Court shall have original jurisdiction. In all the other cases [where federal courts have subject matter jurisdiction], the Supreme Court shall have appellate Jurisdiction . . . with such exceptions, and under such regulations as the Congress shall make.

Section 13 of the Judiciary Act of 1789 built on this constitutional language to specify the original and appellate jurisdiction of the Supreme Court. Subject to a handful of Congressionally-identified exceptions, the Act gave the Supreme Court original jurisdiction over suits where States or foreign ambassadors were parties. In addition, § 13 provided:

> The Supreme Court shall also have appellate jurisdiction from the [federal] circuit courts and courts of the several states [in specified cases]; and shall have power to issue . . . writs of mandamus, in cases warranted by the principles and usages of law, to any courts appointed, or persons holding office, under the authority of the United States.

Marbury's attorney filed his request for a writ of mandamus in the US Supreme Court. Because the statute authorized the Supreme Court to issue writs of mandamus against persons holding federal office, he argued, requests for such writs may originate in the Supreme Court.

When the Court reconvened in February 1803 (after its involuntary hiatus in 1802), its unfinished business included *Marbury*. The Justices took evidence about the executive branch's failure to deliver the sealed commission, and heard arguments from Marbury's attorney. Even though the Court had sent Madison an order to show cause why the writ should not issue, Jefferson instructed Madison not to appear. In light of this deliberate snub, many historians have speculated that even if the Court had issued a writ of mandamus in favor of Marbury, the administration would have ignored it—a result that would have seriously compromised the Court's authority. Marshall's solution became famous as a combination of political and legal cleverness: Rule in favor of the executive branch (giving it no opportunity to ignore an order of the court), but in an opinion announcing significant judicial power for the future.

ITEMS TO CONSIDER WHILE READING *MARBURY v. MADISON*:

A. *Why should a court have the power to issue writs of mandamus against the executive branch?*

B. *What made Marbury's case appropriate for such an order?*

C. *Why would it be unconstitutional for Congress to authorize the Supreme Court to hear Marbury's case as a matter of original jurisdiction?*

D. *Since the Supreme Court held that it lacked original jurisdiction, was the opinion's discussion of mandamus against the executive branch merely dicta?*

E. *What methods of constitutional reasoning are used in the opinion?*

Marbury v. Madison,

5 U.S. 137 (1803)

Opinion of the Court [by Chief Justice Marshall, joined by Justices Paterson, Chase, and Washington. Justices Moore and Cushing did not participate.]

. . . The present motion is for a mandamus [directing Secretary of State James Madison to deliver to William Marbury his commission as a Justice of the Peace for the District of Columbia]. The peculiar delicacy of this case, the novelty of some of its circumstances, and the real difficulty attending the points which occur in it, require a complete exposition of the principles on which the opinion to be given by the court is founded. . . .

In the order in which the court has viewed this subject, the following questions have been considered and decided.

1st. Has the applicant a right to the commission he demands?

2dly. If he has a right, and that right has been violated, do the laws of his country afford him a remedy?

3dly. If they do afford him a remedy, is it a mandamus issuing from this court?

The first object of inquiry is,

1st. Has the applicant a right to the commission he demands? . . .

In order to determine whether he is entitled to this commission, it becomes necessary to enquire whether he has been appointed to the office. . . . It is . . . the opinion of the court, that when a commission has been signed by the President, the appointment is made; and that the commission is complete, when the seal of the United States has been affixed to it by the secretary of state. . . .

To withhold [Marbury's] commission, therefore, is an act deemed by the court not warranted by law, but violative of a vested legal right.

This brings us to the second inquiry; which is,

2dly. If he has a right, and that right has been violated, do the laws of this country afford him a remedy?

The very essence of civil liberty certainly consists in the right of every individual to claim the protection of the laws, whenever he receives an injury. One of the first duties of government is to afford that protection. . . . The government of the United States has been emphatically termed a government of laws, and not of men. It will certainly cease to deserve this high appellation, if the laws furnish no remedy for the violation of a vested legal right. . . .

[But can there be a remedy when the alleged violation occurs at the order of the President?] By the constitution of the United States, the President is invested with certain important political powers, in the exercise of which he is to use his own discretion, and is accountable only to his country in his political character, and to his own conscience. . . . There exists, and can exist, no power to control that discretion. **The subjects are political.** They respect the nation, not individual rights, and being entrusted to the executive, the decision of the executive is conclusive. [And this discretion extends to actions taken by executive branch officers answerable to the President, including the Secretary of State.] The acts of such an officer, as an officer, can never be examinable by the courts.

But when the legislature proceeds to impose on that officer other duties; when he is directed peremptorily to perform certain acts; when the rights of individuals are dependent on the performance of those acts; he is so far the officer of the law; is amenable to the laws for his conduct; and cannot at his discretion sport away the vested rights of others.

■ OBSERVATION

THE SUBJECTS ARE POLITICAL: By identifying certain subjects as political rather than legal, *Marbury* points towards what later became known as the "political question" doctrine, which prevents the judiciary from making decisions that are the exclusive province of the elected (i.e., political) branches. See Ch. 3.D.4.

Marbury v. Madison

The conclusion from this reasoning is, that where the heads of departments are the political or confidential agents of the executive, merely to execute the will of the President, or rather to act in cases in which the executive possesses a constitutional or legal discretion, nothing can be more perfectly clear than that their acts are only politically examinable. But where a specific duty is assigned by law, and individual rights depend upon the performance of that duty, it seems equally clear that the individual who considers himself injured, has a right to resort to the laws of his country for a remedy.

If this be the rule, let us enquire how it applies to the case under the consideration of the court. . . . The question whether a right has vested or not, is, in its nature, judicial, and must be tried by the judicial authority. . . . So, if [Marbury] conceives that, by virtue of his appointment, he has a legal right, either to the commission which has been made out for him, or to a copy of that commission, it is equally a question examinable in a court, and the decision of the court upon it must depend on the opinion entertained of his appointment. . . .

It is then the opinion of the court,

1st. That by signing the commission of Mr. Marbury, the president of the United States appointed him a justice of peace, for the . . . the district of Columbia; and that the seal of the United States, affixed thereto by the secretary of state, is conclusive testimony of the verity of the signature, and of the completion of the appointment; and that the appointment conferred on him a legal right to the office for the space of five years.

2dly. That, having this legal title to the office, he has a consequent right to the commission; a refusal to deliver which, is a plain violation of that right, for which the laws of his country afford him a remedy.

It remains to be inquired whether,

3dly. He is entitled to the remedy for which he applies. This depends on,

1st. The nature of the writ applied for, and,

2dly. The power of this court.

1st. The nature of the writ.

[The current case is not] an attempt to intrude into the cabinet, and to intermeddle with the prerogatives of the executive. It is scarcely necessary for the court to disclaim all pretensions to such a jurisdiction. An extravagance, so absurd and excessive, could not have been entertained for a moment. The province of the court is, solely, to decide on the rights of individuals, not to enquire how the executive, or executive officers, perform duties in which they have a discretion. Questions, in their nature political, or which are, by the constitution and laws, submitted to the executive, can never be made in this court. . . .

If one of the heads of departments commits any illegal act, under color of his office, by which an individual sustains an injury, it cannot be pretended that his office alone exempts him from being sued in the ordinary mode of proceeding, and being compelled to obey the judgment of the law. . . . It is not by the office of the person to whom the writ is directed, but the nature of the thing to be done that the propriety or impropriety of issuing a mandamus, is to be determined. [The nature of delivering the signed and sealed commission is mandatory, not discretionary.] . . . This, then, is a plain case for a mandamus, either to deliver the commission, or a copy of it from the record; and it only remains to be inquired,

2dly. Whether it [the writ of mandamus] can issue from this court.

The act to establish the judicial courts of the United States authorizes the supreme court "to issue writs of mandamus, in cases warranted by the principles and usages of law, to any courts appointed, or persons holding office, under the authority of the United States." [Judiciary Act of 1789, § 13.]

The secretary of state, being a person holding an office under the authority of the United States, is precisely within the letter of the description; and if this court is not authorized to issue a writ of mandamus to such an officer, it must be because the law is unconstitutional, and therefore absolutely incapable of conferring the authority, and assigning the duties which its words purport to confer and assign.

[ORIGINAL JURISDICTION IN THE SUPREME
COURT WOULD BE UNCONSTITUTIONAL]

The constitution vests the whole judicial power of the United States in one supreme court, and such inferior courts as congress shall, from time to time, ordain and establish. [Art. III, § 1.] This power is expressly extended to all cases arising under the laws of the United States [Art. III, § 2, cl. 1]; and consequently, in some form, may be exercised over the present case; because the right claimed is given by a law of the United States.

In the distribution of this power it is declared that "the supreme court shall have original jurisdiction in all cases affecting ambassadors, other public ministers and consuls, and those in which a state shall be a party. In all other cases, the supreme court shall have appellate jurisdiction." [Art. III, § 2, cl. 2.] . . .

If congress remains at liberty to give this court appellate jurisdiction, where the constitution has declared their jurisdiction shall be original; and original jurisdiction where the constitution has declared it shall be appellate; the distribution of jurisdiction, made in the constitution, is form without substance. . . . It cannot be presumed that any clause in the constitution is intended to be without effect; and therefore such a construction is inadmissible, unless the words require it. . . .

To enable this court then to issue a mandamus, it must be shown to be an exercise of appellate jurisdiction, or to be necessary to enable them to exercise appellate jurisdiction. . . . It is the essential criterion of appellate jurisdiction, that it revises and corrects the proceedings in a cause already instituted, and does not create that cause. Although, therefore, a mandamus may be directed to courts, yet to issue such a writ to an officer for the delivery of a paper, is in effect the same as to sustain an original action for that paper, and therefore seems not to belong to appellate, but to original jurisdiction. Neither is it necessary in such a case as this, to enable the court to exercise its appellate jurisdiction.

The authority, therefore, given to the supreme court, by the act establishing the judicial courts of the United States, to issue writs of mandamus to public officers, appears not to be warranted by the constitution; and it becomes necessary to enquire whether a jurisdiction, so conferred, can be exercised.

[THE GOVERNMENT MAY NOT ACT IN VIOLATION OF ITS CONSTITUTION]

The question, whether an act, repugnant to the constitution, can become the law of the land, is a question deeply interesting to the United States; but, happily, not of an intricacy proportioned to its interest. It seems only necessary to recognize certain principles, supposed to have been long and well established, to decide it.

That the people have an original right to establish, for their future government, such principles as, in their opinion, shall most conduce to their own happiness, is the basis, on which the whole American fabric has been erected. The exercise of this original right is a very great exertion; nor can it, nor ought it to be frequently repeated. The principles, therefore, so established, are deemed fundamental. And as the authority from which they proceed [popular sovereignty] is supreme, and can seldom act, [the constitutional principles] are designed to be permanent.

This original and supreme will organizes the government, and assigns, to different departments, their respective powers. It may either stop here; or establish certain limits not to be transcended by those departments.

The government of the United States is of the latter description. The powers of the legislature are defined, and limited; and that those limits may not be mistaken, or forgotten, the constitution is written [as opposed to unwritten]. . . . It is a proposition too plain to be contested, that the constitution controls any legislative act repugnant to it; or, that the legislature may alter the constitution by an ordinary act.

Between these alternatives there is no middle ground. The constitution is either a superior, paramount law, unchangeable by ordinary means, or it is on a level with ordinary legislative acts, and like other acts, is alterable when the legislature shall please to alter it.

If the former part of the alternative be true, then a legislative act contrary to the constitution is not law: if the latter part be true, then written constitutions are absurd attempts, on the part of the people, to limit a power, in its own nature illimitable.

Certainly all those who have framed written constitutions contemplate them as forming the fundamental and paramount law of the nation, and consequently the theory of every such government must be, that an act of the legislature, repugnant to the constitution, is void.

This theory is essentially attached to a written constitution, and is consequently to be considered, by this court, as one of the fundamental principles of our society. It is not therefore to be lost sight of in the further consideration of this subject.

[COURTS MAY NOT GIVE EFFECT TO UNCONSTITUTIONAL LAWS]

If an act of the legislature, repugnant to the constitution, is void, does it, notwithstanding its invalidity, bind the courts, and oblige them to give it effect? Or, in other words, though it be not law, does it constitute a rule as operative as if it was a law? This would be to overthrow in fact what was established in theory; and would seem, at first view, an absurdity too gross to be insisted on. It shall, however, receive a more attentive consideration.

It is emphatically the province and duty of the judicial department **to say what the law is.** Those who apply the rule to particular cases, must of necessity expound and interpret that rule. If two laws conflict with each other, the courts must decide on the operation of each.

■ OBSERVATION

TO SAY WHAT THE LAW IS:
In the most famous sentence from *Marbury v. Madison,* Marshall makes an oblique reference to the Latin origins of the word "jurisdiction," which connotes the power to speak (diction) the law (juris).

So if a law be in opposition to the constitution; if both the law and the constitution apply to a particular case, so that the court must either decide that case conformably to the law, disregarding the constitution; or conformably to the constitution, disregarding the law; the court must determine which of these conflicting rules governs the case. This is of the very essence of judicial duty.

If then the courts are to regard the constitution; and the constitution is superior to any ordinary act of the legislature; the constitution, and not such ordinary act, must govern the case to which they both apply.

Those then who controvert the principle that the constitution is to be considered, in court, as a paramount law, are reduced to the necessity of maintaining that courts must close their eyes on the constitution, and see only the law.

This doctrine would subvert the very foundation of all written constitutions. It would declare that an act, which, according to the principles and theory of our government, is entirely void; is yet, in practice, completely obligatory. It would declare, that if the legislature shall do what is expressly forbidden, such act, notwithstanding the express prohibition, is in reality effectual. It would be giving to the legislature a practical and real omnipotence, with the same breath which professes to restrict their powers within narrow limits. It is prescribing limits, and declaring that those limits may be passed as pleasure.

That it thus reduces to nothing what we have deemed the greatest improvement on political institutions—a written constitution—would of itself be sufficient, in America, where written constitutions have been viewed with so much reverence, for rejecting the construction. But the peculiar expressions of the constitution of the United States furnish additional arguments in favour of its rejection.

The judicial power of the United States is extended to all cases arising under the constitution. [Art III, § 2, cl. 1] Could it be the intention of those who gave this power, to say that, in using it, the constitution should not be looked into? That a case arising under the constitution should be decided without examining the instrument under which it arises? This is too extravagant to be maintained.

In some cases then, the constitution must be looked into by the judges. And if they can open it at all, what part of it are they forbidden to read, or to obey? There are many other parts of the constitution which serve to illustrate this subject.

It is declared that "no tax or duty shall be laid on articles exported from any state." [Art. I, § 9, cl. 5.] Suppose a duty on the export of cotton, of tobacco, or of flour; and a suit instituted to recover it. Ought judgment to be rendered in such a case? Ought the judges to close their eyes on the constitution, and only see the law?

The constitution declares that "no bill of attainder or ex post facto law shall be passed." [Art. I, § 9, cl. 4.] If, however, such a bill should be passed and a person should be prosecuted under it; must the court condemn to death those victims whom the constitution endeavors to preserve?

"No person," says the constitution, "shall be convicted of treason unless on the testimony of two witnesses to the same overt act, or on confession in open court." [Art. III, § 3.] Here the language of the constitution is addressed especially to the courts. It prescribes, directly for them, a rule of evidence not to be departed from. If the legislature should change that rule, and declare one witness, or a confession out of court, sufficient for conviction, must the constitutional principle yield to the legislative act?

From these, and many other selections which might be made, it is apparent, that the framers of the constitution contemplated that instrument, as a rule for the government of courts, as well as of the legislature.

Why otherwise does it direct the judges to take an oath to support it? [Art. VI, § 3.] This oath certainly applies, in an especial manner, to their conduct in their official character. How immoral to impose it on them, if they were to be used as the instruments, and the knowing instruments, for violating what they swear to support? . . . Why does a judge swear to discharge his duties agreeably to the constitution of the United States, if that constitution forms no rule for his government? If it is closed upon him, and cannot be inspected by him? If such be the real state of things, this is worse than solemn mockery. To prescribe, or to take this oath, becomes equally a crime.

It is also not entirely unworthy of observation, that in declaring what shall be the supreme law of the land [Art. VI, § 2], the constitution itself is first mentioned; and not the laws of the United States generally, but those only which shall be made in pursuance of the constitution, have that rank. Thus, the particular phraseology of the constitution of the United States confirms and strengthens the principle, supposed to be essential to all written constitutions, that a law repugnant to the constitution is void; and that courts, as well as other departments, are bound by that instrument.

[To summarize: Marbury filed an original action for mandamus in the Supreme Court, but the Constitution gives it no original jurisdiction over such actions—even if an act of Congress implies otherwise. Marbury's action is therefore dismissed for lack of jurisdiction.]

flashforward

1. ***Marbury's Career.*** William Marbury never re-filed his lawsuit, and never became a justice of the peace. He did not seek public office, but later became a successful D.C.-area banker.

2. ***Congressional Control of the Judiciary Through Impeachment.*** A final strand of the Jeffersonian Republicans' efforts to assert control over the judiciary relied on the impeachment power. In early 1803—as the Supreme Court was hearing arguments in *Marbury v. Madison* and *Stuart v. Laird*—the Republican-dominated Congress debated its first-ever use of the impeachment power. The House of Representatives began by impeaching Circuit District Judge John Pickering of New Hampshire. There was little evidence that he had committed "treason, bribery, or other high crimes and misdemeanors," Art. IV, § 4, but he was alcoholic, senile, and generally not fit for office. The Senate ultimately convicted him. This set a potentially important precedent: if Congress could remove a judge for inability to perform competently, why not remove one for making decisions that Congress considers incorrect? The House pursued this theory in March 1804, voting to impeach Supreme Court Justice Samuel Chase, who was seen as the strongest supporter of Federalist policies on the Court and a pro-prosecution trial judge in cases where the Sedition Act had been used against Republicans. This time, however, the Senate refused to convict. This established a tradition that judges ought not be impeached over policy differences. Ever since, Congress has removed federal judges from office only over allegations of corruption or criminality.

3. *Federal Statutes Found Unconstitutional.* *Marbury* (1803) is widely considered to be the first case to strike down a federal statute as unconstitutional. *Dred Scott* (1856) is the next. The Supreme Court has invalidated federal statutes much more frequently since then. What explains the increase? There are more opportunities now to litigate constitutional questions, because modern Congresses have enacted more legislation that affects more people, and because modern courts provide more opportunities for individuals to challenge those statutes in litigation. Whether the number of decisions striking down federal statutes is excessive may be in the eye of the beholder. It might reflect Congress enacting too many unconstitutional laws, or the Court striking down too many constitutional ones.

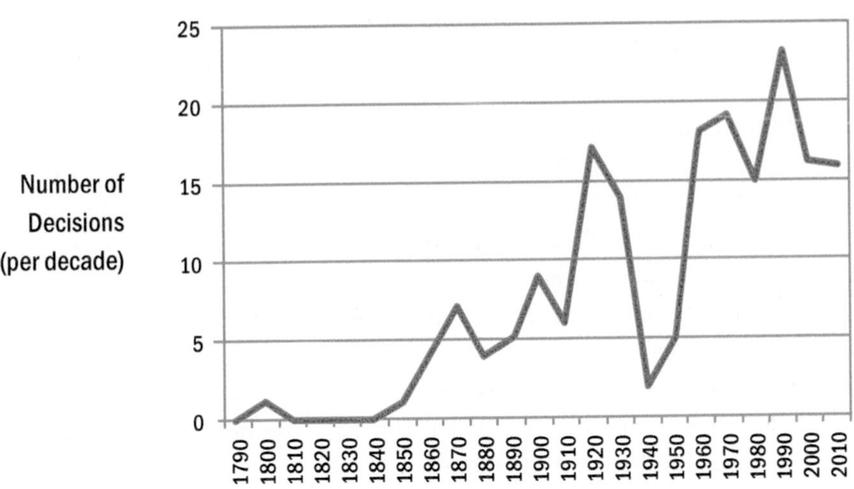

C. Judicial Review of State Court Decisions

The Framers' decision to allow Congress to create or not create federal trial courts, *see* Art. III, § 1 and Art. I, § 8, cl. 9, implies that not all questions of federal law must be litigated in federal court. In fact, it is quite common for federal issues to be ruled upon by state judges presiding over courts of general jurisdiction. This happens, for example, when state criminal defendants argue that the evidence against them was obtained through an unreasonable search in violation of the

Fourth Amendment. State courts are acceptable venues for federal questions because state judges take an oath to uphold the US Constitution, Art. VI, § 3, and the Supremacy Clause directs that "the judges in every State shall be bound [by the supreme law of the land], any thing in the constitution or laws of any State to the contrary," Art. VI, § 2.

Allowing federal legal questions to be decided in state courts runs the risk of non-uniformity, with federal law being interpreted differently in different states. Even worse, states could use their own judiciaries to circumvent federal constitutional requirements. For example, courts in states that were hostile to federal laws could declare those laws to be in violation of the federal Constitution. Or a state court could interpret the federal constitution to uphold locally popular but unconstitutional state laws. Supreme Court Justice Oliver Wendell Holmes said: "I do not think the United States would come to an end if we [the Supreme Court] lost our power to declare an Act of Congress void. I do think the Union would be imperiled if we could not make that declaration as to the laws of the several states."

As early as Section 25 of the Judiciary Act of 1789, Congress's chosen solution to these risks has been for the US Supreme Court to exercise appellate jurisdiction over cases involving federal law after they are decided by the highest courts of the states. *Martin v. Hunter's Lessee*, 14 U.S. 304 (1816), upheld the constitutionality of that statute. *Cohens v. Virginia*, 19 U.S. 264 (1821), similarly ruled that the US Supreme Court could hear an appeal from a state court criminal conviction that involved a potentially dispositive federal defense. The modern statute on the subject is 28 U.S.C. § 1257, which authorizes the US Supreme Court to take appeals of state court decisions "where the validity of a treaty or statute of the United States is drawn into question or where the validity of a statute of any State is drawn in question on the ground of its being repugnant to the [US] Constitution." Over time, the US Supreme Court has found more state statutes to be unconstitutional than federal statutes; part of the reason is that far more state statutes exist.

While the US Supreme Court has the last word on questions of federal law, it has no authority to resolve questions of state law. As a result, in cases that begin in state judicial systems, only the federal issues are subject to US Supreme Court review. Moreover, if the case is capable of being resolved solely on state law grounds, the Supreme Court will avoid ruling on federal grounds.

US Supreme Court Review of State Court Decisions

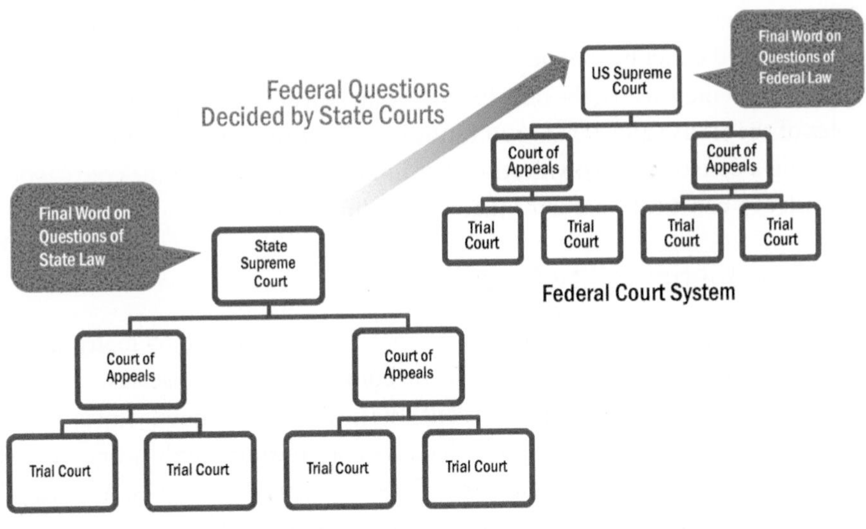

Imagine that a factually innocent criminal defendant is convicted of committing the state crime of burglary, after a trial where the state court judge refused to allow the defendant to be represented by counsel. During appeals within the state system, the defendant may assert state law defenses—there was insufficient evidence to prove the elements of burglary, and that the denial of counsel violates the state constitution—and also a federal defense—that denial of counsel violates the Sixth Amendment. Now imagine that the state supreme court rules (incorrectly) that neither the state constitution nor the US Constitution requires counsel, but also rules (correctly) that the conviction should be overturned due to insufficient evidence. Under *Michigan v. Long*, 463 U.S. 1032 (1983), the US Supreme Court will not take the case, because the decision rested on "adequate and independent state grounds." After all, the defendant deserved to win the appeal and did win it, so federal law is not necessary to resolve the case. The state court's erroneous interpretation of the Sixth Amendment will go uncorrected until the US Supreme Court decides some other case that squarely presents the federal question.

The rule from *Michigan v. Long* is one example of the broader principle that any court should try to **avoid unnecessary constitutional decisions**. The primary reason for this approach is structural. If the US Supreme Court interprets

> ■ OBSERVATION
>
> **AVOID UNNECESSARY CONSTITUTIONAL DECISIONS:** The impulse to avoid unnecessary constitutional decisions is expressed in many forms, such as a preference for resolving a case on statutory grounds rather than constitutional grounds, or on the narrower of two potential constitutional grounds. In addition, ambiguous statutes should be interpreted in a way that avoids potentially unconstitutional results.

a statute incorrectly, Congress can, by a majority vote, alter the statute to generate different results. If the Court interprets an agency regulation incorrectly, the problem could be fixed either by the agency or by Congress. But if the Court interprets the Constitution incorrectly, the only fix may be an amendment requiring two-thirds votes of the House and Senate and ratification by three-fourths of the States. By deciding a case on non-constitutional grounds where possible, the court avoids the risk of a constitutional error that will be difficult to rectify.

D. The Justiciability Requirement

The strong American power of judicial review is limited by many factors, one of which is the requirement that the court take only those cases that are justiciable (suitable for judicial resolution). The justiciability requirement is derived from constitutional language stating that a federal court may only hear cases that involve a concrete "case" or "controversy" between legal adversaries. Art. III, § 2. Imagine that State A passes a law authorizing its treasurer to coin money. This is an obvious violation of Art. I, § 10, cl. 1 ("No State shall . . . coin money"), but a federal court could not, on its own initiative, declare the State law unconstitutional. It must await a case or controversy—a jurisdictionally proper lawsuit between adverse parties. Such a lawsuit might exist if a citizen of State A uses the new State A coins to pay off a $100,000 debt owed to a citizen of State B. A federal court would have subject matter jurisdiction under the diversity of citizenship statute, 28 U.S.C. § 1332, and a ruling on the constitutionality of the State A coins would be necessary to resolve the parties' dispute. Unless the question arises in the context of a case or controversy, federal courts may not rule on the constitutionality of State A's action. Anything they said on the subject would be rejected as an improper **advisory opinion**: that is, an opinion that addresses a legal question as an abstract proposition not grounded in a concrete dispute between adverse parties asking a court to determine their respective rights.

Most law schools offer an elective called Federal Courts that delves into the Article III justiciability requirement in greater detail. The following sections give capsule summaries of a few prominent justiciability doctrines that may arise in connection with cases appearing later in this book.

HISTORY

ADVISORY OPINION: The rule against advisory opinions in federal courts is illustrated by an incident in 1793, when the Washington administration was divided over the best response to the latest war between England and France. Seeking guidance on the options available under the constitution and existing treaties, the administration sent a list of legal questions to the Supreme Court. The Court refused to answer them. In a letter to Washington, the Justices explained that the Court wished to maintain the "lines of separation drawn by the Constitution between the three departments of government," and that it doubted "the propriety of our extrajudicially deciding the questions."

1. Standing

Only a party with a stake in the outcome may litigate it; anyone else lacks "standing" to sue. Consider the example, set forth above, where State A passed a law to coin its own money. Citizens of State A, or State B, or even other countries might be outraged by this constitutional violation, but their mere disagreement with State A's action would not give them standing to litigate. They must experience some personal harm as a result of State A's actions. If they do not, there is no Article III "case" or "controversy." *Valley Forge Christian College v. Americans United for Separation of Church & State, Inc.*, 454 U.S. 464 (1982).

Modern cases about standing consider a number of factors when assessing standing. In all cases, the plaintiff must demonstrate that the lawsuit alleges an "injury in fact" that is "traceable" to conduct of the defendant and would be "redressable" by a court order. *Lujan v. Defenders of Wildlife*, 504 U.S. 555 (1992). These are considered constitutional requirements. In addition, courts sometimes rely on other factors to reject standing, even if the constitutional minimum might be satisfied. Is the litigant asserting his or her own personal rights, or instead the rights of third parties not before the court? Is the litigant asking the court to decide a generalized grievance more appropriately addressed by the political branches? And so on. These judicially-created reasons for rejecting standing are often referred to as "prudential" standing considerations. They could be changed by Congress since they are not considered constitutional requirements. *Bennett v. Spear*, 520 U.S. 154 (1997).

2. Ripeness

There is no case or controversy if a dispute is not yet "ripe" for a decision. For example, if a state senator from State A introduced a bill to authorize the state to coin money, but it had not yet been approved by the state legislature or signed into law by the governor, any dispute about its legality would not be ripe for judicial review. After all, the bill might fail, making any court decision purely advisory. *National Park Hospitality Association v. Department of The Interior*, 538 U.S. 803 (2003) (unripe cases generate advisory opinions).

A case challenging the constitutionality of a criminal statute might not be ripe if there is no reason to believe that the state intends to enforce it. This may happen when a plaintiff sues to invalidate an old statute that has not been relied upon in recent memory, *Poe v. Ullman*, 367 U.S. 497 (1961), or to invalidate a brand-new statute that has not yet had time to be enforced, *Susan B. Anthony List v. Driehaus*, 573 U.S. 149 (2014). In either situation, the ripeness of the challenge will hinge on whether there is a "credible threat of prosecution." If such a threat exists, the plaintiff is forced into an unpalatable choice: refrain from taking action that may be constitutionally protected, or take the action and live under the constant fear of arrest. Being placed in that position is an injury in fact that can be ripe for judicial decision.

3. Mootness

Mootness is the flipside of ripeness. If the parties are no longer in dispute, the case is moot (deriving from an old term meaning "debatable"). Mootness can arise from settlement between the parties, death of a party, change in the law, or change in the facts. Any of these could, in the right circumstances, render a court decision irrelevant because the issues initially presented are no longer live, the parties no longer have a legally cognizable interest in the outcome, and the court's decision would not establish anyone's particular legal rights. *Already, LLC v. Nike, Inc.*, 568 U.S. 85 (2013).

Several exceptions exist to the federal mootness doctrine. A court may hear a case that, while technically moot, is "capable of repetition, yet evading review." A prominent example is *Roe v. Wade*, 410 U.S. 113 (1973), where a pregnant plaintiff challenged a law that prevented her from obtaining a legal abortion. Litigation takes longer than nine months, and Roe's claim became moot after the birth of her baby. However, the situation would be capable of repetition (another pregnancy was possible), but that future case would evade review (any future pregnancy would also be shorter than the time needed to litigate it), so the Court decided the case on the merits.

Another exception to mootness is the "voluntary cessation" doctrine, which explains that a defendant's choice to voluntarily change its behavior for a short time will not render a case moot. Imagine a police department with a policy of handcuffing drivers whenever they are pulled over for speeding tickets. A group of drivers sue, seeking an injunction against the practice on grounds that it violates the Fourth Amendment. The police department might voluntarily stop the handcuffing, but only for as long as it takes to get the case dismissed as moot. If the department retains the ability to resume the allegedly unconstitutional activity, a case or controversy remains. The case will be moot only if the police department satisfies "the formidable burden of showing that it is absolutely clear the allegedly wrongful behavior could not reasonably be expected to recur." *Friends of the Earth, Inc. v. Laidlaw*, 528 U.S. 167 (2000).

4. The Political Question Doctrine

Standing, ripeness, and mootness are old judicial doctrines that existed in one form or another in common law England. A uniquely American limit on justiciability is the rule that federal courts will not resolve "political questions" that the Constitution assigns to other branches of government. For example, Art. I, § 5, cl. 2 says that each house of Congress "may determine the rules of its proceedings." If the Senate enacts a rule regarding the composition of committees, a disappointed Senator would not be able to secure a federal court order reversing the rule. The court is not in a position to rule on the matter, because control over Senate rules has been assigned to one of the political branches. See *Nixon v. United States*, 506 U.S. 224 (1993) (federal judge facing impeachment could not object in court to the Senate's methods for the impeachment trial).

The classic statement of the factors relevant to the political question doctrine appears in *Baker v. Carr*, 369 U.S. 186 (1962). A court should refuse jurisdiction in cases involving "a textually demonstrable constitutional commitment of the issue to a coordinate political department, or a lack of judicially discoverable and manageable standards for resolving it." In *Baker* itself, the Court found that the political question doctrine did not prevent it from ruling that Tennessee's political districting maps violated the Equal Protection Clause.

After *Baker*, federal courts have usually been reluctant to refuse jurisdiction on a political question theory. For example, in *Zivotofsky v. Clinton*, 566 U.S. 189 (2012), the Supreme Court held that the political question doctrine would not prevent a court from deciding a case, even though it touched on questions of foreign policy usually decided by the political branches. (The decision on the merits in *Zivotofsky* appears in Ch. 16.C.2.) However, the Supreme Court has recently relied upon the political question doctrine to reject jurisdiction, finding that claims against states for gerrymandering legislative districts to favor one political party posed non-justiciable political questions. *Rucho v. Common Cause*, 139 S. Ct. 2484 (2019).

Chapter Recap

A. The US Constitution has been interpreted to include a strong power of judicial review, where the judiciary has the power to declare actions of the legislature and executive to be unconstitutional and void. As a result, the judiciary gets the last word on the meaning of the US Constitution.

B. The US Supreme Court also has authority to review decisions of state courts that involve questions of federal law. However, state courts get the last word on the meaning of state law.

C. The court's strong power of judicial review is limited by the justiciability requirement of Article III. Federal courts may not issue advisory opinions purporting to decide legal questions in the abstract. They may only declare governmental actions unconstitutional if doing so is necessary to resolve a concrete case or controversy susceptible to judicial resolution.

CHAPTER 5

Early State-Federal Relations

The central constitutional question for the first few decades under the US Constitution was the implementation of concurrent sovereignty. How could a supreme national government and sovereign state governments exercise authority over the same territory at the same time?

If powers were assigned exclusively to one level of government or the other, coexistence would be easy. The federal government could regulate dogs, state governments could regulate cats, and neither could regulate the other. In a few areas, the US Constitution follows this paradigm of exclusive jurisdiction. For example, the federal government may make treaties with foreign nations, Art. II, § 2, cl. 2, but the states may not, Art. I, § 10, cl. 1.

In most areas, however, the US Constitution does not prevent the states from acting—even in settings where the federal government has enumerated authority. For example, the federal government may impose taxes and create trial courts. So can the states. Concurrent governmental powers are a routine occurrence in modern American life. Income is subject to both federal and state income taxes. Both federal and state criminal laws forbid sales of certain drugs. Factories must abide by both federal and state environmental laws. The problems arise when state and federal governments, exercising concurrent powers, enact laws that conflict with each other.

Many of the ground rules for concurrent sovereignty were established in early 19th-century decisions authored by Chief Justice John Marshall that continue to be cited by lawyers and judges to the present day. In Marshall's day, there was little constitutional precedent to rely upon. As a result, Marshall's opinions tended to rely heavily on close reading of the Constitution's text and careful reasoning about constitutional structure.

BIOGRAPHY

JOHN MARSHALL (1755–1835) held the office of Chief Justice for over 34 years, and is widely considered the most influential Supreme Court justice of all time. He was a cousin to Thomas Jefferson, but they personally loathed each other, were political opponents from rival parties, and adopted drastically different approaches to the Constitution. Marshall's philosophy favored a strong federal government, and within the federal government, a powerful judiciary. Jefferson took a narrow view of the federal government's power and, when president, railed against the judiciary.

A. State Interference with a Federal Entity: *McCulloch v. Maryland*

The most controversial constitutional issue in the early republic was the power of Congress to create a bank. Notice how a variety of actors within the system (not just judges) interpreted the Constitution along the way.

The First Bank of the United States. Debates over the legality of a national bank predate the current US Constitution. In May 1781, only a few months after the ratification of the Articles of Confederation, the Articles Congress created the Bank of North America at the urging of Alexander Hamilton and Robert Morris (nicknamed "The Financier of the Revolution"). The Articles said that Congress should be limited to those powers "expressly delegated" to it, see Ch. 3.A.2, and bank-making and corporation-making were not on the list. Nonetheless, having ready access to a reliable source of funds was so important to the war effort that Congress authorized the bank anyway.

After independence from Britain was secured, a national bank continued to be useful. A bank would make it easier for the government to collect taxes and tariffs and to disburse the collected money. Moreover, the bank could create a money supply over which the government had control. The bank's detractors opposed it for exactly that reason. They were wary of any concentration of economic power in a central bank, let alone one controlled by the government. As Thomas Jefferson later wrote, "banking establishments are more dangerous than standing armies."

In 1790, the first Congress under the new Constitution debated a proposal by Alexander Hamilton (now Washington's Secretary of the Treasury) to create a Bank of the United States. Supporters of the bank argued that the goal of the Constitution was an effective national government, and in particular a government that could be effective at regulating the national economy. This could be seen in the power to collect taxes, coin money, and regulate commerce. Other powers required the government to spend money, such as operating the military and the post office. Finally, the Constitution allowed Congress "to make all laws necessary and proper for carrying into execution" its enumerated powers. This added up to the power to create a bank. Opponents argued that the Constitution does not in so many words give Congress the power to create a bank (or even to create corporations generally). The Framers knew what banks were, and they could have specified bank-making as an enumerated power if they wanted to. Creating a national bank was also not necessary: Congress could deposit its funds with private banks and use privately issued bank notes just like other participants in the economy. The argument that the federal government's enumerated powers should be interpreted narrowly was known as "strict construction."

James Madison, then a member of the House of Representatives, led the opposition to the bank, but he was outvoted. Given the controversy in Congress, President Washington sought legal opinions from three cabinet members before signing the bill into law. Secretary of State Thomas Jefferson and Attorney General Edmund Randolph agreed with Madison that the bank was unconstitutional. **Jefferson, who considered himself a strict constructionist**, wrote: "To take a single step beyond the boundaries thus specially drawn around the powers of Congress is to take possession of a boundless field of power, no longer susceptible of any definition." Secretary of the Treasury Hamilton argued that Congress was within its rights. Hamilton argued that the Constitution enumerated the acceptable goals of legislation, but allowed Congress leeway to select the means it thought would best accomplish those goals. "The means by which national exigencies are to be provided for, national inconveniences obviated, national prosperity promoted, are of such infinite variety, extent and complexity, that there must, of necessity, be great latitude of discretion in the selection of those means." Washington agreed with Hamilton and Congress, and signed the bank into law in 1791.

■ HISTORY

JEFFERSON AND STRICT CONSTRUCTION: Jefferson's commitment to strict construction was put to the test when France offered to sell its interest in the Louisiana territory for $15 million. The United States could gain control over all the land from the Mississippi River to the Rocky Mountains and cement relations with a European ally, all for a bargain price. The only hitch was that under a strict construction of federal power, nothing allowed purchase of territory from another nation. Jefferson encouraged Congress to amend the Constitution, but it proceeded with the purchase without any amendment—and Jefferson went along. France had made an offer he couldn't refuse.

The Second Bank of the United States. By its own terms, the first Bank's charter expired in 1811. Congress created the second Bank of the United States in 1816 after another round of constitutional debate. It was signed into law by now-President James Madison, who by that time had come to agree with its constitutionality.

In 1818, the Bank decided to call in many outstanding loans, leading to a wave of property foreclosures and business failures later known as the Panic of 1819. In response, several states passed laws designed to reduce the power of the

Bank. Maryland enacted a statute requiring all banks not chartered by the state legislature (in other words, the Bank of the United States) to print bank notes on special stamped paper that could only be acquired by paying the state an amount equal to 2% of the value of the notes to be printed. In the alternative, the Bank could pay an annual tax of $15,000. The goal was to drive up the expenses of the Bank and make its money less competitive.

The Bank refused to pay the Maryland tax, and continued to print money on unstamped paper. Maryland filed suit in state court to collect the tax, plus statutory penalties. The nominal defendant was James McCulloch, the head cashier of the Bank's Baltimore branch. As a matter of state law, it was an open-and-shut case: McCulloch had not paid the tax on behalf of the Bank. As a result, the litigation revolved around McCulloch's affirmative defense, namely that the Maryland law violated the US Constitution by impeding the operation of a Congressionally authorized bank. Maryland responded to this defense by arguing (a) Congress had no power to create the Bank of the United States; and (b) even if it had such power, Maryland could tax the national bank just as it could tax any other business entity operating within its borders.

ITEMS TO CONSIDER WHILE READING *MCCULLOCH v. MARYLAND*:

FEDERAL POWER TO CREATE A BANK

A. *What in the Constitution authorized Congress to create a bank? Consider text, structure, history, consequences, and values.*

B. *The Bank had been carefully considered by different Congresses and Presidents over the course of 30 years, all concluding it was constitutional. Did this matter to the Supreme Court? Should it?*

C. *These two passages are the most frequently quoted portions of McCulloch. What do they mean?*

1. *"We must never forget that it is a constitution we are expounding."*
2. *"Let the end be legitimate, let it be within the scope of the constitution, and all means which are appropriate, which are plainly adapted to that end, which are not prohibited, but consist with the letter and spirit of the constitution, are constitutional."*

MARYLAND'S POWER TO TAX A FEDERALLY CREATED BANK

D. *What was the source of Maryland's power to tax banks?*

E. *What in the US Constitution limited Maryland's power to tax the Bank of the United States? Consider text, structure, consequences, and values.*

F. *Why did it matter that Maryland's law may affect people who are not Maryland citizens?*

McCulloch v. Maryland,

17 U.S. 316 (1819)

Chief Justice Marshall delivered the opinion of the court [joined by Justices Washington, Johnson, Livingston, Todd, Duvall, and Story].

In the case now to be determined . . . the constitution of our country, in its most interesting and vital parts, is to be considered; the conflicting powers of the government of the Union and of its members, as marked in that constitution, are to be discussed; and an opinion given, which may essentially influence the great operations of the government. No tribunal can approach such a question without a deep sense of its importance, and of the awful responsibility involved in its decision. But it must be decided peacefully, or remain a source of hostile legislation, perhaps, of hostility of a still more serious nature; and if it is to be so decided, by this tribunal alone can the decision be made. On the supreme court of the United States has the constitution of our country devolved this important duty.

The first question made in the cause is—has congress power to incorporate a bank?

[HISTORY OF THE CONTROVERSY]

It has been truly said, that this can scarcely be considered as an open question, entirely unprejudiced by the former proceedings of the nation respecting it. . . . [But] it will not be denied, that a bold and daring usurpation might be resisted, after an acquiescence still longer and more complete than this. . . .

The power now contested was exercised by the first congress elected under the present constitution. The bill for incorporating the [first] Bank of the United States did not steal upon an unsuspecting legislature, and pass unobserved. Its principle was completely understood, and was opposed with equal zeal and ability. After being resisted, first, in the fair and open field of debate, and afterwards, in the executive cabinet, with as much persevering talent as any measure has ever experienced, and being supported by arguments which convinced minds as pure and as intelligent as this country can boast, it became a law. . . . It would require no ordinary share of intrepidity, to assert that a measure adopted under these circumstances, was a bold and plain usurpation, to which the constitution gave no countenance. These observations belong to the cause; but they are not made under the impression, that, were the question entirely new, the law would be found irreconcilable with the constitution.

[THE ARGUMENT FOR STATE SUPREMACY]

In discussing this question, the counsel for the state of Maryland have deemed it of some importance, in the construction of the constitution, to consider that instrument, not as emanating from the people, but as the act of sovereign and independent states. The powers of the general government, it has been said, are delegated by the states, who alone are truly sovereign; and must be exercised in subordination to the states, who alone possess supreme dominion.

It would be difficult to sustain this proposition. The convention which framed the constitution was indeed elected by the state legislatures. But the instrument, when it came from their hands, was a mere proposal, without obligation, or pretensions to it. It was reported to the then existing congress of the United States, with a request that it might "be submitted to a convention of delegates, chosen in each state by the people thereof, under the recommendation of its legislature, for their assent and ratification." This mode of proceeding was adopted; and by the convention, by congress, and by the state legislatures, the instrument was submitted to the people. They acted upon it in the only manner in which they can act safely, effectively and wisely, on such a subject, by assembling in convention. It is true, they assembled in their several states—and where else should they have assembled? No political dreamer was ever wild enough to think of breaking down the lines which separate the states, and of compounding the American people into one common mass. Of consequence, when they act, they act in their states. But the measures they adopt do not, on that account, cease to be the measures of the people themselves, or become the measures of the state governments.

From these conventions, the constitution derives its whole authority. The [United States] government proceeds directly from the people; is "ordained and established," in the name of the people; and is declared to be ordained, "in order to form a more perfect union, establish justice, insure domestic tranquility, and secure the blessings of liberty to themselves and to their posterity." The assent of the states, in their sovereign capacity, is implied, in calling a [ratifying] convention, and thus submitting that instrument to the people. But the people were at perfect liberty to accept or reject it; and their act was final. It required not the affirmance, and could not be negatived, by the state governments. The constitution, when thus adopted, was of complete obligation, and bound the state sovereignties.

It has been said, that the people had already surrendered all their powers to the state sovereignties, and had nothing more to give. But, surely, the question whether [the people] may resume and modify the powers granted to government, does not remain to be settled in this country. Much more might the legitimacy of the general government be doubted, had it been created by the states. The powers delegated to the state sovereignties were to be exercised by themselves, not by a distinct and independent sovereignty, created by themselves. To the formation of a league, such as was the confederation, the state sovereignties were certainly competent. But when, "in order to form a more perfect union," it was deemed necessary to change this alliance into an effective government, possessing great and sovereign powers, and acting directly on the people, the necessity of referring it to the people, and of deriving its powers directly from them, was felt and acknowledged by all.

The government of the Union, then (whatever may be the influence of this fact on the case), is, emphatically and truly, a government of the people [and not of the states]. In form, and in substance, it emanates from them. Its powers are granted by them, and are to be exercised directly on them, and for their benefit.

[FEDERAL POWER IN GENERAL]

This [United States] government is acknowledged by all, to be one of enumerated powers. The principle, that it can exercise only the powers granted to it, would seem too apparent, to have required to be enforced by all those arguments, which its enlightened friends, while it was depending before the people, found it necessary to urge; that principle is now universally admitted. But the question respecting the extent of the powers actually granted, is perpetually arising, and will probably continue to arise, so long as our system shall exist. . . .

If any one proposition could command the universal assent of mankind, we might expect it would be this—that the government of the Union, though limited in its powers, is supreme within its sphere of action. This would seem to result, necessarily, from its nature. It is the government of all; its powers are delegated by all; it represents all, and acts for all. Though any one state may be willing to control its operations, no state is willing to allow others to control them. The nation, on those subjects on which it can act, must necessarily bind its component parts.

But this question is not left to mere reason: the people have, in express terms, decided it, by saying, "this constitution, and the laws of the United States, which shall be made in pursuance thereof," "shall be the supreme law of the land," and by requiring that the members of the state legislatures, and the officers of the executive and judicial departments of the states, shall take the oath of fidelity to it. [Art. VI, §§ 2–3.] The government of the United States, then, though limited in its powers, is supreme; and its laws, when made in pursuance of the constitution, form the supreme law of the land, "anything in the constitution or laws of any state to the contrary notwithstanding." [Art. VI, § 2.]

Among the enumerated powers, we do not find that of establishing a bank or creating a corporation. But there is no phrase in the instrument which, like the articles of confederation, excludes incidental or implied powers; and which requires that everything granted shall be expressly and minutely described. Even the 10th amendment, which was framed for the purpose of quieting the excessive jealousies which had been excited, omits the word "expressly," and declares only, that the powers "not delegated to the United States, nor prohibited to the states, are reserved to the states or to the people;" thus leaving the question, whether the particular power which may become the subject of contest, has been delegated to the one government, or prohibited to the other, to depend on a fair construction of the whole instrument. The men who drew and adopted this amendment had experienced the embarrassments resulting from the insertion of this word ["expressly"] in the articles of confederation, and probably omitted it, to avoid those embarrassments.

A constitution, to contain an accurate detail of all the subdivisions of which its great powers will admit, and of all the means by which they may be carried into execution, would partake of the prolixity of a legal code, and could scarcely be embraced by the human mind. It would, probably, never be understood by the public. Its nature, therefore, requires, that only its great outlines should be marked, its important objects designated, and the minor ingredients which compose those objects, be deduced from the nature of the objects themselves. That this idea was entertained by the framers of the American constitution, is not only to be inferred from the nature of the instrument, but from the language. Why else were some of the limitations, found in the 9th section of the 1st article, introduced? It is also, in some degree, warranted, by their having omitted to use any restrictive term which might prevent its receiving a fair and just interpretation. In considering this question, then, we must never forget that it is a constitution we are expounding.

Although, among the enumerated powers of government, we do not find the word "bank" or "incorporation," we find the great powers, to lay and collect taxes; to borrow money; to regulate commerce; to declare and conduct a war; and to raise and support armies and navies. The sword and the purse, all the external relations, and no inconsiderable portion of the industry of the nation, are entrusted to its government. . . . A government, entrusted with such ample powers, on the due execution of which the happiness and prosperity of the nation so vitally depends, must also be entrusted with ample means for their execution. The power being given, it is the interest of the nation to facilitate its execution. It can never be their interest, and cannot be presumed to have been their intention, to clog and embarrass its execution, by withholding the most appropriate means.

Throughout this vast republic, from the St. Croix to the Gulf of Mexico, from the Atlantic to the Pacific, revenue is to be collected and expended, armies are to be marched and supported. The exigencies of the nation may require, that the treasure raised in the north should be transported to the south, that raised in the east, conveyed to the west, or that this order should be reversed. Is that construction of the constitution to be preferred, which would render these operations difficult, hazardous and expensive? Can we adopt that construction (unless the words imperiously require it), which would impute to the framers of that instrument, when granting these powers for the public good, the intention of impeding their exercise, by withholding a choice of means? If, indeed, such be the mandate of the constitution, we have only to obey; but that instrument does not profess to enumerate the means by which the powers it confers may be executed; nor does it prohibit the creation of a corporation, if the existence of such a being be essential, to the beneficial exercise of those powers. It is, then, the subject of fair inquiry, how far such means may be employed.

It is not denied [by Maryland], that the powers given to the government imply the ordinary means of execution. That, for example, of raising revenue, and applying it to national purposes, is admitted to imply the power of conveying money from place to place, as the exigencies of the nation may require, and of employing the usual means of conveyance. But it is denied [by Maryland], that the government has its choice of means; or, that it may employ the most convenient means, if, to employ them, it be necessary to erect a corporation. . . . [To the contrary,] the government which has a right to do an act, and has imposed on it, the duty of performing that act, must, according to the dictates of reason, be allowed to select the means; and those who contend that it may not select any appropriate means, that one particular mode of effecting the object is excepted, take upon themselves the burden of establishing that exception. . . .

The power of creating a corporation is never used for its own sake, but for the purpose of effecting something else. No sufficient reason is, therefore, perceived, why it may not pass as incidental to those powers which are expressly given, if it be a direct mode of executing them.

[THE NECESSARY & PROPER CLAUSE GENERALLY]

But the constitution of the United States has not left the right of congress to employ the necessary means, for the execution of the powers conferred on the government, to general reasoning. To its enumeration of powers is added, that of making "all laws which shall be necessary and proper, for carrying into execution the foregoing powers, and all other powers vested by this constitution, in the government of the United States, or in any department thereof." [Art. I, § 8, cl. 18.] The counsel for the state of Maryland have urged various arguments, to prove that this clause, though, in terms, a grant of power, is not so, in effect; but is really restrictive of the general right, which might otherwise be implied, of selecting means for executing the enumerated powers. . . . Congress is not empowered by it to make all laws, which may have relation to the powers conferred on the government, but such only as may be *"necessary and proper"* for carrying them into execution. The word *"necessary"* is considered as controlling the whole sentence, and as limiting the right to pass laws for the execution of the granted powers, to such as are indispensable, and without which the power would be nugatory. That it excludes the choice of means, and leaves to congress, in each case, that only which is most direct and simple.

Is it true, that this is the sense in which the word "necessary" is always used? Does it always import an absolute physical necessity, so strong, that one thing to which another may be termed necessary, cannot exist without that other? We think it does not. If reference be had to its use, in the common affairs of the world, or in approved authors, we find that it frequently imports no more than that one thing is convenient, or useful, or essential to another. To employ the means necessary to an end, is generally understood as employing any means calculated to produce the end, and not as being confined to those single means, without which the end would be entirely unattainable.

Such is the character of human language, that no word conveys to the mind, in all situations, one single definite idea; and nothing is more common than to use words in a figurative sense. Almost all compositions contain words, which, taken in their rigorous sense, would convey a meaning different from that which is obviously intended. It is essential to just construction, that many words which import something excessive, should be understood in a more mitigated sense—in that sense which common usage justifies. The word "necessary" is of this description. It has not a fixed character, peculiar to itself. It admits of all degrees of comparison; and is often connected with other words, which increase or diminish the impression the mind receives of the urgency it imports. A thing may be necessary, very necessary, absolutely or indispensably necessary. To no mind would the same idea be conveyed by these several phrases.

The comment on the word ["necessary"] is well illustrated by the passage cited at the bar, from the 10th section of the 1st article of the constitution. It is, we think, impossible to compare the sentence which prohibits a state from laying "imposts, or duties on imports or exports, except what may be *absolutely* necessary for executing its inspection laws," with that which authorizes congress "to make all laws which shall be necessary and proper for carrying into execution" the powers of the general government, without feeling a conviction, that the convention understood itself to change materially the meaning of the word "necessary," by prefixing the word "absolutely." This word, then, like others, is used in various senses; and, in its construction, the subject, the context, the intention of the person using them, are all to be taken into view.

Let this be done in the case under consideration. The subject is the execution of those great powers on which the welfare of a nation essentially depends. It must have been the intention of those who gave these powers, to insure, so far as human prudence could insure, their beneficial execution. This could not be done, by confiding the choice of means to such narrow limits as not to leave it in the power of congress to adopt any which might be appropriate, and which were conducive to the end. This provision is made in a constitution, intended to endure for ages to come, and consequently, to be adapted to the various crises of human affairs. To have prescribed the means by which government should, in all future time, execute

McCulloch v. Maryland

its powers, would have been to change, entirely, the character of the instrument, and give it the properties of a legal code. It would have been an unwise attempt to provide, by immutable rules, for exigencies which, if foreseen at all, must have been seen dimly, and which can be best provided for as they occur. To have declared, that the best means shall not be used, but those alone, without which the power given would be nugatory, would have been to deprive the legislature of the capacity to avail itself of experience, to exercise its reason, and to accommodate its legislation to circumstances. . . .

[There are other examples where the federal government exercises powers that are not expressly stated in the text of the Constitution.] So, with respect to the whole penal code of the United States: whence arises the power to punish [i.e., to make criminal laws], in cases not prescribed by the constitution? All admit, that the government may, legitimately, punish any violation of its laws; and yet, this is not among the enumerated powers of congress.

The right to enforce the observance of law, by punishing its infraction, might be denied, with the more plausibility, because it is expressly given in some cases. Congress is empowered "to provide for the punishment of counterfeiting the securities and current coin of the United States," [Art. I, § 8, cl. 6] and "to define and punish piracies and felonies committed on the high seas, and offences against the law of nations." [Art. I, § 8, cl. 10] The several powers of congress may exist, in a very imperfect state, to be sure, but they may exist and be carried into execution, although no punishment should be inflicted in cases where **the right to punish** is not expressly given.

Take, for example, the power "to establish post-offices and post-roads." [Art. I, § 8, cl. 7.] This power is executed, by the single act of making the establishment. But, from this has been inferred the power and duty of carrying the mail along the post-road, from one post-office to another. And from this implied power, has again been inferred the right to punish those who steal letters from the post-office, or rob the mail. It may be said, with some plausibility, that the right to carry the mail, and to punish those who rob it, is not indispensably necessary to the establishment of a post-office and post-road. This right is indeed essential to the beneficial exercise of the power, but not indispensably necessary to its existence. So, of the punishment of the crimes of stealing or falsifying a record or process of a court of the United States, or of perjury in such court. To punish these offences, is certainly conducive to the due administration of justice. . . . [Maryland's] limited construction of the word "necessary" must be abandoned, in

OBSERVATION

THE RIGHT TO PUNISH: Other than the specific clauses Marshall notes and the power to set the punishment for treason, Art. III, § 3, cl.2, the Constitution contains no direct mention of a Congressional power to enact criminal laws. However, several provisions seem to assume a power to declare crimes. Art. III, § 2, cl. 3 requires jury trials and allows Congress to specify the venue for trials committed beyond state borders. The Eighth Amendment, by forbidding certain punishments, similarly implies a power to define crimes.

order to punish . . . . [W]hy is [the word "necessary"] not equally comprehensive, when required to authorize the use of means which facilitate the execution of the powers of government, without the infliction of punishment? . . .

But the argument which most conclusively demonstrates the error of the construction contended for by the counsel for the state of Maryland [i.e., that "necessary" means "required for"], is founded on the intention of the convention, as manifested in the whole [Necessary and Proper] clause. . . . This clause, as construed by the state of Maryland, would abridge, and almost annihilate, this useful and necessary right of the legislature to select its means. That this could not be intended, is, we should think, had it not been already controverted, too apparent for controversy.

We think so for the following reasons: 1st. The clause is placed among the powers of congress, not among the limitations on those powers. 2d. Its terms purport to enlarge, not to diminish the powers vested in the government. It purports to be an additional power, not a restriction on those already granted. No reason has been, or can be assigned, for thus concealing [from the ratifying conventions] an intention to narrow the discretion of the national legislature, under words which purport to enlarge it. . . . If, then, their intention had been, by this clause, to [limit all uses of enumerated powers], that intention would have been inserted in another place, and would have been expressed in terms resembling these: "In carrying into execution the foregoing powers, and all others," etc., "no laws shall be passed but such as are necessary and proper." Had the intention been to make this clause restrictive, it would unquestionably have been so in form as well as in effect.

. . . We admit, as all must admit, that the powers of the [federal] government are limited, and that its limits are not to be transcended. But we think the sound construction of the constitution must allow to the national legislature that discretion, with respect to the means by which the powers it confers are to be carried into execution, which will enable that body to perform the high duties assigned to it, in the manner most beneficial to the people. Let the end be legitimate, let it be within the scope of the constitution, and all means which are appropriate, which are plainly adapted to that end, which are not prohibited, but consist with the letter and spirit of the constitution, are constitutional. . . .

[APPLYING THE NECESSARY & PROPER CLAUSE]

[Corporations are a legitimate means to pursue Congress's enumerated ends.] If a corporation may be employed, indiscriminately with other means, to carry into execution the powers of the government, no particular reason can be assigned for excluding the use of a bank, if required for its fiscal operations. To use [a bank], must be within the discretion of congress, if it be an appropriate mode of executing the powers of government. That it is a convenient, a useful, and essential instrument in the prosecution of its fiscal operations, is not now a subject of controversy. All those who have been concerned in the administration of our finances, have concurred in representing its importance and necessity[.] . . .

But were its necessity less apparent, none can deny its being an appropriate measure; and if it is, the degree of its necessity, as has been very justly observed, is to be discussed in another place [than the judicial branch]. Should congress, in the execution of its powers, adopt measures which are prohibited by the constitution; or should congress, under the pretext of executing its powers, pass laws for the accomplishment of objects not entrusted to the government; it would become the painful duty of this tribunal, should a case requiring such a decision come before it, to say, that such an act was not the law of the land. But where the law is not prohibited, and is really calculated to effect any of the objects entrusted to the government, to undertake here to inquire into the degree of its necessity, would be to pass the line which circumscribes the judicial department, and to tread on legislative ground. This court disclaims all pretensions to such a power.

After this declaration, it can scarcely be necessary to say, that the existence of state banks can have no possible influence on the question. No trace is to be found in the constitution, of an intention to create a dependence of the government of the Union on those of the states, for the execution of the great powers assigned to it. Its means are adequate to its ends; and on those means alone was it expected to rely for the accomplishment of its ends. To impose on it the necessity of resorting to means which it cannot control, which another government may furnish or withhold, would render its course precarious, the result of its measures uncertain, and create a dependence on other governments, which might disappoint its most important designs, and is incompatible with the language of the constitution. But were it otherwise, the choice of means implies a right to choose a national bank in preference to state banks, and congress alone can make the election.

After the most deliberate consideration, it is the unanimous and decided opinion of this court, that the act to incorporate the Bank of the United States is a law made in pursuance of the constitution, and is a part of the supreme law of the land. . . .

It being the opinion of the court, that the act incorporating the bank is constitutional; and that the power of establishing a branch in the state of Maryland might be properly exercised by the bank itself, we proceed to inquire—

2. Whether the state of Maryland may, without violating the constitution, tax that branch?

[THE US CONSTITUTION MAY LIMIT STATE TAXING POWERS WHEN THEY COLLIDE WITH FEDERAL INTERESTS]

That the power of taxation is one of vital importance; that it is retained by the states; that it is not abridged by the grant of a similar power to the government of the Union; that it is to be concurrently exercised by the two governments—are truths which have never been denied. But such is the paramount character of the constitution, that its capacity to withdraw any subject from the action of even this power, is admitted. The states are expressly forbidden to lay any duties on imports or exports, except what may be absolutely necessary for executing their inspection laws. If the obligation of this prohibition must be conceded—if it may restrain a state from the exercise of its taxing power on imports and exports—the same paramount character would seem to restrain, as it certainly may restrain, a state from such other exercise of this power, as is in its nature incompatible with, and repugnant to, the constitutional laws of the Union. A law, absolutely repugnant to another, as entirely repeals that other as if express terms of repeal were used.

On this ground, the counsel for the bank place its claim to be exempted from the power of a state to tax its operations. There is no express provision for the case, but the claim has been sustained on a principle which so entirely pervades the constitution, is so intermixed with the materials which compose it, so interwoven with its web, so blended with its texture, as to be incapable of being separated from it, without rending it into shreds. This great principle is, that the constitution and the laws made in pursuance thereof are supreme; that they control the constitution and laws of the respective states, and cannot be controlled by them.

From this, which may be almost termed an axiom, other propositions are deduced as corollaries, on the truth or error of which, and on their application to this case, the cause has been supposed to depend. These are, 1st. That a power to create implies a power to preserve: 2d. That a power to destroy, if wielded by a different hand, is hostile to, and incompatible with these powers to create and to preserve: 3d. That where this repugnancy exists, that authority which is supreme must control, not yield to that over which it is supreme. . . .

The power of congress to create, and of course, to continue, the bank, was the subject of the preceding part of this opinion; and is no longer to be considered as questionable. That the power of taxing it by the states may be exercised so as to destroy it, is too obvious to be denied.

But taxation is said [by Maryland] to be an absolute power, which acknowledges no other limits than those expressly prescribed in the constitution, and like sovereign power of every other description, is entrusted to the discretion of those who use it. But the very terms of this argument admit, that the sovereignty of the state, in the article of taxation itself, is subordinate to, and may be controlled by the constitution of the United States. How far it has been controlled by that instrument, must be a question of construction. In making this construction, no principle, not declared, can be admissible, which would defeat the legitimate operations of a supreme government.

It is of the very essence of supremacy, to remove all obstacles to its action within its own sphere, and so to modify every power vested in subordinate governments, as to exempt its own operations from their own influence. This effect need not be stated in terms. It is so involved in the declaration of supremacy, so necessarily implied in it, that the expression of it could not make it more certain. We must, therefore, keep it in view, while construing the constitution.

McCulloch v. Maryland

[STATE ACTIONS WITH NATIONAL CONSEQUENCES]

The argument on the part of the state of Maryland, is, not that the states may directly resist a law of congress, but that they may exercise their acknowledged powers upon it, and that the constitution leaves them this right, in the confidence that they will not abuse it. Before we proceed to examine this argument, and to subject it to test of the constitution, we must be permitted to bestow a few considerations on the nature and extent of this original right of taxation, which is acknowledged to remain with the states.

It is admitted, that the power of taxing the people and their property, is essential to the very existence of government, and may be legitimately exercised on the objects to which it is applicable, to the utmost extent to which the government may choose to carry it. The only security against the abuse of this power, is found in the structure of the government itself. In imposing a tax, the legislature acts upon its constituents. This is, in general, a sufficient security against erroneous and oppressive taxation.

The people of a state, therefore, give to their government a right of taxing themselves and their property, and as the exigencies of government cannot be limited, they prescribe no limits to the exercise of this right, resting confidently on the interest of the legislator, and on the influence of the constituent over their representative, to guard them against its abuse. But the means employed by the government of the Union have no such security, nor is the right of a state to tax them sustained by the same theory. Those means are not given by the people of a particular state, not given by the constituents of the legislature, which claim the right to tax them, but by the people of all the states. They are given by all, for the benefit of all—and upon theory, should be subjected to that government only which belongs to all. . . .

That the power to tax involves the power to destroy; that the power to destroy may defeat and render useless the power to create; that there is a plain repugnance in conferring on one government a power to control the constitutional measures of another, which other, with respect to those very measures, is declared to be supreme over that which exerts the control, are propositions not to be denied. . . . Would the people of any one state trust those of another with a power to control the most insignificant operations of their state government? We know they would not. Why, then, should we suppose, that the people of any one state should be willing to trust those of another with a power to control the operations of a government to which they have confided their most important and most valuable interests? In the legislature of the Union alone, are all represented. The legislature of the Union alone, therefore, can be trusted by the people with the power of controlling measures which concern all, in the confidence that it will not be abused. . . .

If we apply the principle for which the state of Maryland contends, to the constitution, generally, we shall find it capable of changing totally the character of that instrument. We shall find it capable of arresting all the measures of the government, and of prostrating it at the foot of the states. The American people have declared their constitution and the laws made in pursuance thereof, to be supreme; but this principle would transfer the supremacy, in fact, to the states. If the states may tax one instrument, employed by the government in the execution of its powers, they may tax any and every other instrument. They may tax the mail; they may tax the mint; they may tax patent-rights; they may tax the papers of the custom-house; they may tax judicial process; they may tax all the means employed by the government, to an excess which would defeat all the ends of government. This was not intended by the American people. They did not design to make their government dependent on the states. . . .

It has also been insisted, that, as the power of taxation in the general and state governments is acknowledged to be concurrent, every argument which would sustain the right of the general government to tax banks chartered by the states, will equally sustain the right of the states to tax banks chartered by the general government. But the two cases are not on the same reason. The people of all the states have created the general government, and have conferred upon it the general power of taxation. The people of all the states, and the states themselves, are represented in congress, and, by their representatives, exercise this power. When they tax the chartered institutions of the states, they tax their constituents; and these taxes must be uniform. But when a state taxes the operations of the government of the United States, it acts upon institutions created, not by their own constituents, but by people over whom they claim no control. It acts upon the measures of a government created by others as well as themselves, for the benefit of others in common with themselves. The difference is that which always exists, and always must exist, between the action of the whole on a part, and the action of a part on the whole—between the laws of a government declared to be supreme, and those of a government which, when in opposition to those laws, is not supreme. . . .

The court has bestowed on this subject its most deliberate consideration. The result is a conviction that the states have no power, by taxation or otherwise, to retard, impede, burden, or in any manner control, the operations of the constitutional laws enacted by congress to carry into execution the powers vested in the general government. This is, we think, the unavoidable consequence of that supremacy which the constitution has declared. We are unanimously of opinion, that the law passed by the legislature of Maryland, imposing a tax on the Bank of the United States, is unconstitutional and void.

This opinion does not deprive the states of any resources which they originally possessed. It does not extend to a tax paid by the real property of the bank, in common with the other real property within the state, nor to a tax imposed on the interest which the citizens of Maryland may hold in this institution, in common with other property of the same description throughout the state. But this is a tax on the operations of the bank, and is, consequently, a tax on the operation of an instrument employed by the government of the Union to carry its powers into execution. Such a tax must be unconstitutional.

McCulloch v. Maryland

flash*forward*

1. ***National Banks.*** The second Bank of the United States remained politically contentious long after *McCulloch*. In 1833, President Andrew Jackson effectively killed the institution before its scheduled expiration date by withdrawing all of the government's deposits. There was no other Congressionally-created bank until 1913, when Congress created the Federal Reserve Bank, which continues to supervise the nation's paper money supply.

2. ***Necessary and Proper Criminal Laws.*** As *McCulloch* suggested, the Necessary and Proper Clause is frequently the source of power to enact federal criminal laws. One could argue that the crime of mail theft is not itself contained within "the power . . . to establish post offices and post roads" under Art. I, § 8, cl. 7, but a criminal punishment for interfering with the mail is a "necessary and proper" means of "carrying into execution" the power to establish post offices.

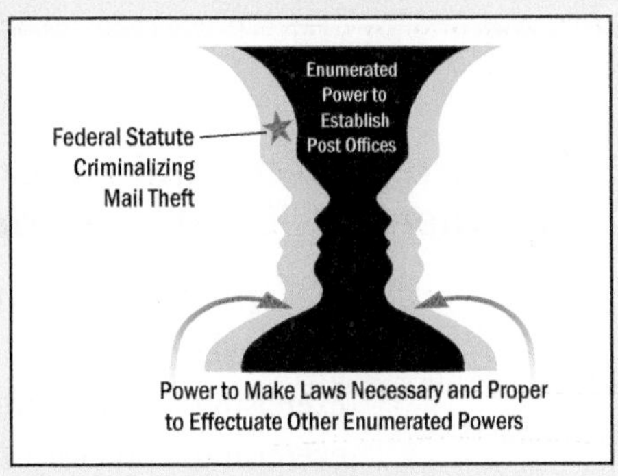

Marshall therefore saw two reasons to read the powers of Congress broadly. First, the structure of a constitution requires it. Second, the text of the US Constitution contains the Necessary and Proper Clause, which effectively builds breathing room around each of the other enumerated powers.

The modern approach to the Necessary and Proper Clause is described in Ch.15.D.

3. *State Regulation of Federal Activities.* As the last paragraph of the *McCulloch* opinion suggests, the federal government is not exempt from every state tax, only those state taxes that single out federal activities for detrimental effect. *McCulloch* said that the federal government could be obliged to pay real estate taxes like any other property owner, and federal employees must pay state income tax on their wages. Separating proper from improper taxes has given rise to a complex body of law known as "intergovernmental tax immunity."

The more general point about federal immunity from state regulation is illustrated by *United States v. Washington*, 142 S. Ct. 1976 (2022), where a state enacted a specialized worker's compensation law applying only to contractors at a specified federal nuclear facility. The relevant question was not whether the state law would indirectly increase costs for the Federal Government; that occurs with a property tax or income tax, which are allowed because costs are passed to the federal government in a "neutral, nondiscriminatory way." A state law violates federal supremacy when it attempts to "regulate the United States directly" or "discriminates against the Federal Government or those with whom it deals." The Washington statute solely targeted a federal program that was being run in a manner the state did not like. In that way, it resembled the law in *McCulloch* and was found unconstitutional.

B. Concurrent State and Federal Regulation of Commerce: *Gibbons v. Ogden*

■ WEBSITE

A fuller version of *Gibbons v. Ogden* is available for download from this casebook's companion website, www.CaplanIntegratedConLaw.com.

In *McCulloch*, the dueling governments appeared to be exercising different powers: the United States was exercising its power to create a bank, while Maryland was exercising its power to tax businesses operating within its borders. State/federal conflicts may also arise when the two levels of government seek to exercise the same type of power concurrently, such as power to regulate economic transactions.

Congress has power "to regulate commerce among the several states," Art. I, § 8, cl. 3, but states also use their sovereign police powers to regulate commerce. Conflicts may arise if the state and federal governments seek to regulate the same commerce differently. Realistically, there is no practical method for the federal government to regulate what crosses the border without having at least some influence over what happens in the state territory on either side of that border.

Similarly, state regulations within borders will often affect what crosses the border and how. The problem of concurrent power to regulate commerce first reached the Supreme Court in *Gibbons v. Ogden* (1824).

The Steamboat Battle. The most prominent American developer of steamboats was Robert Fulton, whose success drew on his engineering skills and his connections to influential investors. These included Robert Livingston, the US Ambassador to France who negotiated the Louisiana Purchase and the Chancellor of New York (an office akin to Chief Justice). In 1807, Fulton and Livingston created a sensation by traveling up the Hudson River by steamboat from New York City to Albany in thirty-two hours—only a third as long as it would take through other methods. Livingston used his political influence to convince the New York legislature to grant him and Fulton a legal monopoly on all steamboat travel in New York waters. No one else could operate steamboats in state waters without permission from Fulton and Livingston, although permission might be obtained for a price. Through a contract, former New Jersey governor Aaron Ogden received a license from Fulton and Livingston in 1814 to run passenger steamboats between New York City and Elizabethtown, New Jersey.

Thomas Gibbons, an estranged business partner of Ogden, was determined to break the New York steamboat monopoly. One of his strategies involved the federal Coasting Licensing Act of 1793. Under that Act, a federal office issued "coasting" licenses, which allowed a ship to fly the US flag (to distinguish it from foreign ships), exempted it from federal fees and duties applicable to foreign ships, and generally entitled it to "the privileges of ships or vessels employed in the coasting trade or fisheries." In 1816, Gibbons procured federal coasting licenses for two passenger steamboats (the *Bellona* and the *Stoudinger*) and began operating them on Ogden's New York-New Jersey route.

Ogden's Lawsuit. Ogden sued in New York state court for an injunction barring Gibbons from operating any steamboats on that route. Considering only state law, it was an open-and-shut case. Fulton and Livingston and their licensee Ogden had a legal monopoly over steamboats in New York waters, which would certainly include the harbor in New York City. Gibbons did not have their permission to land a steamboat in New York harbor, and hence he was violating the monopoly.

Gibbons—represented by the famous attorney **Daniel Webster**—raised several defenses. One was that New York had no authority to regulate commerce at all, because that was exclusively within the power of the federal government. Another was that even if New York had some power to regulate internal commerce, it could not bar interstate commerce authorized by the federal government. Ogden raised two arguments in opposition to these defenses: (a) Congress had no authority to issue coasting licenses to begin with, and (b) even if Congress could issue licenses, the licensing power did not strip New York of its ability to control its own waters.

BIOGRAPHY

DANIEL WEBSTER (1782–1852) of New Hampshire was considered the finest courtroom lawyer and public orator of his day. He prevailed in many important constitutional cases, in part because his philosophy dovetailed with that of John Marshall. Among other important victories, he successfully represented the Bank of the United States in *McCulloch v. Maryland* (1819) and the upstart steamboat operator in *Gibbons v. Ogden* (1824). Later, Webster served as a member of the House of Representatives, US Senator, and Secretary of State. Webster was an admitted elitist who favored urban industrial and banking interests and opposed the right to vote for citizens who did not own property. He disappointed anti-slavery activists with his consistent willingness to compromise with the South.

The state trial court ruled in favor of Ogden, issuing an injunction against Gibbons. The state court of appeals affirmed. The US Supreme Court then granted review, and its decision is summarized below.

Congressional Power to Issue Navigation Licenses. As in *McCulloch*, a central argument against the federal statute in *Gibbons* was that the enumerated powers of Congress were to be "strictly construed" to authorize federal power only in areas unmistakably identified in the text. Marshall's unanimous opinion in *Gibbons* rejected strict construction even more vehemently than the opinion in *McCulloch*. To begin with, said Marshall, strict construction was itself not mandated by anything in the text of the Constitution.

> It has been said, that these [federal] powers ought to be construed strictly. But why ought they to be so construed? [There is not] one sentence in the constitution, which has been pointed out by the gentlemen of the bar, or which we have been able to discern, that prescribes this rule. We do not, therefore, think ourselves justified in adopting it.

Making matters worse, strict construction "would deny to the government those powers which the words of the [Constitution], as usually understood, import." It "would cripple the government, and render it unequal to the object for which it is declared to be instituted." Instead of strict construction of powers, a court should instead construe powers in light of "the language of the instrument which confers them, taken in connection with the purposes for which they were conferred."

The discussion then turned to the meaning of "commerce" as it is used in Art. I, § 8, cl. 3. Ogden argued that "commerce" meant only the selling of goods. By operating a steamship, the argument went, Gibbons was not selling goods; he was transporting goods and passengers. "Navigation" was not "commerce."

Marshall relied on several text-based arguments to conclude that navigation was indeed a type of commerce. He began by asking what the word "commerce" means, and whether it would make any sense to define it as Ogden proposed:

> Commerce, undoubtedly, is traffic [in goods], but it is something more: it is intercourse. It describes the commercial intercourse between nations, and parts of nations, in all its branches, and is regulated by prescribing rules for carrying on that intercourse. The mind can scarcely conceive a system for regulating commerce between nations, which shall exclude all laws concerning navigation, which shall be silent on the admission of the vessels of the one nation into the ports of the other, and be confined to prescribing rules for the conduct of individuals, in the actual employment of buying and selling, or of barter.

Marshall then looked to Constitutional text beyond the Commerce Clause. Art. I, § 9 says that "no preference shall be given, by any regulation of commerce or revenue, to the ports of one State over those of another." If the Commerce Clause truly did not give Congress any power to regulate navigation, there would be no need to have a clause restricting how Congress could impose "regulations of commerce" on ports. "It would be absurd, as well as useless," said Marshall, "to except from a granted power, that which was not granted."

Another text-based argument relied on the validity of a pro-slavery provision in the original Constitution. Today, a legal argument that assumes the rightfulness of the slave trade would be repugnant, but it was an ordinary exercise for lawyers and judges of the early 19th century, many of whom (like Marshall himself) profited from slave labor. The argument proceeded this way: Art. I, § 9, cl. 4 prevented Congress from enacting any law before 1808 that would ban the importation of slaves from abroad, and Art. V made it impossible to amend that provision before 1808. See Ch. 3.B.2.b. Although these pro-slavery provisions did not use the word "commerce," their existence implied that something in the Constitution must give Congress power to ban the importation of slaves—otherwise, why say that Congress could not do so before 1808? The source of power to ban the international slave trade was the Commerce Clause, and specifically its grant of power "to regulate commerce with foreign nations." Congress may regulate "vessels employed in transporting men," said Marshall, a power that extends to those "who pass from place to place voluntarily, and to those who pass involuntarily."

In addition to these text-based arguments, Marshall considered two types of historical arguments, one based on governmental practices after the framing and one based on common understandings at the time of the framing.

> If commerce does not include navigation, the government of the Union has no direct power over that subject, and can make no law prescribing what shall constitute American vessels, or requiring that they shall be navigated by

> American seamen. Yet this power has been exercised from the commencement of the government, has been exercised with the consent of all, and has been understood by all to be a commercial regulation. All America understands, and has uniformly understood, the word "commerce," to comprehend navigation. It was so understood, and must have been so understood, when the constitution was framed. The power over commerce, including navigation, was one of the primary objects for which the people of America adopted their government, and must have been contemplated in forming it. The convention must have used the word in that sense, because all have understood it in that sense; and the attempt to restrict it comes too late.

Ogden next argued that even if Congress had a power to regulate navigation, this power could only affect how ships cross state lines; inside the territory of a state, a ship could be regulated by state law. With federal power limited only to the moment of the border crossing, New York still had control over its own harbors and waterways and could award monopolies over them if it wished.

To refute this argument, Marshall once again began with the text. "The word 'among' means intermingled with. A thing which is among others, is intermingled with them. Commerce among the States, cannot stop at the external boundary line of each State, but may be introduced into the interior" of those states.

Marshall next made a comparison to Congress's power over commerce with foreign nations and Indian tribes. In these scenarios, regulation could not be mystically restricted solely to the moment of border crossing.

> In regulating commerce with foreign nations, the power of Congress does not stop at the jurisdictional lines of the several States. It would be a very useless power, if it could not pass those lines. . . . [If] a foreign voyage may commence or terminate at a port within a State, then the power of Congress may be exercised within a State.
>
> This principle is, if possible, still more clear, when applied to commerce "among the several States." . . . If the trading intercourse be between two States remote from each other, must it not commence in one, terminate in the other, and probably pass through a third? Commerce among the States must, of necessity, be commerce within [the borders of] the States. In the regulation of trade with the Indian tribes, the action of the law, especially when the constitution was made, was chiefly within a State [since tribal lands were found within state borders]. The power of Congress, then, whatever it may be, must be exercised within the territorial jurisdiction of the several States.

The upshot was that Congress, while regulating commerce among states, could control some behavior occurring within states. This result was potentially surprising for advocates of largely unfettered state power over people and property within state borders. To address this concern, Marshall sought to explain how the federal power over commerce "among the states" would not mean the end of all state power over commerce.

> Comprehensive as the word "among" is, it may very properly be restricted to that commerce which concerns more States than one. The phrase is not one which would probably have been selected to indicate the completely interior traffic of a State, because it is not an apt phrase for that purpose; and the enumeration of the particular classes of commerce, to which the power was to be extended, would not have been made, had the intention been to extend the power to every description. The enumeration presupposes something not enumerated; and that something, if we regard the language or the subject of the sentence, must be the exclusively internal commerce of a State.
>
> The genius and character of the whole government seem to be, that its action is to be applied to all the external concerns of the nation, and to those internal concerns which affect the States generally; but not to those which are completely within a particular State, which do not affect other States, and with which it is not necessary to interfere, for the purpose of executing some of the general powers of the government. The completely internal commerce of a State, then, may be considered as reserved for the State itself.

The transportation of goods and passengers from New Jersey to New York by steamship was not "completely interior" or "completely internal" to New York, and hence was not under New York's exclusive control.

Effect of Federal Statute on New York Law. In light of the previous arguments, Gibbons' steamships were engaged in commerce among the states, and thus could be federally regulated. Indeed it was, because Gibbons had obtained a federal coasting license. And when carrying out that commerce, the steamships could use the waterways and ports of New York—over the objection of New York. Marshall correctly predicted that the interaction of state and federal power would be a source of eternal debate. "In our complex system, presenting the rare and difficult scheme of one general government, whose action extends over the whole, but which possesses only certain enumerated powers; and of numerous State governments, which retain and exercise all powers not delegated to the Union, contests respecting power must arise."

In cases posing an unavoidable conflict between state and federal law, the Supremacy Clause, Art. VI, § 2, directs that the federal law will be supreme, state law notwithstanding. This would be so, said Marshall, even if the state law was "enacted in the execution of acknowledged State powers," such as a state's power to regulate its internal harbors and waterways. When state laws "interfere with, or are contrary to the laws of Congress," the act of Congress is supreme. "The law of the State, though enacted in the exercise of powers not controverted, must yield to it."

Here, state law would frustrate the goal of the federal statute. "The laws of New-York, as expounded by the highest tribunal of that State, have, in their application to this case, come into collision with an act of Congress, and deprived a citizen of a right to which that act entitles him." Hence, the decision of the New York courts enjoining Gibbons were reversed.

flashforward

Federal Commerce Power. The Commerce Clause has been the basis for more federal statutes than any other enumerated power. It has also been a source of great constitutional dispute. The basic ideas from *Gibbons* have been widely accepted: (a) When regulating interstate commerce, the federal government may (and probably must) exercise authority over some activities occurring within the territories of states. (b) However, Congress may not regulate commerce that affects only a single state.

Under this framework, federal laws based on the Commerce Clause tend to fall into one or more of these categories:

Cross-border transactions. The federal government may determine whether and how goods or services may cross state borders. In *Gibbons*, for example, Congress could control the transportation of passengers by steamboat across the New York-New Jersey state line.

Infrastructure for cross-border transactions. To regulate cross-border transactions may require regulation of the infrastructure that makes the transactions possible. To facilitate border crossing by the passengers in *Gibbons*, Congress regulated some in-state infrastructure, including the state waters and harbors where the steamboats operated.

In-State activity substantially affecting interstate commerce. Gibbons said that Congress could regulate "commerce which concerns more States than one" but not "internal concerns which are completely within a particular State, which do not affect other States, and with which it is not necessary to interfere for the purpose of executing some of the general powers of the [federal] government." This implies that some transactions occurring within a single state might "concern" or "affect" other states, or "interfere" with federal goals. Perhaps Congress could prevent a corporate merger within one state that would create a monopoly with the ability to raise prices paid in all other states. This basis for commerce regulation has been controversial, with the Supreme Court often changing its view of which laws the theory allows. See Ch. 8.A (narrower interpretation beginning in 1890s) and 9.C.2 (broader interpretation beginning in 1937).

The modern approach to the Commerce Clause is explored in Ch. 15.C.

C. The Federal Bill of Rights and the States: *Barron v. Baltimore*

In Art. I, § 10, the US Constitution places explicit limits on states' sovereign powers, saying that "No state shall . . ." do certain things. Some litigants argued that the 1791 amendments known as the Bill of Rights should similarly be read to prevent states from doing certain things. The text of the Bill of Rights made some of those claims very difficult. It would be inconsistent with freedom of the press for a state to ban all newspapers, but the text of the First Amendment says that "*Congress* shall make no law" abridging freedom of the press. Protections for the press against state governments resided, if anywhere, at the state level.

By contrast, other portions of the federal Bill of Rights do not refer to Congress. The Sixth Amendment begins by saying that in criminal prosecutions, "the accused shall enjoy the right to a speedy and public trial," without specifying who must provide that right. Other portions of the Bill of Rights are phrased in the passive voice, as when the Fourth Amendment says that the right to be free of unreasonable searches and seizures "shall not be violated." (If rewritten in the active voice, the Fourth Amendment would identify *who* "shall not violate" the right.) Imagine that a state, to enforce a ban on newspapers, sends police to unreasonably search an editor's home and office without a warrant. Would this violate the Fourth Amendment? The US Supreme Court finally addressed the applicability of the Bill of Rights to state and local governments in *Barron v. City of Baltimore* (1833).

OBSERVATION

LOCAL GOVERNMENT: The precise relationships between state and local governments are dictated by state constitutions and statutes, with the details potentially varying from state to state. Local government is typically studied in classes on Municipal Law. For the cases in this book, you may assume that local governments are equivalent to state governments with regard to federally protected individual rights.

Barron's Complaint. In a series of public works projects between 1815 and 1821, the **local government** of Baltimore regraded land and diverted streams to create streets and sewers. The work changed runoff patterns, causing silt to run into Baltimore harbor during heavy rains. John Barron owned and operated a wharf in that harbor. The silt deposits made the water under his wharf too shallow for ships to use, ruining the wharf's economic value.

In 1822, Barron sued Baltimore's mayor and city council in a Maryland state court. He argued that the City's actions violated the Takings Clause of the Fifth Amendment, because they had taken the value of his property for public use without just compensation. The county trial court ruled in favor of Barron, but the state court of appeals reversed. Barron then brought the matter to the US Supreme Court.

ITEMS TO CONSIDER WHILE READING *BARRON v. BALTIMORE*:

A. *What are Barron's best arguments for saying that state and local governments must follow the Takings Clause of the Fifth Amendment? What are the best arguments against?*

B. *Identify methods of reasoning used in* Barron. *The decision provides excellent examples of arguments from text, structure, and history.*

C. *Does* Barron *control only the Fifth Amendment Takings Clause, or does it apply more broadly?*

D. *Barron sued under federal law because Maryland law at the time gave him no relief. Should the absence of a state right matter when considering the existence of a federal right?*

Barron v. City of Baltimore,

32 U.S. 243 (1833)

Chief Justice Marshall delivered the opinion of the court [joined by Justices Johnson, Duvall, Story, Thompson, McLean, and Baldwin].

. . . The plaintiff in error [the appellant John Barron] contends that [his claim] comes within that clause in the fifth amendment to the constitution, which inhibits the taking of private property for public use, without just compensation. He insists,

Barron v. City of Baltimore

that this amendment being in favor of the liberty of the citizen, ought to be so construed as to restrain the legislative power of a state, as well as that of the United States. . . .

The question thus presented is, we think, of great importance, but not of much difficulty.

The constitution was ordained and established by the people of the United States for themselves, for their own government, and not for the government of the individual states. Each state established a constitution for itself, and in that constitution, provided such limitations and restrictions on the powers of its particular government, as its judgment dictated. The people of the United States framed such a government for the United States as they supposed best adapted to their situation and best calculated to promote their interests. The powers they conferred on this government were to be exercised by itself; and the limitations on power, if expressed in general terms, are naturally, and, we think, necessarily, applicable to the government created by the instrument. They are limitations of power granted in the instrument itself; not of distinct governments, framed by different persons and for different purposes.

If these propositions be correct, the fifth amendment must be understood as restraining the power of the general government, not as applicable to the states. In their several constitutions, they have imposed such restrictions on their respective governments, as their own wisdom suggested; such as they deemed most proper for themselves. It is a subject on which they judge exclusively, and with which others interfere no further than they are supposed to have a common interest.

The counsel for the plaintiff in error insists, that the constitution was intended to secure the people of the several states against the undue exercise of power by their respective state governments; as well as against that which might be attempted by their general government. . . .

We think [Art. I, § 10] affords a strong, if not a conclusive, argument in support of the opinion already indicated by the court.

The preceding section [Art. I, § 9] contains restrictions which are obviously intended for the exclusive purpose of restraining the exercise of power by the departments of the general government. Some of them use language applicable only to congress; others are expressed in general terms. The third clause, for example, declares, that "no bill of attainder or ex post facto law shall be passed." No language can be more general; yet the demonstration is complete, that it applies solely to the government of the United States. In addition to the general arguments furnished by the instrument itself, some of which have been already suggested, the succeeding section [Art. I, § 10], the avowed purpose of which is to restrain state legislation, contains in terms the very prohibition. It declares, that "no state shall pass any bill of attainder or ex post facto law." This provision, then, of the ninth section, however comprehensive its language, contains no restriction on state legislation.

The ninth section [of Article I] having enumerated, in the nature of a bill of rights, the limitations intended to be imposed on the powers of the general government, the tenth proceeds to enumerate those which were to operate on the state legislatures. These restrictions are brought together in the same section, and are by express words applied to the states. "No state shall enter into any treaty," etc. Perceiving, that in a constitution framed by the people of the United States, for the government of all, no limitation of the action of government on the people would apply to the state government, unless expressed in terms, the restrictions contained in the tenth section are in direct words so applied to the states. . . .

If the original constitution, in the ninth and tenth sections of the first article, draws this plain and marked line of discrimination between the limitations it imposes on the powers of the general government, and on those of the state; if, in every inhibition intended to act on state power, words are employed, which directly express that intent; some strong reason must be assigned for departing from this safe and judicious course, in framing the amendments, before that departure can be assumed.

We search in vain for that reason.

Had the people of the several states, or any of them, required changes in their constitutions; had they required additional safe-guards to liberty from the apprehended encroachments of their particular governments; the remedy was in their own hands, and could have been applied by themselves. A convention could have been assembled by the discontented state, and the required improvements could have been made by itself. The unwieldy and cumbrous machinery of procuring a recommendation from two-thirds of congress, and the assent of three-fourths of their sister states, could never have occurred to any human being, as a mode of doing that which might be effected by the state itself. Had the framers of these [first ten] amendments intended them to be limitations on the powers of the state governments, they would have imitated the framers of the original constitution, and have expressed that intention. Had congress engaged in the extraordinary occupation of improving the constitutions of the several states, by affording the people additional protection from the exercise of power by their own governments, in matters which concerned themselves alone, they would have declared this purpose in plain and intelligible language.

But it is universally understood, it is a part of the history of the day, that the great revolution which established the constitution of the United States, was not effected without immense opposition. Serious fears were extensively entertained, that those powers which the patriot statesmen, who then watched over the interests of our country, deemed essential to union, and to the attainment of those invaluable objects for which union was sought, might be exercised in a manner dangerous to liberty. In almost every convention by which the constitution was adopted, amendments to guard against the abuse of power were recommended.

These amendments demanded security against the apprehended encroachments of the general government not against those of the local governments.

In compliance with a sentiment thus generally expressed, to quiet fears thus extensively entertained, amendments were proposed by the required majority in congress, and adopted by the states. These amendments contain no expression indicating an intention to apply them to the state governments. This court cannot so apply them.

We are of opinion, that the provision in the fifth amendment to the constitution, declaring that private property shall not be taken for public use, without just compensation, is intended solely as a limitation on the exercise of power by the government of the United States, and is not applicable to the legislation of the states. . . .

flashforward

1. *Constitutional Amendments After* Barron. The interpretive principle of *Barron* remains good law: except in those passages where it says otherwise, the US Constitution controls only the US government, not the states. What has changed since *Barron* is the text of the Constitution. In particular, § 1 of the Fourteenth Amendment (ratified 1868), says that "no State shall" do certain forbidden things. Language expressly directed at states can be found in many of the amendments that followed. As a result, states now face federal constitutional limitations that were not present when *Barron* was decided.

2. *The Incorporation Doctrine.* The Due Process Clause of the Fourteenth Amendment says, "No state shall . . . deprive any person of life, liberty, or property, without due process of law." (The Due Process of the Fifth Amendment imposes the same obligation on the federal government.) A series of decisions beginning in the early 20th century established that violating the most important rights found in the Bill of Rights would amount to deprivation of liberty or property without due process of law. Phrased another way, the Due Process Clauses can "incorporate" rights enumerated elsewhere in the Constitution, just as a contract or a complaint in a civil lawsuit might "incorporate" an exhibit attached to it.

If Barron filed his lawsuit today, he would rely on the following logic to assert a claim under the US Constitution:

A. States may not deprive persons of liberty or property without due process of law. Fourteenth Amendment, § 1.

B. The right described in the Takings Clause of the Fifth Amendment—the right to receive just compensation when private property is taken for public use—is incorporated into the meaning of "life, liberty, or property" in the Due Process Clause.

C. Therefore, states must pay just compensation when taking private property for public use.

This logic was adopted in *Chicago, Burlington and Quincy Railroad Co. v. City of Chicago*, 166 U.S. 225 (1897) ("the due process of law enjoined by the Fourteenth Amendment requires compensation to be made or adequately secured to the owner of private property taken for public use under the authority of a state.")

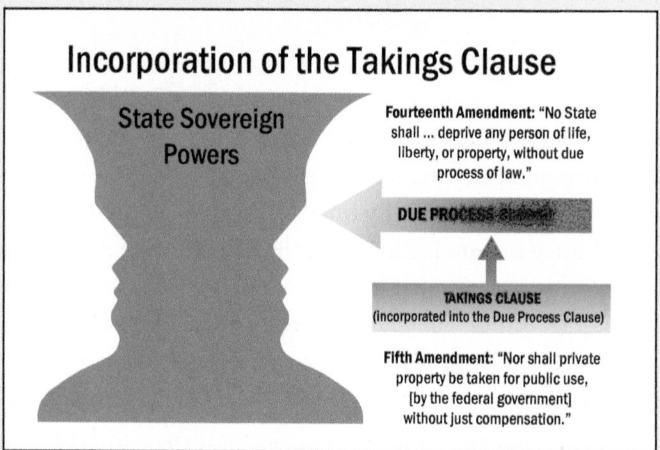
Incorporation of the Takings Clause
State Sovereign Powers
Fourteenth Amendment: "No State shall ... deprive any person of life, liberty, or property, without due process of law."
DUE PROCESS
TAKINGS CLAUSE
(incorporated into the Due Process Clause)
Fifth Amendment: "Nor shall private property be taken for public use, [by the federal government] without just compensation."

In the early-to-mid 20th century, the Supreme Court debated which rights were incorporated into the meaning of "liberty" within the Due Process Clause. After much theoretical jousting, the Court settled on an approach known as "selective incorporation," where only those enumerated rights deemed "fundamental" would be incorporated. The US Supreme Court recently summarized the doctrine in *Timbs v. Indiana*, 139 S.Ct. 682 (2019):

> When ratified in 1791, the [US Constitution's] Bill of Rights applied only to the Federal Government. *Barron v. Baltimore* (1833). The constitutional Amendments adopted in the aftermath of the Civil War, however, fundamentally altered our country's federal system. With only a handful of exceptions, this Court has held that the Fourteenth Amendment's Due Process Clause incorporates the protections contained in the Bill of Rights, rendering them applicable to the States. A Bill of Rights protection is incorporated, we have explained, if it is "fundamental to our scheme of ordered liberty" or "deeply rooted in this Nation's history and tradition."

Incorporation of a right into the Due Process Clause does not end all legal questions. If *Barron* were brought today, a court would next need to decide whether Baltimore had "taken" Barron's property when it caused his part of the harbor to silt up. Takings cases decided against the federal government under the Fifth Amendment would be precedent in a takings case against a state under the Fourteenth, and vice versa. Subject only to a few idiosyncratic exceptions, "incorporated Bill of Rights protections are all to be enforced against the States under the Fourteenth Amendment according to the same standards that protect those personal rights against federal encroachment." *McDonald v. City of Chicago*, 561 U.S. 742 (2010).

3. *Which Rights Are Incorporated?* As of today, the Due Process Clause incorporates so much of the Bill of Rights that it is easier to list the portions not incorporated.

- *Seventh Amendment.* The states are not required to empanel juries in common law civil cases involving more than $20. *Walker v. Sauvinet*, 92 U.S. 90 (1875). This explains the absence of juries in small claims courts. In practice, all states provide for a jury in civil cases where the stakes are high enough, but unlike the $20 figure in the Seventh Amendment, the thresholds may be adjusted without a constitutional amendment.
- *Fifth Amendment Grand Jury Clause.* State prosecutors may bring criminal charges by information, without first obtaining an indictment from a grand jury. *Hurtado v. California*, 110 U.S. 516 (1884). The remaining portions of the Fifth Amendment have all been incorporated.

- *Third Amendment.* No court opinion says that a state is forbidden from quartering soldiers in civilian homes during peacetime, but that is probably because the question has never been litigated. If it were to happen, the Third Amendment would likely be incorporated into the Due Process Clause.

4. *Incorporation Nomenclature.* A state's obligation to respect portions of the federal Bill of Rights arises from the combination of two pieces of text: the text describing a right (like the Sixth Amendment) plus the text requiring states to respect liberty (the Fourteenth Amendment). As a result, some court opinions will use language like "plaintiff brings her claims under the Sixth and Fourteenth Amendments" or "this case involves the state's obligations under the Sixth and Fourteenth Amendments." In such phrases, the reference to the Fourteenth Amendment is a fastidious way of indicating that the case involves state or local government and not the federal government. Other opinions dispense with the reference to the Fourteenth Amendment, as in "this case involves the state's obligations under the Sixth Amendment."

Chapter Recap

A. Sorting out the concurrent sovereignty of the state and federal governments was an early and ongoing source of constitutional disagreement.

B. State laws that conflict with federal statutes violate the Supremacy Clause, as seen in *McCulloch* and *Gibbons*.

C. *McCulloch* announced a broad interpretation of federal powers generally, and the Necessary and Proper Clause in particular, allowing the federal government to utilize a wide range of means to accomplish constitutionally appropriate ends.

D. *Gibbons* announced a broad interpretation of the Commerce Clause, allowing the federal government to regulate some events that occur within the borders of a state as part of a national regulation of interstate commerce.

E. Unless specific language in the text indicates otherwise, limits on government power found in the US Constitution apply only to the federal government, not state governments. *Barron v. Baltimore*. But after *Barron*, the Constitution was amended to include language expressly limiting state governments. The most prominent of these is the Fourteenth Amendment, which says (among other things) that states may not deprive persons of life, liberty, or property without due process of law. The Due Process Clause is now interpreted to incorporate most of the individual rights enumerated elsewhere in the Constitution.

CHAPTER 6

Slavery

Although slavery was abolished by the Thirteenth Amendment in 1865, it is still worth studying in a 21st-century Constitutional Law course.

- Many aspects of our modern constitutional text, and the precedents interpreting it, represent a reaction to the experience of slavery. Just as the contours of a valley can be better understood by reference to the now-vanished glaciers that carved it, today's Constitution is better understood by thinking about the forces that shaped it.
- The most significant slavery cases dealt with the same issues that we struggle with today: the proper methods to interpret imprecise constitutional text, the state/federal balance, and the proper role of the judiciary. If a particular method of reasoning, approach to federalism, or attitude toward judicial review led to a morally repugnant result when applied to slavery, what (if anything) should that mean for our willingness to rely on those methods today?
- Slavery presents an opportunity to consider the mechanisms of constitutional change. The shift from a constitution that protected slavery to one that abolished it was monumental. Lawyers need to be familiar with the processes of constitutional change, because you will be representing clients who seek to make change, oppose it, or simply deal with it when it occurs.

A. Slavery as a Pervasive Legal Institution

Slavery was woven into the daily life and structure of the nation in ways that can be hard to fathom today.

Slavery as an Unremarkable Legal Fact. Think back to *Gibbons v. Ogden* (1824), a legal dispute over the regulation of steamboat traffic between two states that had by that time abandoned slavery. Justice Marshall could make casual reference to Art. I, § 9, cl. 4—which protected the international slave trade—to prove his point that passenger ferries were "commerce." If transporting humans by (slave) ship was not commerce, then there would be no need to say that Congress could not prevent it before 1808. The legal logic is solid, and reliance on a slavery provision to support the reasoning obviously did not trouble Marshall (himself a slave-owning Virginian) or other members of the Court. Indeed, 24 out of the 35 Supreme Court justices appointed before the Civil War were from slave states, and of these most were known to have owned slaves.

Slavery and the Family. Slavery was intertwined with domestic life as well as commercial life. Under 18th-century family law, the father would ordinarily be entitled to custody of children in the event of divorce; after all, the father was the family sovereign and also was in the best financial position to provide for the children given the barriers to women earning a living in the paid economy. However, children born out of wedlock were the sole financial responsibility of the mother, and they could never inherit from their biological father. This would be true whether the pregnancy was the result of consensual extramarital sex, rape, or prostitution. Now add the rules of childbirth within slavery. The child of a slave was a slave, owned by the mother's owner, regardless of the status of the father. This played out in the life of the planter John Wayles of Virginia. His daughter Martha was born within his marriage; she eventually married Thomas Jefferson. Wayles also took his slave Betty Hemings as his personal concubine. The six Wayles-Hemings children became Jefferson's slave property after Wayles' death. Jefferson eventually took the youngest, Sally, to be his concubine with whom he also had six children. Jefferson freed Sally and her children in his will, but they were unable to claim Jefferson's name or any interest in his estate.

In the previous examples, slavery was simply a fact of legal life that dovetailed nicely with other existing law. But occasionally the needs of the slave system came into conflict with other ideals. When that happened, even free speech rights took a back seat to slavery.

Slavery and Speech: The "Gag Rule." In the 1830s and 1840s, abolitionists exercised their First Amendment rights by submitting petitions to Congress, asking it to use its powers under Art. I, § 8, cl. 17 to end slavery in the District of Columbia. An aggravated Senate adopted a rule in 1836 to automatically table anti-slavery petitions without debate, and an even more aggravated House prevented them from being read into the record or mentioned by any House member. This so-called "gag rule" was designed to restrict the speech of House members, and also to discourage the petitions themselves. The gag rule became a matter of continual acrimony and was ultimately repealed in 1844, but only after heroic efforts by then-representative John Quincy Adams.

Slavery and Speech: Postal Censorship. Before telegraphs, telephones, or broadcasting, the US Postal Service was the nation's chief means of communicating ideas over long distances. A federal statute enacted in 1836 required local postmasters to deliver all mail without censorship. Yet many Southern states were convinced that abolitionist writings from the North would encourage unrest and even slave rebellions in the South. Several Southern states banned any publication deemed "incendiary," and local postmasters agreed to censor the incoming mail. The issue never went to litigation, but in 1857 the local postmaster in Yazoo City, Mississippi asked US Attorney General Caleb Cushing for a written opinion on whether he was obligated to deliver a copy of the anti-slavery *Cincinnati Gazette* to a Mississippi subscriber. Cushing did not even consider the First Amendment, analyzing the question this way: "Has a citizen of one of the United States plenary indisputable right to employ the functions and the officers of the Union as the means of enabling him to produce insurrection in another of the United States? Can the officers of the Union lawfully lend its functions to the citizens of one of the States for the purpose of promoting insurrection in another State?" With the question framed that way, the answer was "obviously not." Cushing concluded: "It may be unpleasant to some person in Ohio to find that he is not free to promote insurrection in Mississippi. Nevertheless, even at the risk of not accommodating any such perverse taste, each State of the Union has the right to protect itself against domestic violence, and to invoke to that end the friendly cooperation, or at least the neutrality, of the United States."

B. The Fugitive Slave Clause: *Prigg v. Pennsylvania*

The Fugitive Slave Clause, Art. IV, § 2, cl. 3 reads as follows:

> No person held to service or labor in one state, under the laws thereof, escaping into another, shall, in consequence of any law or regulation therein, be discharged from such service or labor, but shall be delivered up on claim of the party to whom such service or labor may be due.

The text contains none of the language typically used to signal federal power, such as "Congress shall have the power" or "Congress may." The Clause is located in Art. IV, which primarily deals with the obligations of states to each other. Similarly, the Clause does not explicitly speak in terms of an individual "right" to own slaves. Hence, the Clause could be read as solely an obligation for states to return slaves as a matter of interstate comity. But in *Prigg v. Pennsylvania* (1842), it was interpreted as a source for a Congressional power to enact legislation and for an individual right to recapture slaves in ways forbidden by state or federal statutes.

At the time of the framing, all the states—including those that had abolished slavery—had statutes authorizing their judges to order the return of fugitive slaves. But from its earliest days, Congress assumed that it also had power to legislate on the topic of fugitive slaves. The Fugitive Slave Act of 1793, signed into law by President Washington, called for alleged fugitives to be brought before a judge (state or federal) who would rule on the slave's identity. The rules of evidence and burdens of proof were favorable to the putative slave owner, and the alleged slave had no right to a jury, to counsel, or to cross-examine.

After decades of experience under the Fugitive Slave Act, opposition began to arise in the North. One objection was that state judges should not be obliged to administer a federal statute. Another was that the federal statute was slanted against the alleged fugitive, leading to state-facilitated enslavement of free Black people. Finally, the states were alarmed at the rising number of outright kidnappings of free Black people to be sold into slavery without any recourse to judicial procedures. The legislative response took the form of "Personal Liberty Laws" that ordinarily had two components: (a) they updated the states' fugitive slave laws to incorporate greater procedural protections for the alleged slaves; and (b) they made it a crime to kidnap a Black person into slavery without going through a judicial process. The constitutionality of state Personal Liberty Laws came before the US Supreme Court in 1842.

The Kidnapping of Margaret Morgan. The following description from Paul Finkelman, "*Sorting Out Prigg v. Pennsylvania*," 24 Rutgers L.J. 605 (1993), shows how the lines between freedom and slavery could be more distinct in theory than in practice.

> Margaret Morgan's parents had been the slaves of a Maryland master named Ashmore. Although he never formally emancipated them, sometime before 1812 Ashmore allowed Margaret's parents to live as free blacks. Thereafter, Ashmore constantly declared he had set them free. Margaret was born after her parents had been informally set free. Margaret eventually married Jerry Morgan, a free black, and in 1832 they moved just across the Maryland border to Pennsylvania. There they had several children. These children were free under Pennsylvania law and were not subject to the Fugitive Slave Act; they did not fit the constitutional definition of fugitive slaves (persons "escaping into another" state). Margaret's marriage to Jerry Morgan and her subsequent move to Pennsylvania occurred with the apparent acquiescence of Ashmore. Thus, under either Pennsylvania or Maryland law, Margaret might have been legitimately free.

Around 1836, Ashmore died and his estate passed to his niece, Margaret Ashmore Bemis. In February 1837, Margaret's husband, Nathan S. Bemis, Edward Prigg, and two others went to Pennsylvania to find Morgan and bring her back to Maryland. That month, the four slave-catchers seized Morgan and her children and brought them to Maryland. The fact that Bemis and Prigg were immediately able to locate Morgan suggests that she did not see herself as a fugitive slave and had never tried to hide her whereabouts from Ashmore or his niece. That the Morgans lived along the Maryland border also suggests they believed Margaret was a free person.

Bemis and Prigg obtained a warrant from Justice of the Peace Thomas Henderson to apprehend Morgan under Pennsylvania's 1826 [Personal Liberty Law]. They seized Morgan, her children, and her husband Jerry Morgan, even though he was indisputably a free person. When Bemis and Prigg brought the Morgans to Justice of the Peace Henderson, he refused to issue the necessary papers allowing for the Morgans' removal from Pennsylvania. . . . Bemis and Prigg then acted on their own. After releasing Jerry Morgan, they took Margaret and her children to Maryland where "they were sold to a negro trader for shipment to the South."[FN28]

FN28 Margaret and her children were sold, shipped south and disappeared from the records. Her husband, Jerry, was killed as he was returning from a visit to the Pennsylvania Governor, while trying to secure the return of his wife and children.

A Pennsylvania grand jury subsequently indicted the slave-catchers under Pennsylvania's Personal Liberty Law. Initially Maryland refused to comply with an extradition requisition from the governor of Pennsylvania. However, negotiations between the two states led to a compromise. Maryland sent Prigg to Pennsylvania for trial after Pennsylvania officials agreed that in the event of a conviction he would not be incarcerated until after the United States Supreme Court had ruled on the constitutionality of the relevant state and federal laws. Pennsylvania also guaranteed an expedited appeals process from the trial court to the state supreme court. Thus, a trial court convicted Prigg of kidnapping, the Pennsylvania Supreme Court affirmed in a *pro forma* opinion, and Prigg appealed to the United States Supreme Court.

The Supreme Court knew that *Prigg* was a high-profile case with important ramifications for an issue of growing interstate disagreement. When decided, the case had seven separate opinions—the most of any US Supreme Court opinion to that date.

ITEMS TO CONSIDER WHILE READING *PRIGG*:

A. *Did Congress have power to enact the Fugitive Slave Act of 1793? Construct arguments for and against, focusing on text and constitutional structure.*

B. *Is the individual right to recapture slaves through self-help supported by the text of the Fugitive Slave Clause? By other constitutional text? By other methods of reasoning?*

C. *If the individual right to recapture slaves exists without the need of any legislation, what is the purpose of the Fugitive Slave Act of 1793?*

D. *How did Pennsylvania's Personal Liberty Law interfere with (a) slave owners' rights; and (b) the federal Fugitive Slave Act?*

Prigg v. Pennsylvania,

41 U.S. 539 (1842)

Justice Story delivered the opinion of the court [joined by Chief Justice Taney, and Justices Catron, McKinley, Thompson, Baldwin, Wayne, and Daniel.]

[The opinion began by stating the facts and describing the primary arguments of counsel.]

Before, however, we proceed to the points more immediately before us, it may be well, in order to clear the case of difficulty, to say, that in the exposition of this part of the constitution, we shall limit ourselves to those considerations which appropriately and exclusively belong to it, without laying down any rules of interpretation of a more general nature. It will, indeed, probably, be found, when we look to the character of the constitution itself, the objects which it seeks to attain, the powers which it confers, the duties which it enjoins, and the rights which it secures, as well as the known historical fact, that many of its provisions were matters of compromise of opposing interests and opinions, that **no uniform rule of interpretation** can be applied to it, which may not allow, even if it does not positively demand, many modifications, in its actual application to particular clauses. And, perhaps, the safest rule of interpretation, after all, will be found to be to look to the nature and objects of the particular powers, duties and rights, with all the lights and aids of contemporary history; and to give to the

■ OBSERVATION

NO UNIFORM RULE OF INTERPRETATION: Justice Story rejects any "uniform rule of interpretation" for the Constitution. He appears not to be an originalist, since he believes it is legitimate to consider "the lights and aids of contemporary history" (i.e., knowledge and hindsight not available to the founding generation). His reference to "legitimate meaning" implies a textual approach, while the reference to "the nature and objects of the particular powers" implies a structural approach.

words of each just such operation and force, consistent with their legitimate meaning, as may fairly secure and attain the ends proposed.

Prigg v. Pennsylvania

BIOGRAPHY

Appointed to the US Supreme Court by James Madison in 1811, **JOSEPH STORY** (1779–1845) of Massachusetts was—at age 32—the youngest person ever to join the Court. He was a renowned scholar and author of the influential treatise *Commentaries on the Constitution of the United States* (1833). A protégé of John Marshall, Story tended as a Justice to favor expansive powers for the federal government and federal judiciary. Indeed, his decision in *Prigg* seems to have been motivated more by his enthusiasm for federal power than by devotion to slavery itself.

There are two clauses in the constitution upon the subject of fugitives, which stand in juxtaposition with each other, and have been thought mutually to illustrate each other. They are both contained in the second section of the fourth article, and are in the following words: "A person charged in any state with treason, felony or other crime, who shall flee from justice, and be found in another state, shall, on demand of the executive authority of the state from which he fled, be delivered up, to be removed to the state having jurisdiction of the crime." [Art. IV, § 2, cl.2.] "No person held to service or labor in one state, under the laws thereof, escaping into another, shall, in consequence of any law or regulation therein, be discharged from such service or labor; but shall be delivered up, on claim of the party to whom such service or labor may be due." [Art. IV, § 2, cl. 3.]

The last clause is that, the true interpretation whereof is directly in judgment before us. Historically, it is well known, that the object of this clause was to secure to the citizens of the slave-holding states the complete right and title of ownership in their slaves, as property, in every state in the Union into which they might escape from the state where they were held in servitude. The full recognition of this right and title was indispensable to the security of this species of property in all the slave-holding states; and, indeed, was so vital to the preservation of their domestic interests and institutions, that it cannot be doubted, that it constituted a fundamental article, without the adoption of which **the Union could not have been formed**. Its true design was, to guard against the doctrines and principles prevalent in the non-slave-holding

OBSERVATION

THE UNION COULD NOT HAVE BEEN FORMED: Modern historians disagree with Story's assertion that the Fugitive Slave Clause was crucial for the success of the constitutional convention. In fact, the clause was added almost as an afterthought near the end of the convention, and there is no record of any debate on the topic.

states, by preventing them from intermeddling with, or obstructing, or abolishing the rights of the owners of slaves. . . .

How then are we to interpret the language of the clause? The true answer is in such a manner as, consistently with the words, shall fully and completely effectuate the whole objects of it. If, by one mode of interpretation, the right must become shadowy and unsubstantial, and without any remedial power adequate to the end, and, by another mode, it will attain its just end and secure its manifest purpose, it would seem, upon principles of reasoning, absolutely irresistible, that the latter ought to prevail. No court of justice can be authorized so to construe any clause of the Constitution as to defeat its obvious ends when another construction, equally accordant with the words and sense thereof, will enforce and protect them.

[OWNER'S RIGHT TO RECAPTURE FUGITIVE SLAVES]

The clause manifestly contemplates the existence of a positive, unqualified right on the part of the owner of the slave which no state law or regulation can in any way qualify, regulate, control, or restrain. The slave is not to be discharged from service or labor in consequence of any state law or regulation. Now certainly, without indulging in any nicety of criticism upon words, it may fairly and reasonably be said that any state law or state regulation which interrupts, limits, delays, or postpones the right of the owner to the immediate possession of the slave and the immediate command of his service and labor operates *pro tanto* a discharge of the slave therefrom. . . .

We have said that the clause contains a positive and unqualified recognition of the right of the owner in the slave, unaffected by any state law or legislation whatsoever, because there is no qualification or restriction of it to be found therein, and we have no right to insert any which is not expressed and cannot be fairly implied. . . . The owner must, therefore, have the right to seize and repossess the slave, which the local laws of his own State confer upon him, as property, and we all know that this right of seizure and recaption is universally acknowledged in all the slaveholding States. Indeed, this is no more than a mere affirmance of the principles of the common law applicable to this very subject. Mr. Justice Blackstone lays it down as unquestionable doctrine.

Recaption or reprisal is another species of remedy by the mere act of the party injured. This happens when anyone hath deprived another of his property in goods or chattels personal, or wrongfully detains one's wife, child or servant, in which case the owner of the goods, and the husband, parent or master, may lawfully claim and retake them wherever he happens to find them, so it be not in a riotous manner or attended with a breach of the peace.

Upon this ground, we have not the slightest hesitation in holding that, under and in virtue of the Constitution, the owner of a slave is clothed with entire authority, in every State in the Union, to seize and recapture his slave whenever he can do it without any breach of the peace or any illegal violence. In this sense and to this extent, this clause of the Constitution may properly be said to execute itself, and to require no aid from legislation, state or national.

[CONGRESSIONAL POWER TO ENACT FUGITIVE SLAVE LEGISLATION]

But the clause of the Constitution does not stop here, nor, indeed, consistently with its professed objects, could it do so. Many cases must arise in which, if the remedy of the owner were confined to the mere right of seizure and recaption, he would be utterly without any adequate redress. He may not be able to lay his hands upon the slave. He may not be able to enforce his rights against persons who either secrete or conceal or withhold the slave. He may be restricted by local legislation as to the mode of proofs of his ownership, as to the courts in which he shall sue, and as to the actions which he may bring or the process he may use to compel the delivery of the slave. Nay, the local legislation may be utterly inadequate to furnish the appropriate redress, by authorizing no process *in rem*, or no specific mode of repossessing the slave, leaving the owner, at best, not that right which the Constitution designed to secure, a specific delivery and repossession of the slave, but a mere remedy in damages, and that, perhaps, against persons utterly insolvent or worthless. The state legislation may be entirely silent on the whole subject, and its ordinary remedial process framed with different views and objects, and this may be innocently, as well as designedly, done[.]

Capture of fugitives Anthony Burns and Thomas Sims in Boston (1851)

If, therefore, the clause of the Constitution had stopped at the mere recognition of the right, without providing or contemplating any means by which it might be established and enforced, in cases where it did not execute itself, it is plain that it would have been, in a great variety of cases, a delusive and empty annunciation. If it did not contemplate any action, either through state or national legislation, as auxiliaries to its more perfect enforcement in the form of remedy, or of protection, then, as there would be no duty on either to aid the right, it would be left to the mere comity of the States to act as they should please, and would depend for its security upon the changing course of public opinion, the mutations of public policy, and the general adaptations of remedies for purposes strictly according to the *lex fori* [law of the forum].

And this leads us to the consideration of the other part of the clause, which implies at once a guarantee and duty. It says, "but he [the slave] shall be delivered up on claim of the party to whom such service or labor may be due." Now we think it exceedingly difficult, if not impracticable, to read this language and not to feel that it contemplated some further remedial redress than that which might be administered at the hands of the owner himself. A claim is to be made! What is a claim? It is, in a just juridical sense, a demand of some matter, as of right, made by one person upon another, to do or to forbear to do some act or thing as a matter of duty. . . . The slave is to be delivered up on the claim. By whom to be delivered up? In what mode to be delivered up? How, if a refusal takes place, is the right of delivery to be enforced? Upon what proofs? What shall be the evidence of a rightful recaption or delivery? When and under what circumstances shall the possession of the owner, after it is obtained, be conclusive of his right, so as to preclude any further inquiry or examination into it by local tribunals or otherwise, while the slave, in possession of the owner, is *in transitu* [in transit] to the State from which he fled?

These and many other questions will readily occur upon the slightest attention to the clause; and it is obvious that they can receive but one satisfactory answer. They require the aid of legislation to protect the right, to enforce the delivery, and to secure the subsequent possession of the slave. If, indeed, the Constitution guaranties the right, and if it requires the delivery upon the claim of the owner (as cannot well be doubted), the natural inference certainly is that the National Government is clothed with the appropriate authority and functions to enforce it. The fundamental principle, applicable to all cases of this sort, would seem to be that, where the end is required, the means are given; and where the duty is enjoined, the ability to perform it is contemplated to exist on the part of the functionaries to whom it is entrusted.

The clause is found in the National Constitution, and not in that of any State. It does not point out any state functionaries, or any state action, to carry its provisions into effect. . . . On the contrary, the natural, if not the necessary, conclusion is, that the National Government, in the absence of all positive provisions to the contrary, is bound, through its own proper departments, legislative, judicial or executive, as the case may require, to carry into effect all the rights and duties imposed upon it by the Constitution. The remark of Mr. Madison, in The Federalist (No. 43), would seem in such cases to apply with peculiar force. "A right implies a remedy, and where else would the remedy be deposited than where it is deposited by the Constitution?"—meaning, as the context shows, in the Government of the United States. . . . Congress, then, may call that power into activity for the very purpose of giving effect to that right; and, if so, then it may prescribe the mode and extent in which it shall be applied, and how and under what circumstances the proceedings shall afford a complete protection and guarantee to the right. . . .

Chief Justice Taney, Concurring. [Omitted]

Justice Thompson, Concurring. [Omitted]

Justice Baldwin, Concurring. [Omitted]

Justice Wayne, Concurring. [Omitted]

Justice Daniel, Concurring. [Omitted]

Justice McLean, Dissenting. [Omitted]

flashforward

1. *Recapturing Fugitive Slaves After* Prigg. A portion of *Prigg* not included in this book stated, in dicta that was widely followed, that state courts were not obligated to hear cases brought under the federal Fugitive Slave Act. (The obligation of state officers to enforce federal law has arisen in recent years under the doctrine against *commandeering*, explored in Ch. 14.B). Despite the nod to state authority, this aspect of *Prigg* ultimately satisfied no one. Given the relatively small number of federal judges available to hear any cases, let alone fugitive slave cases, it was hard for slave owners to invoke the federal statute, to the detriment of the South. But then again, *Prigg*'s protection for the individual right of self-capture made recourse to state or federal judges optional, to the detriment of the North.

Congress ultimately responded with a revised Fugitive Slave Act in 1850. This law created a staff of federal commissioners to decide slave owners' claims. The procedures were even more slanted in favor of slave owners than the 1793 Act: the slave owner was not required to offer any live testimony, and could instead submit an affidavit that could not be cross-examined. Meanwhile, the alleged slave was not allowed to testify. The commissioner would be paid $10 for issuing a certificate of removal, but only $5 for denying it. Many in the North vehemently opposed the new Fugitive Slave Act. Ralph Waldo Emerson encouraged resistance to what he denounced as a "filthy enactment."

2. ***Fugitive Slaves During the Civil War.*** The peculiar logic surrounding fugitive slaves became an issue early in the Civil War, as slaves who resided near the front lines began fleeing their owners and seeking asylum with the Union Army. General George McClellan considered himself obligated to obey the Fugitive Slave Act and return the slaves to their owners. Many of McClellan's subordinates refused to go along. General Benjamin Butler, a lawyer in civilian life, developed an ingenious legal strategy when hundreds of slaves sought refuge in Union-controlled Fort Monroe in eastern Virginia. Because the slaves could be put to military use by the rebels if they were returned, Butler exercised his military power to seize them as "contraband of war" to keep them out of enemy hands. Then, because he had no desire or authority to own slaves, he freed them. Congress incorporated Butler's idea into the Confiscation Act of 1861. The Fugitive Slave Acts of 1793 and 1850 were finally repealed in 1864.

C. Increasing Political Polarization over Slavery

Art. IV, § 3, cl. 2 gives Congress power to "make all needful rules and regulations" respecting federal territory that was not yet organized into states. Before the Civil War, most of the political debate around slavery focused on these territories. Slavery in the territories was important for many reasons. Citizens of free states who considered slavery immoral did not want it to spread any further, nor did they want their national government to enact laws directly supporting slavery. For their part, slave owners wanted the ability to move into new territory, and to do so without forfeiting their existing property or lifestyle. But most of all, both sides assumed—with reason—that slave or free territories would ultimately join the union as slave or free states. Slavery in the territories (or its absence) would be crucial for future control of Congress.

The solution devised under the Articles of Confederation was to maintain a rough parity of numbers between free and slave states, arrayed north and south. The Northwest Ordinance of 1787 implemented that arrangement for the territory between the Ohio and Mississippi Rivers. Under the new Constitution, the Northwest Ordinance was re-enacted, and the Missouri Compromise of 1820 extended the idea to the Louisiana Territory, west of the Mississippi.

In the late 1840s, the United States took control of the remaining territory west of the Rocky Mountains, as a result of the Mexican-American War and the acquisition of the Oregon Territory. This time, however, the previous north/south compromise was not simply extended westward. The Compromise of 1850 opened far more federal territory to possible slavery. The 1850 legislation allowed California to enter the nation as a free state, but it greatly strengthened the Fugitive Slave Act (as described above) and allowed the Utah territory—which would have been free under the Missouri Compromise of 1820—to allow slavery if the residents voted for it. The Compromise of 1850 prompted New York's Senator William Seward to declare: "There is a higher law than the Constitution."

In some circles, Seward's comment became a slogan of resistance. It also reflected one side of a division of opinion among abolitionists as to whether the US Constitution was the problem or the solution. The abolitionist publisher William Lloyd Garrison gave up on the Constitution altogether, describing it as "a covenant with death" and "an agreement with hell." Others, like Lysander Spooner and Frederick Douglass, came to believe through a variety of ingenious arguments that despite appearances, the Constitution empowered Congress to end slavery. Meanwhile in the South, pro-slavery ideology became much more pronounced, increasingly supported by references to holy scripture.

SOUTHERN CHIVALRY _ ARGUMENT VERSUS CLUB'S.
The Caning of Charles Sumner (1856), by John L. Magee

The Kansas-Nebraska Act of 1854 further exacerbated the North-South polarization. The Kansas and Nebraska territories would have been free under the Missouri Compromise, but the new legislation allowed the residents of each territory to vote on whether to allow slavery before statehood. Pro- and anti-slavery forces rushed into Kansas in hopes of controlling the outcome, leading to a small-scale civil war in 1856 that gave the territory the nickname "Bleeding Kansas." During that controversy, Senator Charles Sumner of Massachusetts gave a speech in Congress titled "The Crime Against Kansas" where he compared supporters of slavery to rapists who would despoil virgins. Rep. Preston Brooks of South Carolina responded a few days later by attacking Sumner on Senate floor with a cane, nearly killing him.

In short, both the South and the North came to feel threatened and invaded by the other. As controversy expanded after 1850, some politicians on both sides of the slavery divide hoped that the Supreme Court would resolve the heated question of slavery in the territories. They got their wish with the *Dred Scott* decision of 1857.

D. Slavery in Federal Territory: The *Dred Scott* Decision

Dred Scott was a slave who lived most of his adult life in St. Louis, Missouri. His owner, Dr. John Emerson, was an Army surgeon who had occasional tours of duty at military bases across the Midwest. From 1833 to 1836, Emerson served at Fort Armstrong in the state of Illinois, and from 1836 to 1838 at Fort Snelling in the part of the Wisconsin Territory that is now Minnesota. Scott accompanied Emerson on these assignments. That fact was legally significant because under Missouri law, slaves became free if their owners voluntarily allowed them to live in free jurisdictions.

BIOGRAPHY

DRED SCOTT (c. 1800–1858) was born into slavery in Alabama, and later taken to Missouri by his owner, Peter Blow. After Blow's death in 1832, Scott was sold to Dr. John Emerson. While traveling with Emerson to the Minnesota territory in 1838, Scott married **HARRIET ROBINSON SCOTT** (c. 1820–1876). The fact that they were allowed to marry—a right legally denied to slaves—suggests that they were held in high esteem by their respective owners. No one knows why the Scotts waited until after Emerson's death to seek freedom for themselves and their daughters Eliza and LIzzie. They might not have known about their legal options, they might have felt personally well-treated as urban domestic slaves not required to do heavy agricultural work, or they may have had other unknown reasons.

The Missouri Lawsuit. After Emerson died and his wife Irene inherited his slaves, Scott filed suit for his freedom in Missouri state court. The White male jury unanimously agreed that Scott should be freed. But on appeal, the Missouri Supreme Court abruptly reversed its earlier precedents to hold that Missouri law no longer freed slaves merely because their owners had taken them to free states like Illinois. *Scott v. Emerson*, 15 Mo. 576 (1852). The opinion closed with a full-throated defense of slavery, coupled with sneers against abolitionists and Northern states.

> Times are not now as they were when the former decisions on this subject were made. Since then not only individuals but States have been possessed with a dark and fell spirit in relation to slavery, whose gratification is sought in the pursuit of measures, whose inevitable consequences must be the overthrow and destruction of our government. Under such circumstances it does not behoove the State of Missouri to show the least countenance to any measure

which might gratify this spirit. She is willing to assume her full responsibility for the existence of slavery within her limits, nor does she seek to share or divide it with others. . . . [W]e will not go to [Northern states] to learn law, morality or religion on the subject.

As to the consequences of slavery, they are much more hurtful to the master than the slave. There is no comparison between the slave in the United States and the cruel, uncivilized negro in Africa. When the condition of our slaves is contrasted with the state of their miserable race in Africa; when their civilization, intelligence and instruction in religious truths are considered, and the means now employed to restore them to the country from which they have been torn, bearing with them the blessings of civilized life, we are almost persuaded, that the introduction of slavery amongst us was, in the providence of God, who makes the evil passions of men subservient to His own glory, a means of placing that unhappy race within the pale of civilized nations.

The Federal Lawsuit. The Missouri Supreme Court opinion focused on whether Scott's years in the free state of Illinois would lead to his freedom under Missouri law, but it did not separately consider the distinct legal issues that might arise from Scott's years in the free federal territory of Minnesota. From this, Scott could argue that the question remained open for litigation. The Missouri court system was plainly a lost cause, so Scott needed to find a jurisdictionally acceptable method to bring the theory to a federal court.

Subject matter jurisdiction in federal court was possible as a result of **diversity of citizenship**. At this point, Irene Emerson's ownership interest in the Scotts was under the control of her brother, John Sanford (misspelled as "Sandford" in the US Supreme Court). Sanford was a citizen of New York, and Scott alleged that he was a citizen of Missouri. Sanford asserted as a defense that the court had no jurisdiction: this was not a suit between "citizens of different states" because Scott was not a citizen at all.

■ OBSERVATION

DIVERSITY OF CITIZENSHIP: The federal statutes creating federal trial courts allow them to exercise the power under Art. III, § 2 to decide controversies "between citizens of different states." Even though Scott's theory for freedom involved federal law, Scott could not rely on federal question jurisdiction because Congress did not authorize federal trial courts to hear cases "arising under the constitution and laws of the United States" until 1875.

Scott lost in the federal trial court. The trial judge disregarded Sanford's jurisdictional defense, and instead held a short trial on stipulated facts. Despite the different focus of Scott's legal arguments (emphasizing his presence in the Minnesota territory instead of his presence in the state of Illinois), the judge instructed the jury that Scott's status as a slave had already been decided by the Missouri Supreme Court. The jury had little choice: it concluded that Scott remained a slave.

Scott appealed and the Supreme Court accepted review. The case was first argued in February 1856. In November, James Buchanan of Pennsylvania won the presidential election. Buchanan was known as a "doughface," the term for a Northern politician who supported slavery. The Supreme Court heard re-argument in *Dred Scott* in December 1856. In early 1857, president-elect Buchanan privately lobbied members of the Supreme Court to rule broadly, in hopes that this would pave the way to national harmony. At his inauguration on March 4, 1857, knowing what decision was coming, Buchanan stated that slavery in the territories was ultimately a "judicial question, which legitimately belongs to the Supreme Court of the United States, before whom it is now pending, and will be speedily and finally settled . . . May we not, then, hope that the long agitation on this subject is approaching its end?" The Court announced its decision two days later. There were nine opinions.

ITEMS TO CONSIDER WHILE READING *SCOTT v. SANDFORD*:

A. Scott v. Sandford *is considered one of the worst Supreme Court opinions of all time. What's wrong with it (legally, morally, politically)?*

B. *What methods of reasoning are used in the opinion of Chief Justice Taney? In particular, how does it invoke text, structure, history, consequences, and values?*

C. *The opinion provides two reasons why Dred Scott was not a citizen. Were both necessary? What are the advantages and disadvantages of deciding a case on something other than the narrowest available grounds?*

Scott v. Sandford,

60 U.S. 393 (1857)

Chief Justice Taney delivered the opinion of the court [joined by Justices Wayne, Catron, Daniel, Nelson, Grier, and Campbell].

This case has been twice argued. After the argument at the last term, differences of opinion were found to exist among the members of the court, and as the questions in controversy are of the highest importance, and the court was at that time much pressed by the ordinary business of the term, it was deemed advisable to continue the case and direct a re-argument on some of the points in order that we might have an opportunity of giving to the whole subject a more deliberate consideration. It has accordingly been again argued by counsel, and considered by the court; and I now proceed to deliver its opinion.

There are two leading questions presented by the record:

1. Had the [federal trial court] jurisdiction to hear and determine the case between these parties? And *Scott v. Sandford*

2. If it had jurisdiction, is the judgment it has given erroneous or not? . . .

[Part I—DESCENDANTS OF AFRICAN SLAVES ARE NOT CITIZENS]

[The asserted basis for federal subject matter jurisdiction is that Scott is a purported citizen of Missouri suing a citizen of New York.] It becomes, therefore, our duty to decide whether . . . plaintiff is . . . entitled to sue as a citizen in a court of the United States. . . . The question is simply this: Can a negro, whose ancestors were imported into this country, and sold as slaves, become a member of the political community formed and brought into existence by the Constitution of the United States, and as such become entitled to all the rights, and privileges, and immunities, guaranteed by that instrument to the citizen? One of which rights is the privilege of suing in a court of the United States in the cases specified in [Art. III of] the Constitution. . . .

The situation of this population [Africans imported as slaves and their descendants] was altogether unlike that of the Indian race. The latter, it is true, formed no part of the colonial communities, and never amalgamated with them in social connections or in government. But although they were uncivilized, they were yet a free and independent people, associated together in nations or tribes, and governed by their own laws. . . . These Indian Governments were regarded and treated as foreign Governments, as much so as if an ocean had separated the red man from the white; and their freedom has constantly been acknowledged, from the time of the first emigration to the English colonies to the present day, by the different Governments which succeeded each other. . . .

We proceed to examine the case as presented by the pleadings.

BIOGRAPHY

ROGER TANEY (1777–1864) of Maryland came to prominence through his work for President Andrew Jackson. The two shared a preference for state power over federal power, a political view that had become increasingly strong after the first generation of Federalists left the government. Jackson appointed Taney (pronounced "tawny") to be acting Secretary of War and then Attorney General. In that role, Taney assisted Jackson in withdrawing all federal funds from the second Bank of the United States, effectively killing it. Jackson then nominated Taney to be Secretary of the Treasury, but for the first time the Senate refused to confirm a nominee for a Cabinet position. Later, Jackson appointed Taney to replace John Marshall as Chief Justice in 1835. Although Taney consistently supported the interests of slave states while in the Cabinet and on the Supreme Court, he chose to free his own slaves during his lifetime.

[THE COURT WILL USE A HISTORICAL APPROACH TO INTERPRETATION]

The words "people of the United States" and "citizens" are synonymous terms, and mean the same thing. They both describe the political body who, according to our republican institutions, form the sovereignty, and who hold the power and conduct the Government through their representatives. They are what we familiarly call the "sovereign people," and every citizen is one of this people, and a constituent member of this sovereignty. The question before us is, whether the class of persons described in the plea in abatement compose a portion of this people, and are constituent members of this sovereignty? We think they are not, and that they are not included, and were not intended to be included, under the word "citizens" in the Constitution, and can therefore claim none of the rights and privileges which that instrument provides for and secures to citizens of the United States. On the contrary, they were at that time considered as a subordinate and inferior class of beings, who had been subjugated by the dominant race, and, whether emancipated or not, yet remained subject to their authority, and had no rights or privileges but such as those who held the power and the Government might choose to grant them.

It is not the province of the court to decide upon the justice or injustice, the policy or impolicy, of these laws. The decision of that question belonged to the political or law-making power; to those who formed the sovereignty and framed the Constitution. The duty of the court is, to interpret the instrument they have framed, with the best lights we can obtain on the subject, and to administer it as we find it, according to its true **intent and meaning when it was adopted.**

■ OBSERVATION

INTENT AND MEANING WHEN IT WAS ADOPTED: *Dred Scott* is one of the first self-consciously originalist Supreme Court opinions. Compare this approach to Justice Story in *Prigg*, who said "no uniform rule of interpretation can be applied" to the Constitution.

[STATE LAW DOES NOT CONTROL THE MEANING OF "CITIZEN OF A STATE" IN THE US CONSTITUTION]

In discussing this question, we must not confound the rights of citizenship which a State may confer within its own limits, and the rights of citizenship as a member of the Union. . . . Each State may still confer [state citizenship] upon an alien, or any one it thinks proper, or upon any class or description of persons; yet he would not be a citizen in the sense in which that word is used in the Constitution of the United States, nor entitled to sue as such in one of its courts, nor to the privileges and immunities of a citizen in the other States. The rights which he would acquire would be restricted to the State which gave them. The Constitution has conferred on Congress the right to establish an uniform rule of naturalization, and this right is evidently exclusive, and has always been held by this court to be so. . . . It is very clear, therefore, that no State can, by any act or law of its own, passed since the adoption of the Constitution, introduce a new member into the political community

Scott v. Sandford

created by the Constitution of the United States. It cannot make him a member of this community by making him a member of its own. And for the same reason it cannot introduce any person, or description of persons, who were not intended to be embraced in this new political family, which the Constitution brought into existence, but were intended to be excluded from it. . . .

The court [thinks that] the plaintiff in error could not be a citizen of the State of Missouri, **within the meaning of the Constitution of the United States**, and, consequently, was not entitled to sue in [United States] courts. It is true, every person, and every class and description of persons, who were at the time of the adoption of the Constitution recognized as citizens in the several States, became also citizens of this new political body; but none other; it was formed by them, and for them and their posterity, but for no one else. . . .

It becomes necessary, therefore, to determine who were citizens of the several States when the Constitution was adopted. And in order to do this, we must recur to the Governments and institutions of the thirteen colonies, when they separated from Great Britain and formed new sovereignties, and took their places in the family of independent nations. We must inquire who, at that time, were recognized as the people or citizens of a State, whose rights and liberties had been outraged by the English Government; and who declared their independence, and assumed the powers of Government to defend their rights by force of arms.

> OBSERVATION
>
> **WITHIN THE MEANING OF THE CONSTITUTION OF THE UNITED STATES:** Sanford's jurisdictional defense was that Dred Scott was not a "citizen of a state" for purposes of Art. III. This might appear to be a question for state law, especially since some states had from their founding treated free Black people as citizens. Justice Taney finessed this problem by declaring that the US Constitution included a definition of "citizen of a state" that was independent of any state's legal definition of citizenship.

In the opinion of the court, the legislation and histories of the times, and the language used in the Declaration of Independence, show, that neither the class of persons who had been imported as slaves, nor their descendants, whether they had become free or not, were then acknowledged as a part of the people, nor intended to be included in the general words used in that memorable instrument. . . .

[AFRICANS AND EUROPE]

The public history of every European nation displays it in a manner too plain to be mistaken. They [Africans] had for more than a century before been regarded as beings of an inferior order, and altogether unfit to associate with the white race, either in social or political relations; and so far inferior, that they had no rights which the white man was bound to respect; and that the negro might justly and lawfully be reduced to slavery for his benefit. He was bought and sold, and treated as an ordinary article of merchandise and traffic, whenever a profit could be made by it. This opinion was at that time fixed and universal in the civilized portion of the white race. It was regarded as an axiom in morals as well as in politics, which no one thought of disputing, or supposed to be open to dispute; and men in every grade and position in society daily and habitually acted upon it in their private pursuits, as well as in matters of public concern, without doubting for a moment the correctness of this opinion. . . .

[AFRICANS AND THE AMERICAN COLONIES]

The opinion thus entertained and acted upon in England was naturally impressed upon the colonies they founded on this side of the Atlantic. And, accordingly, a negro of the African race was regarded by them as an article of property, and held, and bought and sold as such, in every one of the thirteen colonies which united in the Declaration of Independence, and afterwards formed the Constitution of the United States. The slaves were more or less numerous in the different colonies, as slave labor was found more or less profitable. But no one seems to have doubted the correctness of the prevailing opinion of the time.

The legislation of the different colonies furnishes positive and indisputable proof of this fact.

It would be tedious, in this opinion, to enumerate the various laws they passed upon this subject. It will be sufficient, as a sample of the legislation which then generally prevailed throughout the British colonies, to give the laws of two of them; one being still a large slaveholding State [Maryland], and the other the first State in which slavery ceased to exist [Massachusetts in 1783].

The province of Maryland, in 1717, passed a law [against interracial marriage].

The other colonial law to which we refer was passed by Massachusetts in 1705. It [banned interracial marriages and allowed for whipping of any "negro or mulatto" who strikes "any person of the English or other Christian nation"].

[These laws] show, too plainly to be misunderstood, the degraded condition of this unhappy race. They were still in force when the Revolution began, and are a faithful index to the state of feeling towards the class of persons of whom they speak, and of the position they occupied throughout the thirteen colonies, in the eyes and thoughts of the men who framed the Declaration of Independence and established the State Constitutions and Governments. They show that a perpetual and impassable barrier was intended to be erected between the white race and the one which they had reduced to slavery, and governed as subjects with absolute and despotic power, and which they then looked upon as so far below them in the scale of created beings, that intermarriages between white persons and negroes or mulattoes were regarded as unnatural and immoral, and punished as crimes, not only in the parties, but in the person who joined them in marriage. And no distinction in this respect was made between the free negro or mulatto and the slave, but this stigma, of the deepest degradation, was fixed upon the whole race. . . .

[AFRICANS AND THE DECLARATION OF INDEPENDENCE]

Scott v. Sandford

The language of the Declaration of Independence is equally conclusive. . . . [It says] "We hold these truths to be self-evident: that all men are created equal; that they are endowed by their Creator with certain unalienable rights; that among them is life, liberty, and the pursuit of happiness; that to secure these rights, Governments are instituted, deriving their just powers from the consent of the governed."

The general words above quoted would seem to embrace the whole human family, and if they were used in a similar instrument at this day would be so understood. But it is too clear for dispute, that the enslaved African race were not intended to be included, and formed no part of the people who framed and adopted this declaration; for if the language, as understood in that day, would embrace them, the conduct of the distinguished men who framed the Declaration of Independence would have been utterly and flagrantly inconsistent with the principles they asserted; and instead of the sympathy of mankind, to which they so confidently appealed, they would have deserved and received universal rebuke and reprobation.

Yet the men who framed this declaration were great men—high in literary acquirements—high in their sense of honor, and incapable of asserting principles inconsistent with those on which they were acting. They perfectly understood the meaning of the language they used, and how it would be understood by others; and they knew that it would not in any part of the civilized world be supposed to embrace the negro race, which, by common consent, had been excluded from civilized Governments and the family of nations, and doomed to slavery. They spoke and acted according to the then established doctrines and principles, and in the ordinary language of the day, and no one misunderstood them. The unhappy black race were separated from the white by indelible marks, and laws long before established, and were never thought of or spoken of except as property, and when the claims of the owner or the profit of the trader were supposed to need protection.

[AFRICANS AND THE CONSTITUTION]

This state of public opinion had undergone no change when the Constitution was adopted, as is equally evident from its provisions and language.

The brief preamble sets forth by whom it was formed, for what purposes, and for whose benefit and protection. It declares that it is formed by the *people* of the United States; that is to say, by those who were members of the different political communities in the several States; and its great object is declared to be to secure the blessings of liberty to themselves and their posterity. It speaks in general terms of the *people* of the United States, and of *citizens* of the several States, when it is providing for the exercise of the powers granted or the privileges secured to the citizen. It does not define what description of persons are intended to be included under these terms, or who shall be regarded as a citizen and one of the people,

It uses them as terms so well understood, that no further description or definition was necessary.

But there are two clauses in the Constitution which point directly and specifically to the negro race as a separate class of persons, and show clearly that they were not regarded as a portion of the people or citizens of the Government then formed.

One of these clauses reserves to each of the thirteen States the right to import slaves until the year 1808, if it thinks proper. And the importation which it thus sanctions was unquestionably of persons of the race of which we are speaking, as the traffic in slaves in the United States had always been confined to them. And by the other provision the States pledge themselves to each other to maintain the right of property of the master, by delivering up to him any slave who may have escaped from his service, and be found within their respective territories. . . . And these two provisions show, conclusively, that neither the description of persons therein referred to, nor their descendants, were embraced in any of the other provisions of the Constitution; for certainly these two clauses were not intended to confer on them or their posterity the blessings of liberty, or any of the personal rights so carefully provided for the citizen.

[AFRICANS AND EARLY FEDERAL STATUTES]

. . . To all this mass of proof we have still to add, that Congress has repeatedly legislated upon the same construction of the Constitution that we have given. [Two laws] which were passed almost immediately after the Government went into operation, will be abundantly sufficient to show this. [These] are particularly worthy of notice, because many of the men who assisted in framing the Constitution, and took an active part in procuring its adoption, were then in the halls of legislation, and certainly understood what they meant when they used the words "people of the United States" and "citizen" in that well-considered instrument.

The first of these acts is the naturalization law, which was passed at the second session of the first Congress, March 26, 1790, and confines the right of becoming citizens "to aliens being free white persons." Now, the Constitution does not limit the power of Congress in this respect to white persons. And they may, if they think proper, authorize the naturalization of any one, of any color, who was born under allegiance to another Government. But the language of the law above quoted, shows that citizenship at that time was perfectly understood to be confined to the white race; and that they alone constituted the sovereignty in the Government. . . . It would seem to have been used merely because it followed out the line of division which the Constitution has drawn between the citizen race, who formed and held the Government, and the African race, which they held in subjection and slavery, and governed at their own pleasure.

Another of the early laws of which we have spoken, is the first militia law, which was passed in 1792, at the first session of the second Congress. The language of this law is equally plain and significant with the one just mentioned. It directs that every "free able-bodied white male citizen" shall be enrolled in the militia. The word "white" is evidently used to exclude the African race, and the word "citizen" to exclude unnaturalized foreigners; the latter forming no part of the sovereignty, owing it no allegiance, and therefore under no obligation to defend it. The African race, however, born in the country, did owe allegiance to the Government, whether they were slave or free; but it is repudiated, and rejected from the duties and obligations of citizenship in marked language. . . .

[SOCIETAL CHANGES CANNOT CHANGE ORIGINAL MEANING]

No one, we presume, supposes that any change in public opinion or feeling, in relation to this unfortunate race, in the civilized nations of Europe or in this country, should induce the court to give to the words of the Constitution a more liberal construction in their favor than they were intended to bear when the instrument was framed and adopted. Such an argument would be altogether inadmissible in any tribunal called on to interpret it. If any of its provisions are deemed unjust, there is a mode prescribed in the instrument itself by which it may be amended; but while it remains unaltered, it must be construed now as it was understood at the time of its adoption. It is not only the same in words, but the same in meaning, and delegates the same powers to the Government, and reserves and secures the same rights and privileges to the citizen; and as long as it continues to exist in its present form, it speaks not only in the same words, but with the same meaning and intent with which it spoke when it came from the hands of its framers, and was voted on and adopted by the people of the United States. Any other rule of construction would abrogate the judicial character of this court, and make it the mere reflex of the popular opinion or passion of the day. This court was not created by the Constitution for such purposes. Higher and graver trusts have been confided to it, and it must not falter in the path of duty. . . .

And upon a full and careful consideration of the subject, the court is of opinion, that, upon the facts stated in the plea in abatement, Dred Scott was not a citizen of Missouri within the meaning of the Constitution of the United States, and not entitled as such to sue in [United States] courts; and, consequently, that the [United States trial court] had no jurisdiction of the case, and that the judgment on the plea in abatement is erroneous.

[Part II—SCOTT WAS NOT A CITIZEN BECAUSE HE WAS STILL A SLAVE]

[Justice Taney next considered an independent reason to find that Scott did not have the right of a state citizen to sue in federal court.] . . . Now, if [the Scotts' time in Minnesota] did not give them their freedom, then by his own admission he is still a slave; and whatever opinions may be entertained in favor of the citizenship of a free person of the African race, no one supposes that a slave is a citizen of the State or of the United States. If, therefore, the acts done by his owner did not make them free persons, he is still a slave, and certainly incapable of suing in the character of a citizen. . . .

In considering this part of the controversy, [the question arises:] Was [Scott], together with his family, free in Missouri by reason of the stay in the [Minnesota] territory of the United States? . . .

The act of Congress [establishing the Missouri Compromise of 1820] declares that slavery and involuntary servitude, except as a punishment for crime, shall be forever prohibited in all that part of the territory ceded by France, under the name of Louisiana, which lies north of thirty-six degrees thirty minutes north latitude, and not included within the limits of Missouri. And the difficulty which meets us at the threshold of this part of the inquiry is, whether Congress was authorized to pass this law under any of the powers granted to it by the Constitution. . . .

[CONGRESS MUST RESPECT INDIVIDUAL RIGHTS IN THE TERRITORIES]

The power to expand the territory of the United States by the admission of new States is plainly given [in Art. IV, § 3]; and in the construction of this power by all the departments of the Government, it has been held to authorize the acquisition of territory, not fit for admission at the time, but to be admitted as soon as its population and situation would entitle it to admission. It is acquired to become a State, and not to be held as a colony and governed by Congress with absolute authority. . . . All we mean to say on this point is, that, as there is no express regulation in the Constitution defining the power which the General Government may exercise over the person or property of a citizen in a Territory thus acquired, the court must necessarily look to the provisions and principles of the Constitution, and its distribution of powers, for the rules and principles by which its decision must be governed.

Taking this rule to guide us, it may be safely assumed that citizens of the United States who migrate to a Territory belonging to the people of the United States, cannot be ruled as mere colonists, dependent upon the will of the General Government, and to be governed by any laws it may think proper to impose. . . . A reference to a few of the provisions of the Constitution will illustrate this proposition. For example, no one, we presume, will contend that Congress can make any law in a Territory respecting the establishment of religion, or the free exercise thereof, or abridging the freedom of speech or of the press, or the right of the people of the Territory peaceably to assemble, and to petition the Government for the redress of grievances. Nor can Congress deny to the people the right to keep and bear arms, nor the right to trial by jury, nor compel any one to be a witness against himself in a criminal proceeding.

Scott v. Sandford

These powers, and others, in relation to rights of person, which it is not necessary here to enumerate, are, in express and positive terms, denied to the General Government; and the rights of private property have been guarded with equal care. Thus the rights of property are united with the rights of person, and placed on the same ground by the fifth amendment to the Constitution, which provides that no person shall be deprived of life, liberty, and property, without due process of law. And an act of Congress which deprives a citizen of the United States of his liberty or property, merely because he came himself or brought his property into a particular Territory of the United States, and who had committed no offence against the laws, could hardly be dignified with the name of due process of law. . . .

[SLAVE OWNERSHIP IS A CONSTITUTIONALLY PROTECTED PROPERTY RIGHT]

It seems, however, to be supposed, that there is a difference between property in a slave and other property, and that different rules may be applied to it in expounding the Constitution of the United States. . . . If the Constitution recognizes the right of property of the master in a slave, and makes no distinction between that description of property and other property owned by a citizen, no tribunal, acting under the authority of the United States, whether it be legislative, executive, or judicial, has a right to draw such a distinction, or deny to it the benefit of the provisions and guarantees which have been provided for the protection of private property against the encroachments of the Government.

Now, as we have already said in an earlier part of this opinion, upon a different point, the right of property in a slave is distinctly and expressly affirmed in the Constitution. The right to traffic in it, like an ordinary article of merchandise and property, was guaranteed to the citizens of the United States, in every State that might desire it, for twenty years. And the Government in express terms is pledged to protect it in all future time, if the slave escapes from his owner. This is done in plain words—too plain to be misunderstood. And no word can be found in the Constitution which gives Congress a greater power over slave property, or which entitles property of that kind to less protection that property of any other description. The only power conferred is the power coupled with the duty of guarding and protecting the owner in his rights.

Upon these considerations, it is the opinion of the court that the act of Congress which prohibited a citizen from holding and owning property of this kind in the territory of the United States north of the line therein mentioned, is not warranted by the Constitution, and is therefore void; and that neither Dred Scott himself, nor any of his family, were made free by being carried into this territory; even if they had been carried there by the owner, with the intention of becoming a permanent resident. . . .

[CONCLUSION]

Upon the whole, therefore, it is the judgment of this court, that it appears by the record before us that the plaintiff in error is not a citizen of Missouri, in the sense in which that word is used in the Constitution; and that the [trial court], for that reason, had no jurisdiction in the case, and could give no judgment in it. Its judgment for the defendant must, consequently, be reversed, and a mandate issued, directing the suit to be dismissed for want of jurisdiction.

Justice Wayne, concurring. [Omitted]

Justice Nelson, concurring. [Omitted]

Justice Grier, concurring. [Omitted]

Justice Daniel, concurring. [Omitted]

Justice Campbell, concurring. [Omitted]

Justice Catron, concurring. [Omitted]

Justice McLean, dissenting. [Omitted]

Justice Curtis, dissenting. [Omitted]

[The dissents of Justices McLean and Curtis addressed many of the same points. Both argued that a "citizen of a State" for purposes of diversity jurisdiction meant anyone considered a citizen under State law, without regard to race. As Justice Curtis said:

> In five of the thirteen original States [New Hampshire, Massachusetts, New York, New Jersey, and North Carolina], colored persons [at the time of the framing] possessed the elective franchise, and were among those by whom the Constitution was ordained and established. If so, it is not true, in point of fact, that the Constitution was made exclusively by the white race. And that it was made exclusively for the white race is, in my opinion, not only an assumption not warranted by anything in the Constitution, but contradicted by its opening declaration, that it was ordained and established by the people of the United States, for themselves and their posterity. And as free colored persons were then citizens of at least five States, and so in every sense part of the people of the United States, they were among those for whom and whose posterity the Constitution was ordained and established.

Justice McLean objected to the majority's assertion that "a colored citizen would not be an agreeable member of society. This is more a matter of taste than of law."

Scott v. Sandford

The dissenters objected that the majority should not have reached the merits, as it essentially did in Part II, if Scott's race meant there could be no diversity jurisdiction. If the constitutionality of the Missouri Compromise were to be reached at all, the enumerated power in Art. IV, § 3 to make "rules and regulations" for the territories should allow Congress to ban slavery in territories. Congresses had done so ever since the Northwest Ordinance of 1787. Justice Curtis concluded that the best reading of constitutional text and history was that "they who framed and adopted the constitution were aware that persons held to service under the laws of a State are property only to the extent and under the conditions fixed by those laws; [and] that they must cease to be available as property, when their owners voluntarily place them permanently within another jurisdiction, where no municipal laws on the subject of slavery exist."

Regarding the Due Process Clause, Justice Curtis noted that its protection for life, liberty, and property could be traced to the Magna Carta of 1215. See Ch. 19.A. If laws against slavery were deprivations of property without due process, this would mean that all slavery-limiting laws—such as the Northwest Ordinance—would have been forbidden takings of property. And so would a ban on the international slave trade, since it would deprive a person of slave property obtained in a slave jurisdiction when the person sought to bring that property to the United States. This view of the Due Process Clause could not be correct, Justice Curtis concluded, because Art. V of the Constitution implied that Congress could, after 1808, use its foreign commerce power to halt the international slave trade.]

flashforward

1. ***The Scotts' Freedom*****.** Dred and Harriet Scott and their children were finally freed from slavery shortly after the Supreme Court announced its decision. The circumstances shed light on both slavery and the status of women.

Recall that at the start of the Scotts' litigation, their owner was Irene Emerson. As a married woman, she was subject to the laws of coverture that placed all her property and other rights with her husband. But as an unmarried widow, she had some rights to control property and to litigate. The general attitude toward single women was that their independence would be temporary. A widow like Irene Emerson would soon remarry or die, at which point her property would come under a man's control. And in fact, her brother Sanford handled the Scott litigation on her behalf (and some accounts indicate that he may have assumed ownership of the Scotts).

In 1850, Emerson married Dr. Calvin Chaffee—a Massachusetts abolitionist elected to the House of Representatives in 1854. Upon her marriage, Emerson's property became Chaffee's. Chaffee claimed to learn for the first time that he was the true owner of the famous Dred Scott only a month before the decision came down in March 1857. He encountered enormous criticism for hypocrisy—an abolitionist who owned a slave!—and chose not to run for re-election in 1858.

Chaffee was eager to disentangle himself from the controversy, and also eager to free the Scotts. Missouri law allowed only a Missouri citizen to free an in-state slave, so Chaffee quitclaimed all interest in the Scotts to Taylor Blow of St. Louis, who had played with Dred Scott when they both were children. (Although the Blow family did not consider themselves abolitionists, they had helped Scott finance his freedom litigation.) As a result of manumission by Blow, the Scotts became free people in May 1857.

2. ***Taney in the Capitol.*** Since 1874, a bust of Chief Justice Taney sat on a pedestal in the US Capitol, near the entrance to the chamber where the Supreme Court sat from 1810 to 1860. In December 2022, Congress directed that the bust be removed. P.L. 117–265. The legislation also stated: "While the removal of Chief Justice Roger Brooke Taney's bust from the Capitol does not relieve the Congress of the historical wrongs it committed to protect the institution of slavery, it expresses Congress's recognition of one of the most notorious wrongs to have ever taken place in one of its rooms," namely, the *Dred Scott* decision. The law also called for installation of a bust of Thurgood Marshall—a Marylander like Taney, but a lawyer for the plaintiffs in *Brown v. Board of Education* (1954) and the first African-American justice on the US Supreme Court.

E. Lincoln and Douglas Debate The *Dred Scott* Decision

Justice Taney and President Buchanan intended for the *Dred Scott* ruling to calm the country's political divisions, but it did not have that effect. The reaction to *Dred Scott* illustrates the eternal debate over judicial power. In a democracy, should judges always get the last word? Do other office holders have a duty to adhere to the Supreme Court's constitutional interpretations?

The topic arose in the 1858 race to be chosen US Senator by the Illinois legislature. Democrat Stephen Douglas was a former Illinois Supreme Court justice and the current incumbent senator. In Congress, Douglas had been the chief architect of the Kansas-Nebraska Act. His challenger was Abraham Lincoln of the Republican Party, which had been founded in 1854 in reaction to the Kansas-Nebraska Act. Republicans abhorred the *Dred Scott* decision, and their party platform continued to call for a ban on slavery in federal territories. In a series of campaign speeches, the two candidates jousted over the substance of slavery, and also over the role of the Supreme Court.

ITEMS TO CONSIDER WHILE READING EXCERPTS FROM LINCOLN AND DOUGLAS:

A. *Lincoln argues that judicial opinions should be understood as deciding a single case, but that the constitutional interpretation used by the court in reaching that decision is not binding on other political actors. What would be the ramifications of this approach?*

B. *Douglas argues that judges should be appointed without regard for their ideology. Is this possible? Desirable?*

C. *Whose position is best aligned with the rule of law?*

The opening speech of Douglas's campaign occurred on July 9, 1858. Douglas was aware that Lincoln was present in the auditorium. During the speech, Douglas accused Lincoln of disrespecting the Supreme Court and, by extension, the rule of law.

> Mr. Lincoln [is engaged in] a crusade against the Supreme Court of the United States on account of the *Dred Scott* decision. I desire to say to you unequivocally, that I take direct and distinct issue with him. I have no warfare to make on the Supreme Court of the United States, either on account of that or any other decision which they have pronounced from that bench. . . . The right and the province of expounding the Constitution, and construing the law, is vested in the judiciary established by the Constitution. As a lawyer, I feel at liberty to appear before the Court and controvert any principle of law while the question is pending before the tribunal; but when the decision is made, my private opinion, your opinion, all other opinions must yield to the majesty of that authoritative adjudication. . . .
>
> I have no idea of appealing from the decision of the Supreme Court upon a constitutional question to the decisions of a tumultuous town meeting. . . . The

> decision of the highest tribunal known to the Constitution of the country must be final till it has been reversed by an equally high authority. . . . I respect the decisions of that august tribunal; I shall always bow in deference to them. I am a law-abiding man. I will sustain the Constitution of my country as our fathers have made it. I will yield obedience to the laws, whether I like them or not, as I find them on the statute book.

Lincoln responded in a Chicago speech the next day:

> I have expressed heretofore, and I now repeat, my opposition to the *Dred Scott* decision, but I should be allowed to state the nature of that opposition, and I ask your indulgence while I do so. What is fairly implied by the term Judge Douglas has used, "resistance to the decision"? I do not resist it. If I wanted to take Dred Scott from his master, I would be interfering with property, and that terrible difficulty that Judge Douglas speaks of, of interfering with property, would arise. But I am doing no such thing as that, but all that I am doing is refusing to obey it as a political rule. If I were in Congress, and a vote should come up on a question whether slavery should be prohibited in a new territory, in spite of that *Dred Scott* decision, I would vote that it should. . . .
>
> The sacredness that Judge Douglas throws around this decision, is a degree of sacredness that has never been before thrown around any other decision. I have never heard of such a thing. . . . [The *Dred Scott* decision] is the first of its kind; it is an astonisher in legal history. It is a new wonder of the world. . . . But Judge Douglas will have it that all hands must take this extraordinary decision, made under these extraordinary circumstances, and give their vote in Congress in accordance with it, yield to it and obey it in every possible sense. Circumstances alter cases. Do not gentlemen here remember the case of that same Supreme Court, some twenty-five or thirty years ago, deciding that a national bank was constitutional [*McCulloch v. Maryland*]? . . . **The bank charter ran out**, and a re-charter was granted by Congress. That re-charter was laid before General Jackson. It was urged upon him, when he denied the constitutionality of the bank, that the Supreme Court had decided that it was constitutional; and that General Jackson then said that the Supreme Court had no right to lay down a rule to govern a co-ordinate branch of the government, the members of which had sworn to support the Constitution—that each member had sworn to support that Constitution as he

HISTORY

THE BANK CHARTER RAN OUT: *McCulloch v. Maryland* (1819) upheld Congress's power to create the second Bank of the United States. The statute creating the bank was set to expire in 1836. Congress passed a bill in 1832 to re-charter the bank for another twenty years, but President Andrew Jackson vetoed it, saying that he would not sign a bill he considered unconstitutional even if Congress and the Supreme Court considered it constitutional. (Shortly thereafter, he withdrew the federal government's deposits from the second Bank, forcing it to dissolve before its scheduled expiration date.)

> understood it. I will venture here to say, that I have heard Judge Douglas say that he approved of General Jackson for that act. What has now become of all his tirade about "resistance to the Supreme Court?"

Douglas answered a week later on July 17, at an event in Springfield:

> [Mr. Lincoln] says that he will not fight the judges or the United States marshals in order to liberate Dred Scott, but that he will not respect that decision, as a rule of law binding on this country, in the future. Why not? Because, he says, it is unjust. How is he going to remedy it? Why, he says he is going to reverse it. . . . He says to the people of Illinois that if you elect him to the Senate he will introduce a bill to re-enact the law which the court pronounced unconstitutional. . . . The court pronounces that law, prohibiting slavery, unconstitutional and void, and Mr. Lincoln is going to pass an act reversing that decision and making it valid. I have never heard before of an appeal being taken from the Supreme Court to the Congress of the United States to reverse its decision. . . .
>
> But Mr. Lincoln intimates that there is another mode by which he can reverse the *Dred Scott* decision. How is that? Why, he is going to appeal to the people to elect a President who will appoint judges who will reverse the *Dred Scott* decision. . . . How are the new judges to be appointed? Why, the Republican President is to call up the candidates and catechize them, and ask them, "How will you decide this case if I appoint you judge?" . . . Then [the President] asks him how he will decide Tom Jones' case, and Bill Wilson's case, and thus catechises the judge as to how he will decide any case which may arise before him. Suppose you get a Supreme Court composed of such judges, who have been appointed by a partisan President upon their giving pledges how they would decide a case before it arises. What confidence would you have in such a court?
>
> Would not your court be prostituted beneath the contempt of all mankind! What man would feel that his liberties were safe; his right of person or property was secure if the supreme bench, that august tribunal, the highest on earth, was brought down to that low, dirty pool wherein the judges give pledges in advance how they will decide all the questions which may be brought before them? It is a proposition to make that court the corrupt, unscrupulous tool of a political party.

Later that same day in Springfield, Lincoln responded:

> [Judge Douglas] would have the citizen conform his vote to that decision; the member of Congress, his; the President, his use of the veto power. He would make it a rule of political action for the people and all the departments of the

> government. I would not. By resisting it as a political rule, I disturb no right of property, create no disorder, excite no mobs. . . .
>
> [Thomas Jefferson said the following in a letter written in 1820.] "To consider the judges as the ultimate arbiters of all constitutional questions is a very dangerous doctrine indeed and one which would place us under the despotism of an oligarchy. Our judges are as honest as other men, and not more so. They have, with others, the same passions for party, for power, and the privilege of their corps. . . . " Thus we see the power claimed for the Supreme Court by Judge Douglas, Mr. Jefferson holds, would reduce us to the despotism of an oligarchy.

F. Secession, Civil War, and Emancipation

In the 1830s and 1840s, the only people talking seriously about seceding from the Union were northern abolitionists. They despaired that any reform could come by continued adherence to what Garrison called "a covenant with death." But by the late 1850s, Southern elites also began to feel that the national government was not sufficiently protecting their interests. This was true even though the South had disproportionate influence over Congress due to the formulas of representation in the Senate (equal representation by state) and in the House (overrepresentation of Southern voters through the Three-Fifths compromise)—which translated into disproportionate influence over the Electoral College that chose the President, and hence over the Supreme Court selected by the President and confirmed by the Senate.

For the South, the breaking point came with the election of 1860. Abraham Lincoln became President after an acrimonious North-South split in the Democratic Party allowed the Republicans to secure a plurality in the popular vote and the Electoral College. On December 20, 1860, South Carolina became the first state to declare that it had seceded from the Union, in a document that was consciously modeled after the Declaration of Independence. In its Declaration of the Causes of Secession, South Carolina explained that it was leaving the United States because the national government had not done enough for the South, and because the Northern states were using their states' rights in ways the South considered detrimental:

> We assert, that fourteen of the States have deliberately refused for years past to fulfill their constitutional obligations [under the Fugitive Slave Clause]. . . . An increasing hostility on the part of the non-slaveholding States to the Institution of Slavery has led to a disregard of their obligations, and the laws of the general government have ceased to effect the objects of the Constitution. . . .

> We affirm that these ends for which this Government was instituted have been defeated, and the Government itself has been made destructive of them by the action of the non-slaveholding States. Those States have assumed the right of deciding upon the propriety of our domestic institutions; and have denied the rights of property established in fifteen of the States and recognized by the Constitution; they have denounced as sinful the institution of Slavery; they have permitted the open establishment among them of societies, whose avowed object is to disturb the peace and to eloign [i.e., to carry away to a distant place] the property of the citizens of other States. They have encouraged and assisted thousands of our slaves to leave their homes; and those who remain, have been incited by emissaries, books and pictures to servile insurrection. . . .
>
> This sectional combination for the subversion of the Constitution, has been aided in some of the States by elevating to citizenship, persons, who, by the Supreme Law of the land, are incapable of becoming citizens [i.e. Black people]; and their votes have been used to inaugurate a new policy, hostile to the South, and destructive of its peace and safety.

At the start of the war, the predominant motivation of the North was to suppress a rebellion and preserve the "perpetual union" that had begun under the Articles of Confederation. Even though slavery was the ultimate source of disagreement between North and South, ending slavery was not initially viewed as a goal of the Union war effort. After all, the border states that remained part of the Union (Missouri, Kentucky, Maryland, and Delaware) continued to have slavery. But as the war continued, the ideological motivation in the North increasingly emphasized opposition to slavery. A turning point came with Lincoln's Emancipation Proclamation of January 1, 1863, which read in part:

> [A]ll persons held as slaves within any State or designated part of a State, the people whereof shall then be in rebellion against the United States, shall be then, thenceforward, and forever free; and the Executive Government of the United States, including the military and naval authority thereof, will recognize and maintain the freedom of such persons, and will do no act or acts to repress such persons, or any of them, in any efforts they may make for their actual freedom.

The proclamation was made by Lincoln "as a fit and necessary war measure" in his capacity as commander-in-chief of the military forces of the United States. The order hearkened back to a military tactic used by both sides during the Revolutionary War, where the British and some of the colonies offered to free slaves who fought on their side. (Indeed, after the British surrendered, several thousand former slaves and their families who had fought for the crown left the colonies to settle in other British territories). Because the Southern states did not consider themselves bound by any actions of the United States government, the Emancipation Proclamation did not have immediate legal effect in those states. It nonetheless had the desired effect of encouraging Southern slaves to take up arms against the Confederacy.

The Emancipation Proclamation has been criticized as lacking in literary flourish. Historian Richard Hofstadter said it "had all the moral grandeur of a bill of lading." Lincoln himself, of course, was quite capable of persuasive rhetoric. In his speech on November 19, 1863 dedicating a war memorial at the site of the Battle of Gettysburg, Lincoln linked opposition to slavery to the earliest American commitments. When seceding, the Southern states had claimed that they were the inheritors of the Declaration of Independence, emphasizing its primary thesis that a sovereign people had a right of revolution to free themselves from a government they deemed tyrannical. But in the Gettysburg Address, Lincoln turned to other language in the Declaration of Independence when he stated that the United States was at the founding "a new nation, conceived in liberty, and dedicated to the proposition that all men are created equal." The *Dred Scott* decision (perhaps accurately?) concluded that for the Founders, "all men" referred only to a subset of the population. But Lincoln claimed to take the Declaration's text at face value, so that "all men" would encompass a broader swath of society.

When the war ended, the victorious government of the United States began to revise the Constitution and laws to make them more consistent with Lincoln's (perhaps revisionist?) description of what they had always stood for. So that "these dead shall not have died in vain," said Lincoln, the nation needed to pursue their "unfinished work:" to create a "new birth of freedom."

Chapter Recap

A. The experience of slavery in the United States shapes many aspects of modern constitutional law.

B. Ironically, some of the first US Supreme Court decisions upholding individual rights involved the right to control slaves: *Prigg v. Pennsylvania* (1842) protected a constitutional right to recapture fugitive slaves without any legal procedures, and *Dred Scott v. Sandford* (1857) protected slavery as part of the constitutional right against deprivation of property without due process of law.

C. In defense of slavery, both *Prigg* and *Dred Scott* proposed a strong view of certain aspects of the US Constitution. Both *Prigg* and *Dred Scott* considered individual rights of slave owners, found in the Constitution, strong enough to invalidate state and federal laws, respectively. In addition, *Prigg* would give Congress powers to legislate in support of an individual right to own slaves, even if that power was not clearly enumerated.

D. Even though federal courts have the power of judicial review, their decisions may provoke political and social resistance.

CHAPTER 7

The Reconstruction Amendments

Although the Declaration of Independence considered it "self-evident" that "all men are created equal," the original US Constitution did not contain the word "equal." Equality can be seen as a value underlying some constitutional provisions, such as the ban on titles of nobility, Art. I, § 9, cl. 8; the ban on religious tests as a condition of holding federal office, Art. VI, § 3; and the obligations of states to extend privileges and immunities to out-of-state citizens, Art. IV, § 2, cl. 1. Equality of some sort is also implicit in foundational concepts of popular sovereignty and republicanism. These partial and oblique commitments to equality in the Constitution were counterbalanced by language denying the equality of slaves and by a system for lawmaking that did not require any consideration of equality as a general matter.

The series of constitutional amendments following the Civil War (known collectively as the Reconstruction Amendments or Civil War Amendments) made equality an explicitly stated national value—and a legal requirement. But writing equality into a legal document does not necessarily make it so. As James Madison noted, it might be a mere "paper barrier" against oppression. Ch. 3.D. Speaking in favor of women's rights in 1900, the suffragist Carrie Chapman Catt echoed Madison, saying: "No written law has ever been more binding than unwritten custom supported by popular opinion." The first several decades of Supreme Court decisions interpreting the equality provisions of the Reconstruction Amendments exemplify the tension between newly-written positive law mandating racial equality and longstanding practices and attitudes that favored other priorities (such as property rights and state government autonomy). As you read the cases that follow, consider the extent to which changes to constitutional text are sufficient to create change on the ground.

A. Reconstruction Amendments and Statutes

When the Confederate states stopped sending Senators and Representatives to Washington, Congress was controlled by Lincoln's Republican Party. After the war, control shifted to the so-called "Radical Republican" wing, which was committed to legal protections for former slaves. To that end, Congress enacted both constitutional amendments and statutes.

The multiple rounds of legislative action following the Civil War reveal how Congress was embroiled in two familiar conflicts built into the Constitution's structure. With regard to federalism, Congress was pitted against the Southern states. With regard to separation of powers, it was pitted against President Andrew Johnson (a Democrat, a former slave owner, and an opponent of Reconstruction).

1. The Thirteenth Amendment (1865)

The Thirteenth Amendment prohibited "slavery" and "involuntary servitude, except as a punishment for crime whereof the party shall have been duly convicted." Mindful of the rule from *Barron v. Baltimore* (1833) (that the US Constitution applies only to the US government unless the text indicates otherwise), the amendment specified that slavery and involuntary servitude "shall not exist within the United States, or any place subject to **their jurisdiction**," i.e. within states and territories. Section 2 of the amendment created a new enumerated power for Congress: the power to enact "appropriate legislation" to enforce the ban on slavery. The amendment passed Congress in January 1865 and was ratified by December 1865.

Many in the North believed that the end of slavery would mean full citizenship for the former slaves. But the Southern states quickly revealed that they would interpret the Thirteenth Amendment as an end to legalized slavery but nothing else. The freed slaves could not be bought and sold as property, but their lives would resemble slavery as much as possible. Congressional investigations in late 1865 and early 1866 revealed how the former slaves continued to be subordinated through governmental and non-governmental means.

■ TERMINOLOGY

THEIR JURISDICTION: The choice of the pronoun "their" instead of "its" reflects how "the United States" was originally viewed as a plural entity. After the Civil War, the current usage evolved, where "the United States" is singular. Thus, in 1846 one might say "The United States *are* at war with Mexico," but by 1942 one might say "The United States *is* at war with Germany." This grammatical shift is a subtle indicator of the public's increasing comfort with a national identity—or to use the original language of the Pledge of Allegiance (1892), "one nation, indivisible."

On the governmental level, all of the former slave states enacted "Black Codes" that rewrote the earlier slave codes by making them applicable to any Black person. Typical provisions of a Black Code prevented Black people from owning real property, weapons, or alcohol. Crimes committed by Black people were subject to heavier punishment than crimes committed by White people. For example, it was typically a capital offense for a Black man to rape a White woman, but not for a White man to rape a Black woman. In court, Black people had limited ability to testify as witnesses. Vagrancy laws made it a crime for Black people to be without a long-term employment contract. If a Black person was convicted of vagrancy, any White man could pay the fine and then force the defendant to work for free to satisfy the debt. And of course, Black people could not vote, given the laws enacted before the Civil War that limited the franchise to free White males. In short, the former slaves were no longer property, but they did not enjoy full **political and civil rights.**

On the non-governmental level, subordination of the Black population was accomplished through violence and discrimination. Bands of White vigilantes were known to kidnap, torture, and kill Black people. During the debate on the law that became the Civil Rights Act of 1866, Senator Charles Sumner received a box containing the severed finger of a Black person, along with a threatening note: "You old son of a bitch, I send you a piece of one of your friends, and if that bill of yours passes I will have a piece of you." Police protection for freed slaves was typically non-existent, since state and local governments continued to be operated by former Confederates opposed to equality.

> ■ TERMINOLOGY
>
> **POLITICAL AND CIVIL RIGHTS:** *Political rights* are those that give a citizen some measure of control over the government: the rights to vote, to hold public office, and to serve on juries. The term *civil rights* has never had a precise definition. As used in the 19th century, *civil rights* were those that allowed a citizen to function effectively within civil society: to own and convey property, to engage in a lawful trade, to enter into enforceable contracts, to sue and be sued, to testify, to obtain police and fire protection, and others. Today, the term *civil rights* most often (but not always) connotes the right to be free of unlawful discrimination, as opposed to a right to engage in specified activities.

Given the pervasive intransigence of the former slave states, Congress recognized that ending legalized slavery in the Thirteenth Amendment would not be enough.

2. The Freedman's Bureau (1865)

In 1865, Congress established a federal agency within the Department of War popularly known as the Freedman's Bureau. Its mission was to help former slaves in areas occupied by the Army by providing food, water, police protection, clothing, housing, education, health care, and employment. The Freedman's Bureau and its White staff were often targets of vigilante violence. In July 1866, Congress passed a statute extending the lifespan of the Bureau to 1872. President Andrew Johnson vetoed the bill, but Congress overrode him. The Bureau's supporters argued that it was authorized by Congress's enumerated powers over the military, while its opponents claimed it was beyond Congress's powers altogether.

3. Civil Rights Act of 1866

In March 1866, Congress passed the **Civil Rights Act**, which was designed to dismantle the Black Codes and reduce vigilantism. Section 1 stated that citizens of "every race and color, without regard to any previous condition of slavery" had the right to make contracts, to enforce rights in court, to own property, and to enjoy the "full and equal benefit of all laws" to the same extent "as is enjoyed by white citizens." Section 2 made it a federal crime for persons acting under color of state law to violate the rights found in Section 1.

■ HISTORY

THE CIVIL RIGHTS ACT: The Civil Rights Act of 1866 has gone through several rounds of amendments, but its central provisions remain part of the U.S. Code. Portions of Section 1 evolved into portions of the current 42 U.S.C. § 1981 (equal right to contract and benefit from laws) and § 1982 (equal right to own property). Section 2 evolved into the current 18 U.S.C. § 242, (federal crime for state or local officials to violate Constitutional rights).

President Johnson vetoed the Civil Rights Act, claiming that it was not authorized by the Thirteenth Amendment (because it did not address slavery itself) and not authorized by any other enumerated power—and hence a violation of state sovereignty. (He also claimed, in an argument that revealed much about his mindset, that the statute discriminated against White people.) For the first time in US history, Congress overrode a Presidential veto. The Civil Rights Act was now law, but the experience prompted doubts about the scope of federal power under the Thirteenth Amendment.

4. The Fourteenth Amendment (1866–68)

To deal with this and other post-war questions, Congress appointed a committee led by **Rep. John Bingham** of Ohio to draft another constitutional amendment that ultimately became the Fourteenth. Sections 1 and 5 have proven to be its most frequently invoked provisions.

BIOGRAPHY

Attorney **JOHN BINGHAM** (1815–1900) came from a family of abolitionists. In college, he became lifelong friends with Titus Basfield, a former slave who became the first Black person to earn a degree from an Ohio college. In 1865, Bingham was a prosecutor in the 1865 conspiracy trial over Abraham Lincoln's assassination and in the Senate's 1868 impeachment trial of President Andrew Johnson. While in Congress, Bingham was the primary author of § 1 of the Fourteenth Amendment, which he claimed would combat "State injustice and oppression" and ensure "protection by national law from unconstitutional State enactments."

- The first sentence of § 1 overruled *Dred Scott* by announcing that all persons born or naturalized in the United States are citizens of the United States and of the state where they reside.
- The second sentence of § 1, taking account of *Barron v. Baltimore* (1833), specifies that "no State shall"—
  - "abridge the privileges or immunities of citizens of the United States;" or
  - "deprive any person of life, liberty, or property, without due process of law;" or
  - "deny to any person within its jurisdiction the equal protection of the laws."
- Section 5 says that "Congress shall have the power" to enforce the Fourteenth Amendment through "appropriate legislation."

Congress passed the Fourteenth Amendment in June 1866, and it was ratified by July 1868.

5. The Military Reconstruction Act (1867)

Tennessee ratified the Fourteenth Amendment and became the first seceding state to be readmitted to the Union. But other Southern states refused to ratify, egged on by President Johnson. The continuing intransigence from the South convinced the Republicans that sterner action was needed, and after their landslide victory in the election of 1866, they had the veto-proof control of the House and Senate to pursue it.

Using its power under Art. IV, § 4—"the United States shall guarantee to every State in this Union a republican form of government"—Congress authorized the commanders of the military occupation to dissolve existing state governments or override their individual decisions. Military occupation would end if the state took steps toward reconciliation. Among other things, each state would need to ratify the Fourteenth Amendment and adopt a new state constitution guaranteeing Black people the right to vote.

President Johnson vetoed the Reconstruction Act, but was overridden.

6. Impeachment (1868)

Johnson's disputes with Congress over the conduct of Reconstruction culminated in the House of Representatives impeaching him in February 1868, the first ever impeachment of a President. The Senate came within one vote of removing Johnson from office. Needless to say, Johnson did not run for re-election in November. He was replaced as President by the war hero and Republican Ulysses S. Grant.

7. The Fifteenth Amendment (1870)

Fearing that the South would eventually backslide on the state constitutional voting rights provisions required by the Reconstruction Act, Congressional Republicans began work on a voting rights amendment for the US Constitution. John Bingham proposed an amendment that would forbid disenfranchisement on the basis of "race, color, nativity, property, education, or religious beliefs," but this proved too sweeping at a time of nativism when many states did not allow immigrants from China and other countries to vote. As passed by Congress in 1869 and ratified in 1870, the Fifteenth Amendment stated that neither the United States nor the states may deny or abridge the right to vote "**on account of race**, color, or previous condition of servitude."

■ HISTORY

ON ACCOUNT OF RACE: Many abolitionists were women, and the 19th-century social movements for the rights of black people and of women tended to work in concert. But some feminists opposed the Fifteenth Amendment. By preventing disenfranchisement on the basis of race, it seemed to invite disenfranchisement on the basis of sex—following the pattern begun in § 2 of the Fourteenth Amendment, which would take away House seats from states that failed to enfranchise "male inhabitants."

Consistent with the earlier pattern, states hostile to voting rights for Black people found ways to avoid the Fifteenth Amendment. Most enacted voter qualification statutes that avoided express reliance on race but had much the same end result. New bases for disenfranchisement were written into state laws, such as poll taxes, literacy tests, onerous residency or registration requirements, and other devices.

State laws that claimed to obey the letter of the Fifteenth Amendment while violating its spirit did not lead to another constitutional amendment. The readmitted Southern states had acquired sufficient political power to prevent it, and the North had lost its appetite for Reconstruction. Reconstruction finally ended as part of a compromise to settle the exceedingly close presidential election of 1876. In exchange for throwing their Electoral College support to the Republican Rutherford B. Hayes, Southern states were rewarded with a promise to remove the last remaining federal troops from the South.

B. Decisions Upholding Individual Rights Claims

The titanic political battles over Reconstruction and race relations in the 1860s occurred outside the courts. The Supreme Court's first opportunities to apply the Reconstruction Amendments did not arise until the 1870s.

In two cases—still frequently cited today—the Supreme Court was willing to overturn state government actions that unambiguously discriminated on the basis of race. But as described in Ch. 7.C, the Court often applied the Reconstruction Amendments in less protective ways.

1. Racially Discriminatory Statutes: *Strauder v. West Virginia*

When Virginia seceded from the Union in 1861, its mountainous western region was unwilling to secede with it. The territory that became the state of West Virginia had relatively few slaves, because it was not geographically well suited to plantation agriculture. However, West Virginia's willingness to do without slavery did not mean that it was willing to afford full political rights to its Black citizens. In particular, West Virginia law summoned only White males for jury service.

Taylor Strauder was once a slave, but after emancipation he lived and worked as a carpenter in Wheeling, WV. He had a jealous temper, and after hearing rumors that his wife Annie was having affairs—including affairs with White men—he murdered her in front of her nine-year-old daughter. The main question for trial was whether Strauder acted with premeditation, which would mean the difference between first-degree and second-degree murder. The all-White jury convicted Strauder of first-degree murder and sentenced him to death.

The case arrived in the US Supreme Court through a new procedural device enacted by the Reconstruction Congress. Under this statute, now found in amended form at 28 U.S.C. § 1443, a state court defendant could petition to remove a prosecution to federal court. The state court was to grant the petition for removal if the defendant "is denied or cannot enforce in the judicial tribunals of the State . . . any right secured to him by any law providing for the equal civil rights of citizens of the United States." Strauder's chief issue on appeal was that the state court denied his petition to remove.

ITEMS TO CONSIDER WHILE READING *STRAUDER:*

A. *Why did the state law violate the Fourteenth Amendment?*

B. *Should an African-American criminal defendant have a constitutional right to a jury that includes at least one African-American member? If not, should it matter whether the jury pool is all White?*

C. *According to the Supreme Court in* Strauder, *would it be constitutional to draw jurors from a pool consisting only of men? Property owners? College graduates?*

D. *What authorizes Congress to give federal courts control over a state criminal case?*

Strauder v. West Virginia,

100 U.S. 303 (1879)

Justice Strong delivered the opinion of the court [joined by Chief Justice Waite and Justices Swayne, Miller, Bradley, Hunt, and Harlan].

The plaintiff in error [Taylor Strauder], a colored man, was indicted for murder in the Circuit Court of Ohio County, in West Virginia, on the 20th of October, 1874, and upon trial was convicted and sentenced. [The state supreme court affirmed.] It is now, in substance, averred that at the trial in the State court the defendant (now plaintiff in error) was denied rights to which he was entitled under the Constitution and laws of the United States.

In the Circuit Court of the State, before the trial of the indictment was commenced, the defendant presented his petition, verified by his oath, praying for a removal of the cause into [federal court], assigning, as ground for the removal, that "by virtue of the laws of the State of West Virginia no colored man was eligible to be a member of the **grand jury** or to serve on a **petit jury** in the State; that white men are so eligible, and that by reason of his being a colored man and having been a slave, he had reason to believe, and did believe, he could not have the full and equal benefit of all laws and proceedings in the State of West Virginia for the security of his person as is enjoyed by white citizens, and that he had less chance of enforcing in the courts of the State his rights on the prosecution, as a citizen of the United States, and that the probabilities of a denial of them to him as such citizen on every trial which might take place on the indictment in the courts of the State were much more enhanced than if he was a white man." This petition was denied by the State court, and the cause was forced to trial. . . .

■ TERMINOLOGY

GRAND JURY AND PETIT JURY: A grand jury decides whether the prosecutor has probable cause to bring charges against a criminal defendant. The petit jury decides guilt or innocence at trial.

The law of the State to which reference was made . . . is as follows: "All white male persons who are twenty-one years of age and who are citizens of this State shall be liable to serve as jurors, except as herein provided." The persons excepted are State officials.

In this court, several errors have been assigned, and the controlling questions underlying them all are . . . whether, by the Constitution and laws of the United States, every citizen of the United States has a right to a trial of an indictment against him by a jury selected and impanelled without discrimination against his race or color, because of race or color and, second, if he has such a right, and is denied its enjoyment by the State in which he is indicted, may he cause the case to be removed into [a federal court]?

[SECTION 1 OF THE FOURTEENTH AMENDMENT]

Strauder v. West Virginia

It is to be observed that the first of these questions is not whether a colored man, when an indictment has been preferred against him, has a right to a grand or a petit jury composed in whole or in part of persons of his own race or color, but it is whether, in the composition or selection of jurors by whom he is to be indicted or tried, all persons of his race or color may be excluded by law, solely because of their race or color, so that by no possibility can any colored man sit upon the jury. . . .

The Fourteenth Amendment . . . is one of a series of constitutional provisions having a common purpose; namely, securing to a race recently emancipated, a race that through many generations had been held in slavery, all the civil rights that the superior race enjoy. The true spirit and meaning of the amendments . . . cannot be understood without keeping in view the history of the times when they were adopted, and the general objects they plainly sought to accomplish. At the time when they were incorporated into the Constitution, it required little knowledge of human nature to anticipate that those who had long been regarded as an inferior and subject race would, when suddenly raised to the rank of citizenship, be looked upon with jealousy and positive dislike, and that State laws might be enacted or enforced to perpetuate the distinctions that had before existed. Discriminations against them had been habitual. It was well known that in some States laws making such discriminations then existed, and others might well be expected. The colored race, as a race, was abject and ignorant, and in that condition was unfitted to command the respect of those who had superior intelligence. Their training had left them mere children, and as such they needed the protection which a wise government extends to those who are unable to protect themselves. They especially needed protection against unfriendly action in the States where they were resident.

It was in view of these considerations the Fourteenth Amendment was framed and adopted. It was designed to assure to the colored race the enjoyment of all the civil rights that under the law are enjoyed by white persons, and to give to that race the protection of the general [federal] government, in that enjoyment, whenever it should be denied by the States. It not only gave citizenship and the privileges of citizenship to persons of color, but it denied to any State the power to withhold from them the equal protection of the laws, and authorized Congress to enforce its provisions by appropriate legislation. . . .

If this is the spirit and meaning of the amendment, whether it means more or not, it is to be construed liberally, to carry out the purposes of its framers. . . . It ordains that no State shall deprive any person of life, liberty, or property, without due process of law, or deny to any person within its jurisdiction the equal protection of the laws. What is this but declaring that the law in the States shall be the same for the black as for the white; that all persons, whether colored or white, shall stand equal before the laws of the States, and, in regard to the colored race, for whose protection the amendment was primarily designed, that no discrimination shall be made against them by law because of their color? The words of the amendment, it is true, are prohibitory, but they contain a necessary implication of a positive immunity, or right, most valuable to the colored race—the right to exemption from unfriendly legislation against them distinctively as colored—exemption from legal discriminations, implying inferiority in civil society, lessening the security of their enjoyment of the rights which others enjoy, and discriminations which are steps towards reducing them to the condition of a subject race.

That the West Virginia statute respecting juries . . . is such a discrimination ought not to be doubted. Nor would it be if the persons excluded by it were white men. If in those States where the colored people constitute a majority of the entire population a law should be enacted excluding all white men from jury service, thus denying to them the privilege of participating equally with the blacks in the administration of justice, we apprehend no one would be heard to claim that it would not be a denial to white men of the equal protection of the laws. Nor if a law should be passed excluding all naturalized Celtic Irishmen, would there be any doubt of its inconsistency with the spirit of the amendment. The very fact that colored people are singled out and expressly denied by a statute all right to participate in the administration of the law, as jurors, because of their color, though they are citizens, and may be in other respects fully qualified, is practically a brand upon them, affixed by the law, an assertion of their inferiority, and a stimulant to that race prejudice which is an impediment to securing to individuals of the race that equal justice which the law aims to secure to all others.

The right to a trial by jury is guaranteed to every citizen of West Virginia **by the Constitution of that State**, and the constitution of juries is a very essential part of the protection such a mode of trial is intended to secure. The very idea of a jury is a body of men composed of the peers or equals of the person whose rights it is selected or summoned to determine; that is, of his neighbors, fellows, associates, persons having the same legal status in society as that which he holds. . . .

In view of these considerations, it is hard to see why the statute of West Virginia should not be regarded as discriminating against a colored man when he is put upon trial for an alleged criminal offence against the State. . . . Is not protection of life and liberty against race or color prejudice, a right, a legal right, under the [Fourteenth] constitutional amendment? And how can it be maintained that compelling a colored man to submit to a trial for his life by a jury drawn from a panel from which the State has expressly excluded every man of his race, because of color alone, however well qualified in other respects, is not a denial to him of equal legal protection?

■ OBSERVATION

BY THE CONSTITUTION OF THAT STATE: The state law right to jury trial is mentioned to show how the state courts were, in the words of the removal statute, violating a law "providing for the equal civil rights of citizens of the United States." The opinion does not argue that West Virginia violated the federal Sixth Amendment right to an impartial jury, because the incorporation doctrine had not yet developed.

Strauder v. West Virginia

We do not say that within the limits from which it is not excluded by the amendment a State may not prescribe the qualifications of its jurors, and in so doing make discriminations. It may confine the selection to males, to freeholders, to citizens, to persons within certain ages, or to persons having educational qualifications. We do not believe the Fourteenth Amendment was ever intended to prohibit this. Looking at its history, it is clear it had no such purpose. Its aim was against discrimination because of race or color. . . . We are not now called upon to affirm or deny that it had other purposes.

historical

The Fourteenth Amendment makes no attempt to enumerate the rights it designed to protect. It speaks in general terms, and those are as comprehensive as possible. Its language is prohibitory; but every prohibition implies the existence of rights and immunities, prominent among which is an immunity from inequality of legal protection, either for life, liberty, or property. Any State action that denies this immunity to a colored man is in conflict with the Constitution.

textual

[SECTION 5 OF THE FOURTEENTH AMENDMENT]

Concluding, therefore, that the statute of West Virginia, discriminating in the selection of jurors, as it does, against negroes because of their color, amounts to a denial of the equal protection of the laws to a colored man when he is put upon trial for an alleged offence against the State, it remains only to be considered whether the power of Congress to enforce the provisions of the Fourteenth Amendment by appropriate legislation is sufficient to justify the enactment of [the removal statute]. . . .

Rights and immunities created by or dependent upon the Constitution of the United States can be protected by Congress. The form and manner of the protection may be such as Congress in the legitimate exercise of its legislative discretion shall provide. These may be varied to meet the necessities of the particular right to be protected. But there is [in § 5 of the Fourteenth Amendment] express authority to protect the rights and immunities referred to in [§ 1 of] the Fourteenth Amendment, and to enforce observance of them by appropriate congressional legislation. And one very efficient and appropriate mode of extending such protection and securing to a party the enjoyment of the right or immunity, is a law providing for the removal of his case from a State court, in which the right is denied by the State law, into a Federal court, where it will be upheld. . . . [The removal statute] was an advanced step [to secure § 1 rights], fully warranted, we think, by the fifth section of the Fourteenth Amendment. . . .

There was error, therefore, in proceeding to the trial of the indictment against [Strauder] after his petition was filed, as also in overruling his challenge to the array of the jury, and in refusing to quash the panel. . . .

Justice Field, joined by Justice Clifford, dissenting [in the companion case *Ex Parte Virginia*, 100 U.S. 339 (1879)].

[The dissenters believed that the removal statute was not authorized by any enumerated power. They also disputed Strauder's equal protection theory. "The position that in cases where the rights of colored persons are concerned, justice will not be done to them unless they have a mixed jury, is founded upon the notion that in such cases white persons will not be fair and honest jurors. If this position be correct, there ought not to be any white persons on the jury where the interests of colored persons only are involved. . . . To be consistent, those who hold this notion should contend that in cases affecting members of the colored race only, the juries should be composed entirely of colored persons, and that the presiding judge should be of the same race."]

flashforward

Defining Discrimination. The West Virginia statute in *Strauder* purposely removed all Black persons from the jury pool. The statute in *Virginia v. Rives*, 100 U.S. 313 (1879), did not on its face refer to race; all (male) adult citizens were subject to jury service. But in practice, some Virginia counties always had all-White juries. This was the case in *Rives*, where two Black men claimed self-defense in their prosecution for murder of a White man. Seeking removal to federal court under the statute upheld in *Strauder*, they claimed a right to a jury pool that was at least one-third Black. The Supreme Court unanimously disagreed, finding a dispositive difference between a statute guaranteeing all-White juries and the fact of an all-White jury in a particular case.

> The assertions in the petition for removal, that the grand jury by which the petitioners were indicted, as well as the jury summoned to try them, were composed wholly of the white race, and that their race had never been allowed to serve as jurors in the county of Patrick in any case in which a colored man was interested, fall short of showing that any civil right was denied, or that there had been any discrimination against the defendants because of their color or race. The facts may have been as stated, and yet the jury which indicted them, and the panel summoned to try them, may have been impartially selected.

In the absence of a discriminatory statute, *Rives* required affirmative proof of discrimination in seating a juror, not merely proof of a result in a particular case that was consistent with discrimination.

Such proof was present in *Ex Parte Virginia*, 100 U.S. 339 (1879), a companion case to *Strauder* and *Rives*. Judge J.D. Coles of Pittsylvania County, Virginia had an admitted practice of refusing to seat any Black men as grand jurors or petit jurors; his intentional race discrimination was never disputed. He was prosecuted under an 1875 statute making it a federal crime to exclude citizens from jury service on grounds of race, color, or previous condition of servitude. The same 7–2 majority as in *Strauder* upheld the statute as within Congress's enumerated powers to enforce the Fourteenth Amendment, and rejected the claimed defense of judicial immunity.

Neal v. Delaware, 103 U.S. 370 (1880), involved a Black defendant sentenced to death for raping a White woman. Delaware did not bar Black people from juries by statute, but the state admitted that in practice they were always excluded. Approximately 26,000 of 150,000 inhabitants of Delaware were Black, but none had ever been summoned for jury duty. The state claimed that this was not because of race, but because "the great body of black men residing in this State are utterly unqualified by want of intelligence, experience, or moral integrity to sit on juries." The Supreme Court rejected this "violent presumption," concluding that it was forbidden race discrimination. The opinion also summarized the principles from the jury selection cases decided thus far:

> A colored citizen, party to a trial involving his life, liberty, or property, cannot claim, as matter of right, that his race shall have a representation on the jury, and while a mixed jury in a particular case is not, within the meaning of the Constitution, always or absolutely necessary to the equal protection of the laws, it is a right to which he is entitled, that in the selection of jurors to pass upon his life, liberty, or property, there shall be no exclusion of his race, and no discrimination against them, because of their color.

2. Racially Discriminatory Practices: *Yick Wo v. Hopkins*

Strauder involved a state statute that on its face treated potential jurors differently on the basis of race. Discrimination may also arise through the actions of government officials, even where the text of a statute does not treat races differently. The Supreme Court decided early on that intentionally discriminatory actions of officials, just like intentionally discriminatory statutes, could violate equal protection.

Chinese immigrants had encountered discrimination ever since they began to settle in the Western US following the California Gold Rush of 1848. *Yick Wo v. Hopkins* (1886) arose from the City of San Francisco's effort to regulate laundries, a type of business where Chinese immigrants had been able to thrive. In 1880, San Francisco enacted an ordinance requiring all laundries operating in wooden buildings to obtain a permit from the Board of Supervisors. Lee Yick (misidentified in the opinion as Yick Wo), a native of China who emigrated to the United States in 1861, had operated a laundry in a wooden building for over twenty years. He had obtained all necessary permits in the past, but when they expired in 1885, the Board refused to renew them. He was not alone: Approximately 200 Chinese launderers applied for permits at that time, and the Board denied all of them. Meanwhile, permits were granted to 79 out of 80 White applicants.

Wooden Laundry Building, San Francisco (c. 1875)

The City began an enforcement sweep, shutting down unpermitted Chinese laundries and arresting their owners. They would be released upon payment of a $10 fine, but to set up a legal challenge, Yick Wo refused to pay and filed suit against his jailor, Sheriff Hopkins, seeking release from custody. The California Supreme Court upheld the City's actions, and Yick Wo obtained review from the US Supreme Court.

ITEMS TO CONSIDER WHILE READING *YICK WO*:

A. *Was the San Francisco ordinance unconstitutional as written?*

B. *Should the Equal Protection Clause apply to actions of government officials when they enforce statutes that do not discriminate on their face?*

C. *How can we tell whether government action under a nondiscriminatory statute is nonetheless discriminatory?*

D. *Should the Due Process and Equal Protection Clauses apply to noncitizens?*

Yick Wo v. Hopkins,

118 U.S. 356 (1886)

Justice Matthews [delivered the opinion of the court, joined by Chief Justice Waite and Justices Miller, Field, Bradley, Harlan, Woods, Gray, and Blatchford].

. . . The ordinance drawn in question in the present case . . . does not prescribe a rule and conditions, for the regulation of the use of property for laundry purposes, to which all similarly situated may conform. It allows, without restriction, the use for such purposes of buildings of brick or stone; but, as to wooden buildings, constituting nearly all those in previous use, it divides the owners or occupiers into two classes, not having respect to their personal character and qualifications for the business, nor the situation and nature and adaptation of the buildings themselves, but merely by an arbitrary line, on one side of which are those who are permitted to pursue their industry by the mere will and consent of the supervisors, and on the other those from whom that consent is withheld, at their mere will and pleasure. . . .

The rights of the petitioners, as affected by the proceedings of which they complain, are not less because they are aliens and subjects of the emperor of China. . . . The fourteenth amendment to the constitution is not confined to the protection of citizens. It says: "Nor shall any state deprive any person of life, liberty, or property without due process of law; nor deny to any person within its jurisdiction the equal protection of the laws." These provisions are universal in their application, to all persons within the territorial jurisdiction, without regard to any differences of race, of color, or of nationality; and the equal protection of the laws is a pledge of the protection of equal laws. . . . The questions we have to consider and decide in these cases, therefore, are to be treated as involving the rights of every citizen of the United States equally with those of the strangers and aliens who now invoke the jurisdiction of the court.

It is contended on the part of the petitioners that the ordinances for violations of which they are severally sentenced to imprisonment are void on their face, as being within the prohibitions of the fourteenth amendment, and, in the alternative, if not so, that they are void by reason of their administration, operating unequally, so as to punish in the present petitioners what is permitted to others as lawful, without any distinction of circumstances—an unjust and illegal discrimination, it is claimed, which, though not made expressly by the ordinances, is made possible by them.

When we consider the nature and the theory of our institutions of government, the principles upon which they are supposed to rest, and review the history of their development, we are constrained to conclude that they do not mean to leave room for the play and action of purely personal and arbitrary power. Sovereignty itself is, of course, not subject to law, for it is the author and source of law; but in our system, while sovereign powers are delegated to the agencies of government, sovereignty itself remains with the people, by whom and for whom all government exists and acts. And the law is the definition and limitation of power. It is, indeed, quite true that there must always be lodged somewhere, and in some person or body, the authority of final decision; and in many cases of mere administration, the responsibility is purely political, no appeal lying except to the ultimate tribunal of the public judgment, exercised either in the pressure of opinion, or by means of the suffrage. But the fundamental rights to life, liberty, and the pursuit of happiness, considered as individual possessions, are secured by those maxims of constitutional law which are the monuments showing the victorious progress of the race in securing to men the blessings of civilization under the reign of just and equal laws, so that, in the famous language of the Massachusetts bill of rights, the government of the commonwealth "may be a government of laws and not of men." For the very idea that one man may be compelled to hold his life, or the means of living, or any material right essential to the enjoyment of life, at the mere will of another, seems to be intolerable in any country where freedom prevails, as being the essence of slavery itself.

There are many illustrations that might be given of this truth, which would make manifest that it was self-evident in the light of our system of jurisprudence. The case of the political franchise of voting is one. Though not regarded strictly as a natural right, but as a privilege merely conceded by society, according to its will, under certain conditions, nevertheless it is regarded as a fundamental political right, because [it is] preservative of all rights. . . . It has accordingly been held generally in the states that whether the particular provisions of an act of legislation establishing means for ascertaining the qualifications of those entitled to vote, and making previous registration in lists of such, a condition precedent to the exercise of the right, were or were not reasonable regulations, and accordingly valid or void, was always open to inquiry, as a judicial question.

The same principle has been more freely extended to the quasi legislative acts of inferior municipal bodies, in respect to which it is an ancient jurisdiction of judicial tribunals to pronounce upon the reasonableness and consequent validity of their by-laws. . . .

In the present cases, we are not obliged to reason from the probable to the actual, and pass upon the validity of the ordinances complained of, as tried merely by the opportunities which their terms afford, of unequal and unjust discrimination in their administration; for the cases present the ordinances in actual operation, and the facts shown establish an administration directed so exclusively against a particular class of persons as to warrant and require the conclusion that, whatever may have been the intent of the ordinances as adopted, they are applied by the public authorities charged with their administration, and thus representing the state itself, with a mind so unequal and oppressive as to amount to a practical denial by the state of that equal protection of the laws which is secured to the petitioners, as to all other persons, by the broad and benign provisions of the fourteenth amendment to the constitution of the United States. Though the law itself be fair on its face, and impartial in appearance, yet, if it is applied and administered by public authority with an evil eye and an unequal hand, so as practically to make unjust and illegal discriminations between persons in similar circumstances, material to their rights, the denial of equal justice is still within the prohibition of the constitution. . . .

Yick Wo v. Hopkins

The present cases, as shown by the facts disclosed in the record, are within this class. It appears that both petitioners have complied with every requisite deemed by the law, or by the public officers charged with its administration, necessary for the protection of neighboring property from fire, or as a precaution against injury to the public health. No reason whatever, except the will of the supervisors, is assigned why they should not be permitted to carry on, in the accustomed manner, their harmless and useful occupation, on which they depend for a livelihood; and while this consent of the supervisors is withheld from them, and from 200 others who have also petitioned, all of whom happen to be Chinese subjects, 80 others, not Chinese subjects, are permitted to carry on the same business under similar conditions. The fact of this discrimination is admitted. No reason for it is shown, and the conclusion cannot be resisted that no reason for it exists except hostility to the race and nationality to which the petitioners belong, and which, in the eye of the law, is not justified. The discrimination is therefore illegal, and the public administration which enforces it is a denial of the equal protection of the laws, and a violation of the fourteenth amendment of the constitution. . . .

flashforward

The Chinese Exclusion Act. While San Francisco pursued ordinances against Chinese laundries, Congress enacted the Chinese Exclusion Act of 1882, the first federal law to deny the right to emigrate to the US on the basis of race or nationality. The Supreme Court upheld it and various followup statutes in a series of opinions usually called *The Chinese Exclusion Cases.* Those cases introduced the "plenary power" doctrine, which holds that the Courts may not second-guess most Congressional decisions regarding immigration, allowing it to discriminate on the basis of race or national origin in ways that would violate Equal Protection in other contexts. See *Chae Chan Ping v. US*, 130 U.S. 581 (1889) (Field, J.) (Congress may deny entry to Chinese people); *Fong Yue Ting v. US*, 149 U.S. 698 (1893) (Congress may deport Chinese people). Around the same time, however, the Court ruled in *US v. Wong Kim Ark*, 169 U.S. 649 (1898) that birthright citizenship under the Fourteenth Amendment is not limited to former slaves or their descendants, and may be claimed by Asian-Americans.

The Chinese Exclusion Act was ultimately repealed in 1943, when China was a wartime ally (and when Japanese-Americans were being interned; see Ch. 10.B.2). Decades later, each house of Congress passed a resolution formally apologizing for the Chinese Exclusion Act. S. Res. 201 (112th Congress, October 6, 2011); H.Res 683 (112th Congress, June 18, 2012).

C. Decisions Rejecting Individual Rights Claims

In cases like *Strauder* and *Yick Wo*—where state and local governments obviously gave worse treatment to racial minority groups than to the White majority—the Supreme Court invalidated the discrimination under the Fourteenth Amendment. In many of the most important discrimination cases of the late 1800s, however, the Court allowed alleged discrimination to stand.

Social attitudes of the time explain some of this shift. By the 1890s, equality for former slaves and their descendants was no longer a national priority. To the contrary, racist ideology was extraordinarily influential, to the point where *Plessy v. Ferguson* (1896) could assert confidently that non-White people were "inferior to [White people] socially" and that "legislation is powerless to eradicate racial instincts, or to abolish distinctions based upon physical differences." Jim Crow segregation laws became commonplace across the former slave states, but de facto segregation, discrimination, and racialized thinking were widespread throughout the country.

When race discrimination cases reached the Supreme Court, its attitude toward constitutional structure, principally focused on the balance of power between the state and federal governments, became an important factor. A majority of the Supreme Court believed that a defining feature of the Constitution's structure was local control over matters traditionally deemed local. For these justices, protecting minority populations from oppression was all well and good, but not at the cost of shifting much power away from state and local governments and toward Congress or the US Supreme Court. This attitude was clearly expressed in *The Slaughterhouse Cases* (1872), the first US Supreme Court opinion to consider the meaning of the Fourteenth Amendment.

> In the early history of the organization of the government, its statesmen seem to have divided on the line which should separate the powers of the National government from those of the State governments, and though this line has never been very well defined in public opinion, such a division has continued from that day to this. . . . We do not see in those [Reconstruction] amendments any purpose to destroy the main features of the general system. Under the

pressure of all the excited feeling growing out of the war, our statesmen have still believed that the existence of the State with powers for domestic and local government, including the regulation of civil rights—the rights of person and of property—was essential to the perfect working of our complex form of government . . .

1. The Demise of the Fourteenth Amendment Privileges or Immunities Clause

Many litigants bringing individual rights claims in the years immediately after ratification considered the **Fourteenth Amendment Privileges or Immunities Clause** to be the enactment's centerpiece. Before the Civil War, the US Constitution had little to say regarding states' treatment of their own citizens. Now, "no state shall abridge the privileges or immunities of citizens of the United States." For these litigants, the language implied a minimum set of human rights that the federal government would protect if state or local governments failed to respect them. But what exactly were the privileges or immunities (rights) that US citizens had as an automatic result of being citizens? In a rapid series of decisions led by *The Slaughterhouse Cases* (1872), the Supreme Court ruled that the Clause protected only the ability to be a national citizen—which boiled down to a very small set of rights that were mostly protected already. This definition of "privileges or immunities of citizens of the United States" was so narrow that later generations have said the Clause "was rendered a dead letter as a limitation on a state's ability to restrict rights of its own citizens." *Humphreys v. Clinic for Women, Inc.*, 796 N.E.2d 247, 269 (Ind. 2003) (Boehm, J., dissenting).

■ TERMINOLOGY

FOURTEENTH AMENDMENT PRIVILEGES OR IMMUNITIES CLAUSE: The Fourteenth Amendment's command that states not abridge the "privileges or immunities of citizens of the United States" is distinct from the obligation of states under Art. IV, § 2 to afford citizens of other states the same "privileges and immunities" that are afforded to in-state citizens. Because Art. IV was aimed at interstate discrimination, it allowed a state to decide for itself which privileges and immunities to grant, so long as it also granted them to citizens of other states. By contrast, the language of the Fourteenth Amendment implied that a set of federal-level privileges or immunities existed, and that all states must respect them.

The narrow definition can be seen in a series of cases finding that claimed rights were not "privileges or immunities of citizens of the United States."

a) Right to an Unregulated Livelihood: *The Slaughterhouse Cases*

By the late 1860s, New Orleans earned the reputation as the least healthy big city in America, in large part because unregulated butcher shops dumped animal waste in any handy ditch, leading to deadly outbreaks of cholera in 1866 and yellow fever in 1867. For public

■ WEBSITE

A fuller version of *The Slaughterhouse Cases* is available for download from this casebook's companion website, www.CaplanIntegratedConLaw.com.

health purposes, the state legislature enacted a law where slaughtering could be performed only in a government-regulated central slaughterhouse. A coalition of White butchers who disliked the new law filed suit, claiming that pursuing one's livelihood in the location of one's choice was a "privilege or immunity of citizens of the United States."

This was an aggressive legal position, and its brazenness provoked a 5–4 majority of the Supreme Court to reject it in equally aggressive terms. Before the Fourteenth Amendment, the majority said, "the entire domain of the privileges and immunities of citizens of the States . . . lay within the constitutional and legislative power of the States." This had not changed. The Fourteenth Amendment did not "transfer the security and protection of all the civil rights . . . from the States to the Federal government." The Supreme Court ought not act as "a perpetual censor upon all legislation of the States, on the civil rights of their own citizens." The consequences of any other ruling would be "so serious, so far-reaching and pervading, [and] so great a departure from the structure and spirit of our institutions" that it must be rejected. Otherwise, the Court would "fetter and degrade the State governments by subjecting them to the control of Congress, in the exercise of powers heretofore universally conceded to them of the most ordinary and fundamental character." And any other result would "radically change the whole theory of the relations of the State and Federal governments to each other and of both these governments to the people."

What, then, were the "privileges or immunities of citizens of the United States?" The text had to mean something. For the majority, the term encompassed those rights "which owe their existence to the Federal government [and] its National character." In other words, rights so unique to national citizenship that they had no counterparts among the rights of purely state citizens. This included the right to travel across state lines; to enjoy federal protection on the high seas and in foreign lands; to use navigable waterways; to travel to Washington DC and to petition the national government there; and to visit subtreasuries and other federal office buildings located within states.

It was immediately evident that this set of privileges and immunities was so narrow as to be of little practical use. The dissenters charged the majority with turning the Clause into "a vain and idle enactment, which accomplished nothing, and most unnecessarily excited Congress and the people on its passage."

b) Right to Practice Law: *Bradwell v. Illinois*

The day after announcing *The Slaughterhouse Cases*, the Supreme Court decided *Bradwell v. Illinois*, 83 U.S. 130 (1872). Myra Bradwell of Chicago had applied for a license to practice law. She met all of the written qualifications for the license, and had successfully completed the customary training (apprenticeship in a law office). The Illinois Supreme Court denied her a license because she was female. On appeal, the US Supreme Court held that the right to practice law was not a privilege or immunity of citizens of the United States.

Myra Bradwell (1831–1894)

Bradwell is most famous today for the unapologetic sexism found in Justice Bradley's concurring opinion:

> It certainly cannot be affirmed, as an historical fact, that [the right to pursue lawful employment] has ever been established as one of the fundamental privileges and immunities of the [female] sex. On the contrary, the civil law, as well as nature herself, has always recognized a wide difference in the respective spheres and destinies of man and woman. Man is, or should be, woman's protector and defender. The natural and proper timidity and delicacy which belongs to the female sex evidently unfits it for many of the occupations of civil life. The constitution of the family organization, which is founded in the divine ordinance, as well as in the nature of things, indicates the domestic sphere as that which properly belongs to the domain and functions of womanhood. The harmony, not to say identity, of interest and views which belong, or should belong, to the family institution is repugnant to the idea of a woman adopting a distinct and independent career from that of her husband.

A few years after this loss, Bradwell and her supporters succeeded in changing Illinois law to allow women to be licensed attorneys.

c) Right to Vote: *Minor v. Happersett*

Bradwell was followed by *Minor v. Happersett*, 88 U.S. 162 (1874), where Virginia Minor challenged Missouri's law denying the vote to women. The Supreme Court unanimously explained that women are citizens, but the right to vote was not a "privilege or immunity of citizens of the United States." If voting rights were protected by the Privileges or Immunities Clause of the Fourteenth Amendment, the Court reasoned, there would have been no need to pass the Fifteenth Amendment. In addition, a historical review showed that at the time of the founding, women could not vote and in most states still could not. Because "the Constitution of the United States does not confer the right of suffrage upon any one," the Court concluded that "the constitutions and laws of the several States which commit that important trust to men alone are not necessarily void."

Virginia Minor (1824–1894)

A similar result was reached in a prosecution against Susan B. Anthony, the famous women's suffrage activist. When Anthony voted in a New York election for Congress, she was prosecuted for violating a federal statute making it a crime for a person to knowingly vote in a federal election without a lawful right to vote under state law. "The right of voting, or the privilege of voting, is a right or privilege arising under the constitution of the state," wrote the trial judge, "and not under the constitution of the United States." Therefore nothing in the Fourteenth Amendment Privileges or Immunities Clause prevented the state from limiting voting to men. So certain was the result that the trial judge directed the jury to return a verdict of guilty. *United States v. Anthony*, 24 F. Cas. 829 (C.C.N.D.N.Y. 1873).

d) Enumerated Rights in the Bill of Rights: *United States v. Cruikshank*

Many modern historians believe that one intended function of the Fourteenth Amendment Privileges or Immunities Clause was to require states to respect some or all of the rights found in the federal Bill of Rights. For example, the First Amendment right to freedom of speech or the Sixth Amendment right to assistance of counsel in a criminal trial would be "privileges or immunities of citizens of the United States" that states must honor. The Supreme Court squarely rejected that understanding in *United States v. Cruikshank,* 92 U.S. 542 (1876).

The case arose from one of the worst incidents of White supremacist violence during Reconstruction. Louisiana's population was majority Black. Black voters tended to support the Republican party, while White supremacists favored the Democratic party. Organized gangs of White supremacists, associated with the Ku Klux Klan and similar groups, routinely used violence to suppress the Black vote, terrorize the Black population, and take control of local government notwithstanding the election results. Following a disputed election in 1872, a posse of Black people and their White supporters in Colfax (the seat of government for the majority-Black Grant Parish) formed a defensive line around the courthouse to defend against White paramilitary gangs who had been attacking government buildings in nearby towns to prevent Republican election winners from taking office. On Easter Sunday of 1873, a White army—roughly twice the size and much better armed—attacked the courthouse. They targeted its Black defenders, killing dozens and taking others prisoner. A contingent of White supremacists led by William Cruikshank murdered most of the prisoners after they had surrendered. Overall, somewhere between 60 and 150 Black people and three White people were killed that day. No one knows the true number of Black victims because so many bodies were dumped in the river.

Very few of the White participants were charged with any crime, but three leaders of the White assault, including Cruikshank, were convicted of violating the federal Enforcement Act of 1870 (intended to enforce the individual rights of the Fourteenth Amendment). Among other provisions, the Act made it a crime to "band or conspire together . . . with intent to prevent or hinder [another person's] free exercise and enjoyment of any right or privilege granted or secured to him by the constitution or laws of the United States." The prosecutors argued that Cruikshank's band had prevented or hindered the freedmen of Colfax from exercising US constitutional rights including the right to assemble and petition the government for redress of grievances; the right to bear arms; and the right to vote.

The Supreme Court found that none of these were privileges or immunities of US citizens. Instead, they were natural rights that pre-existed the US Constitution. "The government of the United States when established found [these rights] in existence, with the obligation on the part of the States to afford [them] protection. As no direct power over [them] was granted to Congress, [they remain] subject to State jurisdiction." The murdered Republicans were not petitioning the federal government or voting in a federal election, activities that might be privileges or immunities of US citizens. Moreover, said the Court, the Fourteenth Amendment "adds nothing to the rights of one citizen as against another."

flash*forward*

Incorporation of the Bill of Rights. Even though the Privileges or Immunities Clause of the Fourteenth Amendment was rejected as a method of applying the federal Bill of Rights to the states, the Due Process Clause of the Fourteenth Amendment has since taken over that role through the doctrine of incorporation. Today, a state's Fourteenth Amendment obligation to respect due process incorporates most of the US Constitution's enumerated rights, such as First Amendment freedom of speech or Sixth Amendment right to counsel. See Ch. 5.C (flash-forward following *Barron v. Baltimore*).

However, it took many decades for the incorporation doctrine to become well-accepted law, with the theory not fully cemented until the mid-20th century. States that did not wish to respect the federal Bill of Rights had lifetimes after *Cruikshank* to behave oppressively.

2. Limits on the Civil Rights Enforcement Powers: *The Civil Rights Cases*

In *Slaughterhouse*, *Bradwell*, and *Minor*, the Supreme Court upheld state laws alleged to violate the Fourteenth Amendment Privileges or Immunities Clause. In *Cruikshank*, the Court ruled against Congress's use of its power to enforce that Clause through federal statutes targeting certain state or local behavior. Much of *Cruikshank*'s logic was later applied to Congress's ability to enforce other portions of the Reconstruction Amendments.

The Civil Rights Act of 1875. Each of the Reconstruction Amendments contained a final clause stating that Congress has authority to enforce it "by appropriate legislation." One such law enacted by Congress was the Civil Rights Act of 1875:

> All persons within the jurisdiction of the United States shall be entitled to the full and equal enjoyment of the accommodations, advantages, facilities, and privileges of inns, public conveyances on land or water, theaters, and other places of public amusement; subject only to the conditions and limitations established by law, and applicable alike to citizens of every race and color, regardless of any previous condition of servitude.

Violators were subject to criminal prosecution and civil suits by the victims.

For lawyers and judges accustomed to the traditional legal categories used at the time, the Civil Rights Act of 1875 seemed novel and sweeping. To begin with, it did not fall into the familiar categories of political and civil rights. Political rights related to a citizen's control over the government through voting, office holding, or jury service. Civil rights were loosely understood as the kind of rights that one could historically expect government to protect, such as the right to own property, to litigate, or to enter into enforceable contracts. A public accommodations law was arguably something different. Like the law of torts—which was not customarily viewed under the heading of civil rights—it regulated interactions between private individuals. To be sure, the English common law had required innkeepers and public conveyances not to reject eligible customers arbitrarily. Congress's 1875 **public accommodations law** could be viewed as an extension of the common law, specifying that race discrimination was an arbitrary (and hence forbidden) refusal of service. However, it was undecided at the time whether Congress could expand upon a type of law that had historically been protected by common law at the state level.

> ■ TERMINOLOGY
>
> **PUBLIC ACCOMMODATIONS LAW:** A *public accommodation* is a business open to the general public. Stores, restaurants, hotels, theaters, and mass transportation are prominent examples. The word "public," when used as part of the term "public accommodation," does not mean "owned or operated by the government." Most public accommodations are privately owned businesses.

Five Discrimination Cases. The facts of the five cases consolidated under the title *The Civil Rights Cases* reveal a great deal about American society following the Civil War.

In two of the cases, hotel operators in Kansas and Missouri refused to rent rooms to Black people. In two others, Black patrons were denied entrance to theaters in San Francisco and New York. This indicates that race discrimination was not limited to former slave states. But these four cases were criminal prosecutions, which indicates that the US Justice Department was willing to take enforcement action against discriminators. In the four cases, the lower courts were divided as to the Act's constitutionality.

The fifth case was a civil suit against the Memphis & Charleston Railroad for denying service to Sallie Robinson. In the late 19th century, most passenger trains had two cars. The ladies' car was reserved for women and any men who accompanied them. They were the rough equivalent of first class: They had more comfortable seating, no smoking, wealthier patrons, and separate restrooms for women and men. The other car was the "smoker," analogous to second class, that served men of various socio-economic classes and races. These cars tended to be smokier, dirtier, and more raucous. And they had only one restroom.

Sallie Robinson was described at trial as "a young, good-looking mulatto woman about 28 years old." She was traveling with her nephew, "a young man of light complexion, light hair, and light blue eyes." The conductor barred Robinson and her nephew from the ladies' car, and she suffered the indignity of riding in the male smoker car instead. Robinson sued for damages under the Act. (Given the law of coverture, she could not sue separately from her husband, so both she and her husband were identified as plaintiffs.)

The railroad's defense was that it had not discriminated on the basis of race: Sallie Robinson had been kept out of the ladies' car because the conductor thought she was a prostitute. As reported in the Court's brief factual summary, "the conductor had reason to suspect that the plaintiff, the wife, was an improper person, because she was in company with a young man whom he supposed to be a white man, and on that account inferred that there was some improper connection between them." The trial court instructed the jury that if the railroad acted on this basis, it had not engaged in race discrimination. (None of the parties contested the railroad's ability to keep sex workers out of the ladies' car.) The jury ruled for the railroad.

In the Supreme Court, Robinson's lawyer argued that the jury instructions endorsed race discrimination through mere word play. "What is the difference between denying her 'the full and equal enjoyment' because of her color, and denying the same thing to her because of a belief, that she being colored and her traveling companion white, therefore, she must necessarily be a woman wanting in virtue?

In either case the substantial ground of the denial was because of Mrs. Robinson's color, which must be regarded as the proximate cause of her exclusion."

The Supreme Court avoided deciding what counted as race discrimination in Robinson's case, because it ruled on a separate ground: namely, that Congress's power to forbid race discrimination did not extend to these ordinary examples of it.

ITEMS TO CONSIDER WHILE READING *THE CIVIL RIGHTS CASES*:

A. *Why is the 14th Amendment limited to "state action"? Why is the 13th Amendment not so limited?*

B. *Under the 13th Amendment, why are "mere discriminations on account of race or color" not considered "badges and incidents of slavery?"*

C. *How do the majority and dissenting opinion use the various methods of constitutional reasoning?*

- *With regard to text, which language does the majority focus on? The dissent?*
- *With regard to precedent, are* The Civil Rights Cases *consistent with* Strauder *and* Yick Wo? *With* Slaughterhouse *and* Cruikshank? *With Justice Story's view of Congressional power in* Prigg v. Pennsylvania? *With John Marshall's views about "strict construction" in* McCulloch v. Maryland *and* Gibbons v. Ogden?
- *How do the majority and dissent differ in their treatments of structure, history, consequences, and values?*

The Civil Rights Cases,

109 U.S. 3 (1883)

Justice Bradley [delivered the opinion of the court, joined by Chief Justice Waite and Justices Miller, Field, Hunt, Woods, Matthews, and Gray].

It is obvious that the primary and important question in all the cases is the constitutionality of the law; for if the law is unconstitutional none of the prosecutions can stand. . . .

Has congress constitutional power to make such a law? . . . We have carefully considered those arguments, as was due to the eminent ability of those who put them forward, and have felt, in all its force, the weight of authority which always invests a law that congress deems itself competent to pass. But the responsibility of an independent judgment is now thrown upon this court; and we are bound to exercise it according to the best lights we have.

The Civil Rights Cases

[FOURTEENTH AMENDMENT]

The first section of the fourteenth amendment—which is the one relied on—after declaring who shall be citizens of the United States, and of the several states, is prohibitory in its character, and prohibitory upon the states. It declares that "no state shall make or enforce any law which shall abridge the privileges or immunities of citizens of the United States; nor shall any state deprive any person of life, liberty, or property without due process of law; nor deny to any person within its jurisdiction the equal protection of the laws." It is state action of a particular character that is prohibited. Individual invasion of individual rights is not the subject-matter of the amendment. It has a deeper and broader scope. It nullifies and makes void all state legislation, and state action of every kind, which impairs the privileges and immunities of citizens of the United States, or which injures them in life, liberty, or property without due process of law, or which denies to any of them the equal protection of the laws.

It not only does this, but, in order that the national will, thus declared, may not be a mere *brutum fulmen* [empty threat, from the Latin for "inert thunder"], the last section of the amendment invests congress with power to enforce it by appropriate legislation. To enforce what? To enforce the prohibition. To adopt appropriate legislation for correcting the effects of such prohibited state law and state acts, and thus to render them effectually null, void, and innocuous. This is the legislative power conferred upon congress, and this is the whole of it. It does not invest congress with power to legislate upon subjects which are within the domain of state legislation; but to provide modes of relief against state legislation, or state action, of the kind referred to. It does not authorize congress to create a code of municipal law for the regulation of private rights; but to provide modes of redress against the operation of state laws, and the action of state officers, executive or judicial, when these are subversive of the fundamental rights specified in the amendment. . . .

And so in the present case, until some state law has been passed, or some state action through its officers or agents has been taken, adverse to the rights of citizens sought to be protected by the fourteenth amendment, no legislation of the United States under said amendment, nor any proceeding under such legislation, can be called into activity, for the prohibitions of the amendment are against state laws and acts done under state authority. Of course, legislation may and should be provided in advance to meet the exigency when it arises, but it should be adapted to the mischief and wrong which the amendment was intended to provide against; and that is, state laws or state action of some kind adverse to the rights of the citizen secured by the amendment.

Such legislation cannot properly cover the whole domain of rights appertaining to life, liberty, and property, defining them and providing for their vindication. That would be to establish a code of municipal law regulative of all private rights between man and man in society. It would be to make congress take the place of the state legislatures and to supersede them. It is absurd to affirm that, because the rights of life, liberty, and property (which include all civil rights that men have) are by the amendment sought to be protected against invasion on the part of the state without due process of law, congress may, therefore, provide due process of law for their vindication in every case; and that, because the denial by a state to any persons of the equal protection of the laws is prohibited by the amendment, therefore congress may establish laws for their equal protection. In fine, the legislation which congress is authorized to adopt in this behalf is not general legislation upon the rights of the citizen, but corrective legislation; that is, such as may be necessary and proper for counteracting such laws as the states may adopt or enforce, and which by the amendment they are prohibited from making or enforcing, or such acts and proceedings as the states may commit or take, and which by the amendment they are prohibited from committing or taking. It is not necessary for us to state, if we could, what legislation would be proper for congress to adopt. It is sufficient for us to examine whether the law in question is of that character.

An inspection of the [Civil Rights Act of 1875] shows that it makes no reference whatever to any supposed or apprehended violation of the fourteenth amendment on the part of the states. It is not predicated on any such view. It proceeds *ex directo* [directly] to declare that certain acts committed by individuals shall be deemed offenses, and shall be prosecuted and punished by proceedings in the courts of the United States. It does not profess to be corrective of any constitutional wrong committed by the states; it does not make its operation to depend upon any such wrong committed. It applies equally to cases arising in states which have the justest laws respecting the personal rights of citizens, and whose authorities are ever ready to enforce such laws as to those which arise in states that may have violated the prohibition of the amendment. In other words, it steps into the domain of local jurisprudence, and lays down rules for the conduct of individuals in society towards each other, and imposes sanctions for the enforcement of those rules, without referring in any manner to any supposed action of the state or its authorities.

If this legislation is appropriate for enforcing the prohibitions of the amendment, it is difficult to see where it is to stop. Why may not congress, with equal show of authority, enact a code of laws for the enforcement and vindication of all rights of life, liberty, and property? . . .

We have also discussed the validity of the law in reference to cases arising in the states only; and not in reference to cases arising in the territories [Art. IV, § 3, cl. 2] or the District of Columbia [Art. I, § 8, cl. 17], which are subject to the plenary legislation of congress in every branch of municipal regulation. Whether the law would be a valid one as applied to the territories and the district is not a question for consideration in the cases before us; they all being cases arising within the limits of states. And whether congress, in the exercise of its power to regulate commerce among the several states, might or might not pass a law regulating rights in public conveyances passing from one state to another, is also **a question which is not now before us**, as the sections in question are not conceived in any such view.

The Civil Rights Cases

[THIRTEENTH AMENDMENT]

But the power of congress to adopt direct and primary, as distinguished from corrective, legislation on the subject in hand, is sought, in the second place, from the thirteenth amendment, which abolishes slavery. This amendment declares "that neither slavery, nor involuntary servitude, except as a punishment for crime, whereof the party shall have been duly convicted, shall exist within the United States, or any place subject to their jurisdiction;" and it gives congress power to enforce the amendment by appropriate legislation. . . .

■ OBSERVATION

A QUESTION WHICH IS NOT NOW BEFORE US: The Court does not consider whether enumerated powers other than § 5 of the Fourteenth Amendment would authorize a federal public accommodations law. This hint of things to come was not acted upon for many decades.

By its own unaided force [the Thirteenth Amendment] abolished slavery, and established universal freedom. Still, legislation may be necessary and proper to meet all the various cases and circumstances to be affected by it, and to prescribe proper modes of redress for its violation in letter or spirit. And such legislation may be primary and direct in its character; for the amendment is not a mere prohibition of state laws establishing or upholding slavery, but an absolute declaration that slavery or involuntary servitude shall not exist in any part of the United States.

It is true that slavery cannot exist without law any more than property in lands and goods can exist without law, and therefore the thirteenth amendment may be regarded as nullifying all state laws which establish or uphold slavery. But it has a reflex character also, establishing and decreeing universal civil and political freedom throughout the United States; and it is assumed that the power vested in congress to enforce the article by appropriate legislation, clothes congress with power to pass all laws necessary and proper for abolishing all badges and incidents of slavery in the United States; and upon this assumption it is claimed that this is sufficient authority for declaring by law that all persons shall have equal accommodations and privileges in all inns, public conveyances, and places of public amusement; the argument being that the denial of such equal accommodations and privileges is in itself a subjection to a species of servitude within the meaning of the amendment. Conceding the major proposition to be true, that congress has a right to enact all necessary and proper laws for the obliteration and prevention of slavery, with all its badges and incidents, is the minor proposition also true, that the denial to any person of admission to the accommodations and privileges of an inn, a public conveyance, or a theater, does subject that person to any form of servitude, or tend to fasten upon him any badge of slavery? If it does not, then power to pass the law is not found in the thirteenth amendment. . . .

Is there any similarity between such servitudes [of slavery or feudal vassalage in Europe] and a denial by the owner of an inn, a public conveyance, or a theater, of its accommodations and privileges to an individual, even though the denial be founded on the race or color of that individual? Where does any slavery or servitude, or badge of either, arise from such an act of denial? Whether it might not be a denial of a right which, if sanctioned by the state law, would be obnoxious to the prohibitions of the fourteenth amendment, is another question. But what has it to do with the question of slavery? It may be that by the black code (as it was called) in the times when slavery prevailed, the proprietors of inns and public conveyances were forbidden to receive persons of the African race, because it might assist slaves to escape from the control of their masters. This was merely a means of preventing such escapes, and was no part of the servitude itself. A law of that kind could not have any such object now, however justly it might be deemed an invasion of the party's legal right as a citizen, and amenable to the prohibitions of the fourteenth amendment. . . . The thirteenth amendment has respect, not to distinctions of race, or class, or color, but to slavery. . . .

After giving to these questions all the consideration which their importance demands, we are forced to the conclusion that such an act of refusal [of service by a private business] has nothing to do with slavery or involuntary servitude, and that if it is violative of any right of the party, his redress is to be sought under the laws of the state; or, if those laws are adverse to his rights and do not protect him, his remedy will be found in the corrective legislation which congress has adopted, or may adopt, for counteracting the effect of state laws, or state action, prohibited by the fourteenth amendment. It would be running the slavery argument into the ground to make it apply to every act of discrimination which a person may see fit to make as to the guests he will entertain, or as to the people he will take into his coach or cab or car, or admit to his concert or theater, or deal with in other matters of intercourse or business. . . .

When a man has emerged from slavery, and by the aid of beneficent legislation has shaken off the inseparable concomitants of that state, there must be some stage in the progress of his elevation when he takes the rank of a mere citizen, and ceases to be the special favorite of the laws, and when his rights as a citizen, or a man, are to be protected in the ordinary modes by which other men's rights are protected. There were thousands of free colored people in this country before the abolition of slavery, enjoying all the essential rights of life, liberty, and property the same as white citizens; yet no one, at that time, thought that it was any invasion of their personal status as freemen because they were not admitted to all the privileges enjoyed by white citizens, or because they were subjected to discriminations in the enjoyment of accommodations in inns, public conveyances, and places of amusement. Mere discriminations on account of race or color were not regarded as badges of slavery. If, since that time, the enjoyment of equal rights in all these respects has become established by constitutional enactment, it is not by force of the thirteenth amendment (which merely abolishes slavery) but by force of the fourteenth and fifteenth amendments.

[CONCLUSION]

On the whole, we are of opinion that no countenance of authority for the passage of the law in question can be found in either the thirteenth or fourteenth amendment of the constitution; and no other ground of authority for its passage being suggested, it must necessarily be declared void, at least so far as its operation in the several states is concerned.

Harlan, J., dissenting.

The opinion in these cases proceeds, as it seems to me, upon grounds entirely too narrow and artificial. The substance and spirit of the recent amendments of the constitution have been sacrificed by a subtle and ingenious verbal criticism. It is not the words of the law but the internal sense of it that makes the law. The letter of the law is the body; the sense and reason of the law is the soul. Constitutional provisions, adopted in the interest of liberty, and for the purpose of securing, through national legislation, if need be, rights inhering in a state of freedom, and belonging to American citizenship, have been so construed as to defeat the ends the people desired to accomplish, which they attempted to accomplish, and which they supposed they had accomplished by changes in their fundamental law. By this I do not mean that the determination of these cases should have been materially controlled by considerations of mere expediency or policy. I mean only, in this form, to express an earnest conviction that the court has departed from the familiar rule requiring, in the interpretation of constitutional provisions, that full effect be given to the intent with which they were adopted. . . .

BIOGRAPHY

JOHN MARSHALL HARLAN (1833–1911) came from a slave-owning family in the border state of Kentucky, but he opposed secession, fought for the Union during the Civil War, and later joined the Republican Party. He was appointed to the Supreme Court by President Hayes in 1877. He is most famous today for his lone dissents in support of equal rights in *The Civil Rights Cases* (1883) and *Plessy v. Ferguson (*1896), and in support of federal lawmaking authority in *US v. E.C. Knight* (1895). His grandson, John Marshall Harlan II, became a US Supreme Court justice in 1955.

[THE CITIZENSHIP CLAUSE]

The [majority's] assumption that [the Fourteenth Amendment] consists wholly of prohibitions upon State laws and State proceedings in hostility to its provisions, is unauthorized by its language. The first clause of the first section—"all persons born or naturalized in the United States, and subject to the jurisdiction thereof, are citizens of the United States, and of the State wherein they reside"—is of a distinctly affirmative character. In its application to the colored race, previously liberated, it created and granted, as well citizenship of the United States, and citizenship of the State in which they respectively resided. It introduced all of that race, whose ancestors had been imported and sold as slaves, at once, into the political community known as the "People of the United States." They became, instantly, citizens of the United States, and of their respective states. . . .

The citizenship thus acquired by that race, in virtue of an affirmative grant by the nation, may be protected, not alone by the judicial branch of the government, but by Congressional legislation of a primary direct character; this, because the power of Congress is not restricted to the enforcement of prohibitions upon State laws or State action. It is, in terms distinct and positive, to enforce "the provisions of this article" of amendment; not simply those of a prohibitive character, but the provisions—all of the provisions—affirmative and prohibitive, of the amendment. It is, therefore, a grave misconception to suppose that the fifth section of the amendment has reference exclusively to express prohibitions upon State laws or State action. If any right was created by that amendment, the grant of power, through appropriate legislation, to enforce its provisions authorizes Congress, by means of legislation operating throughout the entire Union, to guard, secure, and protect that right.

It is, therefore, an essential inquiry what, if any, right, privilege, or immunity was given by the nation to colored persons when they were made citizens of the State in which they reside? . . . There is one, if there be no others—exemption from race discrimination in respect of any civil right belonging to citizens of the white race in the same State. That, surely, is their constitutional privilege when within the jurisdiction of other States. And such must be their constitutional right, in their own State, unless the recent amendments be splendid baubles, thrown out to delude those who deserved fair and generous treatment at the hands of the nation.

Citizenship in this country necessarily imports equality of civil rights among citizens of every race in the same State. It is fundamental in American citizenship that, in respect of such rights, there shall be no discrimination by the State, or its officers, or by individuals, or corporations exercising public functions or authority, against any citizen because of his race or previous condition of servitude. . . . If, then, exemption from discrimination in respect of civil rights is a new constitutional right, secured by the grant of State citizenship to colored citizens of the United States,—and I do not see how this can now be questioned—why may not the nation, by means of its own legislation of a primary direct character, guard, protect, and enforce that right? It is a right and privilege which the nation conferred. It did not come from the States in which those colored citizens reside. . . .

[COURTS SHOULD NOT UNDULY RESTRAINT CONGRESS]

This court has always given a broad and liberal construction to the Constitution, so as to enable Congress, by legislation, to enforce rights secured by that instrument. The legislation Congress may enact, in execution of its power to enforce the provisions of this amendment, is that which is appropriate to protect the right granted. . . . But it is for Congress, not the judiciary, to say that legislation is appropriate—that is best adapted to the end to be attained. The judiciary may not, with safety to our institutions, enter the domain of legislative discretion, dictate the means which Congress shall employ in the exercise of its granted powers. That would be sheer usurpation of the functions of a co-ordinate department, which, if often repeated, and permanently acquiesced in, would work a radical change in our system of government. . . .

"The sound construction of the Constitution," said Chief Justice Marshall, "must allow to the national legislature that discretion, with respect to the means by which the powers it confers are to be carried into execution, which will enable that body to perform the high duties assigned to it in the manner most beneficial to the people. Let the end be legitimate, let it be within the scope of the Constitution, and all means which are appropriate, which are plainly adapted to that end, which are not prohibited, but consist with the letter and spirit of the Constitution, are constitutional." *McCulloch v. Maryland* (1819). . . .

[CONGRESS HAS POWER TO ENACT EQUALITY LEGISLATION]

I agree that government has nothing to do with social, as distinguished from technically legal, rights of individuals. No government ever has brought, or ever can bring, its people into social intercourse against their wishes. . . . The rights which congress, by the act of 1875, endeavored to secure and protect are legal, not social, rights. The right, for instance, of a colored citizen to use the accommodations of a public highway upon the same terms as are permitted to white citizens is no more a social right than his right, under the law, to use the public streets of a city, or a town, or a turnpike road, or a public market, or a post-office, or his right to sit in a public building with others, of whatever race, for the purpose of hearing the political questions of the day discussed. Scarcely a day passes without our seeing in this court-room citizens of the white and black races sitting side by side watching the progress of our business. It would never occur to any one that the presence of a colored citizen in a court-house or court-room was an invasion of the social rights of white persons who may frequent such places. And yet such a suggestion would be quite as sound in law—I say it with all respect—as is the suggestion that the claim of a colored citizen to use, upon the same terms as is permitted to white citizens, the accommodations of public highways, or public inns, or places of public amusement, established under the license of the law, is an invasion of the social rights of the white race. . . .

My brethren say that when a man has emerged from slavery, and by the aid of beneficent legislation has shaken off the inseparable concomitants of that state, there must be some stage in the progress of his elevation when he takes the rank of a mere citizen, and ceases to be the special favorite of the laws, and when his rights as a citizen, or a man, are to be protected in the ordinary modes by which other men's rights are protected. It is, I submit, scarcely just to say that the colored race has been the special favorite of the laws. What the nation, through congress, has sought to accomplish in reference to that race is, what had already been done in every state in the Union for the white race, to secure and protect rights belonging to them as freemen and citizens; nothing more. The one underlying purpose of congressional legislation has been to enable the black race to take the rank of mere citizens. The difficulty has been to compel a recognition of their legal right to take that rank, and to secure the enjoyment of privileges belonging, under the law, to them as a component part of the people for whose welfare and happiness government is ordained. At every step in this direction the nation has been confronted with class tyranny . . . .

Today it is the colored race which is denied, by corporations and individuals wielding public authority, rights fundamental in their freedom and citizenship. At some future time it may be some other race that will fall under the ban. If the constitutional amendments be enforced, according to the intent with which, as I conceive, they were adopted, there cannot be, in this republic, any class of human beings in practical subjection to another class, with power in the latter to dole out to the former just such privileges as they may choose to grant. The supreme law of the land has decreed that no authority shall be exercised in this country upon the basis of discrimination, in respect of civil rights, against freemen and citizens because of their race, color, or previous condition of servitude. To that decree—for the due enforcement of which, by appropriate legislation, congress has been invested with express power—everyone must bow, whatever may have been, or whatever now are, his individual views as to the wisdom or policy, either of the recent changes in the fundamental law, or of the legislation which has been enacted to give them effect.

For the reasons stated I feel constrained to withhold my assent to the opinion of the court.

flash*forward*

1. *State Action Under the Fourteenth Amendment.* As a statement of Congressional power to enact laws under § 5 of the Fourteenth Amendment, *The Civil Rights Cases* remain good law today. The Fourteenth Amendment limits the actions of state and local government (known as "state action") as performed by governmental agents (known as "state actors"). It does not control the actions of private citizens, except for a few small categories of private citizens who are deemed state actors. See Ch. 21. When using its Fourteenth Amendment enforcement power, Congress must aim its legislation at state action, not private action.

The statute upheld in *Strauder v. West Virginia* (1879) is an example of a federal statute that forbids deprivation of Fourteenth Amendment rights by the states. The statute allowed a defendant to remove a case from state court to federal court if it was clear that the state courts would not respect "any right secured to him by any law providing for the equal civil rights of citizens of the United States." 28 U.S.C. § 1443. The disregard of equality rights by state courts is a form of state action that Congress may correct.

Another example is the 1871 statute now codified at 42 U.S.C. § 1983:

> Every person who, under color of any statute, ordinance, regulation, custom, or usage, of any State or Territory or the District of Columbia, subjects, or causes to be subjected, any citizen of the United States or other person within the jurisdiction thereof to the deprivation of any rights, privileges, or immunities secured by the Constitution and laws, shall be liable to the party injured in an action at law, suit in equity, or other proper proceeding for redress[.]

An action is taken "under color of state law" when it is performed by a state actor. Hence, even after *The Civil Rights Cases*, § 1983 is a constitutional use of Congress's enumerated power to ensure that states do not violate the rights found in § 1 of the Fourteenth Amendment. Section 1983 has proven to be one of the most heavily used federal civil rights laws.

2. *Badges and Incidents of Slavery Under the Thirteenth Amendment.* Congress may directly ban private activity that is the equivalent of slavery. Recent federal statutes against human trafficking are based on this power. *United States v. Kozminski,* 487 U.S. 931 (1988) (prosecution for holding farm laborers in involuntary servitude).

Congress may also ban the "badges and incidents" of slavery, a term that has not been defined in much detail. In the 1960s and 1970s, the Supreme Court used the Thirteenth Amendment to uphold some previously unchallenged Reconstruction-era statutes. E.g., *Jones v. Albert H. Mayer, Inc.*, 392 U.S. 409 (1968) (upholding 42 U.S.C. § 1982—part of the Civil Rights Act of 1866); *Griffin v. Breckenridge*, 403 U.S. 88 (1971) (upholding 42 U.S.C. § 1985(3)—part of the Ku Klux Klan Act of 1871); *Runyon v. McCrary*, 427 U.S. 160 (1976) (upholding 42 U.S.C. § 1981—also part of the Civil Rights Act of 1866). The Supreme Court has not shown much interest in applying Thirteenth Amendment theories to later-enacted civil rights laws. However, lower courts have ruled that a federal law against bias-motivated crimes is properly targeted to badges or incidents of slavery. See *United States v. Diggins*, 36 F.4th 302 (1st Cir. 2022).

3. Government-Enforced Segregation: *Plessy v. Ferguson*

Long before the Civil War, Black and White people tended to be separated from each other in public spaces. As seen in *The Civil Rights Cases*, the practice of reserving the best facilities for White people was often the product of social custom, occasionally enforced by private violence. After Reconstruction, many states supplemented social customs with laws mandating various forms of racial segregation. Historian C. Vann Woodward argued that the ultimate purpose of the "Jim Crow" segregation laws (a term taken from a disparaging epithet for African-Americans) was to placate poor White people by giving them a way to feel superior even as they were denied economic opportunities. Whatever their complicated origins, segregation laws were consistently upheld by a US Supreme Court that refused to acknowledge that segregation was a method to impose inequality.

In *Pace v. Alabama*, 106 U.S. 583 (1883), the Supreme Court upheld a statute forbidding interracial cohabitation. Tony Pace, a Black man, lived together with Mary Cox, a White woman. For living "in a state of adultery or fornication" involving different races, they were convicted and sentenced to two years of hard labor. In an opinion that was only three paragraphs long, the Supreme Court unanimously upheld the statute against an equal protection challenge, reasoning that because the law imposed the same punishment on both partners, it did not discriminate on the basis of race.

The most notorious opinion upholding segregation was *Plessy v. Ferguson*, 163 U.S. 537 (1896). The suit challenged Louisiana's Separate Car Act of 1890, requiring passenger railroads to establish separate cars for the "white and colored races." The railroads tended to oppose such laws since they would impose greater costs on them. But their opposition was no match for the political push to segregate public spaces where White and Black people might be in physical proximity to each other for extended lengths of time.

The Separate Car Act was strongly resented by people of color in New Orleans, a city that for centuries had a significant community of prosperous and socially mobile multi-racial people. An activist group called the Citizens Committee to Test the Constitutionality of the Separate Car Law formed to challenge the law in court. The first test case involved **Daniel Desdunes,** but it failed for jurisdictional reasons. (Desdunes was removed from an interstate train bound for Alabama, and the trial judge ruled that the Separate Car Act applied only to travel within Louisiana.) The second litigant was **Homer Plessy**, who boarded a train from New Orleans to a nearby town within state borders.

BIOGRAPHY

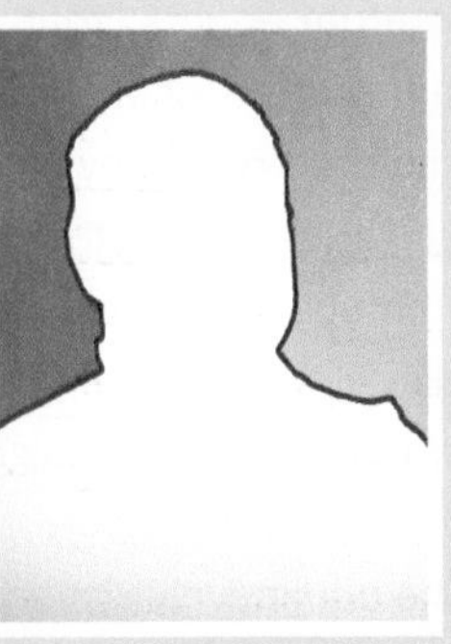

The Citizens Committee decided that the ideal litigant would be a light-skinned multi-racial person nonetheless considered "colored" under state law. The exclusion of someone this close to white, they believed, would show the absurdity of the Separate Car Act. **DANIEL DESDUNES** (1870–1929) and **HOMER PLESSY** (1862–1926) both fit the bill. They were "octoroons"—persons considered 1/8 black who might have been able to pass for white. Both were born into relatively prosperous French-speaking Creole families. No photos of Plessy are known to exist. He ultimately led a quiet life as an insurance salesman. Daniel Desdunes later moved to Omaha, where he earned regional fame as a leader of jazz bands.

ITEMS TO CONSIDER WHILE READING *PLESSY v. FERGUSON*:

A. *Why did the Separate Car Act not violate the Thirteenth Amendment? The Equal Protection Clause?*

B. *Why, according to the majority, might a law separating people by hair color be a violation of the Equal Protection Clause?*

C. *Would a victory for Plessy result in "enforced commingling of the two races"?*

D. *Was* Plessy *consistent with* Strauder? Yick Wo? The Civil Rights Cases?

E. Plessy *was later overruled. What was wrong with it?*

Plessy v. Ferguson,

163 U.S. 537 (1896)

Mr. Justice Brown delivered the opinion of the court [joined by Chief Justice Fuller and Justices Field, Gray, Shiras, White, and Peckham].

This case turns upon the constitutionality of an act of the general assembly of the state of Louisiana, passed in 1890, providing for separate railway carriages for the white and colored races.

The first section of the statute enacts "that all railway companies carrying passengers in their coaches in this state, shall provide equal but separate accommodations for the white, and colored races, by providing two or more passenger coaches for each passenger train, or by dividing the passenger coaches by a partition so as to secure separate accommodations: provided, that this section shall not be construed to apply to street railroads. No person or persons shall be permitted to occupy seats in coaches, other than the ones assigned to them, on account of the race they belong to." . . .

The information filed in the criminal district court charged, in substance, that Plessy, being a passenger between two stations within the state of Louisiana, was assigned by officers of the company to the coach used for the race to which he belonged, but he insisted upon going into a coach used by the race to which he did not belong. Neither in the information nor plea was his particular race or color averred.

[Plessy brought an action in a Louisiana appellate court, seeking a writ of prohibition that would require the trial judge, John Ferguson, to dismiss the charges. The writ was not granted.] The petition for the writ of prohibition averred that petitioner was seven-eighths Caucasian and one-eighth African blood; that the mixture of colored blood was not discernible in him; and that he was entitled to every right, privilege, and immunity secured to citizens of the United States of the white race; and that, upon such theory, he took possession of a vacant seat in a coach where passengers of the white race were accommodated, and was ordered by the conductor to vacate said coach, and take a seat in another, assigned to persons of the colored race, and, having refused to comply with such demand, he was forcibly ejected, with the aid of a police officer, and imprisoned in the parish jail to answer a charge of having violated the above act.

The constitutionality of this act is attacked upon the ground that it conflicts both with the thirteenth amendment of the constitution, abolishing slavery, and the fourteenth amendment, which prohibits certain restrictive legislation on the part of the states.

1. That it does not conflict with the thirteenth amendment, which abolished slavery and involuntary servitude, except as a punishment for crime, is too clear for argument. Slavery implies involuntary servitude—a state of bondage; the ownership of mankind as a chattel, or, at least, the control of the labor and services of one man for the benefit of another, and the absence of a legal right to the disposal of his own person, property, and services. . . . A statute which implies merely a legal distinction between the white and colored races—a distinction which is founded in the color of the two races, and which must always exist so long as white men are distinguished from the other race by color—has no tendency to destroy the legal equality of the two races, or re-establish a state of involuntary servitude. Indeed, we do not understand that the thirteenth amendment is strenuously relied upon by the plaintiff in error in this connection.

2. . . . The object of the [Fourteenth] amendment was undoubtedly to enforce the absolute equality of the two races before the law, but, in the nature of things, it could not have been intended to abolish distinctions based upon color, or to enforce social, as distinguished from political, equality, or a commingling of the two races upon terms unsatisfactory to either. Laws permitting, and even requiring, their separation, in places where they are liable to be brought into contact, do not necessarily imply the inferiority of either race to the other, and have been generally, if not universally, recognized as within the competency of the state legislatures in the exercise of their police power.

The most common instance of this is connected with the establishment of separate schools for white and colored children, which have been held to be a valid exercise of the legislative power even by courts of states where the political rights of the colored race have been longest and most earnestly enforced. [The majority then discussed *Roberts v. City of Boston*, 59 Mass. 198 (1849), where the highest Massachusetts state court upheld segregated public elementary schools.] Similar laws have been enacted by Congress under its general power of legislation over the District of Columbia, as well as by the legislatures of many of the states, and have been generally, if not uniformly, sustained by the courts.

■ OBSERVATION

FREEDOM OF CONTRACT: At this time, the Supreme Court was declining to enforce the Fourteenth Amendment in favor of the Black population, but was beginning to find that the right to enter into contracts was a form of liberty protected by the Due Process Clause. See Ch. 8.C.1.

Laws forbidding the intermarriage of the two races may be said in a technical sense to interfere with the **freedom of contract**, and yet have been universally recognized as within the police power of the state . . . .

It is also suggested by the learned counsel for the plaintiff in error [Plessy] that the same argument that will justify the state legislature in requiring railways to provide separate accommodations for the two races will also authorize them to require separate cars to be provided for people whose hair is of a certain color, or who are aliens, or who belong to certain nationalities, or to enact laws requiring colored people to walk upon one side of the street, and white people upon the other, or requiring white men's houses to be painted white, and colored men's black, or their vehicles or business signs to be of different colors, upon the theory that one side of the street is as good as the other, or that a house or vehicle of one color is as good as one of another color. The reply to all this is that every exercise of the police power must be reasonable, and extend only to such laws as are enacted in good faith for the promotion of the public good, and not for the annoyance or oppression of a particular class. Thus, in *Yick Wo v. Hopkins* (1886), it was held by this court that a municipal ordinance of the city of San Francisco, to regulate the carrying on of public laundries within the limits of the municipality, violated the provisions of the constitution of the United States, if it conferred upon the municipal authorities arbitrary power, at their own will, and without regard to discretion, in the legal sense of the term, to give or withhold consent as to persons or places, without regard to the competency of the persons applying or the propriety of the places selected for the carrying on of the business. It was held to be a covert attempt on the part of the municipality to make an arbitrary and unjust discrimination against the Chinese race. While this was the case of a municipal ordinance, a like principle has been held to apply to acts of a state legislature passed in the exercise of the police power.

So far, then, as a conflict with the fourteenth amendment is concerned, the case reduces itself to the question whether the statute of Louisiana is a reasonable regulation, and with respect to this there must necessarily be a large discretion on the part of the legislature. In determining the question of reasonableness, it is at liberty to act with reference to the established usages, customs, and traditions of the people, and with a view to the promotion of their comfort, and the preservation of the public peace and good order. Gauged by this standard, we cannot say that a law which authorizes or even requires the separation of the two races in public conveyances is unreasonable, or more obnoxious to the fourteenth amendment than the acts of congress requiring separate schools for colored children in the District of Columbia, the constitutionality of which does not seem to have been questioned, or the corresponding acts of state legislatures. . . .

We consider the underlying fallacy of the plaintiff's argument to consist in the assumption that the enforced separation of the two races stamps the colored race with a badge of inferiority. If this be so, it is not by reason of anything found in the act, but solely because the colored race chooses to put that construction upon it. The argument necessarily assumes that if, as has been more than once the case, and is not unlikely to be so again, the colored race should become the dominant power in the state legislature, and should enact a law in precisely similar terms, it would thereby relegate the white race to an inferior position. We imagine that the white race, at least, would not acquiesce in this assumption.

The argument also assumes that social prejudices may be overcome by legislation, and that equal rights cannot be secured to the negro except by an enforced commingling of the two races. We cannot accept this proposition. . . . Legislation is powerless to eradicate racial instincts, or to abolish distinctions based upon physical differences, and the attempt to do so can only result in accentuating the difficulties of the present situation. If the civil and political rights of both races be equal, one cannot be inferior to the other civilly or politically. If one race be inferior to the other socially, the constitution of the United States cannot put them upon the same plane.

It is true that the question of the proportion of colored blood necessary to constitute a colored person, as distinguished from a white person, is one upon which there is a difference of opinion in the different states; some holding that any visible admixture of black blood stamps the person as belonging to the colored race; others, that it depends upon the preponderance of blood; and still others, that the predominance of white blood must only be in the proportion of three-fourths. But these are questions to be determined under the laws of each state, and are not properly put in issue in this case. Under the allegations of his petition, it may undoubtedly become a question of importance whether, under the laws of Louisiana, the petitioner belongs to the white or colored race.

Justice Brewer did not hear the argument or participate in the decision of this case.

Justice Harlan, dissenting.

. . . In respect of civil rights, common to all citizens, the constitution of the United States does not, I think, permit any public authority to know the race of those entitled to be protected in the enjoyment of such rights. Every true man has pride of race, and under appropriate circumstances, when the rights of others, his equals before the law, are not to be affected, it is his privilege to express such pride and to take such action based upon it as to him seems proper. But I deny that any legislative body or judicial tribunal may have regard to the race of citizens when the civil rights of those citizens are involved. Indeed, such legislation as that here in question is inconsistent not only with that equality of rights which pertains to citizenship, national and state, but with the personal liberty enjoyed by everyone within the United States. . . .

It was said in argument that the statute of Louisiana does not discriminate against either race, but prescribes a rule applicable alike to white and colored citizens. But this argument does not meet the difficulty. Everyone knows that the statute in question had its origin in the purpose, not so much to exclude white persons from railroad cars occupied by blacks, as to exclude colored people from coaches occupied by or assigned to white persons. Railroad corporations of Louisiana did not make discrimination among whites in the matter of accommodation for travelers. The thing to accomplish was, under the guise of giving equal accommodation for whites and blacks, to compel the latter to keep to themselves while traveling in railroad passenger coaches. No one would be so wanting in candor as to assert the contrary.

The fundamental objection, therefore, to the statute, is that it interferes with the personal freedom of citizens. "Personal liberty," [Blackstone] said, "consists in the power of locomotion, of changing situation, or removing one's person to whatsoever places one's own inclination may direct, without imprisonment or restraint, unless by due course of law." If a white man and a black man choose to occupy the same public conveyance on a public highway, it is their right to do so; and no government, proceeding alone on grounds of race, can prevent it without infringing the personal liberty of each.

It is one thing for railroad carriers to furnish, or to be required by law to furnish, equal accommodations for all whom they are under a legal duty to carry. It is quite another thing for government to forbid citizens of the white and black races from traveling in the same public conveyance, and to punish officers of railroad companies for permitting persons of the two races to occupy the same passenger coach. If a state can prescribe, as a rule of civil conduct, that whites and blacks shall not travel as passengers in the same railroad coach, why may it not so regulate the use of the streets of its cities and towns as to compel white citizens to keep on one side of a street, and black citizens to keep on the other? Why may it not, upon like grounds, punish whites and blacks who ride together in street cars or in open vehicles on a public road or street? Why may it not require sheriffs to assign whites to one side of a court room, and blacks to the other? And why may it not also prohibit the commingling of the two races in the galleries of legislative halls or in public assemblages convened for the consideration of the political questions of the day? Further, if this statute of Louisiana is consistent with the personal liberty of citizens, why may not the state require the separation in railroad coaches of native and naturalized citizens of the United States, or of Protestants and Roman Catholics? . . .

The white race deems itself to be the dominant race in this country. And so it is, in prestige, in achievements, in education, in wealth, and in power. So, I doubt

Plessy v. Ferguson

not, it will continue to be for all time, if it remains true to its great heritage, and holds fast to the principles of constitutional liberty. But in view of the constitution, in the eye of the law, there is in this country no superior, dominant, ruling class of citizens. There is no caste here. Our constitution is color-blind, and neither knows nor tolerates classes among citizens. In respect of civil rights, all citizens are equal before the law. The humblest is the peer of the most powerful. The law regards man as man, and takes no account of his surroundings or of his color when his civil rights as guaranteed by the supreme law of the land are involved. It is therefore to be regretted that this high tribunal, the final expositor of the fundamental law of the land, has reached the conclusion that it is competent for a state to regulate the enjoyment by citizens of their civil rights solely upon the basis of race.

In my opinion, the judgment this day rendered will, in time, prove to be quite as pernicious as the decision made by this tribunal in the *Dred Scott* case. . . .

If evils will result from the commingling of the two races upon public highways established for the benefit of all, they will be infinitely less than those that will surely come from state legislation regulating the enjoyment of civil rights upon the basis of race. We boast of the freedom enjoyed by our people above all other peoples. But it is difficult to reconcile that boast with a state of the law which, practically, puts the brand of servitude and degradation upon a large class of our fellow citizens—our equals before the law. The thin disguise of "equal" accommodations for passengers in railroad coaches will not mislead anyone, nor atone for the wrong this day done. . . .

flash*forward*

1. *The Scope of Jim Crow Laws.* The first segregation laws tended to focus on rail transportation, likely because it was a setting where people needed to be in close quarters with each other for an extended period of time. They quickly spread to virtually every public setting in the South, from waiting rooms to restaurants to parks to theaters to swimming pools to restrooms and even drinking fountains. In practice, many facilities that were not required by law to be racially segregated were divided anyway as a matter of social custom.

2. *Separate but Equal*. The Louisiana statute in *Plessy* called for "equal but separate accommodations for the white and colored races." Ultimately, the phrase "separate but equal," became shorthand for the theory upholding segregation laws. In practice, of course, it was a rarity for the White and colored cars of a train to be of comparable quality. This fact was widely known (as shown in this cartoon from 1904), but courts were not vigilant in policing the equality of separate facilities.

Cartoon by John T. McCutchen (1904)

Sometimes, however, "separate but equal" accommodations were a step up from no accommodations at all. In *McCabe v. Atchison, Topeka & Santa Fe Railroad. Co.*, 235 U.S. 151 (1914), a railroad subject to Oklahoma's new railway segregation law provided no sleeping cars for Black passengers, claiming that it would be economically infeasible for them to maintain separate quarters when so few Black customers could afford them. Five Black clergymen filed suit, demanding equal access to sleeping cars, even if they were separate. The Supreme Court dismissed the suit on ripeness grounds. Nonetheless, the Court included dicta signaling support for the plaintiffs' theory.

> Whether or not particular facilities shall be provided may doubtless be conditioned upon there being a reasonable demand therefor; but, if facilities are provided, substantial equality of treatment of persons traveling under like conditions cannot be refused. It is the individual who is entitled to the equal protection of the laws, and if he is denied by a common carrier, acting in the matter under the authority of a state law, a facility or convenience in the course of his journey which, under substantially the same circumstances, is furnished to another traveler, he may properly complain that his constitutional privilege has been invaded.

3. *Proxies for Race*. Just as *Plessy* perceived no racism in segregation laws, other decisions in succeeding years perceived no racism in laws that relied on proxies for race. In *Williams v. Mississippi*, 170 U.S. 213 (1898), a Black defendant, Henry Williams, was indicted by an all-White grand jury and convicted and sentenced to death by an all-White trial jury in a county that never summoned Black people for jury service. This would seem to contradict *Strauder v. West Virginia* (1879), which spoke eloquently about Supreme Court distinguished it. The statute in *Strauder* said that only White men were eligible for jury duty, while the statute in *Williams* said that only the right to trial before a jury of one's peers, but the increasingly formalistic registered voters were eligible for jury duty, all of whom in the county were White. The defendant argued unsuccessfully that in this setting, being a voter was a proxy for being White. To register as a voter, one needed to pay the poll tax, not be convicted of any disenfranchising crime, and to pass a literacy test. The Supreme Court found that these requirements were not race-based because "they reach weak and vicious white men as well as weak and vicious black men."

Williams further argued that even if the voting restriction was neutral on its face, the literacy test was administered in a discriminatory fashion, analogizing to *Yick Wo v. Hopkins* (1886). As in many Southern states, an applicant for voting in Mississippi would be asked to read portions of the Constitution and explain their meaning to the registrar, who had authority to decide which questions to ask and to decide what constituted an acceptable answer—a process that allowed for arbitrary exclusion of Black people from the voting rolls. The Supreme Court unanimously found *Yick Wo* inapplicable because "it has not been shown that [the Mississippi statutes'] actual administration was evil; only that evil was possible under them."

Southern states quickly began to write other proxies for race into their voter registration requirements, such as laws that gave automatic registration to property owners or people who had fought in the Civil War. The only proxies for race that the Supreme Court ever found to be discriminatory in this era were the "grandfather clauses" that would give the vote only to persons whose ancestors had the right to vote before Emancipation. In those cases, the link between the statutory requirement and race was too plain to ignore. *Guinn v. United States*, 238 U.S. 347 (1915); *Myers v. Anderson*, 238 U.S. 368 (1915).

4. *Throwing in the Towel.* Cases like *Plessy* revealed that the Supreme Court—with the exception of Justice Harlan—was no longer interested in enforcing equal rights for Black people. The Court's surrender is poignantly illustrated by *Giles v. Harris*, 189 U.S. 475 (1903). In 1902, Alabama changed its state constitution to impose a welter of new voter registration requirements that had the practical effect of preserving the vote for previously-registered White voters while denying any meaningful chance to register for future Black voters. When prospective Black voters sued to add their names to the voting rolls, the Supreme Court (in a 6–3 opinion authored by Justice Oliver Wendell Holmes) rejected the claim, holding that even if race discrimination was proven, a court could not be expected to do anything about it.

> [The Court has] little practical power to deal with the people of the state in a body. The [plaintiffs allege] that the great mass of the white population intends to keep the blacks from voting. To meet such an intent, something more than ordering the plaintiff's name to be inscribed upon the [voter registration rolls] will be needed. If the conspiracy and the intent exist, a name on a piece of paper will not defeat them. Unless we are prepared to supervise the voting in that state by officers of the court, it seems to us that all that the plaintiff could get from equity would be an empty form. Apart from damages to the individual, relief from a great political wrong, if done, as alleged, by the people of a state and the state itself, must be given by them or by the legislative and political department of the government of the United States.

5. *Plessy's Pardon.* After the US Supreme Court ruled that Louisiana was entitled to prosecute Plessy, he was convicted and fined $25 by the local trial court in 1897. In 2022, to mark the 125th anniversary of the conviction, the governor of Louisiana issued a posthumous pardon to Plessy that praised "the heroism and patriotism of his unselfish sacrifice to advocate for and to demand equality and human dignity for *all* of Louisiana's citizens."

Chapter Recap

A. After the Civil War, the US Constitution was amended and major legislation enacted to make equality an explicit national value and a binding legal requirement. The Reconstruction Amendments expressly imposed limits on state and local governments, for the first time extending the US Constitution's Bill of Rights beyond the federal government. The Fourteenth Amendment also added a guarantee of "equal protection of the laws," adding the word "equal" to the Constitution for the first time.

B. Under the new constitutional amendments, the Supreme Court announced that state or local statutes (*Strauder*) or government practices (*Yick Wo*) that unequivocally gave worse treatment to racial minorities than to the White majority were unconstitutional.

C. But when deciding constitutional rights cases later in the 19th Century, the Supreme Court sought to preserve the pre-war status quo where state governments had nearly exclusive control over the everyday rights and obligations of citizens. Specifically:

- In *The Slaughterhouse Cases* and their progeny, the Supreme Court gave such a narrow interpretation to the Privileges or Immunities Clause of the Fourteenth Amendment that it became legally irrelevant.
- *The Civil Rights Cases* declared racial discrimination by private persons to be beyond the scope of Congress's power to enforce the Reconstruction Amendments. Under the Fourteenth Amendment, Congress could only legislate against state or local government practices, not against private conduct. Under the Thirteenth Amendment, Congress could pass laws against private action amounting to a "badge and incident of slavery," but the most prevalent forms of discrimination were declared not to be badges or incidents of slavery.
- Cases like *Plessy v. Ferguson* that adopted the "separate but equal" theory held that government-mandated racial segregation did not violate the Equal Protection Clause.

CHAPTER 8

The Lochner *Era*

From roughly 1885 to 1937—a period often called "The *Lochner* Era" after the decision in *Lochner v. New York* (1905)—the US Supreme Court invalidated important economic legislation enacted by Congress and state legislatures. Although these decisions involved a variety of constitutional provisions, the majority's interpretations tended to converge on the same result: It would be difficult for either level of government to regulate business practices.

The Supreme Court used three approaches to constrict the government's ability to enact economic laws. First was a narrow view of enumerated powers of the federal government, particularly under the Commerce Clause and Taxing Clause. Second was a broad view of federalism that required Congress to refrain from exercising its powers in order to protect a zone of power for the states. Third was a broad view of an individual right to enter into economic transactions—often called freedom of contract—that was considered part of the "liberty" protected by the Due Process Clause. Relying on these interlocking principles, the Supreme Court struck down various economic regulations, although it was never entirely predictable which laws would be found invalid.

Lochner-Era Interpretations Constricting Federal Power

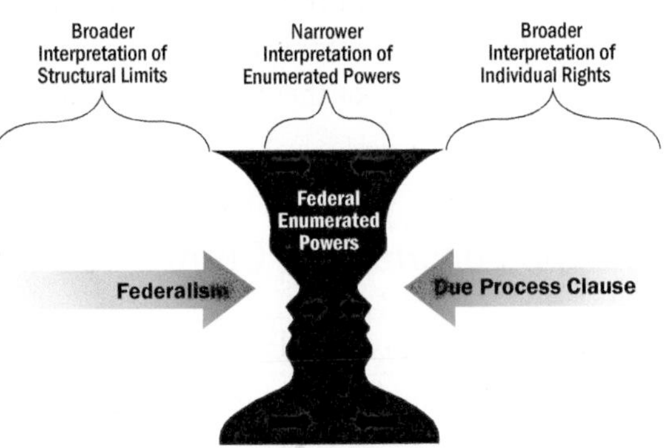

Most of the cases arose from the same basic scenario. Starting in the late 19th century, public and political support had come to favor economic reform legislation, collected under the general heading of **Progressivism**. The Progressive agenda included antitrust laws to prevent or dismantle monopolies; controls over wages and hours; recognition of labor unions as legitimate organizations rather than criminal conspiracies; health and safety regulations for workplaces and rental housing; consumer protection; and pure food and drug laws. Many of these laws were challenged in court by private financial interests (usually a corporation or other business entity, but sometimes a private individual) who argued that the regulations violated the US Constitution.

■ HISTORY

PROGRESSIVISM: Some policies favored by Progressives were sufficiently popular to become constitutional amendments. The Sixteenth Amendment (ratified 1913) authorized a federal income tax that would raise more revenue from wealthy people than from poor ones. The Seventeenth Amendment (ratified 1913) authorized direct election of US Senators, moving the choice from state legislators to state voters. The Nineteenth Amendment (ratified 1920) guaranteed women the right to vote in federal and state elections. In addition, the Eighteenth Amendment (ratified 1919) gave Congress the power to ban alcohol. The social movement for alcohol prohibition predated the Progressive movement, but many Progressives favored it. Alcohol prohibition proved to be a disaster, so the Eighteenth Amendment was repealed by the 21st Amendment (ratified 1933).

Many of the cases in this chapter—including *Lochner*—are today considered part of the "anti-canon" of overruled cases that are famous for being wrong. Two main reasons exist to study certain cases that are no longer good law.

- The repudiation of anti-canonical cases—such as the replacement of *Dred Scott* (1856) with the Fourteenth Amendment (1868) and the overruling of *Plessy v. Ferguson* (1896) by *Brown v. Board of Education* (1954)—functions as a cautionary tale or legal parable. An effective modern lawyer can develop arguments based not only on what made the good decisions good, but what made the bad decisions bad. An anti-canonical case may be cited in a brief or a judicial opinion, as when Justice Harlan's dissent predicted that the decision in *Plessy v. Ferguson* "will, in time, prove to be quite as pernicious as the decision made by this tribunal in the *Dred Scott* case."
- Every overruled decision had arguments in its favor. Those arguments tend to reappear over time, and sometimes even become incorporated into new decisions. Effective lawyers need to recognize eternal debates and swings of the pendulum, as ideas fall out of favor and then back in again.

A. The *Lochner*-Era Commerce Clause

In *Gibbons v. Ogden* (1824), Chief Justice Marshall interpreted the Commerce Clause to be broad in scope and powerful enough to sweep away contrary state laws. As discussed in the Flash-Forward following *Gibbons*, see Ch. 5.B, Marshall's opinion seemed to authorize Commerce Clause legislation in three general situations.

1. Congress could regulate transactions that cross state borders (like the transportation of passengers by steamboat in *Gibbons*).

2. Congress could regulate in-state infrastructure that facilitates those transactions (like the in-state waters and harbors where the steamboats operated).

3. Some language in *Gibbons* suggested that Congress could regulate in-state activities that "concern" or "affect" other states.

By and large, Congress did not use the Commerce Clause to enact many statutes until the end of the 19th century. Most commerce was regulated, if at all, through state and local laws. But as the economy grew larger and more interconnected as a result of new communication and transportation technologies, Congress began to implement nationwide solutions to some economic problems. This new wave of legislation included the Interstate Commerce Act of 1887 (regulating railroads); the Sherman Antitrust Act of 1890 (regulating monopolies, price-fixing, and other anti-competitive business practices), the Pure Food and Drug Act of 1906 (regulating product safety); the Mann-Elkins Act of 1910 (giving Interstate Commerce Commission authority over telegraph, telephone, and radio communications); and the Clayton Antitrust Act of 1914 (expanding on the Sherman Act).

Opponents of federal control over the economy argued that Congress was venturing beyond its enumerated powers. Congress was no longer regulating flows of goods and services across borders, the argument went, but was regulating what occurred inside states. In light of *Gibbons*, the critics had to acknowledge that Congressional regulation of cross-border transactions would inevitably require some federal control over some things that occurred within state boundaries. But they argued that the federal government could only pass laws with "indirect" effects within states, where the indirect effects were small-scale by-products of regulating the borders. If a federal law amounted to "direct" regulation of in-state activity, the argument went, it exceeded the Commerce Clause.

This theory required courts to distinguish between acceptable federal statutes having "indirect" effects on in-state activity and unacceptable federal statutes whose effects on in-state activity were too "direct." This was never a simple task, but for many decades (before the direct/indirect distinction was finally abandoned, see Ch. 9.C.2) a majority of the Supreme Court had confidence that the line was both manageable and necessary to preserve the Constitution's structure. Without that boundary, the Court believed, Congress could use the Commerce Clause to enact exactly the same kinds of laws that states typically passed, effectively reducing states' ability to decide such matters for themselves.

During this period, the Court sometimes referred to the Tenth Amendment in support of its view that the Constitution prevented Congress from passing laws in areas traditionally regulated by the states. The Tenth Amendment reads: "The powers not delegated to the United States by the Constitution, nor prohibited by it to the States, are reserved to the States respectively, or to the people." This language does not indicate which powers are (or are not) delegated to the United States; the answer to that question is found elsewhere in the Constitution. But during the *Lochner* era, the Supreme Court often spoke of the Tenth Amendment as if it were written back to front. The Court began with a vision of which unenumerated powers were "reserved" to state governments, and from this concluded that such powers were "not delegated to the United States." As you read the following cases, notice how the Court's beliefs about the correct state/federal balance affect its interpretation of Congress's enumerated powers.

1. Protecting Monopolies: *US v. E.C. Knight Co.*

■ WEBSITE

A fuller version of *E.C. Knight* is available for download from this casebook's companion website, www.CaplanIntegratedConLaw.com

US v. E.C. Knight Co., 156 U.S. 1 (1895), was the federal government's first major attempt to block a monopolistic merger under the Sherman Antitrust Act of 1890. As of early 1892, six companies controlled all of the sugar refineries in the United States.

COMPANY	LOCATION	MARKET SHARE
American Sugar Refining Co.	NJ	65%
E. C. Knight Co. Franklin Sugar Refining Co. Spreckels' Sugar Refining Co. Delaware Sugar House	PA	33%
Revere Sugar Refinery	MA	2%

In March 1892, American Sugar Refining bought out all four Pennsylvania companies, leaving as its only US competitor the economically insignificant Revere. The Justice Department sought to unwind the transaction as a violation of the Sherman Act. A federal trial court refused to enjoin the acquisitions, and the Supreme Court affirmed in an 8–1 opinion by Chief Justice Fuller.

The Court assumed for purposes of argument that the acquisition would result in a monopoly in violation of the Sherman Act. This left a constitutional question: namely, as the Court framed it, whether the sugar monopoly "can be directly suppressed" by an act of Congress.

To answer that question, the Court began by considering the powers it believed states should have. Prior cases had upheld the power of states to regulate monopolies. And even more broadly, "the power of a state to protect the lives, health, and property of its citizens, and to preserve good order and the public morals . . . is a power originally and always belonging to the states, not surrendered by them to the general government, nor directly restrained by the constitution of the United States, and essentially exclusive [to the states]." As said later in the opinion, "preservation of the autonomy of the states" is "required by our **dual form of government**." Since the Sherman Act was regulating something that state laws had traditionally regulated, the Court was skeptical of it at the outset.

■ TERMINOLOGY

DUAL FORM OF GOVERNMENT: The term "dual federalism" was once used for the theory that federal and state powers ought not overlap, so that state governments had exclusive power over certain areas (such as in-state sugar refining), barring any federal lawmaking in that area.

Against this backdrop of presumed state exclusivity, the Court considered the boundaries of Congressional power under the Commerce Clause. The fact that sugar is "a necessary of life" that most of the US population can obtain only through interstate commerce was not enough to make sugar manufacturing a national concern. The path from a sugar plantation to a refinery to a wholesaler to a retailer to a consumer consisted of many separate links, and Congress had authority only over those links that crossed state borders, or were "directly" connected to such links. The industrial activity of converting sugar cane into refined sugar did not cross any borders and had no "direct" connection to anything that did.

"Commerce Succeeds to Manufacture"

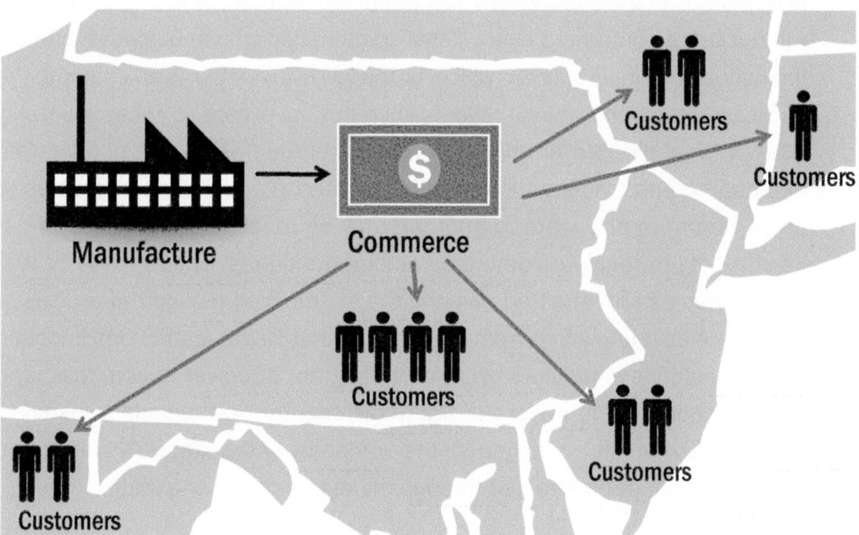

> Commerce succeeds to manufacture, and is not a part of it. . . . Contracts to buy, sell, or exchange goods to be transported among the several states, the transportation and its instrumentalities, and articles bought, sold, or exchanged for the purposes of such transit among the states, or put in the way of transit, may be regulated; but this is because they form part of interstate trade or commerce. The fact that an article is manufactured for export to another state does not of itself make it an article of interstate commerce, and the intent of the manufacturer does not determine the time when the article or product passes from the control of the state and belongs to commerce.

In the Court's view, the requested injunction would not regulate an interstate monopoly whose overall business activities crossed state lines and had power to affect prices nationwide. Instead, the injunction would regulate individual manufacturing plants, none of which played any direct role in cross-border transactions. Admittedly, the monopoly "might unquestionably tend to restrain external as well as domestic trade, but the restraint would be an indirect result" of in-state activities like the operation of a sugar factory. Since the sugar factory had only indirect effects on other states, Congress could not regulate it directly.

Only Justice Harlan dissented. He began by noting that federal power was as much a part of the Constitution's structure as state power. "The just authority of the general government is essential as well to the safety of the states as to the attainment of the important ends for which that government was ordained by the people of the United States." He saw the sugar monopoly as a cross-border enterprise that would, in the absence of federal regulation, imperil the public.

> The citizens of the several states composing the Union are entitled of right to buy goods in the state where they are manufactured, or in any other state, without being confronted by an illegal combination whose business extends throughout the whole country, which, by the law everywhere, is an enemy to the public interests, and which prevents such buying, except at prices arbitrarily fixed by it. . . . Whatever improperly obstructs the free course of interstate intercourse and trade, as involved in the buying and selling of articles to be carried from one state to another, may be reached by congress under its authority to regulate commerce among the states. The exercise of that authority so as to make trade among the states in all recognized articles of commerce absolutely free from unreasonable or illegal restrictions imposed by combinations is justified by an express grant of power to congress, and would redound to the welfare of the whole country. I am unable to perceive that any such result would imperil the autonomy of the states, especially as that result cannot be attained through the action of any one state.

2. Protecting Industrial Child Labor: *Hammer v. Dagenhart*

One Progressive reform that enjoyed considerable popular support was a ban on industrial child labor. The tug-of-war between Congress and the Supreme Court over child labor laws reveals how for any one social problem, there may be more than one potential legal response.

In 1916, Congress passed the first national child labor law, which said that "no producer, manufacturer, or dealer shall ship or deliver for shipment in interstate or foreign commerce" any of the following items:

- products of mines or quarries that employ children under age 16
- products of factories that employ children under age 14
- products of factories that employ children between age 14 and 16 (a) for more than eight hours a day; (b) for more than six days per week; or (c) at any time between 7:00 pm and 6:00 am.

Shortly before the federal law went into effect, the Fidelity Manufacturing Company in Charlotte, North Carolina announced that it would lay off the underage laborers at its cotton mill. Litigation ensued.

ITEMS TO CONSIDER WHILE READING *HAMMER v. DAGENHART*:

A. *Make sure you understand the statute. Does it ban child labor in the US? Ban all sales of products produced using child labor? Something else?*

B. *What methods of reasoning appear in the majority and dissenting opinions? In particular:*

- *What are the contrasting views of constitutional structure? What in the text supports (or fails to support) those competing structures?*
- *Is* Dagenhart *fairly distinguished from the cases that upheld federal statutes regulating cross-border transactions (such as* The Lottery Case, Hipolite Egg, Hoke, *and* James Clark Distilling*)?*

C. *Should Congress's motives in enacting a law affect its constitutionality?*

D. Dagenhart *was later overruled. What was wrong with it?*

Hammer v. Dagenhart,
247 U.S. 251 (1918)

Justice Day delivered the opinion of the Court [joined by Chief Justice White and Justices Van Devanter, Pitney, and McReynolds].

A bill was filed in the United States District Court for the Western District of North Carolina by a father [Roland Dagenhart] in his own behalf and as next friend of his **two minor sons** [Reuben and John], one under the age of fourteen years and the other between the ages of fourteen and sixteen years, employees in a cotton mill at Charlotte, North Carolina, to enjoin [W.C. Hammer, the US Attorney for the Western District of North Carolina from enforcing] the act of Congress [enacted in 1916] intended to prevent interstate commerce in the products of child labor.

> ■ HISTORY
>
> **TWO MINOR SONS:** Although Roland Dagenhart lent his family name to the litigation, the lawsuit was financed and orchestrated by David Clark, the politically ambitious publisher of a trade magazine for the cotton industry. Defendant Fidelity Manufacturing made no effort to defend the law; its announcement that it would lay off its child labor was likely a collusive step to facilitate the litigation. As adults, the Dagenhart children expressed regret over their involvement.

The District Court held the act unconstitutional and entered a decree enjoining its enforcement. This appeal brings the case here. The attack upon the act rests upon [several] propositions: First: It is not a regulation of interstate and foreign commerce; [and] second: It contravenes the Tenth Amendment to the Constitution[.] . . .

The power essential to the passage of this act, the government contends, is found in the commerce clause of the Constitution which authorizes Congress to regulate commerce with foreign nations and among the states.

In *Gibbons v. Ogden* (1824) Chief Justice Marshall, speaking for this court, and defining the extent and nature of the commerce power, said, "It is the power to regulate; that is, to prescribe the rule by which commerce is to be governed." In other words, the power is one to control the means by which commerce is carried on, which is directly the contrary of the assumed right to forbid commerce from moving and thus destroying it as to particular commodities. But it is insisted that adjudged cases in this court establish the doctrine that the power to regulate given to Congress incidentally includes the authority to prohibit the movement of ordinary commodities and therefore that the subject is not open for discussion. The cases

Child factory labor in Macon, GA (1909)

demonstrate the contrary. They rest upon the character of the particular subjects dealt with and the fact that the scope of governmental authority, state or national, possessed over them is such that the authority to prohibit is as to them but the exertion of the power to regulate.

Hammer v. Dagenhart

The first of these cases is *Champion v. Ames,* 188 U. S. 321 (1903), the so-called *Lottery Case*, in which it was held that Congress might pass a law having the effect to keep the channels of commerce free from use in the transportation of tickets used in the promotion of lottery schemes. In *Hipolite Egg Co. v. United States,* 220 U. S. 45 (1911), this court sustained the power of Congress to pass the Pure Food and Drug Act, which prohibited the introduction into the states by means of interstate commerce of impure foods and drugs. In *Hoke v. United States*, 227 U. S. 308 (1913), this court sustained the constitutionality of the so-called White Slave Traffic Act [also known as the Mann Act], whereby the transportation of a woman in interstate commerce for the purpose of prostitution was forbidden. . . . In *Clark Distilling Co. v. Western Maryland Railway Co.*, 242 U. S. 311 (1917), the power of Congress over the transportation of intoxicating liquors was sustained. . . .

In each of these instances the use of interstate transportation was necessary to the accomplishment of harmful results. In other words, although the power over interstate transportation was to regulate, that could only be accomplished by prohibiting the use of the facilities of interstate commerce to effect the evil intended.

This element is wanting in the present case. The thing intended to be accomplished by this statute is the denial of the facilities of interstate commerce to those manufacturers in the states who employ children within the prohibited ages. The act in its effect does not regulate transportation among the states, but aims to standardize the ages at which children may be employed in mining and manufacturing within the states. The goods shipped are of themselves harmless. . . . When offered for shipment, and before transportation begins, the labor of their production is over, and the mere fact that they were intended for interstate commerce transportation does not make their production subject to federal control under the commerce power.

Commerce consists of intercourse and traffic and includes the transportation of persons and property, as well as the purchase, sale and exchange of commodities. The making of goods and the mining of coal are not commerce, nor does the fact that these things are to be afterwards shipped, or used in interstate commerce, make their production a part thereof.

Over interstate transportation, or its incidents, the regulatory power of Congress is ample, but the production of articles, intended for interstate commerce, is a matter of local regulation. . . . If it were otherwise, all manufacture intended for interstate shipment would be brought under federal control to the practical exclusion of the authority of the states, a result certainly not contemplated by the framers of the Constitution when they vested in Congress the authority to regulate commerce among the States.

It is further contended that the authority of Congress may be exerted to control interstate commerce in the shipment of child-made goods because of the effect of the circulation of such goods in other states where the evil of this class of labor has been recognized by local legislation, and the right to thus employ child labor has been more rigorously restrained than in the state of production. In other words, that the unfair competition, thus engendered, may be controlled by closing the channels of interstate commerce to manufacturers in those states where the local laws do not meet what Congress deems to be the more just standard of other states.

There is no power vested in Congress to require the states to exercise their police power so as to prevent possible unfair competition. Many causes may co-operate to give one state, by reason of local laws or conditions, an economic advantage over others. The commerce clause was not intended to give to Congress a general authority to equalize such conditions. In some of the states laws have been passed fixing minimum wages for women, in others the local law regulates the hours of labor of women in various employments. Business done in such states may be at an economic disadvantage when compared with states which have no such regulations; surely, this fact does not give Congress the power to deny transportation in interstate commerce to those who carry on business where the hours of labor and the rate of compensation for women have not been fixed by a standard in use in other states and approved by Congress.

The grant of power of Congress over the subject of interstate commerce was to enable it to regulate such commerce, and not to give it authority to control the states in their exercise of the police power over local trade and manufacture. The grant of authority over a purely federal matter was not intended to destroy the local power always existing and carefully reserved to the states in the Tenth Amendment to the Constitution. . . .

That there should be limitations upon the right to employ children in mines and factories in the interest of their own and the public welfare, all will admit. That such employment is generally deemed to require regulation is shown by the fact that the brief of counsel states that every state in the Union has a law upon the subject, limiting the right to thus employ children. In North Carolina, the state wherein is located the factory in which the employment was had in the present case, no child under twelve years of age is permitted to work.

It may be desirable that such laws be uniform, but our federal government is one of enumerated powers; "this principle," declared Chief Justice Marshall in *McCulloch v. Maryland* (1819), "is universally admitted." . . . In interpreting the Constitution it must never be forgotten that the nation is made up of states to which are entrusted the powers of local government. And to them and to the people the powers not expressly delegated to the national government are reserved. The power of the states to regulate their purely internal affairs by such laws as seem wise to the local authority is inherent and has never been surrendered to the general government. To sustain this statute would not be in our judgment a recognition of the lawful exertion of congressional authority over interstate commerce, but would sanction an invasion by the federal power of the control of a matter purely local in its character, and over which no authority has been delegated to Congress in conferring the power to regulate commerce among the states. . . .

In our view the necessary effect of this act is, by means of a prohibition against the movement in interstate commerce of ordinary commercial commodities to regulate the hours of labor of children in factories and mines within the states, a purely state authority. Thus the act in a two-fold sense is repugnant to the Constitution. It not only transcends the authority delegated to Congress over commerce but also exerts a power as to a purely local matter to which the federal authority does not extend. The far reaching result of upholding the act cannot be more plainly indicated than by pointing out that if Congress can thus regulate matters entrusted to local authority by prohibition of the movement of commodities in interstate commerce, all freedom of commerce will be at an end, and the power of the states over local matters may be eliminated, and thus our system of government be practically destroyed.

Justice Holmes, dissenting [joined by Justices McKenna, Brandeis, and Clarke].

The single question in this case is whether Congress has power to prohibit the shipment in interstate or foreign commerce of any product of a cotton mill situated in the United States [that employs child labor]. The objection urged against the power is that the States have exclusive control over their methods of production and that Congress cannot meddle with them, and taking the proposition in the sense of direct intermeddling I agree to it and suppose that no one denies it. But if an act is within the powers specifically conferred upon Congress, it seems to me that it is not made any less constitutional because of the indirect effects that it may have, however obvious it may be that it will have those effects, and that we are not at liberty upon such grounds to hold it void.

The first step in my argument is to make plain what no one is likely to dispute—that the statute in question is within the power expressly given to Congress if considered only as to its immediate effects and that if invalid it is so only upon some collateral ground. The statute confines itself to prohibiting the carriage of certain goods in interstate or foreign commerce. Congress is given power to regulate such commerce in unqualified terms. It would not be argued today that the power to regulate does not include the power to prohibit. Regulation means the prohibition of something, and when interstate commerce is the matter to be regulated I cannot doubt that the regulation may prohibit any part of such commerce that Congress sees fit to forbid. At all events it is established by the *Lottery Case* and others that have followed it that a law is not beyond the regulative power of Congress merely because it prohibits certain transportation out and out. So I repeat that this statute in its immediate operation is clearly within the Congress's constitutional power.

The question then is narrowed to whether the exercise of its otherwise constitutional power by Congress can be pronounced unconstitutional because of its possible reaction upon the conduct of the States in a matter upon which I have admitted that they are free from direct control. I should have thought that that matter had been disposed of so fully as to leave no room for doubt. I should have thought that the most conspicuous decisions of this Court had made it clear that the power to regulate commerce and other constitutional powers could not be cut down or qualified by the fact that it might interfere with the carrying out of the domestic policy of any State. . . .

The Pure Food and Drug Act which was sustained in *Hipolite Egg Co. v. United States* . . . applies not merely to articles that the changing opinions of the time condemn as intrinsically harmful but to others innocent in themselves[.] . . . It does not matter whether the supposed evil precedes or follows the transportation. It is enough that in the opinion of Congress the transportation encourages the evil. . . .

The Act does not meddle with anything belonging to the States. They may regulate their internal affairs and their domestic commerce as they like. But when they seek to send their products across the State line they are no longer within their rights. If there were no Constitution and no Congress their power to cross the line would depend upon their neighbors. Under the Constitution such commerce belongs not to the States but to Congress to regulate. It may carry out its views of public policy whatever indirect effect they may have upon the activities of the States. Instead of being encountered by a prohibitive tariff at her boundaries the State encounters the public policy of the United States which it is for Congress to express. The public policy of the United States is shaped with a view to the benefit of the nation as a whole. If, as has been the case within the memory of men still living, a State should take a different view of the propriety of sustaining a lottery from that which generally prevails, I cannot believe that the fact would require a different decision from that reached in *Champion v. Ames*. Yet in that case it would be said with quite as much force as in this that Congress was attempting to intermeddle with the State's domestic affairs. The national welfare as understood by Congress may require a different attitude within its sphere from that of some self-seeking State. It seems to me entirely constitutional for Congress to enforce its understanding by all the means at its command.

flashforward

1. ***From Child Labor to Adult Labor.*** The narrow view of the Commerce Clause seen in *E.C. Knight* and *Dagenhart* led to the invalidation of several federal statutes designed to protect the interests of organized labor, including a statute forbidding railroads from firing employees who join unions, *Adair v. United States*, 208 U.S. 161 (1908), and a statute requiring railroads to provide accident insurance for employees, *Howard v. Illinois Central Railroad*, 207 U.S. 463 (1908). During the economically prosperous and politically conservative 1920's, the Supreme Court had few occasions to consider the validity of federal labor legislation, because not much was enacted.

2. ***From the Commerce Clause to the Taxing Clause.*** After *Dagenhart* prevented Congress from using its commerce power to regulate child labor, Congress attempted to regulate it through the tax code. The results are seen below in *Bailey v. Drexel Furniture* (1922). See Ch. 8.B.2.

B. The *Lochner*-Era Taxing Power

A leading concern of the Framers was the lack of an independent source of revenue for the national government under the Articles of Confederation. Under that system, Congress could make polite requests for the states to give it money, but the requests were often ignored. The power "to lay and collect taxes, duties, imposts, and excises" became the first power described in Art. I, § 8. Alexander Hamilton defended the tax power in The Federalist #31, arguing that because "no possible limits can be assigned" to the dangers involved in national defense, the power to finance a response to those dangers "ought to know no other bounds than the exigencies of the nation and the resources of the community."

The Supreme Court decided relatively few federal tax cases in the 19th century, because Congress imposed relatively few taxes other than tariffs on imports, which were expressly authorized as "duties" under Art. I, § 8, cl. 1. The Court began to get involved only as the government began to explore other forms of revenue.

1. Federal Income Tax: *Pollock* and the Sixteenth Amendment

The first federal tax on incomes was levied during the Civil War and repealed when hostilities ended. Congress enacted a peacetime income tax in 1894, in response to a major recession that began in 1893. As part of an overall package designed to lower tariffs while maintaining federal revenue, Congress imposed a

2% tax on income over $4,000 per year to replace the federal revenue lost as a result of the tariff reduction. The tax would likely have affected fewer than 10% of US households.

■ TERMINOLOGY
TAX PROPORTIONALITY CLAUSE: As discussed in Chapter 3.B.2.b., the requirement that direct taxes be proportional to population was designed to protect the wealth of Southern slave owners. In *Pollock*, it now protected the wealth of Northern industrialists.

The constitutional objection to the income tax was that it was a "direct" tax not in proportion to the census, in violation of the **Tax Proportionality Clause,** Art. I, § 9, cl. 4. The tax was admittedly not proportional to the census: taxpayers in a higher-income state like New York would pay more per capita than taxpayers from a lower-income state like Nebraska. The question turned on whether an income tax is a "direct" tax, a term traditionally applied only to capitations (head taxes) and taxes on real property. In *Pollock v. Farmers' Loan & Trust Co.*, 158 U.S. 601 (1895), a 5–4 majority of the Supreme Court held that a tax on any income derived from interest, rent, or dividends was akin to a direct tax on property, because that income was ultimately derived from property. In dissent, Justice Brown complained that "the decision involves nothing less than a surrender of the taxing power to the moneyed class. . . . It is certainly a strange commentary upon the Constitution of the United States and upon a democratic government that Congress has no power to lay a tax which is one of the main sources of revenue of nearly every civilized state."

In response to *Pollock,* Congress passed the Sixteenth Amendment in 1909, which was ratified by 1913. The Amendment does not change the general rule that direct taxes must be proportional to population, but it makes an exception for "taxes on incomes, from whatever source derived." These may be imposed "without apportionment among the several States, and without regard to any census or enumeration."

2. Taxation as a Tool of Social Regulation: *Bailey v. Drexel Furniture*

The power to tax is independent of other enumerated powers. This means the federal government may impose a tax whether or not the items taxed are part of interstate commerce. For example, the federal tax on gasoline is owed even if the oil was pumped, refined, and sold within a single state. After *Dagenhart,* Congress relied on this logic as the basis for a different type of legislation against industrial child labor. In 1919 it enacted a law requiring a payment to the government equal to 10% of the net profits of any business that employed child labor. An affected business fought the new statute, arguing that the payment was not one of the "taxes, duties, imposts and excises" authorized by Art. I, § 8, cl. 1.

Federal Child Labor Statutes

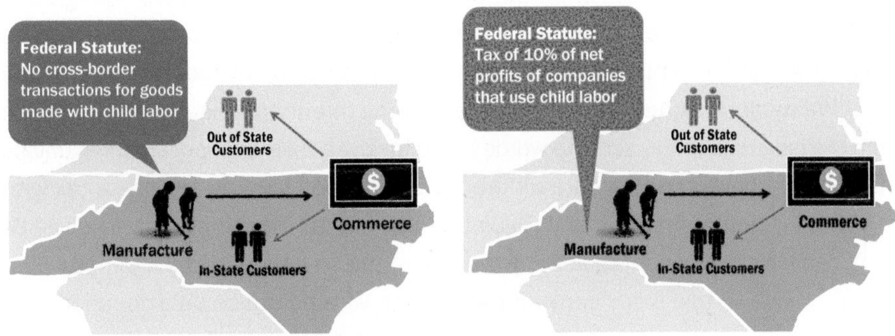

Hammer v. Dagenhart (1918) *Bailey v. Drexel Furniture* (1922)

ITEMS TO CONSIDER WHILE READING
BAILEY v. DREXEL FURNITURE:

A. *What is the difference between a penalty and a tax? What in the text of the Constitution mandates a distinction between the two?*

B. *Why was the law in* Drexel Furniture *not a tax?*

C. *Should Congressional motive matter to a court when deciding whether a law is a tax? Should the terminology used in the statute matter?*

Bailey v. Drexel Furniture Co.,

(The Child Labor Tax Case), 259 U.S. 20 (1922)

Mr. Chief Justice Taft delivered the opinion of the Court [joined by Justices McKenna, Holmes, Day, Van Devanter, Pitney, McReynolds, and Brandeis].

This case presents the question of the constitutional validity of the Child Labor Tax Law. The plaintiff below, the Drexel Furniture Company, is engaged in the manufacture of furniture in the Western district of North Carolina. On September 20, 1921, it received a notice from [J.W.] Bailey, United States collector of internal revenue for the district, that it had been assessed $6,312.79 for having during the taxable year 1919 employed and permitted to work in its factory a boy under 14 years of age, thus incurring the tax of 10 percent on its net profits for that year. The company paid the tax under protest, and, after rejection of its claim for a refund, brought this suit. Judgment was entered for the company against the collector for the full amount, with interest. . . . [The Supreme Court granted review.]

The law is attacked on the ground that it is a regulation of the employment of child labor in the states—an exclusively state function under the federal Constitution and within the reservations of the Tenth Amendment. It is defended on the ground that it is a mere excise tax levied by the Congress of the United States under its broad power of taxation conferred by section 8, article 1, of the federal Constitution.

We must construe the law and interpret the intent and meaning of Congress from the language of the act. The words are to be given their ordinary meaning unless the context shows that they are differently used. Does this law impose a tax with only that incidental restraint and regulation which a tax must inevitably involve? Or does it regulate by the use of the so-called tax as a penalty? If a tax, it is clearly an **excise**. If it were an excise on a commodity or other thing of value, we might not be permitted under previous decisions of this court to infer solely from its heavy burden that the act intends a prohibition instead of a tax. But this act is more. It provides a heavy exaction for a departure from a detailed and specified course of conduct in business. That course of business is that employers shall employ in mines and quarries, children of an age greater than 16 years; in mills and factories, children of an age greater than 14 years, and shall prevent children of less than 16 years in mills and factories from working more than 8 hours a day or 6 days in the week.

TERMINOLOGY

EXCISE: An excise is a tax on the sale of goods or performance of an activity.

If an employer departs from this prescribed course of business, he is to pay to the government one-tenth of his entire net income in the business for a full year. The amount is not to be proportioned in any degree to the extent or frequency of the departures, but is to be paid by the employer in full measure whether he employs 500 children for a year, or employs only one for a day. Moreover, if he does not know the child is within the named age limit, he is not to pay; that is to say, it is only where he knowingly departs from the prescribed course that payment is to be exacted. Scienters are associated with penalties, not with taxes. The employer's factory is to be subject to inspection at any time not only by the taxing officers of the Treasury, the Department normally charged with the collection of taxes, but also by the Secretary of Labor and his subordinates, whose normal function is the advancement and protection of the welfare of the workers. In the light of these features of the act, a court must be blind not to see that the so-called tax is imposed to stop the employment of children within the age limits prescribed. Its prohibitory and regulatory effect and purpose are palpable. All others can see and understand this. How can we properly shut our minds to it?

It is the high duty and function of this court in cases regularly brought to its bar to decline to recognize or enforce seeming laws of Congress, dealing with subjects not entrusted to Congress, but left or committed by the supreme law of the land to the control of the states. We cannot avoid the duty, even though it require us to refuse to give effect to legislation designed to promote the highest good. The good sought in unconstitutional legislation is an insidious feature, because it leads citizens and legislators of good purpose to promote it, without thought of the serious breach it will make in the ark of our covenant, or the harm which will come from breaking down recognized standards. In the maintenance of local self-government, on the one hand, and the national power, on the other, our country has been able to endure and prosper for near a century and a half. . . .

The difference between a tax and a penalty is sometimes difficult to define, and yet the consequences of the distinction in the required method of their collection often are important. Where the sovereign enacting the law has power to impose both tax and penalty, the difference between revenue production and mere regulation may be immaterial, but not so when one sovereign can impose a tax only, and the power of regulation rests in another. Taxes are occasionally imposed in the discretion of the Legislature on proper subjects with the primary motive of obtaining revenue from them and with the incidental motive of discouraging them by making their continuance onerous. They do not lose their character as taxes because of the incidental motive. But there comes a time in the extension of the penalizing features of the so-called tax when it loses its character as such and becomes a mere penalty, with the characteristics of regulation and punishment. Such is the case in the law before us. Although Congress does not invalidate the contract of employment or expressly declare that the employment within the mentioned ages is illegal, it does exhibit its intent practically to achieve the latter result by adopting the criteria of wrongdoing and imposing its principal consequence on those who transgress its standard.

The case before us cannot be distinguished from that of *Hammer v. Dagenhart*, 247 U. S. 251 (1918). Congress there enacted a law to prohibit transportation in interstate commerce of goods made at a factory in which there was employment of children within the same ages and for the same number of hours a day and days in a week as are penalized by the act in this case. . . . In the case at the bar, Congress in the name of a tax which on the face of the act is a penalty seeks to do the same thing, and the effort must be equally futile. . . .

Justice Clarke dissents [without opinion].

flashforward

1. ***Taxes and Penalties.*** As seen in *Drexel Furniture*, no single fact determines whether a law demanding a payment to the government is a tax. Only where the totality of the circumstances indicate that the law was designed to punish and deter misconduct—rather than to raise revenue—will a court conclude that a purported tax is actually a penalty.

For example, the Prohibition-era statute in *United States v. Constantine*, 296 U.S. 287 (1935), imposed a federal tax of $1,000 on the manufacturing or sale of liquor in violation of local law. When Prohibition was in force, the 18th Amendment authorized Congress to punish liquor law violations, but Prohibition ended with the ratification of the 21st Amendment in 1933. When *Constantine* reached the Supreme Court after the repeal of Prohibition, the statute could be justified, if at all, as an exercise of the federal taxing power. A majority of the Court concluded that it could not. The tax would be owed only if a person violated state law, and the amount was much higher than any comparable federal tax on lawful liquor businesses—forty times higher in Constantine's case. A statute making a person pay far more money, solely because **the taxed conduct was illegal** under local law, seemed to be a penalty, not a tax.

> ■ OBSERVATION
>
> **THE TAXED CONDUCT WAS ILLEGAL:** Notwithstanding the *Constantine* principle, Al Capone was convicted of evading income taxes on his illegal earnings in 1931. The difference was in the statute: Capone violated a statute that called for him to report and pay taxes on all income, no matter what the source. Such a law was enacted to raise revenue, unlike the law in *Constantine* that purported to tax only illegal earnings.

The modern approach to the Taxing Clause is explored in Ch. 15.A.

2. ***Another Federal Approach to Child Labor.*** In response to *Dagenhart* and *Drexel Furniture*, Congress passed in 1924 a proposed constitutional amendment to ban child labor. Over the next dozen years, it was ratified by 28 states: a majority, but short of the three fourths margin necessary to amend the Constitution under Art. V. See Appendix B. After *Dagenhart* was overruled by *United States v. Darby* (1941), see Ch. 9.C.2.b., there was no longer a need to pursue a constitutional amendment.

C. The *Lochner*-Era Due Process Clause

Because the cases in the previous sections involved federal statutes, they were litigated in terms of enumerated powers and federalism. But those concerns would impose no limits on state governments. An opponent of economic legislation at the state level, who sought to invalidate it under the US Constitution, would need to frame the argument in terms of individual rights. A state version of *E.C. Knight* would be about the individual right to buy sugar refineries; a state version of *Dagenhart* would be about the individual right to staff factories with child labor. Both cases could be said to involve the right to enter freely into economic transactions—freedom of contract. The Supreme Court first announced that freedom of contract was protected by the Due Process Clause of the Fourteenth Amendment (applicable to states), which then had parallel effects on the Due Process Clause of the Fifth Amendment (applicable to the federal government).

The Two Due Process Clauses

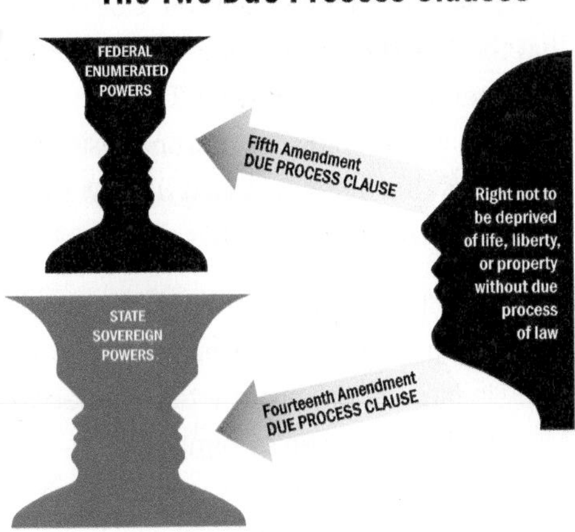

1. Freedom of Contract: *Lochner v. New York*

The Origins of Freedom of Contract. The text of the Constitution explicitly protects certain economic interests. The new government of the United States agreed to pay off debts accrued under the Articles of Confederation. Art. VI, § 1. States were barred from passing laws that would relieve borrowers from the obligation to repay their creditors, Art. I, § 10, cl. 1 (although Congress could create a national bankruptcy law, Art. I, § 8, cl. 4). The Takings Clause of the Fifth Amendment required the government to pay just compensation when private property was taken for public use. And the Third Amendment rule against quartering soldiers in private homes during peacetime and the Fourth Amendment rule against unreasonable searches of "houses, papers, and effects" also protected interests associated with property ownership.

During the *Lochner* era, the Supreme Court went beyond these forms of property protection to announce a broader idea: "Generally speaking, every citizen has a right freely to contract for the price of his labor, services, or property." *Frisbie v. United States*, 157 U.S. 160 (1895). The ability to enforce contracts—like the ability to own property or to file lawsuits—was understood in the 19th century to be a civil right (i.e., a right of citizens that deserved some level of governmental protection). Contracts were crucial for virtually any economic transaction, because without them anyone could be cheated with impunity. Slaves had been legally barred from protecting their interests through enforceable contracts. The Reconstruction Congress considered the right to contract sufficiently important to be protected in § 1 of the Civil Rights Act of 1866 (now 42 U.S.C. § 1981), guaranteeing all persons "the same right . . . to make and enforce contracts . . . as is enjoyed by white citizens."

Dicta in various Supreme Court opinions of the late 19th century speculated that the "liberty" protected by the Due Process Clause included "liberty of contract." In *Allgeyer v. Louisiana*, 165 U.S. 578 (1897), the Supreme Court for the first time held that a state statute regulating insurance contracts was unconstitutional because it violated this unenumerated liberty. In a widely-quoted passage, the opinion gave a partial description of what the Due Process Clause protected:

> The "liberty" mentioned in [the Due Process Clause] means, not only the right of the citizen to be free from the mere physical restraint of his person, as by incarceration, but the term is deemed to embrace the right of the citizen to be free in the enjoyment of all his faculties; to be free to use them in all lawful ways; to live and work where he will; to earn his livelihood by any lawful calling; to pursue any livelihood or avocation; and for that purpose to enter into all contracts which may be proper, necessary, and essential to his carrying out to a successful conclusion the purposes above mentioned.

State Police Power as Limit on Freedom of Contract. There was an obvious problem with the idea that the Constitution barred laws that limited freedom of contract: such laws had been around for centuries. Many contracts were legally unenforceable, such as contracts charging usurious rates of interest, contracts containing other unconscionable terms, or contracts made with persons lacking legal capacity. Some contracts could even be made criminal, like contracts to lie under oath (suborning perjury) or contracts to have sex for money (prostitution). Indeed, almost any law regulating an economic transaction could be seen as an interference with freedom of contract. A state statute banning fireworks would also ban contracts to exchange fireworks for money. A law banning slaughterhouses in residential neighborhoods would ban any number of contracts that the owners might want to pursue in that location, including contracts to hire butchers and contracts to buy and sell meat. Yet such a law was upheld in *The Slaughterhouse Cases* (1872), see Ch. 7.C.1.a.

To deal with this difficulty, opinions involving freedom of contract argued that the freedom could be limited through laws enacted pursuant to state police power (the power to pass laws for the health, safety, welfare, and morals of the community). Thus, the Court was willing to uphold a number of laws that undoubtedly restricted the ability of people to enter into some contracts, including a Utah statute setting maximum working hours for coal miners, *Holden v. Hardy*, 169 U.S. 366 (1898); a Chicago ordinance banning sale of cigarettes without a license,

Gundling v. Chicago, 177 U.S. 183 (1900); and a Tennessee statute requiring that wages paid in company scrip must be redeemable for cash, *Knoxville Iron Co. v. Harbison*, 183 U.S. 13 (1901). Each of these laws was deemed a suitable use of the police power to limit freedom of contract.

But this explanation had its own problems. First, it was entirely circular, declaring that people may enter into any contract they wish, unless the state's police power said they couldn't. Second, federal supremacy should mean that a right protected by the US Constitution ought not be controlled by state law principles. Yet the emerging doctrine said that state police power marked the edge of a federal right. Third, the doctrine purported to give federal courts control over the meaning of police powers under state law. As said in *Lawton v. Steele*, 152 U.S. 133 (1894), a state's "determination as to what is a proper exercise of its police powers is not final or conclusive, but is subject to the supervision of the [federal] courts." *Lawton v. Steele*, 152 U.S. 133 (1894). This inverted ordinary federalism principles, where states would have the last word on the meaning of their own powers.

Critics of *Lochner*, then and now, argued that an ill-defined rule that "people have a right to contract except when they don't" could be abused by result-oriented judges. In practice, the laws found to be violations of freedom of contract tended to be laws that adjusted the relative bargaining power of workers and employers. The Supreme Court was skeptical that such laws could ever serve the welfare of the public. The state law challenged in *Lochner* was just such a law.

The Bake Shop Act. In response to public concern over unsafe and unsanitary bakeries, particularly those operating in the basements of urban tenements, the state of New York enacted the Bake Shop Act of 1895. The law required that all commercial bakeries meet standards for drainage and plumbing, restrooms, fire safety, and sanitation. Those portions of the law were not challenged. The controversial provision limited hours of work: "No employee shall be required or permitted to work in a biscuit, bread, or cake bakery or confectionery establishment more than sixty hours in any one week, or more than ten hours in any one day." This portion of the Act was favored by organized labor and those larger bakeries who had reached agreements with their unionized workers. The law would require more changes on the part of smaller non-unionized bakeries, whose largely immigrant labor force worked long hours for low pay, often being on call 24 hours a day and sometimes sleeping in the bakery itself.

The Lochner Family

Joseph Lochner, a baker from Utica, New York, was prosecuted in 1901 for having an employee named Armand Schmitter work more than sixty hours in a week. Lochner was convicted in a state trial court and fined $50. The intermediate court of appeals upheld the conviction on a 3–2 vote, and New York's highest court affirmed on a 4-3 vote. The US Supreme Court granted review.

ITEMS TO CONSIDER WHILE READING *LOCHNER*:

A. *What made the Bake Shop Act unconstitutional?*

B. *What distinguishes the maximum hour law in* Lochner *from the maximum hour law in* Holden v. Hardy? *From the mandatory vaccination law in* Jacobson v. Massachusetts *(discussed within* Lochner*)?*

C. *Why does it matter whether the New York statute is viewed as a "health law" or a "labor law"?*

D. *Justice Holmes' dissent became very famous, Justice Harlan's dissent less so. What is the difference between the dissents? Why did Holmes' dissent prove to be more influential?*

E. Lochner *is a notorious case, with a reputation that rivals* Dred Scott *for unpopularity. What's wrong with it?*

Lochner v. New York,

198 U.S. 45 (1905)

Justice Peckham delivered the opinion of the court [joined by Chief Justice Fuller and Justices Brewer, Brown, and McKenna].

. . . The mandate of the statute, that "no employee shall be required or permitted to work," is the substantial equivalent of an enactment that "no employee shall contract or agree to work," more than ten hours per day; and, as there is no provision for special emergencies, the statute is mandatory in all cases. It is not an act merely fixing the number of hours which shall constitute a legal day's work, but an absolute prohibition upon the employer permitting, under any circumstances, more than ten hours' work to be done in his establishment. The employee may desire to earn the extra money which would arise from his working more than the prescribed time, but this statute forbids the employer from permitting the employee to earn it.

The statute necessarily interferes with the right of contract between the employer and employees, concerning the number of hours in which the latter may labor in the bakery of the employer. The general right to make a contract in relation to his business is part of the liberty of the individual protected by the 14th Amendment of the Federal Constitution. *Allgeyer v. Louisiana* (1897). Under that provision no state can deprive any person of life, liberty, or property without due process of law. The right to purchase or to sell labor is part of the liberty protected by this amendment, unless there are circumstances which exclude the right. There are, however, certain powers, existing in the sovereignty of each state in the Union, somewhat vaguely termed police powers, the exact description and limitation of which have not been attempted by the courts. Those powers, broadly stated, and without, at present, any attempt at a more specific limitation, relate to the safety, health, morals, and general welfare of the public. Both property and liberty are held on such reasonable conditions as may be imposed by the governing power of the state in the exercise of those powers, and with such conditions the 14th Amendment was not designed to interfere.

The state, therefore, has power to prevent the individual from making certain kinds of contracts, and in regard to them the Federal Constitution offers no protection. If the contract be one which the state, in the legitimate exercise of its police power, has the right to prohibit, it is not prevented from prohibiting it by the 14th Amendment. Contracts in violation of a statute, either of the Federal or state government, or a contract to let one's property for immoral purposes, or to do any other unlawful act, could obtain no protection from the Federal Constitution, as coming under the liberty of person or of free contract. Therefore, when the state, by its legislature, in the assumed exercise of its police powers, has passed an act which seriously limits the right to labor or the right of contract in regard to their means of livelihood between persons who are [legally competent] (both employer and employee), it becomes of great importance to determine which shall prevail—the right of the individual to labor for such time as he may choose, or the right of the state to prevent the individual from laboring, or from entering into any contract to labor, beyond a certain time prescribed by the state.

This court has recognized the existence and upheld the exercise of the police powers of the states in many cases which might fairly be considered as border ones, and it has, in the course of its determination of questions regarding the asserted invalidity of such statutes, on the ground of their violation of the rights secured by the Federal Constitution, been guided by rules of a very liberal nature, the application of which has resulted, in numerous instances, in upholding the validity of state statutes thus assailed. Among the later cases where the state law has been upheld by this court is that of *Holden v. Hardy*, 169 U. S. 366 (1898). A provision in the act of the legislature of Utah was there under consideration, the act limiting the employment of workmen in all underground mines or workings, to eight hours per day, "except in cases of emergency, where life or property is in imminent danger." It also limited the hours of labor in smelting and other institutions for the reduction or refining of ores or metals to eight hours per day, except in like cases of emergency. The act was held to be a valid exercise of the police powers of the state. A review of many of the cases on the subject, decided by this and other courts, is given in the opinion. It was held that the kind of employment, mining, smelting, etc., and the character of the employees in such kinds of labor, were such as to make it reasonable and proper for the state to interfere to prevent the employees from being constrained by the rules laid down by the proprietors in regard to labor. The following citation from the observations of the supreme court of Utah in that case was made by the judge writing the opinion of this court, and approved: "The law in question is confined to the protection of that class of people engaged in labor in underground mines, and in smelters and other works wherein ores are reduced and refined. This law applies only to the classes subjected by their employment to the peculiar conditions and effects attending underground mining and work in smelters, and other works for the reduction and refining of ores. Therefore it is not necessary to discuss or decide whether the legislature can fix the hours of labor in other employments."

It will be observed that, even with regard to that class of labor, the Utah statute provided for cases of emergency wherein the provisions of the statute would not apply. The statute now before this court has no emergency clause in it, and, if the statute is valid, there are no circumstances and no emergencies under which the slightest violation of the provisions of the act would be innocent. There is nothing in *Holden v. Hardy* which covers the case now before us. . . .

■ WEBSITE

A version of *Jacobson v. Massachusetts* is available for download from this casebook's companion website, www.CaplanIntegratedConLaw.com.

The latest case decided by this court, involving the police power, is that of *Jacobson v. Massachusetts*, 197 U. S. 11 (1905). It related to compulsory vaccination, and the law was held valid as a proper exercise of the police powers with reference to the public health. It was stated in the opinion that it was a case "of an adult who, for aught that appears, was himself in perfect health and a fit subject of vaccination, and yet, while remaining in the community, refused to obey the statute and the regulation, adopted in execution of its provisions, for the protection of the public health and the public safety, confessedly endangered by the presence of a dangerous disease." That case is also far from covering the one now before the court. . . .

It must, of course, be conceded that there is a limit to the valid exercise of the police power by the state. There is no dispute concerning this general proposition. Otherwise the 14th Amendment would have no efficacy and the legislatures of the states would have unbounded power, and it would be enough to say that any piece of legislation was enacted to conserve the morals, the health, or the safety of the people; such legislation would be valid, no matter how absolutely without foundation the claim might be. The claim of the police power would be a mere pretext—become another and delusive name for the supreme sovereignty of the state to be exercised free from constitutional restraint. This is not contended for. In every case that comes before this court, therefore, where legislation of this character is concerned, and where the protection of the Federal Constitution is sought, the question necessarily arises: Is this a fair, reasonable, and appropriate exercise of the police power of the state, or is it an unreasonable, unnecessary, and arbitrary interference with the right of the individual to his personal liberty, or to enter into those contracts in relation to labor which may seem to him appropriate or necessary for the support of himself and his family? Of course the liberty of contract relating to labor includes both parties to it. The one has as much right to purchase as the other to sell labor. . . .

The question whether this act is valid as a labor law, pure and simple, may be dismissed in a few words. There is no reasonable ground for interfering with the liberty of person or the right of free contract, by determining the hours of labor, in the occupation of a baker. There is no contention that bakers as a class are not equal in intelligence and capacity to men in other trades or manual occupations, or that they are not able to assert their rights and care for themselves without the protecting arm of the state, interfering with their independence of judgment and of action. They are in no sense wards of the state. Viewed in the light of a purely labor law, with no reference whatever to the question of health, we think that a law like the one before us involves neither the safety, the morals, nor the welfare, of the public, and that the interest of the public is not in the slightest degree affected by such an act. The law must be upheld, if at all, as a law pertaining to the health of the individual engaged in the occupation of a baker. It does not affect any other portion of the public than those who are engaged in that occupation. Clean and wholesome bread does not depend upon whether the baker works but ten hours per day or only sixty hours a week. The limitation of the hours of labor does not come within the police power on that ground.

It is a question of which of two powers or rights shall prevail—the power of the state to legislate or the right of the individual to liberty of person and freedom of contract. The mere assertion that the subject relates, though but in a remote degree, to the public health, does not necessarily render the enactment valid. The act must have a more direct relation, as a means to an end, and the end itself must be appropriate and legitimate, before an act can be held to be valid which interferes with the general right of an individual to be free in his person and in his power to contract in relation to his own labor. . . .

We think that there can be no fair doubt that the trade of a baker, in and of itself, is not an unhealthy one to that degree which would authorize the legislature to interfere with the right to labor, and with the right of free contract on the part of the individual, either as employer or employee. In looking through statistics regarding all trades and occupations, it may be true that the trade of a baker does not appear to be as healthy as some other trades, and is also vastly more healthy than still others. To the common understanding the trade of a baker has never been regarded as an unhealthy one. Very likely physicians would not recommend the exercise of that or of any other trade as a remedy for ill health. Some occupations are more healthy than others, but we think there are none which might not come under the power of the legislature to supervise and control the hours of working therein, if the mere fact that the occupation is not absolutely and perfectly healthy is to confer that right upon the legislative department of the government. It might be safely affirmed that almost all occupations more or less affect the health. There must be more than the mere fact of the possible existence of some small amount of unhealthiness to warrant legislative interference with liberty. It is unfortunately true that labor, even in any department, may possibly carry with it the seeds of unhealthiness. But are we all, on that account, at the mercy of legislative majorities? A printer, a tinsmith, a locksmith, a carpenter, a cabinetmaker, a dry goods clerk, a bank's, a lawyer's, or a physician's clerk, or a clerk in almost any kind of business, would all come under the power of the legislature, on this assumption. No trade, no occupation, no mode of earning one's living, could escape this all-pervading power, and the acts of the legislature in limiting the hours of labor in all employments would be valid, although such limitation might seriously cripple the ability of the laborer to support himself and his family.

In our large cities there are many buildings into which the sun penetrates for but a short time in each day, and these buildings are occupied by people carrying on the business of bankers, brokers, lawyers, real estate, and many other kinds of business, aided by many clerks, messengers, and other employees. Upon the assumption of the validity of this act under review, it is not possible to say that an act, prohibiting lawyers' or bank clerks, or others, from contracting to labor for their employers more than eight hours a day would be invalid. It might be said that it is unhealthy to work more than that number of hours in an apartment lighted by artificial light during the working hours of the day; that the occupation of the bank clerk, the lawyer's clerk, the real estate clerk, or the broker's clerk, in such offices is therefore unhealthy, and the legislature, in its paternal wisdom, must, therefore, have the right to legislate on the subject of, and to limit, the hours for such labor; and, if it exercises that power, and its validity be questioned, it is sufficient to say, it has reference to the public health; it has reference to the health of the employees condemned to labor day after day in buildings where the sun never shines; it is a health law, and therefore it is valid, and cannot be questioned by the courts. . . .

We mention these extreme cases because the contention is extreme. We do not believe in the soundness of the views which uphold this law. On the contrary, we think that such a law as this, although passed in the assumed exercise of the police power, and as relating to the public health, or the health of the employees named, is not within that power, and is invalid. The act is not, within any fair meaning of the term, a health law, but is an illegal interference with the rights of individuals, both employers and employees, to make contracts regarding labor upon such terms as they may think best, or which they may agree upon with the other parties to such contracts. Statutes of the nature of that under review, limiting the hours in which grown and intelligent men may labor to earn their living, are mere meddlesome interferences with the rights of the individual, and they are not saved from condemnation by the claim that they are passed in the exercise of the police power and upon the subject of the health of the individual whose rights are interfered with, unless there be some fair ground, reasonable in and of itself, to say that there is material

Lochner v. New York

danger to the public health, or to the health of the employees, if the hours of labor are not curtailed. . . .

All that [the state] could properly do has been done by it with regard to the conduct of bakeries, as provided for in the other sections of the act, above set forth. These several sections provide for the inspection of the premises where the bakery is carried on, with regard to furnishing proper wash rooms and water closets, apart from the bake room, also with regard to providing proper drainage, plumbing, and painting; the sections, in addition, provide for the height of the ceiling, the cementing or tiling of floors, where necessary in the opinion of the factory inspector, and for other things of that nature; alterations are also provided for, and are to be made where necessary in the opinion of the inspector, in order to comply with the provisions of the statute. These various sections may be wise and valid regulations, and they certainly go to the full extent of providing for the cleanliness and the healthiness, so far as possible, of the quarters in which bakeries are to be conducted. Adding to all these requirements a prohibition to enter into any contract of labor in a bakery for more than a certain number of hours a week is, in our judgment, so wholly beside the matter of a proper, reasonable, and fair provision as to run counter to that liberty of person and of free contract provided for in the Federal Constitution. . . .

This interference on the part of the legislatures of the several states with the ordinary trades and occupations of the people seems to be on the increase. . . . It is impossible for us to shut our eyes to the fact that many of the laws of this character, while passed under what is claimed to be the police power for the purpose of protecting the public health or welfare, are, in reality, passed from **other motives**. We are justified in saying so when, from the character of the law and the subject upon which it legislates, it is apparent that the public health or welfare bears but the most remote relation to the law. . . .

OBSERVATION

OTHER MOTIVES: The majority believes that the real motive was to adjust the relative bargaining power of workers and employers—and that this is illegitimate.

Justice Holmes dissenting:

I regret sincerely that I am unable to agree with the judgment in this case, and that I think it my duty to express my dissent.

This case is decided upon an economic theory which a large part of the country does not entertain. If it were a question whether I agreed with that theory, I should desire to study it further and long before making up my mind. But I do not conceive that to be my duty, because I strongly believe that my agreement or disagreement has nothing to do with the right of a majority to embody their opinions in law.

BIOGRAPHY

OLIVER WENDELL HOLMES, JR. (1841–1935) was named for his father, a famous Massachusetts physician, poet, and founder of *The Atlantic* magazine. The younger Holmes was raised in the abolitionist milieu of Boston intellectuals and fought for the Union in the Civil War. He gained notice as a justice on the Massachusetts Supreme Court, and was appointed to the US Supreme Court by President Roosevelt in 1902. On the strength of his dissent in *Lochner,* he began to be known as "The Great Dissenter." In addition to being an influential judge, Holmes was a scholar whose views had enormous impact on modern legal theory. His lecture *The Path of the Law,* 10 Harv. L. Rev. 457 (1897), is one of the founding works of the legal realist movement.

It is settled by various decisions of this court that state constitutions and state laws may regulate life in many ways which we as legislators might think as injudicious, or if you like as tyrannical, as this, and which, equally with this, interfere with the liberty to contract. Sunday laws and usury laws are ancient examples. A more modern one is the prohibition of lotteries. The liberty of the citizen to do as he likes so long as he does not interfere with the liberty of others to do the same, which has been a shibboleth for some well-known writers, is interfered with by school laws, by the post office, by every state or municipal institution which takes his money for purposes thought desirable, whether he likes it or not. The 14th Amendment does not enact Mr. Herbert Spencer's **Social Statics**.

■ HISTORY

SOCIAL STATICS: Holmes refers to an 1851 book by Herbert Spencer, a British libertarian who argued in favor of *laissez faire* economics (opposition to governmental regulation of the economy). Spencer also coined the term "survival of the fittest" as a description of natural selection, which was seized upon by Social Darwinists.

The other day we sustained the Massachusetts vaccination law. *Jacobson v. Massachusetts* (1905). United States and state statutes and decisions cutting down the liberty to contract by way of combination [in restraint of trade] are familiar to this court. . . . The decision sustaining an eight-hour law for miners is still recent. *Holden v. Hardy* (1898). Some of these laws embody convictions or prejudices which judges are likely to share. Some may not. But a Constitution is not intended to embody a particular economic theory, whether of paternalism and the organic relation of the citizen to the state or of *laissez faire*. It is made for people of fundamentally differing views, and the accident of our finding certain opinions natural and familiar, or novel, and even shocking, ought not to conclude our judgment upon the question whether statutes embodying them conflict with the Constitution of the United States.

General propositions do not decide concrete cases. The decision will depend on a judgment or intuition more subtle than any articulate major premise. But I think that the proposition just stated, if it is accepted, will carry us far toward the end. Every opinion tends to become a law. I think that the word "liberty," in the 14th Amendment, is perverted when it is held to prevent the natural outcome of a dominant opinion, unless it can be said that a rational and fair man necessarily would admit that the statute proposed would infringe fundamental principles as they have been understood by the traditions of our people and our law. It does not need research to show that no such sweeping condemnation can be passed upon the statute before us. A reasonable man might think it a proper measure on the score of health. Men whom I certainly could not pronounce unreasonable would uphold it as a first installment of a general regulation of the hours of work. Whether in the latter aspect it would be open to the charge of inequality I think it unnecessary to discuss.

Lochner v. New York

Justice Harlan (with whom Justices White and Day concurred), dissenting:

While this court has not attempted to mark the precise boundaries of what is called the police power of the state, the existence of the power has been uniformly recognized, equally by the Federal and State courts. All the cases agree that this power extends at least to the protection of the lives, the health, and the safety of the public against the injurious exercise by any citizen of his own rights. . . . I take it to be firmly established that what is called the liberty of contract may, within certain limits, be subjected to regulations designed and calculated to promote the general welfare, or to guard the public health, the public morals, or the public safety. "The liberty secured by the Constitution of the United States to every person within its jurisdiction does not import," this court has recently said, "an absolute right in each person to be at all times and in all circumstances wholly freed from restraint. There are manifold restraints to which every person is necessarily subject for the common good." *Jacobson v. Massachusetts*.

Granting, then, that there is a liberty of contract which cannot be violated even under the sanction of direct legislative enactment, but assuming, as according to settled law we may assume, that such liberty of contract is subject to such regulations as the state may reasonably prescribe for the common good and the well-being of society, what are the conditions under which the judiciary may declare such regulations to be in excess of legislative authority and void? Upon this point there is no room for dispute; for the rule is universal that a legislative enactment, Federal or state, is never to be disregarded or held invalid unless it be, beyond question, plainly and palpably in excess of legislative power. . . . If there be doubt as to the validity of the statute, that doubt must therefore be resolved in favor of its validity, and the courts must keep their hands off, leaving the legislature to meet the responsibility for unwise legislation. If the end which the legislature seeks to accomplish be one to which its power extends, and if the means employed to that end, although not the wisest or best, are yet not plainly and palpably unauthorized by law, then the court cannot interfere. . . .

Let these principles be applied to the present case. . . . It is plain that this statute was enacted in order to protect the physical well-being of those who work in bakery and confectionery establishments. It may be that the statute had its origin, in part, in the belief that employers and employees in such establishments were not upon an equal footing, and that the necessities of the latter often compelled them to submit to such exactions as unduly taxed their strength. Be this as it may, the statute must be taken as expressing the belief of the people of New York that, as a general rule, and in the case of the average man, labor in excess of sixty hours during a week in such establishments may endanger the health of those who thus labor. Whether or not this be wise legislation it is not the province of the court to inquire. . . .

It must be remembered that this statute does not apply to all kinds of business. It applies only to work in bakery and confectionery establishments, in which, as all know, the air constantly breathed by workmen is not as pure and healthful as that to be found in some other establishments or out of doors. Professor Hirt in his treatise on the *Diseases of the Workers* has said: "The labor of the bakers is among the hardest and most laborious imaginable, because it has to be performed under conditions injurious to the health of those engaged in it. It is hard, very hard, work, not only because it requires a great deal of physical exertion in an overheated workshop and during unreasonably long hours, but more so because of the erratic demands of the public, compelling the baker to perform the greater part of his work at night, thus depriving him of an opportunity to enjoy the necessary rest and sleep—a fact which is highly injurious to his health." Another writer says:

> The constant inhaling of flour dust causes inflammation of the lungs and of the bronchial tubes. The eyes also suffer through this dust, which is responsible for the many cases of running eyes among the bakers. The long hours of toil to which all bakers are subjected produce rheumatism, cramps, and swollen legs. The intense heat in the workshops induces the workers to resort to cooling drinks, which, together with their habit of exposing the greater part of their bodies to the change in the atmosphere, is another source of a number of diseases of various organs. Nearly all bakers are palefaced and of more delicate health than the workers of other crafts, which is chiefly due to their hard work and their irregular and unnatural mode of living, whereby the power of resistance against disease is greatly diminished. The average age of a baker is below that of other workmen; they seldom live over their fiftieth year, most of them dying between the ages of forty and fifty. During periods of epidemic diseases the bakers are generally the first to succumb to the disease, and the number swept away during such periods far exceeds the number of other crafts in comparison to the men employed in the respective industries. . . .

I do not stop to consider whether any particular view of this economic question presents the sounder theory. What the precise facts are it may be difficult to say. It is enough for the determination of this case, and it is enough for this court to know, that the question is one about which there is room for debate and for an honest difference of opinion. . . .

Lochner v. New York

flash*forward*

1. ***The Unpredictable Freedom of Contract.*** In years following *Lochner*, the Supreme Court decided a cascade of cases challenging regulations that were alleged to intrude excessively on constitutionally protected freedom of contract. The challenges succeeded or failed depending on the court's shifting majorities and the facts of each case. The principles distinguishing fair from foul legislation were murky. The inconsistency and unpredictability of the court's rulings became a major objection to doctrine. The critics argued that there must be a flaw in any theory that would uphold maximum hour laws for miners (*Holden v. Hardy*) but not for bakers (*Lochner*).

2. ***Women's Rights Under* Lochner.** One principle partially explaining some of the disparate outcomes was the court's belief that protecting vulnerable people was a valid use of the police power. By contrast, protection of people who were not particularly vulnerable was not in the public interest, and hence was beyond the police power and a mere interference with freedom of contract. On the theory that women represented a vulnerable group in legitimate need of state protection, the Supreme Court unanimously upheld laws setting maximum working hours for women, *Muller v. Oregon*, 208 U.S. 412 (1908), and forbidding them from working in restaurants at night, *Radice v. New York*, 264 U.S. 292 (1924).

The paternalistic impulses visible in *Muller* and *Radice* did not carry the majority in *Adkins v. Children's Hospital of the District of Columbia*, 261 U.S. 525 (1923), which struck down a minimum wage law for women as a violation of the Due Process Clause of the Fifth Amendment. The 5–3 majority opinion by Justice Sutherland contained a vocal restatement of the *Lochner* principle: Freedom of contract is "the general rule and restraint [of contract] the exception, and the exercise of legislative authority to abridge it can be justified only by the existence of exceptional circumstances."

No exceptional circumstances could justify a minimum wage law. Salary was not directly linked to working conditions, so the government's authority to create a safe workplace was not implicated. Although this *Lochner*-esque reasoning was sufficient to resolve the case, the need to distinguish *Muller* led to this discussion of sex equality:

> In the *Muller* case the validity of an Oregon statute, forbidding the employment of any female in certain industries more than 10 hours during any one day was upheld. The decision proceeded upon the theory that the difference between the sexes may justify a different rule respecting hours of labor in the case of women than in the case of men. It is pointed out that these consist in differences of physical structure, especially in respect of the maternal functions, and also in the fact that historically woman has always been dependent upon man, who has established his control by superior physical strength. . . .
>
> But the ancient inequality of the sexes, otherwise than physical, as suggested in the *Muller* case has continued with diminishing intensity. In view of the great—not to say revolutionary—changes which have taken place since that utterance, in the contractual, political, and civil status of women, culminating in the Nineteenth Amendment [guaranteeing women's right to vote, ratified in 1920], it is not unreasonable to say that these differences have now come almost, if not quite, to the vanishing point. In this aspect of the matter, while the physical differences must be recognized in appropriate cases, and legislation fixing hours or conditions of work may properly take them into account, we cannot accept the doctrine that women of mature age require or may be subjected to restrictions upon their liberty of contract which could not lawfully be imposed in the case of men under similar circumstances. To do so would be to ignore all the implications to be drawn from the present day trend of legislation, as well as that of common thought and usage, by which woman is accorded emancipation from the old doctrine that she must be given special protection or be subjected to special restraint in her contractual and civil relationships.

Chief Justice Taft's dissent found itself simultaneously defending the modern-sounding principle of governmental power over economic matters *and* the antique-sounding principle of female vulnerability.

> I am not sure from a reading of the opinion whether the court thinks the authority of *Muller v. Oregon* is shaken by the adoption of the Nineteenth Amendment. The Nineteenth Amendment did not change the physical strength or limitations of women upon which the decision in *Muller v. Oregon* rests. The amendment did give women political power and makes more certain that legislative provisions for their protection will be in accord with their interests as they see them. But I do not think we are warranted in varying [our existing] constitutional construction based on physical differences between men and women, because of the amendment.

2. Other Due Process Rights

In *Lochner*, the Supreme Court relied on unenumerated rights under the Due Process Clause to invalidate state economic legislation that was considered politically liberal, with the results benefitting politically conservative business interests. But in other contexts, protection of unenumerated rights did not necessarily generate politically conservative outcomes. In particular, arguing for freedom to act—as opposed to arguing for equality—proved to be useful for some minority groups.

a) Residential Segregation: *Buchanan v. Warley*

The city of Louisville, Kentucky enacted an ordinance barring any person from moving onto a block where a majority of the residents were of a different race. Although plainly designed to enforce racial segregation, the statute did not violate equal protection as interpreted in *Plessy v. Ferguson*: White people could not move into non-White neighborhoods, and vice versa, making the law formally neutral. However, in *Buchanan v. Warley*, 245 U.S. 60 (1917), the Supreme Court unanimously ruled that the Louisville ordinance violated the Fourteenth Amendment for reasons other than equal protection.

> The right which the ordinance annulled was the civil right of a white man to dispose of his property if he saw fit to do so to a person of color and of a colored person to make such disposition to a white person. . . . We think this attempt to prevent the alienation of the property in question to a person of color was not a legitimate exercise of the police power of the state, and is in direct violation of the fundamental law enacted in the Fourteenth Amendment of the Constitution preventing state interference with property rights except by due process of law.

In *Dred Scott*, property was aligned with gross inequality, but in *Buchanan*, property was aligned with equality.

b) Foreign Language Education: *Meyer v. Nebraska*

The Europeans who immigrated to Britain's North American colonies in the 1600s and 1700s were overwhelmingly English-speaking Protestants. Not until the mid-1800s were there large waves of immigrants to the US whose native language was not English or whose religion was not Protestant, beginning in the 1840s with Germans and Irish, in the 1850s with Chinese (on the west coast), and by 1900 an increasing flow from Italy, Poland, Russia, and other countries in southern and eastern Europe. While many American communities welcomed immigrants, nativist opposition movements were also quick to arise, starting in the 1850s with the anti-immigrant and anti-Catholic "Know Nothing" Party.

Robert T. Meyer (1878–1972)

The private schools operating in some immigrant communities became a source of concern for nativists, who argued that these unregulated schools discouraged assimilation into American culture and preserved un-American beliefs. In the 1890s, a dozen states had passed laws requiring all schools (both public and private) to teach primary subjects in English. The US entry into WWI in 1917 reignited the issue, with German immigrants considered domestic enemies. There were calls to ban all use of German, even in church services. The nativist agitation continued after the war. Several states that had not previously enacted language laws did so, including Nebraska, which passed a law preventing any school from teaching any foreign language to students below the eighth grade.

Robert Meyer taught in the religious school founded in 1873 by the German-speaking Zion Lutheran Church in Hampton, Nebraska. Under pressure during the war, the school abandoned all German for a few years, but by 1920 it had resumed a German language class during the lunch recess (scheduled so the school could claim it was an extracurricular activity and not part of the curriculum). When the county attorney visited Meyer's class, the teacher had a choice. "I knew that if I changed into English language, he would say nothing. If I went on in German, he would arrest me. I told myself that I must not flinch. And I did not flinch. I went on in German." In the US Supreme Court, Meyer's case was argued alongside similar cases from Iowa and Ohio.

ITEMS TO CONSIDER WHILE READING *MEYER v. NEBRASKA*:

A. *The paragraph that begins "While this court has not attempted to define . . . " contains a frequently quoted list of concepts included within the meaning of* *"liberty." How does this list differ from the list of liberties offered in* Allgeyer (described in Ch. 8.C.1)*? Is the list cogent, or is it a mish-mash?*

B. *Which liberty does the court protect in* Meyer*? The right to speak a foreign language? To control the education of one's children? To earn a living by contracting to teach foreign languages? To operate a private school? Something else?*

C. *Would it have been possible for the Court to decide* Meyer *as it did without precedents like* Lochner*?*

Meyer v. Nebraska,

262 U.S. 390 (1923)

Justice McReynolds delivered the opinion of the Court [joined by Chief Justice Taft and Justices McKenna, Van Devanter, Brandeis, Butler, and Sanford].

Plaintiff in error [Robert T. Meyer] was tried and convicted in the district court for Hamilton county, Nebraska, under an information which charged that on May 25, 1920, while an instructor in Zion Parochial School he unlawfully taught the subject of reading in the German language to Raymond Parpart, a child of 10 years, who had not attained and successfully passed the eighth grade. The information is based upon "An act relating to the teaching of foreign languages in the state of Nebraska," approved April 9, 1919, which follows:

> Section 1. No person, individually or as a teacher, shall, in any private, denominational, parochial or public school, teach any subject to any person in any language than the English language.
>
> Sec. 2. Languages, other than the English language, may be taught as languages only after a pupil shall have attained and successfully passed the eighth grade . . .
>
> Sec. 3. Any person who violates any of the provisions of this act shall be deemed guilty of a misdemeanor and upon conviction, shall be subject to a fine of not less than twenty-five dollars ($25), nor more than one hundred dollars ($100), or be confined in the county jail for any period not exceeding thirty days for each offense.
>
> Sec. 4. Whereas, an emergency exists, this act shall be in force from and after its passage and approval.

The Supreme Court of the state affirmed the judgment of conviction. It declared the offense charged and established was "the direct and intentional teaching of the German language as a distinct subject to a child who had not passed the eighth grade," in the parochial school maintained by Zion Evangelical Lutheran Congregation, a collection of Biblical stories being used therefore. And it held that the statute forbidding this did not conflict with the Fourteenth Amendment, but was a valid exercise of the police power. The following excerpts from the opinion sufficiently indicate the reasons advanced to support the conclusion:

> The salutary purpose of the statute is clear. The Legislature had seen the baneful effects of permitting foreigners, who had taken residence in this country, to rear and educate their children in the language of their native land. The result of that condition was found to be inimical to our own safety. To allow the children of foreigners, who had emigrated here, to be taught from early childhood the language of the country of their parents was to rear them with that language as their mother tongue. It was to educate them so that they must always think in that language, and, as a consequence, naturally inculcate in them the ideas and sentiments foreign to the best interests of this country. The statute, therefore, was intended not only to require that the education of all children be conducted in the English language, but that, until they had grown into that language and until it had become a part of them, they should not in the schools be taught any other language. The obvious purpose of this statute was that the English language should be and become the mother tongue of all children reared in this state. The enactment of such a statute comes reasonably within the police power of the state. . . .

The problem for our determination is whether the statute as construed and applied unreasonably infringes the liberty guaranteed to the plaintiff in error by the Fourteenth Amendment[.]

While this court has not attempted to define with exactness the liberty thus guaranteed, the term has received much consideration and some of the included things have been definitely stated. Without doubt, it denotes not merely freedom from bodily restraint but also the right of the individual to contract, to engage in any of the common occupations of life, to acquire useful knowledge, to marry, establish a home and bring up children, to worship God according to the dictates of his own conscience, and generally to enjoy those privileges long recognized at common law as essential to the orderly pursuit of happiness by free men. The established doctrine is that this liberty may not be interfered with, under the guise of protecting the public interest, by legislative action which is arbitrary or without reasonable relation to some purpose within the competency of the state to effect. Determination by the Legislature of what constitutes proper exercise of police power is not final or conclusive but is subject to supervision by the courts.

The American people have always regarded education and acquisition of knowledge as matters of supreme importance which should be diligently promoted. The [Northwest] Ordinance of 1787 declares: "Religion, morality and knowledge being necessary to good government and the happiness of mankind, schools and the means of education shall forever be encouraged."

Corresponding to the right of control, it is the natural duty of the parent to give his children education suitable to their station in life; and nearly all the states, including Nebraska, enforce this obligation by compulsory [education] laws.

Practically, education of the young is only possible in schools conducted by especially qualified persons who devote themselves thereto. The calling always has been regarded as useful and honorable, essential, indeed, to the public welfare. Mere knowledge of the German language cannot reasonably be regarded as harmful. Heretofore it has been commonly looked upon as helpful and desirable. Plaintiff in error taught this language in school as part of his occupation. His right thus to teach and the right of parents to engage him so to instruct their children, we think, are within the liberty of the amendment.

The challenged statute forbids the teaching in school of any subject except in English; also the teaching of any other language until the pupil has attained and successfully passed the eighth grade, which is not usually accomplished before the age of twelve. The Supreme Court of the state has held that "the so-called ancient or dead languages" are not "within the spirit or the purpose of the act." Latin, Greek, Hebrew are not proscribed; but German, French, Spanish, Italian, and every other alien speech are within the ban. Evidently the Legislature has attempted materially to interfere with the calling of modern language teachers, with the opportunities of pupils to acquire knowledge, and with the power of parents to control the education of their own.

It is said the purpose of the legislation was to promote civic development by inhibiting training and education of the immature in foreign tongues and ideals before they could learn English and acquire American ideals, and "that the English language should be and become the mother tongue of all children reared in this state." It is also affirmed that the foreign born population is very large, that certain communities commonly use foreign words, follow foreign leaders, move in a foreign atmosphere, and that the children are thereby hindered from becoming citizens of the most useful type and the public safety is imperiled.

That the state may do much, go very far, indeed, in order to improve the quality of its citizens, physically, mentally and morally, is clear; but the individual has certain fundamental rights which must be respected. The protection of the Constitution extends to all, to those who speak other languages as well as to those born with English on the tongue. Perhaps it would be highly advantageous if all had ready understanding of our ordinary speech, but this cannot be coerced by methods which conflict with the Constitution—a desirable end cannot be promoted by prohibited means.

For the welfare of his Ideal Commonwealth, Plato suggested a law which should provide:

> That the wives of our guardians are to be common, and their children are to be common, and no parent is to know his own child, nor any child his parent. The proper officers will take the offspring of the good parents to the pen or fold, and there they will deposit them with certain nurses who dwell in a separate quarter; but the offspring of the inferior, or of the better when they chance to be deformed, will be put away in some mysterious, unknown place, as they should be.'

In order to submerge the individual and develop ideal citizens, Sparta assembled the males at seven into barracks and entrusted their subsequent education and training to official guardians. Although such measures have been deliberately approved by men of great genius their ideas touching the relation between individual and state were wholly different from those upon which our institutions rest; and it hardly will be affirmed that any Legislature could impose such restrictions upon the people of a state without doing violence to both letter and spirit of the Constitution.

The desire of the Legislature to foster a homogeneous people with American ideals prepared readily to understand current discussions of civic matters is easy to appreciate. Unfortunate experiences during the late war and aversion toward every character of truculent adversaries were certainly enough to quicken that aspiration. But the means adopted, we think, exceed the limitations upon the power of the state and conflict with rights assured to plaintiff in error. The interference is plain enough and no adequate reason therefor in time of peace and domestic tranquility has been shown.

The power of the state to compel attendance at some school and to make reasonable regulations for all schools, including a requirement that they shall give instructions in English, is not questioned. Nor has challenge been made of the state's power to prescribe a curriculum for institutions which it supports. Those matters are not within the present controversy. Our concern is with the prohibition approved by the [Nebraska] Supreme Court. . . . Mere abuse incident to an occupation ordinarily useful is not enough to justify its abolition, although regulation may be entirely proper. No emergency has arisen which renders knowledge by a child of some language other than English so clearly harmful as to justify its inhibition with the consequent infringement of rights long freely enjoyed. We are constrained to conclude that the statute as applied is arbitrary and without reasonable relation to any end within the competency of the state.

As the statute undertakes to interfere only with teaching which involves a modern language, leaving complete freedom as to other matters, there seems no adequate foundation for the suggestion that the purpose was to protect the child's health by limiting his mental activities. It is well known that proficiency in a foreign language seldom comes to one not instructed at an early age, and experience shows that this is not injurious to the health, morals or understanding of the ordinary child.

The judgment of the court below must be reversed and the cause remanded for further proceedings not inconsistent with this opinion.

Meyer v. Nebraska

Justice Holmes [dissenting, joined by Justice Sutherland]. [The dissent appeared with the companion case of *Bartels v. Iowa,* 262 U.S. 404 (1923).]

We all agree, I take it, that it is desirable that all the citizens of the United States should speak a common tongue, and therefore that the end aimed at by the statute is a lawful and proper one. The only question is whether the means adopted deprive teachers of the liberty secured to them by the Fourteenth Amendment. It is with hesitation and unwillingness that I differ from my brethren with regard to a law like this but I cannot bring my mind to believe that in some circumstances, and circumstances existing it is said in Nebraska, the statute might not be regarded as a reasonable or even necessary method of reaching the desired result.

The part of the act with which we are concerned deals with the teaching of young children. Youth is the time when familiarity with a language is established and if there are sections in the State where a child would hear only Polish or French or German spoken at home I am not prepared to say that it is unreasonable to provide that in his early years he shall hear and speak only English at school. But if it is reasonable it is not an undue restriction of the liberty either of teacher or scholar. No one would doubt that a teacher might be forbidden to teach many things, and the only criterion of his liberty under the Constitution that I can think of is whether, considering the end in view, the statute passes the bounds of reason and assumes the character of a merely arbitrary fiat. I think I appreciate the objection to the law but it appears to me to present a question upon which men reasonably might differ and therefore I am unable to say that the Constitution of the United States prevents the experiment being tried.

c) Mandatory Public Education: *Pierce v. Society of Sisters*

In 1922, while *Meyer* was on appeal, voters in Oregon approved a statute **requiring all children to attend public schools**. The stated purpose of the law was to encourage assimilation by exposing all students to a standardized curriculum. In so doing, it would effectively eliminate the state's private schools—most of which were Catholic. The most vociferous advocate in favor of the law was the Ku Klux Klan, which enjoyed a huge increase in membership in the 1920s in Oregon and elsewhere, as the formerly anti-Black organization broadened its agenda to also oppose immigrants and Catholics. Klan publications portrayed Catholic schools as un-American.

■ OBSERVATION

REQUIRING ALL CHILDREN TO ATTEND PUBLIC SCHOOLS: The Oregon law should be distinguished from compulsory education laws, which require all parents to provide a minimum amount of education to their children. Today, all states have compulsory education laws, but they allow parents to choose between public schools, private schools, or home schooling.

The Society of Sisters of the Holy Names of Jesus and Mary, an order of Catholic nuns that ran several parochial schools in Oregon, challenged the law. As in *Meyer*, the Supreme Court's opinion in *Pierce v. Society of Sisters*, 268 U.S. 510 (1925), did not allude to the discriminatory motivation behind the statute, or to the law's effect on religious freedom. Instead, it unanimously invalidated the Oregon law as a violation of an unenumerated liberty protected by the Due Process Clause.

> No question is raised concerning the power of the state reasonably to regulate all schools [public and private], to inspect, supervise and examine them, their teachers and pupils; to require that all children of proper age attend some school, that teachers shall be of good moral character and patriotic disposition, that certain studies plainly essential to good citizenship must be taught, and that nothing be taught which is manifestly inimical to the public welfare.
>
> The inevitable practical result of enforcing the act under consideration would be destruction of appellees' primary schools, and perhaps all other private primary schools for normal children within the state of Oregon. Appellees are engaged in a kind of undertaking not inherently harmful, but long regarded as useful and meritorious. . . .
>
> Under the doctrine of *Meyer v. Nebraska*, we think it entirely plain that the [Oregon] Act of 1922 unreasonably interferes with the liberty of parents and guardians to direct the upbringing and education of children under their control. As often heretofore pointed out, rights guaranteed by the Constitution may not be abridged by legislation which has no reasonable relation to some purpose within the competency of the state. The fundamental theory of liberty upon which all governments in this Union repose excludes any general power of the state to standardize its children by forcing them to accept instruction from public teachers only. The child is not the mere creature of the state; those who nurture him and direct his destiny have the right, coupled with the high duty, to recognize and prepare him for additional obligations.

flashforward

***The Longevity of* Meyer *and* Pierce.** As explained in the next chapter, the idea that the Due Process Clause protects freedom of contract has been rejected. But the idea that it protects one's right to educate one's children or to send them to private schools is well established. *Meyer* and *Pierce* remain good law, and are most people's favorite *Lochner*-era decisions. They continue to be cited regularly. E.g., *Obergefell v. Hodges*, 135 S.Ct. 2584 (2015); *Lawrence v. Texas*, 539 U.S. 558 (2003); *Troxel v. Granville*, 530 U.S. 57 (2000).

d) Eugenic Sterilization: *Buck v. Bell*

America had an infatuation with eugenics in the 1920s and 1930s. The eugenics movement was related to Social Darwinism, the notion that stratification between social and economic classes reflected genetic differences rather than manmade social structures. Eugenicists sought to perfect society by encouraging reproduction and childbirth by "fit" populations while discouraging reproduction by "unfit" ones. As defined by eugenicists, the biologically "unfit" tended to be poor, rural, and uneducated. If these backward populations had fewer children, they argued, a variety of problems that were believed to have genetic origins—criminality, poverty, immorality, violence, stupidity, and general ill health—would disappear from the gene pool within a few generations.

Some states encouraged voluntary sterilization, but others were more aggressive, proposing laws that would require sterilization of institutionalized persons. At the time, state mental hospitals were often filled with people civilly committed on the basis of **feeble-mindedness**. One supposedly feeble-minded woman committed to an asylum in Virginia was Carrie Buck. Historians have since determined that Buck was of normal intelligence, and was institutionalized—and later involuntarily sterilized—on the basis of shockingly little evidence. She had been civilly committed as a teenager because her foster family was ashamed that she had become pregnant (even though the pregnancy was the result of a rape). Testimony at her trial consisted largely of opinion evidence that the entire Buck family was part of the "shiftless, ignorant, and worthless class of anti-social whites."

> ■ TERMINOLOGY
>
> **FEEBLE-MINDEDNESS:** Although considered pejorative today, "feeble-minded" was accepted as a scientific term in the early 20th century. Subsets of the feeble-minded included "idiots" (persons so intellectually disabled that they cannot speak), "imbeciles" (persons whose intellect corresponds to that of a young child), and "morons" (persons who are not as intelligent as they should be). As seen in Carrie Buck's case, a person could be declared "feeble-minded" in the 1920s even if they would not today be diagnosed as having an intellectual disability.

The Supreme Court's short opinion considered two constitutional objections to the sterilization law. The first was a freedom argument: Sterilization for eugenic purposes is an unconstitutional abridgment of Carrie Buck's freedom in violation of the Due Process Clause. The second was an equality argument: It is unconstitutional to sterilize only the feeble-minded people who have been civilly committed to state institutions, but not similarly-situated feeble-minded people who have not been institutionalized.

ITEMS TO CONSIDER WHILE READING *BUCK v. BELL*:

A. *For the Court, why did the statute not violate the Due Process Clause? The Equal Protection Clause?*

B. *Justice Holmes concludes that forced sterilization is no different than the forced vaccination upheld in* Jacobson v. Massachusetts *(1905) (discussed in* Lochner*). Are* Buck *and* Jacobson *distinguishable?*

C. Lochner *is considered one of the worst Supreme Court decisions of all time. So is* Buck. *Can they both be wrong?*

Buck v. Bell,

274 U.S. 200 (1927)

Justice Holmes delivered the opinion of the Court [joined by Chief Justice Taft and Justices Van Devanter, McReynolds, Brandeis, Sanford, and Stone].

This is a writ of error to review a judgment of the Supreme Court of Appeals of the State of Virginia, affirming a judgment of the Circuit Court of Amherst County, by which the defendant in error [Dr. J.H. Bell], the superintendent of the State Colony for Epileptics and Feeble Minded, was ordered to perform the operation of salpingectomy [tying of the fallopian tubes] upon Carrie Buck, the plaintiff in error, for the purpose of making her sterile. The case comes here upon the contention that the statute authorizing the judgment is void under the Fourteenth Amendment as denying to the plaintiff in error due process of law and the equal protection of the laws.

Carrie Buck is a feeble-minded white woman who was committed to the State Colony above mentioned in due form. She is the daughter of a feeble-minded mother in the same institution, and the mother of an illegitimate feeble-minded child. She was eighteen years old at the time of the trial of her case in the Circuit Court in the latter part of 1924. An Act of Virginia approved March 20, 1924 recites that the health of the patient and the welfare of society may be promoted in certain cases by the sterilization of mental defectives, under careful safeguard, etc.; that the sterilization may be effected in males by vasectomy and in females by salpingectomy, without serious pain or substantial danger to life; that the Commonwealth is supporting in various institutions many defective persons who if now discharged would become a menace but if incapable of procreating might be discharged with safety and become self-supporting with benefit to themselves and to society; and that experience has shown that heredity plays an important part in the transmission of insanity, imbecility, etc. The statute then enacts that whenever the superintendent of certain institutions including the above named State Colony shall be of opinion that it is for the best interest of the patients and of society that an inmate under

Carrie Buck (1906–1983)

his care should be sexually sterilized, he may have the operation performed upon any patient afflicted with hereditary forms of insanity, imbecility, etc., on complying with the very careful provisions by which the act protects the patients from possible abuse. . . . There can be no doubt that so far as procedure is concerned the rights of the patient are most carefully considered, and as every step in this case was taken in scrupulous compliance with the statute and after months of observation, there is no doubt that in that respect the plaintiff in error has had due process at law.

The attack is not upon the procedure but upon the substantive law. It seems to be contended that in no circumstances could such an order be justified. It certainly is contended that the order cannot be justified upon the existing grounds. The judgment [of the trial court] finds the facts that have been recited and that Carrie Buck "is the probable potential parent of socially inadequate offspring, likewise afflicted, that she may be sexually sterilized without detriment to her general health and that her welfare and that of society will be promoted by her sterilization," and thereupon makes the order. In view of the general declarations of the Legislature and the specific findings of the Court obviously we cannot say as matter of law that the grounds do not exist, and if they exist they justify the result. We have seen more than once that **the public welfare may call upon the best citizens for their lives.** It would be strange if it could not call upon those who already sap the strength of the State for these lesser sacrifices, often not felt to be such by those concerned, in order to prevent our being swamped with incompetence. It is better for all the world, if instead of waiting to execute degenerate offspring for crime, or to let them starve for their imbecility, society can prevent those who are manifestly unfit from continuing their kind. The principle that sustains compulsory vaccination is broad enough to cover cutting the Fallopian tubes. *Jacobson v. Massachusetts*, 197 U.S. 11 (1905). Three generations of imbeciles are enough.

> OBSERVATION
>
> **THE PUBLIC WELFARE MAY CALL UPON THE BEST CITIZENS FOR THEIR LIVES:** Holmes, a proud Civil War veteran, alludes here to deaths of soldiers in warfare.

But, it is said, however it might be if this reasoning were applied generally, it fails when it is confined to the small number who are in the institutions named and is not applied to the multitudes outside. It is the usual last resort of constitutional arguments to point out **shortcomings of this sort**. But the answer is that the law does all that is needed when it does all that it can, indicates a policy, applies it to all within the lines, and seeks to bring within the lines all similarly

> OBSERVATION
>
> **SHORTCOMINGS OF THIS SORT:** Properly understood in context, this sentence does not mean that all Equal Protection Clause arguments are "the usual last resort" of lawyers with losing cases. Holmes is rejecting what today would be called an "under-inclusiveness" argument: namely, that Virginia's statute is fatally under-inclusive because it sterilizes only some feeble-minded people and not all of them. For Holmes, this argument is no more effective than a driver pulled over for speeding who says, "Officer, why don't you ticket those other speeders instead?"

situated so far and so fast as its means allow. Of course so far as the operations enable those who otherwise must be kept confined to be returned to the world, and thus open the asylum to others, the equality aimed at will be more nearly reached.

Justice Butler dissents [without opinion].

Chapter Recap

A. In the late 19th and early 20th centuries, the Supreme Court held that many Progressive-era economic regulations violated the Constitution. Many of its anti-regulatory decisions of the period are today viewed as mistaken.

B. The Court gave narrow interpretations to Congress's enumerated powers to regulate interstate commerce and to tax. These interpretations were made (in part) with an eye toward maximizing the power of states.

C. The Court interpreted the Due Process Clauses of the Fifth and Fourteenth Amendments to protect an individual right of freedom of contract. This doctrine limited the ability of the federal government and the states to enact economic reform legislation.

D. While the *Lochner* era is best known for its hostility to economic regulation, the Supreme Court sometimes (but not always) used its broad interpretation of the Due Process Clause to protect other unenumerated rights.

E. Even during the *Lochner* era, prominent voices encouraged greater judicial deference to legislatures. Often these ideas were found in dissents, but they sometimes emerged in majority opinions, depending on the case and the author.

CHAPTER 9

The New Deal Revolution

The pillars of the *Lochner* era—broad due process protection for freedom of contract, broad concern over federalism, and narrow scope for the federal government's enumerated powers—came crashing down in a few short months in early 1937. The cases from this short but intense period merit study for two main reasons. First, they remain binding precedents that set the stage for modern constitutional law. Second, they vividly illustrate the processes of constitutional change.

A. The New Deal Meets the Four Horsemen

The Great Depression began in 1929, bringing economic dislocation on a scale not seen before or since. At its worst point in 1933, over 25% of the US labor force was unemployed. International trade and industrial production had fallen to roughly half of their previous levels. Of the nation's 25,000 banks, approximately 11,000 had failed. On a single day in 1932, one-quarter of all the land in Mississippi changed ownership in foreclosure sales. Hundreds of thousands of people became homeless, and poverty was widespread. As the Depression wore on, people began to wonder if it would lead to political instability: a Communist revolution as in Russia, or a Fascist takeover as in Italy and Germany.

Franklin D. Roosevelt, a Democrat, was elected President in 1932; he defeated Republican Herbert Hoover, who was perceived as having done too little to alleviate the crisis. Working with a Democratic majority in Congress, Roosevelt enacted a series of laws that he claimed represented "a new deal for America" by giving the government a stronger role in managing the economy. New Deal statutes expanded the scope of federal government activity far beyond anything that had been undertaken before. Some were anti-poverty initiatives that expanded the welfare state—with Social Security being the most prominent. Others were economic stimulus programs like the Tennessee Valley Authority or the Works Progress Administration, which spent government money to encourage more economic activity. Others sought to directly regulate large sectors of the economy that were perceived as failing, including banking and agriculture.

During Roosevelt's first term in office, several of the more ambitious New Deal statutes were invalidated by the US Supreme Court. The court's conservative wing (consisting of Justices Pierce Butler, James McReynolds, George Sutherland, and Willis Van Devanter) became popularly known as "the Four Horsemen" for their regular bloc voting against New Deal statutes. The Four Horsemen were often able to prevail by picking up a fifth vote from Chief Justice Charles Evans Hughes or Justice Owen Roberts. Between 1933 and 1936, the Supreme Court struck down some of the administration's most prized initiatives, including the Agricultural Adjustment Act, the Federal Farm Bankruptcy Act, and the National Industrial Recovery Act. The following sections show how the *Lochner*-era reasoning was continued or expanded in this period.

1. A Narrow View of the Commerce Clause: *Schechter Poultry*

Earlier in the *Lochner* era, the Supreme Court attempted to draw a line between transactions deemed to have "direct" impact on interstate commerce (which Congress could regulate) and those with only "indirect" interstate impact (which Congress could not regulate). Conversely, the federal government was allowed to impose regulations on interstate commerce that affected local commerce, so long as their impact was "indirect."

Unfortunately, terms like "direct" and "indirect" do not define themselves. Why were the in-state effects of a federal ban on interstate shipment of a product tolerably "indirect" when the banned goods were lottery tickets in *Champion v. Ames*, but intolerably "direct" when they were products made with child labor in *Dagenhart*? As these criticisms of the direct/indirect dichotomy mounted in the early 1930s, a majority of the Supreme Court continued to insist that the line between direct and indirect effects on interstate commerce was constitutionally proper.

A.L.A. Schechter Poultry Corp. v. United States, 295 U.S. 495 (1935), struck down the National Industrial Recovery Act of 1934. NIRA was an ambitious law that gave a federal agency wide leeway to impose comprehensive regulatory codes on industries. (Indeed, one of the constitutional objections to the law was that Congress had essentially delegated all lawmaking authority to the agency without providing any instructions or limitations on its authority.) The Live Poultry Code challenged in *Schechter Poultry* set maximum hours and minimum wages for poultry workers and regulated the quality and volume of chickens that could be sold.

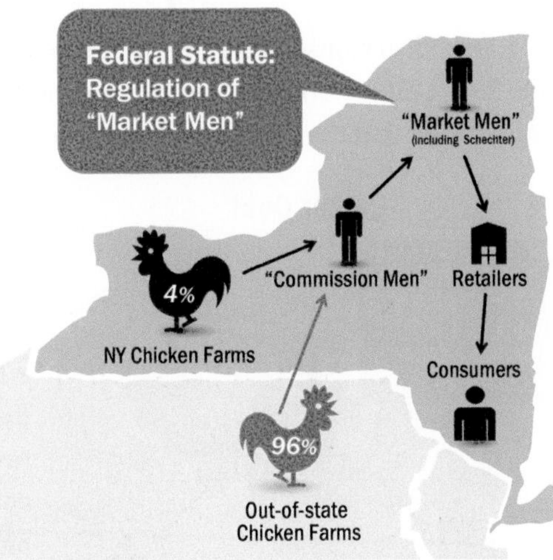

Almost all of the live chickens sold in New York City—96%—came from out of state, purchased by "commission men" who then sold them to "market men" who operated slaughterhouses. Once butchered, the chickens were sold to retailers who then sold them to the end customers. Other than the purchase of out-of-state chickens by commission men, the Supreme Court considered the other transactions in the chain to be purely intrastate matters beyond the scope of the Commerce Clause.

> Much is made of the fact that almost all the poultry coming to New York is sent there from other states. But the code provisions, as here applied, do not concern the transportation of the poultry from other states to New York, or the transactions of the commission men or others to whom it is consigned, or the sales made by such consignees to defendants. When defendants had made their purchases, whether at the West Washington Market in New York City or at the railroad terminals serving the city, or elsewhere, the poultry was trucked to their slaughterhouses in Brooklyn for local disposition. The interstate transactions in relation to that poultry then ended. Defendants held the poultry at their slaughterhouse markets for slaughter and local sale to retail dealers and butchers who in turn sold directly to consumers. Neither the slaughtering nor the sales by defendants were transactions in interstate commerce.

2. A Narrow View of Commerce and Taxation: *Carter Coal*

After the demise of NIRA in *Schechter Poultry*, Congress tried to salvage the code for the coal industry. The Coal Conservation Act of 1935 set minimum and maximum prices for coal sold at each mine, and guaranteed the right of miners to unionize. Congress sought to distinguish this new law from the one invalidated in *Schechter Poultry*. To avoid the problem of excessive delegation, Congress specified the sort of code that the administrative agency could enforce, limiting it to a single industry. Unlike poultry, which had the capacity to be local, the coal industry was nationwide in scope. Finally, the code was binding only on companies that agreed to participate. However, the choice to join the code was not free of government influence. Companies who did not adopt the code would pay a 15% federal tax on sales of coal, but only a 1.5% tax if they signed.

The Coal Conservation Act was challenged in *Carter v. Carter Coal Co.*, 298 U.S. 238 (1936). Consistent with *Bailey v. Drexel Furniture* (1921), the Supreme Court ruled that the law was not really a tax.

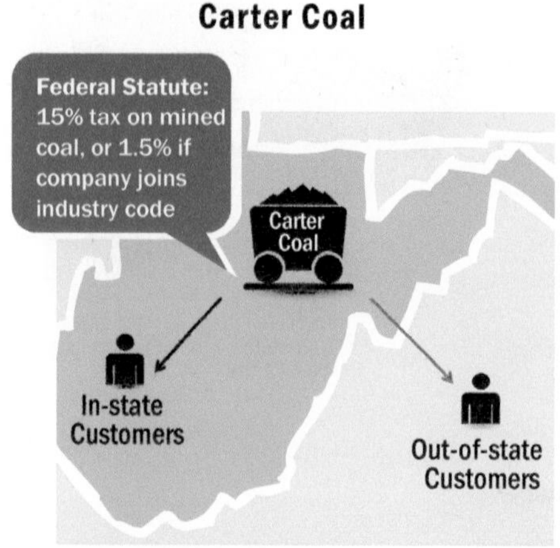

> The so-called excise tax of 15 percent on the sale price of coal at the mine, . . . with its [immense discount for companies who adopted the code], is clearly not a tax but a penalty. . . . It is very clear that the "excise tax" is not imposed for revenue but exacted as a penalty to compel compliance with the regulatory provisions of the act. The whole purpose of the exaction is to coerce what is called an agreement—which, of course, it is not, for it lacks the essential element of consent. One who does a thing in order to avoid a monetary penalty does not agree; he yields to compulsion precisely the same as though he did so to avoid a term in jail.

The Taxing Clause does not authorize Congress to impose penalties, but the Commerce Clause does—as seen in the civil and criminal penalties that arise when one ships lottery tickets or spoiled eggs across state lines. As an alternative basis, Congress asserted that the Coal Conservation Act was a proper use of the Commerce Clause because, in the language of the Act's preamble, production and distribution of coal "bear upon and directly affect its interstate commerce." The Supreme Court rejected the argument. Just as *Schechter Poultry* held that chickens exited the realm of interstate commerce soon after they were sold across state lines, *Carter Coal* held that coal did not enter the realm of interstate commerce when it was mined—even if it was mined for the purpose of interstate sale.

> That commodities produced or manufactured within a state are intended to be sold or transported outside the state does not render their production or manufacture subject to federal regulation under the commerce clause. . . . The possibility, or even certainty of exportation of a product or article from a state did not determine it to be in interstate commerce before the commencement of its movement from the state. To hold otherwise would nationalize all industries, it would nationalize and withdraw from state jurisdiction and deliver to federal commercial control the fruits of California and the South, the wheat of the West and its meats, the cotton of the South, the shoes of Massachusetts and the woolen industries of other states at the very inception of their production or growth . . . .

The majority was unpersuaded by Congress's declaration that coal mining and distribution "directly affect" interstate commerce. However, its explanation of what made an effect direct rather than indirect was murky.

> That the production of every commodity intended for interstate sale and transportation has some effect upon interstate commerce may be, if it has not already been, freely granted; and we are brought to the final and decisive inquiry, whether here that effect is direct. . . . The distinction between direct and indirect effects of intrastate transactions upon interstate commerce must be recognized as a fundamental one, essential to the maintenance of our constitutional system.
>
> Whether the effect of a given activity or condition is direct or indirect is not always easy to determine. The word "direct" implies that the activity or condition invoked or blamed shall operate proximately—not mediately, remotely, or collaterally—to produce the effect. It connotes the absence of an efficient intervening agency or condition. And the extent of the effect bears no logical relation to its character. The distinction between a direct and an indirect effect turns, not upon the magnitude of either the cause or the effect, but entirely upon the manner in which the effect has been brought about.

In short: making a product to sell across state lines was only indirectly related to actually selling it across state lines. Hence the federal government could not regulate how the product was made, no matter how big an effect the making or initial selling of the product had on interstate commerce.

3. A Narrow View of the Taxing and Spending Clauses: *United States v. Butler*

The Agricultural Adjustment Act of 1933 was the first federal statute to pay farmers to produce less, in an effort to stabilize prices by reducing oversupply. In *United States v. Butler*, 297 U.S. 1 (1936), the Four Horsemen plus two allies invalidated the Act. Their internally contradictory opinion agreed with the government that Congress had power to spend tax money to provide for "the general welfare of the United States," and that the taxing and spending could be for purposes that were not among Congress's enumerated powers. Despite this authority, the Act was unconstitutional because regardless of the means chosen, Congress simply had no business regulating farms which were themselves not crossing state lines and hence a purely local matter.

> The act invades the reserved rights of the states. It is a statutory plan to regulate and control agricultural production, a matter beyond the powers delegated to the federal government. The tax, the appropriation of the funds raised, and the direction for their disbursement, are but parts of the plan. They are but

> means to an unconstitutional end. . . . [Congress] may not indirectly accomplish [unconstitutional] ends by taxing and spending to purchase compliance.

4. A Broad View of Freedom of Contract

In addition to its rejection of federal economic regulations, the Four Horsemen and their occasional allies continued to invalidate some but not all state economic regulations under the Due Process Clause, on grounds that they violated freedom of contract. For example, six-member majorities of the Supreme Court invalidated an Oklahoma statute forbidding sale of ice without a license, *New State Ice Co. v. Liebmann*, 285 U.S. 262 (1932), and a Virginia statute requiring railroads to replace grade crossings with overpasses, *Southern Railway Co. v. Virginia*, 290 U.S. 190 (1933). In *Morehead v. New York ex rel. Tipaldo*, 298 U.S. 587 (1936), a 5–4 majority invalidated New York's minimum wage law for women, reaffirming its earlier 5–4 decision in *Adkins v. Children's Hospital* (1923).

B. Hints Before the Fall

The demise of *Lochner* did not come completely out of the blue. The signs of a reversal are always easier to see with hindsight, but several indicators suggested that change might be coming.

1. Language in Dissents

Opposition to *Lochner* was consistently expressed in dissenting opinions. The dissenters were unwilling to accept previous decisions as binding precedents, and continued to dissent on principle.

In the early years, the most well-regarded dissents were written by Justice Holmes, but after his retirement, his ideas continued to be expressed by others in the minority. One passage from Justice Brandeis's dissent in *New State Ice Co. v. Liebmann*, 285 U.S. 262 (1932), continues to be cited today for its metaphor of states as laboratories of democracy, whose innovations should not be stifled by overreaching federal courts.

> Denial of the right to experiment [in things social and economic] may be fraught with serious consequences to the nation. It is one of the happy incidents of the federal system that a single courageous state may, if its citizens choose, serve as a laboratory; and try novel social and economic experiments without risk to the rest of the country. This Court has the power to prevent an experiment. We may strike down the statute which embodies it on the ground that, in our opinion, the measure is arbitrary, capricious, or unreasonable. . . . But, in the exercise of this high power, we must be ever on our guard, lest we erect our prejudices into legal principles.

2. Language in Majority Opinions

Lochner's concepts always contained some wiggle room that allowed the Supreme Court to uphold some economic regulations. When temporary majorities formed in support of a particular statute, the writing justice might include language that could be cited in later opinions to challenge the underlying theory. The most prominent example was *Nebbia v. New York*, 291 U.S. 502 (1934), a 5–4 decision that upheld a New York statute setting minimum prices for milk. An arguably similar Minnesota statute had been invalidated in *Fairmont Creamery Co. v. Minnesota*, 274 U.S. 1 (1927), but that case was decided before the Depression began to change people's minds about the importance of economic regulation. *Nebbia* included this passage that is hard to reconcile with *Lochner* and *Adkins*:

> So far as the requirement of due process is concerned, and in the absence of other constitutional restriction, a state is free to adopt whatever economic policy may reasonably be deemed to promote public welfare, and to enforce that policy by legislation adapted to its purpose. The courts are without authority either to declare such policy, or, when it is declared by the legislature, to override it. If the laws passed are seen to have a reasonable relation to a proper legislative purpose, and are neither arbitrary nor discriminatory, the requirements of due process are satisfied[.]

Although this language seemed to be a direct challenge to *Lochner* and *Adkins*, the Court did not declare the cases to be overruled. Indeed, when *Morehead v. New York ex rel. Tipaldo*, 298 U.S. 587 (1936), struck down New York's minimum wage law for women two years later, it did not even cite *Nebbia*. But as with dissents, seeds planted in majority opinions may later sprout.

3. Academic and Journalistic Criticism

Federal judges are given life tenure to ensure they have the independence to follow the law even in the face of popular pressure. However, independence does not mean that judges are unaware of how their decisions are received. Widespread public disapproval may cause judges to reconsider. The Court's penchant for invalidating laws drew increased criticism into the 1930s. The most prominent legal scholars of the day were raised on the legal realist tradition spearheaded by Justice Holmes, so mainstream academic writing tended to be critical of the court's decisions. Similar criticisms could be found in the popular press.

4. Political Pushback

The most important outside pressures on the Court came from political actors.

a) Continued Legislation and Enforcement

There would be no litigation over the constitutionality of economic regulation if legislatures did not continue to pass reform legislation, or if executive branch officers or state courts did not continue to enforce those laws that had not been specifically invalidated. By continuing to legislate and enforce in ways the Court was likely to disapprove of, these actors signaled their skepticism for the Court's rulings (much as Abraham Lincoln said he would do with regard to the *Dred Scott* decision). The continuing flow of cases provided ammunition for those on the Court who wished to change its doctrines.

b) The Court-Packing Plan

The Supreme Court's opposition to the New Deal prompted a form of political pushback from the President that was unusual for its high stakes and public visibility. During his campaign for re-election in 1936, Roosevelt raised oblique challenges against the Supreme Court, saying that the US Constitution was not intended to "block humanity's advance" but instead should be "a living force for the expression of the national will with respect to national needs." The election doubtless turned on many more issues than the Supreme Court, but it was clear that Roosevelt and the New Deal Democrats enjoyed huge popular support. Roosevelt took over 60% of the popular vote, and won in the Electoral College by a margin of 523 to 8. (His Republican opponent Alf Landon took only Vermont and Maine.) In Congress, Democrats controlled the House 322 to 88 and the Senate 71 to 25.

On March 9, 1937, Roosevelt devoted the first radio address of his second term to the problem of the Supreme Court.

> The American people have learned from the depression. For in the last three national elections an overwhelming majority of them voted a mandate that the Congress and the President begin the task of providing that protection—not after long years of debate, but now. The Courts, however, have cast doubts on the ability of the elected Congress to protect us against catastrophe by meeting squarely our modern social and economic conditions. . . .
>
> I want to talk with you very simply about the need for present action in this crisis—the need to meet the unanswered challenge of one-third of a nation ill-nourished, ill-clad, ill-housed.

> Last Thursday [in my inauguration speech] I described the American form of Government as a three horse team provided by the Constitution to the American people so that their field might be plowed. The three horses are, of course, the three branches of government—the Congress, the Executive and the Courts. Two of the horses are pulling in unison today; the third is not.
>
> Those who have intimated that the President of the United States is trying to drive that team, overlook the simple fact that the President, as Chief Executive, is himself one of the three horses. It is the American people themselves who are in the driver's seat. It is the American people themselves who want the furrow plowed. It is the American people themselves who expect the third horse to pull in unison with the other two. . . .
>
> Since the rise of the modern movement for social and economic progress through legislation, the Court has more and more often and more and more boldly asserted a power to veto laws passed by the Congress and State Legislatures in complete disregard of this original limitation. In the last four years the sound rule of giving statutes the benefit of all reasonable doubt has been cast aside. The Court has been acting not as a judicial body, but as a policy-making body. . . .
>
> The Court in addition to the proper use of its judicial functions has improperly set itself up as a third house of the Congress—a super-legislature, as one of the justices has called it—reading into the Constitution words and implications which are not there, and which were never intended to be there. We have, therefore, reached the point as a nation where we must take action to save the Constitution from the Court and the Court from itself. We must find a way to take an appeal from the Supreme Court to the Constitution itself. We want a Supreme Court which will do justice under the Constitution and not over it. In our courts we want a government of laws and not of men.

To reassert political branch control over the Supreme Court, Roosevelt proposed adding new members to the Court. The Constitution does not indicate the size of the Supreme Court, and the number of justices had been changed during the administrations of John Adams, Thomas Jefferson, Andrew Jackson, Abraham Lincoln, and Ulysses S. Grant. Roosevelt proposed legislation allowing the President to appoint an additional Supreme Court justice for any justice who reached 70 years of age without retiring. Given the ages of the sitting justices, Roosevelt would be able to appoint six new justices immediately, four of whom would directly cancel out the votes of the Four Horsemen.

The "Four Horseman" of the US Supreme Court (early 1937)

■ HISTORY

COURT-PACKING: Efforts by Congress and the President to fill the judiciary with political allies have a long history. In 1801, John Adams and his Federalist-controlled Congress created new trial-level judgeships and quickly staffed them with Federalists. When political control passed to Thomas Jefferson and his Republican-controlled Congress, they sought to unpack the courts. This led to the constitutional struggles ultimately resolved in *Marbury v. Madison* (1803) and *Stuart v. Laird* (1803). See Ch. 4.B. Roosevelt's 1937 proposal to increase the size of the Supreme Court to dilute the votes of older justices also had its predecessor. A similar idea had been suggested during the Woodrow Wilson administration by then-attorney general James McReynolds—now one of the Four Horsemen.

The **court-packing** proposal created a huge political furor. Roosevelt's opponents accused him of a power grab; even many New Dealers were bothered by the bill. Ultimately, the court-packing plan never made it out of committee. The urgency for it evaporated when the Supreme Court abruptly reversed itself regarding the Due Process Clause on March 29, and on the Commerce Clause on April 12. For their part, the Justices claimed that their decisions in these cases were not affected by the threat of court reorganization.

C. The Revolution of 1937

1. Reversal on Freedom of Contract: *West Coast Hotel v. Parrish*

Washington's Minimum Wage for Women. In 1913, Washington state created an Industrial Welfare Commission (IWC) and directed it "to establish such standards of wages and conditions of labor for women and minors employed within the State of Washington, as shall be . . . reasonable and not detrimental to health and morals, and which shall be sufficient for the decent maintenance of women." The state supreme court upheld its constitutionality in *Larsen v. Rice*, 100 Wash. 642 (1918) and again in *Spokane Hotel Co. v. Younger*, 113 Wash. 359 (1920). In 1921, the IWC established a minimum wage of $14.50 per 48-hour work week, but after the US Supreme Court struck down the District of Columbia minimum wage law in *Adkins* (1923), the Washington state department of labor stopped enforcing it.

Elsie Parrish's Lawsuit. Elsie Parrish, a mother of six, worked as a maid at the Cascadian Hotel in Wenatchee, Washington between 1933 and 1935. The hotel's owner, West Coast Hotel Co., paid her only 25 cents an hour—$12 per week for a 48-hour work week. After she was laid off in 1935, Parrish calculated that she had been underpaid by $216, so she sued to collect the shortfall. Her trial testimony indicated her precarious economic situation while working for the hotel: "I never made any demand upon the hotel company or any of its agents for the state wage until my discharge. There was nothing ever said about wages. I took what they gave me because I needed the work so badly."

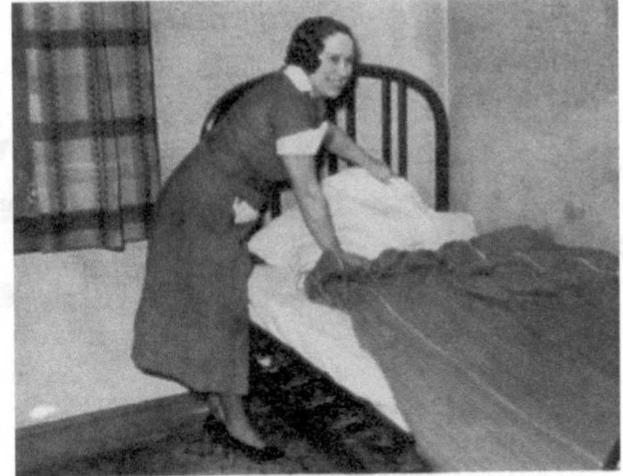
Elsie Parrish (1899–1980)

The state trial judge ruled against her in October 1935, reasoning that the statute violated the Due Process Clause. In his oral ruling, he said the case was controlled by *Adkins*: "The latest pronouncement of the highest court of the land *is* the law of the land, until it is reversed, as I understand it; and even though the court in this state has reached a conclusion that the law is constitutional, if the court of the United States has reached a different conclusion, that of course disposes of the matter."

But on April 2, 1936 the state supreme court unanimously reversed, in an opinion that consisted mostly of lengthy quotations from the dissents in *Adkins* and the majority opinion in *Nebbia*. In addition to implying that *Adkins* was wrong, the state court contended that the US Supreme Court owed greater deference to state laws than federal ones. *Parrish v. West Coast Hotel Co.*, 55 P.2d 1083 (Wash. 1936).

On June 1, 1936, the US Supreme Court decided *Morehead v. New York ex rel. Tipaldo*, 298 U.S. 587 (1936), holding New York's minimum wage law for women unconstitutional. The Court had re-affirmed *Adkins* and applied it against a state law—the opposite of what the Washington Supreme Court proposed. A few months later, the US Supreme Court granted review in *Parrish*. It announced its decision on March 29, 1937.

QUESTIONS TO CONSIDER WHILE READING *WEST COAST HOTEL v. PARRISH*:

A. *Minimum wage laws for women were declared a violation of freedom of contract in* Adkins *(1923). In light of this, was it proper for the Washington Supreme Court to continue to enforce a substantially similar law?*

B. *Compare these two competing descriptions of liberty. What is the threat to liberty in each? What protects liberty in each?*

- *From* Adkins*: "To sustain the individual freedom of action contemplated by the Constitution is not to strike down the common good, but to exalt it; for surely the good of society as a whole cannot be better served than by the preservation against arbitrary restraint of the liberties of its constituent members."*
- *From* Parrish*: "The liberty safeguarded [by the Due Process Clause] is liberty in a social organization which requires the protection of law against the evils which menace the health, safety, morals, and welfare of the people."*

C. *The dissent argues that if minimum wage laws are desired, the correct response is to amend the Constitution, not to overrule* Adkins*. When should a court be willing to overrule a constitutional precedent?*

West Coast Hotel Co. v. Parrish,
300 U.S. 379 (1937)

Chief Justice Hughes delivered the opinion of the Court [joined by Justices Brandeis, Stone, Roberts, and Cardozo].

This case presents the question of the constitutional validity of the minimum wage law of the state of Washington. The act, entitled "Minimum Wages for Women," authorizes the fixing of minimum wages for women and minors. . . .

West Coast Hotel Co. v. Parrish

The appellant conducts a hotel. The appellee Elsie Parrish was employed as a chambermaid and (with her husband) brought this suit to recover the difference between the wages paid her and the minimum wage fixed pursuant to the state law. The minimum wage was $14.50 per week of 48 hours. The appellant challenged the act as repugnant to the due process clause of the Fourteenth Amendment of the Constitution of the United States. The Supreme Court of the state, reversing the trial court, sustained the statute and directed judgment for the plaintiffs. The case is here on appeal.

The appellant relies upon the decision of this Court in *Adkins v. Children's Hospital*, which held invalid the District of Columbia Minimum Wage Act which was attacked under the due process clause of the Fifth Amendment. . . .

The recent case of *Morehead v. New York ex rel. Tipaldo*, came here on certiorari to the New York court which had held the New York minimum wage act for women to be invalid. . . . [This] Court considered that the only question before it was whether the *Adkins* Case was distinguishable and that reconsideration of that decision had not been sought. Upon that point the Court said: "The petition for the writ sought review upon the ground that this case (*Morehead*) is distinguishable from that one (*Adkins*). No application has been made for reconsideration of the constitutional question there decided. . . . [The petitioner] does not ask to be heard upon the question whether the *Adkins* Case should be overruled. . . . "

We think that the question which was not deemed to be open in the *Morehead* Case is open and is necessarily presented here. The Supreme Court of Washington has upheld the minimum wage statute of that state. It has decided that the statute is a reasonable exercise of the police power of the state. In reaching that conclusion, the state court has invoked principles long established by this Court in the application of the Fourteenth Amendment. The state court has refused to regard the decision in the *Adkins* Case as determinative and has pointed to our decisions both before and since that case as justifying its position. We are of the opinion that this ruling of the state court demands on our part a re-examination of the *Adkins* Case. The importance of the question, in which many states having similar laws are concerned, the close division by which the decision in the *Adkins* Case was reached, and the economic conditions which have supervened, and in the light of which the reasonableness of the exercise of the protective power of the state must be considered, make it not only appropriate, but we think imperative, that in deciding the present case the subject should receive fresh consideration. . . .

The principle which must control our decision is not in doubt. The constitutional provision invoked is the due process clause of the Fourteenth Amendment governing the states, as the [Fifth Amendment] due process clause invoked in the *Adkins* Case governed Congress. In each case the violation alleged by those attacking minimum wage regulation for women is deprivation of freedom of contract. What is this freedom? The Constitution does not speak of freedom of contract. It speaks of liberty and prohibits the deprivation of liberty without due process of law. In prohibiting that deprivation, the Constitution does not recognize an absolute and uncontrollable liberty. Liberty in each of its phases has its history and connotation. But the liberty safeguarded is liberty in a social organization which requires the protection of law against the evils which menace the health, safety, morals, and welfare of the people. Liberty under the Constitution is thus necessarily subject to the restraints of due process, and regulation which is reasonable in relation to its subject and is adopted in the interests of the community is due process.

This essential limitation of liberty in general governs freedom of contract in particular. . . . There is no absolute freedom to do as one wills or to contract as one chooses. The guaranty of liberty does not withdraw from legislative supervision that wide department of activity which consists of the making of contracts, or deny to government the power to provide restrictive safeguards. Liberty implies the absence of arbitrary restraint, not immunity from reasonable regulations and prohibitions imposed in the interests of the community.

This power under the Constitution to restrict freedom of contract has had many illustrations. That it may be exercised in the public interest with respect to contracts between employer and employee is undeniable. . . . In dealing with the relation of employer and employed, the Legislature has necessarily a wide field of discretion in order that there may be suitable protection of health and safety, and that peace and good order may be promoted through regulations designed to insure wholesome conditions of work and freedom from oppression. . . .

It is manifest that this established principle is peculiarly applicable in relation to the employment of women in whose protection the state has a special interest. That phase of the subject received elaborate consideration in *Muller v. Oregon* (1908), where the constitutional authority of the state to limit the working hours of women was sustained. . . . This array of precedents and the principles they applied were thought by the dissenting Justices in the *Adkins* Case to demand that the minimum wage statute be sustained. The validity of the distinction made by the Court between a minimum wage and a maximum of hours in limiting liberty of contract was especially challenged. That challenge persists and is without any satisfactory answer. . . .

We think that the views thus expressed are sound and that the decision in the Adkins Case was a departure from the true application of the principles governing the regulation by the state of the relation of employer and employed. . . . With full recognition of the earnestness and vigor which characterize the prevailing opinion in the *Adkins* Case, we find it impossible to reconcile that ruling with these well-considered declarations [from other cases]. What can be closer to the public interest than the health of women and their protection from unscrupulous and overreaching employers? And if the protection of women is a legitimate end of the exercise of state power, how can it be said that the requirement of the payment of

West Coast Hotel Co. v. Parrish

a minimum wage fairly fixed in order to meet the very necessities of existence is not an admissible means to that end? The Legislature of the state was clearly entitled to consider the situation of women in employment, the fact that they are in the class receiving the least pay, that their bargaining power is relatively weak, and that they are the ready victims of those who would take advantage of their necessitous circumstances. The Legislature was entitled to adopt measures to reduce the evils of the "sweating system," the exploiting of workers at wages so low as to be insufficient to meet the bare cost of living, thus making their very helplessness the occasion of a most injurious competition. The Legislature had the right to consider that its minimum wage requirements would be an important aid in carrying out its policy of protection. The adoption of similar requirements by many states evidences a deep-seated conviction both as to the presence of the evil and as to the means adapted to check it. Legislative response to that conviction cannot be regarded as arbitrary or capricious and that is all we have to decide. Even if the wisdom of the policy be regarded as debatable and its effects uncertain, still the Legislature is entitled to its judgment.

There is an additional and compelling consideration which recent economic experience has brought into a strong light. The exploitation of a class of workers who are in an unequal position with respect to bargaining power and are thus relatively defenseless against the denial of a living wage is not only detrimental to their health and well being, but casts a direct burden for their support upon the community. What these workers lose in wages the taxpayers are called upon to pay. The bare cost of living must be met. We may take judicial notice of the unparalleled demands for relief which arose during the recent period of depression and still continue to an alarming extent despite the degree of economic recovery which has been achieved. It is unnecessary to cite official statistics to establish what is of common knowledge through the length and breadth of the land. While in the instant case no factual brief has been presented, there is no reason to doubt that the state of Washington has encountered the same social problem that is present elsewhere. The community is not bound to provide what is in effect a subsidy for unconscionable employers. The community may direct its law-making power to correct the abuse which springs from their selfish disregard of the public interest.

The argument that the legislation in question constitutes an arbitrary discrimination, because it does not extend to men, is unavailing. This Court has frequently held that the legislative authority, acting within its proper field, is not bound to extend its regulation to all cases which it might possibly reach. The Legislature is free to recognize degrees of harm and it may confine its restrictions to those classes of cases where the need is deemed to be clearest. If the law presumably hits the evil where it is most felt, it is not to be overthrown because there are other instances to which it might have been applied. There is no doctrinaire requirement that the legislation should be couched in all embracing terms. This familiar principle has repeatedly been applied to legislation which singles out women, and particular classes of women, in the exercise of the state's protective power. Their relative need in the presence of the evil, no less than the existence of the evil itself, is a matter for the legislative judgment.

Our conclusion is that the case of *Adkins v. Children's Hospital* should be, and it is, overruled. The judgment of the Supreme Court of the state of Washington is affirmed.

Justice Sutherland, dissenting [joined by Justices Van Devanter, McReynolds, and Butler].

I think the judgment of the court below should be reversed.

The principles and authorities relied upon to sustain the judgment were considered in *Adkins v. Children's Hospital* and *Morehead v. New York ex rel. Tipaldo*, . . . A sufficient answer to all that is now said will be found in the opinions of the court in those cases. Nevertheless, in the circumstances, it seems well to restate our reasons and conclusions.

Under our form of government, where the written Constitution, by its own terms, is the supreme law, some agency, of necessity, must have the power to say the final word as to the validity of a statute assailed as unconstitutional. The Constitution makes it clear that the power has been entrusted to this court when the question arises in a controversy within its jurisdiction; and so long as the power remains there, its exercise cannot be avoided without betrayal of the trust. . . .

It is urged that the question involved should now receive fresh consideration, among other reasons, because of the economic conditions which have supervened; but the meaning of the Constitution does not change with the ebb and flow of economic events. We frequently are told in more general words that the Constitution must be construed in the light of the present. If by that it is meant that the Constitution is made up of living words that apply to every new condition which they include, the statement is quite true. But to say, if that be intended, that the words of the Constitution mean today what they did not mean when written—that is, that they do not apply to a situation now to which they would have applied then—is to rob that instrument of the essential element which continues it in force as the people have made it until they, and not their official agents, have made it otherwise. . . .

If the Constitution, intelligently and reasonably construed in the light of these principles, stands in the way of desirable legislation, the blame must rest upon that instrument, and not upon the court for enforcing it according to its terms. The remedy in that situation—and the only true remedy—is to amend the Constitution. [M]uch of the benefit expected from written Constitutions would be lost if their provisions were to be bent to circumstances or modified by public opinion. . . .

The Washington statute, like the one for the District of Columbia, fixes minimum wages for adult women. Adult men and their employers are left free to bargain

West Coast Hotel Co. v. Parrish

as they please; and it is a significant and an important fact that all state statutes to which our attention has been called are of like character. The common-law rules restricting the power of women to make contracts have, under our system, long since practically disappeared. Women today stand upon a legal and political equality with men. There is no longer any reason why they should be put in different classes in respect of their legal right to make contracts; nor should they be denied, in effect, the right to compete with men for work paying lower wages which men may be willing to accept. And it is an arbitrary exercise of the legislative power to do so. . . .

An appeal to the principle that the Legislature is free to recognize degrees of harm and confine its restrictions accordingly, is but to beg the question, which is—Since the contractual rights of men and women are the same, does the legislation here involved, by restricting only the rights of women to make contracts as to wages, create an arbitrary discrimination? We think it does. Difference of sex affords no reasonable ground for making a restriction applicable to the wage contracts of all working women from which like contracts of all working men are left free. Certainly a suggestion that the bargaining ability of the average woman is not equal to that of the average man would lack substance. The ability to make a fair bargain, as every one knows, does not depend upon sex. . . .

2. Reversal on the Commerce Clause

The Supreme Court repudiated the restrictive vision of the Commerce Clause seen in *E.C. Knight* and *Dagenhart*, beginning with a decision only a few weeks after Parrish.

a) Federal Regulation of Multi-State Businesses: *NLRB v. Jones & Laughlin Steel Corp.*

National Labor Relations Board v. Jones & Laughlin Steel Corp., 301 U.S. 1 (1937), also authored by Chief Justice Hughes, upheld the National Labor Relations Act of 1935. The statute outlawed unfair labor practices "affecting commerce," and created the National Labor Relations Board (NLRB) to enforce the Act. Jones & Laughlin was a Pennsylvania corporation that owned and operated facilities in several states. A labor union alleged that Jones & Laughlin had engaged in unfair labor practices by firing union leaders and intimidating workers to prevent union membership. The NLRB agreed that unfair labor practices had occurred, and it ordered the company to pay back wages to the fired workers and change its policies.

The company argued that what happened within its Pennsylvania manufacturing plants was beyond the federal government's reach. The Supreme Court was unwilling to view the company's activities within Pennsylvania in isolation. Its steel plants "might be likened to the heart of a self-contained, highly integrated body. They draw in the raw materials from Michigan, Minnesota, West Virginia, and Pennsylvania in part through arteries and by means controlled by the

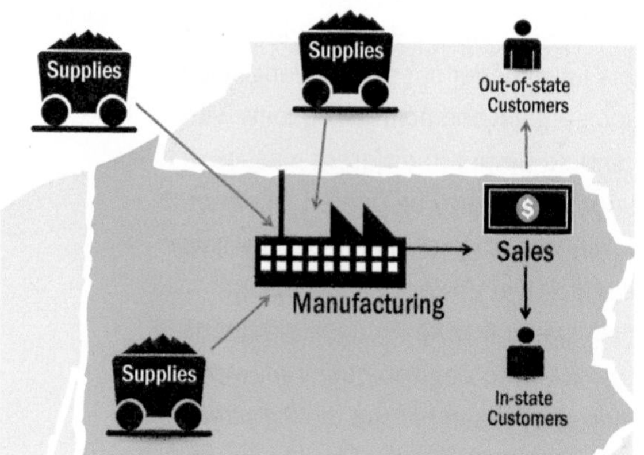

respondent; they transform the materials and then pump them out to all parts of the nation through the vast mechanism which the respondent has elaborated." The Court continued, however, to say that it did not wish to continue the old debates about which activities should be considered "directly" related to a narrow definition of "commerce among the states."

> The fundamental principle is that the power to regulate commerce is the power to enact all appropriate legislation for its protection or advancement; to adopt measures to promote its growth and insure its safety; to foster, protect, control, and restrain. That power is plenary and may be exerted to protect interstate commerce no matter what the source of the dangers which threaten it. Although activities may be intrastate in character when separately considered, if they have such a close and substantial relation to interstate commerce that their control is essential or appropriate to protect that commerce from burdens and obstructions, Congress cannot be denied the power to exercise that control. . . . Whatever amounts to more or less constant practice, and threatens to obstruct or unduly to burden the freedom of interstate commerce is within the regulatory power of Congress under the commerce clause, and it is primarily for Congress to consider and decide the fact of the danger and to meet it.

The combination of *Parrish* with *Jones & Laughlin* was immediately recognized as an enormous change in constitutional interpretation. It was also widely viewed as a victory for representative democracy. The nation's elected

Cartoon by John F. Knott (May 26, 1937)

representatives could make laws without being subjected to a veto by a small group of isolated life-tenured judges. The Court had gotten in step with the nation. Congress and the President, representing the people, wanted greater federal regulation of business, and the Court would allow them to have it.

b) Federal Regulation of Smaller Businesses: *U.S. v. Darby*

The Four Horsemen dissented in *Jones & Laughlin,* but all of them left the court through death or retirement during Roosevelt's second term. By the time Roosevelt died in office in 1945, he had appointed seven out of the nine sitting justices.

Roosevelt's imprint on the Court can be seen in *United States v. Darby*, 312 U.S. 100 (1941), which unanimously upheld the Fair Labor Standards Act of 1938. Among other things, this Act established minimum wages and maximum hours for employees "engaged in interstate commerce or in the production of goods for interstate commerce." The defendant, Fred W. Darby, operated a lumber mill in Georgia and sold the finished wood to both in-state and out-of-state customers. He was criminally prosecuted for violating the Act, but the federal trial court held the Act unconstitutional and quashed the indictment.

ITEMS TO CONSIDER WHILE READING
UNITED STATES v. DARBY:

A. *The government asserted that it wished to prevent certain goods from traveling in interstate commerce. Was this a mere pretext to conceal a motive to raise local wages? Does it matter if it was?*

B. *What allowed Congress to directly regulate the wages of factory workers in* Darby, *as opposed to merely barring the interstate transportation of finished goods?*

C. *Summarize the defendant's argument under the Tenth Amendment, and the Court's reasons for rejecting it.*

D. *Does the Act violate any of the defendant's individual rights?*

United States v. Darby,
312 U.S. 100 (1941)

Justice Stone delivered the opinion of the Court [joined by Chief Justice Hughes and Justices Roberts, Black, Reed, Frankfurter, Douglas, and Murphy].

The two principal questions raised by the record in this case are, first, whether Congress has constitutional power to prohibit the shipment in interstate commerce of lumber manufactured by employees whose wages are less than a prescribed minimum or whose weekly hours of labor at that wage are greater than a prescribed maximum, and, second, whether it has power to prohibit the employment of workmen in the production of goods "for interstate commerce" at other than prescribed wages and hours. . . .

The Fair Labor Standards Act set up a comprehensive legislative scheme for preventing the shipment in interstate commerce of certain products and commodities produced in the United States under labor conditions as respects wages and hours which fail to conform to standards set up by the Act. Its purpose, as we judicially know from the declaration of policy in § 2(a) of the Act, and the reports of Congressional committees proposing the legislation, is to exclude from interstate commerce goods produced for the commerce and to prevent their production for interstate commerce, under conditions detrimental to the maintenance of the minimum standards of living necessary for health and general well-being; and to prevent the use of interstate commerce as the means of competition in the distribution of goods so produced, and as the means of spreading and perpetuating such substandard labor conditions among the workers of the several states. . . .

The indictment charges that appellee [Fred W. Darby] is engaged, in the state of Georgia, in the business of acquiring raw materials, which he manufactures into finished lumber with the intent, when manufactured, to ship it in interstate commerce to customers outside the state, and that he does in fact so ship a large part of the lumber so produced. There are numerous counts charging appellee with the shipment in interstate commerce from Georgia to points outside the state of lumber in the production of which, for interstate commerce, appellee has employed workmen at less than the prescribed minimum wage or more than the prescribed maximum hours without payment to them of any wage for overtime. Other counts charge the employment by appellee of workmen in the production of lumber for interstate commerce at wages of less than 25 cents an hour or for more than the maximum hours per week without payment to them of the prescribed overtime wage. . . .

[*Darby*] challenged the validity of the Fair Labor Standards Act under the Commerce Clause, Art. 1, § 8, cl. 3, and the Fifth and Tenth Amendments. The district court quashed the indictment in its entirety upon the broad grounds that the Act, which it interpreted as a regulation of manufacture within the states, is unconstitutional. It declared that manufacture is not interstate commerce and that the regulation by the Fair Labor Standards Act of wages and hours of employment of those engaged in the manufacture of goods [that] may or will be . . . sold in interstate commerce . . . is not within the congressional power to regulate interstate commerce. . . .

[I]

[Validity of the ban on interstate shipment of goods manufactured under substandard labor conditions.] While manufacture is not of itself interstate commerce

United States v. Darby

the shipment of manufactured goods interstate is such commerce and the prohibition of such shipment by Congress is indubitably a regulation of the commerce. The power to regulate commerce is the power "to prescribe the rule by which commerce is to be governed." *Gibbons v. Ogden* (1824). It extends not only to those regulations which aid, foster and protect the commerce, but embraces those which prohibit it. It is conceded that the power of Congress to prohibit transportation in interstate commerce includes noxious articles, stolen articles, kidnapped persons, and articles such as intoxicating liquor or convict-made goods, traffic in which is forbidden or restricted by the laws of the state of destination.

But it is said that the present prohibition falls within the scope of none of these categories; that while the prohibition is nominally a regulation of the commerce, its motive or purpose is regulation of wages and hours of persons engaged in manufacture, the control of which has been reserved to the states and upon which Georgia and some of the states of destination have placed no restriction; that the effect of the present statute is not to exclude the prescribed articles from interstate commerce in aid of state regulation . . . but instead, under the guise of a regulation of interstate commerce, it undertakes to regulate wages and hours within the state contrary to the policy of the state which has elected to leave them unregulated. . . .

[Congressional] regulation is not a forbidden invasion of state power merely because either its motive or its consequence is to restrict the use of articles of commerce within the states of destination and is not prohibited unless by other Constitutional provisions. It is no objection to the assertion of the power to regulate interstate commerce that its exercise is attended by the same incidents which attend the exercise of the police power of the states. *U.S. v. Carolene Products Co.*, 304 U.S. 14 (1938).

The motive and purpose of the present regulation are plainly to make effective the Congressional conception of public policy that interstate commerce should not be made the instrument of competition in the distribution of goods produced under substandard labor conditions, which competition is injurious to the commerce and to the states from and to which the commerce flows. The motive and purpose of a regulation of interstate commerce are matters for the legislative judgment upon the exercise of which the Constitution places no restriction and over which the courts are given no control. . . . Whatever their motive and purpose, regulations of commerce which do not infringe some constitutional prohibition are within the plenary power conferred on Congress by the Commerce Clause. Subject only to that limitation, presently to be considered, we conclude that the prohibition of the shipment interstate of goods produced under the forbidden substandard labor conditions is within the constitutional authority of Congress.

In the more than a century which has elapsed since the decision of *Gibbons v. Ogden* (1824), these principles of constitutional interpretation have been so long and repeatedly recognized by this Court as applicable to the Commerce Clause, that there would be little occasion for repeating them now were it not for the decision of this Court twenty-two years ago in *Hammer v. Dagenhart* (1918). In that case it was held by a bare majority of the Court over the powerful and now classic dissent of Mr. Justice Holmes setting forth the fundamental issues involved, that Congress was without power to exclude the products of child labor from interstate commerce. The reasoning and conclusion of the Court's opinion there cannot be reconciled with the conclusion which we have reached, that the power of Congress under the Commerce Clause is plenary to exclude any article from interstate commerce subject only to the specific prohibitions of the Constitution. . . . The conclusion is inescapable that *Hammer v. Dagenhart* was a departure from the principles which have prevailed in the interpretation of the commerce clause both before and since the decision and that such vitality, as a precedent, as it then had has long since been exhausted. It should be and now is overruled.

Comparison of *Dagenhart* and *Darby*

Hammer v. Dagenhart (1918):
Law unconstitutional

US v. Darby (1941):
Law constitutional

[II]

Validity of the wage and hour requirements. Section 15(a)(2) and §§ 6 and 7 require employers to conform to the wage and hour provisions with respect to all employees engaged in the production of goods for interstate commerce. As appellee's employees are not alleged to be "engaged in interstate commerce" the validity of the prohibition turns on the question whether the employment, under other than the prescribed labor standards, of employees engaged in the production of goods for interstate commerce is so related to the commerce and so affects it as to be within the reach of the power of Congress to regulate it. . . .

The obvious purpose of the Act was not only to prevent the interstate transportation of the proscribed product, but to stop the initial step toward transportation, production with the purpose of so transporting it. Congress was not unaware that most manufacturing businesses shipping their product in interstate commerce make it in their shops without reference to its ultimate destination and then after manufacture select some of it for shipment interstate and some intrastate according to the daily demands of their business, and that it would be practically impossible, without disrupting manufacturing businesses, to restrict the prohibited kind of production to the particular pieces of lumber, cloth, furniture or the like which later move in interstate rather than intrastate commerce. . . .

The power of Congress over interstate commerce is not confined to the regulation of commerce among the states. It extends to those activities intrastate which so affect interstate commerce or the exercise of the power of Congress over it as to make regulation of them appropriate means to the attainment of a legitimate end, the exercise of the granted power of Congress to regulate interstate commerce. *McCulloch v. Maryland* (1819) . . . Congress, having by the present Act adopted the policy of excluding from interstate commerce all goods produced for the commerce which do not conform to the specified labor standards, it may choose the means reasonably adapted to the attainment of the permitted end, even though they involve control of intrastate activities. . . .

Our conclusion is unaffected by the Tenth Amendment which provides: "The powers not delegated to the United States by the Constitution, nor prohibited by it to the States, are reserved to the States respectively, or to the people." The amendment states but a truism that all is retained which has not been surrendered. There is nothing in the history of its adoption [See Ch. 3.D] to suggest that it was more than declaratory of the relationship between the national and state governments as it had been established by the Constitution before the amendment or that its purpose was other than to allay fears that the new national government might seek to exercise powers not granted, and that the states might not be able to exercise fully their reserved powers.

From the beginning and for many years the amendment has been construed as not depriving the national government of authority to resort to all means for the exercise of a granted power which are appropriate and plainly adapted to the permitted end. *McCulloch v. Maryland* (1819); *The Lottery Case* (1903). . . .

[III]

Validity of the wage and hour provisions under the Fifth Amendment. . . . Since our decision in *West Coast Hotel Co. v. Parrish* (1937), it is no longer open to question that the fixing of a minimum wage is within the legislative power and that the bare fact of its exercise is not a denial of due process under the Fifth more than under the Fourteenth Amendment. Nor is it any longer open to question that it is within the legislative power to fix maximum hours. Similarly the statute is not objectionable because applied alike to both men and women. . . .

c) Federal Regulation of Much Smaller Businesses: *Wickard v. Filburn*

Darby involved a business owner who sold lumber to out-of-state customers. By contrast, *Wickard v. Filburn* involved a producer who claimed that he had no plans to sell anything out of state.

Regulating Agricultural Commodities. The Depression had devastated the agricultural economy. The combination of reduced demand (no one had much money to spend, even on food) and oversupply had driven the prices of farm-produced goods to less than 40% of their previous level. Through a series of laws, Roosevelt and the New Dealers sought to control both supply and demand. On the demand side, the government committed to purchase crops at a minimum price that exceeded current market levels. On the supply side, the government would limit the amount farmers produced, by paying them to cap their production, or simply by setting a quota. In *United States v. Butler*, 297 U.S. 1 (1936), the Four Horsemen plus two allies invalidated the Agricultural Adjustment Act of 1933, but after the Supreme Court's reversals in 1937, Congress passed the similarly-structured Agricultural Adjustment Act of 1938. This statute actually went further than its predecessor, setting mandatory production quotas that would go into effect if a supermajority of farmers voted to comply.

Roscoe Filburn (1902–1987)

Roscoe Filburn's Farm. Using its authority under the new AAA, the Department of Agriculture proposed limits on production of wheat for 1941, and a nationwide referendum of wheat farmers approved the quota. According to the formula, Ohio farmer Roscoe Filburn was allowed to plant 11.1 acres. Instead, he planted 23. It was unclear from the record exactly what Filburn planned to do with the excess. He may have wanted to sell it, but if prices were low he may have been better off keeping it on the farm. There, he could have used it as livestock feed, stored it as seed for next year's crop, or ground it into flour to be eaten by his family. Filburn argued that growing wheat and consuming it on the same farm, without any wheat or money changing hands, could not be "commerce among the several states."

For its part, the Department of Agriculture did not care what Filburn did with the wheat. It sought to control the national supply of a commodity for which there was an interstate and international market. To do that, it limited the total amount of wheat that could be grown, and Filburn had gone over his allotment. As the government's brief argued, "The question is not whether Congress can regulate consumption on the farm, but whether, as a means of regulating the amount of wheat marketed and the interstate price structure, Congress has the power to control the total available supply of wheat, including that which is consumed on the farm."

ITEMS TO CONSIDER WHILE READING *WICKARD v. FILBURN*:

A. *Why can the federal government control the amount of wheat grown by a small farmer?*

B. *What effect(s) would Filburn's small amount of excess wheat have on interstate commerce if he sold it locally? If he never sold it?*

C. *Are any economic activities by definition outside of Congress's commerce power?*

D. *After* Filburn, *what can farmers do to ensure that their farms will not be subject to federal law?*

Wickard v. Filburn,

317 U.S. 111 (1942)

Justice Jackson delivered the opinion of the Court [joined by Chief Justice Stone and Justices Roberts, Black, Reed, Frankfurter, Douglas, and Murphy].

The appellee [farmer Roscoe Filburn] filed his complaint against the Secretary of Agriculture of the United States [Claude Wickard], three members of the County Agricultural Conservation Committee for Montgomery County, Ohio, and a member of the State Agricultural Conservation Committee for Ohio. He sought to enjoin enforcement against himself of the marketing penalty imposed . . . upon that part of his 1941 wheat crop which was . . . in excess of the marketing quota established for his farm. He also sought a declaratory judgment that the wheat marketing quota provisions of the Act as amended and applicable to him were unconstitutional because not sustainable under the Commerce Clause. . . .

The appellee for many years past has owned and operated a small farm in Montgomery County, Ohio, maintaining a herd of dairy cattle, selling milk, raising poultry, and selling poultry and eggs. It has been his practice to raise a small acreage of winter wheat, sown in the fall and harvested in the following July; to sell a portion of the crop; to feed part to poultry and livestock on the farm, some of which is sold;

to use some in making flour for home consumption; and to keep the rest for the following seeding. The intended disposition of the crop here involved has not been expressly stated.

In July of 1940, pursuant to the Agricultural Adjustment Act of 1938, as then amended, there were established for the appellee's 1941 crop a wheat acreage allotment of 11.1 acres. . . . He sowed, however, 23 acres, and harvested from his 11.9 acres of excess acreage 239 bushels, which under the terms of the Act . . . constituted farm marketing excess, subject to a penalty of 49 cents a bushel, or $117.11 in all. The appellee has not paid the penalty . . .

The general scheme of the Agricultural Adjustment Act of 1938 as related to wheat is to control the volume moving in interstate and foreign commerce in order to avoid surpluses and shortages and the consequent abnormally low or high wheat prices and obstructions to commerce. Within prescribed limits and by prescribed standards the Secretary of Agriculture is directed to ascertain and proclaim each year a national acreage allotment for the next crop of wheat, which is then apportioned to the states and their counties, and is eventually broken up into allotments for individual farms. Loans and payments to wheat farmers are authorized in stated circumstances. . . .

The Act provides further that whenever it appears that the total supply of wheat as of the beginning of any marketing year, beginning July 1, will exceed a normal year's domestic consumption and export by more than 35 per cent, the Secretary shall [propose a marketing quota, which will become effective only if two-thirds of the affected farmers agree to it.] . . . Pursuant to the Act, the referendum of wheat growers was held on May 31, 1941. According to the required published statement of the Secretary of Agriculture, 81 per cent of those voting favored the marketing quota, with 19 per cent opposed.

The court below held, with one judge dissenting, that the [fine against Filburn was improper.] The Secretary and his co-defendants have appealed.

I [Omitted.]

II

It is urged that under the Commerce Clause of the Constitution, Congress does not possess the power it has in this instance sought to exercise. The question would merit little consideration since our decision in *United States v. Darby* (1941), sustaining the federal power to regulate production of goods for commerce except for the fact that this Act extends federal regulation to production not intended in any part for commerce but wholly for consumption on the farm. . . . Appellee says that this is a regulation of production and consumption of wheat. Such activities are, he urges, beyond the reach of Congressional power under the Commerce Clause, since they are local in character, and their effects upon interstate commerce are at most "indirect." In answer the Government argues that the statute regulates neither production nor consumption, but only marketing; and, in the alternative, that if the Act does go beyond the regulation of marketing it is sustainable as a "necessary and proper" implementation of the power of Congress over interstate commerce.

Wickard v. Filburn

The Government's concern lest the Act be held to be a regulation of production or consumption rather than of marketing is attributable to a few dicta and decisions of this Court which might be understood to lay it down that activities such as "production," "manufacturing," and "mining" are strictly "local" and, except in special circumstances which are not present here, cannot be regulated under the commerce power because their effects upon interstate commerce are, as matter of law, only "indirect." Even today, when this power has been held to have great latitude, there is no decision of this Court that such activities may be regulated where no part of the product is intended for interstate commerce or intermingled with the subjects thereof. We believe that a review of the course of decision under the Commerce Clause will make plain, however, that questions of the power of Congress are not to be decided by reference to any formula which would give controlling force to nomenclature such as "production" and "indirect" and foreclose consideration of the actual effects of the activity in question upon interstate commerce.

At the beginning Chief Justice Marshall described the Federal commerce power with a breadth never yet exceeded. *Gibbons v. Ogden* (1824). He made emphatic the embracing and penetrating nature of this power by warning that effective restraints on its exercise must proceed from political rather than from judicial processes. . . . It was not until 1887 with the enactment of the Interstate Commerce Act that the interstate commerce power began to exert positive influence in American law and life. This first important federal resort to the commerce power was followed in 1890 by the Sherman Anti-Trust Act and, thereafter, mainly after 1903, by many others. These statutes ushered in new phases of adjudication, which required the Court to approach the interpretation of the Commerce Clause in the light of an actual exercise by Congress of its power thereunder.

When it first dealt with this new legislation, the Court . . . allowed but little scope to the power of Congress. *United States v. E. C. Knight Co.* (1895). . . . Even while important opinions in this line of restrictive authority were being written, however, other cases called forth broader interpretations of the Commerce Clause destined to supersede the earlier ones, and to bring about a return to the principles first enunciated by Chief Justice Marshall in *Gibbons v. Ogden*. . . . The Court's recognition of the relevance of the economic effects in the application of the Commerce Clause . . . has made the mechanical application of legal formulas no longer feasible. Once an economic measure of the reach of the power granted to Congress in the Commerce Clause is accepted, questions of federal power cannot be decided simply by finding the activity in question to be "production" nor can consideration of its economic effects be foreclosed by calling them "indirect." . . .

Whether the subject of the regulation in question was "production," "consumption," or "marketing" is, therefore, not material for purposes of deciding the question of federal power before us. That an activity is of local character may help in a doubtful case to determine whether Congress intended to reach it. . . . But even if appellee's activity be local and though it may not be regarded as commerce, it may still, whatever its nature, be reached by Congress if it exerts a **substantial economic effect on interstate commerce** and this irrespective of whether such effect is what might at some earlier time have been defined as "direct" or "indirect." . . .

■ OBSERVATION

SUBSTANTIAL ECONOMIC EFFECT ON INTERSTATE COMMERCE: Building upon ideas seen in earlier cases including *Darby*, the court here expresses its support for the third category of valid federal laws regulating commerce among the states. Congress may use the commerce clause to regulate cross-border transactions, in-state infrastructure facilitating cross-border transactions, and in-state conduct that that substantially affects the volume or quality of cross-border transactions.

The effect of consumption of homegrown wheat on interstate commerce is due to the fact that it constitutes the most variable factor in the disappearance of the wheat crop. Consumption on the farm where grown appears to vary in an amount greater than 20 per cent of average production. The total amount of wheat consumed as food [in commerce] varies but relatively little, and use as seed is relatively constant.

The maintenance by government regulation of a price for wheat undoubtedly can be accomplished as effectively by sustaining or increasing the demand as by limiting the supply. The effect of the statute before us is to restrict the amount which may be produced for market and the extent as well to which one may forestall resort to the market by producing to meet his own needs. That appellee's own contribution to the demand for wheat may be trivial by itself is not enough to remove him from the scope of federal regulation where, as here, his contribution, taken together with that of many others similarly situated, is far from trivial.

Aggregation of Similarly Situated Economic Actors

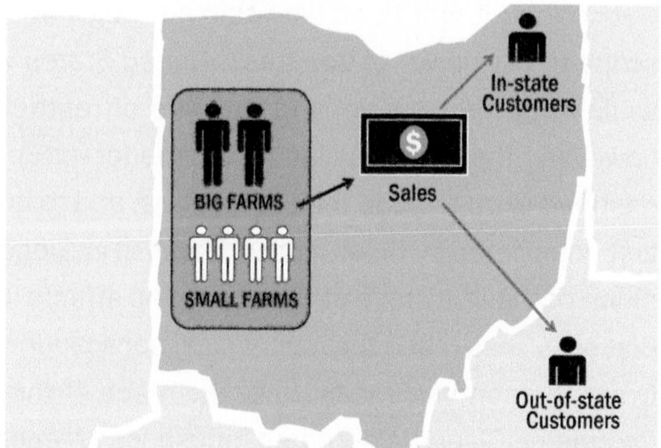

It is well established by decisions of this Court that the power to regulate commerce includes the power to regulate the prices at which commodities in that commerce are dealt in and practices affecting such prices. One of the primary purposes of the Act in question was to increase the market price of wheat and to that end to limit the volume thereof that could affect the market. It can hardly be denied that a factor of such volume and variability as home-consumed wheat would have a substantial influence on price and market conditions. This may arise because being in marketable condition such wheat overhangs the market and if induced by rising prices tends to flow into the market and check price increases. But if we assume that it is never marketed, it supplies a need of the man who grew it which would otherwise be reflected by purchases in the open market. Home-grown wheat in this sense competes with wheat in commerce. The stimulation of commerce is a use of the regulatory function quite as definitely as prohibitions or restrictions thereon. This record leaves us in no doubt that Congress may properly have considered that wheat consumed on the farm where grown if wholly outside the scheme of regulation would have a substantial effect in defeating and obstructing its purpose to stimulate trade therein at increased prices.

It is said, however, that this Act, forcing some farmers into the market to buy what they could provide for themselves, is an unfair promotion of the markets and prices of specializing wheat growers. It is of the essence of regulation that it lays a restraining hand on the self-interest of the regulated and that advantages from the regulation commonly fall to others. The conflicts of economic interest between the regulated and those who advantage by it are wisely left under our system to resolution by the Congress under its more flexible and responsible legislative process. Such conflicts rarely lend themselves to judicial determination. And with the wisdom, workability, or fairness, of the plan of regulation we have nothing to do.

III [Omitted]

3. Relaxation on the Tax Power: *Sonzinsky v. United States*

During the *Lochner* era, the Supreme Court had been suspicious of purported tax laws that sought to regulate conduct beyond the proper reach of the Commerce Clause. This principle had been applied as recently as *United States v. Butler*, 297 U.S. 1 (1936), to invalidate the first Agricultural Adjustment Act. *Butler* was full of mixed signals, however: it also stated that the Taxing Clause was independent of the commerce power, so that Congress could choose to tax goods that it could not directly regulate under the Commerce Clause.

On March 29, 1937—the same day it decided *Parrish*—the Supreme Court upheld a federal tax on gun dealers in *Sonzinsky v. United States*, 300 U.S. 506 (1937). The tax raised only about $4,000 per year, probably less than it cost to administer. Nonetheless, even this small amount represented "some revenue" for the government; in the absence of other punitive features, that was sufficient to justify it as a tax. The language of the opinion emphasized the breadth of Congressional power over taxation, and the limited role of the federal courts in supervising that power.

> In the exercise of its constitutional power to lay taxes, Congress may select the subjects of taxation, choosing some and omitting others. Its power extends

> to the imposition of [taxes] upon the doing of business. Petitioner does not deny that Congress may tax his business as a dealer in firearms. He insists that the present levy is not a true tax, but a penalty imposed for the purpose of suppressing traffic in a certain noxious type of firearms. . . . On its face [the statute] is only a taxing measure, and we are asked to say that the tax, by virtue of its deterrent effect on the activities taxed, operates as a regulation which is beyond the congressional [taxing] power.
>
> Every tax is in some measure regulatory. To some extent it interposes an economic impediment to the activity taxed as compared with others not taxed. But a tax is not any the less a tax because it has a regulatory effect, and it has long been established that an Act of Congress which on its face purports to be an exercise of the taxing power is not any the less so because the tax is burdensome or tends to restrict or suppress the thing taxed.
>
> Inquiry into the hidden motives which may move Congress to exercise a power constitutionally conferred upon it is beyond the competency of courts. They will not undertake, by collateral inquiry as to the measure of the regulatory effect of a tax, to ascribe to Congress an attempt, under the guise of taxation, to exercise another power denied by the Federal Constitution.

Sonzinsky was unanimous, reflecting the general attitude—even among the Four Horsemen—that Congress should have primary control over tax policy. Unusual features must be present before a law would be invalidated as a penalty in tax clothing.

On May 24, 1937, a majority of the Supreme Court upheld the constitutionality of the Social Security Act, one of the most important federal tax programs of the New Deal. *See Steward Machine Co. v. Davis*, 301 U.S. 548 (1937); *Helvering v. Davis*, 301 U.S. 619 (1937).

Chapter Recap

A. As government began to enact more economic reform legislation in response to the Great Depression, the Supreme Court invalidated many popular laws in 1935 and 1936 by continuing to rely on the dominant theories of the *Lochner* era: a narrow view of Congress's enumerated powers and a broad view of the freedom to contract.

B. The Supreme Court abandoned its previous interpretations in a series of decisions beginning in 1937, setting the stage for the modern approach where courts are deferential to state and federal economic regulations. Specifically:

1. *West Coast Hotel v. Parrish* (1937) rejected the idea that the Due Process Clause protected a freedom to contract.
2. *NLRB v. Jones & Laughlin Steel* (1937), *U.S. v. Darby* (1941), and *Wickard v. Filburn* (1942) established that the Commerce Clause allowed the federal government to regulate many activities that had previously been viewed as too local to implicate interstate commerce. In-state conduct with substantial economic effect on cross-border transactions was a legitimate target for federal lawmaking.
3. *U.S. v. Sonzinsky* (1937) signaled a relaxation of the Court's supervision over federal tax policy.

CHAPTER 10

Levels of Scrutiny

The battle over the constitutionality of economic regulations can be seen as a debate about the intensity of judicial review. In cases like *Lochner* and *Dagenhart*, the majority tended to scrutinize statutes very carefully. Was there a strong need for the law? Was the legislature acting for proper motives? Was the law precisely tailored to achieve its goals? Were the law's side effects acceptable? By contrast, the dissenters advocated relatively little scrutiny. It is not for the Court to decide if legislation is necessary, or well-intentioned, or well-designed, they argued: these are decisions for the political branches.

The New Deal Revolution seemed to reflect a complete triumph for a low level of judicial scrutiny of legislation. "Activist" conservative ideologues had improperly thwarted the democratic process for decades, according to this view, and the new liberal majority would ensure that the judiciary would not get in the way of the people's representatives.

A frequently-cited example of this approach to judicial review is *Williamson v. Lee Optical of Oklahoma*, 348 U.S. 483 (1955). Oklahoma statutes gave different powers to ophthalmologists (physicians who specialize in eye care), optometrists (who may administer eye exams and prescribe glasses, but not treat eye diseases), and opticians (who grind lenses and fit them into frames). The statutes did not allow opticians to do much without a prescription from an ophthalmologist or optometrist, including making new lenses to replace broken ones, or taking existing lenses and fitting them into new frames. Unhappy opticians sued for violation of constitutional rights. By treating opticians worse than optometrists and ophthalmologists, for example, it denied them equal protection of the laws. The Supreme Court unanimously disagreed, deferring to the legislature's decisions treating some professions differently than others.

> Evils in the same field may be of different dimensions and proportions, requiring different remedies. Or so the legislature may think. Or the reform may take one step at a time, addressing itself to the phase of the problem which seems most acute to the legislative mind. The legislature may select one phase of one field and apply a remedy there, neglecting the others.

The opticians also claimed the law was so irrational that it amounted to a deprivation of liberty and property without due process of law. Again, the Supreme Court unanimously disagreed.

> The Oklahoma law may exact a needless, wasteful requirement in many cases. But it is for the legislature, not the courts, to balance the advantages and disadvantages of the new requirement. . . . The law need not be in every respect logically consistent with its aims to be constitutional. It is enough that there is an evil at hand for correction, and that it might be thought that the particular legislative measure was a rational way to correct it.
>
> The day is gone when this Court uses the Due Process Clause of the Fourteenth Amendment to strike down state laws, regulatory of business and industrial conditions, because they may be unwise, improvident, or out of harmony with a particular school of thought. . . . For protection against abuses by legislatures the people must resort to the polls, not to the courts.

How far should this logic go? If *all* abuses by legislatures must be remedied through elections, then there is no more judicial review. An answer to this question began to emerge in the late 1930s and early 1940s: stronger forms of judicial review (collectively known as "heightened scrutiny") are proper in some cases, but not in others.

A. "Rational Basis" Scrutiny for Most Laws

1. The Basic Rule: *Carolene Products*

A widely admired statement as to which kinds of laws deserved more careful judicial review is found in dicta from a footnote in *United States v. Carolene Products Co.* (1938). Although the opinion became famous for its footnote, the case as a whole is worth studying as an example of the many different legal arguments that might be raised against a single statute.

The Filled Milk Act of 1923. "Filled milk" is a canned mixture of skim milk and vegetable oil that is a cheaper alternative to evaporated whole milk. Congress passed the Filled Milk Act of 1923 to restrict the product, using the following language:

> It is declared that filled milk . . . is an adulterated article of food, injurious to the public health, and its sale constitutes a fraud upon the public. It shall be unlawful for any person to manufacture within any Territory or possession, or within the District of Columbia, or to ship or deliver for shipment in interstate or foreign commerce, any filled milk.

In the legislative history, the Act's sponsors claimed that filled milk was unhealthy because it lacked important nutrients present in whole milk. Filled milk makers argued that the product was every bit as healthy as other products that substituted vegetable oil for milk fat but were not banned (like margarine). The law was not justified by health concerns, they argued, but was special interest legislation enacted as a favor to the politically influential dairy industry.

The statute arrived in the Supreme Court after the Carolene Products Co. of Litchfield, Illinois was prosecuted for selling filled milk across state lines. As framed by the Supreme Court, the central question was how much a federal court must defer to Congress's judgment. Should it hold a trial to determine whether the ban on filled milk was justified? Or should it take Congress's word for it?

ITEMS TO CONSIDER WHILE READING *CAROLENE PRODUCTS*:

THE OPINION

A. *The section titled "First" involves the Commerce Clause. Why does the Act fall within Congress's commerce power?*

B. *The section titled "Second" focuses on a* Lochner*-style due process objection. Why did the statute not violate the Due Process Clause under a* Lochner*-era approach? And under a post-1937 approach?*

C. *The section titled "Second" also briefly resolves a challenge under the Equal Protection Clause. How did the Act allegedly treat people unequally? Why did the equal protection argument fail?*

D. *The section titled "Third" addresses the defendant's objections to the Act's legislative findings that filled milk is adulterated, unsafe, and fraudulent. The defendant wanted a trial on the sufficiency of the findings, so that the jury could acquit if it considered the statute to be unsound. The Court has two basic responses. (1) The findings are irrelevant at trial, because they are not elements of the offense. (2) The findings were correct—or at least correct enough. Focus on the second response. What evidence does a court need to conclude that Congress's factual assumptions are correct?*

E. *Should the result be different if the defendant could prove that Congress never held any hearings or gathered any evidence about whether filled milk was* *bad for human health? That there was no legislative history of any sort? That Congress banned filled milk solely as a political favor to the dairy industry? Or that Congress had been bribed?*

FOOTNOTE 4

F. *When might the presumption of constitutionality not apply? Why not?*

G. *Are there other types of laws, not mentioned in the footnote, whose constitutionality should not be presumed?*

United States v. Carolene Products Co.,

304 U.S. 144 (1938)

Justice Stone delivered the opinion of the Court [joined by Chief Justice Hughes and Justices Brandeis and Roberts].

The question for decision is whether the Filled Milk Act of Congress of March 4, 1923, which prohibits the shipment in interstate commerce of skimmed milk compounded with any fat or oil other than milk fat, so as to resemble milk or cream, transcends the power of Congress to regulate interstate commerce or infringes the Fifth Amendment.

Back cover of "60 New Recipes for Milnut" (1939)

Appellee [Carolene Products Co.] was indicted in the District Court for Southern Illinois for violation of the act by the shipment in interstate commerce of certain packages of "Milnut," a compound of condensed skimmed milk and coconut oil made in imitation or semblance of condensed milk or cream. The indictment states, in the words of the statute, that Milnut "is an adulterated article of food, injurious to the public health[.]" [The trial court granted Defendant's motion to dismiss the indictment, and the Supreme Court granted review.]

[COMMERCE POWER]

First. [Appellee assails the statute as beyond the power of Congress over interstate commerce, and hence an invasion of a field of action said to be reserved to the states by the Tenth Amendment.] The power to regulate commerce . . .

extends to the prohibition of shipments in such commerce. The power "is complete in itself, may be exercised to its utmost extent, and acknowledges no limitations, other than are prescribed in the Constitution." *Gibbons v. Ogden* (1824). Hence Congress is free to exclude from interstate commerce articles whose use in the states for which they are destined it may reasonably conceive to be injurious. . . . Such regulation is not a forbidden invasion of state power either because its motive or its consequence is to restrict the use of articles of commerce within the states of destination, and is not prohibited unless by [a constitutional provision limiting Congressional action, such as the Bill of Rights]. And it is no objection to the exertion of the power to regulate interstate commerce that its exercise is attended by the same incidents which attend the exercise of the police power of the states. The prohibition of the shipment of filled milk in interstate commerce is a permissible regulation of commerce, subject only to the restrictions of the [Bill of Rights].

[DUE PROCESS]

Second. [Appellee also complains that the statute deprives it of its property without due process of law.] The prohibition of shipment of appellee's product in interstate commerce does not infringe the Fifth Amendment. Twenty years ago this Court, in *Hebe Co. v. Shaw,* 248 U.S. 297 (1919), held that a state law which forbids the manufacture and sale of a product . . . made of condensed skimmed milk compounded with coconut oil, is not forbidden by the Fourteenth Amendment. The power of the Legislature to secure a minimum of particular nutritive elements in a widely used article of food and to protect the public from fraudulent substitutions, was not doubted; and the Court thought that there was ample scope for the legislative judgment that prohibition of the offending article was an appropriate means of preventing injury to the public.

We see no persuasive reason for departing from that ruling here, where the Fifth Amendment is concerned; and since none is suggested, we might rest decision wholly on the presumption of constitutionality. But affirmative evidence also sustains the statute. In twenty years evidence has steadily accumulated of the danger to the public health from the general consumption of foods which have been stripped of elements essential to the maintenance of health. The Filled Milk Act was adopted by Congress after committee hearings, in the course of which eminent scientists and health experts testified. An extensive investigation was made of the commerce in milk compounds in which vegetable oils have been substituted for natural milk fat, and of the effect upon the public health of the use of such compounds as a food substitute for milk. The conclusions drawn from evidence presented at the hearings were embodied in reports of the House Committee on Agriculture and the Senate Committee on Agriculture and Forestry. Both committees concluded, as the statute itself declares, that the use of filled milk as a substitute for pure milk is generally injurious to health and facilitates fraud on the public.

There is nothing in the Constitution which compels a Legislature, either national or state, to ignore such evidence, nor need it disregard the other evidence which amply supports the conclusions of the Congressional committees that the danger is greatly enhanced where an inferior product, like appellee's, is indistinguishable from a valuable food of almost universal use, thus making fraudulent distribution easy and protection of the consumer difficult. . . .

[EQUAL PROTECTION]

[Appellee also complains that the statute denies to it equal protection of the laws.] Appellee raises no valid objection to the present statute by arguing that its prohibition has not been extended to oleomargarine or other butter substitutes in which vegetable fats or oils are substituted for butter fat. The . . . equal protection clause . . . does not compel . . . Legislatures to prohibit all like evils, or none. A Legislature may hit at an abuse which it has found, even though it has failed to strike at another.

[JUDICIAL REVIEW OF LEGISLATIVE JUDGMENT]

Third. [Appellee also objects that the statute purports to make binding and conclusive upon appellee the legislative declaration that appellee's product "is an adulterated article of food, injurious to the public health, and its sale constitutes a fraud on the public."] We may assume for present purposes that no pronouncement of a Legislature can forestall attack upon the constitutionality of the prohibition which it enacts by applying opprobrious epithets to the prohibited act, and that a statute would deny due process which precluded the disproof in judicial proceedings of all facts which would show or tend to show that a statute depriving the suitor of life, liberty, or property had a rational basis.

But such we think is not the purpose or construction of the statutory characterization of filled milk as injurious to health and as a fraud upon the public. There is no need to consider it here as more than a declaration of the legislative findings deemed to support and justify the action taken as a constitutional exertion of the legislative power, aiding informed judicial review, as do the reports of legislative committees, by revealing the rationale of the legislation. Even in the absence of such aids, the existence of facts supporting the legislative judgment is to be presumed, for regulatory legislation affecting ordinary commercial transactions is not to be pronounced unconstitutional unless in the light of the facts made known or generally assumed it is of such a character as to preclude the assumption that it rests upon some rational basis within the knowledge and experience of the legislators.[FN4] The present statutory findings affect appellee no more than the reports of the Congressional committees and since in the absence of the statutory findings they would be presumed, their incorporation in the statute is no more prejudicial than surplusage.

FN4 There may be narrower scope for operation of the presumption of constitutionality when legislation appears on its face to be within a specific prohibition of the Constitution, such as those of the first ten Amendments, which are deemed equally specific when held to be embraced within the Fourteenth.

It is unnecessary to consider now whether legislation which restricts those political processes which can ordinarily be expected to bring about repeal of undesirable legislation, is to be subjected to more exacting judicial scrutiny under the general prohibitions of the Fourteenth Amendment than are most other types of legislation. [As examples, see earlier cases turning] on restrictions upon the right to vote; on restraints upon the dissemination of information; on interferences with political organizations; [or on] prohibition of peaceable assembly.

Nor need we enquire whether similar considerations enter into the review of statutes directed at particular religious, *Pierce v. Society of Sisters* (1925), or national, *Meyer v. Nebraska* (1923), or racial minorities; whether prejudice against discrete and insular minorities may be a special condition, which tends seriously to curtail the operation of those political processes ordinarily to be relied upon to protect minorities, and which may call for a correspondingly more searching judicial inquiry.

Where the existence of a rational basis for legislation whose constitutionality is attacked depends upon facts beyond the sphere of judicial notice, such facts may properly be made the subject of judicial inquiry, and the constitutionality of a statute predicated upon the existence of a particular state of facts may be challenged by showing to the court that those facts have ceased to exist. . . . But by their very nature such inquiries, where the legislative judgment is drawn in question, must be restricted to the issue whether any state of facts either known or which could reasonably be assumed affords support for it. Here the demurrer challenges the validity of the statute on its face and it is evident from all the considerations presented to Congress, and those of which we may take judicial notice, that the question is at least debatable whether commerce in filled milk should be left unregulated, or in some measure restricted, or wholly prohibited. As that decision was for Congress, neither the finding of a court arrived at by weighing the evidence, nor the verdict of a jury can be substituted for it.

The prohibition of shipment in interstate commerce of appellee's product, as described in the indictment, is a constitutional exercise of the power to regulate interstate commerce. As the statute is not unconstitutional on its face, the demurrer should have been overruled and the judgment will be reversed.

Justice Cardozo and Justice Reed took no part in the consideration or decision of this case.

Justice Black concurs in the result and in all of the opinion except the part marked "Third."

Justice Butler [concurring]. [Omitted]

Justice McReynolds thinks that the judgment should be affirmed [but wrote no opinion].

flash*forward*

1. ***Rational Basis Review.*** The opinion in *Carolene Products* is one of the leading statements of the level of scrutiny that later became known as "rational basis review." The standard is "a paradigm of judicial restraint" that presumes laws to be constitutional unless proven otherwise, and requires only "plausible" (not impeccable) reasons for legislative actions. *F.C.C. v. Beach Communications, Inc.*, 508 U.S. 307 (1993). To be rational, a law needs a rationale—some justification that is not irrational. Many cases use the term "reasonable" as a synonym for "rational." When used in this way, a reasonable law is one justified by a reason, i.e., is not irrational or, as it is sometimes said, arbitrary. Overall, the reasons supporting a law do not have to be extraordinarily persuasive; they just need to be not crazy or evil.

2. ***The Famous Footnote.*** Footnote 4 proposes in dicta some possible exceptions to the general rule of rational basis review. Some laws, the footnote suggested, would be presumed unconstitutional and the government would have the burden of satisfying some sort of heightened scrutiny. Footnote 4 is not an exclusive or legally binding list; the Supreme Court has applied heightened scrutiny to some laws that do not seem to fall within its categories. Nonetheless, the footnote has been influential on a more abstract level, by indicating that heightened scrutiny is proper for some kinds of cases; and by identifying a set of paradigm cases where heightened scrutiny would be proper.

Professor John Hart Ely, in his influential book *Democracy and Distrust: A Theory of Judicial Review* (1981), proposed an explanation for the examples chosen for Footnote 4. Ely argued that heightened scrutiny is proper for laws that are alleged to interfere with the proper functioning of the democratic process. The people of a republic should accept the decisions of elected legislators—even the bad decisions—when the law-making process is capable of replacing bad decisions with good ones. Such a system would allow the public to communicate its preferences to the legislature and, if necessary, to vote the rascals out and replace them with legislators who will pass better laws. Because the democratic process has the ability to correct its errors, the proper role for a judge reviewing legislation is to ensure that the law-making process functions properly. Judges should not impose their own policy preferences, but they should engage in **representation reinforcement**, i.e., decisions that will help representative democracy operate properly. For Ely, this concept explains why *Carolene Products* identified "legislation which restricts . . . political processes" as a suitable target for heightened scrutiny. If a law leads to unequal voting rights, or inhibits free speech on political topics, the political process cannot be trusted. The theory also explains why heightened scrutiny is proper for laws that discriminate against "particular religious, or national, or racial minorities." When "prejudice against discrete and insular minorities" exists, adequate representation of minority interests cannot develop and a biased political process will be unable to correct its errors.

■ OBSERVATION

REPRESENTATION REINFORCEMENT: *McCulloch v. Maryland* contained an early version of the idea that courts should step in when the ordinary machinery of democratic representation will be unable to correct errors. For Justice Marshall, the Maryland law imposing taxes on the Bank of the United States involved a fatal problem of representation. The Maryland tax hampered a federal law that had been enacted by the representatives of all citizens of the United States. Yet the affected citizens would not be in a position to fix the problem, because most of them had no electoral voice within Maryland.

3. *The Battle over Filled Milk—Part II*. After the loss in the Supreme Court, the owner of Carolene Products Co., Charlie Hauser, added cod liver oil to the product. He claimed that this took the product outside the statutory definition of "filled milk" and remedied the alleged vitamin deficiency that led Congress to ban filled milk in the first place. He sold the new formula across state lines for several more years.

When he was prosecuted a second time, the Supreme Court rejected Hauser's argument that the new formula did not fit the statutory definition of filled milk. *Carolene Products Co. v. United States* (*Carolene Products II*), 323 U.S. 18 (1944). Hauser did not serve his one-year sentence, however, because President Roosevelt pardoned him in January 1945.

2. Equality and Freedom Under Rational Basis: *Railway Express Agency*

Railway Express Agency, Inc. v. New York, 336 U.S. 106 (1949), is an often-cited example of the rational basis approach in action. The challenged law was undoubtedly imperfect, but the Supreme Court insisted that for ordinary business regulations the Constitution did not require perfection.

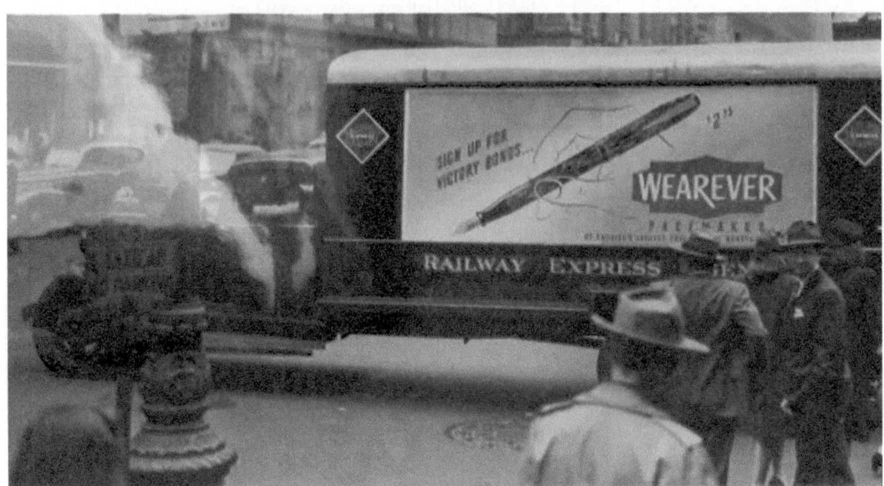

Railway Express Agency truck with advertisement for Wearever Pens, early 1940s

The Railway Express Agency (REA), which existed from 1917 to 1975, was a nationwide package delivery service, similar to today's UPS and FedEx. Once packages were delivered to a rail depot, the company's green trucks with a red diamond logo would deliver the packages to their local destinations. Since the early 1930s, the company had earned additional income by selling billboard space on the sides of the trucks. After WWII, the City of New York began to enforce a local regulation forbidding truck-mounted advertising for anything other than the business that owned the truck. This meant REA trucks could show the company's red diamond logo or a billboard encouraging people to use REA for delivery, but not signs for any other company's products or services. The City's stated justification for the law was that a proliferation of mobile advertising was a distraction to drivers and thus a traffic hazard. There was no hard evidence that truck advertising caused accidents; the law may well have been adopted for aesthetic purposes.

A divided New York court of appeals upheld the law, but some judges dissented, saying that forbidding "these unobjectionable advertisements on defendants' trucks is so entirely unrelated to traffic control as to be arbitrary as matter of law," i.e., a forbidden deprivation of liberty without due process of law. Justice Douglas's opinion for a unanimous US Supreme Court rejected the Due Process Clause argument, adopting the logic of *Carolene Products*:

> We do not sit to weigh evidence on the due process issue in order to determine whether the regulation is sound or appropriate; nor is it our function to pass judgment on its wisdom. We would be trespassing on one of the most intensely local and specialized of all municipal problems if we held that this regulation had no relation to the traffic problem of New York City. It is the judgment of the local authorities that it does have such a relation. And nothing has been advanced which shows that to be palpably false.

REA also argued under the Equal Protection Clause that the law unreasonably distinguished between similarly situated businesses. If advertisements on trucks were a traffic hazard because they distract drivers, this should be true even for a company advertising its own products on its own trucks. The majority rejected this argument, again deferring to lawmakers' choices.

> The local authorities may well have concluded that those who advertised their own wares on their trucks do not present the same traffic problem in view of the nature or extent of the advertising which they use. It would take a degree of omniscience which we lack to say that such is not the case. If that judgment is correct, the advertising displays that are exempt have less incidence on traffic than those of appellants.
>
> We cannot say that that judgment is not an allowable one. [The regulation] does not contain the kind of discrimination against which the Equal Protection Clause affords protection. . . . And the fact that New York City sees fit to eliminate from traffic this kind of distraction but does not touch what may be even greater ones in a different category, such as the vivid displays on Times Square, is immaterial. It is no requirement of equal protection that all evils of the same genus be eradicated or none at all.

Justice Jackson concurred in a thoughtful opinion that emphasized potential differences between freedom arguments under the Due Process Clause and equality arguments under the Equal Protection Clause.

> The burden should rest heavily upon one who would persuade us to use the due process clause to strike down a substantive law or ordinance. Even its provident use against municipal regulations frequently disables all government—state, municipal and federal—from dealing with the conduct in question because the requirement of due process is also applicable to State and Federal Governments. Invalidation of a statute or an ordinance on due process grounds leaves ungoverned and ungovernable conduct which many people find objectionable.

> Invocation of the equal protection clause, on the other hand, does not disable any governmental body from dealing with the subject at hand. It merely means that the prohibition or regulation must have a broader impact. I regard it as a salutary doctrine that cities, states and the Federal Government must exercise their powers so as not to discriminate between their inhabitants except upon some reasonable differentiation fairly related to the object of regulation. This equality is not merely abstract justice. The framers of the Constitution knew, and we should not forget today, that there is no more effective practical guaranty against arbitrary and unreasonable government than to require that the principles of law which officials would impose upon a minority must be imposed generally. Conversely, nothing opens the door to arbitrary action so effectively as to allow those officials to pick and choose only a few to whom they will apply legislation and thus to escape the political retribution that might be visited upon them if larger numbers were affected. Courts can take no better measure to assure that laws will be just than to require that laws be equal in operation. . . . Hence, for my part, I am more receptive to attack on local ordinances for denial of equal protection than for denial of due process[.]

Taxes provide a good example for Justice Jackson's theory that in practice, equal laws tend to be less onerous. A legislature that has discretion to impose a tax only on a disfavored and poorly-represented minority is likely to set the rate high; after all, it will not affect the legislators or their friends and donors. But if the tax must be applied equally to all people, legislators will be personally affected and they will hear complaints from more people. As a result, they will likely choose a lower tax rate than they would if the tax were solely imposed on an under-represented few.

Significantly, Justice Jackson did not advocate that equal protection challenges to economic regulations should involve heightened scrutiny. He agreed with the majority that New York's truck advertising law only had to be rational, not perfect.

flashforward

Business Regulations and Constitutional Rights. *Railway Express Agency* fits into a long line of cases where business owners raised various combinations of Due Process Clause and Equal Protection Clause objections to laws that treated some businesses differently than others. Its predecessors include *The Slaughterhouse Cases* (1872) (licensed v. unlicensed butchers) (Ch. 7.C.1.a) and *Carolene Products* (1938) (Ch. 10.A.1) (filled milk v. margarine). Its successors include *Williamson v. Lee Optical* (1955) (opticians v. ophthalmologists and optometrists); *Ferguson v. Skrupa*, 372 U.S. 726 (1963) (attorneys v. non-attorney debt adjusters); *City of New Orleans v. Dukes* (1976) (Ch. 17.C.1) (new v. old businesses in historic district); *City of Dallas v. Stanglin* (1989) (Ch. 17.C.2) (dance halls v. skating rinks); and *F.C.C. v. Beach Communications, Inc.*, 508 U.S. 307 (1993) (cable TV service for separately owned buildings v. jointly owned buildings).

B. Heightened Scrutiny Under the Equal Protection Clause

1. Unequal Distribution of Fundamental Rights: *Skinner v. Oklahoma*

Carolene Products cemented the idea that ordinary business regulations should be upheld unless they lacked a rational basis. But in the early 1940s the Supreme Court considered some cases where such deference seemed out of place. Footnote 4 to *Carolene Products* suggested that laws restricting genuinely important individual rights ought to require a reason that is more than merely better than crazy; in that setting, the government might need strong reasons to limit rights. In particular, the laws would need to further important government purposes and use means that further those purposes without imposing unacceptable side effects.

Skinner v. Oklahoma (1942) was one of the first such decisions. *Skinner* involved another iteration of the debate over eugenic sterilization, seen previously in *Buck v. Bell* (1927) [Ch. 8.C.2.d]. Oklahoma enacted a statute imposing involuntary sterilization as a punishment for certain repeat felons, on the theory that a predisposition toward "criminality" was an inheritable trait that should be removed from the gene pool. The opinion in *Skinner* points toward the modern rule that different types of inequality should receive different levels of judicial scrutiny. See Ch. 18.

ITEMS TO CONSIDER WHILE READING *SKINNER*:

A. *Why does the majority opinion decide the case under the Equal Protection Clause?*

B. *Does* Skinner *overrule* Buck v. Bell*?*

C. *Justice Douglas writes: "When the law lays an unequal hand on those who have committed intrinsically the same quality of offense and sterilizes one and not the other, it has made as invidious a discrimination as if it had selected a particular race or nationality for oppressive treatment." What makes the two discriminations similar to each other?*

D. *Justice Douglas wrote the opinions in both* Skinner *and* Williamson. *In* Williamson, *the state of Oklahoma was allowed to treat opticians differently from optometrists; but in* Skinner, *the state was not allowed to treat chicken thieves differently from embezzlers. Are these results consistent with each other?*

Skinner v. Oklahoma,

316 U.S. 535 (1942)

Justice Douglas delivered the opinion of the Court [joined by Justices Roberts, Black, Reed, Frankfurter, Murphy, Byrnes, and Jackson].

This case touches a sensitive and important area of human rights. Oklahoma deprives certain individuals of a right which is basic to the perpetuation of a race—the right to have offspring. Oklahoma has decreed the enforcement of its law against petitioner, overruling his claim that it violated the Fourteenth Amendment. Because that decision raised grave and substantial constitutional questions, we granted the petition for certiorari.

The statute involved is Oklahoma's Habitual Criminal Sterilization Act. That Act defines an "habitual criminal" as a person who, having been convicted two or more times for crimes "amounting to felonies involving **moral turpitude**" either in an Oklahoma court or in a court of any other State, is thereafter convicted of such a felony in Oklahoma and is sentenced to a term of imprisonment in an Oklahoma penal institution. Machinery is provided for the institution by the Attorney General of a proceeding against such a person in the Oklahoma courts for a

TERMINOLOGY

MORAL TURPITUDE: "Crime of moral turpitude" is a term of art whose meaning varies across different jurisdictions and different statutes. As a general matter, the phrase means "crimes that are especially reprehensible," with the precise list sorted out on a case-by-case basis. Most jurisdictions agree that crimes of dishonesty (like fraud) and sex crimes are crimes of moral turpitude.

Skinner v. Oklahoma

judgment that such person shall be rendered sexually sterile. Notice, an opportunity to be heard, and the right to a jury trial are provided. The issues triable in such a proceeding are narrow and confined. If the court or jury finds that the defendant is an "habitual criminal" and that he "may be rendered sexually sterile without detriment to his or her general health," then the court "shall render judgment to the effect that said defendant be rendered sexually sterile" by the operation of vasectomy in case of a male and of salpingectomy [tubal ligation] in case of a female. Only one other provision of the Act is material here and that is § 195 which provides that "offenses arising out of the violation of the prohibitory laws [alcohol prohibition], revenue acts, embezzlement, or political offenses, shall not come or be considered within the terms of this Act."

Petitioner [Jack T. Skinner] was convicted in 1926 of the crime of stealing chickens and was sentenced to the Oklahoma State Reformatory. In 1929 he was convicted of the crime of robbery with fire arms and was sentenced to the reformatory. In 1934 he was convicted again of robbery with firearms and was sentenced to the penitentiary. He was confined there in 1935 when the Act was passed. In 1936 the Attorney General instituted proceedings against him. Petitioner in his answer challenged the Act as unconstitutional by reason of the Fourteenth Amendment. A jury trial was had. The court instructed the jury that the crimes of which petitioner had been convicted were felonies involving moral turpitude and that the only question for the jury was whether the operation of vasectomy could be performed on petitioner without detriment to his general health. The jury found that it could be. A judgment directing that the operation of vasectomy be performed on petitioner was affirmed by the Supreme Court of Oklahoma by a five to four decision.

Several objections to the constitutionality of the Act have been pressed upon us. It is urged that the Act cannot be sustained as an exercise of the police power in view of the state of scientific authorities respecting inheritability of criminal traits. It is argued that due process is lacking because under this Act, unlike the act upheld in *Buck v. Bell* (1927), the defendant is given no opportunity to be heard on the issue as to whether he is the probable potential parent of socially undesirable offspring. It is also suggested that the Act is penal in character and that the sterilization provided for is cruel and unusual punishment and violative of the Fourteenth Amendment. We pass those points without intimating an opinion on them, for there is a feature of the Act which clearly condemns it. That is its failure to meet the requirements of the equal protection clause of the Fourteenth Amendment.

We do not stop to point out all of the inequalities in this Act. A few examples will suffice. In Oklahoma grand larceny is a felony. Larceny is grand larceny when the property taken exceeds $20 in value. Embezzlement is punishable "in the manner prescribed for feloniously stealing property of the value of that embezzled." Hence he who embezzles property worth more than $20 is guilty of a felony. A clerk who appropriates over $20 from his employer's till and a stranger who steals the same amount are thus both guilty of felonies. If the latter repeats his act and is convicted three times, he may be sterilized. But the clerk is not subject to the pains and penalties of the Act no matter how large his embezzlements nor how frequent his convictions. A person who enters a chicken coop and steals chickens commits a felony and he may be sterilized if he is thrice convicted. If, however, he is a bailee of the property and fraudulently appropriates it, he is an embezzler. Hence no matter how habitual his proclivities for embezzlement are and no matter how often his conviction, he may not be sterilized. . . .

It was stated in *Buck v. Bell* that the claim that state legislation violates the equal protection clause of the Fourteenth Amendment is "the usual last resort of constitutional arguments." Under our constitutional system the States in determining the reach and scope of particular legislation need not provide abstract symmetry. They may mark and set apart the classes and types of problems according to the needs and as dictated or suggested by experience. . . . The Constitution does not require things which are different in fact or opinion to be treated in law as though they were the same. Thus, if we had here only a question as to a State's classification of crimes, such as embezzlement or larceny, no substantial federal question would be raised. For a State is not constrained in the exercise of its police power to ignore experience which marks a class of offenders or a family of offenses for special treatment. Nor is it prevented by the equal protection clause from confining its restrictions to those classes of cases where the need is deemed to be clearest. As stated in *Buck v. Bell*, "the law does all that is needed when it does all that it can, indicates a policy, applies it to all within the lines, and seeks to bring within the lines all similarly situated so far and so fast as its means allow."

But the instant legislation runs afoul of the equal protection clause, though we give Oklahoma that large deference which the rule of the foregoing cases requires. We are dealing here with legislation which involves one of the basic civil rights of man. Marriage and procreation are **fundamental** to the very existence and survival of the race. The power to sterilize, if exercised, may have subtle, far reaching and devastating effects. In evil or reckless hands it can cause races or types which are inimical to the dominant group to wither and disappear. There is no redemption for the individual whom the law touches. Any experiment which the State conducts is to his irreparable injury. He is forever deprived of a basic liberty.

> ■ TERMINOLOGY
>
> **FUNDAMENTAL:** *Skinner* was an early case to use the term "fundamental" to identify unenumerated rights protected through some form of heightened scrutiny. Although they did not use the term, *Lochner* and *Parrish* could be said to disagree over whether freedom of contract was a fundamental right.

We mention these matters not to reexamine the scope of the police power of the States. We advert to them merely in emphasis of our view that **strict scrutiny** of the classification which a State makes in a sterilization law is essential, lest unwittingly or otherwise invidious discriminations are made against groups or types of individuals in violation of the constitutional guaranty of just and equal laws. The guaranty of "equal protection of the laws is a pledge of the protection of equal laws." *Yick Wo v. Hopkins* (1886). When the law lays an unequal hand on those who have committed intrinsically the same quality of offense and sterilizes one and not the other, it has made as an invidious a discrimination as if it had selected a particular race or nationality for oppressive treatment. Sterilization of those who have thrice committed grand larceny with immunity for those who are embezzlers is a clear, pointed, unmistakable discrimination. Oklahoma makes no attempt to say that he who commits larceny by trespass or trick or fraud has biologically inheritable traits which he who commits embezzlement lacks.... We have not the slightest basis for inferring that that line [between the offenses] has any significance in eugenics nor that the inheritability of criminal traits follows the neat legal distinctions which the law has marked between those two offenses. In terms of fines and imprisonment the crimes of larceny and embezzlement rate the same under the Oklahoma code. Only when it comes to sterilization are the pains and penalties of the law different. The equal protection clause would indeed be a formula of empty words if such conspicuously artificial lines could be drawn. In *Buck v. Bell,* the Virginia statute was upheld though it applied only to feebleminded persons in institutions of the State. But it was pointed out that "so far as the operations enable those who otherwise must be kept confined to be returned to the world, and thus open the asylum to others, the equality aimed at will be more nearly reached." Here there is no such saving feature. Embezzlers are forever free. Those who steal or take in other ways are not. If such a classification were permitted, the technical common law concept of a "trespass" based on distinctions which are very largely dependent upon history for explanation could readily become a rule of human genetics....

Skinner v. Oklahoma

■ TERMINOLOGY

STRICT SCRUTINY: *Skinner* is the first Supreme Court case to use the term "strict scrutiny." In later decades, the term acquired a more technical meaning, but at its inception it simply connoted heightened scrutiny—something other than the rational basis review of *Carolene Products.*

Chief Justice Stone, concurring.

I concur in the result, but I am not persuaded that we are aided in reaching it by recourse to the equal protection clause.... [I would resolve the case as a matter of due process.] Although petitioner here was given a hearing to ascertain whether sterilization would be detrimental to his health, he was given none to discover whether his criminal tendencies are of an inheritable type. Undoubtedly a state may, after appropriate inquiry, constitutionally interfere with the personal liberty of the individual to prevent the transmission by inheritance of his socially injurious tendencies. *Buck v. Bell.* But until now we have not been called upon to say that it may do so without giving him a hearing and opportunity to challenge the existence as to him of the only facts which could justify so drastic a measure....

Justice Jackson, concurring.

I join the Chief Justice in holding that the hearings provided are too limited in the context of the present Act to afford due process of law. I also agree with the opinion of Mr. Justice Douglas that the scheme of classification set forth in the Act denies equal protection of the law. I disagree with the opinion of each in so far as it rejects or minimizes the grounds taken by the other. . . .

flash*forward*

1. *Oklahoma Legislation After* Skinner. The Supreme Court's decision in *Skinner* gave the state legislature some options. It could choose to eugenically sterilize people convicted of certain crimes, if it could show (as it did not in *Skinner*) that those people were chosen on the basis of reasons that could withstand strict scrutiny. Or it could choose to sterilize all people convicted of crimes. The latter choice would affect far more families, and also the bootleggers, tax evaders, and embezzlers exempted from the statute in *Skinner.* As it happened, the legislature did not attempt to enact any further legislation on the subject. This makes *Skinner* a good example of Justice Jackson's observation in *Railway Express Agency* that "there is no more effective practical guaranty against arbitrary and unreasonable government than to require that the principles of law which officials would impose a minority must be imposed generally."

2. *Eugenic Sterilization After* Skinner *and* Buck. Although *Skinner* limited the use of eugenic sterilization as part of the criminal justice system, some states continued to sterilize institutionalized people considered mentally unfit to procreate. The practice finally died out as a result of political and social decisions, not legal ones. North Carolina, whose eugenics program lasted the longest, issued a formal apology in 2002, and authorized restitution payments to survivors in 2012. However, most states still allow for involuntary sterilization of incompetent persons on a case-by-case basis. These sterilizations are not based on eugenics, but require a finding that the procedure will be in the incompetent person's best interests.

2. Racially Discriminatory Laws: The Japanese Internment Cases

Under the emerging notion that different kinds of laws might receive different kinds of scrutiny, race discrimination would seem to be a natural candidate for heightened scrutiny. This approach might explain why *Strauder v. West Virginia* (1879) said that a state could not bar African-Americans from juries, but it could "confine the selection to males, to freeholders, to citizens, to persons within certain ages, or to persons having educational qualifications." To use modern terminology, *Strauder* implied that laws involving race would get heightened scrutiny, but laws involving the other listed characteristics would not.

The Court's first major opportunity to consider race discrimination after the New Deal Revolution involved the laws interning the Japanese during World War II. The cases are significant for many reasons, but pay special attention to their treatment of levels of scrutiny: which type of scrutiny does the Court use? And once the level of scrutiny is chosen, how is the case decided?

The Internment Orders. Art. I, § 8, cl. 4 gives the federal government power over immigration and naturalization. The first immigration statute in 1790 made naturalization an option only for "free white persons." Notwithstanding significant immigration of East Asians in the 19th and early 20th centuries, the naturalization laws had not been amended to include Asians. *Ozawa v. United States*, 260 U.S. 178 (1922) held that then-existing immigration statutes did not allow immigrants born in Japan to ever become naturalized US citizens, even though they were lawfully allowed to reside here. Under § 1 of the Fourteenth Amendment, however, their US-born children were US citizens.

On December 7, 1941, the government of Japan attacked the US military installations at Pearl Harbor. The US declared war against Japan the next day; war against Japan's allies Germany and Italy quickly followed. On February 19, 1942, President Roosevelt issued Executive Order 9066, which authorized the military to designate areas within the United States "from which any or all persons may be excluded" or otherwise restricted. On March 21, Congress made it a crime to disobey any military order issued pursuant to Executive Order 9066.

General John L. DeWitt, the military commander in charge of the west coast of the United States, used his authority under the Executive Order to issue a series of commands to the civilian population. His first order, on March 24, imposed a nighttime curfew applicable to "all alien Germans, all alien Italians, and all persons of Japanese ancestry." The latter category—persons of Japanese ancestry—applied both to lawful resident aliens and their native-born US citizen children and grandchildren.

The curfew order was followed on May 3 by orders directing that "all persons of Japanese ancestry, both alien and non-alien" were "excluded" from designated areas, which included all coastal areas and major cities on the west coast. Excluded persons were required to report to suburban "assembly centers," from which most were sent to rural "relocation camps" like Manzanar and Tule Lake in California, Gila River in Arizona, and Minidoka in Idaho.

a) Curfew Decisions from 1943: *Hirabayashi* and *Yasui*

Two native-born US citizens of Japanese ancestry were convicted of violating the curfew: Gordon Hirabayashi (a college student from Seattle), and Minoru Yasui (an attorney from Portland). Each had purposefully violated the curfew to challenge its legality. The US Supreme Court upheld the constitutionality of the curfew in companion cases decided in 1943. The lengthier decision in *Hirabayashi v. United States*, 320 U.S. 81 (1943), did not purport to apply heightened scrutiny. Instead, it said that racial classifications were "in most circumstances irrelevant and therefore prohibited" (i.e., because it would be irrational to rely on irrelevancy) but that the wartime situation "afforded a rational basis for the decision which [the government] made."

> A curfew was an appropriate measure against sabotage. It is an obvious protection against the perpetration of sabotage most readily committed during the hours of darkness. . . . But appellant insists that the exercise of the power is inappropriate and unconstitutional because it discriminates against citizens of Japanese ancestry[.] . . . Distinctions between citizens solely because of their ancestry are by their very nature odious to a free people whose institutions are founded upon the doctrine of equality. For that reason, legislative classification or discrimination based on race alone has often been held to be a denial of equal protection. *Yick Wo v. Hopkins* (1887). We may assume that these considerations would be controlling here were it not for the fact that the danger of espionage and sabotage, in time of war and of threatened invasion, calls upon the military authorities to scrutinize every relevant fact bearing on the loyalty of populations in the danger areas.

Gordon Hirabayashi (1918–2012)

Minoru Yasui (1916–1986)

> Because racial discriminations are in most circumstances irrelevant and therefore prohibited, it by no means follows that, in dealing with the perils of war, Congress and the Executive are wholly precluded from taking into account those facts and circumstances which are relevant to measures for our national defense and for the successful prosecution of the war, and which may in fact place citizens of one ancestry in a different category from others. "We must never forget, that it is a *constitution* we are expounding," "a constitution intended to endure for ages to come, and, consequently, to be adapted to the various crises of human affairs." *McCulloch v. Maryland* (1819). The adoption by Government, in the crisis of war and of threatened invasion, of measures for the public safety, based upon the recognition of facts and circumstances which indicate that a group of one national extraction may menace that safety more than others, is not wholly beyond the limits of the Constitution and is not to be condemned merely because in other and in most circumstances racial distinctions are irrelevant.

> Here the aim of Congress and the Executive was the protection against sabotage of war materials and utilities in areas thought to be in danger of Japanese invasion and air attack. . . . We cannot say that these facts and circumstances, considered in the particular war setting, could afford no ground for differentiating citizens of Japanese ancestry from other groups in the United States. The fact alone that attack on our shores was threatened by Japan rather than another enemy power set these citizens apart from others who have no particular associations with Japan. . . . We cannot close our eyes to the fact, demonstrated by experience, that in time of war residents having ethnic affiliations with an invading enemy may be a greater source of danger than those of a different ancestry. Nor can we deny that Congress, and the military authorities acting with its authorization, have constitutional power to appraise the danger in the light of facts of public notoriety. We need not now attempt to define the ultimate boundaries of the war power. We decide only the issue as we have defined it—we decide only that the curfew order as applied, and at the time it was applied, was within the boundaries of the war power. In this case it is enough that circumstances within the knowledge of those charged with the responsibility for maintaining the national defense afforded a rational basis for the decision which they made. Whether we would have made it is irrelevant.

In Yasui's appeal, the Supreme Court stated that "the conviction must be sustained for the reasons stated in the *Hirabayashi* case." *Yasui v. United States*, 320 U.S. 115 (1943).

b) Exclusion Decision from 1944: *Korematsu v. United States*

Fred Korematsu, a US citizen born to immigrant parents, was an ironworker in the San Francisco Bay area. He refused to comply with the exclusion order (preventing him from living in San Francisco) and an assembly order (directing him to report to an assembly center for transfer to an internment camp). When apprehended, Korematsu was convicted of violating the exclusion order.

Fred Korematsu (1919–2005)

When his case went to the Supreme Court, the majority carefully limited its ruling to Korematsu's conviction for failing to obey the exclusion order. In this way, it purported to avoid a ruling on the internment itself, even though in practice exclusion and internment were part of the same program.

ITEMS TO CONSIDER WHILE READING
KOREMATSU v. UNITED STATES:

A. *What sort of scrutiny does the majority say should be used?*

B. *Does the majority apply that scrutiny correctly?*

C. *Should it matter that the exclusion order was given by a military commander during wartime?*

D. *Should it matter whether the order applies to US citizens of Japanese ancestry in addition to Japanese aliens residing lawfully in the US?*

Korematsu v. United States,

323 U.S. 214 (1944)

Justice Black delivered the opinion of the Court [joined by Chief Justice Stone and Justices Reed, Frankfurter, Douglas, and Rutledge].

The petitioner, an American citizen of Japanese descent, was convicted in a federal district court for remaining in San Leandro, California, a "Military Area," contrary to Civilian Exclusion Order No. 34 of the Commanding General of the Western Command, U.S. Army, which directed that after May 9, 1942, all persons of Japanese ancestry should be excluded from that area. No question was raised as to petitioner's loyalty to the United States. The Circuit Court of Appeals affirmed, and the importance of the constitutional question involved caused us to grant certiorari.

It should be noted, to begin with, that all legal restrictions which curtail the civil rights of a single racial group are immediately suspect. That is not to say that all such restrictions are unconstitutional. It is to say that courts must subject them to the most rigid scrutiny. Pressing public necessity may sometimes justify the existence of such restrictions; racial antagonism never can. . . .

Exclusion Order No. 34, which the petitioner knowingly and admittedly violated was one of a number of military orders and proclamations, all of which were substantially based upon Executive Order No. 9066. That order, issued after we were at war with Japan, declared that "the successful prosecution of the war requires every possible protection against espionage and against sabotage to national-defense material, national-defense premises, and national-defense utilities." . . .

In the light of the principles we announced in the *Hirabayashi* case, we are unable to conclude that it was beyond the war power of Congress and the Executive to exclude those of Japanese ancestry from the West Coast war area at the time they did. True, exclusion from the area in which one's home is located is a far greater deprivation than constant confinement to the home from 8 p.m. to 6 a.m. Nothing short of apprehension by the proper military authorities of the gravest imminent danger to the public safety can constitutionally justify either. But exclusion from a threatened area, no less than curfew, has a definite and close relationship to the prevention of espionage and sabotage. The military authorities, charged with the primary responsibility of defending our shores, concluded that curfew provided inadequate protection and ordered exclusion. They did so, as pointed out in our *Hirabayashi* opinion, in accordance with Congressional authority to the military to say who should, and who should not, remain in the threatened areas. . . .

Here, as in the *Hirabayashi* case, we cannot reject as unfounded the judgment of the military authorities and of Congress that there were disloyal members of that [Japanese-American] population, whose number and strength could not be precisely and quickly ascertained. We cannot say that the war-making branches of the Government did not have ground for believing that in a critical hour such persons could not readily be isolated and separately dealt with, and constituted a menace to the national defense and safety, which demanded that prompt and adequate measures be taken to guard against it.

Like curfew, exclusion of those of Japanese origin was deemed necessary because of the presence of an unascertained number of disloyal members of the group, most of whom we have no doubt were loyal to this country. It was because we could not reject the finding of the military authorities that it was impossible to bring about an immediate segregation of the disloyal from the loyal that we sustained the validity of the curfew order as applying to the whole group. In the instant case, temporary exclusion of the entire group was rested by the military on the same ground. The judgment that exclusion of the whole group was for the same reason a military imperative answers the contention that the exclusion was in the nature of group punishment based on antagonism to those of Japanese origin. That there were members of the group who retained loyalties to Japan has been confirmed by investigations made subsequent to the exclusion. Approximately five thousand American citizens of Japanese ancestry refused to swear unqualified allegiance to the United States and to renounce allegiance to the Japanese Emperor, and several thousand evacuees requested repatriation to Japan.

We uphold the exclusion order as of the time it was made and when the petitioner violated it. In doing so, we are not unmindful of the hardships imposed by it upon a large group of American citizens. But hardships are part of war, and war is an aggregation of hardships. All citizens alike, both in and out of uniform, feel the impact of war in greater or lesser measure. Citizenship has its responsibilities as well as its privileges, and in time of war the burden is always heavier. Compulsory exclusion of large groups of citizens from their homes, except under circumstances of direst emergency and peril, is inconsistent with our basic governmental institutions. But when under conditions of modern warfare our shores are threatened by hostile forces, the power to protect must be commensurate with the threatened danger. . . .

It is said that we are dealing here with the case of imprisonment of a citizen in a concentration camp solely because of his ancestry, without evidence or inquiry concerning his loyalty and good disposition towards the United States. Our task would be simple, our duty clear, were this a case involving the imprisonment of a loyal citizen in a concentration camp because of racial prejudice. Regardless of the true nature of the assembly and relocation centers—and we deem it unjustifiable to call them concentration camps with all the ugly connotations that term implies—we are dealing specifically with nothing but an exclusion order. To cast this case into outlines of racial prejudice, without reference to the real military dangers which were presented, merely confuses the issue. Korematsu was not excluded from the Military Area because of hostility to him or his race. He was excluded because we are at war with the Japanese Empire, because the properly constituted military authorities feared an invasion of our West Coast and felt constrained to take proper security measures, because they decided that the military urgency of the situation demanded that all citizens of Japanese ancestry be segregated from the West Coast temporarily, and finally, because Congress, reposing its confidence in this time of war in our military leaders—as inevitably it must—determined that they should have the power to do just this. There was evidence of disloyalty on the part of some, the military authorities considered that the need for action was great, and time was short. We cannot—by availing ourselves of the calm perspective of hindsight—now say that at that time these actions were unjustified.

Justice Frankfurter, concurring. [Omitted]

Justice Roberts, [dissenting].

I dissent, because I think the indisputable facts exhibit a clear violation of Constitutional rights.

This is not a case of keeping people off the streets at night as was *Hirabayashi v. United States* (1943), nor a case of temporary exclusion of a citizen from an area for his own safety or that of the community, nor a case of offering him an opportunity to go temporarily out of an area where his presence might cause danger to himself or to his fellows. On the contrary, it is the case of convicting a citizen as a punishment for not submitting to imprisonment in a concentration camp, based on his ancestry, and solely because of his ancestry, without evidence or inquiry concerning his loyalty and good disposition towards the United States. If this be a correct statement of the facts disclosed by this record, and facts of which we take judicial notice, I need hardly labor the conclusion that Constitutional rights have been violated. . . .

The Government has argued this case as if the only order outstanding at the time the petitioner was arrested and informed against was Exclusion Order No. 34 ordering him to leave the area in which he resided, which was the basis of the information against him. That argument has evidently been effective. The opinion

Korematsu v. United States

refers to the *Hirabayashi* case to show that this court has sustained the validity of a curfew order in an emergency. The argument then is that exclusion from a given area of danger, while somewhat more sweeping than a curfew regulation, is of the same nature—a temporary expedient made necessary by a sudden emergency. This, I think, is a substitution of an hypothetical case for the case actually before the court. I might agree with the court's disposition of the hypothetical case. The liberty of every American citizen freely to come and to go must frequently, in the face of sudden danger, be temporarily limited or suspended. The civil authorities must often resort to the expedient of excluding citizens temporarily from a locality. The drawing of fire lines in the case of a conflagration, the removal of persons from the area where a pestilence has broken out, are familiar examples. If the exclusion worked by Exclusion Order No. 34 were of that nature the *Hirabayashi* case would be authority for sustaining it. But . . . the exclusion was but a part of an over-all plan for forceable detention. This case cannot, therefore, be decided on any such narrow ground as the possible validity of a Temporary Exclusion Order under which the residents of an area are given an opportunity to leave and go elsewhere in their native land outside the boundaries of a military area. To make the case turn on any such assumption is to shut our eyes to reality. . . .

Justice Murphy, dissenting.

This exclusion of "all persons of Japanese ancestry, both alien and non-alien," from the Pacific Coast area on a plea of military necessity in the absence of martial law ought not to be approved. Such exclusion goes over the very brink of constitutional power and falls into the ugly abyss of racism.

In dealing with matters relating to the prosecution and progress of a war, we must accord great respect and consideration to the judgments of the military authorities who are on the scene and who have full knowledge of the military facts. The scope of their discretion must, as a matter of necessity and common sense, be wide. And their judgments ought not to be overruled lightly by those whose training and duties ill-equip them to deal intelligently with matters so vital to the physical security of the nation.

At the same time, however, it is essential that there be definite limits to military discretion, especially where martial law has not been declared. Individuals must not be left impoverished of their constitutional rights on a plea of military necessity that has neither substance nor support. Thus, like other claims conflicting with the asserted constitutional rights of the individual, the military claim must subject itself to the judicial process of having its reasonableness determined and its conflicts with other interests reconciled. What are the allowable limits of military discretion, and whether or not they have been overstepped in a particular case, are judicial questions. . . .

It must be conceded that the military and naval situation in the spring of 1942 was such as to generate a very real fear of invasion of the Pacific Coast, accompanied by fears of sabotage and espionage in that area. The military command was therefore justified in adopting all reasonable means necessary to combat these dangers. In adjudging the military action taken in light of the then apparent dangers, we must not erect too high or too meticulous standards; it is necessary only that the action have some reasonable relation to the removal of the dangers of invasion, sabotage and espionage. But the exclusion, either temporarily or permanently, of all persons with Japanese blood in their veins has no such reasonable relation. And that relation is lacking because the exclusion order necessarily must rely for its reasonableness upon the assumption that all persons of Japanese ancestry may have a dangerous tendency to commit sabotage and espionage and to aid our Japanese enemy in other ways. It is difficult to believe that reason, logic or experience could be marshalled in support of such an assumption.

That this forced exclusion was the result in good measure of this erroneous assumption of racial guilt rather than bona fide military necessity is evidenced by the Commanding General's Final Report on the evacuation from the Pacific Coast area. In it he refers to all individuals of Japanese descent as "subversive," as belonging to "an enemy race" whose "racial strains are undiluted," and as constituting "over 112,000 potential enemies at large today" along the Pacific Coast. In support of this blanket condemnation of all persons of Japanese descent, however, no reliable evidence is cited to show that such individuals were generally disloyal, or had generally so conducted themselves in this area as to constitute a special menace to defense installations or war industries, or had otherwise by their behavior furnished reasonable ground for their exclusion as a group. . . .

The main reasons relied upon by those responsible for the forced evacuation, therefore, do not prove a reasonable relation between the group characteristics of Japanese Americans and the dangers of invasion, sabotage and espionage. The reasons appear, instead, to be largely an accumulation of much of the misinformation, half-truths and insinuations that for years have been directed against Japanese Americans by people with racial and economic prejudices—the same people who have been among the foremost advocates of the evacuation. A military judgment based upon such racial and sociological considerations is not entitled to the great weight ordinarily given the judgments based upon strictly military considerations. Especially is this so when every charge relative to race, religion, culture, geographical location, and legal and economic status has been substantially discredited by independent studies made by experts in these matters. . . .

No adequate reason is given for the failure to treat these Japanese Americans on an individual basis by holding investigations and hearings to separate the loyal from the disloyal, as was done in the case of persons of German and Italian ancestry. It is asserted merely that the loyalties of this group "were unknown and time was

Korematsu v. United States

of the essence." Yet nearly four months elapsed after Pearl Harbor before the first exclusion order was issued; nearly eight months went by until the last order was issued; and the last of these "subversive" persons was not actually removed until almost eleven months had elapsed. Leisure and deliberation seem to have been more of the essence than speed. . . .

Nor is there any denial of the fact that not one person of Japanese ancestry was accused or convicted of espionage or sabotage after Pearl Harbor while they were still free, a fact which is some evidence of the loyalty of the vast majority of these individuals and of the effectiveness of the established methods of combatting these evils. It seems incredible that under these circumstances it would have been impossible to hold loyalty hearings for the mere 112,000 persons involved—or at least for the 70,000 American citizens—especially when a large part of this number represented children and elderly men and women. Any inconvenience that may have accompanied an attempt to conform to procedural due process cannot be said to justify violations of constitutional rights of individuals.

I dissent, therefore, from this legalization of racism. Racial discrimination in any form and in any degree has no justifiable part whatever in our democratic way of life. It is unattractive in any setting but it is utterly revolting among a free people who have embraced the principles set forth in the Constitution of the United States. All residents of this nation are kin in some way by blood or culture to a foreign land. Yet they are primarily and necessarily a part of the new and distinct civilization of the United States. They must accordingly be treated at all times as the heirs of the American experiment and as entitled to all the rights and freedoms guaranteed by the Constitution.

Justice Jackson, dissenting.

Korematsu was born on our soil, of parents born in Japan. The Constitution makes him a citizen of the United States by nativity and a citizen of California by residence. No claim is made that he is not loyal to this country. There is no suggestion that apart from the matter involved here he is not law-abiding and well disposed. Korematsu, however, has been convicted of an act not commonly a crime. It consists merely of being present in the state whereof he is a citizen, near the place where he was born, and where all his life he has lived. . . .

Now, if any fundamental assumption underlies our system, it is that guilt is personal and not inheritable. . . . But here is an attempt to make an otherwise innocent act a crime merely because this prisoner is the son of parents as to whom he had no choice, and belongs to a race from which there is no way to resign. If Congress in peace-time legislation should enact such a criminal law, I should suppose this Court would refuse to enforce it.

But the "law" which this prisoner is convicted of disregarding is not found in an act of Congress, but in a military order. Neither the Act of Congress nor the

Executive Order of the President, nor both together, would afford a basis for this conviction. It rests on the orders of General DeWitt. And it is said that if the military commander had reasonable military grounds for promulgating the orders, they are constitutional and become law, and the Court is required to enforce them. There are several reasons why I cannot subscribe to this doctrine.

It would be impracticable and dangerous idealism to expect or insist that each specific military command in an area of probable operations will conform to conventional tests of constitutionality. When an area is so beset that it must be put under military control at all, the paramount consideration is that its measures be successful, rather than legal. . . . No court can require such a commander in such circumstances to act as a reasonable man; he may be unreasonably cautious and exacting. Perhaps he should be. But a commander in temporarily focusing the life of a community on defense is carrying out a military program; he is not making law in the sense the courts know the term. He issues orders, and they may have a certain authority as military commands, although they may be very bad as constitutional law.

But if we cannot confine military expedients by the Constitution, neither would I distort the Constitution to approve all that the military may deem expedient. This is what the Court appears to be doing, whether consciously or not. I cannot say, from any evidence before me, that the orders of General DeWitt were not reasonably expedient military precautions, nor could I say that they were. But even if they were permissible military procedures, I deny that it follows that they are constitutional. If, as the Court holds, it does follow, then we may as well say that any military order will be constitutional and have done with it. . . .

A judicial construction of the due process clause that will sustain this order is a far more subtle blow to liberty than the promulgation of the order itself. A military order, however unconstitutional, is not apt to last longer than the military emergency. Even during that period a succeeding commander may revoke it all. But once a judicial opinion rationalizes such an order to show that it conforms to the Constitution, or rather rationalizes the Constitution to show that the Constitution sanctions such an order, the Court for all time has validated the principle of racial discrimination in criminal procedure and of transplanting American citizens. The principle then lies about like a loaded weapon ready for the hand of any authority that can bring forward a plausible claim of an urgent need. . . . A military commander may overstep the bounds of constitutionality, and it is an incident. But if we review and approve, that passing incident becomes the doctrine of the Constitution. . . .

My duties as a justice as I see them do not require me to make a military judgment as to whether General DeWitt's evacuation and detention program was a reasonable military necessity. I do not suggest that the courts should have attempted to interfere with the Army in carrying out its task. But I do not think they may be asked to execute a military expedient that has no place in law under the Constitution. I would reverse the judgment and discharge the prisoner.

flashforward

1. ***The End of Internment.*** On the same day it decided *Korematsu* in December 1944, the Supreme Court ordered Ms. Mitsuye Endo of Sacramento released from an internment camp in Utah. *Ex parte Endo*, 323 U.S. 283 (1944). *Endo* was not a constitutional decision: It interpreted the relevant Executive Orders and military orders not to allow continued detention of a person like Endo who had demonstrated loyalty to the United States. The war—and the internment—ended a few months later.

Mitsuye Endo (1920–2006)

2. ***Expungement and Apology.*** In the 1980s, Hirabayashi and Korematsu obtained writs of *coram nobis*, rarely-issued orders to expunge wrongful convictions after the sentences have been served. Their legal teams demonstrated that the curfew, exclusion, and internment orders were not based on genuine military need, but instead were driven by racism. (General DeWitt was quoted in a San Francisco newspaper in 1943 saying, "It makes no difference whether the Japanese is theoretically a citizen. A Jap is a Jap.") Written evidence of the racism within Gen. DeWitt's command had been intentionally concealed from the judiciary. (It was later discovered that the government also concealed a 1942 document from the Office of Naval Intelligence called the Ringle Report, which concluded that only a small percentage of Japanese Americans posed a potential security threat, and that the most dangerous ones were already known to the government or in custody.) This proof of prosecutorial misconduct justified the expungement of the convictions. See *Korematsu v. United States*, 584 F. Supp. 1406 (N.D. Cal. 1984); *Hirabayashi v. United States*, 828 F.2d 591 (9th Cir. 1987).

In response to the evidence uncovered through the coram nobis cases, Congress passed the Civil Liberties Act of 1988, P.L. 100–383, which authorized compensation for the former internees. The Act included the following statement from Congress:

> The Congress recognizes that . . . a grave injustice was done to both citizens and permanent resident aliens of Japanese ancestry by the evacuation, relocation, and internment of civilians during World War II. . . . These actions were carried out without adequate security reasons and without any acts of espionage or sabotage documented by the Commission, and were motivated largely by racial prejudice, wartime hysteria, and a failure of political leadership. The excluded individuals of Japanese ancestry suffered enormous damages, both material and intangible, and there were incalculable losses in education and job training, all of which resulted in significant human suffering for which appropriate compensation has not been made. For these fundamental violations of the basic civil liberties and constitutional rights of these individuals of Japanese ancestry, the Congress apologizes on behalf of the Nation.

3. ***Supreme Court Repudiation of* Korematsu.** In *Trump v. Hawaii*, 138 S.Ct. 2392 (2018), both the majority and dissenting justices included dicta in their opinions rejecting *Korematsu*. According to the majority: "*Korematsu* was gravely wrong the day it was decided, has been overruled in the court of history, and—to be clear—has no place in law under the Constitution."

■ WEBSITE

A fuller version of *Trump v. Hawaii* is available for download from this casebook's companion website, www.CaplanIntegratedConLaw.com.

Trump examined a presidential order barring persons from certain predominantly-Muslim countries from entering the US. A divided Supreme Court held 5–4 that the order was not forbidden religious discrimination. The majority and dissent both agreed that the result in *Korematsu* should be repudiated, but they differed on the lesson to be drawn from it. The majority said that it was "objectively unlawful" and "morally repugnant" for the government to order "the forcible relocation of U.S. citizens to concentration camps, solely and explicitly on the basis of race." The dissenters described *Korematsu*'s error differently: as "blindly accepting the Government's misguided invitation to sanction a discriminatory policy motivated by animosity toward a disfavored group, all in the name of a superficial claim of national security."

C. Heightened Scrutiny for Enumerated Rights: The Flag Salute Cases

Footnote 4 of *Carolene Products* suggested several reasons to give heightened scrutiny to laws alleged to violate First Amendment rights. To begin with, the First Amendment is "a specific prohibition of the Constitution" (an enumerated right). Next, interference with freedom of speech, press, assembly, and petition "restricts those political processes which can ordinarily be expected to bring about repeal of undesirable legislation." Finally, the footnote decried discrimination against "particular religious minorities." Cases combining speech and religion should test the Court's willingness to put Footnote 4 into practice.

A pair of famous cases involving the Pledge of Allegiance in public schools presented just such a combination. Believers in the Jehovah's Witnesses religion refused to salute the US flag or recite the Pledge of Allegiance, which they considered acts of idolatry. As the religion spread, more and more conflicts arose between Witness families and local school districts who insisted that students participate in flag rituals.

1. The Court Stays out: *Minersville School District v. Gobitis*

The Supreme Court first considered the issue in *Minersville School District v. Gobitis*, 310 U.S. 586 (1940). The Gobitis family of Minersville, Pennsylvania, sent their children to a private school to avoid the mandatory recitation of the Pledge in the local public schools. Because they could scarcely afford the tuition, they sought an injunction allowing the children to attend public school without being punished for staying silent during the Pledge. The Supreme Court ruled 8–1 against the family. Justice Frankfurter's opinion stressed the lessons of 1937 (courts should be extremely reluctant to interfere with legislation) and of *McCulloch v. Maryland* (governments should have latitude to choose means reasonably related to permissible ends).

> The precise issue, then, for us to decide is whether the legislatures of the various states and the authorities in a thousand counties and school districts of this country are barred from determining the appropriateness of various means to evoke that unifying sentiment without which there can ultimately be no liberties, civil or religious. To stigmatize legislative judgment in providing for this universal gesture of respect for the symbol of our national life in the setting of the common school as a lawless inroad on that freedom of conscience which the Constitution protects, would amount to no less than the pronouncement of pedagogical and psychological dogma in a field where courts possess no marked and certainly no controlling competence. The influences which help toward a common feeling for the common country are manifold. Some may seem harsh and others no doubt are foolish. Surely, however, the end is

> legitimate. And the effective means for its attainment are still so uncertain and so unauthenticated by science as to preclude us from putting the widely prevalent belief in flag-saluting beyond the pale of legislative power. . . .
>
> The wisdom of training children in patriotic impulses by those compulsions which necessarily pervade so much of the educational process is not for our independent judgment. Even were we convinced of the folly of such a measure, such belief would be no proof of its unconstitutionality. For ourselves, we might be tempted to say that the deepest patriotism is best engendered by giving unfettered scope to the most crotchety beliefs. Perhaps it is best, even from the standpoint of those interests which ordinances like the one under review seek to promote, to give to the least popular sect leave from conformities like those here in issue. But the court-room is not the arena for debating issues of educational policy. It is not our province to choose among competing considerations in the subtle process of securing effective loyalty to the traditional ideals of democracy, while respecting at the same time individual idiosyncrasies among a people so diversified in racial origins and religious allegiances. So to hold would in effect make us the school board for the country. That authority has not been given to this Court, nor should we assume it.

Gobitis drew national attention to the nonconformity of the Jehovah's Witnesses, and social pressure mounted to make them conform. Assaults, kidnappings, lynchings, and even torture of Witnesses occurred across several states. In one instance, a perpetrator reportedly told police that Witnesses were being run out of town because "they're traitors—the Supreme Court says so. Ain't you heard?"

2. The Court Dives in: *West Virginia State Board of Education v. Barnette*

After *Gobitis*, some states enacted laws requiring a flag salute in all public schools, even if the matter had previously been decided at the school district level. In West Virginia, the new law was challenged in a class action brought by Jehovah's Witness households.

Barnette is usually cited for its First Amendment holding, namely that the government may not compel people to say certain things. It appears here because so much of the opinion deals with the propriety of judicial review and the proper level of scrutiny. Focus on the debate between the majority and dissent over these topics.

ITEMS TO CONSIDER WHILE READING *BARNETTE*:

A. *Why does the majority believe it is appropriate for the judiciary to invalidate the decisions of local elected officials?*

B. *What prevents courts from abusing that power?*

C. *Justice Frankfurter argues that "the function of this Court does not differ in passing on the constitutionality of legislation challenged under different Amendments." In other words, strict enforcement of free speech is as troublesome as strict enforcement of the unenumerated right to contract under* Lochner. *Is the* Barnette *decision* Lochner *all over again?*

West Virginia State Board of Education v. Barnette,

319 U.S. 624 (1943)

Justice Jackson delivered the opinion of the Court [joined by Chief Justice Stone and Justices Black, Douglas, Murphy, and Byrnes].

Following the decision by this Court in *Minersville School District v. Gobitis,* 310 U.S. 586 (1940), the West Virginia legislature amended its statutes to require all schools therein to conduct courses of instruction in history, civics, and in the Constitutions of the United States and of the State "for the purpose of teaching, fostering and perpetuating the ideals, principles and spirit of Americanism, and increasing the knowledge of the organization and machinery of the government." . . . The Board of Education on January 9, 1942, adopted a resolution containing recitals taken largely from the Court's *Gobitis* opinion and ordering that the salute to the flag become "a regular part of the program of activities in the public schools," that all teachers and pupils "shall be required to participate in the salute honoring the Nation represented by the Flag; provided, however, that refusal to salute the Flag be regarded as an Act of insubordination, and shall be dealt with accordingly." . . .

Failure to conform is "insubordination" dealt with by expulsion. Readmission is denied by statute until compliance. Meanwhile the expelled child is "unlawfully absent" and may be proceeded against as a delinquent. His parents or guardians are liable to prosecution, and if convicted are subject to fine not exceeding $50 and jail term not exceeding thirty days.

Appellees [Walter Barnette, Paul Stull, and Lucy McClure], citizens of the United States and of West Virginia, brought suit in the United States District Court for themselves and others similarly situated asking its injunction to restrain enforcement of these laws and regulations against Jehovah's Witnesses. The Witnesses are an unincorporated body teaching that the obligation imposed by law of God is superior to that of laws enacted by temporal government. Their religious beliefs include a literal version of Exodus 20:4, which says: "Thou shalt not make unto thee any graven image, or any likeness of anything that is in heaven above, or that is in the earth beneath, or that is in the water under the earth; thou shalt not bow down thyself to them nor serve them." They consider that the flag is an "image" within this command. For this reason they refuse to salute it.

Children of this faith have been expelled from school and are threatened with exclusion for no other cause. Officials threaten to send them to reformatories maintained for criminally inclined juveniles. Parents of such children have been prosecuted and are threatened with prosecutions for causing delinquency.

The Board of Education moved to dismiss the complaint setting forth these facts and alleging that the law and regulations are an unconstitutional denial of religious freedom, and of freedom of speech, and are invalid under the "due process" and "equal protection" clauses of the Fourteenth Amendment to the Federal Constitution. The [trial court] restrained enforcement as to the plaintiffs and those of that class. [47 F. Supp. 251 (S.D.W. Va. 1942).] The Board of Education brought the case here by direct appeal.

This case calls upon us to reconsider a precedent decision, as the Court throughout its history often has been required to do. . . . The *Gobitis* decision . . . assumed, as did the argument in that case and in this, that power exists in the State to impose the flag salute discipline upon school children in general. . . . We [now] re-examine specific grounds assigned for the *Gobitis* decision.

1. It was said that the flag-salute controversy confronted the Court with "the problem which **Lincoln cast in memorable dilemma**: "Must a government of necessity be too strong for the liberties of its people, or too weak to maintain its own existence?" and that the answer must be in favor of strength.

We think these issues may be examined free of pressure or restraint growing out of such considerations.

It may be doubted whether Mr. Lincoln would have thought that the strength of government to maintain itself would be impressively vindicated by our confirming power of the state to expel a handful of children from school. Such oversimplification, so handy in political debate, often lacks the precision necessary to postulates of judicial reasoning. If validly applied to this problem, the utterance cited would resolve every issue of power in favor of those in authority

■ HISTORY

LINCOLN'S DILEMMA: Justice Frankfurter's opinion in *Gobitis* quoted Lincoln's speech to Congress of July 7, 1861, where he argued that the secession of the Southern states "presents to the whole family of man the question whether a constitutional republic or democracy—a government of the people, by the same people—can, or cannot, maintain its territorial integrity against its own domestic foes. It presents the question whether discontented individuals, too few in numbers to control administration according to organic law, in any case, can always break up their Government, and thus practically put an end to free government upon the earth. It forces us to ask: Is there, in all republics, this inherent and fatal weakness? Must a government, of necessity, be too strong for the liberties of its own people, or too weak to maintain its own existence?"

West Virginia State Board of Education v. Barnette

and would require us to override every liberty thought to weaken or delay execution of their policies.

Government of limited power need not be anemic government. Assurance that rights are secure tends to diminish fear and jealousy of strong government, and by making us feel safe to live under it makes for its better support. Without promise of a limiting Bill of Rights it is doubtful if our Constitution could have mustered enough strength to enable its ratification. To enforce those rights today is not to choose weak government over strong government. It is only to adhere as a means of strength to individual freedom of mind in preference to officially disciplined uniformity for which history indicates a disappointing and disastrous end.

The subject now before us exemplifies this principle. Free public education, if faithful to the ideal of secular instruction and political neutrality, will not be partisan or enemy of any class, creed, party, or faction. If it is to impose any ideological discipline, however, each party or denomination must seek to control, or failing that, to weaken the influence of the educational system. Observance of the limitations of the Constitution will not weaken government in the field appropriate for its exercise.

2. It was also considered in the *Gobitis* case that functions of educational officers in states, counties and school districts were such that to interfere with their authority "would in effect make us the school board for the country."

The Fourteenth Amendment, as now applied to the States, protects the citizen against the State itself and all of its creatures—Boards of Education not excepted. These have, of course, important, delicate, and highly discretionary functions, but none that they may not perform within the limits of the Bill of Rights. That they are educating the young for citizenship is reason for scrupulous protection of Constitutional freedoms of the individual, if we are not to strangle the free mind at its source and teach youth to discount important principles of our government as mere platitudes.

Such Boards are numerous and their territorial jurisdiction often small. But small and local authority may feel less sense of responsibility to the Constitution, and agencies of publicity may be less vigilant in calling it to account. The action of Congress in making flag observance voluntary and respecting the conscience of the objector in a matter so vital as raising the Army contrasts sharply with these local regulations in matters relatively trivial to the welfare of the nation. There are village tyrants as well as **village Hampdens**, but none who acts under color of law is beyond reach of the Constitution.

3. The *Gobitis* opinion reasoned that this is a field "where courts possess no marked and certainly no controlling competence," that it is committed to the legislatures as well as the courts to guard cherished liberties and that it is

TERMINOLOGY

VILLAGE HAMPDENS: John Hampden (1594–1643) was a member of Parliament who opposed Charles I during the English Civil War. In the 1751 poem "Elegy Written in a Country Churchyard" by Thomas Gray, the phrase "village Hampden" was used to symbolize local resistance to unjust royal authority.

constitutionally appropriate to "fight out the wise use of legislative authority in the forum of public opinion and before legislative assemblies rather than to transfer such a contest to the judicial arena," since all the "effective means of inducing political changes are left free."

The very purpose of a Bill of Rights was to withdraw certain subjects from the vicissitudes of political controversy, to place them beyond the reach of majorities and officials and to establish them as legal principles to be applied by the courts. One's right to life, liberty, and property, to free speech, a free press, freedom of worship and assembly, and other fundamental rights may not be submitted to vote; they depend on the outcome of no elections.

■ OBSERVATION
AN INSTRUMENT FOR TRANSMITTING: Justice Jackson alludes here to the doctrine of incorporation.

In weighing arguments of the parties it is important to distinguish between the due process clause of the Fourteenth Amendment as **an instrument for transmitting** the principles of the First Amendment and those cases in which it is applied for its own sake. The test of legislation which collides with the Fourteenth Amendment, because it also collides with the principles of the First, is much more definite than the test when only the Fourteenth is involved. Much of the vagueness of the due process clause disappears when the specific prohibitions of the First become its standard. The right of a State to regulate, for example, a public utility may well include, so far as the due process test is concerned, power to impose all of the restrictions which a legislature may have a "rational basis" for adopting. But freedoms of speech and of press, of assembly, and of worship may not be infringed on such slender grounds. They are susceptible of restriction only to prevent grave and immediate danger to interests which the state may lawfully protect. It is important to note that while it is the Fourteenth Amendment which bears directly upon the State it is the more specific limiting principles of the First Amendment that finally govern this case.

Nor does our duty to apply the Bill of Rights to assertions of official authority depend upon our possession of marked competence in the field where the invasion of rights occurs. True, the task of translating the majestic generalities of the Bill of Rights, conceived as part of the pattern of liberal government in the eighteenth century, into concrete restraints on officials dealing with the problems of the twentieth century, is one to disturb self-confidence. These principles grew in soil which also produced a philosophy that the individual was the center of society, that his liberty was attainable through mere absence of governmental restraints, and that government should be entrusted with few controls and only the mildest supervision over men's affairs. We must transplant these rights to a soil in which the *laissez-faire* concept or principle of non-interference has withered at least as to economic affairs, and social advancements are increasingly sought through closer integration of society and through expanded and strengthened governmental controls. These changed conditions often deprive precedents of reliability and cast us more than we would choose upon our own judgment. But we act in these matters not by authority of our competence but by force of our commissions. We cannot, because of modest estimates of our competence in such specialties as public education, withhold the judgment that history authenticates as the function of this Court when liberty is infringed.

West Virginia State Board of Education v. Barnette

[4.] **Lastly,** and this is the very heart of the *Gobitis* opinion, it reasons that "National unity is the basis of national security," that the authorities have "the right to select appropriate means for its attainment," and hence reaches the conclusion that such compulsory measures toward "national unity" are constitutional. Upon the verity of this assumption depends our answer in this case.

National unity as an end which officials may foster by persuasion and example is not in question. The problem is whether under our Constitution compulsion as here employed is a permissible means for its achievement.

Struggles to coerce uniformity of sentiment in support of some end thought essential to their time and country have been waged by many good as well as by evil men. Nationalism is a relatively recent phenomenon but at other times and places the ends have been racial or territorial security, support of a dynasty or regime, and particular plans for saving souls. As first and moderate methods to attain unity have failed, those bent on its accomplishment must resort to an ever-increasing severity. As governmental pressure toward unity becomes greater, so strife becomes more bitter as to whose unity it shall be. Probably no deeper division of our people could proceed from any provocation than from finding it necessary to choose what doctrine and whose program public educational officials shall compel youth to unite in embracing. Ultimate futility of such attempts to compel coherence is the lesson of every such effort from the Roman drive to stamp out Christianity as a disturber of its pagan unity, the Inquisition, as a means to religious and dynastic unity, the Siberian exiles as a means to Russian unity, down to the fast failing efforts of **our present totalitarian enemies**. Those who begin coercive elimination of dissent soon find themselves exterminating dissenters. Compulsory unification of opinion achieves only the unanimity of the graveyard.

It seems trite but necessary to say that the First Amendment to our Constitution was designed to avoid these ends by avoiding these beginnings. There is no mysticism in the American concept of the State or of the nature or origin of its authority. We set up government by consent of the governed, and the Bill of Rights denies those in power any legal opportunity to coerce that consent. Authority here is to be controlled by public opinion, not public opinion by authority.

■ OBSERVATION

LASTLY: Parts 1, 2, and 3 of Barnette are focused on the propriety of judicial review. The last portion of the opinion applies the First Amendment, but in language that has resonance for many individual rights.

■ HISTORY

OUR PRESENT TOTALITARIAN ENEMIES: *Barnette* was decided in the midst of World War II.

The case is made difficult not because the principles of its decision are obscure but because the flag involved is our own. Nevertheless, we apply the limitations of the Constitution with no fear that freedom to be intellectually and spiritually diverse or even contrary will disintegrate the social organization. To believe that patriotism will not flourish if patriotic ceremonies are voluntary and spontaneous instead of a compulsory routine is to make an unflattering estimate of the appeal of our institutions to free minds. We can have intellectual individualism and the rich cultural diversities that we owe to exceptional minds only at the price of occasional eccentricity and abnormal attitudes. When they are so harmless to others or to the State as those we deal with here, the price is not too great. But freedom to differ is not limited to things that do not matter much. That would be a mere shadow of freedom. The test of its substance is the right to differ as to things that touch the heart of the existing order.

If there is any fixed star in our constitutional constellation, it is that no official, high or petty, can prescribe what shall be orthodox in politics, nationalism, religion, or other matters of opinion or force citizens to confess by word or act their faith therein. If there are any circumstances which permit an exception, they do not now occur to us.

We think the action of the local authorities in compelling the flag salute and pledge transcends constitutional limitations on their power and invades the sphere of intellect and spirit which it is the purpose of the First Amendment to our Constitution to reserve from all official control.

The decision of this Court in *Minersville School District v. Gobitis* [is] overruled, and the judgment enjoining enforcement of the West Virginia Regulation is affirmed.

Justices Black and Douglas, concurring.

We are substantially in agreement with the opinion just read, but since we originally joined with the Court in the *Gobitis* case, it is appropriate that we make a brief statement of reasons for our change of view.

Reluctance to make the Federal Constitution **a rigid bar against state regulation** of conduct thought inimical to the public welfare was the controlling influence which moved us to consent to the *Gobitis* decision. Long reflection convinced us that although the principle is sound, its application in the particular case was wrong. We believe that the statute before us fails to accord full scope to the freedom of religion secured to the appellees by the First and Fourteenth Amendments. . . .

■ OBSERVATION

A RIGID BAR AGAINST STATE REGULATION: Justices Black and Douglas allude to the *Lochner*-era due process cases.

Justice Murphy, concurring. [Omitted.]

West Virginia State Board of Education v. Barnette

Justices Roberts and Reed adhere to the views expressed by the Court in *Minersville School District v. Gobitis*, and are of the opinion that the judgment below should be reversed.

Justice Frankfurter, dissenting.

One who belongs to the most **vilified and persecuted minority** in history is not likely to be insensible to the freedoms guaranteed by our Constitution. Were my purely personal attitude relevant I should whole-heartedly associate myself with the general libertarian views in the Court's opinion, representing as they do the thought and action of a lifetime. But as judges we are neither Jew nor Gentile, neither Catholic nor agnostic. We owe equal attachment to the Constitution and are equally bound by our judicial obligations whether we derive our citizenship from the earliest or the latest immigrants to these shores. As a member of this Court I am not justified in writing my private notions of policy into the Constitution, no matter how deeply I may cherish them or how mischievous I may deem their disregard. . . .

■ HISTORY

VILIFIED AND PERSECUTED MINORITY: Justice Frankfurter was Jewish.

Not so long ago we were admonished that "the only check upon our own exercise of power is our own sense of self-restraint. For the removal of unwise laws from the statute books appeal lies, not to the courts, but to the ballot and to the processes of democratic government." *United States v. Butler* (1936) (Stone, J., dissenting). . . .

The admonition that judicial self-restraint alone limits arbitrary exercise of our authority is relevant every time we are asked to nullify legislation. The Constitution does not give us greater veto power when dealing with one phase of "liberty" than with another[.] . . . In neither situation is our function comparable to that of a legislature or are we free to act as though we were a super-legislature. . . . This Court has recognized, what hardly could be denied, that all the provisions of the first ten Amendments are "specific" prohibitions, *United States v. Carolene Products Co.*, note 4 (1938). But each specific Amendment, in so far as embraced within the Fourteenth Amendment, must be equally respected, and the function of this Court does not differ in passing on the constitutionality of legislation challenged under different Amendments.

When Mr. Justice Holmes, speaking for this Court, wrote that "it must be remembered that legislatures are ultimate guardians of the liberties and welfare of the people in quite as great a degree as the courts," he went to the very essence of our constitutional system and the democratic conception of our society. . . . Responsibility for legislation lies with legislatures, answerable as they are directly to the people, and this Court's only and very narrow function is to determine whether within the broad grant of authority vested in legislatures they have exercised a judgment for which reasonable justification can be offered. . . .

We are not reviewing merely the action of a local school board. . . . Practically we are passing upon the political power of each of the forty-eight states [and Congress]. . . . To suggest that we are here concerned with the heedless action of some village tyrants is to distort the augustness of the constitutional issue and the reach of the consequences of our decision. . . .

This is no dry, technical matter. It cuts deep into one's conception of the democratic process—it concerns no less the practical differences between the means for making these accommodations that are open to courts and to legislatures. . . . If the function of this Court is to be essentially no different from that of a legislature, if the considerations governing constitutional construction are to be substantially those that underlie legislation, then indeed judges should not have life tenure and they should be made directly responsible to the electorate. . . .

I think I appreciate fully the objections to the law before us. But to deny that it presents a question upon which men might reasonably differ appears to me to be intolerance. And since men may so reasonably differ, I deem it beyond my constitutional power to assert my view of the wisdom of this law against the view of the State of West Virginia. . . .

Chapter Recap

A. In the late 1930s and 1940s a theory began to arise that courts should apply different levels of judicial scrutiny to different types of laws.

B. *Carolene Products* established the baseline, where ordinary economic regulations would be reviewed only to ensure they had a rational basis. In dicta, Footnote 4 of that decision suggested that heightened scrutiny might apply in cases involving enumerated constitutional rights, restrictions affecting the political process, and laws that harm "discrete and insular minorities."

C. *Skinner* introduced the term "strict scrutiny" and applied it to a law that unequally distributed "fundamental" rights.

D. The Court was slow to use heightened scrutiny in cases of race discrimination, at least when applied to wartime discrimination against the Japanese. *Hirabayashi* purported to apply rational basis review. *Korematsu* stated that heightened scrutiny should be used for racially discriminatory laws, but it found that the government's actions satisfied that scrutiny.

E. After going back and forth on the question of mandatory flag salutes, the Supreme Court in *Barnette* indicated its willingness to use a forceful level of scrutiny for enumerated (First Amendment) rights.

CHAPTER 11

The Civil Rights Era and the Warren Court

In the late 19th and early 20th centuries, the most discussed political and legal issues arose from the transformation of the United States from a predominantly rural and agricultural society to an increasingly urban and industrial one: unionization, working conditions, poverty, and an expanded role for the government in economic regulation. Race relations, the issue so prominent during Reconstruction, had been effectively dropped from the nation's legal agenda. Nonetheless, social and political pressure had been building for change, growing even more quickly after World War II. For example, the US military that had defeated the Nazis was itself racially segregated, but President Truman desegregated the armed forces by executive order in 1947.

At the Supreme Court, dramatic movements in the law relating to race occurred during the tenure of Chief Justice Earl Warren (1953–1969), along with changes involving many other individual rights. In many areas, decisions of the Warren Court gave force to previously unprotected (or underprotected) constitutional rights. The scope of these rulings—sometimes called "the rights revolution"—extends beyond the material in this chapter, and is often studied in courses on First Amendment, Criminal Procedure, and Election Law. Some of the highlights include unreasonable search and seizure under the Fourth Amendment; self-incrimination under the Fifth Amendment; the right to counsel under the Sixth Amendment; the Establishment, Free Exercise, and Free Speech Clauses of the First Amendment; voting rights under the Equal Protection Clause and the Fifteenth Amendment; cruel and unusual punishment under the Eighth Amendment; and more.

This chapter focuses on the constitutional law of race relations in the 1950s and 1960s. These years saw extensive grassroots political activity by millions of Americans who involved themselves in the civil rights movement in ways both large and small, pro and con. Changes in the culture affected the law—and vice versa.

BIOGRAPHY

A former Republican governor of California, **EARL WARREN** (1891–1974) was appointed to the Supreme Court by President Eisenhower in 1952. As attorney general of California during World War II, Warren had agitated in favor of the internment of Japanese-Americans. Later in life, he wrote that he "deeply regretted the removal order and my own testimony advocating it, because it was not in keeping with our American concept of freedom and the rights of citizens."

A. The Multifaceted Legal Campaign for Equal Rights

As with any momentous constitutional change, the demise of legally-mandated racial segregation did not come out of the blue. Footnote 4 of *Carolene Products* (1938) suggested that laws discriminating against "particular racial minorities" might deserve heightened scrutiny, and *Korematsu* (1944) at least gave lip service to that idea. If these hints took hold, Jim Crow laws would be in serious constitutional trouble. But in the years before the Equal Protection Clause was interpreted with any vigor, other areas of the law could be used to alleviate some of the effects of discrimination. The National Association for the Advancement of Colored People (NAACP), formed in 1909 by a racially integrated group that included W.E.B. Du Bois and Ida B. Wells, pursued a multi-pronged legal strategy that sought incremental progress by litigating winnable discrete issues, as opposed to a high-stakes legal assault aimed exclusively at redefining the Equal Protection Clause.

1. Mob Violence and Criminal Justice

Some of the NAACP's earliest victories involved those aspects of the criminal justice system that fell most heavily on Black people.

Private violence was an ever-present threat to racial minorities in late 19th and early 20th centuries. The Ku Klux Klan had reformulated in 1915, and claimed to have 6 million members by 1924. Black neighborhoods were often attacked and burned by White mobs during race riots (the most famous occurring in Colfax, Louisiana in 1873; Springfield, Illinois in 1908; Tulsa, Oklahoma in 1921; and Rosewood, Florida in 1923). Similar riots targeting Chinese and Mexican immigrants occurred in California. Nationwide, but especially in the South, Black people suspected of crimes against White victims were routinely lynched by gangs of vigilantes.

These two syndromes (race riots and lynching of the criminal accused) combined in the Elaine Massacre in Eastern Arkansas. On September 30, 1919, a group of Black tenant farmers met in a church to discuss forming a union to get better prices for their crops. Some White men approached with hostile intent, shots were fired, and a White man ended up dead (although it is unclear who fired the fatal shots). In the week that followed, roving White gangs shot and killed over two hundred Black people. Yet all of the criminal prosecutions that followed the rioting were of Black defendants.

Twelve Black men were arrested and charged with murdering one of their White attackers. A lynch mob gathered outside the jail where they were held; this often resulted in the prisoners being taken from police custody to a nearby tree for hanging without trial. To placate the mob, representatives of the governor promised that if the vigilantes held off, the defendants would be found guilty and executed in due course. As described in *Moore v. Dempsey*, 261 U.S. 86 (1923), the resulting trials were a sham:

> On November 3 the petitioners were brought into Court, informed that a certain lawyer was appointed their counsel and were placed on trial before a white jury—blacks being systematically excluded from both grand and petit juries. The Court and neighborhood were thronged with an adverse crowd that threatened the most dangerous consequences to anyone interfering with the desired result. The counsel did not venture to demand delay or a change of venue, to challenge a juryman or to ask for separate trials. He had had no preliminary consultation with the accused, called no witnesses for the defense although they could have been produced, and did not put the defendants on the stand. The trial lasted about three-quarters of an hour and in less than five minutes the jury brought in a verdict of guilty of murder in the first degree. According to the allegations and affidavits there never was a chance for the petitioners to be acquitted; no juryman could have voted for an acquittal and continued to live in Phillips County and if any prisoner by any chance had been acquitted by a jury he could not have escaped the mob.
>
> The averments as to the prejudice by which the trial was environed have some corroboration in appeals to the Governor, about a year later, earnestly urging him not to interfere with the execution of the petitioners. . . . A part of the American Legion protested against a contemplated commutation of the sentence of four of the petitioners and repeats that a "solemn promise was given by the leading citizens of the community that if the guilty parties were not lynched, and let the law take its course, that justice would be done and the majesty of

> the law upheld." A meeting of the Helena Rotary Club attended by members representing, as it said, seventy-five of the leading industrial and commercial enterprises of Helena, passed a resolution approving and supporting the action of the American Legion post. The Lions Club of Helena at a meeting attended by members said to represent sixty of the leading industrial and commercial enterprises of the city passed a resolution to the same effect.

The Supreme Court found that the trials violated basic requirements of procedural fairness: "the whole proceeding is a mask [in which] counsel, jury and judge were swept to the fatal end by an irresistible wave of public passion." The Court granted writs of habeas corpus ordering the state to give defendants new (and hopefully fair) trials. After remand, all the defendants were freed.

flash*forward*

Procedural Due Process. Today, the legal theory in *Moore v. Dempsey* would be called "procedural due process," because it used the Due Process Clause to challenge the procedures used to enforce a law. The *Moore* defendants did not have any constitutional objection to the substance of the Arkansas statute against murder—there was nothing wrong with its substance—but they had valid objections to the unfair procedures used to enforce the law against them. This differs from "substantive due process" cases like *Lochner v. New York* or *Meyer v. Nebraska*, where individuals used the Due Process Clause to challenge the substance of a law, but had no complaints about the methods used to enforce it.

See Ch. 19 for the modern approach to procedural due process, and Ch. 20 for the modern approach to substantive due process.

A less deadly but more famous instance of the Supreme Court insisting on procedural fairness as a means to racial justice involved the "Scottsboro Boys." Seven Black teenagers in Scottsboro, Alabama were accused of raping two White women. Their trial was held under the constant threat of mob violence. At trial, the defendants were not represented by counsel. In *Powell v. Alabama*, 287 U.S. 45 (1932), the Court ruled for the first time that states were obligated to respect the Sixth Amendment right to counsel (incorporating it into the meaning of "liberty" in the Fourteenth Amendment Due Process Clause). In both *Moore* and *Powell*, the racial overtones were hard to miss, even though they were not Equal Protection Clause cases.

2. Residential Segregation

The portion of the Civil Rights Act of 1866 now codified as 42 U.S.C. § 1982 forbids race discrimination in the ownership of property. Nonetheless, a wide array of legal (and non-legal) mechanisms had been used to keep Black people from moving into White neighborhoods. In this area, Supreme Court decisions of the early 20th century tended towards integration, albeit not in ways that were a match for social pressures.

The Supreme Court held in *Buchanan v. Warley* (1917) [see Ch. 8.C.2.a] that a Louisville ordinance limiting the sale of property on racial grounds represented a deprivation of property without due process of law. See Ch. 8.C.2.a. It reiterated that holding in one-line *per curiam* decisions in *Harmon v. Tyler*, 273 U.S. 668 (1927) and *City of Richmond v. Deans*, 281 U.S. 704 (1930). Notwithstanding these decisions, residential segregation continued as a result of nominally private practices, such as binding real estate covenants—whose terms became part of the legal description of the property—forbidding sale to non-Whites (and in some cases non-Christians). In *Corrigan v. Buckley*, 271 U.S. 323 (1926), the Supreme Court held that enforcement of such a covenant did not implicate the Constitution, because nothing in the Due Process Clause "prohibited private individuals from entering into contracts respecting the control and disposition of their own property." The NAACP continued to fight restrictive covenants using a number of legal theories. *Hansberry v. Lee*, 311 U.S. 32 (1940)—a case often studied in Civil Procedure classes—invalidated a covenant because the earlier class action judgment upholding it could not be used against later Black owners whose interests had not been adequately represented. The Court ultimately found a way to apply the Equal Protection Clause directly to the problem of restrictive covenants in *Shelley v. Kraemer*, 334 U.S. 1 (1948). Entering into a contract not to sell one's property to Black buyers might be a private contract, the Court reasoned, but a court order to rescind a sale was state action that violated the Equal Protection Clause. See Ch. 21.B.1.

B. Desegregation of Public Schools

The NAACP's long-term strategy to revive the Equal Protection Clause focused on public education. The strategy began with suits to enforce the "equal" part of the "separate but equal" formula. These cases had goals beyond merely obtaining equivalent quality of education for Black students. Truly equal separate educational facilities would be extremely expensive; increasing the financial cost of segregation would encourage governments to abandon it. Over time such cases could document a chronic inability or unwillingness of governments to equalize their facilities, calling into question whether "separate but equal" could ever be achieved.

The first few decades of litigation involved state-run colleges and universities. The decisions in *Missouri ex rel. Gaines v. Canada,* 305 U.S. 337 (1938) and *Sipuel v. Board of Regents*, 332 U.S. 631 (1948), ordered states to improve the facilities at state-run Black colleges and universities so that they matched the White facilities. The companion cases of *Sweatt v. Painter,* 339 U.S. 629 (1950), and *McLaurin v. Oklahoma State Regents*, 339 U.S. 637 (1950), involved graduate schools. Heman Sweatt was barred from the University of Texas law school (and every other law school in the state) because of his race. The trial court gave the State an opportunity to create a parallel law school for Black students. Plans for the new school revealed that it would have no full-time faculty, no library or librarian, and would not be accredited by the time Sweatt attended. The Supreme Court, finding that Sweatt had not been given "legal education equivalent to that offered by the State to students of other races," ordered him admitted to the University of Texas. George McLaurin sought a Ph.D. in education from the University of Oklahoma. The University admitted him, but placed extraordinary restrictions on his ability to function as a student. For example, he was not allowed to sit in the same class with White students, and instead was placed at a desk outside the door. The Supreme Court ordered an end to such restrictions. "Having been admitted to a state-supported graduate school, [McLaurin] must receive the same treatment at the hands of the state as students of other races." The Court recognized that its orders might not be a panacea.

George McLaurin at the University of Oklahoma (1948)

> It may be argued that [McLaurin] will be in no better position when these restrictions are removed, for he may still be set apart by his fellow students. This we think irrelevant. There is a vast difference—a Constitutional difference—between restrictions imposed by the state which prohibit the intellectual commingling of students, and the refusal of individuals to commingle where the state presents no such bar. The removal of the state restrictions will not necessarily abate individual and group predilections, prejudices and choices. But at the very least, the state will not be depriving appellant of the opportunity to secure acceptance by his fellow students on his own merits.

This reasoning from *McLaurin* contrasts sharply with *Plessy v. Ferguson.* The opinion in *Plessy* believed that segregation laws were an inevitable expression of the natural order—so much so that it would amount to "enforced commingling of the two races" for such laws to be invalidated. The *McLaurin* decision viewed segregation laws that "prohibit the intellectual commingling of students" as a deviation from a natural order where each person interacts with others "on his own merits." This evolution indicated that the Supreme Court might be receptive to the second planned stage of the NAACP's litigation campaign: the argument in *Brown v. Board of Education* that "separate but equal" should be overruled.

1. Desegregation in State Schools: *Brown v. Board of Education*

In June 1952, the Supreme Court granted review of NAACP cases that challenged segregation in public school districts in Delaware, Virginia, South Carolina, Kansas, and the District of Columbia. Significantly, when they reached the Supreme Court, the United States Solicitor General filed an amicus brief urging that *Plessy* should be overruled because racial segregation in the United States was giving a propaganda advantage to the Soviet Union.

The four state cases were decided together under the caption *Brown v. Board of Education*. The plaintiffs in *Brown* included the Topeka, Kansas family of Oliver Brown, a Protestant minister who was active with the local branch of the NAACP. The Brown family lived in an integrated neighborhood only seven blocks away from the nearest elementary school, but because it was limited to White students, young Linda Brown had to spend over an hour and twenty minutes to reach her segregated school, a journey that required a ride on a bus that could be reached only by walking through a railway switching yard.

In these cases, the schools for Black students were likely not equal, but the Court accepted as fact the legal fiction that the districts had achieved equality of facilities (or were close to doing so). This allowed the opinion to focus on the legality of segregation itself. Arguing for the NAACP, future Supreme Court Justice **Thurgood Marshall** made the most of that opportunity in oral argument:

BIOGRAPHY

THURGOOD MARSHALL (1908–1993) of Maryland—the first African-American appointed to the US Supreme Court—was the grandson of slaves. Realizing he would not be admitted to the all-White University of Maryland law school, he attended the law school at private, historically Black Howard University, where he graduated first in his class. He joined the staff of the NAACP in 1936, and began arguing and winning cases before the US Supreme Court while still in his early 30s. He was appointed to the Second Circuit by President Kennedy in 1961. President Lyndon Johnson named him Solicitor General of the United States (the chief Supreme Court lawyer for the executive branch) in 1965, and appointed him to the US Supreme Court in 1967.

> I got the feeling on hearing the [districts' oral argument] that when you put a white child in a school with a whole lot of colored children, the child would fall apart or something. Everybody knows that is not true.
>
> Those same kids in Virginia and South Carolina—and I have seen them do it—they play in the streets together, they play on their farm together, they go down the road together, they separate to go to school, they come out of school and play ball together. [Yet] they have to be separated in school.
>
> There is some magic to it. You can have them voting together, you can have them not restricted because of law in the houses they live in [under *Buchanan v. Warley* and *Shelley v. Kraemer*]. You can have them going to the same state university and the same college [under *Sweatt* and *McLaurin*], but if they go to elementary and high school, the world will fall apart.

ITEMS TO CONSIDER WHILE READING *BROWN v. BOARD OF EDUCATION:*

A. *What made the segregated schools in* Brown *unequal?*

B. *Did* Brown *overrule* Plessy v. Ferguson*?*

C. *Which methods of constitutional reasoning predominate in* Brown*?*

D. Brown *relied in part on research by psychologists and sociologists. See esp. FN11. But* Carolene Products *said that legislatures, not courts, should decide public policy questions that involve contested scientific questions. What dangers, if any, arise from* Brown's *reliance on social science research to justify its conclusion?*

E. *Chief Justice Warren was adamant that the decision be unanimous. Why was this important? How might it have affected the language of the opinion?*

Brown v. Board of Education,

347 U.S. 483 (1954)

Chief Justice Warren delivered the opinion of the Court [joined by Justices Black, Reed, Frankfurter, Douglas, Jackson, Burton, Clark, and Minton].

These cases come to us from the States of Kansas, South Carolina, Virginia, and Delaware. They are premised on different facts and different local conditions, but a common legal question justifies their consideration together in this consolidated opinion.

Brown v. Board of Education

In each of the cases, minors of the Negro race, through their legal representatives, seek the aid of the courts in obtaining admission to the public schools of their community on a nonsegregated basis. In each instance, they have been denied admission to schools attended by white children under laws requiring or permitting segregation according to race. This segregation was alleged to deprive the plaintiffs of the equal protection of the laws under the Fourteenth Amendment. In each of the cases other than the Delaware case, a three-judge federal district court denied relief to the plaintiffs on the so-called "separate but equal" doctrine announced by this Court in *Plessy v. Ferguson* (1896). Under that doctrine, equality of treatment is accorded when the races are provided substantially equal facilities, even though these facilities be separate. In the Delaware case, the Supreme Court of Delaware adhered to that doctrine, but ordered that the plaintiffs be admitted to the white schools because of their superiority to the Negro schools.

The plaintiffs contend that segregated public schools are not "equal" and cannot be made "equal," and that hence they are deprived of the equal protection of the laws. Because of the obvious importance of the question presented, the Court took jurisdiction. Argument was heard in the 1952 Term, and **reargument** was heard this Term on certain questions propounded by the Court.

Reargument was largely devoted to the circumstances surrounding the adoption of the Fourteenth Amendment in 1868. It covered exhaustively consideration of the Amendment in Congress, ratification by the states, then existing practices in racial segregation, and the views of proponents and opponents of the Amendment. This discussion and our own investigation convince us that, although these sources cast some light, it is not enough to resolve the problem with which we are faced. At best, they are inconclusive. The most avid proponents of the post-War Amendments undoubtedly intended them to remove all legal distinctions among "all persons born or naturalized in the United States." Their opponents, just as certainly, were antagonistic to both the letter and the spirit of the Amendments and wished them to have the most limited effect. What others in Congress and the state legislatures had in mind cannot be determined with any degree of certainty.

■ HISTORY

REARGUMENT: According to internal Supreme Court records, the Court may have been prepared to rule in favor of the school districts after the first argument in the fall of 1952. Nonetheless, in early 1953, the Court asked for further briefing and argument. In September 1953, Chief Justice Fred Vinson died and was replaced by Earl Warren. Reargument was held in December 1953, with an unusual ten hours of argument stretched over three days.

An additional reason for the inconclusive nature of the Amendment's history, with respect to segregated schools, is the status of public education at that time. In the South, the movement toward free common schools, supported by general taxation, had not yet taken hold. Education of white children was largely in the hands of private groups. Education of Negroes was almost nonexistent, and practically all of the race were illiterate. In fact, any education of Negroes was forbidden by law in some states. Today, in contrast, many Negroes have achieved outstanding success in the arts and sciences as well as in the business and professional world. It is true that public school education at the time of the Amendment had advanced further in the North, but the effect of the Amendment on Northern States was generally ignored in the congressional debates. Even in the North, the conditions of public education did not approximate those existing today. The curriculum was usually rudimentary; ungraded schools were common in rural areas; the school term was but three months a year in many states; and compulsory school attendance was virtually unknown. As a consequence, it is not surprising that there should be so little in the history of the Fourteenth Amendment relating to its intended effect on public education.

In the first cases in this Court construing the Fourteenth Amendment, decided shortly after its adoption, the Court interpreted it as proscribing all state-imposed discriminations against the Negro race. [Footnote citing *Strauder v. West Virginia* (1879).] The doctrine of "separate but equal" did not make its appearance in this court until 1896 in the case of *Plessy v. Ferguson*, involving not education but transportation. American courts have since labored with the doctrine for over half a century. In this Court, there have been six cases involving the "separate but equal" doctrine in the field of public education. In *Cumming v. Board of Education of Richmond County*, 175 U.S. 528 (1899), and *Gong Lum v. Rice*, 275 U.S. 78 (1927), the validity of the doctrine itself was not challenged. In more recent cases, all on the graduate school level, inequality was found in that specific benefits enjoyed by white students were denied to Negro students of the same educational qualifications. *State of Missouri ex rel. Gaines v. Canada*, 305 U.S. 337 (1938); *Sipuel v. Board of Regents of University of Oklahoma*, 332 U.S. 631 (1948); *Sweatt v. Painter*, 339 U.S. 629 (1950); *McLaurin v. Oklahoma State Regents*, 339 U.S. 637 (1950). In none of these cases was it necessary to re-examine the doctrine to grant relief to the Negro plaintiff. And in *Sweatt v. Painter*, the Court expressly reserved decision on the question whether *Plessy v. Ferguson* should be held inapplicable to public education.

In the instant cases, that question is directly presented. Here, unlike *Sweatt v. Painter*, there are findings below that the Negro and white schools involved have been equalized, or are being equalized, with respect to buildings, curricula, qualifications and salaries of teachers, and other "tangible" factors. Our decision, therefore, cannot turn on merely a comparison of these tangible factors in the Negro and white schools involved in each of the cases. We must look instead to the effect of segregation itself on public education.

In approaching this problem, we cannot turn the clock back to 1868 when the Amendment was adopted, or even to 1896 when *Plessy v. Ferguson* was written. We must consider public education in the light of its full development and its present place in American life throughout the Nation. Only in this way can it be determined if segregation in public schools deprives these plaintiffs of the equal protection of the laws.

Brown v. Board of Education

Today, education is perhaps the most important function of state and local governments. Compulsory school attendance laws and the great expenditures for education both demonstrate our recognition of the importance of education to our democratic society. It is required in the performance of our most basic public responsibilities, even service in the armed forces. It is the very foundation of good citizenship. Today it is a principal instrument in awakening the child to cultural values, in preparing him for later professional training, and in helping him to adjust normally to his environment. In these days, it is doubtful that any child may reasonably be expected to succeed in life if he is denied the opportunity of an education. Such an opportunity, where the state has undertaken to provide it, is a right which must be made available to all on equal terms.

We come then to the question presented: Does segregation of children in public schools solely on the basis of race, even though the physical facilities and other "tangible" factors may be equal, deprive the children of the minority group of equal educational opportunities? We believe that it does.

In *Sweatt v. Painter*, in finding that a segregated law school for Negroes could not provide them equal educational opportunities, this Court relied in large part on "those qualities which are incapable of objective measurement but which make for greatness in a law school." In *McLaurin v. Oklahoma State Regents*, the Court, in requiring that a Negro admitted to a white graduate school be treated like all other students, again resorted to intangible considerations: "his ability to study, to engage in discussions and exchange views with other students, and, in general, to learn his profession." Such considerations apply with added force to children in grade and high schools. To separate them from others of similar age and qualifications solely because of their race generates a feeling of inferiority as to their status in the community that may affect their hearts and minds in a way unlikely ever to be undone. The effect of this separation on their educational opportunities was well stated by a finding in the Kansas case by a court which nevertheless felt compelled to rule against the Negro plaintiffs:

> Segregation of white and colored children in public schools has a detrimental effect upon the colored children. The impact is greater when it has the sanction of the law; for the policy of separating the races is usually interpreted as denoting the inferiority of the negro group. A sense of inferiority affects the motivation of a child to learn. Segregation with the sanction of law, therefore, has a tendency to retard the educational and mental development of Negro children and to deprive them of some of the benefits they would receive in a racially integrated school system.

Whatever may have been the extent of psychological knowledge at the time of *Plessy v. Ferguson*, this finding is amply supported by modern authority.[FN11] Any language in *Plessy v. Ferguson* contrary to this finding is rejected.

FN11 **K. B. Clark**, *Effect of Prejudice and Discrimination on Personality Development* (Midcentury White House Conference on Children and Youth, 1950); Witmer and Kotinsky, *Personality in the Making* (1952), c. VI; Deutscher and Chein, *The Psychological Effects of Enforced Segregation: A Survey of Social Science Opinion*, 26 J.PSYCHOL. 259 (1948); Chein, *What are the Psychological Effects of Segregation Under Conditions of Equal Facilities?*, 3 Int. J. OPINION AND ATTITUDE RES. 229 (1949); Brameld, "Educational Costs," in *Discrimination and National Welfare* (MacIver, ed., 1949), 44-48; Frazier, The *Negro in the United States* (1949), 674-681. And see generally Myrdal, *An American Dilemma* (1944).

HISTORY

K.B. CLARK: Psychologists Kenneth and Mamie Clark performed an influential experiment with school children that was entered into evidence in the trial courts. Shown a White-skinned doll and a Black-skinned doll, Black children attending segregated schools were likely to say that the White doll was "nice," that the Black doll "looks bad," and that they would rather play with the White doll. This was the first psychological study to be cited in a Supreme Court opinion.

We conclude that in the field of public education the doctrine of "separate but equal" has no place. Separate educational facilities are inherently unequal. Therefore, we hold that the plaintiffs and others similarly situated for whom the actions have been brought are, by reason of the segregation complained of, deprived of the equal protection of the laws guaranteed by the Fourteenth Amendment. This disposition makes unnecessary any discussion whether such segregation also violates the Due Process Clause of the Fourteenth Amendment.

Because these are class actions, because of the wide applicability of this decision, and because of the great variety of local conditions, the formulation of decrees in these cases presents problems of considerable complexity. On reargument, the consideration of appropriate relief was necessarily subordinated to the primary question—the constitutionality of segregation in public education. We have now announced that such segregation is a denial of the equal protection of the laws. In order that we may have the full assistance of the parties in formulating decrees, the cases will be restored to the docket, and the parties are requested to present further argument [regarding remedy]. . . .

2. Desegregation in Federal Schools: *Bolling v. Sharpe*

The opinion in *Brown* consolidated class actions from four states. The fifth case decided that day, *Bolling v. Sharpe*, involved the segregated schools of the District of Columbia.

ITEMS TO CONSIDER WHILE READING
BOLLING v. SHARPE:

A. *What's the difference between* Brown *and* Bolling?

B. *Why is race discrimination in public education a deprivation of liberty (and not just a denial of equality)?*

Bolling v. Sharpe,

347 U.S. 497 (1954)

Mr. Chief Justice Warren delivered the opinion of the Court [joined by Justices Black, Reed, Frankfurter, Douglas, Jackson, Burton, Clark, and Minton].

This case challenges the validity of segregation in the public schools of the District of Columbia. . . . We have this day held that the Equal Protection Clause of the Fourteenth Amendment prohibits the states from maintaining racially segregated public schools. *Brown v. Board of Education.* The legal problem in the District of Columbia is somewhat different, however. The Fifth Amendment, which is applicable in the District of Columbia, does not contain an equal protection clause as does the Fourteenth Amendment which applies only to the states. But the concepts of equal protection and due process, both stemming from our American ideal of fairness, are not mutually exclusive. The "equal protection of the laws" is a more explicit safeguard of prohibited unfairness than "due process of law," and, therefore, we do not imply that the two are always interchangeable phrases. But, as this Court has recognized, discrimination may be so unjustifiable as to be violative of due process.

Classifications based solely upon race must be scrutinized with particular care, since they are contrary to our traditions and hence constitutionally suspect. As long ago as 1896, this Court declared the principle "that the constitution of the United States, in its present form, forbids, so far as civil and political rights are concerned, discrimination by the general government, or by the states, against any citizen because of his race." *Gibson v. Mississippi*, 162 U.S. 565 (1896). And in *Buchanan v. Warley* (1917), the Court held that a statute which limited the right of a property owner to convey his property to a person of another race was, as an unreasonable discrimination, a denial of due process of law.

Although the Court has not assumed to define "liberty" with any great precision, that term is not confined to mere freedom from bodily restraint. Liberty under law extends to the full range of conduct which the individual is free to pursue, and it cannot be restricted except for a proper governmental objective. Segregation in public education is not reasonably related to any proper governmental objective, and thus it imposes on Negro children of the District of Columbia a burden that constitutes an arbitrary deprivation of their liberty in violation of the Due Process Clause.

In view of our decision that the Constitution prohibits the states from maintaining racially segregated public schools, it would be unthinkable that the same Constitution would impose a lesser duty on the Federal Government. We hold that racial segregation in the public schools of the District of Columbia is a denial of the due process of law guaranteed by the Fifth Amendment to the Constitution. . . .

flash*forward*

1. *Fifth Amendment Incorporation.* The legal puzzle in *Bolling v. Sharpe* is similar to the one that existed after *Barron v. Baltimore* (1833) (Ch. 5.C). In *Barron*, an individual sought to stop a state from doing something the Constitution's text would have prevented the federal government from doing. In *Bolling*, individuals sought to stop the federal government from doing something the Constitution's text would have prevented the states from doing. The solution to both puzzles is for the word "liberty" in the Due Process Clauses to incorporate rights enumerated elsewhere in the Constitution.

Incorporation can be seen in *West Virginia Board of Education v. Barnette* (1943) (Ch. 10.C.2), which involved freedom of speech. The Fourteenth Amendment Due Process Clause says that no state may deprive people of "liberty." That term incorporates the right to freedom of speech—even though the First Amendment, where freedom of speech is enumerated, applies on its face only to Congress. *Bolling* relied on the same incorporation concept. The Fifth Amendment Due Process Clause says the federal government may not deprive people of "liberty." That term incorporates the right to equal protection of the laws, even though the Constitution enumerates that right as part of a Fourteenth Amendment that applies on its face to the states.

Incorporation of the Equal Protection Clause

Federal Enumerated Powers

Fifth Amendment: "No person shall ... be deprived [by the federal government] of life, liberty, or property, without due process of law."

DUE PROCESS CLAUSE

EQUAL PROTECTION CLAUSE
(incorporated into the Due Process Clause)

Fourteenth Amendment:
"No State shall ... deny to any person ... the equal protection of the laws"

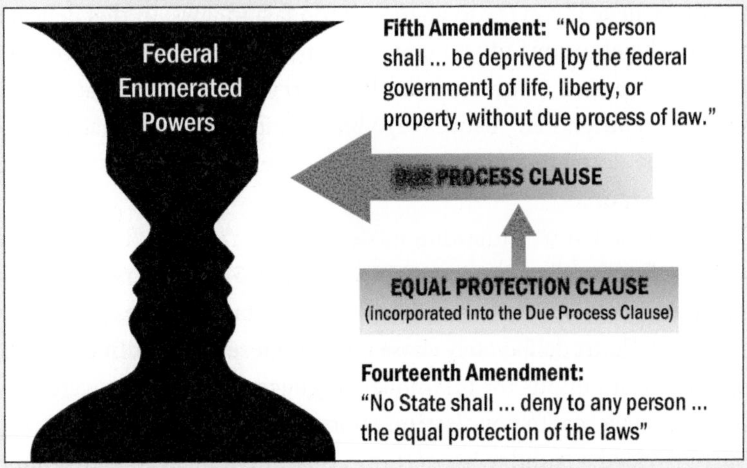

2. *Segregation Beyond Schools.* *Brown* and *Bolling* spoke only about public education, but they sent a clear signal regarding government-mandated segregation generally. Lower federal courts quickly began using *Brown* as authority to strike down segregation laws for public facilities other than schools. The Supreme Court chose not to issue opinions in any of these cases, but affirmed a steady stream of them without opinion. *Muir v. Louisville Park Theatrical Association*, 347 U.S. 971 (1954) (amphitheater in Louisville, Kentucky); *Holmes v. Atlanta*, 350 U.S. 879 (1955) (public golf courses in Atlanta, Georgia); *Baltimore City v. Dawson*, 350 U.S. 877 (1955) (public beaches in Baltimore City, Maryland); *Gayle v. Browder*, 352 U.S. 903 (1956) (city busses in Montgomery, Alabama); *New Orleans City Park Improvement Ass'n v. Detiege*, 358 U.S. 54 (1959) (city parks in New Orleans, Louisiana). The message became clear that racial segregation laws violated the Equal Protection Clause in any setting.

3. Implementing Desegregation

a) "All Deliberate Speed": *Brown v. Board of Education II*

The closing passage in *Brown* scheduled a third round of oral argument, this time focused on the proper remedy. Although the court's jurisdiction extended only to the five cases before it, the chosen remedy would become a template for every school district in the nation. The NAACP argued that the court should set a rapid deadline for full desegregation. The districts argued for a lengthier transition period of indefinite duration, to minimize disruption of the existing educational systems. President Eisenhower shared the districts' concerns, publicly stating: "I personally believe if you try to go too far too fast in laws, in this delicate field, that involves the emotions of so many millions of Americans, you're making a mistake." The Supreme Court had another worry: No matter what remedy was ordered, it might be ignored. Justice Hugo Black, originally from Alabama, foresaw resistance to the decision and counselled his colleagues not to issue any orders they could not enforce.

The Supreme Court's unanimous decision on remedy, *Brown v. Board of Education of Topeka (Brown II)*, 349 U.S. 294 (1955), took a modest path. The Supreme Court would not craft any injunctions itself, but would leave the task to the trial courts. The Court deliberately chose not to impose any deadlines. Instead—in the opinion's most famous (or infamous) language—trial courts were to ensure that plaintiffs had access to nondiscriminatory schools "with all deliberate speed." The Court provided a laundry list of things that might be needed to comply:

> [T]he defendants [must] make a prompt and reasonable start toward full compliance with [*Brown I*]. Once such a start has been made, the courts may find that additional time is necessary to carry out the ruling in an effective manner. The burden rests upon the defendants to establish that such time is necessary in the public interest and is consistent with good faith compliance at the earliest practicable date. To that end, the courts may consider problems related to administration, arising from the physical condition of the school plant, the school transportation system, personnel, revision of school districts and attendance areas into compact units to achieve a system of determining admission to the public schools on a nonracial basis, and revision of local laws and regulations which may be necessary in solving the foregoing problems. They will also consider the adequacy of any plans the defendants may propose to meet these problems and to effectuate a transition to a racially nondiscriminatory school system. During this period of transition, the courts will retain jurisdiction of these cases.

The Court contrasted these administrative problems—which it considered legitimate reasons for a slow transition—with outright political resistance to desegregation. "It should go without saying," the Court said, "that the vitality of these constitutional principles [from *Brown I*] cannot be allowed to yield simply because of disagreement with them." That disagreement did not take long to materialize.

b) Overcoming "Massive Resistance"

White segregationists pledged to defeat school integration through a self-titled program of "massive resistance." Southern resistance to Reconstruction provided a model. After a decade of federal occupation, Reconstruction had ended in 1876 without any lasting reduction in White control over Southern society. The school desegregation orders might encounter the same fate: with enough resistance, the federal government would eventually lose interest and the South could continue its accustomed ways.

As part of the campaign for massive resistance to *Brown*, a segregationist network emerged known as Citizens Councils (or more commonly, White Citizens Councils). These and similar groups often claimed to uphold constitutional values. As US Senator James Eastland of Mississippi put it at a regional conference of the Citizens' Councils:

> All the people of the south are in favor of segregation. And Supreme Court or no Supreme Court, we are going to maintain segregated schools down in Dixie! The political trend is against us, but the overriding trend of the importance of preserving that fundamental principle—that the states are sovereign—they must not be crushed in an overwhelming central government—is gaining strength.

Incidents in Arkansas illustrate the response to *Brown*. They also demonstrate how constitutional and social change arise not only from court opinions, but from the deeds of other government actors and ordinary people. Although the events described here are dramatic, they were not isolated. Cities and towns throughout the South clashed vigorously—and often violently—over school segregation in the 1950s and 1960s, and related controversies continue to the present.

1) Voluntary Desegregation in Hoxie

The all-White school board in Hoxie, Arkansas (population 1,800) chose not to wait to be forced into integration by court order. It voluntarily voted to desegregate its school system for the 1955–56 school year that followed *Brown II*. Superintendent K.A. Vance said that the decision was "right in the sight of God," was required by law, and would also save the money currently spent on maintaining a dual school system. A favorable story about Hoxie's voluntary desegregation appeared in *Life* magazine, including photos of Black grade schoolers calmly entering school with their White classmates. According to Roy Wilkins of the NAACP: "So much emphasis has been placed in so many quarters on the resistance to desegregation in the public schools, that *Life* story of Hoxie comes as a refreshing reassurance of the basic decency of the American people."

Segregationists were less pleased with what the article showed, and decided to make Hoxie a target. Groups affiliated with the Citizens' Councils came to Hoxie, threatening to form a picket line around the formerly all-White schools to keep

Black students out. The school board and superintendent received death threats, delivered by phone and in person. Shots were fired into the homes of leaders of the Black community. White families were urged to keep their children away from school, and on some days White attendance fell by nearly 50%. Segregationists gave a series of inflammatory public speeches, such as one where a leader of the Citizens' Council said that the Fourteenth Amendment was "a damnable, iniquitous fraud," predicted that "blood would run knee-deep all over Arkansas," and praised guns and ropes as useful tools to keep "the nigger out of the white bedroom."

The Hoxie school district took an unusual step in response: it sued the organizers of the Citizens' Councils for conspiracy to violate civil rights under the Ku Klux Klan Act of 1871, now codified at 42 U.S.C. § 1985(3). The trial court ruled in favor of the school district, and the Eighth Circuit affirmed. The members of the school board, the court wrote, "are under a duty to obey the [US] Constitution. Art. VI, cl. 2. They are bound by oath or affirmation to support it and are mindful of their obligation. It follows as a necessary corollary that they have a federal right to be free from direct and deliberate interference with the performance of the constitutionally imposed duty." *Brewer v. Hoxie School District*, 238 F.2d 91 (8th Cir. 1956). The injunction had the intended calming effect in Hoxie, and the school board never rescinded its decision to desegregate.

First-term Arkansas Governor Orval Faubus had stayed out of the Hoxie controversy, saying that it was a local matter. Faubus had a reputation as a moderate on racial issues; among other things he had desegregated the state bus system. But he faced re-election in 1958, and one of his past opponents had been Jim Johnson—the segregationist and advocate of interposition. Faubus calculated that he needed the segregationist vote to remain in office. The next time a school controversy arose, Faubus would not keep his distance.

2) *The Little Rock Nine:* Cooper v. Aaron

After *Brown II*, the school board in the state capital of Little Rock proposed a plan that would take at least six years to desegregate the junior high and high schools. The NAACP challenged the slow pace of the plan, but in 1956 a federal court upheld it as acceptable forward movement with "all deliberate speed." In so doing, the court ruled that the school district must proceed with the proposed plan—converting it from a voluntary effort to one mandated by a federal court order. Later that year, voters added Amendment 44 to the state constitution which directed that the state legislature

> "shall take appropriate action and pass laws opposing in every Constitutional manner the Un-Constitutional desegregation decisions of May 17, 1954 and May 31, 1955 of the United States Supreme Court, including interposing the

sovereignty of the State of Arkansas to the end of **nullification** of these and all deliberate, palpable and dangerous invasions of or encroachments upon rights and powers not delegated to the United States . . . and those rights and powers reserved to the States and to the People."

■ TERMINOLOGY

NULLIFICATION: In the early 19th century, some states advanced the now-discredited theory that states had authority to prohibit in-state enforcement of, and hence nullify, federal laws the state considered to be in violation of the US Constitution. The most prominent incident involving nullification occurred in 1832–33, when South Carolina sought to block in-state collection of federal tariffs. Both the state and federal governments took steps toward mobilizing troops over the dispute before a political compromise reduced the tariff.

The Little Rock desegregation plan was scheduled to begin with a pilot project during the 1957–58 school year, where nine African-American students with strong academic backgrounds would attend the all-White Central High School. On September 2, 1957, Governor Faubus announced that he would call out the Arkansas National Guard to prevent the students from entering. This meant that Arkansas was using military force to resist a federal court order. On the first day of school on September 4, the Arkansas National Guard—joined by an angry White mob—kept the Little Rock Nine from entering the school. Presidential cajoling and a court order persuaded Faubus to withdraw the National Guard, but he continued to encourage resistance. On September 23, the Little Rock Nine were finally able to enter the school building—although it involved sneaking in a side door to avoid an angry White crowd. Learning that the students had entered, the crowd turned ugly, assaulting Black journalists and threatening to kidnap and lynch the Black students. For their own safety, the Nine were driven from campus by Little Rock police. The ugly display, widely reported in the media, forced Eisenhower to act. On September 25 he sent federal paratroopers to escort the students into the school, announcing that "mob rule cannot be allowed to override the decisions of our courts." Federal troops remained a fixture at the school throughout the school year, offering personal protection to the nine students.

Elizabeth Eckford attempts to enter Central High School, September 1957

In early 1958, the school board petitioned the federal court for permission to postpone the rest of the desegregation plan for at least two years. On June 20, the trial court agreed: the "chaos, bedlam and turmoil" surrounding

Central High had caused an "adverse effect upon the educational program," and continuing with desegregation would impose an intolerable financial burden on the school district to pay for the armed security that the local police could not provide. The Eighth Circuit reversed on August 18, ordering the school district to proceed with the plan. The case was appealed to the Supreme Court on an expedited schedule; the opening of school was postponed awaiting the results of the appeal. On September 12, the day after oral argument, the Court announced that it would affirm the Eighth Circuit, and a written opinion issued on September 29.

The unanimous opinion, *Cooper v. Aaron*, 358 U.S. 1 (1958), insisted that "the constitutional rights of [students] are not to be sacrificed or yielded to the violence and disorder which have followed upon the actions of the Governor and Legislature." The Court also took on the legal underpinnings of the resistance movement, which claimed that the states were not bound by US Supreme Court interpretations of the US Constitution.

> The controlling legal principles are plain. . . . The constitutional rights of children not to be discriminated against in school admission on grounds of race or color declared by this Court in the *Brown* case can neither be nullified openly and directly by state legislators or state executive or judicial officers, nor nullified indirectly by them through evasive schemes for segregation whether attempted ingeniously or ingenuously.
>
> What has been said, in the light of the facts developed, is enough to dispose of the case. However, we should answer the premise of the actions of the Governor and Legislature that they are not bound by our holding in the *Brown* case. It is necessary only to recall some basic constitutional propositions which are settled doctrine.
>
> Article VI of the Constitution makes the Constitution the "supreme Law of the Land." In 1803, Chief Justice Marshall, speaking for a unanimous Court, referring to the Constitution as "the fundamental and paramount law of the nation," declared in the notable case of *Marbury v. Madison* that "It is emphatically the province and duty of the judicial department to say what the law is." This decision declared the basic principle that the federal judiciary is supreme in the exposition of the law of the Constitution, and that principle has ever since been respected by this Court and the Country as a permanent and indispensable feature of our constitutional system. It follows that the interpretation of the Fourteenth Amendment enunciated by this Court in the *Brown* case is the supreme law of the land, and Art. VI of the Constitution makes it of binding effect on the States "any Thing in the Constitution or Laws of any State to the Contrary notwithstanding." Every state legislator and executive and judicial officer is solemnly committed by oath taken pursuant to Art. VI, § 3 "to support this Constitution." . . . No state legislator or executive or judicial

officer can war against the Constitution without violating his undertaking to support it. Chief Justice Marshall spoke for a unanimous Court in saying that: "If the legislatures of the several states may, at will, annul the judgments of the courts of the United States, and destroy the rights acquired under those judgments, the constitution itself becomes a solemn mockery." *United States v. Peters*, 9 U.S. 115 (1809). A Governor who asserts a power to nullify a federal court order is similarly restrained. If he had such power, said Chief Justice Hughes, in 1932, also for a unanimous Court, "it is manifest that the fiat of a state Governor, and not the Constitution of the United States, would be the supreme law of the land; that the restrictions of the Federal Constitution upon the exercise of state power would be but impotent phrases." *Sterling v. Constantin*, 287 U.S. 378 (1932).

It is, of course, quite true that the responsibility for public education is primarily the concern of the States, but it is equally true that such responsibilities, like all other state activity, must be exercised consistently with federal constitutional requirements as they apply to state action. The Constitution created a government dedicated to equal justice under law. The Fourteenth Amendment embodied and emphasized that ideal. State support of segregated schools through any arrangement, management, funds, or property cannot be squared with the Amendment's command that no State shall deny to any person within its jurisdiction the equal protection of the laws. The right of a student not to be segregated on racial grounds in schools so maintained is indeed so fundamental and pervasive that it is embraced in the concept of due process of law. *Bolling v. Sharpe*, 347 U.S. 497 (1954). The basic decision in *Brown* was unanimously reached by this Court only after the case had been briefed and twice argued and the issues had been given the most serious consideration. Since the first *Brown* opinion three new Justices have come to the Court. They are at one with the Justices still on the Court who participated in that basic decision as to its correctness, and that decision is now unanimously reaffirmed. The principles announced in that decision and the obedience of the States to them, according to the command of the Constitution, are indispensable for the protection of the freedoms guaranteed by our fundamental charter for all of us. Our constitutional ideal of equal justice under law is thus made a living truth.

The Supreme Court's opinion was lauded in many quarters as a defense of the rule of law, but (as is often the case) the court decision was not the end of the matter. While *Cooper* was pending, the Arkansas legislature authorized the governor to shut down any school if federal troops were stationed there or if "an efficient educational system cannot be maintained because of integration of the races." Faubus issued an executive order closing all four of the Little Rock high schools that were scheduled to be integrated in the 1958–59 school year. The postponement that *Cooper* refused to authorize was occurring anyway. But after a year without high schools, Little Rock began to **rethink its commitment to segregation** now that White families were personally experiencing the costs of maintaining it. In early 1959, an extreme segregationist who had joined the school board was removed from office through a recall election. The Little Rock Chamber of Commerce issued a statement urging Little Rock to reopen its schools because continuing the controversy would be bad for business. The four closed high schools reopened in fall of 1959, and the desegregation plan slowly resumed. In a symbolic act, the people of Arkansas repealed Amendment 44 in 1990.

OBSERVATION

RETHINK ITS COMMITMENT TO SEGREGATION: The aftermath of *Cooper v. Aaron* illustrates Justice Jackson's idea from *Railway Express Agency* (1949): "there is no more effective practical guaranty against arbitrary and unreasonable government than to require that the principles of law which officials would impose upon a minority must be imposed generally" because "political retribution" is more likely to occur when larger numbers of citizens are affected by unjust laws.

flashforward

Desegregation. Achieving *Brown*'s vision of integrated public schooling has proven difficult. Some of the more recent legal battles over school segregation are explored in Ch. 18.C.4.b.2.

C. Interracial Marriage: *Loving v. Virginia*

Virginia's Racial Integrity Act. Many of the segregation laws invalidated by the Warren Court had been enacted after the Civil War as a way to repress the newly freed Black population. Laws banning interracial marriage were much older. Virginia, for example, had laws against such marriages dating back to 1691. The state updated and strengthened its ban in the state's Racial Integrity Act of 1924, part of the wave of eugenically-motivated legislation that included the sterilization law upheld in *Buck v. Bell* (1927).

The Act made it a crime for any "white person" to marry a "colored person." The statute defined a "colored person" as a person "in whom there is ascertainable any Negro blood." The title of "white person" applied "only to such person as has no trace whatever of any blood other than Caucasian; but persons who have one-sixteenth or less of the blood of the American Indian and have no other non-Caucasic blood shall be deemed to be white persons." According to a pamphlet published by the Virginia Bureau of Vital Statistics, the one-sixteenth proviso was motivated by the state's desire "to recognize as an integral and honored part of the white race the descendants of John Rolfe and Pocahontas."

The Loving Family. The Court finally agreed to reach the issue in the aptly-named *Loving v. Virginia* (1967). Richard Loving and Mildred Jeter of Central Point, Virginia wanted to marry, but state law forbade it. Under the statute's definitions, Richard was a "white person" and Mildred was a "colored person" because her ancestors included both African-Americans and Native Americans. They married in Washington DC in 1958, but continued to live in Virginia. When their marriage was discovered, they were prosecuted under the portion of the statute that barred Virginians from traveling to other states to avoid the ban on interracial marriage.

Mildred Loving (1939–2008) and Richard Loving (1933–1975)

QUESTIONS TO CONSIDER WHILE READING *LOVING v. VIRGINIA*:

A. *Virginia's law limited the choice of spouses for both "white" and "colored" people alike. Given the similar treatment of the groups, why did it violate equal protection?*

B. *Which level of scrutiny does the court apply?*

C. *Both* Dred Scott *and* Plessy *pointed to colonial-era bans on interracial marriage to support their conclusions. How does* Loving *deal with the long history of such laws?*

D. *When* Loving *was decided, sixteen states had laws against interracial marriage. Should it matter if that number were larger? Smaller?*

E. Loving *discusses both equal protection and due process. What exactly is the due process argument? Is it necessary to the opinion?*

Loving v. Virginia,

388 U.S. 1 (1967)

Mr. Chief Justice Warren delivered the opinion of the Court [joined by Justices Black, Douglas, Clark, Harlan, Brennan, Stewart, White, and Fortas].

This case presents a constitutional question never addressed by this Court: whether a statutory scheme adopted by the State of Virginia to prevent marriages between persons solely on the basis of racial classifications violates the Equal Protection and Due Process Clauses of the Fourteenth Amendment. For reasons which seem to us to reflect the central meaning of those constitutional commands, we conclude that these statutes cannot stand consistently with the Fourteenth Amendment.

In June 1958, two residents of Virginia, Mildred Jeter, a Negro woman, and Richard Loving, a white man, were married in the District of Columbia pursuant to its laws. Shortly after their marriage, the Lovings returned to Virginia and established their marital abode in Caroline County. At the October Term, 1958, of the Circuit Court of Caroline County, a grand jury issued an indictment charging the Lovings with violating Virginia's ban on interracial marriages. On January 6, 1959, the Lovings pleaded guilty to the charge and were sentenced to one year in jail; however, the trial judge suspended the sentence for a period of 25 years on the condition that the Lovings leave the State and not return to Virginia together for 25 years. He stated in an opinion that:

> Almighty God created the races white, black, yellow, malay and red, and he placed them on separate continents. And but for the interference with his arrangement there would be no cause for such marriages. The fact that he separated the races shows that he did not intend for the races to mix.

After their convictions, the Lovings took up residence in the District of Columbia. On November 6, 1963, they filed a motion in the state trial court to vacate the judgment and set aside the sentence on the ground that the statutes which they had violated were repugnant to the Fourteenth Amendment. [The trial court denied their motion, and Virginia's highest court affirmed. The US Supreme Court granted review.]

Loving v. Virginia

The two statutes under which appellants were convicted and sentenced are part of a comprehensive statutory scheme aimed at prohibiting and punishing interracial marriages. . . . The Lovings have never disputed in the course of this litigation that Mrs. Loving is a "colored person" or that Mr. Loving is a "white person" within the meanings given those terms by the Virginia statutes.

Virginia is now one of sixteen States which prohibit and punish marriages on the basis of racial classifications.[FN5] Penalties for miscegenation arose as an incident to slavery and have been common in Virginia since the colonial period. The present statutory scheme dates from the adoption of the Racial Integrity Act of 1924, passed during the period of extreme nativism which followed the end of the First World War. The central features of this Act, and current Virginia law, are the absolute prohibition of a "white person" marrying other than another "white person," a prohibition against issuing marriage licenses until the issuing official is satisfied that the applicants' statements as to their race are correct, certificates of "racial composition" to be kept by both local and state registrars, and the carrying forward of earlier prohibitions against racial intermarriage.

FN5 After the initiation of this litigation, Maryland repealed its prohibitions against interracial marriage, leaving Virginia and 15 other States with statutes outlawing interracial marriage: [Alabama, Arkansas, Delaware, Florida, Georgia, Kentucky, Louisiana, Mississippi, Missouri, North Carolina, Oklahoma, South Carolina, Tennessee, Texas, West Virginia]. Over the past 15 years, 14 States have repealed laws outlawing interracial marriages: Arizona, California, Colorado, Idaho, Indiana, Maryland, Montana, Nebraska, Nevada, North Dakota, Oregon, South Dakota, Utah, and Wyoming. The first state court to recognize that miscegenation statutes violate the [US] Equal Protection Clause was the Supreme Court of California. *Perez v. Sharp*, 198 P.2d 17 (Cal. 1948).

I

In upholding the constitutionality of these provisions in the decision below, the Supreme Court of Appeals of Virginia referred to its 1955 decision in ***Naim v. Naim***, 87 S.E.2d 749 (Va. 1955), as stating the reasons supporting the validity of these laws. In *Naim*, the state court concluded that the State's legitimate purposes were "to preserve the racial integrity of its citizens," and to prevent "the corruption of blood," "a mongrel breed of citizens," and "the obliteration of racial pride," obviously an endorsement of the doctrine of White Supremacy. The court also reasoned that marriage has traditionally been subject to state regulation without federal

HISTORY

NAIM v. NAIM: The US Supreme Court had an opportunity to rule on the constitutionality of the Virginia statute in *Naim*, a case involving a marriage between a white woman and a Chinese man. The Court ducked the case on procedural grounds. 350 U.S. 985 (1956). It is now widely believed that the Court avoided the case as too controversial to handle so soon after *Brown v. Board of Education*.

intervention, and, consequently, the regulation of marriage should be left to exclusive state control by the Tenth Amendment.

While the state court is no doubt correct in asserting that marriage is a social relation subject to the State's police power, the State does not contend in its argument before this Court that its powers to regulate marriage are unlimited notwithstanding the commands of the Fourteenth Amendment. Nor could it do so in light of *Meyer v. State of Nebraska* (1923) and *Skinner v. State of Oklahoma* (1942). Instead, the State argues that the meaning of the Equal Protection Clause, as illuminated by the statements of the Framers, is only that state penal laws containing an interracial element as part of the definition of the offense must apply equally to whites and Negroes in the sense that members of each race are punished to the same degree. Thus, the State contends that, because its miscegenation statutes punish equally both the white and the Negro participants in an interracial marriage, these statutes, despite their reliance on racial classifications do not constitute an invidious discrimination based upon race. The second argument advanced by the State assumes the validity of its equal application theory. The argument is that, if the Equal Protection Clause does not outlaw miscegenation statutes because of their reliance on racial classifications, the question of constitutionality would thus become whether there was any rational basis for a State to treat interracial marriages differently from other marriages. On this question, the State argues, the scientific evidence is substantially in doubt and, consequently, this Court should defer to the wisdom of the state legislature in adopting its policy of discouraging interracial marriages.

Because we reject the notion that the mere "equal application" of a statute containing racial classifications is enough to remove the classifications from the Fourteenth Amendment's proscription of all invidious racial discriminations, we do not accept the State's contention that these statutes should be upheld if there is any possible basis for concluding that they serve a rational purpose. The mere fact of equal application does not mean that our analysis of these statutes should follow the approach we have taken in cases involving no racial discrimination [as] where the Equal Protection Clause has been arrayed against a statute discriminating between the kinds of advertising which may be displayed on trucks. *Railway Express Agency, Inc. v. New York* (1949). . . . In these [types of] cases, involving distinctions not drawn according to race, the Court has merely asked whether there is any rational foundation for the discriminations, and has deferred to the wisdom of the state legislatures. In the case at bar, however, we deal with statutes containing racial classifications, and the fact of equal application does not immunize the statute from the very heavy burden of justification which the Fourteenth Amendment has traditionally required of state statutes drawn according to race.

The State argues that statements in the Thirty-ninth Congress about the time of the passage of the Fourteenth Amendment indicate that the Framers did not intend the Amendment to make unconstitutional state miscegenation laws. Many

Loving v. Virginia

of the statements alluded to by the State concern the debates over the Freedmen's Bureau Bill, which President Johnson vetoed, and the Civil Rights Act of 1866, enacted over his veto. While these statements have some relevance to the intention of Congress in submitting the Fourteenth Amendment, it must be understood that they pertained to the passage of specific statutes and not to the broader, organic purpose of a constitutional amendment. As for the various statements directly concerning the Fourteenth Amendment, we have said in connection with a related problem, that although these historical sources "cast some light" they are not sufficient to resolve the problem; "at best, they are inconclusive[.]" *Brown v. Board of Education* (1954). *See also, Strauder v. West Virginia* (1880). We have rejected the proposition that the debates in the Thirty-ninth Congress or in the state legislatures which ratified the Fourteenth Amendment supported the theory advanced by the State, that the requirement of equal protection of the laws is satisfied by penal laws defining offenses based on racial classifications so long as white and Negro participants in the offense were similarly punished.

The State finds support for its "equal application" theory in the decision of the Court in *Pace v. Alabama*, 106 U.S. 583 (1883). In that case, the Court upheld a conviction under an Alabama statute forbidding adultery or fornication between a white person and a Negro which imposed a greater penalty than that of a statute proscribing similar conduct by members of the same race. The Court reasoned that the statute could not be said to discriminate against Negroes because the punishment for each participant in the offense was the same. However, as recently as the 1964 Term, in rejecting the reasoning of that case, we stated: "*Pace* represents a limited view of the Equal Protection Clause which has not withstood analysis in the subsequent decisions of this Court." ***McLaughlin v. Florida***, 379 U.S. 184 (1964). As we there demonstrated, the Equal Protection Clause requires the consideration of whether the classifications drawn by any statute constitute an arbitrary and invidious discrimination. The clear and central purpose of the Fourteenth Amendment was to eliminate all official state sources of invidious racial discrimination in the States.

■ HISTORY

McLAUGHLIN v. FLORIDA: In *McLaughlin*, the Supreme Court held that a state law criminalizing interracial cohabitation, but not other cohabitation, violated the Equal Protection Clause. *McLauglin* expressly overruled *Pace*, but unlike *Loving*, the case did not involve marriage laws.

There can be no question but that Virginia's miscegenation statutes rest solely upon distinctions drawn according to race. The statutes proscribe generally accepted conduct if engaged in by members of different races. Over the years, this Court has consistently repudiated "distinctions between citizens solely because of their ancestry" as being "odious to a free people whose institutions are founded upon the doctrine of equality." *Hirabayashi v. United States* (1943). At the very least, the Equal Protection Clause demands that racial classifications, especially suspect in criminal statutes, be subjected to the "most rigid scrutiny," *Korematsu v. United States* (1944), and, if they are ever to be upheld, they must be shown to be necessary to the accomplishment of some permissible state objective, independent of the racial discrimination which it was the object of the Fourteenth Amendment to eliminate. Indeed, two members of this Court have already stated that they "cannot conceive of a valid legislative purpose which makes the color of a person's skin the test of whether his conduct is a criminal offense." *McLaughlin*, 379 U.S. at 198 (1964) (Stewart, J., joined by Douglas, J., concurring).

There is patently no legitimate overriding purpose independent of invidious racial discrimination which justifies this classification. The fact that Virginia prohibits only interracial marriages involving white persons demonstrates that the racial classifications must stand on their own justification, as measures designed to maintain White Supremacy.[FN11] We have consistently denied the constitutionality of measures which restrict the rights of citizens on account of race. There can be no doubt that restricting the freedom to marry solely because of racial classifications violates the central meaning of the Equal Protection Clause.

FN11 Appellants point out that the State's concern in these statutes, as expressed in the words of the 1924 Act's title, "An Act to Preserve Racial Integrity," extends only to the integrity of the white race. While Virginia prohibits whites from marrying any nonwhite (subject to the exception for the descendants of Pocahontas), Negroes, Orientals, and any other racial class may intermarry without statutory interference. Appellants contend that this distinction renders Virginia's miscegenation statutes arbitrary and unreasonable even assuming the constitutional validity of an official purpose to preserve "racial integrity." We need not reach this contention because we find the racial classifications in these statutes repugnant to the Fourteenth Amendment, even assuming an even-handed state purpose to protect the "integrity" of all races.

II.

These statutes also deprive the Lovings of liberty without due process of law in violation of the Due Process Clause of the Fourteenth Amendment. The freedom to marry has long been recognized as one of the vital personal rights essential to the orderly pursuit of happiness by free men.

Marriage is one of the "basic civil rights of man," fundamental to our very existence and survival. *Skinner v. Oklahoma* (1942). To deny this fundamental freedom on so unsupportable a basis as the racial classifications embodied in these statutes, classifications so directly subversive of the principle of equality at the heart of the Fourteenth Amendment, is surely to deprive all the State's citizens of liberty without due process of law. The Fourteenth Amendment requires that the freedom of choice to marry not be restricted by invidious racial discriminations. Under our Constitution, the freedom to marry or not marry a person of another race resides with the individual and cannot be infringed by the State.

Justice Stewart, concurring. [Omitted.]

Chapter Recap

A. Racial inequality in early 20th-century America was maintained through many legal doctrines, but many doctrines were also used to challenge it.

B. *Brown v. Board of Education* (1954) led to the demise of the "separate but equal" concept that had dominated the Equal Protection Clause since the 19th century.

C. *Brown*'s companion case, *Bolling v. Sharpe* (1954), used the incorporation concept to hold that the federal government's Fifth Amendment obligation not to deprive "liberty" without due process incorporated the right of equal protection found in the Fourteenth Amendment.

D. *Loving v. Virginia* (1967) established that statutes forbidding interracial marriage violate both equal protection and due process.

CHAPTER 12

Master Class: The Big Picture

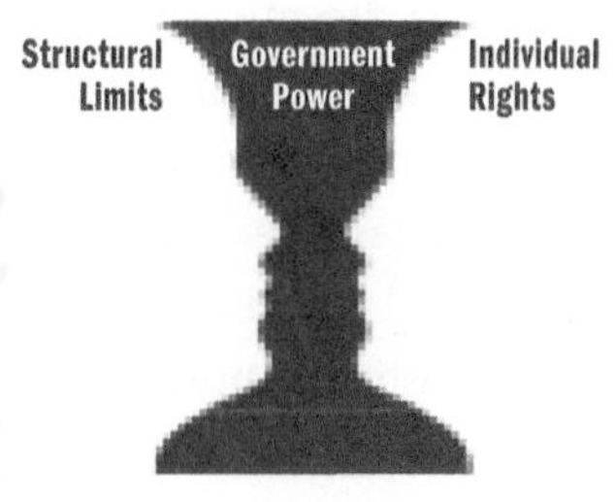

By the close of the Warren Court (around 1970), broad consensus had developed over the most prominent features of the US Constitutional system.

Regarding powers, State governments had authority to make laws in all areas, subject only to limitations found in state constitutions or the US Constitution. Among the federally-imposed limits was the Supremacy Clause, which ensured that federal lawmaking would override contrary state laws. The federal government could act only in enumerated areas, but because the US Constitution was intended to create a government that could accomplish its goals, those enumerated areas tended to be understood broadly. In particular, *Lochner*-era doctrines making it difficult for the national government to regulate the economy through the commerce, taxing, and spending powers had been repudiated. And that repudiation arose, in part, from a concern that the judiciary should not overstep its role within the separation of powers.

Regarding individual rights, the US Constitution's Bill of Rights on its face limited the federal government. But because (almost all of) those rights were incorporated into the meaning of "liberty" in the Fourteenth Amendment Due Process Clause, the States were also obligated to respect them. The precise contours of the rights protected by the US Constitution developed over time. For due process and equal protection (the most broadly-phrased rights that could potentially be invoked against a huge range of laws), courts began to use different levels of scrutiny depending on the right asserted. Most of the time, courts would be quite deferential, upholding laws if any rational basis could support them. This spelled the end of *Lochner*'s since-repudiated strong protection for the unenumerated freedom of contract. For race discrimination or intrusion into fundamental rights, a court would use heightened scrutiny, requiring the government to offer stronger reasons to justify the alleged intrusion on rights.

This big picture can be seen at work in the constitutional challenges to the Civil Rights Act of 1964. As with most significant constitutional law disputes, the controversy involved the interaction among several doctrines.

A. The Civil Rights Act of 1964

Brown and *Loving* struck down laws that mandated racial segregation, but by themselves they did not limit race discrimination by private parties like landlords or shopkeepers. States had authority to enact laws against private discrimination, and by the mid-20th century, many in the North and West had already done so. But the segregated South had no such laws.

Under *The Civil Rights Cases* (1883), Congress's power to employ § 5 of the Fourteenth Amendment to enforce the Equal Protection Clause extended only to discriminatory state action, not private action. This restriction on the Fourteenth Amendment's enforcement power was a significant concern for Congress when it began to explore federal civil rights legislation in the early 1960s. In the hearings and debates, proponents argued that the Fourteenth Amendment ought to give Congress power to enact an anti-discrimination law, but if nothing else, the law could be justified under the Commerce Clause because discrimination reduced economic activity and interfered with the flow of goods and services among states.

After a titanic legislative battle that included record-breaking weeks of filibusters in the Senate, Congress passed the Civil Rights Act of 1964. Among other things, the statute prohibited race discrimination in places of public accommodation (Title II), in employment (Title VII), and in any program receiving federal funds (Title VI).

Title II announced that "All persons shall be entitled to the full and equal enjoyment of the goods, services, facilities, privileges, advantages, and accommodations of any place of public accommodation, as defined in this section, without discrimination or segregation on the ground of race, color, religion, or national origin." 42 U.S.C. § 2000a(1). The definition of "places of public accommodation" included lodgings, restaurants, and theaters where their operations "affect commerce." § 2000a(b).

The Act was swiftly challenged by businesses wishing to refuse service to non-White customers, or to serve them only under segregated conditions.

B. Hotels and Commerce: *Heart of Atlanta Motel*

Race discrimination in hotels and motels was a long-standing problem, as seen in *The Civil Rights Cases* (1883), where two of the collected cases involved refusals to rent hotel rooms in Kansas and Missouri. Ch. 7.C.2. In the mid-20th century, many Black travelers relied on the publication known as "The Green Book" to identify those lodgings that would be willing to house them. In Congressional debates, Senator Hubert Humphrey pointed to the Green Book and a similar guide for pet owners to show that in Charleston, South Carolina, there were ten hotels that allowed dogs, but none that allowed Blacks.

Title II of the Civil Rights Act of 1964 expressly guaranteed a right of non-discriminatory access to hotels. It specified that a place of public accommodation "affects commerce" if it is an "inn, hotel, motel, or other establishment which provides lodging to transient guests, other than an establishment located within a building which contains not more than five rooms for rent or hire and which is actually occupied by the proprietor of such establishment at his residence." § 2000a(b)(1) & (c)(1).

As of 1963, 14 of the major hotels in central Atlanta had agreed to integrate, but the Heart of Atlanta Motel pointedly refused. On the day President Lyndon Johnson signed the Civil Rights Act into law, the hotel filed suit challenging its constitutionality.

At oral argument in the Supreme Court, the Solicitor General Archibald Cox focused on evidence from the Congressional hearings substantiating the economic impacts of discrimination in public accommodations.

> Solicitor General Cox: Title II was addressed to a grave commercial problem. . . . The testimony before Congress provided literally overwhelming evidence that discrimination by hotels and motels impedes interstate travel. . . .
>
> [A study by the Department of Commerce found] not only that interstate travel was made incredibly more difficult for Negroes . . . by reason of discrimination in hotels or motels, but that its volume as a whole was sharply curtailed by the unavailability of adequate public accommodation. . . .
>
> On a motor trip between Washington D.C. and Miami, Florida, the average distance that was found between accommodations of reasonable quality open to Negroes was 141 miles. And when we think of the frequency by such we go by other hotels and motels open to everyone, the significance of a three or four-hour drive between the hope of accommodation is very significant indeed. And it further appeared that those accommodations that were available to Negroes were on the whole likely to be small, so that after driving three or four hours one might well find a No Vacancy sign, and have another equally lengthy drive ahead of it. . . .

> Segregation in hotels and motels has an even more dramatic effect upon the sites chosen for conventions which of course account for a large volume of interstate travel. . . . The Atlanta Convention Bureau, within one day after 14 Atlanta hotels desegregated, received commitments—not feelers but commitments—from organizations expecting over 3000 delegates which would not have gone to Atlanta if segregation were continued to be practiced. Again, New Orleans found an American Legion Convention expecting 50,000 people transferred to another city because New Orleans could not guarantee equal public accommodations.
>
> Finally, this kind of restraint has a most marked effect upon the volume of interstate travel. It won't do to say "well, people will go somewhere else." . . . Any practice that distorts the flow of commerce, that prevents it from flowing freely if Congress thinks it's desirable to flow freely, is itself a restraint on interstate commerce. . . .

The hotel was represented by its owner, Moreton Rolleston—who was also a lawyer. His argument downplayed the Commerce Clause, focusing more on an individual rights argument.

> Mr. Rolleston: The fundamental question, I submit, is whether or not Congress has the power to take away the liberty of an individual to run his business as he sees fit in the selection and choice of his customers. This is the real important issue. And the fact of alleged civil rights of the Negroes involved is purely incidental, because if Congress can exercise these controls over the right of individuals, it is possible that there's no limit to Congress' power to appropriate private property and liberty. . . .
>
> In my opinion, the argument of counsel and of the government that this is done to relieve a burden on interstate commerce is so much hogwash. The purpose of Congress was to pass a law which some way or other, they could control discrimination by individuals in the whole United States. . . .
>
> I didn't come here to talk about commerce. I didn't come here to argue the question of whether or not this motel has an effect on commerce. Certainly everything that happens in this country has an effect on commerce. But I did perceive, I hope, that in the writings of members of this Court there is still the great facet of personal liberty that this Court stands for. . . .
>
> I believe that the rights of individuals, the rights of people, the personal liberty of a person to do what he wants to run his business is more important and more paramount than the commerce of the United States. . . . There is a paramount duty on Congress to protect the individual liberty over and above trade.

ITEMS TO CONSIDER WHILE READING *HEART OF ATLANTA MOTEL*:

A. *Which enumerated powers could Congress rely upon to enact the Civil Rights Act of 1964? Does it matter which power Congress uses to justify its actions?*

B. *Was Congressional reliance on the Commerce Clause a pretext? If so, should that matter?*

C. *How should a court determine whether an in-state practice (like race discrimination at a hotel) has substantial effect on interstate commerce?*

D. *Assuming Congress has enumerated power to enact this law, does it violate any individual rights of business owners?*

E. *What can a business like the Heart of Atlanta Motel do to avoid being subject to federal laws?*

Heart of Atlanta Motel, Inc. v. United States,

379 U.S. 241 (1964)

Justice Clark delivered the opinion of the Court [joined by Chief Justice Warren and Justices Black, Douglas, Harlan, Brennan, Stewart, White, and Goldberg].

This is a declaratory judgment action [by Heart of Atlanta Motel, Inc.] attacking the constitutionality of Title II of the Civil Rights Act of 1964. [The trial court upheld the Act.] We affirm the judgment.

1. The Factual Background and Contentions of the Parties

The case comes here on admissions and stipulated facts. Appellant owns and operates the Heart of Atlanta Motel which has 216 rooms available to transient guests. The motel is located on Courtland Street, two blocks from downtown Peachtree Street. It is readily accessible to interstate highways 75 and 85 and state highways 23 and 41. Appellant solicits patronage from outside the State of Georgia through various national advertising media, including magazines of national circulation; it maintains over 50 billboards and highway signs within the State, soliciting patronage for the motel; it accepts convention trade from outside Georgia and approximately 75% of its registered guests are from out of State. Prior to passage of the Act the motel had followed a practice of refusing to rent rooms to Negroes, and it alleged that it intended to continue to do so. In an effort to perpetuate that policy this suit was filed.

The appellant contends that Congress in passing this Act exceeded its power to regulate commerce under Art. I, § 8, cl. 3, of the Constitution of the United States; that the Act violates the Fifth Amendment because appellant is deprived of the right to choose its customers and operate its business as it wishes, resulting in a taking of its liberty and property without due process of law . . . ; and, finally, that by requiring appellant to rent available rooms to Negroes against its will, Congress is subjecting it to involuntary servitude in contravention of the Thirteenth Amendment. . . .

2. The History of the Act

Congress first evidenced its interest in civil rights legislation in the Civil Rights or Enforcement Act of April 9, 1866. There followed four Acts, with a fifth, the Civil Rights Act of March 1, 1875, culminating the series. In 1883 this Court struck down the public accommodations sections of the 1875 Act in *The Civil Rights Cases*. No major legislation in this field had been enacted by Congress for 82 years when **the Civil Rights Act of 1957** became law. It was followed by **the Civil Rights Act of 1960.** Three years later, on June 19, 1963, the late President Kennedy called for civil rights legislation in a message to Congress to which he attached a proposed bill. Its stated purpose was "to promote the general welfare by eliminating discrimination based on race, color, religion, or national origin in public accommodations through the exercise by Congress of the powers conferred upon it to enforce the provisions of the fourteenth and fifteenth amendments, to regulate commerce among the several States, and to make laws necessary and proper to execute the powers conferred upon it by the Constitution."

■ HISTORY

CIVIL RIGHTS ACTS OF 1957 AND 1960: These voting rights bills were enacted under Congress's enumerated power to enforce the Fifteenth Amendment. While well-intentioned, they did not have their desired effect and were largely superseded by the Voting Rights Act of 1965. See Ch. 15.E.3.

Bills were introduced in each House of the Congress, embodying the President's suggestion. However, it was not until July 2, 1964, upon the recommendation of President Johnson, that the Civil Rights Act of 1964, here under attack, was finally passed.

After extended hearings each of these bills was favorably reported to its respective house. Although each bill originally incorporated extensive findings of fact these were eliminated from the bills as they were reported. The House passed its bill in January 1964 and sent it to the Senate. Through a bipartisan coalition of Senators [Hubert] Humphrey [D-MN] and [Everett] Dirksen [R-IL], together with other Senators, a substitute was worked out in informal conferences. . . . This expedited procedure prevented the usual report on the substitute bill in the Senate as well as a Conference Committee report ordinarily filed in such matters. Our only frame of reference as to the legislative history of the Act is, therefore, the hearings, reports and debates on the respective bills in each house. . . .

3. Title II of the Act [Omitted]

Heart of Atlanta Motel, Inc. v. United States

4. Application of Title II to Heart of Atlanta Motel

It is admitted that the operation of the motel brings it within the provisions . . . of the Act and that appellant refused to provide lodging for transient Negroes because of their race or color and that it intends to continue that policy unless restrained.

The sole question posed is, therefore, the constitutionality of the Civil Rights Act of 1964 as applied to these facts. The legislative history of the Act indicates that Congress based the Act on § 5 and the Equal Protection Clause of the Fourteenth Amendment as well as its power to regulate interstate commerce under Art. I, § 8, cl. 3, of the Constitution.

The Senate Commerce Committee made it quite clear that the fundamental object of Title II was to vindicate "the deprivation of personal dignity that surely accompanies denials of equal access to public establishments." At the same time, however, it noted that such an objective has been and could be readily achieved "by congressional action based on the commerce power of the Constitution." Our study of the legislative record, made in the light of prior cases, has brought us to the conclusion that Congress possessed ample power in this regard, and we have therefore not considered the other grounds relied upon. This is not to say that the remaining authority upon which it acted was not adequate, a question upon which we do not pass, but merely that since the commerce power is sufficient for our decision here we have considered it alone. . . .

5. *The Civil Rights Cases* and their Application

In light of our ground for decision, it might be well at the outset to discuss the *Civil Rights Cases*, which declared provisions of the Civil Rights Act of 1875 unconstitutional. We think that decision inapposite, and without precedential value in determining the constitutionality of the present Act. Unlike Title II of the present legislation, the 1875 Act broadly proscribed discrimination in "inns, public conveyances on land or water, theaters, and other places of public amusement," without limiting the categories of affected businesses to those impinging upon interstate commerce. In contrast, the applicability of Title II is carefully limited to enterprises having a direct and substantial relation to the interstate flow of goods and people, except **where state action is involved**. Further, the fact that certain kinds of businesses may not in 1875 have been sufficiently involved in interstate commerce to warrant bringing them within the ambit of the commerce

■ OBSERVATION

WHERE STATE ACTION IS INVOLVED: Title II's definition reached business establishments if they "affect commerce" or "if discrimination or segregation by it is supported by State action." The second formula took advantage of § 5 of the Fourteenth Amendment, which allows federal laws targeting discriminatory state action whether or not it affects interstate commerce. (There was no allegation that the Heart of Atlanta Motel's discrimination was supported by state action.)

power is not necessarily dispositive of the same question today. Our populace had not reached its present mobility, nor were facilities, goods and services circulating as readily in interstate commerce as they are today. Although the principles which we apply today are those first formulated by Chief Justice Marshall in *Gibbons v. Ogden* (1824), the conditions of transportation and commerce have changed dramatically, and we must apply those principles to the present state of commerce. The sheer increase in volume of interstate traffic alone would give discriminatory practices which inhibit travel a far larger impact upon the Nation's commerce than such practices had on the economy of another day.

Finally, there is language in the *Civil Rights Cases* which indicates that the Court did not fully consider whether the 1875 Act could be sustained as an exercise of the commerce power. Though the Court observed that "no one will contend that the power to pass it was contained in the constitution before the adoption of the last three amendments (Thirteenth, Fourteenth, and Fifteenth)," the Court went on specifically to note that the Act was not "conceived" in terms of the commerce power[.] . . . Since the commerce power was not relied on by the Government and was without support in the record it is understandable that the Court narrowed its inquiry and excluded the Commerce Clause as a possible source of power. In any event, it is clear that such a limitation renders the opinion devoid of authority for the proposition that the Commerce Clause gives no power to Congress to regulate discriminatory practices now found substantially to affect interstate commerce. We, therefore, conclude that the *Civil Rights Cases* have no relevance to the basis of decision here where the Act explicitly relies upon the commerce power, and where the record is filled with testimony of obstructions and restraints resulting from the discriminations found to be existing. We now pass to that phase of the case.

6. The Basis of Congressional Action

While the Act as adopted carried no congressional findings the record of its passage through each house is replete with evidence of the burdens that discrimination by race or color places upon interstate commerce. This testimony included the fact that our people have become increasingly mobile with millions of people of all races traveling from State to State; that Negroes in particular have been the subject of discrimination in transient accommodations, having to travel great distances to secure the same; that often they have been unable to obtain accommodations and have had to call upon friends to put them up overnight, and that these conditions had become so acute as to require the listing of available lodging for Negroes in a special guidebook which was itself dramatic testimony to the difficulties Negroes encounter in travel. These exclusionary practices were found to be nationwide, the Under Secretary of Commerce testifying that there is "no question that this discrimination in the North still exists to a large degree" and in the West and Midwest as well.

This testimony indicated a qualitative as well as quantitative effect on interstate travel by Negroes. The former was the obvious impairment of the Negro traveler's pleasure and convenience that resulted when he continually was uncertain of finding lodging. As for the latter, there was evidence that this uncertainty stemming from racial discrimination had the effect of discouraging travel on the part of a substantial portion of the Negro community. This was the conclusion not only of the Under Secretary of Commerce but also of the Administrator of the Federal Aviation Agency who wrote the Chairman of the Senate Commerce Committee that it was his "belief that air commerce is adversely affected by the denial to a substantial segment of the traveling public of adequate and desegregated public accommodations." We shall not burden this opinion with further details since the voluminous testimony presents overwhelming evidence that discrimination by hotels and motels impedes interstate travel.

Heart of Atlanta Motel, Inc. v. United States

7. The Power of Congress Over Interstate Travel.

The power of Congress to deal with these obstructions depends on the meaning of the Commerce Clause. Its meaning was first enunciated 140 years ago by the great Chief Justice John Marshall in *Gibbons v. Ogden*. [A lengthy quote from *Gibbons* followed.] In short, the determinative test of the exercise of power by the Congress under the Commerce Clause is simply whether the activity sought to be regulated is "commerce which concerns more States than one" and has a real and substantial relation to the national interest. Let us now turn to this facet of the problem.

That . . . the movement of persons through more States than one [is part of commerce] was settled as early as 1849, in the *Passenger Cases (Smith v. Turner)*, 48 U.S. 283 (1849), where Mr. Justice McLean stated: "That the transportation of passengers is a part of commerce is not now an open question." Again in 1913 Mr. Justice McKenna, speaking for the Court, said: "Commerce among the states, we have said, consists of intercourse and traffic between their citizens, and includes the transportation of persons and property." *Hoke v. United States*, 227 U.S. 308 (1913). . . . Nor does it make any difference whether the transportation is commercial in character. . . .

The same interest in protecting interstate commerce which led Congress to deal with segregation in interstate carriers and the white-slave traffic has prompted it to extend the exercise of its power to gambling, *Lottery Case (Champion v Ames)*, 188 U.S. 321 (1903); to criminal enterprises; to deceptive practices in the sale of products; to fraudulent security transactions; to misbranding of drugs; to wages and hours, *United States v. Darby* (1941); to members of labor unions, *National Labor Relations Board v. Jones & Laughlin Steel Corp.* (1937); to crop control, *Wickard v. Filburn* (1942); to discrimination against shippers; to the protection of small business from injurious price cutting; to resale price maintenance; to professional football; and to racial discrimination by owners and managers of terminal restaurants.

That Congress was legislating against moral wrongs in many of these areas rendered its enactments no less valid. In framing Title II of this Act Congress was also dealing with what it considered a moral problem. But that fact does not detract from the overwhelming evidence of the disruptive effect that racial discrimination has had on commercial intercourse. It was this burden which empowered Congress to enact appropriate legislation, and, given this basis for the exercise of its power, Congress was not restricted by the fact that the particular obstruction to interstate commerce with which it was dealing was also deemed a moral and social wrong.

It is said that the operation of the motel here is of a purely local character. But, assuming this to be true, if it is interstate commerce that feels the pinch, it does not matter how local the operation which applies the squeeze. As Chief Justice Stone put it in *United States v. Darby*:

> The power of Congress over interstate commerce is not confined to the regulation of commerce among the states. It extends to those activities intrastate which so affect interstate commerce or the exercise of the power of Congress over it as to make regulation of them appropriate means to the attainment of a legitimate end, the exercise of the granted power of Congress to regulate interstate commerce.

Thus the power of Congress to promote interstate commerce also includes the power to regulate the local incidents thereof, including local activities in both the States of origin and destination, which might have a substantial and harmful effect upon that commerce. One need only examine the evidence which we have discussed above to see that Congress may—as it has—prohibit racial discrimination by motels serving travelers, however "local" their operations may appear.

[INDIVIDUAL RIGHTS]

Nor does the Act deprive appellant of liberty or property under the Fifth Amendment. The commerce power invoked here by the Congress is a specific and plenary one authorized by the Constitution itself. The only questions are: (1) whether Congress had a rational basis for finding that racial discrimination by motels affected commerce, and (2) if it had such a basis, whether the means it selected to eliminate that evil are reasonable and appropriate. If they are, appellant has no "right" to select its guests as it sees fit, free from governmental regulation.

There is nothing novel about such legislation. Thirty-two States now have it on their books either by statute or executive order and many cities provide such regulation. Some of these Acts go back fourscore years. It has been repeatedly held by this Court that such laws do not violate the Due Process Clause of the Fourteenth Amendment. Perhaps the first such holding was in the *Civil Rights Cases* themselves, where Mr. Justice Bradley for the Court inferentially found that innkeepers, "by the laws of all the States, so far as we are aware, are bound, to the extent of their

Heart of Atlanta Motel, Inc. v. United States

facilities, to furnish proper accommodation to all unobjectionable persons who in good faith apply for them."

As we have pointed out, States now have such provisions and no case has been cited to us where the attack on a state statute has been successful, either in federal or state courts. Indeed, in some cases the Due Process and Equal Protection Clause objections have been specifically discarded in this Court. As a result the constitutionality of such state statutes stands unquestioned. The authority of the Federal government over interstate commerce does not differ . . . in extent or character from that retained by the states over intrastate commerce.

It is doubtful if in the long run appellant will suffer economic loss as a result of the Act. Experience is to the contrary where discrimination is completely obliterated as to all public accommodations. But whether this be true or not is of no consequence since this Court has specifically held that the fact that a member of the class which is regulated may suffer economic losses not shared by others has never been a barrier to such legislation. Likewise in a long line of cases this Court has rejected the claim that the prohibition of racial discrimination in public accommodations interferes with personal liberty. Neither do we find any merit in the claim that the Act is a taking of property without just compensation. The cases are to the contrary.

We find no merit in the remainder of appellant's contentions, including that of "involuntary servitude." As we have seen, 32 States prohibit racial discrimination in public accommodations. These laws but codify the **common-law innkeeper rule** which long predated the Thirteenth Amendment. It is difficult to believe that the Amendment was intended to abrogate this principle. Indeed, the opinion of the Court in the *Civil Rights Cases* is to the contrary as we have seen, it having noted with approval the laws of "all the States" prohibiting discrimination. We could not say that the requirements of the Act in this regard are in any way akin to African slavery.

We, therefore, conclude that the action of the Congress in the adoption of the Act as applied here to a motel which concededly serves interstate travelers is within the power granted it by the Commerce Clause of the Constitution, as interpreted by this Court for 140 years. It may be argued that Congress could have pursued other methods to eliminate the obstructions it found in interstate commerce caused by racial discrimination. But this is a matter of policy that rests entirely with the Congress not with the courts. How obstructions in commerce may be removed—what means are to be employed—is within the sound and exclusive discretion of the Congress. It is subject only to one caveat—that the means chosen by

■ HISTORY

COMMON-LAW INNKEEPER RULE: English law dating as far back as the 1400s imposed upon innkeepers a duty to serve all customers, allowing them to refuse service only on reasonable grounds such as boisterousness or past refusal to pay. American jurisdictions that tolerated hotel discrimination had ceased reliance on the innkeeper rule, but other states continued to enforce it (or similar obligations imposed by statute).

it must be reasonably adapted to the end permitted by the Constitution. We cannot say that its choice here was not so adapted. The Constitution requires no more.

Justice Black, concurring.

[Congress's authority in this case flows not from the Commerce Clause alone, but from that clause in conjunction with the Necessary and Proper Clause.] It has long been held that the Necessary and Proper Clause, Art. I, § 8, cl. 18, adds to the commerce power of Congress the power to regulate local instrumentalities operating within a single State if their activities burden the flow of commerce among the States. . . .

Justice Douglas, concurring.

Though I join the Court's opinions [in *Heart of Atlanta Motel* and *Katzenbach v. McClung*], I am somewhat reluctant here . . . to rest solely on the Commerce Clause. My reluctance is not due to any conviction that Congress lacks power to regulate commerce in the interests of human rights. It is rather my belief that the right of people to be free of state action that discriminates against them because of race, like the right of persons to move freely from State to State occupies a more protected position in our constitutional system than does the movement of cattle, fruit, steel and coal across state lines. . . . Hence I would prefer to rest on the assertion of legislative power contained in § 5 of the Fourteenth Amendment which states: "The Congress shall have power to enforce, by appropriate legislation, the provisions of this article"—a power which the Court concedes was exercised at least in part in this Act.

A decision based on the Fourteenth Amendment would have a more settling effect, making unnecessary litigation over whether a particular restaurant or inn is within the commerce definitions of the Act or whether a particular customer is an interstate traveler. Under my construction, the Act would apply to all customers in all the enumerated places of public accommodation. And that construction would put an end to all obstructionist strategies and finally close one door on a bitter chapter in American history. . . .

Justice Goldberg, concurring. [Omitted.]

flashforward

Statutes to Enforce the Fourteenth Amendment. *Heart of Atlanta Motel* chose to distinguish *The Civil Rights Cases* and not overrule them. This left intact the principle that § 5 of the Fourteenth Amendment authorized federal laws only when they targeted denial of due process or equal protection by state or local governments. Although some concurrences from *Heart of Atlanta Motel* objected to that limitation, it has since been reaffirmed in *United States v. Morrison* (2000). See Ch. 15.C.2.b.

C. Restaurants and Commerce: *Katzenbach v. McClung*

Title II of the Civil Rights Act of 1964 reached "any restaurant, cafeteria, lunchroom, lunch counter, soda fountain, or other facility principally engaged in selling food for consumption on the premises" if "its operations affect commerce." 42 U.S.C. § 2000a(b)(2). Congress went on to specify that an eatery affects commerce if "it serves or offers to serve interstate travelers" or "a substantial portion of the food which it serves . . . has moved in commerce." 42 U.S.C. § 2000a(c)(2).

It was fairly easy in *Heart of Atlanta Motel* to see how motels could affect interstate commerce, because by definition they host travelers. The connection to interstate commerce of a local restaurant serving local customers was less obvious. Congress's power to ban discrimination in restaurants was challenged by Ollie McClung Sr. and Jr. of Birmingham, Alabama, the owners of Ollie's Barbeque. As was common practice during the Jim Crow era, the McClungs allowed White customers to eat in the restaurant's seating area, but Black customers could only get take-out orders from a counter facing the street.

ITEMS TO CONSIDER WHEN READING *KATZENBACH v. MCCLUNG*:

A. *What makes a restaurant different from, or similar to, a motel in its potential to affect interstate commerce?*

B. *Must Congress allow a business an opportunity to prove that its individual conduct had no substantial effect on interstate commerce?*

Katzenbach v. McClung,
379 U.S. 294 (1964)

Justice Clark delivered the opinion of the Court [joined by Chief Justice Warren and Justices Black, Douglas, Harlan, Brennan, Stewart, White, and Goldberg].

This case was argued with *Heart of Atlanta Motel v. United States*, decided this date, in which we upheld the constitutional validity of Title II of the Civil Rights Act of 1964 against an attack by hotels, motels, and like establishments. This complaint for injunctive relief [by Ollie McClung Sr. and Jr.] against appellants [government officials including Acting US Attorney General Nicholas Katzenbach] attacks the constitutionality of the Act as applied to a restaurant. The [trial court issued an injunction] restraining appellants from enforcing the Act against the restaurant. . . . We now reverse the judgment.

1. [Omitted]

2. The Facts.

Ollie's Barbecue is a family-owned restaurant in Birmingham, Alabama, specializing in barbecued meats and homemade pies, with a seating capacity of 220 customers. It is located on a state highway 11 blocks from an interstate one and a somewhat greater distance from railroad and bus stations. The restaurant caters to a family and white-collar trade with a take-out service for Negroes. It employs 36 persons, two-thirds of whom are Negroes.

In the 12 months preceding the passage of the Act, the restaurant purchased locally approximately $150,000 worth of food, $69,683 or 46% of which was meat that it bought from a local supplier who had procured it from outside the State. The District Court expressly found that a substantial portion of the food served in the restaurant had moved in interstate commerce. The restaurant has refused to serve Negroes in its dining accommodations since its original opening in 1927, and since July 2, 1964, it has been operating in violation of the Act. The court below concluded that if it were required to serve Negroes it would lose a substantial amount of business. . . .

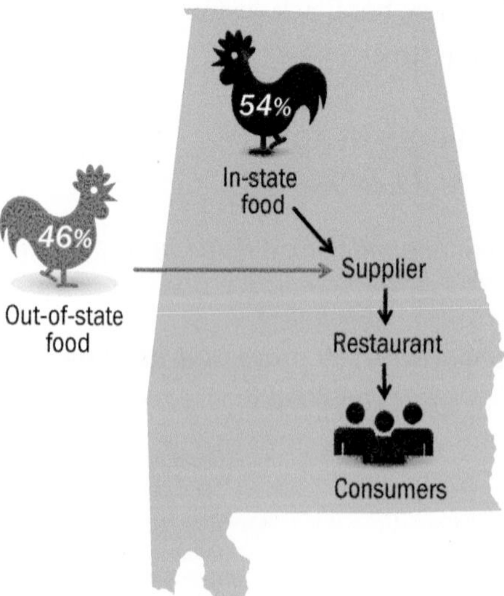

Katzenbach v. McClung

3. The Act As Applied.

. . . There is no claim that interstate travelers frequented the restaurant. The sole question, therefore, narrows down to whether Title II, as applied to a restaurant annually receiving about $70,000 worth of food which has moved in commerce, is a valid exercise of the power of Congress. . . .

4. The Congressional Hearings.

As we noted in *Heart of Atlanta Motel* both Houses of Congress conducted prolonged hearings on the Act. . . . The record is replete with testimony of the burdens placed on interstate commerce by racial discrimination in restaurants. A comparison of per capita spending by Negroes in restaurants, theaters, and like establishments indicated less spending, after discounting income differences, in areas where discrimination is widely practiced. This condition, which was especially aggravated in the South, was attributed . . . to racial segregation. This diminutive spending springing from a refusal to serve Negroes and their total loss as customers has, regardless of the absence of direct evidence, a close connection to interstate commerce. The fewer customers a restaurant enjoys the less food it sells and consequently the less it buys. In addition, the Attorney General testified that this type of discrimination imposed "an artificial restriction on the market" and interfered with the flow of merchandise. In addition, there were many references to discriminatory situations causing wide unrest and having a depressant effect on general business conditions in the respective communities.

Moreover there was an impressive array of testimony that discrimination in restaurants had a direct and highly restrictive effect upon interstate travel by Negroes. This resulted, it was said, because discriminatory practices prevent Negroes from buying prepared food served on the premises while on a trip, except in isolated and unkempt restaurants and under most unsatisfactory and often unpleasant conditions. This obviously discourages travel and obstructs interstate commerce for one can hardly travel without eating. Likewise, it was said, that discrimination deterred professional, as well as skilled, people from moving into areas where such practices occurred and thereby caused industry to be reluctant to establish there.

We believe that this testimony afforded ample basis for the conclusion that established restaurants in such areas sold less interstate goods because of the discrimination, that interstate travel was obstructed directly by it, that business in general suffered and that many new businesses refrained from establishing there as a result of it. Hence the District Court was in error in concluding that there was no connection between discrimination and the movement of interstate commerce. The court's conclusion that such a connection is outside "common experience" flies in the face of stubborn fact.

It goes without saying that, viewed in isolation, the volume of food purchased by Ollie's Barbecue from sources supplied from out of state was insignificant when compared with the total foodstuffs moving in commerce. But, as our late Brother Jackson said for the Court in *Wickard v. Filburn* (1942): "That appellee's own contribution to the demand for wheat may be trivial by itself is not enough to remove him from the scope of federal regulation where, as here, his contribution, taken together with that of many others similarly situated, is far from trivial."

We noted in *Heart of Atlanta Motel* that a number of witnesses attested to the fact that racial discrimination was not merely a state or regional problem but was one of nationwide scope. Against this background, we must conclude that while the focus of the legislation was on the individual restaurant's relation to interstate commerce, Congress appropriately considered the importance of that connection with the knowledge that the discrimination was but representative of many others throughout the country, the total incidence of which if left unchecked may well become far-reaching in its harm to commerce.

With this situation spreading as the record shows, Congress was not required to await the total dislocation of commerce. . . . Congress was entitled to provide reasonable preventive measures. . . .

5. The Power of Congress to Regulate Local Activities.

Article I, § 8, cl. 3, confers upon Congress the power "to regulate commerce . . . among the several States" and Clause 18 of the same Article grants it the power "to make all Laws which shall be necessary and proper for carrying into execution the foregoing Powers." This grant, as we have pointed out in *Heart of Atlanta Motel*, extends to those activities intrastate which so affect interstate commerce, or the exertion of the power of Congress over it, as to make regulation of them appropriate means to the attainment of a legitimate end, the effective execution of the granted power to regulate interstate commerce.

Much is said about a restaurant business being local but "even if appellee's activity be local and though it may not be regarded as commerce, it may still, whatever its nature, be reached by Congress if it exerts a substantial economic effect on interstate commerce." *Wickard v. Filburn*. The activities that are beyond the reach of Congress are "those which are completely which a particular State, which do not affect other States, and with which it is not necessary to interfere, for the purpose of executing some of the general powers of the government." *Gibbons v. Ogden* (1824). This rule is as good today as it was when Chief Justice Marshall laid it down almost a century and a half ago. . . .

The appellees contend that Congress has arbitrarily created a conclusive presumption that all restaurants meeting the criteria set out in the Act "affect commerce." Stated another way, they object to the omission of a provision for a case-by-case determination—judicial or administrative—that racial discrimination in

Katzenbach v. McClung

a particular restaurant affects commerce. . . . But where we find that the legislators, in light of the facts and testimony before them, have a rational basis for finding a chosen regulatory scheme necessary to the protection of commerce, our investigation is at an end. The only remaining question—one answered in the affirmative by the court below—is whether the particular restaurant either serves or offers to serve interstate travelers or serves food a substantial portion of which has moved in interstate commerce. . . .

Here, of course, Congress had included no formal findings. But their absence is not fatal to the validity of the statute, see *United States v. Carolene Products Co.* (1938), for the evidence presented at the hearings fully indicated the nature and effect of the burdens on commerce which Congress meant to alleviate.

Confronted as we are with the facts laid before Congress, we must conclude that it had a rational basis for finding that racial discrimination in restaurants had a direct and adverse effect on the free flow of interstate commerce. Insofar as the sections of the Act here relevant are concerned, Congress prohibited discrimination only in those establishments having a close tie to interstate commerce, i.e., those, like the McClungs', serving food that has come from out of the State. . . . The absence of direct evidence connecting discriminatory restaurant service with the flow of interstate food, a factor on which the appellees place much reliance, is not, given the evidence as to the effect of such practices on other aspects of commerce, a crucial matter.

The power of Congress in this field is broad and sweeping; where it keeps within its sphere and violates no express constitutional limitation it has been the rule of this Court, going back almost to the founding days of the Republic, not to interfere. The Civil Rights Act of 1964, as here applied, we find to be plainly appropriate in the resolution of what the Congress found to be a national commercial problem of the first magnitude. We find it in no violation of any express limitations of the Constitution and we therefore declare it valid.

The judgment is therefore reversed.

flash*forward*

The "Nexus" Requirement. Like any Commerce Clause cases, *Heart of Atlanta Motel* and *McClung* asked how the conduct regulated by a federal statute related to interstate commerce. Modern Commerce Clause cases sometimes speak of the connection or "nexus" between an allegedly local activity and the greater interstate economy. A court must ultimately be satisfied that a sufficient nexus exists. although as seen in the New Deal cases and the 1964 cases that nexus may be proven in light of rules about aggregation of similarly-situated actors.

Must the nexus to interstate commerce also appear in the text of the statute? Sometimes, Congress will define the desired nexus to interstate commerce. Title II of the Civil Rights Act of 1964, for example, explains that a restaurant or gas station is covered when "a substantial portion of the food which it serves, or gasoline or other products which it sells, has moved in commerce." 42 U.S.C. § 2000a(c)(2). Provisions restricting the reach of a statute only to large businesses implicitly serves a similar function, on the understanding that the larger the business, the more likely it has a nexus with interstate commerce. This explains why, for example, Title VII of the Civil Rights Act of 1964 prohibits discrimination by employers with fifteen or more employees. 42 U.S.C. § 2000e(b).

Some statutes contain a generic reference to commerce that might need to be elaborated in case law. For example, a federal statute made it a crime for anyone convicted of a felony to "receive, possess, or transport in commerce or affecting commerce . . . any firearm." Former 18 U.S.C. App. 1 § 1202(a). In *Scarborough v. United States*, 431 U.S. 563 (1977), the Supreme Court held that possessing a firearm that had been in another state at any point in its history satisfied the nexus requirement—even if there was no longer a present nexus between the possession and interstate commerce.

Harder questions arise if the statute has no express nexus language or any explicit reference to commerce. In *Perez v. United States*, 402 U.S. 146 (1971), a defendant was convicted under a federal statute forbidding "extortionate credit transactions," better known as loan-sharking. The statute defined the elements of the federal crime, but none of the elements included limiting words like "in commerce" or "affecting commerce." The Supreme Court concluded that "extortionate credit transactions, though purely intrastate, may in the judgment of Congress affect interstate commerce." Evaluating the purpose of the statute and the economic reality in which it operated, the Court found a sufficient nexus to interstate commerce even though the usual magic words did not appear on the face of the statute.

Part II: Structural Limits

Structural Limits

Part II sharpens the focus on the left side of the diagram, representing structural limits on government power. A structural limit is one that forbids an action by one level or branch of government to protect the role of another level or branch. A state may be prevented from doing something that falls within the federal government's purview (or vice versa). Or the legislative branch may be prevented from doing something that would unduly interfere with the authority of the executive branch (or vice versa). To a great extent, structural limits revolve around the question of "Who decides?"

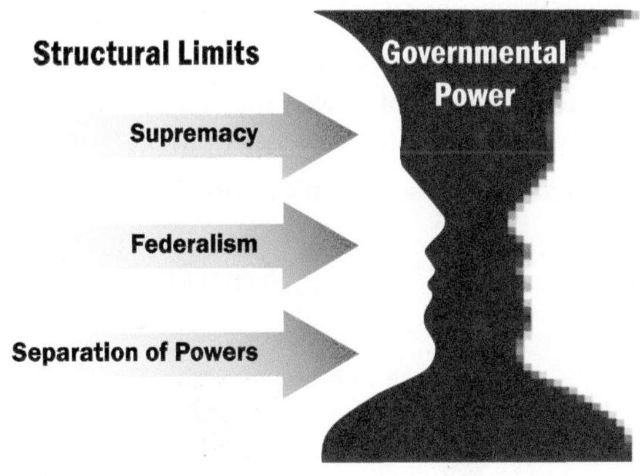

A. The Parts of the Picture

Part II explores three major structural limits.

Supremacy. The US Constitution, federal laws, and federal treaties are "the supreme law of the land," and anything contrary to them in state laws must yield. Art. VI, § 2. This means that the supremacy of federal law acts as a structural limit on the powers of state governments. Two commonly litigated areas of supremacy are preemption (where a federal statute or regulation supersedes inconsistent state laws), Ch. 13.A, and the dormant commerce clause doctrine (where the Constitution itself supersedes state laws that impede interstate commerce), Ch. 13.B.

Federalism. "Federalism" refers to a system where a national government and local governments exercise sovereignty over the same territory. In more recent decades, the term has come to mean something more specific in US law: a structural limitation on the national government that prevents it from taking actions that would imperil the sovereignty of the states. The clearest example of federalism as a limit on the powers of the federal government is the doctrine known as *commandeering*, which forbids federal laws requiring states to implement federal programs against their will. Ch. 14.B. In other settings, federalism appears not as a specific rule but as a general approach to constitutional reasoning, prioritizing the question of how federal law affects state autonomy. Federalism as a method of reasoning may reveal itself in virtually any setting where courts consider federal power, including statutory interpretation or state sovereign immunity (commonly studied in classes on Federal Courts). Ch. 14.C. In particular, arguments from federalism commonly arise in modern cases interpreting the enumerated powers of Congress. Ch. 15.

Separation of Powers. Each level of government (state and federal) is divided into legislative, executive, and judicial branches. Actions that might be constitutional if performed by one branch (such as a tax imposed by the legislature) could be an unconstitutional violation of separation of powers if performed by another (such as a tax imposed by the executive). If one branch seems to have more than its intended share of power, the system falls out of balance. As with federalism, separation of powers may arise in many different legal settings, operating more as a general standard than as a precise legal rule. Ch. 16.

Separation of Powers

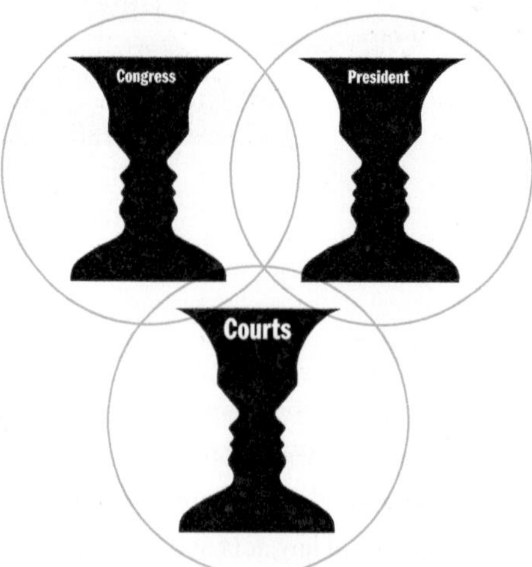

Overlapping but Balanced Allocation of Power Among Branches

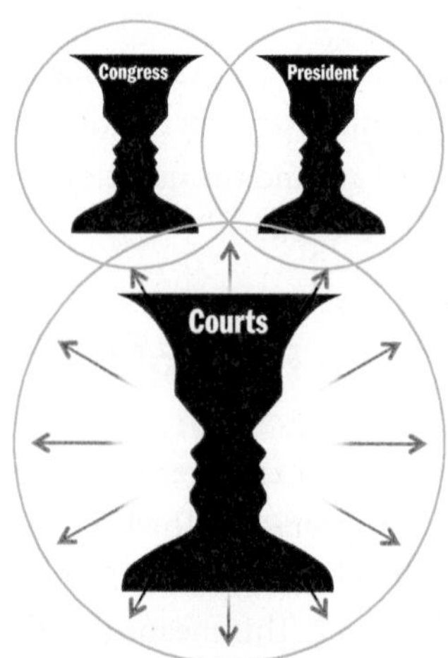

Imbalanced Allocation of Power Among Branches

Since each structural limit protects the interests of a different level or branch of government, it is important to identify which action by which government actor is challenged in a given situation. In a case involving an action by the federal government (or one of its branches), the relevant structural limits would be federalism and the federal separation of powers found in the US Constitution. In a case challenging action of a state government (or one of its branches), the relevant structural limitations would be the supremacy of federal law and the state separation of powers found in the state constitution. (The US Constitution is silent regarding separation of powers within state governments.)

Different Structural Limits for State and Federal Governments

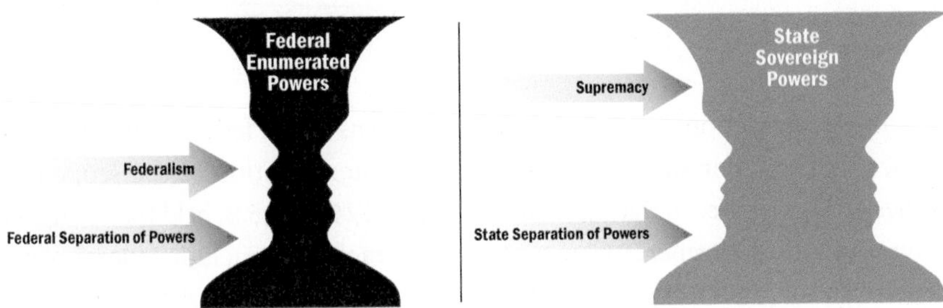

B. Interaction of the Parts

The structural limits studied in Part II must be understood as part of the bigger picture, where decisions involving one part of the diagram will affect other parts. As an example, consider *New York v. United States*, 505 U.S. 144 (1992), where Congress passed a statute that effectively required states to enact laws to dispose of nuclear waste. The Supreme Court held that the statute violated the structural limit of federalism. Even though the federal government may have power under the Commerce Clause to regulate transactions involving nuclear waste, it may not exercise that power in a way that violates federalism by unduly controlling state governments. The decision in *New York* had some necessary corollaries, as seen in the following diagram. Broader federalism means that the preemptive effect of federal legislation under the Supremacy Clause is narrower. As a practical matter, the powers of the state and federal government also change, with a narrower scope for the federal enumerated powers (Congress can do one less thing under the Commerce Clause) and a broader scope for the state's sovereign powers (states are subject to one less federal restriction).

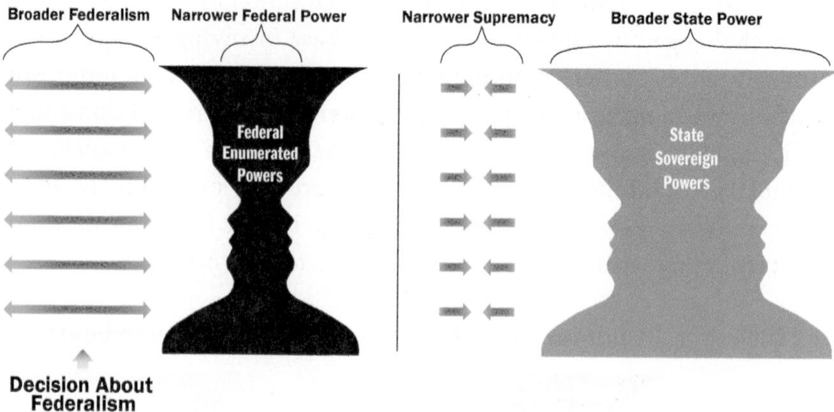

These interactions help explain why concerns about federalism have arisen in cases that on their surface require only an interpretation of the scope of an enumerated power. Recall that *Gibbons v. Ogden* (1824), Ch. 5.B, held that Congress's power under the Commerce Clause was broad enough to include federal control over navigation, including which ships could dock in state harbors. This ruling about an enumerated power meant that Congress could use its supremacy to impose more restrictions on the states, effectively reducing state power. It also meant that any federalism limit on the federal government was lessened, since under the Tenth Amendment as interpreted in *US v. Darby* (1941), Ch. 9.C.2.b, the states are reserved only those powers not delegated to the federal government.

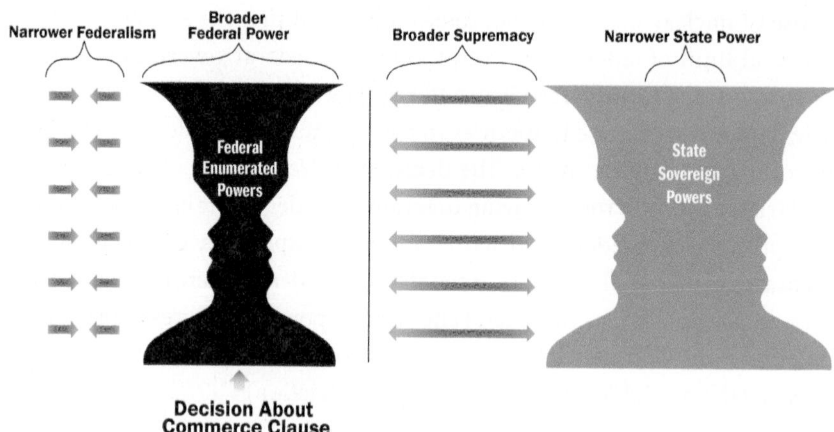

These interactions are not limited to the left side of the diagram. Judicial concern about individual rights may also affect a decision involving structural limitations. For example, in *Hammer v. Dagenhart* (1919) (federal statute restricting industrial child labor), Ch. 8.A.2, a question looming in the background was whether employers and child laborers had a constitutional right to enter into employment contracts. *Dagenhart* was not decided on the basis of individual rights. Nonetheless, a court's solicitude toward a rights argument could affect its decision with regard to the scope of the Commerce Clause and the strength of any federalism interest. In *National Federation of Independent Business v. Sebelius* (2012), Ch. 17.B.2, Chief Justice Roberts explained how a concern for individual rights might affect reasoning elsewhere: "By denying any one government complete jurisdiction over all the concerns of public life, federalism protects the liberty of the individual from arbitrary power."

Concern About Individual Rights May Influence Structural Decisions

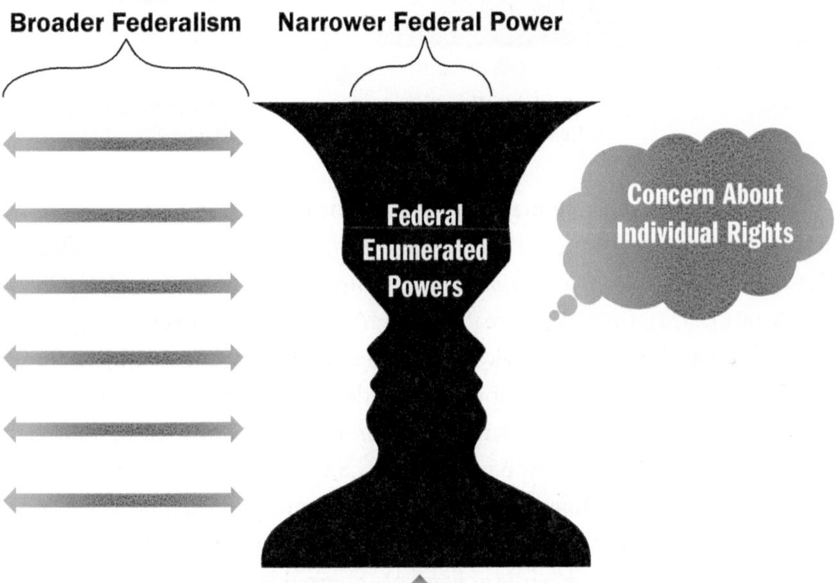

Federalism is not the only structural concern in such cases, however. All instances of judicial review implicate separation of powers. Protecting federalism (and by implication individual rights) against Congressional legislation requires a court to invalidate an act of the people's elected representatives. This is no small matter, as seen by the constitutional crisis of the *Lochner* era. In the *Dagenhart* example, the gains for state power and for the parties to a child labor contract were in effect accomplished through a transfer of power from the legislature to the courts, as illustrated in the following diagram.

Trade-off Between Federalism and Separation of Powers in *Dagenhart*

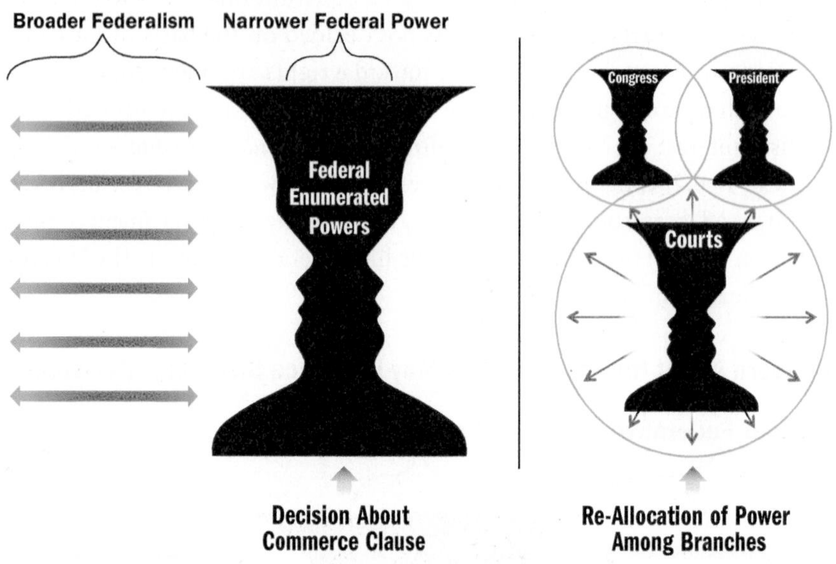

Interactions like these may become significant even in cases that are not, strictly speaking, constitutional. In *National Federation of Independent Business v. Department of Labor, Occupational Safety and Health Administration (OSHA)*, 142 S.Ct. 661 (2022), the statute creating OSHA authorized it to enact regulations to foster "safe and healthful working conditions," 29 U.S.C. § 651(b), including the enactment of emergency temporary standards if "employees are exposed to grave danger from exposure to substances or agents determined to be toxic or physically harmful or from new hazards," 29 U.S.C. § 655(c)(1). The legal question was whether this statute allowed OSHA to issue an emergency temporary standard requiring large employers to require their employees to either (a) take COVID tests every week and wear a mask while at work or (b) provide proof of vaccination. The Supreme Court held (6–3) that the statute did not authorize this type of regulation. Structural concerns—the "who decides" questions that dominate Part II of this book—strongly motivated the justices.

The dissent by three justices said:

> Underlying everything else in this dispute is a single, simple question: Who decides how much protection, and of what kind, American workers need from COVID-19? An agency with expertise in workplace health and safety, acting as Congress and the President authorized? Or a court, lacking any knowledge

of how to safeguard workplaces, and insulated from responsibility for any damage it causes?

By contrast, a concurrence by three justices said:

> The central question we face today is: Who decides? . . . The only question is whether an administrative agency in Washington, one charged with overseeing workplace safety, may mandate the vaccination or regular testing of 84 million people. Or whether, as 27 States before us submit, that work belongs to state and local governments across the country and the people's elected representatives in Congress.

NFIB v. OSHA was more explicit than most opinions in voicing the "who decides" questions, it was not unique in offering different possible answers to them.

C. The Historical Setting

Part I was organized chronologically, but Parts II and III are organized by topic.

Within Part II, **Chapter 13** (Supremacy) examines the two areas where federal supremacy is most likely to be implicated: preemption and the dormant commerce clause doctrine. **Chapter 14** (Federalism) examines federalism as a restraint on the federal government. **Chapter 15** (Enumerated Powers) explores the modern case law regarding Congress's enumerated powers, where federalism arguments are often raised. **Chapter 16** (Separation of Powers) looks at struggles among branches of the federal government. **Chapter 17** (The Affordable Care Act) is a "Master Class"—an opportunity to think deeply about an important case that combines many of the issues explored in Part II.

Shifts in the Political Climate. With a few exceptions, the cases in Part II date from the 1970s to the present, when the Supreme Court was presided over by Chief Justices Warren Burger (1969–1986), William Rehnquist (1986–2005), and John Roberts (2005–present). At the risk of oversimplifying, the general tenor of the Supreme Court's constitutional decisions in these decades has been a reaction to the constitutional interpretations that became dominant during the New Deal and the civil rights movement.

In the middle third of the 20th century, most Supreme Court justices were appointed by presidents who were liberal Democrats (Roosevelt, Truman, Kennedy, and Johnson) or moderate Republicans (Eisenhower). Their legal outlooks were affected by the dominant legal and political issues of their time: the New Deal and the civil rights movement. Legislatively, these years saw landmark federal legislation that had daily impact on ordinary Americans: Social Security in the 1930s, the GI Bill in the 1940s, federal highway and infrastructure building in the 1950s, and the Medicare, Civil Rights, and Voting Rights Acts in the 1960s.

The 1960s ended with social and political turmoil, much of It centered around popular opposition to the war in Vietnam. At least at the level of the presidency, the nation reacted by favoring increasingly conservative Republicans (Nixon, Ford, Reagan, George H.W. Bush, George W. Bush, and Trump), or moderate Democrats (Carter, Clinton, Obama). As exemplified by President Reagan, the dominant political discourse emphasized deregulation of the economy and a smaller role for government generally. (This was true even though in practice the federal budget continued to grow.) Some of the more lasting legislation in these years involved deregulation of some industries, tax cuts, and reductions in welfare benefits for the poor.

As the nation's politics became less liberal, so did the nominees to the Supreme Court. By the start of the Roberts Court, a majority bloc of justices favored positions generally viewed as conservative. Justice John Paul Stevens, a Ford appointee who served from 1976 to 2010, commented on the shift in the Court's philosophical makeup in 2007, when he wrote: "It is my firm conviction that no Member of the Court that I joined in 1975 would have agreed with today's decision." *Parents Involved in Community Schools v. Seattle School Dist. No. 1*, 551 U.S. 701 (2007) (Stevens, J., dissenting). Much of the shift away from the Warren Court's approach revealed itself in individual rights cases that will be studied in Part III. For the structural topics covered in Part II, the biggest shifts began under Chief Justice Rehnquist, when the Court developed an interest in preserving state autonomy as against the federal government. This overarching concern for state prerogatives became known as "the New Federalism."

Shifts in Judicial Writing Styles. You are likely to notice a difference, beginning in approximately the mid-1970s, in how Supreme Court decisions are written. The opinions have a more modern structure and feel, more closely resembling the style of legal argument you are perfecting in your Legal Writing classes. This means, among other things, that they tend to have a more transparent structure than earlier opinions, with sections set apart by Roman numerals, which are in turn divided into subsections. The vocabulary is more familiar to modern ears. The sentence lengths—while still longer than one would find in a newspaper or magazine—are shorter than in earlier eras. The justices tend to be more explicit about stating legal rules in a form easily quotable in future opinions. They also include far more quotations from earlier opinions, string cites, footnotes and other conspicuous displays of legal scholarship. (For ease of reading, this book edits out most of the visual clutter that accompanies internal quotations and citations.)

Some other institutional changes have contributed to newer Supreme Court opinions (at least in highly-charged cases) that are much longer than in earlier times. The Court decides fewer cases than it used to: In the early 1980s it granted review in around 150 cases per year, but by 2020 it tended to decide only half as many. Each justice's staff of law clerks has also increased over time. With more time and staff available, the justices have developed an ethic of discussing nearly every argument raised in parties' briefs, plus arguments found in amicus briefs (and in concurring or dissenting opinions, if any). The resulting opinions go into greater detail than they once did, which requires greater length.

Finally, the Court in recent decades has placed less importance on presenting a united front to the public. Unlike Chief Justice Warren, who considered it crucial for *Brown v. Board of Education* (1954) to be unanimous, the recent Chiefs have allowed individual justices to have their own say. Multiple concurring and dissenting opinions have become common. Consider this statement from Justice Rehnquist's dissent in *Kassel v. Consolidated Freightways Corp. of Delaware*, 450 U.S. 662 (1981), a case decided on a (4–2)–3 vote.

> It is not a particularly pleasant task for the author of a dissent joined by two other Members of the Court to take issue with a statement made by the author of a concurrence in that same case which is joined by only one Member of the Court. Such fragmentation, particularly between two opinions neither of which command the adherence of a majority of the Court, cannot help but further unsettle what certainty there may be in the legal principles which govern our decision of . . . cases such as this and lay a foundation for similar uncertainty in other sorts of constitutional adjudication. Nonetheless, I feel obliged to take up the cudgels, however unwillingly, because Justice Brennan's concurrence, joined by Justice Marshall, is mistaken not only in its analysis but also in its efforts to interpret the meaning of today's decision.

The independence of each justice to write separate opinions has led to more cases decided without a clear majority opinion. As a result, one of the skills that modern constitutional lawyers must develop is the ability to decode fractured decisions, searching for common ground across multiple opinions.

CHAPTER 13

Supremacy

The Supremacy Clause, Art. VI, § 2, declares that the US Constitution, the federal laws created through that Constitution, and US treaties with foreign nations "shall be the supreme law of the land," notwithstanding "any thing in the constitution or laws of any state to the contrary." The form the state law takes does not matter: a state statute, a state agency regulation, a state common law tradition, and even the state constitution are inferior to supreme federal law. When state and federal law conflict, federal law prevails. The tricky question is whether a conflict exists.

Supremacy as a Structural Limit on State Governments

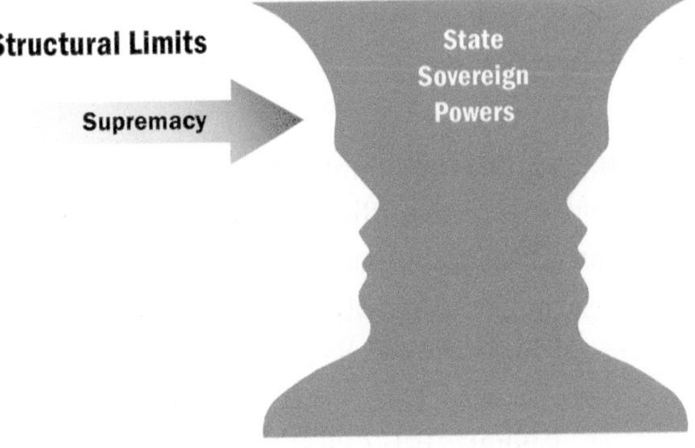

This chapter presents the two most frequently litigated topics involving the Supremacy Clause. *Preemption* occurs when state laws conflict with federal statutes. The *dormant commerce clause doctrine* relies on language in the Constitution to preempt state laws that impose undue burdens on interstate commerce, even in the absence of federal statutes.

flashback

Although they did not use the modern vocabulary, several cases from Part I involved federal supremacy.

In *McCulloch v. Maryland* (1819), the federal law creating the Bank of the United States preempted the Maryland statute seeking to impose a potentially crippling tax on that bank.

In *Gibbons v. Ogden* (1824), the federal statute through which Thomas Gibbons obtained a license for interstate passenger steamboats preempted the state law giving Aaron Ogden a monopoly over some of those routes. In dicta, the court's opinion considered whether the Constitution prohibits all state regulation of interstate commerce, a topic that is now analyzed under the dormant commerce clause doctrine.

In *Prigg v. Pennsylvania* (1842), the federal Fugitive Slave Act preempted inconsistent procedures from Pennsylvania's Personal Liberty Law.

A. Preemption

If Congress has enumerated power to legislate in an area, the positive law it enacts will preempt conflicting state laws. (To "preempt"—sometimes spelled with a hyphen, as in "pre-empt"—means to take the place of, override, or supersede.) State laws may conflict with federal ones in several ways, depending on the details of the relevant laws and the contexts in which they operate.

1. Kickstarter: Federal Preemption

DISCLAIMER: *This Kickstarter is a checklist to help identify relevant issues. It is not a list of elements. Nothing requires judges to write their opinions (or lawyers to write their briefs) in Kickstarter order.*

Federal Preemption **kickstarter**

USE WHEN: *A State law unduly conflicts with federal statutes or regulations.*

A. Express Preemption.

B. Implied Preemption.

1. Implied Conflict Preemption.

a. *Impossibility Preemption.*

b. *Obstacle Preemption.*

2. *Implied Field Preemption.*

KICKSTARTER USER'S GUIDE

The Supremacy Clause leaves no doubt that federal laws will outweigh inconsistent state laws. The challenge in preemption cases is to decide whether a state law is, in fact, inconsistent with a federal one. The Supreme Court has described several scenarios where this may occur, as summarized in *Pacific Gas & Electric Co. v. State Energy Resources Conservation & Development Comm'n*, 461 U.S. 190 (1983):

> It is well-established that within Constitutional limits Congress may preempt state authority by so stating in express terms. [This is typically called *express preemption.*] Absent explicit preemptive language, Congress' intent to supersede state law altogether may be found from a scheme of federal regulation so pervasive as to make reasonable the inference that Congress left no room to supplement it. . . . [This is typically called *implied field preemption.*] Even where Congress has not entirely displaced state regulation in a specific area, state law is preempted to the extent that it actually conflicts with federal law. Such a conflict arises when compliance with both federal and state regulations is a physical impossibility, [typically called *impossibility preemption* or sometimes *direct conflict preemption*], or where state law stands as an obstacle to the accomplishment and execution of the full purposes and objectives of Congress [typically called *obstacle preemption*].

Item A. *Express Preemption.* Whenever it legislates within its enumerated powers, Congress could choose to include a *preemption clause*—express language indicating how the federal statute will interact with state laws. For example, the Employee Retirement Income Security Act of 1974 (ERISA) expressly says, subject to some exceptions, that the Act "shall supersede any and all State laws insofar as they may now or hereafter relate to any employee benefit plan." 29 U.S.C. § 1144(a). The Motor Carrier Act of 1980 expressly says, subject to some exceptions, that a state "may not enact or enforce a law, regulation, or other provision . . . related to a price, route, or service of any motor carrier . . . with respect to the transportation of property." 49 U.S.C. § 14501(c)(1). These examples show that Congress may signal the intent to preempt state laws without using the magic word "preemption."

Congress may, if it wishes, express an intention *not* to preempt state laws. For example, the Federal Labor Standards Act of 1938 (the law upheld in *Darby*), creates a nationwide minimum wage. To remove any doubt about whether state or local government had authority to set higher minimum wages, Congress included an express non-preemption clause (sometimes called a saving clause), which says that "no provision of this [Act] shall excuse noncompliance with any . . . state law or municipal ordinance establishing a minimum wage higher than the minimum wage established under this [Act]." 29 U.S.C. § 218(a).

As with any statutory language, a preemption or non-preemption clause might require case-by-case interpretation. For example, a large body of ERISA preemption cases consider whether particular state laws "relate to" an employee benefit plan. See, e.g., *Egelhoff v. Egelhoff*, 532 U.S. 141 (2001) (state law terminating a spouse's entitlement to retirement benefits upon divorce is preempted), *California Division of Labor Standards Enforcement v. Dillingham Construction, Inc.*, 519 U.S. 316 (1997) (state law requiring payment of prevailing wages by public contractors is not preempted); *Shaw v. Delta Air Lines*, 463 U.S. 85 (1983) (state law requiring employers to pay sick-leave to employees who miss work due to pregnancy is preempted in part and not preempted in part). If a preemption clause is not written clearly, it may result in confusion or split decisions. The Immigration Reform and Control Act of 1986, for example, expressly preempted "any State or local law imposing civil or criminal sanctions (other than through licensing and similar laws) upon those who employ" unauthorized aliens. 8 U.S.C. § 1324a(h)(2). Uncertainty over what counts as a law "similar" to a licensing law led to a 5–3 decision of the Supreme Court, where portions of the majority opinion were joined by only four justices. *Chamber of Commerce of US v. Whiting*, 563 U.S. 582 (2011).

Item B. *Implied Preemption.* When a state law is alleged to conflict with a federal statute in ways not resolved by an express preemption clause, a court must determine whether the statute, taken as a whole, implies that certain state laws should be preempted. This inquiry may involve the usual methods of reasoning: the statute's text and structure, any precedents interpreting it or similar statutes, the history leading to the enactment of the statute and the history of its earlier enforcement, the consequences of allowing the state law to operate, and the impact of the decision on important societal values.

Two matters of constitutional structure inevitably arise when a court decides an implied preemption case. First, preemption of state law by federal law reduces the autonomy of state government to pass the laws it prefers. At least while the federal statute remains on the books, the state's power is reduced, which may give rise to concerns about federalism. Second, implied preemption requires a court to decide a question that Congress has the authority to decide for itself. This may give rise to concerns about separation of powers. For these reasons, the Supreme Court has said that implied preemption should not be found lightly. "In preemption analysis, courts should assume that the historic police powers of the States are not superseded unless that was the clear and manifest purpose of Congress." *Arizona v. United States*, 567 U.S. 387, 400 (2012).

Express non-preemption clauses are enacted to ensure that Courts do not infer preemption where Congress did not mean to imply it. This can be seen in the language of the McCarran-Ferguson Act of 1945, 15 U.S.C. § 1011.

> Congress hereby declares that the continued regulation and taxation by the several States of the business of insurance is in the public interest, and that silence on the part of the Congress shall not be construed to impose any barrier to the regulation or taxation of such business by the several States.

Phrased another way, McCarran-Ferguson instructs courts considering state insurance laws to rule only on the basis of express preemption, not on any form of implied preemption.

Congress sometimes directs courts to use certain types of implied preemption and not others. For example, the preemption clause of the Controlled Substances Act of 1970, 21 U.S.C. § 903, says:

> No provision of this subchapter shall be construed as indicating an intent on the part of the Congress to occupy the field in which that provision operates, including criminal penalties, to the exclusion of any State law on the same subject matter which would otherwise be within the authority of the State, unless there is a positive conflict between that provision of this subchapter and that State law so that the two cannot consistently stand together.

In other words, Congress does not occupy the entire field of laws regulating drugs, but it wants courts to preempt state laws that create "a positive conflict," as arises in the implied preemption scenarios of impossibility preemption and obstacle preemption.

Item B.1. *Implied Conflict Preemption.* The two categories of implied conflict preemption serve two different goals.

- Impossibility preemption protects individuals. It would be unfair to place people in a situation where it is physically or legally impossible to follow both state law and federal law. In these cases, preempting the state law resolves the individual's impossible situation.

- Obstacle preemption protects the federal government. Even if a state law places no individual in an impossible situation, it may impede Congress's chosen policies. In these cases, preempting the state law protects the supreme federal power.

These categories are not mutually exclusive. A given state law might be unconstitutional as a result of impossibility preemption, obstacle preemption, or both. The categories may also be relevant even in cases involving express preemption or field preemption. This would occur if a state law creates impossibility or obstacles in ways not predicted in advance by an express preemption clause or an earlier case defining an occupied field.

Item B.1.a. *Impossibility Preemption.* Impossibility preemption, sometimes called "direct conflict," occurs when it is physically or legally impossible for a person to obey both the federal and state statutes. Impossibility is uncommon, but it may arise in two scenarios.

First, a state law may require a person to do something that federal law forbids, or vice versa. Fortunately, it is hard to come up with real-life examples. Imagine that a state, facing a plague of locusts, required all citizens to carry a specific pesticide at all times and use it on any locusts they encountered—but federal law made that pesticide illegal. It is physically impossible to both carry the pesticide and not carry it. No matter what a person does, at least one law is being broken.

Second, both levels of government may regulate an activity that is otherwise lawful, but the details of the regulation create impossible demands on persons engaged in the activity. If a federal law required cigarette packages to contain warning labels, it would be impossible for a cigarette maker to obey a state law forbidding warning labels, and vice versa. It is physically impossible for the seller to both include and not include a warning label. Admittedly, a cigarette maker could avoid violating either law by not selling any cigarettes at all, but neither the state government nor the federal government intended to ban the product. To ensure that differences in the details of regulation do not create impossible situations for those pursuing otherwise lawful conduct, the state law will be preempted. *Mutual Pharmaceutical Co. v. Bartlett*, 570 U.S. 471 (2013) ("our preemption cases presume that a manufacturer's ability to stop selling does not turn impossibility into possibility.")

There is no impossibility if one law sets a minimum or maximum standard that differs from, but overlaps with, a different standard in the other law. For example, a federal law may make it illegal to discharge more than 100 gallons per week of a certain chemical into a river, while state law makes it illegal to discharge more than 50 gallons per week of that chemical. There is no impossibility, because a person or company that obeys the stricter state law will not violate the weaker federal law.

What if one level of government bans conduct but the other level does not? This is fairly common: Many things may violate state law but not federal law, or vice versa. There is no impossibility preemption in this situation. To begin with, every preemption theory requires both a federal law and a state law. If the state has no law, there is nothing to preempt; if the federal government has no law, there is nothing to do the preempting. Moreover, no one is placed in an impossible situation when only one level of government bans conduct. A person who obeys the law banning the conduct does not violate the law of the other level, since that level does not require anyone to perform the banned activity. Using the language of impossibility preemption, it is physically possible to obey the law of one level without violating the law of the other, and no otherwise lawful conduct is made impossible as a result of conflicting regulatory details. See *Merck Sharp & Dohme Corp. v. Albrecht*, 139 S. Ct. 1668 (2019) (there is no "impossibility where the laws of one sovereign permit an activity that the laws of the other sovereign restrict or even prohibit").

Item B.1.b. *Obstacle Preemption.* Obstacle preemption occurs when state law acts as an obstacle to, or undercuts the effect of, federal law. This theory dates at least to *McCulloch v. Maryland* (1819), which said "It is of the very essence of supremacy, to remove all obstacles to its action within its own sphere." As a result, States could not "retard, impede, [or] burden" the ability of Congress to carry out its otherwise constitutional policy decisions. With that said, mere differences between state and federal law are not enough to establish obstacle preemption. The state law must differ from federal law in a substantial way that in practice will undermine federal goals.

To decide whether a state law creates an obstacle to federal law, a court must consider two questions, both of which involve subjective judgment.

First, the court must decide what Congress wished to accomplish by enacting the federal statute. This may be evident from the face of the statute, or it may require an evaluation of legislative history. Complicating this inquiry is the fact that a law may have more than one purpose. For example, the federal food stamp program has the twin goals of feeding indigent people and stabilizing prices for agricultural commodities by increasing demand.

Second, the court must decide whether the state law will, as a practical matter, undermine or impede the federal purpose(s). The state law must be a significant obstacle, not a mere difference in details.

As an example, consider whether the federal law requiring a health warning on cigarette packages would preempt a state law that required cigarette manufacturers to include a label reading: "Ignore the federal warning. Cigarettes are good for you." It would be physically possible to include both labels on a package, so this is not a case of impossibility preemption. Should there be obstacle preemption? The purpose of the federal law is to convince potential purchasers that cigarettes are dangerous. The state law significantly frustrates this purpose by interposing a contrary message at the point of purchase.

Obstacle preemption is the most common form of implied preemption. But since it requires judges to intuit Congressional purposes and predict how Congress would react to (possibly unforeseen) state laws, the outcomes may be harder to predict than cases of impossibility preemption.

Item B.2. *Implied Field Preemption.* If Congress chooses to "occupy a field," there can be no state or local laws on the subject. The ERISA preemption statute, discussed in Item A above, is an express version of field preemption: if a state or local law "relates to" employee benefits, it is preempted even if it would pass the tests for impossibility and obstacle preemption. When Congress occupies a field, it wants to ensure national uniformity of regulation. Any local lawmaking within the occupied field—no matter how benign it may seem—violates the federal desire for uniformity. Case law uses a two-part method for implied field preemption.

First, the Court must decide if Congress has implied an intention to occupy the field. This may occur where "the scheme of federal regulation [is] so pervasive as to make reasonable the inference that Congress left no room for the States to supplement it" or where "the Act of Congress [touches] a field in which the federal interest is so dominant that the federal system will be assumed to preclude enforcement of state laws on the same subject." *Rice v. Santa Fe Elevator Corp.*, 331 U.S. 218, 230 (1947).

Federal aviation statutes are an example of a system so pervasive and so important to national interests that it occupies the field. As explained in *Northwest Airlines, Inc. v. Minnesota*, 322 U.S. 292 (1944) (Jackson, J., concurring):

> Federal control [of aviation] is intensive and exclusive. Planes do not wander about in the sky like vagrant clouds. They move only by federal permission, subject to federal inspection, in the hands of federally certified personnel and under an intricate system of federal commands. The moment a ship taxis onto a runway it is caught up in an elaborate and detailed system of controls.

Second, the Court must decide whether the state law falls within the occupied field. A state law establishing an independent air traffic control system would obviously encroach upon the federally occupied field of aviation regulation. It may be less obvious whether a local noise ordinance falls within that field. But if the noise ordinance is used to control aircraft noise, it falls within the field and is preempted. *City of Burbank v. Lockheed Air Terminal Inc.*, 411 U.S. 624 (1973).

Both steps of implied field preemption analysis involve some subjective judgment. This can be seen in cases involving the Atomic Energy Act of 1954. In *Pacific Gas & Electric Co. v. State Energy Resources Conservation & Development Commission,* 461 U.S. 190 (1983), the Supreme Court concluded, in light of the breadth and detail of the federal statute and the great importance control of nuclear power had for the nation, that the Act occupied a field. The Court described the field as "radiological safety aspects involved in the construction and operation of a nuclear plant." In a series of opinions, the Court then considered which state laws fell within that field. See *Id.* (state law denying electric generating licenses for nuclear power plants without adequate waste disposal capacity was not within the occupied field, because it regulated the economics of the power plant and not its radiological safety); *Silkwood v. Kerr-McGee Corp.*, 464 U.S. 238 (1984) (state tort action for negligence at a nuclear power plant was not within the occupied field); *English v. General Electric Co.*, 496 U.S. 72 (1990) (state tort action for firing nuclear plant worker who reported safety violations to federal government was not within the occupied field).

Given the vagaries of implied field preemption and its potentially sweeping effect on state law, modern courts are reluctant to say that a statute implies (without expressly saying so) that Congress occupies a field. Most of the decisions finding implied field preemption date from the mid-20th century, when the Supreme Court—dominated by New Deal and Warren Court appointees who were supportive of federal regulation—found that many new and detailed federal programs impliedly occupied various fields. Once a precedent holds that a statute occupies a field, courts will consider the field occupied until Congress says otherwise.

2. Preemption and Immigration: *Garcia v. Kansas*

Art. I, § 8, cl. 4 gives Congress the enumerated power to "establish an uniform rule of naturalization," and Congress has used this power to enact a lengthy and complex body of immigration statutes. However, no express preemption clause or earlier court decision says that these federal statutes occupy the entire field of laws that apply to non-citizens present within the United States. Some smaller sub-fields are occupied, however. *Hines v. Davidowitz*, 312 U.S. 52 (1940) held that the subject of "alien-registration requirements" was occupied by the federal government. Registering one's presence with the federal government, and having documents as proof of that fact, are part of a "single integrated and all-embracing system" that touches on foreign relations, a topic of national importance. The state law in *Hines* set up a parallel state system, and was therefore preempted because it fell within the occupied field.

The federal immigration system prohibits non-citizens from employment in the United States without a federal work permit. In recent decades, acting on a belief that the federal government is not adequately enforcing its immigration laws, some states have enacted their own laws about unauthorized presence and work by non-citizens. Many rounds of litigation have examined whether such laws are preempted.

Arizona. *Arizona v. United States*, 567 U.S. 387 (2012) considered several portions of a new Arizona law (known as S.B. 1070) against different types of preemption arguments.

■ WEBSITE
A fuller version of *Arizona v. United States* is available for download from this casebook's companion website, www.CaplanIntegratedConLaw.com.

One of the Arizona provisions outlawed "willful failure to complete or carry and alien registration document in violation of 8 U.S.C. §§ 1304(e) or 1306(a)." In effect, that provision added a new state-law penalty for violating the federal registration system. It would not be impossible for the non-citizen to comply simultaneously with both laws. And Arizona did not create an obstacle for the federal government, since both governments sought to achieve compliance. However, a majority of the US Supreme Court held that Arizona's law was preempted because it fell within the occupied field of alien registration requirements. The field was known to be occupied as a result of *Hines*, a precedent dating to the New Deal.

Another provision of S.B. 1070 made it a crime for a non-citizen without a federal work permit "to knowingly apply for work . . . or perform work" in Arizona. This section was not part of the occupied field of alien registration. Nonetheless, it was preempted because it was found to pose an obstacle to other Congressional goals. The Supreme Court surveyed the language, structure, and history of the relevant federal statutes governing work permits, noting that they imposed penalties solely on employers, not employees. From this, the majority concluded that "Congress made a deliberate choice not to impose criminal penalties on aliens who seek, or engage in, unauthorized employment." State-level criminal penalties on the workers posed an obstacle to this federal policy, and thus were preempted.

Kansas. In *Kansas v. Garcia* (2020), the Supreme Court considered prosecutions of non-citizens for submitting false documents to procure employment. Unlike Arizona's S.B. 1090, which on its face applied only to non-citizens, the Kansas laws against fraud and identity theft applied on their face to all persons. The defendants argued that as applied to them in this setting, the Kansas laws were similarly preempted, because they amounted to a state penalty on employees for working without a permit.

ITEMS TO CONSIDER WHILE READING *KANSAS v. GARCIA*:

A. *Work through the various categories of preemption in the Kickstarter. Which categories, if any, do the Kansas statutes violate?*

B. *Is implied preemption possible under a federal law that contains an express preemption clause that does not reach the allegedly preempted state statute?*

C. *Is* Garcia *consistent with* Arizona*?*

Kansas v. Garcia,

140 S.Ct. 791 (2020)

Justice Alito delivered the opinion of the Court [joined by Chief Justice Roberts and Justices Thomas, Gorsuch, and Kavanaugh].

Kansas law makes it a crime to commit "identity theft" or engage in fraud to obtain a benefit. Respondents [Ramiro Garcia, Donaldo Morales, and Guadalupe Ochoa-Lara]—three aliens who are not authorized to work in this country—were convicted under these provisions for fraudulently using another person's Social Security number on state and federal tax-withholding forms that they submitted when they obtained employment. The Supreme Court of Kansas held that a provision of the [federal] Immigration Reform and Control Act of 1986 (IRCA) expressly preempts the Kansas statutes at issue insofar as they provide a basis for these prosecutions. We reject this reading of the provision in question, as well as respondents' alternative arguments based on implied preemption. We therefore reverse.

I

A

The foundation of our laws on immigration and naturalization is the Immigration and Nationality Act (INA), which sets out the terms and conditions of admission to the country and the subsequent treatment of aliens lawfully in the country. As initially enacted, the INA did not prohibit the employment of illegal aliens, and this Court held that federal law left room for the States to regulate in this field. See *De Canas v. Bica*, 424 U.S. 351 (1976).

With the enactment of IRCA [in 1986], Congress took a different approach. IRCA made it unlawful to hire an alien knowing that he or she is unauthorized to work in the United States. 8 U.S.C. §§ 1324a(a)(1)(A), (h)(3). To enforce this prohibition, IRCA requires employers to comply with a federal employment verification system. Using a federal work-authorization form (I-9), employers must attest that they have verified that an employee is not an unauthorized alien by examining approved documents such as a United States passport or alien registration card. This requirement applies to the hiring of any individual regardless of citizenship or nationality. Employers who fail to comply may face civil and criminal sanctions. . . .

IRCA concomitantly imposes duties on all employees, regardless of citizenship. No later than their first day of employment, all employees must complete an I-9 and attest that they fall into a category of persons who are authorized to work in the United States. In addition, under penalty of perjury, every employee must provide certain personal information—specifically: name, residence address, birth date, Social Security number, e-mail address, and telephone number. It is a federal crime for an employee to provide false information on an I-9 or to use fraudulent documents to show authorization to work. See 18 U.S.C. §§ 1028, 1546. Federal law does not make it a crime for an alien to work without authorization, and this Court has held that state laws criminalizing such conduct are preempted. *Arizona v. United States* (2012). But if an alien works illegally, the alien's immigration status may be adversely affected.

While IRCA imposes these requirements on employers and employees, it also limits the use of I-9 forms. A provision entitled "Limitation on use of attestation form," § 1324a(b)(5), provides that I-9 forms and "any information contained in or appended to such form[s] may not be used for purposes other than for enforcement of" the INA or other specified provisions of federal law, including those prohibiting the making of a false statement in a federal matter (18 U.S.C. § 1001), identity theft (§ 1028), immigration-document fraud (§ 1546), and perjury (§ 1621). In addition, 8 U.S.C. § 1324a(d)(2)(F) prohibits use of "the employment verification system" "for law enforcement purposes," apart from the enforcement of the aforementioned federal statutes.

Although IRCA expressly regulates the use of I-9's and documents appended to that form, no provision of IRCA directly addresses the use of other documents, such as federal and state tax-withholding forms, that an employee may complete upon beginning a new job. [The federal withholding form is known as a W-4, and its Kansas counterpart is the K-4. It is a federal crime for an employee to submit a fraudulent W-4. 26 U.S.C. § 7205.] . . .

B

Like other States, Kansas has laws against fraud, forgeries, and identity theft. These statutes apply to citizens and aliens alike and are not limited to conduct that occurs in connection with employment. The Kansas identity-theft statute criminalizes the "using" of any "personal identifying information" belonging to another person with the intent to "defraud that person, or anyone else, in order to receive any benefit." Kan. Stat. Ann. § 21–6107(a)(1). . . . Kansas courts have interpreted the statute to cover the use of another person's Social Security number to receive the benefits of employment.

Kansas's false-information statute criminalizes, among other things, "making, generating, distributing or drawing" a "written instrument" with knowledge that it "falsely states or represents some material matter" and "with intent to defraud, obstruct the detection of a theft or felony offense or induce official action." Kan. Stat. Ann. § 21–5824.

The respondents in the three cases now before us are aliens who are not authorized to work in this country but nevertheless secured employment by using the identity of other persons on the I-9 forms that they completed when they applied for work. They also used these same false identities when they completed their W-4's and K-4's. All three respondents were convicted under one or both of the Kansas laws just mentioned for fraudulently using another person's Social Security number on tax-withholding forms. . . .

C and D [Omitted]

II

The Supremacy Clause provides that the Constitution, federal statutes, and treaties constitute "the supreme Law of the Land." Art. VI, cl. 2. . . . In some cases, a federal statute may expressly preempt state law. But it has long been established that preemption may also occur by virtue of restrictions or rights that are inferred from statutory law. And recent cases have often held state laws to be impliedly preempted.

In these [three] cases, respondents do not contend that the Kansas statutes under which they were convicted are preempted in their entirety. Instead, they argue that these laws must yield only insofar as they apply to an unauthorized alien's use of false documents on forms submitted for the purpose of securing employment. In making this argument, respondents invoke all three categories of preemption identified in our cases. They defend the Kansas Supreme Court's holding that provisions of IRCA expressly bar their prosecutions. And they also argue that the decision below is supported by "field" or "conflict" preemption or some combination of the two. We consider these arguments in turn.

III

We begin with the argument that the state criminal statutes under which respondents were convicted are expressly preempted. . . .

The Kansas Supreme Court [based] its holding on . . . § 1324a(b)(5), which is far more than a preemption provision. This provision broadly restricts any use of an I-9, information contained in an I-9, and any documents appended to an I-9. Thus, unlike a typical preemption provision, it applies not just to the States but also to the Federal Government and all private actors.

The Kansas Supreme Court thought that the prosecutions in these cases ran afoul of this provision because the charges were based on respondents' use in their W-4's and K-4's of the same false Social Security numbers that they also inserted on their I-9's. Taken at face value, this theory would mean that no information placed on an I-9—including an employee's name, residence address, date of birth, telephone number, and e-mail address—could ever be used by any entity or person for any reason [because it would be use of information "contained in" an I-9 for purposes other than enforcement of specified federal statutes].

This interpretation is flatly contrary to standard English usage. A tangible object can be "contained in" only one place at any point in time, but an item of information is different. It may be "contained in" many different places, and it is not customary to say that a person uses information that is contained in a particular source unless the person makes use of that source.

Consider a person's e-mail address, one of the bits of information that is called for on an I-9. A person's e-mail address may be "contained in" a great many places. . . . Suppose that John used his e-mail address five years ago to purchase a pair of shoes and that the vendor has that address in its files. Suppose that John now sends an e-mail to Mary and that Mary sends an e-mail reply. No one would say that Mary has used information contained in the files of the shoe vendor. . . . Accordingly, the mere fact that an I-9 contains an item of information, such as a name or address, does not mean that information "contained in" the I-9 is used whenever that name or address is later employed. . . .

For all these reasons, there is no express preemption in these cases.

IV

We therefore proceed to consider respondents' alternative argument that the Kansas laws, as applied, are preempted by implication. This argument, like all preemption arguments, must be grounded in the text and structure of the statute at issue.

A

Respondents contend, first, that the Kansas statutes, as applied, fall into a field that is implicitly reserved exclusively for federal regulation. In rare cases, the Court has found that Congress legislated so comprehensively in a particular field that it left no room for supplementary state legislation, but that is certainly not the situation here.

In order to determine whether Congress has implicitly ousted the States from regulating in a particular field, we must first identify the field in which this is said to have occurred. In their merits brief in this Court, respondents' primary submission is that IRCA preempts "the field of fraud on the federal employment verification system," but this argument fails because . . . the submission of tax withholding forms is not part of that system.

At some points in their brief, respondents define the supposedly preempted field more broadly as the "field relating to the federal employment verification system," but this formulation does not rescue the argument. The submission of tax withholding forms is fundamentally unrelated to the federal employment verification system because, as explained, those forms serve entirely different functions. The employment verification system is designed to prevent the employment of unauthorized aliens, whereas tax withholding forms help to enforce income tax laws. And using another person's Social Security number on tax forms threatens harm that has no connection with immigration law. . . .

It is true that employees generally complete their W-4's and K-4's at roughly the same time as their I-9's, but IRCA plainly does not foreclose all state regulation of information that must be supplied as a precondition of employment. New employees may be required by law to provide all sorts of information that has nothing to do with authorization to work in the United States, such as information about age (for jobs with a minimum age requirement), educational degrees, licensing, criminal records, drug use, and personal information needed for a background check. IRCA surely does not preclude States from requiring and regulating the submission of all such information. . . .

Contrary to respondents' suggestion, IRCA certainly does not bar all state regulation regarding the "use of false documents when an unauthorized alien seeks employment." Nor does IRCA exclude a State from the entire "field of employment verification." For example, IRCA certainly does not prohibit a public school system from requiring applicants for teaching positions to furnish legitimate teaching certificates. And it does not prevent a police department from verifying that a prospective officer does not have a record of abusive behavior.

Respondents argue that field preemption in these cases follows directly from our decision in Arizona, but that is not so. In *Arizona*, relying on our prior decision in *Hines v. Davidowitz*, 312 U.S. 52 (1941), we held that federal immigration law occupied the field of alien registration. "Federal law," we observed, "makes a single sovereign responsible for maintaining a comprehensive and unified system to keep track of aliens within the Nation's borders." But federal law does not create a comprehensive and unified system regarding the information that a State may require employees to provide.

In sum, there is no basis for finding field preemption in these cases.

B

We likewise see no ground for holding that the Kansas statutes at issue [impliedly] conflict with federal law. It is certainly possible to comply with both IRCA and the Kansas statutes, and respondents do not suggest otherwise. They instead maintain that the Kansas statutes, as applied in their prosecutions, stand as an obstacle to the accomplishment and execution of the full purposes of IRCA—one of which is purportedly that the initiation of any legal action against an unauthorized alien for using a false identity in applying for employment should rest exclusively within the prosecutorial discretion of federal authorities. Allowing Kansas to bring prosecutions like these, according to respondents, would risk upsetting federal enforcement priorities and frustrating federal objectives, such as obtaining the cooperation of unauthorized aliens in making bigger cases.

Respondents analogize these cases to our holding in *Arizona*—that a state law making it a crime for an unauthorized alien to obtain employment conflicted with IRCA, which does not criminalize that conduct—but respondents' analogy is unsound. In *Arizona*, the Court inferred that Congress had made a considered decision that it was inadvisable to criminalize the conduct in question. In effect, the Court concluded that IRCA implicitly conferred a right to be free of criminal (as opposed to civil) penalties for working illegally, and thus a state law making it a crime to engage in that conduct conflicted with this federal right.

Nothing similar is involved here. In enacting IRCA, Congress did not decide that an unauthorized alien who uses a false identity on tax-withholding forms should not face criminal prosecution. On the contrary, federal law makes it a crime to use fraudulent information on a W-4.

The mere fact that state laws like the Kansas provisions at issue overlap to some degree with federal criminal provisions does not even begin to make a case for conflict preemption. From the beginning of our country, criminal law enforcement has been primarily a responsibility of the States, and that remains true today. In recent times, the reach of federal criminal law has expanded, and there are now many instances in which a prosecution for a particular course of conduct could be brought by either federal or state prosecutors. Our federal system would be turned upside down if we were to hold that federal criminal law preempts state law whenever they overlap, and there is no basis for inferring that federal criminal statutes preempt state laws whenever they overlap. Indeed, in the vast majority of cases where federal and state laws overlap, allowing the States to prosecute is entirely consistent with federal interests.

In the present cases, there is certainly no suggestion that the Kansas prosecutions frustrated any federal interests. . . . The Federal Government fully supports Kansas's position in this Court. In the end, however, the possibility that federal enforcement priorities might be upset is not enough to provide a basis for preemption. The Supremacy Clause gives priority to "the Laws of the United States," not the criminal law enforcement priorities or preferences of federal officers. Art. VI, cl. 2. . . .

[CONCLUSION]

For these reasons, the judgments of the Supreme Court of Kansas are reversed, and these cases are remanded for further proceedings not inconsistent with this opinion.

Justice Thomas, with whom Justice Gorsuch joins, concurring. [Omitted.]

Justice Breyer, with whom Justices Ginsburg, Sotomayor, and Kagan join, concurring in part and dissenting in part.

I agree with the majority that nothing in the Immigration Reform and Control Act of 1986 (IRCA), expressly preempts Kansas' criminal laws as they were applied in the prosecutions at issue here. But I do not agree with the majority's conclusion about implied preemption.

Kansas v. Garcia

When we confront a question of implied preemption, the words of the statute are especially unlikely to determine the answer by themselves. Nonetheless, in my view, IRCA's text, together with its structure, context, and purpose, make it clear and manifest that Congress has occupied at least the narrow field of policing fraud committed to demonstrate federal work authorization. That is to say, the Act reserves to the Federal Government—and thus takes from the States—the power to prosecute people for misrepresenting material information in an effort to convince their employer that they are authorized to work in this country.

The Act creates . . . a comprehensive scheme to combat the employment of illegal aliens. To that end, the statute's text sets forth highly detailed requirements [for employers and employees]. . . .

Congress, we explained [in *Arizona*], made a deliberate choice not to impose criminal penalties on aliens who merely seek, or engage in, unauthorized employment. . . . We ultimately held in *Arizona* that the States thus may not make criminal what Congress did not, for any such state law would interfere with the careful balance struck by Congress with respect to unauthorized employment of aliens. Given that obstacle to the regulatory system Congress chose, we concluded that the state law at issue conflicted with the federal Act and was therefore preempted.

State laws that police fraud committed to demonstrate federal work authorization are similarly preempted. . . . The Act makes clear that only the Federal Government may prosecute people for misrepresenting their federal work-authorization status. . . . The Act takes from the States the most direct means of policing work-authorization fraud. It prohibits States from using for that purpose both the I-9 and the federal employment verification system more generally. Those . . . provisions strongly suggest that the Act occupies the field of policing fraud committed to demonstrate federal work authorization. Otherwise, their express prohibitions would not constrain the States in any meaningful way. States could evade the Act simply by creating their own work-authorization form with the same requirements as the I-9, requiring employees to submit that form at the same time as the I-9, and prosecuting employees who make misrepresentations on the state form. No one contends that the States may do that. . . .

For these reasons, I would hold that federal law impliedly preempted Kansas' criminal laws as they were applied in these cases. Because the majority takes a different view, with respect, I dissent.

B. The Dormant Commerce Clause Doctrine

The **dormant commerce clause doctrine** is an application of federal supremacy that invalidates state laws that unduly burden the free flow of goods and services in interstate commerce. The doctrine is a form of implied preemption—but the source of preemption is not one or more federal statutes, but the commerce-related portions of the Constitution itself.

> TERMINOLOGY
>
> **DORMANT COMMERCE CLAUSE DOCTRINE:** The phrase "dormant commerce clause" can be confusing for newcomers. It is derived from John Marshall's opinion in *Willson v. Blackbird Creek Marsh Co.*, 27 U.S. 245 (1829), which suggested in dicta that Congress's power to regulate interstate commerce could override state laws even "in its dormant state." The power is "dormant" if Congress has not exercised it to enact statutes. This book avoids referring to a "Dormant Commerce Clause," because no such clause exists. Instead, it speaks of "the dormant commerce clause doctrine" (in lower case).

Under the Articles of Confederation, nothing prevented states from enacting laws to aid in-state businesses against out-of-state competitors. In some states, tariffs, taxes, blockades, and other protectionist devices made out-of-state goods unavailable or uncompetitive. The protectionism sometimes led to retaliation and small-scale trade wars. See Ch. 3.A.3. In response, the US Constitution included many provisions designed to avoid trade wars and unfair economic competition between states, replacing them with something resembling a national free trade zone. Some provisions give the federal government authority over certain economic matters; others forbid harmful forms of economic regulation by both federal and state governments; and some require a level interstate playing field.

- Congress may regulate commerce among the states and with foreign nations and Indian tribes. Art I, § 8, cl. 3.
- Congress may coin money, Art I, § 8, cl. 5, but states may not coin money or issue paper money, Art. I, § 10, cl. 1.
- Federal laws may not give preferences for ports of one state over another, or impose duties on vessels traveling between states. Art. I, § 9, cl. 5.
- States may not impose imposts or duties on imports or exports except as absolutely necessary for executing their inspection laws, unless such imposts or duties receive Congressional approval and federal supervision. Art. I, § 10, cl. 2.
- States may not lay any "duty of tonnage" (a charge on ships entering ports) Art. I, § 10, cl. 3.
- States must give non-state citizens the same "privileges and immunities" offered to state citizens. Art. IV, § 2.

From the early 19th century onwards, the Supreme Court has held that protectionism by the states is incompatible with the overall structure of the Constitution. The Supreme Court described the idea behind the doctrine in *H. P. Hood & Sons, Inc. v. Du Mond*, 336 U.S. 525, 539 (1949):

> Our system, fostered by the Commerce Clause, is that every farmer and every craftsman shall be encouraged to produce by the certainty that he will have free access to every market in the Nation, that no home embargoes will withhold his export, and no foreign state will by customs duties or regulations exclude them. Likewise, every consumer may look to the free competition from every producing area in the Nation to protect him from exploitation by any. Such was the vision of the Founders; such has been the doctrine of this Court which has given it reality.

The dormant commerce clause doctrine presumes that this vision of national free trade may be effectuated not only by Congress through legislation, but by the federal courts through decisions on the validity of state laws. As recently explained in *South Dakota v. Wayfair, Inc.*, 138 S. Ct. 2080 (2018):

> Although the Commerce Clause is written as an affirmative grant of authority to Congress, this Court has long held that in some instances it imposes limitations on the States absent congressional action. Of course, when Congress exercises its power to regulate commerce by enacting legislation, the legislation controls. But this Court has observed that in general Congress has left it to the courts to formulate the rules to preserve the free flow of interstate commerce.

flashback

Hints of what became the dormant commerce clause doctrine were seen in *Gibbons v. Ogden* (1824). Gibbons (the steamboat operator with the federal license) argued in part that New York had no power to pass any laws that had the effect of regulating interstate commerce. Congress's power to regulate interstate commerce must be exclusive, the argument went, because only one government may be a "regulator" of that commerce. Justice Marshall's opinion in *Gibbons* hinted that "there is great force in this argument," but that it was not necessary to go so far: "The sole question is, can a State regulate commerce with foreign nations and among the States, while Congress is regulating it?" In other words, *Gibbons* was decided as a matter of statutory preemption. Justice Johnson's concurrence adopted Gibbons' argument: he would hold unconstitutional any state statute having the effect of regulating interstate commerce.

If the dormant commerce clause doctrine is a form of implied preemption at the constitutional level, what is its scope: conflict or field? One can find language, especially in 19th century opinions, that could be read to suggest that the federal government occupies the field of interstate commerce. As it exists today, the dormant commerce clause doctrine most closely resembles obstacle preemption. State laws with effects on interstate commerce are not per se forbidden—but they will be unconstitutional if they impose significant obstacles to the implied national policy in favor of free interstate trade. (If Congress wishes, it may adopt a different national policy by enacting statutes expressly authorizing states to regulate. Such statutes might resemble the McCarran-Ferguson Act of 1945, described in Ch. 12.A.1. In the absence of such statutes, courts will presume that Congress wants to follow a constitutional baseline of freely flowing interstate commerce.)

1. Kickstarter: The Dormant Commerce Clause Doctrine

DISCLAIMER: *This Kickstarter is a checklist to help identify relevant issues. It is not a list of elements. Nothing requires judges to write their opinions (or lawyers to write their briefs) in Kickstarter order.*

The Dormant Commerce Clause Doctrine

USE WHEN: *A state law that is neither preempted nor expressly authorized by federal statute unduly burdens interstate commerce.*

A. *Does a state law burden interstate commerce?*

B. *Is the state entitled to enact the law because it is a participant in the relevant market?*

C. *Does the state law on its face discriminate against interstate commerce?*

   1. *If yes, the law is unconstitutional unless it is the least discriminatory way to achieve a legitimate purpose.*

   2. *If no, the law is constitutional unless it was enacted with discriminatory purpose or its burden on commerce clearly exceeds any legitimate purpose.*

KICKSTARTER USER'S GUIDE

Taken together, the cases involving the dormant commerce clause doctrine are not fully consistent with each other. There is no universally agreed-upon formula that would explain every case, so the items in this Kickstarter may well differ from those found in other casebooks or treatises. With that said, the following items are likely to lead you to ask the right questions, even though some cases exist that seem to diverge from this pattern.

Item A. *Burdens on Interstate Commerce.* As seen in the post-1937 cases interpreting Congress's power under the Commerce Clause, most economic transactions will (when they are considered in the aggregate) have some effect on the flow of goods and services in interstate commerce. Viewed through that lens, a huge variety of state laws will also have effects on interstate commerce. But the mere fact that a state law has some effect on interstate commerce is not enough to trigger the dormant commerce clause doctrine. Instead, the state law must burden interstate commerce, somehow making cross-border transactions more difficult.

Quite often, state laws burdening interstate commerce will benefit in-state residents over out-of-state residents. But that is not the defining issue for this threshold question. Instead, the doctrine will be triggered if the state law is bad for interstate commerce itself, not for particular people who might be engaged in it. Burdens on interstate commerce will arise from laws that make it impossible or infeasible for out-of-state vendors to sell goods or services in a state, or for in-state vendors to sell goods or services out of state. Burdens may also arise if a state makes its infrastructure unavailable or unattractive for interstate commerce. For example, a state law banning trucks over 55 feet long when all surrounding states set a maximum of 65 feet could make trucking through the state infeasible. See *Kassel v. Consolidated Freightways Corp. of Delaware,* 450 U.S. 662 (1981).

Item B. *The Market Participant Exception.* State governments impose regulations, but they are also buyers and sellers of goods and services. As some of the largest buyers and sellers in the economy, state governments will affect interstate commerce simply through their large economic influence. Is it forbidden protectionism for a state to buy only from in-state vendors (as when a state government prefers to buy locally-made goods), or to offer a discount to in-state purchasers (as when a state university charges less for in-state tuition)? The Supreme Court has decided that a state does not violate the dormant commerce clause doctrine when it acts as a participant in the market—that is, when it buys or sells. According to *Reeves, Inc. v. Stake,* 447 U.S. 429 (1980), the basic distinction "between States as market participants and States as market regulators makes good sense and sound law. [The dormant commerce clause doctrine] responds principally to state taxes and regulatory measures impeding free private trade in the national marketplace. [The Constitution does not] limit the ability of the States themselves to operate freely in the free market."

The market participant exception to the dormant commerce clause doctrine can be illustrated by a state law directing all state agencies to buy their furniture from in-state manufacturers. The "buy local" rule would give an economic advantage to in-state manufacturers and reduce the volume of cross border transactions, but it would not be a regulation of commerce. If instead a state law required the state's private businesses to buy locally produced furniture, the state would be regulating commerce rather than participating in it. For examples of states acting as market participants, *see, e.g., Reeves, Inc. v. Stake*, 447 U.S. 429 (1980) (state-owned cement plant is allowed to sell to only in-state customers); *White v. Massachusetts Council of Construction Employers, Inc.*, 460 U.S. 204 (1983) (city is allowed to prefer contractors whose employees live in the city).

Item C. *Facial v. Non-Facial Burdens.* If the threshold questions in Items A and B are met, the dormant commerce clause doctrine is triggered. The Supreme Court has announced two different approaches to judicial review under the doctrine. Just as the Equal Protection Clause considers some kinds of discrimination to be more constitutionally troubling than others, the dormant commerce clause doctrine distinguishes between different types of commerce-burdening laws. State laws that burden interstate commerce explicitly, through facial discrimination against interstate transactions, will be judged strictly. State laws that do not target interstate commerce on their face, but nonetheless have a burdensome effect on interstate commerce, are judged more deferentially.

Item C.1. *Facial Discrimination Against Interstate Commerce.* A state law that on its face treats out-of-state businesses differently from in-state businesses, or that otherwise expressly prevents interstate commerce, will almost always violate the dormant commerce clause doctrine. For example, *Crutcher v. Kentucky*, 141 U.S. 47 (1891), invalidated a state law that would issue business licenses to out-of-state companies only if they had $150,000 in capital, when no similar requirement existed for in-state companies. *Hughes v. Oklahoma*, 441 U.S. 322 (1979), invalidated a law that banned the out-of-state transport or sale of minnows captured within the state. A state may not hinder interstate commerce by hoarding resources for its own citizens.

Laws that facially discriminate against interstate commerce will be unconstitutional unless the state can demonstrate that no less discriminatory alternative would achieve the state's legitimate local interests. Of the few situations where such laws are upheld, most involve quarantines for health and safety reasons. For example, *Maine v. Taylor*, 477 U.S. 131 (1986), upheld a state law banning importation of out-of-state minnows. Minnows from other states were known to carry parasites that had not yet invaded Maine, so the burden on interstate commerce was justified, even though it was intentional.

Item C.2. *Facially Neutral Statutes with Discriminatory Effects.* A state law that does not discriminate against interstate commerce on its face will ordinarily be constitutional even if it has the effect of preventing some interstate transactions. For example, a state may decide to ban fireworks for public safety reasons, even though the law prevents potential cross-border sales of fireworks. Such laws are ordinary uses of the police power and do not contravene the dormant commerce clause doctrine.

A facially nondiscriminatory law will violate the dormant commerce clause doctrine in two situations. First, if it was enacted for the purpose of hindering interstate commerce: protectionism in disguise. Second, if the burdens on interstate commerce clearly exceed any legitimate local benefits. For example, in *Bibb v. Navajo Freight Lines, Inc.*, 359 U.S. 520 (1959), Illinois required all trucks on the state's roads to use a certain type of mud flap not required anywhere else. The law burdened interstate commerce because it would be awkward, expensive, and time-consuming for trucks to stop at the border to reconfigure their mud flaps. The statute did not discriminate against interstate commerce on its face; it applied to all trucks regardless of their place of origin. Still, the US Supreme Court struck it down, because the modest benefits of the mud flap were clearly outweighed by the burden the law would place on interstate commerce.

2. Facial Discrimination Against Interstate Commerce: *City of Philadelphia v. New Jersey*

The dormant commerce clause doctrine is most stringent when applied to a law that discriminates on its face between in-state and out-of-state commerce.

ITEMS TO CONSIDER WHILE READING *CITY OF PHILADELPHIA v. NEW JERSEY*

A. *Work through the items in the Kickstarter.*

B. *Why is New Jersey's ban on out-of-state garbage not constitutionally acceptable as a health and safety regulation?*

City of Philadelphia v. New Jersey,
437 U.S. 617 (1978)

Justice Stewart delivered the opinion of the Court [joined by Justices Brennan, White, Marshall, Blackmun, Powell, and Stevens].

A New Jersey law prohibits the importation of most "solid or liquid waste which originated or was collected outside the territorial limits of the State." In this case we are required to decide whether this statutory prohibition violates the Commerce Clause of the United States Constitution.

I

The statutory provision in question is ch. 363 of 1973 N.J. Laws, which took effect in early 1974. In pertinent part it provides:

> No person shall bring into this State any solid or liquid waste which originated or was collected outside the territorial limits of the State, except garbage to be fed to swine in the State of New Jersey, until the commissioner [of the State Department of Environmental Protection] shall determine that such action can be permitted without endangering the public health, safety and welfare and has promulgated regulations permitting and regulating the treatment and disposal of such waste in this State.

As authorized by ch. 363, the Commissioner promulgated regulations permitting four categories of waste to enter the State. Apart from these narrow exceptions, however, New Jersey closed its borders to all waste from other States.

Immediately affected by these developments were the operators of private landfills in New Jersey, and several cities in other States [including Philadelphia] that had agreements with these operators for waste disposal. They brought suit against New Jersey and its Department of Environmental Protection in state court, attacking the statute and regulations on a number of state and federal grounds. In an oral opinion granting the plaintiffs' motion for summary judgment, the trial court declared the law unconstitutional because it discriminated against interstate commerce. The New Jersey Supreme Court consolidated this case with another reaching the same conclusion. It found that ch. 363 advanced vital health and environmental objectives with no economic discrimination against, and with little burden upon, interstate commerce, and that the law was therefore permissible under the Commerce Clause of the Constitution. The court also found no congressional intent to pre-empt ch. 363 by enacting [various environmental statutes]. . . .

The plaintiffs then appealed to this Court. . . . . We agree with the New Jersey court that the state law has not been pre-empted by federal legislation. The dispositive question, therefore, is whether the law is constitutionally permissible in light of the Commerce Clause of the Constitution.

II

Before it addressed the merits of the appellants' claim, the New Jersey Supreme Court questioned whether the interstate movement of those wastes banned by ch. 363 is "commerce" at all within the meaning of the Commerce Clause. Any doubts on that score should be laid to rest at the outset.

The state court expressed the view that there may be two definitions of "commerce" for constitutional purposes. When relied on to support some exertion of federal control or regulation, the Commerce Clause permits a "very sweeping concept" of commerce. But when relied on to strike down or restrict state legislation, that Clause and the term "commerce" have a "much more confined reach." . . .

We think the state court misread our cases, and thus erred in assuming that they require a two-tiered definition of commerce. . . . All objects of interstate trade merit Commerce Clause protection; none is excluded by definition at the outset. . . . Just as Congress has power to regulate the interstate movement of these wastes, States are not free from constitutional scrutiny when they restrict that movement.

III

A

Although the Constitution gives Congress the power to regulate commerce among the States, many subjects of potential federal regulation under that power inevitably escape congressional attention because of their local character and their number and diversity. In the absence of federal legislation, these subjects are open to control by the States so long as they act within the restraints imposed by the Commerce Clause itself. The bounds of these restraints appear nowhere in the words of the Commerce Clause, but have emerged gradually in the decisions of this Court giving effect to its basic purpose. . . . This principle that our economic unit is the Nation, which alone has the gamut of powers necessary to control of the economy, including the vital power of erecting customs barriers against foreign competition, has as its corollary that the states are not separable economic units. . . . One state in its dealings with another may not place itself in a position of economic isolation.

The opinions of the Court through the years have reflected an alertness to the evils of economic isolation and protectionism, while at the same time recognizing that incidental burdens on interstate commerce may be unavoidable when a State legislates to safeguard the health and safety of its people. Thus, where simple economic protectionism is effected by state legislation, a virtually per se rule of invalidity has been erected. The clearest example of such legislation is a law that overtly blocks the flow of interstate commerce at a State's borders. But where other legislative objectives are credibly advanced and there is no patent discrimination against interstate trade, the Court has adopted a much more flexible approach[.] Where the statute regulates evenhandedly to effectuate a legitimate local public interest, and its effects on interstate commerce are only incidental, it will be upheld unless the burden imposed on such commerce is clearly excessive in relation to the putative local benefits. If a legitimate local purpose is found, then the question becomes one of degree. And the extent of the burden that will be tolerated will of course depend on the nature of the local interest involved, and on whether it could be promoted as well with a lesser impact on interstate activities.

The crucial inquiry, therefore, must be directed to determining whether ch. 363 is basically a protectionist measure, or whether it can fairly be viewed as a law directed to legitimate local concerns, with effects upon interstate commerce that are only incidental.

B

The purpose of ch. 363 is set out in the statute itself as follows:

> The Legislature finds and determines that the volume of solid and liquid waste continues to rapidly increase, that the treatment and disposal of these wastes continues to pose an even greater threat to the quality of the environment of New Jersey, that the available and appropriate land fill sites within the State are being diminished, that the environment continues to be threatened by the treatment and disposal of waste which originated or was collected outside the State, and that the public health, safety and welfare require that the treatment and disposal within this State of all wastes generated outside of the State be prohibited.

The New Jersey Supreme Court accepted this statement of the state legislature's purpose. The state court additionally found that New Jersey's existing landfill sites will be exhausted within a few years; that to go on using these sites or to develop new ones will take a heavy environmental toll, both from pollution and from loss of scarce open lands; that new techniques to divert waste from landfills to other methods of disposal and resource recovery processes are under development, but that these changes will require time; and finally, that the extension of the lifespan of existing landfills, resulting from the exclusion of out-of-state waste, may be of crucial importance in preventing further virgin wetlands or other undeveloped lands from being devoted to landfill purposes. Based on these findings, the court concluded that ch. 363 was designed to protect, not the State's economy, but its environment, and that its substantial benefits outweigh its slight burden on interstate commerce.

The appellants strenuously contend that ch. 363, while "outwardly cloaked in the currently fashionable garb of environmental protection, is actually no more than a legislative effort to suppress competition and stabilize the cost of solid waste disposal for New Jersey residents." They cite passages of legislative history suggesting that the problem addressed by ch. 363 is primarily financial: Stemming the flow of out-of-state waste into certain landfill sites will extend their lives, thus delaying the day when New Jersey cities must transport their waste to more distant and expensive sites. . . .

This dispute about ultimate legislative purpose need not be resolved, because its resolution would not be relevant to the constitutional issue to be decided in this case. Contrary to the evident assumption of the state court and the parties, the evil of protectionism can reside in legislative means as well as legislative ends. Thus, it does not matter whether the ultimate aim of ch. 363 is to reduce the waste disposal costs of New Jersey residents or to save remaining open lands from pollution, for we assume New Jersey has every right to protect its residents' pocketbooks as well as their environment. And it may be assumed as well that New Jersey may pursue those ends by slowing the flow of all waste into the State's remaining landfills, even though interstate commerce may incidentally be affected. But whatever New Jersey's ultimate purpose, it may not be accomplished by discriminating against articles of commerce coming from outside the State unless there is some reason, apart from their origin, to treat them differently. Both on its face and in its plain effect, ch. 363 violates this principle of nondiscrimination. . . .

The appellees argue that not all laws which facially discriminate against out-of-state commerce are forbidden protectionist regulations. In particular, they point to quarantine laws, which this Court has repeatedly upheld even though they appear to single out interstate commerce for special treatment. In the appellees' view, ch. 363 is analogous to such health-protective measures, since it reduces the exposure of New Jersey residents to the allegedly harmful effects of landfill sites.

It is true that certain quarantine laws have not been considered forbidden protectionist measures, even though they were directed against out-of-state commerce. But those quarantine laws banned the importation of articles such as diseased livestock that required destruction as soon as possible because their very movement risked contagion and other evils. Those laws thus did not discriminate against interstate commerce as such, but simply prevented traffic in noxious articles, whatever their origin.

The New Jersey statute is not such a quarantine law. There has been no claim here that the very movement of waste into or through New Jersey endangers health, or that waste must be disposed of as soon and as close to its point of generation as possible. The harms caused by waste are said to arise after its disposal in landfill sites, and at that point, as New Jersey concedes, there is no basis to distinguish out-of-state waste from domestic waste. If one is inherently harmful, so is the other. Yet New Jersey has banned the former while leaving its landfill sites open to the latter. The New Jersey law blocks the importation of waste in an obvious effort to saddle those outside the State with the entire burden of slowing the flow of refuse into New Jersey's remaining landfill sites. That legislative effort is clearly impermissible under the Commerce Clause of the Constitution.

Today, cities in Pennsylvania and New York find it expedient or necessary to send their waste into New Jersey for disposal, and New Jersey claims the right to close its borders to such traffic. Tomorrow, cities in New Jersey may find it expedient or necessary to send their waste into Pennsylvania or New York for disposal, and those States might then claim the right to close their borders. The Commerce Clause will protect New Jersey in the future, just as it protects her neighbors now, from efforts by one State to isolate itself in the stream of interstate commerce from a problem shared by all.

Justice Rehnquist, with whom Chief Justice Burger joins, dissenting.

. . . The question presented in this case is whether New Jersey must also [in addition to disposing of its own waste] continue to receive and dispose of solid waste from neighboring States, even though these will inexorably increase the health problems [associated with landfills]. The Court answers this question in the affirmative. New Jersey must either prohibit all landfill operations, leaving itself to cast about for a presently nonexistent solution to the serious problem of disposing of the waste generated within its own borders, or it must accept waste from every portion of the United States, thereby multiplying the health and safety problems which would result if it dealt only with such wastes generated within the State. Because past precedents establish that the Commerce Clause does not present appellees with such a Hobson's choice, I dissent.

The Court recognizes that States can prohibit the importation of items "which, on account of their existing condition, would bring in and spread disease, pestilence, and death, such as rags or other substances infected with the germs of yellow fever or the virus of small-pox, or cattle or meat or other provisions that are diseased or decayed or otherwise, from their condition and quality, unfit for human use or consumption." *Bowman v. Chicago & Northwestern R. Co.*, 125 U.S. 465 (1888). As the Court points out, such "quarantine laws have not been considered forbidden protectionist measures, even though they were directed against out-of-state commerce."

In my opinion, these cases are dispositive of the present one. Under them, New Jersey may require germ-infected rags or diseased meat to be disposed of as best as possible within the State, but at the same time prohibit the importation of such items for disposal at the facilities that are set up within New Jersey for disposal of such material generated within the State. The physical fact of life that New Jersey must somehow dispose of its own noxious items does not mean that it must serve as a depository for those of every other State. Similarly, New Jersey should be free under our past precedents to prohibit the importation of solid waste because of the health and safety problems that such waste poses to its citizens. The fact that New Jersey continues to, and indeed must continue to, dispose of its own solid waste does not mean that New Jersey may not prohibit the importation of even more solid waste into the State. I simply see no way to distinguish solid waste, on the record of this case, from germ-infected rags, diseased meat, and other noxious items. . . .

3. Facially Neutral Statutes with Discriminatory Effects: *Hunt v. Washington State Apple Advertising Commission*

The most contentious and least predictable area within the dormant commerce clause doctrine involves state laws that do not on their face discriminate against interstate commerce, but have adverse effects on the flow of goods and services across borders. *Hunt* is a frequently cited case of this type.

Apple Grading Systems. The US Department of Agriculture grades the quality of produce. After government inspection, producers may use the grades (e.g., "USDA prime" or "USDA choice") in their marketing. However, some states or growers prefer to use other grading systems that they believe better communicate the quality of the goods. The state of Washington developed a grading system for apples that is more stringent than the federal counterpart. On a scale from highest to lowest quality, the rankings are as follows:

- Washington Extra Fancy
- US Extra Fancy
- Washington Fancy
- US Fancy
- US No. 1
- US No. 1 Hail (same as US No. 1, but with skin damage from hailstones)

In *Hunt*, a North Carolina law mandated that boxes of apples sold in or shipped into the state be marked with the USDA grades or none at all.

ITEMS TO CONSIDER WHILE READING *HUNT*:

A. *Work through the items in the Kickstarter.*

B. *Should the court have decided the case on the basis that North Carolina enacted its law with protectionist intent?*

C. *Do laws like North Carolina's pose a danger to the nation of constitutional proportions?*

Hunt v. Washington State Apple Advertising Commission,

432 U.S. 333 (1977)

Chief Justice Burger delivered the opinion of the Court [joined by Justices Brennan, Stewart, White, Marshall, Blackmun, Powell, and Stevens].

In 1973, North Carolina enacted a statute which required all closed containers of apples sold, offered for sale, or shipped into the State to bear "no grade other than the applicable U.S. grade or standard." In an action brought by the Washington

State Apple Advertising Commission [against North Carolina governor James B. Hunt and other defendants], a . . . Federal District Court invalidated the statute insofar as it prohibited the display of Washington State apple grades on the ground that it unconstitutionally discriminated against interstate commerce. . . .

I

Washington State is the Nation's largest producer of apples, its crops accounting for approximately 30% of all apples grown domestically and nearly half of all apples shipped in closed containers in interstate commerce. As might be expected, the production and sale of apples on this scale is a multimillion dollar enterprise which plays a significant role in Washington's economy. Because of the importance of the apple industry to the State, its legislature has undertaken to protect and enhance the reputation of Washington apples by establishing a stringent, mandatory inspection program, administered by the State's Department of Agriculture, which requires all apples shipped in interstate commerce to be tested under strict quality standards and graded accordingly. In all cases, the Washington State grades, which have gained substantial acceptance in the trade, are the equivalent of, or superior to, the comparable grades and standards adopted by the United States Department of Agriculture (USDA). Compliance with the Washington inspection scheme costs the State's growers approximately $1 million each year. . . .

In 1972, the North Carolina Board of Agriculture adopted an administrative regulation, unique in the 50 States, which in effect required all closed containers of apples shipped into or sold in the State to display either the applicable USDA grade or none at all. State grades were expressly prohibited. In addition to its obvious consequence prohibiting the display of Washington State apple grades on containers of apples shipped into North Carolina, the regulation presented the Washington apple industry with a marketing problem of potentially nationwide significance. Washington apple growers annually ship in commerce approximately 40 million closed containers of apples, nearly 500,000 of which eventually find their way into North Carolina, stamped with the applicable Washington State variety and grade. It is the industry's practice to purchase these containers preprinted with the various apple varieties and grades, prior to harvest. After these containers are filled with apples of the appropriate type and grade, a substantial portion of them are placed in cold-storage warehouses where the grade labels identify the product and facilitate its handling. These apples are then shipped as needed throughout the year; after February 1 of each year, they constitute approximately two-thirds of all apples sold in fresh markets in this country.

Since the ultimate destination of these apples is unknown at the time they are placed in storage, compliance with North Carolina's unique regulation would have required Washington growers to obliterate the printed labels on containers shipped to North Carolina, thus giving their product a damaged appearance. Alternatively, they could have changed their marketing practices to accommodate the needs of

Hunt v. Washington State Apple Advertising Commission

the North Carolina market, i.e., repack apples to be shipped to North Carolina in containers bearing only the USDA grade, and/or store the estimated portion of the harvest destined for that market in such special containers. As a last resort, they could discontinue the use of the preprinted containers entirely. None of these costly and less efficient options was very attractive to the industry. Moreover, in the event a number of other States followed North Carolina's lead, the resultant inability to display the Washington grades could force the Washington growers to abandon the State's expensive inspection and grading system which their customers had come to know and rely on over the 60-odd years of its existence.

With these problems confronting the industry, the Washington State Apple Advertising Commission petitioned the North Carolina Board of Agriculture to amend its regulation to permit the display of state grades. An administrative hearing was held on the question but no relief was granted. Indeed, North Carolina hardened its position shortly thereafter by enacting the regulation into law:

> All apples sold offered for sale, or shipped into this State in closed containers shall bear on the container, bag or other receptacle, no grade other than the applicable U.S. grade or standard or the marking "unclassified," "not graded" or "grade not determined." . . .

Unsuccessful in its attempts to secure administrative relief, the Commission instituted this action challenging the constitutionality of the statute in the United States District Court for the Eastern District of North Carolina. . . . After a hearing, the District Court . . . held that the statute unconstitutionally discriminated against commerce, insofar as it affected the interstate shipment of Washington apples, and enjoined its application. This appeal followed[.]

II–III

[The Commission has standing to sue, and the Court has subject matter jurisdiction.]

IV

We turn finally to the appellants' claim that the District Court erred in holding that the North Carolina statute violated the Commerce Clause insofar as it prohibited the display of Washington State grades on closed containers of apples shipped into the State. Appellants [the North Carolina defendants] do not really contest the District Court's determination that the challenged statute burdened the Washington apple industry by increasing its costs of doing business in the North Carolina market and causing it to lose accounts there. Rather, they maintain that any such burdens on the interstate sale of Washington apples were far outweighed by the local benefits flowing from what they contend was a valid exercise of North Carolina's inherent police powers designed to protect its citizenry from fraud and deception in the marketing of apples.

Prior to the statute's enactment, appellants point out, apples from 13 different States were shipped into North Carolina for sale. Seven of those States, including the State of Washington, had their own grading systems which, while differing in their standards, used similar descriptive labels (e.g., fancy, extra fancy, etc.). This multiplicity of inconsistent state grades, as the District Court itself found, posed dangers of deception and confusion not only in the North Carolina market, but in the Nation as a whole. The North Carolina statute, appellants claim, was enacted to eliminate this source of deception and confusion by replacing the numerous state grades with a single uniform standard. Moreover, it is contended that North Carolina sought to accomplish this goal of uniformity in an evenhanded manner as evidenced by the fact that its statute applies to all apples sold in closed containers in the State without regard to their point of origin. Nonetheless, appellants argue that the District Court gave "scant attention" to the obvious benefits flowing from the challenged legislation and to the long line of decisions from this Court holding that the States possess "broad powers" to protect local purchasers from fraud and deception in the marketing of foodstuffs.

As the appellants properly point out, not every exercise of state authority imposing some burden on the free flow of commerce is invalid. Although the Commerce Clause acts as a limitation upon state power even without congressional implementation, our opinions have long recognized that in the absence of conflicting legislation by Congress, there is a residuum of power in the state to make laws governing matters of local concern which nevertheless in some measure affect interstate commerce or even, to some extent, regulate it.

Moreover, as appellants correctly note, that "residuum" is particularly strong when the State acts to protect its citizenry in matters pertaining to the sale of foodstuffs. By the same token, however, a finding that state legislation furthers matters of legitimate local concern, even in the health and consumer protection areas, does not end the inquiry. Such a view, we have noted, would mean that the Commerce Clause of itself imposes no limitations on state action save for the rare instance where a state artlessly discloses an avowed purpose to discriminate against interstate goods. Rather, when such state legislation comes into conflict with the Commerce Clause's overriding requirement of a national "common market," we are confronted with the task of effecting an accommodation of the competing national and local interests. We turn to that task.

As the District Court correctly found, the challenged statute has the practical effect of not only burdening interstate sales of Washington apples, but also discriminating against them. This discrimination takes various forms. The first, and most obvious, is the statute's consequence of raising the costs of doing business in the North Carolina market for Washington apple growers and dealers, while leaving those of their North Carolina counterparts unaffected. As previously noted, this disparate effect results from the fact that North Carolina apple producers, unlike their Washington competitors, were not forced to alter their marketing practices in order to comply with the statute. They were still free to market their wares under the USDA grade or none at all as they had done prior to the statute's enactment. Obviously, the increased costs imposed by the statute would tend to shield the local apple industry from the competition of Washington apple growers and dealers who are already at a competitive disadvantage because of their great distance from the North Carolina market.

Second, the statute has the effect of stripping away from the Washington apple industry the competitive and economic advantages it has earned for itself through its expensive inspection and grading system. The record demonstrates that the Washington apple-grading system has gained nationwide acceptance in the apple trade. Indeed, it contains numerous affidavits from apple brokers and dealers located both inside and outside of North Carolina who state their preference, and that of their customers, for apples graded under the Washington, as opposed to the USDA, system because of the former's greater consistency, its emphasis on color, and its supporting mandatory inspections. Once again, the statute had no similar impact on the North Carolina apple industry and thus operated to its benefit.

Third, by prohibiting Washington growers and dealers from marketing apples under their State's grades, the statute has a leveling effect which insidiously operates to the advantage of local apple producers. As noted earlier, the Washington State grades are equal or superior to the USDA grades in all corresponding categories. Hence, with free market forces at work, Washington sellers would normally enjoy a distinct market advantage vis-a-vis local producers in those categories where the Washington grade is superior. However, because of the statute's operation, Washington apples which would otherwise qualify for and be sold under the superior Washington grades will now have to be marketed under their inferior USDA counterparts. Such "downgrading" offers the North Carolina apple industry the very sort of protection against competing out-of-state products that the Commerce Clause was designed to prohibit. At worst, it will have the effect of an embargo against those Washington apples in the superior grades as Washington dealers withhold them from the North Carolina market. At best, it will deprive Washington sellers of the market premium that such apples would otherwise command.

Despite the statute's facial neutrality, the Commission suggests that its discriminatory impact on interstate commerce was not an unintended byproduct and there are some indications in the record to that effect. The most glaring is the response of the North Carolina Agriculture Commissioner to the Commission's request for an exemption following the statue's passage in which he indicated that before he could support such an exemption, he would "want to have the sentiment from our apple producers since they were mainly responsible for this legislation being passed." Moreover, we find it somewhat suspect that North Carolina singled out only closed containers of apples, the very means by which apples are transported in commerce, to effectuate the statute's ostensible consumer protection purpose when apples are not generally sold at retail in their shipping containers. However, we need not ascribe an economic protection motive to the North Carolina Legislature to resolve this case; we conclude that the challenged statute cannot stand insofar as it prohibits the display of Washington State grades even if enacted for the declared purpose of protecting consumers from deception and fraud in the marketplace.

When discrimination against commerce of the type we have found is demonstrated, the burden falls on the State to justify it both in terms of the local benefits flowing from the statute and the unavailability of nondiscriminatory alternatives adequate to preserve the local interests at stake. North Carolina has failed to sustain that burden on both scores.

The several States unquestionably possess a substantial interest in protecting their citizens from confusion and deception in the marketing of foodstuffs, but the challenged statute does remarkably little to further that laudable goal at least with respect to Washington apples and grades. The statute, as already noted, permits the marketing of closed containers of apples under no grades at all. Such a result can hardly be thought to eliminate the problems of deception and confusion created by the multiplicity of differing state grades; indeed, it magnifies them by depriving purchasers of all information concerning the quality of the contents of closed apple containers. Moreover, although the statute is ostensibly a consumer protection measure, it directs its primary efforts, not at the consuming public at large, but at apple wholesalers and brokers who are the principal purchasers of closed containers of apples. And those individuals are presumably the most knowledgeable individuals in this area. Since the statute does nothing at all to purify the flow of information at the retail level, it does little to protect consumers against the problems it was designed to eliminate. Finally, we note that any potential for confusion and deception created by the Washington grades was not of the type that led to the statute's enactment. Since Washington grades are in all cases equal or superior to their USDA counterparts, they could only "deceive" or "confuse" a consumer to his benefit, hardly a harmful result.

In addition, it appears that nondiscriminatory alternatives to the outright ban of Washington State grades are readily available. For example, North Carolina could effectuate its goal by permitting out-of-state growers to utilize state grades only if they also marked their shipments with the applicable USDA label. In that case, the USDA grade would serve as a benchmark against which the consumer could evaluate the quality of the various state grades. If this alternative was for some reason inadequate to eradicate problems caused by state grades inferior to those adopted by the USDA, North Carolina might consider banning those state grades which, unlike Washington's could not be demonstrated to be equal or superior to the corresponding USDA categories. Concededly, even in this latter instance, some potential for "confusion" might persist. However, it is the type of "confusion" that the national interest in the free flow of goods between the States demands be tolerated.

Hunt v. Washington State Apple Advertising Commission

Justice Rehnquist took no part in the consideration or decision of the case.

4. Facial Discrimination, the Market Participant Exception, and Some Basic Questions: *Camps Newfound/Owatonna v. City of Harrison*

Although the dormant commerce clause doctrine originated in the early 19th century, its use steadily expanded in the late 20th century. The increase reflects the growing volume of interstate economic activity, and also the growing amount of state-imposed economic regulation. In the following case, the majority and the dissents grapple over the fundamentals of the doctrine: how much national uniformity should the Constitution be interpreted to require in the name of free trade?

ITEMS TO CONSIDER WHILE READING *CAMPS NEWFOUND/OWATONNA:*

A. *Work through the items in the Kickstarter.*

B. *In Part II, the majority says, "Congress unquestionably has the power to repudiate or substantially modify" the operation of the dormant commerce clause doctrine. How could Congress do this, given that the Supreme Court has final authority for interpreting the Constitution?*

C. *Justice Thomas's dissent argues that the dormant commerce clause doctrine should be abandoned. What would be the result for the nation if the Supreme Court were to do so?*

D. *The dormant commerce clause doctrine allows private commercial interests to invoke the US Constitution to invalidate unwanted state-level regulation. Is the doctrine a modern-day* Lochner?

Camps Newfound/Owatonna, Inc. v. Town of Harrison,

520 U.S. 564 (1997)

Justice Stevens delivered the opinion of the Court [joined by Justices O'Connor, Kennedy, Souter, and Breyer].

The question presented is whether an otherwise generally applicable state property tax violates the Commerce Clause of the United States Constitution, because its exemption for property owned by charitable institutions excludes organizations operated principally for the benefit of nonresidents.

I

Petitioner is a Maine nonprofit corporation that operates a summer camp for the benefit of children of the Christian Science faith. The regimen at the camp [a term that refers collectively to Camp Newfound for girls and Camp Owatonna for boys] includes supervised prayer, meditation, and church services designed to help the children grow spiritually and physically in accordance with the tenets of their religion. About 95 percent of the campers are not residents of Maine.

The camp is located in the town of Harrison (Town); it occupies 180 acres on the shores of a lake about 40 miles northwest of Portland. Petitioner's revenues include camper tuition averaging about $400 per week for each student, contributions from private donors, and income from a "modest endowment." In recent years, the camp has had an annual operating deficit of approximately $175,000. From 1989 to 1991, it paid over $20,000 in real estate and personal property taxes each year.

The Maine statute at issue provides a general exemption from real estate and personal property **taxes** for benevolent and charitable institutions incorporated in the State. With respect to institutions that are "in fact conducted or operated principally for the benefit of persons who are not residents of Maine," however, a charity may only qualify for a more limited tax benefit, and then only if the weekly charge for services provided does not exceed $30 per person. Because most of the campers come from out of State, petitioner could not qualify for a complete exemption. And, since the weekly tuition was roughly $400, petitioner was ineligible for any charitable tax exemption at all.

[The state trial court in Maine ruled in favor of the camp. The Maine Supreme court reversed, and the US Supreme Court granted review.] For the reasons that follow, we now reverse.

■ OBSERVATION

TAXES: Like other state laws, state taxes are subject to the dormant commerce clause doctrine. See *Quill, Inc. v. North Dakota*, 504 U.S. 198 (1992); *Complete Auto Transit, Inc. v. Brady,* 430 U.S. 274 (1977). Whether the tax unconstitutionally burdens interstate commerce will depend on the facts of the case.

II

Camps Newfound/Owatonna, Inc. v. Town of Harrison

During the first years of our history as an independent confederation, the National Government [under the Articles of Confederation] lacked the power to regulate commerce among the States. Because each State was free to adopt measures fostering its own local interests without regard to possible prejudice to nonresidents, what Justice Johnson characterized as a "conflict of commercial regulations, destructive to the harmony of the States", ensued. See *Gibbons v. Ogden* (1824) (opinion concurring in judgment). In his view, this "was the immediate cause that led to the forming of a [constitutional] convention." "If there was any one object riding over every other in the adoption of the constitution, it was to keep the commercial intercourse among the States free from all invidious and partial restraints."

We have subsequently endorsed Justice Johnson's appraisal of the central importance of federal control over interstate and foreign commerce and, more narrowly, his conclusion that the Commerce Clause had not only granted Congress express authority to override restrictive and conflicting commercial regulations adopted by the States, but that it also had immediately effected a curtailment of state power. In short, the Commerce Clause even without implementing legislation by Congress is a limitation upon the power of the States. . . . Although Congress unquestionably has the power to repudiate or substantially modify that course of adjudication, it has not done so.

This case involves an issue that we have not previously addressed—the disparate real estate tax treatment of a nonprofit service provider based on the residence of the consumers that it serves. The Town argues that our dormant Commerce Clause jurisprudence is wholly inapplicable to this case, because interstate commerce is not implicated here and Congress has no power to enact a tax on real estate. We first reject these arguments, and then explain why we think our prior cases make it clear that if profit-making enterprises were at issue, Maine could not tax petitioner more heavily than other camp operators simply because its campers come principally from other States. We next address the novel question whether a different rule should apply to a discriminatory tax exemption for charitable and benevolent institutions. Finally, we reject the Town's argument that the exemption should either be viewed as a permissible subsidy or as a purchase of services by the State acting as a "market participant."

III

We are unpersuaded by the Town's argument that the dormant Commerce Clause is inapplicable here, either because campers are not "articles of commerce," or, more generally, because the camp's "product is delivered and 'consumed' entirely within Maine." Even though petitioner's camp does not make a profit, it is unquestionably engaged in commerce, not only as a purchaser, see *Katzenbach v. McClung* (1964), but also as a provider of goods and services. It markets those services, together with an opportunity to enjoy the natural beauty of an inland lake in Maine, to campers who are attracted to its facility from all parts of the Nation. . . .

Summer camps are comparable to hotels that offer their guests goods and services that are consumed locally. In *Heart of Atlanta Motel, Inc. v. United States* (1964), we recognized that interstate commerce is substantially affected by the activities of a hotel that solicits patronage from outside the State of Georgia through various national advertising media, including magazines of national circulation. In that case, we held that commerce was substantially affected by private race discrimination that limited access to the hotel and thereby impeded interstate commerce in the form of travel. Official discrimination that limits the access of nonresidents to summer camps creates a similar impediment. Even when business activities are purely local, if "it is interstate commerce that feels the pinch, it does not matter how local the operation which applies the squeeze." *Id.* . . .

The Town also argues that the dormant Commerce Clause is inapplicable because a real estate tax is at issue. We disagree. A tax on real estate, like any other tax, may impermissibly burden interstate commerce. We may assume as the Town argues (though the question is not before us) that Congress could not impose a national real estate tax. It does not follow that the States may impose real estate taxes in a manner that discriminates against interstate commerce. A State's power to lay and collect taxes, comprehensive and necessary as that power is, cannot be exerted in a way which involves a discrimination against [interstate] commerce. . . .

We therefore turn to the question whether our prior cases preclude a State from imposing a higher tax on a camp that serves principally nonresidents than on one that limits its services primarily to residents.

IV

There is no question that were this statute targeted at profit-making entities, it would violate the dormant Commerce Clause. State laws discriminating against interstate commerce on their face are virtually per se invalid. It is not necessary to look beyond the text of this statute to determine that it discriminates against interstate commerce. The Maine law expressly distinguishes between entities that serve a principally interstate clientele and those that primarily serve an intrastate market, singling out camps that serve mostly in-staters for beneficial tax treatment, and penalizing those camps that do a principally interstate business. As a practical matter, the statute encourages affected entities to limit their out-of-state clientele, and penalizes the principally nonresident customers of businesses catering to a primarily interstate market.

If such a policy were implemented by a statutory prohibition against providing camp services to nonresidents, the statute would almost certainly be invalid. . . . Avoiding this sort of "economic Balkanization," and the retaliatory acts of other

States that may follow, is one of the central purposes of our negative Commerce Clause jurisprudence. . . . By encouraging economic isolationism, prohibitions on out-of-state access to in-state resources serve the very evil that the dormant Commerce Clause was designed to prevent. . . .

V

The unresolved question presented by this case is whether a different rule should apply to tax exemptions for charitable and benevolent institutions. Though we have never had cause to address the issue directly, the applicability of the dormant Commerce Clause to the nonprofit sector of the economy follows from our prior decisions.

Our cases have frequently applied laws regulating commerce to not-for-profit institutions. . . . We have similarly held that federal antitrust laws are applicable to the anticompetitive activities of nonprofit organizations. The nonprofit character of an enterprise does not place it beyond the purview of federal laws regulating commerce. . . . We see no reason why the nonprofit character of an enterprise should exclude it from the coverage of either the affirmative or the negative aspect of the Commerce Clause. There are a number of lines of commerce in which both for-profit and nonprofit entities participate. Some educational institutions, some hospitals, some child care facilities, some research organizations, and some museums generate significant earnings; and some are operated by not-for-profit corporations. . . .

For purposes of Commerce Clause analysis, any categorical distinction between the activities of profit-making enterprises and not-for-profit entities is therefore wholly illusory. Entities in both categories are major participants in interstate markets. And, although the summer camp involved in this case may have a relatively insignificant impact on the commerce of the entire Nation, the interstate commercial activities of nonprofit entities as a class are unquestionably significant. See *Wickard v. Filburn* (1942). . . .

VI

. . . Finally, the Town argues that its discriminatory tax exemption scheme falls within the "market-participant" exception. That doctrine differentiates between a State's acting in its distinctive governmental capacity, and a State's acting in the more general capacity of a market participant; only the former is subject to the limitations of the negative Commerce Clause.

In *Hughes v. Alexandria Scrap Corp.*, 426 U.S. 794 (1976), we concluded that the State of Maryland had, in effect, entered the market for abandoned automobile hulks as a purchaser because it was using state funds to provide bounties for their removal from Maryland streets and junkyards. In *Reeves, Inc. v. Stake*, 447 U.S. 429 (1980), the State of South Dakota similarly participated in the market for cement as a seller of the output of the cement plant that it had owned and operated for many years. And in *White v. Massachusetts Council of Construction Employers, Inc.*, 460 U.S. 204 (1983), the city of Boston had participated in the construction industry by funding certain projects. These three cases stand for the proposition that, for purposes of analysis under the dormant Commerce Clause, a State acting in its proprietary capacity as a purchaser or seller may favor its own citizens over others.

Maine's tax exemption statute cannot be characterized as a proprietary activity falling within the market-participant exception. . . . A tax exemption is not the sort of direct state involvement in the market that falls within the market-participation doctrine. . . .

VII

[T]he facts of this particular case, viewed in isolation, do not appear to pose any threat to the health of the national economy. Nevertheless, history, including the history of commercial conflict that preceded the Constitutional Convention as well as the uniform course of Commerce Clause jurisprudence animated and enlightened by that early history, provides the context in which each individual controversy must be judged. The history of our Commerce Clause jurisprudence has shown that even the smallest scale discrimination can interfere with the project of our Federal Union. As Justice Cardozo recognized [in *Baldwin v. G.A.F. Seelig, Inc.*, 294 U.S. 511 (1935)], to countenance discrimination of the sort that Maine's statute represents would invite significant inroads on our national solidarity: "The Constitution was framed under the dominion of a political philosophy less parochial in range. It was framed upon the theory that the peoples of the several states must sink or swim together, and that in the long run prosperity and salvation are in union and not division."

Justice Scalia, with whom Chief Justice Rehnquist and Justices Thomas and Ginsburg join, dissenting.

The Court's negative Commerce Clause jurisprudence has drifted far from its moorings. Originally designed to create a national market for commercial activity, it is today invoked to prevent a State from giving a tax break to charities that benefit the State's inhabitants. In my view, Maine's tax exemption, which excuses from taxation only that property used to relieve the State of its burden of caring for its residents, survives even our most demanding Commerce Clause scrutiny.

I

We have often said that the purpose of our negative Commerce Clause jurisprudence is to create a national market. . . . In our zeal to advance this policy, however, we must take care not to overstep our mandate, for the Commerce Clause was not intended to cut the States off from legislating on all subjects relating to the health, life, and safety of their citizens, though the legislation might indirectly affect the commerce of the country. . . .

II [Omitted.]

III

. . . Facially discriminatory or not, [Maine's tax] exemption is no more an artifice of economic protectionism than any state law which dispenses public assistance only to the State's residents. Our cases have always recognized the legitimacy of limiting state-provided welfare benefits to bona fide residents. . . . States have restricted public assistance to their own bona fide residents since colonial times, and such self-interested behavior (or, put more benignly, application of the principle that charity begins at home) is inherent in the very structure of our federal system. We have therefore upheld against equal protection challenge continuing residency requirements for municipal employment, and bona fide residency requirements for free primary and secondary schooling. . . .

If a State that provides social services directly may limit its largesse to its own residents, I see no reason why a State that chooses to provide some of its social services indirectly—by compensating or subsidizing private charitable providers—cannot be similarly restrictive. . . .

Justice Thomas, with whom Justice Scalia joins, and with whom Chief Justice Rehnquist joins as to Part I, dissenting.

The tax at issue here is a tax on real estate, the quintessential asset that does not move in interstate commerce. Maine exempts from its otherwise generally applicable property tax, and thereby subsidizes, certain charitable organizations that provide the bulk of their charity to Maine's own residents. [The majority's invalidation of Maine's law] works a significant, unwarranted, and, in my view, improvident expansion in our "dormant," or "negative," Commerce Clause jurisprudence. For that reason, I join Justice Scalia's dissenting opinion.

I write separately, however, because I believe that the improper expansion undertaken today is possible only because our negative Commerce Clause jurisprudence, developed primarily to invalidate discriminatory state taxation of interstate commerce, was already both overbroad and unnecessary. . . .

I

The negative Commerce Clause has no basis in the text of the Constitution, makes little sense, and has proved virtually unworkable in application. . . .

To cover its exercise of judicial power in an area for which there is no textual basis, the Court has historically offered two different theories in support of its negative Commerce Clause jurisprudence. The first theory posited was that the

■ OBSERVATION

THE EXCLUSIVITY RATIONALE: Justice Thomas alludes to the theory from Justice Johnson's concurrence in *Gibbons v. Ogden*.

Commerce Clause itself constituted an exclusive grant of power to Congress. **The "exclusivity" rationale** was likely wrong from the outset, however. It was seriously questioned even in early cases. And, in any event, the Court has long since repudiated the notion that the Commerce Clause operates as an exclusive grant of power to Congress, and thereby forecloses state action respecting interstate commerce. . . .

The second theory offered to justify creation of a negative Commerce Clause is that Congress, by its silence, pre-empts state legislation. In other words, we presumed that congressional "inaction" was equivalent to a declaration that inter-State commerce shall be free and untrammeled. To the extent that the "pre-emption-by-silence" rationale ever made sense, it, too, has long since been rejected by this Court in virtually every analogous area of the law. . . . Even where Congress has legislated in an area subject to its authority, our pre-emption jurisprudence explicitly rejects the notion that mere congressional silence on a particular issue may be read as preempting state law. . . . To be sure, we have overcome our reluctance to preempt state law in two types of situations: (1) where a state law directly conflicts with a federal law; and (2) where Congress, through extensive legislation, can be said to have pre-empted the field. But those two forms of pre-emption provide little aid to defenders of the negative Commerce Clause. Conflict pre-emption only applies when there is a direct clash between an Act of Congress and a state statute, but the very premise of the negative Commerce Clause is the absence of congressional action. . . .

In sum, neither of the Court's proffered theoretical justifications—exclusivity or preemption-by-silence—currently supports our negative Commerce Clause jurisprudence, if either ever did. Despite the collapse of its theoretical foundation, I suspect we have nonetheless adhered to the negative Commerce Clause because we believed it necessary to check state measures contrary to the perceived spirit, if not the actual letter, of the Constitution. . . . Any test that requires us to assess (1) whether a particular statute serves a "legitimate" local public interest; (2) whether the effects of the statute on interstate commerce are merely "incidental" or "clearly excessive in relation to the putative benefits"; (3) the "nature" of the local interest; and (4) whether there are alternative means of furthering the local interest that have a "lesser impact" on interstate commerce, and even then makes the question "one of degree," surely invites us, if not compels us, to function more as legislators than as judges. . . .

In my view, none of this policy-laden decisionmaking is proper. Rather, the Court should confine itself to interpreting the text of the Constitution, which itself seems to prohibit in plain terms certain of the more egregious state taxes on interstate commerce . . . and leaves to Congress the policy choices necessary for any further regulation of interstate commerce.

Camps Newfound/ Owatonna, Inc. v. Town of Harrison

II–III [Omitted.]

Chapter Recap

A. The Supremacy Clause ensures that federal law will override state law in cases of conflict. Preemption and the dormant commerce clause doctrine are two frequently litigated aspects of the Supremacy Clause.

B. Federal statutes will preempt state laws if they contain express preemption clauses, or if a preemptive effect is implied.

   1. Federal statutes will impliedly preempt conflicting state laws. State laws may conflict with federal statutes in two ways. (a) If they make it impossible for a person to simultaneously obey both state and federal law. (b) If they create obstacles to the achievement of federal policy.

   2. Federal statutes will impliedly preempt any state law that is enacted in a field that has been fully occupied by federal legislation.

C. The dormant commerce clause doctrine is a form of obstacle preemption arising directly from the US Constitution. If Congress has not legislated, the doctrine restricts the ability of states to enact laws hindering the free flow of goods or services in interstate commerce.

CHAPTER 14

Federalism

As seen in the previous chapter, the Supremacy Clause limits the ability of state governments to enact laws that conflict with federal laws or the US Constitution. *Federalism* is the label usually given to the opposite scenario, where powers or prerogatives of states limit the ability of the federal government to enact laws using its enumerated powers. A pure federalism decision would occur if Congress passed a law that was undoubtedly within its enumerated powers, but the Supreme Court nonetheless found it unconstitutional because it intruded excessively into the autonomy of the states. This occurs in the commandeering cases in this chapter. Court decisions about the scope of federal enumerated powers may also be greatly influenced by the spirit of federalism, as in a decision holding that a statute is not within Congress's enumerated powers because the federal power should be interpreted in a way that preserves state power. Cases of this sort can be found in Ch. 15.

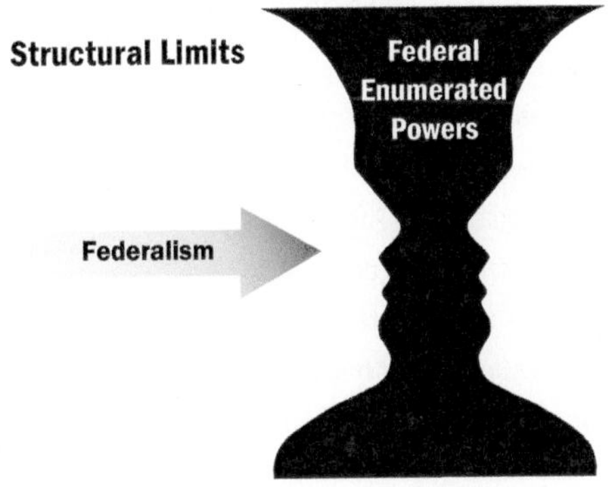

Federalism-based limits on the powers of the federal government have been, and continue to be, the subject of disagreement within the Supreme Court. This is in part because federalism doctrines are not squarely controlled by any text. There is no general "Federalism Clause" corresponding to the Supremacy Clause. Instead, federalism principles are deduced from the Constitution's structure, the nation's history, and judicial attitudes about consequences and values—all of which are subject to debate.

A. The Enigmatic Tenth Amendment

The Tenth Amendment reads: "The powers not delegated to the United States by the Constitution, nor prohibited by it to the States, are reserved to the States respectively, or to the people." This text is sufficiently enigmatic that it cannot, by itself, resolve concrete cases. It does not indicate which powers are (or are not) delegated to the United States; the answer to that question is found elsewhere in the Constitution. As a result, the Tenth Amendment is best read as textual evidence that the Constitution's overall structure includes states whose sovereign powers are not limited by the enumeration that controls the federal government. Judges must then decide, relying on methods of reasoning not expressly stated in the Constitution's text, what importance to assign to this structural fact.

During the *Lochner* era, the Supreme Court sometimes spoke of the Tenth Amendment as if it were written back to front. The Court began with a vision of which unenumerated powers were "reserved" to state governments, and then concluded that any such **state powers** must by definition be "not delegated to the United States." This approach yielded decisions like *Hammer v. Dagenhart* (1919), Ch. 8.A.2, where federal power under the Commerce Clause to control the goods that cross state borders was required to yield to states' unenumerated power over child labor, and *United States v. Butler* (1936), Ch. 9.A.3, where federal power under the Taxing Clause and Spending Clause was required to yield to the states' unenumerated power over agriculture. As expressed by the Four Horsemen in their dissent in *NLRB v. Jones & Laughlin Steel* (1937): "The Constitution still recognizes the existence of states with indestructible powers; the Tenth Amendment was supposed to put them beyond controversy."

■ TERMINOLOGY

STATE POWERS: The phrase "states' rights" should be approached cautiously. The term is inapposite, because only individuals have rights; governments have powers. *Compare, e.g.,* Fourth Amendment (the people have a "right" to be secure in their persons, houses, papers, and effects) *with* Art. I, § 8, cl. 1 (Congress shall have the "power" to legislate in enumerated areas). The Tenth Amendment reserves non-federal "powers" to the states. In political discourse, "states' rights" has historically been associated with slavery and Jim Crow, since it was more often asserted as a justification for those state practices than for benign ones.

This vision was rejected in *United States v. Darby* (1941), which observed that the Tenth Amendment "states but a truism that all is retained which has not been surrendered." In other words, the Tenth Amendment should be read front to back. Ask first what powers are available to the federal government and proceed accordingly. Next, if the question arises, recognize that states may exercise powers that the federal government does not have. This view was consistent with James Madison's statement in 1791 that the Tenth Amendment "may be deemed unnecessary; but there can be no harm in making such a declaration."

Darby's view of the Tenth Amendment remains good law, as seen in *Garcia v. San Antonio Metropolitan Transit Authority*, 469 U.S. 528 (1985): "The Constitution does not carve out express elements of state sovereignty that Congress may not employ its delegated powers to displace. . . . The fact that the States remain sovereign as to all powers not vested in Congress or denied them by the Constitution offers no guidance about where the frontier between state and federal power lies. In short, we [federal judges] have no license to employ freestanding conceptions of state sovereignty when measuring congressional authority." This means that "States must find their protection from congressional regulation through the national political process, not through judicially defined spheres of unregulable state activity." *South Carolina v. Baker*, 486 U.S. 1003 (1988).

Today's post-*Darby* opinions will occasionally mention the Tenth Amendment when discussing federalism. However, most treat the Amendment as a reminder that state powers are a recognized part of the constitutional structure, not as a free-standing basis to invalidate a federal law.

B. Federal Control over State Governments: The Rule Against Commandeering

Federalism as an independent limit on Congress's ability to exercise enumerated powers appears most clearly in a line of cases announcing a rule against *commandeering*. These cases do not allow the federal government to require states to implement federal regulatory programs, even if the federal government would have enumerated power to enact them directly.

1. Kickstarter: Commandeering

DISCLAIMER: *This Kickstarter is a checklist to help identify relevant issues. It is not a list of elements. Nothing requires judges to write their opinions (or lawyers to write their briefs) in Kickstarter order.*

Commandeering **kickstarter**

A. *The federal government may not directly compel state governments to enact or administer federal regulatory programs, even in areas where Congress has enumerated power to legislate.*

KICKSTARTER USER'S GUIDE

Item A. *The Rule Against Commandeering.* The case law setting forth a rule against the federal government commandeering state governments is fairly recent, but an analogy involving older technology helps illustrate it. Under Art. I,

§ 8, cl. 7, Congress has the authority to establish post offices. This means Congress can create a federal postal service, purchase equipment necessary to process the mail and hire employees to deliver it. Commandeering would occur if Congress ordered the states to purchase equipment to handle the US mail, or directed state employees to deliver US mail. This would not be a permissible means of achieving the federal government's enumerated ends.

Not every law that affects the operation of state government will be commandeering. Many federal laws apply to state governments, such as environmental regulations, minimum wage laws, or anti-discrimination statutes. Commandeering occurs when the federal government commands state governments to "enact" or "administer" a "regulatory program"—i.e., a program that regulates private citizens—that the federal government could enact and administer itself. The federal government may ban cocaine and use federal law enforcement resources to enforce the ban, but it cannot require states to ban cocaine or require state or local police to enforce the federal anti-cocaine law. (In practice, state and local police often choose to enforce many federal criminal laws, but this is a matter of state and local preference, not a federal mandate.)

Regulating Private People and Entities

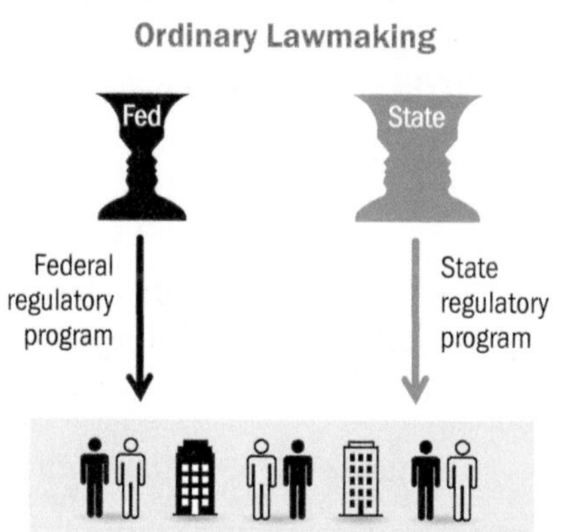

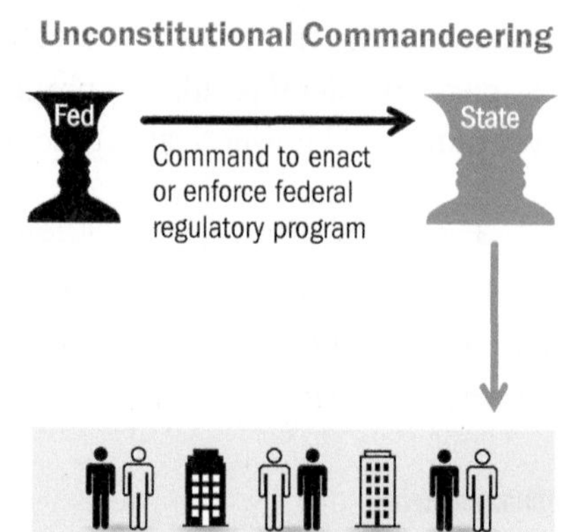

The rule against commandeering is based in part on a theory of political accountability. If the federal government could require states to enact or administer unpopular legislation, voters could be misled into directing their anger against state government when the federal government is to blame. "Citizens must have some means of knowing which of the two governments to hold accountable." *United States v. Lopez*, 514 U.S. 549, 576 (1995) (Kennedy, J., concurring).

2. Commandeering State Legislatures: *New York* and *Murphy*

The modern rule against commandeering was first announced in *New York v. United States*, 505 U.S. 144 (1992), where a federal statute for management of low-level radioactive waste was interpreted to require state governments to enact laws dictated by Congress. New York sued, claiming that Congress cannot coerce states into enacting laws. The Supreme Court (6–3) agreed that the statute was unconstitutional, because "Congress may not simply commandeer the legislative processes of the States."

> The Federal Government may not compel the States to enact or administer a federal regulatory program. The Constitution permits both the Federal Government and the States to enact legislation regarding the disposal of low level radioactive waste. The Constitution enables the Federal Government to pre-empt state regulation contrary to federal interests, and it permits the Federal Government to hold out incentives to the States as a means of encouraging them to adopt suggested regulatory schemes. It does not, however, authorize Congress simply to direct the States to provide for the disposal of the radioactive waste generated within their borders. While there may be many constitutional methods of achieving regional self-sufficiency in radioactive waste disposal, the method Congress has chosen is not one of them.

The majority acknowledged that the rule against commandeering "is not derived from the text of the Tenth Amendment itself," but that it arose from the overall structure of the US Constitution, which includes sovereign states as part of the design.

Murphy v. NCAA, 138 S.Ct. 1461 (2018), is a more recent example of Congress commanding state governments to enact laws. The case involved a federal statute to limit sports gambling. Congress could have used its Commerce Clause power to directly forbid sports gambling by individuals. Instead, Congress made it unlawful for a State or local government to "authorize by law" any sports gambling. By taking control of state lawmaking apparatus, Congress had engaged in forbidden commandeering—and it was irrelevant that the Constitution would have allowed Congress to pursue its goals by other means. *Murphy* offered an explanation of why this formalism was beneficial:

> ■ WEBSITE
> A fuller version of *Murphy v. NCAA* is available for download from this casebook's companion website, www.CaplanIntegratedConLaw.com.

> The anticommandeering rule promotes political accountability. When Congress itself regulates, the responsibility for the benefits and burdens of the regulation is apparent. Voters who like or dislike the effects of the regulation know who to credit or blame. By contrast, if a State imposes regulations only because it has been commanded to do so by Congress, responsibility is blurred.

> [Also], the anticommandeering principle prevents Congress from shifting the costs of regulation to the States. If Congress enacts a law and requires enforcement by the Executive Branch, it must appropriate the funds needed to administer the program. It is pressured to weigh the expected benefits of the program against its costs. But if Congress can compel the States to enact and enforce its program, Congress need not engage in any such analysis.

3. Commandeering State Executive Officials: *Printz v. United States*

The Supreme Court interpreted the federal statutes in *New York* and *Murphy* as commands for state legislatures to pass federally-desired laws. *Printz v. United States* considered similar objections to a federal statute that directed state or local police to perform tasks as part of a federal gun control statute.

ITEMS TO CONSIDER WHILE READING *PRINTZ*:

A. *Which enumerated powers authorized Congress to require background checks for gun purchases? (Disregard any limits that might be imposed by the Second Amendment.)*

B. *Is the rule against commandeering a necessary result of the Constitution's text? Its structure? Something else?*

C. *Who gives the better interpretation of historical evidence, the majority or the dissenters? Should it matter for constitutional purposes if no previous federal statute had required similar action by local law enforcement officers?*

Printz v. United States,

521 U.S. 898 (1997)

Justice Scalia delivered the opinion of the Court [joined by Justices Rehnquist, O'Connor, Kennedy, and Thomas].

The question presented in these cases is whether certain interim provisions of the Brady Handgun Violence Prevention Act commanding state and local law enforcement officers to conduct background checks on prospective handgun purchasers and to perform certain related tasks, violate the Constitution.

I

The Gun Control Act of 1968 [makes it unlawful for certain people to buy firearms]. In 1993, Congress amended the Gun Control Act by enacting the Brady

Printz v. United States

Act. The Act requires the Attorney General to establish a national instant background-check system by November 30, 1998, and immediately puts in place certain interim provisions until that system becomes operative. Under the interim provisions, a firearms dealer who proposes to transfer a handgun must [provide information about the prospective sale to the "chief law enforcement officer" (CLEO) of the buyer's residence]. With some exceptions, the dealer must then wait five business days before consummating the sale, unless the CLEO earlier notifies the dealer that he has no reason to believe the transfer would be illegal. . . .

When a CLEO receives the required notice of a proposed transfer from the firearms dealer, the CLEO must "make a reasonable effort to ascertain within 5 business days whether receipt or possession would be in violation of the law, including research in whatever State and local recordkeeping systems are available and in a national system designated by the Attorney General." The Act does not require the CLEO to take any particular action if he determines that a pending transaction would be unlawful; he may notify the firearms dealer to that effect, but is not required to do so. If, however, the CLEO notifies a gun dealer that a prospective purchaser is ineligible to receive a handgun, he must, upon request, provide the would-be purchaser with a written statement of the reasons for that determination. . . .

Petitioners Jay Printz and Richard Mack, the CLEOs for Ravalli County, Montana, and Graham County, Arizona, respectively, filed separate actions challenging the constitutionality of the Brady Act's interim provisions. In each case, the District Court held that the provision requiring CLEOs to perform background checks was unconstitutional[.] A divided panel of the Court of Appeals for the Ninth Circuit reversed, finding none of the Brady Act's interim provisions to be unconstitutional. We granted certiorari.

II

From the description set forth above, it is apparent that the Brady Act purports to direct state law enforcement officers to participate, albeit only temporarily, in the administration of a federally enacted regulatory scheme. Regulated firearms dealers are required to forward Brady Forms not to a federal officer or employee, but to the CLEOs, whose obligation to accept those forms is implicit in the duty imposed upon them to make "reasonable efforts" within five days to determine whether the sales reflected in the forms are lawful. While the CLEOs are subjected to no federal requirement that they prevent the sales determined to be unlawful (it is perhaps assumed that their state-law duties will require prevention or apprehension), they are empowered to grant, in effect, waivers of the federally prescribed 5-day waiting period for handgun purchases by notifying the gun dealers that they have no reason to believe the transactions would be illegal.

Petitioners here object to being pressed into federal service, and contend that congressional action compelling state officers to execute federal laws is unconstitutional. Because there is no constitutional text speaking to this precise question, the answer to the CLEOs' challenge must be sought in historical understanding and practice, in the structure of the Constitution, and in the jurisprudence of this Court. We treat those three sources, in that order, in this and the next two sections of this opinion.

Petitioners contend that compelled enlistment of state executive officers for the administration of federal programs is, until very recent years at least, unprecedented. The Government contends, to the contrary, that the earliest Congresses enacted statutes that required the participation of state officials in the implementation of federal laws. The Government's contention demands our careful consideration, since early congressional enactments provide contemporaneous and weighty evidence of the Constitution's meaning. Indeed, such contemporaneous legislative exposition of the Constitution acquiesced in for a long term of years, fixes the construction to be given its provisions. Conversely if, as petitioners contend, earlier Congresses avoided use of this highly attractive power, we would have reason to believe that the power was thought not to exist.

The Government observes that statutes enacted by the first Congresses required state courts to record applications for citizenship, to transmit abstracts of citizenship applications and other naturalization records to the Secretary of State, and to register aliens seeking naturalization and issue certificates of registry. . . . Other statutes of that era apparently or at least arguably required state courts to perform functions unrelated to naturalization, such as resolving controversies between a captain and the crew of his ship concerning the seaworthiness of the vessel, hearing the claims of slave owners who had apprehended fugitive slaves and issuing certificates authorizing the slave's forced removal to the State from which he had fled, taking proof of the claims of Canadian refugees who had assisted the United States during the Revolutionary War, and ordering the deportation of alien enemies in times of war.

These early laws establish, at most, that the Constitution was originally understood to permit imposition of an obligation on state *judges* to enforce federal prescriptions, insofar as those prescriptions related to matters appropriate for the judicial power. . . . [W]e do not think the early statutes imposing obligations on state courts imply a power of Congress to impress the state executive into its service. Indeed, it can be argued that the numerousness of these statutes, contrasted with the utter lack of statutes imposing obligations on the States' executive (notwithstanding the attractiveness of that course to Congress), suggests an assumed *absence* of such power. . . .

To complete the historical record, we must note that there is not only an absence of executive-commandeering statutes in the early Congresses, but there is an absence of them in our later history as well, at least until very recent years. . . . Even assuming [the newer statutes] represent assertion of the very same congressional power challenged here, they are of such recent vintage that they are no more probative than the statute before us of a constitutional tradition that lends meaning to the text. Their persuasive force is far outweighed by almost two centuries of apparent congressional avoidance of the practice.

III

The constitutional practice we have examined above tends to negate the existence of the congressional power asserted here, but is not conclusive. We turn next to consideration of the structure of the Constitution, to see if we can discern among its essential postulates a principle that controls the present cases.

A

It is incontestible that the Constitution established a system of "dual sovereignty." Although the States surrendered many of their powers to the new Federal Government, they retained "a residuary and inviolable sovereignty," The Federalist No. 39 (J. Madison). This is reflected throughout the Constitution's text, including (to mention only a few examples) the prohibition on any involuntary reduction or combination of a State's territory, Art. IV, § 3; the Judicial Power Clause, Art. III, § 2, and the Privileges and Immunities Clause, Art. IV, § 2, which speak of the "Citizens" of the States; the amendment provision, Article V, which requires the votes of three-fourths of the States to amend the Constitution; and the Guarantee Clause, Art. IV, § 4, which presupposes the continued existence of the states and those means and instrumentalities which are the creation of their sovereign and reserved rights. Residual state sovereignty was also implicit, of course, in the Constitution's conferral upon Congress of not all governmental powers, but only discrete, enumerated ones, Art. I, § 8, which implication was rendered express by the Tenth Amendment's assertion that "[t]he powers not delegated to the United States by the Constitution, nor prohibited by it to the States, are reserved to the States respectively, or to the people."

The Framers' experience under the Articles of Confederation had persuaded them that using the States as the instruments of federal governance was both ineffectual and provocative of federal-state conflict. Preservation of the States as independent political entities being the price of union, . . . the Framers rejected the concept of a central government that would act upon and through the States, and instead designed a system in which the State and Federal Governments would exercise concurrent authority over the people—who were, in Hamilton's words, "the only proper objects of government. . . . The Framers explicitly chose a Constitution that confers upon Congress the power to regulate individuals, not States." . . .

This separation of the two spheres is one of the Constitution's structural protections of liberty. Just as the separation and independence of the coordinate branches of the Federal Government serve to prevent the accumulation of excessive power in any one branch, a healthy balance of power between the States and the Federal Government will reduce the risk of tyranny and abuse from either front. To quote Madison once again [from The Federalist #51]:

> In the compound republic of America, the power surrendered by the people is first divided between two distinct governments, and then the portion allotted to each subdivided among distinct and separate departments. Hence a double security arises to the rights of the people. The different governments will control each other, at the same time that each will be controlled by itself.

The power of the Federal Government would be augmented immeasurably if it were able to impress into its service—and at no cost to itself—the police officers of the 50 States.

B

. . . The dissent of course resorts to the last, best hope of those who defend *ultra vires* congressional action, the Necessary and Proper Clause. It reasons that the power to regulate the sale of handguns under the Commerce Clause, coupled with the power to "make all Laws which shall be necessary and proper for carrying into Execution the foregoing Powers," conclusively establishes the Brady Act's constitutional validity, because the Tenth Amendment imposes no limitations on the exercise of delegated powers but merely prohibits the exercise of powers "not delegated to the United States." What destroys the dissent's Necessary and Proper Clause argument, however, is not the Tenth Amendment but the Necessary and Proper Clause itself. When a "law for carrying into execution" the Commerce Clause violates the principle of state sovereignty reflected in the various constitutional provisions we mentioned earlier, it is not a "law proper for carrying into execution" the Commerce Clause[.] We in fact answered the dissent's Necessary and Proper Clause argument in *New York v. United States* (1992): "Even where Congress has the authority under the Constitution to pass laws requiring or prohibiting certain acts, it lacks the power directly to compel the States to require or prohibit those acts. The Commerce Clause, for example, authorizes Congress to regulate interstate commerce directly; it does not authorize Congress to regulate state governments' regulation of interstate commerce." . . .

IV

Finally, and most conclusively in the present litigation, we turn to the prior jurisprudence of this Court. Federal commandeering of state governments is such a novel phenomenon that this Court's first experience with it did not occur until the 1970's[.] . . . When we were at last confronted squarely with a federal statute that unambiguously required the States to enact or administer a federal regulatory program, our decision should have come as no surprise. At issue in *New York v. United*

States (1992), were [provisions] effectively requiring the States either to legislate pursuant to Congress's directions, or to implement an administrative solution. We concluded that Congress could constitutionally require the States to do neither. "The Federal Government," we held, "may not compel the States to enact or administer a federal regulatory program." . . .

It is an essential attribute of the States' retained sovereignty that they remain independent and autonomous within their proper sphere of authority. It is no more compatible with this independence and autonomy that their officers be dragooned into administering federal law, than it would be compatible with the independence and autonomy of the United States that its officers be impressed into service for the execution of state laws. . . .

Finally, the Government puts forward a cluster of arguments that can be grouped under the heading: "The Brady Act serves very important purposes, is most efficiently administered by CLEOs during the interim period, and places a minimal and only temporary burden upon state officers." . . . We expressly rejected such an approach in *New York*, and what we said bears repeating:

> Much of the Constitution is concerned with setting forth the form of our government, and the courts have traditionally invalidated measures deviating from that form. The result may appear "formalistic" in a given case to partisans of the measure at issue, because such measures are typically the product of the era's perceived necessity. But the Constitution protects us from our own best intentions: It divides power among sovereigns and among branches of government precisely so that we may resist the temptation to concentrate power in one location as an expedient solution to the crisis of the day.

We adhere to that principle today, and conclude categorically, as we concluded categorically in *New York*: "The Federal Government may not compel the States to enact or administer a federal regulatory program." The mandatory obligation imposed on CLEOs to perform background checks on prospective handgun purchasers plainly runs afoul of that rule.

V [Omitted.]

Justice O'Connor, concurring. [Omitted.]

Justice Thomas, concurring. [Omitted.]

Justice Stevens, with whom Justices Souter, Ginsburg, and Breyer join, dissenting.

When Congress exercises the powers delegated to it by the Constitution, it may impose affirmative obligations on executive and judicial officers of state and local governments as well as ordinary citizens. This conclusion is firmly supported by the text of the Constitution, the early history of the Nation, decisions of this Court, and a correct understanding of the basic structure of the Federal Government. . . .

I

The text of the Constitution provides a sufficient basis for a correct disposition of these cases.

Article I, § 8, grants Congress the power to regulate commerce among the States. . . . There can be no question that that provision adequately supports the regulation of commerce in handguns effected by the Brady Act. Moreover, the additional grant of authority in that section of the Constitution "to make all Laws which shall be necessary and proper for carrying into Execution the foregoing Powers" is surely adequate to support the temporary enlistment of local police officers in the process of identifying persons who should not be entrusted with the possession of handguns. In short, the affirmative delegation of power in Article I provides ample authority for the congressional enactment. . . .

The Tenth Amendment imposes no restriction on the exercise of delegated powers. . . . The Amendment confirms the principle that the powers of the Federal Government are limited to those affirmatively granted by the Constitution, but it does not purport to limit the scope or the effectiveness of the exercise of powers that are delegated to Congress. Thus, the Amendment provides no support for a rule that immunizes local officials from obligations that might be imposed on ordinary citizens. Indeed, it would be more reasonable to infer that federal law may impose greater duties on state officials than on private citizens because another provision of the Constitution requires that "all executive and judicial Officers, both of the United States and of the several States, shall be bound by Oath or Affirmation, to support this Constitution." Art. VI, cl. 3. . . .

There is not a clause, sentence, or paragraph in the entire text of the Constitution of the United States that supports the proposition that a local police officer can ignore a command contained in a statute enacted by Congress pursuant to an express delegation of power enumerated in Article I.

II

Under the Articles of Confederation the National Government had the power to issue commands to the several sovereign States, but it had no authority to govern individuals directly. Thus, it raised an army and financed its operations by issuing requisitions to the constituent members of the Confederacy, rather than by creating federal agencies to draft soldiers or to impose taxes.

That method of governing proved to be unacceptable, not because it demeaned the sovereign character of the several States, but rather because it was cumbersome and inefficient. Indeed, a confederation that allows each of its members to determine the ways and means of complying with an overriding requisition is obviously more deferential to state sovereignty concerns than a National Government that uses its own agents to impose its will directly on the citizenry. The basic change in the character of the government that the Framers conceived was designed to enhance the power of the national government, not to provide some new, unmentioned immunity for state officers. . . . Indeed, the historical materials strongly suggest that the founders intended to enhance the capacity of the Federal Government by empowering it—as a part of the new authority to make demands directly on individual citizens—to act through local officials. . . .

The fact that Congress did elect to rely on state judges and the clerks of state courts to perform a variety of executive functions is surely evidence of a contemporary understanding that their status as state officials did not immunize them from federal service. The majority's description of these early statutes is both incomplete and at times misleading. . . . The use of state judges and their clerks to perform executive functions was, in historical context, hardly unusual. As one scholar has noted, "two centuries ago, state and local judges and associated judicial personnel performed many of the functions today performed by executive officers, including such varied tasks as laying city streets and ensuring the seaworthiness of vessels." . . . The majority's insistence that this evidence of federal enlistment of state officials to serve executive functions is irrelevant simply because the assistance of "judges" was at issue rests on empty formalistic reasoning of the highest order. . . .

III

. . . Perversely, the majority's rule seems more likely to damage than to preserve the safeguards against tyranny provided by the existence of vital state governments. By limiting the ability of the Federal Government to enlist state officials in the implementation of its programs, the Court creates incentives for the National Government to aggrandize itself. In the name of State's rights, the majority would have the Federal Government create vast national bureaucracies to implement its policies. This is exactly the sort of thing that the early Federalists promised would not occur, in part as a result of the National Government's ability to rely on the magistracy of the States. *See, e.g.,* The Federalist # 36 (A. Hamilton); #45 (J. Madison).

Nor is there force to the assumption undergirding the Court's entire opinion that if this trivial burden on state sovereignty is permissible, the entire structure of federalism will soon collapse. . . . The Court seems to accept the fact that Congress could require private persons, such as hospital executives or school administrators, to provide arms merchants with relevant information about a prospective purchaser's fitness to own a weapon[.] A structural problem that vanishes when the statute affects private individuals as well as public officials is not much of a structural problem.

IV

[In this section, the dissent disagrees with the majority's reading of *New York v. United States*.]

[In conclusion,] if Congress believes that [this] statute will benefit the people of the Nation, and serve the interests of cooperative federalism better than an enlarged federal bureaucracy, we should respect both its policy judgment and its appraisal of its constitutional power. Accordingly, I respectfully dissent.

Justice Souter, dissenting. [Omitted.]

Justice Breyer, with whom Justice Stevens joins, dissenting. [Omitted.]

4. Regulating State Activities Without Commandeering: *Reno v. Condon*

Not every federal statute that applies to state governments will violate the rule against commandeering. If Congress uses its commerce power to ban use of a certain pesticide, then States may not use that pesticide any more than private parties can. If Congress writes a minimum wage law that by its terms applies to state governments, then the state must pay its employees at least that wage. And when Congress uses its power under § 5 of the Fourteenth Amendment to enact a law requiring state and local employees to respect the federal constitutional rights of citizens (as it did in 42 U.S.C. § 1983), this regulation of state behavior is not commandeering.

What distinguishes commandeering from permissible regulation applicable to state government? The Supreme Court considered that question in *Reno v. Condon* (2000), which involved a privacy law enacted following a highly-publicized tragedy.

Like many states once did, the California Department of Motor Vehicles routinely released, upon request and sometimes for a fee, personal information about licensed drivers and their vehicles (including license plate numbers, home addresses, and physical descriptions). In 1989, TV and movie actress Rebecca Schaeffer was murdered by an obsessed fan who stalked her using information obtained from the California DMV. Congress responded with the Drivers' Privacy Protection Act, which regulated how states handle drivers' personal information.

ITEMS TO CONSIDER WHILE READING *RENO v. CONDON*:

A. *How does the statute in* Reno *differ from the ones in* New York *and* Printz?

B. *Why is federal regulation of a state's activities allowed, but federal commandeering of a state government not allowed?*

C. *Invent a federal statute that would be binding on a state, but not an instance of unconstitutional commandeering.*

Reno v. Condon,

528 U.S. 141 (2000)

Chief Justice Rehnquist delivered the opinion of the Court [joined by Justices Stevens, O'Connor, Scalia, Kennedy, Souter, Thomas, Ginsburg, and Breyer].

The Driver's Privacy Protection Act of 1994 (DPPA or Act) regulates the disclosure of personal information contained in the records of state motor vehicle departments (DMVs). We hold that in enacting this statute Congress did not run afoul of the federalism principles enunciated in *New York v. United States* (1992), and *Printz v. United States* (1997).

The DPPA regulates the disclosure and resale of personal information contained in the records of state DMVs. State DMVs require drivers and automobile owners to provide personal information, which may include a person's name, address, telephone number, vehicle description, Social Security number, medical information, and photograph, as a condition of obtaining a driver's license or registering an automobile. Congress found that many States, in turn, sell this personal information to individuals and businesses. These sales generate significant revenues for the States.

The DPPA establishes a regulatory scheme that restricts the States' ability to disclose a driver's personal information without the driver's consent. The DPPA generally prohibits any state DMV, or officer, employee, or contractor thereof, from "knowingly disclosing or otherwise making available to any person or entity personal information about any individual obtained by the department in connection with a motor vehicle record." 18 U.S.C. § 2721(a). . . . The DPPA's prohibition of nonconsensual disclosures is also subject to a number of statutory exceptions. . . .

The DPPA's provisions do not apply solely to States. The Act also regulates the resale and redisclosure of drivers' personal information by private persons who have obtained that information from a state DMV [through an exception]. 18 U.S.C. § 2721(c). . . .

The DPPA establishes several penalties to be imposed on States and private actors that fail to comply with its requirements. The Act makes it unlawful for any "person" knowingly to obtain or disclose any record for a use that is not permitted under its provisions, or to make a false representation in order to obtain personal information from a motor vehicle record. §§ 2722(a) and (b). Any person who knowingly violates the DPPA may be subject to a criminal fine, §§ 2723(a), 2725(2). Additionally, any person who knowingly obtains, discloses, or uses information from a state motor vehicle record for a use other than those specifically permitted by the DPPA may be subject to liability in a civil action brought by the driver to whom the information pertains. § 2724. While the DPPA defines "person" to exclude States and state agencies, § 2725(2), a state agency that maintains a "policy or practice of substantial noncompliance" with the Act may be subject to a civil penalty imposed by the United States Attorney General of not more than $5,000 per day of substantial noncompliance. § 2723(b).

South Carolina law conflicts with the DPPA's provisions. Under that law, the information contained in the State's DMV records is available to any person or entity that fills out a form listing the requester's name and address and stating that the information will not be used for telephone solicitation. . . .

Following the DPPA's enactment, South Carolina and its Attorney General, respondent [Charlie] Condon, filed suit [against US Attorney General Janet Reno] in the United States District Court for the District of South Carolina. . . . The District Court concluded that the Act is incompatible with the principles of federalism inherent in the Constitution's division of power between the States and the Federal Government. . . . The Court of Appeals for the Fourth Circuit affirmed, concluding that the Act violates constitutional principles of federalism. We granted certiorari, and now reverse. . . .

The United States asserts that the DPPA is a proper exercise of Congress' authority to regulate interstate commerce under the Commerce Clause. . . . We agree with the United States' contention. The motor vehicle information which the States have historically sold is used by insurers, manufacturers, direct marketers, and others engaged in interstate commerce to contact drivers with customized solicitations. The information is also used in the stream of interstate commerce by various public and private entities for matters related to interstate motoring. Because drivers' information is, in this context, an article of commerce, its sale or release into the interstate stream of business is sufficient to support congressional regulation. . . .

But the fact that drivers' personal information is, in the context of this case, an article in interstate commerce does not conclusively resolve the constitutionality of the DPPA. In *New York* and *Printz*, we held federal statutes invalid, not because Congress lacked legislative authority over the subject matter, but because those statutes violated the principles of federalism contained in the Tenth Amendment. In *New York*, Congress commandeered the state legislative process by requiring a state legislature to enact a particular kind of law. We said: "While Congress has substantial powers to govern the Nation directly, including in areas of intimate concern to the States, the Constitution has never been understood to confer upon Congress the ability to require the States to govern according to Congress' instructions."

In *Printz*, we invalidated a provision of the Brady Act which commanded state and local enforcement officers to conduct background checks on prospective handgun purchasers. We said:

> We held in *New York* that Congress cannot compel the States to enact or enforce a federal regulatory program. Today we hold that Congress cannot circumvent that prohibition by conscripting the States' officers directly. The Federal Government may neither issue directives requiring the States to address particular problems, nor command the States' officers, or those of their political subdivisions, to administer or enforce a federal regulatory program.

South Carolina contends that the DPPA violates the Tenth Amendment because it "thrusts upon the States all of the day-to-day responsibility for administering its complex provisions," and thereby makes "state officials the unwilling implementors of federal policy." South Carolina emphasizes that the DPPA requires the State's employees to learn and apply the Act's substantive restrictions, which are summarized above, and notes that these activities will consume the employees' time and thus the State's resources. South Carolina further notes that the DPPA's penalty provisions hang over the States as a potential punishment should they fail to comply with the Act.

We agree with South Carolina's assertion that the DPPA's provisions will require time and effort on the part of state employees, but reject the State's argument that the DPPA violates the principles laid down in either *New York* or *Printz*. We think, instead, that this case is governed by our decision in *South Carolina v. Baker*, 485 U.S. 505 (1988). In *Baker*, we upheld a statute that prohibited States from issuing unregistered bonds because the law regulated state activities, rather than seeking to control or influence the manner in which States regulate private parties. We further noted:

> The National Governor's Association nonetheless contends that § 310 has commandeered the state legislative and administrative process because many state legislatures had to amend a substantial number of statutes in order to issue bonds in registered form and because state officials had to devote substantial effort to determine how best to implement a registered bond system. Such "commandeering" is, however, an inevitable consequence of regulating a state activity. Any federal regulation demands compliance. That a State wishing to engage in certain activity must take administrative and sometimes legislative action to comply with federal standards regulating that activity is a commonplace that presents no constitutional defect.

Like the statute at issue in *Baker*, the DPPA does not require the States in their sovereign capacity to regulate their own citizens. The DPPA regulates the States as the owners of data bases. It does not require the South Carolina Legislature to enact any laws or regulations, and it does not require state officials to assist in the enforcement of federal statutes regulating private individuals. We accordingly conclude that the DPPA is consistent with the constitutional principles enunciated in *New York* and *Printz*.

As a final matter, we turn to South Carolina's argument that the DPPA is unconstitutional because it regulates the States exclusively. The essence of South Carolina's argument is that Congress may only regulate the States by means of generally applicable laws, or laws that apply to individuals as well as States. But we need not address the question whether general applicability is a constitutional requirement for federal regulation of the States, because the DPPA is generally applicable. The DPPA regulates the universe of entities that participate as suppliers to the market for motor vehicle information—the States as initial suppliers of the information in interstate commerce and private resellers or redisclosers of that information in commerce.

C. Federalism as a Method of Legal Reasoning

In the commandeering cases, federalism acts as a structural limit, preventing Congress from making an otherwise acceptable use of an enumerated power. It is even more common for federalism to be used as a method of reasoning. For example, when the court decides whether an enumerated power allows Congress to pass a given statute, a court might (among other arguments) consider how its decision could affect state autonomy.

Federalism as a tool for legal reasoning can be compared to the other usual tools. See Ch. 2.C. A judge committed to federalism believes that constitutional structure is one of the most important methods of reasoning and also that the preservation of state power is one of the most important features of the constitutional structure. Each of these premises can be disputed. Another judge might believe that other methods of reasoning (such as text, precedent, consequences, history, or values) are equally or more helpful in deciding a case, or that other aspects of the Constitution's structure may be equally or more important (such as federal supremacy or separation of powers between the federal judiciary and legislature). Since nothing in the Constitution's text mandates reliance on any particular methods of reasoning, choosing the best ones for the occasion remains a topic of disagreement.

Hammer v. Dagenhart (1918), Ch. 8.A.2, demonstrated the use of federalism as a method of legal reasoning. The Commerce Clause had long been interpreted to give Congress power to regulate which goods cross state borders, and Congress used that power to ban interstate shipment of goods manufactured with child labor. The Supreme Court in *Dagenhart*, influenced by its understanding of federalism, ruled that the Commerce Clause had a previously unknown limitation: namely, that Congress could not regulate cross-border transactions if doing so would have an excessively large impact on in-state activities. Justice Holmes' dissent disagreed. "I should have thought that the most conspicuous decisions of this Court had made it clear that the power to regulate commerce and other constitutional powers could not be cut down or qualified by the fact that it might interfere with the carrying out of the domestic policy of any State." Holmes was posthumously vindicated when *United States v. Darby* (1941), Ch. 9.C.2.b., overruled *Dagenhart*.

When used as a method of legal reasoning, federalism is not limited to constitutional questions. It can also be used when thinking through questions of statutory interpretation. In a set of cases sometimes collected under the heading of "New Federalism," the Rehnquist and Roberts courts have made federalism a priority in many legal areas, not all of them constitutional. For example, *Davis v. Monroe County Board of Education*, 526 U.S. 629 (1999), was a statutory interpretation case that reveals the spirit motivating New Federalism. Title IX of the Education Amendments of 1972, 20 U.S.C. § 1681, forbids sex discrimination by schools receiving federal funds. For many years, Title IX had been interpreted to authorize private lawsuits as a method of enforcement. In particular, *Gebser v. Lago Vista Independent School District*, 524 U.S. 274 (1998), held that Title IX authorized litigation against a recipient school district for deliberate indifference to teacher-on-student sexual harassment. In *Davis*, a family sued a school district for being deliberately indifferent to student-on-student sexual harassment.

In a 5–4 decision, a majority of the Supreme Court held that Title IX authorized the suit. The majority viewed *Davis* as a fairly simple case, with its conclusion resting primarily on existing precedents applying the statute, plus some policy arguments involving consequences and values. Justice Kennedy, however, wrote a lengthy dissent chastising the majority for failing to pay sufficient attention to federalism:

> The Nation's schoolchildren will learn their first lessons about federalism in classrooms where the Federal Government is the ever-present regulator. The Federal Government will have insinuated itself not only into one of the most traditional areas of state concern but also into one of the most sensitive areas of human affairs [sexuality]. This federal control of the discipline of our Nation's schoolchildren is contrary to our traditions and inconsistent with the sensible administration of our schools. . . .
>
> In the final analysis, this case is about federalism. Yet the majority's decision today says not one word about the federal balance. Preserving our federal system is a legitimate end in itself. It is, too, the means to other ends. It ensures that essential choices can be made by a government more proximate to the people than the vast apparatus of federal power. Defining the appropriate role of schools in teaching and supervising children who are beginning to explore their own sexuality and learning how to express it to others is one of the most complex and sensitive issues our schools face. Such decisions are best made by parents and by the teachers and school administrators who can counsel with them. The delicacy and immense significance of teaching children about sexuality should cause the Court to act with great restraint before it displaces state and local governments. Heedless of these considerations, the Court rushes onward[.] . . .
>
> Perhaps the most grave, and surely the most lasting, disservice of today's decision is that it ensures the Court's own disregard for the federal balance soon will be imparted to our youngest citizens. . . . After today, Johnny will find that the routine problems of adolescence are to be resolved by invoking a federal right to demand assignment to a desk two rows away. . . . Federalism and our struggling school systems deserve better from this Court. I dissent.

On the day *Davis* was announced, Justice Kennedy took the unusual step of reading his dissent in full from the bench. Justice O'Connor, the author of the majority opinion (and the first woman appointed to the US Supreme Court), delivered her own oral response: "The dissent urges that the Court's holding today will teach little Johnny a perverse lesson in federalism. In fact, Title IX works to ensure that little Mary may attend class unhindered by severe and pervasive acts of the sexual harassment by her classmates."

Justice Kennedy's dissent in *Davis* shows how federalism can describe a judicial attitude, rather than a precise legal doctrine. While reading the next chapter—which outlines the modern approaches to the most prominent of Congress's enumerated powers—pay attention to how federalism does (or does not) affect the Court's results.

Chapter Recap

A. In its modern usage, the term "federalism" refers to structural limits on the power of the federal government that seek to preserve or expand the authority of state governments. Federalism is a deduction from the overall structure of the Constitution, and not on any specific text—although the Tenth Amendment provides textual evidence that the Constitution's structure includes states with sovereign power.

B. The rule against commandeering is a federalism-based rule that prevents the federal government from ordering states to enact or administer federal regulatory programs, even in areas where Congress has enumerated power to legislate.

C. Federalism is often used as an interpretive tool. When deciding a case that has potential to affect state authority—whether the case arises under the Constitution or under other law—a court committed to preserving state power may invoke the spirit of federalism in its reasoning. This judicial attitude toward federalism became more prominent under Chief Justices Rehnquist and Roberts, as compared to the New Deal and Warren courts.

CHAPTER 15

Enumerated Powers

John Marshall observed in *McCulloch v. Maryland* (1819) that the need to determine the extent of the federal government's enumerated powers "is perpetually arising, and will probably continue to arise, so long as our system shall exist." This chapter outlines the modern understanding of several frequently invoked federal powers—but as Marshall predicted, the prevailing understanding changes over time and remains contested.

In the early 19th century, the Supreme Court understood the enumerated powers to be very broad—but Congress made few federal laws and used little of its available power. When Congress began to legislate more frequently in the late 19th century and early 20th centuries, the *Lochner*-era Supreme Court perceived implied limits to the enumerated powers, leading it to strike down important federal laws. As Congress sought to legislate even more broadly after the Depression and into the 1960s, the New Deal and Warren Courts read the enumerated powers to be as broad, or perhaps even broader, than John Marshall originally described—effectively swinging the pendulum back. Since the 1970s, the Court's understanding has narrowed somewhat, although not to the point seen during the *Lochner* era.

The pendulum is sure to keep swinging in ways large and small. Some powers have received a relatively stable interpretation over time, while others have shifted as the Court and Congress have adjusted their views about which federal actions the Constitution authorizes. At any historical moment there may be disagreements about the proper balance of the relevant interests: uniformity v. variety; national v. local; flexibility v. stability; and legislative power v. judicial power.

flashback

In the early 19th century, advocates of "strict construction" argued that the Constitution required a tight connection between enumerated powers and statutes enacted under them. John Marshall's opinions for the Court in *McCulloch v. Maryland* (1819) and *Gibbons v. Ogden* (1824) disagreed. In *McCulloch*, Marshall argued that the structure of any Constitution requires a fairly broad approach to the powers of the created government. "We must never forget," he said, "that it is a *constitution* we are expounding." A constitution is a document "intended to endure for ages to come, and consequently, to be adapted to the various crises of human affairs." Moreover, the text of the US Constitution nowhere requires that the authorization for subsequently enacted laws "shall be expressly and minutely described;" otherwise the constitution "would partake of the complexity of a legal code, and could scarcely be embraced by the human mind." In *Gibbons*, Marshall wrote for the Court that "we cannot perceive the propriety of this strict construction" because it "would cripple the government, and render it unequal to the object for which it is declared to be instituted."

Despite this, *Lochner*-era cases like *E.C. Knight* (1895) and *Hammer v. Dagenhart* (1918) took a narrow view of many enumerated federal powers. These decisions were not a pure return to the principle of strict construction, but they consciously chose to give a narrower reach to federal power than Congress presumed. Narrow construction of enumerated powers was again rejected during the New Deal. For example, *United States v. Darby* (1941) was willing to uphold a federal wage and hour statute under the Commerce Clause because it was an "appropriate means to the attainment of a legitimate end," citing *McCulloch*'s language of deference to Congress's choices.

Enumerated powers questions can also be framed in terms of judicial review. When Congress passes a law, it presumably thinks its statute is authorized by one of the enumerated powers. If the matter goes to litigation, Courts have an opportunity to express a view. In that case, should the judicial review be basically deferential to Congressional understandings or basically skeptical of them? *McCulloch* and similar cases imply that courts should be deferential. In fact, some opinions will ask whether there is a rational basis (i.e., a reason that is not crazy) to think that a statute is authorized by the enumerated power. When the phrase "rational basis" is used in this context, it is not identical to its use in individual rights cases like *Carolene Products, Railway Express Agency* or those in future chapters. However, it alludes to the same general concept from the New Deal: Courts should not rush to find that Congress has overstepped its authority.

A. The Taxing Clause

One of Congress's enumerated powers is "to lay and collect taxes, duties, imposts and excises." Art. I, § 8, cl. 1. This was a response to previous system under the Articles of Confederation, where the national government could do no more than ask states for funds, not raise them itself. To be viable, Alexander Hamilton argued in The Federalist #30, "the national government [must be able] to raise its own revenues by the ordinary methods of taxation authorized in every well-ordered constitution of civil government." There are relatively few constitutional limitations on the federal power to tax. The most difficult question has proven to be the most basic: what is a tax?

1. Kickstarter: The Taxing Clause

DISCLAIMER: *This Kickstarter is a checklist to help identify relevant issues. It is not a list of elements. Nothing requires judges to write their opinions (or lawyers to write their briefs) in Kickstarter order.*

The Taxing Clause **kickstarter**

A. *Courts will not rule on the wisdom of (1) Congress's decision to impose a tax, or (2) the chosen tax rate.*

B. *To be a "tax," a law requiring payments to the federal government must:*

   1. *raise "some revenue;" and*

   2. *not be a penalty or punishment.*

C. *A federal tax must be uniform throughout the United States, and if it is a "direct tax," be proportional to state population.*

KICKSTARTER USER'S GUIDE

Item A. *Deference to the Legislature.* Unlike most of the powers in Art. I, § 8, the text of the Taxing Clause contains language indicating the purpose of federal taxation: "to pay the debts, and provide for the common defense and general welfare of the United States." Conceivably, courts could have authority to decide whether a particular tax really does contribute to the general welfare. The Supreme Court has rejected that role, allowing Congress to decide whether it is wise to impose a tax, and in what amount.

This deference flows from the notion that tax decisions are fundamentally political, not legal. Setting a tax rate involves arbitrary line-drawing, which requires negotiation and compromise. In theory, courts rely purely on reasoning, leaving the political business of negotiation and compromise to the legislature. No guiding legal principle can allow judges to reason their way to the optimal tax rate.

flashback

McCulloch v. Maryland (1819) argued that the only effective limits on tax rates will arise from the political process:

> It is admitted, that the power of taxing the people and their property is essential to the very existence of government, and may be legitimately exercised . . . to the utmost extent to which the government may choose to carry it. The only security against the abuse of this power is found in the [democratic] structure of the government itself. In imposing a tax, the legislature acts upon its constituents. This is, in general, a sufficient security against erroneous and oppressive taxation. The people . . . rest[ ] confidently on the interest of the legislator, and on the influence of the constituents over their representatives, to guard them against its abuse.

Item B. *The Definition of Tax.* The Taxing Clause allows the federal government to impose taxes, not to regulate or forbid behavior. To be sure, the federal government does have power to regulate or forbid behavior—and punish it with monetary fines—but only by using enumerated powers other than the Taxing Clause, such as the Commerce Clause. Since both taxes and fines take the same general form ("If you do X, you must pay the government Y"), some cases require a court to determine if a law is a penalty in tax clothing.

Several *Lochner*-era cases held that federal laws purporting to impose taxes were actually penalties not authorized by the Taxing Clause:

- The statute in *Bailey v. Drexel Furniture Co.* (1922) imposed a 10% tax on the net profits of companies that sold goods in interstate commerce that were manufactured with child labor. Ch. 8.B.2.
- The statute in *Carter v. Carter Coal Co.* (1936) imposed a 15% excise tax on mined coal that could be reduced to 1.5% if the company agreed to abide by an industry code of conduct. Ch. 9.A.2.
- The statute in *United States v. Constantine* (1935) imposed a federal tax of $1,000 on the manufacturing or sale of liquor when done in violation of state law, an amount 40 times larger than the tax on lawful liquor businesses. Ch. 8.B.2.

Item B.1. *"Some Revenue."* The Constitution does not define the word "tax," but it connotes a law requiring individuals to pay money to finance the expenses of the government. A law must therefore raise revenue to fall within the definition of a tax. The law does not need to raise much revenue; "some revenue" is sufficient. Indeed, a law can still be a tax even if the costs of collection outstrip the revenue raised. *Sonzinsky v. United States*, 300 U.S. 506 (1937). By contrast, laws that require people to pay money directly to others—like contract and tort law—are not taxes because they do not raise even "some revenue" for the government.

Item B.2. *Not a Penalty.* Laws that require individuals to pay money to the government as punishment for misconduct may in practice raise some revenue, but they are penalties rather than taxes. Examples include the fines included in some criminal sentences (subject to the Eighth Amendment ban on "excessive fines"), and the civil judgments that accompany public infractions like parking tickets. In hard cases, it can be difficult to distinguish between taxes and penalties. No bright-line rule separates them, but the laws upheld as taxes (or rejected as penalties) have a family resemblance to each other, sharing many of the following features—even though a complete list of all relevant factors would not be possible:

- *Proportional to the Amount or Value of the Thing Taxed.* Most taxes are set in reference to the amount or value of the thing taxed, as in a gasoline tax of X cents per gallon; an income tax of Y percent of money earned; or a property tax of Z dollars per $1,000 of assessed value. A law does not have to follow any particular mathematical formula to be a tax, and some true taxes collect fixed amounts. By contrast, the law in *Drexel Furniture* (1922) required payment of 10% of the net profits of any factory that used child labor, no matter how much of those profits were traceable to child labor. This law did not tax child labor, but instead imposed a financial penalty on users of child labor that was calculated by reference to something other than the amount or value of the thing supposedly taxed.

- *A Tax-Like Amount.* The legislature has leeway to set the amount of a tax, but a conspicuously large amount due may indicate that the law is a penalty, designed as a hammer. The 10% tax on total profits in *Drexel Furniture* was large for its time, and the tax in *Constantine* on unlawful liquor sales was many times higher than customary taxes for comparable but lawful liquor sales. This does not mean that all high taxes are unconstitutional penalties, or that rates cannot change over time. Highly taxed goods—like cigarettes, alcohol, or gasoline—could in theory be subject to taxes costing more than the product's untaxed market price. As with other factors, the amount of a tax is not dispositive by itself, but may be an indication that the law is best viewed as a penalty.
- *Owed Even if the Taxed Activity Is Performed Without Scienter.* Taxes are usually owed regardless of the mental state in which one performs the taxed activity. For example, income taxes and sales taxes do not vary based on the intentions of the earner or seller. By contrast, a law requiring a payment to the government only if an act is done with some culpable mental state (scienter or *mens rea*) departs from this pattern, making it resemble torts or crimes that often include a mental element. The law in *Drexel Furniture* had a defense for factory owners who did not know that certain employees were underage, making the tax applicable only to those who knowingly hired child labor. The Court observed that "scienters are associated with penalties, not with taxes."
- *Codified and Enforced Like Other Taxes.* Taxes tend to be codified together as part of tax codes, using language similar to other tax laws. They tend not to be located in the criminal code or other regulatory civil codes, and they tend not to be phrased in penal language. They tend to be enforced by departments with responsibility for tax enforcement, like a state Department of Revenue or the federal Department of the Treasury. By contrast, the law in *Bailey* could be enforced by the Treasury and by the Department of Labor—an agency responsible for regulating employer behavior, not for raising revenue.

- *Coercive Purpose or Effect.* The law in *Carter Coal* gave coal mine owners an offer they couldn't refuse: sign onto an industry code, or multiply your tax burden by ten. If, all things considered, a law seems to designed to (and is likely to) coerce behavior rather than raise revenue, it will be a penalty. The historical setting may be a clue to coercive purpose: the tax laws in *Carter Coal* and *Drexel Furniture* were enacted after Congress unsuccessfully attempted to directly regulate the same industries. However, as seen in *US v. Darby* (1941), courts are reluctant to invalidate laws as exceeding enumerated powers solely for reasons of legislative motive.

It is not dispositive, by itself, that the tax reaches conduct that may be unlawful. *Constantine* struck down a law that imposed a supposed tax only for liquor sales that violated state law, but there were other suspicious features about the law indicating that it was a penalty. Other cases have upheld laws imposing taxes on activity that was unlawful in some or most states, so long as the law otherwise resembled a tax. See *United States v. Sanchez*, 340 U.S. 42 (1950) (upholding federal tax on marijuana).

When reading *United States v. Kahriger* (1953), and the more recent decision in *NFIB v. Sebelius* (2014), Ch. 17.B.2, consider what they mean for the definition of a tax under the Taxing Clause.

Item C. *Tax Equality Requirements.* Two rarely-invoked constitutional provisions were designed to prevent Congress from using its taxing power to disadvantage particular states.

Uniformity. The Taxing Clause requires that any federal tax be "uniform throughout the United States." This does not mean that everyone must pay the same dollar amount of tax, but that federal taxes must be calculated the same way wherever the tax might be owed. **Congress cannot impose a different rate** of tax per pound of tobacco grown in Virginia than it does for tobacco grown in other states. Once a single rate is set for tobacco taxes, Virginia will of course pay far more than Alaska (since tobacco cannot grow there), but this does not make the tax non-uniform.

OBSERVATION

CONGRESS CANNOT IMPOSE A DIFFERENT RATE: A progressive income tax, where those with higher incomes pay a higher percentage of tax, does not violate the uniformity requirement so long as it is structured properly. Under a system with higher marginal taxes for higher income brackets, taxpayers might pay a tax of X% on their first $X of income, a higher tax of Y% on their next $Y of income, an even higher tax of Z% on their next $Z of income, and so on. Low wage earners might never earn enough money to owe the higher marginal rates in the Y and Z tax brackets, but the rates are uniform for all.

Proportionality of Direct Taxes. Art. I, § 9, cl. 4 and Art. I, § 2, cl. 3 require direct taxes to be proportional to state population. These provisions were included in the Constitution to ensure that Congress would not tax slave ownership. See Ch. 3.B.2.b. The precise meaning of "direct tax" has been subject to debate: at a minimum, it includes taxes on real property and "capitations" (per person taxes or "poll taxes"). *Pollock v. Farmers' Loan and Trust Co.*, 158 U.S. 601 (1895), held that a tax on income produced from property was a direct tax that must be proportioned equally by population. *Pollock* was overruled by the Sixteenth Amendment (1913), which authorized the federal government to tax "incomes, from whatever source derived," without regard to the census. See Ch. 8.B.1. As a result, the per capita income tax payments in a high-income state may be greater than the per capita payments in a low-income state.

2. Taxes with Deterrent Effects: *U.S. v. Kahriger*

The distinction between taxes and penalties can be difficult because both have deterrent effects. Consider two laws that deter alcohol-related conduct. A "sin tax" per gallon of alcohol will generate revenue for the government while deterring drinking by making it more expensive. A fine on selling alcohol without a license will generate revenue for the government while deterring unlicensed sales. The first law would be a tax and the second a penalty, even though they share many features. Moreover, the legislature might have mixed motives: it may wish to raise revenue *and* deter future activity *and* punish those who engage in the activity. All of this can make it tricky to categorize a law that deters by raising prices.

ITEMS TO CONSIDER WHILE READING *UNITED STATES v. KAHRIGER:*

A. *Work through the items from the Taxing Clause Kickstarter.*

B. *Does Congress's ability to tax an activity depend on whether Congress has the power to directly regulate that activity?*

C. *The last time the Supreme Court ruled that a law purporting to be a tax was instead a non-tax penalty was* Carter Coal *in 1936. The subsequent cases have, like* Kahriger, *refused to find that the challenged laws were not true taxes. In light of this, what would it take for a federal tax to be a penalty today?*

United States v. Kahriger,

345 U.S. 22 (1953)

Justice Reed delivered the opinion of the Court [joined by Chief Justice Vinson and Justices Jackson, Burton, Clark, and Minton].

The issue raised by this appeal is the constitutionality of the occupational tax provisions of the Revenue Act of 1951, which levy a tax on persons engaged in the business of accepting wagers, and require such persons to register with the Collector of Internal Revenue. [The statute purports to impose an excise tax in an amount equal to 10% of the amount wagered. Failure to pay the tax results in a fine of between $1,000 and $5,000, and willful violations may be criminally prosecuted.] The unconstitutionality of the tax is asserted on two grounds. First, it is said that Congress, under the pretense of exercising its power to tax has attempted to penalize illegal intrastate gambling through the regulatory features of the Act, and has thus infringed the police power which is reserved to the states. Secondly, it is urged that the registration provisions of the tax violate the privilege against self-incrimination . . . contrary to the guarantees of the Fifth Amendment.

The case comes here on appeal from the United States District Court for the Eastern District of Pennsylvania, where an information was filed against appellee [Joseph Kahriger] alleging that he was in the business of accepting wagers and that he willfully failed to register for and pay the occupational tax in question. Appellee moved to dismiss on the ground that the sections upon which the information was based were unconstitutional. The District Court sustained the motion on the authority of our opinion in *United States v. Constantine*, 296 U.S. 287 (1935) [which held that a purported tax that applied only to liquor businesses that violated state laws was not a true tax]. . . .

The result below is at odds with the position of the seven other district courts which have considered the matter, and, in our opinion, is erroneous.

In the term following the *Constantine* opinion, this Court pointed out in *Sonzinsky v. United States*, 300 U.S. 506 (1937) (a case involving a tax on a "limited class" of objectionable firearms alleged to be prohibitory in effect and "to disclose unmistakably the legislative purpose to regulate rather than to tax"), that the subject of the tax in *Constantine* was "described or treated as criminal by the taxing statute." The tax in the *Constantine* case was a special additional excise tax of $1,000, placed only on persons who carried on a liquor business in violation of state law. The wagering tax with which we are here concerned applies to all persons engaged in the business of receiving wagers regardless of whether such activity violates state law.

The substance of respondent's position with respect to the Tenth Amendment is that Congress has chosen to tax a specified business which is not within its power to regulate. The precedents are many upholding taxes similar to this wagering tax as a proper exercise of the federal taxing power. . . .

Appellee would have us say that because there is legislative history indicating a congressional motive to suppress wagering,[FN3] this tax is not a proper exercise of such taxing power. In *The License Tax Cases*, 72 U.S. 462 (1866), it was admitted that the federal license "discouraged" the activities. The intent to curtail and hinder, as well as tax, was also manifest in the following cases, and in each of them the tax was upheld: *Veazie Bank v. Fenno*, 75 U.S. 533 (1869) (tax on paper money issued by state banks); *McCray v. United States*, 195 U.S. 27 (1904) (tax on colored oleomargarine); *United States v. Doremus*, 249 U.S. 86 (1919) (tax on narcotics); *Sonzinsky v. United States*, 300 U.S. 506 (1937) (tax on firearms); *United States v. Sanchez*, 340 U.S. 42 (1950) (tax on marijuana).

FN3 There are suggestions in the debates that Congress sought to hinder, if not prevent the type of gambling taxed.

Mr. Hoffman of Michigan: Then I will renew my observation that it might if properly construed be considered an additional penalty on the illegal activities.

Mr. Cooper: Certainly, and we might indulge the hope that the imposition of this type of tax would eliminate that kind of activity. If the local official does not want to enforce the law and no one catches him winking at the law, he may keep on winking at it, but when the Federal Government identifies a law violator and the local newspaper gets hold of it and the local church organizations get hold of it and the people who do want the law enforced get hold of it, they say, "Mr. Sheriff, what about it? We understand that there is a place down here licensed to sell liquor." He says, "Is that so? I will put him out of business."

It is conceded that a federal excise tax does not cease to be valid merely because it discourages or deters the activities taxed. Nor is the tax invalid because the revenue obtained its negligible. Appellee, however, argues that the sole purpose of the statute is to penalize only illegal gambling in the states through the guise of a tax measure. As with the above excise taxes which we have held to be valid, the instant tax has a regulatory effect. But regardless of its regulatory effect, the wagering tax produces revenue. As such it surpasses both the narcotics and firearms taxes which we have found valid.[FN4]

FN4 One of the indicia which appellee offers to support his contention that the wagering tax is not a proper revenue measure is that the tax amount collected under it was $4,371,869 as compared with an expected amount of $400,000,000 a year. The figure of $4,371,869, however, is relatively large when it is compared with the $3,501 collected under the tax on adulterated and process or renovated butter and filled cheese, the $914,910 collected under the tax on narcotics, including marijuana and special taxes, and the $28,911 collected under the tax on firearms transfer and occupational taxes.

It is axiomatic that the power of Congress to tax is extensive and sometimes falls with crushing effect on businesses deemed unessential or inimical to the public welfare, or where, as in dealings with narcotics, the collection of the tax also is difficult. As is well known, the constitutional restraints on taxing are few. . . . The remedy for excessive taxation is in the hands of Congress, not the courts. Speaking of the creation of the Bank of the United States, as an instrument for carrying out federal fiscal policies, this Court said in *McCulloch v. Maryland* (1819):

> Should Congress, in the execution of its powers, adopt measures which are prohibited by the constitution; or should Congress, under the pretext of executing its powers, pass laws for the accomplishment of objects not entrusted to the government; it would become the painful duty of this tribunal, should a case requiring such a decision come before it, to say that such an act was not the law of the land. But where the law is not prohibited, and is really calculated to effect any of the objects entrusted to the government, to undertake here to inquire into the degree of its necessity, would be to pass the line which circumscribes the judicial department, and to tread on legislative ground. This court disclaims all pretensions to such a power.

[Over time, some have argued that the federal] power to lay uniform taxes [must be] curtailed, because its use brings a result beyond the direct legislative power of Congress. . . . [But] the judicial [branch] cannot prescribe to the legislative departments of the government limitations upon the exercise of its acknowledged powers. The tax cases cited above . . . followed that theory. It is hard to understand why the power to tax should raise more doubts because of **indirect effects** than other federal powers. . . . Unless there are provisions, extraneous to any tax need, courts are without authority to limit the exercise of the taxing power. All the provisions of this excise are adapted to the collection of a valid tax.

[The majority also held that prosecution for failure to declare illegal gambling income to the IRS did not violate the Fifth Amendment right against self-incrimination.]

■ OBSERVATION

INDIRECT EFFECTS: This language adds to the repudiation of the portions of *US v. Butler* (1936), Ch. 9.A.3, that took the now-rejected position that Congress could not tax and spend to influence agricultural policy, even if it could generally tax and spend without restriction.

Justice Jackson, concurring.

I concur in the judgment and opinion of the Court, but with such doubt that if the minority agreed upon an opinion which did not impair legitimate use of the taxing power I probably would join it. But we deal here with important and contrasting values in our scheme of government, and it is important that neither be allowed to destroy the other. . . .

Of course, all taxation has a tendency proportioned to its burdensomeness to discourage the activity taxed. One cannot formulate a revenue-raising plan that would not have economic and social consequences. Congress may and should place the burden of taxes where it will least handicap desirable activities and bear most heavily on useless or harmful ones. If Congress may tax one citizen to the point of discouragement for making an honest living, it is hard to say that it may not do the same to another just because he makes a sinister living. If the law-abiding must tell all to the tax collector, it is difficult to excuse one because his business is law-breaking. . . .

The United States has a system of **taxation by confession.** That a people so numerous, scattered and individualistic annually assesses itself with a tax liability, often in highly burdensome amounts, is a reassuring sign of the stability and vitality of our system of self-government. What surprised me in once trying to help administer these laws was not to discover examples of recalcitrance, fraud or self-serving mistakes in reporting, but to discover that such derelictions were so few. It will be a sad day for the revenues if the good will of the people toward their taxing system is frittered away in efforts to accomplish by taxation moral reforms that cannot be accomplished by direct legislation. But the evil that can come from this statute will probably soon make itself manifest to Congress. The evil of a judicial decision impairing the legitimate taxing power by extreme constitutional interpretations might not be transient. Even though this statute approaches the fair limits of constitutionality, I join the decision of the Court.

■ TERMINOLOGY

TAXATION BY CONFESSION: Justice Jackson alludes to the fact that the US tax system relies primarily on voluntary reporting of income and payment of taxes, as opposed to more coercive collection methods. Before becoming Attorney General in 1940 and Supreme Court justice in 1941, Justice Jackson had served as general counsel to the Internal Revenue Service.

Justice Frankfurter, [with whom Justice Douglas concurs in part,] dissenting.

The Court's opinion manifests a natural difficulty in reaching its conclusion. Constitutional issues are likely to arise whenever Congress draws on the taxing power not to raise revenue but to regulate conduct. . . .

When oblique use is made of the taxing power as to matters which substantively are not within the powers delegated to Congress, the Court cannot shut its eyes to what is obviously, because designedly, an attempt to control conduct which the Constitution left to the responsibility of the States, merely because Congress wrapped the legislation in the verbal cellophane of a revenue measure. . . .

What is relevant to judgment here is that, even if the history of this legislation as it went through Congress did not give one the libretto to the song, the context of the circumstances which brought forth this enactment—sensationally exploited disclosures regarding gambling in big cities and small, the relation of this gambling to corrupt politics, the impatient public response to these disclosures, the feeling of ineptitude or paralysis on the part of local law-enforcing agencies—emphatically supports what was revealed on the floor of Congress, namely, that what was formally a means of raising revenue for the Federal Government was essentially an effort to check if not to stamp out professional gambling. . . .

Justice Black, with whom Justice Douglas concurs, dissenting.

[This dissent argued that the statute violated the Fifth Amendment right against self-incrimination.]

flash*forward*

Self-Incrimination. The statute in *Kahriger* required bookmakers to declare to the IRS any illegal income. The declaration could then be used as evidence in a criminal prosecution for illegal bookmaking. Or, as in *Kahriger* itself, the failure to declare could be an independent federal offense.

As seen above, the majority in *Kahriger* ruled that the reporting requirement did not violate the Fifth Amendment right against self-incrimination. That portion of *Kahriger* was overruled by *Marchetti v. United States*, 390 U.S. 39 (1968):

> The issue before us is not whether the United States may tax activities which a State or Congress has declared unlawful. The Court has repeatedly indicated that the unlawfulness of an activity does not prevent its taxation, and nothing that follows is intended to limit or diminish the vitality of those cases. . . . We hold only that those who properly assert the constitutional privilege [against self-incrimination] as to these provisions may not be criminally punished for failure to comply with their [reporting] requirements.

After *Marchetti*, a bookmaker could be prosecuted for willful failure to pay federal taxes on illegally earned income, but could not be separately prosecuted for failure to declare the income.

B. The Spending Clause

The same clause in the Constitution that authorizes taxation says that tax money may be used "to pay the debts and provide for the common defense and general welfare of the United States." Because paying debts and providing for defense and welfare require the spending of money, Courts often refer to Art. I, § 8, cl. 1 as "The Spending Clause." As with the Taxing Clause, there are few constitutional limits on a political decision to spend money.

The Framers understood the great power that flows from control of the purse strings, so they included within the original Constitution a handful of provisions that use spending to create healthy incentives for federal officials. To ensure that members of Congress will direct their loyalties to the federal government and not to any state or private interests, their salaries are to be paid from federal treasury. Art. I, § 6, cl. 1. The Constitution similarly restricts the ability of the President and other officers to receive "emoluments" from any source other than Congress. Art. I, § 9, cl. 8 (foreign emoluments); Art. II, § 2 (domestic emoluments). To avoid one obvious way the budget could be used to destroy the independence of other branches, the Constitution bars Congress from reducing the salaries of the President, Art. II, § 2, and federal judges, Art. III, § 1, during their terms of office. And to ensure that the army stays within civilian control, military appropriations may last no longer than two years. Art. I, § 8, cl. 12. Beyond those limitations, no Constitutional text places any spending decisions off-limits.

Congress has often used the power of the purse to control the federal executive branch, by withholding desired funds or instructing that funds not be used in certain ways. (For example, the Hinchey-Rohrabacher Amendment to the 2014 budget said that "none of the funds made available in this Act to the Department of Justice may be used . . . to prevent [certain] States from implementing their own State laws that authorize the use, distribution, possession, or cultivation of medical marijuana.") Budgetary limits designed to control the federal government are not viewed as a constitutional problem, because Congress is by and large entitled to shape the federal government's policies.

Whether Congress may use the budget to control state governments has been a more controversial question. At the tail end of the *Lochner* era, the Supreme Court held in *US v. Butler* (1936), Ch. 9.A.3, that Congress could not tax and spend to entice farmers to produce fewer crops, because regulation of domestic agriculture was for the states. After 1937, cases like *Wickard v. Filburn* (1942) established that Congress could directly limit crop production under the Commerce Clause. Yet a nagging question remained as to whether, in *Butler*'s terminology, Congress could use the spending power to "purchase compliance" with federal policies that could not be commanded directly.

That debate has largely ended in favor of federal spending. In the decades following World War II, the federal government has routinely used the Spending Clause to achieve national uniformity that it could not command directly. For example, the federal government has no enumerated power to require state schools to administer standardized tests, but it can offer money to states that will become available only if the states' schools administer standardized tests. In recent decades, the Supreme Court has occasionally questioned whether a federal ability to bribe states into taking desired action should be completely unrestrained. Strictly speaking, the concern arises not from the spending, but with the conditions imposed on the recipients. What strings may be attached when the federal government offers money to states?

1. Kickstarter: The Spending Clause

DISCLAIMER: *This Kickstarter is a checklist to help identify relevant issues. It is not a list of elements. Nothing requires judges to write their opinions (or lawyers to write their briefs) in Kickstarter order.*

The Spending Power **kickstarter**

A. *Courts will not rule on the wisdom of Congress's decisions to spend money.*

B. *Congress may impose conditions on state recipients of federal funds where:*

1. *The spending program is in pursuit of the general welfare;*
2. *The conditions are expressed unambiguously;*
3. *The conditions are related to the purpose of the federal program;*
4. *The conditions do not require the recipient to violate the Constitution; and*
5. *The overall bargain must not be coercive upon the recipient.*

KICKSTARTER USER'S GUIDE

Item A. *Deference to the Legislature.* As with taxing decisions, spending decisions are political, arrived at through negotiation and compromise rather than formal legal reasoning. If Congress chooses to spend money to send astronauts to the moon, a court will not second-guess the wisdom of the expenditure.

Item B. *Conditions on Recipients of Federal Funds.* Most federal spending does not take the form of a gift. Instead, money is granted to a recipient on the condition that the recipient do something in return. For a simple purchase of supplies, the government gives money to a seller on the condition that the seller provide the supplies. For more complex federal programs, the government gives money to recipients on the condition that they use the money to perform more complex tasks. For example, under the federal food stamp program the US Department of Agriculture gives money to states, on condition that the states administer the details of the program in a way that gets the food aid to eligible individuals.

The leading case of *South Dakota v. Dole* (1987) described five factors that should be present for a condition on federal spending to be constitutional.

Item B.1. *Common Defense and General Welfare.* Although the text of the Spending Clause says that expenditures must be for common defense and general welfare, courts have been unwilling to second-guess Congress's decision that a particular form of spending serves those purposes. In the words of *South Dakota v. Dole*, courts should "defer substantially" on this question, because it amounts to an inquiry into the wisdom of the spending. No modern case has ever declared that a spending program fails to advance the common defense or general welfare.

Item B.2. *Clarity.* Conditions attached to federal money should not be a surprise to the recipient. To avoid this problem, Congress must be clear in defining the conditions attached to government spending.

Challenges to clarity often arise when a private party sues a recipient of federal funds for allegedly violating the conditions of the grant. For example, a federal statute says that any school receiving federal funds must respect the privacy of student records. From reading the statute, would recipients have fair warning that they might be sued by a student if they inappropriately released a student's records? In a series of cases, the Court has insisted that a private right to sue a recipient of federal funds will exist only under statutes containing a clear statement to that effect. See, e.g., *Pennhurst State School & Hospital v. Halderman*, 451 U.S. 1 (1981); *Gonzaga University v. Doe*, 536 U.S. 273 (2002).

Item B.3. *Germaneness.* The condition should be germane to the purpose of the spending program. For example, Congress should not require a state, as a condition of receiving federal funds for food stamps, to require a state tax on handguns. The condition needs to have a reasonable relationship to the purpose of the spending.

Item B.4. *Constitutional Violations.* The Spending Clause should not be a method to circumvent other limitations in the Constitution. The Eighth Amendment, for example, forbids cruel and unusual punishment by the federal government. Congress should not be able to evade this limitation by offering states money to inflict cruel and unusual punishment of their own.

As a result of this factor, a court decision on the validity of federal spending may result in a ruling on the merits of another part of the Constitution. For example, the statute in *United States v. American Library Association, Inc.*, 539 U.S. 194

(2003), required public libraries receiving federal subsidies for internet access to install filtering software that blocked access to some web sites. To determine if this use of the Spending Clause was allowed, the Court needed to decide if a public library's use of filtering software would violate Free Speech Clause of the First Amendment. (A divided Court determined that it would not.)

Item B.5. *Coerciveness.* If a purported use of the Taxing Clause can be so coercive as to be a penalty, might it be possible for a spending program to amount to coercion? In *South Dakota v. Dole* (1987), the Supreme Court suggested that it might. When reading *South Dakota v. Dole*, and the more recent decision in *NFIB v. Sebelius* (2014), Ch. 17.B.2, consider what circumstances might amount to coercion.

2. Conditions on Federal Grants to State Governments: *South Dakota v. Dole*

The federal statute in *Dole* offered highway money to states on the condition that they raise their drinking ages. Although *Dole* was decided under the Spending Clause, two other constitutional principles lurk in the background.

Voting at Ages 18 and 21. The Twenty-Sixth Amendment (1971) guaranteed that persons 18 and older would not be denied the right to vote on the basis of age. The politics behind this amendment relate to the Vietnam War. At the time, males were subject to the draft at age 18, while most states set their voting age at 21—the age specified in Section 2 of the Fourteenth Amendment. Most people came to believe that anyone old enough to be drafted was old enough to vote, so the necessary supermajorities of Congress and the states passed and ratified the Twenty-Sixth Amendment. Shortly after the Amendment was ratified, many states lowered other statutory age limits to 18, including the drinking age.

Constitutional Amendments 18 and 21. The Eighteenth Amendment (1919) allowed Congress to prohibit the manufacture, sale, or transportation of intoxicating liquors. The Twenty-First Amendment (1933) repealed the Eighteenth Amendment, but included language allowing states to regulate alcohol. *Dole* is one of many cases holding that while the Twenty-First Amendment gives states control over their domestic alcohol policy, that power must be exercised in harmony with, and not as an exception to, other constitutional limits on state power. For example, a state cannot impose restrictions on alcohol advertising that would violate the Free Speech Clause, *44 Liquormart, Inc. v. Rhode Island*, 517 U.S. 484 (1996), nor can it impose restrictions on alcohol sales that would violate the dormant commerce clause doctrine, *Granholm v. Heald*, 544 U.S. 460 (2005).

ITEMS TO CONSIDER WHILE READING *SOUTH DAKOTA v. DOLE*:

A. *Does Congress's ability to spend money on an activity depend on whether Congress has the power to directly regulate that activity?*

B. *The items in the Kickstarter are derived from* Dole. *Why does the spending statute in* Dole *satisfy (or not satisfy) the* Dole *factors?*

C. *Invent hypothetical federal spending programs that would violate different* Dole *factors.*

South Dakota v. Dole,

483 U.S. 203 (1987)

Chief Justice Rehnquist delivered the opinion of the Court [joined by Justices White, Marshall, Blackmun, Powell, Stevens, and Scalia].

Petitioner South Dakota permits persons 19 years of age or older to purchase beer containing up to 3.2% alcohol. In 1984 Congress enacted 23 U.S.C. § 158, which directs the Secretary of Transportation to withhold a percentage of federal highway funds otherwise allocable from States "in which the purchase or public possession of any alcoholic beverage by a person who is less than twenty-one years of age is lawful." The State sued [US Secretary of Transportation Elizabeth Dole] in United States District Court seeking a declaratory judgment that § 158 violates the constitutional limitations on congressional exercise of the spending power and violates the Twenty-first Amendment to the United States Constitution. The District Court rejected the State's claims, and the Court of Appeals for the Eighth Circuit affirmed.

In this Court, the parties direct most of their efforts to defining the proper scope of the Twenty-first Amendment. . . . Despite the extended treatment of the question by the parties, however, we need not decide in this case whether that Amendment would prohibit an attempt by Congress to legislate directly a national minimum drinking age. Here, Congress has acted indirectly under its spending power to encourage uniformity in the States' drinking ages. As we explain below, we find this legislative effort within constitutional bounds even if Congress may not regulate drinking ages directly.

The Constitution empowers Congress to "lay and collect Taxes, Duties, Imposts, and Excises, to pay the Debts and provide for the common Defense and general Welfare of the United States." Art. I, § 8, cl. 1. Incident to this power, Congress may attach conditions on the receipt of federal funds, and has repeatedly employed the power to further broad policy objectives by conditioning receipt of federal moneys upon compliance by the recipient with federal statutory and administrative directives. The breadth of this power was made clear in *United States v. Butler* (1936), where the Court, resolving a longstanding debate over the scope of the Spending Clause, determined that "the power of Congress to authorize expenditure of public moneys for public purposes is not limited by the direct grants of legislative power found in the Constitution." [This quoted language from *Butler* remains good law, even though other aspects of its holding have been abandoned.] Thus, objectives not thought to be within Article I's enumerated legislative fields may nevertheless be attained through the use of the spending power and the conditional grant of federal funds.

South Dakota v. Dole

The spending power is of course not unlimited, but is instead subject to several general restrictions articulated in our cases. The first of these limitations is derived from the language of the Constitution itself: the exercise of the spending power must be in pursuit of "the general welfare." In considering whether a particular expenditure is intended to serve general public purposes, courts should defer substantially to the judgment of Congress. Second, we have required that if Congress desires to condition the States' receipt of federal funds, it must do so unambiguously, enabling the States to exercise their choice knowingly, cognizant of the consequences of their participation. Third, our cases have suggested (without significant elaboration) that conditions on federal grants might be illegitimate if they are unrelated to the federal interest in particular national projects or programs. Finally, we have noted that other constitutional provisions may provide an independent bar to the conditional grant of federal funds.

South Dakota does not seriously claim that § 158 is inconsistent with any of the first three restrictions mentioned above. We can readily conclude that the provision is designed to serve the general welfare, especially in light of the fact that the concept of welfare or the opposite is shaped by Congress. Congress found that the differing drinking ages in the States created particular incentives for young persons to combine their desire to drink with their ability to drive, and that this interstate problem required a national solution. The means it chose to address this dangerous situation were reasonably calculated to advance the general welfare. The conditions upon which States receive the funds, moreover, could not be more clearly stated by Congress. And the State itself, rather than challenging the germaneness of the condition to federal purposes, admits that it has never contended that the congressional action was unrelated to a national concern in the absence of the Twenty-first Amendment. Indeed, the condition imposed by Congress is directly related to one of the main purposes for which highway funds are expended—safe interstate travel. This goal of the interstate highway system had been frustrated by varying drinking ages among the States. A Presidential commission appointed to study alcohol-related accidents and fatalities on the Nation's highways concluded that the lack of uniformity in the States' drinking ages created an incentive to drink and drive because young persons commute to border States where the drinking age is lower. By enacting § 158, Congress conditioned the receipt of federal funds in a way reasonably calculated to address this particular impediment to a purpose for which the funds are expended.

The remaining question about the validity of § 158—and the basic point of disagreement between the parties—is whether the Twenty-first Amendment constitutes an independent constitutional bar to the conditional grant of federal funds. . . . [Our] cases establish that the "independent constitutional bar" limitation on the spending power is not, as petitioner suggests, a prohibition on the indirect achievement of objectives which Congress is not empowered to achieve directly. Instead, we think that the language in our earlier opinions stands for the unexceptionable proposition that the power may not be used to induce the States to engage in activities that would themselves be unconstitutional. Thus, for example, a grant of federal funds conditioned on invidiously discriminatory state action or the infliction of cruel and unusual punishment would be an illegitimate exercise of the Congress' broad spending power. But no such claim can be or is made here. Were South Dakota to succumb to the blandishments offered by Congress and raise its drinking age to 21, the State's action in so doing would not violate the constitutional rights of anyone.

Our decisions have recognized that in some circumstances the financial inducement offered by Congress might be so coercive as to pass the point at which pressure turns into compulsion. Here, however, Congress has directed only that a State desiring to establish a minimum drinking age lower than 21 lose a relatively small percentage of certain federal highway funds. Petitioner contends that the coercive nature of this program is evident from the degree of success it has achieved. We cannot conclude, however, that a conditional grant of federal money of this sort is unconstitutional simply by reason of its success in achieving the congressional objective.

When we consider, for a moment, that all South Dakota would lose if she adheres to her chosen course as to a suitable minimum drinking age is 5% of the funds otherwise obtainable under specified highway grant programs, the argument as to coercion is shown to be more rhetoric than fact. [Every subsidy] when conditioned upon conduct is in some measure a temptation. But to hold that motive or temptation is equivalent to coercion is to plunge the law in endless difficulties. The outcome of such a doctrine is the acceptance of a philosophical determinism by which choice becomes impossible.

Here Congress has offered relatively mild encouragement to the States to enact higher minimum drinking ages than they would otherwise choose. But the enactment of such laws remains the prerogative of the States not merely in theory but in fact. Even if Congress might lack the power to impose a national minimum drinking age directly, we conclude that encouragement to state action found in § 158 is a valid use of the spending power.

Justice Brennan, dissenting.

. . . Regulation of the minimum age of purchasers of liquor falls squarely within the ambit of those powers reserved to the States by the Twenty-first Amendment. Since States possess this constitutional power, Congress cannot condition a federal grant in a manner that abridges this right. . . .

Justice O'Connor, dissenting.

The Court today upholds the National Minimum Drinking Age Amendment as a valid exercise of the spending power conferred by Article I, § 8. But § 158 is not a condition on spending reasonably related to the expenditure of federal funds and cannot be justified on that ground. Rather, it is an attempt to regulate the sale of liquor, an attempt that lies outside Congress' power to regulate commerce because it falls within the ambit of § 2 of the Twenty-first Amendment.

My disagreement with the Court is relatively narrow on the spending power issue: it is a disagreement about the application of a principle rather than a disagreement on the principle itself. I agree with the Court that Congress may attach conditions on the receipt of federal funds to further the federal interest in particular national projects or programs. I also subscribe to the established proposition that the reach of the spending power is not limited by the direct grants of legislative power found in the Constitution. Finally, I agree that there are four separate types of limitations on the spending power: the expenditure must be for the general welfare, the conditions imposed must be unambiguous, they must be reasonably related to the purpose of the expenditure, and the legislation may not violate any independent constitutional prohibition. Insofar as two of those limitations are concerned, the Court is clearly correct that § 158 is wholly unobjectionable. Establishment of a national minimum drinking age certainly fits within the broad concept of the general welfare and the statute is entirely unambiguous. I am also willing to assume, *arguendo*, that the Twenty-first Amendment does not constitute an "independent constitutional bar" to a spending condition.

But the Court's application of the requirement that the condition imposed be reasonably related to the purpose for which the funds are expended is cursory and unconvincing. We have repeatedly said that Congress may condition grants under the spending power only in ways reasonably related to the purpose of the federal program. In my view, establishment of a minimum drinking age of 21 is not sufficiently related to interstate highway construction to justify so conditioning funds appropriated for that purpose. . . .

When Congress appropriates money to build a highway, it is entitled to insist that the highway be a safe one. But it is not entitled to insist as a condition of the use of highway funds that the State impose or change regulations in other areas of the State's social and economic life because of an attenuated or tangential relationship to highway use or safety. Indeed, if the rule were otherwise, the Congress could effectively regulate almost any area of a State's social, political, or economic life on the theory that use of the interstate transportation system is somehow enhanced. If, for example, the United States were to condition highway moneys upon moving the state capital, I suppose it might argue that interstate transportation is facilitated by locating local governments in places easily accessible to interstate highways—or, conversely, that highways might become overburdened if they had to carry traffic to and from the state capital. In my mind, such a relationship is hardly more attenuated than the one which the Court finds supports § 158. . . .

As discussed above, a condition that a State will raise its drinking age to 21 cannot fairly be said to be reasonably related to the expenditure of funds for highway construction. The only possible connection, highway safety, has nothing to do with how the funds Congress has appropriated are expended. Rather than a condition determining how federal highway money shall be expended, it is a regulation determining who shall be able to drink liquor. As such it is not justified by the spending power. . . .

The immense size and power of the Government of the United States ought not obscure its fundamental character. It remains a Government of enumerated powers. *McCulloch v. Maryland* (1819). Because 23 U.S.C. § 158 cannot be justified as an exercise of any power delegated to the Congress, it is not authorized by the Constitution. The Court errs in holding it to be the law of the land, and I respectfully dissent.

C. The Commerce Clause

Beginning in the 1990s, several Commerce Clause opinions of the Supreme Court reintroduced concerns about federalism. To situate these cases, it will be useful to review Commerce Clause doctrine as it stood at the end of the New Deal and Warren Courts. See Chs. 9 & 12.

1. Kickstarter: The Interstate Commerce Clause

DISCLAIMER: *This Kickstarter is a checklist to help identify relevant issues. It is not a list of elements. Nothing requires judges to write their opinions (or lawyers to write their briefs) in Kickstarter order.*

The Interstate Commerce Clause **kickstarter**

Congress has power to regulate "commerce among the several states" in the following general scenarios:

A. Cross-border transactions.

B. Infrastructure for cross-border transactions.

C. In-state activity with substantial effect on interstate commerce.

KICKSTARTER USER'S GUIDE

The power to regulate commerce among the states is used to justify more federal legislation than any other enumerated power. This is so because so much lawmaking deals with matters that in some way connect with the national economy.

When exercising its commerce power, Congress is allowed to pass laws that closely resemble laws that a state might enact under its police powers; so long as Congress is in fact regulating commerce in one of the ways identified below, similarity between federal and state laws is not an obstacle. Federal laws regulating commerce may have significant effects on wholly in-state commerce. See *Gibbons v. Ogden* (1824) (upholding law requiring New York to accept federally licensed ships into its harbors notwithstanding state law). It does not matter if the in-state effects of a federal law are large; there is no longer any requirement that federal laws have only "indirect" or "incidental" impact on local affairs. It also does not matter if Congress chose to regulate interstate commerce with the motive of affecting in-state conditions. See *US v. Darby* (1941) (upholding law forbidding interstate shipment of lumber milled by underpaid workers); *Heart of Atlanta Motel v. US* (1964) (upholding law forbidding local discrimination in places of public accommodation).

Who decides whether a federal law has a suitable connection to interstate commerce? Ultimately, the Supreme Court makes the final call, but the Court takes a deferential approach to the question. As explained in *Hodel v. Virginia Surface Mining & Reclamation Ass'n, Inc.*, 452 U.S. 264, 276 (1981): "The task of a court that is asked to determine whether a particular exercise of congressional power is valid under the Commerce Clause is relatively narrow. The court must defer to a congressional finding that a regulated activity affects interstate commerce, if there is any rational basis for such a finding."

Three general scenarios have been recognized as involving "commerce among the states." The first two have never been controversial, while the third one has been.

Item A. *Cross-Border Transactions.* Congress may regulate goods and services that cross state borders. A "regulation" may also take the form of a complete ban on the interstate transaction. This notion was recognized even during the *Lochner* era, as seen in cases upholding laws against the interstate shipment of tainted food, *Hipolite Egg Co. v. United States*, 220 U.S. 45 (1911), lottery tickets, *Champion v. Ames*, 188 U.S. 321 (1903), and prostitutes, *Hoke v. United States*, 227 U.S. 308 (1913).

Item B. *Infrastructure for Cross-Border Transactions.* The federal government cannot effectively regulate border crossings without also regulating the infrastructure allowing the border crossing to happen—and this infrastructure necessarily lies within the states sharing that border. To use *Gibbons* as an example, for the federal government to ensure passenger steamship traffic between New Jersey and New York requires the federal government to control at least some of what happens in waters and ports within each state. This is why *Gibbons* said, "The power of Congress [to regulate commerce among the several states] must be exercised within the territorial jurisdiction of the several states." This is sometimes accomplished by regulating the infrastructure necessary for cross-border transactions, such as bridges, railroad tracks, and canals—and the trucks, trains, and boats that use them. See *The Daniel Ball*, 77 U.S. 557 (1871) (upholding federal licensing statute that reached boats travelling solely within states if they carry goods coming from or going to other states); *Pensacola Telegraph Co. v. Western Union Telegraph Co.*, 96 U.S. 1 (1877) (upholding federal statute regulating in-state portions of telegraph wires carrying interstate messages). In addition, the Supreme Court upheld—even during the *Lochner* era—federal laws designed to ensure the economic viability of interstate commerce that relies in part on in-state infrastructure. *Swift & Co. v. United States*, 196 U.S. 375 (1905) (upholding federal antitrust action to halt price-fixing conspiracy at stockyards where cattle have crossed or will cross state lines as part of a "current of commerce"); *Houston, East & West Railway v. United States (The Shreveport Rate Case)*, 207 U.S. 463 (1908) (upholding federal law regulating in-state rail rates that discriminate against interstate railways); *Stafford v. Wallace*, 258 U.S. 495 (1922) (upholding federal law governing rates charged in stockyards that act as way stations for shipment of cattle across state lines). During the New Deal, it was held that the Commerce Clause allowed Congress to regulate labor relations in transportation industries to avoid strikes that could endanger transportation. *Virginian Railway Co. v. System Federation No. 40*, 300 U.S. 515 (1937) (railroads); *Washington, Virginia & Maryland Coach Co. v. NLRB*, 301 U.S. 142 (1937) (busses).

Item C. *In-State Activity with Substantial Effect on Interstate Commerce.* This category has been the source of the greatest historical disagreement when interpreting the Commerce Clause. In *Gibbons*, Justice Marshall wrote that the federal commerce power did not reach commerce that "is completely internal, which is carried on between man and man in a State, or between different parts of the same State, and which does not extend to or affect other States." The opinion also stated that the federal government in general may not control "those [actions] which are completely within a particular state, which do not affect other states, and with which it is not necessary to interfere, for the purpose of executing some of the general powers of the government." These passages have been taken to mean that internal transactions that *do* affect other states, or that *do* interfere with the federal government's ability to pursue its economic goals, may be regulated under the Commerce Clause. During the *Lochner* Era, the Supreme Court was reluctant to implement this idea, but the New Deal cases affirmed it. Even in-state activities with a small effect on interstate commerce may be federally regulated if, in the aggregate, they would affect national supply or demand for goods that regularly travel in interstate commerce. See *Wickard v. Filburn* (1942) (upholding federal law limiting the amount of wheat that could be grown on a small farm); *Katzenbach v. McClung* (1964) (upholding federal law against discrimination in local restaurant that sold food that had moved in interstate commerce).

The power of Congress to regulate in-state activity with substantial effects on interstate commerce is frequently described as arising directly from the Commerce Clause, but it may also be viewed as a use of the Necessary and Proper Clause, which gives Congress power to enact laws to help execute the goals of the Commerce Clause. See Ch. 15.D. The end result of both approaches is the same: an enumerated power exists for Congress to regulate these transactions.

Today, the biggest arguments in this area do not involve the legitimacy of Item C, but its application. Majority and dissenting justices have differed over whether a given type of in-state activity actually has substantial effects on interstate commerce. When reading the following cases, and the more recent decision in *NFIB v. Sebelius* (2014), Ch. 17.B.2, consider how they refine—or even change—the New Deal understanding of substantial effects.

2. Crime and Commerce: The New Federalism and the Commerce Clause

In a trio of cases decided between 1996 and 2005, the Rehnquist Court examined federal statutes regulating in-state activity historically regulated by state criminal laws. For the first time since 1936, the Court held that federal laws purporting to rely on the Commerce Clause were beyond Congress's enumerated power.

a) Gun Possession: *United States v. Lopez*

The Gun-Free School Zones Act of 1990 made it a federal offense "for any individual knowingly to possess a firearm at a place that the individual knows, or has reasonable cause to believe, is a school zone." The 5–4 decision in *United States v. Lopez*, 514 U.S. 549 (1995), held that the statute did not "regulate a commercial activity" like manufacturing, buying, or selling. Mere possession at an in-state location did not affect interstate commerce. The reasoning in *Lopez* is summarized within the next opinion, *United States v. Morrison* (2000).

The dissenters in *Lopez* argued that Congress was entitled to consider the aggregate nationwide impact of gun violence near schools. It would be bad for interstate commerce, they argued, if schools became unsafe places for students to learn or teachers to work. Beyond their disagreement with the majority's result, the dissenters were troubled by the reasoning and the tone of the majority opinion. Chief Justice Rehnquist's majority opinion cited pre-1937 cases like *E.C. Knight*,

Schechter Poultry, and *Carter Coal* without indicating that they had been overruled. It emphasized dicta from post-1937 commerce cases like *Jones & Laughlin*, *Darby*, and *Wickard* to suggest that those cases stood for limits on Congress's commerce authority, even though they had not enforced any such limits. And it stated that the Court's role was to maintain "a distinction between what is truly national and what is truly local." Justice Souter's dissent warned of a return to the *Lochner* era: "It seems fair to ask whether the step taken by the Court today does anything but portend a return to the untenable jurisprudence from which the Court extricated itself almost 60 years ago. The answer is not reassuring."

b) Violence Against Women: *United States v. Morrison*

Lopez was followed by *United States v. Morrison*, which considered the validity of one section of the Violence Against Women Act of 1994, which allowed victims of sexual violence to sue their abusers in federal court. Congress claimed that two separate constitutional provisions gave it the power to enact this law: the Commerce Clause and the Fourteenth Amendment Enforcement Clause.

ITEMS TO CONSIDER WHILE READING *MORRISON:*

Commerce Clause

A. *Must an activity be "commercial" for it to affect interstate commerce?*

B. *The dissents in* Lopez *and* Morrison *argued that the majority embraced* Lochner*-era Commerce Clause cases like* E.C. Knight *and* Dagenhart, *and rejected newer decisions like* Darby *and* Heart of Atlanta Motel. *Are the dissenters correct, or are those cases distinguishable?*

C. *In* Lopez, *the majority found it significant that Congress had made no findings to prove that guns near schools affected interstate commerce. In* Morrison, *Congress compiled evidence that violence against women affected interstate commerce. How did the Court handle this evidence? Should the presence or absence of Congressional fact-finding make a difference?*

D. *The majority in* Morrison *reasserts the notion from* Lopez *that courts must maintain "a distinction between what is truly national and what is truly local." Is this distinction important? If it is, is the judiciary the right branch of government to enforce it?*

Fourteenth Amendment Enforcement Clause (§ 5)

E. *Construct arguments for why the challenged provision of the Violence Against Women Act was (or was not) a response to state action.*

United States v. Morrison,
529 U.S. 598 (2000)

Chief Justice Rehnquist delivered the opinion of the Court [joined by Justices O'Connor, Scalia, Kennedy, and Thomas].

In these cases we consider the constitutionality of 42 U.S.C. § 13981, which provides a federal civil remedy for the victims of gender-motivated violence. The United States Court of Appeals for the Fourth Circuit, sitting en banc, struck down § 13981 because it concluded that Congress lacked constitutional authority to enact the section's civil remedy. Believing that these cases are controlled by our decisions in *United States v. Lopez* (1995) and *The Civil Rights Cases* (1883), we affirm.

I

Petitioner Christy Brzonkala enrolled at Virginia Polytechnic Institute (Virginia Tech) in the fall of 1994. In September of that year, Brzonkala met respondents Antonio Morrison and James Crawford, who were both students at Virginia Tech and members of its varsity football team. Brzonkala alleges that, within 30 minutes of meeting Morrison and Crawford, they assaulted and repeatedly raped her. After the attack, Morrison allegedly told Brzonkala, "You better not have any diseases." In the months following the rape, Morrison also allegedly announced in the dormitory's dining room that he "liked to get girls drunk and. . . ." The omitted portions, quoted verbatim in the briefs on file with this Court, consist of boasting, debased remarks about what Morrison would do to women, vulgar remarks that cannot fail to shock and offend.

Brzonkala alleges that this attack caused her to become severely emotionally disturbed and depressed. She sought assistance from a university psychiatrist, who prescribed antidepressant medication. Shortly after the rape Brzonkala stopped attending classes and withdrew from the university. . . .

In December 1995, Brzonkala sued Morrison, Crawford, and Virginia Tech in the United States District Court for the Western District of Virginia. . . . Morrison and Crawford moved to dismiss this complaint on the grounds that it failed to state a claim and that § 13981's civil remedy is unconstitutional. The **United States intervened** to defend § 13981's constitutionality. The District Court . . . dismissed the complaint because it concluded that Congress lacked authority to enact the section under either the Commerce Clause or § 5 of the Fourteenth Amendment. [The Fourth Circuit affirmed by a divided vote.] Because the Court of Appeals invalidated a federal statute on constitutional grounds, we granted certiorari.

■ OBSERVATION

UNITED STATES INTERVENED: The US Department of Justice has authority to intervene as a party in cases where the constitutionality of an act of Congress is called into question. 28 U.S.C. § 2403. The intervention explains why this case is captioned *United States v. Morrison* rather than *Brzonkala v. Morrison.*

Section 13981 was part of the Violence Against Women Act of 1994. It states that "all persons within the United States shall have the right to be free from crimes of violence motivated by gender." 42 U.S.C. § 13981(b). To enforce that right, subsection (c) declares:

> A person (including a person who acts under color of any statute, ordinance, regulation, custom, or usage of any State) who commits a crime of violence motivated by gender and thus deprives another of the right declared in subsection (b) of this section shall be liable to the party injured, in an action for the recovery of compensatory and punitive damages, injunctive and declaratory relief, and such other relief as a court may deem appropriate.

. . . Every law enacted by Congress must be based on one or more of its powers enumerated in the Constitution. . . . Congress explicitly identified the sources of federal authority on which it relied in enacting § 13981. It said that a "Federal civil rights cause of action" is established "pursuant to the affirmative power of Congress under section 5 of the Fourteenth Amendment to the Constitution, as well as under [the Commerce Clause]." 42 U.S.C. § 13981(a). We address Congress' authority to enact this remedy under each of these constitutional provisions in turn.

II

Due respect for the decisions of a coordinate branch of Government demands that we invalidate a congressional enactment only upon a plain showing that Congress has exceeded its constitutional bounds. With this presumption of constitutionality in mind, we turn to the question whether § 13981 falls within Congress' power under [the Commerce Clause].

As we discussed at length in *Lopez*, our interpretation of the Commerce Clause has changed as our Nation has developed. We need not repeat that detailed review of the Commerce Clause's history here; it suffices to say that, in the years since *NLRB v. Jones & Laughlin Steel Corp.* (1937), Congress has had considerably greater latitude in regulating conduct and transactions under the Commerce Clause than our previous case law permitted.

Lopez emphasized, however, that even under our modern, expansive interpretation of the Commerce Clause, Congress' regulatory authority is not without effective bounds.

> Even our modern-era precedents which have expanded congressional power under the Commerce Clause confirm that this power is subject to outer limits. In *Jones & Laughlin Steel*, the Court warned that the scope of the interstate commerce power must be considered in the light of our dual system of government and may not be extended so as to embrace effects upon interstate commerce so indirect and remote that to embrace them, in view of our complex

society, would effectually obliterate the distinction between what is national and what is local and create a completely centralized government.

As we observed in *Lopez*, modern Commerce Clause jurisprudence has identified three broad categories of activity that Congress may regulate under its commerce power. First, Congress may regulate the use of the channels of interstate commerce [to perform cross-border transactions]. Second, Congress is empowered to regulate and protect the instrumentalities [or infrastructure] of interstate commerce . . . even though the threat may come only from intrastate activities. Finally, Congress' commerce authority includes the power to regulate those activities having a substantial relation to interstate commerce, i.e., those activities that substantially affect interstate commerce.

Petitioners . . . seek to sustain § 13981 as a regulation of activity that substantially affects interstate commerce. . . . In *Lopez*, we held that the Gun-Free School Zones Act of 1990, 18 U.S.C. § 922(q)(1)(A), which made it a federal crime to knowingly possess a firearm in a school zone, exceeded Congress' authority under [the third category within] the Commerce Clause. . . . Several significant considerations contributed to our decision.

First, we observed that § 922(q) was a criminal statute that by its terms has nothing to do with "commerce" or any sort of economic enterprise, however broadly one might define those terms. Reviewing our case law, we noted that we have upheld a wide variety of congressional Acts regulating intrastate economic activity where we have concluded that the activity substantially affected interstate commerce. Although we cited only a few examples, we stated that the pattern of analysis is clear. Where economic activity substantially affects interstate commerce, legislation regulating that activity will be sustained.

Both petitioners and Justice Souter's dissent downplay the role that the economic nature of the regulated activity plays in our Commerce Clause analysis. But a fair reading of *Lopez* shows that the noneconomic, criminal nature of the conduct at issue was central to our decision in that case. *Lopez*'s review of Commerce Clause case law demonstrates that in those cases where we have sustained federal regulation of intrastate activity based upon the activity's substantial effects on interstate commerce, the activity in question has been some sort of economic endeavor.

The second consideration that we found important in analyzing § 922(q) was that the statute contained "no express jurisdictional element which might limit its reach to a discrete set of firearm possessions that additionally have an explicit connection with or effect on interstate commerce." Such a jurisdictional element [or nexus language] may establish that the enactment is in pursuance of Congress' regulation of interstate commerce.

Third, we noted that neither § 922(q) nor its legislative history contain[s] express congressional findings regarding the effects upon interstate commerce of gun possession in a school zone. While Congress normally is not required to make formal findings as to the substantial burdens that an activity has on interstate commerce, the existence of such findings may enable us to evaluate the legislative judgment that the activity in question substantially affects interstate commerce, even though no such substantial effect is visible to the naked eye.

Finally, our decision in *Lopez* rested in part on the fact that the link between gun possession and a substantial effect on interstate commerce was attenuated. The United States argued that the possession of guns may lead to violent crime, and that violent crime can be expected to affect the functioning of the national economy[.] The Government also argued that the presence of guns at schools poses a threat to the educational process, which in turn threatens to produce a less efficient and productive work force, which will negatively affect national productivity and thus interstate commerce. We rejected these "costs of crime" and "national productivity" arguments because they would permit Congress to "regulate not only all violent crime, but all activities that might lead to violent crime, regardless of how tenuously they relate to interstate commerce." We noted that, under this but-for reasoning:

> Congress could regulate any activity that it found was related to the economic productivity of individual citizens: family law (including marriage, divorce, and child custody), for example. Under these theories, it is difficult to perceive any limitation on federal power, even in areas such as criminal law enforcement or education where States historically have been sovereign. Thus, if we were to accept the Government's arguments, we are hard pressed to posit any activity by an individual that Congress is without power to regulate.

With these principles underlying our Commerce Clause jurisprudence as reference points, the proper resolution of the present cases is clear. Gender-motivated crimes of violence are not, in any sense of the phrase, economic activity. While we need not adopt a categorical rule against aggregating the effects of any noneconomic activity in order to decide these cases, thus far in our Nation's history our cases have upheld Commerce Clause regulation of intrastate activity only where that activity is economic in nature.

Like the Gun-Free School Zones Act at issue in *Lopez*, § 13981 contains no jurisdictional element establishing that the federal cause of action is in pursuance of Congress' power to regulate interstate commerce. Although *Lopez* makes clear that such a jurisdictional element would lend support to the argument that § 13981 is sufficiently tied to interstate commerce, Congress elected to cast § 13981's remedy over a wider, and more purely intrastate, body of violent crime.

In contrast with the lack of congressional findings that we faced in *Lopez*, § 13981 is supported by numerous findings regarding the serious impact that gender-motivated violence has on victims and their families. But the existence of congressional findings is not sufficient, by itself, to sustain the constitutionality of

Commerce Clause legislation. As we stated in *Lopez*, "Simply because Congress may conclude that a particular activity substantially affects interstate commerce does not necessarily make it so." Rather, whether particular operations affect interstate commerce sufficiently to come under the constitutional power of Congress to regulate them is ultimately a judicial rather than a legislative question, and can be settled finally only by this Court.

In these cases, Congress' findings are substantially weakened by the fact that they rely so heavily on a method of reasoning that we have already rejected as unworkable if we are to maintain the Constitution's enumeration of powers. Congress found that gender-motivated violence affects interstate commerce "by deterring potential victims from traveling interstate, from engaging in employment in interstate business, and from transacting with businesses, and in places involved in interstate commerce; by diminishing national productivity, increasing medical and other costs, and decreasing the supply of and the demand for interstate products." Given these findings and petitioners' arguments, the concern that we expressed in *Lopez* that Congress might use the Commerce Clause to completely obliterate the Constitution's distinction between national and local authority seems well founded. The reasoning that petitioners advance seeks to follow the but-for causal chain from the initial occurrence of violent crime (the suppression of which has always been the prime object of the States' police power) to every attenuated effect upon interstate commerce. If accepted, petitioners' reasoning would allow Congress to regulate any crime as long as the nationwide, aggregated impact of that crime has substantial effects on employment, production, transit, or consumption. Indeed, if Congress may regulate gender-motivated violence, it would be able to regulate murder or any other type of violence since gender-motivated violence, as a subset of all violent crime, is certain to have lesser economic impacts than the larger class of which it is a part. . . .

We accordingly reject the argument that Congress may regulate noneconomic, violent criminal conduct based solely on that conduct's aggregate effect on interstate commerce. The Constitution requires a distinction between what is truly national and what is truly local. In recognizing this fact we preserve one of the few principles that has been consistent since the Clause was adopted. The regulation and punishment of intrastate violence that is not directed at the instrumentalities, channels, or goods involved in interstate commerce has always been the province of the States. Indeed, we can think of no better example of the police power, which the Founders denied the National Government and reposed in the States, than the suppression of violent crime and vindication of its victims.

III

Because we conclude that the Commerce Clause does not provide Congress with authority to enact § 13981, we address petitioners' alternative argument that the section's civil remedy should be upheld as an exercise of Congress' remedial power under § 5 of the Fourteenth Amendment. As noted above, Congress expressly invoked the Fourteenth Amendment as a source of authority to enact § 13981.

The principles governing an analysis of congressional legislation under § 5 are well settled. Section 5 states that Congress may "enforce" by "appropriate legislation" the constitutional guarantee that no State shall deprive any person of "life, liberty, or property, without due process of law," nor deny any person "equal protection of the laws." Section 5 is a positive grant of legislative power that includes authority to prohibit conduct which is not itself unconstitutional and to intrude into legislative spheres of autonomy previously reserved to the States. However, as broad as the congressional enforcement power is, it is not unlimited. In fact, as we discuss in detail below, several limitations inherent in § 5's text and constitutional context have been recognized since the Fourteenth Amendment was adopted.

Petitioners' § 5 argument is founded on an assertion that there is pervasive bias in various state justice systems against victims of gender-motivated violence. This assertion is supported by a voluminous congressional record. Specifically, Congress received evidence that many participants in state justice systems are perpetuating an array of erroneous stereotypes and assumptions. Congress concluded that these discriminatory stereotypes often result in insufficient investigation and prosecution of gender-motivated crime, inappropriate focus on the behavior and credibility of the victims of that crime, and unacceptably lenient punishments for those who are actually convicted of gender-motivated violence. Petitioners contend that this bias denies victims of gender-motivated violence the equal protection of the laws and that Congress therefore acted appropriately in enacting a private civil remedy against the perpetrators of gender-motivated violence to both remedy the States' bias and deter future instances of discrimination in the state courts. . . .

The language and purpose of the Fourteenth Amendment place certain limitations on the manner in which Congress may attack discriminatory conduct. These limitations are necessary to prevent the Fourteenth Amendment from obliterating the Framers' carefully crafted balance of power between the States and the National Government. Foremost among these limitations is the time-honored principle that the Fourteenth Amendment, by its very terms, prohibits only state action. The principle has become firmly embedded in our constitutional law that the action inhibited by the first section of the Fourteenth Amendment is only such action as may fairly be said to be that of the States. That Amendment erects no shield against merely private conduct, however discriminatory or wrongful.

Shortly after the Fourteenth Amendment was adopted, we decided . . . *The Civil Rights Cases*, 109 U.S. 3 (1883). . . . In those consolidated cases, we held that the public accommodation provisions of the Civil Rights Act of 1875, which applied to purely private conduct, were beyond the scope of the § 5 enforcement power.

The force of the doctrine of *stare decisis* behind these decisions stems not only from the length of time they have been on the books, but also from the insight attributable to the Members of the Court at that time. Every Member had been appointed by President Lincoln, Grant, Hayes, Garfield, or Arthur—and each of their judicial appointees obviously had intimate knowledge and familiarity with the events surrounding the adoption of the Fourteenth Amendment. . . .

Petitioners alternatively argue that, unlike the situation in *The Civil Rights Cases*, here there has been gender-based disparate treatment by state authorities, whereas in those cases there was no indication of such state action. There is abundant evidence, however, to show that the Congresses that enacted the Civil Rights Acts of 1871 and 1875 had a purpose similar to that of Congress in enacting § 13981: There were state laws on the books bespeaking equality of treatment, but in the administration of these laws there was discrimination against newly freed slaves. . . .

But even if that distinction were valid, we do not believe it would save § 13981's civil remedy. For the remedy is simply not "corrective in its character, adapted to counteract and redress the operation of such prohibited state laws or proceedings of state officers," *Civil Rights Cases*, or, as we have phrased it in more recent cases, prophylactic legislation under § 5 must have a "congruence and proportionality between the injury to be prevented or remedied and the means adopted to that end." *City of Boerne v. Flores* (1997) [Ch. 15.E.2]. Section 13981 is not aimed at proscribing discrimination by officials which the Fourteenth Amendment might not itself proscribe; it is directed not at any State or state actor, but at individuals who have committed criminal acts motivated by gender bias.

In the present cases, for example, § 13981 visits no consequence whatever on any Virginia public official involved in investigating or prosecuting Brzonkala's assault. The section is, therefore, unlike any of the § 5 remedies that we have previously upheld. . . . For these reasons, we conclude that Congress' power under § 5 does not extend to the enactment of § 13981.

IV

Petitioner Brzonkala's complaint alleges that she was the victim of a brutal assault. But Congress' effort in § 13981 to provide a federal civil remedy can be sustained neither under the Commerce Clause nor under § 5 of the Fourteenth Amendment. If the allegations here are true, no civilized system of justice could fail to provide her a remedy for the conduct of respondent Morrison. But under our federal system that remedy must be provided by the Commonwealth of Virginia, and not by the United States.

Justice Thomas, concurring.

The majority opinion correctly applies our decision in *United States v. Lopez* (1995), and I join it in full. I write separately only to express my view that the very notion of a "substantial effects" test under the Commerce Clause is inconsistent with the original understanding of Congress' powers and with this Court's early Commerce Clause cases. By continuing to apply this rootless and malleable standard, however circumscribed, the Court has encouraged the Federal Government to persist in its view that the Commerce Clause has virtually no limits. Until this Court replaces its existing Commerce Clause jurisprudence with a standard more consistent with the original understanding, we will continue to see Congress appropriating state police powers under the guise of regulating commerce.

Justice Souter, with whom Justices Stevens, Ginsburg, and Breyer join, dissenting.

The Court says both that it leaves Commerce Clause precedent undisturbed and that the Civil Rights Remedy of the Violence Against Women Act of 1994 exceeds Congress's power under that Clause. I find the claims irreconcilable and respectfully dissent.

I

Our cases, which remain at least nominally undisturbed, stand for the following propositions. Congress has the power to legislate with regard to activity that, in the aggregate, has a substantial effect on interstate commerce. The fact of such a substantial effect is not an issue for the courts in the first instance, but for the Congress, whose institutional capacity for gathering evidence and taking testimony far exceeds ours. By passing legislation, Congress indicates its conclusion, whether explicitly or not, that facts support its exercise of the commerce power. The business of the courts is to review the congressional assessment, not for soundness but simply for the rationality of concluding that a jurisdictional basis exists in fact. Any explicit findings that Congress chooses to make, though not dispositive of the question of rationality, may advance judicial review by identifying factual authority on which Congress relied. Applying those propositions in these cases can lead to only one conclusion.

One obvious difference from *United States v. Lopez* (1995) is the mountain of data assembled by Congress, here showing the effects of violence against women on interstate commerce. Passage of the Act in 1994 was preceded by four years of hearings. . . . With respect to domestic violence, Congress received evidence for the following findings:

- "Three out of four American women will be victims of violent crimes sometime during their life."

- "Violence is the leading cause of injuries to women ages 15 to 44."
- "As many as 50 percent of homeless women and children are fleeing domestic violence."
- "Since 1974, the assault rate against women has outstripped the rate for men by at least twice for some age groups and far more for others."
- "Battering is the single largest cause of injury to women in the United States."
- "An estimated 4 million American women are battered each year by their husbands or partners."
- "Over 1 million women in the United States seek medical assistance each year for injuries sustained from their husbands or other partners."
- "Between 2,000 and 4,000 women die every year from domestic abuse."
- "Arrest rates may be as low as 1 for every 100 domestic assaults."
- "Partial estimates show that violent crime against women costs this country at least 3 billion—not million, but billion—dollars a year."
- "Estimates suggest that we spend $5 to $10 billion a year on health care, criminal justice, and other social costs of domestic violence."

The evidence as to rape was similarly extensive, supporting these conclusions:

- "The incidence of rape rose four times as fast as the total national crime rate over the past 10 years."
- "According to one study, close to half a million girls now in high school will be raped before they graduate."
- "One hundred twenty–five thousand college women can expect to be raped during this—or any—year."
- "Three-quarters of women never go to the movies alone after dark because of the fear of rape and nearly 50 percent do not use public transit alone after dark for the same reason."
- "Forty-one percent of judges surveyed believed that juries give sexual assault victims less credibility than other crime victims."
- "Less than 1 percent of all rape victims have collected damages."
- "An individual who commits rape has only about 4 chances in 100 of being arrested, prosecuted, and found guilty of any offense."
- "Almost one-quarter of convicted rapists never go to prison and another quarter received sentences in local jails where the average sentence is 11 months."

- "Almost 50 percent of rape victims lose their jobs or are forced to quit because of the crime's severity."

Based on the data thus partially summarized, Congress found that "crimes of violence motivated by gender have a substantial adverse effect on interstate commerce, by deterring potential victims from traveling interstate, from engaging in employment in interstate business, and from transacting with business, and in places involved, in interstate commerce, by diminishing national productivity, increasing medical and other costs, and decreasing the supply of and the demand for interstate products."

Congress thereby explicitly stated the predicate for the exercise of its Commerce Clause power. Is its conclusion irrational in view of the data amassed? True, the methodology of particular studies may be challenged, and some of the figures arrived at may be disputed. But the sufficiency of the evidence before Congress to provide a rational basis for the finding cannot seriously be questioned.

Indeed, the legislative record here is far more voluminous than the record compiled by Congress and found sufficient in two prior cases upholding Title II of the Civil Rights Act of 1964 against Commerce Clause challenges. *Heart of Atlanta Motel, Inc. v. United States* (1964) and *Katzenbach v. McClung* (1964). . . .

If the analogy to the Civil Rights Act of 1964 is not plain enough, one can always look back a bit further. In *Wickard v. Filburn* (1942), we upheld the application of the Agricultural Adjustment Act to the planting and consumption of homegrown wheat. The effect on interstate commerce in that case followed from the possibility that wheat grown at home for personal consumption could either be drawn into the market by rising prices, or relieve its grower of any need to purchase wheat in the market. The Commerce Clause predicate was simply the effect of the production of wheat for home consumption on supply and demand in interstate commerce. Supply and demand for goods in interstate commerce will also be affected by the deaths of 2,000 to 4,000 women annually at the hands of domestic abusers, and by the reduction in the work force by the 100,000 or more rape victims who lose their jobs each year or are forced to quit. Violence against women may be found to affect interstate commerce and affect it substantially.

II

The Act would have passed muster at any time between *Wickard* in 1942 and *Lopez* in 1995, a period in which the law enjoyed a stable understanding that congressional power under the Commerce Clause, complemented by the authority of the Necessary and Proper Clause, extended to all activity that, when aggregated, has a substantial effect on interstate commerce. . . . The fact that the Act does not pass muster before the Court today is therefore proof, to a degree that *Lopez* was not, that the Court's nominal adherence to the substantial effects test is merely that. Although a new jurisprudence has not emerged with any distinctness, it is clear that some congressional conclusions about obviously substantial, cumulative effects on commerce are being assigned lesser values than the once-stable doctrine would assign them. These devaluations are accomplished not by any express repudiation of the substantial effects test or its application through the aggregation of individual conduct, but by supplanting rational basis scrutiny with a new criterion of review. . . .

A–B [Omitted.]

C

. . . Today's majority . . . finds no significance whatever in the state support for the Act based upon the States' acknowledged failure to deal adequately with gender-based violence in state courts, and the belief of their own law enforcement agencies that national action is essential.

The National Association of Attorneys General supported the Act unanimously, and Attorneys General from 38 States urged Congress to enact the Civil Rights Remedy, representing that "the current system for dealing with violence against women is inadequate." It was against this record of failure at the state level that the Act was passed to provide the choice of a federal forum in place of the state-court systems found inadequate to stop gender-biased violence. . . .

The collective opinion of state officials that the Act was needed continues virtually unchanged, and when the Civil Rights Remedy was challenged in court, the States came to its defense. Thirty-six of them and the Commonwealth of Puerto Rico have filed an amicus brief in support of petitioners in these cases, and only one State has taken respondents' side. It is, then, not the least irony of these cases that the States will be forced to enjoy the new federalism whether they want it or not. For with the Court's decision today, Antonio Morrison, like *Carter Coal*'s James Carter before him, has won the states' rights plea against the states themselves.

III

All of this convinces me that today's ebb of the commerce power rests on error, and at the same time leads me to doubt that the majority's view will prove to be enduring law. . . . This [regime] will end when the majority realizes that the conception of the commerce power for which it entertains hopes would inevitably fail the test expressed in Justice Holmes's statement that "the first call of a theory of law is that it should fit the facts." The facts that cannot be ignored today are the facts of integrated national commerce and a political relationship between States and Nation much affected by their respective treasuries and constitutional modifications adopted by the people. The federalism of some earlier time is no more adequate to account for those facts today than the theory of laissez-faire was able to govern the national economy 70 years ago.

c) Drug Prohibition: *Gonzales v. Raich*

After *Lopez* and *Morrison* declared that the commerce power could be used to regulate only "commercial" activity that substantially affects interstate commerce, many people wondered whether a majority of the Supreme Court was preparing to back away from the substantial effects concept. Justice Thomas's concurrence in *Morrison* invited litigants to raise the question, and soon enough some of them did.

California banned marijuana in 1913, but in 1996 it amended the law to permit medical uses of the drug. Medical marijuana was still a violation of the federal Controlled Substances Act of 1970 (CSA), which forbids all manufacture and possession of marijuana, whether or not it has crossed state lines. The CSA was challenged by Angel Raich and Diane Monson, two Californians who wished to grow their own medical marijuana as allowed by state law. They relied on *Lopez* and *Morrison* to argue that their activity was "truly local" and not commercial because the marijuana would not be sold or bartered, and hence beyond Congress's authority.

The Supreme Court ruled 6–3 to uphold the national ban on marijuana. The majority opinion in *Gonzales v. Raich*, 545 U.S. 1 (2005), found the case to be indistinguishable from *Wickard v. Filburn* (1942).

> Our case law firmly establishes Congress' power to regulate purely local activities that are part of an economic class of activities that have a substantial effect on interstate commerce. As we stated in *Wickard*, "even if appellee's activity be local and though it may not be regarded as commerce, it may still, whatever its nature, be reached by Congress if it exerts a substantial economic effect on interstate commerce." We have never required Congress to legislate with scientific exactitude. When Congress decides that the total incidence of a practice poses a threat to a national market, it may regulate the entire class. In this vein, we have reiterated that when a general regulatory statute bears a substantial relation to commerce, the *de minimis* character of individual instances arising under that statute is of no consequence. . . .
>
> *Wickard* thus establishes that Congress can regulate purely intrastate activity that is not itself "commercial," in that it is not produced for sale, if it concludes that failure to regulate that class of activity would undercut the regulation of the interstate market in that commodity.
>
> The similarities between this case and *Wickard* are striking. Like the farmer in *Wickard*, respondents are cultivating, for home consumption, a fungible commodity for which there is an established, albeit illegal, interstate market. Just as the Agricultural Adjustment Act was designed to control the volume of wheat moving in interstate and foreign commerce in order to avoid surpluses and consequently control the market price, a primary purpose of the CSA is

> to control the supply and demand of controlled substances in both lawful and unlawful drug markets. In *Wickard*, we had no difficulty concluding that Congress had a rational basis for believing that, when viewed in the aggregate, leaving home-consumed wheat outside the regulatory scheme would have a substantial influence on price and market conditions. Here too, Congress had a rational basis for concluding that leaving home-consumed marijuana outside federal control would similarly affect price and market conditions.

Justice Scalia concurred in the result. Although he considered it improper in *Lopez* and *Morrison* for the federal government to regulate noneconomic activity directly under the Commerce Clause, he believed that Congress had power to regulate noneconomic intrastate activities under the Necessary and Proper Clause to prevent those activities from "undercutting" a valid regulation of interstate commerce. He agreed that home cultivation and possession of marijuana could undercut the national policy prohibiting its interstate use.

O'Connor dissented. "There is simply no evidence that homegrown medicinal marijuana users constitute, in the aggregate, a sizable enough class to have a discernible, let alone substantial, impact on the national illicit drug market—or otherwise to threaten the CSA regime." Justice Thomas also dissented, but unlike Justice O'Connor he questioned the substantial effects concept itself. "Respondents Diane Monson and Angel Raich use marijuana that has never been bought or sold, that has never crossed state lines, and that has had no demonstrable effect on the national market for marijuana. If Congress can regulate this under the Commerce Clause, then it can regulate virtually anything—and the Federal Government is no longer one of limited and enumerated powers."

D. The Necessary & Proper Clause

A long-running constitutional debate has asked how close a connection must exist between an enumerated power and the statutes enacted under its authority. Take as an example the Art. I, § 8, cl. 4 power to establish "uniform laws on the subject of bankruptcies throughout the United States." This text plainly authorizes Congress to enact a bankruptcy statute that allows persons or companies to discharge debts they cannot afford to pay. It is also fairly easy to see how that power authorizes Congress to establish a system of bankruptcy courts to administer the Act, and to make it a criminal offense to engage in bankruptcy fraud. At the other end of the spectrum, it is equally plain that the Bankruptcy Clause does not authorize a statute forbidding trans fats in all restaurants within the United States. Trans fats and bankruptcy have nothing to do with each other.

The hard cases fall in between. Imagine that Congress, believing it desirable to reduce the size and power of corporations, enacts a law saying that all corporations must declare bankruptcy if the value of their stock exceeds $500 billion. Is this within Congress's bankruptcy power? On the one hand, it is a law involving bankruptcy. On the other hand, the law does not create or regulate a bankruptcy process, but instead regulates corporations that would not otherwise need debt relief. In answering this question about the scope of an enumerated power, it will be helpful to consider a more general question: should the powers in the Constitution be interpreted narrowly—which inevitably gives courts a greater role in policing which laws are passed? Or should they be interpreted broadly, giving Congress greater leeway to enact its desired policies? The Necessary and Proper Clause weighs in favor of the broader interpretation.

flashback

In *McCulloch v. Maryland* (1819), John Marshall used the Necessary and Proper Clause to bolster his argument that the enumerated powers of Congress should be interpreted broadly. By its terms, the Clause allows for a variety of laws to be enacted in aid of enumerated federal purposes, so that Congress could "perform the high duties assigned to it, in the manner most beneficial to the people." This led to a frequently-quoted description of how the Clause operates within the greater constitutional structure: "Let the end be legitimate, let it be within the scope of the Constitution, and all means which are appropriate, which are plainly adapted to that end, which are not prohibited, but consist with the letter and spirit of the Constitution, are constitutional." In other words, the Constitution enumerates goals, and Congress may, within reason, choose the means to pursue those goals.

1. Kickstarter: The Necessary and Proper Clause

DISCLAIMER: *This Kickstarter is a checklist to help identify relevant issues. It is not a list of elements. Nothing requires judges to write their opinions (or lawyers to write their briefs) in Kickstarter order.*

Necessary and Proper Clause **kickstarter**

A. Identify a textually-supported power of the federal government.

1. "Foregoing powers" from Art. I, § 8.

2. "Other powers" vested in Congress.

3. *"Other powers" vested in federal departments and officers.*

B. *Determine if the means chosen by the statute are "rationally related" to the implementation of that power.*

KICKSTARTER USER'S GUIDE

As interpreted ever since *McCulloch*, the Necessary and Proper Clause involves ends and means. To be authorized by the Clause, a law must serve suitable ends through suitable means.

Item A. *Enumerated Ends.* The Necessary and Proper Clause authorizes the enactment of laws for carrying into execution powers indicated elsewhere in the Constitution.

Item A.1. *"Foregoing Powers."* The Necessary and Proper Clause is the 18th clause within Article I, § 8. This means the "foregoing" powers are those listed in clauses 1 through 17. John Marshall in *McCulloch* invoked as an example a statute making it a federal crime to steal mail. Although punishing postal crimes is not expressly enumerated as a federal power, the power "to establish post offices and post roads" is. Art. I, § 8, cl. 5. The law against mail theft could help execute that foregoing power, by ensuring that the post offices and post roads can be used for their intended purposes. Using that logic, *McCulloch* concluded that the Bank of the United States would help carry into execution several foregoing powers within Art. I, § 8, including the power to tax (clause 1), to borrow money (clause 2), to regulate commerce (clause 3), and to raise and support armies and navies (clauses 12 and 13).

Item A.2. *"Other Powers" of Congress.* The Necessary and Proper Clause speaks of "other powers" that are "vested by this Constitution" in the United States government. At a minimum, this would include powers of Congress found in the Constitution but not in the "foregoing" list of powers in Art. I, § 8.

Many other portions of the Constitution say that Congress "shall have power" to do various things. For example, Congress "shall have power" to make laws regulating federal territory and property, Art. IV, § 3, cl. 2, "shall have power" to declare the punishment for treason, Art. III, § 3, cl. 2, and "shall have power" to enforce the Constitution's ban on slavery, Amendment 13, cl. 2. In other places, the Constitution uses different words to indicate a Congressional power. Allocating seats in the House of Representatives requires a census that must be taken every ten years "in such manner as [Congress] shall by law direct." Art. I, § 2, cl. 3. Congress "may by law provide for" succession if the President or Vice President leave office or are incapacitated. Art. II, § 1, cl. 6. States may not keep ships of war in time of peace "without the consent of Congress," Art. I, § 10, cl.

3, which indicates a Congressional power to give or withhold consent over this type of state law.

Could the reference to "other powers vested by this Constitution in the government of the United States" allude to powers not enumerated *anywhere* in the text? The Supreme Court has forcefully rejected this notion. To be an "other power," there must be at least some text (beyond the word "other" in the Necessary and Proper Clause) to indicate that the power is within the Constitution's design. For example, Congress routinely issues subpoenas that require witnesses to provide information to Congress, under threat of criminal prosecution for contempt of Congress. While the textual authority for legislative subpoenas is not as transparently clear as in those clauses saying "Congress shall have power," there is no doubt from the text and structure of the Constitution that Congress has power to legislate. E.g., Art. I, § 7, cl. 2. Congress needs good information in order to enact wise legislation, so the subpoena power helps carry into execution Congress's authority to pass bills.

flashback

Prigg v. Pennsylvania (1842), Ch. 6.B, held that Congress could enact a federal fugitive slave statute, even though the text of the Fugitive Slave Clause did not expressly identify this as an enumerated power. (It says only that fugitive slaves "shall be delivered up on claim" of the purported slave owner, without specifying whether state or federal governments would be in charge of the process.) Although the Court did not rely on the Necessary and Proper Clause for its holding, it used analogous reasoning: "If, indeed, the Constitution guaranties the right [to recover fugitive slaves], the natural inference certainly is that the national government is clothed with the appropriate authority and functions to enforce it." *Prigg* may represent the furthest the Supreme Court has ever gone in inferring a Congressional power from text that only weakly implied it.

Item A.3. *"Other Powers" of US Departments and Officials.* Congress may enact laws to carry into execution Congress's powers—and the powers of other "departments" and "officials" of the federal government. This explains the ability of Congress to enact legislation governing the other branches. For example, Congress has enacted many laws that control the operation of the federal courts, including statutes setting the number of justices on the US Supreme Court, the subject matter jurisdiction of the trial courts, and the appealability of cases from trial courts to appellate courts. The "other power" that these laws help carry into execution is "the judicial power" that Art. III, § 1 vests in the Supreme Court and lower courts. See, e.g., *Jinks v. Richland County*, 538 U.S. 456 (2003) (upholding statute that facilitates supplemental jurisdiction).

Congress may also legislate in ways that regulate "the executive power" that Art. II, § 1 vests in the President (and the President in turn delegates to subordinates). The Necessary and Proper Clause authorizes statutes like the Freedom of Information Act—which requires executive agencies to make most of their internal documents available to the public—and the Civil Service Act—which controls how most executive branch employees are hired, paid, and fired, thus limiting the President's ability to award government jobs as political favors. Once laws are enacted under the authority of the Necessary and Proper Clause, the President "shall take care that the laws be faithfully executed" under Art. II, § 3.

Conceivably, a statute controlling how some judicial or executive powers are to be performed could violate the structural limit of separation of powers. This would occur if Congress sought to control functions assigned exclusively to another branch. For example, the Constitution's assignment of the pardoning power to the President in Art. II, § 2, cl. 1 would limit Congress's ability to use the Necessary and Proper Clause to enact a law directing the President to pardon specified federal prisoners. Limits based on separation of powers are the subject of Ch. 16.

Item B. *Appropriate Means.* In addition to serving a suitable end (or goal), a law relying on the Necessary and Proper Clause must use means that are "necessary and proper" for executing that end. (Historically, most court opinions have treated "necessary and proper" as a single term of art, although some recent opinions—usually concurrences or dissents—have attempted to assign separate meanings to "necessary" and "proper.") As explained in *McCulloch*, laws need not be indispensable or inevitable to be "necessary and proper." Instead, laws may be "convenient" or "useful" methods for achieving a legitimate goal. The term is understood "as employing any means calculated to produce the end, and not as being confined to those single means, without which the end would be entirely unattainable." Modern cases have used terms like "rationally related" or "means-ends rationality" to express the required level of connection between ends and means. See *US v. Comstock*, 560 U.S. 126 (2010); *Sabri v. United States*, 541 U.S. 600 (2004). As seen in cases dating at least to *Carolene Products v. United States* (1938), terms like "rational" and "reasonable" imply substantial deference to the legislature. If a reasonable legislature could believe, without being irrational, that the chosen means serve the ends, then the connection is sufficient.

As always, concrete examples can illuminate a potentially vague legal standard like "rationally related."

(a) *Sabri* upheld a statute making it a federal crime to bribe state, local, or tribal officials whose governmental entities receive more than $10,000 in federal funds—even if the bribery did not directly relate to the use of those funds. "Congress has authority under the Spending Clause to appropriate federal moneys to promote the general welfare," the Court explained, "and it has corresponding authority under the Necessary and Proper Clause to see to it that taxpayer dollars [are] not frittered away" or imperiled by being controlled by "corrupt" or "derelict" local officers. The anti-bribery statute addresses the problem "by rational means, to safeguard the integrity of the state, local, and tribal recipients of federal dollars."

(b) *Jinks* upheld a federal subject matter jurisdiction statute that would toll the statute of limitations for state-law claims while those claims were under consideration by a federal court. Although "federal courts can assuredly exist and function in the absence" of that statute, it nonetheless promoted "fair and efficient operation of the federal courts" by removing a barrier that discouraged some litigants from bringing their claims to federal court. This made the statute "necessary and proper for carrying into execution Congress's power 'to constitute tribunals inferior to the supreme Court,' and to assure that those tribunals may fairly and efficiently exercise 'the judicial power of the United States'."

(c) Finally, many opinions in Commerce Clause cases note that the Necessary and Proper Clause helps justify the expansive New Deal interpretation, where "commerce among the states" is interpreted to include in-state activities having substantial effect on interstate commerce. Hence, *Gonzales v. Raich* (2005) combined the two clauses when it explained that "the power vested in Congress by Article I, § 8, of the Constitution 'to make all laws which shall be necessary and proper for carrying into execution' its authority to 'regulate commerce with foreign nations, and among the several states' includes the power to prohibit the local cultivation and use of marijuana."

Which laws would lack a rational relationship to an enumerated power? Even a generally deferential court would strike down some laws for having no rational connection between ends and means. For example, a law requiring all citizens to wear polka-dotted shirts on Thursdays would not be a necessary and proper means to execute the enumerated power to coin money under Art. I, § 8, cl. 3. But not all Supreme Court justices in recent years have been willing to limit judicial review to such outlandish cases. After all, if the judiciary becomes too deferential, Congress could use the Necessary and Proper Clause to enact virtually any law, no matter how tenuous its relationship with an enumerated power. If the Necessary and Proper Clause expands each enumerated power beyond recognition, then the Constitution's enumeration of federal powers becomes a mirage, and the federal government has the equivalent of police powers. This has been a topic of debate ever since the ratification debates of the 1780s, where critics derided the Necessary and Proper Clause as "the Sweeping Clause" or "the Elastic Clause."

Reflecting this concern, some recent opinions have asked whether the connection between means and ends is "too attenuated" to be rational. They have also asked whether the challenged statute would amount to an end-run around limits that were supposed to constrain Congress (in particular the limits implied by the enumeration of federal powers, the absence of federal police power, and the structural feature of federalism). Reasonable judges have differed over exactly how far is too far for Congress to go, even under a generally deferential approach.

2. Public Safety Legislation: *United States v. Comstock*

Many of the cases that expressly discuss the Necessary and Proper Clause involve federal criminal laws. Because the Constitution only enumerates a few areas for Congress to "punish"—such as the power in Art. I, § 8, cl. 6 "to provide for the punishment of counterfeiting" or the power in Art. I, § 8, cl. 10 "to define and punish piracies and felonies committed on the high seas"—federal crimes involving other offenses must be justified through the Necessary and Proper Clause. Federal drug laws, for example, are necessary and proper methods to enforce Congress's power to control the interstate trade in controlled substances. *U.S. v. Comstock* (2010) involved a law that relied on the Necessary and Proper Clause to go a step beyond criminal punishment.

ITEMS TO CONSIDER WHILE READING *COMSTOCK*:

A. *A threshold question: Which enumerated power(s) allow Congress to criminalize possession of child pornography?*

B. *Work through the items in the Kickstarter to determine if the Necessary and Proper Clause allows Congress to civilly commit people previously convicted of that crime.*

C. *Justice Kennedy's concurrence notes that the "rational relationship" between means and ends under the Necessary and Proper Clause is not necessarily the same as the "rational relationship" required when challenging legislation under the Equal Protection and Due Process Clauses. Should judicial review be calibrated differently between enumerated powers and individual rights?*

D. *Invent hypothetical federal statutes whose constitutionality depends on the Necessary & Proper Clause.*

United States v. Comstock,

560 U.S. 126 (2010)

Justice Breyer delivered the opinion of the Court [joined by Chief Justice Roberts and Justices Stevens, Ginsburg, and Sotomayor].

A federal civil-commitment statute authorizes the Department of Justice to detain a mentally ill, sexually dangerous federal prisoner beyond the date the prisoner would otherwise be released. 18 U.S.C. § 4248 [Adam Walsh Child Protection and Safety Act of 2006]. We have previously examined similar statutes enacted under state law to determine whether they violate the Due Process Clause. See ***Kansas v. Hendricks***, 521 U.S. 346 (1997); ***Kansas v. Crane***, 534 U.S. 407 (2002). But this case presents a different question. Here we ask whether the Federal Government has the authority under Article I of the Constitution to enact this federal civil-commitment program or whether its doing so falls beyond the reach of a government of enumerated powers. We conclude that the Constitution grants Congress the authority to enact § 4248 as "necessary and proper for carrying into Execution" the powers "vested by" the "Constitution in the Government of the United States." Art. I, § 8, cl. 18.

■ HISTORY

***HENDRICKS* AND *CRANE*:** These cases considered state laws ordering civil detention of sex offenders after their criminal sentences expired. *Hendricks* upheld the general concept behind such laws, while *Crane* required the government to prove, as a precondition of commitment, that the offender lacked control over harmful impulses.

I

The federal statute before us allows a district court to order the civil commitment of an individual who is currently "in the custody of the [Federal] Bureau of Prisons," if that individual (1) has previously "engaged or attempted to engage in sexually violent conduct or child molestation," (2) currently "suffers from a serious mental illness, abnormality, or disorder," and (3) "as a result of" that mental illness, abnormality, or disorder is "sexually dangerous to others," in that "he would have serious difficulty in refraining from sexually violent conduct or child molestation if released."

In order to detain such a person, the Government (acting through the Department of Justice) must certify to a federal district judge that the prisoner meets the conditions just described. . . . When such a certification is filed, the statute automatically stays the individual's release from prison, thereby giving the Government an opportunity to prove its claims at a hearing through psychiatric (or other) evidence. The statute provides that the prisoner shall be represented by counsel and shall have an opportunity at the hearing to testify, to present evidence, to subpoena witnesses on his behalf, and to confront and cross-examine the Government's witnesses.

If the Government proves its claims by "clear and convincing evidence," the court will order the prisoner's continued commitment in the custody of the Attorney General, who must "make all reasonable efforts to cause" the State where that person was tried, or the State where he is domiciled, to "assume responsibility for his custody, care, and treatment." If either State is willing to assume that responsibility, the Attorney General "shall release" the individual "to the appropriate official" of that State. But if, "notwithstanding such efforts, neither such State will assume such responsibility," then "the Attorney General shall place the person for treatment in a suitable [federal] facility."

Confinement in the federal facility will last until either (1) the person's mental condition improves to the point where he is no longer dangerous (with or without appropriate ongoing treatment), in which case he will be released; or (2) a State assumes responsibility for his custody, care, and treatment, in which case he will be transferred to the custody of that State. The statute establishes a system for ongoing psychiatric and judicial review of the individual's case, including judicial hearings at the request of the confined person at six-month intervals.

In November and December 2006, the Government instituted proceedings in the Federal District Court for the Eastern District of North Carolina against the five respondents in this case [including lead defendant Graydon Earl Comstock, Jr., who] had previously pleaded guilty in federal court to possession of child pornography. . . . Each of the five respondents moved to dismiss the civil-commitment proceeding on constitutional grounds. They claimed that the commitment proceeding [violated various constitutional rights.] And, finally, they claimed that, in enacting the statute, Congress exceeded the powers granted to it by Article I, § 8 of the Constitution, including those granted by the Commerce Clause and the Necessary and Proper Clause.

The District Court [and] the Court of Appeals for the Fourth Circuit [held that Congress lacked authority to enact the statute]. . . . The Government sought certiorari, and we granted its request, limited to the question of Congress' authority under Article I, § 8 of the Constitution. Since then, two other Courts of Appeals have considered that same question, each deciding it in the Government's favor, thereby creating a split of authority among the Circuits.

II

The question presented is whether the Necessary and Proper Clause, Art. I, § 8, cl. 18, grants Congress authority sufficient to enact the statute before us. In resolving that question, we assume, but we do not decide, that other provisions of the Constitution—such as the Due Process Clause—do not prohibit civil commitment in these circumstances. In other words, we assume for argument's sake that the

Federal Constitution would permit a State to enact this statute, and we ask solely whether the Federal Government, exercising its enumerated powers, may enact such a statute as well. On that assumption, we conclude that the Constitution grants Congress legislative power sufficient to enact § 4248. We base this conclusion on five considerations, taken together.

First, the Necessary and Proper Clause grants Congress broad authority to enact federal legislation. Nearly 200 years ago, this Court stated that the Federal Government "is acknowledged by all to be one of enumerated powers," *McCulloch v. Maryland* (1819), which means that every law enacted by Congress must be based on one or more of those powers. But, at the same time, "a government, entrusted with such" powers "must also be entrusted with ample means for their execution." *Id.* Accordingly, the Necessary and Proper Clause makes clear that the Constitution's grants of specific federal legislative authority are accompanied by broad power to enact laws that are "convenient, or useful" or "conducive" to the authority's "beneficial exercise." Chief Justice Marshall emphasized that the word "necessary" does not mean "absolutely necessary." In language that has come to define the scope of the Necessary and Proper Clause, he wrote:

> Let the end be legitimate, let it be within the scope of the constitution, and all means which are appropriate, which are plainly adapted to that end, which are not prohibited, but consist with the letter and spirit of the constitution, are constitutional.

We have since made clear that, in determining whether the Necessary and Proper Clause grants Congress the legislative authority to enact a particular federal statute, we look to see whether the statute constitutes a means that is rationally related to the implementation of a constitutionally enumerated power. *Sabri v. United States,* 541 U.S. 600 (2004) (using term "means-ends rationality" to describe the necessary relationship); see *Gonzales v. Raich* (2005) (holding that because "Congress had a rational basis" for concluding that a statute implements Commerce Clause power, the statute falls within the scope of congressional "authority to 'make all Laws which shall be necessary and proper' to 'regulate Commerce among the several States' ").

Of course, as Chief Justice Marshall stated, a federal statute, in addition to being authorized by Art. I, § 8, must also "not [be] prohibited" by the Constitution. But as we have already stated, the present statute's validity under provisions of the Constitution other than the Necessary and Proper Clause is an issue that is not before us. Under the question presented, the relevant inquiry is simply whether the means chosen are reasonably adapted to the attainment of a legitimate end under the commerce power or under other powers that the Constitution grants Congress the authority to implement.

We have also recognized that the Constitution addresses the choice of means primarily to the judgment of Congress. If it can be seen that the means adopted are really calculated to attain the end, the degree of their necessity, the extent to which they conduce to the end, the closeness of the relationship between the means adopted and the end to be attained, are matters for congressional determination alone.

Thus, the Constitution, which nowhere speaks explicitly about the creation of federal crimes beyond those related to "counterfeiting," Art. I, § 8, cl. 6, "treason," Art. III, § 3, cl. 2, or "Piracies and Felonies committed on the high Seas" or "against the Law of Nations," Art. I, § 8, cl. 10, nonetheless grants Congress broad authority to create such crimes. And Congress routinely exercises its authority to enact criminal laws in furtherance of, for example, its enumerated powers to regulate interstate and foreign commerce, to enforce civil rights, to spend funds for the general welfare, to establish federal courts, to establish post offices, to regulate bankruptcy, to regulate naturalization, and so forth.

Similarly, Congress, in order to help ensure the enforcement of federal criminal laws enacted in furtherance of its enumerated powers, can cause a prison to be erected at any place within the jurisdiction of the United States, and direct that all persons sentenced to imprisonment under the laws of the United States shall be confined there. Moreover, Congress, having established a prison system, can enact laws that seek to ensure that system's safe and responsible administration by, for example, requiring prisoners to receive medical care and educational training, and can also ensure the safety of the prisoners, prison workers and visitors, and those in surrounding communities by, for example, creating further criminal laws governing entry, exit, and smuggling, and by employing prison guards to ensure discipline and security.

Neither Congress' power to criminalize conduct, nor its power to imprison individuals who engage in that conduct, nor its power to enact laws governing prisons and prisoners, is explicitly mentioned in the Constitution. But Congress nonetheless possesses broad authority to do each of those things in the course of "carrying into Execution" the enumerated powers "vested by" the "Constitution in the Government of the United States"—authority granted by the Necessary and Proper Clause.

Second, the civil-commitment statute before us constitutes a modest addition to a set of federal prison-related mental-health statutes that have existed for many decades. We recognize that even a longstanding history of related federal action does not demonstrate a statute's constitutionality. A history of involvement, however, can nonetheless be helpful in reviewing the substance of a congressional statutory scheme, and, in particular, the reasonableness of the relation between the new statute and pre-existing federal interests.

Here, Congress has long been involved in the delivery of mental health care to federal prisoners, and has long provided for their civil commitment. In 1855 it established Saint Elizabeth's Hospital in the District of Columbia to provide treatment to "the insane of the army and navy and of the District of Columbia." [Combined with later statutes enacted in 1857, 1874, and 1882,] Congress created a national, federal civil-commitment program under which any person who was either charged with or convicted of any federal offense in any federal court could be confined in a federal mental institution.

These statutes did not raise the question presented here, for they all provided that commitment in a federal hospital would end upon the completion of the relevant terms of federal imprisonment as set forth in the underlying criminal sentence or statute. But [statutes enacted in 1949 and 1984 authorized civil commitment following the completion of a criminal sentence for mentally ill federal prisoners who posed a danger to others].

In 2006, Congress enacted the particular statute before us. It differs from earlier statutes in that it focuses directly upon persons who, due to a mental illness, are sexually dangerous. Notably, many of these individuals were likely already subject to civil commitment under § 4246, which, since 1949, has authorized the post-sentence detention of federal prisoners who suffer from a mental illness and who are thereby dangerous (whether sexually or otherwise). Aside from its specific focus on sexually dangerous persons, § 4248 is similar to the provisions first enacted in 1949. In that respect, it is a modest addition to a longstanding federal statutory framework, which has been in place since 1855.

Third, Congress reasonably extended its longstanding civil-commitment system to cover mentally ill and sexually dangerous persons who are already in federal custody, even if doing so detains them beyond the termination of their criminal sentence. For one thing, the Federal Government is the custodian of its prisoners. As federal custodian, it has the constitutional power to act in order to protect nearby (and other) communities from the danger federal prisoners may pose. . . . If a federal prisoner is infected with a communicable disease that threatens others, surely it would be "necessary and proper" for the Federal Government to take action, pursuant to its role as federal custodian, to refuse (at least until the threat diminishes) to release that individual among the general public, where he might infect others (even if not threatening an interstate epidemic). And if confinement of such an individual is a "necessary and proper" thing to do, then how could it not be similarly "necessary and proper" to confine an individual whose mental illness threatens others to the same degree?

Moreover, § 4248 is reasonably adapted to Congress' power to act as a responsible federal custodian (a power that rests, in turn, upon federal criminal statutes that legitimately seek to implement constitutionally enumerated authority). Congress could have reasonably concluded that federal inmates who suffer from a mental illness that causes them to "have serious difficulty in refraining from sexually violent conduct" would pose an especially high danger to the public if released. And

Congress could also have reasonably concluded . . . that a reasonable number of such individuals would likely not be detained by the States if released from federal custody, in part because the Federal Government itself severed their claim to legal residence in any State by incarcerating them in remote federal prisons. Here Congress' desire to address [these specific challenges], taken together with its responsibilities as a federal custodian, supports the conclusion that § 4248 satisfies review for means-end rationality, i.e., that it satisfies the Constitution's insistence that a federal statute represent a rational means for implementing a constitutional grant of legislative authority.

Fourth, the statute properly accounts for state interests. Respondents and the dissent contend that § 4248 violates the Tenth Amendment because it invades the province of state sovereignty in an area typically left to state control. But the Tenth Amendment's text is clear: "The powers not delegated to the United States by the Constitution, nor prohibited by it to the States, are reserved to the States respectively, or to the people." The powers "delegated to the United States by the Constitution" include those specifically enumerated powers listed in Article I along with the implementation authority granted by the Necessary and Proper Clause. Virtually by definition, these powers are not powers that the Constitution "reserved to the States." If a power is delegated to Congress in the Constitution, the Tenth Amendment expressly disclaims any reservation of that power to the States.

Nor does this statute invade state sovereignty or otherwise improperly limit the scope of powers that remain with the States. To the contrary, it requires accommodation of state interests: The Attorney General must inform the State in which the federal prisoner is domiciled or was tried that he is detaining someone with respect to whom those States may wish to assert their authority, and he must encourage those States to assume custody of the individual. He must also immediately release that person to the appropriate official of either State if such State will assume such responsibility. And either State has the right, at any time, to assert its authority over the individual, which will prompt the individual's immediate transfer to state custody. Respondents contend that the States are nonetheless "powerless to prevent the detention of their citizens under § 4248, even if detention is contrary to the States' policy choices." But that is not the most natural reading of the statute, and the solicitor general acknowledges that the federal Government would have no appropriate role with respect to an individual covered by the statute once the transfer to State responsibility and State control has occurred. . . .

Fifth, the links between § 4248 and an enumerated Article I power are not too attenuated. Neither is the statutory provision too sweeping in its scope. Invoking the cautionary instruction that we may not pile inference upon inference in order to sustain congressional action under Article I, respondents argue that, when legislating pursuant to the Necessary and Proper Clause, Congress' authority can be no more than one step removed from a specifically enumerated power. But this argument is irreconcilable with our precedents. . [In *Greenwood v. United States*, 350 U.S. 366 (1956)] we upheld the (likely indefinite) civil commitment of a mentally incompetent federal defendant who was accused of robbing a United States Post Office. The underlying enumerated Article I power was the power to "Establish Post Offices and Post Roads." Art. I, § 8, cl. 7. But, as Chief Justice Marshall recognized in *McCulloch*,

> the power "to establish post offices and post roads" is executed by the single act of making the establishment. From this has been inferred the power and duty of carrying the mail along the post road, from one post office to another. And, from this implied power, has again been inferred the right to punish those who steal letters from the post office, or rob the mail.

And, as we have explained, from the implied power to punish we have further inferred both the power to imprison and, in *Greenwood*, the federal civil-commitment power.

Our necessary and proper jurisprudence contains multiple examples of similar reasoning. For example, . . . in *United States v. Hall*, 98 U.S. 343 (1879), we held that the Necessary and Proper Clause grants Congress the power, in furtherance of Art. I, § 8, cls. 11–13, to award pensions to the wounded and disabled soldiers of the armed forces and their dependents, and from that implied power we further inferred the implied power to pass laws to punish anyone who fraudulently appropriated such pensions. . . . Thus, we must reject respondents' argument that the Necessary and Proper Clause permits no more than a single step between an enumerated power and an Act of Congress. . . .

To be sure, as we have previously acknowledged, the Federal Government undertakes activities today that would have been unimaginable to the Framers in two senses; first, because the Framers would not have conceived that any government would conduct such activities; and second, because the Framers would not have believed that the Federal Government, rather than the States, would assume such responsibilities. Yet the powers conferred upon the Federal Government by the Constitution were phrased in language broad enough to allow for the expansion of the Federal Government's role.

The Framers demonstrated considerable foresight in drafting a Constitution capable of such resilience through time. As Chief Justice Marshall observed nearly 200 years ago, the Necessary and Proper Clause is part of "a constitution intended to endure for ages to come, and, consequently, to be adapted to the various crises of human affairs." *McCulloch*.

[CONCLUSION]

We . . . conclude that the statute is a "necessary and proper" means of exercising the federal authority that permits Congress to create federal criminal laws, to punish their violation, to imprison violators, to provide appropriately for those imprisoned, and to maintain the security of those who are not imprisoned but who may be affected by the federal imprisonment of others. The Constitution consequently authorizes Congress to enact the statute.

We do not reach or decide any claim that the statute or its application denies equal protection of the laws, procedural or substantive due process, or any other rights guaranteed by the Constitution. Respondents are free to pursue those claims on remand, and any others they have preserved.

Justice Kennedy, concurring in the judgment.

. . . When the inquiry is whether a federal law has sufficient links to an enumerated power to be within the scope of federal authority, the analysis depends not on the number of links in the congressional-power chain but on the strength of the chain.

Concluding that a relation can be put into a verbal formulation that fits somewhere along a causal chain of federal powers is merely the beginning, not the end, of the constitutional inquiry. The inferences must be controlled by some limitations lest, as Thomas Jefferson warned, congressional powers become completely unbounded by linking one power to another ad infinitum in a veritable game of "this is the house that Jack built." Letter from Thomas Jefferson to Edward Livingston (Apr. 30, 1800).

This separate writing serves two purposes. The first is to withhold assent from certain statements and propositions of the Court's opinion. The second is to caution that the Constitution does require the invalidation of congressional attempts to extend federal powers in some instances.

I

The Court concludes that, when determining whether Congress has the authority to enact a specific law under the Necessary and Proper Clause, we look "to see whether the statute constitutes a means that is rationally related to the implementation of a constitutionally enumerated power."

The terms "rationally related" and "rational basis" must be employed with care, particularly if either is to be used as a stand-alone test. The phrase "rational basis" most often is employed to describe the standard for determining whether legislation that does not proscribe fundamental liberties nonetheless violates the Due Process Clause. Referring to this due process inquiry, and in what must be one of the most deferential formulations of the standard for reviewing legislation in all the Court's precedents, the Court has said: "But the law need not be in every respect logically consistent with its aims to be constitutional. It is enough that there is an evil at hand for correction, and that it might be thought that the particular legislative measure was a rational way to correct it." *Williamson v. Lee Optical* (1955). This formulation was in a case presenting a due process challenge and a challenge to a State's exercise of its own powers, powers not confined by the principles that control the limited nature of our National Government. The phrase, then, should not be extended uncritically to the issue before us.

The operative constitutional provision in this case is the Necessary and Proper Clause. This Court has not held that the *Lee Optical* test, asking if "it might be thought that the particular legislative measure was a rational way to correct" an evil, is the proper test in this context. Rather, under the Necessary and Proper Clause, application of a "rational basis" test should be at least as exacting as it has been in the Commerce Clause cases, if not more so. Indeed, the cases the Court cites in the portion of its opinion referring to "rational basis" are predominantly Commerce Clause cases, and none are due process cases.

There is an important difference between the two questions, but the Court does not make this distinction clear. [Commerce Clause cases] require a tangible link to commerce, not a mere conceivable rational relation, as in *Lee Optical*. Simply because Congress may conclude that a particular activity substantially affects interstate commerce does not necessarily make it so. The rational basis referred to in the Commerce Clause context is a demonstrated link in fact, based on empirical demonstration. While undoubtedly deferential, this may well be different from the rational-basis test as *Lee Optical* described it. . . .

A separate concern stems from the Court's explanation of the Tenth Amendment. I had thought it a basic principle that the powers reserved to the States consist of the whole, undefined residuum of power remaining after taking account of powers granted to the National Government. The Constitution delegates limited powers to the National Government and then reserves the remainder for the States (or the people), not the other way around, as the Court's analysis suggests. And the powers reserved to the States are so broad that they remain undefined. Residual power, sometimes referred to (perhaps imperfectly) as the police power, belongs to the States and the States alone.

It is correct in one sense to say that if the National Government has the power to act under the Necessary and Proper Clause then that power is not one reserved to the States. But the precepts of federalism embodied in the Constitution inform which powers are properly exercised by the National Government in the first place. It is of fundamental importance to consider whether essential attributes of state sovereignty are compromised by the assertion of federal power under the Necessary and Proper Clause; if so, that is a factor suggesting that the power is not one properly within the reach of federal power. . . .

II

As stated at the outset, in this case Congress has acted within its powers to ensure that an abrupt end to the federal detention of prisoners does not endanger third parties. Federal prisoners often lack a single home State to take charge of them due to their lengthy prison stays, so it is incumbent on the National Government to act. This obligation, parallel in some respects to duties defined in tort law, is not to put in motion a particular force (here an unstable and dangerous person) that endangers others. Having acted within its constitutional authority to detain the person, the National Government can acknowledge a duty to ensure that an abrupt end to the detention does not prejudice the States and their citizens. . . .

With these observations, I concur in the judgment of the Court.

Justice Alito, concurring in the judgment.

. . . I entirely agree with the dissent that the Necessary and Proper Clause empowers Congress to enact only those laws that carry into execution one or more of the federal powers enumerated in the Constitution, but § 4248 satisfies that requirement because it is a necessary and proper means of carrying into execution the enumerated powers that support the federal criminal statutes under which the affected prisoners were convicted. . . .

Justice Thomas, with whom Justice Scalia joins in all but Part III-A-1-b, dissenting.

The Court holds today that Congress has power under the Necessary and Proper Clause to enact a law authorizing the Federal Government to civilly commit "sexually dangerous persons" beyond the date it lawfully could hold them on a charge or conviction for a federal crime. I disagree. The Necessary and Proper Clause empowers Congress to enact only those laws that "carry into Execution" one or more of the federal powers enumerated in the Constitution. Art. I, § 8, cl. 18. Because § 4248 executes no enumerated power, I must respectfully dissent.

I [Omitted]

II

. . . No enumerated power in Article I, § 8, expressly delegates to Congress the power to enact a civil-commitment regime for sexually dangerous persons, nor does any other provision in the Constitution vest Congress or the other branches of the Federal Government with such a power. Accordingly, § 4248 can be a valid exercise of congressional authority only if it is "necessary and proper for carrying into Execution" one or more of those federal powers actually enumerated in the Constitution.

Section 4248 does not fall within any of those powers. The Government identifies no specific enumerated power or powers as a constitutional predicate for § 4248, and none are readily discernable. Indeed, not even the Commerce Clause—the enumerated power this Court has interpreted most expansively—can justify federal civil detention of sex offenders. Under the Court's precedents, Congress may not regulate noneconomic activity (such as sexual violence) based solely on the effect such activity may have, in individual cases or in the aggregate, on interstate commerce. *United States v. Morrison* (2000). That limitation forecloses any claim that § 4248 carries into execution Congress' Commerce Clause power, and the Government has never argued otherwise.

This Court, moreover, consistently has recognized that the power to care for the mentally ill and, where necessary, the power to protect the community from the dangerous tendencies of some mentally ill persons, are among the numerous powers that remain with the States. As a consequence, we have held that States may take measures to restrict the freedom of the dangerously mentally ill—including those who are sexually dangerous—provided that such commitments satisfy due process and other constitutional requirements.

Section 4248 closely resembles the involuntary civil-commitment laws that States have enacted under their **parens patriae** and general police powers. Indeed, it is clear, on the face of the Act and in the Government's arguments urging its constitutionality, that § 4248 is aimed at protecting society from acts of sexual violence, not toward "carrying into Execution" any enumerated power or powers of the Federal Government. See Adam Walsh Child Protection and Safety Act of 2006, (entitled "An Act to protect children from sexual exploitation and violent crime" [and containing a] (statement of purpose declaring that the Act was promulgated "to protect the public from sex offenders"); Brief for United States (asserting the Federal Government's power to *"protect the public from harm* that might result upon these prisoners' release, even when that harm might arise from conduct that is *otherwise beyond the general regulatory powers of the federal government"* (emphasis added)).

■ TERMINOLOGY

PARENS PATRIAE: Derived from the Latin for "parent of the country," the *parens patriae* power is exercised when a government acts on behalf of persons unable to legally act on their own. It is most often invoked for laws relating to children, the mentally ill, or the legally incompetent. Today, *parens patriae* is viewed as a subset of the "police power" to enact laws for the health, safety, welfare, and morals of the community.

To be sure, protecting society from violent sexual offenders is certainly an important end. Sexual abuse is a despicable act with untold consequences for the victim personally and society generally. But the Constitution does not vest in Congress the authority to protect society from every bad act that might befall it.

In my view, this should decide the question. Section 4248 runs afoul of our settled understanding of Congress' power under the Necessary and Proper Clause. Congress may act under that Clause only when its legislation "carries into Execution" one of the Federal Government's enumerated powers. Section 4248 does not execute any enumerated power. Section 4248 is therefore unconstitutional.

III [Omitted]

E. The Civil Rights Enforcement Clauses

The Bill of Rights ratified in 1791 did not add to federal enumerated powers. To the contrary, it identified a set of individual rights that would limit those powers. The Reconstruction Amendments were different. The opening sections of the Thirteenth, Fourteenth, and Fifteenth Amendments identified individual rights (limits on government), but their closing sections provided that "Congress shall have power to enforce" those rights through "appropriate legislation." The same pattern was followed in subsequent voting rights amendments (Nineteenth, Twenty-Fourth, and Twenty-Sixth).

Ever since *The Civil Rights Cases* (1883), the Supreme Court has held that laws enacted under these provisions may be aimed only at "state action" (i.e., governmental rather than private action). Otherwise, there was little case law interpreting these enumerated powers. During the Civil Rights Era, opinions of the Warren Court indicated that courts should, as a general matter, defer to Congress on whether a law governing state action is authorized by Congress's enumerated civil rights powers. Typically, legislation under these Amendments will be "appropriate" if a rational (not unreasonable) connection exists between Congress's chosen means and the Constitution's enumerated civil rights ends. This approach was explicitly modeled on the approach to the Necessary and Proper Clause under *McCulloch v. Maryland* (1819).

However, in recent decades the Supreme Court has announced federalism-based limitations on the civil rights enforcement powers—at least in certain settings. Since there have been relatively few decisions in the area, the full impact of these cases remains to be seen.

1. Kickstarter: Civil Rights Enforcement Clauses

DISCLAIMER: *This Kickstarter is a checklist to help identify relevant issues. It is not a list of elements. Nothing requires judges to write their opinions (or lawyers to write their briefs) in Kickstarter order.*

Power to Enforce Civil Rights Amendments kickstarter

A. Congress has enumerated power to enact "appropriate legislation" to enforce the individual rights announced in the Thirteenth, Fourteenth, Fifteenth, Nineteenth, Twenty-Fourth and Twenty-Sixth Amendments, (collectively known as the Civil Rights Amendments).

B. The power is subject to (at least) these limitations.

1. Except for the Thirteenth Amendment, federal statutes to enforce the Civil Rights Amendments must remedy state action, not private action.

2. *Under § 5 of the Fourteenth Amendment, federal statutes must be "congruent and proportional" remedies to state actions that the Supreme Court would agree violate § 1 of the Fourteenth Amendment.*
3. *Under § 2 of the Fifteenth Amendment, federal voting rights statutes might not be rational if they treat states differently from each other but are not clearly responsive to current conditions.*

KICKSTARTER USER'S GUIDE

Item A. *Enumerated Power.* Each of the Civil Rights Amendments announces an individual right in its first section, but all conclude with language enumerating a Congressional power to enforce the right. These enforcement powers use language nearly identical to the following: "The Congress shall have power to enforce this article [Amendment] by appropriate legislation."

Subject to a handful of exceptions described below, courts use a deferential standard to determine if legislation is "appropriate." This deference is constructed by analogy to the means-ends ideas that *McCulloch v. Maryland* (1819) announced in connection with the Necessary and Proper Clause. As a result, the Civil Rights Amendments allow Congress "to exercise its discretion in determining whether and what legislation is needed," *Katzenbach v. Morgan*, 384 U.S. 641 (1966), and it may enact any statutes "adapted to carry out the objects the amendments have in view," *Ex Parte Virginia*, 100 U.S. 339 (1879). As explained in *Strauder v. West Virginia* (1879): "Rights and immunities created by or dependant upon the Constitution of the United States can be protected by Congress. The form and manner of the protection may be such as Congress in the legitimate exercise of its legislative discretion shall provide. These may be varied to meet the necessities of the particular right to be protected."

Item B. *Limitations.* Due to the state action requirement, Item B.1, statutes to enforce the Civil Rights Amendments will by definition regulate state and local governments. This means that litigation over the constitutionality of these laws will highlight competing views about federalism: How a judge feels about the proper balance of state and federal power is likely to arise in cases where the federal government seeks to regulate state governments. Items B.2 and B.3 are based on recent Supreme Court cases under the Fourteenth and Fifteenth Amendments that seem to modify the basic *McCulloch* approach. The extent to which either case applies to the other civil rights enforcement powers is currently subject to debate.

Item B.1. *State Action.* The state action requirement under the Fourteenth Amendment is commonly associated with *The Civil Rights Cases* (1883). That opinion held that Congress has power under § 5 to enforce "the provisions of this article," where "this article" refers to the Fourteenth Amendment. Because § 1 of the Fourteenth Amendment creates rights against states ("No state shall. . . "), federal laws enforcing it must target behavior of state and local government, not of private entities. *Heart of Atlanta Motel* (1964) chose not to revisit this rule, and it was reiterated in *US v. Morrison* (2000). Perhaps the most prominent example of a civil rights enforcement statute that targets state action is 42 U.S.C. § 1983, which allows plaintiffs to sue state actors for violating rights protected by the US Constitution.

The state action requirement in the later Voting Rights Amendments—Fifteenth for race, Nineteenth for sex, Twenty-Fourth for payment of poll taxes, and Twenty-Sixth for age over 18—follows from their text. Each says that the relevant voting right may not be abridged "by the United States or by any State."

The Thirteenth Amendment is an exception to the state action requirement. As explained in *The Civil Rights Cases*, when that Amendment declared that "neither slavery nor involuntary servitude . . . shall exist," it eradicated slavery whether perpetrated by government or by private actors. Thus, the Thirteenth Amendment allows Congress to pass laws against human trafficking. *United States v. Kozminski*, 487 U.S. 931 (1988).

Item B.2. *Congruence and Proportionality Under the Fourteenth Amendment.* The decision in *City of Boerne v. Flores* (1997) held that statutes enacted under § 5 of the Fourteenth Amendment must be "congruent and proportional" remedies for state actions that would be recognized by the Supreme Court as violations of § 1 of the Fourteenth Amendment. In this context, "congruent" implies "having the same shape as," while "proportional" implies "being approximately the same size as." Hence, a federal statute would not be congruent if it bars a state from doing things the Supreme Court believes do not violate § 1 of the Fourteenth Amendment. A statute would not be proportional if it imposed far more of a restriction on state sovereignty than the Court believes is necessary to remedy state violations of § 1 of the Fourteenth Amendment.

Item B.3. *Equal State Sovereignty Under the Fifteenth Amendment.* In its opinion upholding the constitutionality of the Voting Rights Act of 1965, *South Carolina v. Katzenbach*, 383 U.S. 301 (1966), the Supreme Court held that statutes enacted under the Fifteenth Amendment must be rationally related to the goal of equal voting rights. *Shelby County v. Holder* (2013) elaborated on this position, holding that a voting rights law treating some states differently from others would lack rationality if it did not respond to "current needs."

2. Fourteenth Amendment Congruence and Proportionality: *City of Boerne v. Flores*

The decision in *City of Boerne v. Flores* (1997) announced an important limitation on Congress's powers under § 5 of the Fourteenth Amendment, namely that it authorized only statutes that are "congruent and proportional" to problems that the Supreme Court considers to be Fourteenth Amendment violations. In other words, it is not enough if Congress—but not the Supreme Court—deems a state action to be a violation of § 1 of the Fourteenth Amendment. Understanding *Boerne* (pronounced "Bernie") requires background about the Free Exercise Clause of the First Amendment.

■ WEBSITE
A fuller version of *City of Boerne* is available for download from this casebook's companion website, www.CaplanIntegratedConLaw.com.

The Free Exercise Clause and RFRA. The statute in *City of Boerne* arose from a disagreement about the meaning of the Free Exercise Clause of the First Amendment. A line of cases from the mid-20th century considered whether religiously observant people were constitutionally entitled to an exemption from generally applicable laws having the effect of restricting their religion (such as a ban on alcohol that would prevent Catholics and Jews from using wine in religious ceremonies). Although the results of such cases were not always consistent, the Supreme Court had for decades given a form of heightened scrutiny to such laws, saying that a burden on religious conduct would violate the Free Exercise Clause unless the absence of religious exemptions was narrowly tailored to a compelling government interest. *Sherbert v. Verner*, 374 U.S. 398 (1963); *Wisconsin v. Yoder*, 406 U.S. 205 (1972).

This changed with *Employment Division v. Smith*, 494 U.S. 872 (1990). Oregon had banned all possession and use of peyote, with no exception for the peyote ceremonies of the Native American Church. In a 5–4 decision that took most observers by surprise, the Supreme Court ruled that religious exemptions were not constitutionally required. Instead, "free exercise does not relieve an individual of the obligation to comply with a valid and neutral law of general applicability." *Employment Division v. Smith*, 494 U.S. 872 (1990). Thus, Oregon had no constitutional obligation to allow an exception for religious peyote ceremonies.

A huge range of voices across the political spectrum objected that *Smith* inadequately protected religious freedom, especially for minority religions. Congress responded with the Religious Freedom Restoration Act of 1993 (RFRA). The statute began with legislative findings setting forth a different view of religious freedom than the Supreme Court had announced in *Smith*.

1. The framers of the Constitution, recognizing free exercise of religion as an unalienable right, secured its protection in the First Amendment to the Constitution;

2. Laws "neutral" toward religion may burden religious exercise as surely as laws intended to interfere with religious exercise;

3. Governments should not substantially burden religious exercise without compelling justification;

4. In *Employment Division v. Smith*, 494 U.S. 872 (1990), the Supreme Court virtually eliminated the requirement that the government justify burdens on religious exercise imposed by laws neutral toward religion; and

5. The compelling interest test as set forth in prior Federal court rulings [such as *Sherbert v. Verner* (1963) and *Wisconsin v. Yoder* (1972)] is a workable test for striking sensible balances between religious liberty and competing prior governmental interests.

The substance of RFRA stated that no level of government (state or federal) may "substantially burden" a person's exercise of religion—even if the burden results from a religiously-neutral rule of general applicability—unless the government can demonstrate that the burden "is in furtherance of a compelling governmental interest" and "is the least restrictive means of furthering that compelling governmental interest."

Congress believed that RFRA was a constitutionally acceptable exercise of the Fourteenth Amendment Enforcement Clause. Its argument ran this way: (a) As a result of incorporation, free exercise of religion was a form of "liberty" that states could not deprive without due process of law under § 1 of the Fourteenth Amendment. (b) Section 5 of the Fourteenth Amendment authorized Congress to "enforce" that guarantee of liberty. (c) Congress's view of how religious liberty should be protected was a valid basis for legislating, even if the Supreme Court's view of the topic differed.

ITEMS TO CONSIDER WHILE READING *CITY OF BOERNE v. FLORES:*

A. *Under most enumerated powers,. Congress has wide discretion to choose its desired means, but under* City of Boerne, *a statute enacted under the Fourteenth Amendment Enforcement Clause must be "congruent and proportional" to the rights protected by § 1 of the Fourteenth Amendment. What explains the difference?*

B. *Why was RFRA not a "congruent and proportional" response to violations of § 1 of the Fourteenth Amendment?*

C. *To what extent is* Boerne *a decision about federalism? About separation of powers?*

City of Boerne v. Flores,

521 U.S. 507 (1997)

Justice Kennedy delivered the opinion of the Court [joined by Chief Justice Rehnquist and Justices Stevens, Thomas, Ginsburg and Scalia (except that Justice Scalia did not join part III-A-1)].

A decision by local zoning authorities to deny a church a building permit was challenged under the Religious Freedom Restoration Act of 1993 (RFRA or Act). The case calls into question the authority of Congress to enact RFRA. We conclude the statute exceeds Congress' power.

I

Situated on a hill in the city of Boerne, Texas, some 28 miles northwest of San Antonio, is St. Peter Catholic Church. Built in 1923, the church's structure replicates the mission style of the region's earlier history. The church seats about 230 worshipers, a number too small for its growing parish. Some 40 to 60 parishioners cannot be accommodated at some Sunday masses. In order to meet the needs of the congregation the Archbishop of San Antonio [Patrick Flores] gave permission to the parish to plan alterations to enlarge the building.

A few months later, the Boerne City Council passed an ordinance authorizing the city's Historic Landmark Commission to prepare a preservation plan with proposed historic landmarks and districts. Under the ordinance, the commission must preapprove construction affecting historic landmarks or buildings in a historic district.

St. Peter Catholic Church in Boerne, Texas

Soon afterwards, the Archbishop applied for a building permit so construction to enlarge the church could proceed. City authorities, relying on the ordinance and the designation of a historic district (which, they argued, included the church), denied the application. The Archbishop brought this suit challenging the permit denial in the United States District Court for the Western District of Texas.

The complaint contained various claims, but to this point the litigation has centered on RFRA and the question of its constitutionality. The Archbishop relied upon RFRA as one basis for relief from the refusal to issue the permit. The District Court concluded that by enacting RFRA Congress exceeded the scope of its enforcement power under § 5 of the Fourteenth Amendment. The court certified its order for interlocutory appeal and the Fifth Circuit reversed, finding RFRA to be constitutional. We granted certiorari, and now reverse.

II

Congress enacted RFRA in direct response to the Court's decision in *Employment Division v. Smith* (1990). . . . [The correctness of *Smith* was] debated by Members of Congress in hearings and floor debates. Many criticized the Court's reasoning, and this disagreement resulted in the passage of RFRA. . . .

III

A

. . . Congress relied on its Fourteenth Amendment enforcement power in enacting the most far-reaching and substantial of RFRA's provisions, those which impose its requirements on the States. . . . The parties disagree over whether RFRA is a proper exercise of Congress' § 5 power "to enforce" by "appropriate legislation" the constitutional guarantee [in § 1] that no State shall deprive any person of "life, liberty, or property, without due process of law" nor deny any person "equal protection of the laws."

In defense of the Act, respondent the Archbishop contends, with support from the United States, that RFRA is permissible enforcement legislation. Congress, it is said, is only protecting by legislation one of the liberties guaranteed by the Fourteenth Amendment's Due Process Clause, the free exercise of religion, beyond what is necessary under *Smith*. It is said the congressional decision to dispense with proof of deliberate or overt discrimination and instead concentrate on a law's effects accords with the settled understanding that § 5 includes the power to enact legislation designed to prevent, as well as remedy, constitutional violations. It is further contended that Congress' § 5 power is not limited to remedial or preventive legislation.

All must acknowledge that § 5 is a positive grant of legislative power to Congress. In *Ex parte Virginia*, 100 U.S. 339 (1879), we explained the scope of Congress' § 5 power in the following broad terms:

> Whatever legislation is appropriate, that is, adapted to carry out the objects the amendments have in view, whatever tends to enforce submission to the prohibitions they contain, and to secure to all persons the enjoyment of perfect equality of civil rights and the equal protection of the laws against State denial or invasion, if not prohibited, is brought within the domain of congressional power.

Legislation which deters or remedies constitutional violations can fall within the sweep of Congress' enforcement power even if in the process it prohibits conduct which is not itself unconstitutional and intrudes into legislative spheres of autonomy previously reserved to the States. For example, the Court upheld a suspension of literacy tests and similar voting requirements under Congress' parallel power to enforce the provisions of the Fifteenth Amendment as a measure to combat racial discrimination in voting, *South Carolina v. Katzenbach*, 383 U.S. 301 (1966), despite the facial constitutionality of the tests under *Lassiter v. Northampton County Bd. Of Elections*, 360 U.S. 45 (1959). We have also concluded that other measures protecting voting rights are within Congress' power to enforce the Fourteenth and Fifteenth Amendments, despite the burdens those measures placed on the States.

It is also true, however, that as broad as the congressional enforcement power is, it is not unlimited. In assessing the breadth of § 5's enforcement power, we begin with its text. Congress has been given the power "to enforce" the "provisions of this article." We agree with respondent, of course, that Congress can enact legislation under § 5 enforcing the constitutional right to the free exercise of religion. . . .

Congress' power under § 5, however, extends only to "enforcing" the provisions of the Fourteenth Amendment. The Court has described this power as "remedial." The design of the Amendment and the text of § 5 are inconsistent with the suggestion that Congress has the power to decree the substance of the Fourteenth Amendment's restrictions on the States. Legislation which alters the meaning of the Free Exercise Clause cannot be said to be enforcing the Clause. Congress does not enforce a constitutional right by changing what the right is. It has been given the power "to enforce," not the power to determine what constitutes a constitutional violation. Were it not so, what Congress would be enforcing would no longer be, in any meaningful sense, the "provisions of *this article* [the Fourteenth Amendment]."

While the line between measures that remedy or prevent unconstitutional actions and measures that make a substantive change in the governing law is not easy to discern, and Congress must have wide latitude in determining where it lies, the distinction exists and must be observed. There must be a congruence and proportionality between the injury to be prevented or remedied and the means adopted to that end. Lacking such a connection, legislation may become substantive in operation and effect. History and our case law support drawing the distinction, one apparent from the text of the Amendment.

1

[The drafting history of the Fourteenth Amendment supports our conclusion.]

2

The remedial and preventive nature of Congress' enforcement power, and the limitation inherent in the power, were confirmed in our earliest cases on the Fourteenth Amendment. In *The Civil Rights Cases* (1883), . . . the Court said that the Fourteenth Amendment did not authorize Congress to pass "general legislation upon the rights of the citizen, but corrective legislation, that is, such as may be necessary and proper for counteracting such laws as the States may adopt or enforce, and which, by the amendment, they are prohibited from making or enforcing." The power to "legislate generally" upon life, liberty, and property, as opposed to the "power to provide modes of redress" against offensive state action, was "repugnant" to the Constitution. [Our Court's early] treatment of Congress' § 5 power as corrective or preventive, not definitional, has not been questioned. . . .

3

. . . [Our case law indicates that] if Congress could define its own powers by altering the Fourteenth Amendment's meaning, no longer would the Constitution be "superior paramount law, unchangeable by ordinary means." It would be "on a level with ordinary legislative acts, and, like other acts, . . . alterable when the legislature shall please to alter it." *Marbury v. Madison* (1803). Under this approach, it is difficult to conceive of a principle that would limit congressional power. Shifting legislative majorities could change the Constitution and effectively circumvent the difficult and detailed amendment process contained in Article V.

We now turn to consider whether RFRA can be considered enforcement legislation under § 5 of the Fourteenth Amendment.

B

Respondent contends that RFRA is a proper exercise of Congress' remedial or preventive power. The Act, it is said, is a reasonable means of protecting the free exercise of religion as defined by *Smith*. It prevents and remedies laws which are enacted with the unconstitutional object of targeting religious beliefs and practices. To avoid the difficulty of proving such violations, it is said, Congress can simply invalidate any law which imposes a substantial burden on a religious practice unless it is justified by a compelling interest and is the least restrictive means of accomplishing that interest. If Congress can prohibit laws with discriminatory effects in order to prevent racial discrimination in violation of the Equal Protection Clause, then it can do the same, respondent argues, to promote religious liberty.

While preventive rules are sometimes appropriate remedial measures, there must be a congruence between the means used and the ends to be achieved. The appropriateness of remedial measures must be considered in light of the evil presented. Strong measures appropriate to address one harm may be an unwarranted response to another, lesser one. . . .

RFRA's legislative record lacks examples of modern instances of generally applicable laws passed because of religious bigotry. . . . Congress' concern was with the incidental burdens imposed, not the object or purpose of the legislation. This lack of support in the legislative record, however, is not RFRA's most serious shortcoming. Judicial deference, in most cases, is based not on the state of the legislative record

Congress compiles but on due regard for the decision of the body constitutionally appointed to decide. As a general matter, it is for Congress to determine the method by which it will reach a decision.

Regardless of the state of the legislative record, RFRA cannot be considered remedial, preventive legislation, if those terms are to have any meaning. RFRA is so out of proportion to a supposed remedial or preventive object that it cannot be understood as responsive to, or designed to prevent, unconstitutional behavior. It appears, instead, to attempt a substantive change in constitutional protections. Preventive measures prohibiting certain types of laws may be appropriate when there is reason to believe that many of the laws affected by the congressional enactment have a significant likelihood of being unconstitutional. Remedial legislation under § 5 should be adapted to the mischief and wrong which the Fourteenth Amendment was intended to provide against. . . .

The stringent test RFRA demands of state laws reflects a lack of proportionality or congruence between the means adopted and the legitimate end to be achieved. . . . Requiring a State to demonstrate a compelling interest and show that it has adopted the least restrictive means of achieving that interest is the most demanding test known to constitutional law. If "compelling interest" really means what it says, many laws will not meet the test. The test would open the prospect of constitutionally required religious exemptions from civic obligations of almost every conceivable kind. Laws valid under *Smith* would fall under RFRA without regard to whether they had the object of stifling or punishing free exercise. . . . [Under any interpretation of RFRA, the statute] would require searching judicial scrutiny of state law with the attendant likelihood of invalidation. This is a considerable congressional intrusion into the States' traditional prerogatives and general authority to regulate for the health and welfare of their citizens. . . .

Our national experience teaches that the Constitution is preserved best when each part of the Government respects both the Constitution and the proper actions and determinations of the other branches. When the Court has interpreted the Constitution, it has acted within the province of the Judicial Branch, which embraces the duty to say what the law is. When the political branches of the Government act against the background of a judicial interpretation of the Constitution already issued, it must be understood that in later cases and controversies the Court will treat its precedents with the respect due them under settled principles, including stare decisis, and contrary expectations must be disappointed. RFRA was designed to control cases and controversies, such as the one before us; but as the provisions of the federal statute here invoked are beyond congressional authority, it is this Court's precedent, not RFRA, which must control. . . .

Justice Stevens, concurring.

[Justice Stevens concurred in the majority opinion, but also argued that RFRA violated the Establishment Clause by favoring the religious over the non-religious.]

Justice Scalia, with whom Justice Stevens joins, concurring in part.

[Justice Scalia's concurrence responded to the dissents by arguing that *Smith* was properly decided.]

Justice O'Connor, with whom Justice Breyer joins [in part], dissenting.

. . . I agree with much of the reasoning set forth in Part III-A of the Court's opinion. Indeed, if I agreed with the Court's standard in *Smith*, I would join the opinion. As the Court's careful and thorough historical analysis shows, Congress lacks the power to decree the substance of the Fourteenth Amendment's restrictions on the States. Rather, its power under § 5 of the Fourteenth Amendment extends only to enforcing the Amendment's provisions. In short, Congress lacks the ability independently to define or expand the scope of constitutional rights by statute. Accordingly, whether Congress has exceeded its § 5 powers turns on whether there is a congruence and proportionality between the injury to be prevented or remedied and the means adopted to that end. This recognition does not, of course, in any way diminish Congress' obligation to draw its own conclusions regarding the Constitution's meaning. Congress, no less than this Court, is called upon to consider the requirements of the Constitution and to act in accordance with its dictates. But when it enacts legislation in furtherance of its delegated powers, Congress must make its judgments consistent with this Court's exposition of the Constitution and with the limits placed on its legislative authority by provisions such as the Fourteenth Amendment.

The Court's analysis of whether RFRA is a constitutional exercise of Congress' § 5 power, set forth in Part III-B of its opinion, is premised on the assumption that *Smith* correctly interprets the Free Exercise Clause. This is an assumption that I do not accept. [The remainder of the Justice O'Connor's opinion argued that *Smith* was incorrect.]

Justice Souter, dissenting.

[Justice Souter argued that *Smith* was incorrect.]

Justice Breyer, dissenting. [Omitted]

flashforward

1. ***Congruence and Proportionality for Equal Protection Legislation.*** Whether a statute enacted to enforce the Equal Protection Clause against state and local governments is congruent and proportional tends to correlate with whether the form of discrimination targeted by the statute would be subject to heightened scrutiny if it were challenged directly by a private plaintiff in court. For example, the Age Discrimination in Employment Act (ADEA) and the Americans with Disabilities Act (ADA) each target forms of discrimination that do not receive heightened scrutiny, and the Court found that applying these statutes against states was not "congruent and proportional" to recognized equal protection violations. *Kimel v. Florida Board of Regents*, 528 U.S. 62 (2000) (ADEA); *Board of Trustees v. Garrett*, 531 U.S. 356 (2001) (ADA). The Family Medical Leave Act seeks to alleviate sex discrimination, which does receive heightened scrutiny, and the Court upheld it as a congruent and proportional response to state discrimination permitted by § 5. *Nevada Dep't of Human Resources v. Hibbs*, 538 U.S. 721 (2003). For the modern approach to levels of scrutiny under the Equal Protection Clause, see Ch. 18.A.

2. ***RFRA and Federal Regulations.*** Although *City of Boerne* held that Congress could not rely on § 5 of the Fourteenth Amendment to require states to give extra protection for free exercise of religion, Congress may instruct federal agencies to give such protection. As a result, the portions of RFRA that apply to federal regulations continue to be enforced. See, e.g., *Burwell v. Hobby Lobby Stores, Inc.*, 573 U.S. 682 (2014) (RFRA requires a religious exception to a federal regulation mandating contraceptive coverage in employee health insurance plans).

3. ***Congruence and Proportionality Outside the Fourteenth Amendment.*** In *Eldred v. Ashcroft*, 537 U.S. 186 (2003), the Supreme Court declined to apply the Fourteenth Amendment "congruence and proportionality" standard to copyright laws enacted under Art. I, § 8, cl. 8. "We have never applied that standard outside the § 5 context," the Court said. "It does not hold sway for judicial review of legislation enacted, as copyright laws are, pursuant to Article I authorization."

3. Fifteenth Amendment Voting Rights: *Shelby County v. Holder*

The Fifteenth Amendment forbids denial or abridgement of the right to vote on the basis of race, and authorizes Congress to enact "appropriate" legislation to that end. From its earliest days, the term "appropriate" under the Fifteenth Amendment had been interpreted to allow Congress, "in the legitimate exercise of its legislative discretion" to pass "varied" laws suited to their situation and purpose. *United States v. Reese*, 92 U.S. 214 (1875) (federal prosecution of county officials who rejected ballots of Black voters). "Congress may use any rational means to effectuate the constitutional prohibition of racial discrimination in voting." *South Carolina v. Katzenbach*, 383 U.S. 301 (1966).

■ WEBSITE

A fuller version of *Shelby County* is available for download from this casebook's companion website, www.CaplanIntegratedConLaw.com.

Bloody Sunday and the Voting Rights Act. For most of the 20th century, there had been a palpable need for voting rights enforcement. To take one example, Dallas County, Alabama was 57% Black in 1961, but less than 1% of the Black population was registered to vote. No Black people held county office. Civil rights activists had made many attempts to register Black voters in recent years, but the efforts were as likely to lead to arrest as to successful registration. At one point in 1964, city leaders in Selma (the county seat of Dallas County) persuaded a state court judge to issue an injunction preventing any group of three or more civil rights workers from assembling anywhere within the city limits.

In early 1965, civil rights groups planned a march from Selma to the state capitol in Montgomery to present a petition in favor of voting rights legislation to Governor George Wallace. On March 7, 1965—"Bloody Sunday"—police attacked the marchers with horses, nightsticks, and tear gas as they tried to cross Selma's Edmund Pettus Bridge. Televised footage of the assault provoked nationwide outrage and drew more people to Alabama to continue the protest. Armed with a federal court injunction against further interference, over 25,000 marchers ultimately reached Montgomery on March 25. The events surrounding the march demonstrated the deep hostility to equal voting rights in many Southern communities, and convinced Congress to enact the federal Voting Rights Act of 1965 (the VRA).

Unlike previous federal voting rights efforts, the VRA did not limit itself to banning specific discriminatory voting practices. Instead, it authorized courts to invalidate any governmental practice—whatever form it took—that denied or abridged the right to vote "on account of race or color" (words borrowed directly from the Fifteenth Amendment). Moreover, Congress knew that one discriminatory practice could be easily replaced by another with similar effects; this had happened many times in the past. For this reason, § 5 required problem jurisdictions not to make any changes to their voting laws without first obtaining "preclearance" from the Department of Justice or a court, which would allow the change if it would not impact voting on the basis of race.

The preclearance obligation did not apply nationwide, but only to the jurisdictions identified in § 4(b), which were mostly—but not entirely—former slave states. The preclearance requirement, and its geographical application only to certain jurisdictions with discriminatory histories, was upheld as "appropriate" (rational, reasonable) Fifteenth Amendment legislation in *South Carolina v. Katzenbach*, 383 U.S. 301 (1966). Congress reauthorized the Voting Rights Act in 1970, 1975, 1982, and 2006, each time with wide bipartisan support and presidential endorsement.

Shelby County v. Holder. During these decades, the covered jurisdictions routinely objected to the selective preclearance requirement. They ultimately prevailed in *Shelby County v. Holder*, 570 U.S. 529 (2013). In a 5–4 decision, the Supreme Court's majority held that the passage of time made the formerly constitutional preclearance formula unconstitutional when Congress reauthorized the VRA in 2006.

The majority began by asserting that the "current burdens" the VRA imposed on the affected states "must be justified by current needs." The burdens were associated with federalism: federal oversight over the traditional state prerogative of conducting elections. Moreover, the majority considered it constitutionally dubious that preclearance was required for some states but not others. Turning to current needs, the majority concluded that by the time of the *Shelby County* litigation, minority voting strength in the states subject to preclearance resembled or even surpassed that in states not required to obtain preclearance. The majority conceded that the Fifteenth Amendment required only "rational means" to its ends, but it concluded that "the coverage formula met that test in 1965, but no longer does so."

The four-justice dissent argued that the majority had not displayed the deference to Congress demanded by a *McCulloch*-like standard. It was for Congress, not the courts, to decide if circumstances had changed to the point where the statute ought to change. In this case, Congress had made a laudable (or at the very least, rational) decision when it extended a successful law into the future. "Volumes of evidence supported Congress' determination that the prospect of retrogression was real. Throwing out preclearance when it has worked and is continuing to work to stop discriminatory changes is like throwing away your umbrella in a rainstorm because you are not getting wet."

Thus far, the reasoning in *Shelby County* has not been applied outside its Fifteenth Amendment voting rights context.

Chapter Recap

A. The scope of the enumerated powers of Congress is a frequently recurring question in constitutional law.

B. A broad interpretation of enumerated powers gives Congress more leeway to legislate. This corresponds to less authority for the federal judiciary (which must adopt a general posture of deference) and for states (whose ability to legislate will face more limitations as a result of preemption). Conversely, a narrow interpretation of enumerated powers gives Congress less leeway to legislate, and more authority to the federal judiciary and the states.

C. Each of the enumerated powers explored in this chapter—based on the Taxing Clause, the Spending Clause, the Commerce Clause, the Necessary and Proper Clause, and the Civil Rights Enforcement Clauses—has its own case law. In general, the modern Supreme Court interprets enumerated powers fairly broadly. But with regard to federal powers that have the greatest potential impact on state prerogatives—namely, the Commerce Clause and the Civil Rights Enforcement Clauses—the Supreme Court has in recent decades announced limits on the powers that are designed primarily to maintain state authority.

CHAPTER 16

Separation of Powers

In The Federalist #47, James Madison wrote that "the accumulation of all powers, legislative, executive and judicial in the same hands, whether of one, a few, or many, and whether hereditary, self-appointed, or elective, may justly be pronounced the very definition of tyranny." To avoid an over-concentration of power, the Constitution splits power in several ways. The federal government was split from the states. The federal government was also split into branches. And by placing some individual rights beyond the reach of government altogether, control over daily life was split between the government and the people.

Separation of Powers as a Structural Limit on Federal Action

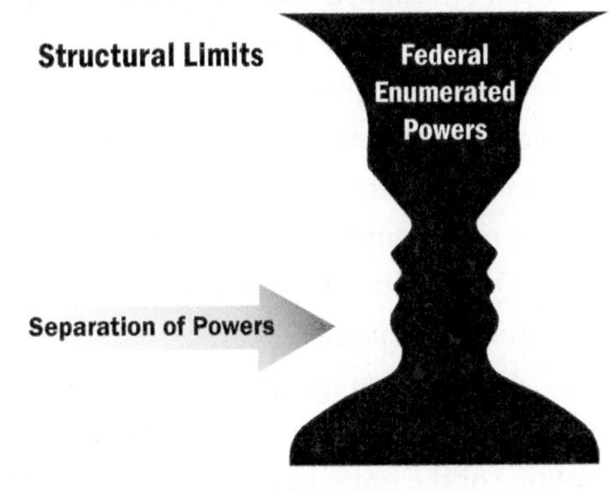

When modern cases speak of *separation of powers*, they usually refer to the division of the federal government into three branches. (A similar separation of powers exists within state governments, with the details controlled by state law.) Separation of powers is a structural limit akin to supremacy and federalism, because it poses a "who decides" question. A particular governmental action might be allowed in general, but be unconstitutional if performed by the wrong branch of government.

In the diagram on this page, the federal government is presented as a single unit. Another way to visualize some separation of powers problems is to depict each branch of government separately, with some actions falling either inside or outside the powers of each branch. As shown on the next page, the power to declare war is within the power of the Legislative branch, but outside the powers of the Executive and Judicial branches. This conclusion arises from text in different parts of the Constitution. Art. I, § 8, cl. 11 says Congress shall have the power "to declare war." Art. II, § 2 says the President "shall be commander in chief of the army and navy of the United States," thus having power to conduct the war that Congress declares. Art. III, § 1 says "the judicial power of the United States shall be vested" in a body of judges, and no reasonable interpretation of "the judicial power" would include the ability to declare war.

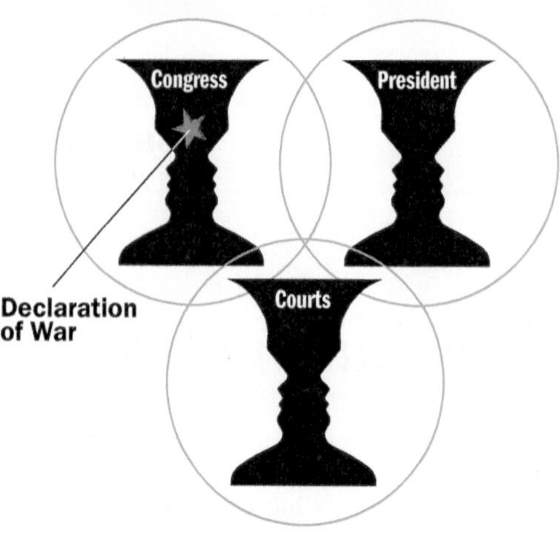

Not all separation of powers questions are as easy. The Framers intentionally chose a system of incomplete separation of powers, characterized by areas of overlap where more than one branch could claim some authority. If any one player threatened to become too powerful, others would have an incentive to respond. As Madison envisioned it in The Federalist #51: "The great security against a gradual concentration of the several powers in the same [branch], consists in giving to those who administer each [branch], the necessary constitutional means, and personal motives, to resist encroachments of the others. . .Ambition must be made to counteract ambition." A structure that includes some overlapping powers creates built-in opportunities for the branches to act as "checks and balances" against each other. Or as political scientist Edward Corwin put it, the Constitution creates "an invitation to struggle."

Because struggle (or phrased more optimistically, healthy competition) is part of the constitutional design, not every instance of inter-branch conflict means that one of the branches has violated the Constitution. Instead, it may well mean that the branches are using the tools the Constitution gives them to resolve their policy disagreements. As a result, most battles between the President and Congress will be resolved politically, and not through court decisions. Judicial opinions devoted solely to separation of powers are fairly rare, and those that exist tend to be fact-specific. With that in mind, the goal of this chapter is not to present firmly-crystallized rules, but to teach the language of separation of powers as it is spoken by judges and constitutional lawyers.

A. Kickstarter: Separation of Powers

DISCLAIMER: *This Kickstarter is a checklist to help identify relevant issues. It is not a list of elements. Nothing requires judges to write their opinions (or lawyers to write their briefs) in Kickstarter order.*

Separation of Powers **kickstarter**

USE WHEN: *One branch of government takes action beyond its authority.*

A. *TEXT: Does the Constitution's text explicitly or impliedly assign this function exclusively to a single branch?*

B. *STRUCTURE: Would it be inconsistent with the Constitution's structure to uphold the branch's action? Consider, among other things:*

   1. *Is a branch seeking to act outside its usual areas of responsibility?*
   2. *Will the challenged action of one branch interfere with the ability of other branches to act in their usual areas of responsibility?*
   3. *Does one branch have a greater institutional competence for this type of action?*

C. *OTHER METHODS: Consider other methods of constitutional reasoning, including precedent, history, consequences, and values.*

KICKSTARTER USER'S GUIDE

Separation of powers is a general standard, not a precise legal rule. As a result, the disclaimer before this Kickstarter should be heeded even more closely than usual: There is no single correct method for approaching separation of powers problems. With that said, the usual methods of constitutional reasoning frequently appear in separation of powers cases, and for that reason they are the backbone of this Kickstarter.

Item A. *Textual Assignment.* Sometimes the text of the Constitution is sufficiently clear on its own to resolve some separation of powers questions. For example, if the President sought to dictate when Congress voted on a bill, it would violate Art. I, § 5, cl. 2, which says that "each house" of Congress—not the President—"may determine the rules of its proceedings." If Congress were to issue a pardon to a person convicted of a federal crime, it would not be authorized by any enumerated legislative power, and would also conflict with Art. II, § 2, cl. 1, which says the President "shall have power to grant reprieves and pardons for offences against the United States."

Recent attempts to alter the customary lawmaking process have violated separation of powers for reasons that can be readily linked to portions of the Constitution's text. In *INS v. Chadha*, 462 U.S. 919 (1983), Congress created an executive branch agency and authorized it to enact regulations. This is a typical arrangement, except that in *Chadha* Congress also claimed the ability to reverse the agency's regulations by a majority vote of a single house. The Supreme Court held that this "legislative veto" of the agency's action was a form of Congressional lawmaking, and hence must use the textually defined lawmaking procedures of bicameralism and presentment from Art. I, § 7, cl. 2. In *Clinton v. City of New York*, 524 U.S. 417 (1998), Congress purported to allow the President to selectively veto only some portions of a budget. The Supreme Court held that this "line-item veto" violated the Constitution's system for Presidential vetoes of legislation.

The previous examples could all be resolved by reference to relatively concrete and specific passages of text. On a more general level, the text assigns broad roles for each branch through language known as the Vesting Clauses.

- "All legislative Powers herein granted shall be vested in a Congress of the United States, which shall consist of a Senate and House of Representatives." Art. I, § 1.
- "The executive Power shall be vested in a President of the United States of America." Art. II, § 1.
- "The judicial Power of the United States shall be vested in one supreme Court, and in such inferior Courts as the Congress may from time to time ordain and establish." Art. III, § 1. See also Art. I, § 8, cl. 9 (Congressional power to create inferior courts).

The Vesting Clauses do not define the crucial terms "legislative," "executive," and "judicial," but the basic divisions can be illustrated with criminal statutes. The legislature establishes the government's policy, by declaring that a certain act is illegal. The executive carries out that policy by investigating and prosecuting persons suspected of committing the crime. The judiciary resolves the dispute between the prosecutor and the defendant over the question of guilt.

As helpful as the Vesting Clauses may be for setting the stage, the labels they contain will not resolve all questions. Take a mundane example: whether the housekeeping staff at the White House should use eco-friendly cleaning products. The President could argue that this falls within the executive power: the White House is the executive mansion and office building; many events that the Constitution assigns to the President occur there, including receiving ambassadors, Art. II, § 3. Thus "the executive power" vested in the President should include the power to decide how to clean the White House. But Congress also has "the legislative power" to mandate how federal office buildings are cleaned. Its source of enumerated power would include the Spending Clause—since money would be used to hire the cleaners and buy the products—and the Necessary and Proper Clause, which allows Congress to pass laws to carry into execution the powers that the Constitution vests in "any department or officer" of the United States. Art. I, § 8, cl. 18. In short, Congress can legitimately claim that its legislative power gives it at least some say over how the executive power is exercised. In this setting, like many others, it becomes necessary to go beyond the text to consider other factors.

Item B. *Structural Concerns.* At its heart, separation of powers is a structural concern. While the text indicates what the structure is, it is also possible to reason from the structure towards outcomes in particular cases. There is no fixed list of ways to reason from structure, but several of them suggest themselves.

Item B.1. *Arrogation of Power.* A branch may violate separation of powers if it performs functions beyond its assigned powers. This is sometimes referred to as "arrogation" of power, or "aggrandizement" of a branch. In cases where the text controls, it is an easy matter to detect arrogation. If Congress were to issue a pardon, it would be arrogating one of the President's powers to itself. Arrogation is more debatable where the text is silent or ambiguous.

Item B.2. *Interference with Another Branch.* A branch may violate separation of powers if it acts within its usual areas of responsibility, but in ways that hinder other branches in their usual areas of responsibility. In *United States v. Nixon*, 418 U.S. 683 (1974), for example, the judicial branch issued a subpoena, a function clearly within its powers. But since the subpoena was directed to the President, it had the potential to hinder the autonomous exercise of executive powers. Courts consider the extent of interference on a case-by-case basis.

Item B.3. *Institutional Competence.* A relatively modern approach to separation of powers asks which branch can most effectively perform the contested function. Consider a policy question that ultimately involves line-drawing, like choosing a tax rate or a speed limit. Courts are not well situated for this type of policy decision, because judges are supposed to interpret laws through legal reasoning, not pick arbitrary numbers (or, on a multi-member court, negotiate their way to a compromise). A single decision-maker like the President is also not ideal for this kind of decision, because there is no guarantee that the person will consider all of the competing interests or carefully deliberate on the correct result. But a legislature is institutionally competent to make such judgments. It consists of many members who represent different regions of the nation, so they will bring more competing views to the table. They must deliberate with each other to reach an agreement that is acceptable to a majority. Yet they are not required (as a court would be) to write a reasoned opinion justifying their ultimate decision as a product of logic rather than politics.

Item C. *Other Methods of Reasoning.* Text and structure tend to dominate separation of powers cases, but other methods of reasoning are available and frequently used.

Courts will of course consider relevant precedent where it exists. Where it does not, the history of pre- and post-ratification practices of the branches may be relevant. Courts may focus on the consequences for constitutional structure (as well as the inevitable concern over the consequences flowing from the immediate decision). In a similar way, courts considering values tend to emphasize those values that relate to constitutional structure. For many justices, separation of powers is itself an independent constitutional value—of equal importance to values like freedom and fairness.

B. Tension Between the Judicial and Legislative Branches

Virtually any case involving judicial review of legislation can be portrayed in terms of separation of powers. Although separation of powers was not discussed in so many words in *West Coast Hotel v. Parrish* (1937) and *U.S. v. Darby* (1941), the repudiation of the *Lochner* era during the New Deal was all about the relative powers of Congress and Court. In *West Virginia State Board of Education v. Barnette* (1943), Justice Frankfurter felt the separation of powers concerns strongly, even in a case involving individual rights enumerated in the First Amendment. "Our function [is not] comparable to that of a legislature," he wrote in his dissent, "[nor] are we free to act as though we were a super-legislature." Debates within the Supreme Court about how much authority the judiciary should have can be found in virtually every difficult constitutional case. Like federalism, separation of powers can be everywhere—if a Court decides to look for it.

***Lochner* Era: Judicial Power Interfering with the Political Branches**

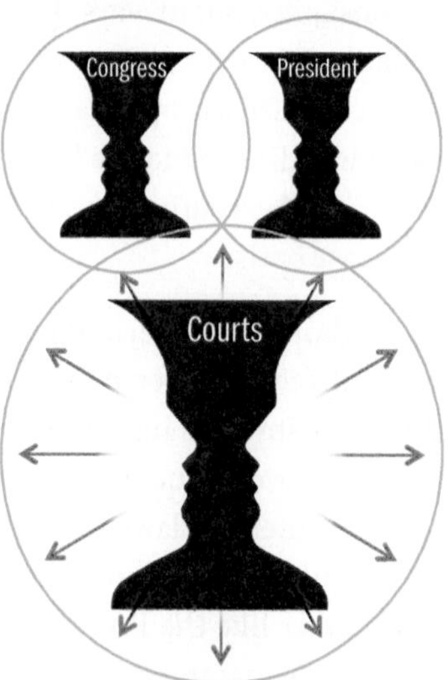

Less common are situations where Congress impermissibly interferes with the judicial power. As a general matter, Congress has considerable authority over the federal courts. Art. I, § 8, cl. 9 allows Congress to create lower courts, including laws defining subject matter jurisdiction and venue (subject to some limits found in Art. III, § 2). As explained in Ch. 14.D, the Necessary and Proper Clause authorizes Congress to pass laws that allow other "departments or officers" of the federal government to perform their functions, such as a law deciding how many justices should sit on the Supreme Court. No federal judge takes office without the advise and consent of the Senate. And of course, Congress is in charge of spending for all three branches. Yet there is a point at which Congressional control over the federal courts would be so complete that there would no longer be a separate and independent judicial branch. *Plaut v. Spendthrift Farm, Inc.*, 514 U.S. 211 (1995) was one of the rare examples of this problem. Congress passed a law that would allow the losing parties in litigation to reopen final judgments of federal courts. The Supreme Court held that this violated separation of powers: after the judiciary decides a case, Congress cannot overrule that result. Nor could Congress dictate how courts exercise the judicial power in the midst of litigation. As stated in *Bank Markazi v. Peterson*, 578 U.S. 212 (2016): "Congress could not enact a statute directing that, in *Smith v. Jones*, Smith wins."

***Plaut v. Spendthrift Farm*: Congressional Power Interfering with the Judiciary**

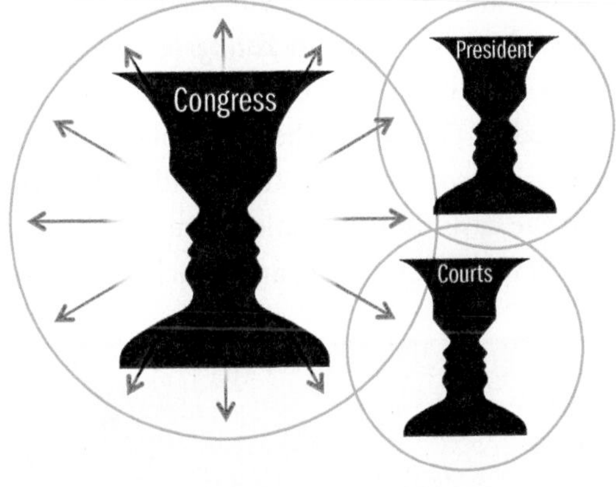

C. Tension Between the Legislative and Executive Branches

The Constitution does not provide much detail about the powers of the President. The Art. II Vesting Clause begins by saying that "the executive power" shall be vested in a President, but it does not attempt to define what "the executive power" is. Sections 2 and 3 of Art. II specify some powers that are within the President's discretion: acting as commander-in-chief of the armed forces; seeking opinions from the Cabinet; granting reprieves and pardons; negotiating treaties; appointing and commissioning ambassadors, judges, and other federal officers, and recommending legislation to Congress. Art. II, § 3 also contains an even shorter list of things the President "shall" do: give a State of the Union message; receive ambassadors from other nations; and "take care that the laws be faithfully executed."

The Constitution's abbreviated description of the Presidency, combined with an American public that generally favors an active leader, has tended to result in Presidents claiming that "the executive power" is not limited to the specific tasks in Art. II. They argue that they should be able to do anything that is "executive" in nature, even if not enumerated. This approach has potential to conflict with any Congress that wishes to pursue its power under the Necessary and Proper Clause to make laws governing the executive branch.

If the aims of Congress and the President diverge, there are two potentially useful ways to think about the problem. One asks whether the Constitution assigns a particular power exclusively to one branch or the other, or if instead the allocation of power is concurrent or unclear. The other, suggested in Justice Jackson's concurrence in *Youngstown Sheet & Tube Co. v. Sawyer* (1952) (often called *The Steel Seizure Case*), asks how the President's actions differ from policies adopted by Congress. The following chart combines the two approaches, using Justice Jackson's method that divides executive actions into three zones. As you read the cases in this section, use the chart to consider which branch ought to prevail in each situation, and which cases fit where.

CONSTITUTION'S ASSIGNMENT OF POWER	ZONE 1: PRESIDENT ACTS CONSISTENTLY WITH STATUTE	ZONE 2: PRESIDENT ACTS WHEN CONGRESS IS SILENT	ZONE 3: PRESIDENT ACTS CONTRARY TO STATUTE
Exclusively Legislative			
Concurrent or Unclear			
Exclusively Executive			

1. Executive Action Without Statutory Authorization: *The Steel Seizure Case*

Executive Orders. In the abstract, an "executive order" is any instruction from the President to the people who work in the executive branch. If the President orally tells the White House janitors to use eco-friendly cleaning products, this would be an executive order, just as any business executive could issue orders to staff. As the term is typically used in the modern federal government, an "Executive Order" is a written document from the President containing instructions on how executive branch agencies are to go about their business. They tend to be carefully written with the input of counsel, and are published in the Federal Register. Congress sometimes directly authorizes the President to make executive orders on specified subjects. See, e.g., 8 U.S.C. § 1182(f) (President may issue a "proclamation" to impose restrictions on the entry of specified groups of aliens into the United States); 50 U.S.C. § 1702 (President may give "instructions" to freeze United States assets of foreign governments or nationals). Even in the absence of specific authorization, the ability to give instructions to subordinates is understood to be part of the executive power.

Presidents may issue orders to subordinates that will affect how the government treats private citizens. In Executive Order 10925 (1961), President Kennedy ordered all executive branch departments to ensure that their contracts with outside vendors contained clauses forbidding race discrimination and requiring agencies to take "affirmative action" to eliminate race discrimination. This order was issued several years before Congress enacted Title VI of the Civil Rights Act of 1964, which forbade race discrimination in any program receiving federal funds. In Executive Order 13672 (2014), President Obama directed federal agencies not to discriminate in employment on the basis of sexual orientation. As of this writing, Congress has passed no law against such discrimination, but the President chose to eliminate it from agencies under his control.

flashback

The internment of Japanese-Americans during World War II flowed from Executive Order 9066 (1942), where President Roosevelt authorized the military to remove Japanese-Americans from their homes. The Supreme Court was never called upon to decide if the internment violated separation of powers, because Congress swiftly passed statutes enforcing the Executive Order. See Ch. 10.B.2. Of course, even if an Executive Order does not violate separation of powers, it may be unconstitutional for other reasons.

Wartime Seizure of Defense Industries. The US government does not, as a rule, operate its own manufacturing plants, so it must purchase war supplies from private industry. If the necessary supplies are unavailable due to strikes, lockouts, or other labor unrest, the government could face a shortage of military equipment. To deal with this problem, the federal government has sometimes seized control of important factories when shutdowns appeared imminent. The seizures allowed the government to operate the factories on its own terms.

During World War I, President Wilson seized many businesses, sometimes acting under statutes specifically authorizing the seizures, and sometimes through executive orders. During World War II, after several industry seizures that occurred without statutory authorization, Congress passed the War Labor Disputes Act of 1943, authorizing President Roosevelt to take similar action. There was a political subtext to these seizures: The Presidents during these wars were Democrats whose electoral constituencies included organized labor. During the seizures, the government often prevented strikes by raising wages for employees, and then released the industries back to their owners only after receiving assurances that the new and more expensive labor contracts would be honored.

After World War II, Congress enacted the Taft-Hartley Act of 1947, a major renovation of the law governing labor unions. Among other things, it replaced the previous statutes authorizing individualized industrial seizures with a more general framework that allowed the President to prevent, for 80 days, any threatened strike that would "imperil the national health or safety." During that cooling-off period, negotiations could continue in hopes of averting a strike. Other statutes relevant to seizures included a portion of the Selective Service Act amendments of 1948 (authorizing the President to seize plants that fail to honor outstanding government contracts) and the Defense Production Act of 1951 (authorizing the President to condemn property necessary to the national defense).

Truman and the Steel Plants. In late 1951, during the Korean War, the United Steelworkers of America announced that it would seek a new contract with steel companies. Despite a government-imposed price ceiling during the war, the steel mills were quite profitable and the union believed the industry could afford a raise. The mill owners refused to negotiate unless the government raised the price ceiling, which it was unwilling to do. After several months of stalemate, the Union announced on April 4, 1952 that a strike would begin on April 9.

On April 8, President Truman issued Executive Order 10340, which in relevant part read as follows:

> 1. The Secretary of Commerce is hereby authorized and directed to take possession of all or such of the plants, facilities, and other property of the companies named in the list attached hereto, or any part thereof, as he may deem necessary in the interests of national defense; and to operate or to arrange for the operation thereof and to do all things necessary for, or incidental to, such operation. . . .
>
> 3. The Secretary of Commerce shall determine and prescribe terms and conditions of employment under which the plants, facilities, and other properties possession of which is taken pursuant to this order shall be operated. The Secretary of Commerce shall recognize the rights of workers to bargain collectively through representatives of their own choosing and to engage in

> concerted activities for the purpose of collective bargaining, adjustment of grievances, or other mutual aid or protection, provided that such activities do not interfere with the operation of such plants, facilities, and other properties.
>
> 4. Except so far as the Secretary of Commerce shall otherwise provide from time to time, the managements of the plants, facilities, and other properties possession of which is taken pursuant to this order shall continue their functions, including the collection and disbursement of funds in the usual and ordinary course of business in the names of their respective companies and by means of any instrumentalities used by such companies. . . .
>
> 6. Whenever in the judgment of the Secretary of Commerce further possession and operation by him of any plant, facility, or other property is no longer necessary or expedient in the interest of national defense, and the Secretary has reason to believe that effective future operation is assured, he shall return the possession and operation of such plant, facility, or other property to the company in possession and control thereof at the time possession was taken under this order.

In a message to Congress, Truman said that he considered this action to be within his executive power, but he indicated willingness to comply with any decisions that Congress chose to make: "The Congress can, if it wishes, reject the course of action I have followed in this matter." Congress took no action in response.

For the steel companies, Paragraph 4 of the Executive Order meant business as usual in the short run. But they feared that under Paragraph 3, the government would negotiate new contracts with the Union, which the companies would need to accept if they wished to have their factories returned to them under Paragraph 6. As a result, they filed suit against the Executive Order the day it was issued.

At oral argument on the motion for a preliminary injunction, attorneys for the President staked out an aggressive legal position. Instead of arguing against an injunction on equitable grounds, or arguing that the President's actions fell within the spirit of existing statutes, they argued that the seizure was authorized by the President's inherent power to take necessary action in times of emergency.

> Judge Pine: So you contend the Executive has unlimited power in time of emergency?
>
> Counsel: He has the power to take such action as is necessary to meet the emergency.
>
> Judge Pine: If the emergency is great, [the Executive power] is unlimited, is it?
>
> Counsel: I suppose if you carry it to its logical conclusion, that is true. But I do want to point out that there are two limitations on the Executive power. One is the ballot box and the other is impeachment.

The trial court granted a preliminary injunction against the seizure on April 30. The Supreme Court granted expedited review.

ITEMS TO CONSIDER WHILE READING *YOUNGSTOWN SHEET & TUBE CO. v. SAWYER*:

A. *Should the President have power to take emergency actions not authorized by statute?*

B. *Justice Jackson's concurrence is the most famous and most frequently quoted portion of the* Youngstown *decision, especially the portion where he considers three different types of executive action (action consistent with statute, action where no statute exists, and action contrary to statute). Which is the right category for the steel seizure? Use the chart on page 538.*

C. *Justice Black's majority opinion finds that seizure of a factory is inherently legislative. What makes it legislative? And why has the majority opinion proven less influential than Justice Jackson's concurrence?*

D. *What distinguishes the various concurring and dissenting opinions?*

Youngstown Sheet & Tube Co. v. Sawyer,

343 U.S. 579 (1952)

Justice Black delivered the opinion of the Court [joined by Justices Frankfurter, Jackson, Burton, and Douglas].

We are asked to decide whether the President was acting within his constitutional power when he issued an order directing the Secretary of Commerce [Charles Sawyer] to take possession of and operate most of the Nation's steel mills. The mill owners argue that the President's order amounts to lawmaking, a legislative function which the Constitution has expressly confided to the Congress and not to the President. The Government's position is that the order was made on findings of the President that his action was necessary to avert a national catastrophe which would inevitably result from a stoppage of steel production, and that in meeting this grave emergency the President was acting within the aggregate of his constitutional powers as the Nation's Chief Executive and the Commander in Chief of the Armed Forces of the United States. . . .

I [Omitted.]

II

The President's power, if any, to issue the order must stem either from an act of Congress or from the Constitution itself. There is no statute that expressly authorizes the President to take possession of property as he did here. Nor is there any act of Congress to which our attention has been directed from which such a power can fairly be implied. Indeed, we do not understand the Government to rely on statutory authorization for this seizure. There are two statutes which do authorize the President to take both personal and real property under certain conditions [the Selective Service Act amendments of 1948 and the Defense Production Act of 1951]. However, the Government admits that these conditions were not met and that the President's order was not rooted in either of the statutes. The Government refers to the seizure provisions of one of these statutes (§ 201(b) of the Defense Production Act) as "much too cumbersome, involved, and time-consuming for the crisis which was at hand."

Moreover, the use of the seizure technique to solve labor disputes in order to prevent work stoppages was not only unauthorized by any congressional enactment; prior to this controversy, Congress had refused to adopt that method of settling labor disputes. When the Taft-Hartley Act was under consideration in 1947, Congress rejected an amendment which would have authorized such governmental seizures in cases of emergency. Apparently it was thought that the technique of seizure, like that of compulsory arbitration, would interfere with the process of collective bargaining. Consequently, the plan Congress adopted in that Act did not provide for seizure under any circumstances. Instead, the plan sought to bring about settlements by use of the customary devices of mediation, conciliation, investigation by boards of inquiry, and public reports. In some instances temporary injunctions were authorized to provide cooling-off periods. All this failing, unions were left free to strike after a secret vote by employees as to whether they wished to accept their employers' final settlement offer.

It is clear that if the President had authority to issue the order he did, it must be found in some provisions of the Constitution. And it is not claimed that express constitutional language grants this power to the President. The contention is that presidential power should be implied from the aggregate of his powers under the Constitution. Particular reliance is placed on provisions in Article II which say that "the executive power shall be vested in a President;" that "he shall take care that the laws be faithfully executed"; and that he "shall be Commander in Chief of the army and navy of the United States."

The order cannot properly be sustained as an exercise of the President's military power as Commander in Chief of the Armed Forces. The Government attempts to do so by citing a number of cases upholding broad powers in military commanders engaged in day-to-day fighting in a theater of war. Such cases need not concern us here. Even though "theater of war" be an expanding concept, we cannot with faithfulness to our constitutional system hold that the Commander in Chief of the Armed Forces has the ultimate power as such to take possession of private property in order to keep labor disputes from stopping production. This is a job for the Nation's lawmakers, not for its military authorities.

Nor can the seizure order be sustained because of the several constitutional provisions that grant executive power to the President. In the framework of our Constitution, the President's power to see that the laws are faithfully executed refutes the idea that he is to be a lawmaker. The Constitution limits his functions in the lawmaking process to the recommending of laws he thinks wise and the vetoing of laws he thinks bad. And the Constitution is neither silent nor equivocal about who shall make laws which the President is to execute. The first section of the first article says that "All legislative Powers herein granted shall be vested in a Congress of the United States." After granting many powers to the Congress, Article I goes on to provide that Congress may "make all Laws which shall be necessary and proper for carrying into Execution the foregoing Powers and all other Powers vested by this Constitution in the Government of the United States, or in any Department or Officer thereof."

The President's order does not direct that a congressional policy be executed in a manner prescribed by Congress—it directs that a presidential policy be executed in a manner prescribed by the President. The preamble of the order itself, like that of many statutes, sets out reasons why the President believes certain policies should be adopted, proclaims these policies as rules of conduct to be followed, and again, like a statute, authorizes a government official to promulgate additional rules and regulations consistent with the policy proclaimed and needed to carry that policy into execution. The power of Congress to adopt such public policies as those proclaimed by the order is beyond question. It can authorize the taking of private property for public use. It can make laws regulating the relationships between employers and employees, prescribing rules designed to settle labor disputes, and fixing wages and working conditions in certain fields of our economy. The Constitution did not subject this law-making power of Congress to presidential or military supervision or control.

It is said that other Presidents without congressional authority have taken possession of private business enterprises in order to settle labor disputes. But even if this be true, Congress has not thereby lost its exclusive constitutional authority to make laws necessary and proper to carry out the powers vested by the Constitution "in the Government of the United States, or in any Department or Officer thereof."

The Founders of this Nation entrusted the law making power to the Congress alone in both good and bad times. It would do no good to recall the historical events, the fears of power and the hopes for freedom that lay behind their choice. Such a review would but confirm our holding that this seizure order cannot stand.

[Statement of] Justice Frankfurter. [Omitted.]

Youngstown Sheet & Tube Co. v. Sawyer

Justice Jackson, concurring in the judgment and opinion of the Court.

That comprehensive and undefined presidential powers hold both practical advantages and grave dangers for the country will impress anyone who [like myself] has served as legal adviser to a President in time of transition and public anxiety. While an interval of detached reflection may temper teachings of that experience, they probably are a more realistic influence on my views than the conventional materials of judicial decision which seem unduly to accentuate doctrine and legal fiction. . . .

A judge, like an executive adviser, may be surprised at the poverty of really useful and unambiguous authority applicable to concrete problems of executive power as they actually present themselves. Just what our forefathers did envision, or would have envisioned had they foreseen modern conditions, must be divined from materials almost as enigmatic as the dreams Joseph was called upon to interpret for Pharaoh. A century and a half of partisan debate and scholarly speculation yields no net result but only supplies more or less apt quotations from respected sources on each side of any question. They largely cancel each other. And court decisions are indecisive because of the judicial practice of dealing with the largest questions in the most narrow way.

BIOGRAPHY

ROBERT H. JACKSON (1892–1954) entered the practice of law through the old-fashioned path of apprenticeship, and was the last member of the US Supreme Court not to have a law degree. In his earliest cases in upstate New York, farmers might clash over the health of a horse or the breed of a cow, with verdicts as low as $15. As solicitor general and then attorney general under President Franklin D. Roosevelt, he pursued the winning legal theories that upheld New Deal legislation after 1937. Roosevelt appointed Jackson to the Supreme Court in 1941. After the end of World War II in 1945, Jackson took an unusual leave of absence from the Court to act as chief US prosecutor of Nazi war criminals at the Nuremberg trials.

The actual art of governing under our Constitution does not and cannot conform to judicial definitions of the power of any of its branches based on isolated clauses or even single Articles torn from context. While the Constitution diffuses power the better to secure liberty, it also contemplates that practice will integrate the dispersed powers into a workable government. It enjoins upon its branches separateness but interdependence, autonomy but reciprocity. Presidential powers are not fixed but fluctuate, depending upon their disjunction or conjunction with those of Congress. We may well begin by a somewhat over-simplified grouping of practical situations in which a President may doubt, or others may challenge, his powers, and by distinguishing roughly the legal consequences of this factor of relativity.

1. When the President acts pursuant to an express or implied authorization of Congress, his authority is at its maximum, for it includes all that he possesses in his own right plus all that Congress can delegate. In these circumstances, and in these only, may he be said (for what it may be worth), to personify the federal sovereignty. If his act is held unconstitutional under these circumstances, it usually means that the Federal Government as an undivided whole lacks power. A seizure executed by the President pursuant to an Act of Congress would be supported by the strongest of presumptions and the widest latitude of judicial interpretation, and the burden of persuasion would rest heavily upon any who might attack it.

2. When the President acts in absence of either a congressional grant or denial of authority, he can only rely upon his own independent powers, but there is a zone of twilight in which he and Congress may have concurrent authority, or in which its distribution is uncertain. Therefore, congressional inertia, indifference or quiescence may sometimes, at least as a practical matter, enable, if not invite, measures on independent presidential responsibility. In this area, any actual test of power is likely to depend on the imperatives of events and contemporary imponderables rather than on abstract theories of law.

3. When the President takes measures incompatible with the expressed or implied will of Congress, his power is at its lowest ebb, for then he can rely only upon his own constitutional powers minus any constitutional powers of Congress over the matter. Courts can sustain exclusive Presidential control in such a case only by disabling the Congress from acting upon the subject. Presidential claim to a power at once so conclusive and preclusive must be scrutinized with caution, for what is at stake is the equilibrium established by our constitutional system.

Into which of these classifications does this executive seizure of the steel industry fit? It is eliminated from the first by admission, for it is conceded that no congressional authorization exists for this seizure. . . .

Can it then be defended under flexible tests available to the second category? It seems clearly eliminated from that class because Congress has not left seizure of private property an open field but has covered it by three statutory policies inconsistent with this seizure. In cases where the purpose is to supply needs of the Government itself, two courses are provided: one, seizure of a plant which fails to comply with obligatory orders placed by the Government [under the Selective Service Act], another, condemnation of facilities, including temporary use under the power of eminent domain [under the Defense Production Act]. The third is applicable where it is the general economy of the country that is to be protected rather than exclusive governmental interests [under the Taft-Hartley Act]. None of these were invoked. In choosing a different and inconsistent way of his own, the President cannot claim that it is necessitated or invited by failure of Congress to legislate upon the occasions, grounds and methods for seizure of industrial properties.

This leaves the current seizure to be justified only by the severe tests under the third grouping, where it can be supported only by any remainder of executive power after subtraction of such powers as Congress may have over the subject. In short, we can sustain the President only by holding that seizure of such strike-bound industries is within his domain and beyond control by Congress. Thus, this Court's first review of such seizures occurs under circumstances which leave Presidential power most vulnerable to attack and in the least favorable of possible constitutional postures.

I did not suppose, and I am not persuaded, that history leaves it open to question, at least in the courts, that the executive branch, like the Federal Government as a whole, possesses only delegated powers. The purpose of the Constitution was not only to grant power, but to keep it from getting out of hand. However, because the President does not enjoy unmentioned powers does not mean that the mentioned ones should be narrowed by a niggardly [stingy] construction. Some clauses could be made almost unworkable, as well as immutable, by refusal to indulge some latitude of interpretation for changing times. I have heretofore, and do now, give to the enumerated powers the scope and elasticity afforded by what seem to be reasonable practical implications instead of the rigidity dictated by a doctrinaire textualism.

The Solicitor General seeks the power of seizure in three clauses of the Executive Article.

[*Art. II, § 1, cl. 1.*] The first read[s], "The executive Power shall be vested in a President of the United States of America." Lest I be thought to exaggerate, I quote the interpretation which his brief puts upon it: "In our view, this clause constitutes a grant of all the executive powers of which the Government is capable." If that be true, it is difficult to see why the forefathers bothered to add several specific items, including some trifling ones.[FN9]

FN9 "He may require the Opinion, in writing, of the principal Officer in each of the executive Departments, upon any Subject relating to the Duties of their respective Offices" Art. II, § 2. He "shall Commission all the Officers of the United States." Art. II, § 3. Matters such as those would seem to be inherent in the Executive if anything is.

The example of such unlimited executive power that must have most impressed the forefathers was the prerogative exercised by George III, and the description of its evils in the Declaration of Independence leads me to doubt that they were creating their new Executive in his image. Continental European examples were no more appealing. And if we seek instruction from our own times, we can match it only from the executive powers in those governments we disparagingly describe as totalitarian. I cannot accept the view that this clause is a grant in bulk of all conceivable executive power but regard it as an allocation to the presidential office of the generic powers thereafter stated.

[*Art. II, § 2, cl. 1.*] The clause on which the Government next relies is that "The President shall be Commander in Chief of the Army and Navy of the United States" . . . Does that empower the Commander-in-Chief to seize industries he thinks necessary to supply our army? The Constitution expressly places in Congress power "to raise and support Armies" [Art. I, § 8, cl. 12] and "to provide and maintain a Navy" [Art. I, § 8, cl. 13]. This certainly lays upon Congress primary responsibility for supplying the armed forces. Congress alone controls the raising of revenues and their appropriation and may determine in what manner and by what means they shall be spent for military and naval procurement. I suppose no one would doubt that Congress can take over war supply as a Government enterprise. On the other hand, if Congress sees fit to rely on free private enterprise collectively bargaining with free labor for support and maintenance of our armed forces can the Executive because of lawful disagreements incidental to that process, seize the facility for operation upon Government-imposed terms?

There are indications that the Constitution did not contemplate that the title Commander-in-Chief of the Army and Navy will constitute him also Commander-in-Chief of the country, its industries and its inhabitants. He has no monopoly of 'war powers,' whatever they are. While Congress cannot deprive the President of the command of the army and navy, only Congress can provide him an army or navy to command. It is also empowered to make rules for the "Government and Regulation of land and naval forces," [Art. I, § 8, cl. 14] by which it may to some unknown extent impinge upon even command functions. . . .

[*Art. II, § 3.*] The third clause in which the Solicitor General finds seizure powers is that "he shall take care that the laws be faithfully executed." That authority must be matched against words of the Fifth Amendment that "no person shall be deprived of life, liberty, or property, without due process of law." One gives a governmental authority that reaches so far as there is law, the other gives a private right that authority shall go no farther. These signify about all there is of the principle that ours is a government of laws, not of men, and that we submit ourselves to rulers only if under rules.

[*Inherent Powers*] The Solicitor General lastly grounds support of the seizure upon nebulous, inherent powers never expressly granted but said to have accrued to the office from the customs and claims of preceding administrations. The plea is for a resulting power to deal with a crisis or an emergency according to the necessities of the case, the unarticulated assumption being that necessity knows no law. . . .

The appeal . . . that we declare the existence of inherent powers *ex necessitate* [from necessity] to meet an emergency asks us to do what many think would be wise, although it is something the forefathers omitted. They knew what emergencies were, knew the pressures they engender for authoritative action, knew, too, how they afford a ready pretext for usurpation. We may also suspect that they suspected that emergency powers would tend to kindle emergencies. Aside from suspension of the privilege of the writ of habeas corpus in time of rebellion or invasion, when the public safety may require it, they made no express provision for exercise of extraordinary authority because of a crisis. I do not think we rightfully may so amend their work, and, if we could, I am not convinced it would be wise to do so, although many modern nations have forthrightly recognized that war and economic crises may upset the normal balance between liberty and authority. Their experience with emergency powers may not be irrelevant to the argument here that we should say that the Executive, of his own volition, can invest himself with undefined emergency powers.

Cartoon by Jim Lange, Daily Oklahoman (1952).

Germany, after the First World War, framed the Weimar Constitution, designed to secure her liberties in the Western tradition. However, the President of the Republic, without concurrence of the Reichstag, was empowered temporarily to suspend any or all individual rights if public safety and order were seriously disturbed or endangered. This proved a temptation to every government, whatever its shade of opinion, and in 13 years suspension of rights was invoked on more than 250 occasions. Finally, Hitler persuaded President Von Hindenberg to suspend all such rights, and they were never restored. . . .

This contemporary foreign experience may be inconclusive as to the wisdom of lodging emergency powers somewhere in a modern government. But it suggests that emergency powers are consistent with free government only when their control is lodged elsewhere than in the Executive who exercises them. That is the safeguard that would be nullified by our adoption of the "inherent powers" formula. Nothing in my experience convinces me that such risks are warranted by any real necessity, although such powers would, of course, be an executive convenience. . . .

I have no illusion that any decision by this Court can keep power in the hands of Congress if it [Congress] is not wise and timely in meeting its problems. A crisis that challenges the President equally, or perhaps primarily, challenges Congress. If not good law, there was worldly wisdom in the maxim attributed to Napoleon that "The tools belong to the man who can use them." We may say that power to legislate for emergencies belongs in the hands of Congress, but only Congress itself can prevent power from slipping through its fingers. . . .

Justice Burton, concurring in both the opinion and judgment of the Court. [Omitted.]

Justice Clark, concurring in the judgment of the Court.

. . . The limits of presidential power are obscure. However, Article II, no less than Article I, is part of "a constitution intended to endure for ages to come, and, consequently, to be adapted to the various crises of human affairs." *McCulloch v. Maryland* (1819). Some of our Presidents, such as Lincoln, felt that measures otherwise unconstitutional might become lawful by becoming indispensable to the preservation of the Constitution through the preservation of the nation. Others, such as Theodore Roosevelt, thought the President to be capable, as a "steward" of the people, of exerting all power save that which is specifically prohibited by the Constitution or the Congress. In my view . . . the Constitution does grant to the President extensive authority in times of grave and imperative national emergency. In fact, to my thinking, such a grant may well be necessary to the very existence of the Constitution itself. As Lincoln aptly said, "is it possible to lose the nation and yet preserve the Constitution?" In describing this authority I care not whether one calls it "residual," "inherent," "moral," "implied," "aggregate," "emergency," or otherwise. I am of the conviction that those who have had the gratifying experience of being **the President's lawyer** have used one or more of these adjectives only with the utmost of sincerity and the highest of purpose.

I conclude that where Congress has laid down specific procedures to deal with the type of crisis confronting the President, he must follow those procedures in meeting the crisis; but that in the absence of such action by Congress, the President's independent power to act depends upon the gravity of the situation confronting the nation. I cannot sustain the seizure in question because here, Congress had prescribed methods to be followed by the President in meeting the emergency at hand. . . .

■ HISTORY

THE PRESIDENT'S LAWYER: Justice Tom Clark (1899–1977) served as Attorney General under Presidents Roosevelt and Truman before being appointed to the Supreme Court in 1949.

Justice Douglas, concurring.

There can be no doubt that the emergency which caused the President to seize these steel plants was one that bore heavily on the country. But the emergency did not create power; it merely marked an occasion when power should be exercised. And the fact that it was necessary that measures be taken to keep steel in production does not mean that the President, rather than the Congress, had the constitutional authority to act. The Congress, as well as the President, is trustee of the national welfare. The President can act more quickly than the Congress. The President with the armed services at his disposal can move with force as well as with speed. All executive power—from the reign of ancient kings to the rule of modern dictators—has the outward appearance of efficiency.

Legislative power, by contrast, is slower to exercise. There must be delay while the ponderous machinery of committees, hearings, and debates is put into motion. That takes time; and while the Congress slowly moves into action, the emergency may take its toll in wages, consumer goods, war production, the standard of living of the people, and perhaps even lives. Legislative action may indeed often be cumbersome, time-consuming, and apparently inefficient. But as Mr. Justice Brandeis stated in his dissent in *Myers v. United States*, 272 U.S. 52 (1926): "The doctrine of the separation of powers was adopted by the Convention of 1787 not to promote efficiency but to preclude the exercise of arbitrary power. The purpose was not to avoid friction, but, by means of the inevitable friction incident to the distribution of the governmental powers among three departments, to save the people from autocracy."

We therefore cannot decide this case by determining which branch of government can deal most expeditiously with the present crisis. The answer must depend on the allocation of powers under the Constitution. . . .

The legislative nature of the action taken by the President seems to me to be clear. When the United States takes over an industrial plant to settle a labor controversy, it is condemning property. The seizure of the plant is a taking in the constitutional sense. A permanent taking would amount to the nationalization of the industry. A temporary taking falls short of that goal. But though the seizure is only for a week or a month, the condemnation is complete and the United States must pay compensation for the temporary possession [under the Takings Clause of the Fifth Amendment]. . . . The President has no power to raise revenues. That power is in the Congress by Article I, Section 8 of the Constitution. The President might seize and the Congress by subsequent action might ratify the seizure. But until and unless Congress acted, no condemnation would be lawful. The branch of government that has the power to pay compensation for a seizure is the only one able to authorize a seizure or make lawful one that the President had effected. That seems to me to be the necessary result of the condemnation provision in the Fifth Amendment. It squares with the theory of checks and balances expounded by Mr. Justice Black in the opinion of the Court in which I Join. . . .

We pay a price for our system of checks and balances, for the distribution of power among the three branches of government. It is a price that today may seem exorbitant to many. Today a kindly President uses the seizure power to effect a wage increase and to keep the steel furnaces in production. Yet tomorrow another President might use the same power to prevent a wage increase, to curb trade unionists, to regiment labor as oppressively as industry thinks it has been regimented by this seizure.

Justice Frankfurter, concurring.

. . . [The Framers] did not make the judiciary the overseer of our government. . . . Rigorous adherence to the narrow scope of the judicial function is especially demanded in controversies that arouse appeals to the Constitution. The attitude with which this Court must approach its duty when confronted with such issues is precisely the opposite of that normally manifested by the general public. So-called constitutional questions seem to exercise a mesmeric influence over the popular mind. This eagerness to settle—preferably forever—a specific problem on the basis of the broadest possible constitutional pronouncements may not unfairly be called one of our minor national traits. . . .

The path of duty for this Court, it bears repetition, lies in the opposite direction. . . . A basic rule is the duty of the Court not to pass on a constitutional issue at all, however narrowly it may be confined, if the case may, as a matter of intellectual honesty, be decided without even considering delicate problems of power under the Constitution. . . .

So here our first inquiry must be not into the powers of the President, but into the powers of a District Judge to issue a temporary injunction in the circumstances of this case. . . . [Such a power exists on these facts.] And so, with the utmost unwillingness, with every desire to avoid judicial inquiry into the powers and duties of the other two branches of the government, I cannot escape consideration of the legality of Executive Order No. 10340. . . .

The question before the Court comes in this setting. Congress has frequently—at least 16 times since 1916—specifically provided for executive seizure of production, transportation, communications, or storage facilities. In every case it has qualified this grant of power with limitations and safeguards. This body of enactments . . . demonstrates that Congress deemed seizure so drastic a power as to require that it be carefully circumscribed [by statute] whenever the President was vested with this extraordinary authority. . . .

Chief Justice Vinson, with whom Justices Reed and Minton join, dissenting.

. . . Some members of the Court are of the view that the President is without power to act in time of crisis in the absence of express statutory authorization. Other members of the Court [Justices Burton and Clark] affirm on the basis of their reading of certain statutes. Because we cannot agree that affirmance is proper on any ground, and because of the transcending importance of the questions presented not only in this critical litigation but also to the powers the President and of future Presidents to act in time of crisis, we are compelled to register this dissent.

I

. . . The central fact of this case [is] that the Nation's entire basic steel production would have shut down completely if there had been no Government seizure.

Even ignoring for the moment whatever confidential information the President may possess as the Nation's organ for foreign affairs, the uncontroverted affidavits in this record amply support the finding that a work stoppage would immediately jeopardize and imperil our national defense. . . .

II

The steel mills were seized for a public use. The power of eminent domain, invoked in that case, is an essential attribute of sovereignty and has long been recognized as a power of the Federal Government. . . .

Admitting that the Government could seize the mills, plaintiffs claim that the implied power of eminent domain can be exercised only under an Act of Congress; under no circumstances, they say, can that power be exercised by the President unless he can point to an express provision in enabling legislation. This was the view adopted by the District Judge when he granted the preliminary injunction. . . . Under this view, the President is left powerless at the very moment when the need for action may be most pressing and when no one, other than he, is immediately capable of action. Under this view, he is left powerless because a power not expressly given to Congress is nevertheless found to rest exclusively with Congress. . . .

The whole of the "executive Power" is vested in the President. . . . This comprehensive grant of the executive power to a single person was bestowed soon after the country had thrown the yoke of monarchy. Only by instilling initiative and vigor in all of the three departments of Government, declared Madison, could tyranny in any form be avoided. Hamilton added: "Energy in the Executive is a leading character in the definition of good government. . . ." It is thus apparent that the Presidency was deliberately fashioned as an office of power and independence. Of course, the Framers created no autocrat capable of arrogating any power unto himself at any time. But neither did they create an automaton impotent to exercise the powers of Government at a time when the survival of the Republic itself may be at stake.

In passing upon the grave constitutional question presented in this case, we must never forget, as Chief Justice Marshall admonished, that the Constitution is "intended to endure for ages to come, and consequently, to be adapted to the various crises of human affairs," and that "its means are adequate to its ends." *McCulloch v. Maryland* (1819). Cases do arise presenting questions which could not have been foreseen by the Framers. In such cases, the Constitution has been treated as a living document adaptable to new situations. But we are not called upon today to expand the Constitution to meet a new situation. For, in this case, we need only look to history and time-honored principles of constitutional law—principles that have been applied consistently by all branches of the Government throughout our history. It is those who assert the invalidity of the Executive Order who seek to amend the Constitution in this case.

III

A review of executive action demonstrates that our Presidents have on many occasions exhibited the leadership contemplated by the Framers when they made the President Commander in Chief, and imposed upon him the trust to "take Care that the Laws be faithfully executed." With or without explicit statutory authorization, Presidents have at such times dealt with national emergencies by acting promptly and resolutely to enforce legislative programs, at least to save those programs until Congress could act. Congress and the courts have responded to such executive initiative with consistent approval.

Our first President displayed at once the leadership contemplated by the Framers. When the national revenue laws were openly flouted in some sections of Pennsylvania [in the so-called "Whiskey Rebellion"], President Washington, without waiting for a call from the state government, summoned the militia and took decisive steps to secure the faithful execution of the laws. . . . Jefferson's initiative in the Louisiana Purchase, the Monroe Doctrine, and Jackson's removal of Government deposits from the Bank of the United States further serve to demonstrate by deed what the Framers described by word when they vested the whole of the executive power in the President. . . .

In an action furnishing a most apt precedent for this case, President Lincoln without statutory authority directed the seizure of rail and telegraph lines leading to Washington. Many months later, Congress recognized and confirmed the power of the President to seize railroads and telegraph lines and provided criminal penalties for interference with Government operation. This Act did not confer on the President any additional powers of seizure. Congress plainly rejected the view that the President's acts had been without legal sanction until ratified by the legislature. Sponsors of the bill declared that its purpose was only to confirm the power which the President already possessed. Opponents insisted a statute authorizing seizure was unnecessary and might even be construed as limiting existing Presidential powers.

[The dissent described other industrial seizures by Presidents Lincoln, Hayes, Cleveland, Theodore Roosevelt, Taft, Wilson, and Franklin Roosevelt.]

This is but a cursory summary of executive leadership. But it amply demonstrates that Presidents have taken prompt action to enforce the laws and protect the country whether or not Congress happened to provide in advance for the particular method of execution. . . .

IV–V [Omitted.]

VI

. . . As the District Judge stated [in granting the preliminary injunction], this is no time for "timorous" judicial action. But neither is this a time for timorous executive action. Faced with the duty of executing the defense programs which Congress had enacted and the disastrous effects that any stoppage in steel production would have on those programs, the President acted to preserve those programs by seizing the steel mills. There is no question that the possession was other than temporary in character and subject to congressional direction—either approving, disapproving or regulating the manner in which the mills were to be administered and returned to the owners. The President immediately informed Congress of his action and clearly stated his intention to abide by the legislative will. No basis for claims of arbitrary action, unlimited powers or dictatorial usurpation of congressional power appears from the facts of this case. On the contrary, judicial, legislative and executive precedents throughout our history demonstrate that in this case the President acted in full conformity with his duties under the Constitution. Accordingly, we would reverse the order of the District Court.

flash*forward*

Averting Strikes After Youngstown. Events in late 2022 illustrate a President and Congress responding to labor disputes in a crucial industry without violating *Youngstown*. Railworkers' unions had been in unsuccessful contract negotiations with the major freight railroads. With mediation assistance from the Biden administration, labor and management negotiators finally reached a tentative agreement. Most of the affected unions voted to accept the agreement, but several did not because the contract included no paid sick leave. A strike deadline was looming.

"Let me be clear," the President said on November 28. "A rail shutdown would devastate our economy. Without freight rail, many U.S. industries would shut down. . . . Where the economic impact of a shutdown would hurt millions of other working people and families, I believe Congress must use its powers to adopt this deal." He concluded by saying: "Congress should get this bill to my desk well in advance of December 9th so we can avoid disruption."

On November 30, the House, invoking Congressional power under the Commerce Clause, voted 290–137 to declare that the tentative agreement "shall be binding" on the parties. The next day, the Senate concurred on a vote of 80–15. The President signed P.L. 117–26 into law on December 2.

2. Executive Action Contrary to Statute: *Zivotofsky v. Kerry*

Many of the President's enumerated powers involve foreign relations: appointing ambassadors (subject to Senate confirmation), receiving ambassadors of other nations, negotiating treaties (subject to Senate ratification), and conducting warfare as commander in chief. Historically, Congress has given the President wide discretion to pursue matters of state with relatively few statutory restrictions. Is this deference to the President a matter of policy, or is it required by the Constitution? This question was at the heart of *Zivotofsky v. Kerry* (2015), which involved disagreement between Congress and the President over the words printed in the passports of US citizens born in Jerusalem.

Passports and Disputed Territory. The State Department issues passports to US citizens that serve as proof of citizenship and authorization to enter the country. By long tradition, passports list the citizen's place of birth.

For citizens born within a State or a US territory, the passports list the State or territory of birth. By statute, a child born abroad to married US citizens is also a US citizen at birth. 8 U.S.C. § 1401(c). (The situation is more complicated for children born abroad to unmarried parents, only one of whom is a US citizen. See *Nguyen v. INS* (2001) and *U.S. v. Morales-Santana* (2017), Ch. 18.C.3.b.3.) For citizens born in other countries, the passports list the nation with sovereignty over the place of birth, or upon request of the citizen the city will be listed instead (e.g., "Paris" instead of "France"). For citizens born in places that are subject to an international dispute where more than one nation claims sovereignty, the State Department's practice has been to list only the city of birth. Jerusalem is one such disputed place, controlled in practice by the nation of Israel (which treats Jerusalem as its capitol city), but also claimed at various times by other nations (Jordan) and peoples (Palestinians).

In *Zivotofsky*, the State Department sought to continue its existing practice of listing "Jerusalem" as the birthplace. Congress, however, sought to require the Department—if the citizen requested it—to list "Israel."

ITEMS TO CONSIDER WHILE READING *ZIVOTOFSKY v. KERRY*:

A. *Which legislative power in Art. I could Congress rely upon to enact the statute challenged in* Zivotofsky?

B. *Using Justice Jackson's framework from* Youngstown, *which zone does the President's action occupy? Within that zone, what would it take for Congress or the President to prevail in litigation? Use the chart on page 538.*

C. *Which executive power did the President rely upon to argue that the statute violated separation of powers? Why did the President believe Congress's action interfered with that exclusive power?*

D. *Does* Zivotofsky *hold that Presidents enjoy exclusive power over all questions of foreign relations?*

E. *How would the dispute be resolved if the federal courts refused to decide it?*

Zivotofsky v. Kerry,

576 U.S. 1 (2015)

Justice Kennedy delivered the opinion of the Court [joined by Justices Ginsburg, Breyer, Sotomayor, and Kagan].

A delicate subject lies in the background of this case. That subject is Jerusalem. Questions touching upon the history of the ancient city and its present legal and international status are among the most difficult and complex in international affairs. In our constitutional system these matters are committed to the Legislature and the Executive, not the Judiciary. As a result, in this opinion the Court does no more, and must do no more, than note the existence of international debate and tensions respecting Jerusalem. Those matters are for Congress and the President to discuss and consider as they seek to shape the Nation's foreign policies.

The Court addresses two questions to resolve the interbranch dispute now before it. First, it must determine whether the President has the exclusive power to grant formal recognition to a foreign sovereign. Second, if he has that power, the Court must determine whether Congress can command the President and his Secretary of State to issue a formal statement that contradicts the earlier recognition. The statement in question here is a congressional mandate that allows a United States citizen born in Jerusalem to direct the President and Secretary of State, when issuing his passport, to state that his place of birth is "Israel."

I

A

. . . In 1948, President Truman formally recognized Israel in a signed statement of "recognition." . . . Neither President Truman nor any later United States President has issued an official statement or declaration acknowledging any country's sovereignty over Jerusalem. Instead, the Executive Branch has maintained that the status of Jerusalem should be decided not unilaterally but in consultation with all concerned. . . .

Understanding that passports will be construed as reflections of American policy, the State Department's Foreign Affairs Manual [FAM] instructs its employees, in general, to record the place of birth on a passport as the country having "present sovereignty over the actual area of birth." If a citizen objects to the country listed as sovereign by the State Department, he or she may list the city or town of birth rather than the country. The FAM, however, does not allow citizens to list a sovereign that conflicts with Executive Branch policy. Because the United States does not recognize any country as having sovereignty over Jerusalem, the FAM instructs employees to record the place of birth for citizens born there as "Jerusalem."

In 2002, Congress passed the Act at issue here, the Foreign Relations Authorization Act [for] Fiscal Year 2003. Section 214 of the Act is titled "United States Policy with Respect to Jerusalem as the Capital of Israel." The subsection that lies at the heart of this case, § 214(d), addresses passports. That subsection seeks to override the FAM by allowing citizens born in Jerusalem to list their place of birth as "Israel." . . .

When he signed the Act into law, President George W. Bush issued a statement declaring his position that § 214 would, "if construed as mandatory rather than advisory, impermissibly interfere with the President's constitutional authority to formulate the position of the United States, speak for the Nation in international affairs, and determine the terms on which recognition is given to foreign states." The President concluded, "U.S. policy regarding Jerusalem has not changed."

Some parties were not reassured by the President's statement. A cable from the United States Consulate in Jerusalem noted that the Palestine Liberation Organization Executive Committee, Fatah Central Committee, and the Palestinian Authority Cabinet had all issued statements claiming that the Act "undermines the role of the U.S. as a sponsor of the peace process." In the Gaza Strip and elsewhere residents marched in protest. . . .

B

In 2002, petitioner Menachem Binyamin Zivotofsky was born to United States citizens living in Jerusalem. In December 2002, Zivotofsky's mother visited the American Embassy in Tel Aviv to request both a passport . . . for her son. She asked that his place of birth be listed as "Jerusalem, Israel." The Embassy clerks explained that, pursuant to State Department policy, the passport would list only "Jerusalem." Zivotofsky's parents objected and, as his guardians, brought suit on his behalf in the United States District Court for the District of Columbia, seeking to enforce § 214(d). . . .

After Zivotofsky brought suit [against the Secretary of State, who is now John Kerry], the District Court dismissed his case, reasoning that it presented a nonjusticiable **political question** and that Zivotofsky lacked standing. The Court of Appeals for the District of Columbia Circuit reversed on the

■ HISTORY

POLITICAL QUESTION: A "political question" is one that can only be resolved by the elected political branches and not the judiciary. Federal courts will refuse jurisdiction over political questions if there is "a textually demonstrable constitutional commitment of the issue to a coordinate political department, or a lack of judicially discoverable and manageable standards for resolving it." *Baker v. Carr,* 369 U.S. 186 (1962). See Ch. 4.D.4.

standing issue, 444 F.3d 614 (2006), but later affirmed the District Court's political question determination, 571 F.3d 1227 (2009).

This Court granted certiorari, vacated the judgment, and remanded the case. Whether § 214(d) is constitutional, the Court held, is not a question reserved for the political branches. In reference to Zivotofsky's claim the Court observed "the Judiciary must decide if Zivotofsky's interpretation of the statute is correct, and whether the statute is constitutional"—not whether Jerusalem is, in fact, part of Israel. *Zivotofsky v. Clinton,* 566 U.S. 189 (2012) (*Zivotofsky* I).

On remand the Court of Appeals held the statute unconstitutional. It determined that "the President exclusively holds the power to determine whether to recognize a foreign sovereign," and that "section 214(d) directly contradicts a carefully considered exercise of the Executive branch's recognition power."

This Court again granted certiorari.

II

In considering claims of Presidential power this Court refers to Justice Jackson's familiar tripartite framework from *Youngstown Sheet & Tube Co. v. Sawyer,* (1952) (concurring opinion). The framework divides exercises of Presidential power into three categories: First, when "the President acts pursuant to an express or implied authorization of Congress, his authority is at its maximum, for it includes all that he possesses in his own right plus all that Congress can delegate." Second, "in absence of either a congressional grant or denial of authority" there is a "zone of twilight in which he and Congress may have concurrent authority," and where "congressional inertia, indifference or quiescence may" invite the exercise of executive power. Finally, when "the President takes measures incompatible with the expressed or implied will of Congress, he can rely only upon his own constitutional powers minus any constitutional powers of Congress over the matter." To succeed in this third category, the President's asserted power must be both "exclusive" and "conclusive" on the issue.

In this case the Secretary contends that § 214(d) infringes on the President's exclusive recognition power by requiring the President to contradict his recognition position regarding Jerusalem in official communications with foreign sovereigns. In so doing the Secretary acknowledges the President's power is "at its lowest ebb." Because the President's refusal to implement § 214(d) falls into Justice Jackson's third category, his claim must be "scrutinized with caution," and he may rely solely on powers the Constitution grants to him alone.

To determine whether the President possesses the exclusive power of recognition the Court examines the Constitution's text and structure, as well as precedent and history bearing on the question.

A

Recognition is a formal acknowledgment that a particular entity possesses the qualifications for statehood or that a particular regime is the effective government of a state. It may also involve the determination of a state's territorial bounds. . . . Recognition is thus useful, even necessary, to the existence of a state.

Despite the importance of the recognition power in foreign relations, the Constitution does not use the term "recognition," either in Article II or elsewhere. The Secretary asserts that the President exercises the recognition power based on the Reception Clause, which directs that the President "shall receive Ambassadors and other public Ministers." Art. II, § 3. As Zivotofsky notes, the Reception Clause received little attention at the Constitutional Convention. In fact, during the ratification debates, Alexander Hamilton claimed that the power to receive ambassadors was "more a matter of dignity than of authority," a ministerial duty largely "without consequence." The Federalist #69.

At the time of the founding, however, prominent international scholars suggested that receiving an ambassador was tantamount to recognizing the sovereignty of the sending state. It is a logical and proper inference, then, that a Clause directing the President alone to receive ambassadors would be understood to acknowledge his power to recognize other nations.

This in fact occurred early in the Nation's history when President Washington recognized the French Revolutionary Government by receiving its ambassador. After this incident the import of the Reception Clause became clear—causing Hamilton to change his earlier view. He wrote that the Reception Clause "includes the power of judging, in the case of a revolution of government in a foreign country, whether the new rulers are competent organs of the national will, and ought to be recognised, or not." As a result, the Reception Clause provides support, although not the sole authority, for the President's power to recognize other nations.

The inference that the President exercises the recognition power is further supported by his additional Article II powers. It is for the President, "by and with the Advice and Consent of the Senate," to "make Treaties, provided two thirds of the Senators present concur." Art. II, § 2, cl. 2. In addition, "he shall nominate, and by and with the Advice and Consent of the Senate, shall appoint Ambassadors" as well as "other public Ministers and Consuls." *Id.*

As a matter of constitutional structure, these additional powers give the President control over recognition decisions. . . . Beyond that, the President himself has the power to open diplomatic channels simply by engaging in direct diplomacy with foreign heads of state and their ministers. The Constitution thus assigns the President means to effect recognition on his own initiative. Congress, by contrast, has no constitutional power that would enable it to initiate diplomatic relations with a foreign nation. Because these specific Clauses confer the recognition power on the President, the Court need not consider whether or to what extent the Vesting

Clause, which provides that the "executive Power" shall be vested in the President, provides further support for the President's action here. Art. II, § 1, cl. 1.

The text and structure of the Constitution grant the President the power to recognize foreign nations and governments. The question then becomes whether that power is exclusive. The various ways in which the President may unilaterally effect recognition—and the lack of any similar power vested in Congress—suggest that it is. So, too, do functional considerations. Put simply, the Nation must have a single policy regarding which governments are legitimate in the eyes of the United States and which are not. Foreign countries need to know, before entering into diplomatic relations or commerce with the United States, whether their ambassadors will be received; whether their officials will be immune from suit in federal court; and whether they may initiate lawsuits here to vindicate their rights. These assurances cannot be equivocal.

Recognition is a topic on which the Nation must speak with one voice. That voice must be the President's. Between the two political branches, only the Executive has the characteristic of unity at all times. And with unity comes the ability to exercise, to a greater degree, "decision, activity, secrecy, and dispatch." The Federalist #70. The President is capable, in ways Congress is not, of engaging in the delicate and often secret diplomatic contacts that may lead to a decision on recognition. He is also better positioned to take the decisive, unequivocal action necessary to recognize other states at international law. These qualities explain why the Framers listed the traditional avenues of recognition—receiving ambassadors, making treaties, and sending ambassadors—as among the President's Article II powers. . . .

It remains true, of course, that many decisions affecting foreign relations—including decisions that may determine the course of our relations with recognized countries—require congressional action. Congress may "regulate Commerce with foreign Nations," "establish an uniform Rule of Naturalization," "define and punish Piracies and Felonies committed on the high Seas, and Offences against the Law of Nations," "declare War," "grant Letters of Marque and Reprisal," and "make Rules for the Government and Regulation of the land and naval Forces." U.S. Const., Art. I, § 8. In addition, the President cannot make a treaty or appoint an ambassador without the approval of the Senate. Art. II, § 2, cl. 2. The President, furthermore, could not build an American Embassy abroad without congressional appropriation of the necessary funds. Art. I, § 8, cl. 1. Under basic separation-of-powers principles, it is for the Congress to enact the laws, including "all Laws which shall be necessary and proper for carrying into Execution" the powers of the Federal Government. § 8, cl. 18.

In foreign affairs, as in the domestic realm, the Constitution "enjoins upon its branches separateness but interdependence, autonomy but reciprocity." *Youngstown,* (Jackson, J., concurring). Although the President alone effects the formal act of recognition, Congress' powers, and its central role in making laws, give it substantial authority regarding many of the policy determinations that precede and follow the act of recognition itself. If Congress disagrees with the President's recognition policy, there may be consequences. Formal recognition may seem a hollow act if it is not accompanied by the dispatch of an ambassador, the easing of trade restrictions, and the conclusion of treaties. And those decisions require action by the Senate or the whole Congress.

In practice, then, the President's recognition determination is just one part of a political process that may require Congress to make laws. The President's exclusive recognition power encompasses the authority to acknowledge, in a formal sense, the legitimacy of other states and governments, including their territorial bounds. Albeit limited, the exclusive recognition power is essential to the conduct of Presidential duties. The formal act of recognition is an executive power that Congress may not qualify. If the President is to be effective in negotiations over a formal recognition determination, it must be evident to his counterparts abroad that he speaks for the Nation on that precise question.

A clear rule that the formal power to recognize a foreign government subsists in the President therefore serves a necessary purpose in diplomatic relations. All this, of course, underscores that Congress has an important role in other aspects of foreign policy, and the President may be bound by any number of laws Congress enacts. In this way ambition counters ambition, ensuring that the democratic will of the people is observed and respected in foreign affairs as in the domestic realm. See The Federalist #51.

B

. . . [Earlier opinions indicate that] the Court has long considered recognition to be the exclusive prerogative of the Executive.

The Secretary now urges the Court to define the executive power over foreign relations in even broader terms. He contends that under the Court's precedent the President has "exclusive authority to conduct diplomatic relations," along with "the bulk of foreign-affairs powers." In support of his submission that the President has broad, undefined powers over foreign affairs, the Secretary quotes ***United States v. Curtiss-Wright Export Corp.***, 299 U.S. 304 (1936), which described the President as "the sole organ of the federal government in the field of international relations." This Court declines to acknowledge that unbounded power. A formulation broader than the rule that the President alone determines what nations to formally recognize as legitimate—and that he consequently controls his statements on matters of recognition—presents different issues and is unnecessary to the resolution of this case.

■ HISTORY

CURTISS-WRIGHT: In this case, the defendant corporation was indicted for violating President Franklin Roosevelt's embargo on arms shipments to South America. The opinion of Justice Sutherland in *Curtiss-Wright* is famous for its broad statements of exclusive Presidential authority over foreign affairs. It has led to the joke that when the President cites the case, it amounts to saying "*Curtiss-Wright*, so I'm right."

The *Curtiss-Wright* case does not extend so far as the Secretary suggests. . . . In a world that is ever more compressed and interdependent, it is essential the congressional role in foreign affairs be understood and respected. For it is Congress that makes laws, and in countless ways its laws will and should shape the Nation's course. The Executive is not free from the ordinary controls and checks of Congress merely because foreign affairs are at issue. It is not for the President alone to determine the whole content of the Nation's foreign policy.

That said, judicial precedent and historical practice teach that it is for the President alone to make the specific decision of what foreign power he will recognize as legitimate, both for the Nation as a whole and for the purpose of making his own position clear within the context of recognition in discussions and negotiations with foreign nations. Recognition is an act with immediate and powerful significance for international relations, so the President's position must be clear. Congress cannot require him to contradict his own statement regarding a determination of formal recognition. . . .

C

Having examined the Constitution's text and this Court's precedent, it is appropriate to turn to accepted understandings and practice. In separation-of-powers cases this Court has often put significant weight upon historical practice. Here, history is not all on one side, but on balance it provides strong support for the conclusion that the recognition power is the President's alone. . . . The major historical examples . . . establish no more than that some Presidents have chosen to cooperate with Congress, not that Congress itself has exercised the recognition power. . . .

III

As the power to recognize foreign states resides in the President alone, the question becomes whether § 214(d) infringes on the Executive's consistent decision to withhold recognition with respect to Jerusalem. [Congressional action is] unlawful when it prevents the Executive Branch from accomplishing its constitutionally assigned functions.

Section 214(d) . . . requires the President, through the Secretary, to identify citizens born in Jerusalem who so request as being born in Israel. But according to the President, those citizens were not born in Israel. As a matter of United States policy, neither Israel nor any other country is acknowledged as having sovereignty over Jerusalem. In this way, § 214(d) directly contradicts the carefully calibrated and longstanding Executive branch policy of neutrality toward Jerusalem.

If the power over recognition is to mean anything, it must mean that the President not only makes the initial, formal recognition determination but also that he may maintain that determination in his and his agent's statements. This conclusion is a matter of both common sense and necessity. If Congress could command the President to state a recognition position inconsistent with his own, Congress could override the President's recognition determination. . . .

As Justice Jackson wrote in *Youngstown,* when a Presidential power is exclusive, it "disables the Congress from acting upon the subject." Here, the subject is quite narrow: The Executive's exclusive power extends no further than his formal recognition determination. But as to that determination, Congress may not enact a law that directly contradicts it. This is not to say Congress may not express its disagreement with the President in myriad ways. For example, it may enact an embargo, decline to confirm an ambassador, or even declare war. But none of these acts would alter the President's recognition decision. . . .

The flaw in § 214(d) is further underscored by the undoubted fact that the purpose of the statute was to infringe on the recognition power—a power the Court now holds is the sole prerogative of the President. The statute is titled "United States Policy with Respect to Jerusalem as the Capital of Israel." The House Conference Report proclaimed that § 214 "contains four provisions related to the recognition of Jerusalem as Israel's capital." And, indeed, observers interpreted § 214 as altering United States policy regarding Jerusalem—which led to protests across the region. From the face of § 214, from the legislative history, and from its reception, it is clear that Congress wanted to express its displeasure with the President's policy by, among other things, commanding the Executive to contradict his own, earlier stated position on Jerusalem. This Congress may not do.

It is true, as Zivotofsky notes, that Congress has substantial authority over passports. . . . The problem with § 214(d), however, lies in how Congress exercised its authority over passports. It was an improper act for Congress to aggrandize its power at the expense of another branch by requiring the President to contradict an earlier recognition determination in an official document issued by the Executive Branch. To allow Congress to control the President's communication in the context of a formal recognition determination is to allow Congress to exercise that exclusive power itself. As a result, the statute is unconstitutional.

[CONCLUSION]

In holding § 214(d) invalid the Court does not question the substantial powers of Congress over foreign affairs in general or passports in particular. This case is confined solely to the exclusive power of the President to control recognition determinations, including formal statements by the Executive Branch acknowledging the legitimacy of a state or government and its territorial bounds. Congress cannot command the President to contradict an earlier recognition determination in the issuance of passports.

Justice Breyer, concurring.

I continue to believe that this case presents a political question inappropriate for judicial resolution. See *Zivotofsky v. Clinton* (2012) (Breyer, J., dissenting). But because precedent precludes resolving this case on political question grounds, I join the Court's opinion.

Justice Thomas, concurring in the judgment in part and dissenting in part. [Omitted.]

Chief Justice Roberts, with whom Justice Alito joins, dissenting.

Today's decision is a first: Never before has this Court accepted a President's direct defiance of an Act of Congress in the field of foreign affairs. . . . The Executive may disregard "the expressed or implied will of Congress" only if the Constitution grants him a power "at once so conclusive and preclusive" as to "disable the Congress from acting upon the subject." *Youngstown* (Jackson, J., concurring). . . . For our first 225 years, no President prevailed when contradicting a statute in the field of foreign affairs. . . .

Ultimately, the only power that could support the President's position is the one the majority purports to reject: the exclusive authority to conduct diplomatic relations. The Government offers a single citation for this allegedly exclusive power: *United States v. Curtiss-Wright Export Corp.* (1936). . . .

The expansive language in *Curtiss-Wright* casting the President as the "sole organ" of the Nation in foreign affairs certainly has attraction for members of the Executive Branch. The Solicitor General invokes the case no fewer than ten times in his brief. But our precedents have never accepted such a sweeping understanding of executive power. . . . [Today] the Court takes the perilous step—for the first time in our history—of allowing the President to defy an Act of Congress in the field of foreign affairs. I respectfully dissent.

Justice Scalia, with whom Chief Justice Roberts and Justice Alito join, dissenting.

Before this country declared independence, the law of England entrusted the King with the exclusive care of his kingdom's foreign affairs. The royal prerogative included the sole power of sending ambassadors to foreign states, and receiving them at home, the sole authority to make treaties, leagues, and alliances with foreign states and princes, the sole prerogative of making war and peace, and the sole power of raising and regulating fleets and armies. The People of the United States had other ideas when they organized our Government. They considered a sound structure of balanced powers essential to the preservation of just government, and international relations formed no exception to that principle. . . .

This case arises out of a dispute between the Executive and Legislative Branches about whether the United States should treat Jerusalem as a part of Israel. The Constitution contemplates that the political branches will make policy about the territorial claims of foreign nations the same way they make policy about other international matters: The President will exercise his powers on the basis of his views, Congress its powers on the basis of its views. That is just what has happened here.

I

. . . Before turning to Presidential power under Article II, I think it well to establish the statute's basis in congressional power under Article I. Congress's power to "establish an uniform Rule of Naturalization," Art. I, § 8, cl. 4, enables it to grant American citizenship to someone born abroad. The naturalization power also enables Congress to furnish the people it makes citizens with papers verifying their citizenship—-[such as] a passport (which certifies citizenship for purposes of international travel). As the Necessary and Proper Clause confirms, every congressional power carries with it all those incidental powers which are necessary to its complete and effectual execution. Even on a miserly understanding of Congress's incidental authority, Congress may make grants of citizenship effectual by providing for the issuance of certificates authenticating them.

One would think that if Congress may grant Zivotofsky a passport . . . it may also require these papers to record his birthplace as "Israel." The birthplace specification promotes the document's citizenship-authenticating function by identifying the bearer, distinguishing people with similar names but different birthplaces from each other, helping authorities uncover identity fraud, and facilitating retrieval of the Government's citizenship records. To be sure, recording Zivotofsky's birthplace as "Jerusalem" rather than "Israel" would fulfill these objectives, but when faced with alternative ways to carry its powers into execution, Congress has the "discretion" to choose the one it deems "most beneficial to the people." *McCulloch v. Maryland* (1819). It thus has the right to decide that recording birthplaces as "Israel" makes for better foreign policy. Or that regardless of international politics, a passport or birth report should respect its bearer's conscientious belief that Jerusalem belongs to Israel. . . .

II

The Court frames this case as a debate about recognition. Recognition is a sovereign's official acceptance of a status under international law. A sovereign might recognize a foreign entity as a state, a regime as the other state's government, a place as part of the other state's territory, rebel forces in the other state as a belligerent power, and so on. President Truman recognized Israel as a state in 1948, but Presidents have consistently declined to recognize Jerusalem as a part of Israel's (or any other state's) sovereign territory.

The Court holds that the Constitution makes the President alone responsible for recognition and that § 214(d) invades this exclusive power. I agree that the Constitution *empowers* the President to extend recognition on behalf of the United States, but I find it a much harder question whether it makes that power exclusive.

The Court tells us that the weight of historical evidence supports exclusive executive authority over "the formal determination of recognition." But even with its attention confined to formal recognition, the Court is forced to admit that "history is not all on one side." To take a stark example, Congress legislated in 1934 to grant independence to the Philippines, which were then an American colony. In the course of doing so, Congress directed the President to "recognize the independence of the Philippine Islands as a separate and self-governing nation" and to "acknowledge the authority and control over the same of the government instituted by the people thereof." Constitutional? . . . Fortunately, I have no need to confront these matters today—nor does the Court—because § 214(d) plainly does not concern recognition. . . .

Section 214(d) does not require the Secretary to make a formal declaration about Israel's sovereignty over Jerusalem. And nobody suggests that international custom infers acceptance of sovereignty from the birthplace designation on a passport or birth report, as it does from bilateral treaties or exchanges of ambassadors. . . . Making a notation in a passport or birth report does not encumber the Republic with any international obligations. It leaves the Nation free (so far as international law is concerned) to change its mind in the future. That would be true even if the statute required *all* passports to list "Israel." But in fact it requires only those passports to list "Israel" for which the citizen (or his guardian) *requests* "Israel"; all the rest, under the Secretary's policy, list "Jerusalem." It is utterly impossible for this deference to private requests to constitute an act that unequivocally manifests an intention to grant recognition. . . .

The best indication that § 214(d) does not concern recognition comes from the State Department's policies concerning Taiwan. According to the Solicitor General, the United States "acknowledges the Chinese position" that Taiwan is a part of China, but "does not take a position" of its own on that issue. Even so, the State Department has for a long time recorded the birthplace of a citizen born in Taiwan as "China." It indeed *insisted* on doing so until Congress passed a law (on which § 214(d) was modeled) giving citizens the option to have their birthplaces recorded as "Taiwan." The Solicitor General explains that the designation "China" "involves a geographic description, not an assertion that Taiwan is part of sovereign China." Quite so. Section 214(d) likewise calls for nothing beyond a "geographic description"; it does not require the Executive even to assert, never mind formally recognize, that Jerusalem is a part of sovereign Israel. Since birthplace specifications in citizenship documents are matters within Congress's control, Congress may treat Jerusalem as a part of Israel when regulating the recording of birthplaces, even if the President does not do so when extending recognition. . . .

III

The Court complains that § 214(d) requires the Secretary of State to issue official documents implying that Jerusalem is a part of Israel; that it appears in a section of the statute bearing the title "United States Policy with Respect to Jerusalem as the Capital of Israel"; and that foreign observers interpreted it as altering United States policy regarding Jerusalem. But these features do not show that § 214(d) recognizes Israel's sovereignty over Jerusalem. They show only that the law displays symbolic support for Israel's territorial claim. That symbolism may have tremendous significance as a matter of international diplomacy, but it makes no difference as a matter of constitutional law.

Even if the Constitution gives the President sole power to extend recognition, it does not give him sole power to make all decisions relating to foreign disputes over sovereignty. To the contrary, a fair reading of Article I allows Congress to decide for itself how its laws should handle these controversies. Read naturally, power to "regulate Commerce with foreign Nations," § 8, cl. 3, includes power to regulate imports from Gibraltar as British goods or as Spanish goods. Read naturally, power to "regulate the Value . . . of foreign Coin," § 8, cl. 5, includes power to honor (or not) currency issued by Taiwan. And so on for the other enumerated powers. . . .

The Constitution likewise does not give the President exclusive power to determine which claims to statehood and territory are legitimate in the eyes of the United States. Congress may express its own views about these matters by declaring war, restricting trade, denying foreign aid, and much else besides. . . .

In the final analysis, the Constitution may well deny Congress power to recognize—the power to make an international commitment accepting a foreign entity as a state, a regime as its government, a place as a part of its territory, and so on. But whatever else § 214(d) may do, it plainly does not make (or require the President to make) a commitment accepting Israel's sovereignty over Jerusalem.

IV

. . . The Court . . . announces a rule that is blatantly gerrymandered to the facts of this case. It concludes that, in addition to the exclusive power to make the "formal recognition determination," the President holds an ancillary exclusive power "to control formal statements by the Executive Branch acknowledging the legitimacy of a state or government and its territorial bounds." It follows, the Court explains, that Congress may not "require the President to contradict an earlier recognition determination in an official document issued by the Executive Branch." So requiring imports from Jerusalem to be taxed like goods from Israel is fine, but requiring Customs to issue an official invoice to that effect is not? Nonsense. . . .

In the end, the Court's decision does not rest on text or history or precedent. It instead comes down to "functional considerations"—principally the Court's perception that the Nation "must speak with one voice" about the status of Jerusalem. The vices of this mode of analysis go beyond mere lack of footing in the Constitution. Functionalism of the sort the Court practices today will *systematically* favor the unitary President over the plural Congress in disputes involving foreign affairs. It is possible that this approach will make for more effective foreign policy, perhaps as effective as that of a monarchy. It is certain that, in the long run, it will erode the structure of separated powers that the People established for the protection of their liberty.

Zivotofsky v. Kerry

V [Omitted.]

flashforward

Subsequent Presidential Action. Starting with Israel's founding in 1948, the State Department had located the US embassy for Israel in Tel Aviv, not Jerusalem. This was a manifestation of the neutrality described in *Zivotofsky.* The Jerusalem Embassy Act of 1995 directed that the US Embassy should be moved to Jerusalem by 1999—although the Act allowed the President to postpone the move for six months by notifying Congress that a delay "is necessary to protect the national security interests of the United States." When *Zivotofsky* was litigated, all Presidents had given such notification once every six months, so the embassy had not yet moved.

In early 2018, President Trump acceded to the Jerusalem Embassy Act, moving the embassy to Jerusalem. In late 2020, he acceded to § 214(d) and directed that passports list Israel as the place of birth on request of US citizens born in Jerusalem. The first recipient was Menachem Zivotofsky.

D. Tension Between the Judicial and Executive Branches

The core function of the judicial branch is to decide cases and controversies between adverse parties. At a minimum, this involves exercising jurisdiction over defendants: haling them into court and issuing adverse judgments against them if they lose, all against their will. The judiciary also routinely exerts authority over witnesses: ordering them to testify or to produce documents or physical evidence pursuant to subpoenas. And in overseeing search warrants and grand jury proceedings, courts have a role in investigating those who may become criminal defendants.

The cases in this section consider the separation of powers problems that arise when the judiciary asserts these traditional powers against the President. Any exercise of judicial power over the President reduces executive branch autonomy. But if the President can claim an exemption from duties the law ordinarily imposes on defendants and witnesses, it encroaches on the judiciary's autonomy. (Because Congress, like the judiciary, has the power to issue subpoenas for testimony or documents, see Ch. 15.D.1, this section will also consider analogous legislative powers.)

1. The President as Defendant

At common law, monarchs enjoyed sovereign immunity. See Ch. 3.A.1. Under modern US law, some forms of sovereign immunity limit an individual's ability to sue the government itself. For suits against government officials as individuals—such as a suit for damages against a government officer for violating individual rights—some forms of personal immunity from suit exist, typically arising from statutes or the common law of torts. The text of the Constitution includes only one explicit immunity provision: The **Speech or Debate Clause** provides that members of Congress "shall in all cases, except treason, felony and breach of the peace, be privileged from arrest during their attendance at the session of their respective Houses, and in going to and returning from the same; and for any speech or debate in either House, they shall not be questioned in any other place." Art. I, § 6, cl. 1.

No similar immunity clause exists for the President. With regard to criminal charges, Art. I, § 3, cl. 7 says that once an official is removed from office upon conviction in a Senate impeachment trial, "the party convicted shall nevertheless be liable and subject to indictment, trial, judgment and punishment, according to law." From this, it is clear that a President has no permanent immunity from prosecution for crimes committed in office.

■ HISTORY

THE SPEECH OR DEBATE CLAUSE: The Speech or Debate Clause has its roots in the English Bill of Rights of 1689, which read in part: "The freedom of speech and debates or proceedings in Parliament ought not to be impeached or questioned in any court or place out of Parliament." This protection was desired to end the practice of members of Parliament being criminally prosecuted for their legislative speeches.

Civil lawsuits against a President may be divided between those that sue the President in an official capacity and in an individual capacity. (This distinction is usually studied in classes dedicated to Federal Courts or Constitutional Torts.) An official-capacity suit seeks an injunction ordering the holder of an office to act—or not act—in ways mandated by law or by the Constitution. No damages are awarded. Such suits occur regularly, and may involve the President as a defendant as well as other government officers. E.g., *Arpaio v. Obama*, 797 F.3d 11 (D.C. Cir. 2015); *National Treasury Employees Union v. Nixon*, 492 F.2d 587 (D.C. Cir. 1974). If the defendant is a high-ranking official who implements Presidential policy, the case may be an official-capacity suit against the President in all but name. See *Marbury v. Madison* (1803) (Secretary of State James Madison sued for actions directed by President Jefferson) and *Youngstown Sheet & Tube Co. v. Sawyer* (1952) (Secretary of Commerce Charles Sawyer sued for actions directed by President Truman).

An individual-capacity suit seeks a remedy against an identified person, not against an office. Claims for money damages will be individual-capacity suits. The Supreme Court has twice ruled on the constitutionality of civil suits seeking damages against Presidents in their individual capacities.

a) Suits over Conduct in Office: *Nixon v. Fitzgerald*

A. Ernest Fitzgerald was a management analyst for the Air Force who made public allegations of wasteful spending. After he lost his job, he filed a civil damages action against President Richard Nixon and other high-ranking administration officials for violating his First Amendment free speech rights. The President argued that he should enjoy absolute immunity from civil suits for damages arising out of the President's actions while in office. In *Nixon v. Fitzgerald*, 457 U.S. 731 (1982) a 5–4 majority of the US Supreme Court agreed.

> ■ WEBSITE
>
> A fuller version of *Nixon v. Fitzgerald* is available for download from this casebook's companion website, www.CaplanIntegratedConLaw.com.

> Because of the singular importance of the President's duties, diversion of his energies by concern with private lawsuits would raise unique risks to the effective functioning of government. As is the case with prosecutors and judges—for whom absolute immunity now is established—a President must concern himself with matters likely to arouse the most intense feelings. Yet, as our decisions have recognized, it is in precisely such cases that there exists the greatest public interest in providing an official the maximum ability to deal fearlessly and impartially with the duties of his office. This concern is compelling where the officeholder must make the most sensitive and far-reaching decisions entrusted to any official under our constitutional system. Nor can the sheer prominence of the President's office be ignored. In view of the visibility of his office and the effect of his actions on countless people, the President would be an easily identifiable target for suits for civil damages. Cognizance of this personal vulnerability frequently could distract a President from his public duties, to the detriment of not only the President and his office but also the Nation that the Presidency was designed to serve.

The majority concluded that the President's decisions while in office should not be influenced by the fear of an individual-capacity civil suit, whether that suit is filed during or after the term of office. The absolute immunity attaches to any action "within the President's constitutional and statutory authority," and indeed to any allegedly wrongful acts falling "within the outer perimeter of his authority." This formula means that the President could not be sued for firing an employee in violation of the First Amendment. By contrast, immunity would not extend to actions not involving presidential authority, such failure to pay a personal debt or negligence committed by a sitting president while on vacation.

b) Suits over Conduct out of Office: *Clinton v. Jones*

The absolute immunity of *Nixon v. Fitzgerald* would not bar a suit against a sitting President for actions that occurred before taking office. Even so, lawsuits against a sitting President can be costly and burdensome distractions from the responsibilities of the office, even if the suits involve non-presidential conduct. This was the subject of *Clinton v. Jones,* 520 U.S. 681 (1997).

■ WEBSITE

A fuller version of *Clinton v. Jones* is available for download from this casebook's companion website, www.CaplanIntegratedConLaw.com.

Paula Jones alleged that in 1991, future President Bill Clinton sexually harassed her when he was the governor of Arkansas. She filed suit in 1994, during Clinton's first term as President. The President argued for a blanket rule of temporary immunity that would delay any civil suit until after the President left office. The Supreme Court unanimously held that Jones's lawsuit need not be delayed.

> The principal rationale for affording certain public servants immunity from suits for money damages arising out of their official acts is inapplicable to unofficial conduct. . . . The point of immunity for such officials is to forestall an atmosphere of intimidation that would conflict with their resolve to perform their designated functions in a principled fashion. . . .
>
> This reasoning provides no support for an immunity for unofficial conduct. . . . We have never suggested that the President, or any other official, has an immunity that extends beyond the scope of any action taken in an official capacity.

The Court recognized that defending against a civil suit would involve some distraction from the President's important official duties, but this was not justification for a baseline rule that all civil suits against a President should be postponed. Plaintiffs are entitled to seek redress for private wrongs, and delays may make it difficult to prove their case. Instead of issuing continuances as a matter of course, judges hearing such cases should, on a case-by-case basis, take the President's busy schedule and heavy responsibilities into consideration on matters of scheduling and discovery. On the record presented to it, the Court saw no reason to postpone discovery and trial of the Jones lawsuit, and remanded for **further proceedings**.

■ HISTORY

FURTHER PROCEEDINGS: On remand, the President sat for a deposition by Jones's lawyers, during which he falsely denied having a sexual relationship with White House intern Monica Lewinsky. Upon learning of the false testimony during his second term in office, the House of Representatives impeached the President for perjury and obstruction of justice. In early 1999, the Senate fell 17 votes short of the necessary two-thirds vote to convict, so the President served out his full term. Meanwhile, the Jones lawsuit was dismissed on summary judgment—although the trial judge also sanctioned the President for contempt of court.

2. The President as Suspect

Even though a president enjoys absolute immunity from civil damage actions based on official acts, a president may (as described above) be subject to impeachment or criminal prosecution for acts in office, and for civil suits not subject to absolute immunity. For obvious reasons, presidents prefer not to face investigations that could lead to such proceedings. Their arguments have combined separation of powers concepts with privileges rooted in the law of evidence.

a) Executive Privilege: *United States v. Nixon*

A basic rule of evidence is that a court may command testimony from any witness. Exceptions exist for evidence protected by testimonial privileges, like those for communications between attorney and client, spouse and spouse, doctor and patient, or priest and penitent. One such testimonial privilege is the "executive privilege," which allows high-ranking executive branch officers to keep secret the internal advice and deliberations exchanged privately among the officer and close advisors when debating decisions. The justification for executive privilege is the same as for the other privileges: to facilitate open and honest communication without fear that a party to the conversation will later be forced to reveal what was said.

■ WEBSITE

A fuller version of *United States v. Nixon* is available for download from this casebook's companion website, www.CaplanIntegratedConLaw.com.

The precise contours of executive privilege are murky; the privilege tends to be asserted and debated outside of court more than inside. But it was litigated to the Supreme Court level in *United States v. Nixon*, 418 U.S. 683 (1974), also known as the Watergate Tapes case.

President Richard Nixon ran for re-election in 1972. In June of that year, the main offices of the Democratic National Committee in the Watergate building were burglarized. The defendants were five men with links to the President: some worked for the campaign itself and others were part of a clandestine team of private detectives known as "The Plumbers" (so named because they were formed to stop leaks of information from the White House). In a series of Oval Office conversations that were captured on audiotape, President Nixon discussed how to prevent the investigation into the burglary from affecting the him. Methods included paying "hush money" to witnesses and attempting to dissuade the FBI with phony claims that the CIA was already handling the burglary as a matter of national security.

Nixon was re-elected in a landslide in November 1972, but public questions about the break-in increased when the Watergate burglars went to trial in January 1973. Over the course of a year, investigations of the Nixon administration proceeded down two paths. First, a federal special prosecutor gathered evidence to submit to a grand jury. (The grand jury ultimately approved criminal charges against several administration officials, including former Attorney General John Mitchell, for conspiracy to obstruct justice. The President was not a defendant in those cases, but had been described as an "unindicted co-conspirator.") Second, Congressional committees convened televised hearings to uncover similar information.

In April 1974, the special prosecutor issued a subpoena to the President to produce the taped conversations. At this stage, the President was technically a witness, asked to produce evidence in the trial of a third party. But it was clear that the President was also being investigated as a suspect. And if the tapes could be subpoenaed by the special prosecutor, they could be obtained by Congress, which was beginning to debate impeachment.

Nixon refused to produce the tapes, arguing that private conversations among the President and staff were *per se* protected by executive privilege. The US Supreme Court unanimously disagreed.

> Neither the doctrine of separation of powers, nor the need for confidentiality of high-level communications, without more, can sustain an absolute, unqualified Presidential privilege of immunity from judicial process under all circumstances. . . .
>
> The impediment that an absolute, unqualified privilege would place in the way of the primary constitutional duty of the Judicial Branch to do justice in criminal prosecutions would plainly conflict with the function of the courts under Art. III. . . . A President's acknowledged need for confidentiality in the communications of his office is general in nature, whereas the constitutional need for production of relevant evidence in a criminal proceeding is specific and central to the fair adjudication of a particular criminal case in the administration of justice. Without access to specific facts a criminal prosecution may be totally frustrated. . . .
>
> We conclude that when the ground for asserting [executive] privilege as to subpoenaed materials sought for use in a criminal trial is based only on the generalized interest in confidentiality, it cannot prevail over the fundamental demands of due process of law in the fair administration of criminal justice. The generalized assertion of privilege must yield to the demonstrated, specific need for evidence in a pending criminal trial.

Although the Court rejected an absolute executive privilege, it indicated that the President could withhold evidence on a claim of executive privilege if he established that disclosure of specific material would create concrete harms to the functioning of the executive branch. This would occur, for example, when the information sought would reveal military or diplomatic secrets. The Supreme Court ordered Nixon to **turn over the tapes** to the

■ HISTORY

TURN OVER THE TAPES: The Supreme Court issued its opinion on July 24, 1974. Realizing that any remaining privilege claims would fail in the trial court, President Nixon publicly released the tapes on August 5. They were widely viewed as strong evidence of obstruction of justice. With impeachment by the full House and conviction by the Senate looming, Nixon resigned the Presidency effective August 9.

trial court, which was to determine whether they met the Court's standard for executive privilege.

b) Non-Privileged Personal Information: *The Trump Cases*

Before running for President in 2016, Donald Trump was known as a real estate developer, hotel owner, and television personality. Rumors had circulated for years that Trump and his businesses had engaged in white-collar crimes including tax evasion, fraud, and laundering money from Russian oligarchs. After taking office, the President's detractors pursued investigations into two alleged instances of wrongdoing in connection with the 2016 presidential campaign.

- First, in the months before the election, it became known that operatives of the Russian government, in an effort to discredit Trump's Democratic opponent Hillary Clinton, had hacked into email accounts of the Democratic National Committee and published the stolen files on the internet. A few weeks after taking office in 2017, now-President Trump fired the director of the FBI, allegedly for pursuing too vigorously the investigations into Russian election activity. (There was some talk of impeachment over this incident, but it was ultimately not pursued. A special prosecutor concluded that the Trump campaign had met with Russian agents but not conspired with them, and reached no conclusion about whether firing the FBI director constituted obstruction of justice.)
- Second, it became known in 2018 that then-candidate Trump, acting through his lawyer Michael Cohen, had secretly paid women tens of thousands of dollars shortly before the election to keep secret their extramarital affairs with Trump—payments that may have violated campaign finance laws. The special prosecutor's investigation led to Cohen pleading guilty in 2018 to various federal crimes including campaign finance violations, tax fraud, bank fraud, and lying to Congress. Cohen publicly stated that he violated campaign finance laws at then-candidate Trump's direction.

As with Watergate, investigations into these scandals proceeded along parallel tracks: criminal and political. In one, a state prosecutor in New York sought to investigate whether Trump or people associated with him and his businesses had violated state laws, including evasion of state taxes and violations of state campaign finance laws. In the other, Congress sought to investigate a variety of Trump's alleged financial misdeeds. In both tracks, subpoenas were issued to third party accountants and bankers for copies of the President's past financial records, including his tax returns.

While the President's objections to these subpoenas worked their way through the courts, another scandal erupted. In September 2019, it was revealed that the President had withheld funds appropriated for military aid to Ukraine to persuade that country to provide political ammunition against former Vice President Joe Biden, the likely Democratic nominee for President in 2020. The House of Representatives voted to impeach in late 2019, but in February 2020 the Senate voted 48–52 to convict, falling 19 votes short of the necessary two-thirds.

Against this backdrop, the Supreme Court considered the propriety of the New York and Congressional subpoenas. Its decisions were announced in July 2020, as the presidential election campaign between President Trump and former Vice President Biden was underway.

ITEMS TO CONSIDER WHILE READING *TRUMP v. VANCE*:

A. *Is* Vance *distinguishable from* US v. Nixon*? In particular:*

- *Should it make a constitutional difference if a grand jury subpoena seeks documents regarding the President's actions in office as opposed to his private actions before being elected?*
- *Should it make a constitutional difference if a grand jury subpoena involving the President's personal information issues from a state criminal proceeding as opposed to a federal one?*

B. *In practical terms, what is the difference between the results of the majority and the separate opinions?*

Trump v. Vance,

140 S.Ct. 2412 (2020)

Chief Justice Roberts delivered the opinion of the Court [joined by Justices Ginsburg, Breyer, Sotomayor and Kagan].

In our judicial system, "the public has a right to every man's evidence."[FN1] Since the earliest days of the Republic, "every man" has included the President of the United States. Beginning with Jefferson and carrying on through Clinton, Presidents have uniformly testified or produced documents in criminal proceedings when called upon by federal courts. This case involves—so far as we and the parties can tell—the first state criminal subpoena directed to a President. The President contends that the subpoena is unenforceable. We granted certiorari to decide whether Article II and the Supremacy Clause categorically preclude, or require a heightened standard for, the issuance of a state criminal subpoena to a sitting President.

FN1 This maxim traces at least as far back as Lord Chancellor Hardwicke, in a 1742 parliamentary debate.

Trump v. Vance

I

In the summer of 2018, the New York County District Attorney's Office [headed by Cyrus Vance, Jr.] opened an investigation into what it opaquely describes as "business transactions involving multiple individuals whose conduct may have violated state law." A year later, the office—acting on behalf of a grand jury—served a subpoena duces tecum (essentially a request to produce evidence) on Mazars USA, LLP, the personal accounting firm of President Donald J. Trump. The subpoena directed Mazars to produce financial records relating to the President and business organizations affiliated with him, including tax returns and related schedules, from 2011 to the present.

The President, acting in his personal capacity, sued the district attorney and Mazars in Federal District Court to enjoin enforcement of the subpoena. He argued that, under Article II and the Supremacy Clause, a sitting President enjoys absolute immunity from state criminal process. He asked the court to issue a declaratory judgment that the subpoena is invalid and unenforceable while the President is in office and to permanently enjoin the district attorney from taking any action to enforce the subpoena. Mazars, concluding that the dispute was between the President and the district attorney, took no position on the legal issues raised by the President. . . .

The Second Circuit . . . agreed with the District Court's denial of a preliminary injunction. Drawing on the 200-year history of Presidents being subject to federal judicial process, the Court of Appeals concluded that "presidential immunity does not bar the enforcement of a state grand jury subpoena directing a third party to produce non-privileged material, even when the subject matter under investigation pertains to the President." It also rejected the argument raised by the United States as amicus curiae that a state grand jury subpoena must satisfy a heightened showing of need. . . . We granted certiorari.

II

In the summer of 1807, all eyes were on Richmond, Virginia. Aaron Burr, the former Vice President, was on trial for treason. Fallen from political grace after his fatal duel with Alexander Hamilton [in July 1804], and with a murder charge pending in New Jersey, Burr followed the path of many down-and-out Americans of his day—he headed West in search of new opportunity. But Burr was a man with outsized ambitions. Together with General James Wilkinson, the Governor of the Louisiana Territory, he hatched a plan to establish a new territory in Mexico, then controlled by Spain. Both men anticipated that war between the United States and

Spain was imminent, and when it broke out they intended to invade Spanish territory at the head of a private army.

But while Burr was rallying allies to his cause, tensions with Spain eased and rumors began to swirl that Burr was conspiring to detach States by the Allegheny Mountains from the Union. Wary of being exposed as the principal co-conspirator, Wilkinson took steps to ensure that any blame would fall on Burr. He sent a series of letters to President Jefferson accusing Burr of plotting to attack New Orleans and revolutionize the Louisiana Territory.

Jefferson, who despised his former running mate Burr for trying to steal the 1800 presidential election from him, was predisposed to credit Wilkinson's version of events. The President sent a special message to Congress identifying Burr as the "prime mover" in a plot "against the peace and safety of the Union." According to Jefferson, Burr contemplated either the "severance of the Union" or an attack on Spanish territory. Jefferson acknowledged that his sources contained a "mixture of rumors, conjectures, and suspicions" but, citing Wilkinson's letters, he assured Congress that Burr's guilt was "beyond question."

The trial that followed was the greatest spectacle in the short history of the republic, complete with a Founder-studded cast. People flocked to Richmond to watch, massing in tents and covered wagons along the banks of the James River, nearly doubling the town's population of 5,000. Burr's defense team included Edmund Randolph and Luther Martin, both former delegates at the Constitutional Convention and renowned advocates. Chief Justice John Marshall, who had recently squared off with the Jefferson administration in *Marbury v. Madison* (1803), presided . . . . Meanwhile Jefferson, intent on conviction, orchestrated the prosecution from afar, dedicating Cabinet meetings to the case, peppering the prosecutors with directions, and spending nearly $100,000 from the Treasury on the five-month proceedings.

In the lead-up to trial, Burr, taking aim at his accusers, moved for a subpoena duces tecum directed at Jefferson. The draft subpoena required the President to produce an October 21, 1806 letter from Wilkinson and accompanying documents, which Jefferson had referenced in his message to Congress. The prosecution opposed the request, arguing that a President could not be subjected to such a subpoena and that the letter might contain state secrets. Following four days of argument, Marshall announced his ruling to a packed chamber.

The President, Marshall declared, does not "stand exempt from the general provisions of the constitution" or, in particular, the Sixth Amendment's guarantee that those accused have compulsory process for obtaining witnesses for their defense. *United States v. Burr*, 25 F. Cas. 30 (CC Va. 1807). At common law the single reservation to the duty to testify in response to a subpoena was the case of the king, whose dignity was seen as incompatible with appearing under the process of the court. But, as Marshall explained, a king is born to power and can do no wrong.

The President, by contrast, is "of the people" and subject to the law. According to Marshall, the sole argument for exempting the President from testimonial obligations was that his "duties as chief magistrate demand his whole time for national objects." But, in Marshall's assessment, those demands were not unremitting. And should the President's duties preclude his attendance at a particular time and place, a court could work that out upon the return of the subpoena.

Trump v. Vance

Marshall also rejected the prosecution's argument that the President was immune from a subpoena duces tecum [for documents] because executive papers might contain state secrets. A subpoena duces tecum, he said, may issue to any person to whom an ordinary subpoena [for testimony] may issue. . . . As for the propriety of introducing any papers [into evidence], that would depend on the character of the paper, not on the character of the person who holds it. Marshall acknowledged that the papers sought by Burr could contain information the disclosure of which would endanger the public safety, but stated that, again, such concerns would have due consideration upon the return of the subpoena.

While the arguments unfolded, Jefferson, who had received word of the motion, wrote to the prosecutor indicating that he would—subject to the prerogative to decide which executive communications should be withheld—"furnish on all occasions, whatever the purposes of justice may require." His personal attendance, however, was out of the question, for it would leave the nation without the "sole branch which the constitution requires to be always in function."

Before Burr received the subpoenaed documents, Marshall rejected the prosecution's core legal theory for treason and **Burr was accordingly acquitted**. Jefferson, however, was not done. Committed to salvaging a conviction, he directed the prosecutors to proceed with a misdemeanor (yes, misdemeanor) charge for inciting war against Spain. Burr then renewed his request for Wilkinson's October 21 letter, which he later received a copy of, and subpoenaed a second letter, dated November 12, 1806, which the prosecutor claimed was privileged. Acknowledging that the President may withhold information to protect public safety, Marshall instructed that Jefferson should "state the particular reasons" for withholding the letter. *United States v. Burr*, 25 F. Cas. 187 (CC Va. 1807). The court, paying "all proper respect" to those reasons, would then decide whether to compel disclosure. But that decision was averted when the misdemeanor trial was cut short after it became clear that the prosecution lacked the evidence to convict.

HISTORY

BURR WAS ACCORDINGLY ACQUITTED: The prosecution did not have two witnesses to the same overt act, as required by Art. III § 3 for any federal treason conviction.

In the two centuries since the Burr trial, successive Presidents have accepted Marshall's ruling that the Chief Executive is subject to subpoena. [While in office, Presidents Monroe, Grant, Ford, Carter, and Clinton all sat for depositions as witnesses in federal criminal matters.]

The bookend to Marshall's ruling came in 1974 when the question he never had to decide—whether to compel the disclosure of official communications over the objection of the President—came to a head. That spring, the Special Prosecutor appointed to investigate the break-in of the Democratic National Committee Headquarters at the Watergate complex filed an indictment charging seven defendants associated with President Nixon and naming Nixon as an unindicted co-conspirator. As the case moved toward trial, the Special Prosecutor secured a subpoena duces tecum directing Nixon to produce, among other things, tape recordings of Oval Office meetings. Nixon moved to quash the subpoena, claiming that the Constitution provides an absolute privilege of confidentiality to all presidential communications. This Court rejected that argument in *United States v. Nixon* (1974), a decision we later described as "unequivocally and emphatically endorsing" Marshall's holding that Presidents are subject to subpoena. *Clinton v. Jones* (1997).

The *Nixon* Court readily acknowledged the importance of preserving the confidentiality of communications between high Government officials and those who advise and assist them. "Human experience," the Court explained, "teaches that those who expect public dissemination of their remarks may well temper candor with a concern for appearances and for their own interests to the detriment of the decisionmaking process." Confidentiality thus promoted the "public interest in candid, objective, and even blunt or harsh opinions in Presidential decisionmaking."

But, like Marshall two centuries prior, the Court recognized the countervailing interests at stake. Invoking the common law maxim that "the public has a right to every man's evidence," the Court observed that the public interest in fair and accurate judicial proceedings is at its height in the criminal setting, where our common commitment to justice demands that guilt shall not escape nor innocence suffer. Because these dual aims would be defeated if judgments were founded on a partial or speculative presentation of the facts, the *Nixon* Court recognized that it was "imperative" that compulsory process be available for the production of evidence needed either by the prosecution or the defense.

The Court thus concluded that the President's "generalized assertion of privilege must yield to the demonstrated, specific need for evidence in a pending criminal trial." Two weeks later, President Nixon dutifully released the tapes.

III

The history surveyed above all involved federal criminal proceedings. Here we are confronted for the first time with a subpoena **issued to the President** by a local grand jury operating under the supervision of a state court.

■ OBSERVATION

ISSUED TO THE PRESIDENT: As the fact section noted, the subpoena was issued to a third party who held information about the President. To sharpen the constitutional issue, the opinion treats the subpoena as if it were issued to the President directly.

In the President's view, that distinction makes all the difference. He argues that the Supremacy Clause gives a sitting President absolute immunity from state criminal subpoenas because compliance with those subpoenas would categorically impair a President's performance of his Article II functions. The Solicitor General, arguing on behalf of the United States, agrees with much of the President's reasoning but does not commit to his bottom line. Instead, the Solicitor General urges us to resolve this case by holding that a state grand jury subpoena for a sitting President's personal records must, at the very least, "satisfy a heightened standard of need," which the Solicitor General contends was not met here.

A

We begin with the question of absolute immunity. No one doubts that Article II guarantees the independence of the Executive Branch. As the head of that branch, the President occupies a unique position in the constitutional scheme. His duties, which range from faithfully executing the laws to commanding the Armed Forces, are of unrivaled gravity and breadth. Quite appropriately, those duties come with protections that safeguard the President's ability to perform his vital functions.

In addition, the Constitution guarantees the entire independence of the General Government from any control by the respective States. As we have often repeated, "States have no power to retard, impede, burden, or in any manner control the operations of the constitutional laws enacted by Congress." *McCulloch v. Maryland* (1819). It follows that States also lack the power to impede the President's execution of those laws.

Marshall's ruling in *Burr*, entrenched by 200 years of practice and our decision in *Nixon*, confirms that federal criminal subpoenas do not rise to the level of constitutionally forbidden impairment of the Executive's ability to perform its constitutionally mandated functions. But the President, joined in part by the Solicitor General, argues that state criminal subpoenas pose a unique threat of impairment and thus demand greater protection. To be clear, the President does not contend here that this subpoena, in particular, is impermissibly burdensome. Instead he makes a categorical argument about the burdens generally associated with state criminal subpoenas, focusing on three: diversion, stigma, and harassment. We address each in turn.

1

The President's primary contention, which the Solicitor General supports, is that complying with state criminal subpoenas would necessarily divert the Chief Executive from his duties. He grounds that concern in *Nixon v. Fitzgerald* (1978), which recognized a President's absolute immunity from damages liability predicated on his official acts. In explaining the basis for that immunity, this Court observed that the prospect of such liability could distract a President from his public duties, to the detriment of not only the President and his office but also the Nation that the Presidency was designed to serve. The President contends that the diversion occasioned by a state criminal subpoena imposes an equally intolerable burden on a President's ability to perform his Article II functions.

But *Fitzgerald* did not hold that distraction was sufficient to confer absolute immunity. We instead drew a careful analogy to the common law absolute immunity of judges and prosecutors, concluding that a President, like those officials, must deal fearlessly and impartially with the duties of his office—not be made unduly cautious in the discharge of those duties by the prospect of civil liability for official acts. Indeed, we expressly rejected immunity based on distraction alone 15 years later in *Clinton v. Jones*. There, President Clinton argued that the risk of being distracted by the need to participate in litigation entitled a sitting President to absolute immunity from civil liability, not just for official acts, as in *Fitzgerald*, but for private conduct as well. We disagreed with that rationale, explaining that the dominant concern in *Fitzgerald* was not mere distraction but the distortion of the Executive's decision-making process with respect to official acts that would stem from worry as to the possibility of damages. The Court recognized that Presidents constantly face myriad demands on their attention, some private, some political, and some as a result of official duty. But, the Court concluded, "while such distractions may be vexing to those subjected to them, they do not ordinarily implicate constitutional concerns."

The same is true of criminal subpoenas. Just as a properly managed civil suit is generally unlikely to occupy any substantial amount of a President's time or attention, two centuries of experience confirm that a properly tailored criminal subpoena will not normally hamper the performance of the President's constitutional duties. If anything, we expect that in the mine run of cases, where a President is subpoenaed during a proceeding targeting someone else, as Jefferson was, the burden on a President will ordinarily be lighter than the burden of defending against a civil suit.

The President, however, believes the district attorney is investigating him and his businesses. In such a situation, he contends, the toll that criminal process exacts from the President is even heavier than the distraction at issue in *Fitzgerald* and *Clinton*, because criminal litigation poses unique burdens on the President's time and will generate a considerable if not overwhelming degree of mental preoccupation.

But the President is not seeking immunity from the diversion occasioned by the prospect of future criminal liability. Instead he concedes—consistent with the position of the Department of Justice—that state grand juries are free to investigate a sitting President with an eye toward charging him after the completion of his term. The President's objection therefore must be limited to the additional distraction caused by the subpoena itself. But that argument runs up against the 200 years of precedent establishing that Presidents, and their official communications, are subject to judicial process, even when the President is under investigation.

2

The President next claims that the stigma of being subpoenaed will undermine his leadership at home and abroad. Notably, the Solicitor General does not endorse this argument, perhaps because we have twice denied absolute immunity claims by Presidents in cases involving allegations of serious misconduct. See *Clinton*; *Nixon*. But even if a tarnished reputation were a cognizable impairment, there is nothing inherently stigmatizing about a President performing the citizen's normal duty of furnishing information relevant to a criminal investigation. Nor can we accept that the risk of association with persons or activities under criminal investigation can absolve a President of such an important public duty. Prior Presidents have weathered these associations in federal cases, and there is no reason to think any attendant notoriety is necessarily greater in state court proceedings. . . .

Additionally, while the current suit has cast the Mazars subpoena into the spotlight, longstanding rules of grand jury secrecy aim to prevent the very stigma the President anticipates. Of course, disclosure restrictions are not perfect. But those who make unauthorized disclosures regarding a grand jury subpoena do so at their peril. See, e.g., N. Y. Penal Law Ann. § 215.70 (designating unlawful grand jury disclosure as a felony).

3

Finally, the President and the Solicitor General warn that subjecting Presidents to state criminal subpoenas will make them easily identifiable targets for harassment. But we rejected a nearly identical argument in *Clinton*, where then-President Clinton argued that permitting civil liability for unofficial acts would generate a large volume of politically motivated harassing and frivolous litigation. The President and the Solicitor General nevertheless argue that state criminal subpoenas pose a heightened risk and could undermine the President's ability to deal fearlessly and impartially with the States. They caution that, while federal prosecutors are accountable to and removable by the President, the 2,300 district attorneys in this country are responsive to local constituencies, local interests, and local prejudices, and might use criminal process to register their dissatisfaction with the President. What is more, we are told, the state courts supervising local grand juries may not exhibit the same respect that federal courts show to the President as a coordinate branch of Government.

We recognize, as does the district attorney, that harassing subpoenas could, under certain circumstances, threaten the independence or effectiveness of the Executive. Even so, in *Clinton* we found that the risk of harassment was not serious because federal courts have the tools to deter and, where necessary, dismiss vexatious civil suits. And, while we cannot ignore the possibility that state prosecutors may have political motivations, here again the law already seeks to protect against the predicted abuse.

First, grand juries are prohibited from engaging in arbitrary fishing expeditions and initiating investigations out of malice or an intent to harass. These protections, as the district attorney himself puts it, "apply with special force to a President, in light of the office's unique position as the head of the Executive Branch." And, in the event of such harassment, a President would be entitled to the protection of federal courts. The policy against federal interference in state criminal proceedings, while strong, allows intervention in those cases where the District Court properly finds that the state proceeding is motivated by a desire to harass or is conducted in bad faith.

Second, contrary to Justice Alito's characterization, our holding does not allow States to run roughshod over the functioning of the Executive Branch. The Supremacy Clause prohibits state judges and prosecutors from interfering with a President's official duties. Any effort to manipulate a President's policy decisions or to retaliate against a President for official acts through issuance of a subpoena, would thus be an unconstitutional attempt to influence a superior sovereign exempt from such obstacles. We generally assume that state courts and prosecutors will observe constitutional limitations. Failing that, federal law allows a President to challenge any allegedly unconstitutional influence in a federal forum, as the President has done here.

Given these safeguards and the Court's precedents, we cannot conclude that absolute immunity is necessary or appropriate under Article II or the Supremacy Clause. . . . On that point the Court is unanimous.

B

We next consider whether a state grand jury subpoena seeking a President's private papers must satisfy a heightened need standard. [Ordinarily, a subpoena for evidence in a state criminal matter may issue if it seeks to obtain relevant evidence.] The Solicitor General would require a threshold showing that the evidence sought is "critical" for specific charging decisions and that the subpoena is a "last resort," meaning the evidence is not available from any other source and is needed now, rather than at the end of the President's term. Justice Alito, largely embracing those criteria, agrees that a state criminal subpoena to a President should not be allowed unless a heightened standard is met.

We disagree, for three reasons. First, such a heightened standard would extend protection designed for official documents to the President's private papers. As the Solicitor General and Justice Alito acknowledge, their proposed test is derived from executive privilege cases that trace back to *Burr.* There, Marshall explained that if Jefferson invoked presidential privilege over executive communications, the court would not proceed against the president as against an ordinary individual but would instead require an affidavit from the defense that would clearly show the paper to be essential to the justice of the case. The Solicitor General and Justice Alito would have us apply a similar standard to a President's personal papers. But this argument does not account for the relevant passage from *Burr*: "If there be a paper in the possession of the executive, which is not of an official nature, he must stand, as respects that paper, in nearly the same situation with any other individual." And it is only "nearly "—and not "entirely"—because the President retains the right to assert privilege over documents that, while ostensibly private, "partake of the character of an official paper."

Second, neither the Solicitor General nor Justice Alito has established that heightened protection against state subpoenas is necessary for the Executive to fulfill his Article II functions. Beyond the risk of harassment, which we addressed above, the only justification they offer for the heightened standard is protecting Presidents from "unwarranted burdens." In effect, they argue that even if federal subpoenas to a President are warranted whenever evidence is material, state subpoenas are warranted only when the evidence is essential. But that double standard has no basis in law. For if the state subpoena is not issued to manipulate, the documents themselves are not protected, and the Executive is not impaired, then nothing in Article II or the Supremacy Clause supports holding state subpoenas to a higher standard than their federal counterparts.

Finally, in the absence of a need to protect the Executive, the public interest in fair and effective law enforcement cuts in favor of comprehensive access to evidence. Requiring a state grand jury to meet a heightened standard of need would hobble the grand jury's ability to acquire all information that might possibly bear on its investigation. And, even assuming the evidence withheld under that standard were preserved until the conclusion of a President's term, in the interim the State would be deprived of investigative leads that the evidence might yield, allowing memories to fade and documents to disappear. This could frustrate the identification, investigation, and indictment of third parties (for whom applicable statutes of limitations might lapse). More troubling, it could prejudice the innocent by depriving the grand jury of exculpatory evidence.

Rejecting a heightened need standard does not leave Presidents with "no real protection" [as Justice Alito worries]. To start, a President may avail himself of the same protections available to every other citizen. These include the right to challenge the subpoena on any grounds permitted by state law, which usually include bad faith and undue burden or breadth. And, as in federal court, "the high respect that is owed to the office of the Chief Executive should inform the conduct of the entire proceeding, including the timing and scope of discovery." *Clinton* (Breyer, J., concurring in judgment) (stressing the need for courts presiding over suits against the President to "schedule proceedings so as to avoid significant interference with the President's ongoing discharge of his official responsibilities"); *Nixon* ("Where a subpoena is directed to a President appellate review should be particularly meticulous.").

Furthermore, although the Constitution does not entitle the Executive to absolute immunity or a heightened standard, he is not relegated only to the challenges available to private citizens. A President can raise subpoena-specific constitutional challenges, in either a state or federal forum. As previously noted, he can challenge the subpoena as an attempt to influence the performance of his official duties, in violation of the Supremacy Clause. This avenue protects against local political machinations interposed as an obstacle to the effective operation of a federal constitutional power.

In addition, the Executive can—as the district attorney concedes—argue that compliance with a particular subpoena would impede his constitutional duties. Incidental to the functions confided in Article II is the power to perform them, without obstruction or impediment. As a result, once the President sets forth and explains a conflict between judicial proceeding and public duties, or shows that an order or subpoena would significantly interfere with his efforts to carry out those duties, the matter changes. At that point, a court should use its inherent authority to quash or modify the subpoena, if necessary to ensure that such interference with the President's duties would not occur.

[CONCLUSION]

Two hundred years ago, a great jurist of our Court established that no citizen, not even the President, is categorically above the common duty to produce evidence when called upon in a criminal proceeding. We reaffirm that principle today and hold that the President is neither absolutely immune from state criminal subpoenas seeking his private papers nor entitled to a heightened standard of need. The guard furnished to this high officer lies where it always has—in the conduct of a court applying established legal and constitutional principles to individual subpoenas in a manner that preserves both the independence of the Executive and the integrity of the criminal justice system.

The arguments presented here and in the Court of Appeals were limited to absolute immunity and heightened need. The Court of Appeals, however, has directed that the case be returned to the District Court, where the President may raise further arguments as appropriate. We affirm the judgment of the Court of Appeals and remand the case for further proceedings consistent with this opinion.

Justice Kavanaugh, with whom Justice Gorsuch joins, concurring in the judgment.

The Court today unanimously concludes that a President does not possess absolute immunity from a state criminal subpoena, but also unanimously agrees that this case should be remanded to the District Court, where the President may raise constitutional and legal objections to the subpoena as appropriate. I agree with those two conclusions. . . .

Trump v. Vance

The question here, then, is how to balance the State's interests and the Article II interests. The longstanding precedent that has applied to federal criminal subpoenas for official, privileged Executive Branch information is *United States v. Nixon* (1974). That landmark case requires that a prosecutor establish a "demonstrated, specific need" for the President's information. *Id.*, see also ***In re Sealed Case***, 121 F.3d 729, (D.C. Cir. 1997). . . .

Because this case again entails a clash between the interests of the criminal process and the Article II interests of the Presidency, I would apply the longstanding *Nixon* "demonstrated, specific need" standard to this case. . . .

In the end, much may depend on how the majority opinion's various standards are applied in future years and decades. It will take future cases to determine precisely how much difference exists between (i) the various standards articulated by the majority opinion, (ii) the overarching *Nixon* "demonstrated, specific need" standard that I would adopt, and (iii) Justice Thomas's and Justice Alito's other proposed standards. In any event, in my view, lower courts in cases of this sort involving a President will almost invariably have to begin by delving into why the State wants the information; why and how much the State needs the information, including whether the State could obtain the information elsewhere; and whether compliance with the subpoena would unduly burden or interfere with a President's official duties. . . .

HISTORY

IN RE SEALED CASE: This Court of Appeals decision involved a subpoena to White House counsel during an investigation of corruption by a former Secretary of Agriculture. The Court said: "We conclude that *Nixon*'s demonstrated, specific need standard has two components. A party seeking to overcome a claim of presidential privilege must demonstrate: first, that each discrete group of the subpoenaed materials likely contains important evidence; and second, that this evidence is not available with due diligence elsewhere."

Justice Thomas, dissenting. [Omitted.]

Justice Alito, dissenting.

. . . Constitutionally speaking, the President never sleeps. The President must be ready, at a moment's notice, to do whatever it takes to preserve, protect, and defend the Constitution and the American people. Without a President who is able at all times to carry out the responsibilities of the office, our constitutional system could not operate, and the country would be at risk. . . .

It is not enough to recite sayings like "no man is above the law" and "the public has a right to every man's evidence." These sayings are true—and important—but they beg the question. The law applies equally to all persons, including a person who happens for a period of time to occupy the Presidency. But there is no question that the nature of the office demands in some instances that the application of laws be adjusted at least until the person's term in office ends. . . .

In light of the above, a subpoena like the one now before us should not be enforced unless it meets a test that takes into account the need to prevent interference with a President's discharge of the responsibilities of the office. . . . We should not treat this subpoena like an ordinary grand jury subpoena and should not relegate a President to the meager defenses that are available when an ordinary grand jury subpoena is challenged. But that, at bottom, is the effect of the Court's decision.

The Presidency deserves greater protection. Thus, in a case like this one, a prosecutor should be required (1) to provide at least a general description of the possible offenses that are under investigation, (2) to outline how the subpoenaed records relate to those offenses, and (3) to explain why it is important that the records be produced and why it is necessary for production to occur while the President is still in office. . . .

ITEMS TO CONSIDER WHILE READING *TRUMP v. MAZARS*:

A. *What is the source of Congress's power to issue subpoenas?*

B. *Should the enforceability of a subpoena for a President's information differ if it is issued by Congress rather than a court? Consider the differences, if any, between the standards announced in* Vance *and* Mazars.

C. *Justice Thomas argues that the subpoena could be proper if the House was considering impeachment, but not if it was considering legislation. Is this distinction sensible?*

Trump v. Mazars USA, LLP,

140 S.Ct. 2019 (2020)

Chief Justice Roberts delivered the opinion of the Court [joined by Justices Ginsburg, Breyer, Sotomayor, Kagan, Gorsuch and Kavanaugh].

Over the course of five days in April 2019, three committees of the U.S. House of Representatives issued four subpoenas seeking information about the finances of President Donald J. Trump, his children, and affiliated businesses. We have held that the House has authority under the Constitution to issue subpoenas to assist it in carrying out its legislative responsibilities. The House asserts that the financial information sought here—encompassing a decade's worth of transactions by the President and his family—will help guide legislative reform in areas ranging from money laundering and terrorism to foreign involvement in U. S. elections. The President contends that the House lacked a valid legislative aim and instead sought these records to harass him, expose personal matters, and conduct law enforcement activities beyond its authority. The question presented is whether the subpoenas exceed the authority of the House under the Constitution.

We have never addressed a congressional subpoena for the President's information. Two hundred years ago, it was established that Presidents may be subpoenaed during a federal criminal proceeding, *United States v. Burr*, 25 F. Cas. 30 (CC Va. 1807) (Marshall, Cir. J.), and earlier today we extended that ruling to state criminal proceedings, *Trump v. Vance* (2020). Nearly fifty years ago, we held that a federal prosecutor could obtain information from a President despite assertions of executive privilege, *United States v. Nixon* (1974), and more recently we ruled that a private litigant could subject a President to a damages suit and appropriate discovery obligations in federal court, *Clinton v. Jones* (1997).

This case is different. Here the President's information is sought not by prosecutors or private parties in connection with a particular judicial proceeding, but by committees of Congress that have set forth broad legislative objectives. Congress and the President—the two political branches established by the Constitution—have an ongoing relationship that the Framers intended to feature both rivalry and reciprocity. That distinctive aspect necessarily informs our analysis of the question before us.

I

A

Each of the three committees sought overlapping sets of financial documents, but each supplied different justifications for the requests. [Documents were sought from businesses that held financial records relating to the President, his children, their immediate family members, and several affiliated business entities. These included two banks—Deutsche Bank and Capital One—and the President's personal accounting firm, Mazars USA, LLP.] . . .

The Financial Services Committee issued these subpoenas pursuant to House Resolution 206, which called for "efforts to close loopholes that allow corruption, terrorism, and money laundering to infiltrate our country's financial system." Such loopholes, the resolution explained, had allowed "illicit money, including from Russian oligarchs," to flow into the United States through "anonymous shell companies" using investments such as "luxury high-end real estate." The House also invokes the oversight plan of the Financial Services Committee, which stated that the Committee intends to review banking regulation and "examine the implementation, effectiveness, and enforcement" of laws designed to prevent money laundering and the financing of terrorism. The plan further provided that the Committee would "consider proposals to prevent the abuse of the financial system" and "address any vulnerabilities identified" in the real estate market. . . .

The Intelligence Committee subpoenaed Deutsche Bank as part of an investigation into foreign efforts to undermine the U. S. political process. Committee Chairman Adam Schiff had described that investigation in a previous statement, explaining that the Committee was examining alleged attempts by Russia to influence the 2016 election; potential links between Russia and the President's campaign; and whether the President and his associates had been compromised by foreign actors or interests. Chairman Schiff added that the Committee planned "to develop legislation and policy reforms to ensure the U. S. government is better positioned to counter future efforts to undermine our political process and national security." . . .

[The Oversight and Reform Committee argued that] recent testimony by the President's former personal attorney Michael Cohen, along with several documents prepared by Mazars and supplied by Cohen, raised questions about whether the President had accurately represented his financial affairs. Chairman Cummings asserted that the Committee had full authority to investigate whether the President: (1) may have engaged in illegal conduct before and during his tenure in office, (2) has undisclosed conflicts of interest that may impair his ability to make impartial policy decisions, (3) is complying with the **Emoluments Clauses** of the Constitution and (4) has accurately reported his finances to the Office of Government Ethics and other federal entities. "The Committee's interest in these matters," Chairman Cummings concluded, "informs its review of multiple laws and legislative proposals under our jurisdiction."

TERMINOLOGY

EMOLUMENTS CLAUSES: To help ensure loyalty, the Constitution limits the ability of the President and other officers to receive "emoluments" from sources other than Congress. Art. I, § 9, cl. 8 (foreign emoluments); Art. II, § 2 (domestic emoluments). A debate during the Trump Presidency asked whether money his hotels earned from foreign dignitaries were forbidden emoluments.

B

Petitioners—the President in his personal capacity, along with his children and affiliated businesses—filed two suits challenging the subpoenas [in the federal district courts for the District of Columbia and the Southern District of New York]. In both cases, petitioners contended that the subpoenas lacked a legitimate legislative purpose and violated the separation of powers. The President did not, however, resist the subpoenas by arguing that any of the requested records were protected by executive privilege. For relief, petitioners asked for declaratory judgments and injunctions preventing Mazars and the banks from complying with the subpoenas. Although named as defendants, Mazars and the banks took no positions on the legal issues in these cases, and the House committees intervened to defend the subpoenas.

Petitioners' challenges failed [in the trial courts and their respective Courts of Appeal]. We granted certiorari in both cases and stayed the judgments below pending our decision.

II

A

The question presented is whether the subpoenas exceed the authority of the House under the Constitution. Historically, disputes over congressional demands for presidential documents have not ended up in court. Instead, they have been hashed out in the hurly-burly, the give-and-take of the political process between the legislative and the executive.

That practice began with George Washington and the early Congress. In 1792, a House committee requested Executive Branch documents pertaining to General St. Clair's campaign against the Indians in the Northwest Territory, which had concluded in an utter rout of federal forces when they were caught by surprise near the present-day border between Ohio and Indiana. Since this was the first such request from Congress, President Washington called a Cabinet meeting, wishing to take care that his response "be rightly conducted" because it could "become a precedent."

The meeting, attended by the likes of Alexander Hamilton, Thomas Jefferson, Edmund Randolph, and Henry Knox, ended with the Cabinet of "one mind": The House had authority to institute inquiries and call for papers but the President could exercise a discretion over disclosures, communicating such papers as the public good would permit and refusing the rest. President Washington then dispatched Jefferson to speak to individual congressmen and "bring them by persuasion into the right channel." The discussions were apparently fruitful, as the House later narrowed its request and the documents were supplied without recourse to the courts.

[Similar negotiations resulted in delivery of some but not all requested papers by Presidents Jefferson, Reagan, and Clinton.] Congress and the President maintained this tradition of negotiation and compromise—without the involvement of this Court—until the present dispute. . . .

This dispute therefore represents a significant departure from historical practice. Although the parties agree that this particular controversy is justiciable, we recognize that it is the first of its kind to reach this Court; that disputes of this sort can raise important issues concerning relations between the branches; that related disputes involving congressional efforts to seek official Executive Branch information recur on a regular basis, including in the context of deeply partisan controversy; and that Congress and the Executive have nonetheless managed for over two centuries to resolve such disputes among themselves without the benefit of guidance from us. Such longstanding practice is a consideration of great weight in cases concerning the allocation of power between the two elected branches of Government, and it imposes on us a duty of care to ensure that we not needlessly disturb the compromises and working arrangements that those branches themselves have reached. With that in mind, we turn to the question presented.

B

Congress has no enumerated constitutional power to conduct investigations or issue subpoenas, but we have held that each House has power to secure needed information in order to legislate. This power of inquiry—with process to enforce it—is an essential and appropriate auxiliary to the legislative function. Without information, Congress would be shooting in the dark, unable to legislate wisely or effectively. The congressional power to obtain information is "broad" and "indispensable." *Watkins v. United States*, 354 U. S. 178 (1957). It encompasses inquiries into the administration of existing laws, studies of proposed laws, and surveys of defects in our social, economic or political system for the purpose of enabling the Congress to remedy them.

Because this power is justified solely as an adjunct to the legislative process, it is subject to several limitations. Most importantly, a congressional subpoena is valid only if it is "related to, and in furtherance of, a legitimate task of the Congress." *Watkins v. United States*, 354 U.S. 178 (1957). The subpoena must serve a "**valid legislative purpose**," *Quinn v. United States*, 349 U.S. 155 (1955); it must concern a subject on which legislation could be had.

Furthermore, Congress may not issue a subpoena for the purpose of law enforcement, because those powers are assigned under our Constitution to the Executive and the Judiciary. Thus Congress may not use subpoenas to "try" someone before a committee for any crime or wrongdoing. Congress has no general power to inquire into private affairs and compel disclosures, and there is no congressional power to expose for the sake of exposure. Investigations conducted solely for the personal aggrandizement of the investigators or to "punish" those investigated are indefensible.

■ HISTORY

VALID LEGISLATIVE PURPOSE: The cases requiring valid legislative purpose for Congressional subpoenas arose in the 1950s, when Congressional committees convened highly-publicized hearings seeking to identify private persons as current or former members of the Communist Party. In cases challenging actions of the House Un-American Activities Committee (HUAC) or Senate committees led by Sen. Joseph McCarthy and others, the Supreme Court considered when Congress's power to gather information for its work might be abused beyond constitutional limits.

Finally, recipients of legislative subpoenas retain their constitutional rights throughout the course of an investigation. And recipients have long been understood to retain common law and constitutional privileges with respect to certain materials, such as attorney-client communications and governmental communications protected by executive privilege.

C

The President contends, as does the Solicitor General appearing on behalf of the United States, that the usual rules for congressional subpoenas do not govern here because the President's papers are at issue. They argue for a more demanding standard based in large part on cases involving the *Nixon* tapes—recordings of conversations between President Nixon and close advisers discussing the break-in at the Democratic National Committee's headquarters at the Watergate complex. The tapes were subpoenaed by a Senate committee and the Special Prosecutor investigating the break-in, prompting President Nixon to invoke executive privilege and leading to two cases addressing the showing necessary to require the President to comply with the subpoenas.

Those cases, the President and the Solicitor General now contend, establish the standard that should govern the House subpoenas here. Quoting *Nixon*, the President asserts that the House must establish a "demonstrated, specific need" for the financial information, just as the Watergate special prosecutor was required to do in order to obtain the tapes. . . . The President and the Solicitor General [further] argue that the House must show that the financial information is "demonstrably critical" to its legislative purpose.

We disagree that these demanding standards apply here. Unlike the cases before us, *Nixon* . . . involved Oval Office communications over which the President asserted executive privilege. That privilege safeguards the public interest in candid, confidential deliberations within the Executive Branch; it is fundamental to the operation of Government. As a result, information subject to executive privilege deserves the greatest protection consistent with the fair administration of justice. We decline to transplant that protection root and branch to cases involving nonprivileged, private information, which by definition does not implicate sensitive Executive Branch deliberations.

The standards proposed by the President and the Solicitor General—if applied outside the context of privileged information—would risk seriously impeding Congress in carrying out its responsibilities. The President and the Solicitor General would apply the same exacting standards to all subpoenas for the President's information, without recognizing distinctions between privileged and nonprivileged information, between official and personal information, or between various legislative objectives. Such a categorical approach would represent a significant departure from the longstanding way of doing business between the branches, giving short shrift to Congress's important interests in conducting inquiries to obtain the information it needs to legislate effectively. Confounding the legislature in that effort would be contrary to the principle that:

> It is the proper duty of a representative body to look diligently into every affair of government and to talk much about what it sees. It is meant to be the eyes and the voice, and to embody the wisdom and will of its constituents. Unless Congress have and use every means of acquainting itself with the acts and the disposition of the administrative agents of the government, the country must be helpless to learn how it is being served. *United States v. Rumely*, 345 U. S. 41 (1953)

Legislative inquiries might involve the President in appropriate cases; as noted, Congress's responsibilities extend to "every affair of government." Because the President's approach does not take adequate account of these significant congressional interests, we do not adopt it.

D

The House meanwhile would have us ignore that these suits involve the President. Invoking our precedents concerning investigations that did not target the President's papers, the House urges us to uphold its subpoenas because they "relate to a valid legislative purpose" or "concern a subject on which legislation could be had." That approach is appropriate, the House argues, because the cases before us are not "momentous separation-of-powers disputes." . . .

The House's approach fails to take adequate account of the significant separation of powers issues raised by congressional subpoenas for the President's information. Congress and the President have an ongoing institutional relationship as the "opposite and rival" political branches established by the Constitution. The Federalist #51. As a result, congressional subpoenas directed at the President differ markedly from congressional subpoenas we have previously reviewed, and they bear little resemblance to criminal subpoenas issued to the President in the course of a specific investigation. Unlike those subpoenas, congressional subpoenas for the President's information unavoidably pit the political branches against one another.

Far from accounting for separation of powers concerns, the House's approach aggravates them by leaving essentially no limits on the congressional power to subpoena the President's personal records. Any personal paper possessed by a President could potentially "relate to" a conceivable subject of legislation, for Congress has broad legislative powers that touch a vast number of subjects. The President's financial records could relate to economic reform, medical records to health reform, school transcripts to education reform, and so on. Indeed, at argument, the House was unable to identify any type of information that lacks some relation to potential legislation.

Without limits on its subpoena powers, Congress could "exert an imperious control" over the Executive Branch and aggrandize itself at the President's expense, just as the Framers feared. The Federalist #71. And a limitless subpoena power would transform the established practice of the political branches. Instead of negotiating over information requests, Congress could simply walk away from the bargaining table and compel compliance in court.

The House and the courts below suggest that these separation of powers concerns are not fully implicated by the particular subpoenas here, but we disagree. We would have to be "blind" not to see what "all others can see and understand": that the subpoenas do not represent a run-of-the-mill legislative effort but rather a clash between rival branches of government over records of intense political interest for all involved. *Rumely* (quoting *Bailey v. Drexel Furniture a/k/a The Child Labor Tax Case* (1922)).

The interbranch conflict here does not vanish simply because the subpoenas seek personal papers or because the President sued in his personal capacity. The President is the only person who **alone composes a branch of government**. As a result, there is not always a clear line between his personal and official affairs. "The interest of the man" is often "connected with the constitutional rights of the place." The Federalist #51. Given the close connection between the Office of the President and its occupant, congressional demands for the President's papers can implicate the relationship between the branches regardless whether those papers are personal or official. Either way, a demand may aim to harass the President or render him "complaisant to the humors of the Legislature." The Federalist #71. In fact, a subpoena for personal papers may pose a heightened risk of such impermissible purposes, precisely because of the documents' personal nature and their less evident connection to a legislative task. No one can say that the controversy here is less significant to the relationship between the branches simply because it involves personal papers. Quite the opposite. That appears to be what makes the matter of such great consequence to the President and Congress.

■ OBSERVATION

ALONE COMPOSES A BRANCH OF GOVERNMENT: The Court alludes to the Vesting Clause of Art. II, § 1, which states: "The executive power shall be vested in a President of the United States of America." Compare Art. I, § 1 (vesting legislative power in "a Congress" consisting of the House and Senate) and Art. III, § 1 (vesting judicial power in "one supreme Court, and in such inferior Courts as the Congress may from time to time ordain and establish").

In addition, separation of powers concerns are no less palpable here simply because the subpoenas were issued to third parties. Congressional demands for the President's information present an interbranch conflict no matter where the information is held—it is, after all, the President's information. Were it otherwise, Congress could sidestep constitutional requirements any time a President's information is entrusted to a third party—as occurs with rapidly increasing frequency. Indeed, Congress could declare open season on the President's information held by schools, archives, internet service providers, e-mail clients, and financial institutions. The Constitution does not tolerate such ready evasion; it deals with substance, not shadows.

E

Congressional subpoenas for the President's personal information implicate weighty concerns regarding the separation of powers. Neither side, however, identifies an approach that accounts for these concerns. For more than two centuries, the political branches have resolved information disputes using the wide variety of means that the Constitution puts at their disposal. The nature of such interactions would be transformed by judicial enforcement of either of the approaches suggested by the parties, eroding a deeply embedded traditional way of conducting government.

A balanced approach is necessary, one that takes a "considerable impression" from "the practice of the government," *McCulloch v. Maryland* (1819), and resists the pressure inherent within each of the separate Branches to exceed the outer limits of its power, We therefore conclude that, in assessing whether a subpoena directed at the President's personal information is "related to, and in furtherance of, a legitimate task of the Congress," *Watkins*, courts must perform a careful analysis that takes adequate account of the separation of powers principles at stake, including both the significant legislative interests of Congress and the unique position of the President. Several special considerations inform this analysis.

First, courts should carefully assess whether the asserted legislative purpose warrants the significant step of involving the President and his papers. Occasions for constitutional confrontation between the two branches should be avoided whenever possible. Congress may not rely on the President's information if other sources could reasonably provide Congress the information it needs in light of its particular legislative objective. The President's unique constitutional position means that Congress may not look to him as a case study for general legislation.

Unlike in criminal proceedings, where the very integrity of the judicial system would be undermined without full disclosure of all the facts, efforts to craft legislation involve predictive policy judgments that are not hampered in quite the same way when every scrap of potentially relevant evidence is not available, While we certainly recognize Congress's important interests in obtaining information through appropriate inquiries, those interests are not sufficiently powerful to justify access to the President's personal papers when other sources could provide Congress the information it needs.

Second, to narrow the scope of possible conflict between the branches, courts should insist on a subpoena no broader than reasonably necessary to support Congress's legislative objective. The specificity of the subpoena's request serves as an important safeguard against unnecessary intrusion into the operation of the Office of the President.

Third, courts should be attentive to the nature of the evidence offered by Congress to establish that a subpoena advances a valid legislative purpose. The more detailed and substantial the evidence of Congress's legislative purpose, the better. That is particularly true when Congress contemplates legislation that raises sensitive constitutional issues, such as legislation concerning the Presidency. In such cases, it is impossible to conclude that a subpoena is designed to advance a valid legislative purpose unless Congress adequately identifies its aims and explains why the President's information will advance its consideration of the possible legislation.

Fourth, courts should be careful to assess the burdens imposed on the President by a subpoena. We have held that burdens on the President's time and attention stemming from judicial process and litigation, without more, generally do not cross constitutional lines. But burdens imposed by a congressional subpoena should be carefully scrutinized, for they stem from a rival political branch that has an ongoing relationship with the President and incentives to use subpoenas for institutional advantage.

Other considerations may be pertinent as well; one case every two centuries does not afford enough experience for an exhaustive list.

When Congress seeks information needed for intelligent legislative action, it unquestionably remains the duty of all citizens to cooperate. Congressional subpoenas for information from the President, however, implicate special concerns regarding the separation of powers. The courts below did not take adequate account of those concerns. The judgments of the Courts of Appeals for the D. C. Circuit and the Second Circuit are vacated, and the cases are remanded for further proceedings consistent with this opinion.

Justice Thomas, dissenting.

. . . The Committees do not argue that these subpoenas were issued pursuant to the House's impeachment power. Instead, they argue that the subpoenas are a valid exercise of their legislative powers. . . . I would hold that Congress has no power to issue a legislative subpoena for private, nonofficial documents—whether they belong to the President or not. Congress may be able to obtain these documents as part of an investigation of the President, but to do so, it must proceed under the impeachment power. Accordingly, I would reverse the judgments of the Courts of Appeals. . . .

Congress' legislative powers do not authorize it to engage in a nationwide inquisition with whatever resources it chooses to appropriate for itself. The majority's solution—a nonexhaustive four-factor test of uncertain origin—is better than nothing. But the power that Congress seeks to exercise here has even less basis in the Constitution than the majority supposes. . . .

Justice Alito, dissenting.

Justice Thomas makes a valuable argument about the constitutionality of congressional subpoenas for a President's personal documents. In these cases, however, I would assume for the sake of argument that such subpoenas are not categorically barred. Nevertheless, legislative subpoenas for a President's personal documents are inherently suspicious. Such documents are seldom of any special value in considering potential legislation, and subpoenas for such documents can easily be used for improper non-legislative purposes. Accordingly, courts must be very sensitive to separation of powers issues when they are asked to approve the enforcement of such subpoenas. . . .

The Court recognizes that the decisions below did not give adequate consideration to separation of powers concerns. Therefore, after setting out a non-exhaustive list of considerations for the lower courts to take into account, the Court vacates the judgments of the Courts of Appeals and sends the cases back for reconsideration. I agree that the lower courts erred and that these cases must be remanded, but I do not think that the considerations outlined by the Court can be properly satisfied unless the House is required to show more than it has put forward to date.

Specifically, the House should provide a description of the type of legislation being considered, and while great specificity is not necessary, the description should be sufficient to permit a court to assess whether the particular records sought are of any special importance. The House should also spell out its constitutional authority to enact the type of legislation that it is contemplating, and it should justify the scope of the subpoenas in relation to the articulated legislative needs. In addition, it should explain why the subpoenaed information, as opposed to information available from other sources, is needed. Unless the House is required to make a showing along these lines, I would hold that enforcement of the subpoenas cannot be ordered. Because I find the terms of the Court's remand inadequate, I must respectfully dissent.

flash*forward*

1. ***The Vance Subpoenas.*** On remand in *Trump v. Vance*, lower courts applying the standards announced by the Supreme Court found upheld the subpoenas. 480 F.Supp.3d 460 (S.D.N.Y. 2020), aff'd, 977 F.3d 198 (2d Cir. 2020). The requested documents were provided to state investigators after President Trump left office in January 2021. In July 2021, state charges of criminal tax evasion and fraud were filed against the business known as The Trump Organization and its chief financial officer; they were convicted in 2022. As this volume goes to print, State investigations into the former President's business conduct continue.

2. *The Mazars Subpoenas.* On remand in *Trump v. Mazars*, the third-party subpoenas that had been litigated to the Supreme Court were found to be enforceable, so long as their scope was narrowed to focus on a specific set of transactions. 39 F.4th 774 (D.C. Cir. 2022). Meanwhile, pursuant to a pre-existing statute, the chair of the House Ways and Means Committee requested the President's tax returns directly from the Department of the Treasury. Applying the standards announced by the Supreme Court in *Mazars*, lower courts held that the request had a legitimate legislative purpose—namely, to determine if the IRS was properly applying its regulations for tax audits of presidents. *Committee on Ways & Means v. Department of the Treasury*, 45 F.4th 324 (D.C. Cir. 2022), *motion for stay denied*, 2022 WL 17098419 (U.S. 2022).

3. *The January 6 Committee Subpoenas.* President Trump did not leave office quietly after losing his bid for re-election in 2020. His false insistence that he was the true winner led to a violent mob charging the Capitol building on January 6, 2021, as a joint session of Congress certified the results of the Electoral College vote. The President's actions led to a second impeachment by the House of Representatives on January 13; he left office on January 20; and at the close of the trial on February 13, the Senate voted 57–43 to convict (ten votes short of the required two-thirds). Although he had left office, a conviction would have disqualified him from any future "office of honor, trust or profit under the United States." Art. I, § 3, cl. 7.

In May 2021, the House of Representatives formed a Select Committee to Investigate the January 6th Attack on the US Capitol. Relying on a pre-existing statute, the Committee requested documents from the National Archives, which takes custody of official papers of former presidents. Trump filed suit to prevent the disclosure, but that suit failed with the Court finding no basis for any claim of executive privilege. *Trump v. Thompson*, 20 F.4th 10 (D.C. Cir. 2021), *motion for stay denied*, 142 S.Ct. 680 (2022).

As this volume goes to print, the January 6 Committee asked the Department of Justice to bring criminal charges against the former President, a possibility already being investigated by a special prosecutor. State prosecutors in Georgia were also considering criminal charges over attempts to subvert that state's election results.

Chapter Recap

A. Separation of powers prevents one branch of the federal government from unduly interfering with functions assigned to others. However, the Constitution purposely includes areas of overlap between branches, which means that not every instance of conflict between branches will violate separation of powers.

B. Separation of powers questions may arise in many distinct factual and legal settings. As a result, separation of powers is best viewed as an overarching standard, rather than a precise legal rule.

C. The usual methods of constitutional reasoning may be useful in separation of powers cases, with text and structure receiving the most attention.

CHAPTER 17

Master Class: Structural Limits

In 2010, Congress passed the Affordable Care Act (the ACA, nicknamed "Obamacare") after considerable political tumult. Litigation over the Act's constitutionality culminated in *National Federation of Independent Businesses v. Sebelius* (2012). The decision is important in itself, and also provides an excellent review of concepts studied to date. Like most important constitutional law decisions, it involves more than one set of legal doctrines.

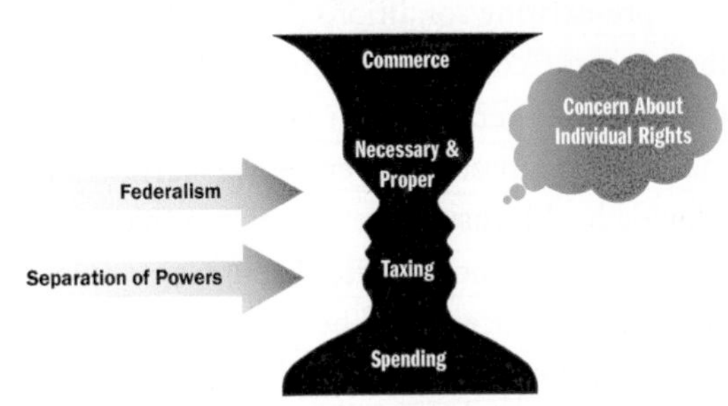

A. Background on the Affordable Care Act

Sebelius focused on those portions of the ACA that were designed to provide health insurance to more individuals.

1. The ACA and Private Health Insurance

Congress did not create a national, government-run, "single-payer" health insurance plan like those in Britain, France, Canada, and many other Western democracies. Instead, it followed a model used in Germany and the State of Massachusetts (and that had been advocated by some within the Republican Party in the early 1990s as an alternative to a national system proposed by President

Clinton). The ACA sought to make private health insurance more affordable by increasing the number of people insured.

Health insurance spreads the cost of treatment across a pool of insured persons. Some of them will pay more in premiums than they receive in benefits, and others less, but on average a well-structured pool will collect enough in premiums to pay for all contracted benefits, with enough left over to pay the costs of the program plus some profit for the insurer. A for-profit insurer will prefer a pool with younger, healthier people who do not incur large medical bills. However, those customers often do not buy health insurance because they calculate that in the short run the cost of insurance outweighs the benefits. The insurer will also prefer to avoid older, sicker people who face large medical bills; this is why health insurers had traditionally refused to issue policies to patients with pre-existing conditions. The result: the people who most need insurance either couldn't get it due to pre-existing conditions, or couldn't afford to pay for it because the absence of healthy people in the pools forced insurers to charge high premiums.

The ACA sought to address these problems through a grand bargain with the insurers. Private insurance companies would no longer be allowed to exclude persons with pre-existing conditions ("guaranteed issue") or charge them higher premiums than others ("community-rating"). In exchange, government would take two steps to bring younger, healthier people into the insurance pools. First, the "employer mandate" required those employers large enough to affect interstate commerce to provide health insurance for their employees. Second, the "individual mandate" required anyone not insured through an employer to obtain health insurance. Those lacking insurance would be required to make a "shared responsibility payment" as part of their annual federal income taxes. The constitutional challenge to the individual mandate was the focus of *NFIB v. Sebelius.*

2. The ACA and Medicaid

Recognizing that some people would not be able to afford private insurance—even if premiums fell as a result of the ACA—Congress also greatly expanded the existing Medicaid program. First enacted in 1965 alongside Medicare (a government-financed health insurance plan for the elderly), Medicaid provided government-financed health insurance for the poor. Medicaid was administered as a federal-state partnership. The federal government provided most of the money and established the ground rules, while states would administer the program's day-to-day functions.

The details of Medicaid changed frequently over the years, with a general trend towards expanding coverage for more and more people. The ACA expanded Medicaid eligibility much further than previous expansions. In *Sebelius*, some state governments that preferred the existing Medicaid program sued to stop the expansion.

B. Litigation Against the Affordable Care Act

A number of civil suits challenged the constitutionality of the basic provisions of the ACA. Regarding the individual mandate, the Sixth and DC Circuits found it constitutional, *Thomas More Law Center v. Obama*, 651 F.3d 529 (6th Cir. 2011); *Seven-Sky v. Holder*, 661 F.3d 1 (D.C. Cir. 2011), the Eleventh Circuit found it unconstitutional, *Florida v. US Dep't of Health & Human Services*, 648 F.3d 1235 (11th Cir. 2011), and the Fourth Circuit concluded that it lacked jurisdiction, *Liberty University, Inc. v. Geithner*, 671 F.3d 391 (4th Cir. 2011). Only the Eleventh Circuit considered the Medicaid expansion, and found it to be constitutional.

The Supreme Court granted review of the Eleventh Circuit case, under the title *National Federation of Independent Business v. Sebelius.*

1. Law and Politics in the Fifth Circuit

The Supreme Court heard oral arguments in Sebelius on March 26–29, 2012. Media interest in the arguments was intense. On Monday, April 2, 2012, President Barack Obama was asked about the case during a press conference.

> PRESIDENT OBAMA: Ultimately, I'm confident that the Supreme Court will not take what would be an unprecedented, extraordinary step of overturning a law that was passed by a strong majority of a democratically elected Congress. And I'd just remind conservative commentators that for years what we've heard is, the biggest problem on the bench was judicial activism or a lack of judicial restraint—that an unelected group of people would somehow overturn a duly constituted and passed law. Well, this is a good example. And I'm pretty confident that this Court will recognize that and not take that step.
>
> Q: . . . Do you have contingency plans?
>
> PRESIDENT OBAMA: As I said, we are confident . . . that this will be upheld. I'm confident that this will be upheld because it should be upheld. And, again, that's not just my opinion; that's the opinion of a whole lot of constitutional law professors and academics and judges and lawyers who have examined this law, even if they're not particularly sympathetic to this particular piece of legislation or my presidency.

On April 3, 2012, the Fifth Circuit heard oral argument in *Physician Hospitals of America v. Sebelius*, 691 F.3d 649 (5th Cir. 2012), a challenge to portions of the ACA that did not involve the individual mandate. The argument included this exchange:

> JUDGE JERRY SMITH: Does the Department of Justice recognize that federal courts have the authority in appropriate circumstances to strike federal statutes because of one or more constitutional infirmities?

DEPARTMENT OF JUSTICE ATTORNEY DANA KAERSVANG: Yes, your honor. . . .

JUDGE SMITH: I'm referring to statements by the President in the past few days to the effect, and I'm sure you've heard about them, that it is somehow inappropriate for what he termed "unelected judges" to strike acts of Congress that have enjoyed—and he was referring, of course to Obamacare—to what he termed a broad consensus and majorities in both houses of Congress. That has troubled a number of people who have read it as somehow a challenge to the federal courts, or to their authority, or to the appropriateness of the concept of judicial review. And that's not a small matter.

So I want to be sure that you're telling us that the attorney general and the Department of Justice do recognize the authority of the federal courts through unelected judges to strike acts of Congress or portions thereof in appropriate cases.

MS. KAERSVANG: *Marbury v. Madison* is the law, your honor. And it would not make sense in this circumstance to strike down this statute.

JUDGE SMITH: All right. Well, I would like to have from you by noon on Thursday, that's about 48 hours from now, a letter stating what is the position of the attorney general and the Department of Justice in regard to the recent statements by the president, stating specifically and in detail, in reference to those statements, what the authority is of the federal courts in this regard in terms of judicial review. That letter needs to be at least three pages, single-spaced, no less, and it needs to be specific. It needs to make specific reference to the president's statements and to, again, the position of the attorney general and the Department of Justice.

ITEMS TO CONSIDER WHEN READING THE ATTORNEY GENERAL'S LETTER:

A. *Were the President's comments about the judiciary appropriate?*

B. *Was the Fifth Circuit's order for a written explanation of the President's comments appropriate?*

C. *What is the appropriate tone for a litigant to take in responding to such an order?*

OFFICE OF THE ATTORNEY GENERAL
WASHINGTON, DC 20530

April 5, 2012

Judge Jerry E. Smith
Judge Emilio M. Garza
Judge Leslie H. Southwick

RE: *Physician Hospitals of America v. Sebelius*, No. 11-40631

Dear Judge Smith, Judge Garza, and Judge Southwick:

[This Court] requested a response to questions raised at oral argument in this case, *Physician Hospitals of America v. Sebelius*. From the electronic recording of the argument, I understand the Court to have requested the views of the Department of Justice regarding judicial review of the constitutionality of Acts of Congress. The Court indicated that its inquiry was prompted by recent statements of the President.

The longstanding, historical position of the United States regarding judicial review of the constitutionality of federal legislation has not changed and was accurately stated by counsel for the government at oral argument in this case a few days ago. The Department has not in this litigation, nor in any other litigation of which I am aware, ever asked this or any other Court to reconsider or limit long-established precedent concerning judicial review of the constitutionality of federal legislation.

The government's brief cites jurisdictional bars to the instant suit and urges that Plaintiffs' constitutional claims are insubstantial. At no point has the government suggested that the Court would lack authority to review Plaintiffs' constitutional claims if the Court were to conclude that jurisdiction exists. . . .

1. The power of the courts to review the constitutionality of legislation is beyond dispute. The Supreme Court resolved this question in *Marbury v. Madison*, 5 U.S. 137 (1803). In that case, the Court held that "it is emphatically the province and duty of the judicial department to say what the law is."

The Supreme Court has further explained that this power may only be exercised in appropriate cases. "If a dispute is not a proper case or controversy, the courts have no business deciding it, or expounding the law in the course of doing so." *DaimlerChrysler Corp. v. Cuno*, 547 U.S. 332 (2006). In the case before this Court—*Physician Hospitals of America v. Sebelius*, No. 11-40631—we have argued that this Court lacks jurisdiction to hear the case.

Where a plaintiff properly invokes the jurisdiction of a court and presents a justiciable challenge, there is no dispute that courts properly review the constitutionality of Acts of Congress.

2. In considering such challenges, Acts of Congress are presumptively constitutional, and the Supreme Court has stressed that the presumption of constitutionality

accorded to Acts of Congress is strong. See, e.g., *Gonzales v. Raich*, 545 U.S. 1 (2005) (noting that the "congressional judgment" at issue was "entitled to a strong presumption of validity"). The Supreme Court has explained: "This is not a mere polite gesture. It is a deference due to deliberate judgment by constitutional majorities of the two Houses of Congress that an Act is within their delegated power or is necessary and proper to execution of that power." *Five Gambling Devices Labeled in Part "Mills" and Bearing Serial Nos. 593221*, 346 U.S. 441 (1953). In light of the presumption of constitutionality, it falls to the party seeking to overturn a federal law to show that it is clearly unconstitutional. See, e.g., *Salazar v. Buono*. 559 U.S. 700 (2010) (' "Respect for a coordinate branch of Government forbids striking down an Act of Congress except upon a clear showing of unconstitutionality").

3. While duly recognizing the courts' authority to engage in judicial review, the Executive Branch has often urged courts to respect the legislative judgments of Congress.

The Supreme Court has often acknowledged the appropriateness of reliance on the political branches' policy choices and judgments. The Court accords great weight to the decisions of Congress in part because "the Congress is a coequal branch of government whose Members take the same oath [judges] do to uphold the Constitution of the United States." *Rostker v. Goldberg*, 453 U.S. 57 (1981). These principles of deference are fully applicable when Congress legislates in the commercial sphere. The courts accord particular deference when evaluating the appropriateness of the means Congress has chosen to exercise its enumerated powers, including the Commerce Clause, to accomplish constitutional ends. *See, e.g., NLRB v. Jones & Laughlin Steel Corp.*, 301 U.S. 1 (1937); *McCulloch v. Maryland*, 17 U.S. 316 (1819). See also *Thomas More Law Center v. Obama*, 651 F.3d 529 (6th Cir. 2011) (Opinion of Sutton, J.); *Seven-Sky v. Holder*, 661 F.3d 1 (D.C. Cir. 2011) (Opinion of Silberman, J.)

The President's remarks were fully consistent with the principles described herein.

Sincerely,
Eric H. Holder, Jr.
Attorney General

2. The Supreme Court Decides: *NFIB v. Sebelius*

The Supreme Court announced its opinion on June 28, 2012.

ITEMS TO CONSIDER WHILE READING *NFIB v. SEBELIUS:*

General Questions

A. *Do a careful head count to see which propositions of law are supported by a majority. A table will help.*

JUSTICE (By Seniority)	INDIVIDUAL MANDATE: Commerce Clause	INDIVIDUAL MANDATE: Necessary and Proper Clause	SHARED RESPONSIBILITY PAYMENT: Taxing Clause	MEDICAID EXPANSION: Spending Clause
Roberts, C.J.				
Scalia				
Kennedy				
Thomas				
Ginsburg				
Breyer				
Alito				
Sotomayor				
Kagan				

B. *Does existing precedent squarely control the outcome of this case? Or was it a matter of first impression?*

C. *In what ways, if any, is this a case about individual rights? About separation of powers?*

Commerce Clause

D. *What does the individual mandate regulate? The failure to purchase health insurance? The choice to finance one's future health care expenditures through savings (known as "self-insurance")? Something else?*

E. *However defined, does the thing regulated by the individual mandate constitute "commercial" activity as defined by* Lopez *and* Morrison*?*

Necessary & Proper Clause

F. *What are the arguments for and against viewing the individual mandate as a necessary and proper means for pursuing Commerce Clause ends?*

Taxing Clause

G. *Is the shared responsibility payment a tax or a penalty?*

H. *In light of his holding regarding the Taxing Clause, was it necessary for Chief Justice Roberts to rule on the arguments involving the Commerce Clause and the Necessary and Proper Clause?*

Spending Clause

I. *What part(s) of the* Dole *test did the Medicaid expansion flunk, and why?*

J. *What could Congress do to ensure that an expansion of Medicaid would be constitutional?*

National Federation of Independent Businesses v. Sebelius,

567 U.S. 519 (2012)

Chief Justice Roberts announced the judgment of the Court and delivered the opinion of the Court with respect to Parts I, II, and III-C, an opinion with respect to Part IV, in which Justice Breyer and Justice Kagan join, and an opinion with respect to Parts III-A, III-B, and III-D.

Today we resolve constitutional challenges to two provisions of the Patient Protection and Affordable Care Act of 2010: the individual mandate, which requires individuals to purchase a health insurance policy providing a minimum level of coverage; and the Medicaid expansion, which gives funds to the States on the condition that they provide specified health care to all citizens whose income falls below a certain threshold. We do not consider whether the Act embodies sound policies. That judgment is entrusted to the Nation's elected leaders. We ask only whether Congress has the power under the Constitution to enact the challenged provisions.

■ OBSERVATION

INTRODUCTION: The introduction to the opinion of Chief Justice Roberts lays out general principles that may be useful for review. If it seems overly familiar, skim the introduction and begin with Roman Numeral I.

In our federal system, the National Government possesses only limited powers; the States and the people retain the remainder. Nearly two centuries ago, Chief Justice Marshall observed that "the question respecting the extent of the powers actually

National Federation of Independent Businesses v. Sebelius

granted" to the Federal Government "is perpetually arising, and will probably continue to arise, as long as our system shall exist." *McCulloch v. Maryland* (1819). In this case we must again determine whether the Constitution grants Congress powers it now asserts, but which many States and individuals believe it does not possess. Resolving this controversy requires us to examine both the limits of the Government's power, and our own limited role in policing those boundaries.

The Federal Government is acknowledged by all to be one of enumerated powers. That is, rather than granting general authority to perform all the conceivable functions of government, the Constitution lists, or enumerates, the Federal Government's powers. Congress may, for example, "coin Money," "establish Post Offices," and "raise and support Armies." Art. I, § 8, cls. 5, 7, 12. The enumeration of powers is also a limitation of powers, because "the enumeration presupposes something not enumerated." *Gibbons v. Ogden* (1824). The Constitution's express conferral of some powers makes clear that it does not grant others. And the Federal Government can exercise only the powers granted to it.

Today, the restrictions on government power foremost in many Americans' minds are likely to be affirmative prohibitions, such as contained in the Bill of Rights. These affirmative prohibitions come into play, however, only where the Government possesses authority to act in the first place. If no enumerated power authorizes Congress to pass a certain law, that law may not be enacted, even if it would not violate any of the express prohibitions in the Bill of Rights or elsewhere in the Constitution.

Indeed, the Constitution did not initially include a Bill of Rights at least partly because the Framers felt the enumeration of powers sufficed to restrain the Government. As Alexander Hamilton put it, "the Constitution is itself, in every rational sense, and to every useful purpose, a Bill of Rights." *The Federalist* #84. And when the Bill of Rights was ratified, it made express [in the Tenth Amendment] what the enumeration of powers necessarily implied: "The powers not delegated to the United States by the Constitution are reserved to the States respectively, or to the people." The Federal Government has expanded dramatically over the past two centuries, but it still must show that a constitutional grant of power authorizes each of its actions. *U.S. v. Comstock* (2010).

The same does not apply to the States, because the Constitution is not the source of their power. The Constitution may restrict state governments—as it does, for example, by forbidding them to deny any person the equal protection of the laws. But where such prohibitions do not apply, state governments do not need constitutional authorization to act. The States thus can and do perform many of the vital functions of modern government—punishing street crime, running public schools, and zoning property for development, to name but a few—even though the Constitution's text does not authorize any government to do so. Our cases refer to this general power of governing, possessed by the States but not by the Federal Government, as the "police power."

State sovereignty is not just an end in itself: Rather, federalism secures to citizens the liberties that derive from the diffusion of sovereign power. Because the police power is controlled by 50 different States instead of one national sovereign, the facets of governing that touch on citizens' daily lives are normally administered by smaller governments closer to the governed. The Framers thus ensured that powers which in the ordinary course of affairs, concern the lives, liberties, and properties of the people were held by governments more local and more accountable than a distant federal bureaucracy. The independent power of the States also serves as a check on the power of the Federal Government: By denying any one government complete jurisdiction over all the concerns of public life, federalism protects the liberty of the individual from arbitrary power.

This case concerns two powers that the Constitution does grant the Federal Government, but which must be read carefully to avoid creating a general federal authority akin to the police power. The Constitution authorizes Congress to "regulate Commerce with foreign Nations, and among the several States, and with the Indian Tribes." Art. I, § 8, cl. 3. Our precedents read that to mean that Congress may regulate the channels of interstate commerce, persons or things in interstate commerce, and those activities that substantially affect interstate commerce. The power over activities that substantially affect interstate commerce can be expansive. That power has been held to authorize federal regulation of such seemingly local matters as a farmer's decision to grow wheat for himself and his livestock, and a loan shark's extortionate collections from a neighborhood butcher shop. See *Wickard v. Filburn* (1942); *Perez v. United States*, 402 U.S. 146 (1971).

Congress may also "lay and collect taxes, duties, imposts and excises, to pay the debts and provide for the common defense and general welfare of the United States." Art. I, § 8, cl. 1. Put simply, Congress may tax and spend. This grant gives the Federal Government considerable influence even in areas where it cannot directly regulate. The Federal Government may enact a tax on an activity that it cannot authorize, forbid, or otherwise control. And in exercising its spending power, Congress may offer funds to the States, and may condition those offers on compliance with specified conditions. These offers may well induce the States to adopt policies that the Federal Government itself could not impose. See, e.g., *South Dakota v. Dole*, 483 U.S. 203 (1987) (conditioning federal highway funds on States raising their drinking age to 21).

The reach of the Federal Government's enumerated powers is broader still because the Constitution authorizes Congress to "make all Laws which shall be necessary and proper for carrying into Execution the foregoing Powers." Art. I, § 8, cl. 18. We have long read this provision to give Congress great latitude in exercising its powers: "Let the end be legitimate, let it be within the scope of the constitution, and all means which are appropriate, which are plainly adapted to that end, which are not prohibited, but consist with the letter and spirit of the constitution, are constitutional." *McCulloch*.

Our permissive reading of these powers is explained in part by a general reticence to invalidate the acts of the Nation's elected leaders. Proper respect for a coordinate branch of the government requires that we strike down an Act of Congress only if the lack of constitutional authority to pass the act in question is clearly demonstrated. Members of this Court are vested with the authority to interpret the law; we possess neither the expertise nor the prerogative to make policy judgments. Those decisions are entrusted to our Nation's elected leaders, who can be thrown out of office if the people disagree with them. It is not our job to protect the people from the consequences of their political choices.

Our deference in matters of policy cannot, however, become abdication in matters of law. "The powers of the legislature are defined and limited; and that those limits may not be mistaken, or forgotten, the constitution is written." *Marbury v. Madison* (1803). Our respect for Congress's policy judgments thus can never extend so far as to disavow restraints on federal power that the Constitution carefully constructed. The peculiar circumstances of the moment may render a measure more or less wise, but cannot render it more or less constitutional. And there can be no question that it is the responsibility of this Court to enforce the limits on federal power by striking down acts of Congress that transgress those limits.

The questions before us must be considered against the background of these basic principles.

I

In 2010, Congress enacted the Patient Protection and Affordable Care Act. The Act aims to increase the number of Americans covered by health insurance and decrease the cost of health care. The Act's 10 titles stretch over 900 pages and contain hundreds of provisions. This case concerns constitutional challenges to two key provisions, commonly referred to as the individual mandate and the Medicaid expansion.

The individual mandate requires most Americans to maintain "minimum essential" health insurance coverage. 26 U.S.C. § 5000A. The mandate does not apply to some individuals, such as prisoners and undocumented aliens. Many individuals will receive the required coverage through their employer, or from a government program such as Medicaid or Medicare. But for individuals who are not exempt and do not receive health insurance through a third party, the means of satisfying the requirement is to purchase insurance from a private company.

Beginning in 2014, those who do not comply with the mandate must make a "shared responsibility payment" to the Federal Government. That payment, which

> ■ OBSERVATION
>
> **THE ACT DESCRIBES AS A "PENALTY":**
>
> A portion of the ACA codified as part of the federal tax code reads as follows:
>
> 26 U.S.C. § 5000A(b) Shared responsibility payment.
>
> (1) In general. If a taxpayer . . . fails to meet the requirement of [obtaining health insurance] for 1 or more months, then . . . there is hereby imposed on the taxpayer a penalty. . . .
>
> (2) Inclusion with return. Any penalty imposed by this section . . . shall be included with a taxpayer's return . . .

the Act describes as a "penalty," is calculated as a percentage of household income, subject to a floor based on a specified dollar amount and a ceiling based on the average annual premium the individual would have to pay for qualifying private health insurance. In 2016, for example, the penalty will be 2.5 percent of an individual's household income, but no less than $695 and no more than the average yearly premium for insurance that covers 60 percent of the cost of 10 specified services (e.g., prescription drugs and hospitalization). The Act provides that the penalty will be paid to the Internal Revenue Service with an individual's taxes, and "shall be assessed and collected in the same manner" as tax penalties, such as the penalty for claiming too large an income tax refund. The Act, however, bars the IRS from using several of its normal enforcement tools, such as criminal prosecutions and levies. And some individuals who are subject to the mandate are nonetheless exempt from the penalty—for example, those with income below a certain threshold and members of Indian tribes.

On the day the President signed the Act into law, Florida and 12 other States filed a complaint in the Federal District Court for the Northern District of Florida. Those plaintiffs—who are both respondents and petitioners here, depending on the issue—were subsequently joined by 13 more States, several individuals, and the National Federation of Independent Business. The plaintiffs alleged, among other things, that the individual mandate provisions of the Act exceeded Congress's powers under Article I of the Constitution. The District Court agreed, holding that Congress lacked constitutional power to enact the individual mandate. [The Court of Appeals for the Eleventh Circuit affirmed in relevant part.] . . .

The second provision of the Affordable Care Act directly challenged here is the Medicaid expansion. Enacted in 1965, Medicaid offers federal funding to States to assist pregnant women, children, needy families, the blind, the elderly, and the disabled in obtaining medical care. In order to receive that funding, States must comply with federal criteria governing matters such as who receives care and what services are provided at what cost. By 1982 every State had chosen to participate in Medicaid. Federal funds received through the Medicaid program have become a substantial part of state budgets, now constituting over 10 percent of most States' total revenue.

The Affordable Care Act expands the scope of the Medicaid program and increases the number of individuals the States must cover. For example, the Act requires state programs to provide Medicaid coverage to adults with incomes up to

133 percent of the federal poverty level, whereas many States now cover adults with children only if their income is considerably lower, and do not cover childless adults at all. The Act increases federal funding to cover the States' costs in expanding Medicaid coverage, although States will bear a portion of the costs on their own. If a State does not comply with the Act's new coverage requirements, it may lose not only the federal funding for those requirements, but all of its federal Medicaid funds.

Along with their challenge to the individual mandate, the state plaintiffs in the Eleventh Circuit argued that the Medicaid expansion exceeds Congress's constitutional powers. The Court of Appeals unanimously held that the Medicaid expansion is a valid exercise of Congress's power under the Spending Clause. And the court rejected the States' claim that the threatened loss of all federal Medicaid funding violates the Tenth Amendment by coercing them into complying with the Medicaid expansion.

We granted certiorari to review the judgment of the Court of Appeals for the Eleventh Circuit with respect to both the individual mandate and the Medicaid expansion. . . .

II

[The Tax Anti-Injunction Act, which forbids suits "for the purpose of restraining the assessment or collection of any tax," 26 U.S.C. § 7421(a), does not prevent jurisdiction over the suit.]

III

The Government advances two theories for the proposition that Congress had constitutional authority to enact the individual mandate. First, the Government argues that Congress had the power to enact the mandate under the Commerce Clause. Under that theory, Congress may order individuals to buy health insurance because the failure to do so affects interstate commerce, and could undercut the Affordable Care Act's other reforms. Second, the Government argues that if the commerce power does not support the mandate, we should nonetheless uphold it as an exercise of Congress's power to tax. According to the Government, even if Congress lacks the power to direct individuals to buy insurance, the only effect of the individual mandate is to raise taxes on those who do not do so, and thus the law may be upheld as a tax.

A

The Government's first argument is that the individual mandate is a valid exercise of Congress's power under the Commerce Clause and the Necessary and Proper Clause. According to the Government, the health care market is characterized by a significant cost-shifting problem. Everyone will eventually need health care at a time and to an extent they cannot predict, but if they do not have insurance, they often will not be able to pay for it. Because state and federal laws nonetheless require hospitals to provide a certain degree of care to individuals without regard to their ability to pay, hospitals end up receiving compensation for only a portion of the services they provide. To recoup the losses, hospitals pass on the cost to insurers through higher rates, and insurers, in turn, pass on the cost to policy holders in the form of higher premiums. Congress estimated that the cost of uncompensated care raises family health insurance premiums, on average, by over $1,000 per year.

In the Affordable Care Act, Congress addressed the problem of those who cannot obtain insurance coverage because of preexisting conditions or other health issues. It did so through the Act's "guaranteed-issue" and "community-rating" provisions. These provisions together prohibit insurance companies from denying coverage to those with such conditions or charging unhealthy individuals higher premiums than healthy individuals.

The guaranteed-issue and community-rating reforms do not, however, address the issue of healthy individuals who choose not to purchase insurance to cover potential health care needs. In fact, the reforms sharply exacerbate that problem, by providing an incentive for individuals to delay purchasing health insurance until they become sick, relying on the promise of guaranteed and affordable coverage. The reforms also threaten to impose massive new costs on insurers, who are required to accept unhealthy individuals but prohibited from charging them rates necessary to pay for their coverage. This will lead insurers to significantly increase premiums on everyone.

The individual mandate was Congress's solution to these problems. By requiring that individuals purchase health insurance, the mandate prevents cost-shifting by those who would otherwise go without it. In addition, the mandate forces into the insurance risk pool more healthy individuals, whose premiums on average will be higher than their health care expenses. This allows insurers to subsidize the costs of covering the unhealthy individuals the reforms require them to accept. The Government claims that Congress has power under the Commerce and Necessary and Proper Clauses to enact this solution.

1

The Government contends that the individual mandate is within Congress's power because the failure to purchase insurance has a substantial and deleterious effect on interstate commerce by creating the cost-shifting problem. The path of our Commerce Clause decisions has not always run smooth, but it is now well established that Congress has broad authority under the Clause. We have recognized, for example, that the power of Congress over interstate commerce is not confined to the regulation of commerce among the states, but extends to activities that have a substantial effect on interstate commerce. *United States v. Darby* (1941). Congress's power, moreover, is not limited to regulation of an activity that by itself

National Federation of Independent Businesses v. Sebelius

substantially affects interstate commerce, but also extends to activities that do so only when aggregated with similar activities of others. *Wickard.*

Given its expansive scope, it is no surprise that Congress has employed the commerce power in a wide variety of ways to address the pressing needs of the time. But Congress has never attempted to rely on that power to compel individuals not engaged in commerce to purchase an unwanted product. Legislative novelty is not necessarily fatal; there is a first time for everything. But sometimes the most telling indication of a severe constitutional problem is the lack of historical precedent for Congress's action. At the very least, we should pause to consider the implications of the Government's arguments when confronted with such new conceptions of federal power.

The Constitution grants Congress the power to "regulate Commerce." The power to regulate commerce presupposes the existence of commercial activity to be regulated. If the power to "regulate" something included the power to create it, many of the provisions in the Constitution would be superfluous. For example, the Constitution gives Congress the power to "coin Money," in addition to the power to "regulate the Value thereof." And it gives Congress the power to "raise and support Armies" and to "provide and maintain a Navy," in addition to the power to "make Rules for the Government and Regulation of the land and naval Forces." If the power to regulate the armed forces or the value of money included the power to bring the subject of the regulation into existence, the specific grant of such powers would have been unnecessary. The language of the Constitution reflects the natural understanding that the power to regulate assumes there is already something to be regulated.

Our precedent also reflects this understanding. As expansive as our cases construing the scope of the commerce power have been, they all have one thing in common: They uniformly describe the power as reaching "activity." It is nearly impossible to avoid the word when quoting them. See, e.g., *US v. Lopez* (1995) ("Where economic *activity* substantially affects interstate commerce, legislation regulating that activity will be sustained"); *Wickard v. Filburn* (1942) ("Even if appellee's *activity* be local and though it may not be regarded as commerce, it may still, whatever its nature, be reached by Congress if it exerts a substantial economic effect on interstate commerce); *NLRB v. Jones & Laughlin Steel Corp.* (1937) ("Although *activities* may be intrastate in character when separately considered, if they have such a close and substantial relation to interstate commerce that their control is essential or appropriate to protect that commerce from burdens and obstructions, Congress cannot be denied the power to exercise that control").

The individual mandate, however, does not regulate existing commercial activity. It instead compels individuals to become active in commerce by purchasing a product, on the ground that their failure to do so affects interstate commerce. Construing the Commerce Clause to permit Congress to regulate individuals precisely because they are doing nothing would open a new and potentially vast domain to congressional authority. Every day individuals do not do an infinite number of things. In some cases they decide not to do something; in others they simply fail to do it. Allowing Congress to justify federal regulation by pointing to the effect of inaction on commerce would bring countless decisions an individual could potentially make within the scope of federal regulation, and—under the Government's theory—empower Congress to make those decisions for him.

Applying the Government's logic to the familiar case of *Wickard v. Filburn* shows how far that logic would carry us from the notion of a government of limited powers. In *Wickard*, the Court famously upheld a federal penalty imposed on a farmer for growing wheat for consumption on his own farm. That amount of wheat caused the farmer to exceed his quota under a program designed to support the price of wheat by limiting supply. The Court rejected the farmer's argument that growing wheat for home consumption was beyond the reach of the commerce power. It did so on the ground that the farmer's decision to grow wheat for his own use allowed him to avoid purchasing wheat in the market. That decision, when considered in the aggregate along with similar decisions of others, would have had a substantial effect on the interstate market for wheat.

Wickard has long been regarded as perhaps the most far reaching example of Commerce Clause authority over intrastate activity, but the Government's theory in this case would go much further. Under *Wickard* it is within Congress's power to regulate the market for wheat by supporting its price. But price can be supported by increasing demand as well as by decreasing supply. The aggregated decisions of some consumers not to purchase wheat have a substantial effect on the price of wheat, just as decisions not to purchase health insurance have on the price of insurance. Congress can therefore command that those not buying wheat do so, just as it argues here that it may command that those not buying health insurance do so. The farmer in *Wickard* was at least actively engaged in the production of wheat, and the Government could regulate that activity because of its effect on commerce. The Government's theory here would effectively override that limitation, by establishing that individuals may be regulated under the Commerce Clause whenever enough of them are not doing something the Government would have them do.

Indeed, the Government's logic would justify a mandatory purchase to solve almost any problem. To consider a different example in the health care market, many Americans do not eat a balanced diet. That group makes up a larger percentage of the total population than those without health insurance. The failure of that group to have a healthy diet increases health care costs, to a greater extent than the failure of the uninsured to purchase insurance. Those increased costs are borne in part by other Americans who must pay more, just as the uninsured shift costs to the insured. Congress addressed the insurance problem by ordering everyone to buy insurance. Under the Government's theory, Congress could address the diet problem by ordering everyone to buy vegetables.

People, for reasons of their own, often fail to do things that would be good for them or good for society. Those failures—joined with the similar failures of others—can readily have a substantial effect on interstate commerce. Under the Government's logic, that authorizes Congress to use its commerce power to compel citizens to act as the Government would have them act.

That is not the country the Framers of our Constitution envisioned. . . . Congress already enjoys vast power to regulate much of what we do. Accepting the Government's theory would give Congress the same license to regulate what we do not do, fundamentally changing the relation between the citizen and the Federal Government. . . . The Framers gave Congress the power to regulate commerce, not to compel it, and for over 200 years both our decisions and Congress's actions have reflected this understanding. There is no reason to depart from that understanding now. . . .

The Government regards it as sufficient to trigger Congress's authority that almost all those who are uninsured will, at some unknown point in the future, engage in a health care transaction. Asserting that "there is no temporal limitation in the Commerce Clause," the Government argues that because "everyone subject to this regulation is in or will be in the health care market," they can be "regulated in advance."

The proposition that Congress may dictate the conduct of an individual today because of prophesied future activity finds no support in our precedent. We have said that Congress can anticipate the effects on commerce of an economic activity. But we have never permitted Congress to anticipate that activity itself in order to regulate individuals not currently engaged in commerce. Each one of our cases, including those cited by Justice Ginsburg, involved preexisting economic activity. See, e.g., *Wickard* (producing wheat); *Raich* (growing marijuana).

Everyone will likely participate in the markets for food, clothing, transportation, shelter, or energy; that does not authorize Congress to direct them to purchase particular products in those or other markets today. The Commerce Clause is not a general license to regulate an individual from cradle to grave, simply because he will predictably engage in particular transactions. Any police power to regulate individuals as such, as opposed to their activities, remains vested in the States. . . .

2

The Government next contends that Congress has the power under the Necessary and Proper Clause to enact the individual mandate because the mandate is an integral part of a comprehensive scheme of economic regulation—the guaranteed-issue and community-rating insurance reforms. Under this argument, it is not necessary to consider the effect that an individual's inactivity may have on interstate commerce; it is enough that Congress regulate commercial activity in a way that requires regulation of inactivity to be effective.

The power to "make all Laws which shall be necessary and proper for carrying into Execution" the powers enumerated in the Constitution vests Congress with authority to enact provisions "incidental to the [enumerated] power, and conducive to its beneficial exercise," McCulloch. Although the Clause gives Congress authority to legislate on that vast mass of incidental powers which must be involved in the constitution, it does not license the exercise of any great substantive and independent powers beyond those specifically enumerated. Instead, the Clause is merely a declaration, for the removal of all uncertainty, that the means of carrying into execution those powers otherwise granted are included in the grant.

As our jurisprudence under the Necessary and Proper Clause has developed, we have been very deferential to Congress's determination that a regulation is "necessary." We have thus upheld laws that are "convenient or useful" or "conducive to the authority's beneficial exercise." *Comstock*. But we have also carried out our responsibility to declare unconstitutional those laws that undermine the structure of government established by the Constitution. Such laws, which are not "consistent with the letter and spirit of the constitution," *McCulloch*, are not "*proper* [means] for carrying into Execution" Congress's enumerated powers. Rather, they are, "in the words of *The Federalist* [#33], "merely acts of usurpation" which "deserve to be treated as such."

Applying these principles, the individual mandate cannot be sustained under the Necessary and Proper Clause as an essential component of the insurance reforms. Each of our prior cases upholding laws under that Clause involved exercises of authority derivative of, and in service to, a granted power. For example, we have upheld provisions permitting continued confinement of those already in federal custody when they could not be safely released, *Comstock*; criminalizing bribes involving organizations receiving federal funds, *Sabri v. United States*, 541 U.S. 600 (2004); and tolling state statutes of limitations while cases are pending in federal court, *Jinks v. Richland County*, 538 U.S. 456 (2003). The individual mandate, by contrast, vests Congress with the extraordinary ability to create the necessary predicate to the exercise of an enumerated power.

This is in no way an authority that is "narrow in scope," *Comstock*, or "incidental" to the exercise of the commerce power, *McCulloch*. Rather, such a conception of the Necessary and Proper Clause would work a substantial expansion of federal authority. . . . Even if the individual mandate is "necessary" to the Act's insurance reforms, such an expansion of federal power is not a "proper" means for making those reforms effective. . . .

National Federation of Independent Businesses v. Sebelius

B

That is not the end of the matter. Because the Commerce Clause does not support the individual mandate, it is necessary to turn to the Government's second argument: that the mandate may be upheld as within Congress's enumerated power to "lay and collect Taxes." . . . The Government asks us to read the mandate not as ordering individuals to buy insurance, but rather as imposing a tax on those who do not buy that product.

The text of a statute can sometimes have more than one possible meaning. To take a familiar example, a law that reads **"no vehicles in the park"** might, or might not, ban bicycles in the park. And it is well established that if a statute has two possible meanings, one of which violates the Constitution, courts should adopt the meaning that does not do so. . . .

> HISTORY
>
> **NO VEHICLES IN THE PARK:** In 1958, law professors H.L.A. Hart of Oxford University and Lon Fuller of Harvard University debated how best to interpret a legal rule that said "no vehicles in the park." It seems to forbid automobiles, but what about bicycles? Wheelchairs? Toy airplanes? A decommissioned tank placed in the park as a war memorial? See H.L.A. Hart, *Positivism and the Separation of Law and Morals,* 71 HARV. L. REV. 593 (1958) and Lon Fuller, *Positivism and Fidelity to Law—A Reply to Professor Hart,* 71 HARV. L. REV. 630 (1958).

The most straightforward reading of the mandate is that it commands individuals to purchase insurance. After all, it states that individuals "shall" maintain health insurance. Congress thought it could enact such a command under the Commerce Clause, and the Government primarily defended the law on that basis. But, for the reasons explained above, the Commerce Clause does not give Congress that power. Under our precedent, it is therefore necessary to ask whether the Government's alternative reading of the statute—that it only imposes a tax on those without insurance—is a reasonable one.

Under the mandate, if an individual does not maintain health insurance, the only consequence is that he must make an additional payment to the IRS when he pays his taxes. That, according to the Government, means the mandate can be regarded as establishing a condition—not owning health insurance—that triggers a tax—the required payment to the IRS. Under that theory, the mandate is not a legal command to buy insurance. Rather, it makes going without insurance just another thing the Government taxes, like buying gasoline or earning income. And if the mandate is in effect just a tax hike on certain taxpayers who do not have health insurance, it may be within Congress's constitutional power to tax.

The question is not whether that is the most natural interpretation of the mandate, but only whether it is a fairly possible one. As we have explained, every reasonable construction must be resorted to, in order to save a statute from unconstitutionality. The Government asks us to interpret the mandate as imposing a tax, if it would otherwise violate the Constitution. Granting the Act the full measure of deference owed to federal statutes, it can be so read, for the reasons set forth below.

C

The exaction the Affordable Care Act imposes on those without health insurance looks like a tax in many respects. The "shared responsibility payment," as the statute entitles it, is paid into the Treasury by "taxpayers" when they file their tax returns. It does not apply to individuals who do not pay federal income taxes because their household income is less than the filing threshold in the Internal Revenue Code. For taxpayers who do owe the payment, its amount is determined by such familiar factors as taxable income, number of dependents, and joint filing status. The requirement to pay is found in the Internal Revenue Code and enforced by the IRS, which—as we previously explained—must assess and collect it "in the same manner as taxes." This process yields the essential feature of any tax: it produces at least some revenue for the Government. *U.S. v. Kahriger* (1953). Indeed, the payment is expected to raise about $4 billion per year by 2017.

It is of course true that the Act describes the payment as a "penalty," not a "tax." But . . . that label . . . does not determine whether the payment may be viewed as an exercise of Congress's taxing power. . . . Our precedent reflects this: In 1922, we decided [a challenge] to the "Child Labor Tax." . . . [A]lthough labeled a tax, [we found it] was not in fact authorized by Congress's taxing power. *Bailey v. Drexel Furniture* (1922). That constitutional question was not controlled by Congress's choice of label. . . .

The same analysis [used in *Drexel Furniture*] here suggests that the shared responsibility payment may for constitutional purposes be considered a tax, not a penalty: First, for most Americans the amount due will be far less than the price of insurance, and, by statute, it can never be more. It may often be a reasonable financial decision to make the payment rather than purchase insurance, unlike the "prohibitory" financial punishment in *Drexel Furniture*. Second, the individual mandate contains no scienter requirement. Third, the payment is collected solely by the IRS through the normal means of taxation—except that the Service is not allowed to use those means most suggestive of a punitive sanction, such as criminal prosecution. The reasons the Court in *Drexel Furniture* held that what was called a "tax" there was a penalty support the conclusion that what is called a "penalty" here may be viewed as a tax.

None of this is to say that the payment is not intended to affect individual conduct. Although the payment will raise considerable revenue, it is plainly designed to expand health insurance coverage. But taxes that seek to influence conduct are nothing new. Some of our earliest federal taxes [tariffs] sought to deter the purchase of imported manufactured goods in order to foster the growth of domestic industry. Today, federal and state taxes can compose more than half the retail price of cigarettes, not just to raise more money, but to encourage people to quit smoking. And we have upheld such obviously regulatory measures as taxes on selling marijuana and sawed-off shotguns. Indeed, "every tax is in some measure regulatory. To some extent it interposes an economic impediment to the activity taxed as compared with others not taxed." *U.S. v. Sonzinsky* (1937). That § 5000A seeks to shape decisions about whether to buy health insurance does not mean that it cannot be a valid exercise of the taxing power.

In distinguishing penalties from taxes, this Court has explained that if the concept of penalty means anything, it means punishment for an unlawful act or omission. While the individual mandate clearly aims to induce the purchase of health insurance, it need not be read to declare that failing to do so is unlawful. Neither the Act nor any other law attaches negative legal consequences to not buying health insurance, beyond requiring a payment to the IRS. The Government agrees with that reading, confirming that if someone chooses to pay rather than obtain health insurance, they have fully complied with the law.

Indeed, it is estimated that four million people each year will choose to pay the IRS rather than buy insurance. We would expect Congress to be troubled by that prospect if such conduct were unlawful. That Congress apparently regards such extensive failure to comply with the mandate as tolerable suggests that Congress did not think it was creating four million outlaws. It suggests instead that the shared responsibility payment merely imposes a tax citizens may lawfully choose to pay in lieu of buying health insurance. . . .

There may, however, be a more fundamental objection to a tax on those who lack health insurance. Even if only a tax, the payment under § 5000A(b) remains a burden that the Federal Government imposes for an omission, not an act. If it is troubling to interpret the Commerce Clause as authorizing Congress to regulate those who abstain from commerce, perhaps it should be similarly troubling to permit Congress to impose a tax for not doing something.

[Several] considerations allay this concern. First, and most importantly, it is abundantly clear the Constitution does not guarantee that individuals may avoid taxation through inactivity. A capitation [a tax per person], after all, is a tax that everyone must pay simply for existing, and capitations are expressly contemplated by the Constitution [in Art. I, § 9]. . . . Congress's use of the Taxing Clause to encourage buying something is, by contrast, not new. Tax incentives already promote, for example, purchasing homes and professional educations. . . .

[Next,] although the breadth of Congress's power to tax is greater than its power to regulate commerce, the taxing power does not give Congress the same degree of control over individual behavior. Once we recognize that Congress may regulate a particular decision under the Commerce Clause, the Federal Government can bring its full weight to bear. Congress may simply command individuals to do as it directs. An individual who disobeys may be subjected to criminal sanctions. . . .

By contrast, Congress's authority under the taxing power is limited to requiring an individual to pay money into the Federal Treasury, no more. If a tax is properly paid, the Government has no power to compel or punish individuals subject to it. We do not make light of the severe burden that taxation—especially taxation motivated by a regulatory purpose—can impose. But imposition of a tax nonetheless leaves an individual with a lawful choice to do or not do a certain act, so long as he is willing to pay a tax levied on that choice.

The Affordable Care Act's requirement that certain individuals pay a financial penalty for not obtaining health insurance may reasonably be characterized as a tax. Because the Constitution permits such a tax, it is not our role to forbid it, or to pass upon its wisdom or fairness.

D

Justice Ginsburg questions the necessity of rejecting the Government's commerce power argument, given that § 5000A can be upheld under the taxing power. But the statute reads more naturally as a command to buy insurance than as a tax, and I would uphold it as a command if the Constitution allowed it. It is only because the Commerce Clause does not authorize such a command that it is necessary to reach the taxing power question. And it is only because we have a duty to construe a statute to save it, if fairly possible, that § 5000A can be interpreted as a tax. Without deciding the Commerce Clause question, I would find no basis to adopt such a saving construction.

The Federal Government does not have the power to order people to buy health insurance. Section 5000A would therefore be unconstitutional if read as a command. The Federal Government does have the power to impose a tax on those without health insurance. Section 5000A is therefore constitutional, because it can reasonably be read as a tax.

IV

A

The States also contend that the Medicaid expansion exceeds Congress's authority under the Spending Clause. They claim that Congress is coercing the States to adopt the changes it wants by threatening to withhold all of a State's Medicaid grants, unless the State accepts the new expanded funding and complies with the conditions that come with it. This, they argue, violates the basic principle that the "Federal Government may not compel the States to enact or administer a federal regulatory program." *New York v. United States* (1992).

There is no doubt that the Act dramatically increases state obligations under Medicaid. The current Medicaid program requires States to cover only certain discrete categories of needy individuals—pregnant women, children, needy families, the blind, the elderly, and the disabled. There is no mandatory coverage for most childless adults, and the States typically do not offer any such coverage. The States also enjoy considerable flexibility with respect to the coverage levels for parents of needy families. On average States cover only those unemployed parents who make less than 37 percent of the federal poverty level, and only those employed parents who make less than 63 percent of the poverty line.

The Medicaid provisions of the Affordable Care Act, in contrast, require States to expand their Medicaid programs by 2014 to cover all individuals under the age of 65 with incomes below 133 percent of the federal poverty line. The Act also establishes a new "essential health benefits" package, which States must provide to all new Medicaid recipients—a level sufficient to satisfy a recipient's obligations under the individual mandate. The Affordable Care Act provides that the Federal Government will pay 100 percent of the costs of covering these newly eligible individuals through 2016. In the following years, the federal payment level gradually decreases, to a minimum of 90 percent. In light of the expansion in coverage mandated by the Act, the Federal Government estimates that its Medicaid spending will increase by approximately $100 billion per year, nearly 40 percent above current levels.

The Spending Clause grants Congress the power "to pay the Debts and provide for the . . . general Welfare of the United States." We have long recognized that Congress may use this power to grant federal funds to the States, and may condition such a grant upon the States' taking certain actions that Congress could not require them to take. . . .

At the same time, our cases have recognized limits on Congress's power under the Spending Clause to secure state compliance with federal objectives. We have repeatedly characterized Spending Clause legislation as much in the nature of a contract. The legitimacy of Congress's exercise of the spending power thus rests on whether the State voluntarily and knowingly accepts the terms of the contract. Respecting this limitation is critical to ensuring that Spending Clause legislation does not undermine the status of the States as independent sovereigns in our federal system. That system rests on what might at first seem a counter-intuitive insight, that freedom is enhanced by the creation of two governments, not one. For this reason, the Constitution has never been understood to confer upon Congress the ability to require the States to govern according to Congress' instructions. Otherwise the two-government system established by the Framers would give way to a system that vests power in one central government, and individual liberty would suffer.

That insight has led this Court to strike down federal legislation that commandeers a State's legislative or administrative apparatus for federal purposes. See, e.g., *Printz v. US* (1997) (striking down federal legislation compelling state law enforcement officers to perform federally mandated background checks on handgun purchasers); *New York v. US* (1992) (invalidating provisions of an Act that would compel a State to either take title to nuclear waste or enact particular state waste regulations). It has also led us to scrutinize Spending Clause legislation to ensure that Congress is not using financial inducements to exert a power akin to undue influence. Congress may use its spending power to create incentives for States to act in accordance with federal policies. But when pressure turns into compulsion, the legislation runs contrary to our system of federalism. The Constitution simply does not give Congress the authority to require the States to regulate. That is true whether Congress directly commands a State to regulate or indirectly coerces a State to adopt a federal regulatory system as its own. . . .

Congress may attach appropriate conditions to federal taxing and spending programs to preserve its control over the use of federal funds. In the typical case we look to the States to defend their prerogatives by adopting the simple expedient of not yielding to federal blandishments when they do not want to embrace the federal policies as their own. The States are separate and independent sovereigns. Sometimes they have to act like it.

The States, however, argue that the Medicaid expansion is far from the typical case. They object that Congress has "crossed the line distinguishing encouragement from coercion," *New York*, in the way it has structured the funding: Instead of simply refusing to grant the new funds to States that will not accept the new conditions, Congress has also threatened to withhold those States' existing Medicaid funds. The States claim that this threat serves no purpose other than to force unwilling States to sign up for the dramatic expansion in health care coverage effected by the Act.

Given the nature of the threat and the programs at issue here, we must agree. We have upheld Congress's authority to condition the receipt of funds on the States' complying with restrictions on the use of those funds, because that is the means by which Congress ensures that the funds are spent according to its view of the "general Welfare." Conditions that do not here govern the use of the funds, however, cannot be justified on that basis. When, for example, such conditions take the form of threats to terminate other significant independent grants, the conditions are properly viewed as a means of pressuring the States to accept policy changes.

In *South Dakota v. Dole* (1987), we considered a challenge to a federal law that threatened to withhold five percent of a State's federal highway funds if the State did not raise its drinking age to 21. The Court found that the condition was "directly related to one of the main purposes for which highway funds are expended—safe interstate travel." At the same time, the condition was not a restriction on how the highway funds—set aside for specific highway improvement and maintenance efforts—were to be used.

We accordingly asked whether the financial inducement offered by Congress was so coercive as to pass the point at which pressure turns into compulsion. By "financial inducement" the Court meant the threat of losing five percent of highway funds; no new money was offered to the States to raise their drinking ages. We found that the inducement was not impermissibly coercive, because Congress was offering only "relatively mild encouragement to the States." We observed that "all South Dakota would lose if she adheres to her chosen course as to a suitable minimum drinking age is 5%" of her highway funds. In fact, the federal funds at stake constituted less than half of one percent of South Dakota's budget at the time. . . . Whether to accept the drinking age change remained the prerogative of the States not merely in theory but in fact.

In this case, the financial inducement Congress has chosen is much more than "relatively mild encouragement"—it is a gun to the head. Section 1396c of the Medicaid Act provides that if a State's Medicaid plan does not comply with the Act's requirements, the Secretary of Health and Human Services may declare that further payments will not be made to the State. A State that opts out of the Affordable Care Act's expansion in health care coverage thus stands to lose not merely a relatively small percentage of its existing Medicaid funding, but all of it. Medicaid spending accounts for over 20 percent of the average State's total budget, with federal funds covering 50 to 83 percent of those costs. . . . It is easy to see how the *Dole* Court could conclude that the threatened loss of less than half of one percent of South Dakota's budget left that State with a prerogative to reject Congress's desired policy, not merely in theory but in fact. The threatened loss of over 10 percent of a State's overall budget, in contrast, is economic dragooning that leaves the States with no real option but to acquiesce in the Medicaid expansion.

Justice Ginsburg claims that *Dole* is distinguishable because here "Congress has not threatened to withhold funds earmarked for any other program." But that begs the question: The States contend that the expansion is in reality a new program and that Congress is forcing them to accept it by threatening the funds for the existing Medicaid program. We cannot agree that existing Medicaid and the expansion dictated by the Affordable Care Act are all one program simply because Congress styled them as such. If the expansion is not properly viewed as a modification of the existing Medicaid program, Congress's decision to so title it is irrelevant.

Here, the Government claims that the Medicaid expansion is properly viewed merely as a modification of the existing program because the States agreed that Congress could change the terms of Medicaid when they signed on in the first place. The Government observes that the Social Security Act, which includes the original Medicaid provisions, contains a clause expressly reserving "the right to alter, amend, or repeal any provision" of that statute. 42 U.S.C. § 1304. So it does. But if Congress intends to impose a condition on the grant of federal moneys, it must do so unambiguously. *Pennhurst State School & Hospital v. Halderman*, 451 U.S. 1 (1981). A State confronted with statutory language reserving the right to "alter" or "amend" the pertinent provisions of the Social Security Act might reasonably assume that Congress was entitled to make adjustments to the Medicaid program as it developed. Congress has in fact done so, sometimes conditioning only the new funding, other times both old and new.

The Medicaid expansion, however, accomplishes a shift in kind, not merely degree. The original program was designed to cover medical services for four particular categories of the needy: the disabled, the blind, the elderly, and needy families with dependent children. Previous amendments to Medicaid eligibility merely altered and expanded the boundaries of these categories. Under the Affordable Care Act, Medicaid is transformed into a program to meet the health care needs of the entire non-elderly population with income below 133 percent of the poverty level. It is no longer a program to care for the neediest among us, but rather an element of a comprehensive national plan to provide universal health insurance coverage. . . .

[We need not] attempt to fix the outermost line where persuasion gives way to coercion. . . . It is enough for today that wherever that line may be, this statute is surely beyond it. Congress may not simply conscript state agencies into the national bureaucratic army, and that is what it is attempting to do with the Medicaid expansion.

B [Omitted.]

[CONCLUSION]

The Affordable Care Act is constitutional in part and unconstitutional in part. . . .

The Framers created a Federal Government of limited powers, and assigned to this Court the duty of enforcing those limits. The Court does so today. But the Court does not express any opinion on the wisdom of the Affordable Care Act. Under the Constitution, that judgment is reserved to the people.

Justice Ginsburg, with whom Justice Sotomayor joins, and with whom Justice Breyer and Justice Kagan join as to Parts I, II, III, and IV, concurring in part, concurring in the judgment in part, and dissenting in part.

I agree with the Chief Justice that the Anti-Injunction Act does not bar the Court's consideration of this case, and that the minimum coverage provision is a proper exercise of Congress' taxing power. I therefore join Parts I, II, and III-C of the Chief Justice's opinion. Unlike the Chief Justice, however, I would hold, alternatively, that the Commerce Clause authorizes Congress to enact the minimum coverage provision. I would also hold that the Spending Clause permits the Medicaid expansion exactly as Congress enacted it.

I

. . .

Since 1937, our precedent has recognized Congress' large authority to set the Nation's course in the economic and social welfare realm. The Chief Justice's crabbed reading of the Commerce Clause harks back to the era in which the Court routinely thwarted Congress' efforts to regulate the national economy in the interest of those who labor to sustain it. It is a reading that should not have staying power.

National Federation of Independent Businesses v. Sebelius

A

In enacting the Patient Protection and Affordable Care Act (ACA), Congress comprehensively reformed the national market for health-care products and services. By any measure, that market is immense. Collectively, Americans spent $2.5 trillion on health care in 2009, accounting for 17.6% of our Nation's economy. Within the next decade, it is anticipated, spending on health care will nearly double.

The health-care market's size is not its only distinctive feature. Unlike the market for almost any other product or service, the market for medical care is one in which all individuals inevitably participate. Virtually every person residing in the United States, sooner or later, will visit a doctor or other health-care professional. Most people will do so repeatedly. . . .

B

The large number of individuals without health insurance, Congress found, heavily burdens the national health-care market. . . . Those with health insurance subsidize the medical care of those without it. As economists would describe what happens, the uninsured "free ride" on those who pay for health insurance.

The size of this subsidy is considerable. Congress found that the cost-shifting just described increases family insurance premiums by on average over $1,000 a year. Higher premiums, in turn, render health insurance less affordable, forcing more people to go without insurance and leading to further cost-shifting. . . .

C

States cannot resolve the problem of the uninsured on their own. Like Social Security benefits, a universal health-care system, if adopted by an individual State, would be bait to the needy and dependent elsewhere, encouraging them to migrate and seek a haven of repose. An influx of unhealthy individuals into a State with universal health care would result in increased spending on medical services. To cover the increased costs, a State would have to raise taxes, and private health-insurance companies would have to increase premiums. Higher taxes and increased insurance costs would, in turn, encourage businesses and healthy individuals to leave the State.

States that undertake health-care reforms on their own thus risk placing themselves in a position of economic disadvantage as compared with neighbors or competitors. Facing that risk, individual States are unlikely to take the initiative in addressing the problem of the uninsured, even though solving that problem is in all States' best interests. Congress' intervention was needed to overcome this collective-action impasse.

D

Aware that a national solution was required, Congress could have taken over the health-insurance market by establishing a tax-and-spend federal program like Social Security. Such a program, commonly referred to as a single-payer system (where the sole payer is the Federal Government), would have left little, if any, room for private enterprise or the States. Instead of going this route, Congress enacted the ACA, a solution that retains a robust role for private insurers and state governments. To make its chosen approach work, however, Congress had to use some new tools, including a requirement that most individuals obtain private health insurance coverage. As explained below, by employing these tools, Congress was able to achieve a practical, altogether reasonable, solution. . . .

Whatever one thinks of the policy decision Congress made, it was Congress' prerogative to make it. Reviewed with appropriate deference, the minimum coverage provision, allied to the guaranteed-issue and community-rating prescriptions, should survive measurement under the Commerce and Necessary and Proper Clauses.

II

A

The Commerce Clause, it is widely acknowledged, was the Framers' response to the central problem that gave rise to the Constitution itself. Under the Articles of Confederation, the Constitution's precursor, the regulation of commerce was left to the States. This scheme proved unworkable, because the individual States, understandably focused on their own economic interests, often failed to take actions critical to the success of the Nation as a whole. . . .

B

Consistent with the Framers' intent, we have repeatedly emphasized that Congress' authority under the Commerce Clause is dependent upon practical considerations, including actual experience. We afford Congress the leeway to undertake to solve national problems directly and realistically.

Until today, this Court's pragmatic approach to judging whether Congress validly exercised its commerce power was guided by two familiar principles. First, Congress has the power to regulate economic activities that substantially affect interstate commerce. *Gonzales v. Raich* (2005). This capacious power extends even to local activities that, viewed in the aggregate, have a substantial impact on interstate commerce. *Wickard v. Filburn* (1942); *Jones & Laughlin Steel Corp.* (1937).

Second, we owe a large measure of respect to Congress when it frames and enacts economic and social legislation. When appraising such legislation, we ask only (1) whether Congress had a "rational basis" for concluding that the regulated activity substantially affects interstate commerce, and (2) whether there is a "reasonable connection between the regulatory means selected and the asserted ends."

In answering these questions, we presume the statute under review is constitutional and may strike it down only on a plain showing that Congress acted irrationally.

C

Straightforward application of these principles would require the Court to hold that the minimum coverage provision is proper Commerce Clause legislation. Beyond dispute, Congress had a rational basis for concluding that the uninsured, as a class, substantially affect interstate commerce. Those without insurance consume billions of dollars of health-care products and services each year. Those goods are produced, sold, and delivered largely by national and regional companies who routinely transact business across state lines. The uninsured also cross state lines to receive care. Some have medical emergencies while away from home. Others, when sick, go to a neighboring State that provides better care for those who have not prepaid for care.

Not only do those without insurance consume a large amount of health care each year; critically, as earlier explained, their inability to pay for a significant portion of that consumption drives up market prices, foists costs on other consumers, and reduces market efficiency and stability. Given these far-reaching effects on interstate commerce, the decision to forgo insurance is hardly inconsequential or equivalent to "doing nothing," it is, instead, an economic decision Congress has the authority to address under the Commerce Clause. . . .

D

Rather than evaluating the constitutionality of the minimum coverage provision in the manner established by our precedents, the Chief Justice relies on a newly minted constitutional doctrine. The commerce power does not, the Chief Justice announces, permit Congress to "compel individuals to become active in commerce by purchasing a product."

1

a

The Chief Justice's novel constraint on Congress' commerce power gains no force from our precedent and for that reason alone warrants disapprobation. But even assuming, for the moment, that Congress lacks authority under the Commerce Clause to "compel individuals not engaged in commerce to purchase an unwanted product," such a limitation would be inapplicable here. Everyone will, at some point, consume health-care products and services. Thus, if the Chief Justice is correct that an insurance-purchase requirement can be applied only to those who "actively" consume health care, the minimum coverage provision fits the bill. . . .

It is Congress' role, not the Court's, to delineate the boundaries of the market the Legislature seeks to regulate. The Chief Justice defines the health-care market as including only those transactions that will occur either in the next instant or within some (unspecified) proximity to the next instant. But Congress could reasonably have viewed the market from a long-term perspective, encompassing all transactions virtually certain to occur over the next decade, not just those occurring here and now. . . .

Our decisions thus acknowledge Congress' authority, under the Commerce Clause, to direct the conduct of an individual today (the farmer in *Wickard*, stopped from growing excess wheat; the plaintiff in *Raich*, ordered to cease cultivating marijuana) because of a prophesied future transaction (the eventual sale of that wheat or marijuana in the interstate market). Congress' actions are even more rational in this case, where the future activity (the consumption of medical care) is certain to occur, the sole uncertainty being the time the activity will take place. . . .

b

In any event, the Chief Justice's limitation of the commerce power to the regulation of those actively engaged in commerce finds no home in the text of the Constitution or our decisions. Article I, § 8, of the Constitution grants Congress the power "to regulate Commerce . . . among the several States." Nothing in this language implies that Congress' commerce power is limited to regulating those actively engaged in commercial transactions. Indeed, as the D.C. Circuit observed, at the time the Constitution was framed, to "regulate" meant, among other things, "to require action." . . .

Nor does our case law toe the activity versus inactivity line. In *Wickard*, for example, we upheld the penalty imposed on a farmer who grew too much wheat, even though the regulation had the effect of compelling farmers to purchase wheat in the open market. Forcing some farmers into the market to buy what they could provide for themselves was, the Court held, a valid means of regulating commerce. . . .

This Court's former endeavors to impose categorical limits on the commerce power have not fared well. In several pre-New Deal cases, the Court . . . sought to distinguish activities having a "direct" effect on interstate commerce, and for that reason, subject to federal regulation, from those having only an "indirect" effect, and therefore not amenable to federal control. See, e.g., *Schechter Poultry Corp. v. United States* (1935).

These line-drawing exercises were untenable, and the Court long ago abandoned them. . . . Failing to learn from this history, the Chief Justice plows ahead with his formalistic distinction between those who are "active in commerce," and those who are not.

It is not hard to show the difficulty courts (and Congress) would encounter in distinguishing statutes that regulate "activity" from those that regulate "inactivity." . . . Take this case as an example. An individual who opts not to purchase insurance from a private insurer can be seen as actively selecting another form of insurance: self-insurance. The minimum coverage provision could therefore be described as regulating activists in the self-insurance market. Wickard is another example. Did the statute there at issue target activity (the growing of too much wheat) or inactivity (the farmer's failure to purchase wheat in the marketplace)? If anything, the Court's analysis suggested the latter.

At bottom, the Chief Justice's and the joint dissenters' view that an individual cannot be subject to Commerce Clause regulation absent voluntary, affirmative acts that enter him or her into, or affect, the interstate market expresses a concern for individual liberty that is more redolent of Due Process Clause arguments. Plaintiffs have abandoned any argument pinned to substantive due process, however, and now concede that the provisions here at issue do not offend the Due Process Clause.

2–3 [Omitted.]

III

A

. . . The Necessary and Proper Clause empowers Congress to enact laws in effectuation of its commerce power that are not within its authority to enact in isolation. Hence, a complex regulatory program can survive a Commerce Clause challenge without a showing that every single facet of the program is independently and directly related to a valid congressional goal. It is enough that the challenged provisions are an integral part of the regulatory program and that the regulatory scheme when considered as a whole satisfies this test.

Recall that one of Congress' goals in enacting the Affordable Care Act was to eliminate the insurance industry's practice of charging higher prices or denying coverage to individuals with preexisting medical conditions. The commerce power allows Congress to ban this practice, a point no one disputes.

Congress knew, however, that simply barring insurance companies from relying on an applicant's medical history would not work in practice. Without the individual mandate, Congress learned, guaranteed-issue and community-rating requirements would trigger an adverse-selection death-spiral in the health-insurance market: Insurance premiums would skyrocket, the number of uninsured would increase, and insurance companies would exit the market. When complemented by an insurance mandate, on the other hand, guaranteed issue and community rating would work as intended, increasing access to insurance and reducing uncompensated care. The minimum coverage provision is thus an essential part of a larger regulation of economic activity; without the provision, the regulatory scheme would be undercut. Put differently, the minimum coverage provision, together with the guaranteed-issue and community-rating requirements, is reasonably adapted to the attainment of a legitimate end under the commerce power: the elimination of pricing and sales practices that take an applicant's medical history into account.

B

Asserting that the Necessary and Proper Clause does not authorize the minimum coverage provision, the Chief Justice focuses on the word "proper." A mandate to purchase health insurance is not "proper" legislation, the Chief Justice urges, because the command undermines the structure of government established by the Constitution. If long on rhetoric, the Chief Justice's argument is short on substance.

The Chief Justice cites only two cases in which this Court concluded that a federal statute impermissibly transgressed the Constitution's boundary between state and federal authority: *Printz v. United States* (1997), and *New York v. United States* (1992). The statutes at issue in both cases, however, compelled state officials to act on the Federal Government's behalf. "Federal laws conscripting state officers," the Court reasoned, "violate state sovereignty and are thus not in accord with the Constitution." *Printz*.

The minimum coverage provision, in contrast, acts directly upon individuals, without employing the States as intermediaries. The provision is thus entirely consistent with the Constitution's design.

Lacking case law support for his holding, the Chief Justice nevertheless declares the minimum coverage provision not "proper" because it is less "narrow in scope" than other laws this Court has upheld under the Necessary and Proper Clause. The Chief Justice's reliance on cases [like *Comstock*, *Sabri*, *Jinks*, and *McCulloch*] in which this Court has *affirmed* Congress' broad authority to enact federal legislation under the Necessary and Proper Clause is underwhelming.

Nor does the Chief Justice pause to explain *why* the power to direct either the purchase of health insurance or, alternatively, the payment of a penalty collectible as a tax is more far-reaching than other implied powers this Court has found meet under the Necessary and Proper Clause. These powers include the power to enact criminal laws; the power to imprison, including civil imprisonment, *Comstock*, and the power to create a national bank, *McCulloch*.

In failing to explain why the individual mandate threatens our constitutional order, the Chief Justice disserves future courts. How is a judge to decide, when ruling on the constitutionality of a federal statute, whether Congress employed an "independent power" or merely a "derivative" one? Whether the power used is "substantive" or just "incidental"? The instruction the Chief Justice, in effect, provides lower courts: You will know it when you see it. . . .

IV

In the early 20th century, this Court regularly struck down economic regulation enacted by the peoples' representatives in both the States and the Federal Government. The Chief Justice's Commerce Clause opinion, and even more so the joint dissenters' reasoning, bear a disquieting resemblance to those long-overruled decisions.

National Federation of Independent Businesses v. Sebelius

Ultimately, the Court upholds the individual mandate as a proper exercise of Congress' power to tax and spend for the general welfare of the United States. I concur in that determination, which makes the Chief Justice's Commerce Clause essay all the more puzzling. Why should the Chief Justice strive so mightily to hem in Congress' capacity to meet the new problems arising constantly in our ever-developing modern economy? I find no satisfying response to that question in his opinion.

V

. . .

A [Omitted.]

B

The Spending Clause authorizes Congress "to pay the Debts and provide for the . . . general Welfare of the United States." To ensure that federal funds granted to the States are spent to provide for the general welfare in the manner Congress intended, Congress must of course have authority to impose limitations on the States' use of the federal dollars. This Court, time and again, has respected Congress' prescription of spending conditions, and has required States to abide by them. In particular, we have recognized Congress' prerogative to condition a State's receipt of Medicaid funding on compliance with the terms Congress set for participation in the program.

Congress' authority to condition the use of federal funds is not confined to spending programs as first launched. The legislature may, and often does, amend the law, imposing new conditions grant recipients henceforth must meet in order to continue receiving funds. . . . That is what makes this such a simple case, and the Court's decision [on the Medicaid expansion] so unsettling. . . .

C

The Chief Justice asserts that the Medicaid expansion creates a "new health care program." Moreover, States could "hardly anticipate" that Congress would "transform the program so dramatically." Therefore, the Chief Justice maintains, Congress' threat to withhold "old" Medicaid funds based on a State's refusal to participate in the "new" program is a "threat to terminate another independent grant." And because the threat to withhold a large amount of funds from one program "leaves the States with no real option but to acquiesce [in a newly created program]," the Chief Justice concludes, the Medicaid expansion is unconstitutionally coercive.

1

The starting premise on which the Chief Justice's coercion analysis rests is that the ACA did not really "extend" Medicaid; instead, Congress created an entirely new program to co-exist with the old. The Chief Justice calls the ACA new, but in truth, it simply reaches more of America's poor than Congress originally covered. . . .

Endeavoring to show that Congress created a new program, the Chief Justice . . . asserts that, in covering those earning no more than 133% of the federal poverty line, the Medicaid expansion, unlike pre-ACA Medicaid, does not "care for the neediest among us." What makes that so? Single adults earning no more than $14,856 per year—133% of the current federal poverty level—surely rank among the Nation's poor. . . .

Consider also that Congress could have repealed Medicaid. Thereafter, Congress could have enacted Medicaid II, a new program combining the pre-2010 coverage with the expanded coverage required by the ACA. By what right does a court stop Congress from building up without first tearing down?

2

The Chief Justice finds the Medicaid expansion vulnerable because it took participating States by surprise. . . . [There is no surprise.] Section 2001 does not take effect until 2014. The ACA makes perfectly clear what will be required of States that accept Medicaid funding after that date: They must extend eligibility to adults with incomes no more than 133% of the federal poverty line. . . .

If I understand [The Chief Justice's] point correctly, it was incumbent on Congress, in 1965, to warn the States clearly of the size and shape potential changes to Medicaid might take. And absent such notice, sizable changes could not be made mandatory. Our decisions do not support such a requirement. . . .

In any event, from the start, the Medicaid Act put States on notice that the program could be changed: "The right to alter, amend, or repeal any provision of [Medicaid]," the statute has read since 1965, "is hereby reserved to the Congress." 42 U.S.C. § 1304. The effect of these few simple words has long been settled. By reserving the right to alter, amend, or repeal a spending program, Congress has given special notice of its intention to retain full and complete power to make such alterations and amendments as come within the just scope of legislative power. . . .

The Chief Justice nevertheless would rewrite § 1304 to countenance only the "right to alter somewhat," or "amend, but not too much." Congress, however, did not so qualify § 1304. Indeed, Congress retained discretion to "repeal" Medicaid, wiping it out entirely. . . . No State could reasonably have read § 1304 as reserving to Congress authority to make adjustments only if modestly sized. . . .

3

The Chief Justice ultimately asks whether "the financial inducement offered by Congress passed the point at which pressure turns into compulsion." The financial inducement Congress employed here, he concludes, crosses that threshold: The threatened withholding of "existing Medicaid funds" is "a gun to the head" that forces States to acquiesce. . . .

When future Spending Clause challenges arrive, as they likely will in the wake of today's decision, how will litigants and judges assess whether a State has a legitimate choice whether to accept the federal conditions in exchange for federal funds? Are courts to measure the number of dollars the Federal Government might withhold for noncompliance? The portion of the State's budget at stake? And which State's—or States'—budget is determinative: the lead plaintiff, all challenging States (26 in this case, many with quite different fiscal situations), or some national median? Does it matter that Florida, unlike most States, imposes no state income tax, and therefore might be able to replace foregone federal funds with new state revenue? Or that the coercion state officials in fact fear is punishment at the ballot box for turning down a politically popular federal grant? The coercion inquiry, therefore, appears to involve political judgments that defy judicial calculation. . . .

At bottom, my colleagues' position is that the States' reliance on federal funds limits Congress' authority to alter its spending programs. This gets things backwards: Congress, not the States, is tasked with spending federal money in service of the general welfare. And each successive Congress is empowered to appropriate funds as it sees fit. When the 110th Congress reached a conclusion about Medicaid funds that differed from its predecessors' view, it abridged no State's right to existing, or pre-existing funds. For, in fact, there are no such funds. There is only money States anticipate receiving from future Congresses.

D [Omitted.]

Justices Scalia, Kennedy, Thomas, and Alito, dissenting. [This opinion is known as "the Joint Dissent."]

. . . What is absolutely clear, affirmed by the text of the 1789 Constitution, by the Tenth Amendment ratified in 1791, and by innumerable cases of ours in the 220 years since, is that there are structural limits upon federal power—upon what it can prescribe with respect to private conduct, and upon what it can impose upon the sovereign States. Whatever may be the conceptual limits upon the Commerce Clause and upon the power to tax and spend, they cannot be such as will enable the Federal Government to regulate all private conduct and to compel the States to function as administrators of federal programs. . . .

I

The Individual Mandate

[The Joint Dissent argued that Congress lacks power to enact the individual mandate under the Commerce Clause and the Necessary and Proper Clause, for reasons similar to those in the opinion of Chief Justice Roberts.]

II

The Taxing Power

. . . Our cases establish a clear line between a tax and a penalty: a tax is an enforced contribution to provide for the support of government; a penalty is an exaction imposed by statute as punishment for an unlawful act. In a few cases, this Court has held that a "tax" imposed upon private conduct was so onerous as to be in effect a penalty. But we have never held—never—that a penalty imposed for violation of the law was so trivial as to be in effect a tax. We have never held that any exaction imposed for violation of the law is an exercise of Congress' taxing power—even when the statute calls it a tax, much less when (as here) the statute repeatedly calls it a penalty. When an act adopts the criteria of wrongdoing and then imposes a monetary penalty as the principal consequence on those who transgress its standard, it creates a regulatory penalty, not a tax.

So the question is, quite simply, whether the exaction here is imposed for violation of the law. It unquestionably is. The minimum-coverage provision is found in 26 U.S.C. § 5000A, entitled "Requirement to maintain minimum essential coverage." It commands that every "applicable individual shall ensure that the individual is covered under minimum essential coverage." And the immediately following provision states that, "if an applicable individual fails to meet the requirement of subsection (a), there is hereby imposed a penalty." . . .

The fact that Congress (in its own words) "imposed a penalty" for failure to buy insurance is alone sufficient to render that failure unlawful. . . . We never have classified as a tax an exaction imposed for violation of the law, and so too, we never have classified as a tax an exaction described in the legislation itself as a penalty. To be sure, we have sometimes treated as a tax a statutory exaction (imposed for something other than a violation of law) which bore an agnostic label that does not entail the significant constitutional consequences of a penalty—such as "license" or "surcharge." But we have never—never—treated as a tax an exaction which faces up to the critical difference between a tax and a penalty, and explicitly denominates the exaction a "penalty." Eighteen times in § 5000A itself and elsewhere throughout the Act, Congress called the exaction in § 5000A(b) a "penalty." . . .

For all these reasons, to say that the Individual Mandate merely imposes a tax is not to interpret the statute but to rewrite it. Judicial tax-writing is particularly troubling. Taxes have never been popular, and in part for that reason, the Constitution requires tax increases to originate in the House of Representatives. [Art. I, § 7, cl. 1.] That is to say, they must originate in the legislative body most accountable to the people, where legislators must weigh the need for the tax against the terrible price they might pay at their next election, which is never more than two years off. . . .

III

The Anti-Injunction Act [Omitted.]

IV

The Medicaid Expansion

[The Joint Dissent argued that the Medicaid expansion is a coercive use of federal spending, for reasons similar to those in the Chief Justice's opinion.]

V

Severability [Omitted.]

[CONCLUSION]

The Constitution, though it dates from the founding of the Republic, has powerful meaning and vital relevance to our own times. The constitutional protections that this case involves are protections of structure. Structural protections—notably, the restraints imposed by federalism and separation of powers—are less romantic and have less obvious a connection to personal freedom than the provisions of the Bill of Rights or the Civil War Amendments. Hence they tend to be undervalued or even forgotten by our citizens. It should be the responsibility of the Court to teach otherwise, to remind our people that the Framers considered structural protections of freedom the most important ones, for which reason they alone were embodied in the original Constitution and not left to later amendment. The fragmentation of power produced by the structure of our Government is central to liberty, and when we destroy it, we place liberty at peril. Today's decision should have vindicated, should have taught, this truth; instead, our judgment today has disregarded it.

Justice Thomas, dissenting.

I dissent for the reasons stated in our joint opinion, but I write separately to say a word about the Commerce Clause. The joint dissent and the Chief Justice correctly apply our precedents to conclude that the Individual Mandate is beyond the power granted to Congress under the Commerce Clause and the Necessary and Proper Clause. Under those precedents, Congress may regulate economic activity that substantially affects interstate commerce. I adhere to my view that the very notion of a "substantial effects" test under the Commerce Clause is inconsistent with the original understanding of Congress' powers and with this Court's early Commerce Clause cases. As I have explained, the Court's continued use of that test has encouraged the Federal Government to persist in its view that the Commerce Clause has virtually no limits. The Government's unprecedented claim in this suit that it may regulate not only economic activity but also inactivity that substantially affects interstate commerce is a case in point.

flashforward

Changing the Amount Due. As part of a tax reform package in December 2017, Congress set the cost of the "shared responsibility payment" for individuals without health insurance to zero. This change led some litigants to argue that it rendered the ACA unconstitutional, because there was no longer any tax to justify the individual mandate (to the extent one still existed after *NFIB v. Sebelius*) as an exercise of the Taxing Clause. The Supreme Court held that no one had standing to challenge a law whose only method of enforcement was a tax of zero. *California v. Texas*, 141 S.Ct. 2104 (2021).

Part III: Individual Rights

Individual Rights

Part III sharpens focus on the right side of the diagram, representing the boundary between government power and individual rights. When enforced, rights limit how the government may use its powers. For example, Art. I, § 8, cls. 12 & 14 give Congress the enumerated powers to "raise and support Armies" and "to make rules for [their] government and regulation." These enumerated powers, either by themselves or in combination with the Necessary and Proper Clause, authorize Congress to pass laws to house the troops. But that power is limited by the Third Amendment, which creates an individual right not to have soldiers quartered in one's home during peacetime. Like other individual rights, the Third Amendment prevents Congress from exercising its enumerated powers in certain forbidden ways.

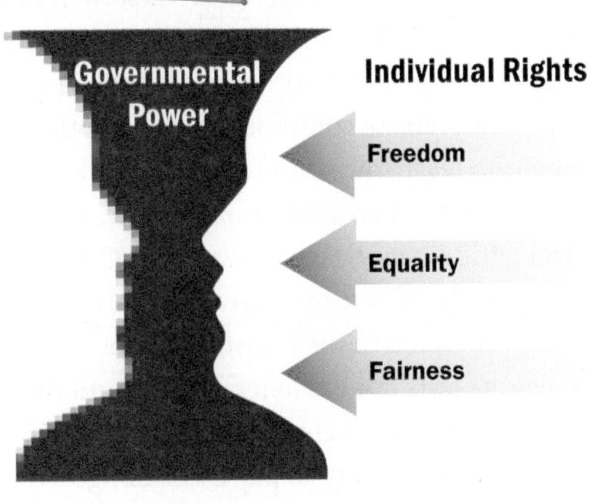

The Third Amendment's results could in theory be accomplished through the language enumerating Congress's power. If the Constitution said "Congress shall have power in peacetime to quarter soldiers in government-owned barracks," courts would not allow the government to quarter soldiers in private homes during peacetime. But even when a conversation about powers and a conversation about rights converge on the same result, the first conversation will tend to focus on the government's purposes (military preparedness), while the second conversation will tend to focus on the individual's interests (privacy of the home). Compared to an enumerated powers case, an individual rights case may well interpret different parts of the Constitution's text, cite different precedents, emphasize different structural features, hearken back to different history, consider different consequences, and invoke different values.

A. The Parts of the Picture

By and large, the rights protected by the US Constitution reflect three overlapping constitutional values: *freedom, equality,* and *fairness.*

Freedom calls for the government to allow people to do what they want: an absence of legal compulsion. Enumerated freedoms include the First Amendment rights of religion, speech, assembly, and petition, the Second Amendment right to keep and bear arms, and the Thirteenth Amendment ban on slavery.

Part III studies *substantive due process* as its primary example of a freedom right. The doctrine of substantive due process protects against deprivations of unenumerated fundamental rights. As seen in Part I, substantive due process—as a tool to enforce freedom of contract—was used to invalidate economic regulations during the *Lochner* Era. Although that use of substantive due process was rejected in 1937, the doctrine continues to protect other unenumerated rights, such as the freedoms to teach one's children a foreign language, *Meyer v. Nebraska* (1923), or to send them to a private school, *Pierce v. Society of Sisters* (1925), or to use birth control within a marriage, *Griswold v. Connecticut* (1965).

Equality calls for the government to treat people similarly to each other. Equality provisions in the Constitution include the ban on titles of nobility, the ban on religious tests to hold federal office, and the various amendments preventing the right to vote from being abridged on the basis of race, color, previous condition of servitude, sex, ability to pay a tax, or age over 18.

Part III studies the *Equal Protection Clause* as its primary example of an equality right. Because the Equal Protection Clause is written in broad language that requires equality across many factual settings, an intricate set of legal rules has arisen around it.

Fairness calls for the government to conduct its business honorably, even in those inevitable situations where it must limit individuals' freedom or equality. A central concept animating the fairness rights is the *rule of law.* The rule of law requires the government to act according to agreed-upon principles applied through agreed-upon procedures—and not to act arbitrarily to satisfy the whims of those currently in power. As stated in *Marbury v. Madison* (1803): "the government of the United States has been emphatically termed a government of laws, and not of men." Fairness appears in the Constitution in the many criminal procedure protections found in Art. III and in the Fourth, Fifth, and Sixth Amendments. The Takings Clause of the Fifth Amendment reflects fairness in another context, by requiring just compensation when private property is taken for public use.

Part III studies *procedural due process* as its primary example of a fairness right. This doctrine is a blanket guarantee of fair procedures across many factual settings.

B. Interaction of the Parts

Relationships Among Rights. Freedom, equality, and fairness are not mutually exclusive. Equality implicates freedom and fairness, because we view some forms of inequality as inherently unfair, and because most government-imposed inequalities involve reduction in someone's freedom. The rule of law implicates fairness, equality, and freedom, because scrupulously following written rules is fair in individual cases, will result in like cases being treated alike, and restricts the government's practical ability to restrict freedom. All of this means that a single constitutional right may protect multiple values. The abolition of slavery undoubtedly serves fairness, freedom, and equality together. Cruel and unusual punishment can be seen as unfair (excessive and arbitrary), unequal (unusual), and a threat to freedom (by giving individuals more reasons to be fearful of those in power).

Individual Rights Protect Overlapping Constitutional Value

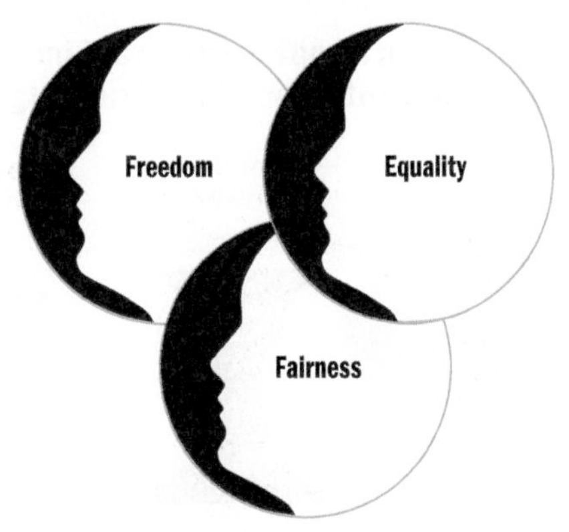

Given their complex interactions, the three categories of rights should be viewed as tools to generate ideas, and not as a rigid framework limiting the options for advocacy. Thinking about these categories can help a lawyer explain why a right is important. It can also help a lawyer decide which arguments to emphasize. For example, the ban on interracial marriage in *Loving v. Virginia* (1967) was challenged as a violation of equality and a violation of freedom. The railway segregation law in *Plessy v. Ferguson* (1896) could be viewed as a violation of racial equality, or of the freedom to sit where one wishes, or of the freedom to associate with whom one wishes, or perhaps as a deprivation of the full property value of one's railway ticket. Deciding which potential arguments to emphasize requires knowledge of each legal doctrine, an understanding of the similarities and differences among doctrines, and a sense of the values held most dear by the decision-makers in a given time and place.

Relationship of Rights and Structure. The individual rights studied in Part III are protected by the US Constitution against infringement by the federal government and by the states (often through the incorporation of rights into the Due Process Clause of the Fourteenth Amendment). As a result, when the Supreme Court issues a decision enforcing an incorporated right, it represents an identical limit on the powers of both the state and federal governments. See Ch. 5.C.

Although the substance of rights is the same whether they are applied directly or through incorporation, the enforcement of individual rights has an impact on state sovereignty that differs from its impact on federal sovereignty. A state must obey its state constitution and the applicable parts of the US Constitution. The people of a state can alter their own constitution, but acting alone they cannot change the US Constitution. Judges concerned about federalism may therefore be hesitant to recognize federal constitutional rights that could limit state power. In addition, the decision to recognize federal constitutional rights is made by the federal judiciary, unlike the decision to enact federal statutory rights, which is made by Congress. Judges concerned about separation of powers between the legislative and judicial branches may similarly feel cautious when ruling on individual rights. If they control the outcome, these two structural concerns have the inevitable effect of broadening the power of states and political branches.

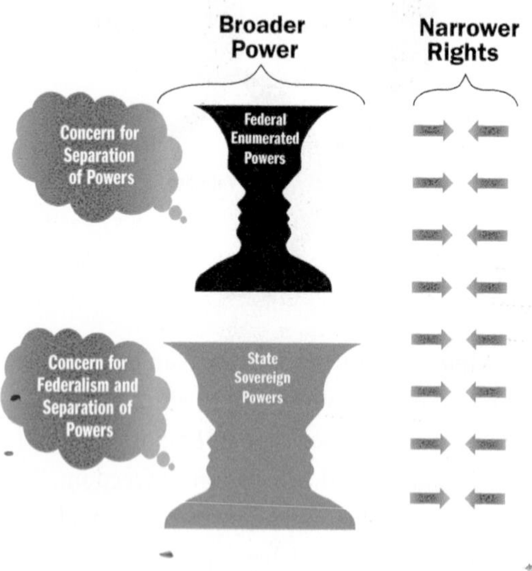

Tinker v. Des Moines Independent School District, 393 U.S. 503 (1969), reveals how structural concerns—the "who decides" questions—can matter even in cases litigated in terms of individual rights. The public school district in *Tinker* learned that students were planning to wear black armbands to school as a protest against the Vietnam War; in response, the district adopted a rule banning armbands. By holding that the First Amendment protected the students' right to wear armbands, the Supreme Court decided that each individual student—and not the elected school board—could decide whether armbands would be worn. But viewed another way, the ruling placed the power to decide with the judiciary—not the legislature or the executive—and to the federal Constitution—not state or local law.

Justice Black's dissent emphasized these structural concerns; for him, school districts should decide dress code questions, not courts or individuals.

> The Court's holding in this case ushers in what I deem to be an entirely new era in which the power to control pupils by the elected officials of state supported public schools in the United States is in ultimate effect transferred to the Supreme Court. . . .
>
> I, for one, am not fully persuaded that school pupils are wise enough, even with this Court's expert help from Washington, to run the 23,390 public school systems in our 50 States. I wish, therefore, wholly to disclaim any purpose on my part to hold that the Federal Constitution compels the teachers, parents, and elected school officials to surrender control of the American public school system to public school students.

Tinker exemplifies a conundrum: for a government to intrude minimally on individual rights may require a strong judiciary that intrudes on the powers of democratically elected legislatures and executives. This tension seen in individual rights cases—between big government and a big judiciary—was heavily contested during the *Lochner* Era. The optimal balance continues to be debated and recalibrated in individual rights cases today.

C. The Historical Setting

As with any court decisions, the cases in Part III arose in a concrete historical setting. Under Chief Justice Warren (1954–1969), the Supreme Court saw itself as a protector and supporter of a wide variety of individual rights. In some areas involving equality, criminal procedure, expression, and religion, these years saw the first serious efforts to enforce many of the enumerated rights. Since then, the Supreme Court has had to decide how far to continue down that path.

From the 1970s onward, the nation as a whole became more politically conservative (although also more socially tolerant of some individual differences). In keeping with the times, the judicial politics of the Burger, Rehnquist, and Roberts Courts can be seen as reactions to, or reconsiderations of, the principles that animated the Warren Court. In some areas, notably freedom of speech, recent decisions have generally continued the rights-protective trajectory established by the Warren Court. In other areas, notably criminal procedure, they have been more likely to favor the government's position.

Recent Courts have also had to confront questions that had not previously been litigated. Under the Equal Protection Clause, for example, the enormous achievements of the Warren Court in cases like *Brown v. Board of Education*

(1954) and *Loving v. Virginia* (1967) involved a single racial classification between "white" and "colored." Since then, other social groups have emulated the civil rights movement to pursue legal equality, including women; racial minorities other than African-Americans; people with disabilities; the poor; immigrants; and lesbian, gay, bisexual, and transgender (LGBT) people. New theories began to be litigated, including challenges to racially neutral laws that burdened minorities as applied, and challenges to government efforts to take affirmative action to improve the economic, political, and social position of minority groups. The equality questions of these years were more complex than the stark discrimination of the Jim Crow era. And they were being decided by courts that were increasingly concerned about federalism, separation of powers, and other structural limitations studied in Part II.

Within Part III, **Chapter 18** (Equality Rights) explores the modern approach to the Equal Protection Clause. **Chapter 19** (Fairness Rights) examines procedural due process as a guarantee of fairness in administrative and judicial procedures. **Chapter 20** (Freedom Rights) considers how substantive due process can be used to protect unenumerated rights. **Chapter 21** (Exceptions to the State Action Doctrine) considers a topic that might arise in any individual rights case: whether private actors might ever be the equivalent of the government, and hence be obligated to respect constitutional rights. **Chapter 22** (Master Class) uses the recent history of gay rights litigation as a tool to review everything studied earlier. These cases show how legal doctrines can combine—and change—in pursuit of constitutional goals.

CHAPTER 18

Equality Rights

Although the Declaration of Independence considered it "self-evident" that "all men are created equal," the word "equal" did not enter the US Constitution until 1868, when the Fourteenth Amendment declared that no State shall deny "the equal protection of the laws." Because the Equal Protection Clause is incorporated into the Due Process Clause of the Fifth Amendment, the federal government may not deny the equal protection of the laws, either. *Bolling v. Sharpe* (1954).

Most laws have the potential to treat some people differently than others. A law requiring a medical school degree as a condition for a license to practice medicine distinguishes between medical school graduates and non-medical school graduates. Laws against homicide distinguish between killers and non-killers, and the degrees of homicide distinguish among those who kill with premeditation, those who kill during the course of a felony, those who kill in the heat of passion, and those who do not intend to kill at all. Oklahoma's law from *Williamson v. Lee Optical* (1955) distinguished optometrists from opticians, and the federal law in *Carolene Products* (1938) distinguished sellers of filled milk from sellers of other dairy products. All of these laws could be said to impose inequality, but they do not violate the Equal Protection Clause.

Equal Protection Limits Both State and Federal Governments

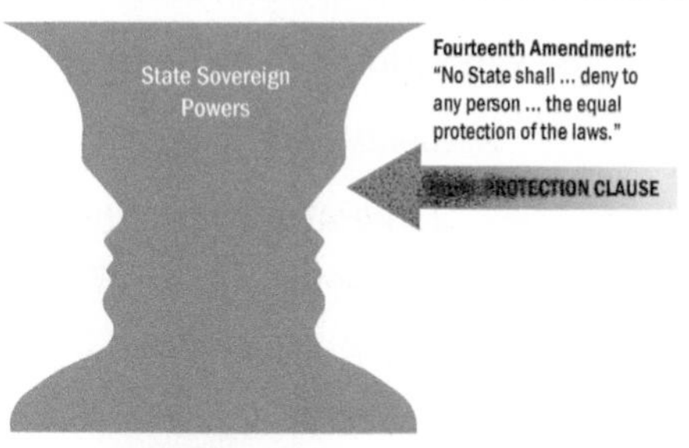

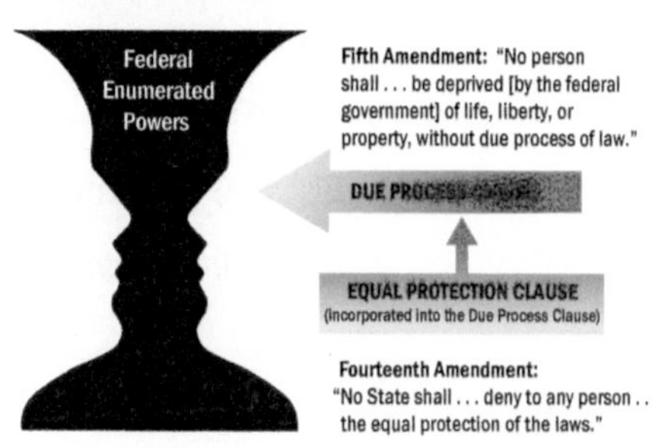

Federal Enumerated Powers
Fifth Amendment: "No person shall . . . be deprived [by the federal government] of life, liberty, or property, without due process of law."
DUE PROC
EQUAL PROTECTION CLAUSE
(incorporated into the Due Process Clause)
Fourteenth Amendment: "No State shall . . . deny to any person . . . the equal protection of the laws."

One way to express the law's tolerance for certain types of inequality is to say that the government must treat like things alike, but it may treat unlike things differently. Of course, that formula requires a judgment call about which things are like and unlike each other, and in what settings. For purposes of issuing drivers' licenses, we believe that adult men are similarly situated to adult women; a law giving licenses only to one sex would be an unconstitutional form of inequality. Yet we believe that adults and children are not similarly situated in their ability to drive, so laws denying licenses to children are constitutional. Meanwhile, adults are like children for other purposes: both are protected against unreasonable search and seizure, and (if they are US citizens) both are entitled to obtain passports allowing them to return to the country after foreign travel.

The task of equal protection law, therefore, is to develop a framework for deciding when equality is constitutionally required—or phrased another way, when inequality can be justified. To do this, the Equal Protection Clause builds on the New Deal concept of levels of scrutiny. Courts will give careful scrutiny to laws that rely on suspicious forms of inequality, but show deference to the government's choices when they involve forms of inequality considered tolerable.

A. Kickstarter: Equal Protection

DISCLAIMER: *This Kickstarter is a checklist to help identify relevant issues. It is not a list of elements. Nothing requires judges to write their opinions (or lawyers to write their briefs) in Kickstarter order.*

Equal Protection **kickstarter**

USE WHEN: *Government treats similarly situated people differently.*

A. *Identify the inequality.*
   1. *WHAT burden or benefit does the law distribute unequally? (Fundamental Rights prong).*
   2. *WHO is affected by the law's classifications? (Suspect Classifications prong).*

B. *Select the proper level of scrutiny for the type of inequality.*

C. *Apply the scrutiny.*
   1. *ENDS: Government Interest.*
   2. *MEANS: Tailoring.*

KICKSTARTER USER'S GUIDE

The modern approach to the Equal Protection Clause requires the government to justify inequalities imposed by law or other state action. At the outset, this means government action that treats all people the same will not violate the Equal Protection Clause—even if the law is harsh, reflects bad motives, or violates some other constitutional right. For example, the city of Jackson, Mississippi in the late 1960s closed all its public swimming pools to avoid operating racially integrated ones. This policy was burdensome and mean-spirited, but it did not violate the Equal Protection Clause, because no one in Jackson—regardless of race, national origin, sex, or any other classification—could use a public swimming pool. *Palmer v. Thompson* (1971) (Ch. 18.C.2.b.3).

Any equal protection violation must therefore involve a classification between people. A law classifies whenever it creates two or more groups, or classes, of people: those who do (and do not) suffer from a government-imposed burden—or alternately, those who do (and do not) enjoy a government-bestowed benefit. The primary error of the now-abandoned "separate but equal" doctrine was its failure to acknowledge that the race-based classifications of Jim Crow segregation laws imposed inequality. *Plessy v. Ferguson* (1896), for example, was satisfied that Louisiana's Separate Car Act provided formal equality; the majority saw no inequality because all people—both White and non-White—were barred from sitting in integrated rail cars. The accomplishment of *Brown v. Board of Education* (1954) and *Loving v. Virginia* (1967) was to recognize how in practice, segregation imposed a burden of social stigma, subordination, and psychological harm on racial minorities and not on White people.

Item A. *Identify the Inequality.* As *Loving* said, "the Equal Protection Clause requires consideration of . . . the classifications drawn by any statute." Begin by carefully describing the inequality imposed by the law. WHAT does the law distribute unequally? And WHO is burdened or benefitted by that inequality? The answers to either question might make heightened scrutiny appropriate. Under what is often called the "fundamental rights prong" of Equal Protection, a law that unequally distributes fundamental rights will be scrutinized more skeptically than a law involving non-fundamental rights. Under the "suspect classifications prong," a law will be scrutinized more skeptically if it divides people on the basis of a disfavored classification like race or national origin.

flashback

The two prongs of modern equal protection law can be illustrated with cases studied in Part I. Although it did not speak in terms of suspect or non-suspect classifications, *Strauder v. West Virginia* (1879) alluded to the idea: It held that barring citizens from jury service on the basis of race would violate the Equal Protection Clause, while proposing in dicta that barring them on the basis of education would not. Strict scrutiny was invoked for laws that classified on the basis of national origin in *Korematsu v. United States* (1944) and on the basis of race in *Loving v. Virginia* (1967). Meanwhile, ordinary economic regulations that classified on the basis of a person's business or occupation were upheld if they had a rational basis in *Carolene Products* (1938) and *Williamson v. Lee Optical* (1955).

The fundamental rights prong of equal protection was introduced in *Skinner v. Oklahoma* (1942). Because the eugenic sterilization law in that case impacted a fundamental right, the court used strict scrutiny, requiring the state to make a strong showing to justify the classification used in the law (some three-time felons v. others).

Depending on the facts, a law might impose inequality with regard to a fundamental right, on the basis of a suspect classification, or both, or neither. As described in Item B, heightened scrutiny would be proper when a law's classification involves either a fundamental right or a suspect classification. The following chart shows hypothetical laws involving each combination. Three of the four would be subjected to heightened scrutiny.

	FUNDAMENTAL RIGHT	NON-FUNDAMENTAL RIGHT
Suspect Classification	"People of Japanese ancestry are not allowed to procreate."	"People of Japanese ancestry are not allowed to work as stockbrokers."
Non-Suspect Classification	"People convicted of embezzlement are not allowed to procreate."	"People convicted of embezzlement are not allowed to work as stockbrokers."

Item A.1. *Fundamental Rights Prong.* Any equal protection challenge begins with a statute, regulation, or government practice that distributes burdens or benefits unequally. It is usually not difficult to identify WHAT is unequally distributed. In the equal protection cases presented in Part I, the rights unequally distributed included ability to serve on a jury in *Strauder v. West Virginia* (1879), a license to operate a laundry in a wooden building in *Yick Wo v. Hopkins* (1886), the right to procreate in *Skinner v. Oklahoma* (1942), the right to live in one's own home rather than in an internment camp in *Korematsu v. United States* (1944), the right to fit lenses into frames without a prescription in *Williamson v. Lee Optical* (1955), and the right to marry in *Loving v. Virginia* (1967). Heightened scrutiny will be used when the thing unequally distributed is a fundamental right. Whether a right is "fundamental" is often hotly contested. Like most difficult constitutional questions, various methods of legal reasoning might be used when answering it: text, precedent, structure, history, consequences, and values. With regard to precedent, for example, *Skinner* said that procreation was a fundamental right, and *Loving* said the same for marriage. By contrast, freedom from ordinary economic regulations is not a fundamental right, as shown in the substantive due process decision *West Coast Hotel v. Parrish* (1937), which held that the Constitution did not protect freedom of contract at all. *Parrish* explains why the economic regulation in *Williamson* did not involve a fundamental right: the freedom to sell eyeglasses as one wishes amounts to the freedom to enter into contracts as one wishes.

As the *Parrish* example shows, a right that is (or is not) fundamental under substantive due process will also be (or not be) fundamental under this prong of the Equal Protection Clause. Many of the cases giving the deepest consideration to the presence or absence of fundamental rights appear in Ch. 20, so the methods in those cases may also be used in an equal protection setting.

Item A.2. *Suspect Classifications Prong.* Where the fundamental rights prong focuses on WHAT is being distributed unequally, the **suspect classifications** prong asks WHO is burdened or benefitted. The usual vocabulary in this area asks *on what basis* a law classifies people. The law in *Strauder* classified on the basis of race, and the law in *Korematsu* classified on the basis of national origin (a concept closely tied to race). A law giving drivers' licenses only to men but not women classifies on the basis of sex, while a law giving them only to adults but not children classifies on the basis of age. The law in *Williamson v. Lee Optical* giving different rights to optometrists than to opticians classified on the basis of occupation. Once the

TERMINOLOGY

SUSPECT CLASSIFICATIONS: Some lawyers and judges speak of "suspect classes," as in the sentence "Racial minorities are a suspect class." There is nothing suspect (suspicious) about racial minorities as a class of people; instead, there is something suspect about laws that classify on the basis of race. To avoid unintended offense, be careful to speak of "suspect classifications" rather than "suspect classes." Another option is to use the term "protected class" to refer to a class that has historically been burdened by suspect classifications.

law's classification is identified, a court can determine the appropriate level of scrutiny, as described in Item B.

The terms *disparate treatment* and *disparate impact* will sometimes arise when identifying the classifications imposed by a law. A law imposes *disparate treatment* when its classifications appear unambiguously on the law's face (as in the examples in the previous paragraph). Such laws *treat* people differently, depending on which class they fall into. Some laws pose a trickier problem, known as *disparate impact.* This scenario arises when a law has adverse *impact* on an identifiable class that is not mentioned on the face of the law. For example, some states during the Jim Crow era would register people to vote if their grandparents had been registered to vote. On their face these laws said nothing about race, but in practice its impacts were intensely racial, since descendants of slaves—all of whom were Black—would be denied the right to vote. Such laws imposed disparate treatment on the basis of a grandparent's voting status, but it imposed disparate impact on the basis of race. Should we say that the law classifies on the basis of race (thus triggering strict scrutiny in Item B)? The answer depends on the government's purpose. If the legislature adopted a law for the discriminatory purpose of achieving a racially disparate impact, then the law will be scrutinized as a racial classification even though it does not invoke race on its face. See *Washington v. Davis* (1976) (Ch. 18.C.2.b.1).

Item B. *Level of Scrutiny.* Once the inequality has been described using the vocabulary from Item A, the court will select the appropriate level of scrutiny. As seen in New Deal cases like *Carolene Products*, most laws are presumed constitutional and courts will overturn them only if they lack any rational basis. But heightened scrutiny is proper if a law unequally distributes fundamental rights or relies on suspect classifications; in those situations the government needs a better reason for imposing inequality. The chart on the next page summarizes which types of classifications get which type of scrutiny.

The left-hand column represents the fundamental rights prong described in Item A.1 of the Kickstarter, which asks WHAT is being distributed unequally. A law not involving fundamental rights will be judged for rational basis. But when a law unequally allocates "the exercise of a fundamental right . . . the prior decisions of this Court require the application of the strict standard of judicial review." *San Antonio Independent School District v. Rodriguez* (1973) (Ch. 18.D.2).

The next column represents the suspect classifications prong described in Item A.2 of the Kickstarter, which asks WHO is affected by the unequal distribution. For much of the mid-20th century, courts envisioned only two levels of scrutiny under the Equal Protection Clause: rational basis and strict scrutiny. Rational basis was used for most classifications (including classifications on the basis of sex). Strict scrutiny was reserved for laws that relied on the suspect classifications of race and national origin. In the mid-1970s, the Supreme Court held that sex classifications should be judged under what has come to be called intermediate scrutiny. Intermediate scrutiny is also used for laws that classify on the basis of birth outside of marriage (formerly known as "illegitimacy"). These are sometimes called "quasi-suspect" classifications.

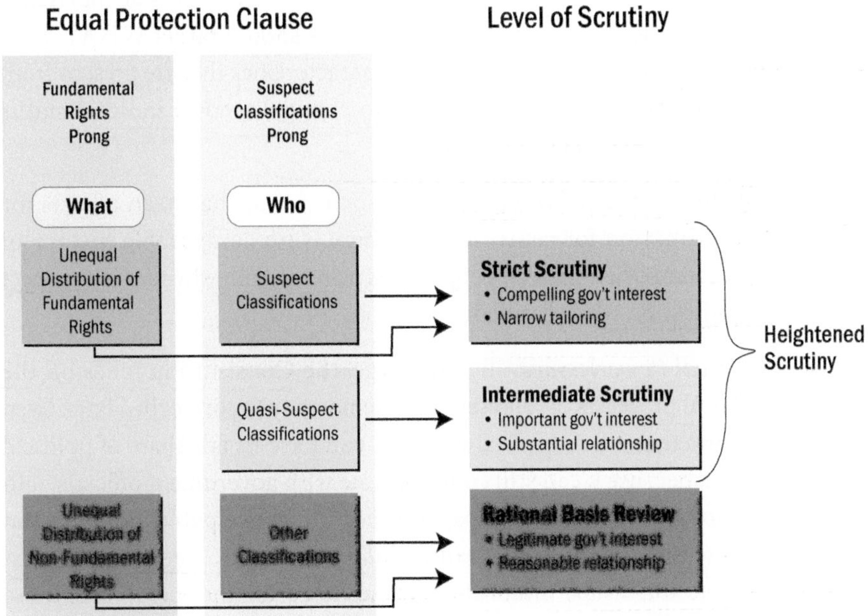

Strict scrutiny and intermediate scrutiny resemble each other more than either one resembles rational basis review. As a result, the two are often grouped together under the general heading of "heightened scrutiny." Phrased another way: heightened scrutiny is the term for any scrutiny more stringent than rational basis review.

Language in some cases suggests that all classifications other than race, **national origin**, sex, or birth outside marriage will be reviewed only for rational basis. But that list might not be fixed for all time. After all, sex classifications were once reviewed for rational basis, but now receive intermediate scrutiny. On that logic, various groups have argued that laws harming them should be understood to

■ TERMINOLOGY

NATIONAL ORIGIN: National origin refers to the country where one's ancestors lived, and is distinct from nationality or citizenship. During WWII, the government interned people of Japanese ancestry, even if they were native-born US citizens. The internment law was based on national origin, not nationality. Today, laws that classify on the basis of national origin receive strict scrutiny, with one exception: When Congress enacts immigration laws pursuant to Art. I, § 8, cl. 4, it may prefer aliens from some countries but not others, or impose different conditions on visas for visitors depending upon their countries of origin. However, strict scrutiny is used for laws classifying on the basis of national origin if enacted by a state or by Congress for purposes other than immigration.

classify in ways that are suspect or quasi-suspect. To decide, as a matter of first impression, whether a given classification triggers heightened scrutiny, courts often consider a number of factors, none of which is dispositive on its own.

- *Conduct v. Status.* It is usually acceptable to attach legal consequences to a person's voluntary *conduct*, but not to a *status* beyond the person's control (like one's race, national origin, sex, or birth outside marriage). Phrased another way: legal classifications should target WHAT YOU DO rather than WHO YOU ARE. Characteristics that are present from birth or are immutable (resistant to change) tend to indicate status rather than conduct.
- *History of Subordination.* In our society, race has been a basis for subordination for centuries, but there is no comparable history of oppression of left-handed people. This helps explain why race is a suspect classification while handedness is not.
- *Political Powerlessness.* By and large, the Constitution relies on the political processes of representative democracy to correct bad laws. Even a group that is a numerical minority can have its fair share of political power, because it can still communicate with government officials, join coalitions with other groups, and seek to change public opinion. But as suggested in Footnote 4 of *Carolene Products*, "prejudice against discrete and insular minorities . . . tends to curtail the operation of those political processes ordinarily to be relied upon to protect minorities." Deep-seated prejudice can lock a group out of the connections that would allow its voice to be heard politically. Stronger judicial review can be an appropriate response for laws that reflect such defects in the political process. See Ch. 4.A.
- *Visibility and Isolation.* The terms "discrete" and "insular" from Footnote 4 describe features shared by many historically subordinated groups.
    - A "discrete" group is separate and easily identifiable. Readily visible characteristics like race may draw a discriminatory response from a hostile majority, while a hidden characteristic (like high blood pressure) may not.
    - An "insular" group is separated from mainstream society, without access to people in power. A group whose members are not insular (like children) regularly interact with people in power, who may then legislate with the group's interests in mind.

- *Stereotypes.* Groups defined by suspect classifications are often subject to inaccurate or demeaning stereotypes. Laws that consciously or unconsciously embody or perpetuate such stereotypes may deserve heightened scrutiny.
- *Likelihood of Valid Justifications.* The levels of scrutiny reflect estimates of the likelihood that a type of law will be constitutionally appropriate. Laws that classify on the basis of race will almost always be unjust, while a meaningful number of laws that classify on the basis of occupation—like licensing or workplace safety laws—may do so for benign reasons. As a result, race-based laws get heightened scrutiny, while occupation-based laws do not. In a sense, this is the ultimate Equal Protection Clause question: If society believes that a certain classification should not be relied upon absent exceptional circumstances, then that classification should be deemed suspect.

In addition to these factors, the usual methods of constitutional reasoning (text, precedent, structure, history, consequences, and values) may be relevant when deciding if a classification should trigger heightened scrutiny. In particular, structural concerns over federalism and separation of powers may arise, because declaring a classification suspect can effectively move final decision-making authority from state or federal political branches to the federal judiciary.

Item C. *Apply the Scrutiny.* Every level of scrutiny considers two things: the strength of the government's interests (its goals or ends) and the necessity of using the chosen classification to pursue those interests (its methods or means). Modern opinions interpreting the Equal Protection Clause typically invoke standard terms to describe the ends and means at each level of scrutiny.

(a) A law imposing inequality will have a rational basis if it relies on a classification that is "reasonably related" to a "legitimate" government interest. In keeping with the purpose of rational basis review, the words are intended to connote deference. The government's purpose does not have to be extraordinarily important, but merely "legitimate" (i.e., not illegitimate). The government's chosen classification does not have to be the best of all possible alternatives, but merely a choice that is "reasonable" (i.e., not unreasonable or irrational).

(b) Under strict scrutiny, the government's ends must be "compelling" (very strong) and its chosen means must be "narrowly tailored" to those ends (necessary—or close to it—as a way to accomplish the government's ends).

(c) Intermediate scrutiny falls somewhere in between, requiring "important" ends and "substantially related" means.

This standardized terminology should not imply a false sense of precision. It ultimately requires judgment, rather than a formula, to decide whether government interests are "compelling" instead of merely "important" or "legitimate," or whether the chosen means are "narrowly tailored" to the ends instead of "substantially related" or "reasonably related" to them. Precedents involving similar facts will be the best guides.

Item C.1. *Government Interests.* When assessing the strength of the government's interests, two general patterns emerge. At the low end of the scale, it is not legitimate to impose burdens on a disliked group simply because it is disliked. Phrased another way, animus is irrational. At the high end of the scale, the goals of national security, crime control, and public health are usually considered compelling.

Item C.2. *Tailoring.* The fit between means and ends is usually called *tailoring.* ("Narrow tailoring" are the magic words only under strict scrutiny.) No single formula can distinguish well-tailored from poorly-tailored laws, but two techniques are often used to help judge the adequacy of the tailoring.

One approach asks whether the government's interests could be served as well or better by a less discriminatory alternative (i.e., a law that did not rely on the challenged classification). Imagine that a state facing a shortage of gasoline rations it on the basis of race, with White customers able to buy gas on some days, Black customers on other days, Latinos on other days, and so on. Even though race-based gas rationing helps alleviate the shortage, assigning random numbers to gas buyers would be equally or more effective, while not relying on a suspect classification.

Another approach asks whether the challenged law is under-inclusive (failing to solve the whole problem), over-inclusive (prohibiting conduct that is not part of the problem), or both. Imagine a law denying drivers' licenses to anyone over age 70, on the theory that older drivers cause accidents. It is under-inclusive because by itself it does not solve the entire problem of unsafe drivers; there are plenty of unsafe drivers under age 70. It is over-inclusive because it prevents driving by those people over age 70 who are able to drive safely. Like many rules of thumb, this law uses something easy to measure (age) as proxy for something else that is more important but harder to measure (driving ability).

Once less-discriminatory alternatives and areas of over- and under-inclusiveness are identified, their significance will vary with the applicable level of scrutiny. The logic of the suspect classifications prong is that the government should avoid disfavored classifications, so whenever heightened scrutiny applies less discriminatory alternatives are preferred. The logic of the fundamental rights prong is that unequal distribution of important rights should be avoided unless it is truly necessary, and significant under- or over-inclusiveness calls that necessity into question. By contrast, rational basis review is used for classifications that are not inherently suspicious, so there is no obligation to avoid relying on them.

Under-inclusiveness is typically not cause to invalidate a law under rational basis, because at that level of scrutiny, "a legislature may hit at an abuse which it has found, even though it has failed to strike at another." *Carolene Products.* Over-inclusiveness "may exact a needless, wasteful requirement in many cases," said *Williamson v. Lee Optical,* but under rational basis review "it is for the legislature, not the courts, to balance the advantages and disadvantages."

As an exercise, assume that **the following cartoon** depicts a government-operated swimming pool. What are the government interests served by the bathing-cap rule? Is a sex-based classification well tailored to those interests? Try assessing the law at each of the three levels of scrutiny: under which (if any) would the rule be constitutional?

Dave Berg (1971) From: MAD #137 © E.C. Publications, Inc.

B. Identifying Levels of Scrutiny in Court Opinions

Because judges have discretion over the wording of their opinions, not all Equal Protection Clause decisions expressly indicate their level of scrutiny. For example, an opinion might say that the government's interest is "strong" without specifying whether that term correlates with "compelling" or "important." If an opinion says a law has no rational basis, this may imply that rational basis is the correct level of scrutiny, or it may mean that the government would lose the case at any level of scrutiny.

When reading ambiguously-worded opinions, consider the features that typically appear in opinions where the level of scrutiny is known. The rational basis cases have a family resemblance to each other, as do the heightened scrutiny cases. Few opinions will exhibit every feature on the following list, and no single combination of factors is mandatory. But a predominance of one set of traits will be a valuable clue.

FEATURES COMMONLY SEEN IN RATIONAL BASIS CASES	FEATURES COMMONLY SEEN IN HEIGHTENED SCRUTINY CASES
▪ Court adopts general posture of deference to the government	▪ Court adopts general posture of skepticism toward the government
▪ Court presumes laws like the challenged law are constitutional	▪ Court presumes laws like the challenged law are unconstitutional
▪ Court accepts at face value the description of government interests offered by the government's attorneys during litigation	▪ Court seeks to determine government's true purposes for enacting law through evidence in the record
▪ Court hypothesizes potentially legitimate government interests for the law not evident from its face or its legislative history	▪ Court unlikely to hypothesize government interests as a way to salvage a challenged law
▪ Court considers only the rationality of the governmental justification, without regard to the burden imposed on the individual	▪ Court contrasts the government's interest with the burden imposed on the individual
▪ Court does not consider less discriminatory alternatives	▪ Court requires government to use less discriminatory alternatives
▪ Court is highly tolerant of over-inclusiveness and under-inclusiveness	▪ Court is troubled by over-inclusiveness and under-inclusiveness
▪ Court does not require much proof that the challenged law will actually work	▪ Court carefully considers whether the challenged law will accomplish its stated purpose
▪ Court is not concerned with the social message conveyed by the law	▪ Court objects to laws that reinforce invidious stereotypes
▪ Court emphasizes separation of powers, federalism, and the value of legislative experimentation and change	▪ Court emphasizes supremacy of constitutional rights, the structural importance of judicial review, and the value of eternal principles
▪ Court says it is not using heightened scrutiny	▪ Court says it is not using the rational basis test
▪ Court uses words like "deference," "reasonableness," and "rationality."	▪ Court uses words like "strict," "stringent," and "heavy burden."

Under this framework, it is evident that *Williamson v. Lee Optical* (1955) used the rational basis test even though the opinion did not include the phrases "rational basis" or "legitimate government interest." Consider this paragraph dealing with the argument that Oklahoma unfairly treated opticians differently from sellers of ready-to-wear glasses.

> Evils in the same field may be of different dimensions and proportions, requiring different remedies. Or so the legislature may think. Or the reform may take one step at a time, addressing itself to the phase of the problem which seems most acute to the legislative mind. The legislature may select one phase of one field and apply a remedy there, neglecting the others.

The opinion in *Loving v. Virginia* did not include the tell-tale phrase "strict scrutiny." It also deviated from the usual strict scrutiny formula of "narrowly tailored to a compelling interest," stating instead that the Equal Protection Clause allows only those racial classifications that are "necessary to the accomplishment of some permissible state objective, independent of . . . racial discrimination." Despite these verbal variations, there is no doubt from the following paragraph that *Loving* is a heightened scrutiny opinion.

> [In cases] involving distinctions not drawn according to race, the Court has merely asked whether there is any rational foundation for the discriminations, and has deferred to the wisdom of the state legislatures. In the case at bar, however, we deal with statutes containing racial classifications, and the fact of equal application does not immunize the statute from the very heavy burden of justification which the Fourteenth Amendment has traditionally required of state statutes drawn according to race.

The fact that different cases employ different verbal formulas can give rise to two types of legal debate. (1) Later cases may disagree on the level of scrutiny used in a precedent. (2) In a divided decision, a concurrence or dissent may argue that the lead opinion does not properly apply its stated level of scrutiny. Overall, lawyers should be alert to the language that judges use to describe levels of scrutiny, but should not be alarmed by minor variations.

C. The Suspect Classifications Prong

1. Rational Basis Review

a) Rational Basis Review of Economic Legislation: *City of New Orleans v. Dukes*

Laws regulating business—whether motivated by economic, social, health, aesthetic, or other reasons—are common applications of state police powers. In its discussion of a due process argument, *Carolene Products* stated that "regulatory legislation affecting ordinary commercial transactions is not to be pronounced unconstitutional" unless it lacks a rational basis. The same principle applies to challenges under the Equal Protection Clause.

New Orleans v. Dukes involved a local ordinance designed to protect the ambiance of the French Quarter, the historic section of New Orleans that is renowned for its 18th and 19th century architecture. The ordinance, in the interests of historic preservation, banned pushcarts that sold food, but with an exception that protected hot dog carts operated by the Lucky Dog company, notable for their garish mid-20th century design. Nancy Dukes, owner of a competing hot dog stand driven out of the Quarter by the ordinance, challenged the de facto hot dog monopoly the city had awarded Lucky Dog.

ITEMS TO CONSIDER WHILE READING *CITY OF NEW ORLEANS v. DUKES:*

A. *Work through the items from the Kickstarter. In particular, what are the arguments for saying that the ordinance was (or was not) adequately tailored?*

B. *If the Court concluded that the ordinance violated equal protection, what would be the proper remedy: allowing Dukes (and all others) to operate in the French Quarter, or barring Lucky Dogs from doing so?*

City of New Orleans v. Dukes,

427 U.S. 297 (1976)

Per Curiam [joined by Chief Justice Burger and Justices Brennan, Stewart, White, Blackmun, Powell, and Rehnquist].

The question presented by this case is whether the provision of a New Orleans ordinance, as amended in 1972, that excepts from the ordinance's prohibition against vendors' selling of foodstuffs from pushcarts in the Vieux Carré, or French Quarter, "vendors who have continuously operated the same business within the Vieux Carré for eight or more years prior to January 1, 1972" denied appellee vendor equal protection of the laws in violation of the Fourteenth Amendment.

Appellee [Nancy Dukes] operates a vending business from pushcarts throughout New Orleans but had carried on that business in the Vieux Carré for only two years when the ordinance was amended in 1972 and barred her from continuing operations there. She . . . filed an action in the District Court for the Eastern District of Louisiana . . . to challenge the application of the ordinance's "grandfather

City of New Orleans v. Dukes

clause"—the eight-years-or-more provision—as a denial of equal protection. . . . On cross-motions for summary judgment, the District Court, without opinion, granted appellant city's motion. The Court of Appeals for the Fifth Circuit reversed. . . . We hold that we have jurisdiction of appellant's appeal, and on the merits reverse the judgment of the Court of Appeals.

The Vieux Carré of the city of New Orleans is the heart of that city's considerable tourist industry and an integral component of the city's economy. The sector plays a special role in the city's life, and pursuant to the Louisiana State Constitution, ch. 8 of Art. V of the city's Home Rule Charter grants the New Orleans City Council power to enact ordinances designed to preserve its distinctive charm, character, and economic vitality.

Chapter 46 of the Code of the City of New Orleans sets up a comprehensive scheme of permits for the conduct of various businesses in the city. In 1972, the Code was amended to restrict the validity of many of these permits to points outside the Vieux Carré. However, even as to those occupations—including all pushcart food vendors—which were to be banned from the Vieux Carré during seasons other than Mardi Gras, the City Council made the "grandfather provision" exception. Two pushcart food vendors, one [Lucky Dogs] engaged in the sale of hot dogs and the other an ice cream vendor, had operated in the Vieux Carré for 20 or more years and therefore qualified under the "grandfather clause" and continued to operate there.

The Court of Appeals recognized the "City Council's legitimate authority generally to regulate business conducted on the public streets and sidewalks of the Vieux Carré in order to preserve the appearance and custom valued by the Quarter's residents and attractive to tourists," but nevertheless found that the Council's justification for the "grandfather" exception was "insufficient to support the discrimination imposed" and thus deprived appellee of equal protection. . . . The Court of Appeals focused on the "exclusionary character" of the ordinance and its concomitant "creation of a protected monopoly for the favored class member." The " pivotal defect" in the statutory scheme was perceived to be the fact that the favored class members need not "continue to operate in a manner more consistent with the traditions of the Quarter than would any other operator," and the fact that there was no reason to believe that length of operation "instills in the (favored) licensed vendors (or their likely transient operators) the kind of appreciation for the conservation of the Quarter's tradition" that would cause their operations to become or remain consistent with that tradition. Because these factors demonstrated the "insubstantiality of the relation between the nature of the discrimination and the legitimate governmental interest in conserving the traditional assets of the Vieux Carré," the ordinance was declared violative of equal protection as applied and the case was remanded for a determination of the severability of the "grandfather clause" from the remainder of the ordinance.

I

[The Supreme Court has jurisdiction over the appeal.]

II

The record makes abundantly clear that the amended ordinance, including the "grandfather provision," is solely an economic regulation aimed at enhancing the vital role of the French Quarter's tourist-oriented charm in the economy of New Orleans.

When local economic regulation is challenged solely as violating the Equal Protection Clause, this Court consistently defers to legislative determinations as to the desirability of particular statutory discriminations. Unless a classification trammels fundamental personal rights or is drawn upon inherently suspect distinctions such as race, religion, or alienage, our decisions presume the constitutionality of the statutory discriminations and require only that the classification challenged be rationally related to a legitimate state interest. States are accorded wide latitude in the regulation of their local economies under their police powers, and rational distinctions may be made with substantially less than mathematical exactitude. Legislatures may implement their program step by step, in such economic areas, adopting regulations that only partially ameliorate a perceived evil and deferring complete elimination of the evil to future regulations. See, e.g., *Williamson v. Lee Optical Co.* (1955). In short, the judiciary may not sit as a super-legislature to judge the wisdom or desirability of legislative policy determinations made in areas that neither affect fundamental rights nor proceed along suspect lines; in the local economic sphere, it is only the invidious discrimination, the wholly arbitrary act, which cannot stand consistently with the Fourteenth Amendment.

The Court of Appeals held in this case, however, that the "grandfather provision" failed even the rationality test. We disagree. The city's classification rationally furthers the purpose which the Court of Appeals recognized the city had identified as its objective in enacting the provision, that is, as a means "to preserve the appearance and custom valued by the Quarter's residents and attractive to tourists." The legitimacy of that objective is obvious. The City Council plainly could further that objective by making the reasoned judgment that street peddlers and hawkers tend to interfere with the charm and beauty of a historic area and disturb tourists and disrupt their enjoyment of that charm and beauty, and that such vendors in the Vieux Carré, the heart of the city's tourist industry, might thus have a deleterious effect on the economy of the city. They therefore determined that to ensure the economic vitality of that area, such businesses should be substantially curtailed in the Vieux Carré, if not totally banned.

It is suggested that the "grandfather provision," allowing the continued operation of some vendors was a totally arbitrary and irrational method of achieving the city's purpose. But rather than proceeding by the immediate and absolute abolition of all pushcart food vendors, the city could rationally choose initially to eliminate vendors of more recent vintage. This gradual approach to the problem is not constitutionally impermissible. . . . We are guided by the familiar principles that a statute is not invalid under the Constitution because it might have gone farther than it did, that a legislature need not strike at all evils at the same time, and that reform may take one step at a time, addressing itself to the phase of the problem which seems most acute to the legislative mind.

City of New Orleans v. Dukes

The city could reasonably decide that newer businesses were less likely to have built up substantial reliance interests in continued operation in the Vieux Carré and that the two vendors who qualified under the "grandfather clause"—both of whom had operated in the area for over 20 years rather than only eight—had themselves become part of the distinctive character and charm that distinguishes the Vieux Carré. We cannot say that these judgments so lack rationality that they constitute a constitutionally impermissible denial of equal protection. . . .

Justice Marshall concurs in the judgment [without opinion].

Justice Stevens took no part in the consideration or decision of this case.

b) Rational Basis Review of Social Legislation: *City of Dallas v. Stanglin*

The Twilight Skating Rink opened in 1961 in a blue-collar (and mostly White) residential neighborhood in Dallas. By the late 1970s, roller skating had become a less popular pastime, so owner Charles "Mike" Stanglin experimented with the business model. Some nights were devoted to dancing, with music provided by a local DJ who specialized in funk and soul music. The dance nights became extremely popular, with hundreds of (mostly Black) teenagers attending. In response to complaints about traffic and noise, the City passed a new ordinance requiring any dance hall with teenage customers to obtain a special license with restrictive provisions. These included a rule allowing only customers between ages 14 and 18, even if no alcohol was served on the premises. Stanglin sued, arguing that it was irrational to keep teenagers aged 18 and 19 from dancing together, when the city allowed them to skate, bowl, dine, or go to movies together.

ITEMS TO CONSIDER WHILE READING *CITY OF DALLAS v. STANGLIN:*

A. *Work through the items from the Kickstarter. Specifically:*

1. *WHAT is distributed unequally? Why might it be (or not be) a fundamental right?*

2. *WHO is affected by the inequality? On what bases does the law classify people, and are any of them suspect?*

B. *Is the Dallas ordinance best viewed as raising a question of equality (as the majority saw it) or a question of freedom (as the concurrence saw it)?*

City of Dallas v. Stanglin,

490 U.S. 19 (1989)

Chief Justice Rehnquist delivered the opinion of the Court [joined by Justices Brennan, White, Marshall, O'Connor, Scalia, and Kennedy].

Petitioner city of Dallas adopted an ordinance restricting admission to certain dance halls to persons between the ages of 14 and 18. Respondent [Mike Stanglin], the owner of one of these "teenage" dance halls, sued to contest the constitutional validity of the ordinance. The Texas Court of Appeals held that the ordinance violated the First Amendment right of persons between the ages of 14 and 18 to associate with persons outside that age group [and violated the Equal Protection Clause]. We now reverse[.]

In 1985, in response to requests for dance halls open only to teenagers, the city of Dallas authorized the licensing of "Class E" dance halls. The purpose of the ordinance was to provide a place where teenagers could socialize with each other, but not be subject to the potentially detrimental influences of older teenagers and young adults. The provision of the ordinance at issue here, restricts the ages of admission to Class E dance halls to persons between the ages of 14 and 18. . . . Parents, guardians, law enforcement, and dance-hall personnel are excepted from the ordinance's age restriction. The ordinance also limits the hours of operation of Class E dance halls to between 1 p.m. and midnight daily when school is not in session.

Respondent operates the Twilight Skating Rink in Dallas and obtained a license for a Class E dance hall. He divided the floor of his roller-skating rink into two sections with moveable plastic cones or pylons. On one side of the pylons, persons between the ages of 14 and 18 dance, while on the other side, persons of all ages skate to the same music—usually soul and "funk" music played by a disc jockey. No age or hour restrictions are applicable to the skating rink. Respondent does not serve alcohol on the premises, and security personnel are present. The Twilight does not have a selective admissions policy. It charges between $3.50 and $5 per person for admission to the dance hall and between $2.50 and $5 per person for admission to the skating rink. Most of the patrons are strangers to each other, and the establishment serves as many as 1,000 customers per night.

Respondent sued in the District Court of Dallas County to enjoin enforcement of the age and hour restrictions of the ordinance. He contended that the ordinance violated . . . equal protection under the United States and Texas Constitutions, and that it unconstitutionally infringed the rights of persons between the ages of 14

City of Dallas v. Stanglin

and [18] to associate with persons outside that age bracket. The trial court upheld the ordinance, finding that it was rationally related to the city's legitimate interest in ensuring the safety and welfare of children.

The Texas Court of Appeals upheld the ordinance's time restriction, but it struck down the age restriction. . . . We granted certiorari, and now reverse.

The dispositive question in this case is the level of judicial "scrutiny" to be applied to the city's ordinance. Unless laws create suspect classifications or impinge upon constitutionally protected rights, it need only be shown that they bear some rational relationship to a legitimate state purpose. Respondent does not contend that dance-hall patrons are a "suspect classification," but he does urge that the ordinance in question interferes with associational rights of such patrons guaranteed by the First Amendment.

[The Court concludes that the First Amendment right of association does not extend to the ability to mingle with strangers in a dance hall.]

The Dallas ordinance, therefore, implicates no suspect class and impinges on no constitutionally protected right. The question remaining is whether the classification engaged in by the city survives "rational-basis" scrutiny under the Equal Protection Clause. The city has chosen to impose a rule that separates 14- to 18-year-olds from what may be the corrupting influences of older teenagers and young adults. Ray Couch, an urban planner for the city's Department of Planning and Development, testified: "Older kids [whom the ordinance prohibits from entering Class E dance halls] can access drugs and alcohol, and they have more mature sexual attitudes, more liberal sexual attitudes in general. And we're concerned about mixing up these older individuals with youngsters that have not fully matured." A Dallas police officer, Wesley Michael, testified that the age restriction was intended to discourage juvenile crime.

Respondent claims that this restriction has no real connection with the City's stated interests and objectives. Except for saloons and teenage dance halls, respondent argues, teenagers and adults in Dallas may associate with each other, including at the skating area of the Twilight Skating Rink. Respondent also states, as did the court below, that the city can achieve its objectives through increased supervision, education, and prosecution of those who corrupt minors.

We think respondent's arguments misapprehend the nature of rational-basis scrutiny, which is the most relaxed and tolerant form of judicial scrutiny under the Equal Protection Clause. A State does not violate the Equal Protection Clause merely because the classifications made by its laws are imperfect. If the classification has some reasonable basis, it does not offend the Constitution simply because the classification is not made with mathematical nicety or because in practice it results in some inequality. The problems of government are practical ones and may justify, if they do not require, rough accommodations—illogical, it may be, and unscientific. The rational-basis standard is true to the principle that the Fourteenth Amendment gives the federal courts no power to impose upon the States their views of what constitutes wise economic or social policy.

We think that similar considerations support the age restriction at issue here. As we said in *New Orleans v. Dukes* (1976): "In the local economic sphere, it is only the invidious discrimination, the wholly arbitrary act, which cannot stand consistently with the Fourteenth Amendment." The city could reasonably conclude, as Couch stated, that teenagers might be susceptible to corrupting influences if permitted, unaccompanied by their parents, to frequent a dance hall with older persons. See 7 E. McQuillin, Law of Municipal Corporations § 24.210 (3d ed. 1981) ("Public dance halls have been regarded as being in that category of businesses and vocations having potential evil consequences"). The city could properly conclude that limiting dance-hall contacts between juveniles and adults would make less likely illicit or undesirable juvenile involvement with alcohol, illegal drugs, and promiscuous sex. It is true that the city allows teenagers and adults to roller-skate together, but skating involves less physical contact than dancing. The differences between the two activities may not be striking, but differentiation need not be striking in order to survive rational-basis scrutiny.

We hold that the Dallas ordinance does not infringe on any constitutionally protected right of association, and that a rational relationship exists between the age restriction for Class E dance halls and the city's interest in promoting the welfare of teenagers. The judgment of the Court of Appeals is therefore reversed, and the cause is remanded for further proceedings not inconsistent with this opinion.

Justice Stevens, with whom Justice Blackmun joins, concurring in the judgment.

In my opinion the opportunity to make friends and enjoy the company of other people—in a dance hall or elsewhere—is an aspect of liberty protected by the Fourteenth Amendment. For that reason, I believe the critical issue in this case involves substantive due process rather than the First Amendment right of association. Nonetheless, I agree with the Court that the city has adequately justified the ordinance's modest impairment of the liberty of teenagers. . . . I therefore join the Court's judgment.

c) Rational Basis Review of Government Benefits Programs: *U.S. Department of Agriculture v. Moreno*

Any social welfare law that distributes subsidies to individuals will contain a definition of eligible persons. This effectively creates a classification between those who may and may not receive the subsidies. Government subsidies are not a "fundamental right" for equal protection purposes, since the government is under no obligation to provide them to anyone. For this reason, the plaintiffs ineligible for food stamps in *Moreno* argued that the law violated the suspect classifications prong of the Equal Protection Clause.

ITEMS TO CONSIDER WHILE READING
USDA v. MORENO:

A. *Work through the items from the Kickstarter.*

B. *How does the majority determine the purpose of the statute (relevant to assessing ends and means)?*

C. *Why does the first paragraph of the opinion refer to the Due Process Clause of the Fifth Amendment?*

U.S. Dep't of Agriculture v. Moreno,
413 U.S. 528 (1973)

Justice Brennan delivered the opinion of the Court [joined by Justices Douglas, Stewart, White, Marshall, Blackmun, and Powell].

This case requires us to consider the constitutionality of § 3(e) of the Food Stamp Act of 1964, which, with certain exceptions, excludes from participation in the food stamp program any household containing an individual who is unrelated to any other member of the household. In practical effect, § 3(e) creates two classes of persons for food stamp purposes: one class is composed of those individuals who live in households all of whose members are related to one another, and the other class consists of those individuals who live in households containing one or more members who are unrelated to the rest. The latter class of persons is denied federal food assistance. [The district court] held this classification invalid as violative of the Due Process Clause of the Fifth Amendment. . . . We affirm.

I

The federal food stamp program was established in 1964 in an effort to alleviate hunger and malnutrition among the more needy segments of our society. Eligibility for participation in the program is determined on a household rather than an individual basis. An eligible household purchases sufficient food stamps to provide that household with a nutritionally adequate diet. The household pays for the stamps at a reduced rate based upon its size and cumulative income. The food stamps are then used to purchase food at retail stores, and the Government redeems the stamps at face value, thereby paying the difference between the actual cost of the food and the amount paid by the household for the stamps.

As initially enacted, § 3(e) defined a "household" as "a group of related or non-related individuals, who are not residents of an institution or boarding house, but are living as one economic unit sharing common cooking facilities and for whom food is customarily purchased in common." In January 1971, however, Congress redefined the term "household" so as to include only groups of related individuals. Pursuant to this amendment, the Secretary of Agriculture promulgated regulations rendering ineligible for participation in the program any "household" whose members are not "all related to each other."

Appellees in this case consist of several groups of individuals who allege that, although they satisfy the income eligibility requirements for federal food assistance, they have nevertheless been excluded from the program solely because the persons in each group are not "all related to each other." Appellee Jacinta Moreno, for example is a 56-year-old diabetic who lives with Ermina Sanchez and the latter's three children. They share common living expenses, and Mrs. Sanchez helps to care for appellee. Appellee's monthly income, derived from public assistance, is $75; Mrs. Sanchez receives $133 per month from public assistance. The household pays $135 per month for rent, gas and electricity, of which appellee pays $50. Appellee spends $10 per month for transportation to a hospital for regular visits, and $5 per month for laundry. That leaves her $10 per month for food and other necessities. Despite her poverty, appellee has been denied federal food assistance solely because she is unrelated to the other members of her household. Moreover, although Mrs. Sanchez and her three children were permitted to purchase $108 worth of food stamps per month for $18, their participation in the program will be terminated if appellee Moreno continues to live with them. . . .

[Moreno, Sanchez, and four] other groups of appellees instituted a class action against the Department of Agriculture, its Secretary, and two other departmental officials, seeking declaratory and injunctive relief against the enforcement of the 1971 amendment of § 3(e) and its implementing regulations. In essence, appellees contend, and the District Court held, that the "unrelated person" provision of § 3(e) creates an irrational classification in violation of the equal protection component of the Due Process Clause of the Fifth Amendment. We agree.

II

Under traditional equal protection analysis, a legislative classification must be sustained, if the classification itself is rationally related to a legitimate governmental interest. The purposes of the Food Stamp Act were expressly set forth in the congressional "declaration of policy":

> It is hereby declared to be the policy of Congress to safeguard the health and well-being of the Nation's population and raise levels of nutrition among low-income households. The Congress hereby finds that the limited food purchasing power of low-income households contributes to hunger and malnutrition among members of such households. The Congress further finds that increased utilization of food in establishing and maintaining adequate national levels of nutrition will promote the distribution in a beneficial manner of our

agricultural abundances and will strengthen our agricultural economy, as well as result in more orderly marketing and distribution of food. To alleviate such hunger and malnutrition, a food stamp program is herein authorized which will permit low-in-come households to purchase a nutritionally adequate diet through normal channels of trade.

The challenged statutory classification (households of related persons versus households containing one or more unrelated persons) is clearly irrelevant to the stated purposes of the Act. As the District Court recognized, the relationships among persons constituting one economic unit and sharing cooking facilities have nothing to do with their abilities to stimulate the agricultural economy by purchasing farm surpluses, or with their personal nutritional requirements.

Thus, if it is to be sustained, the challenged classification must rationally further some legitimate governmental interest other than those specifically stated in the congressional declaration of policy. Regrettably, there is little legislative history to illuminate the purposes of the 1971 amendment of § 3(e). The legislative history that does exist, however, indicates that that amendment was intended to prevent so-called "hippies" and "hippie communes" from participating in the food stamp program. See 116 Cong. Rec. 44439 (1970) (Sen. Holland). The challenged classification clearly cannot be sustained by reference to this congressional purpose. For if the constitutional conception of equal protection of the laws means anything, it must at the very least mean that a bare congressional desire to harm a politically unpopular group cannot constitute a legitimate governmental interest. As a result, a purpose to discriminate against hippies cannot, in and of itself and without reference to (some independent) considerations in the public interest, justify the 1971 amendment.

Although apparently conceding this point, the Government maintains that the challenged classification should nevertheless be upheld as rationally related to the clearly legitimate governmental interest in minimizing fraud in the administration of the food stamp program. In essence, the Government contends that, in adopting the 1971 amendment, Congress might rationally have thought (1) that households with one or more unrelated members are more likely than fully related households to contain individuals who abuse the program by fraudulently failing to report sources of income or by voluntarily remaining poor; and (2) that such households are relatively unstable, thereby increasing the difficulty of detecting such abuses. But even if we were to accept as rational the Government's wholly unsubstantiated assumptions concerning the differences between related and unrelated households we still could not agree with the Government's conclusion that the denial of essential federal food assistance to all otherwise eligible households containing unrelated members constitutes a rational effort to deal with these concerns.

At the outset, it is important to note that the Food Stamp Act itself contains provisions, wholly independent of § 3(e), aimed specifically at the problems of fraud and of the voluntarily poor. For example, with certain exceptions, § 5(c) of the Act renders ineligible for assistance any household containing "an able-bodied adult person between the ages of eighteen and sixty-five" who fails to register for, and accept, offered employment. Similarly, § 14(b) and (c) specifically impose strict criminal penalties upon any individual who obtains or uses food stamps fraudulently. The existence of these provisions necessarily casts considerable doubt upon the proposition that the 1971 amendment could rationally have been intended to prevent those very same abuses.

Moreover, in practical effect, the challenged classification simply does not operate so as rationally to further the prevention of fraud. As previously noted, § 3(e) defines an eligible "household" as "a group of related individuals (1) living as one economic unit (2) sharing common cooking facilities (and 3) for whom food is customarily purchased in common." Thus, two unrelated persons living together and meeting all three of these conditions would constitute a single household ineligible for assistance. If financially feasible, however, these same two individuals can legally avoid the "unrelated person" exclusion simply by altering their living arrangements so as to eliminate any one of the three conditions. By so doing, they effectively create two separate households both of which are eligible for assistance. Indeed, as the California Director of Social Welfare has explained:

> The "related household" limitations will eliminate many households from eligibility in the Food Stamp Program. It is my understanding that the Congressional intent of the new regulations are specifically aimed at the "hippies" and "hippie communes." Most people in this category can and will alter their living arrangements in order to remain eligible for food stamps. However, the [indigent] mothers who try to raise their standard of living by sharing housing will be affected. They will not be able to utilize the altered living patterns in order to continue to be eligible without giving up their advantage of shared housing costs.

Thus, in practical operation, the 1971 amendment excludes from participation in the food stamp program, not those persons who are likely to abuse the program, but, rather, only those persons who are so desperately in need of aid that they cannot even afford to alter their living arrangements so as to retain their eligibility. Traditional equal protection analysis does not require that every classification be drawn with precise mathematical nicety. But the classification here in issue is not only imprecise, it is wholly without any rational basis. The judgment of the District Court holding the unrelated person provision invalid under the Due Process Clause of the Fifth Amendment is therefore affirmed.

U.S. Dep't of Agriculture v. Moreno

Justice Douglas, concurring. [Omitted.]

Justice Rehnquist, with whom Chief Justice Burger concurs, dissenting.

. . . The Court's opinion would make a very persuasive congressional committee report arguing against the adoption of the limitation in question. Undoubtedly, Congress attacked the problem with a rather blunt instrument and, just as undoubtedly, persuasive arguments may be made that what we conceive to be its purpose will not be significantly advanced by the enactment of the limitation. But questions such as this are for Congress, rather than for this Court; our role is limited to the determination of whether there is any rational basis on which Congress could decide that public funds made available under the food stamp program should not go to a household containing an individual who is unrelated to any other member of the household.

I do not believe that asserted congressional concern with the fraudulent use of food stamps is, when interpreted in the light most favorable to sustaining the limitation, quite as irrational as the Court seems to believe. . . . I do not think it is unreasonable for Congress to conclude that the basic unit which it was willing to support with federal funding through food stamps is some variation on the family as we know it—a household consisting of related individuals. This unit provides a guarantee which is not provided by households containing unrelated individuals that the household exists for some purpose other than to collect federal food stamps.

Admittedly, as the Court points out, the limitation will make ineligible many households which have not been formed for the purpose of collecting federal food stamps, and will at the same time not wholly deny food stamps to those households which may have been formed in large part to take advantage of the program. But, as the Court concedes, "traditional equal protection analysis does not require that every classification be drawn with precise mathematical nicety." . . . The fact that the limitation will have unfortunate and perhaps unintended consequences . . . does not make it unconstitutional.

2. Strict Scrutiny

Footnote 4 of *Carolene Products* suggested in dicta that "more searching judicial inquiry" should be given to "statutes directed at particular religious, or national, or racial minorities" because "prejudice against discrete and insular minorities" has an adverse influence on "the operation of [democratic] political processes." During the years of the Warren Court, the "searching judicial inquiry" proposed in Footnote 4 was applied so vigorously that Professor Gerald Gunther quipped in 1972 that strict scrutiny was "strict in theory but fatal in fact." The reality is more complicated, but there is no mistaking that modern doctrine requires very persuasive justifications for any law relying on classifications deemed suspect.

The earliest decisions applying the Equal Protection Clause did not purport to rely on levels of scrutiny. If race discrimination was present, it was unconstitutional. *See Strauder v. West Virginia* (1879) and *Yick Wo v. Hopkins* (1886). Today's use of strict scrutiny for racial classifications evolved during and after WWII. Initially, *Hirabayashi v. United States* (1943) said that racial classifications were "in most circumstances irrelevant" (i.e., lacking rationality), but wartime conditions "afforded a rational basis" to discriminate against persons of Japanese ancestry. By contrast, *Korematsu v. United States* (1944) stated that "all legal restrictions which curtail the civil rights of a single racial group are immediately suspect" and that "courts must subject them to the most rigid scrutiny." By the time of *Loving v. Virginia* (1967), a unanimous Court said that "statutes containing racial classifications" face a "very heavy burden of justification" and not the rational basis review used for cases "involving distinctions not drawn according to race."

a) Laws Imposing Disparate Treatment

After the dismantling of Jim Crow laws in the 1950s and 1960s, it has been rare for the Supreme Court to consider a statute that on its face treats racial minorities worse than the White majority. The strength of judicial opposition to racial classifications can be seen in the following two cases, where the government's race-based decisions might not have been driven solely by racial animus.

1) *Race-Based Judicial Action:* Palmore v. Sidoti

Palmore involved a child custody decision following a divorce. Although the details of family law vary from state to state, judges are typically required to make the custody decision that will be "in the best interests of the child."

ITEMS TO CONSIDER WHILE READING
PALMORE v. SIDOTI:

A. *Work through the items from the Kickstarter.*

B. *Factually, was it clear error for the trial court to conclude (under existing social conditions at the time and place) that a child raised by an interracial couple would suffer from societal prejudice? If that factual finding was not clearly erroneous, why was it improper for the trial court to consider it?*

Palmore v. Sidoti,

466 U.S. 429 (1984)

Chief Justice Burger delivered the opinion of the Court [joined by Justices Brennan, White, Marshall, Blackmun, Powell, Rehnquist, Stevens, and O'Connor].

We granted certiorari to review a judgment of a state court divesting a natural mother of the custody of her infant child because of her remarriage to a person of a different race.

I

When petitioner Linda Sidoti Palmore and respondent Anthony J. Sidoti, both Caucasians, were divorced in May 1980 in Florida, the mother was awarded custody of their 3-year-old daughter.

In September 1981 the father sought custody of the child by filing a petition to modify the prior judgment because of changed conditions. The change was that the child's mother was then cohabiting with a Negro, Clarence Palmore, Jr., whom she married two months later. Additionally, the father made several allegations of instances in which the mother had not properly cared for the child.

After hearing testimony from both parties and considering a court counselor's investigative report, . . . the court made a finding that "there is no issue as to either party's devotion to the child, adequacy of housing facilities, or respectability of the new spouse of either parent."

The court then addressed the recommendations of the court counselor, who had made an earlier report "in [another] case coming out of this circuit also involving the social consequences of an interracial marriage. ***Niles v. Niles***, 299 So.2d 162 (1974)." From this vague reference to that earlier case, the court turned to the present case and noted the counselor's recommendation for a change in custody because "the wife has chosen for herself and for her child, a life-style unacceptable to the father and to society. The child is, or at school age will be, subject to environmental pressures not of choice."

> HISTORY
>
> ***NILES v. NILES***: In *Niles*, the Second District Court of Appeal for the state of Florida wrote: "The effect of an interracial marriage upon a particular child is but one of many factors which may be considered in determining the person in whose custody the child's best interest would be served."

The court then concluded that the best interests of the child would be served by awarding custody to the father. The court's rationale is contained in the following:

> The father's evident resentment of the mother's choice of a black partner is not sufficient to wrest custody from the mother. . . . [However,] this Court feels that despite the strides that have been made in bettering relations between

> the races in this country, it is inevitable that Melanie will, if allowed to remain in her present situation and attains school age and thus more vulnerable to peer pressures, suffer from the social stigmatization that is sure to come.

The Second District Court of Appeal affirmed without opinion. [This was the highest state court to rule on the matter.] We granted certiorari, and we reverse.

II

The judgment of a state court determining or reviewing a child custody decision is not ordinarily a likely candidate for review by this Court. However, the court's opinion, after stating that the "father's evident resentment of the mother's choice of a black partner is not sufficient" to deprive her of custody, then turns to what it regarded as the damaging impact on the child from remaining in a racially mixed household. This raises important federal concerns arising from the Constitution's commitment to eradicating discrimination based on race.

. . . The court correctly stated that the child's welfare was the controlling factor. But that court was entirely candid and made no effort to place its holding on any ground other than race. Taking the court's findings and rationale at face value, it is clear that the outcome would have been different had petitioner married a Caucasian male of similar respectability.

A core purpose of the Fourteenth Amendment was to do away with all governmentally imposed discrimination based on race. See *Strauder v. West Virginia* (1879). Classifying persons according to their race is more likely to reflect racial prejudice than legitimate public concerns; the race, not the person, dictates the category. Such classifications are subject to the most exacting scrutiny; to pass constitutional muster, they must be justified by a compelling governmental interest and must be necessary to the accomplishment of their legitimate purpose.

The State, of course, has a duty of the highest order to protect the interests of minor children, particularly those of tender years. In common with most states, Florida law mandates that custody determinations be made in the best interests of the children involved. The goal of granting custody based on the best interests of the child is indisputably a substantial governmental interest for purposes of the Equal Protection Clause.

It would ignore reality to suggest that racial and ethnic prejudices do not exist or that all manifestations of those prejudices have been eliminated. There is a risk that a child living with a stepparent of a different race may be subject to a variety of pressures and stresses not present if the child were living with parents of the same racial or ethnic origin.

The question, however, is whether the reality of private biases and the possible injury they might inflict are permissible considerations for removal of an infant child from the custody of its natural mother. We have little difficulty concluding that they

Palmore v. Sidoti

are not. The Constitution cannot control such prejudices but neither can it tolerate them. Private biases may be outside the reach of the law, but the law cannot, directly or indirectly, give them effect. Public officials sworn to uphold the Constitution may not avoid a constitutional duty by bowing to the hypothetical effects of private racial prejudice that they assume to be both widely and deeply held.

This is by no means the first time that acknowledged racial prejudice has been invoked to justify racial classifications. In *Buchanan v. Warley* (1917), for example, this Court invalidated a Kentucky law forbidding Negroes to buy homes in white neighborhoods. [We said:] "It is urged that this proposed segregation will promote the public peace by preventing race conflicts. Desirable as this is, and important as is the preservation of the public peace, this aim cannot be accomplished by laws or ordinances which deny rights created or protected by the Federal Constitution."

Whatever problems racially mixed households may pose for children in 1984 can no more support a denial of constitutional rights than could the stresses that residential integration was thought to entail in 1917. The effects of racial prejudice, however real, cannot justify a racial classification removing an infant child from the custody of its natural mother found to be an appropriate person to have such custody.

2) *Race-Based Administrative Action:* Johnson v. California

Johnson v. California involves racial segregation in prisons. As a general matter, prisoners have far fewer constitutional rights than non-incarcerated people: they are not allowed to travel as they wish, they are subject to warrantless searches, they may be punished for speech that would be protected outside prison, and much more. The usual standard for assessing prison rules that impinge on constitutional rights comes from *Turner v. Safley*, 482 U.S. 78 (1987), where prisoners challenged prison rules limiting their ability to marry while incarcerated and to write letters to other inmates. The Supreme Court held as follows: "when a prison regulation impinges on inmates' constitutional rights, the regulation is valid if it is reasonably related to legitimate penological interests. In our view, such a standard is necessary if prison administrators and not the courts, are to make the difficult judgments concerning institutional operations." Using this standard—which resembles rational basis review more than strict scrutiny—*Turner* upheld the ban on inmate-to-inmate correspondence, but overturned the ban on marriage while incarcerated.

ITEMS TO CONSIDER WHILE READING *JOHNSON v. CALIFORNIA*:

A. *Work through the items from the Kickstarter.*

B. *How would counsel for plaintiff and for the state complete this sentence: "This is a case about _______."*

c. *Should courts use a more deferential level of scrutiny for laws that rely on race for reasons other than animus?*

Johnson v. California,

543 U.S. 499 (2005)

Justice O'Connor delivered the opinion of the Court [joined by Justices Kennedy, Souter, Ginsburg, and Breyer].

The California Department of Corrections (CDC) has an unwritten policy of racially segregating prisoners in double cells in reception centers for up to 60 days each time they enter a new correctional facility. We consider whether strict scrutiny is the proper standard of review for an equal protection challenge to that policy.

I

A

CDC institutions house all new male inmates and all male inmates transferred from other state facilities in reception centers for up to 60 days upon their arrival. During that time, prison officials evaluate the inmates to determine their ultimate placement. Double-cell assignments in the reception centers are based on a number of factors, predominantly race. In fact, the CDC has admitted that the chances of an inmate being assigned a cellmate of another race are "pretty close" to zero percent. The CDC further subdivides prisoners within each racial group. Thus, Japanese-Americans are housed separately from Chinese-Americans, and northern California Hispanics are separated from southern California Hispanics.

The CDC's asserted rationale for this practice is that it is necessary to prevent violence caused by racial gangs. It cites numerous incidents of racial violence in CDC facilities and identifies five major prison gangs in the State: Mexican Mafia, Nuestra Familia, Black Guerrilla Family, Aryan Brotherhood, and Nazi Low Riders. The CDC also notes that prison-gang culture is violent and murderous. An associate warden testified that if race were not considered in making initial housing assignments, she is certain there would be racial conflict in the cells and in the yard. Other prison officials also expressed their belief that violence and conflict would result if prisoners were not segregated. The CDC claims that it must therefore segregate all inmates while it determines whether they pose a danger to others.

With the exception of the double cells in reception areas, the rest of the state prison facilities—dining areas, yards, and cells—are fully integrated. After the initial 60-day period, prisoners are allowed to choose their own cellmates. The CDC usually grants inmate requests to be housed together, unless there are security reasons for denying them.

B

Johnson v. California

Garrison Johnson is an African-American inmate in the custody of the CDC. He has been incarcerated since 1987 and, during that time, has been housed at a number of California prison facilities. Upon his arrival at Folsom prison in 1987, and each time he was transferred to a new facility thereafter, Johnson was double-celled with another African-American inmate.

Johnson filed a complaint pro se in the United States District Court for the Central District of California on February 24, 1995, alleging that the CDC's reception-center housing policy violated his right to equal protection under the Fourteenth Amendment by assigning him cellmates on the basis of his race. . . . The District Court granted summary judgment to the defendants. . . . The Court of Appeals for the Ninth Circuit affirmed. It held that the constitutionality of the CDC's policy should be reviewed under the deferential standard we articulated in *Turner v. Safley*, 482 U.S. 78 (1987)—not strict scrutiny. . . . We granted certiorari to decide which standard of review applies.

II

A

We have held that all racial classifications imposed by government must be analyzed by a reviewing court under strict scrutiny. Under strict scrutiny, the government has the burden of proving that racial classifications are narrowly tailored measures that further compelling governmental interests. We have insisted on strict scrutiny in every context, even for so-called "benign" racial classifications, such as race-conscious university admissions policies, race-based preferences in government contracts, and race-based districting intended to improve minority representation.

The reasons for strict scrutiny are familiar. Racial classifications raise special fears that they are motivated by an invidious purpose. Thus, we have admonished time and again that, absent searching judicial inquiry into the justification for such race-based measures, there is simply no way of determining what classifications are in fact motivated by illegitimate notions of racial inferiority or simple racial politics. We therefore apply strict scrutiny to all racial classifications to "smoke out" illegitimate uses of race by assuring that government is pursuing a goal important enough to warrant use of a highly suspect tool.

The CDC claims that its policy should be exempt from our categorical rule because it is "neutral"—that is, it "neither benefits nor burdens one group or individual more than any other group or individual." In other words, strict scrutiny should not apply because all prisoners are "equally" segregated. The CDC's argument ignores our repeated command that racial classifications receive close scrutiny even when they may be said to burden or benefit the races equally. Indeed, we rejected the notion that separate can ever be equal—or "neutral"—50 years ago in *Brown v. Board of Education* (1954), and we refuse to resurrect it today. . . .

The need for strict scrutiny is no less important here, where prison officials cite racial violence as the reason for their policy. As we have recognized in the past, racial classifications threaten to stigmatize individuals by reason of their membership in a racial group and to incite racial hostility. Indeed, by insisting that inmates be housed only with other inmates of the same race, it is possible that prison officials will breed further hostility among prisoners and reinforce racial and ethnic divisions. By perpetuating the notion that race matters most, racial segregation of inmates may exacerbate the very patterns of violence that it is said to counteract.

The CDC's policy is unwritten. Although California claimed at oral argument that two other States follow a similar policy, this assertion was unsubstantiated, and we are unable to confirm or deny its accuracy. Virtually all other States and the Federal Government manage their prison systems without reliance on racial segregation. Federal regulations governing the Federal Bureau of Prisons (BOP) expressly prohibit racial segregation. The United States contends that racial integration actually leads to less violence in BOP's institutions and better prepares inmates for re-entry into society. Indeed, the United States argues, based on its experience with the BOP, that it is possible to address concerns of prison security through individualized consideration without the use of racial segregation, unless warranted as a necessary and temporary response to a race riot or other serious threat of race-related violence. As to transferees, in particular, whom the CDC has already evaluated at least once, it is not clear why more individualized determinations are not possible.

Because the CDC's policy is an express racial classification, it is immediately suspect. We therefore hold that the Court of Appeals erred when it failed to apply strict scrutiny to the CDC's policy and to require the CDC to demonstrate that its policy is narrowly tailored to serve a compelling state interest.

B

The CDC invites us to make an exception to the rule that strict scrutiny applies to all racial classifications, and instead to apply the deferential standard of review articulated in *Turner v. Safley*, 482 U.S. 78 (1987), because its segregation policy applies only in the prison context. We decline the invitation. In *Turner*, we considered a claim by Missouri prisoners that regulations restricting inmate marriages and inmate-to-inmate correspondence were unconstitutional. We rejected the prisoners' argument that the regulations should be subject to strict scrutiny, asking instead whether the regulation that burdened the prisoners' fundamental rights was "reasonably related" to "legitimate penological interests."

We have never applied *Turner* to racial classifications. *Turner* itself did not involve any racial classification[.] We think this unsurprising, as we have applied *Turner*'s reasonable-relationship test only to rights that are inconsistent with proper incarceration. This is because certain privileges and rights must necessarily be limited in the prison context. Thus, for example, we have relied on *Turner* in addressing First Amendment challenges to prison regulations, including restrictions on freedom of association, limits on inmate correspondence, restrictions on inmates' access to courts, restrictions on receipt of subscription publications, and work rules limiting prisoners' attendance at religious services. We have also applied *Turner* to some due process claims, such as involuntary medication of mentally ill prisoners, and restrictions on the right to marry.

The right not to be discriminated against based on one's race is not susceptible to the logic of *Turner*. It is not a right that need necessarily be compromised for the sake of proper prison administration. On the contrary, compliance with the Fourteenth Amendment's ban on racial discrimination is not only consistent with proper prison administration, but also bolsters the legitimacy of the entire criminal justice system. Race discrimination is especially pernicious in the administration of justice. And public respect for our system of justice is undermined when the system discriminates based on race. When government officials are permitted to use race as a proxy for gang membership and violence without demonstrating a compelling government interest and proving that their means are narrowly tailored, society as a whole suffers. . . .

The CDC protests that strict scrutiny will handcuff prison administrators and render them unable to address legitimate problems of race-based violence in prisons. Not so. . . . Strict scrutiny does not preclude the ability of prison officials to address the compelling interest in prison safety. Prison administrators, however, will have to demonstrate that any race-based policies are narrowly tailored to that end.

The fact that strict scrutiny applies says nothing about the ultimate validity of any particular law; that determination is the job of the court applying strict scrutiny. At this juncture, no such determination has been made. On remand, the CDC will have the burden of demonstrating that its policy is narrowly tailored with regard to new inmates as well as transferees. Prisons are dangerous places, and the special circumstances they present may justify racial classifications in some contexts. Such circumstances can be considered in applying strict scrutiny, which is designed to take relevant differences into account.

III

We do not decide whether the CDC's policy violates the Equal Protection Clause. We hold only that strict scrutiny is the proper standard of review and remand the case to allow the Court of Appeals for the Ninth Circuit, or the District Court, to apply it in the first instance. The judgment of the Court of Appeals is reversed, and the case is remanded for further proceedings consistent with this opinion.

Chief Justice Rehnquist took no part in the decision of this case.

Justice Ginsburg, with whom Justices Souter and Breyer join, concurring. [Omitted.]

Justice Stevens, dissenting.

In my judgment a state policy of segregating prisoners by race during the first 60 days of their incarceration, as well as the first 60 days after their transfer from one facility to another, violates the Equal Protection Clause of the Fourteenth Amendment. . . . I therefore agree with the submission of the United States as amicus curiae that the Court should hold the policy unconstitutional on the current record [and not remand for further proceedings]. . . .

Justice Thomas, with whom Justice Scalia joins, dissenting.

The questions presented in this case require us to resolve two conflicting lines of precedent. On the one hand, as the Court stresses, this Court has said that all racial classifications reviewable under the Equal Protection Clause must be strictly scrutinized. On the other, this Court has no less categorically said that the relaxed standard of review we adopted in *Turner v. Safley*, 482 U.S. 78 (1987), applies to all circumstances in which the needs of prison administration implicate constitutional rights.

Emphasizing the former line of cases, the majority resolves the conflict in favor of strict scrutiny. I disagree. The Constitution has always demanded less within the prison walls. Time and again, even when faced with constitutional rights no less "fundamental" than the right to be free from state-sponsored racial discrimination, we have deferred to the reasonable judgments of officials experienced in running this Nation's prisons. There is good reason for such deference in this case. California oversees roughly 160,000 inmates in prisons that have been a breeding ground for some of the most violent prison gangs in America—all of them organized along racial lines. . . . The majority is concerned with sparing inmates the indignity and stigma of racial discrimination. California is concerned with their safety and saving their lives. I respectfully dissent.

I—II [Omitted.]

III

The majority claims that strict scrutiny is the applicable standard of review based on this Court's precedents and its general skepticism of racial classifications. It is wrong on both scores.

A [Discussion of precedents omitted.]

B

The majority offers various other reasons for applying strict scrutiny. None is persuasive. The majority's main reason is that "*Turner*'s reasonable-relationship test applies only to rights that are inconsistent with proper incarceration." According to the majority, the question is thus whether a right "need necessarily be compromised for the sake of proper prison administration." . . .

Inquiring whether a given right is consistent with "proper prison administration" calls for precisely the sort of judgments that *Turner* said courts were ill equipped to make. In none of the cases in which the Court deferred to the judgments of prison officials under *Turner* did it examine whether "proper" prison security and discipline permitted greater speech or associational rights; expanded access to the courts; broader freedom from bodily restraint; or additional free exercise rights. . . . And with good reason: As *Turner* pointed out, these judgments are better left in the first instance to the officials who run our Nation's prisons, not to the judges who run its courts. . . .

IV [Omitted.]

[CONCLUSION]

Petitioner Garrison Johnson challenges not permanent, but temporary, segregation of only a portion of California's prisons. Of the 17 years Johnson has been incarcerated, California has assigned him a cellmate of the same race for no more than a year (and probably more like four months); Johnson has had black cellmates during the other 16 years, but by his own choice. Nothing in the record demonstrates that if Johnson (or any other prisoner) requested to be housed with a person of a different race, it would be denied (though Johnson's gang affiliation with the Crips might stand in his way). Moreover, Johnson concedes that California's prisons are racially violent places, and that he lives in fear of being attacked because of his race. Perhaps on remand the CDC's policy will survive strict scrutiny, but in the event that it does not, Johnson may well have won a Pyrrhic victory.

flashforward

Johnson *on Remand*. After the Supreme Court's remand order, the *Johnson* litigation settled, with the California Department of Corrections agreeing not to presumptively assign prisoners on the basis of race.

b) Laws Imposing Disparate Impact

The distinction between disparate treatment and disparate impact has become a central concept in modern discrimination law, both under the Equal Protection Clause and many statutes. The dichotomy tracks other terminology sometimes seen in equality cases, such as the difference between *de jure* discrimination (imposed by law) and *de facto* discrimination (occurring in fact), and the difference between laws that are discriminatory on their face and discriminatory as applied.

For the approach to the Equal Protection Clause outlined in the Kickstarter, the law of disparate impact determines which classifications are contained in a challenged statute. Imagine a city fire department with a policy that all firefighters must be at least six feet tall. This policy imposes disparate treatment on the basis of height, but it will have disparate impact on the basis of sex, since far fewer women than men are over six feet tall. If the Equal Protection Clause cares only about disparate treatment, the policy would be examined for rational basis (because height is not a suspect or quasi-suspect classification). But if the Equal Protection Clause cares about disparate impact, then the law would be examined using heightened scrutiny (because sex is a quasi-suspect classification).

1) *The Requirement of Discriminatory Purpose:* Washington v. Davis

Different bodies of discrimination law may have different approaches to the question of disparate impact. Under the Equal Protection Clause, the leading decision is *Washington v. Davis* (1976), but the case was decided against a backdrop of earlier decisions interpreting statutes.

Disparate Impact Under Title VII. Title VII of the Civil Rights Act of 1964, 42 U.S.C. § 2000e–2, forbids employment discrimination on the basis of race, color, religion, sex, or national origin by any employer "engaged in an industry affecting commerce" and having fifteen or more employees. *Griggs v. Duke Power Co.*, 401 U.S. 424 (1971), involved a North Carolina company that had, before enactment of Title VII, openly restricted Black employees to the lowest-paying jobs with the worst chances for promotion. After the Act became effective, the company dropped its explicit racial restrictions but added new job qualifications. To be eligible for better positions, an applicant had to be a high school graduate and earn passing scores on the Wonderlic Personnel Test (which purports to measure general intelligence) and the Bennett Mechanical Comprehension Test. Neither test was designed to measure one's ability to perform the tasks required by Duke Power, and the record indicated that many people without high school diplomas performed well on the job. However, the tests had the effect of disproportionately disqualifying Black applicants.

A unanimous Supreme Court stated that even if the employer did not intend to discriminate, "good intent or absence of discriminatory intent does not redeem employment procedures or testing mechanisms that operate as built-in headwinds for minority groups and are unrelated to measuring job capability." By passing Title VII, Congress required "the removal of artificial, arbitrary, and unnecessary barriers to employment when the barriers operate invidiously to discriminate on the basis of racial or other impermissible classification."

> The Act proscribes not only overt discrimination but also practices that are fair in form, but discriminatory in operation. The touchstone is business necessity. If an employment practice which operates to exclude Negroes cannot be shown to be related to job performance, the practice is prohibited.

After *Griggs*, federal regulations were enacted to codify the principle that under Title VII, it would be a form of employment discrimination to use tests with racially discriminatory impact if they had not been "validated," i.e., shown to be related to job performance.

Test 21 of the Civil Service Commission. Plaintiffs in *Washington v. Davis* were African-Americans who wished to be police officers for the District of Columbia, a predominantly Black city with a predominantly White police force. Their discrimination lawsuit did not rely on Title VII, because the statute did not at that time apply to civil service employees of the District of Columbia. Instead, plaintiffs alleged that the District had violated the US Constitution, 42 U.S.C. § 1981 (a reconstruction-era statute forbidding race discrimination in contracts), and a section of the DC Municipal Code.

By the time the case advanced to the Supreme Court, it focused on the police department's reliance on the Civil Service Commission's Test 21 to screen applicants for the police academy. Test 21 was created in the 1940s as a general test of verbal ability for all civil service jobs, and was not designed specifically to test police aptitude. However, the DC police department had been relying on Test 21 since 1948. The record indicated that in the late 1960s and early 1970s—the period challenged in the lawsuit—Black applicants received failing scores on Test 21 four times more often than White applicants (57% v. 13%).

ITEMS TO CONSIDER WHILE READING EXCERPTS FROM TEST 21:

A. *Why might White applicants tend to score better on Test 21 than Black applicants?*

B. *Is Test 21 a good way to predict future performance as a police officer? If not, what methods would be better?*

Excerpts from Test 21:

- **Of the following reasons, the one that best explains the continued sale of records in spite of the popularity of the radio is that the:**

A) records make available the particular selections desired when they are desired

B) appreciation of records is more widespread than appreciation of radio

C) collection of records provides an interesting hobby

D) newest records are almost unbreakable

E) sound effect of records is superior to that of the radio.

- **BOUNTY means most nearly:**

A) generosity

B) limit

C) service

D) fine

E) duty

- **The saying "Straight trees are the first to be felled" means most nearly:**

A) Honest effort is always rewarded.

B) The best are the first chosen.

C) Ill luck passes no one by.

D) The highest in rank have farthest to fall.

E) The stubborn are soon broken.

- **SMILE is related to HAPPINESS as FROWN is related to:**

A) Surprise

B) Ridicule

C) Face

D) Displeasure

E) Inquiry

- **(Reading) "Although the types of buildings in ghetto areas vary from the one-story shack to the large tenement building, they are alike in that they are all drab, unsanitary, in disrepair, and often structurally unsound." The quotation best supports the statement that all buildings in ghetto areas are:**

A) overcrowded

B) undesirable as living quarters

C) well-constructed

D) about to be torn down

E) seldom inspected

- **A tenant who holds a long-term lease on a building will be most likely to gain by the transaction if during the period covered by the lease:**

A) business rentals vary considerably
B) real estate becomes cheaper
C) prices in general are increased
D) living costs are lowered
E) the tax rate is decreased

- **PROMONTORY means most nearly:**

A) marsh
B) monument
C) headland
D) boundary
E) plateau

- **The saying "The first blow is as much as two" means most nearly:**

A) He who takes the initiative gains a distinct advantage.
B) One hard blow is more effective than numerous lighter ones.
C) In any struggle the stronger participant makes the first move.
D) The wise man takes advantage of every opportunity.
E) He who strikes first will win the battle.

- **SPEAK is related to SHOUT as DAMAGE is related to:**

A) sue
B) repay
C) destroy
D) condemn
E) repair

- **(Reading) "Adhering to old traditions, old methods, and old policies at a time when new circumstances demand a new course of action may be praiseworthy from a sentimental point of view, but success is won most frequently by facing the facts and acting in accordance with the logic of the facts." The quotation best supports the statement that success is attained through:**

A) recognizing necessity and adjusting to it
B) using methods that have proved successful
C) exercising will power
D) remaining on a job until it is completed
E) considering each new problem separately

ITEMS TO CONSIDER WHILE READING *WASHINGTON v. DAVIS:*

A. *Work through the items from the Kickstarter. Specifically, did the District of Columbia's recruiting and hiring criteria classify people by test score or by race? What additional facts might be necessary to answer that question?*

B. *Must discrimination be shown in each individual case, or is it sufficient to show that a group has been adversely discriminated against?*

C. *The legislature's motive for enacting a law is not considered relevant when asking whether a law falls within Congress's power under the Commerce Clause. Why should the government's intent to discriminate matter under the Equal Protection Clause?*

D. *Given that Congress (in Title VII as interpreted in* Griggs*) and the executive branch (in post-*Griggs *regulations) agree that it is discriminatory to base hiring decisions on unvalidated tests with racially disparate impact, why does the Supreme Court not adopt the same standard under the Equal Protection Clause?*

Washington v. Davis,

426 U.S. 229 (1976)

Justice White delivered the opinion of the Court [joined by Chief Justice Burger and Justices Stewart, Blackmun, Powell, Rehnquist, and Stevens].

This case involves the validity of a qualifying test administered to applicants for positions as police officers in the District of Columbia Metropolitan Police Department. The test was sustained by the District Court but invalidated by the Court of Appeals. We are in agreement with the District Court and hence reverse the judgment of the Court of Appeals.

I

This action began on April 10, 1970, when two Negro police officers [including lead plaintiff Alfred E. Davis] filed suit against the then Commissioner of the District of Columbia, the Chief of the District's Metropolitan Police Department [defendant Walter E. Washington], and the Commissioners of the United States Civil Service Commission, [alleging racial discrimination in promotion].

[Additional plaintiffs] [George] Harley and [John D.] Sellers were permitted to intervene, their amended complaint asserting that their applications to become officers in the Department had been rejected, and that the Department's recruiting procedures discriminated on the basis of race against black applicants by a series of practices including, but not limited to, a written personnel test which excluded a disproportionately high number of Negro applicants. These practices were asserted to violate respondents' rights under the due process clause of the Fifth Amendment to the United States Constitution, under 42 U.S.C. § 1981 and under D.C. Code § 1-320. . . .

[Cross-motions for summary judgment were filed regarding the Department's recruiting practices.] According to the findings and conclusions of the District Court, to be accepted by the Department and to enter an intensive 17-week training program, the police recruit was required to satisfy certain physical and character standards, to be a high school graduate or its equivalent, and to receive a grade of at least 40 out of 80 on Test 21, which is "an examination that is used generally throughout the federal service," which "was developed by the Civil Service Commission, not the Police Department," and which was "designed to test verbal ability, vocabulary, reading and comprehension."

The validity of Test 21 was the sole issue before the court on the motions for summary judgment. The District Court noted that there was no claim of an intentional discrimination or purposeful discriminatory acts but only a claim that Test 21 bore no relationship to job performance and has a highly discriminatory impact in screening out black candidates. Respondents' evidence, the District Court said, warranted three conclusions: (a) The number of black police officers, while substantial, is not proportionate to the population mix of the city. (b) A higher percentage of blacks fail the Test than whites. (c) The Test has not been validated to establish its reliability for measuring subsequent job performance. . . .

The court nevertheless concluded that on the undisputed facts respondents were not entitled to relief. . . . The District Court rejected the assertion that Test 21 was culturally slanted to favor whites and was satisfied that the undisputable facts prove the test to be reasonably and directly related to the requirements of the police recruit training program and that it is neither so designed nor operated to discriminate against otherwise qualified blacks. It was thus not necessary to show that Test 21 was not only a useful indicator of training school performance but had also been validated in terms of job performance. "The lack of job performance validation does not defeat the Test, given its direct relationship to recruiting and the valid part it plays in this process." The District Court ultimately concluded that "the proof is wholly lacking that a police officer qualifies on the color of his skin rather than ability" and that the Department "should not be required on this showing to lower standards or to abandon efforts to achieve excellence."

Having lost on both constitutional and statutory issues in the District Court, respondents brought the case to the Court of Appeals. . . . The tendered constitutional issue was whether the use of Test 21 invidiously discriminated against Negroes and hence denied them due process of law contrary to the commands of the Fifth Amendment. The Court of Appeals, addressing that issue, announced that it would be guided by *Griggs v. Duke Power Co.*, 401 U.S. 424 (1971), a case involving the interpretation and application of Title VII of the Civil Rights Act of 1964, and held that the statutory standards elucidated in that case were to govern the due process question tendered in this one. The court went on to declare that lack of discriminatory intent in designing and administering Test 21 was irrelevant; the critical fact was rather that a far greater proportion of blacks (four times as many) failed the test than did whites. . . . We granted the petition for certiorari, filed by the District of Columbia officials.

II

Because the Court of Appeals erroneously applied the legal standards applicable to Title VII cases in resolving the constitutional issue before it, we reverse its judgment in respondents' favor. . . . As the Court of Appeals understood Title VII, employees or applicants proceeding under it need not concern themselves with the employer's possibly discriminatory purpose but instead may focus solely on the racially differential impact of the challenged hiring or promotion practices. This is not the constitutional rule. We have never held that the constitutional standard for adjudicating claims of invidious racial discrimination is identical to the standards applicable under Title VII, and we decline to do so today.

The central purpose of the Equal Protection Clause of the Fourteenth Amendment is the prevention of official conduct discriminating on the basis of race. It is also true that the Due Process Clause of the Fifth Amendment contains an equal protection component prohibiting the United States from invidiously discriminating between individuals or groups. *Bolling v. Sharpe* (1954). But our cases have not embraced the proposition that a law or other official act, without regard to whether it reflects a racially discriminatory purpose, is unconstitutional solely because it has a racially disproportionate impact.

Almost 100 years ago, *Strauder v. West Virginia* (1880) established that the exclusion of Negroes from grand and petit juries in criminal proceedings violated the Equal Protection Clause, but the fact that a particular jury or a series of juries does not statistically reflect the racial composition of the community does not in itself make out an invidious discrimination forbidden by the Clause. "A purpose to discriminate must be present which may be proven by systematic exclusion of eligible jurymen of the proscribed race or by unequal application of the law to such an extent as to show intentional discrimination." *Akins v. Texas*, 325 U.S. 398 (1945). A defendant in a criminal case is entitled to require that the State not deliberately and systematically deny to members of his race the right to participate as jurors in the administration of justice. . . .

This is not to say that the necessary discriminatory racial purpose must be express or appear on the face of the statute, or that a law's disproportionate impact is irrelevant in cases involving Constitution-based claims of racial discrimination.

Washington v. Davis

A statute, otherwise neutral on its face, must not be applied so as invidiously to discriminate on the basis of race. *Yick Wo v. Hopkins* (1886). It is also clear from the cases dealing with racial discrimination in the selection of juries that the systematic exclusion of Negroes is itself such an unequal application of the law as to show intentional discrimination. A prima facie case of discriminatory purpose may be proved as well by the absence of Negroes on a particular jury combined with the failure of the jury commissioners to be informed of eligible Negro jurors in a community, or with racially non-neutral selection procedures. With a prima facie case made out, the burden of proof shifts to the State to rebut the presumption of unconstitutional action by showing that permissible racially neutral selection criteria and procedures have produced the monochromatic result.

Necessarily, an invidious discriminatory purpose may often be inferred from the totality of the relevant facts, including the fact, if it is true, that the law bears more heavily on one race than another. It is also not infrequently true that the discriminatory impact in the jury cases for example, the total or seriously disproportionate exclusion of Negroes from jury venires may for all practical purposes demonstrate unconstitutionality because in various circumstances the discrimination is very difficult to explain on nonracial grounds. Nevertheless, we have not held that a law, neutral on its face and serving ends otherwise within the power of government to pursue, is invalid under the Equal Protection Clause simply because it may affect a greater proportion of one race than of another. Disproportionate impact is not irrelevant, but it is not the sole touchstone of an invidious racial discrimination forbidden by the Constitution. Standing alone, it does not trigger the rule that racial classifications are to be subjected to the strictest scrutiny and are justifiable only by the weightiest of considerations. . . .

Various Courts of Appeals have held in several contexts, including public employment, that the substantially disproportionate racial impact of a statute or official practice standing alone and without regard to discriminatory purpose, suffices to prove racial discrimination violating the Equal Protection Clause absent some justification going substantially beyond what would be necessary to validate most other legislative classifications. The cases impressively demonstrate that there is another side to the issue; but, with all due respect, to the extent that those cases rested on or expressed the view that proof of discriminatory racial purpose is unnecessary in making out an equal protection violation, we are in disagreement.

As an initial matter, we have difficulty understanding how a law establishing a racially neutral qualification for employment is nevertheless racially discriminatory and denies any person equal protection of the laws simply because a greater proportion of Negroes fail to qualify than members of other racial or ethnic groups. Had respondents, along with all others who had failed Test 21, whether white or black, brought an action claiming that the test denied each of them equal protection of the laws as compared with those who had passed with high enough scores to qualify them as police recruits, it is most unlikely that their challenge would have been sustained. Test 21, which is administered generally to prospective Government employees, concededly seeks to ascertain whether those who take it have acquired a particular level of verbal skill; and it is untenable that the Constitution prevents the Government from seeking modestly to upgrade the communicative abilities of its employees rather than to be satisfied with some lower level of competence, particularly where the job requires special ability to communicate orally and in writing. Respondents, as Negroes, could no more successfully claim that the test denied them equal protection than could white applicants who also failed. The conclusion would not be different in the face of proof that more Negroes than whites had been disqualified by Test 21. That other Negroes also failed to score well would, alone, not demonstrate that respondents individually were being denied equal protection of the laws by the application of an otherwise valid qualifying test being administered to prospective police recruits.

Nor on the facts of the case before us would the disproportionate impact of Test 21 warrant the conclusion that it is a purposeful device to discriminate against Negroes and hence an infringement of the constitutional rights of respondents as well as other black applicants. As we have said, the test is neutral on its face and rationally may be said to serve a purpose the Government is constitutionally empowered to pursue. . . .

Under Title VII, Congress provided that when hiring and promotion practices disqualifying substantially disproportionate numbers of blacks are challenged, discriminatory purpose need not be proved, and that it is an insufficient response to demonstrate some rational basis for the challenged practices. It is necessary, in addition, that they be "validated" in terms of job performance in any one of several ways, perhaps by ascertaining the minimum skill, ability, or potential necessary for the position at issue and determining whether the qualifying tests are appropriate for the selection of qualified applicants for the job in question. However this process proceeds, it involves a more probing judicial review of, and less deference to, the seemingly reasonable acts of administrators and executives than is appropriate under the Constitution where special racial impact, without discriminatory purpose, is claimed. We are not disposed to adopt this more rigorous standard for the purposes of applying the Fifth and the Fourteenth Amendments in cases such as this.

A rule that a statute designed to serve neutral ends is nevertheless invalid, absent compelling justification, if in practice it benefits or burdens one race more than another would be far-reaching and would raise serious questions about, and perhaps invalidate, a whole range of tax, welfare, public service, regulatory, and licensing statutes that may be more burdensome to the poor and to the average black than to the more affluent white.

Given that rule, such consequences would perhaps be likely to follow. However, in our view, extension of the rule beyond those areas where it is already applicable by reason of statute, such as in the field of public employment, should await legislative prescription.

III

We also hold that [summary judgment in favor of defendants was proper on the statutory claims].

Justice Stewart joins Parts I and II of the Court's opinion.

Justice Stevens, concurring.

While I agree with the Court's disposition of this case, I add these comments on the constitutional issue discussed in Part II. . . .

Frequently the most probative evidence of intent will be objective evidence of what actually happened rather than evidence describing the subjective state of mind of the actor. For normally the actor is presumed to have intended the natural consequences of his deeds. This is particularly true in the case of governmental action which is frequently the product of compromise, of collective decisionmaking, and of mixed motivation. It is unrealistic, on the one hand, to require the victim of alleged discrimination to uncover the actual subjective intent of the decisionmaker or, conversely, to invalidate otherwise legitimate action simply because an improper motive affected the deliberation of a participant in the decisional process. A law conscripting clerics should not be invalidated because an atheist voted for it.

My point in making this observation is to suggest that the line between discriminatory purpose and discriminatory impact is not nearly as bright, and perhaps not quite as critical, as the reader of the Court's opinion might assume. I agree, of course, that a constitutional issue does not arise every time some disproportionate impact is shown. On the other hand, when the disproportion is as dramatic as in . . . *Yick Wo v. Hopkins* (1886), it really does not matter whether the standard is phrased in terms of purpose or effect. Therefore, although I accept the statement of the general rule in the Court's opinion, I am not yet prepared to indicate how that standard should be applied in the many cases which have formulated the governing standard in different language. . . .

Justice Brennan, with whom Justice Marshall joins, dissenting.

[The dissent argued that summary judgment should not have been granted on the statutory claims in Part III. Because plaintiffs' success under the statutes would have been sufficient to resolve the appeal, the dissent did not believe it appropriate to discuss the constitutional questions.]

flashforward

1. ***Disparate Impact Under Other Civil Rights Amendments.*** The *Washington v. Davis* rule—that a neutral law that imposes racially disparate impact will be assessed as a racial classification only upon proof of discriminatory purpose—has been applied to comparable equality provisions in the Constitution. See *Rogers v. Lodge*, 458 U.S. 613 (1981) (Fifteenth Amendment).

2. ***Disparate Impact Under Statutes.*** If it wishes, and if authorized by an enumerated power, Congress may enact laws that treat practices imposing racially disparate impact as statutorily forbidden forms of discrimination. Examples include Title VII of the Civil Rights Act of 1964 under *Griggs* and the Voting Rights Act of 1965 under *Thornburg v. Gingles*, 478 U.S. 30 (1986). But see *Alexander v. Sandoval*, 532 U.S. 275 (2001) (Title VI of Civil Rights Act of 1964 is not violated by practices with disparate impact standing alone).

2) *Proving Discriminatory Purpose*

Several Supreme Court decisions following *Washington v. Davis* elaborated on the concept of discriminatory purpose.

a) Methods of Proof: *Village of Arlington Heights v. Metropolitan Housing Development Corp.*

The Plaintiff in *Village of Arlington Heights v. Metropolitan Housing Development Corp.*, 429 U.S. 252 (1977), was a nonprofit organization that sought to build affordable housing in largely White suburbs outside Chicago, in hopes of reducing racially segregated housing patterns. The government of the overwhelmingly White village of Arlington Heights denied a zoning variance that would be needed for a project to go forward.

The Supreme Court explained that courts had an obligation to ensure the absence of discriminatory purpose:

> *Washington v. Davis* does not require a plaintiff to prove that the challenged action rested solely on racially discriminatory purposes. Rarely can it be said that a legislature or administrative body operating under a broad mandate made a decision motivated solely by a single concern, or even that a particular purpose was the "dominant" or "primary" one. In fact, it is because legislators and administrators are properly concerned with balancing numerous competing considerations that courts refrain from reviewing the merits of their decisions,

> absent a showing of arbitrariness or irrationality. But racial discrimination is not just another competing consideration. When there is a proof that a discriminatory purpose has been a motivating factor in the decision, this judicial deference is no longer justified.

Arlington Heights is most often cited for its (non-exclusive) list of factors that could be considered as evidence of discriminatory purpose.

Clear Pattern of Impact. Although disparate impact is not sufficient by itself to violate the Equal Protection Clause under *Washington v. Davis*, it can be evidence of discriminatory purpose. "Sometimes a clear pattern, unexplainable on grounds other than race, emerges from the effect of the state action even when the governing legislation appears neutral on its face." This factor draws on the sentiments of Justice Stevens' concurrence in *Washington v. Davis*. Nonetheless, using disparate impact as proof of discriminatory purpose would, if carried to an extreme, eliminate the purpose requirement altogether. This means that cases where impact can prove purpose will be "rare." The Court needs a pattern so "stark" that it resembles *Yick Wo* (1886), where almost all White applicants but no Chinese applicants received laundry licenses.

Historical Background. The general history of race relations in the area can be significant. In a jurisdiction that has seen a "series of official actions taken for invidious purposes," a new action with racially disparate impact is more likely to have discriminatory purpose.

Procedural Irregularities. As a general matter, courts are willing to tolerate laws that they consider unwise because they trust that the legislature has used valid procedures to reach its decision. Conversely, "departures from the normal procedural sequence also might afford evidence that improper purposes are playing a role." For example, if a city usually sends legislation through a committee to take public comments, it may indicate discriminatory purpose if the city skipped that customary procedure and rushed to a rapid vote in favor of a law having racially disparate impact.

Substantive Irregularities. If the substance of the law imposing disparate impact is significantly different from the substance of most other laws, this can be a clue that discriminatory purpose existed. When a city that routinely grants zoning variances for construction projects denies a variance for the one project that was likely to provide housing for racial minorities, the trier of fact could validly conclude that it was not a coincidence. Moreover, "if the factors usually considered important by the decisionmaker strongly favor a decision contrary to the one reached," discriminatory purpose could be the explanation.

Legislative History. A court may consider the events giving rise to the government's action, along with any legislative history. "Contemporary statements by members of the decisionmaking body, minutes of its meetings, or reports" may be probative.

Applying these factors, the Supreme Court found no discriminatory purpose in *Arlington Heights.* (1) The denial of the zoning variance had disparate impact on the basis of race, because the population of potential black residents had greater need for low-income housing. But the statistical showing of greater need by one racial group did not amount to a "clear" or "stark" pattern that could prove discriminatory purpose. (2) Although the village was overwhelmingly White, it did not have a history of racist lawmaking. (3) The village followed its usual zoning procedures, and in fact had provided some extra procedural opportunities for the plaintiff. There was one deviation from the usual procedures, but the Court deemed it insignificant. (4) The zoning denial was consistent with other land use decisions within the village. "If the property involved here always had been zoned R-5 but suddenly was changed to R-3 when the town learned of MHDC's plans to erect integrated housing, we would have a far different case." But the challenged zoning decision was consistent with past practice. (5) Viewed as a whole, the legislative history revealed a concern over property values in the nearby single-family neighborhood, which was viewed as a legitimate and non-racial motivation. During public comment periods, "some of the comments, both from opponents and supporters, addressed what was referred to as the 'social issue:' the desirability or undesirability of introducing at this location in Arlington Heights low- and moderate-income housing, housing that would probably be racially integrated." Even though some public comments suggested a potential racial motivation, the legislative history as a whole did not indicate discriminatory purpose.

b) Because of, Not in Spite of: *Personnel Administrator of Massachusetts v. Feeney*

In *Personnel Administrator of Massachusetts v. Feeney*, 442 U.S. 256 (1979), the plaintiff Helen Feeney challenged a law giving preferences to veterans when hiring for state jobs. Because over 98% of the veterans in Massachusetts were male, and over one-quarter of the Massachusetts population were veterans, women were disproportionately kept out of state employment by the law. The case hinged on whether the law should be viewed as a classification on the basis of veteran status (judged for rational basis) or as a classification on the basis of sex (judged with heightened scrutiny, see Ch. 18.C.3).

> ■ WEBSITE
> A fuller version of *Personnel Administrator v. Feeney* is available for download from this casebook's companion website, www.CaplanIntegratedConLaw.com.

The Supreme Court found no constitutional violation. The majority explained that disparate impact in the absence of discriminatory purpose was a problem for the legislature to resolve.

> The equal protection guarantee of the Fourteenth Amendment does not take from the States all power of classification. Most laws classify, and many affect

> certain groups unevenly, even though the law itself treats them no differently from all other members of the class described by the law. When the basic classification is rationally based, uneven effects upon particular groups within a class are ordinarily of no constitutional concern. The calculus of effects, the manner in which a particular law reverberates in a society, is a legislative and not a judicial responsibility. In assessing an equal protection challenge, a court is called upon only to measure the basic validity of the legislative classification. When some other independent right is not at stake, and when there is no reason to infer antipathy, it is presumed that even improvident decisions will eventually be rectified by the democratic process.

For the majority, "the Fourteenth Amendment guarantees equal laws, not equal results."

The Court acknowledged that "any state law overtly or covertly designed to prefer males over females in public employment would require an exceedingly persuasive justification to withstand a constitutional challenge under the Equal Protection Clause of the Fourteenth Amendment." But the Massachusetts veteran's preference was not such a law:

> The decision to grant a preference to veterans was of course "intentional." So, necessarily, did an adverse impact upon nonveterans follow from that decision. And it cannot seriously be argued that the Legislature of Massachusetts could have been unaware that most veterans are men. It would thus be disingenuous to say that the adverse consequences of this legislation for women were unintended, in the sense that they were not volitional or in the sense that they were not foreseeable.
>
> "Discriminatory purpose," however, implies more than intent as volition or intent as awareness of consequences. It implies that the decisionmaker, in this case a state legislature, selected or reaffirmed a particular course of action at least in part "because of," not merely "in spite of," its adverse effects upon an identifiable group. Yet, nothing in the record demonstrates that this preference for veterans was originally devised or subsequently re-enacted because it would accomplish the collateral goal of keeping women in a stereotypic and predefined place in the Massachusetts Civil Service.

c) Mixed Legislative Motives

Although *Feeney* makes it challenging to prove that discriminatory purpose exists, it does not require that discrimination be the *sole* purpose motivating a legislature. As *Feeney* said, what matters is whether the government acted "at least in part" out of discriminatory purpose. This is consistent with the observation in *Arlington Heights* that legislation ordinarily reflects many motives, but that more careful judicial review is proper if discriminatory purpose is "*a* motivating factor" (emphasis added). When that impermissible factor is part of the mix, heightened scrutiny will be proper.

This approach is sometimes expressed in terms of a shifting burden, as mentioned in *Washington v. Davis*: Once an individual shows disparate impact plus proof that discrimination was among the motivating factors, "the burden of proof shifts to the State to rebut the presumption of unconstitutional action by showing that permissible racially neutral selection criteria and procedures have produced the [racially disparate] result." This burden-shifting method is used in related areas of law that consider mixed motives. For example, public employees fired from their jobs may prevail under the First Amendment if they can show that retaliation against constitutionally protected speech was "a motivating factor" in the firing, but the employer will have a defense if it can show "by a preponderance of the evidence that it would have reached the same decision" even without bad intent. *Mt. Healthy Board of Education v. Doyle*, 429 U.S. 274 (1977). See also *McDonnell Douglas Corp. v. Green*, 411 U.S. 792 (1973) (similar approach under Title VII).

d) Cases Finding Discriminatory Purpose

Washington v. Davis, Arlington Heights, and *Feeney* found no discriminatory purpose on their facts. Indeed, it has been rare for the Supreme Court to find discriminatory purpose in a disparate impact case. A finding of discriminatory purpose has been most likely in cases where voting rights have been denied in jurisdictions with a long history of race-based voter suppression.

Hunter v. Underwood, 471 U.S. 222 (1985), involved a provision of the **Alabama Constitution of 1901** that permanently denied the vote to any person convicted of a "crime involving moral turpitude." State court decisions and attorney general opinions had thereafter defined a wide variety of crimes—including many misdemeanors—as involving moral turpitude, including writing bad checks (the crime that cost the *Hunter* plaintiffs their right to vote). Shortly after enactment, the Alabama moral turpitude law disenfranchised over ten times as many Black voters as White ones. As recently as the early 1980s, it still disenfranchised 1.7 Black voters for every White one. The US Supreme Court unanimously found that the disparate impact was intentional. Historical records showed that Alabama's all-White constitutional convention was thoroughly racist in its outlook. The president of the convention said this in his opening address: "And what is it that we want to do? Why it is, within the limits imposed by the

■ HISTORY

ALABAMA CONSTITUTION OF 1901: *Hunter v. Underwood* represents a marked shift from the Supreme Court's first encounter with voter disenfranchisement under the Alabama Constitution of 1901. In *Giles v. Harris*, 189 U.S. 475 (1903), the Supreme Court refused to consider the merits, saying that even if discrimination existed, the Court was not "prepared to supervise the voting in that state by officers of the court." See Ch. 7:C.2.b.

Federal Constitution, to establish White supremacy in this State." In the debates, delegates repeatedly said they were interested in disenfranchising Black voters and not White ones. The Supreme Court concluded: "[the] original enactment was motivated by a desire to discriminate against blacks on account of race and the section continues to this day to have that effect. As such, it violates equal protection under *Arlington Heights*."

Rogers v. Lodge, 458 U.S. 613 (1982), found discriminatory purpose in the at-large system for electing County Commissioners in Burke County, Georgia, where the candidates supported by Black voters had never held office. Dividing the county into fairly-apportioned districts would allow some candidates favored by Black voters to be elected. The Court identified many past patterns as proof of discriminatory purpose in the at-large voting system, including the complete lack of Black elected officials, long-standing efforts to discourage Black voter registration, exclusion of Black voters from political party participation, and widespread local discrimination with regard to education, employment, and criminal justice. The Court explained: "Evidence of historical discrimination is relevant to drawing an inference of purposeful discrimination, particularly in cases such as this one where the evidence shows that discriminatory practices were commonly utilized, that they were abandoned when enjoined by courts or made illegal by civil rights legislation, and that they were replaced by laws and practices which, though neutral on their face, serve to maintain the status quo."

Lower courts have been slightly more likely than the Supreme Court to find discriminatory purpose on modern facts outside the context of voting rights in the old South. *Floyd v. City of New York*, 959 F.Supp.2d 540 (S.D.N.Y. 2013), held that the New York Police Department policy to "stop and frisk" pedestrians without probable cause violated the Equal Protection Clause—even though it was racially neutral on its face.

> The NYPD has known for more than a decade that its officers were conducting unjustified stops and frisks and were disproportionately stopping blacks and Hispanics. Despite this notice, the NYPD expanded its use of stop and frisk by seven-fold between 2002 and 2011. This increase was achieved by pressuring commanders . . . to increase the numbers of stops. The commanders, in turn, pressured mid-level managers and line officers to increase stop activity by rewarding high stoppers and denigrating or punishing those with lower numbers of stops. . . .
>
> I find that the NYPD instituted a policy of indirect racial profiling by directing its commanders and officers to focus their stop activity on "the right people"—the demographic groups that appear most often in a precinct's crime complaints. This policy led inevitably to impermissibly targeting blacks and Hispanics for stops and frisks at a higher rate than similarly situated whites.

3) *Discriminatory Purpose Without Disparate Treatment or Impact:* Palmer v. Thompson

As bad as discriminatory purpose may be, it is not constitutionally dispositive by itself. A government motive to discriminate matters under the Equal Protection Clause only when it leads to laws that impose disparate treatment or disparate impact on a disfavored class.

During the Jim Crow era, the city of Jackson, Mississippi operated racially segregated recreation facilities. In response to a federal court order, the City desegregated its public parks, auditoriums, golf course, and the city zoo. But rather than allow multi-racial swimming, the City in 1963 drained and permanently closed its four White-only and one Black-only swimming pools. In *Palmer v. Thompson*, 403 U.S. 217 (1971), the Supreme Court held 5–4 that acts taken with discriminatory purpose would not violate equal protection unless they created inequality.

> Neither the Fourteenth Amendment nor any Act of Congress purports to impose an affirmative duty on a State to begin to operate or to continue to operate swimming pools. Furthermore, this is not a case where whites are permitted to use public facilities while blacks are denied access. It is not a case where a city is maintaining different sets of facilities for blacks and whites and forcing the races to remain separate in recreational or educational activities. . . .
>
> Petitioners have also argued that respondents' action violates the Equal Protection Clause because the decision to close the pools was motivated by a desire to avoid integration of the races. But no case in this Court has held that a legislative act may violate equal protection solely because of the motivations of the men who voted for it. . . . Here the record indicates only that Jackson once ran segregated public swimming pools and that no public pools are now maintained by the city. . . . It shows no state action affecting blacks differently from whites.

The Equal Protection Clause gave Jackson a choice: operate racially integrated swimming pools or none at all. For a time, the city chose to operate none at all, but eventually the people of Jackson wearied of paying this cost. A political decision was reached in 1975 to reopen the pools to the entire public—a result predicted by Justice Jackson's concurrence in *Railway Express Agency v. New York* (1949). See Ch. 10.A.2.

3. Intermediate Scrutiny

Cases from the mid-20th century envisioned an Equal Protection Clause with two levels of scrutiny, now known as rational basis review and strict scrutiny. Laws classifying on the basis of sex initially received only rational basis review, but in the 1970s the Supreme Court changed course, deciding that sex classifications would receive what has come to be known as intermediate scrutiny. The evolution of intermediate scrutiny is a valuable study in constitutional change.

a) The Path to Intermediate Scrutiny

The law of coverture that denied women most political and civil rights, see Ch. 3.B.2.a., began to change in the mid-19th century through legislation. By 1900, most states enacted laws permitting married women to own property independently of their husbands, and a few even experimented with voting rights for women. But the Equal Protection Clause did not become a force for sex equality until the 1970s.

flashback

When the Fourteenth Amendment entered the Constitution in 1868, women quickly began to use it as a legal tool for sex equality, but the US Supreme Court showed little interest. See Ch. 7.C.1. *Bradwell v. Illinois* (1872) found no constitutional violation in a state denying women the ability to practice law. *Minor v. Happersett* (1872) found no constitutional violation in a state denying women the right to vote. Dicta from *Strauder v. West Virginia* (1879) implied that all-male juries would be constitutional. The Nineteenth Amendment (ratified in 1920) guaranteed that the right to vote could not be abridged on the basis of sex, but it was never interpreted to require sex equality beyond the voting booth. For example, *West Coast Hotel v. Parrish* (1937) upheld a minimum wage law that applied only to women, with the majority disregarding the dissent's argument that women should have the same rights as men to bargain over their wages.

1) *Gender Roles as a Rational Basis:* Hoyt v. Florida

For most of the 20th century, laws that classified on the basis of sex were examined only for rational basis, and socially assigned gender roles were seen as rational.

This dynamic appeared in *Hoyt v. Florida*, 368 U.S. 57 (1961). Gwendolyn Hoyt of Tampa was charged with murdering her abusive and unfaithful husband. She pleaded not guilty by reason of temporary insanity, on a theory that combined her diagnosis of epilepsy with what today would be called "battered woman's syndrome." Florida law at the time required all men to report for jury duty, but women would be summoned only if they registered as volunteers (which very few did). For Hoyt's trial, the state court sent jury summonses to 60 persons selected at random from a box containing the names of 3,000 men and 35 women. Not surprisingly, the 60 members of the venire were all men, and from this group a trial jury of 12 men was chosen. They found Hoyt guilty of second-degree murder after 25 minutes of deliberation, and she was sentenced to 30 years of hard labor.

On appeal, the US Supreme Court unanimously rejected Hoyt's equal protection challenge. The opinion relied on the rational basis test rather than any form of heightened scrutiny.

At oral argument, counsel for the state argued that laws imposing different standards of jury duty for men and women were fully rational. Even though some women were capable of serving as jurors—Florida allowed them to volunteer, after all—"the reason we have this difference with women is because they are the ones that do have all these infirmities that no amount of ascension on the social scale can erase." When asked to identify the infirmities, counsel replied: "All I mean is the traditional reasons that women have to stay home. In other words to prepare meals, to raise children, keep the house, etcetera." The Supreme Court's opinion used less stark language, but agreed that Florida's classification was rational.

> [We cannot] conclude that Florida's statute is not based on some reasonable classification, and that it is thus infected with unconstitutionality. Despite the enlightened emancipation of women from the restrictions and protections of bygone years, and their entry into many parts of community life formerly considered to be reserved to men, woman is still regarded as the center of home and family life. We cannot say that it is constitutionally impermissible for a State, acting in pursuit of the general welfare, to conclude that a woman should be relieved from the civic duty of jury service unless she herself determines that such service is consistent with her own special responsibilities.

flash*forward*

Women on Juries. *Taylor v. Louisiana*, 419 U.S. 522 (1975), held that statutes automatically exempting women from jury service violated the Sixth Amendment right to trial by a fair cross-section of the community, effectively overruling the result in *Hoyt* without addressing its equal protection reasoning. The Equal Protection Clause was finally applied to women's jury service in *J.E.B. v. Alabama*, 511 U.S. 127 (1994), which held that an attorney's intentional use of peremptory strikes to eliminate women from juries violated equal protection.

2) *An Unconstitutional Sex Classification:* Reed v. Reed

Ten years after *Hoyt*, the US Supreme Court held for the first time that a law classifying on the basis of sex violated the Equal Protection Clause. *Reed v. Reed*, 401 U.S. 71 (1971) was the first of a string of sex equality cases where plaintiffs or amici were represented in the Supreme Court by future justice **Ruth Bader Ginsburg**.

BIOGRAPHY

RUTH BADER GINSBURG (1933–2020) entered Harvard Law School in 1956, one of nine women out of a class of 500. The Dean of Harvard urged Justice Felix Frankfurter to hire her as a law clerk, but he would not hire women. Ginsburg later became the first woman to earn tenure on the faculty of Columbia Law School, a co-author of the first casebook on sex discrimination law, a founder of the Women's Rights Project at the American Civil Liberties Union, and a judge on the US Court of Appeals for the DC Circuit. She was appointed to the US Supreme Court by President Clinton in 1993.

Cecil Reed, rather than his ex-wife Sally Reed, was named administrator of their late son's estate. This choice was required by an Idaho statute that said "of several persons claiming and equally entitled to administer, males must be preferred to females." In court, the State argued that the statute served the rational purpose of being an efficient tie-breaker: given the low stakes usually involved in naming an administrator, Courts should not have to devote resources to holding hearings to decide which parent would be better at the task. The Supreme Court rejected this justification.

■ WEBSITE

A fuller version of *Reed v. Reed* is available for download from this casebook's companion website, www.CaplanIntegratedConLaw.com.

> Clearly the objective of reducing the workload on probate courts by eliminating one class of contests is not without some legitimacy. The crucial question, however, is whether [the Idaho statute] advances that objective in a manner consistent with the command of the Equal Protection Clause. We hold that it does not. To give a mandatory preference to members of either sex over members of the other, merely to accomplish the elimination of hearings on the merits, is to make the very kind of arbitrary legislative choice forbidden by the Equal Protection Clause of the Fourteenth Amendment. . . .

3) *The Argument for Strict Scrutiny:* Frontiero v. Richardson

A debate ensued over which level of scrutiny best explained the result in *Reed*. The Court said that having an easy-to-apply tie-breaker "is not without some legitimacy," which implies a rational (not irrational) basis. Yet Idaho's law was unconstitutional. Perhaps a better explanation of the result was that sex-based classifications are disfavored: they should be avoided unless justified by a strong reason, not merely a rational basis. This would correlate with heightened scrutiny—and perhaps the same sort of strict scrutiny required for laws that classify on the basis of race or national origin.

Sharron Frontiero was a lieutenant in the US Air Force; Joseph Frontiero was her civilian husband. Under existing regulations, a male officer would automatically receive health insurance coverage for his wife as a dependent, regardless of her income. A female officer would receive health insurance for her husband only if his income was less than half of the officer's. Joseph Frontiero's income was too high for him to be counted as a dependent. As a result, Sharron Frontiero lost an employment benefit (spousal health insurance) that would have been available to her if she were male.

In *Frontiero v. Richardson*, 411 U.S. 677 (1973), the Supreme Court ruled 8–1 that the sex-based denial of insurance coverage violated the Equal Protection Clause, but there was no majority reasoning. Justice Brennan's plurality opinion on behalf of four justices argued that sex classifications should receive strict scrutiny.

Joseph and Sharron Frontiero

> There can be no doubt that our Nation has had a long and unfortunate history of sex discrimination. Traditionally, such discrimination was rationalized by an attitude of romantic paternalism which, in practical effect, put women, not on a pedestal, but in a cage. . . . As a result of notions such as these, our statute books gradually became laden with gross, stereotyped distinctions between the sexes and, indeed, throughout much of the 19th century the position of women in our society was, in many respects, comparable to that of blacks under the pre-Civil War slave codes. Neither slaves nor women could hold office, serve on juries, or bring suit in their own names, and married women traditionally were denied the legal capacity to hold or convey property or to serve as legal guardians of their own children. And although blacks were guaranteed the right to vote in 1870, women were denied even that right—which is itself preservative of other basic civil and political rights—until adoption of the Nineteenth Amendment half a century later.
>
> It is true, of course, that the position of women in America has improved markedly in recent decades. Nevertheless, it can hardly be doubted that, in part because of the high visibility of the sex characteristic, women still face pervasive, although at times more subtle, discrimination in our educational institutions, in the job market and, perhaps most conspicuously, in the political arena.

> Moreover, since sex, like race and national origin, is an immutable characteristic determined solely by the accident of birth, the imposition of special disabilities upon the members of a particular sex because of their sex would seem to violate the basic concept of our system that legal burdens should bear some relationship to individual responsibility. And what differentiates sex from such non-suspect statuses as intelligence or physical disability, and aligns it with the recognized suspect criteria, is that the sex characteristic frequently bears no relation to ability to perform or contribute to society. As a result, statutory distinctions between the sexes often have the effect of invidiously relegating the entire class of females to inferior legal status without regard to the actual capabilities of its individual members.

Applying strict scrutiny, the plurality opinion concluded that the law could not survive. The government argued that the civilian husbands of female officers usually had jobs that provided health insurance or sufficient income to purchase it, while the civilian wives of male officers usually did not. Given these prevailing patterns, it would save money and be administratively easier to create a blanket rule instead of making an individualized assessment of need for every family. The plurality responded this way:

> Our prior decisions make clear that, although efficacious administration of governmental programs is not without some importance, the Constitution recognizes higher values than speed and efficiency. . . . On the contrary, any statutory scheme which draws a sharp line between the sexes, solely for the purpose of achieving administrative convenience, necessarily commands dissimilar treatment for men and women who are similarly situated, and therefore involves the very kind of arbitrary legislative choice forbidden by the Constitution.

The other four justices in the majority concurred only in the result and did not join the plurality opinion. Justice Powell's three-justice concurrence expressly refused to adopt strict scrutiny. Justice Stewart's one-sentence concurrence simply said that the statute was "invidious discrimination in violation of the Constitution" and cited *Reed v. Reed,* without specifying what level of scrutiny it required. Justice Rehnquist dissented.

4) The Arrival of Intermediate Scrutiny: **Craig v. Boren**

After several more years without clarity about the level of scrutiny for sex classifications, the Supreme Court resolved the question in *Craig v. Boren,* 429 U.S. 190 (1976). The case adopted the approach now called intermediate scrutiny.

WEBSITE

A fuller version of *Craig v. Boren* is available for download from this casebook's companion website, www.CaplanIntegratedConLaw.com.

The Oklahoma law in *Craig* involved the sale of low-alcohol "near-beer," also known as 3.2% beer. Females could buy it at age 18, but males had to wait to age 21. It was challenged by 18–20 year-old men and a liquor store that wished to sell to them.

The State would likely prevail under rational basis review. The government interest behind the law was traffic safety, preventing deaths and injuries from intoxicated driving. This would be a legitimate or even compelling interest. Turning to tailoring, the state had evidence that between ages 18–20, the sexes were not similarly situated when it came to drinking and driving. Males had more arrests for driving under the influence both in Oklahoma and nationwide. Males suffered more deaths from traffic accidents. Surveys in Oklahoma showed that males were more inclined to drink beer before driving. Under the *Carolene Products* approach to rational basis review, keeping at least one form of alcohol away from 18–20 year-old men was reasonably related to the goal of traffic safety.

The Supreme Court held 7–2 that the law was unconstitutional. A majority of justices in *Frontiero* were unwilling to apply strict scrutiny; yet a series of cases from *Reed* onward found laws to be forbidden sex discrimination even though they were arguably rational. The Court concluded from this pattern that sex-based laws were being judged with a form of heightened scrutiny, even if it did not precisely match the strict scrutiny from race-based cases like *Loving v. Virginia*. "To withstand constitutional challenge," said *Craig*, "previous cases establish that classifications by gender must serve important governmental objectives and must be substantially related to achievement of those objectives."

Fred Gilbert (plaintiffs' attorney), Carolyn Whitener, Ruth Bader Ginsburg, and Curtis Craig in 1996.

The Oklahoma law served "important" government interests, but its reliance on a sex classification was not "substantially related" to those interests.

> [The State's statistical evidence] offers only a weak answer to the equal protection question presented here. The most focused and relevant of the statistical surveys, arrests of 18-20-year-olds for alcohol-related driving offenses, exemplifies the ultimate unpersuasiveness of this evidentiary record. Viewed in terms of the correlation between sex and the actual activity that Oklahoma seeks to regulate (driving while under the influence of alcohol) the statistics broadly establish that 0.18% of females and 2% of males in that age group were arrested for that offense. While such a disparity is not trivial in a statistical sense, it hardly can form the basis for employment of a gender line

as a classifying device. Certainly if maleness is to serve as a proxy for drinking and driving, a correlation of 2% must be considered an unduly tenuous fit. . . .

> Suffice to say that the showing offered by the appellees does not satisfy us that sex represents a legitimate, accurate proxy for the regulation of drinking and driving. . . . The relationship between gender and traffic safety becomes far too tenuous to satisfy *Reed*'s requirement that the gender-based difference be substantially related to achievement of the statutory objective. We hold, therefore, that under Reed, Oklahoma's 3.2% beer statute invidiously discriminates against males 18–20 years of age.

In dissent, Justice Rehnquist argued that the intermediate scrutiny standard "apparently comes out of thin air;" that it was judicially unworkable; and that it intruded into the legislative sphere.

> I would think we have had enough difficulty with the two [existing] standards of review . . . as to counsel weightily against the insertion of still another standard between those two. How is this Court to divine what objectives are important? How is it to determine whether a particular law is "substantially" related to the achievement of such objective, rather than related in some other way to its achievement? Both of the phrases used are so diaphanous and elastic as to invite subjective judicial preferences or prejudices. . . .
>
> I would have thought that if this Court were to leave anything to decision by the popularly elected branches of the Government, where no constitutional claim other than that of equal protection is invoked, it would be the decision as to what governmental objectives to be achieved by law are "important," and which are not. As for the second part of the Court's new test, the Judicial Branch is probably in no worse position than the Legislative or Executive Branches to determine if there is any rational relationship between a classification and the purpose which it might be thought to serve. But the introduction of the adverb "substantially" requires courts to make subjective judgments as to operational effects, for which neither their expertise nor their access to data fits them. . . .

5) Intermediate Scrutiny for Birth Outside Marriage

As it did for sex-based classifications, the Supreme Court gradually felt its way into intermediate scrutiny for laws classifying on the basis of birth outside marriage (formerly called "illegitimacy"). Such statutes tend to involve laws making it difficult or impossible for a child born to an unmarried mother to prove paternity, obtain child support, or inherit from the father. *See Clark v. Jeter*, 486 U.S. 456 (1988) ("Between these extremes of rational basis review and strict scrutiny lies a level of intermediate scrutiny, which generally has been applied to discriminatory classifications based on sex or illegitimacy.")

b) Intermediate Scrutiny in Action

The logic of intermediate scrutiny for sex-based classifications implies that laws may sometimes classify on the basis of sex in situations where racial classifications would not be allowed. Which situations are these? As with many constitutional questions, the answer evolves gradually, on a case-by-case basis.

On the whole, intermediate scrutiny has more in common with strict scrutiny (its companion in the realm of heightened scrutiny) than it does with rational basis review. Some Supreme Court opinions, beginning with *Personnel Administrator of Massachusetts v. Feeney* (1979), have observed that it will take an "exceedingly persuasive justification" to survive intermediate scrutiny—language that might also describe strict scrutiny. As you read the following cases that rule on whether laws pass (or fail) intermediate scrutiny, consider how they would be resolved at lower or higher levels of scrutiny.

1) Sex Classifications in Education: United States v. Virginia

The Virginia Military Institute is a state-operated college offering bachelor's degrees in various subjects, including liberal arts, science, and engineering. The campus's culture and educational methods draw on the model of a 19th-century military academy, emphasizing spartan surroundings, strict discipline, and initiation rituals. VMI differs in many respects from the academies operated by branches of the US military (the Army Academy in West Point, the Naval Academy in Annapolis, and the Air Force Academy in Colorado Springs). Students at the federal academies are active duty service members, while VMI's students are civilians, only some of whom choose to enter the military after graduation. The US military academies began accepting female students in 1975, but VMI did not. When the US Department of Justice sued VMI in 1990, it was the last military college in the US with a males-only admissions policy.

ITEMS TO CONSIDER WHILE READING
UNITED STATES v. VIRGINIA:

A. *Work through the items from the Kickstarter.*

B. *Will admitting women to VMI change the nature of the program? If so, should that matter for constitutional purposes?*

C. *May a state offer separate but equal higher education for men and women? Separate but equal K–12 schools for boys and girls? Sex-segregated K–12 classrooms within otherwise co-ed schools? Sex-segregated home economics or shop classes? Gym classes? Bathrooms?*

D. *Do the rhetorical choices of Justice Scalia make his dissent more or less persuasive?*

United States v. Virginia,

518 U.S. 515 (1996)

Justice Ginsburg delivered the opinion of the Court [joined by Justices Stevens, O'Connor, Kennedy, Souter, and Breyer].

Virginia's public institutions of higher learning include an incomparable military college, Virginia Military Institute (VMI). The United States maintains that the Constitution's equal protection guarantee precludes Virginia from reserving exclusively to men the unique educational opportunities VMI affords. We agree.

I

Founded in 1839, VMI is today the sole single-sex school among Virginia's 15 public institutions of higher learning. VMI's distinctive mission is to produce "citizen-soldiers," men prepared for leadership in civilian life and in military service. VMI pursues this mission through pervasive training of a kind not available anywhere else in Virginia. Assigning prime place to character development, VMI uses an "adversative method" modeled on English public schools and once characteristic of military instruction. VMI constantly endeavors to instill physical and mental discipline in its cadets and impart to them a strong moral code. The school's graduates leave VMI with heightened comprehension of their capacity to deal with duress and stress, and a large sense of accomplishment for completing the hazardous course. . . .

Neither the goal of producing citizen-soldiers nor VMI's implementing methodology is inherently unsuitable to women. And the school's impressive record in producing leaders has made admission desirable to some women. Nevertheless, Virginia has elected to preserve exclusively for men the advantages and opportunities a VMI education affords.

II

A

From its establishment in 1839 as one of the Nation's first state military colleges, VMI has remained financially supported by Virginia and "subject to the control of the [Virginia] General Assembly," Va.Code Ann. § 23–92 . . . . VMI today enrolls about 1,300 men as cadets. Its academic offerings in the liberal arts, sciences, and engineering are also available at other public colleges and universities in Virginia. But VMI's mission is special. It is the mission of the school "to produce educated and honorable men, prepared for the varied work of civil life, imbued with love of learning, confident in the functions and attitudes of leadership, possessing a high sense of public service, advocates of the American democracy and free enterprise system, and ready as citizen-soldiers to defend their country in time of national peril." . . .

VMI cadets live in spartan barracks where surveillance is constant and privacy nonexistent; they wear uniforms, eat together in the mess hall, and regularly participate in drills. Entering students are incessantly exposed to the rat line, "an extreme form of the adversative model," comparable in intensity to Marine Corps boot camp. Tormenting and punishing, the rat line bonds new cadets to their fellow sufferers and, when they have completed the 7-month experience, to their former tormentors . . . .

B

In 1990, prompted by a complaint filed with the Attorney General by a female high-school student seeking admission to VMI, the United States sued the Commonwealth of Virginia and VMI, alleging that VMI's exclusively male admission policy violated the Equal Protection Clause of the Fourteenth Amendment. Trial of the action consumed six days and involved an array of expert witnesses on each side.

In the two years preceding the lawsuit, the District Court noted, VMI had received inquiries from 347 women, but had responded to none of them. "Some women, at least," the court said, "would want to attend the school if they had the opportunity." The court further recognized that, with recruitment, VMI could achieve at least 10% female enrollment—"a sufficient 'critical mass' to provide the female cadets with a positive educational experience." And it was also established that some women are capable of all of the individual activities required of VMI cadets. In addition, experts agreed that if VMI admitted women, the VMI ROTC experience would become a better training program from the perspective of the armed forces, because it would provide training in dealing with a mixed-gender army.

The District Court ruled in favor of VMI, however, and rejected the equal protection challenge pressed by the United States. That court correctly recognized that ***Mississippi Univ. for Women v. Hogan***, 458 U.S. 718 (1982), was the closest guide. There, this Court underscored that a party seeking to uphold government action based on sex must establish an "exceedingly persuasive justification" for the classification. To succeed, the defender of the challenged action must show "at least that the classification serves important governmental objectives and that the discriminatory means employed are substantially related to the achievement of those objectives."

The District Court reasoned that education in a single-gender environment, be it male or female, yields substantial benefits. VMI's school for men brought diversity to an otherwise coeducational Virginia system, and that diversity

■ HISTORY

MISSISSIPPI UNIVERSITY FOR WOMEN v. HOGAN: In this case, the US Supreme Court held that excluding men from a State's all-female nursing school could not be justified as a form of affirmative action for women. "Rather than compensate for discriminatory barriers faced by women," the Court explained, "excluding males from admission to the School of Nursing tends to perpetuate the stereotyped view of nursing as an exclusively woman's job."

was enhanced by VMI's unique method of instruction. If single-gender education for males ranks as an important governmental objective, it becomes obvious, the District Court concluded, that the only means of achieving the objective is to exclude women from the all-male institution—VMI.

"Women are indeed denied a unique educational opportunity that is available only at VMI," the District Court acknowledged. But "VMI's single-sex status would be lost, and some aspects of the school's distinctive method would be altered," if women were admitted: . . . the adversative environment could not survive unmodified. Thus, "sufficient constitutional justification" had been shown, the District Court held, for continuing VMI's single-sex policy.

The Court of Appeals for the Fourth Circuit disagreed and vacated the District Court's judgment. . . . The court suggested these options for the Commonwealth: Admit women to VMI; establish parallel institutions or programs; or abandon state support, leaving VMI free to pursue its policies as a private institution. . . .

C

In response to the Fourth Circuit's ruling, Virginia proposed a parallel program for women: Virginia Women's Institute for Leadership (VWIL). The 4-year, state-sponsored undergraduate program would be located at Mary Baldwin College, a private liberal arts school for women, and would be open, initially, to about 25 to 30 students. Although VWIL would share VMI's mission—to produce "citizen-soldiers"—the VWIL program would differ, as does Mary Baldwin College, from VMI in academic offerings, methods of education, and financial resources. [The most significant differences are described in Part VI.A of this opinion.]

D

Virginia returned to the District Court seeking approval of its proposed remedial plan, and the court decided the plan met the requirements of the Equal Protection Clause. . . . The "controlling legal principles," the District Court decided, "do not require the Commonwealth to provide a mirror image VMI for women." The court anticipated that the two schools would "achieve substantially similar outcomes." It concluded: "If VMI marches to the beat of a drum, then Mary Baldwin marches to the melody of a fife and when the march is over, both will have arrived at the same destination."

A divided Court of Appeals affirmed the District Court's judgment. . . .

III

The cross-petitions in this suit present two ultimate issues. First, does Virginia's exclusion of women from the educational opportunities provided by VMI—extraordinary opportunities for military training and civilian leadership development—deny to women capable of all of the individual activities required of VMI cadets, the equal protection of the laws guaranteed by the Fourteenth Amendment? Second, if VMI's unique situation as Virginia's sole single-sex public institution of higher education offends the Constitution's equal protection principle, what is the remedial requirement?

IV

We note, once again, the core instruction of this Court's pathmarking decisions: Parties who seek to defend gender-based government action must demonstrate an "exceedingly persuasive justification" for that action. . . . Without equating gender classifications, for all purposes, to classifications based on race or national origin, the Court, in post-*Reed* decisions, has carefully inspected official action that closes a door or denies opportunity to women (or to men). To summarize the Court's current directions for cases of official classification based on gender: Focusing on the differential treatment for denial of opportunity for which relief is sought, the reviewing court must determine whether the proffered justification is exceedingly persuasive. The burden of justification is demanding and it rests entirely on the State. The State must show at least that the challenged classification serves important governmental objectives and that the discriminatory means employed are substantially related to the achievement of those objectives. The justification must be genuine, not hypothesized or invented post hoc in response to litigation. And it must not rely on overbroad generalizations about the different talents, capacities, or preferences of males and females.

The heightened review standard our precedent establishes does not make sex a proscribed classification. Supposed "inherent differences" are no longer accepted as a ground for race or national origin classifications. Physical differences between men and women, however, are enduring: The two sexes are not fungible; a community made up exclusively of one sex is different from a community composed of both.

"Inherent differences" between men and women, we have come to appreciate, remain cause for celebration, but not for denigration of the members of either sex or for artificial constraints on an individual's opportunity. Sex classifications may be used to compensate women for particular economic disabilities they have suffered, to promote equal employment opportunity, to advance full development of the talent and capacities of our Nation's people.[FN7] But such classifications may not be used, as they once were, to create or perpetuate the legal, social, and economic inferiority of women.

FN7 Several amici have urged that diversity in educational opportunities is an altogether appropriate governmental pursuit and that single-sex schools can contribute importantly to such diversity. Indeed, it is the mission of some single-sex schools to dissipate, rather than perpetuate, traditional gender classifications. We do not question the Commonwealth's prerogative evenhandedly to support diverse educational opportunities. We address specifically and only an educational opportunity recognized by the District Court and the Court of Appeals as "unique," an opportunity available only at Virginia's premier military institute, the Commonwealth's sole single-sex public university or college. . . . Thus, we are not faced with the question of whether States can provide "separate but equal" undergraduate institutions for males and females.

Measuring the record in this case against the review standard just described, we conclude that Virginia has shown no "exceedingly persuasive justification" for excluding all women from the citizen-soldier training afforded by VMI. We therefore affirm the Fourth Circuit's initial judgment, which held that Virginia had violated the Fourteenth Amendment's Equal Protection Clause. Because the remedy proffered by Virginia—the Mary Baldwin VWIL program—does not cure the constitutional violation, i.e., it does not provide equal opportunity, we reverse the Fourth Circuit's final judgment in this case.

V

. . . Virginia . . . asserts two justifications in defense of VMI's exclusion of women. First, the Commonwealth contends, single-sex education provides important educational benefits, and the option of single-sex education contributes to diversity in educational approaches. Second, the Commonwealth argues, the unique VMI method of character development and leadership training, the school's adversative approach, would have to be modified were VMI to admit women. We consider these two justifications in turn.

A

Single-sex education affords pedagogical benefits to at least some students, Virginia emphasizes, and that reality is uncontested in this litigation. Similarly, it is not disputed that diversity among public educational institutions can serve the public good. But Virginia has not shown that VMI was established, or has been maintained, with a view to diversifying, by its categorical exclusion of women, educational opportunities within the Commonwealth. In cases of this genre, our precedent instructs that "benign" justifications proffered in defense of categorical exclusions will not be accepted automatically; a tenable justification must describe actual state purposes, not rationalizations for actions in fact differently grounded. . . .

Neither recent nor distant history bears out Virginia's alleged pursuit of diversity through single-sex educational options. In 1839, when the Commonwealth established VMI, a range of educational opportunities for men and women was scarcely contemplated. Higher education at the time was considered dangerous for women; reflecting widely held views about women's proper place, the Nation's first universities and colleges—for example, Harvard in Massachusetts, William and Mary in Virginia—admitted only men. VMI was not at all novel in this respect: In admitting no women, VMI followed the lead of the Commonwealth's flagship school, the University of Virginia, founded in 1819. . . .

We find no persuasive evidence in this record that VMI's male-only admission policy is in furtherance of a state policy of diversity. No such policy, the Fourth Circuit observed, can be discerned from the movement of all other public colleges and universities in Virginia away from single-sex education. That court also questioned "how one institution with autonomy, but with no authority over any other state institution, can give effect to a state policy of diversity among institutions." A purpose genuinely to advance an array of educational options, as the Court of Appeals recognized, is not served by VMI's historic and constant plan—a plan to afford a unique educational benefit only to males. However liberally this plan serves the Commonwealth's sons, it makes no provision whatever for her daughters. That is not equal protection.

B

Virginia next argues that VMI's adversative method of training provides educational benefits that cannot be made available, unmodified, to women. Alterations to accommodate women would necessarily be "radical," so "drastic," Virginia asserts, as to transform, indeed "destroy," VMI's program. Neither sex would be favored by the transformation, Virginia maintains: Men would be deprived of the unique opportunity currently available to them; women would not gain that opportunity because their participation would eliminate the very aspects of the program that distinguish VMI from other institutions of higher education in Virginia. . . .

It may be assumed, for purposes of this decision, that most women would not choose VMI's adversative method. . . . [I]t is also probable that many men would not want to be educated in such an environment. Education, to be sure, is not a "one size fits all" business. The issue, however, is not whether women—or men—should be forced to attend VMI; rather, the question is whether the Commonwealth can constitutionally deny to women who have the will and capacity, the training and attendant opportunities that VMI uniquely affords.

The notion that admission of women would downgrade VMI's stature, destroy the adversative system and, with it, even the school, is a judgment hardly proved, a prediction hardly different from other self-fulfilling prophecies once routinely used to deny rights or opportunities. . . . Women's successful entry into the federal military academies, and their participation in the Nation's military forces, indicate that Virginia's fears for the future of VMI may not be solidly grounded. The Commonwealth's justification for excluding all women from "citizen-soldier" training for which some are qualified, in any event, cannot rank as "exceedingly persuasive," as we have explained and applied that standard. . . .

VI

In the second phase of the litigation, Virginia presented its remedial plan—maintain VMI as a male-only college and create VWIL as a separate program for women. . . .

A

. . . Virginia chose not to eliminate, but to leave untouched, VMI's exclusionary policy. For women only, however, Virginia proposed a separate program, different in kind from VMI and unequal in tangible and intangible facilities. . . . Virginia described VWIL as a "parallel program," and asserted that VWIL shares VMI's mission of producing "citizen-soldiers" and VMI's goals of providing "education, military training, mental and physical discipline, character and leadership development." . . . A comparison of the programs said to be "parallel" informs our answer. . . .

VWIL affords women no opportunity to experience the rigorous military training for which VMI is famed. Instead, the VWIL program deemphasizes military education, and uses a "cooperative method" of education "which reinforces self-esteem."

VWIL students participate in ROTC and a "largely ceremonial" Virginia Corps of Cadets, but Virginia deliberately did not make VWIL a military institute. The VWIL House is not a military-style residence and VWIL students need not live together throughout the 4-year program, eat meals together, or wear uniforms during the schoolday. VWIL students thus do not experience the barracks life crucial to the VMI experience, or the spartan living arrangements designed to foster an egalitarian ethic. "The most important aspects of the VMI educational experience occur in the barracks," the District Court found, yet Virginia deemed that core experience nonessential, indeed inappropriate, for training its female citizen-soldiers.

VWIL students receive their "leadership training" in seminars, externships, and speaker series, episodes and encounters lacking the physical rigor, mental stress, minute regulation of behavior, and indoctrination in desirable values made hallmarks of VMI's citizen-soldier training. Kept away from the pressures, hazards, and psychological bonding characteristic of VMI's adversative training, VWIL students will not know the feeling of tremendous accomplishment commonly experienced by VMI's successful cadets.

Virginia maintains that these methodological differences are justified pedagogically, based on "important differences between men and women in learning and developmental needs," "psychological and sociological differences" Virginia describes as "real" and "not stereotypes." The Task Force charged with developing the leadership program for women, drawn from the staff and faculty at Mary Baldwin College, "determined that a military model and, especially VMI's adversative method, would be wholly inappropriate for educating and training most women." . . .

As earlier stated, generalizations about "the way women are," estimates of what is appropriate for most women, no longer justify denying opportunity to women whose talent and capacity place them outside the average description. Notably, Virginia never asserted that VMI's method of education suits most men. It is also revealing that Virginia accounted for its failure to make the VWIL experience the entirely militaristic experience of VMI on the ground that VWIL is planned for women who do not necessarily expect to pursue military careers. By that reasoning, VMI's entirely militaristic program would be inappropriate for men in general or as a group, for only about 15% of VMI cadets enter career military service. . . .

B—C [Omitted.]

VII

. . . A prime part of the history of our Constitution . . . is the story of the extension of constitutional rights and protections to people once ignored or excluded. VMI's story continued as our comprehension of "We the People" expanded. There is no reason to believe that the admission of women capable of all the activities required of VMI cadets would destroy the Institute rather than enhance its capacity to serve the "more perfect Union."

For the reasons stated, the initial judgment of the Court of Appeals is affirmed, the final judgment of the Court of Appeals is reversed, and the case is remanded for further proceedings consistent with this opinion.

Justice Thomas took no part in the consideration or decision of these cases.

Chief Justice Rehnquist, concurring in the judgment.

. . . Two decades ago in *Craig v. Boren* (1976), we announced that to withstand constitutional challenge, "classifications by gender must serve important governmental objectives and must be substantially related to achievement of those objectives." We have adhered to that standard of scrutiny ever since. While the majority adheres to this test today, it also says that the Commonwealth must demonstrate an "exceedingly persuasive justification" to support a gender-based classification. It is unfortunate that the Court thereby introduces an element of uncertainty respecting the appropriate test.

While terms like "important governmental objective" and "substantially related" are hardly models of precision, they have more content and specificity than does the phrase "exceedingly persuasive justification." That phrase is best confined, as it was first used, as an observation on the difficulty of meeting the applicable test, not as a formulation of the test itself. To avoid introducing potential confusion, I would have adhered more closely to our traditional, firmly established, standard that a gender-based classification must bear a close and substantial relationship to important governmental objectives. . . .

United States v. Virginia

Justice Scalia, dissenting.

Today the Court shuts down an institution that has served the people of the Commonwealth of Virginia with pride and distinction for over a century and a half. To achieve that desired result, it rejects (contrary to our established practice) the factual findings of two courts below, sweeps aside the precedents of this Court, and ignores the history of our people. As to facts: It explicitly rejects the finding that there exist "gender-based developmental differences" supporting Virginia's restriction of the "adversative" method to only a men's institution, and the finding that the all-male composition of the Virginia Military Institute (VMI) is essential to that institution's character. As to precedent: It drastically revises our established standards for reviewing sex-based classifications. And as to history: It counts for nothing the long tradition, enduring down to the present, of men's military colleges supported by both States and the Federal Government.

BIOGRAPHY

ANTONIN SCALIA (1936–2016), raised in New York City, was the son and grandson of Italian immigrants. After receiving his law degree, his career ranged from private practice, to the University of Chicago law school, to the U.S. Department of Justice—where he worked in the influential Office of Legal Counsel under Presidents Nixon and Ford—to the University of Chicago law school. President Reagan appointed Scalia to the D.C. Circuit in 1982 and to the US Supreme Court in 1986. Scalia was a vivid and assertive writer, expressly committed to his preferred methods of legal reasoning: textualism for statutes (vehemently opposing citations to legislative history) and originalism for the Constitution. He was known for his big personality, which encompassed both charm and pugnacity.

Much of the Court's opinion is devoted to deprecating the closed-mindedness of our forebears with regard to women's education, and even with regard to the treatment of women in areas that have nothing to do with education. Closed-minded they were—as every age is, including our own, with regard to matters it cannot guess, because it simply does not consider them debatable. The virtue of a democratic system with a First Amendment is that it readily enables the people, over time, to be persuaded that what they took for granted is not so, and to change their laws accordingly. That system is destroyed if the smug assurances of each age are removed from the democratic process and written into the Constitution. So to counterbalance the Court's criticism of our ancestors, let me say a word in their praise: They left us free to change. The same cannot be said of this most illiberal Court, which has embarked on a course of inscribing one after another of the current preferences of the society (and in some cases only the counter-majoritarian preferences of the society's law-trained elite) into our Basic Law. Today it enshrines the notion that no substantial educational value is to be served by an all-men's military academy—so that the decision by the people of Virginia to maintain such an institution denies equal protection to women who cannot attend that institution but can attend others. Since it is entirely clear that the Constitution of the United States—the old one—takes no sides in this educational debate, I dissent.

I—IV [Omitted.]

[CONCLUSION]

. . . In an odd sort of way, it is precisely VMI's attachment to such old-fashioned concepts as manly "honor" that has made it, and the system it represents, the target of those who today succeed in abolishing public single-sex education. The record contains a booklet that all first-year VMI students (the so-called "rats") were required to keep in their possession at all times. Near the end there appears the following period piece, entitled "The Code of a Gentleman":

> Without a strict observance of the fundamental Code of Honor, no man, no matter how "polished," can be considered a gentleman. The honor of a gentleman demands the inviolability of his word, and the incorruptibility of his principles. He is the descendant of the knight, the crusader; he is the defender of the defenseless and the champion of justice, or he is not a Gentleman.
>
> A Gentleman:
>
> Does not discuss his family affairs in public or with acquaintances.
>
> Does not speak more than casually about his girl friend.
>
> Does not go to a lady's house if he is affected by alcohol. He is temperate in the use of alcohol.
>
> Does not lose his temper; nor exhibit anger, fear, hate, embarrassment, ardor or hilarity in public.
>
> Does not hail a lady from a club window.
>
> A gentleman never discusses the merits or demerits of a lady.
>
> Does not mention names exactly as he avoids the mention of what things cost.
>
> Does not borrow money from a friend, except in dire need. Money borrowed is a debt of honor, and must be repaid as promptly as possible. Debts incurred by a deceased parent, brother, sister or grown child are assumed by honorable men as a debt of honor.

> Does not display his wealth, money or possessions.
>
> Does not put his manners on and off, whether in the club or in a ballroom. He treats people with courtesy, no matter what their social position may be.
>
> Does not slap strangers on the back nor so much as lay a finger on a lady.
>
> Does not "lick the boots of those above" nor "kick the face of those below him on the social ladder."
>
> Does not take advantage of another's helplessness or ignorance and assumes that no gentleman will take advantage of him.
>
> A Gentleman respects the reserves of others, but demands that others respect those which are his.
>
> A Gentleman can become what he wills to be.

I do not know whether the men of VMI lived by this code; perhaps not. But it is powerfully impressive that a public institution of higher education still in existence sought to have them do so. I do not think any of us, women included, will be better off for its destruction.

2) *Sex Classifications in the Workplace:* Geduldig v. Aiello

Healthy adult women can become pregnant and bear children, while healthy adult men cannot. This is a genuine biological difference—but when is it justifiable for a law to treat men differently than women because of it? The question is particularly important for women working outside the home, since one reason traditionally given for not hiring women is that they would take more time off the job than men, particularly for maternity leave and child care. *Geduldig* considered whether an employee who takes time off for childbirth should receive the same temporary disability payments that would be available to an employee who takes a similar amount of time off work for heart surgery or a broken leg.

ITEMS TO CONSIDER WHILE READING *GEDULDIG v. AIELLO*:

A. Geduldig *was decided before* Craig v. Boren *adopted intermediate scrutiny. As an exercise, work through the items in the Kickstarter, applying both rational basis scrutiny and intermediate scrutiny.*

B. *Does the California law classify on the basis of sex, or on the basis of pregnancy? Is there a difference?*

C. *What is required to create a workplace that does not discriminate on the basis of sex? Is it enough to have a rule permitting both men and women to hold jobs?*

Or must job expectations be altered so that both men and women are equally likely to succeed?

Geduldig v. Aiello,

417 U.S. 484 (1974)

Justice Stewart delivered the opinion of the Court [joined by Chief Justice Burger and Justices White, Blackmun, Powell, and Rehnquist].

For almost 30 years California has administered a disability insurance system that pays benefits to persons in private employment who are temporarily unable to work because of disability not covered by workmen's compensation. The appellees brought this action to challenge the constitutionality of a provision of the California program that, in defining "disability," excludes from coverage certain disabilities resulting from pregnancy. . . . On the appellees' motion for summary judgment, the District Court . . . held that this provision of the disability insurance program violates the Equal Protection Clause of the Fourteenth Amendment, and therefore enjoined its continued enforcement. . . . We subsequently noted probable jurisdiction of the appeal.

I

California's disability insurance system is funded entirely from contributions deducted from the wages of participating employees. Participation in the program is mandatory unless the employees are protected by a voluntary private plan approved by the State. Each employee is required to contribute one percent of his salary, up to an annual maximum of $85. . . . In return for his one-percent contribution to the Disability Fund, the individual employee is insured against the risk of disability stemming from a substantial number of "mental or physical illnesses and mental or physical injuries." It is not every disabling condition, however, that triggers the obligation to pay benefits under the program. [F]or example, any disability of less than eight days' duration is not compensable, except when the employee is hospitalized. Conversely, no benefits are payable for any single disability beyond 26 weeks. Further, disability is not compensable if it results from the individual's court commitment as a dipsomaniac, drug addict, or sexual psychopath. Finally, § 2626 of the Unemployment Insurance Code excludes from coverage certain disabilities that are attributable to pregnancy. It is this provision that is at issue in the present case.

Appellant [Dwight Geduldig] is the Director of the California Department of Human Resources Development. He is responsible for the administration of the State's disability insurance program. Appellees are four women [Carolyn Aiello, Augustina Armendariz, Elizabeth Johnson, and Jacqueline Jaramillo] who have paid

Geduldig v. Aiello

sufficient amounts into the Disability Fund to be eligible for benefits under the program. Each of the appellees became pregnant and suffered employment disability as a result of her pregnancy. . . .

At all times relevant to this case, § 2626 of the Unemployment Insurance Code provided:

> "Disability" or "disabled" includes both mental or physical illness and mental or physical injury. An individual shall be deemed disabled in any day in which, because of his physical or mental condition, he is unable to perform his regular or customary work. In no case shall the term "disability" or "disabled" include any injury or illness caused by or arising in connection with pregnancy up to the termination of such pregnancy and for a period of 28 days thereafter.

[California courts interpret the statute to allow disability payments for work-related absences caused by medical complications occurring during pregnancy, but not for absences related to "normal" pregnancy.] . . . The District Court, finding that the exclusion of pregnancy-related disabilities [for normal pregnancy] is not based upon a classification having a rational and substantial relationship to a legitimate state purpose, held that the exclusion was unconstitutional under the Equal Protection Clause. . . .

II

It is clear that California intended to establish this benefit system as an insurance program that was to function essentially in accordance with insurance concepts. Since the program was instituted in 1946, it has been totally self-supporting, never drawing on general state revenues to finance disability or hospital benefits. The Disability Fund is wholly supported by the one percent of wages annually contributed by participating employees. At oral argument, counsel for the appellant informed us that in recent years between 90% and 103% of the revenue to the Disability Fund has been paid out in disability and hospital benefits. This history strongly suggests that the one-percent contribution rate, in addition to being easily computable, bears a close and substantial relationship to the level of benefits payable and to the disability risks insured under the program.

Over the years California has demonstrated a strong commitment not to increase the contribution rate above the one-percent level. The State has sought to provide the broadest possible disability protection that would be affordable by all employees, including those with very low incomes. Because any larger percentage or any flat dollar-amount rate of contribution would impose an increasingly regressive levy bearing most heavily upon those with the lowest incomes, the State has resisted any attempt to change the required contribution from the one-percent level. The program is thus structured, in terms of the level of benefits and the risks insured, to maintain the solvency of the Disability Fund at a one-percent annual level of contribution.

In ordering the State to pay benefits for disability accompanying normal pregnancy and delivery, the District Court acknowledged the State's contention that coverage of these disabilities is so extraordinarily expensive that it would be impossible to maintain a program supported by employee contributions if these disabilities are included. There is considerable disagreement between the parties with respect to how great the increased costs would actually be, but they would clearly be substantial. For purposes of analysis the District Court accepted the State's estimate, which was in excess of $100 million annually. . . .

It is evident that a totally comprehensive program would be substantially more costly than the present program and would inevitably require state subsidy, a higher rate of employee contribution, a lower scale of benefits for those suffering insured disabilities, or some combination of these measures. There is nothing in the Constitution, however, that requires the State to subordinate or compromise its legitimate interests solely to create a more comprehensive social insurance program than it already has.

The State has a legitimate interest in maintaining the self-supporting nature of its insurance program. Similarly, it has an interest in distributing the available resources in such a way as to keep benefit payments at an adequate level for disabilities that are covered, rather than to cover all disabilities inadequately. Finally, California has a legitimate concern in maintaining the contribution rate at a level that will not unduly burden participating employees, particularly low-income employees who may be most in need of the disability insurance.

These policies provide an objective and wholly noninvidious basis for the State's decision not to create a more comprehensive insurance program than it has. There is no evidence in the record that the selection of the risks insured by the program worked to discriminate against any definable group or class in terms of the aggregate risk protection derived by that group or class from the program.[FN20] There is no risk from which men are protected and women are not. Likewise, there is no risk from which women are protected and men are not.

FN20 The dissenting opinion to the contrary, this case is thus a far cry from cases like *Reed v. Reed* (1971), and *Frontiero v. Richardson* (1973), involving discrimination based upon gender as such. The California insurance program does not exclude anyone from benefit eligibility because of gender but merely removes one physical condition—pregnancy—from the list of compensable disabilities. . . . The program divides potential recipients into two groups—pregnant women and nonpregnant persons. While the first group is exclusively female, the second includes members of both sexes. The fiscal and actuarial benefits of the program thus accrue to members of both sexes.

Geduldig v. Aiello

The appellee simply contends that, although she has received insurance protection equivalent to that provided all other participating employees, she has suffered discrimination because she encountered a risk that was outside the program's protection. For the reasons we have stated, we hold that this contention is not a valid one under the Equal Protection Clause of the Fourteenth Amendment.

Justice Brennan, with whom Justices Douglas and Marshall join, dissenting.

. . . By singling out for less favorable treatment a gender-linked disability peculiar to women, the State has created a double standard for disability compensation: a limitation is imposed upon the disabilities for which women workers may recover, while men receive full compensation for all disabilities suffered, including those that affect only or primarily their sex, such as prostatectomies, circumcision, hemophilia, and gout. In effect, one set of rules is applied to females and another to males. Such dissimilar treatment of men and women, on the basis of physical characteristics inextricably linked to one sex, inevitably constitutes sex discrimination. . . .

The State has clearly failed to meet [its] burden in the present case. The essence of the State's justification for excluding disabilities caused by a normal pregnancy from its disability compensation scheme is that covering such disabilities would be too costly. To be sure, as presently funded, inclusion of normal pregnancies would be substantially more costly than the present program. The present level of benefits for insured disabilities could not be maintained without increasing the employee contribution rate, raising or lifting the yearly contribution ceiling, or securing state subsidies. But whatever role such monetary considerations may play in traditional equal protection analysis, the State's interest in preserving the fiscal integrity of its disability insurance program simply cannot render the State's use of a suspect classification constitutional. For while a State has a valid interest in preserving the fiscal integrity of its programs, a State may not accomplish such a purpose by invidious distinctions between classes of its citizens. . . .

flashforward

The Pregnancy Discrimination Act. Geduldig interpreted the Equal Protection Clause, and hence applied only to governmental employers. But Title VII of the Civil Rights Act of 1964 forbids employment discrimination on the basis of sex by private employers. In a factually similar case, *General Electric Co. v. Gilbert*, 429 U.S. 125 (1976), the Supreme Court applied the reasoning of *Geduldig* to conclude that "exclusion of pregnancy from a disability-benefits plan providing general coverage is not a gender-based discrimination" under Title VII.

Geduldig and *Gilbert* were widely unpopular. Congress responded with the Pregnancy Discrimination Act of 1978, 42 U.S.C. § 2000e(k). The Act provides in relevant part:

> The terms "because of sex" or "on the basis of sex" [as used in Title VII] include, but are not limited to, because of or on the basis of pregnancy, childbirth, or related medical conditions; and women affected by pregnancy, childbirth, or related medical conditions shall be treated the same for all employment-related purposes, including receipt of benefits under fringe benefit programs, as other persons not so affected but similar in their ability or inability to work . . .

3) Sex Classifications and Citizenship

One theme in modern sex discrimination cases is an opposition to sex-based stereotypes. Genuine differences between the sexes may justify a sex-based law, but socially constructed gender roles should not. In practice, the two may overlap. This can be seen in *Nguyen v. INS* (2000) and *Sessions v. Morales-Santana* (2017), two challenges to statutes that treated biological mothers differently than biological fathers when determining the citizenship of a newborn child.

The Fourteenth Amendment's citizenship clause overruled *Dred Scott* to guarantee that persons born in the United States would be citizens. The Constitution is silent about children of US citizens who are born outside the country. However, Congress has used its enumerated power over naturalization under Art. I, § 8, cl. 4 to enact statutes on the topic.

- If both parents are US citizens, the child will be a US citizen at birth. 8 U.S.C. § 1401(c).

- If only one of the two parents is a US citizen, the child will be a US citizen upon a combination of (a) the parent's length of residency in the US before the child's birth; and (b) proof of parentage. The requirements for each factor differ depending on whether the parents are married and whether the US citizen parent is male or female.

The following chart shows the law as it existed for the parties in *Nguyen* and *Morales-Santana*. If the parents were married, the child would be a US citizen if the US citizen parent (of either sex) had been physically present in the US for ten years, five of them after age 14. No special proof of parentage would be required. If the parents were unmarried, however, the requirements differed based on sex. Citizen fathers would need to show the same length of residency as married parents, but also must prove parentage through a specified combination of legal actions and documents. Citizen mothers would need to show a shorter length of residency and required no special method to prove parentage.

	MARRIED	UNMARRIED
Father is US citizen, mother is alien	Before child's birth, citizen parent of either sex was "physically present" in US for periods totaling at least ten years, five of them after age 14. ▪ 8 U.S.C. § 1401(g)	Before child's birth, citizen father was "physically present" in US for periods totaling at least ten years, five of them after age 14 and Citizen father proves paternity in specified ways before the child turns 18. ▪ 8 U.S.C. § 1409(a), incorporating 8 U.S.C. § 1401(g)
Mother is US citizen, father is alien	Before child's birth, citizen parent of either sex was "physically present" in US for periods totaling at least ten years, five of them after age 14. ▪ 8 U.S.C. § 1401(g)	Before child's birth, citizen mother was "physically present" in US for a continuous period of one year. ▪ 8 U.S.C. § 1409(c)

a) Proof of Parentage: *Nguyen v. INS*

The majority and dissenting opinions in *Nguyen* (pronounced approximately as "nwen") offer different views about which aspects of pregnancy and motherhood are biological, and which are social.

ITEMS TO CONSIDER WHILE READING *NGUYEN v. INS*:

A. *Work through the items from the Kickstarter. Focus on applying the scrutiny, assessing the strength of the government's interests and the degree of tailoring.*

B. *Under what circumstances might a US citizen father and a non-citizen mother have a child born outside the US? Are the circumstances likely to be different for a US citizen mother and a non-citizen father? To the extent they are different, should it matter for constitutional purposes?*

C. *Would a sex-neutral alternative adequately serve the government's interests?*

Nguyen v. INS,

533 U.S. 53 (2001)

Justice Kennedy delivered the opinion of the Court [joined by Chief Justice Rehnquist and Justices Stevens, Scalia, and Thomas].

. . . 8 U.S.C. § 1409 governs the acquisition of United States citizenship by persons born to one United States citizen parent and one noncitizen parent when the parents are unmarried and the child is born outside of the United States or its possessions. The statute imposes different requirements for the child's acquisition of citizenship depending upon whether the citizen parent is the mother or the father. The question before us is whether the statutory distinction is consistent with the equal protection guarantee embedded in the Due Process Clause of the Fifth Amendment.

I

Petitioner Tuan Anh Nguyen was born in Saigon, Vietnam, on September 11, 1969, to copetitioner Joseph Boulais and a Vietnamese citizen. Boulais and Nguyen's mother were not married. Boulais always has been a citizen of the United States, and he was in Vietnam under the employ of a corporation. After he and Nguyen's mother ended their relationship, Nguyen lived for a time with the family of Boulais' new Vietnamese girlfriend. In June 1975, Nguyen, then almost six years of age, came to the United States. He became a lawful permanent resident and was raised in Texas by Boulais.

In 1992, when Nguyen was 22, he pleaded guilty in a Texas state court to two counts of sexual assault on a child. He was sentenced to eight years in prison on each count. Three years later, the United States Immigration and Naturalization Service (INS) initiated deportation proceedings against Nguyen as an alien who had been convicted of two crimes involving moral turpitude, as well as an aggravated felony. Though later he would change his position and argue he was a United States citizen, Nguyen testified at his deportation hearing that he was a citizen of Vietnam. The Immigration Judge found him deportable.

Nguyen v. INS

Nguyen appealed to the Board of Immigration Appeals and, in 1998, while the matter was pending, his father obtained an order of parentage from a state court, based on DNA testing. By this time, Nguyen was 28 years old. The Board dismissed Nguyen's appeal, rejecting his claim to United States citizenship because he had failed to establish compliance with 8 U.S.C. § 1409(a), which sets forth the requirements for one who was born out of wedlock and abroad to a citizen father and a noncitizen mother.

Nguyen and Boulais appealed to the Court of Appeals for the Fifth Circuit, arguing that § 1409 violates equal protection by providing different rules for attainment of citizenship by children born abroad and out of wedlock depending upon whether the one parent with American citizenship is the mother or the father. The court rejected the constitutional challenge to § 1409(a).

[The lower courts disagree on the issue.] We granted certiorari to resolve the conflict. **The father is before the Court** in this case; and, as all agree he has standing to raise the constitutional claim, we now resolve it. We hold that § 1409(a) is consistent with the constitutional guarantee of equal protection.

OBSERVATION

THE FATHER IS BEFORE THE COURT: Nguyen was not discriminated against because of his sex, but Boulais was. (If Boulais had been female, it would have been easier to transmit citizenship to his child.)

II

The general requirement for acquisition of citizenship by a child born outside the United States and its outlying possessions and to parents who are married, one of whom is a citizen and the other of whom is an alien, is set forth in 8 U.S.C. § 1401(g). The statute provides that the child is also a citizen if, before the birth, the citizen parent had been physically present in the United States for a total of five years, at least two of which were after the parent turned 14 years of age.

As to an individual born under the same circumstances, save that the parents are unwed, § 1409(a) sets forth the following [additional] requirements where the father is the citizen parent and the mother is an alien:

(1) a blood relationship between the person and the father is established by clear and convincing evidence,

(2) the father had the nationality of the United States at the time of the person's birth,

(3) Omitted], and

(4) while the person is under the age of 18 years—

(A) the person is legitimated under the law of the person's residence or domicile,

(B) the father acknowledges paternity of the person in writing under oath, or

(C) the paternity of the person is established by adjudication of a competent court.

In addition, § 1409(a) incorporates by reference, as to the citizen parent, the residency requirement of § 1401(g).

When the citizen parent of the child born abroad and out of wedlock is the child's mother, the requirements for the transmittal of citizenship are described in § 1409(c):

> Notwithstanding the provision of subsection (a) of this section, a person born . . . outside the United States and out of wedlock shall be held to have acquired at birth the nationality status of his mother, if the mother had the nationality of the United States at the time of such person's birth, and if the mother had previously been physically present in the United States or one of its outlying possessions for a continuous period of one year.

Section 1409(a) thus imposes a set of requirements on the children of citizen fathers born abroad and out of wedlock to a noncitizen mother that are not imposed under like circumstances when the citizen parent is the mother. All concede the requirements of §§ 1409(a)(4), relating to a citizen father's acknowledgment of a child while he is under 18, were not satisfied in this case. . . .

III

For a gender-based classification to withstand equal protection scrutiny, it must be established at least that the challenged classification serves important governmental objectives and that the discriminatory means employed are substantially related to the achievement of those objectives. For reasons to follow, we conclude § 1409 satisfies this standard. Given that determination, we need not decide whether some lesser degree of scrutiny pertains because the statute implicates Congress' immigration and naturalization power. . . .

A

The first governmental interest to be served is the importance of assuring that a biological parent-child relationship exists. In the case of the mother, the relation is verifiable from the birth itself. The mother's status is documented in most instances by the birth certificate or hospital records and the witnesses who attest to her having given birth.

Nguyen v. INS

In the case of the father, the uncontestable fact is that he need not be present at the birth. If he is present, furthermore, that circumstance is not incontrovertible proof of fatherhood. Fathers and mothers are not similarly situated with regard to the proof of biological parenthood. The imposition of a different set of rules for making that legal determination with respect to fathers and mothers is neither surprising nor troublesome from a constitutional perspective. Section 1409(a)(4)'s provision of three options for a father seeking to establish paternity—legitimation, paternity oath, and court order of paternity—is designed to ensure an acceptable documentation of paternity.

Petitioners argue that [a DNA test would satisfy the] requirement of § 1409(a)(1) that a father provide clear and convincing evidence of parentage [without the need for the time-limited paperwork requirements in § 1409(a)(4)]. . . . The Constitution . . . does not require that Congress elect one particular mechanism from among many possible methods of establishing paternity, even if that mechanism arguably might be the most scientifically advanced method. . . . The requirement of § 1409(a)(4) represents a reasonable conclusion by the legislature that the satisfaction of one of several alternatives will suffice to establish the blood link between father and child required as a predicate to the child's acquisition of citizenship. Given the proof of motherhood that is inherent in birth itself, it is unremarkable that Congress did not require the same affirmative steps of mothers . . .

B

1

The second important governmental interest furthered in a substantial manner by § 1409(a)(4) is the determination to ensure that the child and the citizen parent have some demonstrated opportunity or potential to develop not just a relationship that is recognized, as a formal matter, by the law, but one that consists of the real, everyday ties that provide a connection between child and citizen parent and, in turn, the United States. In the case of a citizen mother and a child born overseas, the opportunity for a meaningful relationship between citizen parent and child inheres in the very event of birth, an event so often critical to our constitutional and statutory understandings of citizenship. The mother knows that the child is in being and is hers and has an initial point of contact with him. There is at least an opportunity for mother and child to develop a real, meaningful relationship.

The same opportunity does not result from the event of birth, as a matter of biological inevitability, in the case of the unwed father. Given the 9-month interval between conception and birth, it is not always certain that a father will know that a child was conceived, nor is it always clear that even the mother will be sure of the father's identity. This fact takes on particular significance in the case of a child born overseas and out of wedlock. One concern in this context has always been with young people, men for the most part, who are on duty with the Armed Forces in foreign countries. . . .

Even if a father knows of the fact of conception, moreover, it does not follow that he will be present at the birth of the child. Thus, unlike the case of the mother, there is no assurance that the father and his biological child will ever meet. Without an initial point of contact with the child by a father who knows the child is his own, there is no opportunity for father and child to begin a relationship. Section 1409 takes the unremarkable step of ensuring that such an opportunity, inherent in the event of birth as to the mother-child relationship, exists between father and child before citizenship is conferred upon the latter. . . .

Petitioners and their amici argue in addition that, rather than fulfilling an important governmental interest, § 1409 merely embodies a gender-based stereotype. Although the above discussion should illustrate that, contrary to petitioners' assertions, § 1409 addresses an undeniable difference in the circumstance of the parents at the time a child is born, it should be noted, furthermore, that the difference does not result from some stereotype, defined as a frame of mind resulting from irrational or uncritical analysis. There is nothing irrational or improper in the recognition that at the moment of birth—a critical event in the statutory scheme and in the whole tradition of citizenship law—the mother's knowledge of the child and the fact of parenthood have been established in a way not guaranteed in the case of the unwed father. This is not a stereotype.

2

Having concluded that facilitation of a relationship between parent and child is an important governmental interest, the question remains whether the means Congress chose to further its objective—the imposition of certain additional requirements upon an unwed father—substantially relate to that end. Under this test, the means Congress adopted must be sustained. . . .

Petitioners argue that § 1409(a)(4) is not effective. In particular, petitioners assert that, although a mother will know of her child's birth, knowledge that one is a parent, no matter how it is acquired, does not guarantee a relationship with one's child. They thus maintain that the imposition of the additional requirements of § 1409(a)(4) only on the children of citizen fathers must reflect a stereotype that women are more likely than men to actually establish a relationship with their children.

This line of argument misconceives the nature of both the governmental interest at issue and the manner in which we examine statutes alleged to violate equal protection. As to the former, Congress would of course be entitled to advance the interest of ensuring an actual, meaningful relationship in every case before citizenship is conferred. Or Congress could excuse compliance with the formal requirements when an actual father-child relationship is proved. It did neither here, perhaps because of the subjectivity, intrusiveness, and difficulties of proof that might attend an inquiry into any particular bond or tie. Instead, Congress enacted an easily administered scheme to promote the different but still substantial interest of ensuring at least an opportunity for a parent-child relationship to develop. Petitioners' argument confuses the means and ends of the equal protection inquiry; § 1409(a)(4) should not be invalidated because Congress elected to advance an interest that is less demanding to satisfy than some other alternative.

Even if one conceives of the interest Congress pursues as the establishment of a real, practical relationship of considerable substance between parent and child in every case, as opposed simply to ensuring the potential for the relationship to begin, petitioners' misconception of the nature of the equal protection inquiry is fatal to their argument. A statute meets the equal protection standard we here apply so long as it is substantially related to the achievement of the governmental objective in question. It is almost axiomatic that a policy which seeks to foster the opportunity for meaningful parent-child bonds to develop has a close and substantial bearing on the governmental interest in the actual formation of that bond. None of our gender-based classification equal protection cases have required that the statute under consideration must be capable of achieving its ultimate objective in every instance.

In this difficult context of conferring citizenship on vast numbers of persons, the means adopted by Congress are in substantial furtherance of important governmental objectives. The fit between the means and the important end is "exceedingly persuasive." We have explained that an "exceedingly persuasive justification" is established by showing at least that the classification serves important governmental objectives and that the discriminatory means employed are substantially related to the achievement of those objectives. Section 1409 meets this standard.

C [Omitted.]

IV [Omitted.]

V

To fail to acknowledge even our most basic biological differences—such as the fact that a mother must be present at birth but the father need not be—risks making the guarantee of equal protection superficial, and so disserving it. Mechanistic classification of all our differences as stereotypes would operate to obscure those misconceptions and prejudices that are real. The distinction embodied in the statutory scheme here at issue is not marked by misconception and prejudice, nor does it show disrespect for either class. The difference between men and women in relation to the birth process is a real one, and the principle of equal protection does not forbid Congress to address the problem at hand in a manner specific to each gender.

Justice Scalia, with whom Justice Thomas joins, concurring. [Omitted.]

Justice O'Connor, with whom Justices Souter, Ginsburg, and Breyer join, dissenting.

In a long line of cases spanning nearly three decades, this Court has applied heightened scrutiny to legislative classifications based on sex. The Court today confronts another statute that classifies individuals on the basis of their sex. While the Court invokes heightened scrutiny, the manner in which it explains and applies this standard is a stranger to our precedents. Because the Immigration and Naturalization Service (INS) has not shown an exceedingly persuasive justification for the sex-based classification embodied in 8 U.S.C. § 1409(a)(4)—i.e., because it has failed to establish at least that the classification substantially relates to the achievement of important governmental objectives—I would reverse the judgment of the Court of Appeals.

I [Omitted.]

II

The Court recites the governing substantive standard for heightened scrutiny of sex-based classifications, but departs from the guidance of our precedents concerning such classifications in several ways. . . . For example, the majority hypothesizes about the interests served by the statute and fails adequately to inquire into the actual purposes of § 1409(a)(4). The Court also does not always explain adequately the importance of the interests that it claims to be served by the provision. The majority also fails carefully to consider whether the sex-based classification is being used impermissibly as a proxy for other, more germane bases of classification, and instead casually dismisses the relevance of available sex-neutral alternatives. And, contrary to the majority's conclusion, the fit between the means and ends of § 1409(a)(4) is far too attenuated for the provision to survive heightened scrutiny. In all, the majority opinion represents far less than the rigorous application of heightened scrutiny that our precedents require.

A

According to the Court, "the first governmental interest to be served is the importance of assuring that a biological parent-child relationship exists." The majority does not elaborate on the importance of this interest, which presumably lies in preventing fraudulent conveyances of citizenship. Nor does the majority demonstrate that this is one of the actual purposes of § 1409(a)(4). . . .

Congress could have required both mothers and fathers to prove parenthood within 30 days or, for that matter, 18 years, of the child's birth. Indeed, whether one conceives the majority's asserted interest as assuring the existence of a biological parent-child relationship, or as ensuring acceptable documentation of that relationship, a number of sex-neutral arrangements . . . would better serve that end. As the majority seems implicitly to acknowledge at one point, a mother will not always have formal legal documentation of birth because a birth certificate may not issue or may subsequently be lost. Conversely, a father's name may well appear on a birth certificate. While it is doubtless true that a mother's blood relation to a child is uniquely "verifiable from the birth itself" to those present at birth, the majority has not shown that a mother's birth relation is uniquely verifiable by the INS, much less that any greater verifiability warrants a sex-based, rather than a sex-neutral, statute.

B

The Court states that "the second important governmental interest furthered in a substantial manner by § 1409(a)(4) is the determination to ensure that the child and the citizen parent have some demonstrated opportunity or potential to develop not just a relationship that is recognized, as a formal matter, by the law, but one that consists of the real, everyday ties that provide a connection between child and citizen parent and, in turn, the United States." The Court again fails to demonstrate that this was Congress' actual purpose in enacting § 1409(a)(4). The majority's focus on "some demonstrated opportunity or potential to develop real, everyday ties" in fact appears to be the type of hypothesized rationale that is insufficient under heightened scrutiny. . . .

Assuming, as the majority does, that Congress was actually concerned about ensuring a "demonstrated opportunity" for a relationship, it is questionable whether such an opportunity qualifies as an "important" governmental interest apart from the existence of an actual relationship. . . . It is difficult to see how, in this citizenship-conferral context, anyone profits from a "demonstrated opportunity" for a relationship in the absence of the fruition of an actual tie. Children who have an "opportunity" for such a tie with a parent, of course, may never develop an actual relationship with that parent. If a child grows up in a foreign country without any postbirth contact with the citizen parent, then the child's never-realized "opportunity" for a relationship with the citizen seems singularly irrelevant to the appropriateness of granting citizenship to that child. Likewise, where there is an actual relationship, it is the actual relationship that does all the work in rendering appropriate a grant of citizenship, regardless of when and how the opportunity for that relationship arose. . . .

Indeed, the idea that a mother's presence at birth supplies adequate assurance of an opportunity to develop a relationship while a father's presence at birth does not would appear to rest only on an overbroad sex-based generalization. A mother may not have an opportunity for a relationship if the child is removed from his or her mother on account of alleged abuse or neglect, or if the child and mother are separated by tragedy, such as disaster or war, of the sort apparently present in this case. There is no reason, other than stereotype, to say that fathers who are present at birth lack an opportunity for a relationship on similar terms. The physical differences between men and women, therefore do not justify § 1409(a)(4)'s discrimination. . . .

C [Omitted.]

III [Omitted.]

[Conclusion]

No one should mistake the majority's analysis for a careful application of this Court's equal protection jurisprudence concerning sex-based classifications. Today's decision instead represents a deviation from a line of cases in which we have vigilantly applied heightened scrutiny to such classifications to determine whether a constitutional violation has occurred. I trust that the depth and vitality of these precedents will ensure that today's error remains an aberration. I respectfully dissent.

b) Duration of Residency: *Sessions v. Morales-Santana*

Unlike the US citizen father in *Nguyen*, the US citizen father in *Morales-Santana* did the necessary paperwork to prove parentage before the child turned 18. However, he could not fulfill the residency requirement, because he had not lived in the United States long enough before the child was born.

ITEMS TO CONSIDER WHILE READING *SESSIONS v. MORALES-SANTANA*:

A. *Work through the items in the Kickstarter.*

B. *Is* Morales-Santana *consistent with* Nguyen v. INS?

C. *How, if at all, does the majority opinion change the intermediate scrutiny standard?*

D. *What remedy should a court provide when it determines that a statute violates equal protection? "Equalize up" by giving everyone the benefits available to the statute's most favored group? "Equalize down" by giving everyone the benefits available to the statute's least favored group? Use some other approach?*

Sessions v. Morales-Santana,

582 U.S. 47 (2017)

Justice Ginsburg delivered the opinion of the Court [joined by Chief Justice Roberts and Justices Kennedy, Breyer, Sotomayor, and Kagan].

This case concerns a gender-based differential in the law governing acquisition of U.S. citizenship by a child born abroad, when one parent is a U.S. citizen, the other, a citizen of another nation. The main rule appears in 8 U.S.C. § 1401(g). Applicable to married couples, § 1401(g) requires a period of physical presence in the United States for the U.S.-citizen parent. The requirement [for purposes of this case] was ten years' physical presence prior to the child's birth. . . . That main rule is rendered applicable to unwed U.S.-citizen fathers by § 1409(a). Congress ordered an exception, however, for unwed U.S.-citizen mothers. Contained in § 1409(c), the exception allows an unwed mother to transmit her citizenship to a child born abroad if she has lived in the United States for just one year prior to the child's birth.

[The petitioner is US Attorney General Jeff Sessions.] The respondent in this case, Luis Ramón Morales-Santana, was born in the Dominican Republic when his father was just 20 days short of meeting § 1401(g)'s physical-presence requirement. Opposing removal to the Dominican Republic, Morales-Santana asserts that the equal protection principle implicit in the Fifth Amendment entitles him to citizenship stature. We hold that the gender line Congress drew is incompatible with the requirement that the Government accord to all persons "the equal protection of the laws." Nevertheless, we cannot convert § 1409(c)'s exception for unwed mothers into the main rule displacing § 1401(g) (covering married couples) and § 1409(a) (covering unwed fathers). We must therefore leave it to Congress to select, going forward, a physical-presence requirement (ten years, one year, or some other period) uniformly applicable to all children born abroad with one U.S.-citizen and one alien parent, wed or unwed. In the interim, the Government must ensure that the laws in question are administered in a manner free from gender-based discrimination.

I

A

We first describe in greater detail the regime Congress constructed. [Refer to the description found in the introduction to *Nguyen*.]

B

Respondent Luis Ramón Morales-Santana moved to the United States at age 13, and has resided in this country most of his life. Now facing deportation, he asserts U.S. citizenship at birth based on the citizenship of his biological father,

José Morales, who accepted parental responsibility and included Morales-Santana in his household.

José Morales was born in Guánica, Puerto Rico, on March 19, 1900. Puerto Rico was then, as it is now, part of the United States, and José became a U.S. citizen under the Organic Act of Puerto Rico. After living in Puerto Rico for nearly two decades, José left his childhood home on February 27, 1919, 20 days short of his 19th birthday, therefore failing to satisfy § 1401(g)'s requirement of five years' physical presence after age 14. He did so to take up employment as a builder-mechanic for a U.S. company in the then-U.S.-occupied Dominican Republic.

By 1959, José . . . was living with Yrma Santana Montilla, a Dominican woman he would eventually marry. In 1962, Yrma gave birth to their child, respondent Luis Morales-Santana. While the record before us reveals little about Morales-Santana's childhood, the Dominican archives disclose that Yrma and José married in 1970, and that José was then added to Morales-Santana's birth certificate as his father. . . . In 1975, when Morales-Santana was 13, he moved to Puerto Rico, and by 1976, the year his father died, he was attending public school in the Bronx, a New York City borough.

C

In 2000, the Government placed Morales-Santana in removal proceedings based on several convictions for offenses under New York State Penal Law, all of them rendered on May 17, 1995. Morales-Santana ranked as an alien despite the many years he lived in the United States, because, at the time of his birth, his father did not satisfy the requirement of five years' physical presence after age 14. An immigration judge rejected Morales-Santana's claim to citizenship derived from the U.S. citizenship of his father, and ordered Morales-Santana's removal to the Dominican Republic. In 2010, Morales-Santana moved to reopen the proceedings, [but] the Board of Immigration Appeals (BIA) denied the motion.

The United States Court of Appeals for the Second Circuit reversed the BIA's decision. Relying on this Court's post-1970 construction of the equal protection principle as it bears on gender-based classifications, the court held unconstitutional the differential treatment of unwed mothers and fathers. To cure the constitutional flaw, the court further held that Morales-Santana derived citizenship through his father, just as he would were his mother the U.S. citizen. . . . We consider the matter anew.

II

Because § 1409 treats sons and daughters alike, Morales-Santana does not suffer discrimination on the basis of *his* gender. He complains, instead, of gender-based discrimination against his father, who was unwed at the time of Morales-Santana's birth and was not accorded the right an unwed U.S.-citizen mother would have to transmit citizenship to her child. Although the Government does not contend otherwise, we briefly explain why Morales-Santana may seek to vindicate his father's right to the equal protection of the laws.

Ordinarily, a party must assert his own legal rights and cannot rest his claim to relief on the legal rights of third parties. But we recognize an exception where, as here, the party asserting the right has a close relationship with the person who possesses the right and there is a hindrance to the possessor's ability to protect his own interests. José Morales' ability to pass citizenship to his son, respondent Morales-Santana, easily satisfies the "close relationship" requirement. So, too, is the "hindrance" requirement well met. José Morales' failure to assert a claim in his own right stems from disability, not disinterest, for José died in 1976, many years before the current controversy arose. Morales-Santana is thus the obvious claimant, the best available proponent, of his father's right to equal protection.

III

Sections 1401 and 1409, we note, date from an era when the lawbooks of our Nation were rife with overbroad generalizations about the way men and women are. See, *e.g., Hoyt v. Florida* (1961) (women are the "center of home and family life," therefore they can be "relieved from the civic duty of jury service"); *Goesaert v. Cleary,* 335 U.S. 464 (1948) (States may draw "a sharp line between the sexes"). Today, laws of this kind are subject to review under the heightened scrutiny that now attends all gender-based classifications. *See, e.g., United States v. Virginia* (1996) (state-maintained military academy may not deny admission to qualified women).

Laws granting or denying benefits on the basis of the sex of the qualifying parent, our post-1970 decisions affirm, differentiate on the basis of gender, and therefore attract heightened review under the Constitution's equal protection guarantee. *Califano v. Westcott,* 443 U.S. 76 (1979) (holding unconstitutional provision of unemployed-parent benefits exclusively to fathers). Accord, *Califano v. Goldfarb,* 430 U.S. 199 (1977) (plurality opinion) (holding unconstitutional a Social Security classification that denied widowers survivors' benefits available to widows); *Weinberger v. Wiesenfeld,* 420 U.S. 636 (1975) (holding unconstitutional a Social Security classification that excluded fathers from receipt of child-in-care benefits available to mothers); *Frontiero v. Richardson* (1973) (plurality opinion) (holding unconstitutional exclusion of married female officers in the military from benefits automatically accorded married male officers); cf. *Reed v. Reed* (1971) (holding unconstitutional a probate-code preference for a father over a mother as administrator of a deceased child's estate).[FN7]

FN7 See Gerald Gunther, In Search of Evolving Doctrine on a Changing Court: A Model for a Newer Equal Protection, 86 Harv. L. Rev. 1, 34 (1972) ("It is difficult to understand Reed without an assumption that some special sensitivity to sex as a classifying factor entered into the analysis. Only by importing some special suspicion of sex-related means can the Reed result be made entirely persuasive.").

Prescribing one rule for mothers, another for fathers, § 1409 is of the same genre as the classifications we declared unconstitutional in *Reed, Frontiero, Wiesenfeld, Goldfarb,* and *Westcott.* As in those cases, heightened scrutiny is in order. Successful defense of legislation that differentiates on the basis of gender, we have reiterated, requires an exceedingly persuasive justification.

A

The defender of legislation that differentiates on the basis of gender must show at least that the challenged classification serves important governmental objectives and that the discriminatory means employed are substantially related to the achievement of those objectives. Moreover, the classification must substantially serve an important governmental interest *today,* for "in interpreting the equal protection guarantee, we have recognized that new insights and societal understandings can reveal unjustified inequality that once passed unnoticed and unchallenged." *Obergefell v. Hodges* (2015). Here, the Government has supplied no exceedingly persuasive justification for § 1409(a) and (c)'s gender-based and gender-biased disparity.

1

History reveals what lurks behind § 1409. Enacted in the Nationality Act of 1940, § 1409 ended a century and a half of congressional silence on the citizenship of children born abroad to unwed parents. During this era, two once habitual, but now untenable, assumptions pervaded our Nation's citizenship laws and underpinned judicial and administrative rulings: In marriage, husband is dominant, wife subordinate; unwed mother is the natural and sole guardian of a nonmarital child.

Under the once entrenched principle of male dominance in marriage, the husband controlled both wife and child. "Dominance of the husband," this Court observed in 1915, "is an ancient principle of our jurisprudence." ***Mackenzie v. Hare,*** 239 U.S. 299 (1915). Through the early 20th century, a male citizen automatically conferred U.S. citizenship on his alien wife. A female citizen, however, was incapable of conferring citizenship on her husband; indeed, she was subject to expatriation if she married an alien. The family of a citizen or a lawfully admitted permanent resident enjoyed statutory exemptions from entry requirements, but only if the citizen or resident was male. And from 1790 until 1934, the foreign-born child of a married couple gained U.S. citizenship only through the father.

■ HISTORY

MACKENZIE v. HARE: In this opinion, the Supreme Court upheld the constitutionality of a 1907 statute that read: "any American woman who marries a foreigner shall take the nationality of her husband."

For unwed parents, the father-controls tradition never held sway. Instead, the mother was regarded as the child's natural and sole guardian. At common law, the mother, and only the mother, was bound to maintain a nonmarital child as its natural guardian. In line with that understanding, in the early 20th century, the State Department sometimes permitted unwed mothers to pass citizenship to their children, despite the absence of any statutory authority for the practice.

In the 1940 Act, Congress discarded the father-controls assumption concerning married parents, but codified the mother-as-sole-guardian perception regarding unmarried parents. . . . This unwed-mother-as-natural-guardian notion renders § 1409's gender-based residency rules understandable. Fearing that a foreign-born child could turn out "more alien than American in character," the [Roosevelt] administration believed that a citizen parent with lengthy ties to the United States would counteract the influence of the alien parent. Concern about the attachment of foreign-born children to the United States explains the treatment of unwed citizen fathers, who, according to the familiar stereotype, would care little about, and have scant contact with, their nonmarital children. For unwed citizen mothers, however, there was no need for a prolonged residency prophylactic: The alien father, who might transmit foreign ways, was presumptively out of the picture.

2

For close to a half century, as earlier observed, this Court has viewed with suspicion laws that rely on overbroad generalizations about the different talents, capacities, or preferences of males and females. In particular, we have recognized that if a statutory objective is . . . to exclude or "protect" members of one gender in reliance on fixed notions concerning that gender's roles and abilities, the objective itself is illegitimate.

In accord with this eventual understanding . . . , the Court has held that no important governmental interest is served by laws grounded, as § 1409(a) and (c) are, in the obsolescing view that unwed fathers are invariably less qualified and entitled than mothers to take responsibility for nonmarital children. Overbroad generalizations of that order, the Court has come to comprehend, have a constraining impact, descriptive though they may be of the way many people still order their lives. Laws according or denying benefits in reliance on stereotypes about women's domestic roles, the Court has observed, may create a self-fulfilling cycle of discrimination that forces women to continue to assume the role of . . . primary family caregiver. Correspondingly, such laws may disserve men who exercise responsibility for raising their children. In light of the equal protection jurisprudence this Court has developed since 1971, § 1409(a) and (c)'s discrete duration-of-residence requirements for unwed mothers and fathers who have accepted parental responsibility is stunningly anachronistic.

B

In urging this Court nevertheless to reject Morales-Santana's equal protection plea, the Government cites . . . decisions of this Court [including] *Nguyen v. INS*. None controls this case. . . .

The provision challenged in . . . *Nguyen* as violative of equal protection requires unwed U.S.-citizen fathers, but not mothers, to formally acknowledge parenthood of their foreign-born children in order to transmit their U.S. citizenship to those children. See § 1409(a)(4). . . . In *Nguyen*, the Court held that imposing a paternal-acknowledgment requirement on fathers was a justifiable, easily met means of ensuring the existence of a biological parent-child relationship, which the mother establishes by giving birth. Morales-Santana's challenge does not renew the contest over § 1409's paternal-acknowledgment requirement . . . and the Government does not dispute that Morales-Santana's father, by marrying Morales-Santana's mother, satisfied that requirement [as it existed at the time].

Unlike the paternal-acknowledgment requirement at issue in *Nguyen* . . . , the physical-presence requirements now before us relate solely to the duration of the parent's prebirth residency in the United States, not to the parent's filial tie to the child. As the Court of Appeals observed in this case, a man needs no more time in the United States than a woman in order to have assimilated citizenship-related values to transmit to his child. And unlike *Nguyen*'s parental-acknowledgment requirement, § 1409(a)'s age-calibrated physical-presence requirements cannot fairly be described as "minimal."

C

Notwithstanding § 1409(a) and (c)'s provenance in traditional notions of the way women and men are, the Government maintains that the statute serves two important objectives: (1) ensuring a connection between the child to become a citizen and the United States and (2) preventing "statelessness," *i.e.*, a child's possession of no citizenship at all. Even indulging the assumption that Congress intended § 1409 to serve these interests, neither rationale survives heightened scrutiny.

1

We take up first the Government's assertion that § 1409(a) and (c)'s gender-based differential ensures that a child born abroad has a connection to the United States of sufficient strength to warrant conferral of citizenship at birth. The Government does not contend, nor could it, that unmarried men take more time to absorb U.S. values than unmarried women do. Instead, it [argues that an unwed mother] is the child's only legally recognized parent at the time of childbirth. An unwed citizen father enters the scene later, as a second parent. A longer physical

Sessions v. Morales-Santana

connection to the United States is warranted for the unwed father, the Government maintains, because of the competing national influence of the alien mother. . . .

Underlying this apparent design is the assumption that the alien father of a nonmarital child born abroad to a U.S.-citizen mother will not accept parental responsibility. . . . Hardly gender neutral, that assumption conforms to the long-held view that unwed fathers care little about, indeed are strangers to, their children. Lump characterization of that kind, however, no longer passes equal protection inspection.

Accepting, arguendo, that Congress intended the diverse physical-presence prescriptions to serve an interest in ensuring a connection between the foreign-born nonmarital child and the United States, the gender-based means scarcely serve the posited end. The scheme permits the transmission of citizenship to children who have no tie to the United States so long as their mother was a U.S. citizen continuously present in the United States for one year at any point in her life *prior* to the child's birth. The transmission holds even if the mother marries the child's alien father immediately after the child's birth and never returns with the child to the United States. At the same time, the legislation precludes citizenship transmission by a U.S.-citizen father who falls a few days short of meeting § 1401(g)'s longer physical-presence requirements, even if the father acknowledges paternity on the day of the child's birth and raises the child in the United States. One cannot see in this driven-by-gender scheme the close means-end fit required to survive heightened scrutiny.

2

The Government maintains that Congress established the gender-based residency differential in § 1409(a) and (c) to reduce the risk that a foreign-born child of a U.S. citizen would be born stateless. This risk, according to the Government, was substantially greater for the foreign-born child of an unwed U.S.-citizen mother than it was for the foreign-born child of an unwed U.S.-citizen father. But there is little reason . . . to believe that a statelessness concern prompted the diverse physical-presence requirements. Nor has the Government shown that the risk of statelessness disproportionately endangered the children of unwed mothers.

As the Court of Appeals pointed out, with one exception [found in a sentence in a Senate Report dealing with a separate provision of the statute], nothing in the congressional hearings and reports on the 1940 and 1952 Acts refers to the problem of statelessness for children born abroad. Reducing the incidence of statelessness was the express goal of *other* sections of the 1940 Act. The justification for § 1409's gender-based dichotomy, however, was not the child's plight, it was the mother's role as the "natural guardian" of a nonmarital child. It will not do to hypothesize or invent governmental purposes for gender classifications *post hoc* in response to litigation. . . .

[The Government argues that due to operation of foreign law, children born abroad to unmarried U.S.-citizen mothers are at risk of statelessness. In fact, that risk is at least at large—and is probably larger—for children of unmarried U.S.-citizen fathers.] One can hardly characterize as gender neutral a scheme allegedly attending to the risk of statelessness for children of unwed U.S.-citizen mothers while ignoring the same risk for children of unwed U.S.-citizen fathers. . . .

In sum, the Government has advanced no exceedingly persuasive justification for § 1409(a) and (c)'s gender-specific residency and age criteria. Those disparate criteria, we hold, cannot withstand inspection under a Constitution that requires the Government to respect the equal dignity and stature of its male and female citizens.

IV

While the equal protection infirmity in retaining a longer physical-presence requirement for unwed fathers than for unwed mothers is clear, this Court is not equipped to grant the relief Morales-Santana seeks, *i.e.*, extending to his father (and, derivatively, to him) the benefit of the one-year physical-presence term § 1409(c) reserves for unwed mothers.

There are two remedial alternatives, our decisions instruct, when a statute benefits one class (in this case, unwed mothers and their children), as § 1409(c) does, and excludes another from the benefit (here, unwed fathers and their children). A court may either declare the statute a nullity and order that its benefits not extend to the class that the legislature intended to benefit, or it may extend the coverage of the statute to include those who are aggrieved by exclusion. When the right invoked is that to equal treatment, the appropriate remedy is a mandate of equal treatment, a result that can be accomplished by withdrawal of benefits from the favored class as well as by extension of benefits to the excluded class. How equality is accomplished is a matter on which the Constitution is silent.

The choice between these outcomes is governed by the legislature's intent, as revealed by the statute at hand. On finding unlawful discrimination, courts may attempt, within the bounds of their institutional competence, to implement what the legislature would have willed had it been apprised of the constitutional infirmity.

Ordinarily, we have reiterated, extension, rather than nullification, is the proper course. Illustratively, in a series of cases involving federal financial assistance benefits, the Court struck discriminatory exceptions denying benefits to discrete groups, which meant benefits previously denied were extended. See, *e.g., Department of Agriculture v. Moreno* (1973) (food stamps); *Frontiero* (plurality opinion) (military spousal benefits). Here, however, the discriminatory exception consists of *favorable* treatment for a discrete group (a shorter physical-presence requirement for unwed U.S.-citizen mothers giving birth abroad). Following the same approach as in those benefits cases—striking the discriminatory exception—leads here to extending the general rule of longer physical-presence requirements to cover the previously favored group.

Sessions v. Morales-Santana

In considering whether the legislature would have struck an exception and applied the general rule equally to all, or instead, would have broadened the exception to cure the equal protection violation . . . a court should measure the intensity of commitment to the residual policy—the main rule, not the exception—and consider the degree of potential disruption of the statutory . . . scheme that would occur by extension as opposed to abrogation.

The residual policy here, the longer physical-presence requirement stated in §§ 1401(g) and 1409, evidences Congress' recognition of the importance of residence in this country as "the talisman of dedicated attachment [to the United States]." And the potential for disruption of the statutory scheme is large. For if § 1409(c)'s one-year dispensation were extended to unwed citizen fathers, would it not be irrational to retain the longer term when the U.S.-citizen parent is married? Disadvantageous treatment of marital children in comparison to nonmarital children is scarcely a purpose one can sensibly attribute to Congress.[FN25]

FN25 Distinctions based on parents' marital status, we have said, are subject to the same heightened scrutiny as distinctions based on gender. *Clark v. Jeter*, 486 U.S. 456 (1988).

Although extension of benefits is customary in federal benefit cases, all indicators in this case point in the opposite direction. Put to the choice, Congress, we believe, would have abrogated § 1409(c)'s exception, preferring preservation of the general rule.

V

. . . The judgment of the Court of Appeals for the Second Circuit is affirmed in part and reversed in part, and the case is remanded for further proceedings consistent with this opinion.

Justice Gorsuch took no part in the consideration or decision of this case.

Justice Thomas, with whom Justice Alito joins, concurring in the judgment in part.

The Court today holds that we are not equipped to remedy the equal protection injury that respondent claims his father suffered under the Immigration and Nationality Act (INA) of 1952. I agree with that holding. As the majority concludes, extending 8 U.S.C. § 1409(c)'s 1-year physical presence requirement to unwed citizen fathers (as respondent requests) is not, under this Court's precedent, an appropriate remedy for any equal protection violation. Indeed, I am skeptical that we even have the power to provide relief of the sort requested in this suit—namely, conferral of citizenship on a basis other than that prescribed by Congress.

The Court's remedial holding resolves this case. Because respondent cannot obtain relief in any event, it is unnecessary for us to decide whether the 1952 version of the INA was constitutional, whether respondent has third-party standing to raise an equal protection claim on behalf of his father, or whether other immigration laws (such as the current versions of §§ 1401(g) and 1409) are constitutional. I therefore concur only in the judgment reversing the Second Circuit.

4. Affirmative Action

Feeney said that "the Fourteenth Amendment guarantees equal laws, not equal results." But it did not say that government was forbidden from going beyond the constitutional minimum through *affirmative action*—a term referring generally to laws that seek to advance racial equality through means other than the mere removal of facially discriminatory legal obstacles.

The phrase "affirmative action" was first used in Executive Order 10925, signed by President John F. Kennedy in 1961. That order created a President's Committee on Equal Employment Opportunity, charged with developing "positive measures for the elimination of any discrimination, direct or indirect, which now exists" in executive branch hiring. It also required that government contractors undertake "affirmative action" to ensure that their employees would be "treated during employment without regard to their race, creed, color, or national origin." In 1965, President Lyndon B. Johnson described affirmative action as "the next and the more profound stage of the battle for civil rights." He described the goals of affirmative action in language that differed from what would later be said in *Feeney*: "We seek not just legal equity, but human ability; not just equality as a right and a theory, but equality as a fact and equality as a result."

flashback

The Freedmen's Bureau (1865–1872), which provided social services to former slaves, can be viewed as an early experiment in affirmative action. See Ch. 7.A.2. A few years after the Bureau closed, a majority of the Supreme Court intimated in *The Civil Rights Cases* (1882) that such efforts were no longer needed: "When a man has emerged from slavery, and by the aid of beneficent legislation has shaken off the inseparable concomitants of that state, there must be some stage in the progress of his elevation when he takes the rank of a mere citizen, and ceases to be the special favorite of the laws, and when his rights as a citizen, or a man, are to be protected in the ordinary modes by which other men's rights are protected."

Some forms of affirmative action are not controversial. The DC Police Department in *Washington v. Davis*, for example, could decide to replace Test 21 with a test better validated and correlated with actual job duties. A public university could ensure that its recruiters spend some of their time at high schools with predominantly minority student populations. However, other forms of affirmative action have led to legal challenges based on a theory of "reverse discrimination" against the White majority. These challenges raise important questions about the true goal of the Equal Protection Clause, with the answers tending to fall into two categories.

Anti-Classification. One approach to the Equal Protection Clause considers the absence of suspect classifications to be an end in itself. Drawing on the metaphor from Justice Harlan's dissent in *Plessy v. Ferguson*, the goal is a "color-blind" constitution where the government would simply not pay any attention to race. Under this view, a program specifically designed to increase minority participation in government programs could be a problem, since the government should not be making race-based decisions in favor of any group, whether the group represents a minority or majority.

Anti-Subordination. Another approach to the Equal Protection Clause argues that its goal is to prevent subordination of minority groups. Under this view, laws that classify on the basis of race are bad to the extent they perpetuate an overclass and an underclass. But an affirmative action program that uses race to further the overall purpose of achieving greater equality among groups is consistent with the Equal Protection Clause.

As summarized in *Johnson v. California* (2005) (Ch. 18.C.2.a.2), race-conscious affirmative action programs trigger strict scrutiny, even though their motivations are far different from the discriminatory laws of the Jim Crow era. *Johnson* said: "We have insisted on strict scrutiny in every context, even for so-called 'benign' racial classifications, such as race-conscious university admissions policies, race-based preferences in government contracts, and race-based districting intended to improve minority representation." As you read the following cases, consider what the anti-classification and anti-subordination approaches imply for the application of strict scrutiny. Specifically, which ends are "compelling" under each approach, and which means are "narrowly tailored" to those ends?

a) Affirmative Action in Government Contracting: *City of Richmond v. J.A. Croson Co.*

One goal of the Kennedy and Johnson affirmative action programs was to ensure that lucrative government contracts were not monopolized by businesses owned by White males. *City of Richmond v. J.A. Croson Co.* (1989) involved a municipal plan with a similar goal.

ITEMS TO CONSIDER WHILE READING *CROSON*:

A. Croson *has no single majority opinion. Make a chart where the columns stand for the numbered sections of the lead opinion. Even if no single opinion has a majority of justices, are there any legal propositions joined by five or more?*

JUSTICE (By Seniority)	I	II	III-A	III-B	IV	V
Rehnquist, C.J.						
Brennan						
White						
Marshall						
Blackmun						
Stevens						
O'Connor						
Scalia						
Kennedy						

B. *Work through the items from the Kickstarter. In particular:*

1. *Is this a case of disparate treatment or disparate impact?*
2. *What level of scrutiny should be used for race-conscious affirmative action programs, and why?*
3. *Which government interests does the court consider sufficiently strong to justify race-conscious affirmative action in contracting? Which ones are not strong enough?*
4. *What does it take for a race-conscious government contracting program to be sufficiently well tailored?*

City of Richmond v. J.A. Croson Co.,

488 U.S. 469 (1989)

Justice O'Connor announced the judgment of the Court and delivered the opinion of the Court with respect to Parts I, III-B, and IV, an opinion with respect to Part II, in which Chief Justice Rehnquist and Justice White join, and an opinion with respect to Parts III-A and V, in which Chief Justice Rehnquist, Justice White, and Justice Kennedy join.

In this case, we confront once again the tension between the Fourteenth Amendment's guarantee of equal treatment to all citizens, and the use of race-based measures to ameliorate the effects of past discrimination on the opportunities enjoyed by members of minority groups in our society. . . .

I

On April 11, 1983, the Richmond City Council adopted the Minority Business Utilization Plan (the Plan). The Plan required prime contractors to whom the city awarded construction contracts to subcontract at least 30% of the dollar amount of the contract to one or more Minority Business Enterprises (MBE's). The 30% set-aside did not apply to city contracts awarded to minority-owned prime contractors.

The Plan defined an MBE as a business at least 51% of which is owned and controlled by minority group members. "Minority group members" were defined as "citizens of the United States who are Blacks, Spanish-speaking, Orientals, Indians, Eskimos, or Aleuts." There was no geographic limit to the Plan; an otherwise qualified MBE from anywhere in the United States could avail itself of the 30% set-aside. The Plan declared that it was "remedial" in nature, and enacted "for the purpose of promoting wider participation by minority business enterprises in the construction of public projects." The Plan expired on June 30, 1988, and was in effect for approximately five years. . . .

The Plan was adopted by the Richmond City Council after a public hearing. Seven members of the public spoke to the merits of the ordinance: five were in opposition, two in favor. Proponents of the set-aside provision relied on a study which indicated that, while the general population of Richmond was 50% black, only 0.67% of the city's prime construction contracts had been awarded to minority businesses in the 5-year period from 1978 to 1983. It was also established that a variety of contractors' associations, whose representatives appeared in opposition to the ordinance, had virtually no minority businesses within their membership. The city's legal counsel indicated his view that the ordinance was constitutional under this Court's [previous] decision[s]. Councilperson Marsh, a proponent of the ordinance, made the following statement:

> There is some information, however, that I want to make sure that we put in the record. I have been practicing law in this community since 1961, and I am familiar with the practices in the construction industry in this area, in the State, and around the nation. And I can say without equivocation, that the general conduct of the construction industry in this area, and the State, and around the nation, is one in which race discrimination and exclusion on the basis of race is widespread.

There was no direct evidence of race discrimination on the part of the city in letting contracts or any evidence that the city's prime contractors had discriminated against minority-owned subcontractors.

Opponents of the ordinance questioned both its wisdom and its legality. They argued that a disparity between minorities in the population of Richmond and the number of prime contracts awarded to MBE's had little probative value in establishing discrimination in the construction industry. Representatives of various contractors' associations questioned whether there were enough MBE's in the Richmond area to satisfy the 30% set-aside requirement. Mr. Murphy noted that only 4.7% of all construction firms in the United States were minority owned and that 41% of these were located in California, New York, Illinois, Florida, and Hawaii. He predicted that the ordinance would thus lead to a windfall for the few minority firms in Richmond. Councilperson Gillespie indicated his concern that many local labor jobs, held by both blacks and whites, would be lost because the ordinance put no geographic limit on the MBE's eligible for the 30% set-aside. Some of the representatives of the local contractor's organizations indicated that they did not discriminate on the basis of race and were in fact actively seeking out minority members. Councilperson Gillespie expressed his concern about the legality of the Plan, and asked that a vote be delayed pending consultation with outside counsel. His suggestion was rejected, and the ordinance was enacted by a vote of six to two, with Councilperson Gillespie abstaining.

On September 6, 1983, the city of Richmond issued an invitation to bid on a project for the provision and installation of certain plumbing fixtures at the city jail. [The J.A. Croson Company bid on the project but was ruled out because it could not satisfy the set-aside.] . . . Shortly thereafter Croson brought this action under 42 U.S.C. § 1983 in the Federal District Court for the Eastern District of Virginia, arguing that the Richmond ordinance was unconstitutional on its face and as applied in this case.

The District Court upheld the Plan in all respects. [The Fourth Circuit reversed.] . . . We now affirm the judgment.

II

The parties and their supporting amici fight an initial battle over the scope of the city's power to adopt legislation designed to address the effects of past discrimination. [A]ppellee [Croson] argues that the city must limit any race-based remedial efforts to eradicating the effects of its own prior discrimination. This is essentially the position taken by the Court of Appeals below. Appellant [the City] argues [that it] enjoys sweeping legislative power to define and attack the effects of prior discrimination in its local construction industry. We find that neither of these two rather stark alternatives can withstand analysis. . . .

A state or local subdivision (if delegated the authority from the State) has the authority to eradicate the effects of private discrimination within its own legislative jurisdiction. This authority must, of course, be exercised within the constraints of § 1 of the Fourteenth Amendment. . . . As a matter of state law, the city of Richmond has legislative authority over its procurement policies, and can use its spending powers to remedy private discrimination, if it identifies that discrimination with the particularity required by the Fourteenth Amendment. . . .

Thus, if the city could show that it had essentially become a "passive participant" in a system of racial exclusion practiced by elements of the local construction industry, we think it clear that the city could take affirmative steps to dismantle such a system. It is beyond dispute that any public entity, state or federal, has a compelling interest in assuring that public dollars, drawn from the tax contributions of all citizens, do not serve to finance the evil of private prejudice.

III

A

The Equal Protection Clause of the Fourteenth Amendment provides that no State shall "deny to any person within its jurisdiction the equal protection of the laws." As this Court has noted in the past, the rights created by the first section of the Fourteenth Amendment are, by its terms, guaranteed to the individual. The rights established are personal rights. The Richmond Plan denies certain citizens the opportunity to compete for a fixed percentage of public contracts based solely upon their race. To whatever racial group these citizens belong, their "personal rights" to be treated with equal dignity and respect are implicated by a rigid rule erecting race as the sole criterion in an aspect of public decisionmaking.

Absent searching judicial inquiry into the justification for such race-based measures, there is simply no way of determining what classifications are "benign" or "remedial" and what classifications are in fact motivated by illegitimate notions of racial inferiority or simple racial politics. Indeed, the purpose of strict scrutiny is to "smoke out" illegitimate uses of race by assuring that the legislative body is pursuing a goal important enough to warrant use of a highly suspect tool. The test also ensures that the means chosen "fit" this compelling goal so closely that there is little or no possibility that the motive for the classification was illegitimate racial prejudice or stereotype.

Classifications based on race carry a danger of stigmatic harm. Unless they are strictly reserved for remedial settings, they may in fact promote notions of racial inferiority and lead to a politics of racial hostility. [T]he standard of review under the Equal Protection Clause is not dependent on the race of those burdened or benefited by a particular classification.

Our . . . adherence to [this] standard of review . . . does not, as Justice Marshall's dissent suggests, indicate that we view "racial discrimination as largely a phenomenon of the past" or that "government bodies need no longer preoccupy themselves with rectifying racial injustice." As we indicate, States and their local subdivisions have many legislative weapons at their disposal both to punish and prevent present discrimination and to remove arbitrary barriers to minority advancement. Rather, our interpretation of § 1 stems from our [belief] that the guarantee of equal protection cannot mean one thing when applied to one individual and something else when applied to a person of another color.

Under the standard proposed by Justice Marshall's dissent, "race-conscious classifications designed to further remedial goals" are forthwith subject to a relaxed standard of review. How the dissent arrives at the legal conclusion that a racial classification is "designed to further remedial goals," without first engaging in an examination of the factual basis for its enactment and the nexus between its scope and that factual basis, we are not told. However, once the "remedial" conclusion is reached, the dissent's standard is singularly deferential, and bears little resemblance to the close examination of legislative purpose we have engaged in when reviewing classifications based either on race or gender. The dissent's watered-down version of equal protection review effectively assures that race will always be relevant in American life, and that the ultimate goal of eliminating entirely from governmental decisionmaking such irrelevant factors as a human being's race will never be achieved.

Even were we to accept a reading of the guarantee of equal protection under which the level of scrutiny varies according to the ability of different groups to defend their interests in the representative process, heightened scrutiny would still be appropriate in the circumstances of this case. One of the central arguments for applying a less exacting standard to "benign" racial classifications is that such measures essentially involve a choice made by dominant racial groups to disadvantage themselves. If one aspect of the judiciary's role under the Equal Protection Clause is to protect "discrete and insular minorities" from majoritarian prejudice or indifference, see *United States v. Carolene Products Co.* (1938), some maintain that these concerns are not implicated when the white majority places burdens upon itself.

In this case, blacks constitute approximately 50% of the population of the city of Richmond. Five of the nine seats on the city council are held by blacks. The concern that a political majority will more easily act to the disadvantage of a minority based on unwarranted assumptions or incomplete facts would seem to militate for, not against, the application of heightened judicial scrutiny in this case. . . .

B

We think it clear that the factual predicate offered in support of the Richmond Plan suffers from . . . two [fatal] defects[.] The District Court found the city council's "findings sufficient to ensure that, in adopting the Plan, it was remedying the present effects of past discrimination in the construction industry." . . . A generalized assertion that there has been past discrimination in an entire industry provides no guidance for a legislative body to determine the precise scope of the injury it seeks to remedy. It has no logical stopping point. Relief for such an ill-defined wrong could extend until the percentage of public contracts awarded to MBE's in Richmond mirrored the percentage of minorities in the population as a whole. . . .

While there is no doubt that the sorry history of both private and public discrimination in this country has contributed to a lack of opportunities for black entrepreneurs, this observation, standing alone, cannot justify a rigid racial quota in the awarding of public contracts in Richmond, Virginia. Like the claim that discrimination in primary and secondary schooling justifies a rigid racial preference in medical school admissions, *Regents of the University of California v. Bakke*, 438 U.S. 265 (1978), an amorphous claim that there has been past discrimination in a particular industry cannot justify the use of an unyielding racial quota.

It is sheer speculation how many minority firms there would be in Richmond absent past societal discrimination[.] Defining these sorts of injuries as "identified discrimination" would give local governments license to create a patchwork of racial preferences based on statistical generalizations about any particular field of endeavor.

These defects are readily apparent in this case. The 30% quota cannot in any realistic sense be tied to any injury suffered by anyone. The District Court relied upon five predicate "facts" in reaching its conclusion that there was an adequate basis for the 30% quota: (1) the ordinance declares itself to be remedial; (2) several proponents of the measure stated their views that there had been past discrimination in the construction industry; (3) minority businesses received 0.67% of prime contracts from the city while minorities constituted 50% of the city's population; (4) there were very few minority contractors in local and state contractors' associations; and (5) in 1977, Congress made a determination that the effects of past discrimination had stifled minority participation in the construction industry nationally.

None of these "findings," singly or together, provide the city of Richmond with a strong basis in evidence for its conclusion that remedial action was necessary.

There is nothing approaching a prima facie case of a constitutional or statutory violation by anyone in the Richmond construction industry.

The District Court accorded great weight to the fact that the city council designated the Plan as "remedial." But the mere recitation of a "benign" or legitimate purpose for a racial classification is entitled to little or no weight. Racial classifications are suspect, and that means that simple legislative assurances of good intention cannot suffice.

The District Court also relied on the highly conclusionary statement of a proponent of the Plan that there was racial discrimination in the construction industry "in this area, and the State, and around the nation." It also noted that the city manager had related his view that racial discrimination still plagued the construction industry in his home city of Pittsburgh. These statements are of little probative value in establishing identified discrimination in the Richmond construction industry. The factfinding process of legislative bodies is generally entitled to a presumption of regularity and deferential review by the judiciary. But when a legislative body chooses to employ a suspect classification, it cannot rest upon a generalized assertion as to the classification's relevance to its goals. A governmental actor cannot render race a legitimate proxy for a particular condition merely by declaring that the condition exists. The history of racial classifications in this country suggests that blind judicial deference to legislative or executive pronouncements of necessity has no place in equal protection analysis. . . .

In this case, the city does not even know how many MBE's in the relevant market are qualified to undertake prime or subcontracting work in public construction projects. Nor does the city know what percentage of total city construction dollars minority firms now receive as subcontractors on prime contracts let by the city. . . .

Justice Marshall apparently views the requirement that Richmond identify the discrimination it seeks to remedy in its own jurisdiction as a mere administrative headache, an "onerous documentary obligation." We cannot agree. . . . Because racial characteristics so seldom provide a relevant basis for disparate treatment, and because classifications based on race are potentially so harmful to the entire body politic, it is especially important that the reasons for any such classification be clearly identified and unquestionably legitimate. The "evidence" relied upon by the dissent, the history of school desegregation in Richmond and numerous congressional reports, does little to define the scope of any injury to minority contractors in Richmond or the necessary remedy. The factors relied upon by the dissent could justify a preference of any size or duration. . . .

In sum, none of the evidence presented by the city points to any identified discrimination in the Richmond construction industry. We, therefore, hold that the city has failed to demonstrate a compelling interest in apportioning public contracting opportunities on the basis of race. To accept Richmond's claim that past societal discrimination alone can serve as the basis for rigid racial preferences would be to open the door to competing claims for "remedial relief" for every disadvantaged group. The dream of a Nation of equal citizens in a society where race is irrelevant to personal opportunity and achievement would be lost in a mosaic of shifting preferences based on inherently unmeasurable claims of past wrongs. Courts would be asked to evaluate the extent of the prejudice and consequent harm suffered by various minority groups. Those whose societal injury is thought to exceed some arbitrary level of tolerability then would be entitled to preferential classifications. We think such a result would be contrary to both the letter and spirit of a constitutional provision whose central command is equality.

The foregoing analysis applies only to the inclusion of blacks within the Richmond set-aside program. There is absolutely no evidence of past discrimination against Spanish-speaking, Oriental, Indian, Eskimo, or Aleut persons in any aspect of the Richmond construction industry. The District Court took judicial notice of the fact that the vast majority of "minority" persons in Richmond were black. It may well be that Richmond has never had an Aleut or Eskimo citizen. The random inclusion of racial groups that, as a practical matter, may never have suffered from discrimination in the construction industry in Richmond suggests that perhaps the city's purpose was not in fact to remedy past discrimination.

If a 30% set-aside was "narrowly tailored" to compensate black contractors for past discrimination, one may legitimately ask why they are forced to share this "remedial relief" with an Aleut citizen who moves to Richmond tomorrow? The gross overinclusiveness of Richmond's racial preference strongly impugns the city's claim of remedial motivation.

IV

As noted by the court below, it is almost impossible to assess whether the Richmond Plan is narrowly tailored to remedy prior discrimination since it is not linked to identified discrimination in any way. We limit ourselves to two observations in this regard.

First, there does not appear to have been any consideration of the use of race-neutral means to increase minority business participation in city contracting. Many of the barriers to minority participation in the construction industry relied upon by the city to justify a racial classification appear to be race neutral. If MBE's disproportionately lack capital or cannot meet bonding requirements, a race-neutral program of city financing for small firms would, a fortiori, lead to greater minority participation. . . . There is no evidence in this record that the Richmond City Council has considered any alternatives to a race-based quota.

Second, the 30% quota cannot be said to be narrowly tailored to any goal, except perhaps outright racial balancing. It rests upon the completely unrealistic assumption that minorities will choose a particular trade in lockstep proportion to their representation in the local population. . . .

Given the [option] of an individualized procedure, the city's only interest in maintaining a quota system rather than investigating the need for remedial action in particular cases would seem to be simple administrative convenience. But the interest in avoiding the bureaucratic effort necessary to tailor remedial relief to those who truly have suffered the effects of prior discrimination cannot justify a rigid line drawn on the basis of a suspect classification. See *Frontiero v. Richardson* (1973) (plurality opinion) ("When we enter the realm of strict judicial scrutiny, there can be no doubt that administrative convenience is not a shibboleth, the mere recitation of which dictates constitutionality"). Under Richmond's scheme, a successful black, Hispanic, or Oriental entrepreneur from anywhere in the country enjoys an absolute preference over other citizens based solely on their race. We think it obvious that such a program is not narrowly tailored to remedy the effects of prior discrimination.

V

Nothing we say today precludes a state or local entity from taking action to rectify the effects of identified discrimination within its jurisdiction. If the city of Richmond had evidence before it that nonminority contractors were systematically excluding minority businesses from subcontracting opportunities it could take action to end the discriminatory exclusion. Where there is a significant statistical disparity between the number of qualified minority contractors willing and able to perform a particular service and the number of such contractors actually engaged by the locality or the locality's prime contractors, an inference of discriminatory exclusion could arise. Under such circumstances, the city could act to dismantle the closed business system by taking appropriate measures against those who discriminate on the basis of race or other illegitimate criteria. In the extreme case, some form of narrowly tailored racial preference might be necessary to break down patterns of deliberate exclusion.

Nor is local government powerless to deal with individual instances of racially motivated refusals to employ minority contractors. Where such discrimination occurs, a city would be justified in penalizing the discriminator and providing appropriate relief to the victim of such discrimination. Moreover, evidence of a pattern of individual discriminatory acts can, if supported by appropriate statistical proof, lend support to a local government's determination that broader remedial relief is justified.

Even in the absence of evidence of discrimination, the city has at its disposal a whole array of race-neutral devices to increase the accessibility of city contracting opportunities to small entrepreneurs of all races. Simplification of bidding procedures, relaxation of bonding requirements, and training and financial aid for disadvantaged entrepreneurs of all races would open the public contracting market to all those who have suffered the effects of past societal discrimination or neglect. Many of the formal barriers to new entrants may be the product of bureaucratic inertia more than actual necessity, and may have a disproportionate effect on the opportunities open to new minority firms. Their elimination or modification would have little detrimental effect on the city's interests and would serve to increase the opportunities available to minority business without classifying individuals on the basis of race. The city may also act to prohibit discrimination in the provision of credit or bonding by local suppliers and banks. Business as usual should not mean business pursuant to the unthinking exclusion of certain members of our society from its rewards.

In the case at hand, the city has not ascertained how many minority enterprises are present in the local construction market nor the level of their participation in city construction projects. The city points to no evidence that qualified minority contractors have been passed over for city contracts or subcontracts, either as a group or in any individual case. Under such circumstances, it is simply impossible to say that the city has demonstrated a strong basis in evidence for its conclusion that remedial action was necessary.

Proper findings in this regard are necessary to define both the scope of the injury and the extent of the remedy necessary to cure its effects. Such findings also serve to assure all citizens that the deviation from the norm of equal treatment of all racial and ethnic groups is a temporary matter, a measure taken in the service of the goal of equality itself. Absent such findings, there is a danger that a racial classification is merely the product of unthinking stereotypes or a form of racial politics. If there is no duty to attempt either to measure the recovery by the wrong or to distribute that recovery within the injured class in an evenhanded way, our history will adequately support a legislative preference for almost any ethnic, religious, or racial group with the political strength to negotiate a piece of the action for its members. Because the city of Richmond has failed to identify the need for remedial action in the awarding of its public construction contracts, its treatment of its citizens on a racial basis violates the dictates of the Equal Protection Clause. Accordingly, the judgment of the Court of Appeals for the Fourth Circuit is affirmed.

Justice Stevens, concurring in part and concurring in the judgment.

A central purpose of the Fourteenth Amendment is to further the national goal of equal opportunity for all our citizens. In order to achieve that goal we must learn from our past mistakes, but I believe the Constitution requires us to evaluate our policy decisions—including those that govern the relationships among different racial and ethnic groups—primarily by studying their probable impact on the future. I therefore do not agree with the premise that seems to underlie today's decision . . . that a governmental decision that rests on a racial classification is never permissible except as a remedy for a past wrong. I do, however, agree with the Court's explanation of why the Richmond ordinance cannot be justified as a remedy for past discrimination, and therefore join Parts I, III-B, and IV of its opinion. . . .

Justice Kennedy, concurring in part and concurring in the judgment. [Omitted.]

Justice Scalia, concurring in the judgment.

I agree with much of the Court's opinion, and, in particular, with Justice O'Connor's conclusion that strict scrutiny must be applied to all governmental classification by race, whether or not its asserted purpose is "remedial" or "benign." I do not agree, however, with Justice O'Connor's dictum suggesting that, despite the Fourteenth Amendment, state and local governments may in some circumstances discriminate on the basis of race in order (in a broad sense) "to ameliorate the effects of past discrimination." The benign purpose of compensating for social disadvantages, whether they have been acquired by reason of prior discrimination or otherwise, can no more be pursued by the illegitimate means of racial discrimination than can other assertedly benign purposes we have repeatedly rejected. . . . The difficulty of overcoming the effects of past discrimination is as nothing compared with the difficulty of eradicating from our society the source of those effects, which is the tendency—fatal to a Nation such as ours—to classify and judge men and women on the basis of their country of origin or the color of their skin. A solution to the first problem that aggravates the second is no solution at all. . . . At least where state or local action is at issue, only a social emergency rising to the level of imminent danger to life and limb—for example, a prison race riot, requiring temporary segregation of inmates—can justify an exception to the principle embodied in the Fourteenth Amendment that "our Constitution is color-blind, and neither knows nor tolerates classes among citizens," *Plessy v. Ferguson* (1896) (Harlan, J., dissenting). . . .

In my view there is only one circumstance in which the States may act by race to "undo the effects of past discrimination": where that is necessary to eliminate their own maintenance of a system of unlawful racial classification. If, for example, a state agency has a discriminatory pay scale compensating black employees in all positions at 20% less than their nonblack counterparts, it may assuredly promulgate an order raising the salaries of all black employees to eliminate the differential. This distinction explains our school desegregation cases, in which we have made plain that States and localities sometimes have an obligation to adopt race-conscious remedies. While there is no doubt that those cases have taken into account the continuing effects of previously mandated racial school assignment, we have held those effects to justify a race-conscious remedy only because we have concluded, in that context, that they perpetuate a dual school system. . . .

A State can, of course, act to undo the effects of past discrimination in many permissible ways that do not involve classification by race. In the particular field of state contracting, for example, it may adopt a preference for small businesses, or even for new businesses—which would make it easier for those previously excluded by discrimination to enter the field. Such programs may well have racially disproportionate impact, but they are not based on race. And, of course, a State may undo the effects of past discrimination in the sense of giving the identified victim of state discrimination that which it wrongfully denied him—for example, giving to a previously rejected black applicant the job that, by reason of discrimination, had been awarded to a white applicant, even if this means terminating the latter's employment. In such a context, the white job-holder is not being selected for disadvantageous treatment because of his race, but because he was wrongfully awarded a job to which another is entitled. That is worlds apart from the system here, in which those to be disadvantaged are identified solely by race. . . .

Justice Marshall, with whom Justices Brennan and Blackmun join, dissenting.

It is a welcome symbol of racial progress when the former capital of the Confederacy acts forthrightly to confront the effects of racial discrimination in its midst. In my view, nothing in the Constitution can be construed to prevent Richmond, Virginia, from allocating a portion of its contracting dollars for businesses owned or controlled by members of minority groups. . . .

A majority of this Court holds today, however, that the Equal Protection Clause of the Fourteenth Amendment blocks Richmond's initiative. The essence of the majority's position is that Richmond has failed to catalog adequate findings to prove that past discrimination has impeded minorities from joining or participating fully in Richmond's construction contracting industry. I find deep irony in second-guessing Richmond's judgment on this point. As much as any municipality in the United States, Richmond knows what racial discrimination is; a century of decisions by this and other federal courts has richly documented the city's disgraceful history of public and private racial discrimination. In any event, the Richmond City Council has supported its determination that minorities have been wrongly excluded from local construction contracting. Its proof includes statistics showing that minority-owned businesses have received virtually no city contracting dollars and rarely if ever belonged to area trade associations; testimony by municipal officials that discrimination has been widespread in the local construction industry; and . . . studies which showed that pervasive discrimination in the Nation's tight-knit construction industry had operated to exclude minorities from public contracting. These are precisely the types of statistical and testimonial evidence which, until today, this Court had credited in cases approving of race-conscious measures designed to remedy past discrimination.

More fundamentally, today's decision marks a deliberate and giant step backward in this Court's affirmative-action jurisprudence. Cynical of one municipality's attempt to redress the effects of past racial discrimination in a particular industry, the majority launches a grapeshot attack on race-conscious remedies in general. The majority's unnecessary pronouncements will inevitably discourage or prevent governmental entities, particularly States and localities, from acting to rectify the scourge of past discrimination. This is the harsh reality of the majority's decision, but it is not the Constitution's command.

I [Omitted.]

II

Agreement upon a means for applying the Equal Protection Clause to an affirmative-action program has eluded this Court every time the issue has come before us. My view has long been that race-conscious classifications designed to further remedial goals must serve important governmental objectives and must be substantially related to achievement of those objectives in order to withstand constitutional scrutiny. Analyzed in terms of this two-pronged standard, Richmond's set-aside . . . is plainly constitutional.

A

1

Turning first to the governmental interest inquiry, Richmond has two powerful interests in setting aside a portion of public contracting funds for minority-owned enterprises. The first is the city's interest in eradicating the effects of past racial discrimination. It is far too late in the day to doubt that remedying such discrimination is a compelling, let alone an important, interest. . . .

Richmond has a second compelling interest in setting aside, where possible, a portion of its contracting dollars. That interest is the prospective one of preventing the city's own spending decisions from reinforcing and perpetuating the exclusionary effects of past discrimination. . . . The majority is wrong to trivialize the continuing impact of government acceptance or use of private institutions or structures once wrought by discrimination. When government channels all its contracting funds to a white-dominated community of established contractors whose racial homogeneity is the product of private discrimination, it does more than place its imprimatur on the practices which forged and which continue to define that community. It also provides a measurable boost to those economic entities that have thrived within it, while denying important economic benefits to those entities which, but for prior discrimination, might well be better qualified to receive valuable government contracts. In my view, the interest in ensuring that the government does not reflect and reinforce prior private discrimination in dispensing public contracts is every bit as strong as the interest in eliminating private discrimination—an interest which this Court has repeatedly deemed compelling. The more government bestows its rewards on those persons or businesses that were positioned to thrive during a period of private racial discrimination, the tighter the deadhand grip of prior discrimination becomes on the present and future. Cities like Richmond may not be constitutionally required to adopt set-aside plans. But there can be no doubt that when Richmond acted affirmatively to stem the perpetuation of patterns of discrimination through its own decisionmaking, it served an interest of the highest order.

2

The remaining question with respect to the "governmental interest" prong of equal protection analysis is whether Richmond has proffered satisfactory proof of past racial discrimination to support its twin interests in remediation and in governmental nonperpetuation. . . . The varied body of evidence on which Richmond relied provides an unquestionably legitimate basis upon which the city council could determine that the effects of past racial discrimination warranted a remedial and prophylactic governmental response. . . .

When the legislatures and leaders of cities with histories of pervasive discrimination testify that past discrimination has infected one of their industries, armchair cynicism like that exercised by the majority has no place. . . . [F]ederal judges, with nothing but their impressions to go on, [ought not] disbelieve the explanations of these local governments and officials. Disbelief is particularly inappropriate here in light of the fact that appellee Croson, which had the burden of proving unconstitutionality at trial, has at no point come forward with any direct evidence that the city council's motives were anything other than sincere. . . .

B

In my judgment, Richmond's set-aside plan also comports with the second prong of the equal protection inquiry, for it is substantially related to the interests it seeks to serve in remedying past discrimination and in ensuring that municipal contract procurement does not perpetuate that discrimination. . . .

III

I would ordinarily end my analysis at this point and conclude that Richmond's ordinance satisfies both the governmental interest and substantial relationship prongs of our Equal Protection Clause analysis. However, I am compelled to add more, for the majority has gone beyond the facts of this case to announce a set of principles which unnecessarily restricts the power of governmental entities to take race-conscious measures to redress the effects of prior discrimination.

A

Today, for the first time, a majority of this Court has adopted strict scrutiny as its standard of Equal Protection Clause review of race-conscious remedial measures. This is an unwelcome development. A profound difference separates governmental actions that themselves are racist, and governmental actions that seek to remedy the effects of prior racism or to prevent neutral governmental activity from perpetuating the effects of such racism.

Racial classifications drawn on the presumption that one race is inferior to another or because they put the weight of government behind racial hatred and separatism warrant the strictest judicial scrutiny because of the very irrelevance of these rationales. By contrast, racial classifications drawn for the purpose of remedying the effects of discrimination that itself was race based have a highly pertinent basis: the tragic and indelible fact that discrimination against blacks and other racial minorities in this Nation has pervaded our Nation's history and continues to scar our society. Because the consideration of race is relevant to remedying the continuing effects of past racial discrimination, and because governmental programs employing racial classifications for remedial purposes can be crafted to avoid stigmatization, such programs should not be subjected to conventional "strict scrutiny"—scrutiny that is strict in theory, but fatal in fact.

In concluding that remedial classifications warrant no different standard of review under the Constitution than the most brutal and repugnant forms of state-sponsored racism, a majority of this Court signals that it regards racial discrimination as largely a phenomenon of the past, and that government bodies need no longer preoccupy themselves with rectifying racial injustice. I, however, do not believe this Nation is anywhere close to eradicating racial discrimination or its vestiges. In constitutionalizing its wishful thinking, the majority today does a grave disservice not only to those victims of past and present racial discrimination in this Nation whom government has sought to assist, but also to this Court's long tradition of approaching issues of race with the utmost sensitivity.

B [Omitted.]

C

Today's decision, finally, is particularly noteworthy for the daunting standard it imposes upon States and localities contemplating the use of race-conscious measures to eradicate the present effects of prior discrimination and prevent its perpetuation. . . . The fact is that Congress' concern in passing the Reconstruction Amendments, and particularly their congressional authorization provisions, was that States would not adequately respond to racial violence or discrimination against newly freed slaves. To interpret any aspect of these Amendments as proscribing state remedial responses to these very problems turns the Amendments on their heads. . . .

IV

The majority today sounds a full-scale retreat from the Court's longstanding solicitude to race-conscious remedial efforts directed toward deliverance of the century-old promise of equality of economic opportunity. The new and restrictive tests it applies scuttle one city's effort to surmount its discriminatory past, and imperil those of dozens more localities. I, however, profoundly disagree with the cramped vision of the Equal Protection Clause which the majority offers today and with its application of that vision to Richmond, Virginia's, laudable set-aside plan. The battle against pernicious racial discrimination or its effects is nowhere near won. I must dissent.

Justice Blackmun, with whom Justice Brennan joins, dissenting. [Omitted.]

b) Affirmative Action in Education

The Supreme Court has wrestled for decades with affirmative action in education. It is helpful to divide these cases into two categories. College and university admissions involve rationing a limited resource: there is not room for everyone who wishes to attend. For K–12 education, states offer seats to all students, so the questions have involved how to assign students within a district.

1) Affirmative Action in Higher Education: **Fisher v. University of Texas**

Ever since race-conscious affirmative action policies in college admissions began to be used in the early 1970s, the Supreme Court has wrestled over their constitutionality. In a series of cases presenting slightly different admissions plans, the Court has repeatedly cautioned that race is a disfavored factor that may be used only for certain purposes and only in certain ways.

Set-Asides at the University of California. In *Regents of University of California v. Bakke*, 438 U.S. 265 (1978), the medical school at UC-Davis reserved 15% of the seats in its entering class for minority applicants. Allan Bakke, a White male whose credentials were strong enough for entry, argued that if these seats had not been reserved on the basis of race, he would have been admitted.

A majority of the Supreme Court ordered that Bakke be admitted to the medical school. Although no opinion was joined by a majority of the court, Justice Powell's lead opinion was later viewed as the rule of the case. Among other things, Justice Powell's opinion considered several reasons that a University might offer to justify a race-conscious admissions program.

(1) A goal of "assuring within its student body some specified percentage of a particular group merely because of its race" is facially invalid, "discrimination for its own sake."

(2) A goal of eliminating "the disabling effects of identified discrimination" is legitimate and substantial, but the discrimination must have been imposed by the university itself. A university admissions program that has an impact on "innocent individuals" like Bakke as a means to redress discrimination elsewhere in society is improper.

(3) A goal of creating a pool of doctors who are willing and able to serve disadvantaged communities is legitimate, but there was not good evidence to show that the minority set-aside would have that result.

(4) Finally, Justice Powell identified one goal that he considered powerful: improving the educational experience. A diverse class leads to a greater range of insight and interactions, and provides benefits to both majority and minority students. However, Justice Powell held that reserving a fixed number of seats for minority students was not well tailored to the goal of a good classroom experience. A less discriminatory alternative would resemble the admissions program at Harvard, which had no fixed quotas, but considered diversity of race a "plus" in an applicant's file, along with other forms of diversity, including geographical diversity, economic status, unique life experiences, and so on.

Plus Factors at the University of Michigan. The Supreme Court revisited *Bakke*'s concept of "plus factors" in a pair of cases challenging admissions programs at the University of Michigan.

Grutter v. Bollinger, 539 U.S. 306 (2003), upheld (5–4) the Michigan law school's admission program modeled on the Harvard plan praised in *Bakke*. The law school sought to admit an entering class with a "critical mass" of minority students (a lesser number might be mere tokenism that leaves these students isolated). Among the pool of students with acceptable academic credentials, admissions officers would undertake a holistic review of the candidates, seeking to assemble a class with wide a range of diversities, including racial diversity. Of the many areas of disagreement between the five-justice majority and the four dissenters was a dispute over the importance of a diverse student body. The majority considered it to be a compelling government interest, while the dissenters vehemently disagreed.

■ WEBSITE
Fuller versions of *Grutter* and *Gratz* are available for download from this casebook's companion website, www.CaplanIntegratedConLaw.com.

The companion case of *Gratz v. Bollinger*, 539 U.S. 244 (2003), invalidated (6–3) the admissions plan for Michigan's undergraduate college. Like the law school, the college wished to obtain the educational benefits of a racially diverse student body. But because the college had a much larger applicant pool, the college had chosen not to undertake individualized, holistic review of each applicant. Instead, points were awarded for various attributes, and being a member of a racial minority was worth 20 points. Because in some cases these 20 race points would mean the difference between acceptance and rejection, the majority found the plan to be unconstitutional. The dissenters did not see a constitutional difference between plus factors that involved numbers and those that did not. "If honesty is the best policy," they wrote, "surely Michigan's accurately described, fully disclosed College affirmative action program is preferable to achieving similar numbers through winks, nods, and disguises."

Plus Factors at the University of Texas. After *Grutter* and *Gratz* were decided, the University of Texas at Austin set as a goal the admission of a racially, culturally, and economically diverse entering class. To ensure that admitted minority students were not mere tokens who have an isolated and uncomfortable educational experience, the University sought to admit a "critical mass" of each group. These goals were pursued through two separate admission tracks.

By state statute, approximately 75% of the seats were reserved for students graduating near the top ten percent of their in-state high school class. Because many school districts in Texas are residentially segregated (see *Rodriguez v. San Antonio School District,* Ch. 18.D.2), this part of the plan ensured that top students from underfunded or predominantly minority schools were admitted, no matter how they compare to students at better funded or predominantly majority schools.

By University policy, the remainder of the seats would go to students selected through a "holistic" review of their applications, considering a number of factors other than the high school grades that controlled the Top Ten Percent statute. The extent to which an applicant's race might contribute to the overall diversity of the class was one factor to be considered, as allowed by *Grutter.*

Admissions Program Challenged in *Fisher v. University of Texas*

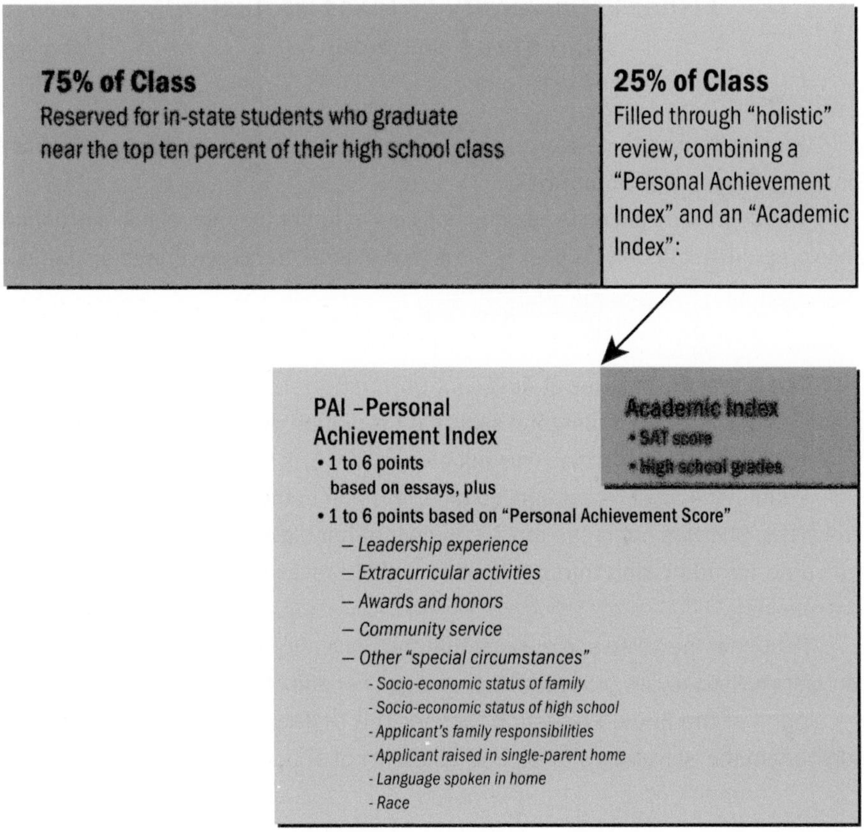

75% of Class
Reserved for in-state students who graduate near the top ten percent of their high school class

25% of Class
Filled through "holistic" review, combining a "Personal Achievement Index" and an "Academic Index":

PAI – Personal Achievement Index
- 1 to 6 points based on essays, plus
- 1 to 6 points based on "Personal Achievement Score"
  - *Leadership experience*
  - *Extracurricular activities*
  - *Awards and honors*
  - *Community service*
  - *Other "special circumstances"*
    - *Socio-economic status of family*
    - *Socio-economic status of high school*
    - *Applicant's family responsibilities*
    - *Applicant raised in single-parent home*
    - *Language spoken in home*
    - *Race*

Academic Index
- SAT score
- High school grades

Abigail Fisher's challenge to the presence of race as one of the holistic variables reached the Supreme Court twice, with *Fisher I* (2013) announcing general principles and *Fisher II* (2016) applying them to the facts.

ITEMS TO CONSIDER WHILE READING *FISHER v. U. OF TEXAS II*:

A. *Apply the Kickstarter to each of the University's admissions formulas: Top Ten Percent and Holistic. Specifically:*

1. *Should strict scrutiny, or some less difficult standard, be used for race-conscious affirmative action plans involving University admissions?*
2. *What does it take for a University to satisfy strict scrutiny?*

B. *The majority and dissent differ over what it means if the race-conscious aspects of the admission program have little numerical impact on the racial makeup of the entering class. If relatively few seats are affected, is this a reason to think the plan is narrowly tailored, or that it is not serving a compelling state interest?*

Fisher v. University of Texas at Austin II,

579 U.S. 365 (2016)

Justice Kennedy delivered the opinion of the Court [joined by Justices Ginsburg, Breyer, and Sotomayor].

The Court is asked once again to consider whether the race-conscious admissions program at the University of Texas is lawful under the Equal Protection Clause.

I

The University of Texas at Austin (or University) relies upon a complex system of admissions that has undergone significant evolution over the past two decades. [The challenged system, which was adopted in 2004, is summarized above.] . . .

Petitioner Abigail Fisher applied for admission to the University's 2008 freshman class. She was not in the top 10 percent of her high school class, so she was evaluated for admission through holistic, full-file review. Petitioner's application was rejected.

Petitioner then filed suit alleging that the University's consideration of race as part of its holistic-review process disadvantaged her and other Caucasian applicants, in violation of the Equal Protection Clause. The District Court entered summary judgment in the University's favor, and the Court of Appeals affirmed.

This Court granted certiorari and vacated the judgment of the Court of Appeals, *Fisher v. University of Texas at Austin*, 570 U.S. 297 (2013) (*Fisher I*), because it had applied an overly deferential "good-faith" standard in assessing the constitutionality of the University's program. The Court remanded the case for the Court of Appeals to assess the parties' claims under the correct legal standard.

Fisher v. University of Texas at Austin II

Without further remanding to the District Court, the Court of Appeals again affirmed the entry of summary judgment in the University's favor. This Court granted certiorari for a second time, and now affirms.

II

Fisher I set forth three controlling principles relevant to assessing the constitutionality of a public university's affirmative-action program. First, because racial characteristics so seldom provide a relevant basis for disparate treatment, race may not be considered by a university unless the admissions process can withstand strict scrutiny. Strict scrutiny requires the university to demonstrate with clarity that its purpose or interest is both constitutionally permissible and substantial, and that its use of the classification is necessary to the accomplishment of its purpose.

Second, *Fisher I* confirmed that the decision to pursue the educational benefits that flow from student body diversity is, in substantial measure, an academic judgment to which some, but not complete, judicial deference is proper. A university cannot impose a fixed quota or otherwise define diversity as some specified percentage of a particular group merely because of its race or ethnic origin. Once, however, a university gives a reasoned, principled explanation for its decision, deference must be given to the University's conclusion, based on its experience and expertise, that a diverse student body would serve its educational goals.

Third, *Fisher I* clarified that no deference is owed when determining whether the use of race is narrowly tailored to achieve the university's permissible goals. A university, *Fisher I* explained, bears the burden of proving a nonracial approach would not promote its interest in the educational benefits of diversity about as well and at tolerable administrative expense. Though narrow tailoring does not require exhaustion of every conceivable race-neutral alternative or require a university to choose between maintaining a reputation for excellence and fulfilling a commitment to provide educational opportunities to members of all racial groups, it does impose on the university the ultimate burden of demonstrating that race-neutral alternatives that are both available and workable do not suffice. . . .

III

The University's program is sui generis. Unlike other approaches to college admissions considered by this Court, it combines holistic review with a percentage plan. This approach gave rise to an unusual consequence in this case: The component of the University's admissions policy that had the largest impact on petitioner's chances of admission was not the school's consideration of race under its holistic-review process but rather the Top Ten Percent Plan. Because petitioner did not graduate in the top 10 percent of her high school class, she was categorically ineligible for more than three-fourths of the slots in the incoming freshman class. . . .

Despite the Top Ten Percent Plan's outsized effect on petitioner's chances of admission, she has not challenged it. For that reason, throughout this litigation, the Top Ten Percent Plan has been taken, somewhat artificially, as a given premise. . . .

IV

In seeking to reverse the judgment of the Court of Appeals, petitioner makes four arguments.

First, she argues that the University has not articulated its compelling interest with sufficient clarity. According to petitioner, the University must set forth more precisely the level of minority enrollment that would constitute a "critical mass." Without a clearer sense of what the University's ultimate goal is, petitioner argues, a reviewing court cannot assess whether the University's admissions program is narrowly tailored to that goal.

As this Court's cases have made clear, however, the compelling interest that justifies consideration of race in college admissions is not an interest in enrolling a certain number of minority students. Rather, a university may institute a race-conscious admissions program as a means of obtaining the educational benefits that flow from student body diversity. As this Court has said, enrolling a diverse student body promotes cross-racial understanding, helps to break down racial stereotypes, and enables students to better understand persons of different races. Equally important, student body diversity promotes learning outcomes, and better prepares students for an increasingly diverse workforce and society.

Increasing minority enrollment may be instrumental to these educational benefits, but it is not, as petitioner seems to suggest, a goal that can or should be reduced to pure numbers. Indeed, since the University is prohibited from seeking a particular number or quota of minority students, it cannot be faulted for failing to specify the particular level of minority enrollment at which it believes the educational benefits of diversity will be obtained.

On the other hand, asserting an interest in the educational benefits of diversity writ large is insufficient. A university's goals cannot be elusory or amorphous—they must be sufficiently measurable to permit judicial scrutiny of the policies adopted to reach them.

The record reveals that in first setting forth its current admissions policy, the University articulated concrete and precise goals. On the first page of its 2004 "Proposal to Consider Race and Ethnicity in Admissions," the University identifies the educational values it seeks to realize through its admissions process: the destruction of stereotypes, the promotion of cross-racial understanding, the preparation of a

Fisher v. University of Texas at Austin II

student body for an increasingly diverse workforce and society, and the cultivation of a set of leaders with legitimacy in the eyes of the citizenry. Later in the proposal, the University explains that it strives to provide an academic environment that offers a robust exchange of ideas, exposure to differing cultures, preparation for the challenges of an increasingly diverse workforce, and acquisition of competencies required of future leaders. All of these objectives, as a general matter, mirror the "compelling interest" this Court has approved in its prior cases. . . . Petitioner's contention that the University's goal was insufficiently concrete is rebutted by the record.

Second, petitioner argues that the University has no need to consider race because it had already achieved critical mass by 2003 using the Top Ten Percent Plan and race-neutral holistic review. [Before 2004, the University used a holistic review formula that did not consider race.] Petitioner is correct that a university bears a heavy burden in showing that it had not obtained the educational benefits of diversity before it turned to a race-conscious plan. The record reveals, however, that, at the time of petitioner's application, the University could not be faulted on this score. Before changing its policy the University conducted months of study and deliberation, including retreats, interviews, and review of data, and concluded that the use of race-neutral policies and programs had not been successful in achieving sufficient racial diversity at the University, . . .

In 2002, 52 percent of undergraduate classes with at least five students had no African-American students enrolled in them, and 27 percent had only one African-American student. In other words, only 21 percent of undergraduate classes with five or more students in them had more than one African-American student enrolled. Twelve percent of these classes had no Hispanic students, as compared to 10 percent in 1996. Though a college must continually reassess its need for race-conscious review, here that assessment appears to have been done with care, and a reasonable determination was made that the University had not yet attained its goals.

Third, petitioner argues that considering race was not necessary because such consideration has had only a minimal impact in advancing the University's compelling interest. Again, the record does not support this assertion. In 2003, 11 percent of the Texas residents enrolled through [race-neutral] holistic review were Hispanic and 3.5 percent were African-American. In 2007, by contrast, 16.9 percent of the Texas [race-conscious] holistic-review freshmen were Hispanic and 6.8 percent were African-American. Those increases—of 54 percent and 94 percent, respectively—show that consideration of race has had a meaningful, if still limited, effect on the diversity of the University's freshman class.

In any event, it is not a failure of narrow tailoring for the impact of racial consideration to be minor. The fact that race consciousness played a role in only a small portion of admissions decisions should be a hallmark of narrow tailoring, not evidence of unconstitutionality.

Petitioner's final argument is that there are numerous other available race-neutral means of achieving the University's compelling interest. A review of the record reveals, however, that, at the time of petitioner's application, none of her proposed alternatives was a workable means for the University to attain the benefits of diversity it sought. For example, petitioner suggests that the University could intensify its outreach efforts to African-American and Hispanic applicants. But the University submitted extensive evidence of the many ways in which it already had intensified its outreach efforts to those students. The University has created three new scholarship programs, opened new regional admissions centers, increased its recruitment budget by half-a-million dollars, and organized over 1,000 recruitment events. Perhaps more significantly . . . the University spent seven years attempting to achieve its compelling interest using race-neutral holistic review. None of these efforts succeeded, and petitioner fails to offer any meaningful way in which the University could have improved upon them at the time of her application. . . .

Petitioner's final suggestion is to uncap the Top Ten Percent Plan, and admit more—if not all—the University's students through a percentage plan. As an initial matter, petitioner overlooks the fact that the Top Ten Percent Plan, though facially neutral, cannot be understood apart from its basic purpose, which is to boost minority enrollment. Percentage plans are adopted with racially segregated neighborhoods and schools front and center stage. It is race consciousness, not blindness to race, that drives such plans. Consequently, petitioner cannot assert simply that increasing the University's reliance on a percentage plan would make its admissions policy more race neutral.

Even if, as a matter of raw numbers, minority enrollment would increase under such a regime, petitioner would be hard-pressed to find convincing support for the proposition that college admissions would be improved if they were a function of class rank alone. That approach would sacrifice all other aspects of diversity in pursuit of enrolling a higher number of minority students. A system that selected every student through class rank alone would exclude the star athlete or musician whose grades suffered because of daily practices and training. It would exclude a talented young biologist who struggled to maintain above-average grades in humanities classes. And it would exclude a student whose freshman-year grades were poor because of a family crisis but who got herself back on track in her last three years of school, only to find herself just outside of the top decile of her class. . . .

In short, none of petitioner's suggested alternatives—nor other proposals considered or discussed in the course of this litigation—have been shown to be available and workable means through which the University could have met its educational goals, as it understood and defined them in 2008. The University has thus met its burden of showing that the admissions policy it used at the time it rejected petitioner's application was narrowly tailored.

[CONCLUSION]

A university is in large part defined by those intangible "qualities which are incapable of objective measurement but which make for greatness." *Sweatt v. Painter*, 339 U.S. 629 (1950). Considerable deference is owed to a university in defining those intangible characteristics, like student body diversity, that are central to its identity and educational mission. But still, it remains an enduring challenge to our Nation's education system to reconcile the pursuit of diversity with the constitutional promise of equal treatment and dignity.

In striking this sensitive balance, public universities, like the States themselves, can serve as laboratories for experimentation. See *New State Ice Co. v. Liebmann*, 285 U.S. 262 (1932) (Brandeis, J., dissenting). The University of Texas at Austin has a special opportunity to learn and to teach. The University now has at its disposal valuable data about the manner in which different approaches to admissions may foster diversity or instead dilute it. The University must continue to use this data to scrutinize the fairness of its admissions program; to assess whether changing demographics have undermined the need for a race-conscious policy; and to identify the effects, both positive and negative, of the affirmative-action measures it deems necessary.

The Court's affirmance of the University's admissions policy today does not necessarily mean the University may rely on that same policy without refinement. It is the University's ongoing obligation to engage in constant deliberation and continued reflection regarding its admissions policies.

Justice Kagan took no part in the consideration or decision of this case.

[Justice Scalia attended oral argument, but died before a decision was issued.]

Justice Thomas, dissenting.

I join Justice Alito's dissent. As Justice Alito explains, the Court's decision today is irreconcilable with strict scrutiny, rests on pernicious assumptions about race, and departs from many of our precedents.

I write separately to reaffirm that "a State's use of race in higher education admissions decisions is categorically prohibited by the Equal Protection Clause." *Fisher I* (Thomas, J., concurring). The Constitution abhors classifications based on race because every time the government places citizens on racial registers and makes race relevant to the provision of burdens or benefits, it demeans us all. That constitutional imperative does not change in the face of a faddish theory that racial discrimination may produce educational benefits. The Court was wrong to hold otherwise in *Grutter v. Bollinger.* I would overrule *Grutter* and reverse the Fifth Circuit's judgment.

Justice Alito, with whom Chief Justice Roberts and Justice Thomas join, dissenting.

Something strange has happened since our prior decision in this case. In that decision, we held that strict scrutiny requires the University of Texas at Austin (UT or University) to show that its use of race and ethnicity in making admissions decisions serves compelling interests and that its plan is narrowly tailored to achieve those ends. . . . The University has still not identified with any degree of specificity the interests that its use of race and ethnicity is supposed to serve. Its primary argument is that merely invoking "the educational benefits of diversity" is sufficient and that it need not identify any metric that would allow a court to determine whether its plan is needed to serve, or is actually serving, those interests. This is nothing less than the plea for deference that we emphatically rejected in our prior decision. Today, however, the Court inexplicably grants that request.

To the extent that UT has ever moved beyond a plea for deference and identified the relevant interests in more specific terms, its efforts have been shifting, unpersuasive, and, at times, less than candid. When it adopted its race-based plan, UT said that the plan was needed to promote classroom diversity. [But the University does not indicate whether diversity is being achieved at the classroom level.] And although UT's records should permit it to determine without much difficulty whether holistic admittees are any more likely than students admitted through the Top Ten Percent Law, to enroll in the classes lacking racial or ethnic diversity, UT either has not crunched those numbers or has not revealed what they show. . . .

UT has also claimed at times that the race-based component of its plan is needed because the Top Ten Percent Plan admits the wrong kind of African-American and Hispanic students, namely, students from poor families who attend schools in which the student body is predominantly African-American or Hispanic. As UT put it in its brief in *Fisher I*, the race-based component of its admissions plan is needed to admit the African-American or Hispanic child of successful professionals in Dallas. . . . The assumption behind [this] reasoning is that most of the African-American and Hispanic students admitted under the race-neutral component of UT's plan were able to rank in the top decile of their high school classes only because they did not have to compete against white and Asian-American students. This insulting stereotype is not supported by the record. African-American and Hispanic students admitted under the Top Ten Percent Plan receive higher college grades than the African-American and Hispanic students admitted under the race-conscious program. . . .

I [Omitted.]

II

UT's race-conscious admissions program cannot satisfy strict scrutiny. . . .

A [Omitted]

B

. . . When UT adopted its challenged policy, it characterized its compelling interest as obtaining a critical mass of underrepresented minorities. [UT] claimed that the use of race-neutral policies and programs has not been successful in achieving a critical mass of racial diversity. But to this day, UT has not explained in anything other than the vaguest terms what it means by critical mass. . . . UT has insisted that critical mass is not an absolute number. Instead, UT prefers a deliberately malleable "we'll know it when we see it" notion of critical mass. It defines "critical mass" as "an adequate representation of minority students so that the educational benefits that can be derived from diversity can actually happen," and it declares that it "will know that it has reached critical mass" when it "sees the educational benefits happening." In other words: Trust us. . . .

To be sure, I agree with the majority that our precedents do not require UT to pinpoint an interest in enrolling a certain number of minority students. But in order for us to assess whether UT's program is narrowly tailored, the University must identify some sort of concrete interest. Classifying and assigning students according to race requires more than an amorphous end to justify it. . . . According to the majority, however, UT has articulated the following "concrete and precise" goals: "the destruction of stereotypes, the promotion of cross-racial understanding, the preparation of a student body for an increasingly diverse workforce and society, and the cultivation of a set of leaders with legitimacy in the eyes of the citizenry." These are laudable goals, but they are not concrete or precise, and they offer no limiting principle for the use of racial preferences. . . .

C

. . . [UT uses] a few crude, overly simplistic racial and ethnic categories. Under the UT plan, both the favored and the disfavored groups are broad and consist of students from enormously diverse backgrounds. Because crude measures of this sort threaten to reduce students to racial chits, UT's reliance on such measures further undermines any claim based on classroom diversity statistics.

For example, students labeled "Asian American," seemingly include individuals of Chinese, Japanese, Korean, Vietnamese, Cambodian, Hmong, Indian and other backgrounds comprising roughly 60% of the world's population. It would be ludicrous to suggest that all of these students have similar backgrounds and similar ideas and experiences to share. So why has UT lumped them together . . . ? UT has no good answer. And UT makes no effort to ensure that it has a critical mass of, say, "Filipino

Americans" or "Cambodian Americans." As long as there are a sufficient number of "Asian Americans," UT is apparently satisfied.

UT's failure to provide any definition of the various racial and ethnic groups is also revealing. UT does not specify what it means to be "African-American," "Hispanic," "Asian American," "Native American," or "White." And UT evidently labels each student as falling into only a single racial or ethnic group, without explaining how individuals with ancestors from different groups are to be characterized. . . . UT's crude classification system is ill suited for the more integrated country that we are rapidly becoming. . . .

D

Even assuming UT is correct that, under *Grutter*, it need only cite a generic interest in the educational benefits of diversity, its plan still fails strict scrutiny because it is not narrowly tailored. . . . The majority argues that [no race-neutral] alternative is a workable means for the University to attain the benefits of diversity it sought. Tellingly, however, the majority devotes only a single, conclusory sentence to the most obvious race-neutral alternative: race-blind, holistic review that considers the applicant's unique characteristics and personal circumstances. Under a system that combines the Top Ten Percent Plan with race-blind, holistic review, UT could still admit "the star athlete or musician whose grades suffered because of daily practices and training," the "talented young biologist who struggled to maintain above-average grades in humanities classes," and the "student whose freshman-year grades were poor because of a family crisis but who got herself back on track in her last three years of school." All of these unique circumstances can be considered without injecting race into the process. . . .

The fact that UT's racial preferences are unnecessary to achieve its stated goals is further demonstrated by their minimal effect on UT's diversity. In 2004, when race was not a factor, 3.6% of non-Top Ten Percent Texas enrollees were African-American and 11.6% were Hispanic. It would stand to reason that at least the same percentages of African-American and Hispanic students would have been admitted through holistic review in 2008 even if race were not a factor. If that assumption is correct, then race was determinative for only 15 African-American students and 18 Hispanic students in 2008 (representing 0.2% and 0.3%, respectively, of the total enrolled first-time freshmen from Texas high schools).

The majority contends that "the fact that race consciousness played a role in only a small portion of admissions decisions should be a hallmark of narrow tailoring, not evidence of unconstitutionality." This argument directly contradicts this Court's precedent. Because racial classifications are a highly suspect tool, they should be employed only as a last resort. Where, as here, racial preferences have only a slight impact on minority enrollment, a race-neutral alternative likely could have reached the same result . . . without gratuitously branding the covers of tens of thousands of applications with a bare racial stamp and telling each student he or she is to be defined by race.

III–IV [Omitted.]

2) *Affirmative Action in K–12 Schools:* PICS v. Seattle School District

The Rise and Fall of School Bussing. The process of desegregating public K–12 schools did not end with *Brown v. Board of Education* (1954) or *Cooper v. Aaron* (1958). Into the 1960s, many school districts, relying on the "all deliberate speed" language from *Brown II*, had made no meaningful change or only token efforts at desegregation. In addition, it was becoming clear that the removal of mandatory segregation laws would not by itself result in integrated schools in cities with highly segregated housing patterns. In a series of decisions in the mid-1960s, the Supreme Court began to insist on more speed. In *Green v. County School Board of New Kent County*, 391 U.S. 430 (1968), the Court declared that the Constitution forbade "dual school systems"—a term connoting districts that remained de facto segregated with racial separation of students, faculty, staff, transportation, extracurricular activities, and facilities.

Trial courts, carrying out their mission under *Brown II* and *Green* to oversee transitions from "dual" to "unitary" systems, began to order more extensive injunctions. *Swann v. Charlotte-Mecklenburg Board of Education*, 402 U.S. 1 (1971), upheld a trial court order that redrew a school district's assignment map and required bussing of students from one part of town to another. In a companion case, *North Carolina Board of Education v. Swann*, 402 U.S. 43 (1971), the Court found that a North Carolina anti-bussing statute was an unconstitutional interference with school districts' Fourteenth Amendment obligations to eliminate segregation.

Mandatory bussing proved to be enormously controversial throughout the 1970s and 1980s, since many families of all races objected to sending their children to distant schools. Bussing also could not prevent (and may have contributed to) a growing pattern of White flight, with White parents removing their children from urban public school systems and into private schools or suburban districts. A combination of Supreme Court decisions had effectively given constitutional protection to White flight. *Pierce v. Society of Sisters* (1925), Ch 8.C.2.c, had ruled that parents had a constitutional right to send their children to private schools, and *Milliken v. Bradley*, 418 U.S. 717 (1974), held that federal courts could not issue desegregation orders that applied across school district boundaries.

After the heyday of bussing, public school districts in cities with segregated housing patterns attempted other means to encourage families to select schools in a way that might result in more integration, including "magnet schools" and voluntary choice systems. Voluntary choice systems that included a racial tie-breaker were challenged in *Parents Involved in Community Schools v. Seattle School District* (2007) *(PICS)*, which consolidated appeals from Seattle, Washington and Jefferson County, Kentucky (outside Louisville).

ITEMS TO CONSIDER WHILE READING *PICS*:

A. *There is no majority opinion in* PICS. *Make a chart visualizing the different positions taken by the justices. Which should be considered the holding?*

B. *Work through the items from the Kickstarter. Specifically:*

1. *Is diversity of students in a classroom a compelling government interest after* PICS*? Is the answer different for universities than for K–12 schools?*
2. *What would make the Seattle plan narrowly tailored?*

C. *What race-conscious affirmative actions would Justice Roberts allow? Justice Kennedy? Justice Breyer?*

D. *All of the opinions in* PICS *claim to be faithful to Justice Harlan's dissent in* Plessy *and the unanimous decision in* Brown. *Which one is most faithful?*

Parents Involved in Community Schools v. Seattle School District No. 1,

551 U.S. 701 (2007)

Chief Justice Roberts announced the judgment of the Court, and delivered the opinion of the Court with respect to Parts I, II, III-A, and III-C, and an opinion with respect to Parts III-B and IV, in which Justice Scalia, Justice Thomas, and Justice Alito join.

The school districts in these cases voluntarily adopted student assignment plans that rely upon race to determine which public schools certain children may attend. The Seattle school district classifies children as white or nonwhite; the Jefferson County school district as black or "other." In Seattle, this racial classification is used to allocate slots in oversubscribed high schools. In Jefferson County, it is used to make certain elementary school assignments and to rule on transfer requests. In each case, the school district relies upon an individual student's race in assigning that student to a particular school, so that the racial balance at the school falls within a predetermined range based on the racial composition of the school district as a whole. Parents of students denied assignment to particular schools under these plans solely because of their race brought suit, contending that allocating children to different public schools on the basis of race violated the

Fourteenth Amendment guarantee of equal protection. The Courts of Appeals below upheld the plans. We granted certiorari, and now reverse.

I

. . .

A

Seattle School District No. 1 operates 10 regular public high schools. In 1998, it adopted the plan at issue in this case for assigning students to these schools. The plan allows incoming ninth graders to choose from among any of the district's high schools, ranking however many schools they wish in order of preference.

Some schools are more popular than others. If too many students list the same school as their first choice, the district employs a series of "tiebreakers" to determine who will fill the open slots at the oversubscribed school. The first tiebreaker selects for admission students who have a sibling currently enrolled in the chosen school. The next tiebreaker depends upon the racial composition of the particular school and the race of the individual student. In the district's public schools approximately 41 percent of enrolled students are white; the remaining 59 percent, comprising all other racial groups, are classified by Seattle for assignment purposes as nonwhite. If an oversubscribed school is not within 10 percentage points of the district's overall white/nonwhite racial balance, it is what the district calls "integration positive," and the district employs a tiebreaker that selects for assignment students whose race "will serve to bring the school into balance." If it is still necessary to select students for the school after using the racial tiebreaker, the next tiebreaker is the geographic proximity of the school to the student's residence.

Seattle has never operated segregated schools—legally separate schools for students of different races—nor has it ever been subject to court-ordered desegregation. It nonetheless employs the racial tiebreaker in an attempt to address the effects of racially identifiable housing patterns on school assignments. Most white students live in the northern part of Seattle, most students of other racial backgrounds in the southern part. Four of Seattle's high schools are located in the north—Ballard, Nathan Hale, Ingraham, and Roosevelt—and five in the south—Rainier Beach, Cleveland, West Seattle, Chief Sealth, and Franklin. One school—Garfield—is more or less in the center of Seattle.

For the 2000-2001 school year, five of these schools were oversubscribed—Ballard, Nathan Hale, Roosevelt, Garfield, and Franklin—so much so that 82 percent of incoming ninth graders ranked one of these schools as their first choice. Three of the oversubscribed schools were "integration positive" because the school's white enrollment the previous school year was greater than 51 percent—Ballard, Nathan Hale, and Roosevelt. Thus, more nonwhite students (107, 27, and 82, respectively) who selected one of these three schools as a top choice received placement at the school than would have been the case had race not been considered, and proximity been the next tiebreaker. Franklin was "integration positive" because its nonwhite enrollment the previous school year was greater than 69 percent; 89 more white students were assigned to Franklin by operation of the racial tiebreaker in the 2000–2001 school year than otherwise would have been. Garfield was the only oversubscribed school whose composition during the 1999–2000 school year was within the racial guidelines, although in previous years Garfield's enrollment had been predominantly nonwhite, and the racial tiebreaker had been used to give preference to white students.

Petitioner Parents Involved in Community Schools (Parents Involved) is a nonprofit corporation comprising the parents of children who have been or may be denied assignment to their chosen high school in the district because of their race. The concerns of Parents Involved are illustrated by Jill Kurfirst, who sought to enroll her ninth-grade son, Andy Meeks, in Ballard High School's special Biotechnology Career Academy. Andy suffered from attention deficit hyperactivity disorder and dyslexia, but had made good progress with hands-on instruction, and his mother and middle school teachers thought that the smaller biotechnology program held the most promise for his continued success. Andy was accepted into this selective program but, because of the racial tiebreaker, was denied assignment to Ballard High School. Parents Involved commenced this suit in the Western District of Washington, alleging that Seattle's use of race in assignments violated the Equal Protection Clause of the Fourteenth Amendment, Title VI of the Civil Rights Act of 1964, and the Washington Civil Rights Act.

The District Court granted summary judgment to the school district [and the Ninth Circuit affirmed.] . . . We granted certiorari.

B

[The facts of the Jefferson County case are omitted. Occasional references to them appear later in the opinion.]

II

[Plaintiffs have standing.]

III

A

Without attempting in these cases to set forth all the interests a school district might assert, it suffices to note that our prior cases, in evaluating the use of racial classifications in the school context, have recognized two interests that qualify as compelling. The first is the compelling interest of remedying the effects of past intentional discrimination. Yet the Seattle public schools have not shown that they were ever segregated by law, and were not subject to court-ordered desegregation decrees. . . .

The second government interest we have recognized as compelling for purposes of strict scrutiny is the interest in diversity in higher education upheld in *Grutter v. Bollinger* (2003). The specific interest found compelling in *Grutter* was student body diversity in the context of higher education. The diversity interest was not focused on race alone but encompassed all factors that may contribute to student body diversity. . . . The entire gist of the analysis in *Grutter* was that the admissions program at issue there focused on each applicant as an individual, and not simply as a member of a particular racial group. The classification of applicants by race upheld in *Grutter* was only as part of a "highly individualized, holistic review." As the Court explained, "the importance of this individualized consideration in the context of a race-conscious admissions program is paramount." The point of the narrow tailoring analysis in which the *Grutter* Court engaged was to ensure that the use of racial classifications was indeed part of a broader assessment of diversity, and not simply an effort to achieve racial balance, which the Court explained would be "patently unconstitutional."

In the present cases, by contrast, race is not considered as part of a broader effort to achieve exposure to widely diverse people, cultures, ideas, and viewpoints; race, for some students, is determinative standing alone. The districts argue that other factors, such as student preferences, affect assignment decisions under their plans, but under each plan when race comes into play, it is decisive by itself. It is not simply one factor weighed with others in reaching a decision, as in *Grutter*; it is *the* factor. Like the University of Michigan undergraduate plan struck down in *Gratz*, the plans here do not provide for a meaningful individualized review of applicants but instead rely on racial classifications in a nonindividualized, mechanical way.

Even when it comes to race, the plans here employ only a limited notion of diversity, viewing race exclusively in white/nonwhite terms in Seattle and black/"other" terms in Jefferson County. The Seattle "Board Statement Reaffirming Diversity Rationale" speaks of the "inherent educational value" in "providing students the opportunity to attend schools with diverse student enrollment." But under the Seattle plan, a school with 50 percent Asian-American students and 50 percent white students but no African-American, Native-American, or Latino students would qualify as balanced, while a school with 30 percent Asian-American, 25 percent African-American, 25 percent Latino, and 20 percent white students would not. It is hard to understand how a plan that could allow these results can be viewed as being concerned with achieving enrollment that is broadly diverse.

. . . In upholding the admissions plan in *Grutter*, . . . this Court relied upon considerations unique to institutions of higher education, noting that in light of the expansive freedoms of speech and thought associated with the university environment, universities occupy a special niche in our constitutional tradition. The Court explained that context matters in applying strict scrutiny, and repeatedly noted that it was addressing the use of race in the context of higher education. The Court in *Grutter* expressly articulated key limitations on its holding—defining a specific type of broad-based diversity and noting the unique context of higher education—but these limitations were largely disregarded by the lower courts in extending *Grutter* to uphold race-based assignments in elementary and secondary schools. The present cases are not governed by *Grutter*.

B

Perhaps recognizing that reliance on *Grutter* cannot sustain their plans, both school districts assert additional interests, distinct from the interest upheld in *Grutter*, to justify their race-based assignments. In briefing and argument before this Court, Seattle contends that its use of race helps to reduce racial concentration in schools and to ensure that racially concentrated housing patterns do not prevent nonwhite students from having access to the most desirable schools. . . . Each school district argues that educational and broader socialization benefits flow from a racially diverse learning environment, and each contends that because the diversity they seek is racial diversity—not the broader diversity at issue in *Grutter*—it makes sense to promote that interest directly by relying on race alone.

The parties and their amici dispute whether racial diversity in schools in fact has a marked impact on test scores and other objective yardsticks or achieves intangible socialization benefits. The debate is not one we need to resolve, however, because it is clear that the racial classifications employed by the districts are not narrowly tailored to the goal of achieving the educational and social benefits asserted to flow from racial diversity. In design and operation, the plans are directed only to racial balance, pure and simple, an objective this Court has repeatedly condemned as illegitimate.

The plans are tied to each district's specific racial demographics, rather than to any pedagogic concept of the level of diversity needed to obtain the asserted educational benefits. In Seattle, the district seeks white enrollment of between 31 and 51 percent (within 10 percent of "the district white average" of 41 percent), and nonwhite enrollment of between 49 and 69 percent (within 10 percent of "the district minority average" of 59 percent). . . . [T]he racial demographics in each district—whatever they happen to be—drive the required "diversity" numbers. The plans here are not tailored to achieving a degree of diversity necessary to realize the asserted educational benefits; instead the plans are tailored, in the words of Seattle's Manager of Enrollment Planning, Technical Support, and Demographics, to "the goal established by the school board of attaining a level of diversity within the schools that approximates the district's overall demographics." . . .

The principle that racial balancing is not permitted is one of substance, not semantics. Racial balancing is not transformed from "patently unconstitutional" to a compelling state interest simply by relabeling it "racial diversity." While the school districts use various verbal formulations to describe the interest they seek to promote—racial diversity, avoidance of racial isolation, racial integration—they offer no definition of the interest that suggests it differs from racial balance. . . .

C

The districts assert, as they must, that the way in which they have employed individual racial classifications is necessary to achieve their stated ends. The minimal effect these classifications have on student assignments, however, suggests that other means would be effective. Seattle's racial tiebreaker results, in the end, only in shifting a small number of students between schools. Approximately 307 student assignments were affected by the racial tiebreaker in 2000–2001; the district was able to track the enrollment status of 293 of these students. Of these, 209 were assigned to a school that was one of their choices, 87 of whom were assigned to the same school to which they would have been assigned without the racial tiebreaker. Eighty-four students were assigned to schools that they did not list as a choice, but 29 of those students would have been assigned to their respective school without the racial tiebreaker, and 3 were able to attend one of the oversubscribed schools due to waitlist and capacity adjustments. In over one-third of the assignments affected by the racial tiebreaker, then, the use of race in the end made no difference, and the district could identify only 52 students who were ultimately affected adversely by the racial tiebreaker in that it resulted in assignment to a school they had not listed as a preference and to which they would not otherwise have been assigned. . . .

While we do not suggest that greater use of race would be preferable, the minimal impact of the districts' racial classifications on school enrollment casts doubt on the necessity of using racial classifications. . . .

IV

. . . Justice Breyer's position comes down to a familiar claim: The end justifies the means. He admits that there is a cost in applying a state-mandated racial label, but he is confident that the cost is worth paying. Our established strict scrutiny test for racial classifications, however, insists on detailed examination, both as to ends and as to means. Simply because the school districts may seek a worthy goal does not mean they are free to discriminate on the basis of race to achieve it, or that their racial classifications should be subject to less exacting scrutiny. . . .

[CONCLUSION]

The parties and their amici debate which side is more faithful to the heritage of *Brown*, but the position of the plaintiffs in *Brown* was spelled out in their brief and could not have been clearer: "[T]he Fourteenth Amendment prevents states from according differential treatment to American children on the basis of their color or race." What do the racial classifications at issue here do, if not accord differential treatment on the basis of race? As counsel who appeared before this Court for the plaintiffs in *Brown* put it: "We have one fundamental contention which we will seek to develop in the course of this argument, and that contention is that no State has any authority under the equal-protection clause of the Fourteenth Amendment to use race as a factor in affording educational opportunities among its citizens." There is no ambiguity in that statement. And it was that position that prevailed in this Court, which emphasized in its remedial opinion [Brown II] that what was "at stake is the personal interest of the plaintiffs in admission to public schools as soon as practicable on a nondiscriminatory basis," and what was required was "determining admission to the public schools on a nonracial basis." What do the racial classifications do in these cases, if not determine admission to a public school on a racial basis?

Before *Brown*, schoolchildren were told where they could and could not go to school based on the color of their skin. The school districts in these cases have not carried the heavy burden of demonstrating that we should allow this once again—even for very different reasons. For schools that never segregated on the basis of race, such as Seattle, or that have removed the vestiges of past segregation, such as Jefferson County, the way to achieve a system of determining admission to the public schools on a nonracial basis, is to stop assigning students on a racial basis. The way to stop discrimination on the basis of race is to stop discriminating on the basis of race.

Justice Thomas, concurring. [Omitted.]

Justice Kennedy, concurring in part and concurring in the judgment.

. . . I agree with The Chief Justice that [plaintiffs have standing] and join Parts I and II of the Court's opinion. I also join Parts III-A and III-C for reasons provided below. My views do not allow me to join the balance of the opinion by The Chief Justice, which seems to me to be inconsistent in both its approach and its implications with the history, meaning, and reach of the Equal Protection Clause. Justice Breyer's dissenting opinion, on the other hand, rests on what in my respectful submission is a misuse and mistaken interpretation of our precedents. This leads it to advance propositions that, in my view, are both erroneous and in fundamental conflict with basic equal protection principles. As a consequence, this separate opinion is necessary to set forth my conclusions in the two cases before the Court.

I

. . . The dissent finds that the school districts have identified a compelling interest in increasing diversity, including for the purpose of avoiding racial isolation.

Parents Involved in Community Schools v. Seattle School District No. 1

The plurality, by contrast, does not acknowledge that the school districts have identified a compelling interest here. For this reason, among others, I do not join Parts III-B and IV. Diversity, depending on its meaning and definition, is a compelling educational goal a school district may pursue. . . .

[But the plans are not narrowly tailored. Seattle] has failed to make an adequate showing in at least one respect. It has failed to explain why, in a district composed of a diversity of races, with fewer than half of the students classified as "white," it has employed the crude racial categories of "white" and "non-white" as the basis for its assignment decisions.

The district has identified its purposes as follows: "(1) to promote the educational benefits of diverse school enrollments; (2) to reduce the potentially harmful effects of racial isolation by allowing students the opportunity to opt out of racially isolated schools; and (3) to make sure that racially segregated housing patterns did not prevent non-white students from having equitable access to the most popular over-subscribed schools." Yet the school district does not explain how, in the context of its diverse student population, a blunt distinction between "white" and "non-white" furthers these goals. . . . Other problems are evident in Seattle's system, but there is no need to address them now. As the district fails to account for the classification system it has chosen, despite what appears to be its ill fit, Seattle has not shown its plan to be narrowly tailored to achieve its own ends; and thus it fails to pass strict scrutiny.

II

. . . [P]arts of the opinion by The Chief Justice imply an all-too-unyielding insistence that race cannot be a factor in instances when, in my view, it may be taken into account. . . . The plurality opinion is at least open to the interpretation that the Constitution requires school districts to ignore the problem of *de facto* resegregation in schooling. I cannot endorse that conclusion. To the extent the plurality opinion suggests the Constitution mandates that state and local school authorities must accept the status quo of racial isolation in schools, it is, in my view, profoundly mistaken.

The statement by Justice Harlan that "our Constitution is color-blind" was most certainly justified in the context of his dissent in *Plessy v. Ferguson* (1896). The Court's decision in that case was a grievous error it took far too long to overrule. *Plessy*, of course, concerned official classification by race applicable to all persons who sought to use railway carriages. And, as an aspiration, Justice Harlan's axiom must command our assent. In the real world, it is regrettable to say, it cannot be a universal constitutional principle.

In the administration of public schools by the state and local authorities it is permissible to consider the racial makeup of schools and to adopt general policies to encourage a diverse student body, one aspect of which is its racial composition.

If school authorities are concerned that the student-body compositions of certain schools interfere with the objective of offering an equal educational opportunity to all of their students, they are free to devise race-conscious measures to address the problem in a general way and without treating each student in different fashion solely on the basis of a systematic, individual typing by race.

School boards may pursue the goal of bringing together students of diverse backgrounds and races through other means, including strategic site selection of new schools; drawing attendance zones with general recognition of the demographics of neighborhoods; allocating resources for special programs; recruiting students and faculty in a targeted fashion; and tracking enrollments, performance, and other statistics by race. These mechanisms are race conscious but do not lead to different treatment based on a classification that tells each student he or she is to be defined by race, so it is unlikely any of them would demand strict scrutiny to be found permissible. Executive and legislative branches, which for generations now have considered these types of policies and procedures, should be permitted to employ them with candor and with confidence that a constitutional violation does not occur whenever a decisionmaker considers the impact a given approach might have on students of different races. Assigning to each student a personal designation according to a crude system of individual racial classifications is quite a different matter; and the legal analysis changes accordingly. . . .

III

The dissent rests on the assumptions that these sweeping race-based classifications of persons are permitted by existing precedents; that its confident endorsement of race categories for each child in a large segment of the community presents no danger to individual freedom in other, prospective realms of governmental regulation; and that the racial classifications used here cause no hurt or anger of the type the Constitution prevents. Each of these premises is, in my respectful view, incorrect. . . .

A—B [Omitted.]

C

. . . Though this may oversimplify the matter a bit, one of the main concerns underlying [some recent opinions in this area by Court of Appeals judges] was this: If it is legitimate for school authorities to work to avoid racial isolation in their schools, must they do so only by indirection and general policies? Does the Constitution mandate this inefficient result? Why may the authorities not recognize the problem in candid fashion and solve it altogether through resort to direct assignments based on student racial classifications? So, the argument proceeds, if race is the problem, then perhaps race is the solution.

The argument ignores the dangers presented by individual classifications, dangers that are not as pressing when the same ends are achieved by more indirect means. When the government classifies an individual by race, it must first define what it means to be of a race. Who exactly is white and who is nonwhite? To be forced to live under a state-mandated racial label is inconsistent with the dignity of individuals in our society. And it is a label that an individual is powerless to change. Governmental classifications that command people to march in different directions based on racial typologies can cause a new divisiveness. The practice can lead to corrosive discourse, where race serves not as an element of our diverse heritage but instead as a bargaining chip in the political process. On the other hand race-conscious measures that do not rely on differential treatment based on individual classifications present these problems to a lesser degree. . . .

[CONCLUSION]

. . . The decision today should not prevent school districts from continuing the important work of bringing together students of different racial, ethnic, and economic backgrounds. Due to a variety of factors—some influenced by government, some not—neighborhoods in our communities do not reflect the diversity of our Nation as a whole. Those entrusted with directing our public schools can bring to bear the creativity of experts, parents, administrators, and other concerned citizens to find a way to achieve the compelling interests they face without resorting to widespread governmental allocation of benefits and burdens on the basis of racial classifications.

Justice Stevens, dissenting.

While I join Justice Breyer's eloquent and unanswerable dissent in its entirety, it is appropriate to add these words.

There is a cruel irony in The Chief Justice's reliance on our decision in *Brown v. Board of Education*. The first sentence in the concluding paragraph of his opinion states: "Before *Brown*, schoolchildren were told where they could and could not go to school based on the color of their skin." This sentence reminds me of Anatole France's observation: "The majestic equality of the law forbids rich and poor alike to sleep under the bridges, to beg in the streets, and to steal their bread." The Chief Justice fails to note that it was only black schoolchildren who were so ordered; indeed, the history books do not tell stories of white children struggling to attend black schools. In this and other ways, The Chief Justice rewrites the history of one of this Court's most important decisions. . . .

The Court has changed significantly since it decided [a case upholding a Massachusetts school desegregation plan] in 1968. It was then more faithful to *Brown* and more respectful of our precedent than it is today. It is my firm conviction that no Member of the Court that I joined in 1975 would have agreed with today's decision.

Justice Breyer, with whom Justices Stevens, Souter, and Ginsburg join, dissenting.

These cases consider the longstanding efforts of two local school boards to integrate their public schools. The school board plans before us resemble many others adopted in the last 50 years by primary and secondary schools throughout the Nation. All of those plans represent local efforts to bring about the kind of racially integrated education that *Brown v. Board of Education* long ago promised—efforts that this Court has repeatedly required, permitted, and encouraged local authorities to undertake. This Court has recognized that the public interests at stake in such cases are "compelling." We have approved of "narrowly tailored" plans that are no less race conscious than the plans before us. And we have understood that the Constitution permits local communities to adopt desegregation plans even where it does not require them to do so.

The plurality pays inadequate attention to this law, to past opinions' rationales, their language, and the contexts in which they arise. As a result, it reverses course and reaches the wrong conclusion. In doing so, it distorts precedent, it misapplies the relevant constitutional principles, it announces legal rules that will obstruct efforts by state and local governments to deal effectively with the growing resegregation of public schools, it threatens to substitute for present calm a disruptive round of race-related litigation, and it undermines *Brown*'s promise of integrated primary and secondary education that local communities have sought to make a reality. This cannot be justified in the name of the Equal Protection Clause.

I

Facts [Omitted.]

II

The Legal Standard

A longstanding and unbroken line of legal authority tells us that the Equal Protection Clause permits local school boards to use race-conscious criteria to achieve positive race-related goals, even when the Constitution does not compel it. Because of its importance, I shall repeat what this Court said about the matter in *Swann v. Charlotte-Mecklenburg Board of Education*, 402 U.S. 1 (1971). Chief Justice Burger, on behalf of a unanimous Court in a case of exceptional importance, wrote:

> School authorities are traditionally charged with broad power to formulate and implement educational policy and might well conclude, for example, that in order to prepare students to live in a pluralistic society each school should have a prescribed ratio of Negro to white students reflecting the proportion for the district as a whole. To do this as an educational policy is within the broad discretionary powers of school authorities.

The statement was not a technical holding in the case. But the Court set forth in *Swann* a basic principle of constitutional law—a principle of law that has found wide acceptance in the legal culture.

Thus, in *North Carolina Board of Education v. Swann*, 402 U.S. 43 (1971), this Court, citing *Swann*, restated the point. "School authorities," the Court said, "have wide discretion in formulating school policy, and as a matter of educational policy school authorities may well conclude that some kind of racial balance in the schools is desirable quite apart from any constitutional requirements." Then-Justice Rehnquist echoed this view in *Bustop, Inc. v. Los Angeles Board of Education*, 439 U.S. 1380 (1978) (opinion in chambers), making clear that he too believed that *Swann*'s statement reflected settled law: "While I have the gravest doubts that a state supreme court was required by the United States Constitution to take the desegregation action that it has taken in this case, I have very little doubt that it was permitted by that Constitution to take such action." These statements nowhere suggest that this freedom is limited to school districts where court-ordered desegregation measures are also in effect. . . .

Courts are not alone in accepting as constitutionally valid the legal principle that *Swann* enunciated—i.e., that the government may voluntarily adopt race-conscious measures to improve conditions of race even when it is not under a constitutional obligation to do so. That principle has been accepted by every branch of government and is rooted in the history of the Equal Protection Clause itself. Thus, Congress has enacted numerous race-conscious statutes that illustrate that principle or rely upon its validity. See, e.g., No Child Left Behind Act of 2001 (authorizing aid to minority institutions). In fact, without being exhaustive, I have counted 51 federal statutes that use racial classifications. I have counted well over 100 state statutes that similarly employ racial classifications. Presidential administrations for the past half century have used and supported various race-conscious measures. See, e.g., Exec. Order No. 10925 (1961) (President Kennedy); Exec. Order No. 11246 (1965) (President Johnson). And during the same time, hundreds of local school districts have adopted student assignment plans that use race-conscious criteria.

That *Swann*'s legal statement should find such broad acceptance is not surprising. For *Swann* is predicated upon a well-established legal view of the Fourteenth Amendment. That view understands the basic objective of those who wrote the Equal Protection Clause as forbidding practices that lead to racial exclusion. The Amendment sought to bring into American society as full members those whom the Nation had previously held in slavery.

There is reason to believe that those who drafted an Amendment with this basic purpose in mind would have understood the legal and practical difference between the use of race-conscious criteria in defiance of that purpose, namely to keep the races apart, and the use of race-conscious criteria to further that purpose, namely to bring the races together. Although the Constitution almost always forbids the former, it is significantly more lenient in respect to the latter. . . .

These and related considerations convinced one Ninth Circuit judge in the Seattle case to apply a standard of constitutionality review that is less than "strict," and to conclude that this Court's precedents do not require the contrary. ("That a student is denied the school of his choice may be disappointing, but it carries no racial stigma and says nothing at all about that individual's aptitude or ability"). That judge is not alone. . . .

In my view, this contextual approach to scrutiny is altogether fitting. I believe that the law requires application here of a standard of review that is not "strict" in the traditional sense of that word, although it does require the careful review I have just described. Apparently Justice Kennedy also agrees that strict scrutiny would not apply in respect to certain "race-conscious" school board policies.

Nonetheless, in light of *Grutter* and other precedents, *see, e.g., Bakke* (opinion of Powell, J.), . . . I shall apply the version of strict scrutiny that those cases embody. I shall consequently ask whether the school boards in Seattle and Louisville adopted these plans to serve a "compelling governmental interest" and, if so, whether the plans are "narrowly tailored" to achieve that interest. If the plans survive this strict review, they would survive less exacting review a fortiori. Hence, I conclude that the plans before us pass both parts of the strict scrutiny test. Consequently I must conclude that the plans here are permitted under the Constitution.

III
Applying the Legal Standard

A
Compelling Interest

The principal interest advanced in these cases to justify the use of race-based criteria goes by various names. Sometimes a court refers to it as an interest in achieving racial "diversity." Other times a court, like the plurality here, refers to it as an interest in racial "balancing." I have used more general terms to signify that interest, describing it, for example, as an interest in promoting or preserving greater racial "integration" of public schools. By this term, I mean the school districts' interest in eliminating school-by-school racial isolation and increasing the degree to which racial mixture characterizes each of the district's schools and each individual student's public school experience.

Regardless of its name, however, the interest at stake possesses three essential elements. First, there is a historical and remedial element: an interest in setting right the consequences of prior conditions of segregation. This refers back to a time when public schools were highly segregated, often as a result of legal or administrative policies that facilitated racial segregation in public schools. It is an interest in continuing to combat the remnants of segregation caused in whole or in part by these school-related policies, which have often affected not only schools, but also housing patterns, employment practices, economic conditions, and social attitudes. It is an interest in maintaining hard-won gains. And it has its roots in preventing what gradually may become the de facto resegregation of America's public schools.

Second, there is an educational element: an interest in overcoming the adverse educational effects produced by and associated with highly segregated schools. Studies suggest that children taken from those schools and placed in integrated settings often show positive academic gains. Other studies reach different conclusions. But the evidence supporting an educational interest in racially integrated schools is well established and strong enough to permit a democratically elected school board reasonably to determine that this interest is a compelling one. . . .

Third, there is a democratic element: an interest in producing an educational environment that reflects the pluralistic society in which our children will live. It is an interest in helping our children learn to work and play together with children of different racial backgrounds. It is an interest in teaching children to engage in the kind of cooperation among Americans of all races that is necessary to make a land of 300 million people one Nation. . . .

In light of this Court's conclusions in *Grutter*, the "compelling" nature of these interests in the context of primary and secondary public education follows here *a fortiori*. Primary and secondary schools are where the education of this Nation's children begins, where each of us begins to absorb those values we carry with us to the end of our days. As Justice Marshall said, "unless our children begin to learn together, there is little hope that our people will ever learn to live together." *Milliken v. Bradley*, 418 U.S. 717 (1974) (dissenting opinion).

And it was *Brown*, after all, focusing upon primary and secondary schools, not *Sweatt v. Painter*, 339 U.S. 629 (1950), focusing on law schools, or *McLaurin v. Oklahoma State Regents for Higher Ed.*, 339 U.S. 637 (1950), focusing on graduate schools, that affected so deeply not only Americans but the world. Hence, I am not surprised that Justice Kennedy finds that "a district may consider it a compelling interest to achieve a diverse student population," including a racially diverse population. . . .

B

Narrow Tailoring

I next ask whether the plans before us are "narrowly tailored" to achieve these "compelling" objectives. I shall not accept the school boards' assurances on faith, and I shall subject the tailoring of their plans to rigorous judicial review. Several factors, taken together, nonetheless lead me to conclude that the boards' use of race-conscious criteria in these plans passes even the strictest "tailoring" test.

First, the race-conscious criteria at issue only help set the outer bounds of broad ranges. They constitute but one part of plans that depend primarily upon other, nonracial elements. To use race in this way is not to set a forbidden quota. . . .

Second, broad-range limits on voluntary school choice plans are less burdensome, and hence more narrowly tailored, than other race-conscious restrictions this Court has previously approved [that involved mandatory bussing]. Indeed, the plans before us are more narrowly tailored than the race-conscious admission plans that this Court approved in *Grutter*. Here, race becomes a factor only in a fraction of students' non-merit-based assignments—not in large numbers of students' merit-based applications. Moreover, the effect of applying race-conscious criteria here affects potentially disadvantaged students less severely, not more severely, than the criteria at issue in *Grutter*. Disappointed students are not rejected from a State's flagship graduate program; they simply attend a different one of the district's many public schools, which in aspiration and in fact are substantially equal. And, in Seattle, the disadvantaged student loses at most one year at the high school of his choice. One will search *Grutter* in vain for similarly persuasive evidence of narrow tailoring as the school districts have presented here.

Third, the manner in which the school boards developed these plans itself reflects "narrow tailoring." Each plan was devised to overcome a history of segregated public schools. Each plan embodies the results of local experience and community consultation. Each plan is the product of a process that has sought to enhance student choice, while diminishing the need for mandatory busing. And each plan's use of race-conscious elements is diminished compared to the use of race in preceding integration plans. . . .

Finally, I recognize that the Court seeks to distinguish *Grutter* from these cases by claiming that *Grutter* arose in the context of higher education. But that is not a meaningful legal distinction. I have explained why I do not believe the Constitution could possibly find "compelling" the provision of a racially diverse education for a 23-year-old law student but not for a 13-year-old high school pupil. And I have explained how the plans before us are more narrowly tailored than those in *Grutter*. I add that one cannot find a relevant distinction in the fact that these school districts did not examine the merits of applications individually. The context here does not involve admission by merit; a child's academic, artistic, and athletic "merits" are not at all relevant to the child's placement. These are not affirmative action plans, and hence "individualized scrutiny" is simply beside the point.

The upshot is that these plans' specific features—(1) their limited and historically diminishing use of race, (2) their strong reliance upon other non-race-conscious elements, (3) their history and the manner in which the districts developed and modified their approach, (4) the comparison with prior plans, and (5) the lack of reasonably evident alternatives—together show that the districts' plans are "narrowly tailored" to achieve their "compelling" goals. In sum, the districts' race-conscious plans satisfy "strict scrutiny" and are therefore lawful.

IV

Direct Precedent [Omitted.]

V

Consequences [Omitted.]

VI

Conclusions

. . . Finally, what of the hope and promise of *Brown*? For much of this Nation's history, the races remained divided. It was not long ago that people of different races drank from separate fountains, rode on separate buses, and studied in separate schools. In this Court's finest hour, *Brown v. Board of Education* challenged this history and helped to change it. For *Brown* held out a promise. It was a promise embodied in three Amendments designed to make citizens of slaves. It was the promise of true racial equality—not as a matter of fine words on paper, but as a matter of everyday life in the Nation's cities and schools. It was about the nature of a democracy that must work for all Americans. It sought one law, one Nation, one people, not simply as a matter of legal principle but in terms of how we actually live. . . .

The last half century has witnessed great strides toward racial equality, but we have not yet realized the promise of *Brown*. To invalidate the plans under review is to threaten the promise of *Brown*. The plurality's position, I fear, would break that promise. This is a decision that the Court and the Nation will come to regret. I must dissent.

D. The Fundamental Rights Prong

Skinner v. Oklahoma (1942) introduced the idea that courts should use strict scrutiny for laws that unequally distribute fundamental rights—even if the laws do not rely on suspect classifications. This concept remains part of modern equal protection law.

The fundamental rights prong of equal protection gives constitutional protection to some unenumerated rights, a trait it shares with substantive due process. See Ch. 20. As a result, it has been subjected to similar criticisms. For example, *Shapiro v. Thompson*, 394 U.S. 618 (1969), relied on the doctrine to invalidate laws that unequally distributed the right of interstate travel (a right the majority deemed fundamental as a result of reasoning that relied on precedent, constitutional structure, history, consequences, and values). Justice Harlan's dissent said: "I know of nothing which entitles this Court to pick out particular human activities, characterize them as 'fundamental,' and give them added protection under an unusually stringent equal protection test." Because "virtually every state statute affects important rights," he said, the doctrine "would go far toward making this Court a super-legislature."

Justice Stewart responded in a concurring opinion: "The Court today does not 'pick out particular human activities, characterize them as 'fundamental,' and give them added protection.' To the contrary, the Court simply recognizes, as it must, an established constitutional right [to interstate travel], and gives to that right no less protection than the Constitution itself demands."

1. Unequal Distribution of Voting Rights: *Harper v. Virginia State Board of Elections*

Harper held that the ability to vote in state elections was a fundamental right that could be distributed unequally only on bases that satisfy heightened scrutiny. Although that result seems intuitive today, it is not a simple question in light of the Constitution's text.

Constitutional Text Relating to Voting. When drafted, the US Constitution envisioned that the new national government would be a republic—a representative democracy—and that the States would be republics as well. See Art. IV, § 4 (Congress has an enumerated power to "guarantee to every State in this Union a republican form of government.") Yet alongside this founding-era commitment to representative democracy was the reality that voting rights were far from universal, with each state granting the vote to far less than half of its adult citizens. See Ch. 3.B.2.a.

The 1787 Constitution contained no language declaring who was eligible to vote. Instead, that was to be a state-level decision. If a state allowed a person to vote for its state house of representatives, then that person could vote for the US House of Representatives. Art. I, § 2, cl. 1. (The Seventeenth Amendment, ratified in 1913, adopted the same approach for the US Senate.) Thus, if a state chose to limit the vote only to propertied White males, it could do so, and for many decades states did just that.

After the Civil War and into the 20th Century, four Voting Rights Amendments were ratified that for the first time directly limited states' power to set voting qualifications. Under the Fifteenth, Nineteenth, Twenty-Fourth, and Twenty-Sixth Amendments, a state may not deny the right to vote on the basis of race, sex, and other enumerated characteristics. These Amendments leave undisturbed a state's ability to restrict the vote for other reasons. The potential for variation can be seen most clearly today for people convicted of felonies: some states never disenfranchise felons; some states permanently disenfranchise them; and most fall somewhere in between.

Poll Taxes as a Qualification for Voting. In the Framers' time, a poll tax was another name for a capitation—a tax per person. See Ch. 3.B.2.b. Congress has never imposed a national capitation, but many states once relied on them as ordinary sources of revenue. Starting in the 1880s and 1890s, many states enacted laws depriving the right to vote for anyone whose poll taxes were not paid in full. By and large, the laws were designed to disenfranchise black voters, although they also affected people of any race who lived in sufficient poverty. In *Breedlove v. Suttles*, 302 U.S. 277 (1937), the Supreme Court unanimously upheld a Georgia law that made payment of the $1 annual poll tax a precondition for voting. "[The] privilege of voting is not derived from the United States [Constitution], but is conferred by the state," the Court said. "Save as restrained by the Fifteenth and Nineteenth Amendments and other provisions of the Federal Constitution, the state may condition suffrage as it deems appropriate."

Poll taxes as a qualification for voting became less politically popular in the decades after *Breedlove*, until the practice was restricted by § 1 of the Twenty-Fourth Amendment (ratified 1964), which reads as follows:

> The right of citizens of the United States to vote in any primary or other election for President or Vice President, for electors for President or Vice President, or for Senator or Representative in Congress, shall not be denied or abridged by the United States or any state by reason of failure to pay any poll tax or other tax.

The plain language of the 24th Amendment banned poll taxes as a voting qualification for federal elections, but was silent about state elections. For that reason, challenges to state-level poll tax qualifications relied on different constitutional provisions. *Harper v. Virginia State Board of Elections* consolidated two different challenges. One, brought by civil rights activist Evelyn Butts of Norfolk, emphasized race discrimination theories: She argued that Virginia's poll tax qualification violated the Equal Protection Clause and the Fifteenth Amendment because of its intentionally designed racially disparate impact. The other, brought by citizens from Fairfax County (Annie Harper, Gladys Berry, Curtis Burr, and Myrtle Burr), made a race-neutral argument that the law unequally distributed a fundamental right.

ITEMS TO CONSIDER WHILE READING *HARPER*:

A. *Work through the items from the Kickstarter. Specifically, since the US Constitution does not itself guarantee a right to vote, what makes voting a "fundamental" right for purposes of the 14th Amendment? Consider various methods of reasoning, such as text, precedent, structure, history, consequences, and values.*

B. *If the Equal Protection Clause (ratified in 1866) forbids the use of poll taxes as a qualification for voting, what function is served by the 24th Amendment (ratified in 1964)?*

C. *How would* Harper *be decided differently under a race discrimination theory? Why might the Court have preferred a fundamental rights theory?*

D. *The dissenters argue that this is* Lochner *all over again. Are they right?*

Harper v. Virginia State Board of Elections,

383 U.S. 663 (1966)

Justice Douglas delivered the opinion of the Court [joined by Chief Justice Warren and Justices Clark, Brennan, White, and Fortas].

These are suits by Virginia residents to have declared unconstitutional Virginia's poll tax [of $1.50]. The . . . District Court, feeling bound by our decision in *Breedlove v. Suttles*, 302 U.S. 277 (1937), dismissed the complaint. The cases came here on appeal . . .

While the right to vote in federal elections is conferred by Art. I, § 2, of the Constitution, the right to vote in state elections is nowhere expressly mentioned. It is argued that the right to vote in state elections is implicit, particularly by reason of the First Amendment and that it may not constitutionally be conditioned upon the payment of a tax or fee. We do not stop to canvass the relation between voting and political expression. For it is enough to say that once the franchise is granted to the electorate, lines may not be drawn which are inconsistent with the Equal Protection Clause of the Fourteenth Amendment. That is to say, the right of suffrage is subject to the imposition of state standards which are not discriminatory and which do not contravene any restriction that Congress, acting pursuant to its constitutional powers, has imposed. . . .

We conclude that a State violates the Equal Protection Clause of the Fourteenth Amendment whenever it makes the affluence of the voter or payment of any fee an electoral standard. Voter qualifications have no relation to wealth nor to paying or not paying this or any other tax. Our cases demonstrate that the Equal Protection Clause of the Fourteenth Amendment restrains the States from fixing voter qualifications which invidiously discriminate. . . .

Long ago in *Yick Wo v. Hopkins* (1886), the Court referred to "the political franchise of voting" as a "fundamental political right, because [it is] preservative of all rights." Recently in *Reynolds v. Sims*, 377 U.S. 533 (1964), we said, "Undoubtedly, the right of suffrage is a fundamental matter in a free and democratic society.

Harper v. Virginia State Board of Elections

Especially since the right to exercise the franchise in a free and unimpaired manner is preservative of other basic civil and political rights, any alleged infringement of the right of citizens to vote must be carefully and meticulously scrutinized." There we were considering charges that voters in one part of the State had greater representation per person in the State Legislature than voters in another part of the State. We concluded:

> A citizen, a qualified voter, is no more nor no less so because he lives in the city or on the farm. This is the clear and strong command of our Constitution's Equal Protection Clause. This is an essential part of the concept of a government of laws and not men. This is at the heart of Lincoln's vision of "government of the people, by the people, and for the people." The Equal Protection Clause demands no less than substantially equal state legislative representation for all citizens, of all places as well as of all races.

We say the same whether the citizen, otherwise qualified to vote, has $1.50 in his pocket or nothing at all, pays the fee or fails to pay it. The principle that denies the State the right to dilute a citizen's vote on account of his economic status or other such factors by analogy bars a system which excludes those unable to pay a fee to vote or who fail to pay.

It is argued that a State may exact fees from citizens for many different kinds of licenses; that if it can demand from all an equal fee for a driver's license, it can demand from all an equal poll tax for voting. But we must remember that the interest of the State, when it comes to voting, is limited to the power to fix qualifications. Wealth, like race, creed, or color, is not germane to one's ability to participate intelligently in the electoral process. Lines drawn on the basis of wealth or property, like those of race, *Korematsu v. United States* (1944), are traditionally disfavored. To introduce wealth or payment of a fee as a measure of a voter's qualifications is to introduce a capricious or irrelevant factor. The degree of the discrimination is irrelevant. In this context—that is, as a condition of obtaining a ballot—the requirement of fee paying causes an "invidious" discrimination, *Skinner v. State of Oklahoma* (1942), that runs afoul of the Equal Protection Clause. Levy "by the poll," is an old familiar form of taxation; and we say nothing to impair its validity so long as it is not made a condition to the exercise of the franchise. *Breedlove v. Suttles* sanctioned its use as a prerequisite of voting. To that extent the *Breedlove* case is overruled.

We agree, of course, with Mr. Justice Holmes that the Due Process Clause of the Fourteenth Amendment "does not enact Mr. Herbert Spencer's *Social Statics*." *Lochner v. New York* (1905) (dissenting). Likewise, the Equal Protection Clause is not shackled to the political theory of a particular era. In determining what lines are unconstitutionally discriminatory, we have never been confined to historic notions of equality, any more than we have restricted due process to a fixed catalogue of what was at a given time deemed to be the limits of fundamental rights. Notions of what constitutes equal treatment for purposes of the Equal Protection Clause do change. This Court in 1896 held that laws providing for separate public facilities for white and Negro citizens did not deprive the latter of the equal protection and treatment that the Fourteenth Amendment commands. *Plessy v. Ferguson*. Seven of the eight Justices then sitting subscribed to the Court's opinion, thus joining in expressions of what constituted unequal and discriminatory treatment that sound strange to a contemporary ear. When, in 1954—more than a half-century later—we repudiated the "separate-but-equal" doctrine of *Plessy* as respects public education we stated: "In approaching this problem, we cannot turn the clock back to 1868 when the Amendment was adopted, or even to 1896 when *Plessy v. Ferguson* was written." *Brown v. Board of Education* (1954). . . .

We have long been mindful that where fundamental rights and liberties are asserted under the Equal Protection Clause, classifications which might invade or restrain them must be closely scrutinized and carefully confined.

Those principles apply here. For to repeat, wealth or fee paying has, in our view, no relation to voting qualifications; the right to vote is too precious, too fundamental to be so burdened or conditioned.

Justice Black, dissenting. [Omitted.]

Justice Harlan, whom Justice Stewart joins, dissenting.

The final demise of state poll taxes, already totally proscribed by the Twenty-Fourth Amendment with respect to federal elections and abolished by the States themselves in all but four States with respect to state elections, is perhaps in itself not of great moment. But that fact that the *coup de grace* has been administered by this Court instead of being left to the affected States or to the federal political process should be a matter of continuing concern to all interested in maintaining the proper role of this tribunal under our scheme of government. . . .

Property qualifications and poll taxes have been a traditional part of our political structure. In the Colonies the franchise was generally a restricted one. Over the years these and other restrictions were gradually lifted, primarily because popular theories of political representation had changed. Often restrictions were lifted only after wide public debate. The issue of woman suffrage, for example, raised questions of family relationships, of participation in public affairs, of the very nature of the type of society in which Americans wished to live; eventually a consensus was reached, which culminated in the Nineteenth Amendment no more than 45 years ago.

Similarly with property qualifications, it is only by fiat that it can be said, especially in the context of American history, that there can be no rational debate as to their advisability. Most of the early Colonies had them; many of the States have had them during much of their histories; and, whether one agrees or not, arguments have been and still can be made in favor of them. . . . These viewpoints, to be sure, ring hollow on most contemporary ears. . . .

Harper v. Virginia State Board of Elections

Property and poll-tax qualifications, very simply, are not in accord with current egalitarian notions of how a modern democracy should be organized. It is of course entirely fitting that legislatures should modify the law to reflect such changes in popular attitudes. However, it is all wrong, in my view, for the Court to adopt the political doctrines popularly accepted at a particular moment of our history and to declare all others to be irrational and invidious, barring them from the range of choice by reasonably minded people acting through the political process. It was not too long ago that Mr. Justice Holmes felt impelled to remind the Court that the Due Process Clause of the Fourteenth Amendment does not enact the laissez-faire theory of society. *Lochner*. The times have changed, and perhaps it is appropriate to observe that neither does the Equal Protection Clause of that Amendment rigidly impose upon America an ideology of unrestrained egalitarianism.[FN11]

FN11 Justice Holmes' admonition [in his *Lochner* dissent] is particularly appropriate: "Some of these laws embody convictions or prejudices which judges are likely to share. Some may not. But a Constitution is not intended to embody a particular economic theory, whether of paternalism and the organic relation of the citizen to the state or of laissez faire. It is made for people of fundamentally differing views, and the accident of our finding certain opinions natural and familiar, or novel, and even shocking, ought not to conclude our judgment upon the question whether statutes embodying them conflict with the Constitution of the United States."

2. Unequal Distribution of Educational Opportunity: *San Antonio Independent School District v. Rodriguez*

In the early 1970s, class actions suits were filed in many states alleging that disparities between rich and poor public school districts within a state constituted a denial of equal protection. These challenges invoked two strands of equal protection argument: suspect classification and unequal distribution of a fundamental right. The California Supreme Court found that funding disparities violated the Fourteenth Amendment's Equal Protection Clause, *Serrano v. Priest*, 487 P.2d 1241 (Cal. 1971), and a federal trial court ruled similarly in Texas. In *Rodriguez*, the US Supreme Court took review of the Texas case.

ITEMS TO CONSIDER WHILE READING *RODRIGUEZ*:

A. *Work through the items from the Kickstarter. Specifically:*

1. *Is* Rodriguez *a race case?*

2. *Is wealth a suspect classification? Is* Rodriguez *consistent with* Harper *on this point?*

3. *Is free education a fundamental right? Is* Rodriguez *consistent with* Meyer *and* Pierce *on this point?*

B. *How would Justice Marshall decide whether a right is fundamental? How does this differ from the majority's approach?*

San Antonio Independent School District v. Rodriguez,

411 U.S. 1 (1973)

Justice Powell delivered the opinion of the Court [joined by Chief Justice Burger, and Justices Stewart, Blackmun, and Rehnquist].

This suit attacking the Texas system of financing public education was initiated by Mexican-American parents whose children attend the elementary and secondary schools in the Edgewood Independent School District, an urban school district in San Antonio, Texas. They brought a class action on behalf of schoolchildren throughout the State who are members of minority groups or who are poor and reside in school districts having a low property tax base. . . . [The trial court found] the Texas school finance system unconstitutional under the Equal Protection Clause of the Fourteenth Amendment. The State appealed, and we noted probable jurisdiction to consider the far-reaching constitutional questions presented. For the reasons stated in this opinion, we reverse the decision of the District Court.

I

. . . Until recent times, Texas was a predominantly rural State and its population and property wealth were spread relatively evenly across the State. Sizable differences in the value of assessable property between local school districts became increasingly evident as the State became more industrialized and as rural-to-urban population shifts became more pronounced. The location of commercial and industrial property began to play a significant role in determining the amount of tax resources available to each school district. These growing disparities in population and taxable property between districts were responsible in part for increasingly notable differences in levels of local expenditure for education. . . .

The school district in which appellees reside, the Edgewood Independent School District, has been compared throughout this litigation with the Alamo Heights Independent School District. This comparison between the least and most affluent districts in the San Antonio area serves to illustrate the manner in which the dual system of finance operates and to indicate the extent to which substantial disparities exist despite the State's impressive progress in recent years. Edgewood is one of seven public school districts in the metropolitan area. Approximately 22,000 students are enrolled in its 25 elementary and secondary schools. The district is situated in the core-city sector of San Antonio in a residential neighborhood that has little commercial or industrial property. The residents are predominantly of Mexican-American descent: approximately 90% of the student population is Mexican-American and over 6% is Negro. The average assessed property value per pupil is $5,960—the lowest in the metropolitan area—and the median family income ($4,686) is also the lowest. . . . [State and local funding combine] per pupil for a state-local total of $248. Federal funds added another $108 for a total of $356 per pupil.

Alamo Heights is the most affluent school district in San Antonio. Its six schools, housing approximately 5,000 students, are situated in a residential community quite unlike the Edgewood District. The school population is predominantly "Anglo," having only 18% Mexican-Americans and less than 1% Negroes. The assessed property value per pupil exceeds $49,000,33 and the median family income is $8,001. . . . [T]he district was able to supply $558 per student. Supplemented by a $36 per-pupil grant from federal sources, Alamo Heights spent $594 per pupil. . . .

This, then, establishes the framework for our analysis. We must decide, first, whether the Texas system of financing public education operates to the disadvantage of some suspect class or impinges upon a fundamental right explicitly or implicitly protected by the Constitution, thereby requiring strict judicial scrutiny. If so, the judgment of the District Court should be affirmed. If not, the Texas scheme must still be examined to determine whether it rationally furthers some legitimate, articulated state purpose and therefore does not constitute an invidious discrimination in violation of the Equal Protection Clause of the Fourteenth Amendment.

II

The District Court's opinion does not reflect the novelty and complexity of the constitutional questions posed by appellees' challenge to Texas' system of school financing. In concluding that strict judicial scrutiny was required, that court relied on decisions dealing with the rights of indigents to equal treatment in the criminal trial and appellate processes, and on cases disapproving wealth restrictions on the right to vote. Those cases, the District Court concluded, established wealth as a suspect classification. Finding that the local property tax system discriminated on the basis of wealth, it regarded those precedents as controlling. It then reasoned, based on decisions of this Court affirming the undeniable importance of education, that there is a fundamental right to education and that, absent some compelling state justification, the Texas system could not stand.

We are unable to agree that this case, which in significant aspects is sui generis, may be so neatly fitted into the conventional mosaic of constitutional analysis under the Equal Protection Clause. Indeed, for the several reasons that follow, we find neither the suspect-classification nor the fundamental-interest analysis persuasive.

A

The wealth discrimination discovered by the District Court in this case, and by several other courts that have recently struck down school-financing laws in other States, is quite unlike any of the forms of wealth discrimination heretofore reviewed by this Court. Rather than focusing on the unique features of the alleged discrimination, the courts in these cases have virtually assumed their findings of a suspect classification through a simplistic process of analysis: since, under the traditional systems of financing public schools, some poorer people receive less expensive educations than other more affluent people, these systems discriminate on the basis of wealth. This approach largely ignores the hard threshold questions, including whether it makes a difference for purposes of consideration under the Constitution that the class of disadvantaged "poor" cannot be identified or defined in customary equal protection terms, and whether the relative—rather than absolute—nature of the asserted deprivation is of significant consequence. Before a State's laws and the justifications for the classifications they create are subjected to strict judicial scrutiny, we think these threshold considerations must be analyzed more closely than they were in the court below.

The case comes to us with no definitive description of the classifying facts or delineation of the disfavored class. Examination of the District Court's opinion and of appellees' complaint, briefs, and contentions at oral argument suggests, however, at least three ways in which the discrimination claimed here might be described. The Texas system of school financing might be regarded as discriminating (1) against "poor" persons whose incomes fall below some identifiable level of poverty or who might be characterized as functionally "indigent," or (2) against those who are relatively poorer than others, or (3) against all those who, irrespective of their personal incomes, happen to reside in relatively poorer school districts. Our task must be to ascertain whether, in fact, the Texas system has been shown to discriminate on any of these possible bases and, if so, whether the resulting classification may be regarded as suspect. . . .

Only appellees' first possible basis for describing the class disadvantaged by the Texas school-financing system—discrimination against a class of definably "poor" persons—might arguably meet the criteria established in these prior cases. Even a cursory examination, however, demonstrates that neither of the two distinguishing characteristics of wealth classifications can be found here. First, in support of their charge that the system discriminates against the "poor," appellees have made no effort to demonstrate that it operates to the peculiar disadvantage of any class fairly definable as indigent, or as composed of persons whose incomes are beneath any designated poverty level. . . . Defining "poor" families as those below the Bureau of the Census poverty level, [a] Connecticut study found, not surprisingly, that the poor were clustered around commercial and industrial areas–those same areas that provide the most attractive sources of property tax income for school districts. Whether a similar pattern would be discovered in Texas is not known, but there is no basis on the record in this case for assuming that the poorest people–defined by reference to any level of absolute impecunity–are concentrated in the poorest districts.

Second, neither appellees nor the District Court addressed the fact that, unlike each of the foregoing cases, lack of personal resources has not occasioned an absolute deprivation of the desired benefit. The argument here is not that the children in districts having relatively low assessable property values are receiving no public education; rather, it is that they are receiving a poorer quality education than that available to children in districts having more assessable wealth. Apart from the unsettled and disputed question whether the quality of education may be determined by the amount of money expended for it, a sufficient answer to appellees' argument is that, at least where wealth is involved, the Equal Protection Clause does not require absolute equality or precisely equal advantages. Nor indeed, in view of the infinite variables affecting the educational process, can any system assure equal quality of education except in the most relative sense. Texas asserts that the Minimum Foundation Program provides an adequate education for all children in the State. By providing 12 years of free public-school education, and by assuring teachers, books, transportation, and operating funds, the Texas Legislature has endeavored to "guarantee, for the welfare of the state as a whole, that all people shall have at least an adequate program of education. This is what is meant by 'A Minimum Foundation Program of Education'." The State repeatedly asserted in its briefs in this Court that it has fulfilled this desire and that it now assures every child in every school district an adequate education. No proof was offered at trial persuasively discrediting or refuting the State's assertion.

For these two reasons–the absence of any evidence that the financing system discriminates against any definable category of "poor" people or that it results in the absolute deprivation of education–the disadvantaged class is not susceptible of identification in traditional terms. . . .

However described, it is clear that appellees' suit asks this Court to extend its most exacting scrutiny to review a system that allegedly discriminates against a large, diverse, and amorphous class, unified only by the common factor of residence in districts that happen to have less taxable wealth than other districts. The system of alleged discrimination and the class it defines have none of the traditional indicia of suspectness: the class is not saddled with such disabilities, or subjected to such a history of purposeful unequal treatment, or relegated to such a position of political powerlessness as to command extraordinary protection from the majoritarian political process.

We thus conclude that the Texas system does not operate to the peculiar disadvantage of any suspect class. But in recognition of the fact that this Court has never heretofore held that wealth discrimination alone provides an adequate basis for invoking strict scrutiny, appellees have not relied solely on this contention. They also assert that the State's system impermissibly interferes with the exercise of a "fundamental" right and that accordingly the prior decisions of this Court require the application of the strict standard of judicial review. It is this question—whether education is a fundamental right, in the sense that it is among the rights and liberties protected by the Constitution—which has so consumed the attention of courts and commentators in recent years.

B

In *Brown v. Board of Education* (1954), a unanimous Court recognized that "education is perhaps the most important function of state and local governments." . . . This theme, expressing an abiding respect for the vital role of education in a free society, may be found in numerous opinions of Justices of this Court writing both before and after *Brown* was decided.

Nothing this Court holds today in any way detracts from our historic dedication to public education. . . . But the importance of a service performed by the State does not determine whether it must be regarded as fundamental for purposes of examination under the Equal Protection Clause. . . . We would, indeed, then be assuming a legislative role and one for which the Court lacks both authority and competence. . . . It is not the province of this Court to create substantive constitutional rights in the name of guaranteeing equal protection of the laws. Thus, the key to discovering whether education is "fundamental" is not to be found in comparisons of the relative societal significance of education as opposed to [other social goods]. Rather, the answer lies in assessing whether there is a right to education explicitly or implicitly guaranteed by the Constitution.

Education, of course, is not among the rights afforded explicit protection under our Federal Constitution. Nor do we find any basis for saying it is implicitly so protected. As we have said, the undisputed importance of education will not alone cause this Court to depart from the usual standard for reviewing a State's social and economic legislation. It is appellees' contention, however, that education is distinguishable from other services and benefits provided by the State because it bears a peculiarly close relationship to other rights and liberties accorded protection under the Constitution. Specifically, they insist that education is itself a fundamental personal right because it is essential to the effective exercise of First Amendment freedoms and to intelligent utilization of the right to vote. In asserting a nexus between speech and education, appellees urge that the right to speak is meaningless unless the speaker is capable of articulating his thoughts intelligently and persuasively. The "marketplace of ideas" is an empty forum for those lacking basic communicative tools. Likewise, they argue that the corollary right to receive information becomes little more than a hollow privilege when the recipient has not been taught to read, assimilate, and utilize available knowledge.

A similar line of reasoning is pursued with respect to the right to vote. Exercise of the franchise, it is contended, cannot be divorced from the educational foundation of the voter. The electoral process, if reality is to conform to the democratic ideal, depends on an informed electorate: a voter cannot cast his ballot intelligently unless his reading skills and thought processes have been adequately developed.

We need not dispute any of these propositions. The Court has long afforded zealous protection against unjustifiable governmental interference with the individual's rights to speak and to vote. Yet we have never presumed to possess either the ability or the authority to guarantee to the citizenry the most effective speech or the most informed electoral choice. That these may be desirable goals of a system of freedom of expression and of a representative form of government is not to be doubted. These are indeed goals to be pursued by a people whose thoughts and beliefs are freed from governmental interference. But they are not values to be implemented by judicial instruction into otherwise legitimate state activities.

Even if it were conceded that some identifiable quantum of education is a constitutionally protected prerequisite to the meaningful exercise of either right, we have no indication that the present levels of educational expenditures in Texas provide an education that falls short. . . .

Furthermore, the logical limitations on appellees' nexus theory are difficult to perceive. How, for instance, is education to be distinguished from the significant personal interests in the basics of decent food and shelter? Empirical examination might well buttress an assumption that the ill-fed, ill-clothed, and ill-housed are among the most ineffective participants in the political process, and that they derive the least enjoyment from the benefits of the First Amendment. . . .

The present case, in another basic sense, is significantly different from any of the cases in which the Court has applied strict scrutiny to state or federal legislation touching upon constitutionally protected rights. Each of our prior cases involved legislation which "deprived," "infringed," or "interfered" with the free exercise of some such fundamental personal right or liberty. A critical distinction between those cases and the one now before us lies in what Texas is endeavoring to do with respect to education. . . . Every step leading to the establishment of the system Texas utilizes today—including the decisions permitting localities to tax and expend locally, and creating and continuously expanding the state aid—was implemented in an effort to extend public education and to improve its quality. Of course, every reform that benefits some more than others may be criticized for what it fails to accomplish. But we think it plain that, in substance, the thrust of the Texas system is affirmative and reformatory and, therefore, should be scrutinized under judicial principles sensitive to the nature of the State's efforts and to the rights reserved to the States under the Constitution.

C

It should be clear, for the reasons stated above and in accord with the prior decisions of this Court, that this is not a case in which the challenged state action must be subjected to the searching judicial scrutiny reserved for laws that create suspect classifications or impinge upon constitutionally protected rights. . . .

It must be remembered, also, that every claim arising under the Equal Protection Clause has implications for the relationship between national and state power under our federal system. Questions of federalism are always inherent in the process of determining whether a State's laws are to be accorded the traditional presumption of constitutionality, or are to be subjected instead to rigorous judicial scrutiny. While the maintenance of the principles of federalism is a foremost consideration in interpreting any of the pertinent constitutional provisions under which this Court examines state action, it would be difficult to imagine a case having a greater potential impact on our federal system than the one now before us, in which we are urged to abrogate systems of financing public education presently in existence in virtually every State.

The foregoing considerations buttress our conclusion that Texas' system of public school finance is an inappropriate candidate for strict judicial scrutiny. These same considerations are relevant to the determination whether that system, with its conceded imperfections, nevertheless bears some rational relationship to a legitimate state purpose. It is to this question that we next turn our attention.

III

. . . Appellees . . . urge that the Texas system is unconstitutionally arbitrary because it allows the availability of local taxable resources to turn on 'happenstance.' They see no justification for a system that allows, as they contend, the quality of education to fluctuate on the basis of the fortuitous positioning of the boundary lines of political subdivisions and the location of valuable commercial and industrial property. But any scheme of local taxation—indeed the very existence of identifiable local governmental units—requires the establishment of jurisdictional boundaries that are inevitably arbitrary. It is equally inevitable that some localities are going to be blessed with more taxable assets than others. Nor is local wealth a static quantity. Changes in the level of taxable wealth within any district may result from any number of events, some of which local residents can and do influence. For instance, commercial and industrial enterprises may be encouraged to locate within a district by various actions—public and private. . . .

In sum, to the extent that the Texas system of school financing results in unequal expenditures between children who happen to reside in different districts, we cannot say that such disparities are the product of a system that is so irrational as to be invidiously discriminatory. . . .

IV

. . . These matters merit . . . continued attention, . . . but the ultimate solutions must come from the lawmakers and from the democratic pressures of those who elect them.

Justice Stewart, concurring.

The method of financing public schools in Texas, as in almost every other State, has resulted in a system of public education that can fairly be described as chaotic and unjust. It does not follow, however, and I cannot find, that this system violates the Constitution of the United States. I join the opinion and judgment of the Court because I am convinced that any other course would mark an extraordinary departure from principled adjudication under the Equal Protection Clause of the Fourteenth Amendment. . . .

Justice Brennan, dissenting. [Omitted.]

Justice White, with whom Justices Douglas and Brennan join, dissenting.

[This dissent argued that the Texas public school financing system lacked rational basis.]

Justice Marshall, with whom Justice Douglas concurs, dissenting.

The Court today decides, in effect, that a State may constitutionally vary the quality of education which it offers its children in accordance with the amount of taxable wealth located in the school districts within which they reside. . . . The majority's holding can only be seen as a retreat from our historic commitment to equality of educational opportunity and as unsupportable acquiescence in a system which deprives children in their earliest years of the chance to reach their full potential as citizens. . . .

In my judgment, the right of every American to an equal start in life, so far as the provision of a state service as important as education is concerned, is far too vital to permit state discrimination on grounds as tenuous as those presented by this record. Nor can I accept the notion that it is sufficient to remit these appellees to the vagaries of the political process which, contrary to the majority's suggestion, has proved singularly unsuited to the task of providing a remedy for this discrimination. I, for one, am unsatisfied with the hope of an ultimate "political" solution sometime in the indefinite future while, in the meantime, countless children unjustifiably receive inferior educations that may "affect their hearts and minds in a way unlikely ever to be undone." *Brown v. Board of Education* (1954). I must therefore respectfully dissent.

I [Omitted]

II

This Court has repeatedly held that state discrimination which either adversely affects a fundamental interest or is based on a distinction of a suspect character must be carefully scrutinized to ensure that the scheme is necessary to promote a substantial, legitimate state interest. The majority today concludes, however, that the Texas scheme is not subject to such a strict standard of review under the Equal Protection Clause. Instead, in its view, the Texas scheme must be tested by nothing more than that lenient standard of rationality which we have traditionally applied to discriminatory state action in the context of economic and commercial matters. . . . I cannot accept such an emasculation of the Equal Protection Clause in the context of this case.

A

To begin, I must once more voice my disagreement with the Court's rigidified approach to equal protection analysis. The Court apparently seeks to establish today that equal protection cases fall into one of two neat categories which dictate the appropriate standard of review—strict scrutiny or mere rationality. But this Court's decisions in the field of equal protection defy such easy categorization. A principled reading of what this Court has done reveals that it has applied a spectrum of standards in reviewing discrimination allegedly violative of the Equal Protection Clause. This spectrum clearly comprehends variations in the degree of care with which the Court will scrutinize particular classifications, depending, I believe, on the constitutional and societal importance of the interest adversely affected and the recognized invidiousness of the basis upon which the particular classification is drawn. . . .

I therefore cannot accept the majority's labored efforts to demonstrate that fundamental interests, which call for strict scrutiny of the challenged classification, encompass only established rights which we are somehow bound to recognize from the text of the Constitution itself. To be sure, some interests which the Court has deemed to be fundamental for purposes of equal protection analysis are themselves constitutionally protected rights [such as freedom of speech and freedom of interstate travel]. But it will not do to suggest that the "answer" to whether an interest is fundamental for purposes of equal protection analysis is always [as the majority says] determined by whether that interest "is a right explicitly or implicitly guaranteed by the Constitution.". . .

San Antonio Independent School District v. Rodriguez

The majority is, of course, correct when it suggests that the process of determining which interests are fundamental is a difficult one. But I do not think the problem is insurmountable. And I certainly do not accept the view that the process need necessarily degenerate into an unprincipled, subjective picking-and-choosing between various interests or that it must involve this Court in creating substantive constitutional rights in the name of guaranteeing equal protection of the laws. Although not all fundamental interests are constitutionally guaranteed, the determination of which interests are fundamental should be firmly rooted in the text of the Constitution. The task in every case should be to determine the extent to which constitutionally guaranteed rights are dependent on interests not mentioned in the Constitution. As the nexus between the specific constitutional guarantee and the nonconstitutional interest draws closer, the nonconstitutional interest becomes more fundamental and the degree of judicial scrutiny applied when the interest is infringed on a discriminatory basis must be adjusted accordingly. . . . Only if we closely protect the related interests from state discrimination do we ultimately ensure the integrity of the constitutional guarantee itself. This is the real lesson that must be taken from our previous decisions involving interests deemed to be fundamental. . . .

B

Since the Court now suggests that only interests guaranteed by the Constitution are fundamental for purposes of equal protection analysis, and since it rejects the contention that public education is fundamental, it follows that the Court concludes that public education is not constitutionally guaranteed. [Actually,] the fundamental importance of education is amply indicated by the prior decisions of this Court, by the unique status accorded public education by our society, and by the close relationship between education and some of our most basic constitutional values. . . .

Education directly affects the ability of a child to exercise his First Amendment rights, both as a source and as a receiver of information and ideas, whatever interests he may pursue in life. . . . Of particular importance is the relationship between education and the political process. Americans regard the public schools as a most vital civic institution for the preservation of a democratic system of government. Education serves the essential function of instilling in our young an understanding of and appreciation for the principles and operation of our governmental processes. Education may instill the interest and provide the tools necessary for political discourse and debate. . . . But of most immediate and direct concern must be the demonstrated effect of education on the exercise of the franchise by the electorate. . . . Data from the Presidential Election of 1968 clearly demonstrate a direct relationship between participation in the electoral process and level of educational attainment; and . . . the quality of education offered may influence a child's decision to enter or remain in school. It is this very sort of intimate relationship between a particular personal interest and specific constitutional guarantees that has heretofore caused the Court to attach special significance, for purposes of equal protection analysis, to [unenumerated] individual interests such as procreation and the exercise of the state franchise. . . .

As this Court held in *Brown v. Board of Education* the opportunity of education, "where the state has undertaken to provide it, is a right which must be made available to all on equal terms." The factors just considered, including the relationship between education and the social and political interests enshrined within the Constitution, compel us to recognize the fundamentality of education and to scrutinize with appropriate care the bases for state discrimination affecting equality of educational opportunity in Texas' school districts. . . .

C–D [Omitted.]

III [Omitted.]

flashforward

The Future of Education Equity Litigation. After *Rodriguez* found no federal constitutional right to an adequate free public education, litigation on the issue continued under state law. Many state supreme courts held that disparities in education violated the equality clauses of state constitutions or state constitutional provisions regarding education that have no federal counterpart. These included decisions in California and Texas, the two states with federal litigation mentioned in *Rodriguez*. See *Serrano v. Priest II*, 557 P.2d 929 (Cal. 1976); *Edgewood Independent School District v. Kirby*, 777 S.W.2d 391 (Tex. 1989). Disputes over what sort of education funding a state constitution requires—and whether court orders are an effective way to ensure it—continue into the 21st century.

E. Other Classifications and Other Methods: *City of Cleburne v. Cleburne Living Center*

In its first 100 years, the Equal Protection Clause was most often applied in cases involving race and class. But in the years after the Warren Court, other groups have sought, with varying levels of success, constitutional protection against discriminatory laws. Sex classifications, once upheld if they had a rational basis, now receive intermediate scrutiny. Are there other classifications that should undergo a similar evolution? This chapter closes with a case that considers a novel classification. As you read it, consider how the Equal Protection Clause should treat the classification—and also whether there should be changes to the prevailing multi-tiered approach to equality questions.

The plaintiffs in *City of Cleburne v. Cleburne Living Center* challenged a decision under a local zoning ordinance. This is a type of lawmaking where different treatment for different parcels of land would ordinarily be reviewed only for rational basis. *Village of Willowbrook v. Olech*, 528 U.S. 562 (2000). However, *Cleburne*'s decision hinged on whether the proposed land use was a "hospital for the feeble-minded." As seen in *Buck v. Bell* (1927), "feeble-minded" was an early 20th century term for people with intellectual disabilities (referred to in *Cleburne* as "mental retardation").

ITEMS TO CONSIDER WHILE READING *CLEBURNE LIVING CENTER*:

A. *Work through the items in the Kickstarter. Specifically, should classifications on the basis of intellectual disability trigger heightened scrutiny? And if they do, should the scrutiny be strict or intermediate?*

B. *What makes classifications on the basis of intellectual disability similar to, or different from, classifications on the basis of race? Of sex?*

C. *What level of scrutiny does the majority claim to be using, and why? Is it actually using that level of scrutiny?*

D. *What differences separate the majority opinion, the concurrence of Justice Stevens, and the concurrence of Justice Marshall?*

City of Cleburne v. Cleburne Living Center,

473 U.S. 432 (1985)

Justice White delivered the opinion of the Court [joined by Chief Justice Burger and Justices Powell, Rehnquist, Stevens, and O'Connor].

A Texas city denied a special use permit for the operation of a group home for the mentally retarded, acting pursuant to a municipal zoning ordinance requiring permits for such homes. The Court of Appeals for the Fifth Circuit held that mental retardation is a "quasi-suspect" classification and that the ordinance violated the Equal Protection Clause because it did not substantially further an important governmental purpose. We hold that a lesser standard of scrutiny is appropriate, but conclude that under that standard the ordinance is invalid as applied in this case.

I

In July 1980, respondent Jan Hannah purchased a building at 201 Featherston Street in the city of Cleburne, Texas, with the intention of leasing it to Cleburne Living Center, Inc. (CLC), for the operation of a group home for the mentally retarded. It was anticipated that the home would house 13 retarded men and women, who would be under the constant supervision of CLC staff members. The house had four bedrooms and two baths, with a half bath to be added. CLC planned to comply with all applicable state and federal regulations. . . .

The city explained that under the zoning regulations applicable to the site, a special use permit, renewable annually, was required for the construction of "hospitals for the insane or feeble-minded, or alcoholics or drug addicts, or penal or correctional institutions." The city had determined that the proposed group home should be classified as a "hospital for the feebleminded." After holding a public hearing on CLC's application, the City Council voted 3 to 1 to deny a special use permit.

CLC then filed suit in Federal District Court against the city and a number of its officials, alleging, *inter alia*, that the zoning ordinance was invalid on its face and as applied because it discriminated against the mentally retarded in violation of the equal protection rights of CLC and its potential residents. . . . Concluding that no fundamental right was implicated and that mental retardation was neither a suspect nor a quasi-suspect classification, the [District] court employed the minimum level of judicial scrutiny applicable to equal protection claims [and entered summary judgment in favor of the City]. . . . The Court of Appeals for the Fifth Circuit reversed, determining that mental retardation was a quasi-suspect classification and that it should assess the validity of the ordinance under intermediate-level scrutiny . . . We granted certiorari.

II [Omitted.]

III

. . . We conclude for several reasons that the Court of Appeals erred in holding mental retardation a quasi-suspect classification calling for a more exacting standard of judicial review than is normally accorded economic and social legislation. First, it is undeniable, and it is not argued otherwise here, that those who are mentally retarded have a reduced ability to cope with and function in the everyday world. Nor are they all cut from the same pattern: as the testimony in this record indicates, they range from those whose disability is not immediately evident to those who must be constantly cared for. They are thus different, immutably so, in relevant respects, and the States' interest in dealing with and providing for them is plainly a legitimate one. How this large and diversified group is to be treated under the law is a difficult and often a technical matter, very much a task for legislators guided by qualified professionals and not by the perhaps ill-informed opinions of the judiciary. Heightened scrutiny inevitably involves substantive judgments about legislative decisions, and we doubt that the predicate for such judicial oversight is present where the classification deals with mental retardation.

Second, the distinctive legislative response, both national and state, to the plight of those who are mentally retarded demonstrates not only that they have unique problems, but also that the lawmakers have been addressing their difficulties in a manner that belies a continuing antipathy or prejudice and a corresponding need for more intrusive oversight by the judiciary. Thus, the Federal Government has not only outlawed discrimination against the mentally retarded in federally funded programs, see § 504 of the Rehabilitation Act of 1973, 29 U.S.C. § 794, but it has also provided the retarded with the right to receive "appropriate treatment, services, and habilitation" in a setting that is least restrictive of their personal liberty." Developmental Disabilities Assistance and Bill of Rights Act, 42 U.S.C. § 6010. In addition, the Government has conditioned federal education funds on a State's assurance that retarded children will enjoy an education that, "to the maximum extent appropriate," is integrated with that of nonmentally retarded children. Education of the Handicapped Act, 20 U.S.C. § 1412. The Government has also facilitated the hiring of the mentally retarded into the federal civil service by exempting them from the requirement of competitive examination. See 5 CFR § 213.3102(t) (1984). . . .

Such legislation thus singling out the retarded for special treatment reflects the real and undeniable differences between the retarded and others. That a civilized and decent society expects and approves such legislation indicates that governmental consideration of those differences in the vast majority of situations is not only legitimate but also desirable. It may be, as CLC contends, that legislation designed to benefit, rather than disadvantage, the retarded would generally withstand examination under a test of heightened scrutiny. The relevant inquiry, however, is whether heightened scrutiny is constitutionally mandated in the first instance. Even assuming that many of these laws could be shown to be substantially related to an important governmental purpose, merely requiring the legislature to justify its efforts in these terms may lead it to refrain from acting at all. . . . Especially given the wide variation in the abilities and needs of the retarded themselves, governmental bodies must have a certain amount of flexibility and freedom from judicial oversight in shaping and limiting their remedial efforts.

Third, the legislative response, which could hardly have occurred and survived without public support, negates any claim that the mentally retarded are politically powerless in the sense that they have no ability to attract the attention of the lawmakers. Any minority can be said to be powerless to assert direct control over the legislature, but if that were a criterion for higher level scrutiny by the courts, much economic and social legislation would now be suspect.

Fourth, if the large and amorphous class of the mentally retarded were deemed quasi-suspect for the reasons given by the Court of Appeals, it would be difficult to find a principled way to distinguish a variety of other groups who have perhaps immutable disabilities setting them off from others, who cannot themselves mandate the desired legislative responses, and who can claim some degree of prejudice from at least part of the public at large. One need mention in this respect only the aging, the disabled, the mentally ill, and the infirm. We are reluctant to set out on that course, and we decline to do so. . . .

Our refusal to recognize the retarded as a quasi-suspect class does not leave them entirely unprotected from invidious discrimination. To withstand equal protection review, legislation that distinguishes between the mentally retarded and others must be rationally related to a legitimate governmental purpose. This standard, we believe, affords government the latitude necessary both to pursue policies designed to assist the retarded in realizing their full potential, and to freely and efficiently engage in activities that burden the retarded in what is essentially an incidental manner. The State may not rely on a classification whose relationship to an asserted goal is so attenuated as to render the distinction arbitrary or irrational. Furthermore, some objectives—such as "a bare desire to harm a politically unpopular group," *United States Dept. of Agriculture v. Moreno* (1973)—are not legitimate state interests. Beyond that, the mentally retarded, like others, have and retain their substantive constitutional rights in addition to the right to be treated equally by the law.

IV

. . . The constitutional issue is clearly posed. The city does not require a special use permit in an R-3 zone for apartment houses, multiple dwellings, boarding and lodging houses, fraternity or sorority houses, dormitories, apartment hotels, hospitals, sanitariums, nursing homes for convalescents or the aged (other than for the insane or feebleminded or alcoholics or drug addicts), private clubs or fraternal orders, and other specified uses. It does, however, insist on a special permit for the Featherston home, and it does so, as the District Court found, because it would be a facility for the mentally retarded. May the city require the permit for this facility when other care and multiple-dwelling facilities are freely permitted?

It is true, as already pointed out, that the mentally retarded as a group are indeed different from others not sharing their misfortune, and in this respect they may be different from those who would occupy other facilities that would be permitted in an R-3 zone without a special permit. But this difference is largely irrelevant unless the Featherston home and those who would occupy it would threaten legitimate interests of the city in a way that other permitted uses such as boarding houses and hospitals would not. Because in our view the record does not reveal any rational basis for believing that the Featherston home would pose any special threat to the city's legitimate interests, we affirm the judgment below insofar as it holds the ordinance invalid as applied in this case.

The District Court found that the City Council's insistence on the permit rested on several factors. First, the Council was concerned with the negative attitude of the majority of property owners located within 200 feet of the Featherston facility, as well as with the fears of elderly residents of the neighborhood. But mere negative attitudes, or fear, unsubstantiated by factors which are properly cognizable in a zoning proceeding, are not permissible bases for treating a home for the mentally retarded differently from apartment houses, multiple dwellings, and the like. It is plain that the electorate as a whole, whether by referendum or otherwise, could not order city action violative of the Equal Protection Clause, and the City may not avoid the strictures of that Clause by deferring to the wishes or objections of some fraction of the body politic. "Private biases may be outside the reach of the law, but the law cannot, directly or indirectly, give them effect." *Palmore v. Sidoti* (1984).

Second, the Council had two objections to the location of the facility. It was concerned that the facility was across the street from a junior high school, and it feared that the students might harass the occupants of the Featherston home. But the school itself is attended by about 30 mentally retarded students, and denying a permit based on such vague, undifferentiated fears is again permitting some portion of the community to validate what would otherwise be an equal protection violation. [Third,] the other objection to the home's location was that it was located on "a five hundred year flood plain." This concern with the possibility of a flood, however, can hardly be based on a distinction between the Featherston home and, for example, nursing homes, homes for convalescents or the aged, or sanitariums or hospitals, any of which could be located on the Featherston site without obtaining a special use permit. The same may be said of another concern of the Council—doubts about the legal responsibility for actions which the mentally retarded might take. If there is no concern about legal responsibility with respect to other uses that would be permitted in the area, such as boarding and fraternity houses, it is difficult to believe that the groups of mildly or moderately mentally retarded individuals who would live at 201 Featherston would present any different or special hazard.

Fourth, the Council was concerned with the size of the home and the number of people that would occupy it. The District Court found, and the Court of Appeals repeated, that "if the potential residents of the Featherston Street home were not mentally retarded, but the home was the same in all other respects, its use would be permitted under the city's zoning ordinance." Given this finding, there would be no restrictions on the number of people who could occupy this home as a boarding house, nursing home, family dwelling, fraternity house, or dormitory. The question is whether it is rational to treat the mentally retarded differently. . . . Those who would live in the Featherston home are the type of individuals who, with supporting staff, satisfy federal and state standards for group housing in the community; and there is no dispute that the home would meet the federal square-footage-per-resident requirement for facilities of this type. In the words of the Court of Appeals, "the City never justifies its apparent view that other people can live under such 'crowded' conditions when mentally retarded persons cannot."

In the courts below the city also urged that the ordinance is aimed at avoiding concentration of population and at lessening congestion of the streets. These concerns obviously fail to explain why apartment houses, fraternity and sorority houses, hospitals and the like, may freely locate in the area without a permit. So, too, the expressed worry about fire hazards, the serenity of the neighborhood, and the avoidance of danger to other residents fail rationally to justify singling out a home such as 201 Featherston for the special use permit, yet imposing no such restrictions on the many other uses freely permitted in the neighborhood.

The short of it is that requiring the permit in this case appears to us to rest on an irrational prejudice against the mentally retarded, including those who would occupy the Featherston facility and who would live under the closely supervised and highly regulated conditions expressly provided for by state and federal law.

Justice Stevens, with whom Chief Justice Burger joins, concurring.

The Court of Appeals disposed of this case as if a critical question to be decided were which of three clearly defined standards of equal protection review should be applied to a legislative classification discriminating against the mentally retarded. In fact, our cases have not delineated three—or even one or two—such well-defined standards. Rather, our cases reflect a continuum of judgmental responses to differing classifications which have been explained in opinions by terms ranging from "strict scrutiny" at one extreme to "rational basis" at the other. I have never been persuaded that these so-called "standards" adequately explain the decisional process. Cases involving classifications based on alienage, illegal residency, illegitimacy, gender, age, or—as in this case—mental retardation, do not fit well into sharply defined classifications.

I am inclined to believe that what has become known as the tiered analysis of equal protection claims does not describe a completely logical method of deciding cases, but rather is a method the Court has employed to explain decisions that actually apply a single standard in a reasonably consistent fashion. In my own approach to these cases, I have always asked myself whether I could find a "rational basis" for the classification at issue. The term "rational," of course, includes a requirement that an impartial lawmaker could logically believe that the classification would serve a legitimate public purpose that transcends the harm to the members of the disadvantaged class. Thus, the word "rational"—for me at least—includes elements of legitimacy and neutrality that must always characterize the performance of the sovereign's duty to govern impartially.

City of Cleburne v. Cleburne Living Center

The rational-basis test, properly understood, adequately explains why a law that deprives a person of the right to vote because his skin has a different pigmentation than that of other voters violates the Equal Protection Clause. It would be utterly irrational to limit the franchise on the basis of height or weight; it is equally invalid to limit it on the basis of skin color. None of these attributes has any bearing at all on the citizen's willingness or ability to exercise that civil right. We do not need to apply a special standard, or to apply "strict scrutiny," or even "heightened scrutiny," to decide such cases.

In every equal protection case, we have to ask certain basic questions. What class is harmed by the legislation, and has it been subjected to a tradition of disfavor by our laws? What is the public purpose that is being served by the law? What is the characteristic of the disadvantaged class that justifies the disparate treatment? In most cases the answer to these questions will tell us whether the statute has a rational basis. The answers will result in the virtually automatic invalidation of racial classifications and in the validation of most economic classifications, but they will provide differing results in cases involving classifications based on alienage, gender, or illegitimacy. But that is not because we apply an "intermediate standard of review" in these cases; rather it is because the characteristics of these groups are sometimes relevant and sometimes irrelevant to a valid public purpose, or, more specifically, to the purpose that the challenged laws purportedly intended to serve. . . .

The record convinces me that [the City acted] because of the irrational fears of neighboring property owners, rather than for the protection of the mentally retarded persons who would reside in respondent's home. . . . Accordingly, I join the opinion of the Court.

Justice Marshall, with whom Justices Brennan and Blackmun join, concurring in the judgment in part and dissenting in part.

The Court holds that all retarded individuals cannot be grouped together as the "feebleminded" and deemed presumptively unfit to live in a community. Underlying this holding is the principle that mental retardation per se cannot be a proxy for depriving retarded people of their rights and interests without regard to variations in individual ability. With this holding and principle I agree. The Equal Protection Clause requires attention to the capacities and needs of retarded people as individuals.

I cannot agree, however, with the way in which the Court reaches its result[.] The Court holds the ordinance invalid on rational-basis grounds and disclaims that anything special, in the form of heightened scrutiny, is taking place. Yet Cleburne's ordinance surely would be valid under the traditional rational-basis test applicable to economic and commercial regulation. In my view, it is important to articulate, as the Court does not, the facts and principles that justify subjecting this zoning ordinance to the searching review—the heightened scrutiny—that actually leads to its invalidation. . . .

I

At the outset, two curious and paradoxical aspects of the Court's opinion must be noted. First, because the Court invalidates Cleburne's zoning ordinance on rational-basis grounds, the Court's wide-ranging discussion of heightened scrutiny is wholly superfluous to the decision of this case. . . .

Second, the Court's heightened-scrutiny discussion is even more puzzling given that Cleburne's ordinance is invalidated only after being subjected to precisely the sort of probing inquiry associated with heightened scrutiny. To be sure, the Court does not label its handiwork heightened scrutiny, and perhaps the method employed must hereafter be called "second order" rational-basis review rather than "heightened scrutiny." But however labeled, the rational basis test invoked today is most assuredly not the rational-basis test of *Williamson v. Lee Optical* (1955).

The Court, for example, concludes that legitimate concerns for fire hazards or the serenity of the neighborhood do not justify singling out respondents to bear the burdens of these concerns, for analogous permitted uses appear to pose similar threats. Yet under the traditional and most minimal version of the rational-basis test, "reform may take one step at a time, addressing itself to the phase of the problem which seems most acute to the legislative mind." *Williamson*. The record is said not to support the ordinance's classifications, but under the traditional standard we do not sift through the record to determine whether policy decisions are squarely supported by a firm factual foundation. Finally, the Court further finds it difficult to believe that the retarded present different or special hazards inapplicable to other groups. In normal circumstances, the burden is not on the legislature to convince the Court that the lines it has drawn are sensible; legislation is presumptively constitutional, and a State is not required to resort to close distinctions or to maintain a precise, scientific uniformity with reference to its goals. . . .

The refusal to acknowledge that something more than minimum rationality review is at work here is, in my view, unfortunate in at least two respects. The suggestion that the traditional rational-basis test allows this sort of searching inquiry creates precedent for this Court and lower courts to subject economic and commercial classifications to similar and searching "ordinary" rational-basis review—a small and regrettable step back toward the days of *Lochner*. Moreover, by failing to articulate the factors that justify today's "second order" rational-basis review, the Court provides no principled foundation for determining when more searching inquiry is to be invoked. Lower courts are thus left in the dark on this important question, and this Court remains unaccountable for its decisions employing, or refusing to employ, particularly searching scrutiny. Candor requires me to acknowledge the particular factors that justify invalidating Cleburne's zoning ordinance under the careful scrutiny it today receives.

II

I have long believed the level of scrutiny employed in an equal protection case should vary with the constitutional and societal importance of the interest adversely affected and the recognized invidiousness of the basis upon which the particular classification is drawn. When a zoning ordinance works to exclude the retarded from all residential districts in a community, these two considerations require that the ordinance be convincingly justified as substantially furthering legitimate and important purposes. . . .

In light of the importance of the interest at stake and the history of discrimination the retarded have suffered, the Equal Protection Clause requires us to do more than review the distinctions drawn by Cleburne's zoning ordinance as if they appeared in a taxing statute or in economic or commercial legislation. The searching scrutiny I would give to restrictions on the ability of the retarded to establish community group homes leads me to conclude that Cleburne's vague generalizations for classifying the "feeble-minded" with drug addicts, alcoholics, and the insane, and excluding them where the elderly, the ill, the boarder, and the transient are allowed, are not substantial or important enough to overcome the suspicion that the ordinance rests on impermissible assumptions or outmoded and perhaps invidious stereotypes.

III—V [Omitted.]

flashforward

1. ***Rational Basis with Bite.*** The majority in *Cleburne* claimed that it was using rational basis review as traditionally understood. The government action was invalidated because animus against a disfavored group is never a rational basis for legislation. As stated in *US Department of Agriculture v. Moreno* (1973), "a bare . . . desire to harm a politically unpopular group cannot constitute a legitimate governmental interest." Class-based ill will is simply irrational.

However, some scholars have come to agree with Justice Marshall that the decision in *Cleburne,* and also that in *Moreno,* were not examples of rational basis as usual. Instead, they argue, when evidence suggests that animus may have been a motivating factor for the government's action, any neutral-sounding justifications for the law will as a practical matter be judged in ways that are usually seen under heightened scrutiny (in particular, seeking out the government's true motives, expressing concern about the impact of the law on the disfavored group, and being less forgiving of under- and over-inclusiveness). Should there be a name for this particular combination, where evidence of animus leads to somewhat more stringent scrutiny in a case that supposedly applies rational basis review? Justice Marshall sarcastically suggested that the *Cleburne* majority had engaged in "second order" rational basis review. Others have called it "rational basis with bite" or "rational basis plus."

The idea that "rational basis with bite" represents a unique standard of review has never been adopted by a majority of the Supreme Court. However, the concept is sometimes mentioned in lower court opinions and legal scholarship. In particular, it has been suggested that some gay rights cases decided after *Cleburne* may fall into this category. See Ch. 22.

2. *Sliding Scale.* Justices Marshall and Stevens proposed that tiers of scrutiny with sharp separations and wildly different standards are unrealistic. Instead, they argued, cases fall on a continuum: as classifications become more burdensome, courts require the government to offer better reasons for using them. As a result, some of the features that accompany heightened scrutiny, see Ch. 18.B, may properly be used more often than traditional doctrine admits. Whatever its merits as a way of explaining outcomes of past cases, this "sliding scale" approach has never been adopted by a majority of the Supreme Court.

Chapter Recap

A. Modern cases have developed a relatively complex set of rules to decide which laws violate the Equal Protection Clause. These rules identify particular types of inequality that deserve more stringent judicial review, distinguishing them from ordinary laws where federal courts are expected to be deferential to decisions of political branches and state governments.

B. The suspect classifications prong of equal protection gives heightened scrutiny to laws that classify people on suspicious grounds like race or sex (whether or not the right involved is fundamental).

1. A law classifies on a particular basis if (1) on its face, the law imposes disparate treatment on that basis, or (2) in practice, the law imposes disparate impact on that basis and the law was adopted with the discriminatory purpose of having that impact.

2. Under existing Supreme Court decisions, laws that classify on the basis of race or national origin (the suspect classifications) receive strict scrutiny; those that classify on the basis of sex or birth outside marriage (sometimes called quasi-suspect classifications) receive intermediate scrutiny; and all others receive rational basis review. Nonetheless, efforts continue to treat additional classifications as suspect or quasi-suspect.

C. The fundamental rights prong of equal protection gives heightened scrutiny to laws that unequally distribute rights deemed fundamental. When such rights are at stake, the government must offer strong justifications for its choice of classifications (whether or not the classifications are based on suspect criteria like race). Laws unequally distributing non-fundamental rights will be judged deferentially under the rational basis test.

D. Under either prong, once the correct level of scrutiny has been identified, a court considers whether the government's interest in using the challenged classification is sufficiently strong, and whether the classification is sufficiently well tailored as a means to serve that interest.

CHAPTER 19

Fairness Rights

Even when the Constitution allows the government to limit freedom and treat some people differently than others (as in a statute making it a crime to practice medicine without a license), the government must act fairly when executing those laws. Most of the Constitution's fairness rights apply in specific factual settings, such as the Takings Clause and the many provisions governing criminal justice. In addition to these specific protections, the Due Process Clause mandates fair procedures across a wide variety of settings. Fair procedures are of constitutional importance because, as stated in *Wisconsin v. Constantineau*, 400 U.S. 433 (1971), "it is procedure that marks much of the difference between rule by law and rule by fiat."

Procedural Due Process Limits Both State and Federal Governments

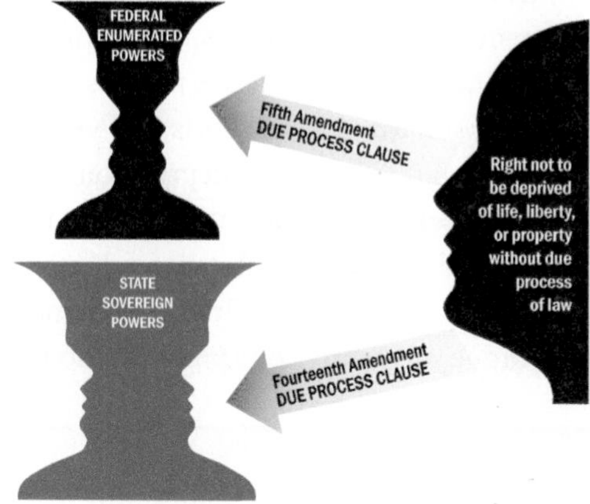

Both the Fifth Amendment (limiting the federal government) and the Fourteenth Amendment (limiting state and local governments) declare that no person shall be "deprived of life, liberty, or property, without due process of law." When either clause is invoked as a guarantee of procedural fairness, the resulting body of law is known today as "procedural due process."

A. Distinguishing Procedural Due Process from Substantive Due Process

The Due Process Clause may be the hardest-working language in the US Constitution. It is invoked to resolve a huge variety of legal disputes, ranging from a public utility terminating a customer's electric service, *Memphis Light, Gas & Water Div. v. Craft*, 436 U.S. 1 (1978), to a high school student's suspension from classes, *Goss v. Lopez*, 419 U.S. 565 (1975), to the jail conditions for pretrial detainees, *Bell v. Wolfish*, 441 U.S. 520 (1979), to the right to use contraceptives, *Griswold v. Connecticut*, 381 U.S. 479 (1965), to the incorporation doctrine, *McDonald v. City of Chicago*, 561 U. S. 742 (2010), and much more. Due process covers a huge territory because at its root, due process is about *fairness*: treating people right, following the rule of law, avoiding arbitrariness and injustice. Modern legal terminology tends to divide these concerns into two categories that consider *how* the government does things and *whether* the government may do them.

Procedural due process is the "how" doctrine. It requires the government to use constitutionally appropriate *procedures* when depriving someone of life, liberty, or property. Procedural due process does not control the government's choice of goals, but it does limit the means used to enforce them. For example, the legislature may decide, without worrying about procedural due process, whether to make sports gambling a crime. But when prosecuting and convicting a person for committing the crime of sports gambling, the executive and judicial branches must abide by procedural due process.

Substantive due process is the "whether" doctrine. It limits the substance of laws that would constitute a deprivation of life, liberty, or property, regardless of the procedures used to enforce them. When banning sports gambling, the legislature would need to consider substantive due process, by asking if the ability to gamble on sports is a constitutionally protected individual right. Phrased another way: one may argue substantive due process if no procedures would ever be good enough.

For the cases studied in Part I, modern terminology would apply the label "substantive due process" to the cases involving unenumerated rights, like freedom of contract in *Lochner v. New York* (1905). It was also seen in some cases upholding unenumerated non-economic rights, like the rights related to family and child-rearing in *Meyer v. Nebraska* (1923) (right to teach German language to children), *Pierce v. Society of Sisters* (1927) (right to send children to private school), and *Loving v. Virginia* (1967) (right to marry). See Chs. 8.C.2 and 11.C.

As a freestanding doctrine, procedural due process began to gain prominence in the 1950s. As a result, procedural due process issues appeared only sporadically in Part I. For example, *Buck v. Bell* (1927) concluded with little discussion that Virginia followed appropriate procedures when deciding to sterilize Carrie Buck. Ch. 8.C.2.c. The majority opinion in *Skinner v. Oklahoma* (1942) identified, but did not rule upon, a potential procedural problem with Oklahoma's criminal sterilization statute (it did not give the defendant an opportunity to prove that his personal form of criminality was not inheritable). Ch. 10.B.1. *Moore v. Dempsey* (1923) was a clear early example of procedural due process, holding that criminal trials conducted under the influence of a racist mob were so fundamentally unfair that they violated the Due Process Clause. Ch. 11.A.1.

Due process is a very old tradition within the Anglo-American legal system, predating representative democracy itself in Britain. In the Magna Carta of 1215, King John, under pressure from barons threatening to remove him from power, agreed that:

> No free man shall be seized or imprisoned, or stripped of his rights or possessions, or outlawed or exiled, or deprived of his standing in any other way, nor will we [the King] proceed with force against him, or send others to do so, except by the lawful judgment of his equals or by the law of the land.

King John Signs the Magna Carta

The requirement that the King respect the "law" of the land implies that the King is subject to rules; like everyone else, he has a duty to abide by pre-established principles that may prevent him from pursuing his desires of the moment. For the law to be of "the land" implies that law arises from the nation and binds the sovereign, and not the other way around.

Like the modern Due Process Clause, this passage from the Magna Carta can be read as a limit on both procedure and substance. Taken as a whole, the paragraph alludes to procedure. The government has authority to do many drastic things to a person, but it must go through certain steps first (such as obtaining a "lawful judgment of his equals"). The "law of the land" can also be read as a limit on the substance of government action. To say that drastic things may not happen unless the law of the land allows them implies that the law of the land might not allow some of those drastic things at all.

The "law of the land" concept has appeared in many other linguistic forms over the years, including "the rights of Englishmen" and the preference for "a government of laws, and not of men" mentioned in *Marbury v. Madison* (1803). In 1354, Parliament enacted a statute that used the phrase "due process of law" where the Magna Carta had used "the law of the land:"

> No man of what state or condition he be, shall be put out of his lands or tenements nor taken, nor disinherited, nor put to death, without he be brought to answer by due process of law.

The word "process" builds on the basic idea of procedural regularity found in the Magna Carta. The word "due" (owed) indicates that the government's adherence to the rule of law is an individual right: something to which persons are entitled.

B. Kickstarter: Procedural Due Process

DISCLAIMER: *This Kickstarter is a checklist to help identify relevant issues. It is not a list of elements. Nothing requires judges to write their opinions (or lawyers to write their briefs) in Kickstarter order.*

Procedural Due Process **kickstarter**

USE WHEN: *The government uses inadequate procedures when making individualized enforcement decisions.*

A. Has the government "deprived" a person of something?

B. Does the thing deprived constitute a "liberty interest" or "property interest"?

C. Was the deprivation "without due process of law" (i.e., did the government follow constitutionally adequate procedures?) If using the formula from Mathews v. Eldridge, consider:

1. The strength of the individual's liberty or property interest.

2. The value of the proposed procedures as a means to avoid wrongful deprivations of liberty or property.

3. The monetary and non-monetary cost to the government of the proposed procedures.

KICKSTARTER USER'S GUIDE

Procedural due process controls *how* the government goes about depriving life, liberty, or property on an individual level. It focuses on the procedures used to adjudicate—i.e., to make individualized decisions about whether a person meets a legal standard, and whether to impose a deprivation as a consequence. Adjudications occur, for example, when a court finds a defendant liable at trial, when the Department of Motor Vehicles rescinds a person's driver's license, or when a school principal suspends a student from school. Individualized adjudications will almost always be performed by the judicial and executive branches.

Procedural due process imposes no similar constraints on the legislative process. Specifically, it does not require the legislature to invite every potentially affected citizen to participate in debate or to cast a vote. *BiMetallic Investment Co. v. State Board of Equalization*, 239 U.S. 441 (1915). The Constitution establishes procedures for federal lawmaking, but the topic is controlled by Art. I, §§ 5–7, and not by procedural due process. (With that said, one might say that a statute violates procedural due process if it requires courts or executive agencies to use unfair adjudicative procedures.)

Modern executive branch agencies sometimes adjudicate (when they make individualized decisions, such as rescinding a driver's license or denying a permit to install a septic tank) and sometimes legislate (when they enact regulations). When agencies act as adjudicators they must respect procedural due process. But as with Congressional legislation, procedural due process does not require agencies to follow any specific procedures when enacting regulations. *Vermont Yankee Nuclear Power Corp. v. NRDC*, 435 U.S. 519 (1978). As it happens, Congress and all states have passed Administrative Procedure Acts that control the agency rule-making process, *e.g.*, 5 U.S.C. § 553, but these limits are the result of statute, not constitutional requirements.

Item A. *Deprivation.* Due process is triggered when the government "deprives" a person of something. At the outset, this means that procedural due process has a state action requirement: procedural due process is an obligation of the government (federal under the Fifth Amendment, states under the Fourteenth), and not of private persons.

Within the realm of state action, only an action putting a person in a worse position will be a "deprivation." The government's failure to improve a person's position (e.g., by providing free education or health care) is not a deprivation. In addition, mere negligence is not a deprivation (although intentional or reckless action may be), *Daniels v. Williams* (1986), Ch. 19.D.1.a, nor is failure to protect a person against privately inflicted harm, *DeShaney v. Winnebago County Department of Social Services* (1989), Ch. 19.D.1.b.

The meaning of "deprivation" operates similarly for both procedural and substantive due process cases.

Item B. *Liberty or Property Interest.* A deprivation will only violate due process if the thing deprived qualifies as "liberty" or "property." (It is usually easy to identify when life is at stake, so that aspect of the Due Process Clause tends not to be much litigated.) In modern terminology, anything that a person wants is an "interest," so the task of a court is to decide whether a person's asserted interest rises to a level enjoying constitutional protection.

The absence of due process protection does not mean the absence of all legal protection. The government is free to enact criminal, tort, or property laws to protect interests that do not count as liberty or property interests under the Due Process Clause. For example, *Paul v. Davis*, 424 U.S. 693 (1976), held that a person's reputation as a law-abiding citizen was not a liberty or property interest—which meant there was no constitutional violation when the Chief of Police falsely described someone as a shoplifter. However, the Chief of Police could be made liable under the state law tort of defamation if the state so chose.

When does an asserted interest count as a "property interest" or "liberty interest"? *Board of Regents v. Roth* (1972), Ch. 19.D.2.a, offered a widely-used explanation of the terms.

Property. People have property interests in the things we usually consider property under ordinary common law principles, including money, real estate, or chattels. But for purposes of procedural due process, people also have property interests when positive law creates an entitlement to a government-bestowed benefit. For example, *Goldberg v. Kelly* (1970), Ch. 19.D.2.b, and *Mathews v. Eldridge* (1976), Ch. 19.D.3 held that the ability to receive future welfare and disability payments were property interests, even though those payments had not yet entered the recipient's possession. The right to continued utility service was a property interest in *Memphis Light, Gas & Water Division v. Craft*, 436 U.S. 1 (1978), even though at common law the service would not be property, but a matter of contract. The key is whether the law creating the benefit gives the government discretion to bestow it or not. No entitlement results from a law authorizing an arts commission to award grants to artists it considers deserving. But an entitlement is created by a law saying that any person who passes a driving test will receive a driver's license. Unlike the artist, the prospective driver is entitled to the government benefit, and the law does not give the government discretion to refuse it.

Liberty. Liberty interests are less cut-and-dried. The liberty inquiry asks whether a person is being deprived of a type of freedom that seems important enough to require procedural protection. No crisply defined test tells which freedoms those are, so precedent provides the best guide.

- At one end of the spectrum are cases holding that certain things are not liberty interests at all, like the right to have a good reputation in Paul v. Davis, or the right of a professor with no contract and no tenure to be hired for an additional year (the facts in Roth).
- At the other end of the spectrum are freedoms important enough to be deemed "fundamental rights," like the right to control a child's education in Meyer and Pierce or the right to marry in Loving. (The right not to be incarcerated is also fundamental right long considered to be part of "liberty," so many procedural due process cases are brought by prisoners.) Any right that is fundamental for purposes of equal protection, see Ch. 18, or substantive due process, see Ch. 20, will be a liberty interest for purposes of procedural due process. But in practice, most non-incarcerated people faced with deprivation of fundamental rights will have greater objections to the substance of a rights-restricting law than to the procedures used to enforce it.
- Falling in between those two poles are freedoms that count as liberty interests for purposes of procedural due process, but are not fundamental rights. Few cases outside of a prison setting explore that territory. One of the rare examples is the right to attend a public K–12 school, *Goss v. Lopez*, 419 U.S. 565 (1975), although that was also found to be a property interest.

Item C. *Adequate Procedures.* If a deprivation of a liberty or property interest is shown, a court must then consider the process "due" (owed) to the individual. An often-cited formula is "notice and an opportunity to be heard"—the person must be told that the deprivation is threatened and be given a chance to provide input to the governmental decision-maker "at a meaningful time and in a meaningful manner." *Armstrong v. Manzo*, 380 U.S. 545 (1965). Deciding whether a given procedure provides a meaningful opportunity to be heard is often fact-intensive and guided by the precedents most factually on point.

In general, the more serious the deprivation, the more rigorous the procedures. Deprivation of life—as in a capital murder trial—requires the most careful procedures known in our system. These go beyond the basics of the Fifth and Sixth Amendments (such as trial by jury) to include heightened requirements for the effective assistance of counsel, adequate funding for necessary expert witnesses, separate deliberations over guilt and punishment, and much more. By contrast, deprivation of a small amount of property—like a $20 parking ticket—requires far less procedure. The notice is little more than a note tucked under the windshield wiper, and the opportunity to be heard in traffic court is far less elaborate than a capital trial.

The factors identified in *Mathews v. Eldridge* (1976) are useful in assessing the adequacy of procedures: the importance of the deprivation to the affected individual; the value of the desired procedures; and the cost of those procedures. Although the *Mathews* factors can be helpful, they are not mandatory; many cases decided after *Mathews* follow a more holistic approach that considers the usual methods of constitutional reasoning (text, precedent, structure, history, consequences, and values).

C. Procedural Due Process for Courts: *Caperton v. Massey Coal*

Because courts are in the business of adjudication, procedural due process is a constant concern for the judiciary. In re Gault, 387 U.S. 1 (1967), explained the constitutional value of adequate court procedures:

> Failure to observe the fundamental requirements of due process has resulted in instances, which might have been avoided, of unfairness to individuals and inadequate or inaccurate findings of fact and unfortunate prescriptions of remedy. Due process of law is the primary and indispensable foundation of individual freedom. It is the basic and essential term in the social compact which defines the rights of the individual and delimits the powers which the state may exercise. As Mr. Justice Frankfurter has said: "The history of American freedom is, in no small measure, the history of procedure." *Malinski v. New York,* 324 U.S. 401 (1945) (concurring opinion). But, in addition, the procedural rules which have been fashioned from the generality of due process are our best instruments for the distillation and evaluation of essential facts from the conflicting welter of data that life and our adversary methods present. It is these instruments of due process which enhance the possibility that truth will emerge from the confrontation of opposing versions and conflicting data. Procedure is to law what "scientific method" is to science.

Entire bodies of law—especially Civil Procedure and Evidence—are rules giving concrete expression to the general standards of procedural due process. Another requirement of judicial due process is an unbiased decision-maker, which was the problem presented by *Caperton v. Massey Coal.*

The Law of Judicial Recusal. Centuries-old common law traditions call for judges to recuse (disqualify) themselves if they have a financial stake in the outcome of a case. Most American jurisdictions have statutes or court rules on the subject that go farther than the common law. For example, 28 U.S.C. § 455 requires federal judges to recuse themselves if they have a financial interest in the case, have personal knowledge of disputed evidentiary facts, have previously represented one of the parties as a lawyer or are presiding over "any proceeding in which his impartiality might reasonably be questioned."

In most jurisdictions, a judge decides for himself or herself whether recusal is necessary. *See, e.g., Cheney v. United States District Court*, 541 U.S. 913 (2004) (US Supreme Court justice denies motion to recuse after going on a hunting trip with the appellant). In *Caperton*, a justice of the West Virginia Supreme Court decided that he was not required to recuse himself under the state code of judicial conduct, which read in relevant part:

> A judge . . . shall avoid impropriety and the appearance of impropriety in all of the judge's activities, and shall act at all times in a manner that promotes public confidence in the integrity and impartiality of the judiciary. . . . The test for appearance of impropriety is whether the conduct would create in reasonable minds a perception that the judge's ability to carry out judicial responsibilities with integrity, impartiality, and competence is impaired.

With the state law question resolved, the issue for the US Supreme Court was whether recusal was required by the Due Process Clause.

ITEMS TO CONSIDER WHILE READING *CAPERTON v. MASSEY COAL*:

A. *Work through the items in the Kickstarter.*

B. *The dissent argues that Tumey v. Ohio and In Re Murchison represent the only situations where the Due Process Clause mandates recusal, while the majority treats them as non-exclusive examples. Which approach to precedent is more persuasive?*

C. *What other methods of constitutional reasoning are revealed in* Caperton*? Specifically, how do structure, history, consequences, and values contribute to the opinions?*

D. *Why are the dissenters so upset about a constitutional ruling that appears to be consistent with existing judicial recusal statutes?*

Caperton v. A.T. Massey Coal Co.,

556 U.S. 868 (2009)

Justice Kennedy delivered the opinion of the Court [joined by Justices Stevens, Souter, Ginsburg, and Breyer].

In this case the Supreme Court of Appeals of West Virginia reversed a trial court judgment, which had entered a jury verdict of $50 million. Five justices heard the case, and the vote to reverse was 3 to 2. The question presented is whether the Due Process Clause of the Fourteenth Amendment was violated when one of the justices in the majority denied a recusal motion. The basis for the motion was that the justice had received campaign contributions in an extraordinary amount from, and through the efforts of, the board chairman and principal officer of the corporation found liable for the damages.

Under our precedents there are objective standards that require recusal when the probability of actual bias on the part of the judge or decisionmaker is too high to be constitutionally tolerable. Applying those precedents, we find that, in all the circumstances of this case, due process requires recusal.

I

In August 2002 a West Virginia jury returned a verdict that found respondents A.T. Massey Coal Co. and its affiliates (hereinafter Massey) liable for fraudulent misrepresentation, concealment, and tortious interference with existing contractual relations. The jury awarded petitioners Hugh Caperton, Harman Development Corp., Harman Mining Corp., and Sovereign Coal Sales (hereinafter Caperton) the sum of $50 million in compensatory and punitive damages.

In June 2004 the state trial court denied Massey's post-trial motions challenging the verdict and the damages award, finding that Massey "intentionally acted in utter disregard of [Caperton's] rights and ultimately destroyed [Caperton's] businesses because, after conducting cost-benefit analyses, [Massey] concluded it was in its financial interest to do so." In March 2005 the trial court denied Massey's motion for judgment as a matter of law.

Don Blankenship is Massey's chairman, chief executive officer, and president. After the verdict but before the appeal, West Virginia held its 2004 judicial elections. Knowing the Supreme Court of Appeals of West Virginia would consider the appeal in the case, Blankenship decided to support an attorney who sought to replace Justice McGraw. Justice McGraw was a candidate for reelection to that court. The attorney who sought to replace him was Brent Benjamin.

In addition to contributing the $1,000 statutory maximum to Benjamin's campaign committee, Blankenship donated almost $2.5 million to "And For The Sake Of The Kids," a political organization [that] opposed McGraw and supported

Caperton v. A.T. Massey Coal Co.

Benjamin. Blankenship's donations accounted for more than two-thirds of the total funds it raised. This was not all. Blankenship spent, in addition, just over $500,000 on independent expenditures—for direct mailings and letters soliciting donations as well as television and newspaper advertisements to support Brent Benjamin.

To provide some perspective, Blankenship's $3 million in contributions were more than the total amount spent by all other Benjamin supporters and three times the amount spent by Benjamin's own committee. Caperton contends that Blankenship spent $1 million more than the total amount spent by the campaign committees of both candidates combined.

Benjamin won. He received 382,036 votes (53.3%), and McGraw received 334,301 votes (46.7%).

In October 2005, before Massey filed its petition for appeal in West Virginia's highest court, Caperton moved to disqualify now-Justice Benjamin under the Due Process Clause and the West Virginia Code of Judicial Conduct, based on the conflict caused by Blankenship's campaign involvement. Justice Benjamin denied the motion in April 2006. He indicated that he "carefully considered the bases and accompanying exhibits proffered by the movants." But he found "no objective information to show that this Justice has a bias for or against any litigant, that this Justice has prejudged the matters which comprise this litigation, or that this Justice will be anything but fair and impartial." In December 2006 Massey filed its petition for appeal to challenge the adverse jury verdict. The West Virginia Supreme Court of Appeals granted review.

In November 2007 that court reversed the $50 million verdict against Massey. The majority opinion, authored by then-Chief Justice Davis and joined by Justices Benjamin and Maynard, found that "Massey's conduct warranted the type of judgment rendered in this case." It reversed, nevertheless, based on two independent grounds—first, that a forum-selection clause contained in a contract to which Massey was not a party barred the suit in West Virginia, and, second, that *res judicata* barred the suit due to an out-of-state judgment to which Massey was not a party. Justice Starcher dissented, stating that the "majority's opinion is morally and legally wrong." Justice Albright also dissented, accusing the majority of "misapplying the law and introducing sweeping new law into our jurisprudence that may well come back to haunt us."

Caperton sought rehearing, and the parties moved for disqualification of three of the five justices who decided the appeal. Photos had surfaced of Justice Maynard vacationing with Blankenship in the French Riviera while the case was pending. Justice Maynard granted Caperton's recusal motion. On the other side Justice Starcher granted Massey's recusal motion, apparently based on his public criticism of Blankenship's role in the 2004 elections. In his recusal memorandum Justice Starcher urged Justice Benjamin to recuse himself as well. He noted that "Blankenship's bestowal of his personal wealth, political tactics, and friendship have created a cancer in the affairs of this Court." Justice Benjamin declined Justice Starcher's suggestion and denied Caperton's recusal motion.

The court granted rehearing. Justice Benjamin, now in the capacity of acting chief justice, selected Judges Cookman and Fox to **replace the recused justices**. Caperton moved a third time for disqualification, arguing that Justice Benjamin had failed to apply the correct standard under West Virginia law—i.e., whether "a reasonable and prudent person, knowing these objective facts, would harbor doubts about Justice Benjamin's ability to be fair and impartial." Caperton also included the results of a public opinion poll, which indicated that over 67% of West Virginians doubted Justice Benjamin would be fair and impartial. Justice Benjamin again refused to withdraw, noting that the "push poll" was "neither credible nor sufficiently reliable to serve as the basis for an elected judge's disqualification."

■ OBSERVATION

REPLACE THE RECUSED JUDGES: Most states and all lower federal courts have a mechanism to substitute other judges for those recused. By contrast, there is no substitution for a recused justice of the US Supreme Court, so the Court decides the case with fewer than nine justices. See, e.g., *Shelley v. Kraemer* (1948) (Ch. 20.B.1).

In April 2008 a divided court again reversed the jury verdict, and again it was a 3-to-2 decision. . . . The dissent [lamented the result on the merits and] also noted "genuine due process implications arising under federal law" with respect to Justice Benjamin's failure to recuse himself. 679 S.E.2d 223.

Four months later—a month after the petition for writ of certiorari was filed in this Court—Justice Benjamin filed a concurring opinion. [*Id.*] He defended the merits of the majority opinion as well as his decision not to recuse. He rejected Caperton's challenge to his participation in the case under both the Due Process Clause and West Virginia law. Justice Benjamin reiterated that he had no "direct, personal, substantial, pecuniary interest in this case." Adopting "a standard merely of appearances," he concluded, "seems little more than an invitation to subject West Virginia's justice system to the vagaries of the day—a framework in which predictability and stability yield to supposition, innuendo, half-truths, and partisan manipulations."

We granted certiorari.

II

It is axiomatic that a fair trial in a fair tribunal is a basic requirement of due process. As the Court has recognized, however, most matters relating to judicial disqualification do not rise to a constitutional level. The early and leading case on the subject is *Tumey v. Ohio*, 273 U.S. 510 (1927). There, the Court stated that "matters of kinship, personal bias, state policy, remoteness of interest, would seem generally to be matters merely of legislative discretion."

The *Tumey* Court concluded that the Due Process Clause incorporated the common-law rule that a judge must recuse himself when he has "a direct, personal, substantial, pecuniary interest" in a case. This rule reflects the maxim that "no man is allowed to be **a judge in his own cause**; because his interest would certainly bias his judgment, and, not improbably, corrupt his integrity." *The Federalist #10* (Madison). Under this rule, disqualification for bias or prejudice was not permitted; those matters were left to statutes and judicial codes. Personal bias or prejudice alone would not be sufficient basis for imposing a constitutional requirement under the Due Process Clause.

Caperton v. A.T. Massey Coal Co.

As new problems have emerged that were not discussed at common law, however, the Court has identified additional instances which, as an objective matter, require recusal. These are circumstances in which experience teaches that the probability of actual bias on the part of the judge or decisionmaker is too high to be constitutionally tolerable. To place the present case in proper context, two instances where the Court has required recusal merit further discussion.

■ HISTORY

A JUDGE IN HIS OWN CAUSE: Legal treatises by Sir Edward Coke (1628) and Sir William Blackstone (1765) hypothesized, as an example of obvious unfairness, a law that would make a man "a judge in his own cause" (his own case). The opinions of Justices Chase and Iredell in *Calder v. Bull*, 3 U.S. 386 (1798), see Ch. 3.E., both used this example, confident that lawyers trained in the common law tradition would be familiar with it.

A

The first involved the emergence of local tribunals where a judge had a financial interest in the outcome of a case, although the interest was less than what would have been considered personal or direct at common law.

This was the problem addressed in *Tumey*. There, the mayor of a village had the authority to sit as a judge (with no jury) to try those accused of violating a state law prohibiting the possession of alcoholic beverages. Inherent in this structure were two potential conflicts. First, . . . the mayor-judge thus received a salary supplement only if he convicted the defendant. Second, sums from the criminal fines were deposited to the village's general treasury fund for village improvements and repairs.

The Court held that the Due Process Clause required disqualification both because of the mayor-judge's direct pecuniary interest in the outcome, and because of his official motive to convict and to graduate the fine to help the financial needs of the village. It so held despite observing that "there are doubtless mayors who would not allow such a consideration as $12 costs in each case to affect their judgment in it." The Court articulated the controlling principle: "Every procedure which would offer a possible temptation to the average man as a judge to forget the burden of proof required to convict the defendant, or which might lead him not to hold the balance nice, clear and true between the State and the accused, denies the latter due process of law." The Court was thus concerned with more than the traditional common-law prohibition on direct pecuniary interest. It was also concerned with a more general concept of interests that tempt adjudicators to disregard neutrality. . . .

B

The second instance requiring recusal that was not discussed at common law emerged in the criminal contempt context, where a judge had no pecuniary interest in the case but was challenged because of a conflict arising from his participation in an earlier proceeding. This Court characterized that first proceeding (perhaps pejoratively) as a "one-man grand jury." *In Re Murchison*, 349 U.S. 133 (1955).

In that first proceeding, and as provided by state law, a judge examined witnesses [in private] to determine whether criminal charges should be brought. The judge called the two petitioners before him [for a secret hearing]. One petitioner answered questions, but the judge found him untruthful and charged him with perjury. The second declined to answer on the ground that he did not have counsel with him, as state law seemed to permit. The judge charged him with contempt. The judge proceeded to try and convict both petitioners.

This Court set aside the convictions on grounds that the judge had a conflict of interest at the trial stage because of his earlier participation followed by his decision to charge them. The Due Process Clause required disqualification. The Court recited the general rule that no man can be a judge in his own case, adding that "no man is permitted to try cases where he has an interest in the outcome." It noted that the disqualifying criteria "cannot be defined with precision. Circumstances and relationships must be considered." These circumstances and the prior relationship required recusal: "Having been a part of the one-man grand jury process a judge cannot be, in the very nature of things, wholly disinterested in the conviction or acquittal of those accused." That is because "as a practical matter it is difficult if not impossible for a judge to free himself from the influence of what took place in his 'grand-jury' secret session." . . .

Following *Murchison* the Court held in *Mayberry v. Pennsylvania*, 400 U.S. 455 (1971), that by reason of the Due Process Clause of the Fourteenth Amendment a defendant in criminal contempt proceedings should be given a public trial before a judge other than the one reviled by the contemnor. The Court reiterated that this rule rests on the relationship between the judge and the defendant: "A judge, vilified as was this Pennsylvania judge, necessarily becomes embroiled in a running, bitter controversy. No one so cruelly slandered is likely to maintain that calm detachment necessary for fair adjudication." . . . The inquiry is an objective one. The Court asks not whether the judge is actually, subjectively biased, but whether the average judge in his position is "likely" to be neutral, or whether there is an unconstitutional "potential for bias."

III

Caperton v. A.T. Massey Coal Co.

. . . Caperton contends that Blankenship's pivotal role in getting Justice Benjamin elected created a constitutionally intolerable probability of actual bias. Though not a bribe or criminal influence, Justice Benjamin would nevertheless feel a debt of gratitude to Blankenship for his extraordinary efforts to get him elected. That temptation, Caperton claims, is as strong and inherent in human nature as was the conflict the Court confronted in *Tumey,* when a mayor-judge (or the city) benefited financially from a defendant's conviction, as well as the conflict identified in *Murchison,* when a judge was the object of a defendant's contempt.

Justice Benjamin was careful to address the recusal motions and explain his reasons why, on his view of the controlling standard, disqualification was not in order. . . . Justice Benjamin conducted a probing search into his actual motives and inclinations; and he found none to be improper. We do not question his subjective findings of impartiality and propriety. Nor do we determine whether there was actual bias. . . .

The difficulties of inquiring into actual bias, and the fact that the inquiry is often a private one, simply underscore the need for objective rules. . . . In lieu of exclusive reliance on [the accused judge's personal inquiry into the judge's actual bias], or on appellate review of the judge's determination respecting actual bias, the Due Process Clause has been implemented by objective standards that do not require proof of actual bias. In defining these standards the Court has asked whether, under a realistic appraisal of psychological tendencies and human weakness, the interest poses such a risk of actual bias or prejudgment that the practice must be forbidden if the guarantee of due process is to be adequately implemented.

We turn to the influence at issue in this case. Not every campaign contribution by a litigant or attorney creates a probability of bias that requires a judge's recusal, but this is an exceptional case. We conclude that there is a serious risk of actual bias—based on objective and reasonable perceptions—when a person with a personal stake in a particular case had a significant and disproportionate influence in placing the judge on the case by raising funds or directing the judge's election campaign when the case was pending or imminent. The inquiry centers on the contribution's relative size in comparison to the total amount of money contributed to the campaign, the total amount spent in the election, and the apparent effect such contribution had on the outcome of the election.

Applying this principle, we conclude that Blankenship's campaign efforts had a significant and disproportionate influence in placing Justice Benjamin on the case. . . .

Massey responds that Blankenship's support, while significant, did not cause Benjamin's victory. In the end the people of West Virginia elected him, and they did so based on many reasons other than Blankenship's efforts. Massey points out that every major state newspaper, but one, endorsed Benjamin. It also contends

■ HISTORY

A SPEECH DURING THE CAMPAIGN: Justice McGraw appeared rambling and disorganized during a Labor Day speech that later went viral under the names "The Rant at Racine" or "The Scream at Racine." According to a West Virginia newspaper columnist, "McGraw sounded as though he was coming unhinged as he ranted about his opponents following him around to take pictures of him to make him look ugly."

that then-Justice McGraw cost himself the election by giving **a speech during the campaign**, a speech the opposition seized upon for its own advantage. . . .

Whether Blankenship's campaign contributions were a necessary and sufficient cause of Benjamin's victory is not the proper inquiry. Much like determining whether a judge is actually biased, proving what ultimately drives the electorate to choose a particular candidate is a difficult endeavor, not likely to lend itself to a certain conclusion. This is particularly true where, as here, there is no procedure for judicial factfinding and the sole trier of fact is the one accused of bias. Due process requires an objective inquiry into whether the contributor's influence on the election under all the circumstances "would offer a possible temptation to the average judge to lead him not to hold the balance nice, clear and true." *Tumey*. In an election decided by fewer than 50,000 votes (382,036 to 334,301), Blankenship's campaign contributions—in comparison to the total amount contributed to the campaign, as well as the total amount spent in the election—had a significant and disproportionate influence on the electoral outcome. And the risk that Blankenship's influence engendered actual bias is sufficiently substantial that it must be forbidden if the guarantee of due process is to be adequately implemented. . . .

Justice Benjamin did undertake an extensive search for actual bias. But, as we have indicated, that is just one step in the judicial process; objective standards may also require recusal whether or not actual bias exists or can be proved. Due process may sometimes bar trial by judges who have no actual bias and who would do their very best to weigh the scales of justice equally between contending parties. The failure to consider objective standards requiring recusal is not consistent with the imperatives of due process. We find that Blankenship's significant and disproportionate influence—coupled with the temporal relationship between the election and the pending case—offer a possible temptation to the average judge to lead him not to hold the balance nice, clear and true. On these extreme facts the probability of actual bias rises to an unconstitutional level.

IV

Our decision today addresses an extraordinary situation where the Constitution requires recusal. Massey and its amici predict that various adverse consequences will follow from recognizing a constitutional violation here—ranging from a flood of recusal motions to unnecessary interference with judicial elections. We disagree. The facts now before us are extreme by any measure. The parties point to no other instance involving judicial campaign contributions that presents a potential for bias comparable to the circumstances in this case.

Caperton v. A.T. Massey Coal Co.

It is true that extreme cases often test the bounds of established legal principles, and sometimes no administrable standard may be available to address the perceived wrong. But it is also true that extreme cases are more likely to cross constitutional limits, requiring this Court's intervention and formulation of objective standards. This is particularly true when due process is violated.

Chief Justice Roberts, with whom Justices Scalia, Thomas, and Alito join, dissenting.

I, of course, share the majority's sincere concerns about the need to maintain a fair, independent, and impartial judiciary—and one that appears to be such. But I fear that the Court's decision will undermine rather than promote these values.

Until today, we have recognized exactly two situations in which the Federal Due Process Clause requires disqualification of a judge: when the judge has a financial interest in the outcome of the case, and when the judge is trying a defendant for certain criminal contempts. Vaguer notions of bias or the appearance of bias were never a basis for disqualification, either at common law or under our constitutional precedents. Those issues were instead addressed by legislation or court rules.

Today, however, the Court enlists the Due Process Clause to overturn a judge's failure to recuse because of a "probability of bias." Unlike the established grounds for disqualification, a probability of bias cannot be defined in any limited way. The Court's new rule provides no guidance to judges and litigants about when recusal will be constitutionally required. This will inevitably lead to an increase in allegations that judges are biased, however groundless those charges may be. The end result will do far more to erode public confidence in judicial impartiality than an isolated failure to recuse in a particular case.

I

There is a presumption of honesty and integrity in those serving as adjudicators. All judges take an oath to uphold the Constitution and apply the law impartially, and we trust that they will live up to this promise. We have thus identified only two situations in which the Due Process Clause requires disqualification of a judge: when the judge has a financial interest in the outcome of the case, *Tumey*, and when the judge is presiding over certain types of criminal contempt proceedings, *Murchison*. . . . Our decisions in this area have also emphasized when the Due Process Clause does not require recusal: "All questions of judicial qualification may not involve constitutional validity. Thus matters of kinship, personal bias, state policy, remoteness of interest, would seem generally to be matters merely of legislative discretion." *Tumey*. Subject to the two well-established exceptions described above, questions of judicial recusal are regulated by common law, statute, or the professional standards of the bench and bar.

In any given case, there are a number of factors that could give rise to a probability or appearance of bias: friendship with a party or lawyer, prior employment experience, membership in clubs or associations, prior speeches and writings, religious affiliation, and countless other considerations. We have never held that the Due Process Clause requires recusal for any of these reasons, even though they could be viewed as presenting a probability of bias. Many state statutes require recusal based on a probability or appearance of bias, but that alone would not be sufficient basis for imposing a constitutional requirement under the Due Process Clause. States are, of course, free to adopt broader recusal rules than the Constitution requires—and every State has—but these developments are not continuously incorporated into the Due Process Clause.

II

In departing from this clear line between when recusal is constitutionally required and when it is not, the majority repeatedly emphasizes the need for an "objective" standard. The majority's analysis is "objective" in that it does not inquire into Justice Benjamin's motives or decisionmaking process. But the standard the majority articulates—probability of bias—fails to provide clear, workable guidance for future cases. At the most basic level, it is unclear whether the new probability of bias standard is somehow limited to financial support in judicial elections, or applies to judicial recusal questions more generally.

But there are other fundamental questions as well. With little help from the majority, courts will now have to determine:

1. How much money is too much money? What level of contribution or expenditure gives rise to a probability of bias?

2. How do we determine whether a given expenditure is "disproportionate"? Disproportionate to what?

3. Are independent, non-coordinated expenditures treated the same as direct contributions to a candidate's campaign? What about contributions to independent outside groups supporting a candidate?

4. Does it matter whether the litigant has contributed to other candidates or made large expenditures in connection with other elections?

5. Does the amount at issue in the case matter? What if this case were an employment dispute with only $10,000 at stake? What if the plaintiffs only sought non-monetary relief such as an injunction or declaratory judgment?

Caperton v. A.T. Massey Coal Co.

6. Does the analysis change depending on whether the judge whose disqualification is sought sits on a trial court, appeals court, or state supreme court?

7. How long does the probability of bias last? Does the probability of bias diminish over time as the election recedes? Does it matter whether the judge plans to run for reelection?

8. What if the disproportionately large expenditure is made by an industry association, trade union, physicians' group, or the plaintiffs' bar? Must the judge recuse in all cases that affect the association's interests? Must the judge recuse in all cases in which a party or lawyer is a member of that group? Does it matter how much the litigant contributed to the association?

9. What if the case involves a social or ideological issue rather than a financial one? Must a judge recuse from cases involving, say, abortion rights if he has received "disproportionate" support from individuals who feel strongly about either side of that issue? If the supporter wants to help elect judges who are "tough on crime," must the judge recuse in all criminal cases?

10. What if the candidate draws "disproportionate" support from a particular racial, religious, ethnic, or other group, and the case involves an issue of particular importance to that group?

11. What if the supporter is not a party to the pending or imminent case, but his interests will be affected by the decision? Does the Court's analysis apply if the supporter "chooses the judge" not in his case, but in someone else's?

12. What if the case implicates a regulatory issue that is of great importance to the party making the expenditures, even though he has no direct financial interest in the outcome (e.g., a facial challenge to an agency rulemaking or a suit seeking to limit an agency's jurisdiction)?

13. Must the judge's vote be outcome determinative in order for his non-recusal to constitute a due process violation?

14. Does the due process analysis consider the underlying merits of the suit? Does it matter whether the decision is clearly right (or wrong) as a matter of state law?

15. What if a lower court decision in favor of the supporter is affirmed on the merits on appeal, by a panel with no debt of gratitude to the supporter? Does that moot the due process claim?

16. What if the judge voted against the supporter in many other cases?

17. What if the judge disagrees with the supporter's message or tactics? What if the judge expressly disclaims the support of this person?

18. Should we assume that elected judges feel a debt of hostility towards major opponents of their candidacies? Must the judge recuse in cases involving individuals or groups who spent large amounts of money trying unsuccessfully to defeat him?

19. If there is independent review of a judge's recusal decision, e.g., by a panel of other judges, does this completely foreclose a due process claim?

20. Does a debt of gratitude for endorsements by newspapers, interest groups, politicians, or celebrities also give rise to a constitutionally unacceptable probability of bias? How would we measure whether such support is disproportionate?

21. Does close personal friendship between a judge and a party or lawyer now give rise to a probability of bias?

22. Does it matter whether the campaign expenditures come from a party or the party's attorney? If from a lawyer, must the judge recuse in every case involving that attorney?

23. Does what is unconstitutional vary from State to State? What if particular States have a history of expensive judicial elections?

24. Under the majority's "objective" test, do we analyze the due process issue through the lens of a reasonable person, a reasonable lawyer, or a reasonable judge?

25. What role does causation play in this analysis? The Court sends conflicting signals on this point. The majority asserts that "whether Blankenship's campaign contributions were a necessary and sufficient cause of Benjamin's victory is not the proper inquiry." But elsewhere in the opinion, the majority considers "the apparent effect such contribution had on the outcome of the election," and whether the litigant has been able to "choose the judge in his own cause." If causation is a pertinent factor, how do we know whether the contribution or expenditure had any effect on the outcome of the election? What if the judge won in a landslide? What if the judge won primarily because of his opponent's missteps?

26. Is the due process analysis less probing for incumbent judges—who typically have a great advantage in elections—than for challengers? *Caperton v. A.T. Massey Coal Co.*

27. How final must the pending case be with respect to the contributor's interest? What if, for example, the only issue on appeal is whether the court should certify a class of plaintiffs? Is recusal required just as if the issue in the pending case were ultimate liability?

28. Which cases are implicated by this doctrine? Must the case be pending at the time of the election? Reasonably likely to be brought? What about an important but unanticipated case filed shortly after the election?

29. When do we impute a probability of bias from one party to another? Does a contribution from a corporation get imputed to its executives, and vice-versa? Does a contribution or expenditure by one family member get imputed to other family members?

30. What if the election is nonpartisan? What if the election is just a yes-or-no vote about whether to retain an incumbent?

31. What type of support is disqualifying? What if the supporter's expenditures are used to fund voter registration or get-out-the-vote efforts rather than television advertisements?

32. Are contributions or expenditures in connection with a primary aggregated with those in the general election? What if the contributor supported a different candidate in the primary? Does that dilute the debt of gratitude?

33. What procedures must be followed to challenge a state judge's failure to recuse? May Caperton claims only be raised on direct review? Or may such claims also be brought in federal district court under 42 U.S.C. § 1983, which allows a person deprived of a federal right by a state official to sue for damages? If § 1983 claims are available, who are the proper defendants? The judge? The whole court? The clerk of court?

34. What about state-court cases that are already closed? Can the losing parties in those cases now seek collateral relief in federal district court under § 1983? What statutes of limitation should be applied to such suits?

35. What is the proper remedy? After a successful *Caperton* motion, must the parties start from scratch before the lower courts? Is any part of the lower court judgment retained?

36. Does a litigant waive his due process claim if he waits until after decision to raise it? Or would the claim only be ripe after decision, when the judge's actions or vote suggest a probability of bias?

37. Are the parties entitled to discovery with respect to the judge's recusal decision?

38. If a judge erroneously fails to recuse, do we apply harmless-error review?

39. Does the judge get to respond to the allegation that he is probably biased, or is his reputation solely in the hands of the parties to the case?

40. What if the parties settle a *Caperton* claim as part of a broader settlement of the case? Does that leave the judge with no way to salvage his reputation?

These are only a few uncertainties that quickly come to mind. Judges and litigants will surely encounter others when they are forced to, or wish to, apply the majority's decision in different circumstances. Today's opinion requires state and federal judges simultaneously to act as political scientists (why did candidate X win the election?), economists (was the financial support disproportionate?), and psychologists (is there likely to be a debt of gratitude?).

The Court's inability to formulate a judicially discernible and manageable standard strongly counsels against the recognition of a novel constitutional right. The need to consider these and countless other questions helps explain why the common law and this Court's constitutional jurisprudence have never required disqualification on such vague grounds as probability or appearance of bias.

III

A

To its credit, the Court seems to recognize that the inherently boundless nature of its new rule poses a problem. But the majority's only answer is that the present case is an "extreme" one, so there is no need to worry about other cases. The Court repeats this point over and over.

But this is just so much whistling past the graveyard. Claims that have little chance of success are nonetheless frequently filed. The success rate for certiorari petitions before this Court is approximately 1.1%, and yet the previous Term some 8,241 were filed. Every one of the *Caperton* motions or appeals or § 1983 actions will claim that the judge is biased, or probably biased, bringing the judge and the judicial system into disrepute. And all future litigants will assert that their case is really the most extreme thus far.

Extreme cases often test the bounds of established legal principles. There is a cost to yielding to the desire to correct the extreme case, rather than adhering to the legal principle. That cost has been demonstrated so often that it is captured in a legal aphorism: Hard cases make bad law. . . .

B

. . . It is an old cliché, but sometimes the cure is worse than the disease. I am sure there are cases where a probability of bias should lead the prudent judge to step aside, but the judge fails to do so. Maybe this is one of them. But I believe that opening the door to recusal claims under the Due Process Clause, for an amorphous probability of bias, will itself bring our judicial system into undeserved disrepute, and diminish the confidence of the American people in the fairness and integrity of their courts. I hope I am wrong.

I respectfully dissent.

Justice Scalia, dissenting.

. . . A Talmudic maxim instructs with respect to the Scripture: "Turn it over, and turn it over, for all is therein." Divinely inspired text may contain the answers to all earthly questions, but the Due Process Clause most assuredly does not. The Court today continues its quixotic quest to right all wrongs and repair all imperfections through the Constitution. Alas, the quest cannot succeed—which is why some wrongs and imperfections have been called nonjusticiable. In the best of all possible worlds, should judges sometimes recuse even where the clear commands of our prior due process law do not require it? Undoubtedly. The relevant question, however, is whether we do more good than harm by seeking to correct this imperfection through expansion of our constitutional mandate in a manner ungoverned by any discernable rule. The answer is obvious.

flash*forward*

1. Caperton *on Remand.* The West Virginia Supreme Court once again considered Massey's appeal on remand, but this time with a court that did not contain Justice Benjamin or the other already-recused justices. It ruled 4–1 in favor of Massey on the forum selection clause issue, concluding that Caperton should have filed in Virginia. 690 S.E.2d 322 (W.V. 2009). The action was refiled in Virginia, where a jury ruled for Caperton in 2014.

2. Caperton *in Fiction.* Before the US Supreme Court ruled, John Grisham published the legal thriller *The Appeal* (2008), where the owner of a chemical company that lost a big jury verdict takes steps to elect a compliant judge to the state supreme court. Asked on *The Today Show* whether the plot was plausible, Grisham said, "It happened a few years ago in West Virginia."

D. Procedural Due Process for Executive Action

Whether it is a clerk in City Hall deciding whether to issue a construction permit, an immigration officer deciding whether to grant political asylum, or a school principal deciding whether to discipline a student, executive branch officers regularly make individualized enforcement decisions. These decisions are usually made pursuant to statutes or regulations designed to provide adequate procedures. Constitutional litigation may result if no written procedures exist, or if the written procedures are inadequate to the task.

1. Deprivation

Any due process violation (procedural or substantive) requires a "deprivation." The first case described below was framed as a procedural due process violation, and the second substantive.

a) Mere Negligence: *Daniels v. Williams*

ITEMS TO CONSIDER WHILE READING
DANIELS v. WILLIAMS:

A. *Work through the items in the Kickstarter.*

B. *What does it take for government action to constitute a deprivation? Why does mere negligence not count?*

C. *In many cases of alleged governmental misconduct, plaintiffs may be able to assert state law theories. Why might a plaintiff prefer to argue the case as a violation of the US Constitution? (One reason is that 42 U.S.C. § 1988 allows prevailing plaintiffs in constitutional rights cases to collect attorneys' fees as part of the judgment.)*

Daniels v. Williams,
474 U.S. 327 (1986)

Justice Rehnquist delivered the opinion of the Court [joined by Chief Justice Burger and Justices Brennan, White, Powell, and O'Connor].

. . . Petitioner [Roy Daniels] seeks to recover damages for back and ankle injuries allegedly sustained when he fell on a prison stairway. He claims that, while an inmate at the city jail in Richmond, Virginia, he slipped on a pillow negligently left on the stairs by respondent [Andrew Williams], a correctional deputy stationed at the jail. Respondent's negligence, the argument runs, "deprived" petitioner of his "liberty" interest in freedom from bodily injury, because respondent maintains that he is entitled to the defense of sovereign immunity in a state tort suit, petitioner is without an adequate state remedy. Accordingly, the deprivation of liberty was without "due process of law." *Daniels v. Williams*

The District Court granted respondent's motion for summary judgment. [The Fourth Circuit affirmed in a divided opinion.] Because of the inconsistent approaches taken by lower courts in determining when tortious conduct by state officials rises to the level of a constitutional tort, and the apparent lack of adequate guidance from this Court, we granted certiorari. We now affirm.

In *Parratt v. Taylor*, 451 U.S. 527 (1981), we granted certiorari, as we had twice before, to decide whether mere negligence will support a claim for relief under 42 U.S.C. § 1983 [the federal statute allowing individuals to sue state employees for violating rights protected by the US Constitution]. . . .

In *Parratt*, . . . we said that the loss of the prisoner's hobby kit, "even though negligently caused, amounted to a deprivation under the Due Process Clause." Justice Powell, concurring in the result, . . . argued that negligent acts by state officials, though causing loss of property, are not actionable under the Due Process Clause. To Justice Powell, mere negligence could not work a deprivation in the constitutional sense. Not only does the word "deprive" in the Due Process Clause connote more than a negligent act, but we should not open the federal courts to lawsuits where there has been no affirmative abuse of power. Upon reflection, we agree and overrule *Parratt* to the extent that it states that mere lack of due care by a state official may "deprive" an individual of life, liberty, or property under the Fourteenth Amendment.

The Due Process Clause of the Fourteenth Amendment provides: "[N]or shall any State deprive any person of life, liberty, or property, without due process of law." Historically, this guarantee of due process has been applied to deliberate decisions of government officials to deprive a person of life, liberty, or property. No decision of this Court before *Parratt* supported the view that negligent conduct by a state official, even though causing injury, constitutes a deprivation under the Due Process Clause. This history reflects the traditional and common-sense notion that the Due Process Clause, like its forebear in the Magna Carta, was intended to secure the individual from the arbitrary exercise of the powers of government. By requiring the government to follow appropriate procedures when its agents decide to "deprive any person of life, liberty, or property," the Due Process Clause promotes fairness in such decisions. And by barring certain government actions regardless of the fairness of the procedures used to implement them, it serves to prevent governmental power from being used for purposes of oppression.

We think that the actions of prison custodians in leaving a pillow on the prison stairs, or mislaying an inmate's property, are quite remote from the concerns just discussed. Far from an abuse of power, lack of due care suggests no more than a failure to measure up to the conduct of a reasonable person. To hold that injury caused by such conduct is a deprivation within the meaning of the Fourteenth Amendment would trivialize the centuries-old principle of due process of law.

The Fourteenth Amendment is a part of a Constitution generally designed to allocate governing authority among the Branches of the Federal Government and between that Government and the States, and to secure certain individual rights against both State and Federal Government. When dealing with a claim that such a document creates a right in prisoners to sue a government official because he negligently created an unsafe condition in the prison, we bear in mind Chief Justice Marshall's admonition that "we must never forget, that it is a *constitution* we are expounding," *McCulloch v. Maryland* (1819) (emphasis in original). Our Constitution deals with the large concerns of the governors and the governed, but it does not purport to supplant traditional tort law in laying down rules of conduct to regulate liability for injuries that attend living together in society. We have previously rejected reasoning that would make of the Fourteenth Amendment a font of tort law to be superimposed upon whatever systems may already be administered by the States. . . . Where a government official's act causing injury to life, liberty, or property is merely negligent, no procedure for compensation is constitutionally required.

That injuries inflicted by governmental negligence are not addressed by the United States Constitution is not to say that they may not raise significant legal concerns and lead to the creation of protectible legal interests. The enactment of tort claim statutes, for example, reflects the view that injuries caused by such negligence should generally be redressed. It is no reflection on either the breadth of the United States Constitution or the importance of traditional tort law to say that they do not address the same concerns. . . .

Justice Blackmun, with whom Justice Marshall joins, [concurring in *Daniels* but dissenting in the companion case of *Davidson v. Cannon*, 474 U.S. 344 (1986), where the plaintiff alleged that a prison negligently failed to protect him from a foreseeable beating by another inmate.]

. . . In *Daniels*, also a § 1983 suit, the Court holds that a pretrial detainee, allegedly injured when he slipped on a pillow negligently left on the jail stairs by a deputy, as a matter of law suffered no deprivation under the Fourteenth Amendment. While I concur in the judgment in *Daniels*, I do not join the Court in extending that result to [*Davidson*]. It is one thing to hold that a commonplace slip and fall, or the loss of a $23.50 hobby kit, see *Parratt v. Taylor*, does not rise to the dignified level of a constitutional violation. It is a somewhat different thing to say that negligence that permits anticipated inmate violence resulting in injury, or perhaps leads to the execution of the wrong prisoner, does not implicate the Constitution's guarantee of due process. When the State incarcerated Daniels, it left intact his own faculties for avoiding a slip and a fall. But the State prevented Davidson from defending himself, and therefore assumed some responsibility to protect him from the dangers to which he was exposed. In these circumstances, I feel that Davidson was deprived of liberty by the negligence of the prison officials. Moreover, the acts of the state officials in this case may well have risen to the level of recklessness. I therefore dissent. . . .

In *Daniels*, the negligence was only coincidentally connected to an inmate-guard relationship; the same incident could have occurred on any staircase. Daniels in jail was as able as he would have been anywhere else to protect himself against a pillow on the stairs. The State did not prohibit him from looking where he was going or from taking care to avoid the pillow.

In contrast, where the State renders a person vulnerable and strips him of his ability to defend himself, an injury that results from a state official's negligence in performing his duty is peculiarly related to the governmental function. Negligence in such a case implicates the misuse of power, possessed by virtue of state law and made possible only because the wrongdoer is clothed with the authority of state law. The deliberate decision not to protect Davidson from a known threat was directly related to the often violent life of prisoners. And protecting inmates from attack is central to one of the State's primary missions in running a prison—the maintenance of internal security.

The Fourteenth Amendment is not trivialized by recognizing that in some situations negligence can lead to a deprivation of liberty. On the contrary, excusing the State's failure to provide reasonable protection to inmates against prison violence demeans both the Fourteenth Amendment and individual dignity.

Justice Stevens, concurring in the judgments [in *Daniels* and *Davidson*].

Two prisoners raise similar claims in these two cases. Both seek to recover for personal injuries suffered, in part, from what they allege was negligence by state officials. Both characterize their injuries as "deprivations of liberty" and both invoke 42 U.S.C. § 1983 as a basis for their claims. . . . I agree with the majority that petitioners cannot prevail under § 1983. I do not agree, however, that it is necessary either to redefine the meaning of "deprive" in the Fourteenth Amendment, or to repudiate the reasoning of *Parratt v. Taylor*, to support this conclusion.

We should begin by identifying the precise constitutional claims that petitioners have advanced. It is not enough to note that they rely on the Due Process Clause of the Fourteenth Amendment, for that Clause is the source of three different kinds of constitutional protection. First, it incorporates specific protections defined in the Bill of Rights. Thus, the State, as well as the Federal Government, must comply with the commands in the First and Eighth Amendments; so too, the State must respect the guarantees in the Fourth, Fifth, and Sixth Amendments. Second, it contains a substantive component, sometimes referred to as "substantive due process," which bars certain arbitrary government actions regardless of the fairness of the procedures used to implement them. Third, it is a guarantee of fair procedure, sometimes referred to as "procedural due process:" the State may not execute, imprison, or fine a defendant without giving him a fair trial, nor may it take property without providing appropriate procedural safeguards. . . . [The claims in these cases] are of the third kind: Daniels and Davidson attack the validity of the procedures that Virginia and New Jersey, respectively, provide for prisoners who seek redress for physical injury caused by the negligence of corrections officers.

I would not reject these claims, as the Court does, by attempting to fashion a new definition of the term "deprivation" and excluding negligence from its scope. No serious question has been raised about the presence of state action in the allegations of negligence, and the interest in freedom from bodily harm surely qualifies as an interest in "liberty." Thus, the only question is whether negligence by state actors can result in a deprivation. "Deprivation," it seems to me, identifies, not the actor's state of mind, but the victim's infringement or loss. The harm to a prisoner is the same whether a pillow is left on a stair negligently, recklessly, or intentionally; so too, the harm resulting to a prisoner from an attack is the same whether his request for protection is ignored negligently, recklessly, or deliberately. In each instance, the prisoner is losing—being "deprived" of—an aspect of liberty as the result, in part, of a form of state action.

Thus, I would characterize each loss as a "deprivation" of liberty. Because the cases raise only procedural due process claims, however, it is also necessary to examine the nature of petitioners' challenges to the state procedures. To prevail, petitioners must demonstrate that the state procedures for redressing injuries of this kind are constitutionally inadequate. Petitioners must show that they contain a defect so serious that we can characterize the procedures as fundamentally unfair, a defect so basic that we are forced to conclude that the deprivation occurred without due process. . . .

[Assuming as true that state tort law was unavailable, the case] puts the question whether a state policy of noncompensability for certain types of harm, in which state action may play a role, renders a state procedure constitutionally defective. In my judgment, a state policy that defeats recovery does not, in itself, carry that consequence. Those aspects of a State's tort regime that defeat recovery are not constitutionally invalid, so long as there is no fundamental unfairness in their operation. Thus, defenses such as contributory negligence or statutes of limitations may defeat recovery in particular cases without raising any question about the constitutionality of a State's procedures for disposing of tort litigation. Similarly, in my judgment, the mere fact that a State elects to provide some of its agents with a sovereign immunity defense in certain cases does not justify the conclusion that its remedial system is constitutionally inadequate. There is no reason to believe that the Due Process Clause of the Fourteenth Amendment and the legislation enacted pursuant to § 5 of that Amendment [i.e., 42 U.S.C. § 1983] should be construed to suggest that the doctrine of sovereign immunity renders a state procedure fundamentally unfair. . . .

Thus, although I believe that the harms alleged by Daniels and proved by Davidson qualify as deprivations of liberty, I am not persuaded that either has raised a violation of the Due Process Clause of the Fourteenth Amendment. I therefore concur in the judgments.

b) Failure to Protect from Third Parties: *DeShaney v. Winnebago County*

DeShaney was litigated as a substantive due process claim, but its logic with regard to deprivations applies to cases involving both procedural and substantive due process.

ITEMS TO CONSIDER WHILE READING
DESHANEY v. WINNEBAGO COUNTY:

A. *Work through the items in the Kickstarter, noting where the majority and dissent approach items differently.*

B. *What explains plaintiff's choice of defendants? Consider who was sued and who was not.*

C. *The majority and dissenting opinions in* DeShaney *devote more than the usual amount of space to consequences. What are the consequences of each approach to due process?*

DeShaney v. Winnebago County Department of Social Services,

489 U.S. 189 (1989)

Chief Justice Rehnquist delivered the opinion of the Court [joined by Justices White, Stevens, O'Connor, Scalia, and Kennedy].

Petitioner is a boy who was beaten and permanently injured by his father, with whom he lived. Respondents are social workers and other local officials who received complaints that petitioner was being abused by his father and had reason to believe that this was the case, but nonetheless did not act to remove petitioner from his father's custody. Petitioner sued respondents claiming that their failure to act deprived him of his liberty in violation of the Due Process Clause of the Fourteenth Amendment to the United States Constitution. We hold that it did not.

I

The facts of this case are undeniably tragic. Petitioner Joshua DeShaney was born in 1979. In 1980, a Wyoming court granted his parents a divorce and awarded custody of Joshua to his father, Randy DeShaney. The father shortly thereafter moved to Neenah, a city located in Winnebago County, Wisconsin, taking the infant Joshua with him. There he entered into a second marriage, which also ended in divorce.

The Winnebago County authorities first learned that Joshua DeShaney might be a victim of child abuse in January 1982, when his father's second wife complained to the police, at the time of their divorce, that he had previously "hit the boy causing marks and was a prime case for child abuse." The Winnebago County Department of Social Services (DSS) interviewed the father, but he denied the accusations, and DSS did not pursue them further. In January 1983, Joshua was admitted to a local hospital with multiple bruises and abrasions. The examining physician suspected child abuse and notified DSS, which immediately obtained an order from a Wisconsin juvenile court placing Joshua in the temporary custody of the hospital. Three days later, the county convened an ad hoc Child Protection Team—consisting of a pediatrician, a psychologist, a police detective, the county's lawyer, several DSS caseworkers, and various hospital personnel—to consider Joshua's situation. At this meeting, the Team decided that there was insufficient evidence of child abuse to retain Joshua in the custody of the court. The Team did, however, decide to recommend several measures to protect Joshua, including enrolling him in a preschool program, providing his father with certain counseling services, and encouraging his father's girlfriend to move out of the home. Randy DeShaney entered into a voluntary agreement with DSS in which he promised to cooperate with them in accomplishing these goals.

Based on the recommendation of the Child Protection Team, the juvenile court dismissed the child protection case and returned Joshua to the custody of his father. A month later, emergency room personnel called the DSS caseworker handling Joshua's case to report that he had once again been treated for suspicious injuries. The caseworker concluded that there was no basis for action. For the next six months, the caseworker made monthly visits to the DeShaney home, during which she observed a number of suspicious injuries on Joshua's head; she also noticed that he had not been enrolled in school, and that the girlfriend had not moved out. The caseworker dutifully recorded these incidents in her files, along with her continuing suspicions that someone in the DeShaney household was physically abusing Joshua, but she did nothing more. In November 1983, the emergency room notified DSS that Joshua had been treated once again for injuries that they believed to be caused by child abuse. On the caseworker's next two visits to the DeShaney home, she was told that Joshua was too ill to see her. Still DSS took no action.

In March 1984, Randy DeShaney beat 4-year-old Joshua so severely that he fell into a life-threatening coma. Emergency brain surgery revealed a series of hemorrhages caused by traumatic injuries to the head inflicted over a long period of time. Joshua did not die, but he suffered brain damage so severe that he is expected to spend the rest of his life confined to an institution for the profoundly retarded. Randy DeShaney was subsequently tried and convicted of child abuse.

Joshua and his mother brought this action under 42 U.S.C. § 1983 in the United States District Court for the Eastern District of Wisconsin against respondents Winnebago County, DSS, and various individual employees of DSS. The complaint alleged that respondents had deprived Joshua of his liberty without due process of law, in violation of his rights under the Fourteenth Amendment, by failing to intervene to protect him against a risk of violence at his father's hands of which they knew or should have known. The District Court granted summary judgment for respondents.

The Court of Appeals for the Seventh Circuit affirmed. . . . Because of the inconsistent approaches taken by the lower courts in determining when, if ever, the failure of a state or local governmental entity or its agents to provide an individual with adequate protective services constitutes a violation of the individual's due process rights, and the importance of the issue to the administration of state and local governments, we granted certiorari. We now affirm.

II

The Due Process Clause of the Fourteenth Amendment provides that "no State shall . . . deprive any person of life, liberty, or property, without due process of law." Petitioners contend that the State deprived Joshua of his liberty interest in freedom from unjustified intrusions on personal security by failing to provide him with adequate protection against his father's violence. The claim is one invoking the substantive rather than the procedural component of the Due Process Clause; petitioners do not claim that the State denied Joshua protection without according him appropriate procedural safeguards, but that it was categorically obligated to protect him in these circumstances.

But nothing in the language of the Due Process Clause itself requires the State to protect the life, liberty, and property of its citizens against invasion by private actors. The Clause is phrased as a limitation on the State's power to act, not as a guarantee of certain minimal levels of safety and security. It forbids the State itself to deprive individuals of life, liberty, or property without due process of law, but its language cannot fairly be extended to impose an affirmative obligation on the State to ensure that those interests do not come to harm through other means. Nor does history support such an expansive reading of the constitutional text. Like its counterpart in the Fifth Amendment, the Due Process Clause of the Fourteenth Amendment was intended to prevent government from abusing its power, or employing it as an instrument of oppression. See *Daniels v. Williams* (1986). Its purpose was to protect the people from the State, not to ensure that the State protected them from each other. The Framers were content to leave the extent of governmental obligation in the latter area to the democratic political processes.

Consistent with these principles, our cases have recognized that the Due Process Clauses generally confer no affirmative right to governmental aid, even where such aid may be necessary to secure life, liberty, or property interests of which the government itself may not deprive the individual. . . . If the Due Process Clause does not require the State to provide its citizens with particular protective services, it follows that the State cannot be held liable under the Clause for injuries that could have been averted had it chosen to provide them. As a general matter, then, we conclude that a State's failure to protect an individual against private violence simply does not constitute a violation of the Due Process Clause.

Petitioners contend, however, that even if the Due Process Clause imposes no affirmative obligation on the State to provide the general public with adequate protective services, such a duty may arise out of certain "special relationships" created or assumed by the State with respect to particular individuals. Petitioners argue that such a "special relationship" existed here because the State knew that Joshua faced a special danger of abuse at his father's hands, and specifically proclaimed, by word and by deed, its intention to protect him against that danger. Having actually undertaken to protect Joshua from this danger—which petitioners concede the State played no part in creating—the State acquired an affirmative "duty," enforceable through the Due Process Clause, to do so in a reasonably competent fashion. Its failure to discharge that duty, so the argument goes, was an abuse of governmental power that so shocks the conscience as to constitute a substantive due process violation.

We reject this argument. It is true that in certain limited circumstances the Constitution imposes upon the State affirmative duties of care and protection with respect to particular individuals. . . . But these cases afford petitioners no help. Taken together, they stand only for the proposition that when the State takes a person into its custody and holds him there against his will, the Constitution imposes upon it a corresponding duty to assume some responsibility for his safety and general well-being. . . . The affirmative duty to protect arises not from the State's knowledge of the individual's predicament or from its expressions of intent to help him, but from the limitation which it has imposed on his freedom to act on his own behalf. In the substantive due process analysis, it is the State's affirmative act of restraining the individual's freedom to act on his own behalf—through incarceration, institutionalization, or other similar restraint of personal liberty—which is the deprivation of liberty triggering the protections of the Due Process Clause, not its failure to act to protect his liberty interests against harms inflicted by other means. . . .

It may well be that, by voluntarily undertaking to protect Joshua against a danger it concededly played no part in creating, the State acquired a duty under state tort law to provide him with adequate protection against that danger. But the claim here is based on the Due Process Clause of the Fourteenth Amendment, which, as we have said many times, does not transform every tort committed by a state actor

DeShaney v. Winnebago County Department of Social Services

into a constitutional violation. . . . Because, as explained above, the State had no constitutional duty to protect Joshua against his father's violence, its failure to do so—though calamitous in hindsight—simply does not constitute a violation of the Due Process Clause.

Judges and lawyers, like other humans, are moved by natural sympathy in a case like this to find a way for Joshua and his mother to receive adequate compensation for the grievous harm inflicted upon them. But before yielding to that impulse, it is well to remember once again that the harm was inflicted not by the State of Wisconsin, but by Joshua's father. The most that can be said of the state functionaries in this case is that they stood by and did nothing when suspicious circumstances dictated a more active role for them. In defense of them it must also be said that had they moved too soon to take custody of the son away from the father, they would likely have been met with charges of improperly intruding into the parent-child relationship, charges based on the same Due Process Clause that forms the basis for the present charge of failure to provide adequate protection.

The people of Wisconsin may well prefer a system of liability which would place upon the State and its officials the responsibility for failure to act in situations such as the present one. They may create such a system, if they do not have it already, by changing the tort law of the State in accordance with the regular lawmaking process. But they should not have it thrust upon them by this Court's expansion of the Due Process Clause of the Fourteenth Amendment.

Justice Brennan, with whom Justices Marshall and Blackmun join, dissenting.

. . . The Court's baseline is the absence of positive rights in the Constitution and a concomitant suspicion of any claim that seems to depend on such rights. From this perspective, the DeShaneys' claim is first and foremost about inaction (the failure, here, of respondents to take steps to protect Joshua), and only tangentially about action (the establishment of a state program specifically designed to help children like Joshua). . . .

I would begin from the opposite direction. I would focus first on the action that Wisconsin has taken with respect to Joshua and children like him, rather than on the actions that the State failed to take. . . . If a State cuts off private sources of aid and then refuses aid itself, it cannot wash its hands of the harm that results from its inaction. . . .

Wisconsin has established a child-welfare system specifically designed to help children like Joshua. Wisconsin law places upon the local departments of social services such as respondent (DSS or Department) a duty to investigate reported instances of child abuse. While other governmental bodies and private persons are largely responsible for the reporting of possible cases of child abuse, Wisconsin law channels all such reports to the local departments of social services for evaluation and, if necessary, further action. Even when it is the sheriff's office or police department that receives a report of suspected child abuse, that report is referred to local social services departments for action, the only exception to this occurs when the reporter fears for the child's immediate safety. In this way, Wisconsin law invites—indeed, directs—citizens and other governmental entities to depend on local departments of social services such as respondent to protect children from abuse. . . .

In these circumstances, a private citizen, or even a person working in a government agency other than DSS, would doubtless feel that her job was done as soon as she had reported her suspicions of child abuse to DSS. Through its child-welfare program, in other words, the State of Wisconsin has relieved ordinary citizens and governmental bodies other than the Department of any sense of obligation to do anything more than report their suspicions of child abuse to DSS. If DSS ignores or dismisses these suspicions, no one will step in to fill the gap. Wisconsin's child-protection program thus effectively confined Joshua DeShaney within the walls of Randy DeShaney's violent home until such time as DSS took action to remove him. Conceivably, then, children like Joshua are made worse off by the existence of this program when the persons and entities charged with carrying it out fail to do their jobs.

It simply belies reality, therefore, to contend that the State "stood by and did nothing" with respect to Joshua. Through its child-protection program, the State actively intervened in Joshua's life and, by virtue of this intervention, acquired ever more certain knowledge that Joshua was in grave danger. . . .

As the Court today reminds us, the Due Process Clause of the Fourteenth Amendment was intended to prevent government from abusing its power, or employing it as an instrument of oppression. My disagreement with the Court arises from its failure to see that inaction can be every bit as abusive of power as action, that oppression can result when a State undertakes a vital duty and then ignores it. Today's opinion construes the Due Process Clause to permit a State to displace private sources of protection and then, at the critical moment, to shrug its shoulders and turn away from the harm that it has promised to try to prevent. Because I cannot agree that our Constitution is indifferent to such indifference, I respectfully dissent.

Justice Blackmun, dissenting.

Today, the Court purports to be the dispassionate oracle of the law, unmoved by "natural sympathy." But, in this pretense, the Court itself retreats into a sterile formalism which prevents it from recognizing either the facts of the case before it or the legal norms that should apply to those facts. As Justice Brennan demonstrates, the facts here involve not mere passivity, but active state intervention in the life of Joshua DeShaney—intervention that triggered a fundamental duty to aid the boy once the State learned of the severe danger to which he was exposed.

DeShaney v. Winnebago County Department of Social Services

... Like the antebellum judges who denied relief to fugitive slaves, the Court today claims that its decision, however harsh, is compelled by existing legal doctrine. On the contrary, the question presented by this case is an open one, and our Fourteenth Amendment precedents may be read more broadly or narrowly depending upon how one chooses to read them. Faced with the choice, I would adopt a sympathetic reading, one which comports with dictates of fundamental justice and recognizes that compassion need not be exiled from the province of judging.

Poor Joshua! Victim of repeated attacks by an irresponsible, bullying, cowardly, and intemperate father, and abandoned by respondents who placed him in a dangerous predicament and who knew or learned what was going on, and yet did essentially nothing except, as the Court revealingly observes, "dutifully recorded these incidents in their files." It is a sad commentary upon American life, and constitutional principles—so full of late of **patriotic fervor** and proud proclamations about "liberty and justice for all"—that this child, Joshua DeShaney, now is assigned to live out the remainder of his life profoundly retarded. Joshua and his mother, as petitioners here, deserve—but now are denied by this Court—the opportunity to have the facts of their case considered in the light of the constitutional protection that 42 U.S.C. § 1983 is meant to provide.

■ HISTORY

PATRIOTIC FERVOR:
Justice Blackmun alludes to an episode from the 1988 Presidential campaign. George H.W. Bush accused his opponent Michael Dukakis of lacking patriotism because, as governor of Massachusetts, Dukakis—abiding by *Barnette*—vetoed a bill mandating recitation of the pledge of allegiance in public schools.

2. Liberty or Property Interest

a) Liberty and Property Distinguished: *Roth v. Board of Regents*

Liberty and property interests need not be mutually exclusive. Some interests may involve both liberty and property—like the right to attend public school in *Goss v. Lopez* (1975)—or neither liberty nor property—like the right to a good reputation in *Paul v. Davis* (1976). Even though it is possible to litigate a case without settling on one category or the other, *Board of Regents v. Roth* sets forth the theory distinguishing the two categories.

Faculty Activism in the Vietnam Era. Dr. David Roth had a one-year contract, without tenure or guarantee of extension, to teach political science at Wisconsin State University at Oshkosh. In November 1968, during Roth's first semester, a group of 94 Black students occupied the office of the University's president. All the demonstrators were suspended after the occupation devolved into a melee, complete with property damage. Roth became an advocate for the student activists, devoting many hours of his International Relations classes to the topic and cancelling several classes to present a petition to the Board of Regents.

In December 1968, the five tenured members of the political science department voted to recommend renewing the contracts of all the non-tenured teachers, but a dean demanded that they reverse the recommendation as to Roth. The group did so, with one voting in favor of Roth, two against, and two abstaining. Roth was thereafter informed that he would not be appointed for the 1969–1970 academic year. He received no explanation of the University's reasons, and had no opportunity at any stage to present arguments in favor of reappointment.

ITEMS TO CONSIDER WHILE READING
BOARD OF REGENTS v. ROTH:

A. *Work through the items in the Kickstarter. Specifically, did Roth have a liberty interest in the deprived thing? A property interest?*

B. *Does the importance of a government benefit affect whether it qualifies as a liberty or property interest?*

C. *Will a public employee ever have a liberty or property interest in continued employment?*

Board of Regents v. Roth,

408 U.S. 564 (1972)

Justice Stewart delivered the opinion of the Court [joined by Chief Justice Burger and Justices White, Blackmun, and Rehnquist].

In 1968 the respondent, David Roth, was hired for his first teaching job as assistant professor of political science at Wisconsin State University-Oshkosh. He was hired for a fixed term of one academic year. The notice of his faculty appointment specified that his employment would begin on September 1, 1968, and would end on June 30, 1969. The respondent completed that term. But he was informed that he would not be rehired for the next academic year.

The respondent had no tenure rights to continued employment. Under Wisconsin statutory law a state university teacher can acquire tenure as a permanent employee only after four years of year-to-year employment. Having acquired tenure, a teacher is entitled to continued employment "during efficiency and good behavior" [and may be fired only for cause]. A relatively new teacher without tenure, however, is under Wisconsin law entitled to nothing beyond his one-year appointment. There are no statutory or administrative standards defining eligibility for re-employment. State law thus clearly leaves the decision whether to rehire a nontenured teacher for another year to the unfettered discretion of university officials.

The procedural protection afforded a Wisconsin State University teacher before he is separated from the University corresponds to his job security. As a matter of statutory law, a tenured teacher cannot be discharged except for cause upon written charges and pursuant to certain procedures. A nontenured teacher, similarly, is protected to some extent during his one-year term. Rules promulgated by the Board of Regents provide that a nontenured teacher dismissed before the end of the year may have some opportunity for review of the dismissal. But the Rules provide no real protection for a nontenured teacher who simply is not re-employed for the next year. He must be informed by February 1 concerning retention or non-retention for the ensuing year. But no reason for non-retention need be given. No review or appeal is provided in such case.

In conformance with these Rules, the President of Wisconsin State University-Oshkosh informed the respondent before February 1, 1969, that he would not be rehired for the 1969–1970 academic year. He gave the respondent no reason for the decision and no opportunity to challenge it at any sort of hearing.

The respondent then brought this action in Federal District Court alleging that the decision not to rehire him for the next year infringed his Fourteenth Amendment rights. He attacked the decision both in substance and procedure. First, he alleged that the true reason for the decision was to punish him for certain statements critical of the University administration, and that it therefore violated his right to freedom of speech.[FN5] Second, he alleged that the failure of University officials to give him notice of any reason for nonretention and an opportunity for a hearing violated his right to procedural due process of law.

FN5 While the respondent alleged that he was not rehired because of his exercise of free speech, the petitioners insisted that the non-retention decision was based on other, constitutionally valid grounds. The District Court came to no conclusion whatever regarding the true reason for the University President's decision. . . .

The District Court granted summary judgment for the respondent on the procedural issue, ordering the University officials to provide him with reasons and a hearing. The Court of Appeals, with one judge dissenting, affirmed this partial summary judgment. We granted certiorari. The only question presented to us at this stage in the case is whether the respondent had a constitutional right to a statement of reasons and a hearing on the University's decision not to rehire him for another year. We hold that he did not.

I

The requirements of procedural due process apply only to the deprivation of interests encompassed by the Fourteenth Amendment's protection of liberty and property. When protected interests are implicated, the right to some kind of prior hearing is paramount. But the range of interests protected by procedural due process is not infinite.

The District Court decided that procedural due process guarantees apply in this case by assessing and balancing the weights of the particular interests involved. It concluded that the respondent's interest in re-employment at Wisconsin State University-Oshkosh outweighed the University's interest in denying him re-employment summarily. Undeniably, the respondent's re-employment prospects were of major concern to him—concern that we surely cannot say was insignificant. And a weighing process has long been a part of any determination of the form of hearing required in particular situations by procedural due process. But, to determine whether due process requirements apply in the first place, we must look not to the weight but to the nature of the interest at stake. We must look to see if the interest is within the Fourteenth Amendment's protection of liberty and property.

"Liberty" and "property" are broad and majestic terms. They are among the great constitutional concepts purposely left to gather meaning from experience. They relate to the whole domain of social and economic fact, and the statesmen who founded this Nation knew too well that only a stagnant society remains unchanged. For that reason, the Court has fully and finally rejected the wooden distinction between "rights" and "privileges" that once seemed to govern the applicability of procedural due process rights. The Court has also made clear that the property interests protected by procedural due process extend well beyond actual ownership of real estate, chattels, or money. By the same token, the Court has required due process protection for deprivations of liberty beyond the sort of formal constraints imposed by the criminal process.

Yet, while the Court has eschewed rigid or formalistic limitations on the protection of procedural due process, it has at the same time observed certain boundaries. For the words "liberty" and "property" in the Due Process Clause of the Fourteenth Amendment must be given some meaning.

II

"While this court has not attempted to define with exactness the liberty . . . guaranteed (by the Fourteenth Amendment), the term has received much consideration and some of the included things have been definitely stated. Without doubt, it denotes not merely freedom from bodily restraint but also the right of the individual to contract, to engage in any of the common occupations of life, to acquire useful knowledge, to marry, establish a home and bring up children, to worship God according to the dictates of his own conscience, and generally to enjoy those privileges long recognized as essential to the orderly pursuit of happiness by free men." *Meyer v. Nebraska*, 262 U.S. 390 (1927). In a Constitution for a free people, there can be no doubt that the meaning of "liberty" must be broad indeed. See, e.g., *Bolling v. Sharpe*, 347 U.S. 497 (1954).

There might be cases in which a State refused to re-employ a person under such circumstances that interests in liberty would be implicated. But this is not such a case. . . . There is no suggestion that the State, in declining to re-employ the respondent, imposed on him a stigma or other disability that foreclosed his freedom to take advantage of other employment opportunities. The State, for example, did not invoke any regulations to bar the respondent from all other public employment in state universities. Had it done so, this, again, would be a different case. For to be deprived not only of present government employment but of future opportunity for it certainly is no small injury. The Court has held, for example, that a State, in regulating eligibility for a type of professional employment, cannot foreclose a range of opportunities in a manner that contravenes Due Process, and, specifically, in a manner that denies the right to a full prior hearing. In the present case, however, this principle does not come into play. . . .

Board of Regents v. Roth

Hence, on the record before us, all that clearly appears is that the respondent was not rehired for one year at one university. It stretches the concept too far to suggest that a person is deprived of "liberty" when he simply is not rehired in one job but remains as free as before to seek another.

III

The Fourteenth Amendment's procedural protection of property is a safeguard of the security of interests that a person has already acquired in specific benefits. These interests—property interests—may take many forms.

Thus, the Court has held that a person receiving welfare benefits under statutory and administrative standards defining eligibility for them has an interest in continued receipt of those benefits that is safeguarded by procedural due process. Similarly, in the area of public employment, the Court has held that a public college professor dismissed from an office held under tenure provisions, and college professors and staff members dismissed during the terms of their contracts, have interests in continued employment that are safeguarded by due process. Only last year, the Court held that this principle proscribing summary dismissal from public employment without hearing or inquiry required by due process also applied to a teacher recently hired without tenure or a formal contract, but nonetheless with a clearly implied promise of continued employment.

Certain attributes of "property" interests protected by procedural due process emerge from these decisions. To have a property interest in a benefit, a person clearly must have more than an abstract need or desire for it. He must have more than a unilateral expectation of it. He must, instead, have a legitimate claim of entitlement to it. It is a purpose of the ancient institution of property to protect those claims upon which people rely in their daily lives, reliance that must not be arbitrarily undermined. It is a purpose of the constitutional right to a hearing to provide an opportunity for a person to vindicate those claims.

Property interests, of course, are not created by the Constitution. Rather they are created and their dimensions are defined by existing rules or understandings that stem from an independent source such as state-law rules or understandings that secure certain benefits and that support claims of entitlement to those benefits. Thus, the welfare recipients in *Goldberg v. Kelly* (1970) had a claim of entitlement to welfare payments that was grounded in the statute defining eligibility for them. The recipients had not yet shown that they were, in fact, within the statutory terms of eligibility. But we held that they had a right to a hearing at which they might attempt to do so.

Just as the welfare recipients' property interest in welfare payments was created and defined by statutory terms, so the respondent's property interest in employment at Wisconsin State University-Oshkosh was created and defined by the terms of his appointment. Those terms secured his interest in employment up to June 30, 1969. But the important fact in this case is that they specifically provided that the respondent's employment was to terminate on June 30. They did not provide for contract renewal absent sufficient cause. Indeed, they made no provision for renewal whatsoever.

Thus, the terms of the respondent's appointment secured absolutely no interest in re-employment for the next year. They supported absolutely no possible claim of entitlement to re-employment. Nor, significantly, was there any state statute or University rule or policy that secured his interest in re-employment or that created any legitimate claim to it. In these circumstances, the respondent surely had an abstract concern in being rehired, but he did not have a property interest sufficient to require the University authorities to give him a hearing when they declined to renew his contract of employment.

IV

Our analysis of the respondent's constitutional rights in this case in no way indicates a view that an opportunity for a hearing or a statement of reasons for nonretention would, or would not, be appropriate or wise in public colleges and universities. For it is a written Constitution that we apply. Our role is confined to interpretation of that Constitution. . . .

Justice Powell took no part in the decision of this case.

Chief Justice Burger, concurring.

[This omitted concurrence appears in the companion case of *Perry v. Sindermann*, 408 U.S. 593 (1972).]

Justice Douglas, dissenting. [Omitted.]

Justice Brennan, with whom Justice Douglas joins, dissenting.

[This omitted dissent appears in the companion case of *Perry v. Sindermann*, 408 U.S. 593 (1972).]

Board of Regents v. Roth

Justice Marshall [joined by Justices Douglas and Brennan], dissenting.

. . . While I agree with Part I of the Court's opinion, setting forth the proper framework for consideration of the issue presented, and also with . . . portions of Parts II and III of the Court's opinion . . . I would go further than the Court does in defining the terms "liberty" and "property."

The prior decisions of this Court, discussed at length in the opinion of the Court, establish a principle that is as obvious as it is compelling—i.e., federal and state governments and governmental agencies are restrained by the Constitution from acting arbitrarily with respect to employment opportunities that they either offer or control. Hence, it is now firmly established that whether or not a private employer is free to act capriciously or unreasonably with respect to employment practices, at least absent statutory or contractual controls, a government employer is different. The government may only act fairly and reasonably. . . .

In my view, every citizen who applies for a government job is entitled to it unless the government can establish some reason for denying the employment. This is the "property" right that I believe is protected by the Fourteenth Amendment and that cannot be denied "without due process of law." And it is also liberty—liberty to work—which is the very essence of the personal freedom and opportunity secured by the Fourteenth Amendment. . . .

Employment is one of the greatest, if not the greatest, benefits that governments offer in modern-day life. When something as valuable as the opportunity to work is at stake, the government may not reward some citizens and not others without demonstrating that its actions are fair and equitable. And it is procedural due process that is our fundamental guarantee of fairness, our protection against arbitrary, capricious, and unreasonable government action. . . .

It may be argued that to provide procedural due process to all public employees or prospective employees would place an intolerable burden on the machinery of government. The short answer to that argument is that it is not burdensome to give reasons when reasons exist. Whenever an application for employment is denied, an employee is discharged, or a decision not to rehire an employee is made, there should be some reason for the decision. It can scarcely be argued that government would be crippled by a requirement that the reason be communicated to the person most directly affected by the government's action. . . .

It might also be argued that to require a hearing and a statement of reasons is to require a useless act, because a government bent on denying employment to one or more persons will do so regardless of the procedural hurdles that are placed in its path. Perhaps this is so, but a requirement of procedural regularity at least renders arbitrary action more difficult. Moreover, proper procedures will surely eliminate some of the arbitrariness that results, not from malice, but from innocent error. Experience teaches that the affording of procedural safeguards, which by their nature serve to illuminate the underlying facts, in itself often operates to prevent erroneous decisions on the merits from occurring. When the government knows it may have to justify its decisions with sound reasons, its conduct is likely to be more cautious, careful, and correct. . . .

Accordingly, I dissent.

flashforward

1. *Property Interests After* Roth. Under *Roth*, property interests exist when substantive law creates an entitlement to a benefit. If the government has discretion over whether to award the benefit, it is not a property interest. After *Roth*, various entitlements have been identified that arise under state or federal law. Government-issued licenses or permits are typically found to involve property interests. These include things like a driver's license, *Bell v. Burson*, 402 U.S. 535 (1971), a horse racing license, *Barry v. Barchi*, 443 U.S. 55 (1979), a lease to mine on public lands, *Texaco, Inc. v. Short*, 454 U.S. 516 (1982), and a license to operate video poker machines, *Cleveland v. United States*, 531 U.S. 12 (2000). Services provided by a government-run utility (such as water, electricity, or gas) are a property interest. *Memphis Light, Gas & Water Div. v. Craft*, 436 U.S. 1 (1978).

2. *Liberty Interests After* Roth. Liberty interests are said to arise from the Due Process Clause itself, which is another way of saying that a right is a liberty interest when a federal court finds it to be one. Without doubt, the right not to be incarcerated is a liberty interest, which means that decisions to revoke parole, *Morrissey v. Brewer*, 408 U.S. 471 (1972), or to rescind time off for good behavior, *Wolff v. McDonnell*, 418 U.S. 539 (1974), are deprivations of liberty that require adequate procedures. Changes in the conditions of confinement (like placement in solitary confinement or denial of recreational privileges) will be deprivations of liberty only where they impose "atypical and significant hardship on the inmate in relation to ordinary incidents of prison life." *Sandin v. Conner*, 515 U.S. 472 (1995). For example, a convicted prisoner has no liberty interest in remaining at a particular prison, and can be transferred to another facility without any advance notice or opportunity to be heard. *Olim v. Wakinekona*, 461 U.S. 238 (1983).

Relatively few procedural due process cases at the Supreme Court level have considered liberty interests of non-incarcerated people. This may be because they are more likely to raise substantive objections to deprivation itself, rather than procedural objections to the methods used when deciding to impose the deprivation.

b) Defining Property Interests: *Goldberg v. Kelly*

Goldberg v. Kelly was a groundbreaking decision that ushered in the modern era of procedural due process. It is relevant to two questions: (a) the definition of a "property interest," and (b) the process that is due before property interests may be deprived.

ITEMS TO CONSIDER WHILE READING
GOLDBERG v. KELLY:

A. *Work through the items in the Kickstarter.*

B. *How does the property interest in Goldberg differ from the common law definition of property?*

C. *What procedures were followed with regard to the deprivation? What procedures did the plaintiffs want the government to use instead? What are the costs and benefits of the proposed procedures?*

Goldberg v. Kelly,

397 U.S. 254 (1970)

Justice Brennan delivered the opinion of the Court [joined by Justices Douglas, Harlan, White, and Marshall].

The question for decision is whether a State that terminates public assistance payments to a particular recipient without affording him the opportunity for an evidentiary hearing prior to termination denies the recipient procedural due process in violation of the Due Process Clause of the Fourteenth Amendment.

This action was brought in the District Court for the Southern District of New York by residents of New York City receiving financial aid under the federally assisted program of Aid to Families with Dependent Children (AFDC) or under New York State's general Home Relief program. [The lead plaintiff was John Kelly.] Their complaint alleged that the New York State and New York City officials administering these programs [including Jack Goldberg] terminated, or were about to terminate, such aid without prior notice and hearing, thereby denying them due process of law. At the time the suits were filed there was no requirement of prior notice or hearing of any kind before termination of financial aid. However, the State and city adopted procedures for notice and hearing after the suits were brought, and the plaintiffs, appellees here, then challenged the constitutional adequacy of those procedures. . . .

[Under the new procedures] a caseworker who has doubts about the recipient's continued eligibility must first discuss them with the recipient. If the caseworker concludes that the recipient is no longer eligible, he recommends termination of aid to a unit supervisor. If the latter concurs, he sends the recipient a letter stating the reasons for proposing to terminate aid and notifying him that within seven days he may request that a higher official review the record, and may support the request with a written statement prepared personally or with the aid of an attorney or other person. If the reviewing official affirms the determination of ineligibility, aid is stopped immediately and the recipient is informed by letter of the reasons for the action. Appellees' challenge to this procedure emphasizes the absence of any provisions for the personal appearance of the recipient before the reviewing official, for oral presentation of evidence, and for confrontation and cross-examination of adverse witnesses. However, the letter does inform the recipient that he may request a post-termination "fair hearing." This is a proceeding before an independent state hearing officer at which the recipient may appear personally, offer oral evidence, confront and cross-examine the witnesses against him, and have a record made of the hearing. If the recipient prevails at the 'fair hearing' he is paid all funds erroneously withheld. A recipient whose aid is not restored by a 'fair hearing' decision may have judicial review. The recipient is so notified.

I

The constitutional issue to be decided, therefore, is the narrow one whether the Due Process Clause requires that the recipient be afforded an evidentiary hearing before the termination of benefits. The District Court held that only a pretermination evidentiary hearing would satisfy the constitutional command, and rejected the argument of the state and city officials that the combination of the post-termination "fair hearing" with the informal pre-termination review disposed of all due process claims. The court said: "While post-termination review is relevant, there is one overpowering fact which controls here. By hypothesis, a welfare recipient is destitute, without funds or assets. Suffice it to say that to cut off a welfare recipient in the face of 'brutal need' without a prior hearing of some sort is unconscionable, unless overwhelming considerations justify it." The court rejected the argument that the need to protect the public's tax revenues supplied the requisite "overwhelming consideration." . . . We affirm.

Goldberg v. Kelly

Appellant does not contend that procedural due process is not applicable to the termination of welfare benefits. Such benefits are a matter of statutory entitlement for persons qualified to receive them.[FN8] Their termination involves state action that adjudicates important rights. The constitutional challenge cannot be answered by an argument that public assistance benefits are a "privilege" and not a "right." Relevant constitutional restraints apply as much to the withdrawal of public assistance benefits as to disqualification for unemployment compensation, or to denial of a tax exemption, or to discharge from public employment. The extent to which procedural due process must be afforded the recipient is influenced by the extent to which he may be condemned to suffer grievous loss, and depends upon whether the recipient's interest in avoiding that loss outweighs the governmental interest in summary adjudication. Accordingly, consideration of what procedures due process may require under any given set of circumstances must begin with a determination of the precise nature of the government function involved as well as of the private interest that has been affected by governmental action.

FN8 It may be realistic today to regard welfare entitlements as more like property than a gratuity. Much of the existing wealth in this country takes the form of rights that do not fall within traditional common-law concepts of property. It has been aptly noted that "Society today is built around entitlement. The automobile dealer has his franchise, the doctor and lawyer their professional licenses, the worker his union membership, contract, and pension rights, the executive his contract and stock options; all are devices to aid security and independence. Many of the most important of these entitlements now flow from government: subsidies to farmers and businessmen, routes for airlines and channels for television stations; long term contracts for defense, space, and education; social security pensions for individuals. Such sources of security, whether private or public, are no longer regarded as luxuries or gratuities; to the recipients they are essentials, fully deserved, and in no sense a form of charity. It is only the poor whose entitlements, although recognized by public policy, have not been effectively enforced." Reich, *Individual Rights and Social Welfare: The Emerging Legal Issues*, 74 Yale L.J. 1245 (1965). See also Reich, *The New Property*, 73 Yale L.J. 733 (1964).

It is true, of course, that some governmental benefits may be administratively terminated without affording the recipient a pre-termination evidentiary hearing. But we agree with the District Court that when welfare is discontinued, only a pre-termination evidentiary hearing provides the recipient with procedural due process. For qualified recipients, welfare provides the means to obtain essential food, clothing, housing, and medical care. Thus the crucial factor in this context—a factor not present in the case of the blacklisted government contractor, the discharged government employee, the taxpayer denied a tax exemption, or virtually anyone else whose governmental entitlements are ended—is that termination of aid pending resolution of a controversy over eligibility may deprive an eligible recipient of the very means by which to live while he waits. Since he lacks independent resources, his situation becomes immediately desperate. His need to concentrate upon finding the means for daily subsistence, in turn, adversely affects his ability to seek redress from the welfare bureaucracy.

Moreover, important governmental interests are promoted by affording recipients a pre-termination evidentiary hearing. From its founding the Nation's basic commitment has been to foster the dignity and well-being of all persons within its borders. We have come to recognize that forces not within the control of the poor contribute to their poverty. This perception, against the background of our traditions, has significantly influenced the development of the contemporary public assistance system. Welfare, by meeting the basic demands of subsistence, can help bring within the reach of the poor the same opportunities that are available to others to participate meaningfully in the life of the community. At the same time, welfare guards against the societal malaise that may flow from a widespread sense of unjustified frustration and insecurity. Public assistance, then, is not mere charity, but a means to "promote the general Welfare, and secure the Blessings of Liberty to ourselves and our Posterity." The same governmental interests that counsel the provision of welfare, counsel as well its uninterrupted provision to those eligible to receive it; pre-termination evidentiary hearings are indispensable to that end.

Appellant does not challenge the force of these considerations but argues that they are outweighed by countervailing governmental interests in conserving fiscal and administrative resources. These interests, the argument goes, justify the delay of any evidentiary hearing until after discontinuance of the grants. Summary adjudication protects the public fisc by stopping payments promptly upon discovery of reason to believe that a recipient is no longer eligible. Since most terminations are accepted without challenge, summary adjudication also conserves both the fisc and administrative time and energy by reducing the number of evidentiary hearings actually held.

We agree with the District Court, however, that these governmental interests are not overriding in the welfare context. The requirement of a prior hearing doubtless involves some greater expense, and the benefits paid to ineligible recipients pending decision at the hearing probably cannot be recouped, since these recipients are likely to be judgment-proof. But the State is not without weapons to minimize these increased costs. Much of the drain on fiscal and administrative resources can be reduced by developing procedures for prompt pre-termination hearings and by skillful use of personnel and facilities. Indeed, the very provision for a post-termination evidentiary hearing in New York's Home Relief program is itself cogent evidence that the State recognizes the primacy of the public interest in correct eligibility determinations and therefore in the provision of procedural safeguards. Thus, the interest of the eligible recipient in uninterrupted receipt of public assistance,

Goldberg v. Kelly

coupled with the State's interest that his payments not be erroneously terminated, clearly outweighs the State's competing concern to prevent any increase in its fiscal and administrative burdens. As the District Court correctly concluded, "the stakes are simply too high for the welfare recipient, and the possibility for honest error or irritable misjudgment too great, to allow termination of aid without giving the recipient a chance, if he so desires, to be fully informed of the case against him so that he may contest its basis and produce evidence in rebuttal."

II

We also agree with the District Court, however, that the pre-termination hearing need not take the form of a judicial or quasi-judicial trial. We bear in mind that the statutory "fair hearing" will provide the recipient with a full administrative review. Accordingly, the pre-termination hearing has one function only: to produce an initial determination of the validity of the welfare department's grounds for discontinuance of payments in order to protect a recipient against an erroneous termination of his benefits. Thus, a complete record and a comprehensive opinion, which would serve primarily to facilitate judicial review and to guide future decisions, need not be provided at the pre-termination stage. We recognize, too, that both welfare authorities and recipients have an interest in relatively speedy resolution of questions of eligibility, that they are used to dealing with one another informally, and that some welfare departments have very burdensome caseloads. These considerations justify the limitation of the pre-termination hearing to minimum procedural safeguards, adapted to the particular characteristics of welfare recipients, and to the limited nature of the controversies to be resolved. We wish to add that we, no less than the dissenters, recognize the importance of not imposing upon the States or the Federal Government in this developing field of law any procedural requirements beyond those demanded by rudimentary due process.

The fundamental requisite of due process of law is the opportunity to be heard. The hearing must be at a meaningful time and in a meaningful manner. In the present context these principles require that a recipient have timely and adequate notice detailing the reasons for a proposed termination, and an effective opportunity to defend by confronting any adverse witnesses and by presenting his own arguments and evidence orally. These rights are important in cases such as those before us, where recipients have challenged proposed terminations as resting on incorrect or misleading factual premises or on misapplication of rules or policies to the facts of particular cases.

We are not prepared to say that the seven-day notice currently provided by New York City is constitutionally insufficient per se, although there may be cases where fairness would require that a longer time be given. Nor do we see any constitutional deficiency in the content or form of the notice. New York employs both a letter and a personal conference with a caseworker to inform a recipient of the precise questions raised about his continued eligibility. Evidently the recipient is told the legal and factual bases for the Department's doubts. This combination is probably the most effective method of communicating with recipients.

The city's procedures presently do not permit recipients to appear personally with or without counsel before the official who finally determines continued eligibility. Thus a recipient is not permitted to present evidence to that official orally, or to confront or cross-examine adverse witnesses. These omissions are fatal to the constitutional adequacy of the procedures.

The opportunity to be heard must be tailored to the capacities and circumstances of those who are to be heard. It is not enough that a welfare recipient may present his position to the decision maker in writing or second-hand through his caseworker. Written submissions are an unrealistic option for most recipients, who lack the educational attainment necessary to write effectively and who cannot obtain professional assistance. Moreover, written submissions do not afford the flexibility of oral presentations; they do not permit the recipient to mold his argument to the issues the decision maker appears to regard as important. Particularly where credibility and veracity are at issue, as they must be in many termination proceedings, written submissions are a wholly unsatisfactory basis for decision. The second-hand presentation to the decisionmaker by the caseworker has its own deficiencies; since the caseworker usually gathers the facts upon which the charge of ineligibility rests, the presentation of the recipient's side of the controversy cannot safely be left to him. Therefore a recipient must be allowed to state his position orally. Informal procedures will suffice; in this context due process does not require a particular order of proof or mode of offering evidence.

In almost every setting where important decisions turn on questions of fact, due process requires an opportunity to confront and cross-examine adverse witnesses. . . . Welfare recipients must therefore be given an opportunity to confront and cross-examine the witnesses relied on by the department.

"The right to be heard would be, in many cases, of little avail if it did not comprehend the right to be heard by counsel." *Powell v. Alabama*, 287 U.S. 45 (1932) [*The Scottsboro Boys Case*]. We do not say that counsel must be provided at the pre-termination hearing, but only that the recipient must be allowed to retain an attorney if he so desires. Counsel can help delineate the issues, present the factual contentions in an orderly manner, conduct cross-examination, and generally safeguard the interests of the recipient. We do not anticipate that this assistance will unduly prolong or otherwise encumber the hearing. Evidently HEW has reached the same conclusion.

Finally, the decisionmaker's conclusion as to a recipient's eligibility must rest solely on the legal rules and evidence adduced at the hearing. To demonstrate compliance with this elementary requirement, the decision maker should state the reasons for his determination and indicate the evidence he relied on, though his statement need not amount to a full opinion or even formal findings of fact and conclusions of law. And, of course, an impartial decision maker is essential. We agree with the District Court that prior involvement in some aspects of a case will not necessarily bar a welfare official from acting as a decision maker. He should not, however, have participated in making the determination under review.

Goldberg v. Kelly

Justice Black, dissenting.

In the last half century the United States, along with many, perhaps most, other nations of the world, has moved far toward becoming a welfare state, that is, a nation that for one reason or another taxes its most affluent people to help support, feed, clothe, and shelter its less fortunate citizens. The result is that today more than nine million men, women, and children in the United States receive some kind of state or federally financed public assistance in the form of allowances or gratuities, generally paid them periodically, usually by the week, month, or quarter. Since these gratuities are paid on the basis of need, the list of recipients is not static, and some people go off the lists and others are added from time to time. These ever-changing lists put a constant administrative burden on government and it certainly could not have reasonably anticipated that this burden would include the additional procedural expense imposed by the Court today. . . .

I do not think that the Fourteenth Amendment should be given such an unnecessarily broad construction. That Amendment came into being primarily to protect Negroes from discrimination, and while some of its language can and does protect others, all know that the chief purpose behind it was to protect ex-slaves. The Court, however, relies upon the Fourteenth Amendment and in effect says that failure of the government to pay a promised charitable installment to an individual deprives that individual of his own property, in violation of the Due Process Clause of the Fourteenth Amendment. It somewhat strains credulity to say that the government's promise of charity to an individual is property belonging to that individual when the government denies that the individual is honestly entitled to receive such a payment. . . .

The Court apparently feels that this decision will benefit the poor and needy. In my judgment the eventual result will be just the opposite. While today's decision requires only an administrative, evidentiary hearing, the inevitable logic of the approach taken will lead to constitutionally imposed, time-consuming delays of a full adversary process of administrative and judicial review. In the next case the welfare recipients are bound to argue that cutting off benefits before judicial review of the agency's decision is also a denial of due process. . . . The inevitable result of such a constitutionally imposed burden will be that the government will not put a claimant on the rolls initially until it has made an exhaustive investigation to determine his eligibility. While this Court will perhaps have insured that no needy person will be taken off the rolls without a full "due process" proceeding, it will also have insured that many will never get on the rolls, or at least that they will remain destitute during the lengthy proceedings followed to determine initial eligibility.

For the foregoing reasons I dissent from the Court's holding. The operation of a welfare state is a new experiment for our Nation. For this reason, among others, I feel that new experiments in carrying out a welfare program should not be frozen into our constitutional structure. They should be left, as are other legislative determinations, to the Congress and the legislatures that the people elect to make our laws.

Chief Justice Burger, with whom Justice Black joins, dissenting.

. . . The Court's action today seems another manifestation of the now familiar constitutionalizing syndrome: once some presumed flaw is observed, the Court then eagerly accepts the invitation to find a constitutionally rooted remedy. If no provision is explicit on the point, it is then seen as implicit or commanded by the vague and nebulous concept of fairness.

I can share the impatience of all who seek instant solutions; there is a great temptation in this area to frame remedies that seem fair and can be mandated forthwith as against administrative or congressional action that calls for careful and extended study. That is thought too slow. But, however cumbersome or glacial, this is the procedure the Constitution contemplated. . . .

Justice Stewart, dissenting.

Although the question is for me a close one, I do not believe that the procedures that New York and California now follow in terminating welfare payments are violative of the United States Constitution.

3. Adequacy of Procedures

a) Procedures for Terminating Disability Benefits: *Mathews v. Eldridge*

If deprivation of a liberty or property interest is shown, the court must consider whether the government used constitutionally adequate procedures. *Mathews v. Eldridge* provides a frequently-used framework for such questions.

ITEMS TO CONSIDER WHILE READING *MATHEWS v. ELDRIDGE*:

A. *Work through the items in the Kickstarter.*

B. Mathews *sets forth three factors to help decide whether procedures were adequate. What are they? Should there be others? Were they properly applied in* Mathews*?*

C. *In* Goldberg v. Kelly, *the Supreme Court held that due process required an evidentiary hearing before the government could cut off welfare payments.*

Mathews *decided that due process did not require a similar hearing before cutting off Social Security disability payments (at least when such a hearing was offered after the cutoff). What explains the difference?*

Mathews v. Eldridge,

424 U.S. 319 (1976)

Justice Powell delivered the opinion of the Court [joined by Chief Justice Burger and Justices Stewart, White, Blackmun, and Rehnquist].

The issue in this case is whether the Due Process Clause of the Fifth Amendment requires that prior to the termination of Social Security disability benefit payments the recipient be afforded an opportunity for an evidentiary hearing.

I

Cash benefits are provided to workers during periods in which they are completely disabled under the disability insurance benefits program created by the 1956 amendments to Title II of the Social Security Act. Respondent [George] Eldridge was first awarded benefits in June 1968. In March 1972, he received a questionnaire from the state agency charged with monitoring his medical condition. Eldridge completed the questionnaire, indicating that his condition had not improved and identifying the medical sources, including physicians, from whom he had received treatment recently. The state agency then obtained reports from his physician and a psychiatric consultant. After considering these reports and other information in his file the agency informed Eldridge by letter that it had made a tentative determination that his disability had ceased in May 1972. The letter included a statement of reasons for the proposed termination of benefits, and advised Eldridge that he might request reasonable time in which to obtain and submit additional information pertaining to his condition.

In his written response, Eldridge disputed one characterization of his medical condition and indicated that the agency already had enough evidence to establish his disability.[FN2] The state agency then made its final determination that he had ceased to be disabled in May 1972. This determination was accepted by the Social Security Administration (SSA), which notified Eldridge in July that his benefits would terminate after that month. The notification also advised him of his right to seek reconsideration by the state agency of this initial determination within six months.

FN2 Eldridge originally was disabled due to chronic anxiety and back strain. He subsequently was found to have diabetes. The tentative determination letter indicated that aid would be terminated because available medical evidence indicated that his diabetes was under control, that there existed no limitations on his back movements which would impose severe functional restrictions, and that he no longer suffered emotional problems that would preclude him from all work for which he was qualified. In his reply letter he claimed to have arthritis of the spine rather than a strained back.

Instead of requesting reconsideration Eldridge commenced this action challenging the constitutional validity of the administrative procedures established by the Secretary of Health, Education, and Welfare [F. David Matthews] for assessing whether there exists a continuing disability. He sought an immediate reinstatement of benefits pending a hearing on the issue of his disability. . . . In support of his contention that due process requires a pretermination hearing, Eldridge relied exclusively upon this Court's decision in *Goldberg v. Kelly* (1970), which established a right to an evidentiary hearing prior to termination of welfare benefits.[FN4] The Secretary contended that *Goldberg* was not controlling since eligibility for disability benefits, unlike eligibility for welfare benefits, is not based on financial need and since issues of credibility and veracity do not play a significant role in the disability entitlement decision, which turns primarily on medical evidence.

FN4 In *Goldberg* the Court held that the pretermination hearing must include the following elements: (1) timely and adequate notice detailing the reasons for a proposed termination; (2) an effective opportunity (for the recipient) to defend by confronting any adverse witnesses and by presenting his own arguments and evidence orally; (3) retained counsel, if desired; (4) an impartial decisionmaker; (5) a decision resting solely on the legal rules and evidence adduced at the hearing; (6) a statement of reasons for the decision and the evidence relied on. In this opinion the term "evidentiary hearing" refers to a hearing generally of the type required in *Goldberg*.

The District Court concluded that the administrative procedures pursuant to which the Secretary had terminated Eldridge's benefits abridged his right to procedural due process. . . . [The Fourth Circuit affirmed.] We reverse.

II

[The District Court had subject matter jurisdiction.]

III

A

Procedural due process imposes constraints on governmental decisions which deprive individuals of liberty or property interests within the meaning of the Due Process Clause of the Fifth or Fourteenth Amendment. The Secretary does not contend that procedural due process is inapplicable to terminations of Social Security disability benefits. He recognizes, as has been implicit in our prior decisions, that the interest of an individual in continued receipt of these benefits is a statutorily created property interest protected by the Fifth Amendment. Rather, the Secretary contends that the existing administrative procedures, detailed below, provide all the process that is constitutionally due before a recipient can be deprived of that interest.

This Court consistently has held that some form of hearing is required before an individual is finally deprived of a property interest. The right to be heard before being condemned to suffer grievous loss of any kind, even though it may not involve the stigma and hardships of a criminal conviction, is a principle basic to our society. The fundamental requirement of due process is the opportunity to be heard at a meaningful time and in a meaningful manner. Eldridge agrees that the review procedures available to a claimant before the initial determination of ineligibility becomes final would be adequate if disability benefits were not terminated until after the evidentiary hearing stage of the administrative process. The dispute centers upon what process is due prior to the initial termination of benefits, pending review.

In recent years this Court increasingly has had occasion to consider the extent to which due process requires an evidentiary hearing prior to the deprivation of some type of property interest even if such a hearing is provided thereafter. In only one case, *Goldberg v. Kelly*, has the Court held that a hearing closely approximating a judicial trial is necessary. In other cases requiring some type of pretermination hearing as a matter of constitutional right the Court has spoken sparingly about the requisite procedures. . . .

These decisions underscore the truism that due process, unlike some legal rules, is not a technical conception with a fixed content unrelated to time, place and circumstances. Due process is flexible and calls for such procedural protections as the particular situation demands. Accordingly, resolution of the issue whether the administrative procedures provided here are constitutionally sufficient requires analysis of the governmental and private interests that are affected. More precisely, our prior decisions indicate that identification of the specific dictates of due process generally requires consideration of three distinct factors: First, the private interest that will be affected by the official action; second, the risk of an erroneous deprivation of such interest through the procedures used, and the probable value, if any, of additional or substitute procedural safeguards; and finally, the Government's interest, including the function involved and the fiscal and administrative burdens that the additional or substitute procedural requirement would entail.

We turn first to a description of the procedures for the termination of Social Security disability benefits and thereafter consider the factors bearing upon the constitutional adequacy of these procedures.

B

[Detailed description of termination procedures omitted.]

C

Despite the elaborate character of the administrative procedures provided by the Secretary, the courts below held them to be constitutionally inadequate, concluding that due process requires an evidentiary hearing prior to termination. In light of the private and governmental interests at stake here and the nature of the existing procedures, we think this was error.

Since a recipient whose benefits are terminated is awarded full retroactive relief if he ultimately prevails, his sole interest is in the uninterrupted receipt of this source of income pending final administrative decision on his claim. His potential injury is thus similar in nature to that of the welfare recipient in *Goldberg*[.]

Only in *Goldberg* has the Court held that due process requires an evidentiary hearing prior to a temporary deprivation. It was emphasized there that welfare assistance is given to persons on the very margin of subsistence. . . . Eligibility for disability benefits, in contrast, is not based upon financial need. Indeed, it is wholly unrelated to the worker's income or support from many other sources, such as earnings of other family members, workmen's compensation awards, tort claims awards, savings, private insurance, public or private pensions, veterans' benefits, food stamps, public assistance, or the many other important programs, both public and private, which contain provisions for disability payments affecting a substantial portion of the work force.

As *Goldberg* illustrates, the degree of potential deprivation that may be created by a particular decision is a factor to be considered in assessing the validity of any administrative decisionmaking process. The potential deprivation here is generally likely to be less than in *Goldberg*, although the degree of difference can be overstated. . . .

The possible length of wrongful deprivation of benefits also is an important factor in assessing the impact of official action on the private interests. The Secretary concedes that the delay between a request for a hearing before an administrative law judge and a decision on the claim is currently between 10 and 11 months. Since a terminated recipient must first obtain a reconsideration decision as a prerequisite to invoking his right to an evidentiary hearing, the delay between the actual cutoff of benefits and final decision after a hearing exceeds one year.

In view of the torpidity of this administrative review process, and the typically modest resources of the family unit of the physically disabled worker, the hardship imposed upon the erroneously terminated disability recipient may be significant. Still, the disabled worker's need is likely to be less than that of a welfare recipient. In addition to the possibility of access to private resources, other forms of government assistance will become available where the termination of disability benefits places a worker or his family below the subsistence level. In view of these potential sources of temporary income, there is less reason here than in Goldberg to depart from the ordinary principle, established by our decisions, that something less than an evidentiary hearing is sufficient prior to adverse administrative action.

D

An additional factor to be considered here is the fairness and reliability of the existing pretermination procedures, and the probable value, if any, of additional procedural safeguards. Central to the evaluation of any administrative process is the nature of the relevant inquiry. In order to remain eligible for benefits the disabled worker must demonstrate by means of "medically acceptable clinical and laboratory diagnostic techniques," that he is unable "to engage in any substantial gainful activity by reason of any medically determinable physical or mental impairment." In short, a medical assessment of the worker's physical or mental condition is required. This is a more sharply focused and easily documented decision than the typical determination of welfare entitlement. In the latter case, a wide variety of information may be deemed relevant, and issues of witness credibility and veracity often are critical to the decisionmaking process. *Goldberg* noted that in such circumstances "written submissions are a wholly unsatisfactory basis for decision."

By contrast, the decision whether to discontinue disability benefits will turn, in most cases, upon routine, standard, and unbiased medical reports by physician specialists, concerning a subject whom they have personally examined. . . . To be sure, credibility and veracity may be a factor in the ultimate disability assessment in some cases. But procedural due process rules are shaped by the risk of error inherent in the truthfinding process as applied to the generality of cases, not the rare exceptions. The potential value of an evidentiary hearing, or even oral presentation to the decisionmaker, is substantially less in this context than in *Goldberg*. . . .

E

In striking the appropriate due process balance the final factor to be assessed is the public interest. This includes the administrative burden and other societal costs that would be associated with requiring, as a matter of constitutional right, an evidentiary hearing upon demand in all cases prior to the termination of disability benefits. The most visible burden would be the incremental cost resulting from the increased number of hearings and the expense of providing benefits to ineligible recipients pending decision. No one can predict the extent of the increase, but the fact that full benefits would continue until after such hearings would assure the exhaustion in most cases of this attractive option. Nor would the theoretical right of the Secretary to recover undeserved benefits result, as a practical matter, in any substantial offset to the added outlay of public funds. The parties submit widely varying estimates of the probable additional financial cost. We only need say that experience with the constitutionalizing of government procedures suggests that the ultimate additional cost in terms of money and administrative burden would not be insubstantial.

Financial cost alone is not a controlling weight in determining whether due process requires a particular procedural safeguard prior to some administrative decision. But the Government's interest, and hence that of the public, in conserving scarce fiscal and administrative resources is a factor that must be weighed. At some point the benefit of an additional safeguard to the individual affected by the administrative action and to society in terms of increased assurance that the action is just, may be outweighed by the cost. Significantly, the cost of protecting those whom the preliminary administrative process has identified as likely to be found undeserving may in the end come out of the pockets of the deserving since resources available for any particular program of social welfare are not unlimited.

But more is implicated in cases of this type than ad hoc weighing of fiscal and administrative burdens against the interests of a particular category of claimants. The ultimate balance involves a determination as to when, under our constitutional system, judicial-type procedures must be imposed upon administrative action to assure fairness. . . . Differences in the origin and function of administrative agencies preclude wholesale transplantation of the rules of procedure, trial and review which have evolved from the history and experience of courts. The judicial model of an evidentiary hearing is neither a required, nor even the most effective, method of decisionmaking in all circumstances. The essence of due process is the requirement that a person in jeopardy of serious loss be given notice of the case against him and opportunity to meet it. All that is necessary is that the procedures be tailored, in light of the decision to be made, to the capacities and circumstances of those who are to be heard, to insure that they are given a meaningful opportunity to present their case. In assessing what process is due in this case, substantial weight must be given to the good-faith judgments of the individuals charged by Congress with the administration of social welfare programs that the procedures they have provided assure fair consideration of the entitlement claims of individuals. This is especially so where, as here, the prescribed procedures not only provide the claimant with an effective process for asserting his claim prior to any administrative action, but also assure a right to an evidentiary hearing, as well as to subsequent judicial review, before the denial of his claim becomes final.

We conclude that an evidentiary hearing is not required prior to the termination of disability benefits and that the present administrative procedures fully comport with due process.

Justice Stevens took no part in the consideration or decision of this case.

Justice Brennan, with whom Justice Marshall concurs, dissenting.

. . . I agree with the District Court and the Court of Appeals that, prior to termination of benefits, Eldridge must be afforded an evidentiary hearing of the type required for welfare beneficiaries under Title IV of the Social Security Act. I would add that the Court's consideration that a discontinuance of disability benefits may cause the recipient to suffer only a limited deprivation is no argument. It is speculative. Moreover, the very legislative determination to provide disability benefits, without any prerequisite determination of need in fact, presumes a need by the recipient which is not this Court's function to denigrate. Indeed, in the present case, it is indicated that because disability benefits were terminated there was a foreclosure upon the Eldridge home and the family's furniture was repossessed, forcing Eldridge, his wife, and their children to sleep in one bed. Finally, it is also no argument that a worker, who has been placed in the untenable position of having been denied disability benefits, may still seek other forms of public assistance.

b) Procedures for Firing Government Employees: *Cleveland Board of Education v. Loudermill*

As the contrast between *Goldberg v. Kelly* (1970) and *Matthews v. Eldridge* (1976) reveals, a frequently litigated procedural due process question is whether procedures must be offered "pre-deprivation" or "post-deprivation." *Loudermill* is a leading statement on that question in the context of public employment. It is also a significant precedent on the definition of property interests in employment, following up on the issue from *Roth*.

ITEMS TO CONSIDER WHILE READING
CLEVELAND BOARD OF EDUCATION v. LOUDERMILL:

A. *Work through the items in the Kickstarter.*

B. *What procedures would the majority opinion require before a tenured employee is fired? What would Justice Marshall's concurrence require instead?*

C. *What options might be available to a public agency that wishes to avoid offering the termination procedures described in Loudermill?*

Cleveland Board of Education v. Loudermill,

470 U.S. 532 (1985)

Justice White delivered the opinion of the Court [joined by Chief Justice Burger and Justices Blackmun, Powell, Stevens, and O'Connor].

In these cases we consider what pretermination process must be accorded a public employee who can be discharged only for cause.

I

In 1979 the Cleveland Board of Education, hired respondent James Loudermill as a security guard. On his job application, Loudermill stated that he had never been convicted of a felony. Eleven months later, as part of a routine examination of his employment records, the Board discovered that in fact Loudermill had been convicted of grand larceny in 1968. By letter dated November 3, 1980, the Board's Business Manager informed Loudermill that he had been dismissed because of his dishonesty in filling out the employment application. Loudermill was not afforded an opportunity to respond to the charge of dishonesty or to challenge his dismissal. . . .

Under Ohio law, Loudermill was a "classified civil servant." Such employees can be terminated only for cause, and may obtain administrative review if discharged. Ohio Rev.Code Ann. § 124.34. Pursuant to this provision, Loudermill filed an appeal with the Cleveland Civil Service Commission. . . . Loudermill argued that he had thought that his 1968 larceny conviction was for a misdemeanor rather than a felony. . . . The full Commission heard argument and orally announced that it would uphold the dismissal. . . .

Although the Commission's decision was subject to judicial review in the state courts, Loudermill instead brought the present suit in the Federal District Court for the Northern District of Ohio. The complaint alleged that § 124.34 was unconstitutional on its face because it did not provide the employee an opportunity to respond to the charges against him prior to removal. As a result, discharged employees were deprived of liberty and property without due process. The complaint also alleged that the provision was unconstitutional as applied because discharged employees were not given sufficiently prompt postremoval hearings.

Before a responsive pleading was filed, the District Court dismissed for failure to state a claim on which relief could be granted. It held that because the very statute that created the property right in continued employment also specified the procedures for discharge, and because those procedures were followed, Loudermill was, by definition, afforded all the process due. The post-termination hearing also adequately protected Loudermill's liberty interests. Finally, the District Court concluded that, in light of the Commission's crowded docket, the delay in processing Loudermill's administrative appeal was constitutionally acceptable.

The other case before us [*Donnelly v. Parma Board of Education*] arises on similar facts and followed a similar course. . . . The Court of Appeals found that both respondents [Loudermill and Donnelly] had been deprived of due process. It disagreed with the District Court's original rationale. Instead, it concluded that the compelling private interest in retaining employment, combined with the value of presenting evidence prior to dismissal, outweighed the added administrative burden of a pretermination hearing. With regard to the alleged deprivation of liberty, and Loudermill's 9-month wait for an administrative decision, the court affirmed the District Court, finding no constitutional violation. . . .

We granted [the] petitions, and now affirm in all respects.

II

Respondents' federal constitutional claim depends on their having had a property right in continued employment. *Board of Regents v. Roth* (1972). If they did, the State could not deprive them of this property without due process.

Property interests are not created by the Constitution, "they are created and their dimensions are defined by existing rules or understandings that stem from an independent source such as state law." *Roth*. The Ohio statute plainly creates such an interest. Respondents were "classified civil service employees," entitled to retain their positions "during good behavior and efficient service," who could not be dismissed "except for misfeasance, malfeasance, or nonfeasance in office." The statute plainly supports the conclusion, reached by both lower courts, that respondents possessed property rights in continued employment. Indeed, this question does not seem to have been disputed below.

The Parma Board argues, however, that the property right is defined by, and conditioned on, the legislature's choice of procedures for its deprivation. The Board stresses that in addition to specifying the grounds for termination, the statute sets out procedures by which termination may take place. The procedures were adhered to in these cases. According to petitioner, to require additional procedures would in effect expand the scope of the property interest itself. . . .

[We reject this argument.] The point is straightforward: the Due Process Clause provides that certain substantive rights—life, liberty, and property—cannot be deprived except pursuant to constitutionally adequate procedures. The categories of substance and procedure are distinct. Were the rule otherwise, the Clause would be reduced to a mere tautology. Property cannot be defined by the procedures provided for its deprivation any more than can life or liberty. The right to due process is conferred, not by legislative grace, but by constitutional guarantee. While the legislature may elect not to confer a property interest in public employment, it may not constitutionally authorize the deprivation of such an interest, once conferred, without appropriate procedural safeguards.

In short, once it is determined that the Due Process Clause applies, the question remains what process is due. The answer to that question is not to be found in the Ohio statute.

III

An essential principle of due process is that a deprivation of life, liberty, or property be preceded by notice and opportunity for hearing appropriate to the nature of the case. We have described the root requirement of the Due Process Clause as being that an individual be given an opportunity for a hearing before he is deprived of any significant property interest. This principle requires some kind of a hearing prior to the discharge of an employee who has a constitutionally protected property interest in his employment. . . . Even decisions finding no constitutional violation in termination procedures have relied on the existence of some pretermination opportunity to respond. . . .

The need for some form of pretermination hearing, recognized in these cases, is evident from a balancing of the competing interests at stake. These are the private interests in retaining employment, the governmental interest in the expeditious removal of unsatisfactory employees and the avoidance of administrative burdens, and the risk of an erroneous termination. See *Mathews v. Eldridge* (1976).

First, the significance of the private interest in retaining employment cannot be gainsaid. We have frequently recognized the severity of depriving a person of the means of livelihood. While a fired worker may find employment elsewhere, doing so will take some time and is likely to be burdened by the questionable circumstances under which he left his previous job.

Second, some opportunity for the employee to present his side of the case is recurringly of obvious value in reaching an accurate decision. Dismissals for cause will often involve factual disputes. Even where the facts are clear, the appropriateness or necessity of the discharge may not be; in such cases, the only meaningful opportunity to invoke the discretion of the decisionmaker is likely to be before the termination takes effect.

The cases before us illustrate these considerations. Both respondents had plausible arguments to make that might have prevented their discharge. The fact that the Commission saw fit to reinstate Donnelly suggests that an error might have been avoided had he been provided an opportunity to make his case to the Board. As for Loudermill, given the Commission's ruling we cannot say that the discharge was mistaken. Nonetheless, in light of the referee's recommendation, neither can we say that a fully informed decisionmaker might not have exercised its discretion and decided not to dismiss him, notwithstanding its authority to do so. In any event, the termination involved arguable issues, and the right to a hearing does not depend on a demonstration of certain success.

The governmental interest in immediate termination does not outweigh these interests. As we shall explain, affording the employee an opportunity to respond prior to termination would impose neither a significant administrative burden nor intolerable delays. Furthermore, the employer shares the employee's interest in avoiding disruption and erroneous decisions; and until the matter is settled, the employer would continue to receive the benefit of the employee's labors. It is preferable to keep a qualified employee on than to train a new one. A governmental employer also has an interest in keeping citizens usefully employed rather than taking the possibly erroneous and counterproductive step of forcing its employees onto the welfare rolls. Finally, in those situations where the employer perceives a significant hazard in keeping the employee on the job, it can avoid the problem by suspending with pay.

IV

The foregoing considerations indicate that the pretermination hearing, though necessary, need not be elaborate. We have pointed out that the formality and procedural requisites for the hearing can vary, depending upon the importance of the interests involved and the nature of the subsequent proceedings. In general, something less than a full evidentiary hearing is sufficient prior to adverse administrative action. Under state law, respondents were later entitled to a full administrative hearing and judicial review. The only question is what steps were required before the termination took effect.

In only one case, *Goldberg v. Kelly* (1970), has the Court required a full adversarial evidentiary hearing prior to adverse governmental action. However, as the *Goldberg* Court itself pointed out, that case presented significantly different considerations than are present in the context of public employment. Here, the pretermination hearing need not definitively resolve the propriety of the discharge. It should be an initial check against mistaken decisions—essentially, a determination of whether there are reasonable grounds to believe that the charges against the employee are true and support the proposed action.

The essential requirements of due process, and all that respondents seek or the Court of Appeals required, are notice and an opportunity to respond. The opportunity to present reasons, either in person or in writing, why proposed action should not be taken is a fundamental due process requirement. The tenured public employee is entitled to oral or written notice of the charges against him, an explanation of the employer's evidence, and an opportunity to present his side of the story. To require more than this prior to termination would intrude to an unwarranted extent on the government's interest in quickly removing an unsatisfactory employee.

V

Our holding rests in part on the provisions in Ohio law for a full post-termination hearing. In his cross-petition Loudermill asserts, as a separate constitutional violation, that his administrative proceedings took too long. The Court of Appeals held otherwise, and we agree. The Due Process Clause requires provision of a hearing at a meaningful time. At some point, a delay in the post-termination hearing would become a constitutional violation. In the present case, however, the complaint merely recites the course of proceedings and concludes that the denial of a speedy resolution violated due process. This reveals nothing about the delay except that it stemmed in part from the thoroughness of the procedures. A 9-month adjudication is not, of course, unconstitutionally lengthy per se. Yet Loudermill offers no indication that his wait was unreasonably prolonged other than the fact that it took nine months. The chronology of the proceedings set out in the complaint, coupled with the assertion that nine months is too long to wait, does not state a claim of a constitutional deprivation.

VI

We conclude that all the process that is due is provided by a pretermination opportunity to respond, coupled with post-termination administrative procedures as provided by the Ohio statute. Because respondents allege in their complaints that they had no chance to respond, the District Court erred in dismissing for failure to state a claim. The judgment of the Court of Appeals is affirmed, and the case is remanded for further proceedings consistent with this opinion.

Justice Marshall, concurring in part and concurring in the judgment. [Omitted.]

Justice Brennan, concurring in part and dissenting in part. [Omitted.]

Justice Rehnquist, dissenting. [Omitted.]

Chapter Recap

A. The Due Process Clause requires the government to use appropriate procedures when depriving a person of life, liberty, or property.

B. Procedural due process applies to adjudicative decisions—typically made by courts and executive branch agencies—that enforce substantive law against individuals on a case-by-case basis.

C. Constitutionally adequate procedures are required whenever the government "deprives" a person of something that qualifies as a "liberty interest" or "property interest." Liberty interests are freedoms that are deemed to require constitutional protection, while property interests are entitlements created by substantive law.

D. If a deprivation of liberty or property interests is threatened, the government must provide the process that is "due" to an individual. The necessary procedures will vary according to the facts, with more serious deprivations requiring more rigorous procedures. The factors identified in *Mathews v. Eldridge* are often used to assess the adequacy of procedures: the burden that the deprivation would impose on the individual, the value of proposed procedures in avoiding unjust deprivations, and the cost of providing the procedures.

CHAPTER 20

Freedom Rights

Laws that abridge protected freedoms are unconstitutional, no matter how equally they apply, or how fair the procedures are for enforcing them. The Bill of Rights enumerates several freedoms, including those protected by the First Amendment (religion, speech, press, assembly, petition), and the Second Amendment (keeping and bearing arms). After the Thirteenth Amendment, the United States became a country where "neither slavery nor involuntary servitude . . . shall exist." But as reflected in the ratification debates of 1787–1788, the Framers envisioned a country whose citizens would have a great many freedoms, perhaps too many to ever fully enumerate. See Ch. 3.D.

Substantive Due Process Limits Both State and Federal Governments

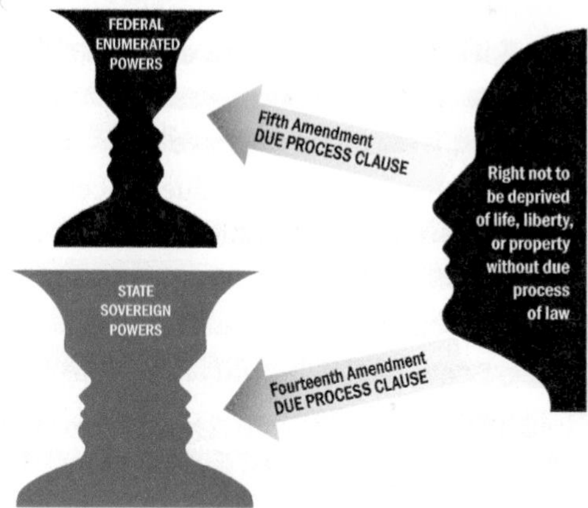

The Framers hoped that the structure of the new government would make it difficult or impossible to enact laws abridging important freedoms. But from the outset (as seen in the debate between Justice Chase and Justice Iredell in *Calder v. Bull* (1798), Ch. 3.E), there was concern that laws unduly restricting freedom might sneak through the system. Under modern interpretations of the Constitution, the Due Process Clauses of the Fifth Amendment (limiting the federal government) and Fourteenth Amendment (limiting state and local governments) will, in narrow circumstances, limit the power of government to abridge unenumerated rights. This use of the Due Process

Clause is known as substantive due process, because it addresses the substance of laws, not the procedures for enforcing them.

A. Kickstarter: Substantive Due Process

DISCLAIMER: *This Kickstarter is a checklist to help identify relevant issues. It is not a list of elements. Nothing requires judges to write their opinions (or lawyers to write their briefs) in Kickstarter order.*

Substantive Due Process **kickstarter**

USE WHEN: *The substance of a law deprives affected people of unenumerated rights.*

- *A. Has the government "deprived" a person of something?*
- *B. Does the thing that was deprived constitute a "fundamental right"?*
  - *1. Identify the right.*
  - *2. Decide if the right is fundamental.*
- *C. Can the government justify the deprivation by satisfying the applicable level of scrutiny?*

KICKSTARTER USER'S GUIDE

Substantive due process asks *whether* the government may deprive a person of life, liberty, or property—as opposed to procedural due process, which asks *how* the government enforces the deprivation. See Ch. 19.A (distinguishing procedural and substantive due process). Substantive due process is concerned with legislation—government actions that establish governmental policy—and not with the methods of adjudication. Acts of the legislature will of course be legislative, but executive branch agencies may also establish the substance of law by enacting formal rules and regulations and by implementing unwritten patterns and practices. The substance of a state's law might also be created by state courts having the power to make common law.

To avoid giving litigants two bites at the apple, a court will not entertain a substantive due process claim if the Constitution already deals with the underlying question through its enumerated rights. For example, in *Graham v. Connor*, 490 U.S. 386 (1989), a plaintiff sued a police officer for excessive use of force, claiming that it was (a) an unreasonable seizure in violation of the Fourth Amendment and (b) a deprivation of liberty under the Due Process Clause. The Supreme Court explained: "because the Fourth Amendment provides an explicit textual source of constitutional protection against this sort of physically intrusive governmental conduct, that Amendment, not the more generalized notion of substantive due process, must be the guide for analyzing these claims." As a result, substantive due process is used only for cases involving unenumerated rights.

Item A. *Deprivation.* The meaning of "deprivation" operates similarly for both procedural and substantive due process cases. Please consult the description from the procedural due process Kickstarter, Ch. 19.B.

Item B. *Fundamental Right.* "Fundamental rights" are a subset of liberty interests. Laws burdening fundamental rights will receive heightened scrutiny, while laws burdening non-fundamental rights will be upheld if they have a rational basis. The case law, taken as a whole, does not reveal a bright-line test for the fundamentality of rights. A court must exercise its best judgment, informed by the usual methods of constitutional reasoning.

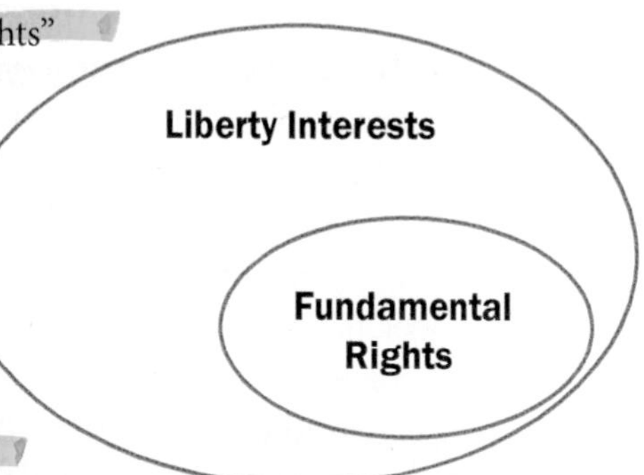

Item B.1. *Identifying the Right.* Good lawyers know that the answer you get depends on the question you ask. This principle matters when considering unenumerated rights, where the question will be some variation of "may the government restrict my right to do X." In *Lochner*, for example, the individuals' claims could be described as the right to work long hours, the right to hire someone to work long hours, the right to make contracts, the right to run one's business, the right to control one's labor, the right to be free of unjustified government regulations, the right to be left alone, and so on. Characterizing rights is an art, not a science.

Recent substantive due process cases have featured sharp disagreements in describing the asserted rights. As a strategic matter, litigants arguing in favor of a fundamental right will often use relatively broad terms that resonate with constitutional text, earlier precedents, and national values. The government, arguing against the fundamental right, will typically describe it narrowly, so that it sounds different from the Framers' vision and beyond any current consensus of national opinion.

For example, the plaintiffs in *Flores v. Reno*, 507 U.S. 292 (1993), were non-citizen children held in immigration detention centers (locked, jail-like facilities) while their families' deportations were being litigated. Community members were willing to act as foster parents for the children so they could leave detention, but federal regulations did not allow it. Counsel for the children identified the asserted right as "freedom from institutional confinement," which they considered a fundamental right—indeed, one of the oldest recognized meanings of the word "liberty." This framing persuaded the four dissenters, but the five justices in the majority disagreed, saying that "the right at issue is the alleged right of a child who has no available parent, close relative, or legal guardian, and for whom the government is responsible, to be placed in the custody of a willing-and-able private custodian rather than of a government-operated or government-selected child care institution." The majority concluded that the Due Process Clause encompassed no right matching that description.

Item B.2. *Whether the Right Is Fundamental.* Deciding whether the asserted right (however characterized) is "fundamental" is the most contentious topic within substantive due process. The narrowest view would argue that the constitution protects only the fundamental rights that are enumerated; unenumerated rights are under the control of the legislature. That reasoning would mean there is no such thing as substantive due process. Whatever its allure, this position conflicts with the Ninth Amendment, which says "The enumeration in the Constitution, of certain rights, shall not be construed to deny or disparage others retained by the people." The central task in a substantive due process case, therefore, is to decide *which* unenumerated rights are protected liberties.

For most modern judges, *Lochner* looms over the substantive due process doctrine as a cautionary tale. Nowadays, it is considered a grave error that the Supreme Court once considered freedom of contract to be a fundamental right that limited the power of government. The revival of substantive due process from the 1960s onward has tended to involve non-economic rights, such as the rights to use contraception, *Griswold v. Connecticut* (1965); to marry, *Loving v. Virginia* (1967);; to share a household with extended family members, *Moore v. City of East Cleveland* (1977); to refuse unwanted life-saving medical treatment, *Cruzan v. Director* (1990); and to form consensual intimate adult relationships, *Lawrence v. Texas* (2003). The economic/non-economic distinction helps explain the continuing influence of the two *Lochner*-era cases dealing with the rights of parents over their childrens' education: *Meyer v. Nebraska* (1923) and *Pierce v. Society of Sisters* (1925). But the realm of non-economic rights is vast, and disagreements remain over which non-economic rights deserve protection from substantive due process.

The text provides relatively little guidance, consisting only of the word "liberty" in the Due Process Clause and the Ninth Amendment's caution that individual rights are not limited to those enumerated. The enumerated rights can, however, provide some clues as a result of the incorporation doctrine. Recall that provisions in the Bill of Rights will be incorporated into the meaning of Fourteenth Amendment "liberty" (and apply to the states) if they involve fundamental rights. See Ch. 5.C. Hence, an unenumerated right that seems similar in content or importance to the incorporated rights may well be fundamental.

Various verbal formulas have been used to indicate how important a right must be for it to be considered fundamental. Many of these descriptions are borrowed from incorporation decisions of the early 20th century, which spoke of rights that are "so rooted in the traditions and conscience of our people as to be ranked as fundamental," *Snyder v. Massachusetts*, 291 U.S. 97 (1934); that constitute "immutable principles of justice which inhere in the very idea of free government," *Twining v. New Jersey*, 211 U.S. 78 (1908); and that are so "implicit in the concept of ordered liberty" that "a fair and enlightened system of justice would be impossible without them," *Palko v. Connecticut*, 302 U.S. 319 (1937). Some of these descriptions are so restrictive that almost nothing would qualify, as with *Palko*'s statement that rights are fundamental if "neither liberty nor justice would exist if they were sacrificed." Applying that standard, *Palko* held that the right against double jeopardy was not fundamental, a holding since overruled by *Benton v. Maryland*, 395 U.S. 784 (1969). More recent cases offering substantive due process protections have used different verbal formulas, asking whether the rights involve the "autonomy of self," *Lawrence v. Texas* (2003); are among "the most intimate and personal choices a person may make in a lifetime, central to personal dignity and autonomy," *Planned Parenthood v. Casey* (1993), overruled by *Dobbs v. Jackson Women's Health Organization* (2022); form part of the "realm of personal liberty which the government may not enter," *id.*, or are "intimate choices that define personal identity and beliefs," *Obergefell v. Hodges* (2015).

In the absence of a single controlling verbal formula, courts will use the usual methods of legal reasoning to determine whether a case implicates fundamental rights, with special emphasis on precedent, the history of laws in the area, consequences, and values. Concerns about governmental structure also play a role: judges who place a high value on state autonomy (federalism) or legislative and executive autonomy (separation of powers) will be less eager to recognize a fundamental right, because doing so would place a realm of lawmaking beyond the reach of states and the federal political branches.

Item C. *Level of Scrutiny.* Laws burdening interests that are not fundamental rights will be scrutinized under the rational basis test. Laws that burden fundamental rights will be reviewed with heightened scrutiny. The correct level of scrutiny for substantive due process cases can be visualized by adding a new column to the right side of the diagram used to illustrate levels of scrutiny under equal protection.

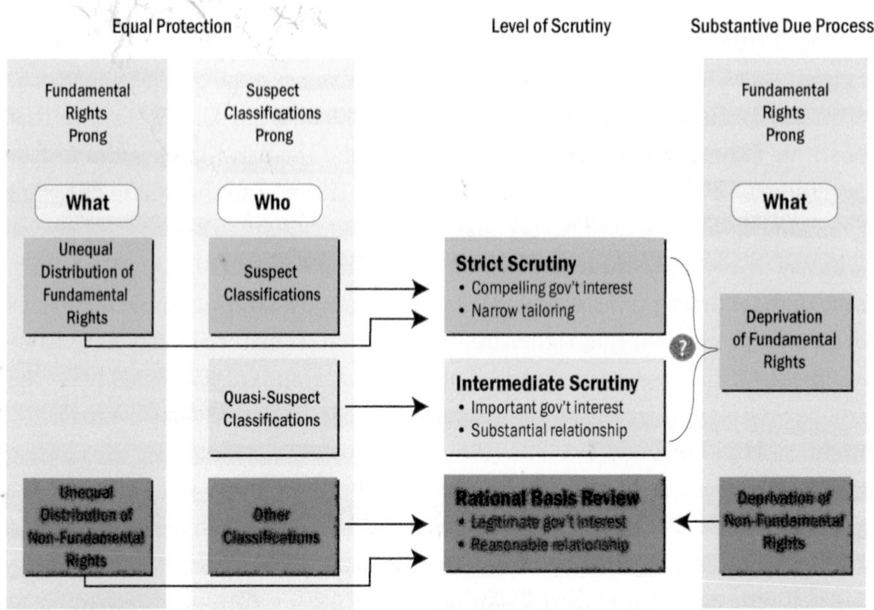

Lawyers and judges have long debated exactly how rigorous heightened scrutiny should be within the context of substantive due process. Many opinions from the 1970s onward state that courts should use "strict scrutiny"—the term originating with *Skinner v. Oklahoma* (1942). As used in equal protection cases like *Johnson v. California* (2005), strict scrutiny requires that laws be "narrowly tailored" to a "compelling" government interest, which implies that courts will be intolerant of under-inclusiveness and over-inclusiveness, and that the government must select means that impose the least feasible restriction on the fundamental right (with the phrase "least restrictive alternative" sometimes used as a parallel to the "least discriminatory alternative" language in equal protection cases). But in recent decades, some substantive due process cases have avoided the term "strict scrutiny" and its related language. Most prominent of these was *Planned Parenthood v. Casey* (1993), which held that laws burdening the right to abortion will be judged for "undue burden," although this was overruled by *Dobbs v. Jackson Women's Health Organization* (2022). A less famous line of cases involve the government's power to force a criminal defendant to take anti-psychotic medication. In that setting, *Riggins v. Nevada*, 504 U.S. 27 (1992), expressly declined to apply strict scrutiny, and *Sell v. United States*, 539 U.S. 166 (2003), asked whether, "taking account of less intrusive alternatives, [the treatment] is necessary significantly to further important governmental trial-related interests"—a formula similar to intermediate scrutiny under the Equal Protection Clause.

Given the variations among the forms of heightened scrutiny applied in substantive due process cases, the careful lawyer will be guided by the precedents most closely on point. It will also be helpful to review the features that tend to be present in cases that purport to apply different levels of scrutiny. See Ch. 18.B.

B. Interaction of Substantive Due Process, Procedural Due Process, and the Fundamental Rights Prong of Equal Protection

Just as the constitutional values of freedom, fairness, and equality overlap with each other, there is overlap among substantive due process, procedural due process, and the fundamental rights prong of equal protection. Substantive due process and procedural due process both arise from the same text. Substantive due process and the fundamental rights prong of equal protection both involve protection for unenumerated rights. It is possible for a single law to be challenged on one, two, or all three theories, depending on the facts.

1. Procedural and Substantive Due Process

The origins of procedural and substantive due process are described in Ch. 19.A. Please (re-)read it now.

Even though both procedural and substantive due process arise from the same constitutional text, their purpose and application are quite different. Both theories require, as a threshold matter, governmental action that counts as a deprivation of something that counts as life, liberty, or property. Past that threshold, the theories diverge. Procedural due process asks *how* the government goes about enforcing a law, while substantive due process asks *whether* the law may be enforced at all. They use different methods to answer each question.

	Procedural Due Process	Substantive Due Process
Interests not constituting liberty or property	n/a	Rational Basis Review
Property interests	*Mathews* Test or Equivalent	Rational Basis Review
Liberty interests—not fundamental rights	*Mathews* Test or Equivalent	Rational Basis Review
Liberty interests—fundamental rights	*Mathews* Test or Equivalent	**Heightened Scrutiny**

A single law might implicate both rights. Imagine a state law that bans elementary schools from teaching German, and that gives the Department of

Education unreviewable power to close schools without any advance notice or hearing if the department believes that they teach German. The enforcement provision of the law violates procedural due process, since it gives a school no opportunity to present its side of the story (perhaps it does not teach German). Also, in light of *Meyer v. Nebraska* (1923), the ban on teaching German violates substantive due process. No matter how good the enforcement procedures might be—even if they required a full-blown jury trial on the merits—the law would still be unconstitutional on a substantive due process theory.

This example also highlights the difference in the remedies available under procedural and substantive due process. If a law violates procedural due process, the usual remedy is to require the government to make its enforcement decision again, but using constitutionally adequate procedures. This explains why a new trial was ordered in *Moore v. Dempsey* (1923), Ch. 11.A.1, rather than dismissal of charges. If a law violates substantive due process, the usual remedy is an injunction or declaration preventing any enforcement of the law. Money damages are also available under both theories to compensate victims for losses resulting from the constitutional violations. However, as a practical matter the damages in purely procedural cases are likely to be smaller. See *Carey v. Piphus*, 435 U.S. 247 (1978) (nominal damage award of a symbolic $1 is proper compensation for procedural due process violation in the absence of actual damages).

2. Substantive Due Process and the Fundamental Rights Prong of Equal Protection

Like substantive due process, the fundamental rights prong of the Equal Protection Clause protects unenumerated rights. See Ch. 18.D. Whether an individual can assert a claim under substantive due process, the fundamental rights prong of equal protection, or both will depend on whether the challenged law puts a fundamental right off-limits for all people, or only for some.

Consider an example based on *Skinner v. Oklahoma* (1942), which found that the right to procreate was fundamental. A state law mandating sterilization for everyone could be challenged under substantive due process, but not equal protection. The challenger's argument in such a case would be about freedom; the argument does not hinge on a comparison between different groups of people. In the real *Skinner*, the state passed a law mandating sterilization only for some three-time felons. The felons could make both equality and freedom arguments. To justify an unequal distribution of the fundamental right to procreate, the state must show that its chosen classification satisfies strict scrutiny: why sterilize some three-time felons and no one else? A three-time felon could also make the same substantive due process argument that would be available against a universal sterilization law: why sterilize anyone? (In the real case, the Supreme Court ruled only on the equal protection argument, but both theories were raised.)

The same logic determines which arguments are available in cases involving unenumerated rights not considered fundamental. A state law requiring helmets when riding motorcycles could not be challenged under the Equal Protection Clause—there is no unequal distribution of rights—but there could be a challenge under substantive due process. (In practice, the challenge would fail, because riding a motorcycle without a helmet is not a fundamental right, and there is a rational basis to believe the helmet law will further public health, safety, and welfare.) Now imagine a law requiring helmets for people over six feet tall when riding motorcycles. A tall motorcyclist could argue both substantive due process (all helmet laws are unconstitutional) and equal protection (this discriminatory helmet law is unconstitutional). While the freedom argument would fail under rational basis review, the equality argument could conceivably win if the law's classification on the basis of height is irrational, lacking a reasonable relationship to the legitimate goals of public safety. Finally, a law requiring only women to wear helmets when riding motorcycles could give rise to these arguments *plus* an argument that the law's sex-based classification flunks heightened scrutiny under the suspect classifications prong of equal protection.

	Equal Protection—Fundamental Rights Prong	Substantive Due Process
Law deprives all persons of non-fundamental interests	n/a	Rational basis review of the deprivation
Law unequally allocates non-fundamental interests	Rational basis review of the classification	Rational basis review of the deprivation
Law deprives all persons of fundamental rights	n/a	Heightened scrutiny of the deprivation
Law unequally allocates fundamental rights	Heightened scrutiny of the classification	Heightened scrutiny of the deprivation

C. Substantive Due Process and Contraception: *Griswold v. Connecticut*

Substantive due process protection for economic rights had fallen out of favor with the collapse of *Lochner* in 1937. In the succeeding decades, substantive due process was occasionally used to invalidate executive action that violated unenumerated rights. *E.g.*, *Rochin v. California*, 342 U.S. 165 (1952) (forcible stomach pumping violates due process). But substantive due process was not used to invalidate a statute for several decades. This changed with *Griswold v. Connecticut* (1965). Remember that under Chief Justice Warren, the Supreme

Court in the 1950s and 1960s protected enumerated individual rights in previously unseen ways. With *Griswold*, the Warren court's commitment to individual rights extended to unenumerated rights.

Poe v. Ullman. A Connecticut law banned all drugs and devices for the purposes of avoiding pregnancy, even for married couples. However, condoms could be readily obtained at drugstores if purchased "for the prevention of disease." This meant that the law, in practice, barred birth control methods requiring a prescription (birth control pills or IUDs) or those distributed by doctors or clinics with the intent that they be used to avoid pregnancy. In other words, it banned birth control methods that could be under the exclusive control of women.

Family planning activists and physicians first challenged the Connecticut law in *Poe v. Ullman*, 367 U.S. 497 (1961), a civil suit brought against the state attorney general. A majority of the Supreme Court held that no case or controversy existed because Connecticut had not enforced the statute in decades. In an influential dissent, Justice Harlan argued that the case was justiciable and that the law violated substantive due process.

> Due process has not been reduced to any formula; its content cannot be determined by reference to any code. The best that can be said is that through the course of this Court's decisions it has represented the balance which our Nation, built upon postulates of respect for the liberty of the individual, has struck between that liberty and the demands of organized society. . . . The supplying of content to this Constitutional concept . . . certainly has not been one where judges have felt free to roam where unguided speculation might take them. The balance of which I speak is the balance struck by this country, having regard to what history teaches are the traditions from which it developed as well as the traditions from which it broke. That tradition is a living thing. A decision of this Court which radically departs from it could not long survive, while a decision which builds on what has survived is likely to be sound. No formula could serve as a substitute, in this area, for judgment and restraint. . . .
>
> Inasmuch as this context is one not of words, but of history and purposes, the full scope of the liberty guaranteed by the Due Process Clause cannot be found in or limited by the precise terms of the specific guarantees elsewhere provided in the Constitution. This "liberty" is not a series of isolated points pricked out in terms of the taking of property; the freedom of speech, press, and religion; the right to keep and bear arms; the freedom from unreasonable searches and seizures; and so on. It is a rational continuum which, broadly speaking, includes a freedom from all substantial arbitrary impositions and purposeless restraints, and which also recognizes, what a reasonable and sensitive judgment must, that certain interests require particularly careful

scrutiny of the state needs asserted to justify their abridgment. *Cf. Skinner v. Oklahoma* (1942); *Bolling v. Sharpe* (1954). . . .

The Griswold Litigation. In response to *Poe*, Planned Parenthood opened an office in New Haven to distribute prescription contraceptives. Connecticut brought charges against its officers. The direct appeal of a criminal conviction always poses a justiciable case or controversy, and the Supreme Court granted review.

ITEMS TO CONSIDER WHILE READING *GRISWOLD*:

A. *Work through the topics in the Kickstarter.*

B. *Why does the majority opinion not rely directly on the Due Process Clause? What does it rely upon instead?*

C. *How do the concurrences differ from the majority opinion and each other?*

D. *Justice Black's dissent argues that this is* Lochner *all over again. Is he right? What do Justices Goldberg and Harlan propose to avoid the problems of* Lochner?

Griswold v. Connecticut,

381 U.S. 479 (1965)

Justice Douglas delivered the opinion of the Court [joined by Chief Justice Warren and Justices Clark, Goldberg, and Brennan.]

Appellant [Estelle] Griswold is Executive Director of the Planned Parenthood League of Connecticut. Appellant [C. Lee] Buxton is a licensed physician and a professor at the Yale Medical School who served as Medical Director for the League at its Center in New Haven—a center open and operating from November 1 to November 10, 1961, when appellants were arrested.

They gave information, instruction, and medical advice to married persons as to the means of preventing conception. They examined the wife and prescribed the best contraceptive device or material for her use. Fees were usually charged, although some couples were serviced free.

The statutes whose constitutionality is involved in this appeal are §§ 53-32 and 54-196 of the General Statutes of Connecticut. The former provides: "Any person who uses any drug, medicinal article

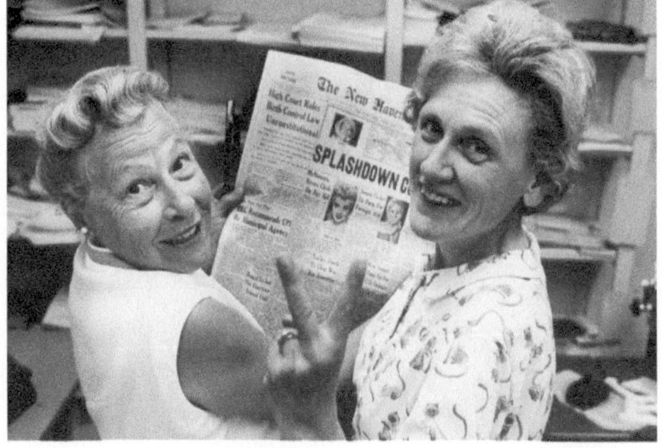

Estelle Griswold (1900–1981) with Cornelia Jahncke

or instrument for the purpose of preventing conception shall be fined not less than fifty dollars or imprisoned not less than sixty days nor more than one year or be both fined and imprisoned." Section 54-196 provides: "Any person who assists, abets, counsels, causes, hires or commands another to commit any offense may be prosecuted and punished as if he were the principal offender."

The appellants were found guilty as accessories and fined $100 each, against the claim that the accessory statute as so applied violated the Fourteenth Amendment. The Appellate Division of the [state] Circuit Court affirmed. The [state] Supreme Court of Errors affirmed that judgment. [We granted review.]

We think that appellants have standing to raise the constitutional rights of the married people with whom they had a professional relationship. . . .

Coming to the merits, we are met with a wide range of questions that implicate the Due Process Clause of the Fourteenth Amendment. Overtones of some arguments suggest that *Lochner v New York* (1905) should be our guide. But we decline that invitation as we did in *West Coast Hotel Co. v. Parrish* (1937), *Williamson v. Lee Optical* (1955) [and their progeny]. We do not sit as a super-legislature to determine the wisdom, need, and propriety of laws that touch economic problems, business affairs, or social conditions. This law, however, operates directly on an intimate relation of husband and wife and their physician's role in one aspect of that relation.

[As an analogy, the next four paragraphs discuss precedents protecting rights that involved expression, but that did not fall squarely within the text of the First Amendment: association, education, and belief.]

The association of people is not mentioned in the Constitution nor in the Bill of Rights. The right to educate a child in a school of the parents' choice—whether public or private or parochial—is also not mentioned. Nor is the right to study any particular subject or any foreign language. Yet the First Amendment has been construed to include certain of those rights.

By *Pierce v. Society of Sisters* (1925), the right to educate one's children as one chooses is made applicable to the States by the force of the First and Fourteenth Amendments. By *Meyer v. Nebraska* (1923), the same dignity is given the right to study the German language in a private school. In other words, the State may not, consistently with the spirit of the First Amendment, contract the spectrum of available knowledge. The right of freedom of speech and press includes not only the right to utter or to print, but the right to distribute, the right to receive, the right to read, and freedom of inquiry, freedom of thought, and freedom to teach—indeed the freedom of the entire university community. Without those peripheral rights the specific rights would be less secure. And so we reaffirm the principle of the *Pierce* and the *Meyer* cases.

Griswold v. Connecticut

In ***NAACP v. Alabama***, 357 U.S. 449 (1958), we protected the freedom to associate and privacy in one's associations, noting that freedom of association was a peripheral First Amendment right. Disclosure of membership lists of a constitutionally valid association, we held, was invalid as entailing the likelihood of a substantial restraint upon the exercise by petitioner's members of their right to freedom of association. In other words, the First Amendment has a penumbra where privacy is protected from governmental intrusion. In like context, we have protected forms of association that are not political in the customary sense but pertain to the social, legal, and economic benefit of the members. . . .

Those cases involved more than the right of "assembly"—a right that extends to all irrespective of their race or ideology. The right of association, like the right of belief, *West Virginia State Board of Education v. Barnette* (1943), is more than the right to attend a meeting; it includes the right to express one's attitudes or philosophies by membership in a group or by affiliation with it or by other lawful means. Association in that context is a form of expression of opinion; and while it is not expressly included in the First Amendment its existence is necessary in making the express guarantees fully meaningful.

■ HISTORY

***NAACP* v. *ALABAMA*:** The Supreme Court held that the state could not demand a list of all members of the NAACP, because it would inhibit membership in the then-controversial civil rights organization. The Court's opinion relied on concepts of "association" that were related, but not identical, to the First Amendment's protections for "speech" and "assembly."

The foregoing cases suggest that specific guarantees in the Bill of Rights have **penumbras**, formed by emanations from those guarantees that help give them life and substance. See *Poe v. Ullman* (1961) (dissenting opinion). Various guarantees create zones of privacy. The right of association contained in the penumbra of the First Amendment is one, as we have seen. The Third Amendment in its prohibition against the quartering of soldiers in any house in time of peace without the consent of the owner is another facet of that privacy. The Fourth Amendment explicitly affirms the "right of the people to be secure in their persons, houses, papers, and effects, against unreasonable searches and seizures." The Fifth Amendment in its Self-Incrimination Clause enables the citizen to create a zone of privacy which government may not force him to surrender to his detriment. The Ninth Amendment provides: "The enumeration in the Constitution, of certain rights, shall not be construed to deny or disparage others retained by the people."

■ TERMINOLOGY

PENUMBRAS: In the science of optics, a penumbra is the fuzzy area of partial shade extending beyond the edges of the shadow cast by an opaque object. Other dictionary definitions of "penumbra" include "a surrounding or adjoining region in which something exists in a lesser degree" and "something that surrounds." Although its legal usage is now associated with *Griswold*, the word had occasionally been used in other Supreme Court opinions. E.g. *Olmstead v. United States*, 277 U.S. 438, 469 (1928) (Holmes, J. dissenting).

The Fourth and Fifth Amendments were described in *Boyd v. United States*, 116 U.S. 616 (1886), as protection against all governmental invasions "of the sanctity of a man's home and the privacies of life." We recently referred in *Mapp v. Ohio*, 367 U.S. 643 (1961) to the Fourth Amendment as creating a "right to privacy, no less important than any other right carefully and particularly reserved to the people."

We have had many controversies over these penumbral rights of privacy and repose. See, e.g., *Skinner v. Oklahoma* (1942) [and other cases]. These cases bear witness that the right of privacy which presses for recognition here is a legitimate one.

The present case, then, concerns a relationship lying within the zone of privacy created by several fundamental constitutional guarantees. And it concerns a law which, in forbidding the use of contraceptives rather than regulating their manufacture or sale, seeks to achieve its goals by means having a maximum destructive impact upon that relationship. Such a law cannot stand in light of the familiar principle, so often applied by this Court, that a governmental purpose to control or prevent activities constitutionally subject to state regulation may not be achieved by means which sweep unnecessarily broadly and thereby invade the area of protected freedoms. Would we allow the police to search the sacred precincts of marital bedrooms for telltale signs of the use of contraceptives? The very idea is repulsive to the notions of privacy surrounding the marriage relationship.

We deal with a right of privacy older than the Bill of Rights—older than our political parties, older than our school system. Marriage is a coming together for better or for worse, hopefully enduring, and intimate to the degree of being sacred. It is an association that promotes a way of life, not causes; a harmony in living, not political faiths; a bilateral loyalty, not commercial or social projects. Yet it is an association for as noble a purpose as any involved in our prior decisions.

Justice Goldberg, whom Chief Justice Warren and Justice Brennan join, concurring.

I agree with the Court that Connecticut's birth-control law unconstitutionally intrudes upon the right of marital privacy, and I join in its opinion and judgment. [I agree] that the concept of liberty protects those personal rights that are fundamental, and is not confined to the specific terms of the Bill of Rights. My conclusion that the concept of liberty is not so restricted and that it embraces the right of marital privacy though that right is not mentioned explicitly in the Constitution is supported both by numerous decisions of this Court, referred to in the Court's opinion, and by the language and history of the Ninth Amendment. In reaching the conclusion that the right of marital privacy is protected, as being within the protected penumbra of specific guarantees of the Bill of Rights, the Court refers to the Ninth Amendment. I add these words to emphasize the relevance of that Amendment to the Court's holding. . . .

Griswold v. Connecticut

While this Court has had little occasion to interpret the Ninth Amendment, it cannot be presumed that any clause in the constitution is intended to be without effect. In interpreting the Constitution, real effect should be given to all the words it uses. The Ninth Amendment to the Constitution may be regarded by some as a recent discovery and may be forgotten by others, but since 1791 it has been a basic part of the Constitution which we are sworn to uphold. To hold that a right so basic and fundamental and so deep-rooted in our society as the right of privacy in marriage may be infringed because that right is not guaranteed in so many words by the first eight amendments to the Constitution is to ignore the Ninth Amendment and to give it no effect whatsoever. . . .

A dissenting opinion [by Justice Black] suggests that my interpretation of the Ninth Amendment somehow broadens the powers of this Court. With all due respect, I believe that it misses the import of what I am saying. I do not take the position . . . that the Ninth Amendment constitutes an independent source of rights protected from infringement by either the States or the Federal Government. Rather, the Ninth Amendment shows a belief of the Constitution's authors that fundamental rights exist that are not expressly enumerated in the first eight amendments and an intent that the list of rights included there not be deemed exhaustive. . . . I do not see how this broadens the authority of the Court; rather it serves to support what this Court has been doing in protecting fundamental rights. . . .

In determining which rights are fundamental, judges are not left at large to decide cases in light of their personal and private notions. Rather, they must look to the traditions and collective conscience of our people to determine whether a principle is so rooted there as to be ranked as fundamental. *Snyder v. Massachusetts*, 291 U.S. 97 (1934). The inquiry is whether a right involved is of such a character that it cannot be denied without violating those "fundamental principles of liberty and justice which lie at the base of all our civil and political institutions." *Powell v. State of Alabama*, 287 U.S. 45 (1932) [the *Scottsboro Boys* case, see Ch. 11.A.1]. Liberty also "gains content from the emanations of specific constitutional guarantees" and "from experience with the requirements of a free society." *Poe v. Ullman* (1961) (dissenting opinion of Justice Douglas).

I agree fully with the Court that, applying these tests, the right of privacy is a fundamental personal right, emanating from the totality of the constitutional scheme under which we live. Mr. Justice Brandeis, dissenting in *Olmstead v. United States*, 277 U.S. 438 (1928), comprehensively summarized the principles underlying the Constitution's guarantees of privacy:

> The protection guaranteed by the (Fourth and Fifth) amendments is much broader in scope. The makers of our Constitution undertook to secure conditions favorable to the pursuit of happiness. They recognized the significance of man's spiritual nature, of his feelings and of his intellect. They knew that only

> a part of the pain, pleasure and satisfactions of life are to be found in material things. They sought to protect Americans in their beliefs, their thoughts, their emotions and their sensations. They conferred, as against the government, the right to be let alone—the most comprehensive of rights and the right most valued by civilized men.

The Connecticut statutes here involved deal with a particularly important and sensitive area of privacy—that of the marital relation and the marital home. . . . Although the Constitution does not speak in so many words of the right of privacy in marriage, I cannot believe that it offers these fundamental rights no protection. The fact that no particular provision of the Constitution explicitly forbids the State from disrupting the traditional relation of the family—a relation as old and as fundamental as our entire civilization—surely does not show that the Government was meant to have the power to do so. Rather, as the Ninth Amendment expressly recognizes, there are fundamental personal rights such as this one, which are protected from abridgment by the Government though not specifically mentioned in the Constitution.

My Brother Stewart, while characterizing the Connecticut birth control law as "an uncommonly silly law," would nevertheless let it stand on the ground that it is not for the courts to substitute their social and economic beliefs for the judgment of legislative bodies, who are elected to pass laws. Elsewhere, I have stated that while I quite agree with Mr. Justice Brandeis that a State may "serve as a laboratory; and try novel social and economic experiments," *New State Ice Co. v. Liebmann* (1923) (dissenting opinion), I do not believe that this includes the power to experiment with the fundamental liberties of citizens. The vice of the dissenters' views is that it would permit such experimentation by the States in the area of the fundamental personal rights of its citizens. I cannot agree that the Constitution grants such power either to the States or to the Federal Government.

The logic of the dissents would sanction federal or state legislation that seems to me even more plainly unconstitutional than the statute before us. Surely the Government, absent a showing of a compelling subordinating state interest, could not decree that all husbands and wives must be sterilized after two children have been born to them. Yet by their reasoning such an invasion of marital privacy would not be subject to constitutional challenge because, while it might be "silly," no provision of the Constitution specifically prevents the Government from curtailing the marital right to bear children and raise a family. While it may shock some of my Brethren that the Court today holds that the Constitution protects the right of marital privacy, in my view it is far more shocking to believe that the personal liberty guaranteed by the Constitution does not include protection against such totalitarian limitation of family size, which is at complete variance with our constitutional concepts. Yet, if upon a showing of a slender basis of rationality, a law outlawing voluntary birth control by married persons is valid, then, by the same reasoning, a law requiring compulsory birth control also would seem to be valid. In my view, however, both types of law would unjustifiably intrude upon rights of marital privacy which are constitutionally protected. . . .

Finally, it should be said of the Court's holding today that it in no way interferes with a State's proper regulation of sexual promiscuity or misconduct. As my Brother Harlan so well stated in his dissenting opinion in *Poe v. Ullman*:

> Adultery, homosexuality and the like are sexual intimacies which the State forbids, but the intimacy of husband and wife is necessarily an essential and accepted feature of the institution of marriage, an institution which the State not only must allow, but which always and in every age it has fostered and protected. It is one thing when the State exerts its power either to forbid extra-marital sexuality or to say who may marry, but it is quite another when, having acknowledged a marriage and the intimacies inherent in it, it undertakes to regulate by means of the criminal law the details of that intimacy.

In sum, I believe that the right of privacy in the marital relation is fundamental and basic—a personal right "retained by the people" within the meaning of the Ninth Amendment. Connecticut cannot constitutionally abridge this fundamental right, which is protected by the Fourteenth Amendment from infringement by the States. I agree with the Court that petitioners' convictions must therefore be reversed.

Justice Harlan, concurring in the judgment.

I fully agree with the judgment of reversal, but find myself unable to join the Court's opinion. . . . In my view, the proper constitutional inquiry in this case is whether this Connecticut statute infringes the Due Process Clause of the Fourteenth Amendment because the enactment violates basic values implicit in the concept of ordered liberty. For reasons stated at length in my dissenting opinion in *Poe v. Ullman*, I believe that it does. While the relevant inquiry may be aided by resort to one or more of the provisions of the Bill of Rights, it is not dependent on them or any of their radiations. The Due Process Clause of the Fourteenth Amendment stands, in my opinion, on its own bottom.

A further observation seems in order respecting the justification of my Brothers Black and Stewart[.] . . . Their approach [rests] on the thesis that by limiting the content of the Due Process Clause of the Fourteenth Amendment to the protection of rights which can be found elsewhere in the Constitution, in this instance in the Bill of Rights, judges will thus be confined to interpretation of specific constitutional provisions, and will thereby be restrained from introducing their own notions of constitutional right and wrong into the vague contours of the Due Process Clause.

While I could not more heartily agree that judicial self restraint is an indispensable ingredient of sound constitutional adjudication, I do submit that the formula suggested for achieving it is more hollow than real. Specific provisions of the Constitution, no less than due process, lend themselves as readily to personal interpretations by judges whose constitutional outlook is simply to keep the Constitution in supposed tune with the times. . . . Judicial self-restraint . . . will be achieved in this area, as in other constitutional areas, only by continual insistence upon respect for the teachings of history, solid recognition of the basic values that underlie our society, and wise appreciation of the great roles that the doctrines of federalism and separation of powers have played in establishing and preserving American freedoms. Adherence to these principles will not, of course, obviate all constitutional differences of opinion among judges, nor should it. Their continued recognition will, however, go farther toward keeping most judges from roaming at large in the constitutional field than will the interpolation into the Constitution of an artificial and largely illusory restriction on the content of the Due Process Clause.

Justice White, concurring in the judgment.

In my view this Connecticut law as applied to married couples deprives them of liberty without due process of law, as that concept is used in the Fourteenth Amendment. . . .

As I read the opinions of the Connecticut courts and the argument of Connecticut in this Court, the State claims but one justification for its anti-use statute. . . . The statute is said to serve the State's policy against all forms of promiscuous or illicit sexual relationships, be they premarital or extramarital, concededly a permissible and legitimate legislative goal.

Without taking issue with the premise that the fear of conception operates as a deterrent to such relationships in addition to the criminal proscriptions Connecticut has against such conduct, I wholly fail to see how the ban on the use of contraceptives by married couples in any way reinforces the State's ban on illicit sexual relationships. . . . Moreover, it would appear that the sale of contraceptives to prevent disease is plainly legal under Connecticut law.

In these circumstances one is rather hard pressed to explain how the ban on use by married persons in any way prevents use of such devices by persons engaging in illicit sexual relations and thereby contributes to the State's policy against such relationships. Neither the state courts nor the State before the bar of this Court has tendered such an explanation. . . . I find nothing in this record justifying the sweeping scope of this statute, with its telling effect on the freedoms of married persons, and therefore conclude that it deprives such persons of liberty without due process of law.

Justice Black, with whom Justice Stewart joins, dissenting.

. . . The Court talks about a constitutional "right of privacy" as though there is some constitutional provision or provisions forbidding any law ever to be passed which might abridge the privacy of individuals. But there is not. . . .

Griswold v. Connecticut

One of the most effective ways of diluting or expanding a constitutionally guaranteed right is to substitute for the crucial word or words of a constitutional guarantee another word or words, more or less flexible and more or less restricted in meaning. This fact is well illustrated by the use of the term "right of privacy" as a comprehensive substitute for the Fourth Amendment's guarantee against unreasonable searches and seizures. Privacy is a broad, abstract and ambiguous concept which can easily be shrunken in meaning but which can also, on the other hand, easily be interpreted as a constitutional ban against many things other than searches and seizures. . . . For these reasons I get nowhere in this case by talk about a constitutional right of privacy as an emanation from one or more constitutional provisions. I like my privacy as well as the next one, but I am nevertheless compelled to admit that government has a right to invade it unless prohibited by some specific constitutional provision. For these reasons I cannot agree with the Court's judgment and the reasons it gives for holding this Connecticut law unconstitutional.

This brings me to the arguments made by my Brothers Harlan, White and Goldberg for invalidating the Connecticut law. Brothers Harlan and White would invalidate it by reliance on the Due Process Clause of the Fourteenth Amendment, but Brother Goldberg . . . relies also on the Ninth Amendment. . . . I think that if properly construed neither the Due Process Clause nor the Ninth Amendment, nor both together, could under any circumstances be a proper basis for invalidating the Connecticut law. I discuss the due process and Ninth Amendment arguments together because on analysis they turn out to be the same thing—merely using different words to claim for this Court and the federal judiciary power to invalidate any legislative act which the judges find irrational, unreasonable or offensive.

The due process argument which my Brothers Harlan and White adopt here is based, as their opinions indicate, on the premise that this Court is vested with power to invalidate all state laws that it consider to be arbitrary, capricious, unreasonable, or oppressive, or this Court's belief that a particular state law under scrutiny has no rational or justifying purpose, or is offensive to a sense of fairness and justice. If these formulas based on natural justice, or others which mean the same thing, are to prevail, they require judges to determine what is or is not constitutional on the basis of their own appraisal of what laws are unwise or unnecessary. The power to make such decisions is of course that of a legislative body. . . .

Of the cases on which my Brothers White and Goldberg rely so heavily, undoubtedly the reasoning of two of them supports their result here—as would that of a number of others which they do not bother to name, e.g., *Lochner v. New York* (1905) and *Adkins v. Children's Hospital* (1923). The two they do cite and quote from, *Meyer v. Nebraska* (1923) and *Pierce v. Society of Sisters* (1925) were both decided in opinions by Mr. Justice McReynolds [one of the "Four Horsemen"] which elaborated the same natural law due process philosophy found in *Lochner v. New York*, one of the cases on which he relied in *Meyer*, along with such other long-discredited decisions as *Adkins v. Children's Hospital*. . . . Without expressing an opinion as to whether either of those cases reached a correct result in light of our later decisions applying the First Amendment to the States through the Fourteenth, I merely point out that the reasoning stated in *Meyer* and *Pierce* was the same natural law due process philosophy which many later opinions repudiated, and which I cannot accept. . . .

My Brother Goldberg has adopted the recent discovery that the Ninth Amendment as well as the Due Process Clause can be used by this Court as authority to strike down all state legislation which this Court thinks violates "fundamental principles of liberty and justice," or is contrary to the "traditions and collective conscience of our people." He also states, without proof satisfactory to me, that in making decisions on this basis judges will not consider their personal and private notions. One may ask how they can avoid considering them. Our Court certainly has no machinery with which to take a Gallup Poll. And the scientific miracles of this age have not yet produced a gadget which the Court can use to determine what traditions are rooted in the "collective conscience of our people." Moreover, one would certainly have to look far beyond the language of the Ninth Amendment to find that the Framers vested in this Court any such awesome veto powers over lawmaking, either by the States or by the Congress. . . .

If any broad, unlimited power to hold laws unconstitutional because they offend what this Court conceives to be the "collective conscience of our people" is vested in this Court by the Ninth Amendment, the Fourteenth Amendment, or any other provision of the Constitution, it was not given by the Framers, but rather has been bestowed on the Court by the Court. This fact is perhaps responsible for the peculiar phenomenon that for a period of a century and a half no serious suggestion was ever made that the Ninth Amendment, enacted to protect state powers against federal invasion, could be used as a weapon of federal power to prevent state legislatures from passing laws they consider appropriate to govern local affairs. Use of any such broad, unbounded judicial authority would make of this Court's members a day-to-day constitutional convention. . . .

I realize that many good and able men have eloquently spoken and written, sometimes in rhapsodical strains, about the duty of this Court to keep the Constitution in tune with the times. The idea is that the Constitution must be changed from time to time and that this Court is charged with a duty to make those changes. For myself, I must with all deference reject that philosophy. The Constitution makers knew the need for change and provided for it. Amendments suggested by the people's elected representatives can be submitted to the people or their selected agents for ratification. That method of change was good for our Fathers, and being somewhat old-fashioned I must add it is good enough for me. And so, I cannot rely on the Due Process Clause or the Ninth Amendment or any mysterious and uncertain natural law concept as a reason for striking down this state law. . . .

In 1798, when this Court was asked to hold another Connecticut law unconstitutional [in *Calder v. Bull*], Justice Iredell said:

> If . . . the Legislature of the Union, or the Legislature of any member of the Union, shall pass a law, within the general scope of their constitutional power, the Court cannot pronounce it to be void, merely because it is, in their judgment, contrary to the principles of natural justice. The ideas of natural justice are regulated by no fixed standard: the ablest and the purest men have differed upon the subject; and all that the Court could properly say, in such an event, would be, that the Legislature (possessed of an equal right of opinion) had passed an act which, in the opinion of the judges, was inconsistent with the abstract principles of natural justice.

I would adhere to that constitutional philosophy in passing on this Connecticut law today. . . . The late Judge Learned Hand, after emphasizing his view that judges should not use the due process formula suggested in the concurring opinions today or any other formula like it to invalidate legislation offensive to their personal preferences, made the statement, with which I fully agree, that: "For myself it would be most irksome to be ruled by a bevy of Platonic Guardians, even if I knew how to choose them, which I assuredly do not."

So far as I am concerned, Connecticut's law as applied here is not forbidden by any provision of the Federal Constitution as that Constitution was written, and I would therefore affirm.

Justice Stewart, whom Justice Black joins, dissenting.

Since 1879 Connecticut has had on its books a law which forbids the use of contraceptives by anyone. I think this is an uncommonly silly law. As a practical matter, the law is obviously unenforceable, except in the oblique context of the present case. As a philosophical matter, I believe the use of contraceptives in the relationship of marriage should be left to personal and private choice, based upon each individual's moral, ethical, and religious beliefs. As a matter of social policy, I think professional counsel about methods of birth control should be available to all, so that each individual's choice can be meaningfully made. But we are not asked in this case to say whether we think this law is unwise, or even asinine. We are asked to hold that it violates the United States Constitution. And that I cannot do. . . .

flashforward

1. Griswold *as a Substantive Due Process Decision.* The majority opinion in *Griswold* considered it important not to rely upon the Due Process Clause, instead finding that the right of married couples to use contraceptives could be tied, albeit indirectly, to other constitutional text. Later decisions have followed Justice Harlan's concurrence, relying directly on a theory of unenumerated liberty protected by the Due Process Clause. *Griswold* itself is now generally understood as a substantive due process case, regularly included in string cites of substantive due process decisions. See e.g., *Lawrence v. Texas* (2003), Ch. 22.E; *County of Sacramento v. Lewis*, 523 U.S. 833 (1998). See also *Roe v. Wade* (1973) (Stewart, J., concurring) ("*Griswold* stands as one in a long line of . . . cases decided under the doctrine of substantive due process, and I now accept it as such").

2. Griswold*'s Impact on Equal Protection.* Connecticut's ban on contraception applied to all persons, so *Griswold* included no equal protection argument. But once a right is deemed fundamental, laws distributing it unequally would face strict scrutiny under the Equal Protection Clause. This logic drove the decision in *Eisenstadt v. Baird*, 405 U.S. 438 (1972), which invalidated (6–1) Massachusetts laws limiting contraceptive sales only to married couples.

> If under *Griswold* the distribution of contraceptives to married persons cannot be prohibited, a ban on distribution to unmarried persons would be equally impermissible. It is true that in *Griswold* the right of privacy in question inhered in the marital relationship. Yet the marital couple is not an independent entity with a mind and heart of its own, but an association of two individuals each with a separate intellectual and emotional makeup. If the right of privacy means anything, it is the right of the individual, married or single, to be free from unwarranted governmental intrusion into matters so fundamentally affecting a person as the decision whether to bear or beget a child. See *Skinner v. Oklahoma* (1942). . . . We hold that by providing dissimilar treatment for married and unmarried persons who are similarly situated, [the Massachusetts laws] violate the Equal Protection Clause.

The passage in *Eisenstadt* about "the decision whether to bear or beget a child" was written with the knowledge that the Court would soon be deciding *Roe v. Wade*. See Ch. 20.F.1.

3. Griswold-*Style "Privacy."* The majority opinion in *Griswold* held that Connecticut's law violated a right to "privacy" that was implied by various enumerated rights. For a decade or so, other fundamental rights opinions of the Supreme Court made that word a centerpiece of their reasoning, with "privacy" meaning something similar to Justice Brandeis's "right to be let alone." This use of "privacy" can be seen in the passage from *Eisenstadt* quoted above and in *Roe v. Wade* (1973). Since then, primary reliance on "privacy" has fallen out of favor, in part because the word has so many possible meanings (publication of private facts, intrusion into seclusion, surveillance in public places, and more). More recent substantive due process cases are more likely to use terms like "autonomy" or "self-determination" when referring to the ability to act free of governmental compulsion. With that said, some state courts continue to use "privacy" in the *Griswold* sense, sometimes as a result of express privacy provisions in state constitutions. See, e.g., Alaska Constitution, Art. I, § 22 ("The right of the people to privacy is recognized and shall not be infringed"); Florida Constitution, Art. I, § 23 ("Right to Privacy: Every natural person has the right to be let alone and free from governmental intrusion into the person's private life except as otherwise provided herein").

D. Substantive Due Process and Family Relationships

The laws governing daily family life—marriage, divorce, parentage, child custody, and housing—have historically been set by state and local governments. It has sometimes proven difficult to apply substantive due process to these traditionally local areas of regulation, as seen in the splintered opinions that follow.

1. Housing and the Extended Family: *Moore v. City of East Cleveland*

East Cleveland, Ohio, founded in 1911, held the summer home of John D. Rockefeller and a strip known as "Millionaire's Row." Like most suburbs established around this time, the city was originally exclusively White. As housing discrimination became legally untenable—see *Shelley v. Kraemer* (1948) (Ch. 21.B.1)—African-Americans began to move into East Cleveland in the 1960s.

The City adopted an ordinance in 1966 forbidding groups other than a "family" to live in certain homes. The City defined a family as follows:

> "Family" means a number of individuals related to the nominal head of the household or to the spouse of the nominal head of the household living as a single housekeeping unit in a single dwelling unit, but limited to the following:
>
> (a) Husband or wife of the nominal head of the household.
>
> (b) Unmarried children of the nominal head of the household or of the spouse of the nominal head of the household, provided, however, that such unmarried children have no children residing with them.
>
> (c) Father or mother of the nominal head of the household or of the spouse of the nominal head of the household.

The Moore Family. The Moores were an African-American extended family living in one side of an East Cleveland duplex. When the lawsuit began, seven-year-old John Moore Jr. lived with his grandmother, Inez Moore, his uncle Dale Moore Sr., and his cousin Dale Moore Jr. Other cousins lived next door. John Jr. had lived with his grandmother ever since his own mother died when he was a baby. By the early 1970s, his father had remarried and moved elsewhere, but the family decided it would be best for John Jr. to remain in the home and neighborhood he had always known.

The Moore Family

(■ = lives in house)

In 1972, when John Jr. was old enough to begin school, Inez sought to register him in their local school district. The district refused to admit him because Inez was not his legal guardian. She responded with a lawsuit that ultimately led to a favorable settlement and a change in policy. But a few months after her suit against the school district was filed, the City's housing inspectors arrived.

ITEMS TO CONSIDER WHILE READING *MOORE v. CITY OF EAST CLEVELAND*:

A. *Work through the items in the Kickstarter.*

B. Moore *has no majority opinion. Make a chart summarizing the various opinions. Which opinion should be considered the holding?*

C. *How do the justices use the various methods of reasoning in their opinions? Focus on precedent: between the plurality and Justice Stewart's dissent, who has the better reading of the earlier cases?*

D. *How would the case be framed and resolved under an equal protection theory?*

Moore v. City of East Cleveland,

431 U.S. 494 (1977)

Justice Powell announced the judgment of the Court, and delivered an opinion in which Justices Brennan, Marshall, and Blackmun joined.

East Cleveland's housing ordinance, like many throughout the country, limits occupancy of a dwelling unit to members of a single family. But the ordinance contains an unusual and complicated definitional section that recognizes as a "family" only a few categories of related individuals. Because her family, living together in her home, fits none of those categories, appellant stands convicted of a criminal offense. The question in this case is whether the ordinance violates the Due Process Clause of the Fourteenth Amendment.

I

Appellant, Mrs. Inez Moore, lives in her East Cleveland home together with her son, Dale Moore Sr., and her two grandsons, Dale, Jr., and John Moore, Jr. The two boys are first cousins rather than brothers; we are told that John came to live with his grandmother and with the elder and younger Dale Moores after his mother's death.

In early 1973, Mrs. Moore received a notice of violation from the city, stating that John was an illegal occupant and directing her to comply with the ordinance. When she failed to remove him from her home, the city filed a criminal charge. Mrs. Moore moved to dismiss, claiming that the ordinance was constitutionally invalid on its face. Her motion was overruled, and upon conviction she was sentenced to five days in jail and a $25 fine. The Ohio Court of Appeals affirmed after giving full consideration to her constitutional claims, and the Ohio Supreme Court denied review. We [granted review].

II

The city argues that our decision in ***Village of Belle Terre v. Boraas***, 416 U.S. 1 (1974), requires us to sustain the ordinance attacked here. Belle Terre, like East Cleveland, imposed limits on the types of groups that could occupy a single dwelling unit. Applying the constitutional standard announced in this Court's leading land-use case, *Euclid v. Ambler Realty Co.*, 272 U.S. 365 (1926),[FN6] we sustained the Belle Terre ordinance on the ground that it bore a rational relationship to permissible state objectives.

FN6 *Euclid* held that land-use regulations violate the Due Process Clause if they are "clearly arbitrary and unreasonable, having no substantial relation to the public health, safety, morals, or general welfare." Later cases have emphasized that the general welfare is not to be narrowly understood; it embraces a broad range of governmental purposes. But our cases have not departed from the requirement that the government's chosen means must rationally further some legitimate state purpose.

HISTORY

VILLAGE OF BELLE TERRE** v.* ***BORAAS: A small and exclusive village on the north shore of Long Island allowed only single-family residences that were home to "one or more persons related by blood, adoption, or marriage." The Supreme Court held (7–2) that it was constitutional for the City to rely on this ordinance to exclude a group of six college housemates attending the nearby State University of New York at Stonybrook.

But one overriding factor sets this case apart from *Belle Terre*. The ordinance there affected only unrelated individuals. It expressly allowed all who were related by "blood, adoption, or marriage" to live together, and in sustaining the ordinance we were careful to note that it promoted "family needs" and "family values." East Cleveland, in contrast, has chosen to regulate the occupancy of its housing by slicing deeply into the family itself. This is no mere incidental result of the ordinance. On its face it selects certain categories of relatives who may live together and declares that others may not. In particular, it makes a crime of a grandmother's choice to live with her grandson in circumstances like those presented here.

When a city undertakes such intrusive regulation of the family, neither *Belle Terre* nor *Euclid* governs; the usual judicial deference to the legislature is inappropriate. This Court has long recognized that freedom of personal choice in matters of marriage and family life is one of the liberties protected by the Due Process Clause of the Fourteenth Amendment. A host of cases, tracing their lineage to *Meyer v. Nebraska* (1923), and *Pierce v. Society of Sisters* (1925), have consistently acknowledged a private realm of family life which the state cannot enter. Of course, the family is not beyond regulation. But when the government intrudes on choices concerning family living arrangements, this Court must examine carefully the importance of the governmental interests advanced and the extent to which they are served by the challenged regulation.

When thus examined, this ordinance cannot survive. The city seeks to justify it as a means of preventing overcrowding, minimizing traffic and parking congestion, and avoiding an undue financial burden on East Cleveland's school system. Although these are legitimate goals, the ordinance before us serves them marginally, at best. For example, the ordinance permits any family consisting only of husband, wife, and unmarried children to live together, even if the family contains a half dozen licensed drivers, each with his or her own car. At the same time it forbids an adult brother and sister to share a household, even if both faithfully use public transportation. The ordinance would permit a grandmother to live with a single dependent son and children, even if his school-age children number a dozen, yet it forces Mrs. Moore to find another dwelling for her grandson John, simply because of the presence of his uncle and cousin in the same household. We need not labor the point. [The ordinance] has but a tenuous relation to alleviation of the conditions mentioned by the city.

III

The city would distinguish the cases based on *Meyer* and *Pierce*. It points out that none of them gives grandmothers any fundamental rights with respect to grandsons, and suggests that any constitutional right to live together as a family extends only to the nuclear family essentially a couple and their dependent children.

To be sure, these cases did not expressly consider the family relationship presented here. They were immediately concerned with freedom of choice with respect to childbearing, or with the rights of parents to the custody and companionship of their own children, or with traditional parental authority in matters of child rearing and education. But unless we close our eyes to the basic reasons why certain rights associated with the family have been accorded shelter under the Fourteenth Amendment's Due Process Clause, we cannot avoid applying the force and rationale of these precedents to the family choice involved in this case. . . .

Substantive due process has at times been a treacherous field for this Court. There are risks when the judicial branch gives enhanced protection to certain substantive liberties without the guidance of the more specific provisions of the Bill of Rights. As the history of the *Lochner* era demonstrates, there is reason for concern lest the only limits to such judicial intervention become the predilections of those who happen at the time to be Members of this Court. That history counsels caution and restraint. But it does not counsel abandonment, nor does it require what the city urges here: cutting off any protection of family rights at the first convenient, if arbitrary boundary: the boundary of the nuclear family.

Appropriate limits on substantive due process come not from drawing arbitrary lines but rather from careful respect for the teachings of history and solid recognition of the basic values that underlie our society. . . . Ours is by no means a tradition limited to respect for the bonds uniting the members of the nuclear family. The tradition of uncles, aunts, cousins, and especially grandparents sharing a household along with parents and children has roots equally venerable and equally deserving of constitutional recognition. Over the years millions of our citizens have grown up in just such an environment, and most, surely, have profited from it. Even if conditions of modern society have brought about a decline in extended family households, they have not erased the accumulated wisdom of civilization, gained over the centuries and honored throughout our history, that supports a larger conception of the family. Out of choice, necessity, or a sense of family responsibility, it has been common for close relatives to draw together and participate in the duties and the satisfactions of a common home. Decisions concerning child rearing, which *Meyer, Pierce* and other cases have recognized as entitled to constitutional protection, long have been shared with grandparents or other relatives who occupy the same household indeed who may take on major responsibility for the rearing of the children. Especially in times of adversity, such as the death of a spouse or economic need, the broader family has tended to come together for mutual sustenance and to maintain or rebuild a secure home life. This is apparently what happened here.

Whether or not such a household is established because of personal tragedy, the choice of relatives in this degree of kinship to live together may not lightly be denied by the State. *Pierce* struck down an Oregon law requiring all children to attend the State's public schools, holding that the Constitution excludes any general power of the State to standardize its children by forcing them to accept instruction from public teachers only. By the same token the Constitution prevents East Cleveland from standardizing its children and its adults by forcing all to live in certain narrowly defined family patterns.

Justice Brennan, with whom Justice Marshall joins, concurring.

I join the plurality's opinion. . . . I write only to underscore the cultural myopia of the arbitrary boundary drawn by the East Cleveland ordinance in the light of the tradition of the American home that has been a feature of our society since our beginning as a Nation: the tradition in the plurality's words "of uncles, aunts, cousins, and especially grandparents sharing a household along with parents and children." The line drawn by this ordinance displays a depressing insensitivity toward the economic and emotional needs of a very large part of our society.

In today's America, the nuclear family is the pattern so often found in much of white suburbia. The Constitution cannot be interpreted, however, to tolerate the imposition by government upon the rest of us of white suburbia's preference in patterns of family living. The extended family that provided generations of early Americans with social services and economic and emotional support in times of hardship, and was the beachhead for successive waves of immigrants who populated our cities, remains not merely still a pervasive living pattern, but under the goad of brutal economic necessity, a prominent pattern virtually a means of survival for large numbers of the poor and deprived minorities of our society. For them compelled pooling of scant resources requires compelled sharing of a household.

The extended form is especially familiar among black families. . . . I do not wish to be understood as implying that East Cleveland's enforcement of its ordinance is motivated by a racially discriminatory purpose: The record of this case would not support that implication. But the prominence of other than nuclear families among ethnic and racial minority groups, including our black citizens, surely demonstrates that the extended family pattern remains a vital tenet of our society. . . .

Justice Stevens, concurring in the judgment.

In my judgment the critical question presented by this case is whether East Cleveland's housing ordinance is a permissible restriction on appellant's right to use her own property as she sees fit. . . .

The city has failed totally to explain the need for a rule which would allow a homeowner to have two grandchildren live with her if they are brothers, but not if they are cousins. Since this ordinance has not been shown to have any substantial relation to the public health, safety, morals, or general welfare of the city of East Cleveland, and since it cuts so deeply into a fundamental right normally associated with the ownership of residential property that of an owner to decide who may reside on his or her property it must fall under the limited standard of review of zoning decisions which this Court preserved in *Euclid*. Under that standard, East Cleveland's unprecedented ordinance constitutes a taking of property without due process and without just compensation.

Chief Justice Burger, dissenting.

It is unnecessary for me to reach the difficult constitutional issue this case presents. [The city's ordinance allows Ms. Moore to apply for a variance.] Appellant's deliberate refusal to use a plainly adequate administrative remedy provided by the city should foreclose her from pressing in this Court any constitutional objections to the city's zoning ordinance. . . .

Justice Stewart, with whom Justice Rehnquist joins, dissenting.

. . . In my view, the appellant's claim that the ordinance in question invades constitutionally protected rights of association and privacy is in large part answered by the *Belle Terre* decision. The argument was made there that a municipality could not zone its land exclusively for single-family occupancy because to do so would interfere with protected rights of privacy or association. We rejected this contention, and held that the ordinance at issue involved no fundamental right guaranteed by the Constitution, such as the right of association or any rights of privacy. . . .

Several decisions of the Court have identified specific aspects of what might broadly be termed "private family life" that are constitutionally protected against state interference. See, e.g., *Roe v. Wade* (1973) (woman's right to decide whether to terminate pregnancy); *Loving v. Virginia* (1967) (freedom to marry person of another race); *Griswold v. Connecticut* (1965); *Eisenstadt v. Baird* (1972) (right to use contraceptives); *Pierce v. Society of Sisters* (1925) (parents' right to send children to private schools); *Meyer v. Nebraska* (1923) (parents' right to have children instructed in foreign language).

Although the appellant's desire to share a single-dwelling unit also involves "private family life" in a sense, that desire can hardly be equated with any of the interests protected in the cases just cited. The ordinance about which the appellant complains did not impede her choice to have or not to have children, and it did not dictate to her how her own children were to be nurtured and reared. The ordinance clearly does not prevent parents from living together or living with their unemancipated offspring.

But even though the Court's previous cases are not directly in point, the appellant contends that the importance of the extended family in American society requires us to hold that her decision to share her residence with her grandsons may not be interfered with by the State. This decision, like the decisions involved in bearing and raising children, is said to be an aspect of family life also entitled to substantive protection under the Constitution. Without pausing to inquire how far under this argument an extended family might extend, I cannot agree. When the Court has found that the Fourteenth Amendment placed a substantive limitation on a State's power to regulate, it has been in those rare cases in which the personal interests at issue have been deemed "implicit in the concept of ordered liberty." The interest that the appellant may have in permanently sharing a single kitchen and a suite of contiguous rooms with some of her relatives simply does not rise to that level. To equate this interest with the fundamental decisions to marry and to bear and raise children is to extend the limited substantive contours of the Due Process Clause beyond recognition. . . .

Viewed in the light of these principles, I do not think East Cleveland's definition of family offends the Constitution. The city has undisputed power to ordain single-family residential occupancy. And that power plainly carries with it the power to say what a family is. Here the city has defined family to include not only father, mother, and dependent children, but several other close relatives as well. The definition is rationally designed to carry out the legitimate governmental purposes identified in the *Belle Terre* opinion: "The police power is not confined to elimination of filth, stench, and unhealthy places. It is ample to lay out zones where family values, youth values, and the blessings of the quiet seclusion and clean air make the area a sanctuary for people." . . .

Moore v. City of East Cleveland

Justice White, dissenting.

. . . The Court has no license to invalidate legislation which it thinks merely arbitrary or unreasonable. . . . Much of the underpinning for the broad, substantive application of the Clause disappeared in the conflict between the Executive and the Judiciary in the 1930s and 1940s, the Court should be extremely reluctant to breathe still further substantive content into the Due Process Clause so as to strike down legislation adopted by a State or city to promote its welfare. Whenever the Judiciary does so, it unavoidably pre-empts for itself another part of the governance of the country without express constitutional authority. . . .

flash*forward*

***The Opinions in* Moore.** Although there was no majority opinion in *Moore*, the four-justice plurality opinion has been quoted with approval in dozens of later cases. By contrast, the concurring opinion from Justice Stevens—providing a crucial fifth vote, but on a property rights theory—has had little impact.

2. Parentage and Visitation: *Michael H. v. Gerald D.*

Decisions about parentage, child support, and child custody are overwhelmingly made in state courts. But on rare occasions, a family law matter will raise issues under the US Constitution.

ITEMS TO CONSIDER WHILE READING
MICHAEL H. v. GERALD D.:

A. *Work through the items in the Kickstarter.*

B. Michael H. *has no majority opinion. Make a chart summarizing the various opinions. Which opinion should be considered the holding?*

C. *Which methods of constitutional reasoning are favored by Justice Scalia's plurality opinion? By Justice Brennan's dissent?*

D. *Explain the concept suggested in Footnote 6 of Justice Scalia's opinion. Why do the opinions of Justices O'Connor (concurring) and Brennan (dissenting) refuse to endorse it?*

Michael H. v. Gerald D.,

491 U.S. 110 (1989)

Justice Scalia announced the judgment of the Court and delivered an opinion, in which Chief Justice Rehnquist joins, and in all but footnote 6 of which Justices O'Connor and Kennedy join.

Under California law, a child born to a married woman living with her husband is presumed to be a child of the marriage. Cal.Evid.Code § 621. The presumption of legitimacy may be rebutted only by the husband or wife, and then only in limited circumstances. The instant appeal presents the claim that this presumption infringes upon the due process rights of a man who wishes to establish his paternity of a child born to the wife of another man, and the claim that it infringes upon the constitutional right of the child to maintain a relationship with her natural father.

I

The facts of this case are, we must hope, extraordinary. On May 9, 1976, in Las Vegas, Nevada, Carole D., an international model, and Gerald D., a top executive in a French oil company, were married. The couple established a home in Playa del Rey, California, in which they resided as husband and wife when one or the other was not out of the country on business. In the summer of 1978, Carole became involved in an adulterous affair with a neighbor, Michael H. In September 1980, she conceived a child, Victoria D., who was born on May 11, 1981. Gerald was listed as father on the birth certificate and has always held Victoria out to the world as his daughter. Soon after delivery of the child, however, Carole informed Michael that she believed he might be the father.

In the first three years of her life, Victoria remained always with Carole, but found herself within a variety of quasi-family units. In October 1981, Gerald moved to New York City to pursue his business interests, but Carole chose to remain in California. At the end of that month, Carole and Michael had blood tests of themselves and Victoria, which showed a 98.07% probability that Michael was Victoria's father. In January 1982, Carole visited Michael in St. Thomas, where his primary business interests were based. There Michael held Victoria out as his child. In March, however, Carole left Michael and returned to California, where she took up residence with yet another man, Scott K. Later that spring, and again in the summer, Carole and Victoria spent time with Gerald in New York City, as well as on vacation in Europe. In the fall, they returned to Scott in California.

In November 1982, rebuffed in his attempts to visit Victoria, Michael filed a filiation action in California Superior Court to establish his paternity and right to

Michael H. v. Gerald D.

visitation. In March 1983, the court appointed an attorney and **guardian ad litem** to represent Victoria's interests. Victoria then filed a cross-complaint asserting that if she had more than one psychological or de facto father, she was entitled to maintain her filial relationship, with all of the attendant rights, duties, and obligations, with both. In May 1983, Carole filed a motion for summary judgment. During this period, from March through July 1983, Carole was again living with Gerald in New York. In August, however, she returned to California, became involved once again with Michael, and instructed her attorneys to remove the summary judgment motion from the calendar.

■ TERMINOLOGY

GUARDIAN AD LITEM: A *guardian ad litem* (from the Latin, "for the suit") is a competent adult who appears in court to assert the interests of a child or incompetent person.

For the ensuing eight months, when Michael was not in St. Thomas he lived with Carole and Victoria in Carole's apartment in Los Angeles and held Victoria out as his daughter. In April 1984, Carole and Michael signed a stipulation that Michael was Victoria's natural father. Carole left Michael the next month, however, and instructed her attorneys not to file the stipulation. In June 1984, Carole reconciled with Gerald and joined him in New York, where they now live with Victoria and two other children since born into the marriage.

In May 1984, Michael and Victoria, through her guardian ad litem, sought visitation rights for Michael. . . . On October 19, 1984, Gerald, who had intervened in the action, moved for summary judgment on the ground that under Cal.Evid.Code § 621 there were no triable issues of fact as to Victoria's paternity. This law provides that "the issue of a wife cohabiting with her husband, who is not impotent or sterile, is conclusively presumed to be a child of the marriage." Cal.Evid.Code § 621(a). The presumption may be rebutted by blood tests, but only if a motion for such tests is made within two years from the date of the child's birth. . . §§ 621(c) and (d). [No such motion was made here.]

On January 28, 1985, having found that affidavits submitted by Carole and Gerald sufficed to demonstrate that the two were cohabiting at conception and birth and that Gerald was neither sterile nor impotent, the Superior Court granted Gerald's motion for summary judgment, rejecting Michael's and Victoria's challenges to the constitutionality of § 621. The court also denied their motions for continued visitation pending the appeal under Cal. Civ. Code § 4601, which provides that a court may, in its discretion, grant "reasonable visitation rights to any person having an interest in the welfare of the child." It found that allowing such visitation would violate the intention of the Legislature by impugning the integrity of the family unit.

On appeal, Michael asserted, *inter alia*, that the Superior Court's application of § 621 had violated his procedural and substantive due process rights. Victoria also raised a due process challenge to the statute, seeking to preserve her de facto relationship with Michael as well as with Gerald. . . . Finally, she asserted a right to continued visitation with Michael under § 4601. After submission of briefs and a hearing, the California Court of Appeal affirmed the judgment of the Superior Court and upheld the constitutionality of the statute. It interpreted that judgment, moreover, as having denied permanent visitation rights under § 4601, [because] once an assertion of biological paternity is "determined to be legally impossible" under § 621, visitation against the wishes of the mother should be denied under § 4601.

The Court of Appeal denied Michael's and Victoria's petitions for rehearing, and, on July 30, 1987, the California Supreme Court denied discretionary review. [We granted review.]

II [Omitted.]

III

We address first the claims of Michael. At the outset, it is necessary to clarify what he sought and what he was denied. California law, like nature itself, makes no provision for dual fatherhood. Michael was seeking to be declared the father of Victoria. The immediate benefit he evidently sought to obtain from that status was visitation rights. But if Michael were successful in being declared the father, other rights would follow—most importantly, the right to be considered as the parent who should have custody. . . .

Michael contends as a matter of substantive due process that, because he has established a parental relationship with Victoria, protection of Gerald's and Carole's marital union is an insufficient state interest to support termination of that relationship. This argument is, of course, predicated on the assertion that Michael has a constitutionally protected liberty interest in his relationship with Victoria.

It is an established part of our constitutional jurisprudence that the term "liberty" in the Due Process Clause extends beyond freedom from physical restraint. See, e.g., *Pierce v. Society of Sisters* (1925); *Meyer v. Nebraska* (1923). Without that core textual meaning as a limitation, defining the scope of the Due Process Clause "has at times been a treacherous field for this Court," giving "reason for concern lest the only limits to judicial intervention become the predilections of those who happen at the time to be Members of this Court." *Moore v. East Cleveland* (1977) [plurality opinion]. . . .

In an attempt to limit and guide interpretation of the Clause, we have insisted not merely that the interest denominated as a "liberty" be "fundamental" (a concept that, in isolation, is hard to objectify), but also that it be an interest traditionally protected by our society. As we have put it, the Due Process Clause affords only those protections "so rooted in the traditions and conscience of our people as to be ranked as fundamental." *Snyder v. Massachusetts*, 291 U.S. 97, 105 (1934). Our cases reflect "continual insistence upon respect for the teachings of history and solid recognition of the basic values that underlie our society." *Griswold v. Connecticut*, (1965) (Harlan, J., concurring in judgment).

This insistence that the asserted liberty interest be rooted in history and tradition is evident, as elsewhere, in our cases according constitutional protection to certain parental rights. Michael reads [our earlier cases dealing with the rights of biological fathers] as establishing that a liberty interest is created by biological fatherhood plus an established parental relationship—factors that exist in the present case as well. We think that distorts the rationale of those cases. As we view them, they rest not upon such isolated factors but upon the historic respect—indeed, sanctity would not be too strong a term—traditionally accorded to the relationships that develop within the unitary family. In *Stanley v. Illinois,* 405 U.S. 645 (1972), for example, we forbade the destruction of such a family when, upon the death of the mother, the State had sought to remove children from the custody of a father who had lived with and supported them and their mother for 18 years. As Justice Powell stated for the plurality in *Moore v. East Cleveland* (1977): "Our decisions establish that the Constitution protects the sanctity of the family precisely because the institution of the family is deeply rooted in this Nation's history and tradition."

Thus, the legal issue in the present case reduces to whether the relationship between persons in the situation of Michael and Victoria has been treated as a protected family unit under the historic practices of our society, or whether on any other basis it has been accorded special protection. We think it impossible to find that it has. In fact, quite to the contrary, our traditions have protected the marital family (Gerald, Carole, and the child they acknowledge to be theirs) against the sort of claim Michael asserts.

The presumption of legitimacy was a fundamental principle of the common law. H. Nicholas, *Adulturine Bastardy* (1836). Traditionally, that presumption could be rebutted only by proof that a husband was incapable of procreation or had had no access to his wife during the relevant period. . . . The primary policy rationale underlying the common law's severe restrictions on rebuttal of the presumption appears to have been an aversion to declaring children illegitimate, thereby depriving them of rights of inheritance and succession and likely making them wards of the state. A secondary policy concern was the interest in promoting the peace and tranquility of States and families, a goal that is obviously impaired by facilitating suits against husband and wife asserting that their children are illegitimate. Even though, as **bastardy laws** became less harsh, judges in both England and the United States retained a strong bias against ruling the children of married women illegitimate.

We have found nothing in the older sources, nor in the older cases, addressing specifically the power of the natural father to assert parental rights over a child born into a woman's existing marriage with another man. Since it is Michael's burden to

■ OBSERVATION

BASTARDY LAWS: Today, laws that discriminate against children born out of wedlock will violate the Equal Protection Clause unless they satisfy intermediate scrutiny. See Ch. 18.C.3.a.5.

establish that such a power (at least where the natural father has established a relationship with the child) is so deeply embedded within our traditions as to be a fundamental right, the lack of evidence alone might defeat his case. But the evidence shows that even in modern times—when, as we have noted, the rigid protection of the marital family has in other respects been relaxed—the ability of a person in Michael's position to claim paternity has not been generally acknowledged. . . .

Moreover, even if it were clear that one in Michael's position generally possesses, and has generally always possessed, standing to challenge the marital child's legitimacy, that would still not establish Michael's case. As noted earlier, what is at issue here is not entitlement to a state pronouncement that Victoria was begotten by Michael. It is no conceivable denial of constitutional right for a State to decline to declare facts unless some legal consequence hinges upon the requested declaration. What Michael asserts here is a right to have himself declared the natural father and thereby to obtain parental prerogatives. What he must establish, therefore, is not that our society has traditionally allowed a natural father in his circumstances to establish paternity, but that it has traditionally accorded such a father parental rights, or at least has not traditionally denied them. . . . Thus, it is ultimately irrelevant, even for purposes of determining current social attitudes towards the alleged substantive right Michael asserts, that the present law in a number of States appears to allow the natural father—including the natural father who has not established a relationship with the child—the theoretical power to rebut the marital presumption. What counts is whether the States in fact award substantive parental rights to the natural father of a child conceived within, and born into, an extant marital union that wishes to embrace the child. We are not aware of a single case, old or new, that has done so. This is not the stuff of which fundamental rights qualifying as liberty interests are made.[FN6] . . .

FN6 Justice Brennan criticizes our methodology in using historical traditions specifically relating to the rights of an adulterous natural father, rather than inquiring more generally "whether parenthood is an interest that historically has received our attention and protection." . . . We do not understand why, having rejected our focus upon the societal tradition regarding the natural father's rights vis-à-vis a child whose mother is married to another man, Justice Brennan would choose to focus instead upon "parenthood." Why should the relevant category not be even more general—perhaps "family relationships"; or "personal relationships"; or even "emotional attachments in general"? Though the dissent has no basis for the level of generality it would select, we do: We refer to the most specific level at which a relevant tradition protecting, or denying protection to, the asserted right can be identified. If, for example, there were no societal tradition, either way, regarding the rights of the natural father of a child adulterously conceived, we would have to consult, and (if possible) reason from, the traditions regarding natural fathers in general. But there is such a more specific tradition, and it unqualifiedly denies protection to such a parent. . . .

The need, if arbitrary decisionmaking is to be avoided, to adopt the most specific tradition as the point of reference—or at least to announce, as Justice Brennan declines to do, some other criterion for selecting among the innumerable relevant traditions that could be consulted—is well enough exemplified by the fact that in the present case Justice Brennan's opinion and Justice O'Connor's opinion, which disapproves this footnote, both appeal to tradition, but on the basis of the tradition they select reach opposite results. Although assuredly having the virtue (if it be that) of leaving judges free to decide as they think best when the unanticipated occurs, a rule of law that binds neither by text nor by any particular, identifiable tradition is no rule of law at all. . . .

We do not accept Justice Brennan's criticism that this result "squashes" the liberty that consists of "the freedom not to conform." It seems to us that reflects the erroneous view that there is only one side to this controversy—that one disposition can expand a liberty of sorts without contracting an equivalent liberty on the other side. Such a happy choice is rarely available. Here, to provide protection to an adulterous natural father is to deny protection to a marital father, and vice versa. If Michael has a "freedom not to conform" (whatever that means), Gerald must equivalently have a "freedom to conform." One of them will pay a price for asserting that "freedom"—Michael by being unable to act as father of the child he has adulterously begotten, or Gerald by being unable to preserve the integrity of the traditional family unit he and Victoria have established. Our disposition does not choose between these two "freedoms," but leaves that to the people of California. Justice Brennan's approach chooses one of them as the constitutional imperative, on no apparent basis except that the unconventional is to be preferred.

IV

We have never had occasion to decide whether a child has a liberty interest, symmetrical with that of her parent, in maintaining her filial relationship. We need not do so here because, even assuming that such a right exists, Victoria's claim must fail. Victoria's due process challenge is, if anything, weaker than Michael's. Her basic claim is not that California has erred in preventing her from establishing that Michael, not Gerald, should stand as her legal father. Rather, she claims a due process right to maintain filial relationships with both Michael and Gerald. This assertion merits little discussion, for, whatever the merits of the guardian ad litem's belief that such an arrangement can be of great psychological benefit to a child, the claim that a State must recognize multiple fatherhood has no support in the history or traditions of this country. Moreover, even if we were to construe Victoria's argument as forwarding the lesser proposition that, whatever her status vis-à-vis Gerald, she has a liberty interest in maintaining a filial relationship with her natural father, Michael, we find that, at best, her claim is the obverse of Michael's and fails for the same reasons. . . .

Justice O'Connor, with whom Justice Kennedy joins, concurring in part.

I concur in all but footnote 6 of Justice Scalia's opinion. This footnote sketches a mode of historical analysis to be used when identifying liberty interests protected by the Due Process Clause of the Fourteenth Amendment that may be somewhat inconsistent with our past decisions in this area. On occasion the Court has characterized relevant traditions protecting asserted rights at levels of generality that might not be the most specific level available. See *Loving v. Virginia* (1967). I would not foreclose the unanticipated by the prior imposition of a single mode of historical analysis.

Justice Stevens, concurring in the judgment.

As I understand this case, it raises [this question]: Does the California statute deny appellants a fair opportunity to prove that Victoria's best interests would be served by granting Michael visitation rights? . . .

On [that] issue I do not agree with Justice Scalia's analysis. He seems to reject the possibility that a natural father might ever have a constitutionally protected interest in his relationship with a child whose mother was married to, and cohabiting with, another man at the time of the child's conception and birth. I think cases like *Stanley v. Illinois*, 405 U.S. 645 (1972) [recognizing parental rights for an unmarried father] demonstrate that enduring family relationships may develop in unconventional settings. I therefore would not foreclose the possibility that a constitutionally protected relationship between a natural father and his child might exist in a case like this. Indeed, I am willing to assume for the purpose of deciding this case that Michael's relationship with Victoria is strong enough to give him a constitutional right to try to convince a trial judge that Victoria's best interest would be served by granting him visitation rights. I am satisfied, however, that the California statute, as applied in this case, gave him that opportunity. . . .

Justice Brennan, with whom Justices Marshall and Blackmun join, dissenting.

In a case that has yielded so many opinions as has this one, it is fruitful to begin by emphasizing the common ground shared by a majority of this Court. Five Members of the Court [the three of us, plus Justices Stevens and White] refuse to foreclose the possibility that a natural father might ever have a constitutionally protected interest in his relationship with a child whose mother was married to, and cohabiting with, another man at the time of the child's conception and birth. [The same] five Justices agree that the flaw inhering in a conclusive presumption that terminates a constitutionally protected interest without any hearing whatsoever is a *procedural* one. Four Members of the Court agree that Michael H. has a liberty interest in his relationship with Victoria [the three of us, plus Justice White], and one assumes for purposes of this case that he does [Justice Stevens].

In contrast, only one other Member of the Court [Chief Justice Rehnquist] fully endorses Justice Scalia's view of the proper method of analyzing questions arising under the Due Process Clause. Nevertheless, because the plurality opinion's exclusively historical analysis portends a significant and unfortunate departure from our prior cases and from sound constitutional decisionmaking, I devote a substantial portion of my discussion to it.

I

Once we recognized that the "liberty" protected by the Due Process Clause of the Fourteenth Amendment encompasses more than freedom from bodily restraint, today's plurality opinion emphasizes, the concept was cut loose from one natural limitation on its meaning. This innovation paved the way, so the plurality hints, for judges to substitute their own preferences for those of elected officials. Dissatisfied with this supposedly unbridled and uncertain state of affairs, the plurality casts about for another limitation on the concept of liberty.

It finds this limitation in "tradition." Apparently oblivious to the fact that this concept can be as malleable and as elusive as "liberty" itself, the plurality pretends that tradition places a discernible border around the Constitution. The pretense is seductive; it would be comforting to believe that a search for tradition involves nothing more idiosyncratic or complicated than poring through dusty volumes on American history. Yet, as Justice White observed in his dissent in *Moore v. East Cleveland* (1977): "What the deeply rooted traditions of the country are is arguable." Indeed, wherever I would begin to look for an interest deeply rooted in the country's traditions, one thing is certain: I would not stop (as does the plurality) at **Bracton, or Blackstone, or Kent**, or even the American Law Reports in conducting my search. Because reasonable people can disagree about the content of particular traditions, and because they can disagree even about which traditions are relevant to the definition of liberty, the plurality has not found the objective boundary that it seeks.

> HISTORY
>
> **BRACTON, OR BLACKSTONE, OR KENT:** This passage alludes to authors of famous legal treatises: the Britons Henry of Bracton (1210–1268) and Sir William Blackstone (1723–1780), and the American James Kent (1763–1847).

Even if we could agree, moreover, on the content and significance of particular traditions, we still would be forced to identify the point at which a tradition becomes firm enough to be relevant to our definition of liberty and the moment at which it becomes too obsolete to be relevant any longer. The plurality supplies no objective means by which we might make these determinations. Indeed, as soon as the plurality sees signs that the tradition upon which it bases its decision (the laws denying putative fathers like Michael standing to assert paternity) is crumbling, it shifts ground and says that the case has nothing to do with that tradition, after all. "What is at issue here," the plurality asserts after canvassing the law on paternity suits, "is not entitlement to a state pronouncement that Victoria was begotten by Michael." But that is precisely what is at issue here, and the plurality's last-minute denial of this fact dramatically illustrates the subjectivity of its own analysis.

It is ironic that an approach so utterly dependent on tradition is so indifferent to our precedents. Citing barely a handful of this Court's numerous decisions defining the scope of the liberty protected by the Due Process Clause to support its reliance on tradition, the plurality acts as though English legal treatises and the American Law Reports always have provided the sole source for our constitutional principles. They have not. Just as common-law notions no longer define the property that the Constitution protects, neither do they circumscribe the liberty that it guarantees. On the contrary, "liberty and property are broad and majestic terms. They are among the great constitutional concepts purposely left to gather meaning from experience. They relate to the whole domain of social and economic fact, and the statesmen who founded this Nation knew too well that only a stagnant society remains unchanged." *Board of Regents v. Roth* (1971). . . .

Today's plurality, however, does not ask whether parenthood is an interest that historically has received our attention and protection; the answer to that question is too clear for dispute. Instead, the plurality asks whether the specific variety of parenthood under consideration—a natural father's relationship with a child whose mother is married to another man—has enjoyed such protection.

If we had looked to tradition with such specificity in past cases, many a decision would have reached a different result. Surely the use of contraceptives by unmarried couples, *Eisenstadt v. Baird*, 405 U.S. 438 (1972), or even by married couples, *Griswold v. Connecticut* (1965); the freedom from an arbitrary transfer from a prison to a psychiatric institution, *Vitek v. Jones*, 445 U.S. 480 (1980); and even the right to raise one's natural but illegitimate children, *Stanley v. Illinois*, 405 U.S. 645 (1972), were not "interests traditionally protected by our society" at the time of their consideration by this Court. If we had asked, therefore, in *Eisenstadt, Griswold, Vitek*, or *Stanley* itself whether the specific interest under consideration had been traditionally protected, the answer would have been a resounding "no." That we did not ask this question in those cases highlights the novelty of the interpretive method that the plurality opinion employs today.

The plurality's interpretive method is more than novel; it is misguided. It ignores the good reasons for limiting the role of tradition in interpreting the Constitution's deliberately capacious language. In the plurality's constitutional universe, we may not take notice of the fact that the original reasons for the conclusive presumption of paternity are out of place in a world in which blood tests can prove virtually beyond a shadow of a doubt who sired a particular child and in which the fact of illegitimacy no longer plays the burdensome and stigmatizing role it once did. Nor, in the plurality's world, may we deny tradition its full scope by pointing out that the rationale for the conventional rule has changed over the years, as has the rationale for Cal.Evid.Code Ann. § 621; instead, our task is simply to identify a rule denying the asserted interest and not to ask whether the basis for that rule—which is the true reflection of the values undergirding it—has changed too often or too recently to call the rule embodying that rationale a tradition. Moreover, by describing the decisive question as whether Michael's and Victoria's interest is one that has been "traditionally protected by our society," rather than one that society traditionally has thought important (with or without protecting it), and by suggesting that our sole function is to "discern the society's views," the plurality acts as if the only purpose of the Due Process Clause is to confirm the importance of interests already protected by a majority of the States. Transforming the protection afforded by the Due Process Clause into a redundancy mocks those who, with care and purpose, wrote the Fourteenth Amendment.

In construing the Fourteenth Amendment to offer shelter only to those interests specifically protected by historical practice, moreover, the plurality ignores the kind of society in which our Constitution exists. We are not an assimilative, homogeneous society, but a facilitative, pluralistic one, in which we must be willing to abide someone else's unfamiliar or even repellent practice because the same tolerant impulse protects our own idiosyncrasies. Even if we can agree, therefore, that "family" and "parenthood" are part of the good life, it is absurd to assume that we can agree on the content of those terms and destructive to pretend that we do. In a community such as ours, liberty must include the freedom not to conform. The plurality today squashes this freedom by requiring specific approval from history before protecting anything in the name of liberty.

The document that the plurality construes today is unfamiliar to me. It is not the living charter that I have taken to be our Constitution; it is instead a stagnant, archaic, hidebound document steeped in the prejudices and superstitions of a time long past. This Constitution does not recognize that times change, does not see that sometimes a practice or rule outlives its foundations. I cannot accept an interpretive method that does such violence to the charter that I am bound by oath to uphold.

II

The plurality's reworking of our interpretive approach is all the more troubling because it is unnecessary. This is not a case in which we face a new kind of interest, one that requires us to consider for the first time whether the Constitution protects it. On the contrary, we confront an interest—that of a parent and child in their relationship with each other—that was among the first that this Court acknowledged in its cases defining the liberty protected by the Constitution, see, e.g., *Meyer v. Nebraska* (1923); *Skinner v. Oklahoma* (1942); and I think I am safe in saying that no one doubts the wisdom or validity of those decisions. Where the interest under consideration is a parent-child relationship, we need not ask, over and over again, whether that interest is one that society traditionally protects. . . .

On four prior occasions, we have considered whether unwed fathers have a constitutionally protected interest in their relationships with their children. See *Stanley v. Illinois*, 405 U.S. 645 (1972); *Quilloin v. Walcott*, 434 U.S. 246 (1978); *Caban v. Mohammed*, 441 U.S. 380 (1979); and *Lehr v. Robertson*, 463 U.S. 248 (1983). Though different in factual and legal circumstances, these cases have produced a unifying theme: although an unwed father's biological link to his child does not, in and of itself, guarantee him a constitutional stake in his relationship with that child, such a link combined with a substantial parent-child relationship will do so. When an unwed father demonstrates a full commitment to the responsibilities of parenthood by coming forward to participate in the rearing of his child, his interest in personal contact with his child acquires substantial protection under the Due Process Clause. . . . This commitment is why Mr. Stanley and Mr. Caban won; why Mr. Quilloin and Mr. Lehr lost; and why Michael H. should prevail today. Michael H. is almost certainly Victoria D.'s natural father, has lived with her as her father, has contributed to her support, and has from the beginning sought to strengthen and maintain his relationship with her. . . .

III [Omitted.]

IV

The atmosphere surrounding today's decision is one of make-believe. Beginning with the suggestion that the situation confronting us here does not repeat itself every day in every corner of the country, moving on to the claim that it is tradition alone that supplies the details of the liberty that the Constitution protects, and passing finally to the notion that the Court always has recognized a cramped vision of the family, today's decision lets stand California's pronouncement that Michael—whom blood tests show to a 98 percent probability to be Victoria's father—is not Victoria's father. When and if the Court awakes to reality, it will find a world very different from the one it expects.

Justice White, with whom Justice Brennan joins, dissenting.

California law, as the plurality describes it, tells us that, except in limited circumstances, California declares it to be "irrelevant for paternity purposes whether a child conceived during, and born into, an existing marriage was begotten by someone other than the husband." This I do not accept, for the fact that Michael H. is the biological father of Victoria is to me highly relevant to whether he has rights, as a father or otherwise, with respect to the child. Because I believe that Michael H. has a liberty interest that cannot be denied without due process of the law, I must dissent. . . .

E. Substantive Due Process and End-of-Life Decisions

By the late 20th century, advances in medical technology created a problem never faced by the Framers: the possibility that a person in an irreversible vegetative state could be kept alive indefinitely by machines. Most legal activity in the area has involved the development of state laws regarding living wills, advance directives, do-not-resuscitate orders, and similar innovations. A few high-profile cases in the area have led to constitutional litigation.

1. Refusal of Life-Sustaining Treatment: *Quinlan* and *Cruzan*

Karen Ann Quinlan entered a vegetative state following a drug overdose in 1975. Her father, acting as her legal representative, asked for her artificial respirator to be removed, but the hospital and doctors refused to comply, arguing that it would conflict with their medical ethics and that it might constitute homicide under New Jersey law. The New Jersey Supreme Court held that Karen's rights under the US and state constitutions protected her decision to refuse life-sustaining treatment, and that the doctors would face no liability for respecting her wishes. *Matter of Quinlan*, 355 A.2d 647 (N.J. 1976).

Quinlan was removed from the respirator in 1976, but she remained alive with artificial feeding and hydration until 1985. Her story provoked the passage of laws in many states to allow advance directives and other mechanisms for families to make similar decisions in the future without litigation.

The first US Supreme Court decision on the topic was *Cruzan v. Director of Missouri Department of Health*, 497 U.S. 261 (1990). Nancy Cruzan fell into a persistent vegetative state after an auto accident in 1983. After all hope for recovery was exhausted, her parents sought to have the life-sustaining treatment withdrawn. The hospital said it would comply with the family's request if there were a court order allowing it. Missouri law would allow life-sustaining treatment to be withdrawn from an incompetent person, but only upon clear and convincing evidence that withdrawal was consistent with the incompetent person's previously expressed wishes. Applying the state statute, the Missouri courts concluded that clear and convincing evidence of Cruzan's wishes had not been shown. The US Supreme Court affirmed. Assuming for purposes of decision a *Quinlan*-like constitutional right to refuse unwanted medical treatment, the majority concluded that Missouri's law did not abridge the right: it simply established an acceptable burden of proof in cases where the patient was not competent to express her own views.

After the Supreme Court's decision, the family presented additional evidence of Cruzan's wishes to a Missouri court, which concluded that clear and convincing evidence had finally been shown that she would have wished the treatments terminated. She died in late 1990 after withdrawal of artificial life support.

2. Aid in Dying: *Glucksberg* and *Quill*

In a pair of cases decided in 1997, the Supreme Court considered end-of-life decision-making that did not involve the withdrawal of artificial life support. In *Washington v. Glucksberg* and *Vacco v. Quill*, mentally competent but terminally ill patients wished to hasten their deaths, typically by receiving a lethal dose of opiates. Since the humane administration of these drugs typically requires the aid of a third party with medical training, questions arose whether a doctor could participate without violating state laws against assisting suicide. By the time the cases came to the Supreme Court, *Glucksberg* focused on a substantive due process theory, while *Quill* focused on equal protection.

ITEMS TO CONSIDER WHILE READING
GLUCKSBERG AND *QUILL*:

A. *Work through the topics from the Kickstarter for each case.*

B. *What are the differences among the various opinions? In particular, how does each describe the right at stake?*

Washington v. Glucksberg,

521 U.S. 702 (1997)

Chief Justice Rehnquist delivered the opinion of the Court [joined by Justices O'Connor, Scalia, Kennedy, and Thomas].

The question presented in this case is whether Washington's prohibition against causing or aiding a suicide offends the Fourteenth Amendment to the United States Constitution. We hold that it does not.

It has always been a crime to assist a suicide in the State of Washington. In 1854, Washington's first Territorial Legislature outlawed "assisting another in the commission of self-murder." Today, Washington law provides: "A person is guilty of promoting a suicide attempt when he knowingly causes or aids another person to attempt suicide." RCW 9A.36.060(1). "Promoting a suicide attempt" is a felony, punishable by up to five years' imprisonment and up to a $10,000 fine. At the same time, Washington's Natural Death Act, enacted in 1979, states that the withholding or withdrawal of life-sustaining treatment at a patient's direction "shall not, for any purpose, constitute a suicide."

Petitioners in this case are the State of Washington and its Attorney General. Respondents Harold Glucksberg, M.D., Abigail Halperin, M.D., Thomas A. Preston, M.D., and Peter Shalit, M.D., are physicians who practice in Washington. These doctors occasionally treat terminally ill, suffering patients, and declare that they would

Washington v. Glucksberg

assist these patients in ending their lives if not for Washington's assisted-suicide ban. In January 1994, respondents, along with three gravely ill, pseudonymous plaintiffs who have since died and Compassion in Dying, a nonprofit organization that counsels people considering physician-assisted suicide, sued in the United States District Court, seeking a declaration that RCW 9A.36.060(1) is, on its face, unconstitutional.

The plaintiffs asserted the existence of a liberty interest protected by the Fourteenth Amendment which extends to a personal choice by a mentally competent, terminally ill adult to commit physician-assisted suicide. Relying primarily on *Planned Parenthood v. Casey* (1992) [an abortion case; see Ch. 20.F] and *Cruzan v. Director* (1990), the District Court agreed, and concluded that Washington's assisted-suicide ban is unconstitutional because it "places an undue burden on the exercise of that constitutionally protected liberty interest." [The Ninth Circuit affirmed the trial court.] We granted certiorari, and now reverse.

I

We begin, as we do in all due process cases, by examining our Nation's history, legal traditions, and practices. In almost every State—indeed, in almost every western democracy—it is a crime to assist a suicide. The States' assisted-suicide bans are not innovations. Rather, they are longstanding expressions of the States' commitment to the protection and preservation of all human life. Indeed, opposition to and condemnation of suicide—and, therefore, of assisting suicide—are consistent and enduring themes of our philosophical, legal, and cultural heritages.

More specifically, for over 700 years, the Anglo-American common-law tradition has punished or otherwise disapproved of both suicide and assisting suicide. In the 13th century, Henry de Bracton, one of the first legal-treatise writers, observed that "just as a man may commit felony by slaying another so may he do so by slaying himself." The real and personal property of one who killed himself to avoid conviction and punishment for a crime were forfeit to the King; however, thought Bracton, "if a man slays himself in weariness of life or because he is unwilling to endure further bodily pain only his movable goods were confiscated." Thus, the principle that suicide of a sane person, for whatever reason, was a punishable felony was introduced into English common law. Centuries later, Sir William Blackstone, whose Commentaries on the Laws of England not only provided a definitive summary of the common law but was also a primary legal authority for 18th- and 19th-century American lawyers, referred to suicide as "self-murder." Blackstone emphasized that "the law has ranked suicide among the highest crimes," although, anticipating later developments, he conceded that the harsh and shameful punishments imposed for suicide "border a little upon severity."

For the most part, the early American Colonies adopted the common-law approach. . . . Over time, however, the American Colonies abolished these harsh common-law penalties. William Penn abandoned the criminal-forfeiture sanction in Pennsylvania in 1701, and the other Colonies (and later, the other States) eventually followed this example. . . .

The movement away from the common law's harsh sanctions did not represent an acceptance of suicide; rather. . . this change reflected the growing consensus that it was unfair to punish the suicide's family for his wrongdoing. Nonetheless, although States moved away from Blackstone's treatment of suicide, courts continued to condemn it as a grave public wrong.

That suicide remained a grievous, though nonfelonious, wrong is confirmed by the fact that colonial and early state legislatures and courts did not retreat from prohibiting assisting suicide. [Justice Zephaniah] Swift, in his early 19th-century treatise on the laws of Connecticut, stated that "if one counsels another to commit suicide, and the other by reason of the advice kills himself, the advisor is guilty of murder as principal." This was the well-established common-law view, as was the similar principle that the consent of a homicide victim is wholly immaterial to the guilt of the person who caused his death. And the prohibitions against assisting suicide never contained exceptions for those who were near death. Rather, [in the words of an Ohio decision from 1872,] "the life of those to whom life had become a burden—of those who were hopelessly diseased or fatally wounded—nay, even the lives of criminals condemned to death, were under the protection of the law, equally as the lives of those who were in the full tide of life's enjoyment, and anxious to continue to live."

The earliest American statute explicitly to outlaw assisting suicide was enacted in New York in 1828, and many of the new States and Territories followed New York's example. . . .

Though deeply rooted, the States' assisted-suicide bans have in recent years been reexamined and, generally, reaffirmed. Because of advances in medicine and technology, Americans today are increasingly likely to die in institutions, from chronic illnesses. Public concern and democratic action are therefore sharply focused on how best to protect dignity and independence at the end of life, with the result that there have been many significant changes in state laws and in the attitudes these laws reflect. Many States, for example, now permit living wills, surrogate health-care decisionmaking, and the withdrawal or refusal of life-sustaining medical treatment. At the same time, however, voters and legislators continue for the most part to reaffirm their States' prohibitions on assisting suicide.

The Washington statute at issue in this case was enacted in 1975 as part of a revision of that State's criminal code. Four years later, Washington passed its Natural Death Act, which specifically stated that the "withholding or withdrawal of life-sustaining treatment shall not, for any purpose, constitute a suicide" and that "nothing in this chapter shall be construed to condone, authorize, or approve mercy killing." In 1991, Washington voters rejected a ballot initiative which, had it passed, would have permitted a form of physician-assisted suicide. . . .

California voters rejected an assisted-suicide initiative similar to Washington's in 1993. On the other hand, in 1994, voters in Oregon enacted, also through ballot initiative, that State's "Death With Dignity Act," which legalized physician-assisted suicide for competent, terminally ill adults. Since the Oregon vote, many proposals to legalize assisted-suicide have been and continue to be introduced in the States' legislatures, but none has been enacted. And just last year, Iowa and Rhode Island joined the overwhelming majority of States explicitly prohibiting assisted suicide. Also, on April 30, 1997, President Clinton signed the Federal Assisted Suicide Funding Restriction Act of 1997, which prohibits the use of federal funds in support of physician-assisted suicide [42 U.S.C. § 14401 et. seq.] . . . Thus, the States are currently engaged in serious, thoughtful examinations of physician-assisted suicide and other similar issues. . . .

Attitudes toward suicide itself have changed since Bracton, but our laws have consistently condemned, and continue to prohibit, assisting suicide. Despite changes in medical technology and notwithstanding an increased emphasis on the importance of end-of-life decisionmaking, we have not retreated from this prohibition. Against this backdrop of history, tradition, and practice, we now turn to respondents' constitutional claim.

II

The Due Process Clause guarantees more than fair process, and the liberty it protects includes more than the absence of physical restraint. The Clause also provides heightened protection against government interference with certain fundamental rights and liberty interests. In a long line of cases, we have held that, in addition to the specific freedoms protected by the Bill of Rights, the liberty specially protected by the Due Process Clause includes the rights to marry, *Loving v. Virginia* (1967); to have children, *Skinner v. Oklahoma* (1942); to direct the education and upbringing of one's children, *Meyer v. Nebraska* (1923); *Pierce v. Society of Sisters* (1925); to marital privacy, *Griswold v. Connecticut* (1965); to use contraception, *Eisenstadt v. Baird* (1972); to bodily integrity, *Rochin v. California*, 342 U.S. 165 (1952), and to abortion, *Planned Parenthood v. Casey* (1993). We have also assumed, and strongly suggested, that the Due Process Clause protects the traditional right to refuse unwanted lifesaving medical treatment. *Cruzan v. Director* (1990).

But we have always been reluctant to expand the concept of substantive due process because guideposts for responsible decisionmaking in this unchartered area are scarce and open-ended. By extending constitutional protection to an asserted right or liberty interest, we, to a great extent, place the matter outside the arena of public debate and legislative action. We must therefore exercise the utmost care whenever we are asked to break new ground in this field, lest the liberty protected by the Due Process Clause be subtly transformed into the policy preferences of the Members of this Court.

Our established method of substantive-due-process analysis has two primary features: First, we have regularly observed that the Due Process Clause specially protects those fundamental rights and liberties which are, objectively, "deeply rooted in this Nation's history and tradition," and "implicit in the concept of ordered liberty," such that "neither liberty nor justice would exist if they were sacrificed." Second, we have required in substantive-due-process cases a careful description of the asserted fundamental liberty interest. . . .

Justice Souter, relying on Justice Harlan's dissenting opinion in *Poe v. Ullman* (1961), would largely abandon this restrained methodology, and instead ask whether Washington's statute sets up one of those "arbitrary impositions" or "purposeless restraints" at odds with the Due Process Clause of the Fourteenth Amendment. In our view, however, the development of this Court's substantive-due-process jurisprudence has been a process whereby the outlines of the liberty specially protected by the Fourteenth Amendment—never fully clarified, to be sure, and perhaps not capable of being fully clarified—have at least been carefully refined by concrete examples involving fundamental rights found to be deeply rooted in our legal tradition. This approach tends to rein in the subjective elements that are necessarily present in due-process judicial review. In addition, by establishing a threshold requirement—that a challenged state action implicate a fundamental right—before requiring more than a reasonable relation to a legitimate state interest to justify the action, it avoids the need for complex balancing of competing interests in every case.

Turning to the claim at issue here, the Court of Appeals stated that "properly analyzed, the first issue to be resolved is whether there is a liberty interest in determining the time and manner of one's death," or, in other words, "is there a right to die?" Similarly, respondents assert a "liberty to choose how to die" and a right to "control of one's final days," and describe the asserted liberty as "the right to choose a humane, dignified death," and "the liberty to shape death." As noted above, we have a tradition of carefully formulating the interest at stake in substantive-due-process cases. For example, although *Cruzan* is often described as a "right to die" case, we were, in fact, more precise: We assumed that the Constitution granted competent persons a "constitutionally protected right to refuse lifesaving hydration and nutrition." The Washington statute at issue in this case prohibits "aiding another person to attempt suicide," and, thus, the question before us is whether the "liberty" specially protected by the Due Process Clause includes a right to commit suicide which itself includes a right to assistance in doing so.

We now inquire whether this asserted right has any place in our Nation's traditions. Here, we are confronted with a consistent and almost universal tradition that has long rejected the asserted right, and continues explicitly to reject it today, even for terminally ill, mentally competent adults. To hold for respondents, we would have to reverse centuries of legal doctrine and practice, and strike down the considered policy choice of almost every State.

Washington v. Glucksberg

Respondents contend, however, that the liberty interest they assert is consistent with this Court's substantive due process line of cases, if not with this Nation's history and practice. Pointing to *Casey* and *Cruzan*, respondents read our jurisprudence in this area as reflecting a general tradition of "self-sovereignty," and as teaching that the liberty protected by the Due Process Clause includes "basic and intimate exercises of personal autonomy." According to respondents, our liberty jurisprudence, and the broad, individualistic principles it reflects, protects the "liberty of competent, terminally ill adults to make end-of-life decisions free of undue government interference." The question presented in this case, however, is whether the protections of the Due Process Clause include a right to commit suicide with another's assistance. With this careful description of respondents' claim in mind, we turn to *Casey* and *Cruzan*. . . .

The right assumed in *Cruzan* . . . was not simply deduced from abstract concepts of personal autonomy. Given the common-law rule that forced medication was a battery, and the long legal tradition protecting the decision to refuse unwanted medical treatment, our assumption was entirely consistent with this Nation's history and constitutional traditions. The decision to commit suicide with the assistance of another may be just as personal and profound as the decision to refuse unwanted medical treatment, but it has never enjoyed similar legal protection. Indeed, the two acts are widely and reasonably regarded as quite distinct. See *Vacco v. Quill*. In *Cruzan* itself, we recognized that most States outlawed assisted suicide—and even more do today—and we certainly gave no intimation that the right to refuse unwanted medical treatment could be some-how transmuted into a right to assistance in committing suicide. . . .

Similarly, respondents emphasize the statement in *Casey* that:

> At the heart of liberty is the right to define one's own concept of existence, of meaning, of the universe, and of the mystery of human life. Beliefs about these matters could not define the attributes of personhood were they formed under compulsion of the State.

By choosing this language, the Court's opinion in *Casey* described, in a general way and in light of our prior cases, those personal activities and decisions that this Court has identified as so deeply rooted in our history and traditions, or so fundamental to our concept of constitutionally ordered liberty, that they are protected by the Fourteenth Amendment. . . . That many of the rights and liberties protected by the Due Process Clause sound in personal autonomy does not warrant the sweeping conclusion that any and all important, intimate, and personal decisions are so protected, and *Casey* did not suggest otherwise.

The history of the law's treatment of assisted suicide in this country has been and continues to be one of the rejection of nearly all efforts to permit it. That being the case, our decisions lead us to conclude that the asserted right to assistance in committing suicide is not a fundamental liberty interest protected by the Due Process Clause. The Constitution also requires, however, that Washington's assisted-suicide ban be rationally related to legitimate government interests. This requirement is unquestionably met here. As the court below recognized, Washington's assisted-suicide ban implicates a number of state interests.

First, Washington has an unqualified interest in the preservation of human life. The State's prohibition on assisted suicide, like all homicide laws, both reflects and advances its commitment to this interest. . . .

Relatedly, all admit that suicide is a serious public-health problem, especially among persons in otherwise vulnerable groups. The State has an interest in preventing suicide, and in studying, identifying, and treating its causes. . . .

The State also has an interest in protecting the integrity and ethics of the medical profession. . . . The American Medical Association, like many other medical and physicians' groups, has concluded that physician-assisted suicide is fundamentally incompatible with the physician's role as healer. And physician-assisted suicide could, it is argued, undermine the trust that is essential to the doctor-patient relationship by blurring the time-honored line between healing and harming.

Next, the State has an interest in protecting vulnerable groups—including the poor, the elderly, and disabled persons—from abuse, neglect, and mistakes. . . . We have recognized the real risk of subtle coercion and undue influence in end-of-life situations. . . . If physician-assisted suicide were permitted, many might resort to it to spare their families the substantial financial burden of end-of-life health-care costs. . . .

Finally, the State may fear that permitting assisted suicide will start it down the path to voluntary and perhaps even involuntary euthanasia. The Court of Appeals struck down Washington's assisted-suicide ban only "as applied to competent, terminally ill adults who wish to hasten their deaths by obtaining medication prescribed by their doctors." Washington insists, however, that the impact of the court's decision will not and cannot be so limited. If suicide is protected as a matter of constitutional right, it is argued, every man and woman in the United States must enjoy it. . . . Thus, it turns out that what is couched as a limited right to "physician-assisted suicide" is likely, in effect, a much broader license, which could prove extremely difficult to police and contain. Washington's ban on assisting suicide prevents such erosion. . . .

We need not weigh exactingly the relative strengths of these various interests. They are unquestionably important and legitimate, and Washington's ban on assisted suicide is at least reasonably related to their promotion and protection. We therefore hold that RCW 9A.36.060(1) does not violate the Fourteenth Amendment, either on its face or "as applied to competent, terminally ill adults who wish to hasten their deaths by obtaining medication prescribed by their doctors."

Throughout the Nation, Americans are engaged in an earnest and profound debate about the morality, legality, and practicality of physician-assisted suicide. Our holding permits this debate to continue, as it should in a democratic society. The decision of the en banc Court of Appeals is reversed, and the case is remanded for further proceedings consistent with this opinion.

Justice Souter, concurring in the judgment.

. . . The question is whether the statute sets up one of those "arbitrary impositions" or "purposeless restraints" at odds with the Due Process Clause of the Fourteenth Amendment. *Poe v. Ullman* (1961) (Harlan, J., dissenting). I conclude that the statute's application to the doctors has not been shown to be unconstitutional, but I write separately to give my reasons. . . .

Respondents claim that a patient facing imminent death, who anticipates physical suffering and indignity, and is capable of responsible and voluntary choice, should have a right to a physician's assistance in providing counsel and drugs to be administered by the patient to end life promptly. . . . I do not understand the argument to rest on any assumption that rights either to suicide or to assistance in committing it are historically based as such. Respondents, rather, acknowledge the prohibition of each historically, but rely on the fact that to a substantial extent the State has repudiated that history. . . .

A legislature has [not] acted arbitrarily when the following conditions are met: there is a serious factual controversy over the feasibility of recognizing the claimed right without at the same time making it impossible for the State to engage in an undoubtedly legitimate exercise of power; facts necessary to resolve the controversy are not readily ascertainable through the judicial process; but they are more readily subject to discovery through legislative factfinding and experimentation. . . . Since there is little experience directly bearing on the issue [the dangers of assisted suicide], the most that can be said is that whichever way the Court might rule today, events could overtake its assumptions [if and when] experimentation in some jurisdictions confirmed or discredited the concerns about progression from assisted suicide to euthanasia.

Legislatures, on the other hand, have superior opportunities to obtain the facts necessary for a judgment about the present controversy. Not only do they have more flexible mechanisms for factfinding than the Judiciary, but their mechanisms include the power to experiment, moving forward and pulling back as facts emerge within their own jurisdictions. . . . We therefore have a clear question about which institution, a legislature or a court, is relatively more competent to deal with an emerging issue as to which facts currently unknown could be dispositive. The answer has to be, for the reasons already stated, that the legislative process is to be preferred. . . .

The Court should accordingly stay its hand to allow reasonable legislative consideration. While I do not decide for all time that respondents' claim should not be recognized, I acknowledge the legislative institutional competence as the better one to deal with that claim at this time.

[The following opinions apply to both *Glucksberg* and *Quill*.]

Justice O'Connor, concurring.

Death will be different for each of us. For many, the last days will be spent in physical pain and perhaps the despair that accompanies physical deterioration and a loss of control of basic bodily and mental functions. Some will seek medication to alleviate that pain and other symptoms.

The Court frames the issue in *Washington v. Glucksberg* as whether the Due Process Clause of the Constitution protects a "right to commit suicide which itself includes a right to assistance in doing so," and concludes that our Nation's history, legal traditions, and practices do not support the existence of such a right. I join the Court's opinions [in *Glucksberg* and *Quill*] because I agree that there is no generalized right to commit suicide. But respondents urge us to address the narrower question whether a mentally competent person who is experiencing great suffering has a constitutionally cognizable interest in controlling the circumstances of his or her imminent death. I see no need to reach that question in the context of the facial challenges to the New York and Washington laws at issue here. The parties and amici agree that in these States a patient who is suffering from a terminal illness and who is experiencing great pain has no legal barriers to obtaining medication, from qualified physicians, to alleviate that suffering, even to the point of causing unconsciousness and hastening death. In this light, even assuming that we would recognize such an interest, I agree that the State's interests in protecting those who are not truly competent or facing imminent death, or those whose decisions to hasten death would not truly be voluntary, are sufficiently weighty to justify a prohibition against physician-assisted suicide.

Every one of us at some point may be affected by our own or a family member's terminal illness. There is no reason to think the democratic process will not strike the proper balance between the interests of terminally ill, mentally competent individuals who would seek to end their suffering and the State's interests in protecting those who might seek to end life mistakenly or under pressure. As the Court recognizes, States are presently undertaking extensive and serious evaluation of physician-assisted suicide and other related issues. In such circumstances, the challenging task of crafting appropriate procedures for safeguarding liberty interests is entrusted to the laboratory of the States in the first instance. . . .

Washington v. Glucksberg

Justice Stevens, concurring in the judgments.

. . . I fully agree with the Court that the "liberty" protected by the Due Process Clause does not include a categorical "right to commit suicide which itself includes a right to assistance in doing so." But just as our conclusion that capital punishment is not always unconstitutional did not preclude later decisions holding that it is sometimes impermissibly cruel, so is it equally clear that a decision upholding a general statutory prohibition of assisted suicide does not mean that every possible application of the statute would be valid. A State, like Washington, that has authorized the death penalty, and thereby has concluded that the sanctity of human life does not require that it always be preserved, must acknowledge that there are situations in which an interest in hastening death is legitimate. Indeed, not only is that interest sometimes legitimate, I am also convinced that there are times when it is entitled to constitutional protection. . . .

While I agree with the Court that *Cruzan* does not decide the issue presented by these cases, *Cruzan* did give recognition, not just to vague, unbridled notions of autonomy, but to the more specific interest in making decisions about how to confront an imminent death. Although there is no absolute right to physician-assisted suicide, *Cruzan* makes it clear that some individuals who no longer have the option of deciding whether to live or to die because they are already on the threshold of death have a constitutionally protected interest that may outweigh the State's interest in preserving life at all costs. The liberty interest at stake in a case like this differs from, and is stronger than, both the common-law right to refuse medical treatment and the unbridled interest in deciding whether to live or die. It is an interest in deciding how, rather than whether, a critical threshold shall be crossed. . . .

Justice Ginsburg, concurring in the judgments.

I concur in the Court's judgments in these cases substantially for the reasons stated by Justice O'Connor in her concurring opinion.

Justice Breyer, concurring in the judgments.

I believe that Justice O'Connor's views, which I share, have greater legal significance than the Court's opinion suggests. I join her separate opinion, except insofar as it joins the majority. And I concur in the judgments. I shall briefly explain how I differ from the Court.

I agree with the Court in *Vacco v. Quill* that the articulated state interests justify the distinction drawn between physician assisted suicide and withdrawal of life-support. I also agree with the Court that the critical question in both of the cases before us is whether the liberty specially protected by the Due Process Clause includes a right of the sort that the respondents assert. I do not agree, however, with the Court's formulation of that claimed liberty interest. The Court describes it as a "right to commit suicide with another's assistance." But I would not reject the

> respondents' claim without considering a different formulation, for which our legal tradition may provide greater support. That formulation would use words roughly like a "right to die with dignity." But irrespective of the exact words used, at its core would lie personal control over the manner of death, professional medical assistance, and the avoidance of unnecessary and severe physical suffering—combined. . . .
>
> I do not believe . . . that this Court need or now should decide whether or a not such a right is "fundamental." That is because, in my view, the avoidance of severe physical pain (connected with death) would have to constitute an essential part of any successful claim and because, as Justice O'Connor points out, the laws before us do not force a dying person to undergo that kind of pain. . . . Were the legal circumstances different—for example, were state law to prevent the provision of palliative care, including the administration of drugs as needed to avoid pain at the end of life—then the law's impact upon serious and otherwise unavoidable physical pain (accompanying death) would be more directly at issue. And as Justice O'Connor suggests, the Court might have to revisit its conclusions in these cases.

Glucksberg's companion case, *Vacco v. Quill*, 521 U.S. 793 (1997), focused on an equal protection theory. Plaintiffs argued that New York's law made an irrational distinction between two groups of terminally ill people: those kept alive by artificial means and those who did not require such equipment. The patients on machines could hasten their deaths by giving instructions to their doctors to disconnect the machines. That choice would be protected under the logic of *Quinlan* and *Cruzan*. The patients not on machines could not hasten their deaths by giving instructions to their doctors to administer lethal drugs. That choice was illegal under the state law against assisting suicide.

The Second Circuit held that the law violated equal protection. Justice Rehnquist's majority opinion rejected that argument:

> Unlike the Court of Appeals, we think the distinction between assisting suicide and withdrawing life-sustaining treatment, a distinction widely recognized and endorsed in the medical profession and in our legal traditions, is both important and logical; it is certainly rational. . . . We disagree with respondents' claim that the distinction between refusing lifesaving medical treatment and assisted suicide is arbitrary and irrational. Granted, in some cases, the line between the two may not be clear, but certainty is not required, even were it possible. Logic and contemporary practice support New York's judgment that the two acts are different, and New York may therefore, consistent with the Constitution, treat them differently. By permitting everyone to refuse unwanted medical treatment while prohibiting anyone from assisting a suicide, New York law follows a longstanding and rational distinction.

flashforward

1. ***Death with Dignity Laws.*** The majority opinion in *Glucksberg* noted that Oregon voters adopted a statute in 1994 allowing physicians to provide aid in dying, but that voters in Washington and California rejected similar proposals in 1991 and 1993. Later, Washington adopted such a statute through a ballot initiative in 2008, and California's legislature enacted one in 2016. State-level activity around the issue continues today, in the form of legislation, ballot proposals, and judicial interpretations of state constitutions and statutes.

2. **Gonzales v. Oregon.** In 2001, the US Attorney General announced that it would violate the federal Controlled Substances Act (CSA) for any doctor to prescribe federally-regulated drugs for the purpose of hastening death. Any doctor who provided aid in dying under the Oregon statute would lose the ability to prescribe drugs and could face federal criminal prosecution. In *Gonzales v. Oregon*, 546 U.S. 243 (2006), the Supreme Court held (6–3) that the Attorney General's interpretation of the statute was improper. In reaching this result, the majority indicated that states should be able to exercise their discretion under *Glucksberg* to adopt varying policies and act as Justice Brandeis's laboratories of democracy.

> The importance of the issue of physician-assisted suicide, which has been the subject of an "earnest and profound debate" across the country, *Glucksberg*, makes the [government's interpretation of the CSA] all the more suspect. . . . The statute and our case law amply support the conclusion that Congress regulates medical practice insofar as it bars doctors from using their prescription-writing powers as a means to engage in illicit drug dealing and trafficking as conventionally understood. Beyond this, however, the statute manifests no intent to regulate the practice of medicine generally. The silence is understandable given the structure and limitations of federalism, which allow the States great latitude under their police powers to legislate as to the protection of the lives, limbs, health, comfort, and quiet of all persons.

F. Substantive Due Process and Abortion

The most prominent—and the most controversial—modern application of substantive due process has involved abortion. As is widely known, the Supreme

Court held in *Roe v. Wade* (1973) and *Planned Parenthood v. Casey* (1993) that substantive due process protected a right to abortion, but these cases were overruled by *Dobbs v. Jackson Women's Health Organization* (2022).

No state statutes regulated abortion during the founding era. But by the middle of the 20th century, all states had laws either forbidding abortion or sharply limiting its availability, typically allowing it only for medical emergencies where continuing the pregnancy placed the patient's life in danger. Despite the prohibitions, safe and legal abortions were available for women who could afford to travel to countries without bans, or to states where cooperative doctors were willing to find the patient's life in danger. For those who could not afford to travel, illegal abortions were widely available, but they were far from safe. In the 1960s, somewhere between 600,000 to 800,000 illegal abortions were performed annually in the United States, leading to 8,000 to 17,000 avoidable maternal deaths annually, and even more injuries. Cook County Hospital in Chicago had a 40-bed "septic abortion ward" devoted to treating women for injuries following amateur abortions.

Against this backdrop of financial disparity and physical danger, an abortion reform movement arose in the 1960s that began to result in legislative reform in some states. In 1968, California decriminalized abortions necessary to preserve maternal health, not just life. In 1970, New York became the first state to legalize all abortions during the first 24 weeks of pregnancy, or thereafter if necessary to save the patient's life. By the time of *Roe v. Wade* in 1973, similar laws had passed in Washington and Alaska. Hawaii had legalized abortion at all stages for any reason. But a large majority of states had more restrictive laws.

1. Abortion Protected: *Roe v. Wade*

A Texas law in force since 1857 criminalized all abortions except those performed with "the purpose of saving the life of the mother." In *Roe v. Wade*, 410 U.S. 113 (1973), the Supreme Court held (7–2) that the statute was unconstitutional.

Justice Blackmun's majority opinion was structured unusually. Much of the opinion spoke not about the interests of pregnant women, but about the beliefs and practices of the medical profession. A lengthy historical section traced medical standards and laws regarding abortion from the ancient Greeks and the Hippocratic Oath, to the Romans, to English common law and statutes, to early American statutes, and then to position papers recently issued by the American Medical Association, the American Public Health Association, and the American Bar Association. In a famous critique of the Roe majority opinion, John Hart Ely—a supporter of abortion rights, but an opponent of overly aggressive judicial review—said that *Roe* "is not constitutional law and gives almost no sense of an obligation to try to be." *The Wages of Crying Wolf: A Comment on Roe v. Wade*, 82 Yale L. J. 920, 947 (1973).

Ultimately, the majority opinion turned to the interests of pregnant women, which were described under the heading of "privacy" as that term had been used in *Griswold* and *Eisenstadt*:

> This right of privacy, whether it be founded in the Fourteenth Amendment's concept of personal liberty and restrictions upon state action, as we feel it is, or, as the District Court determined, in the Ninth Amendment's reservation of rights to the people, is broad enough to encompass a woman's decision whether or not to terminate her pregnancy. The detriment that the State would impose upon the pregnant woman by denying this choice altogether is apparent. Specific and direct harm medically diagnosable even in early pregnancy may be involved. Maternity, or additional offspring, may force upon the woman a distressful life and future. Psychological harm may be imminent. Mental and physical health may be taxed by child care. There is also the distress, for all concerned, associated with the unwanted child, and there is the problem of bringing a child into a family already unable, psychologically and otherwise, to care for it. In other cases, as in this one, the additional difficulties and continuing stigma of unwed motherhood may be involved. All these are factors the woman and her responsible physician necessarily will consider in consultation.

Since control over one's pregnancy was a "fundamental right," a state could restrict it only for compelling reasons using narrowly tailored laws. The majority acknowledged that a State had "important interests in safeguarding health, in maintaining medical standards, and in protecting potential life." But these state interests could not justify an abortion ban until later in pregnancy. The interest in safeguarding maternal health and medical standards did not support abortion bans early in pregnancy, because abortion is actually safer for a woman than continuing with pregnancy would be. The interest in bringing the fetus to term did not become compelling until later in pregnancy when the fetus was well enough developed to survive outside the womb. This point was known as "viability," occurring around 24 weeks (6 months) into a pregnancy. In dividing pregnancy into early and late phases with different legal consequences, the viability concept had a general resemblance to the common-law notion of "quickening"—the time when a fetus could be felt moving in the womb, which occurs around 16 to 18 weeks.

Justice Rehnquist dissented, drawing an analogy to *Lochner*. Abortion regulation was a suitable task for legislatures, he argued, just as labor regulation should have been in the *Lochner* era.

> As in *Lochner* and similar cases applying substantive due process standards to economic and social welfare legislation, the adoption of the compelling state interest standard [for abortion] will inevitably require this Court to examine the legislative policies and pass on the wisdom of these policies in the very

> process of deciding whether a particular state interest put forward may or may not be "compelling." . . . The fact that a majority of the States, reflecting after all the majority sentiment in those States, have had restrictions on abortions for at least a century is a strong indication, it seems to me, that the asserted right to an abortion is not so rooted in the traditions and conscience of our people as to be ranked as fundamental.

2. Abortion Reconsidered: *Planned Parenthood of Southeast Pennsylvania v. Casey*

Roe was not immediately perceived as controversial or partisan. The majority and the dissent each included justices appointed by Democratic and Republican presidents. But in the ensuing decades, opponents of abortion became increasingly politically vocal, both on the streets (through demonstrations near facilities that performed abortions and outside the Supreme Court), and in legislatures (through a steady stream of statutes regulating abortion in various ways). Support or opposition to legalized abortion became a topic of partisan polarization. During nominations of federal judges, Senate questioning increasingly turned toward the nominees' views on abortion, often using coded language about a constitutional right to privacy. US Supreme Court opinions involving abortion began to reveal angry disagreements among justices in the 1980s. Under Presidents Reagan and George H.W. Bush, the Justice Department began submitting amicus briefs calling for *Roe* to be overruled, and in the fractured decision *Webster v. Reproductive Health Services*, 492 U.S. 490 (1989), four justices signaled that they were prepared to do so.

> ■ WEBSITE
> A fuller version of *Planned Parenthood v. Casey* is available for download from this casebook's companion website, www.CaplanIntegratedConLaw.com.

This set the stage for *Planned Parenthood v. Casey*, 505 U.S. 833 (1992), a case that many observers anticipated would overrule *Roe v. Wade*. The suit challenged several provisions Pennsylvania's Abortion Control Act affecting pre-viability abortions. Two provision drew the most attention. One stated that doctors must deliver government-mandated information to the patient and then wait 24 hours for her to consider it. Another stated that a married woman must notify her husband before getting an abortion.

Casey resulted in a splintered decision with no majority opinion. Four justices (Rehnquist, White, Scalia, and Thomas) said they would overrule *Roe* and then uphold both parts of the statute under the rational basis test. Two justices (Blackmun and Stevens) said they would reject both provisions under *Roe*, finding that they were not narrowly tailored to compelling interests. A three-justice plurality opinion—that was later treated as the holding—found that the spousal notification provision was unconstitutional, but that the waiting period provision was not, in an opinion that expressly refused to overrule *Roe*. The plurality was a surprise to many, since it was jointly written by Justices **O'Connor**, Kennedy, and Souter—all of whom were appointed in the 1980s by Republican presidents who had publicly declared opposition to *Roe*.

BIOGRAPHY

SANDRA DAY O'CONNOR—the first woman to serve on the US Supreme Court—was born in 1930 in Texas and grew up on a cattle ranch in Arizona. After graduating from Stanford Law School in 1952, she was rejected from dozens of law firms because of her sex. Her first legal job was as a deputy county attorney in San Mateo, California—without pay, and sharing office space with a secretary. She later became involved in Arizona politics, serving two terms in the state Senate from 1969 to 1975, becoming the first woman in any state to serve as a Senate majority leader. After leaving the legislature, she served as a judge in Arizona trial and appellate courts. She was appointed to the US Supreme Court by President Ronald Reagan in 1981, remaining on the court until her retirement in 2006.

The *Casey* plurality explained itself in different terms than *Roe*. For example, its focus throughout was on the rights of women—including their equality interests—and not the opinions of the medical establishment. Legally, the opinion steered clear of the word "privacy" used prominently in *Griswold* and *Roe*, and instead asked whether restrictions on abortion deprived "liberty" without due process of law. But despite these differences, the plurality stated that "the woman's right to terminate her pregnancy before viability is the most central principle of *Roe v. Wade*. It is a rule of law and a component of liberty we cannot renounce."

The plurality rejected the suggestion that the Due Process clauses protect only enumerated rights. "It is a promise of the Constitution that there is a realm of personal liberty which the government may not enter," as reflected in cases protecting various unenumerated rights relating to marriage, procreation, contraception, family relationships, child rearing, and education. "These matters, involving the most intimate and personal choices a person may make in a lifetime, choices central to personal dignity and autonomy, are central to the liberty protected by" the Due Process clauses.

For the plurality, early-stage abortion was a similar liberty. While reasonable people have differing views about the propriety of abortion, it is a decision of a "deep, personal character." The government may not "resolve these philosophic questions in such a definitive way that a woman lacks all choice in the matter."

> The liberty of the woman is at stake in a sense unique to the human condition and so unique to the law. The mother who carries a child to full term is subject to anxieties, to physical constraints, to pain that only she must bear. . . . Her suffering is too intimate and personal for the State to insist, without more, upon its own vision of the woman's role, however dominant that vision has been in the course of our history and our culture. The destiny of the woman must be shaped to a large extent on her own conception of her spiritual imperatives and her place in society.

With that said, "the woman's liberty is not so unlimited . . . that from the outset the State cannot show its concern for the life of the unborn, and at a later point in fetal development the State's interest in life has sufficient force so that the right of the woman to terminate the pregnancy can be restricted." The dividing line would be viability, "the time at which there is a realistic possibility of maintaining and nourishing a life outside the womb, so that the independent existence of the second life can in reason and all fairness be the object of state protection that now overrides the rights of the woman." The resulting standard looked like this:

- Post-viability, a state could ban abortions simply because it opposes them (so long as it makes exceptions to allow abortions medically necessary to protect the life and health of the patient).
- Pre-viability, a state could not ban abortion. But it could impose regulations on abortion designed to protect patient health, just as it could for other medical procedures. So long as such a law "serves a valid purpose, one not designed to strike at the right itself," it would be allowed even if it "has the incidental effect of making it more difficult or more expensive to procure an abortion." Such laws would be invalid if they imposed an "undue burden," which would exist if a regulation had "the purpose or effect of placing a substantial obstacle in the path of a woman seeking an abortion of a nonviable fetus."

For the plurality, Pennsylvania's spousal notification provision was an undue burden. Evidence at trial established that women in abusive marriages would risk domestic violence if they had to notify their spouses before obtaining an abortion. In a meaningful number of cases, the law would amount to a spousal veto, not merely spousal notification. The plurality considered it improper to treat adult women like children who need the consent of a guardian before making reproductive decisions, or like founding-era women living under coverture with no legal existence separate from their husbands.

By contrast, the plurality held that Pennsylvania's 24-hour waiting period was not an undue burden. Its goal was to ensure that the patient gave meaningful informed consent. The plurality recognized that for many women—especially those with the fewest financial resources or those who must travel long distances—the waiting period could be burdensome, but in their judgment the burden was not substantial enough to become "undue." (This portion of *Casey* overruled *City of Akron v. Akron Center for Reproductive Health, Inc.*, 462 U.S. 416 (1983), which found a mandatory 24-hour waiting period to be unconstitutional.)

Cognizant of the political polarization swirling around the case, the plurality devoted a lengthy section to stare decisis. It emphasized the benefits of consistency and warned that overruling decisions, especially ones as famous as *Roe*, comes at a cost—especially if the public believes the court changed the law merely to reflect political preferences. "A decision to overrule *Roe*'s essential holding under the existing circumstances would address error, if error there was, at the cost of both profound and unnecessary damage to the Court's legitimacy, and to the Nation's commitment to the rule of law."

The plurality opinion was followed by several emotional separate opinions.

Justice Blackmun—the author of *Roe*—lamented that overruling would cast the nation into "darkness" that was, for now, staved off by "a single, flickering flame." He stated: "I fear for the darkness as four Justices anxiously await the single vote necessary to extinguish the light."

Justice Scalia, reiterating arguments from earlier dissents, argued that abortion was not constitutionally protected "because of two simple facts: (1) the Constitution says absolutely nothing about it, and (2) the longstanding traditions of American society have permitted it to be legally proscribed." He asserted that the plurality opinion contained no "reasoned judgment" but was instead "a collection of adjectives that simply decorate a value judgment and conceal a political choice." Not stopping there, he called various aspects of the plurality opinion "Orwellian," "Nietzschean" and "czarist." His opinion concluded by comparing the plurality opinion to *Dred Scott*.

> It is no more realistic for us in this litigation, than it was [in *Dred Scott*], to think that an issue of the sort they both involved—an issue involving life and death, freedom and subjugation—can be speedily and finally settled by the Supreme Court. . . . Quite to the contrary, by foreclosing all democratic outlet for the deep passions this issue arouses, by banishing the issue from the political forum that gives all participants, even the losers, the satisfaction of a fair hearing and an honest fight, by continuing the imposition of a rigid national rule instead of allowing for regional differences, the Court merely prolongs and intensifies the anguish.

3. Abortion Reversed: *Dobbs v. Jackson Women's Health Organization*

In the decades after *Casey*, constitutional litigation over abortion centered on whether particular laws imposed undue burdens. For example, a Montana law requiring that abortions be performed by a physician and not a physician's assistant was not an undue burden, even though this would reduce access to abortion in the state. *Mazurek v. Armstrong*, 520 U.S. 968 (1997).

***Escalating Challenges to* Casey.** A significant turning point involved statutes that banned what they termed "partial birth abortion." In *Stenberg v. Carhart*, 530 U.S. 914 (2000), the Court ruled 5–4 that a Kansas statute imposed an undue burden with a statutory definition of "partial birth abortion" that banned many common abortion methods and had no exception to protect the patient's health. After two new appointments by President George W. Bush changed the Court's personnel, *Gonzales v. Carhart*, 550 U.S. 124 (2007), ruled 5–4 that no undue burden was imposed by a federal statute with slightly different wording that also banned what it called "partial birth abortion" with no exception for maternal health. Justice Kennedy's majority opinion in *Gonzales v. Carhart* contained language suggesting that legislatures retained power to make value judgments about whether specific abortion procedures could be banned because they were perceived to be "gruesome" or "brutal" (terms that some people might apply to any abortion). The majority also used language connoting disdain for abortion generally. For example, dicta in the opinion said that "respect for human life finds an ultimate expression in the bond of love the mother has for her child" and that any woman who later regrets having an abortion will "struggle with grief more anguished and sorrow more profound" if she learns the details of the surgery.

Following *Gonzales*, state governments opposed to abortion steadily enacted new laws affecting previability abortion. For example, Texas and Louisiana required that abortions be performed only in clinics that had architectural features resembling hospital emergency rooms, and by doctors with hospital admitting privileges, even though previability abortions were safe outpatient procedures with far fewer complications and fatalities than other common procedures that were not subject to similar rules (such as colonoscopy, liposuction, or childbirth). These laws would have the effect of shuttering most abortion clinics in their states. The laws were found to be undue burdens in *Whole Woman's Health v. Hellerstedt*, 579 U.S. 582 (2016) (Texas) and *June Medical Services LLC v. Russo*, 140 S.Ct. 2103 (2020) (Louisiana), but each was decided by narrow five-member votes whose rulings prompted increasingly vehement dissents.

Some states enacted laws that were clearly unconstitutional under *Roe* and *Casey*, in hopes that challenges to the statutes would lead to overruling. For example, some states banned abortions long before viability—after 15 weeks, or six weeks, or when a fetal heartbeat could supposedly be detected, or other time periods that could expire before some women realized they were pregnant. Also, 13 states passed "trigger laws" that would ban most abortions if and when *Roe* and *Casey* were ever overruled.

The* Dobbs *Litigation. By 2020, only one medical facility in Mississippi provided non-emergency previability abortions. (This situation was not unique. In several states, complex medical regulations plus social hostility to abortion and abortion providers—some of whom had been stalked and even murdered—combined to sharply limit abortion access as a practical matter. Even for nonsurgical abortions that could be induced with oral medication, access was in some states limited by laws requiring that the pills be dispensed only at an office visit.) The remaining Mississippi clinic brought suit when that state enacted a 15-week law in 2018. Meanwhile, a combination of deaths and retirements on the Supreme Court allowed President Trump, who had promised to nominate abortion opponents, to appoint three new justices in a single presidential term.

ITEMS TO CONSIDER WHILE READING *DOBBS v. JACKSON WOMEN'S HEALTH ORGANIZATION*:

A. *Work through the items in the Kickstarter for Substantive Due Process, noting where the majority and dissent differ.*

B. *Which methods of reasoning do the majority and dissent rely upon? What are the advantages and disadvantages of those choices?*

C. *Consider the role of women's rights in the opinions. Specifically, how would the reasoning proceed if the main arguments focused on sex equality instead of reproductive freedom?*

D. *Which factors do the majority and dissent consider important when deciding to overrule a precedent?*

E. *Any individual rights case could be viewed as a struggle between legislatures and courts, or between legislatures and individuals. Which framework do the majority and dissent adopt? Which is more justifiable?*

Dobbs v. Jackson Women's Health Organization,
142 S.Ct. 2228 (2022)

Justice Alito delivered the opinion of the Court [joined by Justices Thomas, Gorsuch, Kavanaugh, and Barrett].

Abortion presents a profound moral issue on which Americans hold sharply conflicting views. Some believe fervently that a human person comes into being at conception and that abortion ends an innocent life. Others feel just as strongly that any regulation of abortion invades a woman's right to control her own body and prevents women from achieving full equality. Still others in a third group think that abortion should be allowed under some but not all circumstances, and those within this group hold a variety of views about the particular restrictions that should be imposed.

For the first 185 years after the adoption of the Constitution, each State was permitted to address this issue in accordance with the views of its citizens. Then, in 1973, this Court decided Roe v. Wade. Even though the Constitution makes no mention of abortion, the Court held that it confers a broad right to obtain one. . . . Eventually, in *Planned Parenthood of Southeastern Pa. v. Casey* (1992), the Court revisited *Roe*. . . . [The controlling opinion of three justices in Casey] concluded that stare decisis, which calls for prior decisions to be followed in most instances, required adherence to what it called Roe's "central holding"—that a State may not constitutionally protect fetal life before viability—even if that holding was wrong. . . .

Americans continue to hold passionate and widely divergent views on abortion, and state legislatures have acted accordingly. Some have recently enacted laws allowing abortion, with few restrictions, at all stages of pregnancy. Others have tightly restricted abortion beginning well before viability. . . . Before us now is one such state law. The State of Mississippi asks us to uphold the constitutionality of a law that generally prohibits an abortion after the 15th week of pregnancy—several weeks before the point at which a fetus is now regarded as "viable" outside the womb. In defending this law, the State's primary argument is that we should reconsider and overrule *Roe* and *Casey* and once again allow each State to regulate abortion as its citizens wish. On the other side, respondents and **the Solicitor General** ask us to reaffirm *Roe* and *Casey*, and they contend that the Mississippi law cannot stand if we do so. . . .

■ TERMINOLOGY

SOLICITOR GENERAL: The Solicitor General, an attorney within the US Department of Justice, states the position of the executive branch in Supreme Court litigation. Beginning in the late 1980s, solicitors general submitted amicus briefs to the Supreme Court that voiced conflicting views on whether *Roe* should be overruled, varying with the political party of the President who appointed the Solicitor General.

Dobbs v. Jackson Women's Health Organization

We hold that *Roe* and *Casey* must be overruled. . . . It is time to heed the Constitution and return the issue of abortion to the people's elected representatives. The permissibility of abortion, and the limitations, upon it, are to be resolved like most important questions in our democracy: by citizens trying to persuade one another and then voting. That is what the Constitution and the rule of law demand.

I

The law at issue in this case, Mississippi's Gestational Age Act (2018), contains this central provision: "Except in a medical emergency or in the case of a severe fetal abnormality, a person shall not intentionally or knowingly perform or induce an abortion of an unborn human being if the probable gestational age of the unborn human being has been determined to be greater than fifteen (15) weeks."[FN14] . . .

FN14 The Act defines "gestational age" to be "the age of an unborn human being as calculated from the first day of the last menstrual period of the pregnant woman."

Respondents [the plaintiffs below] are an abortion clinic, Jackson Women's Health Organization, and one of its doctors [Sacheen Carr-Ellis]. [Petitioners, the defendants below, are Thomas Dobbs of the Mississippi Department of Health and Kenneth Cleveland of the Mississippi Board of Medical Licensure, sued in their official capacities.] . . . The District Court granted summary judgment in favor of respondents and permanently enjoined enforcement of the Act, reasoning that "viability marks the earliest point at which the State's interest in fetal life is constitutionally adequate to justify a legislative ban on nontherapeutic abortions" and that 15 weeks' gestational age is "prior to viability." The Fifth Circuit affirmed. . . .

II

We begin by considering the critical question whether the Constitution, properly understood, confers a right to obtain an abortion. . . . First, we explain the standard that our cases have used in determining whether the Fourteenth Amendment's reference to "liberty" protects a particular right. Second, we examine whether the right at issue in this case is rooted in our Nation's history and tradition and whether it is an essential component of what we have described as "ordered liberty." Finally, we consider whether a right to obtain an abortion is part of a broader entrenched right that is supported by other precedents.

A

1

Constitutional analysis must begin with the language of the instrument, which offers a "fixed standard" for ascertaining what our founding document means. 1

J. Story, Commentaries on the Constitution of the United States § 399 (1833). The Constitution makes no express reference to a right to obtain an abortion, and therefore those who claim that it protects such a right must show that the right is somehow implicit in the constitutional text.

Roe, however, was remarkably loose in its treatment of the constitutional text. It held that the abortion right, which is not mentioned in the Constitution, is part of a right to privacy, which is also not mentioned. And that privacy right, Roe observed, had been found to spring from no fewer than five different constitutional provisions—the First, Fourth, Fifth, Ninth, and Fourteenth Amendments.

The Court's discussion left open at least three ways in which some combination of these provisions could protect the abortion right. One possibility was that the right was founded in the Ninth Amendment's reservation of rights to the people. Another was that the right was rooted in the First, Fourth, or Fifth Amendment, or in some combination of those provisions [as in the *Griswold* majority opinion]. And a third path was . . . that the right was simply a component of the "liberty" protected by the Fourteenth Amendment's Due Process Clause. *Roe* expressed the "feel[ing]" that the Fourteenth Amendment was the provision that did the work, but its message seemed to be that the abortion right could be found *somewhere* in the Constitution and that specifying its exact location was not of paramount importance. The *Casey* Court did not defend this unfocused analysis and instead grounded its decision solely on the theory that the right to obtain an abortion is part of the "liberty" protected by the Fourteenth Amendment's Due Process Clause.

We discuss this theory in depth below, but before doing so, we briefly address one additional constitutional provision that some of respondents' amici have now offered as yet another potential home for the abortion right: the Fourteenth Amendment's Equal Protection Clause. Neither *Roe* nor *Casey* saw fit to invoke this theory, and it is squarely foreclosed by our precedents, which establish that a State's regulation of abortion is not a sex-based classification and is thus not subject to the "heightened scrutiny" that applies to such classifications. The regulation of a medical procedure that only one sex can undergo does not trigger heightened constitutional scrutiny unless the regulation is a mere pretext designed to effect an invidious discrimination against members of one sex or the other. *Geduldig v. Aiello* (1974). And as the Court has stated, the "goal of preventing abortion" does not constitute "invidiously discriminatory animus" against women. ***Bray v. Alexandria Women's Health Clinic***, 506 U.S. 263 (1993). Accordingly, laws regulating or prohibiting abortion are not subject to

■ HISTORY

BRAY: In *Bray*, a women's health clinic sued protestors who blocked access to the building. The suit relied on 28 U.S.C. § 1985(3), a reconstruction-era statute known as the Ku Klux Klan Act. The Supreme Court ruled that the protesters had not engaged in an unlawful conspiracy to deprive women of the equal protection of the laws, the standard under the Act. Congress responded to Bray by enacting the Free Access to Clinic Entrances (FACE) Act of 1994, which expressly reached obstructions at abortion clinics.

heightened scrutiny. Rather, they are governed by the same standard of review as other health and safety measures. . . .

Dobbs v. Jackson Women's Health Organization

2

The underlying theory [of *Casey*]—that the Fourteenth Amendment's Due Process Clause provides substantive, as well as procedural, protection for "liberty"—has long been controversial. But our decisions have held that the Due Process Clause protects two categories of substantive rights.

The first consists of rights guaranteed by the first eight Amendments. Those Amendments originally applied only to the Federal Government, *Barron v. Baltimore* (1833), but this Court has held that the Due Process Clause of the Fourteenth Amendment **incorporates** the great majority of those rights and thus makes them equally applicable to the States. The second category—which is the one in question here—comprises a select list of fundamental rights that are not mentioned anywhere in the Constitution.

In deciding whether a right falls into either of these categories, the Court has long asked whether the right is "deeply rooted in our history and tradition" and whether it is essential to our Nation's "scheme of ordered liberty." . . . Justice Ginsburg's opinion for the Court in *Timbs v. Indiana*, 139 S.Ct. 682 (2019) is a recent example. In concluding that the Eighth Amendment's protection against excessive fines is "fundamental to our scheme of ordered liberty" and "deeply rooted in this Nation's history and tradition," her opinion traced the right back to Magna Carta, Blackstone's Commentaries, and 35 of the 37 state constitutions in effect at the ratification of the Fourteenth Amendment. . . .

■ TERMINOLOGY

INCORPORATION: The "liberty" protected by the Due Process Clauses includes enumerated rights found elsewhere in the Constitution when those rights are deemed "fundamental." This concept, known as "incorporation," developed slowly over the course of decades. The doctrine is described in Flash-Forwards following *Barron v. Baltimore* (Ch. 5.C) (Fourteenth Amendment incorporation) and *Bolling v. Sharpe* (Ch. 11.B.2) (Fifth Amendment incorporation).

Timbs . . . concerned the question whether the Fourteenth Amendment protects rights that are expressly set out in the Bill of Rights, and it would be anomalous if similar historical support were not required when a putative right is not mentioned anywhere in the Constitution. Thus, in *Washington v. Glucksberg* (1997), which held that the Due Process Clause does not confer a right to assisted suicide, the Court surveyed more than 700 years of Anglo-American common law tradition, and made clear that a fundamental right must be "objectively, deeply rooted in this Nation's history and tradition."

Historical inquiries of this nature are essential whenever we are asked to recognize a new component of the "liberty" protected by the Due Process Clause because the term "liberty" alone provides little guidance. "Liberty" is a capacious term. As Lincoln once said: "We all declare for Liberty; but in using the same word we do not all mean the same thing." . . .

In interpreting what is meant by the Fourteenth Amendment's reference to "liberty," we must guard against the natural human tendency to confuse what that Amendment protects with our own ardent views about the liberty that Americans should enjoy. . . . On occasion, when the Court has ignored the appropriate limits imposed by respect for the teachings of history, it has fallen into the freewheeling judicial policymaking that characterized discredited decisions such as *Lochner v. New York* (1905). The Court must not fall prey to such an unprincipled approach. . . .

B

1

Until the latter part of the 20th century, there was no support in American law for a constitutional right to obtain an abortion. No state constitutional provision had recognized such a right. Until a few years before *Roe* was handed down, no federal or state court had recognized such a right. Nor had any scholarly treatise of which we are aware. And although law review articles are not reticent about advocating new rights, the earliest article proposing a constitutional right to abortion that has come to our attention was published only a few years before *Roe*.

Not only was there no support for such a constitutional right until shortly before *Roe*, but abortion had long been a crime in every single State. At common law, abortion was criminal in at least some stages of pregnancy and was regarded as unlawful and could have very serious consequences at all stages. American law followed the common law until a wave of statutory restrictions in the 1800s expanded criminal liability for abortions. By the time of the adoption of the Fourteenth Amendment, three-quarters of the States had made abortion a crime at any stage of pregnancy, and the remaining States would soon follow.

Roe either ignored or misstated this history, and Casey declined to reconsider *Roe*'s faulty historical analysis. It is therefore important to set the record straight.

2

a

We begin with the common law, under which abortion was a crime at least after "quickening"—i.e., the first felt movement of the fetus in the womb, which usually occurs between the 16th and 18th week of pregnancy.

The eminent common-law authorities (Blackstone, Coke, Hale, and the like) all describe abortion after quickening as criminal. Henry de Bracton's 13th-century treatise explained that if a person has "struck a pregnant woman, or has given her poison, whereby he has caused abortion, if the fetus be already formed and animated, and particularly if it be animated, he commits homicide." [Similar statements can be found in treatises by Sir Edward Coke (1552–1634), Sir Matthew Hale

(1609–1676), and Sir William Blackstone (1723–1780).] . . . Although a pre-quickening abortion was not itself considered homicide, it does not follow that abortion was permissible at common law—much less that abortion was a legal right. . . .

In sum, although common-law authorities differed on the severity of punishment for abortions committed at different points in pregnancy, none endorsed the practice. Moreover, we are aware of no common-law case or authority, and the parties have not pointed to any, that remotely suggests a positive right to procure an abortion at any stage of pregnancy.

b

In this country [up to the 19th century], the historical record is similar. . . .

c

. . . In this country during the 19th century, the vast majority of the States enacted statutes criminalizing abortion at all stages of pregnancy. By 1868, the year when the Fourteenth Amendment was ratified, three-quarters of the States, 28 out of 37, had enacted statutes making abortion a crime even if it was performed before quickening. Of the nine States that had not yet criminalized abortion at all stages, all but one did so by 1910. . . . By the end of the 1950s, according to the Roe Court's own count, statutes in all but four States and the District of Columbia prohibited abortion however and whenever performed, unless done to save or preserve the life of the mother.

This overwhelming consensus endured until the day Roe was decided. At that time, also by the *Roe* Court's own count, a substantial majority—30 States—still prohibited abortion at all stages except to save the life of the mother. And though *Roe* discerned a "trend toward liberalization" in about one-third of the States, those States still criminalized some abortions and regulated them more stringently than *Roe* would allow. . . .

d

The inescapable conclusion is that a right to abortion is not deeply rooted in the Nation's history and traditions. On the contrary, an unbroken tradition of prohibiting abortion on pain of criminal punishment persisted from the earliest days of the common law until 1973. . . .

3

Respondents and their amici have no persuasive answer to this historical evidence. . . . Not only are respondents and their amici unable to show that a constitutional right to abortion was established when the Fourteenth Amendment was adopted, but they have found no support for the existence of an abortion right that predates the latter part of the 20th century—no state constitutional provision, no statute, no judicial decision, no learned treatise. The earliest sources called to our attention are a few district court and state court decisions decided shortly before Roe and a small number of law review articles from the same time period. . . .

C

1

Instead of seriously pressing the argument that the abortion right itself has deep roots, supporters of *Roe* and *Casey* contend that the abortion right is an integral part of a broader entrenched right. *Roe* termed this a right to privacy, and *Casey* described it as the freedom to make "intimate and personal choices" that are "central to personal dignity and autonomy." *Casey* elaborated: "At the heart of liberty is the right to define one's own concept of existence, of meaning, of the universe, and of the mystery of human life."

The Court did not claim that this broadly framed right is absolute, and no such claim would be plausible. While individuals are certainly free to think and to say what they wish about "existence," "meaning," the "universe," and "the mystery of human life," they are not always free to act in accordance with those thoughts. License to act on the basis of such beliefs may correspond to one of the many understandings of "liberty," but it is certainly not "ordered liberty."

Ordered liberty sets limits and defines the boundary between competing interests. *Roe* and *Casey* each struck a particular balance between the interests of a woman who wants an abortion and the interests of what they termed "potential life." But the people of the various States may evaluate those interests differently. . . . Our Nation's historical understanding of ordered liberty does not prevent the people's elected representatives from deciding how abortion should be regulated.

Nor does the right to obtain an abortion have a sound basis in precedent. *Casey* relied on cases involving the right to marry a person of a different race, *Loving v. Virginia* (1967); the right to marry while in prison, *Turner v. Safley*, 482 U.S. 78 (1987); the right to obtain contraceptives, *Griswold v. Connecticut* (1965), *Eisenstadt v. Baird* (1972); the right to reside with relatives, *Moore v. City of East Cleveland* (1977); the right to make decisions about the education of one's children, *Pierce v. Society of Sisters* (1925), *Meyer v. Nebraska* (1923); the right not to be sterilized without consent, *Skinner v. Oklahoma* (1942); and the right in certain circumstances not to undergo involuntary surgery, forced administration of drugs, or other substantially similar procedures, *Winston v. Lee*, 470 U.S. 753 (1985), *Washington v. Harper*, 494 U.S. 210 (1990), *Rochin v. California*, 342 U.S. 165 (1952). Respondents and the Solicitor General also rely on post-*Casey* decisions like *Lawrence v. Texas* (2003) (right to engage in private, consensual sexual acts), and *Obergefell v. Hodges* (2015) (right to marry a person of the same sex).

These attempts to justify abortion through appeals to a broader right to autonomy and to define one's "concept of existence" prove too much. Those criteria, at a high level of generality, could license fundamental rights to illicit drug use, prostitution, and the like. None of these rights has any claim to being deeply rooted in history.

Dobbs v. Jackson Women's Health Organization

What sharply distinguishes the abortion right from the rights recognized in the cases on which *Roe* and *Casey* rely is something that both those decisions acknowledged: Abortion destroys what those decisions call "potential life" and what the law at issue in this case regards as the life of an "unborn human being." None of the other decisions cited by *Roe* and *Casey* involved the critical moral question posed by abortion. They are therefore inapposite. They do not support the right to obtain an abortion, and by the same token, our conclusion that the Constitution does not confer such a right does not undermine them in any way.

2 [Omitted]

D

1 and 2 [Omitted]

3

The most striking feature of the dissent is the absence of any serious discussion of the legitimacy of the States' interest in protecting fetal life. . . . The dissent has much to say about the effects of pregnancy on women, the burdens of motherhood, and the difficulties faced by poor women. These are important concerns. However, the dissent evinces no similar regard for a State's interest in protecting prenatal life. . . .

Our opinion is not based on any view about if and when prenatal life is entitled to any of the rights enjoyed after birth. The dissent, by contrast, would impose on the people a particular theory about when the rights of personhood begin. According to the dissent, the Constitution requires the States to regard a fetus as lacking even the most basic human right—to live—at least until an arbitrary point in a pregnancy has passed. Nothing in the Constitution or in our Nation's legal traditions authorizes the Court to adopt that theory of life.

III

We next consider whether the doctrine of stare decisis counsels continued acceptance of *Roe* and *Casey*. Stare decisis plays an important role in our case law, and we have explained that it serves many valuable ends. . . . We have long recognized, however, that stare decisis is not an inexorable command, and it is at its weakest when we interpret the Constitution. It has been said [quoting Justice

Brandeis] that it is sometimes more important that an issue "be settled than that it be settled right." But when it comes to the interpretation of the Constitution—the great charter of our liberties, which was meant to endure through a long lapse of ages—we place a high value on having the matter "settled right." In addition, when one of our constitutional decisions goes astray, the country is usually stuck with the bad decision unless we correct our own mistake. An erroneous constitutional decision can be fixed by amending the Constitution, but our Constitution is notoriously hard to amend. Therefore, in appropriate circumstances we must be willing to reconsider and, if necessary, overrule constitutional decisions.

Some of our most important constitutional decisions have overruled prior precedents. We mention three. In *Brown v. Board of Education* (1954), the Court repudiated the "separate but equal" doctrine, which had allowed States to maintain racially segregated schools and other facilities. In so doing, the Court overruled the infamous decision in *Plessy v. Ferguson* (1896), along with six other Supreme Court precedents that had applied the separate-but-equal rule.

In *West Coast Hotel Co. v. Parrish* (1937), the Court overruled *Adkins v. Children's Hospital of DC* (1923), which had held that a law setting minimum wages for women violated the "liberty" protected by the Fifth Amendment's Due Process Clause. *West Coast Hotel* signaled the demise of an entire line of important precedents that had protected an individual liberty right against state and federal health and welfare legislation. See *Lochner v. New York* (1905).

Finally, in *West Virginia Board. of Education v. Barnette* (1943), after the lapse of only three years, the Court overruled *Minersville School District v. Gobitis* (1940), and held that public school students could not be compelled to salute the flag in violation of their sincere beliefs. *Barnette* stands out because nothing had changed during the intervening period other than the Court's belated recognition that its earlier decision had been seriously wrong. . . .

No Justice of this Court has ever argued that the Court should never overrule a constitutional decision, but overruling a precedent is a serious matter. . . . In this case, five factors weigh strongly in favor of overruling *Roe* and *Casey*: the nature of their error, the quality of their reasoning, the "workability" of the rules they imposed on the country, their disruptive effect on other areas of the law, and the absence of concrete reliance.

A

The nature of the Court's error. An erroneous interpretation of the Constitution is always important, but some are more damaging than others.

The infamous decision in *Plessy v. Ferguson*, was one such decision. It betrayed our commitment to equality before the law. It was egregiously wrong on the day it was decided, and as the Solicitor General agreed at oral argument, it should have been overruled at the earliest opportunity.

Roe was also egregiously wrong and deeply damaging. For reasons already explained, *Roe*'s constitutional analysis was far outside the bounds of any reasonable interpretation of the various constitutional provisions to which it vaguely pointed.

Roe was on a collision course with the Constitution from the day it was decided, *Casey* perpetuated its errors, and those errors do not concern some arcane corner of the law of little importance to the American people. . . . *Roe* fanned into life an issue that has inflamed our national politics in general, and has obscured with its smoke the selection of Justices to this Court in particular, ever since. . . . As the Court's landmark decision in *West Coast Hotel* illustrates, the Court has previously overruled decisions that wrongly removed an issue from the people and the democratic process. . . .

B

The quality of the reasoning. Under our precedents, the quality of the reasoning in a prior case has an important bearing on whether it should be reconsidered. In Part II, we explained why *Roe* was incorrectly decided, but that decision was more than just wrong. It stood on exceptionally weak grounds [insofar as it ignored history, deviated from precedent, and assumed its own conclusions.]

1

The weaknesses in Roe's reasoning are well-known. . . .

[*Roe*] made little effort to explain how [its] rules could be deduced from any of the sources on which constitutional decisions are usually based. We have already discussed Roe's treatment of constitutional text, and the opinion failed to show that history, precedent, or any other cited source supported its scheme. . . .

An even more glaring deficiency was *Roe*'s failure to justify the critical distinction it drew between pre- and post-viability abortions. Here is the Court's entire explanation:

> With respect to the State's important and legitimate interest in potential life, the compelling point is at viability. This is so because the fetus then presumably has the capability of meaningful life outside the womb.

As Professor Laurence Tribe has written, "clearly, this mistakes a definition for a syllogism." The definition of a "viable" fetus is one that is capable of surviving outside the womb, but why is this the point at which the State's interest becomes compelling? If, as *Roe* held, a State's interest in protecting prenatal life is compelling after viability, why isn't that interest equally compelling before viability? *Roe* did not say, and no explanation is apparent. . . .

2

When *Casey* revisited *Roe* almost 20 years later . . . the Court retained what it called *Roe*'s "central holding"—that a State may not regulate pre-viability abortions for the purpose of protecting fetal life—but it provided no principled defense of the viability line. Instead, it merely rephrased what *Roe* had said, stating that viability marked the point at which "the independent existence of a second life can in reason and fairness be the object of state protection that now overrides the rights of the woman." Why "reason and fairness" demanded that the line be drawn at viability the Court did not explain. . . .

As discussed below, *Casey* also deployed a novel version of the doctrine of stare decisis. This new doctrine did not account for the profound wrongness of the decision in *Roe*, and placed great weight on an intangible form of reliance with little if any basis in prior case law. Stare decisis does not command the preservation of such a decision.

C

Workability. Our precedents counsel that another important consideration in deciding whether a precedent should be overruled is whether the rule it imposes is workable—that is, whether it can be understood and applied in a consistent and predictable manner. *Casey*'s "undue burden" test has scored poorly on the workability scale.

1

Problems begin with the very concept of an "undue burden." As Justice Scalia noted in his *Casey* partial dissent, determining whether a burden is due or undue is "inherently standardless." [The same is true of *Casey*'s language about whether a law's "purpose or effect is to place a *substantial* obstacle in the path of a woman seeking an abortion," and whether a pre-viability regulation on abortion is an "*unnecessary* health regulation."]

2

The difficulty of applying *Casey*'s new rules surfaced in that very case. The controlling opinion found that Pennsylvania's 24-hour waiting period requirement and its informed-consent provision did not impose "undue burdens," but Justice Stevens, applying the same test, reached the opposite result. That did not bode well, and then-Chief Justice Rehnquist aptly observed that "the undue burden standard presents nothing more workable than the [*Roe*] framework." . . .

3 [Omitted]

Dobbs v. Jackson Women's Health Organization

D

Effect on other areas of law. Roe and *Casey* have led to the distortion of many important but **unrelated legal doctrines**, and that effect provides further support for overruling those decisions. . . . The Court's abortion cases have diluted the strict standard for facial constitutional challenges. They have ignored the Court's third-party standing doctrine. They have disregarded standard res judicata principles. They have flouted the ordinary rules on the severability of unconstitutional provisions, as well as the rule that statutes should be read where possible to avoid unconstitutionality. And they have distorted First Amendment doctrines. . . .

■ HISTORY

UNRELATED LEGAL DOCTRINES: The majority alludes to accusations from dissenters that earlier majorities acted out of an excess of zeal to protect abortion rights. See, e.g., dissents in *June Medical Services LLC v. Russo*, 140 S. Ct. 2103 (2020). Before *Dobbs*, these complaints did not command a majority.

E

Reliance interests. We last consider whether overruling *Roe* and *Casey* will upend substantial reliance interests.

1 [Omitted]

2

. . . The controlling opinion in *Casey* . . . wrote that "people had organized intimate relationships and made choices that define their views of themselves and their places in society in reliance on the availability of abortion in the event that contraception should fail" and that "the ability of women to participate equally in the economic and social life of the Nation has been facilitated by their ability to control their reproductive lives." But this Court is ill-equipped to assess generalized assertions about the national psyche. *Casey*'s notion of reliance thus finds little support in our cases, which instead emphasize very concrete reliance interests, like those that develop in cases involving property and contract rights. . . .

The contending sides in this case make impassioned and conflicting arguments about the effects of the abortion right on the lives of women. The contending sides also make conflicting arguments about the status of the fetus. This Court has neither the authority nor the expertise to adjudicate those disputes, and the *Casey* plurality's speculations and weighing of the relative importance of the fetus and mother represent a departure from the original constitutional proposition that courts do not substitute their social and economic beliefs for the judgment of legislative bodies.

Our decision returns the issue of abortion to those legislative bodies, and it allows women on both sides of the abortion issue to seek to affect the legislative process by influencing public opinion, lobbying legislators, voting, and running for office. . . .

3

Unable to show concrete reliance on *Roe* and *Casey* themselves, the Solicitor General suggests that overruling those decisions would threaten the Court's precedents holding that the Due Process Clause protects other rights. (citing *Obergefell*; *Lawrence*; *Griswold*). That is not correct for reasons we have already discussed. As even the *Casey* plurality recognized, abortion is a unique act because it terminates life or potential life. And to ensure that our decision is not misunderstood or mischaracterized, we emphasize that our decision concerns the constitutional right to abortion and no other right. Nothing in this opinion should be understood to cast doubt on precedents that do not concern abortion.

IV

Having shown that traditional stare decisis factors do not weigh in favor of retaining *Roe* or *Casey*, we must address one final argument that featured prominently in the *Casey* plurality opinion.

The argument was cast in different terms, but stated simply, it was essentially as follows. The American people's belief in the rule of law would be shaken if they lost respect for this Court as an institution that decides important cases based on principle, not social and political pressures. . . .

This analysis starts out on the right foot but ultimately veers off course. The *Casey* plurality was certainly right that it is important for the public to perceive that our decisions are based on principle, and we should make every effort to achieve that objective by issuing opinions that carefully show how a proper understanding of the law leads to the results we reach. But we cannot exceed the scope of our authority under the Constitution, and we cannot allow our decisions to be affected by any extraneous influences such as concern about the public's reaction to our work. That is true both when we initially decide a constitutional issue and when we consider whether to overrule a prior decision. . . .

We do not pretend to know how our political system or society will respond to today's decision overruling *Roe* and *Casey*. And even if we could foresee what will happen, we would have no authority to let that knowledge influence our decision. We can only do our job, which is to interpret the law, apply longstanding principles of stare decisis, and decide this case accordingly. . . .

V [Omitted]

VI

We must now decide what standard will govern if state abortion regulations undergo constitutional challenge and whether the law before us satisfies the appropriate standard.

A

Under our precedents, rational-basis review is the appropriate standard for such challenges. As we have explained, procuring an abortion is not a fundamental constitutional right because such a right has no basis in the Constitution's text or in our Nation's history.

It follows that the States may regulate abortion for legitimate reasons, and when such regulations are challenged under the Constitution, courts cannot substitute their social and economic beliefs for the judgment of legislative bodies. See *United States v. Carolene Products Co.* (1938). That respect for a legislature's judgment applies even when the laws at issue concern matters of great social significance and moral substance. See, e.g., *Glucksberg* ("assisted suicide"); *San Antonio Independent School Dist. v. Rodriguez* (1973) ("financing public education").

A law regulating abortion, like other health and welfare laws, is entitled to a strong presumption of validity. It must be sustained if there is a rational basis on which the legislature could have thought that it would serve legitimate state interests. *Williamson v. Lee Optical of Oklahoma* (1955). These legitimate interests include respect for and preservation of prenatal life at all stages of development; the protection of maternal health and safety; the elimination of particularly gruesome or barbaric medical procedures; the preservation of the integrity of the medical profession; the mitigation of fetal pain; and the prevention of discrimination on the basis of race, sex, or disability.

B

These legitimate interests justify Mississippi's Gestational Age Act. . . .

VII

We end this opinion where we began. Abortion presents a profound moral question. The Constitution does not prohibit the citizens of each State from regulating or prohibiting abortion. *Roe* and *Casey* arrogated that authority. We now overrule those decisions and return that authority to the people and their elected representatives.

Justice Thomas, concurring.

I join the opinion of the Court because it correctly holds that there is no constitutional right to abortion. . . . I write separately to emphasize a second, more fundamental reason why there is no abortion guarantee lurking in the Due Process

Clause. . . . The Due Process Clause at most guarantees process. It does not, as the Court's substantive due process cases suppose, forbid the government to infringe certain "fundamental" liberty interests at all, no matter what process is provided.

As I have previously explained, "substantive due process" is an oxymoron that lacks any basis in the Constitution. . . . The resolution of this case is thus straightforward. Because the Due Process Clause does not secure any substantive rights, it does not secure a right to abortion. . . .

For that reason, in future cases, we should reconsider all of this Court's substantive due process precedents, including *Griswold* [right of married persons to obtain contraceptives], *Lawrence* [right to engage in private, consensual sexual acts], and *Obergefell* [right to same-sex marriage]. Because any substantive due process decision is demonstrably erroneous, we have a duty to correct the error. After overruling these demonstrably erroneous decisions, the question would remain whether other constitutional provisions guarantee the myriad rights that our substantive due process cases have generated. . . .

Justice Kavanaugh, concurring. [Omitted]

Chief Justice Roberts, concurring in the judgment.

. . . I agree with the Court that the viability line established by *Roe* and *Casey* should be discarded under a straightforward stare decisis analysis. That line never made any sense. Our abortion precedents describe the right at issue as a woman's right to choose to terminate her pregnancy. That right should therefore extend far enough to ensure a reasonable opportunity to choose, but need not extend any further—certainly not all the way to viability. Mississippi's law allows a woman three months to obtain an abortion, well beyond the point at which it is considered late to discover a pregnancy. I see no sound basis for questioning the adequacy of that opportunity.

But that is all I would say, out of adherence to a simple yet fundamental principle of judicial restraint: If it is not necessary to decide more to dispose of a case, then it is necessary not to decide more. Perhaps we are not always perfect in following that command, and certainly there are cases that warrant an exception. But this is not one of them. Surely we should adhere closely to principles of judicial restraint here, where the broader path the Court chooses entails repudiating a constitutional right we have not only previously recognized, but also expressly reaffirmed applying the doctrine of stare decisis. The Court's opinion is thoughtful and thorough, but those virtues cannot compensate for the fact that its dramatic and consequential ruling is unnecessary to decide the case before us. . . .

Both the Court's opinion and the dissent display a relentless freedom from doubt on the legal issue that I cannot share. . . . I therefore concur only in the judgment.

Justice Breyer, Justice Sotomayor, and Justice Kagan, dissenting.

Dobbs v. Jackson Women's Health Organization

For half a century, *Roe v. Wade* (1973) and *Planned Parenthood of Southeastern Pennsylvania v. Casey* (1992), have protected the liberty and equality of women. *Roe* held, and *Casey* reaffirmed, that the Constitution safeguards a woman's right to decide for herself whether to bear a child. *Roe* held, and *Casey* reaffirmed, that in the first stages of pregnancy, the government could not make that choice for women. The government could not control a woman's body or the course of a woman's life: It could not determine what the woman's future would be. Respecting a woman as an autonomous being, and granting her full equality, meant giving her substantial choice over this most personal and most consequential of all life decisions.

Roe and *Casey* well understood the difficulty and divisiveness of the abortion issue. The Court knew that Americans hold profoundly different views about the morality of terminating a pregnancy, even in its earliest stage. And the Court recognized that "the State has legitimate interests from the outset of the pregnancy in protecting" the "life of the fetus that may become a child." So the Court struck a balance, as it often does when values and goals compete. . . . Today, the Court discards that balance. It says that from the very moment of fertilization, a woman has no rights to speak of. A State can force her to bring a pregnancy to term, even at the steepest personal and familial costs. An abortion restriction, the majority holds, is permissible whenever rational, the lowest level of scrutiny known to the law. And because, as the Court has often stated, protecting fetal life is rational, States will feel free to enact all manner of restrictions. . . .

Whatever the exact scope of the coming laws, one result of today's decision is certain: the curtailment of women's rights, and of their status as free and equal citizens. . . . As of today, this Court holds, a State can always force a woman to give birth, prohibiting even the earliest abortions. . . . Some women, especially women of means, will find ways around the State's assertion of power. Others—those without money or childcare or the ability to take time off from work—will not be so fortunate. Maybe they will try an unsafe method of abortion, and come to physical harm, or even die. Maybe they will undergo pregnancy and have a child, but at significant personal or familial cost. At the least, they will incur the cost of losing control of their lives. The Constitution will, today's majority holds, provide no shield, despite its guarantees of liberty and equality for all.

And no one should be confident that this majority is done with its work. . . . The majority could write just as long an opinion showing, for example, that until the mid-20th century, there was no support in American law for a constitutional right to obtain contraceptives. . . . One piece of evidence on that score seems especially salient: The majority's cavalier approach to overturning this Court's precedents. . . . Stare decisis, this Court has often said, contributes to the actual and perceived integrity of the judicial process by ensuring that decisions are founded in the law rather than in the proclivities of individuals. Today, the proclivities of individuals rule. The Court departs from its obligation to faithfully and impartially apply the law. We dissent.

I

We start with *Roe* and *Casey*, and with their deep connections to a broad swath of this Court's precedents. To hear the majority tell the tale, *Roe* and *Casey* are aberrations: They came from nowhere, went nowhere—and so are easy to excise from this Nation's constitutional law. That is not true. . . .

A

Some half-century ago, *Roe* struck down a state law making it a crime to perform an abortion unless its purpose was to save a woman's life. The *Roe* Court knew it was treading on difficult and disputed ground. It understood that different people's experiences, values, and religious training and beliefs led to opposing views about abortion. But by a 7-to-2 vote, the Court held that in the earlier stages of pregnancy, that contested and contestable choice must belong to a woman, in consultation with her family and doctor. The Court explained that a long line of precedents, founded in the Fourteenth Amendment's concept of personal liberty, protected individual decision-making related to marriage, procreation, contraception, family relationships, and child rearing and education. For the same reasons, the Court held, the Constitution must protect a woman's decision whether or not to terminate her pregnancy. . . . At the same time, though, the Court recognized valid interests of the State in regulating the abortion decision. The Court noted in particular important interests in protecting potential life, maintaining medical standards, and safeguarding the health of the woman. No absolutist account of the woman's right could wipe away those significant state claims.

The Court therefore struck a balance, turning on the stage of the pregnancy at which the abortion would occur. . . . Then, in *Casey*, the Court considered the matter anew, and again upheld *Roe*'s core precepts. . . . Central to that conclusion was a full-throated restatement of a woman's right to choose. Like *Roe*, *Casey* grounded that right in the Fourteenth Amendment's guarantee of liberty. That guarantee encompasses realms of conduct not specifically referenced in the Constitution: Marriage is mentioned nowhere in that document, yet the Court was no doubt correct to protect the freedom to marry against state interference. And the guarantee of liberty encompasses conduct today that was not protected at the time of the Fourteenth Amendment. "It is settled now," the Court said—though it was not always so—that "the Constitution places limits on a State's right to interfere with a person's most basic decisions about family and parenthood, as well as bodily integrity." . . .

We make one initial point about this analysis in light of the majority's insistence that *Roe* and *Casey*, and we in defending them, are dismissive of a "State's interest in protecting prenatal life." Nothing could get those decisions more wrong. As just described, *Roe* and *Casey* invoked powerful state interests in that protection, operative at every stage of the pregnancy and overriding the woman's liberty after viability. The strength of those state interests is exactly why the Court allowed greater restrictions on the abortion right than on other rights deriving from the Fourteenth Amendment. . . . The constitutional regime we have lived in for the last 50 years recognized competing interests, and sought a balance between them. The constitutional regime we enter today erases the woman's interest and recognizes only the State's (or the Federal Government's).

Dobbs v. Jackson Women's Health Organization

B

The majority makes this change based on a single question: Did the reproductive right recognized in *Roe* and *Casey* exist in 1868, the year when the Fourteenth Amendment was ratified? The majority says (and with this much we agree) that the answer to this question is no: In 1868, there was no nationwide right to end a pregnancy, and no thought that the Fourteenth Amendment provided one. . . .

[We disagree with the majority's reliance on, and portrayal of, ancient common law sources stretching back to the 13th century. Regardless,] the majority's core legal postulate . . . is that we in the 21st century must read the Fourteenth Amendment just as its ratifiers did. And that is indeed what the majority emphasizes over and over again. If the ratifiers did not understand something as central to freedom, then neither can we. Or said more particularly: If those people did not understand reproductive rights as part of the guarantee of liberty conferred in the Fourteenth Amendment, then those rights do not exist.

As an initial matter, note a mistake in the just preceding sentence. We referred there to the "people" who ratified the Fourteenth Amendment: What rights did those "people" have in their heads at the time? But, of course, "people" did not ratify the Fourteenth Amendment. Men did. So it is perhaps not so surprising that the ratifiers were not perfectly attuned to the importance of reproductive rights for women's liberty, or for their capacity to participate as equal members of our Nation. Indeed, the ratifiers—both in 1868 and when the original Constitution was approved in 1788—did not understand women as full members of the community embraced by the phrase "We the People." In 1868, the first wave of American feminists were explicitly told—of course by men—that it was **not their time** to seek constitutional protections. (Women would not get even the vote for another half-century.) To be sure, most women in 1868 also had a foreshortened view of their rights: If most men could not then imagine giving women control over their bodies, most women could not imagine having that

■ HISTORY

NOT THEIR TIME: The dissent alludes to § 2 of the Fourteenth Amendment, which created a penalty to dissuade states from disenfranchising former slaves. That section reduces representation in the House for any State that denies the vote "to any of the male inhabitants of such State." Feminists argued unsuccessfully that this provision should not be limited by sex.

kind of autonomy. But that takes away nothing from the core point. Those responsible for the original Constitution, including the Fourteenth Amendment, did not perceive women as equals, and did not recognize women's rights. When the majority says that we must read our foundational charter as viewed at the time of ratification (except that we may also check it against [legal treatises from] the Dark Ages), it consigns women to second-class citizenship. . . .

So how is it that, as *Casey* said, our Constitution, read now, grants rights to women, though it did not in 1868? . . .

The answer is that this Court has rejected the majority's pinched view of how to read our Constitution. "The Founders," we recently wrote, "knew they were writing a document designed to apply to ever-changing circumstances over centuries." *NLRB v. Noel Canning*, 573 U.S. 513 (2014). Or in the words of the great Chief Justice John Marshall, our Constitution is "intended to endure for ages to come," and must adapt itself to a future "seen dimly," if at all. *McCulloch v. Maryland* (1819). That is indeed why our Constitution is written as it is. The Framers (both in 1788 and 1868) understood that the world changes. So they did not define rights by reference to the specific practices existing at the time. Instead, the Framers defined rights in general terms, to permit future evolution in their scope and meaning. And over the course of our history, this Court has taken up the Framers' invitation. It has kept true to the Framers' principles by applying them in new ways, responsive to new societal understandings and conditions. . . .

That does not mean anything goes. The majority wishes people to think there are but two alternatives: (1) accept the original applications of the Fourteenth Amendment and no others, or (2) surrender to judges' own ardent views, ungrounded in law, about the liberty that Americans should enjoy. . . . [To the contrary,] applications of liberty and equality can evolve while remaining grounded in constitutional principles, constitutional history, and constitutional precedents. The second Justice Harlan discussed how to strike the right balance when he explained why he would have invalidated a State's ban on contraceptive use. Judges, he said, are not free to roam where unguided speculation might take them. *Poe v. Ullman*, 367 U.S. 497 (1961) (dissenting opinion). Yet they also must recognize that the constitutional "tradition" of this country is not captured whole at a single moment. Rather, its meaning gains content from the long sweep of our history and from successive judicial precedents—each looking to the last and each seeking to apply the Constitution's most fundamental commitments to new conditions. That is why Americans . . . have a right to marry across racial lines. And it is why, to go back to Justice Harlan's case, Americans have a right to use contraceptives so they can choose for themselves whether to have children.

All that is what *Casey* understood. Casey explicitly rejected the present majority's method. "The specific practices of States at the time of the adoption of the Fourteenth Amendment," Casey stated, do not "mark the outer limits of the substantive sphere of liberty which the Fourteenth Amendment protects." To hold otherwise—as the majority does today—"would be inconsistent with our law." Why? Because the Court has vindicated the principle over and over that (no matter the sentiment in 1868) there is a realm of personal liberty which the government may not enter—especially relating to bodily integrity and family life. . . .

Dobbs v. Jackson Women's Health Organization

Consider first, [as proof of this principle], the line of this Court's cases protecting bodily integrity. "No right," in this Court's time-honored view, "is held more sacred, or is more carefully guarded," than "the right of every individual to the possession and control of his own person." ***Union Pacific Railroad Co. v. Botsford***, 141 U.S. 250 (1891). Or to put it more simply: Everyone, including women, owns their own bodies. So the Court has restricted the power of government to interfere with a person's medical decisions or compel her to undergo medical procedures or treatments. See, e.g., *Winston v. Lee*, 470 U.S. 753 (1985) (forced surgery); *Rochin v. California*, 342 U.S. 165 (1952) (forced stomach pumping); *Washington v. Harper*, 494 U.S. 210 (1990) (forced administration of antipsychotic drugs). . . .

HISTORY

BOTSFORD: This decision held that no existing law required a tort plaintiff to submit to an independent medical examination before trial. (Such exams are now authorized by Federal Rule of Civil Procedure 35.) The full sentence from *Botsford* reads: "No right is held more sacred, or is more carefully guarded by the common law, than the right of every individual to the possession and control of his own person, free from all restraint or interference of others, unless by clear and unquestionable authority of law."

There are few greater incursions on a body than forcing a woman to complete a pregnancy and give birth. For every woman, those experiences involve all manner of physical changes, medical treatments (including the possibility of a cesarean section), and medical risk. Just as one example, an American woman is 14 times more likely to die by carrying a pregnancy to term than by having an abortion. That women happily undergo those burdens and hazards of their own accord does not lessen how far a State impinges on a woman's body when it compels her to bring a pregnancy to term. And for some women, as *Roe* recognized, abortions are medically necessary to prevent harm. . . .

So too, *Roe* and *Casey* fit neatly into a long line of decisions protecting from government intrusion a wealth of private choices about family matters, child rearing, intimate relationships, and procreation. . . . In varied cases, the Court explained that those choices—the most intimate and personal a person can make—reflect fundamental aspects of personal identity; they define the very attributes of personhood. And they inevitably shape the nature and future course of a person's life (and often the lives of those closest to her). So, the Court held, those choices belong to the individual, and not the government. . . .

Faced with all these connections between *Roe/Casey* and judicial decisions recognizing other constitutional rights, the majority tells everyone not to worry. It can (so it says) neatly extract the right to choose from the constitutional edifice without affecting any associated rights. (Think of someone telling you that the Jenga tower simply will not collapse.) . . . According to the majority, no liberty interest is present [in this case]—because (and only because) the law offered no protection to the woman's choice in the 19th century. But here is the rub. The law also did not then (and would not for ages) protect a wealth of other things. It did not protect the rights recognized in *Lawrence* and *Obergefell* to same-sex intimacy and marriage. It did not protect the right recognized in *Loving* to marry across racial lines. It did not protect the right recognized in *Griswold* to contraceptive use. For that matter, it did not protect the right recognized in *Skinner v. Oklahoma* (1942), not to be sterilized without consent. So if the majority is right in its legal analysis, all those decisions were wrong, and all those matters properly belong to the States too—whatever the particular state interests involved. . . .

As a matter of constitutional method, the majority's commitment to replicate in 2022 every view about the meaning of liberty held in 1868 has precious little to recommend it. Our law in this constitutional sphere, as in most, has for decades upon decades proceeded differently. . . . It relies on accumulated judgments, not just the sentiments of one long-ago generation of men (who themselves believed, and drafted the Constitution to reflect, that the world progresses). And by doing so, it includes those excluded from that olden conversation, rather than perpetuating its bounds.

As a matter of constitutional substance, the majority's opinion has all the flaws its method would suggest. Because laws in 1868 deprived women of any control over their bodies, the majority approves States doing so today. . . . Today's decision strips women of agency over what even the majority agrees is a contested and contestable moral issue. It forces her to carry out the State's will, whatever the circumstances and whatever the harm it will wreak on her and her family. In the Fourteenth Amendment's terms, it takes away her liberty. Even before we get to stare decisis, we dissent.

II

By overruling *Roe*, *Casey*, and more than 20 [US Supreme Court] cases reaffirming or applying the constitutional right to abortion, the majority abandons stare decisis, a principle central to the rule of law. . . . Stare decisis is, of course, not an inexorable command; it is sometimes appropriate to overrule an earlier decision. But the Court must have a good reason to do so over and above the belief that the precedent was wrongly decided. . . . Whether or not we agree with a prior precedent is the beginning, not the end, of our analysis—and the remaining principles of stare decisis weigh heavily against overruling *Roe* and *Casey*. . . .

A

Contrary to the majority's view, there is nothing unworkable about *Casey*'s undue burden standard. Its primary focus on whether a State has placed a "substantial obstacle" on a woman seeking an abortion is the sort of inquiry familiar to judges across a variety of contexts. And it has given rise to no more conflict in application than many standards this Court and others unhesitatingly apply every day.

General standards, like the undue burden standard, are ubiquitous in the law, and particularly in constitutional adjudication. When called on to give effect to the Constitution's broad principles, this Court often crafts flexible standards that can be applied case-by-case to a myriad of unforeseeable circumstances. So, for example, the Court asks about undue or substantial burdens on speech, on voting, and on interstate commerce. . . . Applying general standards to particular cases is, in many contexts, just what it means to do law.

And the undue burden standard has given rise to no unusual difficulties. Of course, it has provoked some disagreement among judges. *Casey* knew it would: That much "is to be expected in the application of any legal standard which must accommodate life's complexity." Which is to say: That much is to be expected in the application of any legal standard. . . .

B

When overruling constitutional precedent, the Court has almost always pointed to major legal or factual changes undermining a decision's original basis. . . . The majority throws longstanding precedent to the winds without showing that anything significant has changed to justify its radical reshaping of the law.

1

Subsequent legal developments have only reinforced *Roe* and *Casey*. The Court has continued to embrace all the decisions *Roe* and *Casey* cited, decisions which recognize a constitutional right for an individual to make her own choices about intimate relationships, the family, and contraception. *Roe* and *Casey* have themselves formed the legal foundation for subsequent decisions protecting these profoundly personal choices. . . . While the majority might wish it otherwise, *Roe* and *Casey* are the very opposite of obsolete constitutional thinking.

Moreover, no subsequent factual developments have undermined *Roe* and *Casey*. Women continue to experience unplanned pregnancies and unexpected developments in pregnancies. Pregnancies continue to have enormous physical, social, and economic consequences. Even an uncomplicated pregnancy imposes significant strain on the body, unavoidably involving significant physiological change and excruciating pain. For some women, pregnancy and childbirth can mean life-altering physical ailments or even death. . . .

2

In support of its holding, the majority invokes two watershed cases overruling prior constitutional precedents: *West Coast Hotel Co. v. Parrish* and *Brown v. Board of Education*. But those decisions, unlike today's, responded to changed law and to changed facts and attitudes that had taken hold throughout society. As *Casey* recognized, the two cases are relevant only to show—by stark contrast—how unjustified overturning the right to choose is.

West Coast Hotel overruled *Adkins v. Children's Hospital of DC* (1923), and a whole line of cases beginning with *Lochner v. New York* (1905). *Adkins* had found a state minimum-wage law unconstitutional because, in the Court's view, the law interfered with a constitutional right to contract. But then the Great Depression hit, bringing with it unparalleled economic despair. The experience undermined—in fact, it disproved—*Adkins*'s assumption that a wholly unregulated market could meet basic human needs. . . .

Brown v. Board of Education overruled *Plessy v. Ferguson*, along with its doctrine of "separate but equal." By 1954, decades of Jim Crow had made clear what *Plessy*'s turn of phrase actually meant: inherent inequality. Segregation was not, and could not ever be, consistent with the Reconstruction Amendments, ratified to give the former slaves full citizenship. Whatever might have been thought in *Plessy*'s time, the *Brown* Court explained, both experience and modern authority showed the detrimental effects of state-sanctioned segregation: It "affected children's hearts and minds in a way unlikely ever to be undone." By that point, too, the law had begun to reflect that understanding. . . . Changed facts and changed law required *Plessy*'s end. . . .

If the *Brown* Court had used the majority's method of constitutional construction, it might not ever have overruled *Plessy*, whether 5 or 50 or 500 years later. *Brown* thought that whether the ratification-era history supported desegregation was "at best inconclusive." But even setting that aside, we are not saying that a decision can never be overruled just because it is terribly wrong. Take *West Virginia Board of Education v. Barnette*, which the majority also relies on. That overruling took place just three years after the initial decision, before any notable reliance interests had developed. It happened as well because individual Justices changed their minds, not because a new majority wanted to undo the decisions of their predecessors. Both *Barnette* and *Brown*, moreover, share another feature setting them apart from the Court's ruling today. They protected individual rights with a strong basis in the Constitution's most fundamental commitments; they did not, as the majority does here, take away a right that individuals have held, and relied on, for 50 years. . . .

C

. . . When overruling precedent would dislodge individuals' settled rights and expectations, stare decisis has added force. . . . By characterizing *Casey*'s reliance arguments as "generalized assertions about the national psyche," it reveals how little it knows or cares about women's lives or about the suffering its decision will cause. . . .

Abortion is a common medical procedure and a familiar experience in women's lives. About 18 percent of pregnancies in this country end in abortion, and about one quarter of American women will have an abortion before the age of 45. Those numbers reflect the predictable and life-changing effects of carrying a pregnancy, giving birth, and becoming a parent. As *Casey* understood, people today rely on their ability to control and time pregnancies when making countless life decisions: where to live, whether and how to invest in education or careers, how to allocate financial resources, and how to approach intimate and family relationships. Women may count on abortion access for when contraception fails. They may count on abortion access for when contraception cannot be used, for example, if they were raped. They may count on abortion for when something changes in the midst of a pregnancy, whether it involves family or financial circumstances, unanticipated medical complications, or heartbreaking fetal diagnoses. Taking away the right to abortion, as the majority does today, destroys all those individual plans and expectations. In so doing, it diminishes women's opportunities to participate fully and equally in the Nation's political, social, and economic life. . . .

That is especially so for women without money. When we count the cost of *Roe*'s repudiation on women who once relied on that decision, it is not hard to see where the greatest burden will fall. In States that bar abortion, women of means will still be able to travel to obtain the services they need. It is women who cannot afford to do so who will suffer most. These are the women most likely to seek abortion care in the first place. Women living below the federal poverty line experience unintended pregnancies at rates five times higher than higher income women do, and nearly half of women who seek abortion care live in households below the poverty line. . . .

The Court's failure to perceive the whole swath of expectations *Roe* and *Casey* created reflects an impoverished view of reliance. According to the majority, a reliance interest must be "very concrete," like those involving property or contract. . . . The interests women have in *Roe* and *Casey* are perfectly, viscerally concrete. Countless women will now make different decisions about careers, education, relationships, and whether to try to become pregnant than they would have when Roe served as a backstop. . . .

D

One last consideration counsels against the majority's ruling: the very controversy surrounding *Roe* and *Casey*. . . . *Casey* addressed the national controversy in order to emphasize how important it was, in that case of all cases, for the Court to stick to the law. Would that today's majority had done likewise. . . .

Here, more than anywhere, the Court needs to apply the law—particularly the law of stare decisis. Here, we know that citizens will continue to contest the Court's decision, because men and women of good conscience deeply disagree about abortion. When that contestation takes place—but when there is no legal basis for reversing course—the Court needs to be steadfast, to stand its ground. That is what the rule of law requires. And that is what respect for this Court depends on. . . .

Justice Jackson once called a decision he dissented from a "loaded weapon," ready to hand for improper uses. *Korematsu v. United States* (1944). We fear that today's decision, departing from stare decisis for no legitimate reason, is its own loaded weapon. . . .

III

Power, not reason, is the new currency of this Court's decision-making. . . . Mississippi—and other States too—knew exactly what they were doing in ginning up new legal challenges to *Roe* and *Casey*. . . . Mississippi itself decided in 2019 that it had not gone far enough: The year after enacting the law under review, the State passed a 6-week restriction. A state senator who championed both Mississippi laws said the obvious out loud. "A lot of people thought," he explained, that "finally, we have" a conservative Court "and so now would be a good time to start testing the limits of *Roe*." . . .

Now a new and bare majority of this Court—acting at practically the first moment possible—overrules *Roe* and *Casey*. It converts a series of dissenting opinions expressing antipathy toward *Roe* and *Casey* into a decision greenlighting even total abortion bans. It eliminates a 50-year-old constitutional right that safeguards women's freedom and equal station. It breaches a core rule-of-law principle, designed to promote constancy in the law. In doing all of that, it places in jeopardy other rights, from contraception to same-sex intimacy and marriage. And finally, it undermines the Court's legitimacy. . . .

With sorrow—for this Court, but more, for the many millions of American women who have today lost a fundamental constitutional protection—we dissent.

flashforward

The *Dobbs* majority sought to return abortion decisions to states, which may have their own relevant constitutional provisions. A variety of state constitutional approaches have already developed, but are also subject to change.

1. *Text of State Constitutions.* Most state constitutions have no text specifically mentioning abortion; where state abortion rights have been recognized, they have been based on constitutional text speaking of "due process," "privacy," "equality," "privileges," or other individual rights language. Before *Dobbs*, provisions expressly declaring that the state constitution does not protect a right to abortion had been added to the constitutions of Tennessee (2014), Alabama (2018), West Virginia (2018) and Louisiana (2020). Months after *Dobbs*, voters in five states considered proposals for abortion-specific amendments.

- Voters in California, Michigan, and Vermont added "reproductive freedom" language to their respective bills of rights in November 2022.
- In Kansas, the state Supreme Court had previously found a state constitutional right to abortion under a provision stating: "all men are possessed of equal and inalienable natural rights, among which are life, liberty, and pursuit of happiness." *Hodes & Nauser v. Schmidt*, 440 P.3d 461 (Kan. 2019). In November 2022, voters rejected a proposed "no right to abortion" amendment intended to overrule that decision.
- In Kentucky, there had been no rulings about abortion under the state constitution. After *Dobbs*, litigation had begun in connection with a trigger law. *EMW Women's Surgical Center v. Cameron*, 2022 WL 36512196 (Ky. 2022). In November 2022, with that case pending, voters rejected a proposed "no right to abortion" amendment.

2. *State Court Opinions.* State supreme courts have the final word on the meaning of state constitutions, Ch. 4.C, and they may reach independent results even when interpreting state constitutional clauses with similarly-worded federal counterparts. For example, the Minnesota Bill of Rights contains near-verbatim versions of the federal Due Process Clauses and Fourth Amendment, but also language stating that "government is instituted for the security, benefit and protection of the people" and language guaranteeing "the rights or privileges secured to any citizen." The Minnesota Supreme Court has held that these provisions give rise to a right of privacy (in the *Griswold* sense) that affords "broader protection than the United States Constitution of a woman's fundamental right to reach a private decision on whether to obtain an abortion." *Women of the State of Minnesota by Doe v. Gomez*, 542 N.W.2d 17 (1995) (state Medicaid plan must cover abortion, even if not federally required).

Meanwhile, the Iowa Supreme Court changed its view of how the state due process clause applied to abortion. In 2015, it rejected the undue burden standard from *Casey*, instead requiring that abortion restrictions satisfy strict scrutiny. *Planned Parenthood of the Heartland, Inc. v. Reynolds*, 915 N.W.2d 206 (Iowa 2018) (invalidating 72-hour waiting period). In the ensuing years, four new justices joined the seven-member court. The newly constituted court overruled the earlier decision a week before *Dobbs* was announced, saying that under the Iowa Constitution, abortion was not a fundamental right and strict scrutiny was not required—but leaving open which standard should control instead (undue burden, rational basis, or something else). *Planned Parenthood of the Heartland, Inc. v. Reynolds*, 975 N.W.2d 710 (Iowa 2022). The litigation continues as this edition goes to press.

3. *Mississippi After* Dobbs. In 2007, Mississippi enacted a trigger law that would go into effect if and when the US Supreme Court overruled *Roe v. Wade*. This meant that although *Dobbs* upheld Mississippi's 15-week statute enacted in 2018, the decision had the indirect effect of making the statute irrelevant. Under the new law, "No abortion shall be performed or induced in the State of Mississippi, except in the case where necessary for the preservation of the mother's life or where the pregnancy was caused by rape" that has been formally filed with a law enforcement official.

The Mississippi Supreme Court had previously ruled that several provisions in the state constitution—and particularly its analogue to the Ninth Amendment—combined to create a right to privacy which extended to abortion. *Pro-Choice Mississippi v. Fordice*, 716 So.2d 645 (Miss. 1998). When the trigger law took effect after *Dobbs*, the trial court declined to enjoin it, predicting that the state supreme court would overrule *Fordice* at the first opportunity. *Jackson Women's Health Organization v. Dobbs*, No. 25CH1:22-cv-00739 (Miss. Chancery 2022). The litigation continues as this edition goes to press.

Chapter Recap

A. The Due Process Clause has been interpreted to protect some unenumerated rights against government regulation. The logic behind these interpretations is that certain unenumerated rights are forms of "liberty" that cannot be deprived no matter which procedures might be used. Because this approach limits the substance of laws (not only the procedures through which they are implemented), it is known as substantive due process.

B. Substantive due process protects only those liberty interests that are considered "fundamental." After the rejection of *Lochner*, freedom of contract is not considered a fundamental right. The fundamental rights protected by modern substantive due process have been non-economic.

C. Judges sometimes differ over which rights should be considered fundamental.

D. Although there is consensus that laws burdening fundamental rights will be subjected to heightened scrutiny, the content of that scrutiny varies across factual settings.

CHAPTER 21

Exceptions to the State Action Doctrine

As the law that governs the government, a constitution does not generally govern the actions of private individuals. The term most often used for this concept under the US Constitution is *state action.* (When used in this context, the phrase "state action" means "government action" at any level: federal, state, or local.) If the government conducts an unreasonable search or discriminates on the basis of race, its state action would violate the Fourth Amendment or the Equal Protection Clause. If a private person conducts an unreasonable search or discriminates on the basis of race, there is no state action and no constitutional violation—although there might be a violation of statutes or common law.

State Action and Private Action

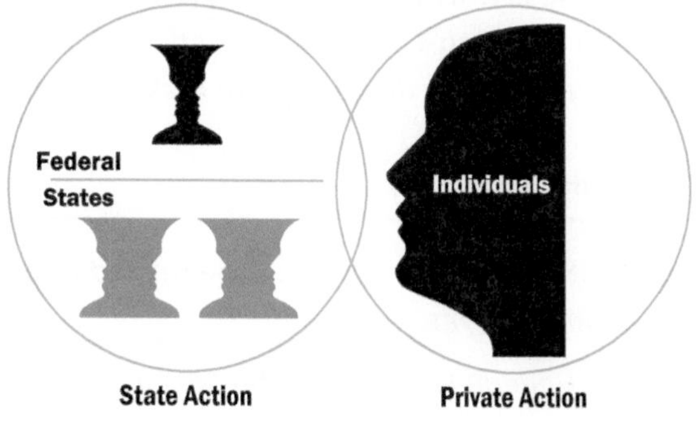

Lugar v. Edmondson Oil Co., 457 U.S. 922 (1982), explained some of the purposes served by the US Constitution's state action requirement.

> Careful adherence to the state action requirement preserves an area of individual freedom by limiting the reach of federal law and federal judicial power. It also avoids imposing on the State, its agencies or officials, responsibility for conduct for which they cannot fairly be blamed. A major consequence is to

require the courts to respect the limits of their own power as directed against state governments and private interests. Whether this is good or bad policy, it is a fundamental fact of our political order.

Although state action is usually easy to distinguish from private action, some (relatively narrow) areas of overlap exist. In those settings, the Supreme Court has made an exception to the state action doctrine, holding that some private persons or entities will have an obligation to respect constitutional rights.

Given the enormous variety of interactions between the government and private parties, the cases involving exceptions to the state action doctrine are difficult to categorize. They tend not to announce bright-line rules. Instead, these cases have a family resemblance, sharing a number of features but in no mandatory combination. As explained in *Brentwood Academy v. TSSAA*, 531 U.S. 288 (2001), the question "is a matter of normative judgment, and the criteria lack rigid simplicity." When making these judgments, "no one fact can function as a necessary condition across the board for finding state action; nor is any set of circumstances absolutely sufficient, for there may be some countervailing reason against attributing activity to the government."

A. Kickstarter: State Action Exceptions

DISCLAIMER: *This Kickstarter is a checklist to help identify relevant issues. It is not a list of elements. Nothing requires judges to write their opinions (or lawyers to write their briefs) in Kickstarter order.*

State Action Exceptions **kickstarter**

USE WHEN: *A private party should be treated as a state actor obligated to respect constitutional rights.*

A. *General Rule: Unless the text indicates otherwise, the US Constitution governs state action, not private action.*

B. *Exception: In some circumstances, private parties will be treated as state actors in light of the government's relationship to the challenged action, to the private actor, or both. In deciding whether state action exists, courts may consider items from this (non-exclusive) list:*

   1. *Whether the private actor performs a function traditionally performed by the government.*

   2. *Whether the government has significant involvement with the private action.*

3. *Whether the private actor exercises a power bestowed by the government.*
4. *Whether the government encouraged or endorsed the alleged violation.*
5. *Whether the alleged violation is a privatized version of governmental conduct already held to be unconstitutional.*
6. *The nature of the alleged constitutional violation.*
7. *The usual methods of constitutional reasoning.*

KICKSTARTER USER'S GUIDE

Under modern law, exceptions to the state action requirement are relatively rare. Far more cases enforce the rule (the Constitution does not regulate private persons) than enforce the narrow exception (sometimes private persons should be treated as if they were the government). The most potentially far-reaching uses of the doctrine were from mid-20th century cases decided by the New Deal and Warren Courts. The Burger, Rehnquist, and Roberts courts have been less likely to find exceptions to the state action requirement. Nonetheless, the earlier cases have not been overruled and it remains current law that exceptions may sometimes be found—even if the necessary facts are likely to be atypical.

Item A. *The General Rule.* The baseline rule—that only the government or its agents are capable of violating the Constitution—derives primarily from the structural fact that a constitution is the law that governs the government. Some portions of constitutional text also reinforce this result, such as the Fourteenth Amendment's directive that "no State" may violate equal protection or due process, or the directives in the Fifteenth, Nineteenth, Twenty-Fourth, and Twenty-Sixth Amendments that voting rights should not be abridged "by the United States or by any State." If it is written that way, constitutional text may apply directly to private parties with no state action requirement. Hence, the Thirteenth Amendment declares that "neither slavery nor involuntary servitude . . . shall exist within the United States," even if it is entirely private.

flashback

In *The Civil Rights Cases* (1883) (Ch. 7.C.2), the Supreme Court held that Congress's enumerated power in § 5 of the Fourteenth Amendment could only be used to enact federal laws against conduct by state actors, not private actors. See also Ch. 15.E. The Supreme Court left this principle untouched in *Heart of Atlanta Motel* (1964) (Ch. 12.D.1), and reiterated it in *United States v. Morrison* (2000) (Ch. 15.C.2.b). Although *The Civil Rights Cases* were the most prominent early announcement of the state action doctrine, similar ideas had been voiced in *United States v. Cruikshank* (1876) (Ch. 7.C.1.d), which said, "The fourteenth amendment prohibits a State from depriving any person of life, liberty, or property, without due process of law; but this adds nothing to the rights of one citizen as against another."

State action exists when a legislature enacts a law. It also exists when executive branch employees act in the course of their official duties. As *Lugar* explained, "state employment is generally sufficient to render the defendant a state actor." The same principle applies to persons who hold government offices, but are not full-time employees performing functions ordinarily viewed as governmental. For example, in *Commonwealth of Pennsylvania v. Board of Directors of City Trusts of Pennsylvania*, 353 U.S. 230 (1957), a donor had created a trust in 1831 to operate a school for "poor white male orphans." The trust and its school were administered by a Board appointed by the City of Philadelphia. "Even though the Board was acting as a trustee" and not in a customary sovereign capacity, its actions constituted "discrimination by the State" in violation of the Equal Protection Clause.

Item B. *Exceptions.* On occasion, private action may be "fairly attributable" to the government. *Lugar v. Edmondson Oil Co.*, 457 U.S. 922 (1982). In such cases, a private party who has been deemed a state actor may be sued civilly if that person's (state) action has violated someone's rights to equal protection, to due process, to freedom of speech or religion, or to other rights guaranteed by the Constitution. In most cases, the statutory vehicle for the liability will be 42 U.S.C. § 1983, the Reconstruction-era statute authorizing civil suits for violations of federal constitutional rights by persons acting "under color of" state law, i.e., by state actors.

Cases asking whether private actors must respect federal constitutional rights tend to be fact-specific. A lawyer with a contract to provide public defender services is not a state actor, but a doctor with a contract to provide health care to prisoners is. Compare *Polk County v. Dodson*, 454 U.S. 312 (1981) with *West v. Atkins*, 487 U.S. 42 (1988). The National Collegiate Athletic Association—the association setting rules for college sporting events—is not a state actor, but the equivalent association for Tennessee high schools is. Compare *NCAA v. Tarkanian*, 488 U.S. 179 (1988) with *Brentwood Academy v. TSSAA*, 531 U.S. 288 (2001).

As these examples indicate, the state action cases do not easily crystallize into bright-line rules. And as one might expect with doctrines that rely on family resemblance or multi-factor balancing, there is no universally agreed-upon method for approaching state action questions. *Lugar* suggested breaking the inquiry into two steps (one focused on the nature of the action, and one focused on the actor's relationship to the government), but later cases have not treated this as mandatory. In the absence of any formula, the most honest description of the sometimes-inconsistent state action cases is that they consider a variety of factors that may point in different directions depending on the facts.

Item B.1. *Traditional Government Functions.* Some state action cases emphasize that functions traditionally performed by the government should be performed according to constitutional standards. This can be seen most vividly in *Marsh v. Alabama*, 326 U.S. 501 (1946), the earliest of the cases recognizing an exception to the state action doctrine. The "company town" of Chickasaw, Alabama, looked just like any other city: it had streets, sidewalks, residential housing, businesses, sewer systems, a post office, and a police officer. But the land and buildings were owned by the private Gulf Shipbuilding Corp., which claimed the right to treat the town as its private property—including the right to order Grace Marsh, a Jehovah's Witness, to stop distributing religious leaflets on the sidewalk in front of the post office. The Supreme Court framed the question this way: "Can those people who live in or come to Chickasaw be denied freedom of press and religion simply because a single company has legal title to all the town?" The answer was no. "Since these facilities are built and operated primarily to benefit the public and since their operation is essentially a public function, it is subject to state regulation." Moreover, "Whether a corporation or a municipality owns or possesses the town, the public in either case has an identical interest in the functioning of the community in such manner that the channels of communication remain free. . . . The managers appointed by the corporation cannot curtail the liberty of press and religion of these people consistently with the purposes of the Constitutional guarantees."

The idea from *Marsh*—that the public is entitled to have governmental functions performed according to governmental standards—leaves room for debate over which functions are inherently governmental. The Supreme Court has said that elections for public office are a traditional government function, so that all-White political party primaries violate the Constitution, even if they are in theory performed by private political associations. *Smith v. Allwright*, 321 U.S. 649 (1944); *Terry v. Adams*, 345 U.S. 461 (1953). By contrast, operating an electrical power plant is not traditionally governmental. In *Jackson v. Metropolitan Edison Co.*, 419 U.S. 345 (1974), the plaintiff objected that a private but heavily regulated electrical utility denied procedural due process by cutting off her power without adequate notice and opportunity to be heard. The Supreme Court held that providing electrical power was not a function "traditionally associated with sovereignty" or "traditionally exclusively reserved" to the government. Some government-run utility companies exist, but most are private—even if they are subject to extensive regulation or benefit from a legal monopoly.

Item B.2. *Government Involvement in Private Action.* Some private action performed in concert with the government may be state action. Different cases use different words for this concept, including but not limited to "entanglement," "entwinement," "involvement," "synergy," "symbiosis," and more.

Burton v. Wilmington Parking Authority, 365 U.S. 715 (1961) is the most famous—and perhaps the most aggressive—example of state action arising from an allegedly symbiotic public/private relationship. The Parking Authority of Wilmington, Delaware (a governmental entity) operated a parking garage with space on the ground floor rented to a private restaurant. William Burton, a Black member of the Wilmington City Council, was refused service at the restaurant because of his race. The restaurant argued that it was a private entity not obligated to obey the Equal Protection Clause, while the Parking Authority argued that the discriminatory actions of a tenant should not be imputed to the landlord. The Supreme Court found enough connection between the two to support a finding of state action. The government issued bonds to buy land and construct a building to serve the general public's need for downtown parking. The government was responsible for maintenance and repairs. The presence of a restaurant encouraged more people to park in the garage (raising more money for the city), and the presence of parking encouraged more people to use the restaurant (which allowed the City to collect more rent). The restaurant argued that it would lose its White customers if it served Black ones, so to the extent the restaurant was profiting from discrimination, the government profited from it as well.

For a modern court to find state action on the basis of the government's involvement with a private actor, the interaction must be extensive. It is doubtful whether *Burton* would come out the same way today. Later cases have found it insufficient that the government issues a license without which the private party could not operate. *Jackson v. Metropolitan Edison Co.*, 419 U.S. 345 (1974) (no state action as a result of license to operate an electrical utility); *Moose Lodge No. 107 v. Irvis*, 407 U.S. 163 (1972) (no state action as a result of a liquor license). It is insufficient that the government heavily regulates the business. *Id.* It is insufficient that the private party derives most of its revenue from government contracts. *Rendell-Baker v. Kohn*, 457 U.S. 830 (1982) (private school receiving over 90% of its funding from the government grants is not a state actor); *Blum v. Yaretsky*, 457 U.S. 991 (1982) (nursing home receiving almost all of its funding through Medicaid reimbursement is not a state actor).

Item B.3. *Power Bestowed by Government.* As the cases in the previous paragraph indicate, it can be important to link the government not just to the private actor, but to the allegedly wrongful action. When a private club like the Moose Lodge discriminates on the basis of race, the discrimination is not a result of the state giving the Lodge a liquor license. By contrast, a private doctor with a contract to provide health care at a prison is able to inflict allegedly cruel and unusual punishment only because the government has put that person in a position to inflict it. *West v. Atkins*, 487 U.S. 42 (1988). The injury was caused "by the exercise of some right or privilege created by the State." *Lugar.*

This factor requires more than mere but-for causation. Such but-for causation was present in Moose Lodge (if the government had not given the lodge a liquor license, it could not have operated a bar where discrimination occurred), but that was insufficient. What matters most is whether the government empowered the private actor to do the specific challenged act.

This concept leads to fact-specific decisions where the outcome may hinge on precisely what the law authorizes private persons to do and precisely what any government agents must do to make it happen. Consider two procedural due process cases where creditors used state law to obtain control over a debtor's goods as a way to obtain payment. In *Flagg Brothers, Inc. v. Brooks*, 436 U.S. 149 (1978), a state's version of the Uniform Commercial Code authorized the owner of a warehouse to sell off a debtor's goods to satisfy debts. There was no state action: the sale happened privately with no involvement of government employees. In *Lugar v. Edmondson Oil Co.*, 457 U.S. 922 (1982), state law allowed a creditor to easily secure a prejudgment writ of attachment of a debtor's property. Here there was state action: the creditor could take control of the property only with the participation of a court clerk to issue the writ and then the sheriff to execute it. As a result, the methods needed to comply with procedural due process.

(These examples show how factors in this Kickstarter may overlap with each other in practice. In *Flagg Brothers* and *Lugar*, it mattered whether the private actor was exercising powers bestowed by state law and whether the private actor worked in concert with state officials.)

Item B.4. *Encouragement or Endorsement.* State action may exist where the government encourages or endorses private action. This theory appeared most prominently during the civil rights movement, and has been used only sparingly since. In *Norwood v. Harrison*, 413 U.S. 455 (1973), the state of Mississippi provided free textbooks to private schools, including those that discriminated on the basis of race. At the time, discriminatory private schools were rapidly growing as a result of White flight from public school systems subject to desegregation orders. In context, the state's facially neutral textbooks-for-private-schools program was an encouragement and endorsement of *de facto* segregation. In *Reitman v. Mulkey*, 387 U.S. 369 (1967), race discrimination by a private landlord was treated as state action because California had amended its state constitution to forbid laws against housing discrimination. Because the landlord was acting in the way seemingly encouraged and endorsed by the state, the action was held to constitutional standards.

Item B.5. *Evasion of Settled Law Through Privatization.* Government should not be able to privatize its way around the Constitution. This can be seen in a series of cases where Texas attempted to have all-White political primaries. During the early 20th century, Texas was overwhelmingly affiliated with the Democratic Party. Because the Democratic nominee would always win the general election, the party primary became the only meaningful election. In 1923, a state statute barred non-White voters from the Democratic primary. The Supreme Court found this to be an obvious violation of the Equal Protection Clause. *Nixon v. Herndon*, 273 U.S. 536 (1927). Texas responded with a statute authorizing the party to determine who could vote in primaries. The Supreme Court invalidated the statute as a forbidden delegation of the decision to discriminate. *Nixon v. Condon*, 286 U.S. 73 (1932). After these cases, the Texas legislature stopped passing laws on the subject, but the Texas Democratic Party continued to use internal mechanisms to forbid non-White voting. The actions of the Party were found to be state action in *Smith v. Allwright*, 321 U.S. 649 (1944), and *Terry v. Adams*, 345 U.S. 461 (1953). As described in Item B.1 above, these cases found a primary election to be an inherently governmental function subject to the Constitution, but the blatant and recurring pattern—where the state relied on non-state entities to further the state's desire to discriminate—also motivated the court's decisions.

Item B.6. *The Nature of the Violation.* Although no court decision says so, the nature of the alleged constitutional violation seems to affect the outcome. Exceptions to the state action doctrine have been more prevalent in cases of race discrimination than in cases alleging violations of procedural due process or freedom of speech. *Burton v. Wilmington Parking Authority* (1961)—where an African-American man could park his car in a city parking garage but not eat in the restaurant located in the same building—shows how the perceived gravity of the wrong may affect the court's view of state action.

> It is irony amounting to grave injustice that in one part of a single building, erected and maintained with public funds by an agency of the State to serve

a public purpose, all persons have equal rights, while in another portion, also serving the public, a Negro is a second-class citizen, offensive because of his race, without rights and unentitled to service, but at the same time fully enjoys equal access to nearby restaurants in wholly privately owned buildings.

Many observers have argued that the Warren Court relied on exceptions to the state action doctrine as a way to attack private race discrimination before civil rights statutes were enacted. After Title II of the Civil Rights Act of 1964 made race discrimination illegal in restaurants, future cases like *Burton* would not need to rely on the Equal Protection Clause. Similarly, once the Fair Housing Act of 1968 was available, a tenant denied housing on the basis of race would not need to rely on the endorsement theory of *Reitman v. Mulkey* (1967). In recent decades, the Supreme Court has been less inclined to expand the state action concept to plug perceived holes in the network of civil rights statutes.

Item B.7. *Methods of Reasoning.* As with most constitutional questions, multiple methods of reasoning can be helpful in state action cases. As explained above, the text and structure of the Constitution support the general rule requiring state action. The exceptions are supported by precedent and by considerations of history (is this an area with a history suggesting that it should be constitutionalized?), consequences (what will be the result if the challenged action is or is not brought within the Constitution?), and values (what harms should the Constitution seek to avoid?).

B. State Action and Courts

The courts make for a good study of the state action doctrine. Courts themselves are operated by the government, but they only act when asked to do so by the parties—who may be non-governmental.

1. Judicial Enforcement of Racially Restrictive Covenants: *Shelley v. Kraemer*

During the Jim Crow era and beyond, efforts to maintain all-White neighborhoods were common. In *Buchanan v. Warley*, 245 U.S. 60 (1917), the Supreme Court found that a Louisville ordinance violated property owners' rights by making it illegal for an owner of residential property in a predominantly White neighborhood to sell to a "colored" person (and vice versa). See Ch. 8.C.2.a. Unconstitutional ordinances like these operated in parallel with another trend: racially restrictive covenants that ran with the land. Under the property laws of most states, adjoining property owners may enter into mutual agreements with each other regarding the use of their property, and the agreements can be binding on future purchasers. In both Northern and Southern cities, it was commonplace in the early 20th century for White neighborhoods and even entire suburbs to have covenants barring sale or rental to non-Whites (and often non-Christians). Among the many unfair results of these covenants was that as the Black population grew in size and prosperity, the housing stock available to it remained small. The law of supply and demand sometimes caused Black tenants or homebuyers to pay higher housing costs than their White counterparts.

Although these covenants were in theory private agreements among landowners, government had an unsavory hand in encouraging their use. The Federal Housing Administration, founded in 1934, issued an underwriting manual, used by the agency and also private lenders, that favored neighborhoods with racially restrictive covenants because they "provide the surest protection against undesirable encroachment and inharmonious use." The FHA also offered subsidies to developers of new subdivisions and suburbs on condition that they impose racially restrictive covenants. As a manual from 1946 put it: "Incompatible racial groups should not be permitted to live in the same communities."

ITEMS TO CONSIDER WHILE READING *SHELLEY v. KRAEMER*:

A. *Work through the items in the Kickstarter, along with any other relevant factors, to determine whether state action should be found.*

B. *Does it violate the Equal Protection Clause for private parties to enter into contracts in which they agree to discriminate on the basis of race?*

C. *If a state court is willing to enforce all contracts with equal vigor—including racially discriminatory contracts—in what way does it violate the Equal Protection Clause?*

D. *Does* Shelley *apply the Bill of Rights to all judicial enforcement of all contracts, or only certain types of enforcement of certain types of contracts?*

Shelley v. Kraemer,

334 U.S. 1 (1948)

Chief Justice Vinson delivered the opinion of the Court [joined by Justices Frankfurter, Douglas, Murphy, Burton, and Black].

These [consolidated] cases present for our consideration questions relating to the validity of court enforcement of private agreements, generally described as restrictive covenants, which have as their purpose the exclusion of persons of designated race or color from the ownership or occupancy of real property. Basic constitutional issues of obvious importance have been raised.

Shelley v. Kraemer

The first of these cases comes to this Court on certiorari to the Supreme Court of Missouri. On February 16, 1911, thirty out of a total of thirty-nine owners of property fronting both sides of Labadie Avenue between Taylor Avenue and Cora Avenue in the city of St. Louis, signed an agreement, which was subsequently recorded, providing in part [that for the next 50 years] "no part of said property or any portion thereof shall be . . . occupied by any person not of the Caucasian race, it being intended hereby to restrict the use of said property . . . against the occupancy as owners or tenants . . . by people of the Negro or Mongolian Race." . . .

On August 11, 1945, pursuant to a contract of sale, petitioners [J.D. and Ethel] Shelley, who are Negroes, for valuable consideration received from one [Josephine] Fitzgerald a warranty deed to the parcel in question. . . . On October 9, 1945, respondents [Louis and Fern Kraemer], as owners of other property subject to the terms of the restrictive covenant, brought suit in Circuit Court of the city of St. Louis praying that petitioners Shelley be restrained from taking possession of the property and that judgment be entered divesting title out of petitioners Shelley and revesting title in the immediate grantor or in such other person as the court should direct. The trial court denied the requested relief on the ground that the [covenant had not been signed by enough property owners].

The home in Shelley v. Kraemer

The Supreme Court of Missouri sitting en banc reversed and directed the trial court to grant the relief for which respondents had prayed. That court held the agreement effective and concluded that enforcement of its provisions violated no rights guaranteed to petitioners by the Federal Constitution. At the time the court rendered its decision, petitioners were occupying the property in question.

[*Shelley v. Kraemer* was consolidated with *Sipes v. McGee*, a factually similar case from Detroit.]

I

. . . It cannot be doubted that among the civil rights intended to be protected from discriminatory state action by the Fourteenth Amendment are the rights to acquire, enjoy, own and dispose of property. Equality in the enjoyment of property rights was regarded by the framers of that Amendment as an essential pre-condition to the realization of other basic civil rights and liberties which the Amendment was intended to guarantee. Thus, § 1 of the Civil Rights Act of 1866 [now codified as 42 U.S.C. § 1982] which was enacted by Congress while the Fourteenth Amendment was also under consideration, provides: "All citizens of the United States shall have the same right, in every State and Territory, as is enjoyed by white citizens thereof to inherit, purchase, lease, sell, hold, and convey real and personal property." This Court has given specific recognition to the same principle. *Buchanan v. Warley* (1917).

It is likewise clear that restrictions on the right of occupancy of the sort sought to be created by the private agreements in these cases could not be squared with the requirements of the Fourteenth Amendment if imposed by state statute or local ordinance. We do not understand respondents to urge the contrary. In the case of *Buchanan v. Warley*, a unanimous Court declared unconstitutional the provisions of a city ordinance which denied to colored persons the right to occupy houses in blocks in which the greater number of houses were occupied by white persons, and imposed similar restrictions on white persons with respect to blocks in which the greater number of houses were occupied by colored persons. During the course of the opinion in that case, this Court stated: "The Fourteenth Amendment and these statutes enacted in furtherance of its purpose operate to qualify and entitle a colored man to acquire property without state legislation discriminating against him solely because of color."

In *Harmon v. Tyler*, 273 U.S. 668 (1927), a unanimous court, on the authority of *Buchanan v. Warley*, declared invalid an ordinance which forbade any Negro to establish a home on any property in a white community or any white person to establish a home in a Negro community, "except on the written consent of a majority of the persons of the opposite race inhabiting such community or portion of the City to be affected." . . .

But the present cases, unlike those just discussed, do not involve action by state legislatures or city councils. Here the particular patterns of discrimination and the areas in which the restrictions are to operate, are determined, in the first instance, by the terms of agreements among private individuals. Participation of the State consists in the enforcement of the restrictions so defined. The crucial issue with which we are here confronted is whether this distinction removes these cases from the operation of the prohibitory provisions of the Fourteenth Amendment.

Since the decision of this Court in *The Civil Rights Cases* (1883), the principle has become firmly embedded in our constitutional law that the action inhibited by the first section of the Fourteenth Amendment is only such action as may fairly be said to be that of the States. That Amendment erects no shield against merely private conduct, however discriminatory or wrongful.

We conclude, therefore, that the restrictive agreements standing alone cannot be regarded as a violation of any rights guaranteed to petitioners by the Fourteenth Amendment. So long as the purposes of those agreements are effectuated by voluntary adherence to their terms, it would appear clear that there has been no action by the State and the provisions of the Amendment have not been violated.

But here there was more. These are cases in which the purposes of the agreements were secured only by judicial enforcement by state courts of the restrictive terms of the agreements. The respondents urge that judicial enforcement of private agreements does not amount to state action; or, in any event, the participation of the State is so attenuated in character as not to amount to state action within the meaning of the Fourteenth Amendment. Finally, it is suggested, even if the States in these cases may be deemed to have acted in the constitutional sense, their action did not deprive petitioners of rights guaranteed by the Fourteenth Amendment. We move to a consideration of these matters.

Shelley v. Kraemer

II

That the action of state courts and of judicial officers in their official capacities is to be regarded as action of the State within the meaning of the Fourteenth Amendment, is a proposition which has long been established by decisions of this Court. That principle was given expression in the earliest cases involving the construction of the terms of the Fourteenth Amendment. Thus, in *Commonwealth of Virginia v. Rives*, 100 U.S. 313 (1880), this Court stated: "It is doubtless true that a State may act through different agencies—either by its legislative, its executive, or its judicial authorities; and the prohibitions of the amendment extend to all action of the State denying equal protection of the laws, whether it be action by one of these agencies or by another." In *Ex parte Virginia*, 100 U.S. 339 (1880), the Court observed: "A State acts by its legislative, its executive, or its judicial authorities. It can act in no other way." In *The Civil Rights Cases* (1883), this Court pointed out that the Amendment makes void "state action of every kind" which is inconsistent with the guaranties therein contained, and extends to manifestations of "state authority in the shape of laws, customs, or judicial or executive proceedings." Language to like effect is employed no less than eighteen times during the course of that opinion.

Similar expressions, giving specific recognition to the fact that judicial action is to be regarded as action of the State for the purposes of the Fourteenth Amendment, are to be found in numerous cases which have been more recently decided. . . . The short of the matter is that from the time of the adoption of the Fourteenth Amendment until the present, it has been the consistent ruling of this Court that the action of the States to which the Amendment has reference, includes action of state courts and state judicial officials. Although, in construing the terms of the Fourteenth Amendment, differences have from time to time been expressed as to whether particular types of state action may be said to offend the Amendment's prohibitory provisions, it has never been suggested that state court action is immunized from the operation of those provisions simply because the act is that of the judicial branch of the state government.

III

Against this background of judicial construction, extending over a period of some three-quarters of a century, we are called upon to consider whether enforcement by state courts of the restrictive agreements in these cases may be deemed to be the acts of those States; and, if so, whether that action has denied these petitioners the equal protection of the laws which the Amendment was intended to insure.

We have no doubt that there has been state action in these cases in the full and complete sense of the phrase. The undisputed facts disclose that petitioners were willing purchasers of properties upon which they desired to establish homes. The owners of the properties were willing sellers; and contracts of sale were accordingly consummated. It is clear that but for the active intervention of the state courts, supported by the full panoply of state power, petitioners would have been free to occupy the properties in question without restraint.

These are not cases, as has been suggested, in which the States have merely abstained from action, leaving private individuals free to impose such discriminations as they see fit. Rather, these are cases in which the States have made available to such individuals the full coercive power of government to deny to petitioners, on the grounds of race or color, the enjoyment of property rights in premises which petitioners are willing and financially able to acquire and which the grantors are willing to sell. The difference between judicial enforcement and nonenforcement of the restrictive covenants is the difference to petitioners between being denied rights of property available to other members of the community and being accorded full enjoyment of those rights on an equal footing. . . .

We have noted that previous decisions of this Court have established the proposition that judicial action is not immunized from the operation of the Fourteenth Amendment simply because it is taken pursuant to the state's common-law policy. Nor is the Amendment ineffective simply because the particular pattern of discrimination, which the State has enforced, was defined initially by the terms of a private agreement. State action, as that phrase is understood for the purposes of the Fourteenth Amendment, refers to exertions of state power in all forms. And when the effect of that action is to deny rights subject to the protection of the Fourteenth Amendment, it is the obligation of this Court to enforce the constitutional commands.

We hold that in granting judicial enforcement of the restrictive agreements in these cases, the States have denied petitioners the equal protection of the laws and that, therefore, the action of the state courts cannot stand. . . . Respondents urge, however, that since the state courts stand ready to enforce restrictive covenants excluding white persons from the ownership or occupancy of property covered by such agreements, enforcement of covenants excluding colored persons may not be deemed a denial of equal protection of the laws to the colored persons who are thereby affected. This contention does not bear scrutiny. The parties have directed our attention to no case in which a court, state or federal, has been called upon to enforce a covenant excluding members of the white majority from ownership or occupancy of real property on grounds of race or color. But there are more fundamental considerations. The rights created by the first section of the Fourteenth Amendment are, by its terms, guaranteed to the individual. The rights established are personal rights. It is, therefore, no answer to these petitioners to say that the courts may also be induced to deny white persons rights of ownership and occupancy on grounds of race or color. Equal protection of the laws is not achieved through indiscriminate imposition of inequalities.

Shelley v. Kraemer

Nor do we find merit in the suggestion that property owners who are parties to these agreements are denied equal protection of the laws if denied access to the courts to enforce the terms of restrictive covenants and to assert property rights which the state courts have held to be created by such agreements. The Constitution confers upon no individual the right to demand action by the State which results in the denial of equal protection of the laws to other individuals. And it would appear beyond question that the power of the State to create and enforce property interests must be exercised within the boundaries defined by the Fourteenth Amendment. *Cf. Marsh v. Alabama*, 326 U.S. 501 (1946). . . .

Justices Reed, Jackson, and Rutledge took no part in the consideration or decision of these cases. [These justices most likely recused themselves because their DC-area homes were subject to racially restrictive covenants.]

2. Peremptory Strikes of Jurors: *Edmonson v. Leesville Concrete*

Historically, trial attorneys have been allowed to remove a fixed number of prospective jurors from a panel peremptorily—that is, without individualized evidence of juror bias. An exception to that longstanding rule was announced in *Batson v. Kentucky*, 476 U.S. 79 (1986), which held that a prosecutor in a criminal trial violated the Equal Protection Clause by using peremptory strikes to eliminate African-Americans from a jury. Cases following *Batson* established a procedure for evaluating peremptory strikes: if a defendant challenges a prosecutor's peremptory strike of a minority juror, the prosecutor has the burden to articulate a race-neutral justification for the strike.

As an agent of the government, the criminal prosecutor is undoubtedly a state actor. *Edmonson* considers the problem in the context of a civil trial, with peremptory strikes made by private attorneys representing private clients.

ITEMS TO CONSIDER WHILE READING *EDMONSON v. LEESVILLE CONCRETE*:

A. *Work through the items in the Kickstarter, along with any other relevant factors, to determine whether state action should be found.*

B. *Why was a private attorney a state actor in* Edmonson *when a public defender employed by the government was not a state actor in* Polk County v. Dodson *(described in* Edmonson*)?*

C. *What other things that attorneys do in court might be state action?*

Edmonson v. Leesville Concrete Co.,

500 U.S. 614 (1991)

Justice Kennedy delivered the opinion of the Court [joined by Justices White, Marshall, Blackmun, Stevens, and Souter].

We must decide in the case before us whether a private litigant in a civil case may use peremptory challenges to exclude jurors on account of their race. Recognizing the impropriety of racial bias in the courtroom, we hold the race-based exclusion violates the equal protection rights of the challenged jurors. This civil case originated in a United States District Court, and we apply the equal protection component of the Fifth Amendment's Due Process Clause. See *Bolling v. Sharpe* (1954).

I

Thaddeus Donald Edmonson, a construction worker, was injured in a job-site accident at Fort Polk, Louisiana, a federal enclave. Edmonson sued Leesville Concrete Company for negligence in the United States District Court for the Western District of Louisiana, claiming that a Leesville employee permitted one of the company's trucks to roll backward and pin him against some construction equipment. Edmonson invoked his Seventh Amendment right to a trial by jury.

During voir dire, Leesville used two of its three peremptory challenges authorized by statute to remove black persons from the prospective jury. Citing our decision in *Batson v. Kentucky*, 476 U.S. 79 (1986), Edmonson, who is himself black, requested that the District Court require Leesville to articulate a race-neutral explanation for striking the two jurors. The District Court denied the request on the ground that *Batson* does not apply in civil proceedings. As empaneled, the jury included 11 white persons and 1 black person. The jury rendered a verdict for Edmonson, assessing his total damages at $90,000. It also attributed 80% of the fault to Edmonson's contributory negligence, however, and awarded him the sum of $18,000.

Edmonson appealed. . . . A divided en banc panel [of the Fifth Circuit] affirmed the judgment of the District Court, holding that a private litigant in a civil case can exercise peremptory challenges without accountability for alleged racial classifications. . . . We granted certiorari, and now reverse the Court of Appeals.

II

A

In *Powers v. Ohio*, 499 U.S. 400 (1991), we held that a criminal defendant, regardless of his or her race, may object to a prosecutor's race-based exclusion of persons from the petit jury. . . .

Powers relied upon over a century of jurisprudence dedicated to the elimination of race prejudice within the jury selection process. See, e.g., *Batson*; *Strauder v. West Virginia* (1879). While these decisions were for the most part directed at discrimination by a prosecutor or other government officials in the context of criminal proceedings, we have not intimated that race discrimination is permissible in civil proceedings. Indeed, discrimination on the basis of race in selecting a jury in a civil proceeding harms the excluded juror no less than discrimination in a criminal trial. In either case, race is the sole reason for denying the excluded venireperson the honor and privilege of participating in our system of justice.

That an act violates the Constitution when committed by a government official, however, does not answer the question whether the same act offends constitutional guarantees if committed by a private litigant or his attorney. The Constitution's protections of individual liberty and equal protection apply in general only to action by the government. Racial discrimination, though invidious in all contexts, violates the Constitution only when it may be attributed to state action. Thus, the legality of the exclusion at issue here turns on the extent to which a litigant in a civil case may be subject to the Constitution's restrictions.

The Constitution structures the National Government, confines its actions, and, in regard to certain individual liberties and other specified matters, confines the actions of the States. With a few exceptions, such as the provisions of the Thirteenth Amendment, constitutional guarantees of individual liberty and equal protection do not apply to the actions of private entities. This fundamental limitation on the scope of constitutional guarantees preserves an area of individual freedom by limiting the reach of federal law and avoids imposing on the State, its agencies or officials, responsibility for conduct for which they cannot fairly be blamed. One great object of the Constitution is to permit citizens to structure their private relations as they choose subject only to the constraints of statutory or decisional law.

To implement these principles, courts must consider from time to time where the governmental sphere ends and the private sphere begins. Although the conduct of private parties lies beyond the Constitution's scope in most instances, governmental authority may dominate an activity to such an extent that its participants must be deemed to act with the authority of the government and, as a result, be subject to constitutional constraints. This is the jurisprudence of state action, which explores the essential dichotomy between the private sphere and the public sphere, with all its attendant constitutional obligations.

We begin our discussion within the framework for state-action analysis set forth in *Lugar v. Edmondson Oil Co.*, 457 U.S. 922 (1982). There we considered the state-action question in the context of a due process challenge to a State's procedure allowing private parties to obtain prejudgment attachments. We asked first whether the claimed constitutional deprivation resulted from the exercise of a right or privilege having its source in state authority, and second, whether the private party charged with the deprivation could be described in all fairness as a state actor.

There can be no question that the first part of the *Lugar* inquiry is satisfied here. By their very nature, peremptory challenges have no significance outside a court of law. Their sole purpose is to permit litigants to assist the government in the selection of an impartial trier of fact. While we have recognized the value of peremptory challenges in this regard, particularly in the criminal context, there is no constitutional obligation to allow them. Peremptory challenges are permitted only when the government, by statute or decisional law, deems it appropriate to allow parties to exclude a given number of persons who otherwise would satisfy the requirements for service on the petit jury. . . . In the case before us, the challenges were exercised under a federal statute . . . . Without this authorization, granted by an Act of Congress itself, Leesville would not have been able to engage in the alleged discriminatory acts.

Given that the statutory authorization for the challenges exercised in this case is clear, the remainder of our state-action analysis centers around the second part of the *Lugar* test, whether a private litigant in all fairness must be deemed a government actor in the use of peremptory challenges. Although we have recognized that this aspect of the analysis is often a factbound inquiry, our cases disclose certain principles of general application. Our precedents establish that, in determining whether a particular action or course of conduct is governmental in character, it is relevant to examine the following: the extent to which the actor relies on governmental assistance and benefits; whether the actor is performing a traditional governmental function; and whether the injury caused is aggravated in a unique way by the incidents of governmental authority. Based on our application of these three principles to the circumstances here, we hold that the exercise of peremptory challenges by the defendant in the District Court was pursuant to a course of state action.

Although private use of state-sanctioned private remedies or procedures does not rise, by itself, to the level of state action, our cases have found state action when private parties make extensive use of state procedures with the overt, significant assistance of state officials. . . .

A private party could not exercise its peremptory challenges absent the overt, significant assistance of the court. The government summons jurors, constrains their freedom of movement, and subjects them to public scrutiny and examination. The party who exercises a challenge invokes the formal authority of the court, which

Edmonson v. Leesville Concrete Co.

must discharge the prospective juror, thus effecting the final and practical denial of the excluded individual's opportunity to serve on the petit jury. Without the direct and indispensable participation of the judge, who beyond all question is a state actor, the peremptory challenge system would serve no purpose. By enforcing a discriminatory peremptory challenge, the court has not only made itself a party to the biased act, but has elected to place its power, property and prestige behind the alleged discrimination. *Burton v. Wilmington Parking Authority* (1961). In so doing, the government has created the legal framework governing the challenged conduct, and in a significant way has involved itself with invidious discrimination.

In determining Leesville's state-actor status, we next consider whether the action in question involves the performance of a traditional function of the government. A traditional function of government is evident here. The peremptory challenge is used in selecting an entity that is a quintessential governmental body, having no attributes of a private actor. The jury exercises the power of the court and of the government that confers the court's jurisdiction. . . . These are traditional functions of government, not of a select, private group beyond the reach of the Constitution.

If a government confers on a private body the power to choose the government's employees or officials, the private body will be bound by the constitutional mandate of race neutrality. At least a plurality of the Court recognized this principle in *Terry v. Adams* (1953). [That case invalidated a nominally private Whites-only primary for a political party.] . . . The principle that the selection of state officials, other than through election by all qualified voters, may constitute state action applies with even greater force in the context of jury selection through the use of peremptory challenges. Though the motive of a peremptory challenge may be to protect a private interest, the objective of jury selection proceedings is to determine representation on a governmental body. Were it not for peremptory challenges, there would be no question that the entire process of determining who will serve on the jury constitutes state action. The fact that the government delegates some portion of this power to private litigants does not change the governmental character of the power exercised. The delegation of authority that in *Terry* occurred without the aid of legislation occurs here through explicit statutory authorization.

We find respondent's reliance on ***Polk County v. Dodson,*** 454 U.S. 312 (1981), unavailing. In that case, we held that a public defender is not a state actor in his general representation of a criminal defendant, even though he may be in his performance of other official duties. While recognizing the employment relation between the public defender and the government, we noted that the relation is otherwise adversarial in nature. . . .

■ HISTORY

POLK COUNTY v. DODSON: In *Polk County,* a public defender withdrew from representing a client because she believed he was pursuing a frivolous appeal. The client sued the county—the defender's employer—arguing that the withdrawal had deprived him of his right to counsel, subjected him to cruel and unusual punishment, and denied him due process of law.

In the ordinary context of civil litigation in which the government is not a party, an adversarial relation does not exist between the government and a private litigant. In the jury-selection process, the government and private litigants work for the same end. Just as a government employee was deemed a private actor because of his purpose and functions in *Dodson*, so here a private entity becomes a government actor for the limited purpose of using peremptories during jury selection. The selection of jurors represents a unique governmental function delegated to private litigants by the government and attributable to the government for purposes of invoking constitutional protections against discrimination by reason of race. . . .

Finally, we note that the injury caused by the discrimination is made more severe because the government permits it to occur within the courthouse itself. Few places are a more real expression of the constitutional authority of the government than a courtroom, where the law itself unfolds. Within the courtroom, the government invokes its laws to determine the rights of those who stand before it. In full view of the public, litigants press their cases, witnesses give testimony, juries render verdicts, and judges act with the utmost care to ensure that justice is done.

Race discrimination within the courtroom raises serious questions as to the fairness of the proceedings conducted there. Racial bias mars the integrity of the judicial system and prevents the idea of democratic government from becoming a reality. In the many times we have addressed the problem of racial bias in our system of justice, we have not questioned the premise that racial discrimination in the qualification or selection of jurors offends the dignity of persons and the integrity of the courts. To permit racial exclusion in this official forum compounds the racial insult inherent in judging a citizen by the color of his or her skin.

B [Omitted.]

III

It remains to consider whether a *prima facie* case of racial discrimination has been established in the case before us, requiring Leesville to offer race-neutral explanations for its peremptory challenges. . . . We leave it to the trial courts in the first instance to develop evidentiary rules for implementing our decision.

Justice O'Connor, with whom Chief Justice Rehnquist and Justice Scalia join, dissenting.

The Court concludes that the action of a private attorney exercising a peremptory challenge is attributable to the government and therefore may compose a constitutional violation. This conclusion is based on little more than that the challenge occurs in the course of a trial. Not everything that happens in a courtroom is state action. A trial, particularly a civil trial, is by design largely a stage on which private parties may act; it is a forum through which they can resolve their disputes in a peaceful and ordered manner. The government erects the platform; it does not thereby become responsible for all that occurs upon it. As much as we would like to eliminate completely from the courtroom the specter of racial discrimination, the Constitution does not sweep that broadly. Because I believe that a peremptory strike by a private litigant is fundamentally a matter of private choice and not state action, I dissent.

I

In order to establish a constitutional violation, Edmonson must first demonstrate that Leesville's use of a peremptory challenge can fairly be attributed to the government. . . . The Court concludes that this standard is met in the present case. It rests this conclusion primarily on two empirical assertions. First, that private parties use peremptory challenges with the "overt, significant participation of the government." Second, that the use of a peremptory challenge by a private party "involves the performance of a traditional function of the government." Neither of these assertions is correct.

A

. . . The Court amasses much ostensible evidence of the Federal Government's "overt, significant assistance" in the peremptory process. Most of this evidence is irrelevant to the issue at hand. The bulk of the practices the Court describes—the establishment of qualifications for jury service, the location and summoning of prospective jurors, the jury wheel, the voter lists, the jury qualification forms, the per diem for jury service—are independent of the statutory entitlement to peremptory strikes, or of their use. All of this Government action is in furtherance of the Government's distinct obligation to provide a qualified jury; the Government would do these things even if there were no peremptory challenges. All of this activity, as well as the trial judge's control over voir dire, is merely prerequisite to the use of a peremptory challenge; it does not constitute participation in the challenge. That these actions may be necessary to a peremptory challenge—in the sense that there could be no such challenge without a venire from which to select—no more makes the challenge state action than the building of roads and provision of public transportation makes state action of riding on a bus.

The entirety of the government's actual participation in the peremptory process boils down to a single fact: "When a lawyer exercises a peremptory challenge, the judge advises the juror he or she has been excused." This is not significant participation. . . .

The alleged state action here is a far cry from that which the Court found, for example, in *Shelley v. Kraemer* (1948). In that case, state courts were called upon to enforce racially restrictive covenants against sellers of real property who did not wish to discriminate. The coercive power of the State was necessary in order to enforce the private choice of those who had created the covenants: "But for the active intervention of the state courts, supported by the full panoply of state power, petitioners would have been free to occupy the properties in question without restraint." Moreover, the courts in *Shelley* were asked to enforce a facially discriminatory contract. In contrast, peremptory challenges are exercised without a reason stated and without inquiry. A judge does not significantly encourage discrimination by the mere act of excusing a juror in response to an unexplained request.

There is another important distinction between *Shelley* and this case. The state courts in *Shelley* used coercive force to impose conformance on parties who did not wish to discriminate. Enforcement of peremptory challenges, on the other hand, does not compel anyone to discriminate; the discrimination is wholly a matter of private choice. Judicial acquiescence does not convert private choice into that of the State. . . .

The Court relies also on *Burton v. Wilmington Parking Authority* (1961). But the decision in that case depended on the perceived symbiotic relationship between a restaurant and the state parking authority from whom it leased space in a public building. The State had so far insinuated itself into a position of interdependence with the restaurant that it had to be recognized as a joint participant in the challenged activity. Among the peculiar facts and circumstances leading to that conclusion was that the State stood to profit from the restaurant's discrimination. As I have shown, the government's involvement in the use of peremptory challenges falls far short of interdependence or joint participation. Whatever the continuing vitality of *Burton* beyond its facts, it does not support the Court's conclusion here.

Jackson v. Metropolitan Edison Co., 419 U.S. 345 (1974), is a more appropriate analogy to this case. Metropolitan Edison terminated Jackson's electrical service under authority granted it by the State, pursuant to a procedure approved by the state utility commission. Nonetheless, we held that Jackson could not challenge the termination procedure on due process grounds. The termination was not state action because the State had done nothing to encourage the particular termination practice. . . . The similarity to this case is obvious. The Court's "overt, significant" government participation amounts to the fact that the government provides the mechanism whereby a litigant can choose to exercise a peremptory challenge. That the government allows this choice and that the judge approves it, does not turn this private decision into state action. . . .

B

The Court errs also when it concludes that the exercise of a peremptory challenge is a traditional government function. In its definition of the peremptory challenge, the Court asserts, correctly, that jurors struck via peremptories otherwise satisfy the requirements for service on the petit jury. Whatever reason a private litigant may have for using a peremptory challenge, it is not the government's

Edmonson v. Leesville Concrete Co.

reason. . . . The Court may be correct that were it not for peremptory challenges, the entire process of determining who will serve on the jury would constitute state action. But there are peremptory challenges, and always have been. The peremptory challenge forms no part of the government's responsibility in selecting a jury.

A peremptory challenge by a private litigant does not meet the Court's standard; it is not a traditional government function. Beyond this, the Court has misstated the law. . . . In order to constitute state action under [the public-function] doctrine, private conduct must not only comprise something that the government traditionally does, but something that only the government traditionally does. Even if one could fairly characterize the use of a peremptory strike as the performance of the traditional government function of jury selection, it has never been exclusively the function of the government to select juries; peremptory strikes are older than the Republic. . . .

C

None of this should be news, as this case is fairly well controlled by *Polk County v. Dodson* (1981). We there held that a public defender, employed by the State, does not act under color of state law when representing a defendant in a criminal trial. In such a circumstance, government employment is not sufficient to create state action. . . . An attorney's job is to advance the undivided interests of his client. This is essentially a private function for which state office and authority are not needed. . . . Our conclusion in *Dodson* was that a public defender does not act under color of state law when performing a lawyer's traditional functions as counsel to a defendant in a criminal proceeding. It cannot be gainsaid that a peremptory strike is a traditional adversarial act; parties use these strikes to further their own perceived interests, not as an aid to the government's process of jury selection. The Court does not challenge the rule of *Dodson*, yet concludes that private attorneys performing this adversarial function are state actors. Where is the distinction? . . . Attorneys in an adversarial relation to the state are not state actors, but that does not mean that attorneys who are not in such a relation are state actors. . . .

II

Beyond "significant participation" and "traditional function," the Court's final argument is that the exercise of a peremptory challenge by a private litigant is state action because it takes place in a courtroom. . . . If *Dodson* stands for anything, it is that the actions of a lawyer in a courtroom do not become those of the government by virtue of their location. This is true even if those actions are based on race.

Racism is a terrible thing. It is irrational, destructive, and mean. Arbitrary discrimination based on race is particularly abhorrent when manifest in a courtroom, a forum established by the government for the resolution of disputes through quiet rationality. But not every opprobrious and inequitable act is a constitutional violation. The Fifth Amendment's Due Process Clause prohibits only actions for which the Government can be held responsible. The Government is not responsible for everything that occurs in a courtroom. The Government is not responsible for a peremptory challenge by a private litigant. I respectfully dissent.

Justice Scalia, dissenting. [Omitted.]

C. State Action and Government-Affiliated Entities

As far back as 1791 when Congress created the Bank of the United States, see *McCulloch v. Maryland* (1819), the government has been creating corporations, boards, and other freestanding entities. One might argue that all government-created entities are state actors: they are created by the government to perform tasks the government wants performed, and "it surely cannot be that government, state or federal, is able to evade the most solemn obligations imposed in the Constitution by simply resorting to the corporate form." *Lebron v. National Railroad Passenger Corp.*, 513 U.S. 374 (1995).

But things are not so simple. Every corporation—public or private, for-profit or non-profit—is a creature of statute that exists only with the permission of the government. The privately-owned electric company in *Jackson v. Metropolitan Edison* and the private school in *Rendell-Baker v. Kohn* were not state actors, even though they owed their corporate existence to the government. This means that the same attention to factual detail seen in other state action cases is also required in cases involving government-created or government-affiliated entities. For example, differences in corporate structure and purpose meant that Amtrak was a state actor for constitutional purposes in *Lebron*, but that Conrail—another federally-created railroad—was not in *The Regional Rail Reorganization Act Cases*, 419 U.S. 102 (1974). The two cases below explore these nuances in the context of sports governance associations.

1. The Olympics: *San Francisco Arts & Athletics, Inc. v. U.S. Olympic Committee*

In 1982, the US Olympic Committee (USOC) sued a nonprofit organization (SFAA) that sought to organize an athletic event to be called the Gay Olympics. Trademark infringement disputes typically raise no constitutional questions, but two constitutional issues entered this case through affirmative defenses. First, USOC's infringement action was premised on provisions of the Amateur Sports Act of 1978 that gave USOC exclusive rights to certain uses of the term "Olympic." Any act of Congress is undoubtedly state action; here, SFAA argued that the statute violated constitutional free speech rights. Second, SFAA alleged that USOC itself was discriminating on the basis of sexual orientation because it had not prevented other groups from using the word "Olympic" as the name of sporting contests (including the Special Olympics and the Police Olympics). An equal protection defense would be available only if USOC was a state actor.

ITEMS TO CONSIDER WHILE READING
SAN FRANCISCO ARTS & ATHLETICS v. USOC:

A. *Work through the items in the Kickstarter, along with any other relevant factors, to determine whether state action should be found.*

B. *Imagine that you are a member of Congress who wanted the US Olympic Committee to adhere to constitutional standards. What language would you include in the statute to accomplish this goal?*

San Francisco Arts & Athletics, Inc. v. U.S. Olympic Committee,

483 U.S. 522 (1987)

Justice Powell delivered the opinion of the Court [joined by Chief Justice Rehnquist and Justices White, Stevens, and Scalia in full, and by Justices Blackmun and O'Connor with regard to Parts I, II, and III].

In this case, we consider the scope and constitutionality of a provision of the Amateur Sports Act of 1978 that authorizes the United States Olympic Committee to prohibit certain commercial and promotional uses of the word "Olympic."

I

Petitioner San Francisco Arts & Athletics, Inc. (SFAA), is a nonprofit California corporation. The SFAA originally sought to incorporate under the name "Golden Gate Olympic Association," but was told by the California Department of Corporations that the word "Olympic" could not appear in a corporate title. After its incorporation in 1981, the SFAA nevertheless began to promote the "Gay Olympic Games," using those words on its letterheads and mailings and in local newspapers. The games were to be a 9-day event to begin in August 1982, in San Francisco, California. The SFAA expected athletes from hundreds of cities in this country and from cities all over the world. The Games were to open with a ceremony "which will rival the traditional Olympic Games." A relay of over 2,000 runners would carry a torch from New York City across the country to Kezar Stadium in San Francisco. The final runner would enter the stadium with the "Gay Olympic Torch" and light the "Gay Olympic Flame." The ceremony would continue with the athletes marching in uniform into the stadium behind their respective city flags. Competition was to occur in 18 different contests, with the winners receiving gold, silver, and bronze medals. To cover the cost of the planned Games, the SFAA sold T-shirts, buttons, bumper stickers, and other merchandise bearing the title "Gay Olympic Games."

Section 110 of the Amateur Sports Act (Act), 36 U.S.C. § 380, grants respondent United States Olympic Committee (USOC) the right to prohibit certain commercial and promotional uses of the word "Olympic" and various Olympic symbols. . . . In August [1982], the USOC brought suit in the Federal District Court for the Northern District of California to enjoin the SFAA's use of the word "Olympic." The District Court . . . granted the USOC summary judgment and a permanent injunction. The Court of Appeals affirmed the judgment of the District Court. . . . We granted certiorari, to review the issues of statutory and constitutional interpretation decided by the Court of Appeals. We now affirm.

I–III

[Congress did not violate the First Amendment when it awarded exclusive rights to USOC.]

IV

The SFAA argues that even if the exclusive use granted by § 110 does not violate the First Amendment, the USOC's [selective] enforcement of that right [against SFAA] is discriminatory in violation of [the equal protection component of] the Fifth Amendment. The fundamental inquiry is whether the USOC is a governmental actor to whom the prohibitions of the Constitution apply. The USOC is a private corporation established under Federal law. In the Act, Congress granted the USOC a corporate charter, imposed certain requirements on the USOC, and provided for some USOC funding through exclusive use of the Olympic words and symbols, and through direct grants.

The fact that Congress granted it a corporate charter does not render the USOC a Government agent. All corporations act under charters granted by a government, usually by a State. They do not thereby lose their essentially private character. Even extensive regulation by the government does not transform the actions of the regulated entity into those of the government. Nor is the fact that Congress has granted the USOC exclusive use of the word "Olympic" dispositive. All enforceable rights in trademarks are created by some governmental act, usually pursuant to a statute or the common law. The actions of the trademark owners nevertheless remain private. Moreover, the intent on the part of Congress to help the USOC obtain funding does not change the analysis. The Government may subsidize private entities without assuming constitutional responsibility for their actions.

This Court also has found action to be governmental action when the challenged entity performs functions that have been traditionally the exclusive prerogative of the Federal Government. Certainly the activities performed by the USOC serve a national interest, as its objects and purposes of incorporation indicate. The fact that a private entity performs a function which serves the public does not make its acts governmental action. The Amateur Sports Act was enacted to correct the disorganization and the serious factional disputes that seemed to plague amateur sports in the United States. The Act merely authorized the USOC to coordinate activities that always have been performed by private entities. Neither the conduct nor the coordination of amateur sports has been a traditional governmental function.

Most fundamentally, this Court has held that a government normally can be held responsible for a private decision only when it has exercised coercive power or has provided such significant encouragement, either overt or covert, that the choice must in law be deemed to be that of the government. The USOC's choice of how to enforce its exclusive right to use the word "Olympic" simply is not a governmental decision. There is no evidence that the Federal Government coerced or encouraged the USOC in the exercise of its right. At most, the Federal Government, by failing to supervise the USOC's use of its rights, can be said to exercise mere approval of or acquiescence in the initiatives of the USOC. This is not enough to make the USOC's actions those of the Government. Because the USOC is not a governmental actor, the SFAA's claim that the USOC has enforced its rights in a discriminatory manner must fail.

V

Accordingly, we affirm the judgment of the Court of Appeals for the Ninth Circuit.

Justice O'Connor, with whom Justice Blackmun joins, concurring in part and dissenting in part.

I agree with the Court's construction of § 110 of the Amateur Sports Act, and with its holding that the statute is within constitutional bounds. Therefore, I join Parts I through III of the Court's opinion. But largely for the reasons explained by Justice Brennan in Part I-B of his dissenting opinion, I believe the United States Olympic Committee and the United States are joint participants in the challenged activity and as such are subject to the equal protection provisions of the Fifth Amendment. Accordingly, I would reverse the Court of Appeals' finding of no Government action and remand the case for determination of petitioners' claim of discriminatory enforcement.

Justice Brennan, with whom Justice Marshall joins, dissenting.

The Court wholly fails to appreciate both the congressionally created interdependence between the United States Olympic Committee (USOC) and the United States, and the significant extent to which § 110 of the Amateur Sports Act of 1978 infringes on [constitutionally protected] speech. I would find that the action of the USOC challenged here is Government action, and that § 110 [violates the First Amendment]. I therefore dissent.

I

For two independent reasons, the action challenged here constitutes Government action. First, the USOC performs important governmental functions and should therefore be considered a governmental actor. Second, there exists a sufficiently close nexus between the Government and the challenged action of the USOC that the action of the latter may be fairly treated as that of the Government itself.

A

. . . The USOC performs a distinctive, traditional governmental function: it represents this Nation to the world community. The USOC is our country's exclusive representative to the International Olympic Committee (IOC), a highly visible and influential international body. The Court overlooks the extraordinary representational responsibility that Congress has placed on the USOC. As the Olympic Games have grown in international visibility and importance, the USOC's role as our national representative has taken on increasing significance.

Although the Olympic ideals are avowedly nonpolitical, Olympic participation is inescapably nationalist. Membership in the IOC is structured not according to athletes or sports, but nations. The athletes the USOC selects are viewed, not as a group of individuals who coincidentally are from the United States, but as the team of athletes that represents our Nation. . . . Every aspect of the Olympic pageant, from the procession of athletes costumed in national uniform, to the raising of national flags and the playing of national anthems at the medal ceremony, to the official tally of medals won by each national team, reinforces the national significance of Olympic participation. Indeed, it was the perception of shortcomings in the Nation's performance that led to the Amateur Sports Act of 1978. In the words of the President's Commission, "the fact is that we are competing less well and other nations competing more successfully because other nations have established excellence in international athletics as a national priority."

Private organizations sometimes participate in international conferences resplendent with billowing flags. But the Olympic Games are unique: at stake are significant national interests that stem not only from pageantry but from politics. Recent experience illustrates the inherent interdependence of national political interests and the decisions of the USOC. In his State of the Union Address of January 23, 1980 (a forum, one need hardly add, traditionally reserved for matters of national import), the President announced his opposition to American participation in the 1980 summer

San Francisco Arts & Athletics, Inc. v. U.S. Olympic Committee

Olympic Games in Moscow. The opposition was not premised on, e.g., the financial straits of a private corporation, but on the implications of participation for American foreign policy. Echoing the President's concerns, the House of Representatives passed a resolution expressing its opposition to American participation. In a speech on April 10, 1980, the President threatened to take legal actions if necessary to enforce the decision not to send a team to Moscow. Shortly thereafter, with the national and international stakes of the USOC's decision set forth by the President and Congress, and with reports in the press of possible cuts in federal aid to the USOC, the USOC announced that the United States would not participate in the 1980 Olympic Games. Although the lesson had been learned long before 1980, this sequence of events laid bare the impact and interrelationship of USOC decisions on the definition and pursuit of the national interest.

■ HISTORY

OLYMPIC GAMES IN MOSCOW: The United States boycotted the 1980 Summer Olympics as a protest against the Soviet Union's invasion of Afghanistan, which began in December 1979.

There is more to the USOC's public role than representation. The current USOC was born out of governmental dissatisfaction with the performance of the United States in international athletic competition. This dissatisfaction led Congress to grant the USOC unprecedented administrative authority over all private American athletic organizations relating to international competition. The legislative history reveals, contrary to the Court's assumption, that no actor in the private sector had ever performed this function, and indeed never could perform it absent enabling legislation. . . .

The function of the USOC is obviously and fundamentally different than that of the private nursing homes in *Blum v. Yaretsky* (1982), or the private school in *Rendell-Baker v. Kohn* (1982), or the private Moose Lodge *in Moose Lodge No. 107 v. Irvis* (1972), or even the public utility in *Jackson v. Metropolitan Edison Co.* (1974). Unlike those entities, which merely provided public services, the USOC has been endowed by the Federal Government with the exclusive power to serve a unique national, administrative, adjudicative, and representational role. The better analogy, then, is to the company town in *Marsh v. Alabama* (1946), or to the private political party in *Terry v. Adams* (1953). Like those entities, the USOC is a private organization on whom the Government has bestowed inherently public powers and responsibilities. Its actions, like theirs, ought to be subject to constitutional limits.

B

Apart from the argument that the USOC is itself a Government actor, there is a second reason to find Government action. At a minimum, this case, like *Burton v. Wilmington Parking Authority* (1961), is one in which the Government has so far insinuated itself into a position of interdependence with the USOC that it must be recognized as a joint participant in the challenged activity.

The action at issue in *Burton* was the refusal of a private restaurant that leased space in a public parking facility to serve a black customer. Central to the Court's analysis was what later cases have termed "the symbiotic relationship" of the restaurant to the parking facility. This relationship provided the sufficiently close nexus between the State and the challenged action of the private entity so that the action of the latter may be fairly treated as that of the State itself.

The USOC and the Federal Government exist in a symbiotic relationship sufficient to provide a nexus between the USOC's challenged action and the Government. First, as in *Burton*, the relationship here confers a variety of mutual benefits. As discussed above, the Act gave the USOC authority and responsibilities that no private organization in this country had ever held. The Act also conferred substantial financial resources on the USOC, authorizing it to seek up to $16 million annually in grants from the Secretary of Commerce, and affording it unprecedented power to control the use of the word "Olympic" and related emblems to raise additional funds. As a result of the Act, the United States obtained, for the first time in its history, an exclusive and effective organization to coordinate and administer all amateur athletics related to international competition, and to represent that program abroad.

Second, in the eye of the public, both national and international, the connection between the decisions of the United States Government and those of the United States Olympic Committee is profound. The President of the United States has served as the Honorary President of the USOC. The national flag flies both literally and figuratively over the central product of the USOC, the United States Olympic Team. . . .

Even more importantly, there is a close financial and legislative link between the USOC's alleged discriminatory exercise of its word-use authority and the financial success of both the USOC and the Government. It would certainly be "irony amounting to grave injustice," *Burton*, if, to finance the team that is to represent the virtues of our political system, the USOC were free to employ Government-created economic leverage to prohibit political speech. Yet that is exactly what petitioners allege. . . .

If petitioner is correct in its allegation that the USOC has used its discretion to discriminate against certain groups, then the situation here, as in *Burton*, is that profits earned by discrimination not only contribute to, but also are indispensable elements in, the financial success of a governmental agency. Indeed, the required nexus between the challenged action and the Government appears even closer here than in *Burton*. While in *Burton* the restaurant was able to pursue a policy of discrimination because the State had failed to impose upon it a policy of nondiscrimination, the USOC could pursue its alleged policy of selective enforcement only because Congress affirmatively granted it power that it would not otherwise have to control the use of the word "Olympic." I conclude, then, that the close nexus between the Government and the challenged action compels a finding of Government action.

San Francisco Arts & Athletics, Inc. v. U.S. Olympic Committee

C

. . . The Government is free, of course, to "privatize" some functions it would otherwise perform. But such privatization ought not automatically release those who perform Government functions from constitutional obligations. Because the USOC performs a Government function, and because its challenged action is inextricably intertwined with the Government, I would reverse the Court of Appeals finding of no Government action, and remand to the District Court for further proceedings.

II

[Dissent with regard to trademark law omitted.]

2. High School Sports: *Brentwood Academy v. TSSAA*

Many sporting activities in the United States are sponsored by public school districts and universities. Most of them participate in nonprofit athletic associations that establish uniform rules for each sport, organize schedules, and operate tournaments. The associations exercise considerable control over member schools. For example, in *NCAA v. Tarkanian*, 488 U.S. 179 (1988), the National Collegiate Athletic Association suspended the basketball program at the University of Nevada at Las Vegas from all league play for two years as a sanction for recruiting violations. The NCAA threatened to increase the sanctions unless the University fully removed head coach Jerry Tarkanian from the athletic department during the suspension. The University suspended Tarkanian without notice or hearing, despite his tenured faculty position. He sued for violation of his due process rights under *Board of Regents v. Roth* (1972) (Ch. 19.D.2.a) and *Cleveland Board of Education v. Loudermill* (1985) (Ch. 19.D.3.b).

The Supreme Court held that the NCAA was not a state actor—but as seen in the following case, that decision did not necessarily apply to all athletic associations.

ITEMS TO CONSIDER WHILE READING *BRENTWOOD ACADEMY v. TSSAA*:

A. *Work through the items in the Kickstarter, along with any other relevant factors, to determine whether state action should be found in* Brentwood Academy.

B. Tarkanian *reached a different result for the NCAA than* Brentwood Academy *reached for its Tennessee counterpart. Are the cases meaningfully distinguishable?*

C. *The dissent objects to the majority's use of the word "entwinement." How much importance should attach to an opinion's choice of words to describe the relationship between the government and a private actor?*

Brentwood Academy v. Tennessee Secondary School Athletic Association,

531 U.S. 288 (2001)

Justice Souter delivered the opinion of the Court [joined by Justices Stevens, O'Connor, Ginsburg, and Breyer].

The issue is whether a statewide association incorporated to regulate interscholastic athletic competition among public and private secondary schools may be regarded as engaging in state action when it enforces a rule against a member school. The association in question here includes most public schools located within the State, acts through their representatives, draws its officers from them, is largely funded by their dues and income received in their stead, and has historically been seen to regulate in lieu of the State Board of Education's exercise of its own authority. We hold that the association's regulatory activity may and should be treated as state action owing to the pervasive entwinement of state school officials in the structure of the association, there being no offsetting reason to see the association's acts in any other way.

I

Respondent Tennessee Secondary School Athletic Association (Association) is a not-for-profit membership corporation organized to regulate interscholastic sport among the public and private high schools in Tennessee that belong to it. No school is forced to join, but without any other authority actually regulating interscholastic athletics, it enjoys the memberships of almost all the State's public high schools (some 290 of them or 84% of the Association's voting membership), far outnumbering the 55 private schools that belong. A member school's team may play or scrimmage only against the team of another member, absent a dispensation.

The Association's rulemaking arm is its legislative council, while its board of control tends to administration. The voting membership of each of these nine-person committees is limited under the Association's bylaws to high school principals, assistant principals, and superintendents elected by the member schools, and the public school administrators who so serve typically attend meetings during regular school hours. Although the Association's staff members are not paid by the State, they are eligible to join the State's public retirement system for its employees. Member schools pay dues to the Association, though the bulk of its revenue is gate receipts at member teams' football and basketball tournaments, many of them held in public arenas rented by the Association.

The constitution, bylaws, and rules of the Association set standards of school membership and the eligibility of students to play in interscholastic games. Each school, for example, is regulated in awarding financial aid, most coaches must have

Brentwood Academy v. Tennessee Secondary School Athletic Association

a Tennessee state teaching license, and players must meet minimum academic standards and hew to limits on student employment. Under the bylaws, "in all matters pertaining to the athletic relations of his school," the principal is responsible to the Association, which has the power "to suspend, to fine, or otherwise penalize any member school for the violation of any of the rules of the Association or for other just cause."

Ever since the Association was incorporated in 1925, Tennessee's State Board of Education (State Board) has (to use its own words) acknowledged the corporation's functions "in providing standards, rules and regulations for interscholastic competition in the public schools of Tennessee." More recently, the State Board cited [the Association's] statutory authority, when it adopted language expressing the relationship between the Association and the State Board. Specifically, in 1972, it went so far as to adopt a rule expressly designating the Association as "the organization to supervise and regulate the athletic activities in which the public junior and senior high schools in Tennessee participate on an interscholastic basis." The Rule provided that "the authority granted herein shall remain in effect until revoked" and instructed the State Board's chairman to designate a person or persons to serve in an ex-officio capacity on the Association's governing bodies." That same year, the State Board specifically approved the Association's rules and regulations, while reserving the right to review future changes. Thus, on several occasions over the next 20 years, the State Board reviewed, approved, or reaffirmed its approval of the recruiting Rule at issue in this case. In 1996, however, the State Board dropped the original rule expressly designating the Association as regulator; it substituted a statement "recognizing the value of participation in interscholastic athletics and the role of the Association in coordinating interscholastic athletic competition," while "authorizing the public schools of the state to voluntarily maintain membership in the Association."

The action before us responds to a 1997 regulatory enforcement proceeding brought against petitioner, Brentwood Academy, a private parochial high school member of the Association. The Association's board of control found that Brentwood violated a rule prohibiting "undue influence" in recruiting athletes, when it wrote to incoming students and their parents about spring football practice. The Association accordingly placed Brentwood's athletic program on probation for four years, declared its football and boys' basketball teams ineligible to compete in playoffs for two years, and imposed a $3,000 fine. When these penalties were imposed, all the voting members of the board of control and legislative council were public school administrators.

Brentwood sued the Association and its executive director in federal court under 42 U.S.C. § 1983, claiming that enforcement of the Rule was state action and a violation of the First and Fourteenth Amendments. . . . The United States Court of Appeals for the Sixth Circuit reversed. . . . We granted certiorari, to resolve the conflict [among lower courts] and now reverse.

II

A

Our cases try to plot a line between state action subject to Fourteenth Amendment scrutiny and private conduct (however exceptionable) that is not. The judicial obligation is not only to preserve an area of individual freedom by limiting the reach of federal law and avoid the imposition of responsibility on a State for conduct it could not control, but also to assure that constitutional standards are invoked when it can be said that the State is responsible for the specific conduct of which the plaintiff complains. . . . Thus, we say that state action may be found if, though only if, there is such a close nexus between the State and the challenged action that seemingly private behavior may be fairly treated as that of the State itself.

What is fairly attributable is a matter of normative judgment, and the criteria lack rigid simplicity. From the range of circumstances that could point toward the State behind an individual face, no one fact can function as a necessary condition across the board for finding state action; nor is any set of circumstances absolutely sufficient, for there may be some countervailing reason against attributing activity to the government.

Our cases have identified a host of facts that can bear on the fairness of such an attribution. We have, for example, held that a challenged activity may be state action when it results from the State's exercise of "coercive power," when the State provides "significant encouragement, either overt or covert," or when a private actor operates as a "willful participant in joint activity with the State or its agents." We have treated a nominally private entity as a state actor when it is controlled by an "agency of the State," when it has been delegated a public function by the State, when it is "entwined with governmental policies," or when government is "entwined in its management or control."

Amidst such variety, examples may be the best teachers, and examples from our cases are unequivocal in showing that the character of a legal entity is determined neither by its expressly private characterization in statutory law, nor by the failure of the law to acknowledge the entity's inseparability from recognized government officials or agencies. *Lebron v. National Railroad Passenger Corporation*, 513 U.S. 374 (1995), held that Amtrak was the Government for constitutional purposes, regardless of its congressional designation as private; it was organized under federal law to attain governmental objectives and was directed and controlled by federal appointees. [Descriptions of *Pennsylvania v. Board of Directors of City Trusts of Philadelphia*, 353 U.S. 230 (1957) and *Evans v. Newton*, 382 U.S. 296 (1966) omitted.]

Brentwood Academy v. Tennessee Secondary School Athletic Association

These examples of public entwinement in the management and control of ostensibly separate trusts or corporations foreshadow this case, as this Court itself anticipated in *National Collegiate Athletic Assn. v. Tarkanian*, 488 U.S. 179 (1988). . . . To be sure, it is not the strict holding in *Tarkanian* that points to our view of this case, for we found no state action on the part of the NCAA. We could see, on the one hand, that the university had some part in setting the NCAA's rules, and the Supreme Court of Nevada had gone so far as to hold that the NCAA had been delegated the university's traditionally exclusive public authority over personnel. But on the other side, the NCAA's policies were shaped not by the University of Nevada alone, but by several hundred member institutions, most of them having no connection with Nevada, and exhibiting no color of Nevada law. Since it was difficult to see the NCAA, not as a collective membership, but as surrogate for the one State, we held the organization's connection with Nevada too insubstantial to ground a state-action claim.

But dictum in *Tarkanian* pointed to a contrary result on facts like ours, with an organization whose member public schools are all within a single State. "The situation would, of course, be different if the Association's membership consisted entirely of institutions located within the same State, many of them public institutions created by the same sovereign." . . .

B

Just as we foresaw in *Tarkanian*, the necessarily fact-bound inquiry leads to the conclusion of state action here. The nominally private character of the Association is overborne by the pervasive entwinement of public institutions and public officials in its composition and workings, and there is no substantial reason to claim unfairness in applying constitutional standards to it.

The Association is not an organization of natural persons acting on their own, but of schools, and of public schools to the extent of 84% of the total. Under the Association's bylaws, each member school is represented by its principal or a faculty member, who has a vote in selecting members of the governing legislative council and board of control from eligible principals, assistant principals, and superintendents.

Although the findings and prior opinions in this case include no express conclusion of law that public school officials act within the scope of their duties when they represent their institutions, no other view would be rational, the official nature of their involvement being shown in any number of ways. Interscholastic athletics obviously play an integral part in the public education of Tennessee, where nearly every public high school spends money on competitions among schools. Since a pickup system of interscholastic games would not do, these public teams need some mechanism to produce rules and regulate competition. The mechanism is an organization overwhelmingly composed of public school officials who select representatives (all of them public officials at the time in question here), who in turn adopt and enforce the rules that make the system work. Thus, by giving these jobs to the Association, the 290 public schools of Tennessee belonging to it can sensibly be seen as exercising their own authority to meet their own responsibilities. Unsurprisingly, then, the record indicates that half the council or board meetings documented here were held during official school hours, and that public schools have largely provided for the Association's financial support. A small portion of the Association's revenue comes from membership dues paid by the schools, and the principal part from gate receipts at tournaments among the member schools. Unlike mere public buyers of contract services, whose payments for services rendered do not convert the service providers into public actors, the schools here obtain membership in the service organization and give up sources of their own income to their collective association. The Association thus exercises the authority of the predominantly public schools to charge for admission to their games; the Association does not receive this money from the schools, but enjoys the schools' moneymaking capacity as its own.

In sum, to the extent of 84% of its membership, the Association is an organization of public schools represented by their officials acting in their official capacity to provide an integral element of secondary public schooling. There would be no recognizable Association, legal or tangible, without the public school officials, who do not merely control but overwhelmingly perform all but the purely ministerial acts by which the Association exists and functions in practical terms. Only the 16% minority of private school memberships prevents this entwinement of the Association and the public school system from being total and their identities totally indistinguishable.

To complement the entwinement of public school officials with the Association from the bottom up, the State of Tennessee has provided for entwinement from top down. State Board members are assigned ex officio to serve as members of the board of control and legislative council, and the Association's ministerial employees are treated as state employees to the extent of being eligible for membership in the state retirement system. . . . The close relationship is confirmed by the Association's enforcement of the same preamendment rules and regulations reviewed and approved by the State Board (including the recruiting Rule challenged by Brentwood), and by the State Board's continued willingness to allow students to satisfy its physical education requirement by taking part in interscholastic athletics sponsored by the Association. . . . The entwinement down from the State Board is therefore unmistakable, just as the entwinement up from the member public schools is overwhelming. Entwinement will support a conclusion that an ostensibly private organization ought to be charged with a public character and judged by constitutional standards; entwinement to the degree shown here requires it.

C [Omitted.]

D

This is not to say that all of the Association's arguments are rendered beside the point by the public officials' involvement in the Association, for after application of the entwinement criterion, or any other, there is a further potential issue, and the Association raises it. Even facts that suffice to show public action (or, standing alone, would require such a finding) may be outweighed in the name of some value at odds with finding public accountability in the circumstances. In *Polk County v. Dodson,* 454 U.S. 312 (1981), a defense lawyer's actions were deemed private even though she was employed by the county and was acting within the scope of her duty as a public defender. Full-time public employment would be conclusive of state action for some purposes, but not when the employee is doing a defense lawyer's primary job; then, the public defender does "not act on behalf of the State; he is the State's adversary." The state-action doctrine does not convert opponents into virtual agents.

The assertion of such a countervailing value is the nub of each of the Association's two remaining arguments, neither of which, however, persuades us. The Association suggests, first, that reversing the judgment here will somehow trigger an epidemic of unprecedented federal litigation. Even if that might be counted as a good reason, . . . the record raises no reason for alarm here. Save for the Sixth Circuit, every Court of Appeals to consider a statewide athletic association like the one here has found it a state actor. . . . No one, however, has pointed to any explosion of § 1983 cases against interscholastic athletic associations in the affected jurisdictions. . . .

Nor do we think there is anything to be said for the Association's contention that there is no need to treat it as a state actor since any public school applying the Association's rules is itself subject to suit under § 1983. . . . Its position boils down to saying that the Association should not be dressed in state clothes because other, concededly public actors are; that Brentwood should be kept out of court because a different plaintiff raising a different claim in a different case may find the courthouse open. . . .

Justice Thomas, with whom Chief Justice Rehnquist, and Justices Scalia and Kennedy join, dissenting.

We have never found state action based upon mere "entwinement." Until today, we have found a private organization's acts to constitute state action only when the organization performed a public function; was created, coerced, or encouraged by the government; or acted in a symbiotic relationship with the government. The majority's holding—that the Tennessee Secondary School Athletic Association's (TSSAA) enforcement of its recruiting rule is state action—not only extends state-action doctrine beyond its permissible limits but also encroaches upon the realm of individual freedom that the doctrine was meant to protect. I respectfully dissent.

I

. . . Although we have used many different tests to identify state action, they all have a common purpose. Our goal in every case is to determine whether an action can fairly be attributed to the State.

A

Regardless of these various tests for state action, common sense dictates that the TSSAA's actions cannot fairly be attributed to the State, and thus cannot constitute state action. The TSSAA was formed in 1925 as a private corporation to organize interscholastic athletics and to sponsor tournaments among its member schools. Any private or public secondary school may join the TSSAA by signing a contract agreeing to comply with its rules and decisions. Although public schools currently compose 84% of the TSSAA's membership, the TSSAA does not require that public schools constitute a set percentage of its membership, and, indeed, no public school need join the TSSAA. The TSSAA's rules are enforced not by a state agency but by its own board of control, which comprises high school principals, assistant principals, and superintendents, none of whom must work at a public school. Of course, at the time the recruiting rule was enforced in this case, all of the board members happened to be public school officials. However, each board member acts in a representative capacity on behalf of all the private and public schools in his region of Tennessee, and not simply his individual school.

The State of Tennessee did not create the TSSAA. The State does not fund the TSSAA and does not pay its employees. In fact, only 4% of the TSSAA's revenue comes from the dues paid by member schools; the bulk of its operating budget is derived from gate receipts at tournaments it sponsors. The State does not permit the TSSAA to use state-owned facilities for a discounted fee, and it does not exempt the TSSAA from state taxation. No Tennessee law authorizes the State to coordinate interscholastic athletics or empowers another entity to organize interscholastic athletics on behalf of the State. The only state pronouncement acknowledging the TSSAA's existence is a rule providing that the State Board of Education permits public schools to maintain membership in the TSSAA if they so choose.

Moreover, the State of Tennessee has never had any involvement in the particular action taken by the TSSAA in this case: the enforcement of the TSSAA's recruiting rule prohibiting members from using "undue influence" on students or their parents or guardians "to secure or to retain a student for athletic purposes." There is no indication that the State has ever had any interest in how schools choose to regulate recruiting. In fact, the TSSAA's authority to enforce its recruiting rule arises solely from the voluntary membership contract that each member school signs, agreeing to conduct its athletics in accordance with the rules and decisions of the TSSAA.

Brentwood Academy v. Tennessee Secondary School Athletic Association

B [Omitted.]

II

Although the TSSAA's enforcement activities cannot be considered state action as a matter of common sense or under any of this Court's existing theories of state action, the majority presents a new theory. Under this theory, the majority holds that the combination of factors it identifies evidences "entwinement" of the State with the TSSAA, and that such entwinement converts private action into state action. The majority does not define "entwinement," and the meaning of the term is not altogether clear. But whatever this new "entwinement" theory may entail, it lacks any support in our state-action jurisprudence. Although the majority asserts that there are three examples of entwinement analysis in our cases, there is no case in which we have rested a finding of state action on entwinement alone.

Two of the cases on which the majority relies do not even use the word "entwinement." See *Lebron v. National Railroad Passenger Corporation* (1995); *Pennsylvania v. Board of Directors of City Trusts of Philadelphia* (1957) . . .

The majority's third example, *Evans v. Newton*, 382 U.S. 296 (1966), . . . at least uses the word "entwined" ("Conduct that is formally private may become so entwined with governmental policies or so impregnated with a governmental character as to become subject to the constitutional limitations placed upon state action"), [but it] did not discuss entwinement as a distinct concept, let alone one sufficient to transform a private entity into a state actor when traditional theories of state action do not. . . .

These cases, therefore, cannot support the majority's "entwinement" theory. Only *Evans* speaks of entwinement at all, and it does not do so in the same broad sense as does the majority. Moreover, these cases do not suggest that the TSSAA's activities can be considered state action, whether the label for the state-action theory is "entwinement" or anything else.

[CONCLUSION]

. . . I am not prepared to say that any private organization that permits public entities and public officials to participate acts as the State in anything or everything it does, and our state-action jurisprudence has never reached that far. The state-action doctrine was developed to reach only those actions that are truly attributable to the State, not to subject private citizens to the control of federal courts hearing § 1983 actions.

I respectfully dissent.

flashforward

Brentwood Academy *on Remand*. In later proceedings, it was held that the TSSAA's rules did not violate Brentwood Academy's free speech rights, and that any procedural due process violation was harmless error. *Tennessee Secondary School Athletic Association v. Brentwood Academy*, 551 U.S. 291 (2007) (*Brentwood II*).

Chapter Recap

A. As a general rule, the Constitution binds only the government, not private parties.

B. An exception to that rule exists, where private parties may in some circumstances be found to be state actors subject to constitutional limitations. The exception will be invoked when the private action should be attributed to the government.

C. The cases examining the exception to the state action doctrine tend to be fact-specific. Cases finding state action tend to share certain recurring features, but no single factor (or combination of factors) is dispositive.

CHAPTER 22

Master Class: Individual Rights

A major theme of this book has been the interaction among constitutional doctrines. Decisions involving one legal theory will affect other legal theories going forward. This dynamic is vividly illustrated by the recent history of litigation involving the rights of gay, lesbian, and bisexual people. The topic makes for a fitting capstone unit that integrates many of the concepts studied in this book.

In the materials that follow, notice how power is exercised by different levels of government (national, state, and local) and by different branches (legislative, executive and judicial). Notice the many legal theories that may limit governmental power, both structurally and with regard to individual rights, and how they interact with each other. Notice how lawyers and lower courts seek to interpret sometimes-ambiguous Supreme Court rulings. Finally, notice how constitutional meaning can be affected not just by people who hold public office, but also by the individuals affected by laws and their enforcement, by the attorneys who represent them, and by the jurors who consider their claims.

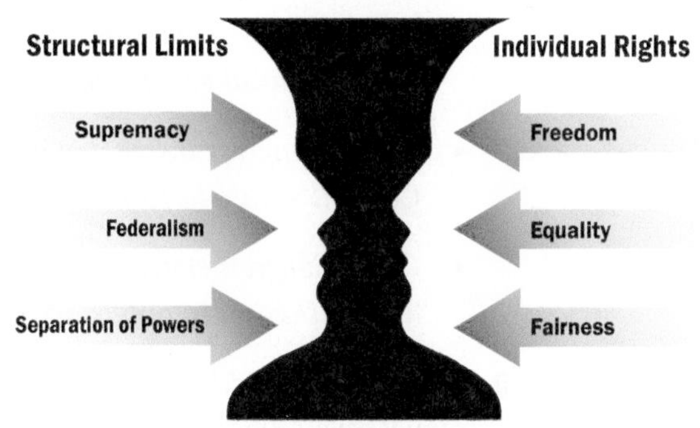

To highlight the process of legal change, this chapter is ordered chronologically. For best results, put yourself in the position of an attorney representing a client at each stage in the evolution of the doctrine. Which theories are available to you, and which are foreclosed? If existing case law seems to present an obstacle, how can you best navigate around it?

A. Anti-Discrimination Statutes (1979): *City of Austin v. Driskill Hotel*

Gay rights have seen dramatic changes within living memory. To greatly oversimplify the beginnings of the story, assume that as of 1970, federal and state governments could act however they wished with regard to sexual orientation. That discretion was routinely exercised in ways harmful to gay people. No American jurisdiction allowed same-sex couples to marry. No American jurisdiction had laws preventing discrimination on the basis of sexual orientation with regard to employment, housing, or public accommodations. And many American jurisdictions had laws making sexual contact between persons of the same sex a felony.

Inspired by the civil rights and feminist movements, an analogous social movement for gay rights began in earnest in the early 1970s. Some of its first victories occurred at the local level, mostly in cities with large or well-organized gay communities. One of these was Austin, Texas, which in 1976 enacted one of the nation's first laws barring discrimination on the basis of sexual orientation.

ITEMS TO CONSIDER WHILE READING *CITY OF AUSTIN v. DRISKILL HOTEL*:

A. *As a review exercise, consider the constitutionality of various laws inspired by the facts of the* Driskill Hotel *case, in terms of constitutional structure and individual rights:*

- *Does Congress have power to enact a law banning same-sex dancing? Does a state or local government?*
- *Could Congress instruct states to repeal laws banning same-sex dancing? Could it withhold federal funds to states having such laws?*
- *Could Congress enact a law similar to Austin's, forbidding sexual orientation discrimination in public accommodations?*

B. *Does a rule forbidding dancing by same-sex couples discriminate on the basis of sexual orientation? If so, does it impose disparate treatment or disparate impact?*

C. *What makes discrimination on the basis of sexual orientation similar to, or different from, discrimination on the basis of race, national origin, sex, or disability?*

D. *In a federalism-based system that allows decentralized lawmaking, the cost of allowing a city like Austin to enact laws that some people consider good is that other cities are allowed to enact laws some people consider bad. When does it become appropriate to insist on uniformity?*

City of Austin v. Driskill Hotel

as described in Carlos A. Ball, From the Closet to the Courtroom (2010)

The Driskill Hotel, in downtown Austin, is one of the most famous buildings in the state of Texas. Built by a wealthy cattleman in 1886, the cream-colored brick and limestone Victorian structure is where most Texas governors in the last century have held their inaugural balls. President Lyndon Johnson and his wife Lady Bird had their first date at the Driskill, and it was there that they watched the results of the 1964 presidential election. In 2000, George W. Bush and his advisors set up camp at the hotel as they waited for courts to determine the outcome of that year's contested presidential election.

The Driskill has been commercially successful for most of its history, except during a brief period in the late 1970s. In 1977, the hotel owners, looking to increase revenues, opened a dance bar called the Cabaret. The disco attracted young people from throughout Austin, some of whom were gay; although the gay clientele at the dance club was not large, the hotel's managers grew concerned that the Cabaret might become a gay dance club. Their solution to this perceived problem was to institute a house rule prohibiting same-sex couples from dancing together. A few days later, a hotel staff member approached two men dancing on the disco floor and asked them to leave the premises.

The Driskill Hotel

If the hotel had instituted its new dance policy two years earlier, it could have done so with legal impunity. In 1976, however, the Austin City Council enacted an ordinance making it a mis-demeanor, punishable by a fine of up to $200, for places of public accommodation to discriminate on the basis of sexual orientation.

Word of the hotel's dance policy quickly spread throughout Austin's LGBT community. A group of local activists approached the couple that had been asked to leave by the hotel's staff to inquire whether they would be interested in taking legal action under the new ordinance. The two men demurred, wanting to avoid the publicity that would inevitably accompany the filing of a legal complaint against the hotel. A few days later, four students at the University of Texas, who were also members of a local gay community group, stepped forward and volunteered to help.

On February 11, 1978, the four students—two men and two women —went to the Cabaret, accompanied by a city attorney and by a member of the Austin Human Rights Commission, the agency charged with enforcing the city's antidiscrimination laws. Shortly after the party of six arrived at the disco, the four students started dancing together, dividing themselves into two different-sex couples. At a predetermined moment during a particular song, the dancers switched partners, transforming themselves into two same-sex couples. A hotel manager quickly approached the students, informing them of the house rule against same-sex dancing. When the students protested that such a rule violated the local ordinance, the manager responded by saying that he did not care. He then ordered the students to stop dancing as same-sex couples or leave the premises.

The following week, the students filed a complaint with the Human Rights Commission, which began an investigation. The hotel refused to cooperate with the investigation, and the Commission—not surprisingly, given that one of its members had observed what occurred on the Cabaret's dance floor—concluded that there was enough evidence to turn the case over to the city attorney's office for prosecution.

When the hotel owners learned that they would likely be prosecuted under the local ordinance, they responded not by changing their policy but by suing the city instead. The lawsuit claimed that the city lacked the authority, under state law, to enact an ordinance prohibiting sexual orientation discrimination. The city attorney assigned the case to a young lawyer named Clayton Strange. Strange, a self-described cowboy who grew up on a cattle ranch in West Texas, knew nothing about gay issues. The first thing he did after being assigned the case was to ask around for the name of a lawyer who might know something about gay rights laws. The name that he kept hearing was that of Matthew Coles, a San Francisco attorney.

Coles had graduated from law school only the year before. As a law student at the University of California's Hastings Law School in the mid-1970s, he had helped to found the San Francisco Gay Democratic Club (later renamed the Harvey Milk Democratic Club). One of the club's first political objectives was to convince the San Francisco Board of Supervisors to enact a gay rights law. There was, however, one slight problem: none of the members knew what a gay rights law should say. It became Coles's responsibility, as the only member of the group with legal training, to figure that out.

Coles contacted city attorneys' offices in most of the roughly two dozen municipalities that then had gay rights laws on their books to request copies of their ordinances. As the material arrived, Coles read through the laws, noting the wording that he thought made the most sense, and typed up a draft law that would prohibit employers, landlords, and owners of public accommodations from discriminating on the basis of sexual orientation. A year later, thanks largely to the lobbying efforts of the San Francisco Gay Democratic Club, the City's Board of Supervisors enacted into law a gay rights ordinance, the origins of which could be traced back to Coles's typewriter.

When Strange reached Coles on the telephone in May 1978, the latter was practicing as a lawyer in San Francisco's predominantly gay Castro district. Strange told Coles about the Driskill Hotel case and asked whether he, as a national expert on municipal gay law, would be willing to help. Although amused at the notion that he, twelve months out of law school, could be an expert at anything, Coles nonetheless agreed.

City of Austin v. Driskill Hotel

Coles's first responsibility was to write a brief defending Austin's authority, under Texas law, to enact a gay rights ordinance. While working on the San Francisco gay rights law the year before, Coles had done extensive research on the authority of municipalities, under **home rule** principles, to enact antidiscrimination ordinances. It was clear to Coles that Austin had acted well within its power under state law when it enacted the gay rights measure and he argued so in his brief. Several months later, the state court agreed with Coles, dismissing the hotel's challenge to the ordinance. The discrimination case was now ready to be tried before a jury.

■ TERMINOLOGY

HOME RULE: Some states allow cities to legislate only on specific topics specified by the state legislature. Other states grant "home rule" to some or all local governments, allowing them to make laws on any subject (similar to a state's sovereign police power). Municipal laws enacted by home rule cities must not violate the state or federal constitutions, and they will be preempted if they conflict with state or federal statutes or regulations.

The day before the trial was scheduled to begin in the summer of 1979, Coles flew to Austin to meet with Strange at the city attorney's office and discuss their trial strategy. Coles knew that the hotel's main defense during the trial would be that its staff had not asked the four college students to stop dancing *because* of their sexual orientation. The hotel's legal position was that it had not violated the city ordinance prohibiting discrimination on the basis of sexual orientation because its house rule applied equally to both gays and straights; patrons, the hotel would argue at the trial, were not allowed to dance with others of the same sex *regardless* of their sexual orientation.

To counter this argument, Coles had lined up four local psychiatrists and psychologists who agreed to testify to the seemingly obvious proposition that club patrons usually dance with members of the sex to whom they are attracted. This testimony would allow Coles to establish that a policy which prohibited individuals of the same sex from dancing together had, in legal terminology, a "disparate impact" on lesbians and gay men, and was therefore illegal under the Austin ordinance.

When Coles, the day before the trial, called the four witnesses whom he had lined up to testify, they all told him that they were no longer willing to help with the case. This turn of events left Coles suspecting that someone had contacted his potential witnesses and convinced them—perhaps even threatened them—not to testify against the hotel. Coles was annoyed, but it was too late—the trial started the next day—to line up new medical experts.

As Coles thought about his predicament, it occurred to him that he might not need medical experts after all. Perhaps the point he wanted to make in court the following day—essentially that people who dance with others of the same sex are usually gay—could be made through the testimony of a dance bar owner. He got on the phone and called a handful of local gay activists, seeking their help. At eleven o'clock that evening, he found himself in the modest home of Bunch King Britten, who had owned two discos in Austin, one gay and one straight. Britten at first was understandably incredulous that a lawyer was in his home late at night asking him to testify the following day about how most people who danced with others of the opposite sex at his straight disco were straight and how most people who danced with others of the same sex at his gay disco were gay. But when Coles explained that the prosecution of the Driskill was an important discrimination case that would test Austin's new antidiscrimination ordinance, Britten agreed to do his part and testify.

The trial began the next morning in the courtroom of municipal court judge Steve Russell. Russell, a Native American of Cherokee descent, was born and raised in Oklahoma. He quit school in the ninth grade, later joined the air force, and eventually acquired his education (including a law degree from the University of Texas) through the GI Bill. Upon completing his legal education, Russell worked as a civil rights lawyer in Austin for several years, after which the city council appointed him to the bench.

In the late 1970s, municipal courts in Texas dealt with minor offenses, such as drinking in public and traffic violations, which carried fines of no more than $200. So when Russell first learned that he would be presiding over the case against the Driskill, he realized immediately that he had an unusual municipal court case in his hands. Suspecting that many potential jurors might be uncomfortable with the topic of homosexuality, the judge asked his assistant to fill the courtroom with as many potential jurors as could be accommodated. A few minutes after 9:00 a.m., on June 10, 1979, Russell walked into his courtroom and addressed a crowd of over sixty potential jurors. He thanked them for their service and informed them that they might be chosen to serve on a case that involved possible discrimination on the basis of sexual orientation. When Russell asked the potential jurors how many might find it difficult to be impartial in a case that involved homosexuality, most of them raised their hands. He proceeded to explain to the jurors that he was not there to pass moral judgments on their personal views of homosexuality. Instead, his job, and that of the lawyers, was to find jurors who were willing to listen to the evidence carefully and to apply the law as written.

From the beginning of the proceedings, Russell created an atmosphere in the courtroom that encouraged the potential jurors to express themselves freely. In fact, at one point, the following colloquy took place between Russell and a potential juror:

> POTENTIAL JUROR: Judge, I believe that every individual person has the right to decide who he wants to serve in his establishment.
>
> JUDGE RUSSELL: I understand that sentiment, sir, but I'm just trying to determine if you can follow the law the way it's written. What about the law that requires everyone to serve blacks?

POTENTIAL JUROR: That's different. Blacks are human beings.

City of Austin v. Driskill Hotel

Although Russell was startled by the man's comment, he politely thanked the potential juror and told him that he was free to leave.

After three hours of careful questioning by Russell and the lawyers, a group of six individuals—three men and three women—was chosen to hear the case. It took only two additional hours to try the case. Two of the college students who had visited the Driskill the year before testified that they had been asked to stop dancing with their same-sex partners. One of the students noted how the hotel's actions "made me feel like a second class citizen. And that made me angry because here they were telling me I could not dance with my life partner of four years." That same student also testified about how difficult it was to be openly gay in a society that was so intolerant and fearful of homosexuality. When asked why he had decided to challenge publicly the Driskill Hotel's policy, the young man replied that his parents had raised him to confront injustice whenever possible.

The hotel's lawyer, while cross-examining Bunch King Britten (Coles's "expert" witness), tried to establish that even if most people who dance with someone of the same sex at a club are gay, that did not mean that a policy that was meant to prevent same-sex dancing was necessarily antigay. The lawyer returned to this point during his closing argument, telling the jurors that they should find the hotel not guilty because its dance policy applied to everyone regardless of their sexual orientation.

In the end, the jurors were not persuaded that an ostensibly neutral policy that prohibited all patrons from dancing with someone of the same sex was not ultimately aimed at gay people. After deliberating for about thirty minutes, they returned to the courtroom to announce a finding of guilt. Judge Russell thanked them and closed the proceedings after fining the hotel $200.

As they walked out of the courthouse, Strange thanked Coles for his help, noting that Coles's obvious trial experience had made a big difference in the case. As a bemused Coles was telling Strange that, in fact, this had been his first trial, he noticed that one of the jurors, a librarian at a local Bible college, was walking a few feet ahead of them. Coles quickened his pace and politely asked the middle-aged woman if he could talk to her about the trial. She agreed. When Coles inquired why the jury had voted to convict the hotel, the woman replied as follows:

> You know, Mr. Coles, there was a lot of discussion during the trial about who dances with whom and the lawyers and the judge went on and on talking about "disparate impact," but none of us really understood any of that. We just figured that if they can stop gay folks from dancing at a disco, then they can deny them jobs, and if they can deny them jobs, then they can deny them housing, and if they can do it to gays, well, the next thing you know, they can do it to Jews. But honestly, Mr. Coles, I am not sure I understood the case at all.

Coles looked at the woman in amazement for a moment, and then replied: "No, ma'am. You understood the case perfectly. Thank you."

B. Substantive Due Process (1986): *Bowers v. Hardwick*

The US Supreme Court's first major statement about gay rights arose from a civil lawsuit brought by litigants challenging § 16–6–2 of the Georgia Code:

> (a) A person commits the offense of sodomy when he performs or submits to any sexual act involving the sex organs of one person and the mouth or anus of another.
>
> (b) A person convicted of the offense of sodomy shall be punished by imprisonment for not less than one nor more than 20 years.

ITEMS TO CONSIDER WHILE READING
BOWERS v. HARDWICK:

A. *Why did the plaintiffs emphasize a freedom theory, rather than an equality theory?*

B. *Work through the items in the substantive due process Kickstarter.*

C. *What impact, if any, should* Hardwick *have on the Equal Protection Clause?*

D. Hardwick *was later overruled. What was wrong with it?*

Bowers v. Hardwick,

478 U.S. 186 (1986)

Justice White delivered the opinion of the Court [joined by Chief Justice Burger and Justices Powell, Rehnquist, and O'Connor].

In August 1982, respondent [Michael] Hardwick (hereafter respondent) was charged with violating the Georgia statute criminalizing sodomy by committing that act with another adult male in the bedroom of respondent's home. After a preliminary hearing, the District Attorney decided not to present the matter to the grand jury unless further evidence developed.

Respondent then brought suit [against Michael Bowers (Attorney General of Georgia), Lewis Slaton (District Attorney for Fulton County), and George Napper (Public Safety Commissioner of Atlanta)] in the Federal District Court, challenging the constitutionality of the statute insofar as it criminalized consensual sodomy.[FN2] He asserted that he was a practicing homosexual, that the Georgia sodomy statute, as administered by the defendants, placed him in imminent danger of arrest, and that the statute for several reasons violates the Federal Constitution. The District Court granted the defendants' motion to dismiss for failure to state a claim.

FN2 John and Mary Doe were also plaintiffs in the action. They alleged that they wished to engage in sexual activity proscribed by § 16-6-2 in the privacy of their home, and that they had been chilled and deterred from engaging in such activity by both the existence of the statute and Hardwick's arrest. The District Court held, however, that because they had neither sustained, nor were in immediate danger of sustaining, any direct injury from the enforcement of the statute, they did not have proper standing to maintain the action. The Court of Appeals affirmed the District Court's judgment dismissing the Does' claim for lack of standing, and the Does do not challenge that holding in this Court. The only claim properly before the Court, therefore, is Hardwick's challenge to the Georgia statute as applied to consensual homosexual sodomy. We express no opinion on the constitutionality of the Georgia statute as applied to other acts of sodomy.

A divided panel of the Court of Appeals for the Eleventh Circuit reversed. [We granted review.]

This case does not require a judgment on whether laws against sodomy between consenting adults in general, or between homosexuals in particular, are wise or desirable. It raises no question about the right or propriety of state legislative decisions to repeal their laws that criminalize homosexual sodomy, or of state-court decisions invalidating those laws on state constitutional grounds. The issue presented is whether the Federal Constitution confers a fundamental right upon homosexuals to engage in sodomy and hence invalidates the laws of the many States that still make such conduct illegal and have done so for a very long time. The case also calls for some judgment about the limits of the Court's role in carrying out its constitutional mandate.

We first register our disagreement with the Court of Appeals and with respondent that the Court's prior cases have construed the Constitution to confer a right of privacy that extends to homosexual sodomy and for all intents and purposes have decided this case. *Pierce v. Society of Sisters* (1925), and *Meyer v. Nebraska* (1923), were described as dealing with child rearing and education; *Skinner v. Oklahoma* (1942), with procreation; *Loving v. Virginia* (1967), with marriage; *Griswold v. Connecticut* (1965) and *Eisenstadt v. Baird* (1972), with contraception; and *Roe v. Wade* (1973), with abortion. The latter three cases were interpreted as construing the Due Process Clause of the Fourteenth Amendment to confer a fundamental individual right to decide whether or not to beget or bear a child.

Accepting the decisions in these cases and the above description of them, we think it evident that none of the rights announced in those cases bears any resemblance to the claimed constitutional right of homosexuals to engage in acts of sodomy that is asserted in this case. No connection between family, marriage, or procreation on the one hand and homosexual activity on the other has been demonstrated, either by the Court of Appeals or by respondent. Moreover, any claim that these cases nevertheless stand for the proposition that any kind of private sexual conduct between consenting adults is constitutionally insulated from state proscription is unsupportable. . . .

Precedent aside, however, respondent would have us announce, as the Court of Appeals did, a fundamental right to engage in homosexual sodomy. This we are quite unwilling to do. It is true that despite the language of the Due Process Clauses of the Fifth and Fourteenth Amendments, which appears to focus only on the processes by which life, liberty, or property is taken, the cases are legion in which those Clauses have been interpreted to have substantive content, subsuming rights that to a great extent are immune from federal or state regulation or proscription. Among such cases are those recognizing rights that have little or no textual support in the constitutional language. *Meyer,* and *Pierce* fall in this category, as do the privacy cases from *Griswold* [onward].

Striving to assure itself and the public that announcing rights not readily identifiable in the Constitution's text involves much more than the imposition of the Justices' own choice of values on the States and the Federal Government, the Court has sought to identify the nature of the rights qualifying for heightened judicial protection. In *Palko v. Connecticut*, 302 U.S. 319 (1937), it was said that this category includes those fundamental liberties that are "implicit in the concept of ordered liberty," such that "neither liberty nor justice would exist if they were sacrificed." A different description of fundamental liberties appeared in *Moore v. East Cleveland* (1977) (opinion of Powell, J.), where they are characterized as those liberties that are "deeply rooted in this Nation's history and tradition."

It is obvious to us that neither of these formulations would extend a fundamental right to homosexuals to engage in acts of consensual sodomy. Proscriptions against that conduct have ancient roots. Sodomy was a criminal offense at common law and was forbidden by the laws of the original thirteen States when they ratified the Bill of Rights. In 1868, when the Fourteenth Amendment was ratified, all but 5 of the 37 States in the Union had criminal sodomy laws. In fact, until 1961, all 50 States outlawed sodomy, and today, 24 States and the District of Columbia continue to provide criminal penalties for sodomy performed in private and between consenting adults. Against this background, to claim that a right to engage in such conduct is "deeply rooted in this Nation's history and tradition" or "implicit in the concept of ordered liberty" is, at best, facetious.

Nor are we inclined to take a more expansive view of our authority to discover new fundamental rights embedded in the Due Process Clause. The Court is most vulnerable and comes nearest to illegitimacy when it deals with judge-made constitutional law having little or no cognizable roots in the language or design of the

Constitution. That this is so was painfully demonstrated by the face-off between the Executive and the Court in the 1930s, which resulted in the repudiation of much of the substantive gloss that the Court had placed on the Due Process Clauses of the Fifth and Fourteenth Amendments. There should be, therefore, great resistance to expand the substantive reach of those Clauses, particularly if it requires redefining the category of rights deemed to be fundamental. Otherwise, the Judiciary necessarily takes to itself further authority to govern the country without express constitutional authority. The claimed right pressed on us today falls far short of overcoming this resistance. . . .

Even if the conduct at issue here is not a fundamental right, respondent asserts that [the law has no basis] other than the presumed belief of a majority of the electorate in Georgia that homosexual sodomy is immoral and unacceptable. This is said to be an inadequate rationale to support the law. The law, however, is constantly based on notions of morality, and if all laws representing essentially moral choices are to be invalidated under the Due Process Clause, the courts will be very busy indeed. Even respondent makes no such claim, but insists that majority sentiments about the morality of homosexuality should be declared inadequate. We do not agree, and are unpersuaded that the sodomy laws of some 25 States should be invalidated on this basis.

Chief Justice Burger, concurring. [Omitted.]

Justice Powell, concurring.

I join the opinion of the Court. I agree with the Court that there is no fundamental right—i.e., no substantive right under the Due Process Clause—such as that claimed by respondent Hardwick, and found to exist by the Court of Appeals. This is not to suggest, however, that respondent may not be protected by the Eighth Amendment of the Constitution. The Georgia statute at issue in this case authorizes a court to imprison a person for up to 20 years for a single private, consensual act of sodomy. In my view, a prison sentence for such conduct—certainly a sentence of long duration—would create a serious Eighth Amendment issue. Under the Georgia statute a single act of sodomy, even in the private setting of a home, is a felony comparable in terms of the possible sentence imposed to serious felonies such as aggravated battery, first-degree arson, and robbery.

In this case, however, respondent has not been tried, much less convicted and sentenced. Moreover, respondent has not raised the Eighth Amendment issue below. For these reasons this constitutional argument is not before us.

Justice Blackmun, with whom Justices Brennan, Marshall, and Stevens join, dissenting.

This case is [not] about "a fundamental right to engage in homosexual sodomy," as the Court purports to declare[.] Rather, this case is about "the most comprehensive of rights and the right most valued by civilized men," namely, "the right to be let alone." ***Olmstead v. United States***, 277 U.S. 438 (1928) (Brandeis, J., dissenting).

■ HISTORY

OLMSTEAD: *Olmstead v. United States* held that the government did not violate the Fourth Amendment by wiretapping a phone line without a warrant, so long as the surveillance equipment could be installed without trespassing. *Olmstead* was ultimately overruled by *Katz v. United States*, 389 U.S. 347 (1967). Today, *Olmstead* is most often cited for Justice Brandeis's dissent, which was also quoted with approval in *Griswold v. Connecticut* (1965) (Ch. 20.C).

The statute at issue denies individuals the right to decide for themselves whether to engage in particular forms of private, consensual sexual activity. The Court concludes that § 1662 is valid essentially because "the laws of many States still make such conduct illegal and have done so for a very long time." But the fact that the moral judgments expressed by statutes like § 1662 may be "natural and familiar ought not to conclude our judgment upon the question whether statutes embodying them conflict with the Constitution of the United States." *Roe v. Wade* (1973), quoting *Lochner v. New York* (1905) (Holmes, J., dissenting). Like Justice Holmes, I believe that "it is revolting to have no better reason for a rule of law than that so it was laid down in the time of Henry IV. It is still more revolting if the grounds upon which it was laid down have vanished long since, and the rule simply persists from blind imitation of the past." Holmes, *The Path of the Law*, 10 Harv.L.Rev. 457, 489 (1897). I believe we must analyze Hardwick's claim in the light of the values that underlie the constitutional right to privacy. If that right means anything, it means that, before Georgia can prosecute its citizens for making choices about the most intimate aspects of their lives, it must do more than assert that the choice they have made is [in the words of a Georgia Supreme Court decision from 1904] an "abominable crime not fit to be named among Christians." . . .

I

In its haste to reverse the Court of Appeals and hold that the Constitution does not "confer a fundamental right upon homosexuals to engage in sodomy," the Court relegates the actual statute being challenged to a footnote and ignores the procedural posture of the case before it. A fair reading of the statute and of the complaint clearly reveals that the majority has distorted the question this case presents.

First, the Court's almost obsessive focus on homosexual activity is particularly hard to justify in light of the broad language Georgia has used. Unlike the Court, the Georgia Legislature has not proceeded on the assumption that homosexuals are so different from other citizens that their lives may be controlled in a way that would not be tolerated if it limited the choices of those other citizens. Rather, Georgia has provided that "a person commits the offense of sodomy when he performs or submits to any sexual act involving the sex organs of one person and the mouth or anus of another." The sex or status of the persons who engage in the act is irrelevant as a matter of state law. In fact, to the extent I can discern a legislative purpose for Georgia's 1968 enactment of § 16-6-2, that purpose seems to have been to broaden the coverage of the law to reach heterosexual as well as homosexual activity. I therefore see no basis for the Court's decision to treat this case as an "as applied" challenge to § 16-6-2, or for Georgia's attempt, both in its brief and at oral argument, to defend § 16-6-2 solely on the grounds that it prohibits homosexual activity. Michael Hardwick's standing may rest in significant part on Georgia's apparent willingness to enforce against homosexuals a law it seems not to have any desire to enforce against heterosexuals. But his claim that § 16-6-2 involves an unconstitutional intrusion into his privacy and his right of intimate association does not depend in any way on his sexual orientation. . . .

II . . .

A

The Court concludes today that none of our prior cases dealing with various decisions that individuals are entitled to make free of governmental interference "bears any resemblance to the claimed constitutional right of homosexuals to engage in acts of sodomy that is asserted in this case." While it is true that these cases may be characterized by their connection to protection of the family, the Court's conclusion that they extend no further than this boundary ignores the warning in *Moore v. East Cleveland* (1977) (plurality opinion), against "closing our eyes to the basic reasons why certain rights associated with the family have been accorded shelter under the Fourteenth Amendment's Due Process Clause." We protect those rights not because they contribute, in some direct and material way, to the general public welfare, but because they form so central a part of an individual's life. The concept of privacy embodies the moral fact that a person belongs to himself and not others nor to society as a whole. And so we protect the decision whether to marry precisely because "marriage is an association that promotes a way of life, not causes; a harmony in living, not political faiths; a bilateral loyalty, not commercial or social projects." *Griswold*. We protect the decision whether to have a child because parenthood alters so dramatically an individual's self-definition, not because of demographic considerations or the Bible's command to be fruitful and multiply. And we protect the family because it contributes so powerfully to the happiness of individuals, not because of a preference for stereotypical households. . . . The ability independently to define one's identity that is central to any concept of liberty cannot truly be exercised in a vacuum; we all depend on the emotional enrichment from close ties with others.

Only the most willful blindness could obscure the fact that sexual intimacy is a sensitive, key relationship of human existence, central to family life, community welfare, and the development of human personality. The fact that individuals define themselves in a significant way through their intimate sexual relationships with others suggests, in a Nation as diverse as ours, that there may be many "right" ways of conducting those relationships, and that much of the richness of a relationship will come from the freedom an individual has to choose the form and nature of these intensely personal bonds.

B

The behavior for which Hardwick faces prosecution occurred in his own home, a place to which the Fourth Amendment attaches special significance. The Court's treatment of this aspect of the case is symptomatic of its overall refusal to consider the broad principles that have informed our treatment of privacy in specific cases. Just as the right to privacy is more than the mere aggregation of a number of entitlements to engage in specific behavior, so too, protecting the physical integrity of the home is more than merely a means of protecting specific activities that often take place there. Even when our understanding of the contours of the right to privacy depends on reference to a place, the essence of a Fourth Amendment violation is not the breaking of a person's doors, and the rummaging of his drawers, but rather is the invasion of his indefeasible right of personal security, personal liberty and private property. . . .

III [Omitted.]

IV

It took but three years for the Court to see the error in its analysis in *Minersville School District v. Gobitis* (1940), and to recognize that the threat to national cohesion posed by a refusal to salute the flag was vastly outweighed by the threat to those same values posed by compelling such a salute. See *West Virginia Board of Education v. Barnette* (1943). I can only hope that here, too, the Court soon will reconsider its analysis and conclude that depriving individuals of the right to choose for themselves how to conduct their intimate relationships poses a far greater threat to the values most deeply rooted in our Nation's history than tolerance of nonconformity could ever do. Because I think the Court today betrays those values, I dissent.

Justice Stevens, with whom Justices Brennan and Marshall join, dissenting. [Omitted.]

flashforward

***Change in Georgia Law After* Hardwick.** In 1998, the Georgia Supreme Court found that the statute upheld in *Hardwick* violated the Due Process Clause of the state constitution. That clause had been interpreted since at least 1905 to include a right to privacy that had been described in various terms, including the right "to be free of unwarranted interference by the public about matters with which the public is not necessarily concerned." *Georgia Power Co. v. Busbin*, 254 S.E.2d 146 (Ga. App. 1979). Reversing a criminal sodomy conviction 12 years after *Hardwick*, the Georgia Supreme Court said: "We cannot think of any other activity that reasonable persons would rank as more private and more deserving of protection from governmental interference than unforced, private, adult sexual activity." *Powell v. State*, 510 S.E.2d 18 (Ga. 1998).

C. Equal Protection (1990): *High Tech Gays v. DISCO*

Because *Bowers v. Hardwick* imposed a significant barrier to gay rights litigation that relied on substantive due process, attention in subsequent years focused on equality theories. (Of course, challenges under state law theories were unaffected by *Bowers*.) *High Tech Gays v. Defense Industrial Security Clearance Office (DISCO)*, 895 F.2d 563 (9th Cir. 1990), exemplifies the questions that began to arise under the Equal Protection Clause.

The plaintiff was an association of civilian employees of firms that did business for the Department of Defense. Its members required security clearances from DISCO to perform their jobs. DISCO subjected gay employees to more lengthy and intrusive background checks than straight employees. It was a case of disparate treatment, not merely disparate impact: DISCO acted intentionally, based on its view that gay people posed greater security risks.

Plaintiffs prevailed in the trial court, with the judge concluding that "gay people are a 'quasi-suspect class' entitled to heightened scrutiny under the equal protection clause." 668 F. Supp. 1361 (N.D. Cal. 1987). On appeal, a three-judge panel of the Ninth Circuit reversed. 895 F.2d 563 (9th Cir. 1990).

> The Supreme Court has ruled that homosexual activity is not a fundamental right protected by substantive due process and that the proper standard of review under the Fifth Amendment is rational basis review. *Bowers v. Hardwick* (1986). The Court explained that the right to privacy inheres only in family

relationships, marriage and procreation, and does not extend to all private sexual conduct between consenting adults. The Court specifically characterized "fundamental liberties" under the Constitution "as those liberties that are deeply rooted in this Nation's history and tradition."

Other circuits are in accord and have held that although the Court in *Hardwick* analyzed the constitutionality of the sodomy statute on a due process rather than equal protection basis, by the Hardwick majority holding that the Constitution confers no fundamental right upon homosexuals to engage in sodomy, and because homosexual conduct can thus be criminalized, homosexuals cannot constitute a suspect or quasi-suspect class entitled to greater than rational basis review for equal protection purposes. . . .

It is apparent that while the Supreme Court has identified that legislative classifications based on race, alienage, or national origin are subject to strict scrutiny and that classifications based upon gender or illegitimacy call for a heightened standard, the Court has never held homosexuality to a heightened standard of review.

To be a "suspect" or "quasi-suspect" class, homosexuals must (1) have suffered a history of discrimination; (2) exhibit obvious, immutable, or distinguishing characteristics that define them as a discrete group; and (3) show that they are a minority or politically powerless, or alternatively show that the statutory classification at issue burdens a fundamental right.

While we do agree that homosexuals have suffered a history of discrimination, we do not believe that they meet the other criteria. Homosexuality is not an immutable characteristic; it is behavioral and hence is fundamentally different from traits such as race, gender, or alienage, which define already existing suspect and quasi-suspect classes. The behavior or conduct of such already recognized classes is irrelevant to their identification.

Moreover, legislatures have addressed and continue to address the discrimination suffered by homosexuals on account of their sexual orientation through the passage of anti-discrimination legislation. Thus, homosexuals are not without political power; they have the ability to and do "attract the attention of the lawmakers," as evidenced by such legislation. Lastly, as previously noted, homosexual conduct is not a fundamental right.

Our review compels us to agree with the other circuits that have ruled on this issue and to hold that homosexuals do not constitute a suspect or quasi-suspect class entitled to greater than rational basis scrutiny under the equal protection component of the Due Process Clause of the Fifth Amendment.

Plaintiffs asked the Ninth Circuit to rehear the case en banc, but the petition was denied. Judge Canby dissented from the Court's refusal to rehear the case. 909 F.2d 375 (9th Cir. 1990).

The class of "homosexuals" clearly qualifies as a suspect category, triggering strict judicial scrutiny of any governmental discrimination against them. The applicable criteria are properly described but improperly applied by the panel: To be a "suspect" or "quasi-suspect" class, homosexuals must (1) have suffered a history of discrimination; (2) exhibit obvious immutable, or distinguishing characteristics that define them as a discrete group; and (3) show that they are a minority or politically powerless.

The panel agrees that the first criterion is met; homosexuals have suffered a history of discrimination. This point should not be put quickly out of mind, however, for this history of discrimination makes it far more likely that differential treatment is simply a resort to old prejudices. As the district court said, lesbians and gays have been the object of some of the deepest prejudice and hatred in American society. That fact tends to make discrimination against them all too easy. We should be careful not to endorse that tendency.

With regard to the second criterion, the panel's opinion states: "Homosexuality is not an immutable characteristic; it is behavioral and hence is fundamentally different from traits such as race, gender, or alienage, which define already existing suspect and quasi-suspect classes."

There are several problems with this conclusion. . . . The Supreme Court has more than once recited the characteristics of a suspect class without mentioning immutability. Aliens, for example, constitute a suspect category, but the condition is not immutable. The real question is whether discrimination on the basis of the class's distinguishing characteristic amounts to an unfair branding or resort to prejudice, not necessarily whether the characteristic is immutable.

Immutability, of course, does make discrimination more clearly unfair. There is every reason to regard homosexuality as an immutable characteristic for equal protection purposes. It is not enough to say that the category is behavioral. One can make behavioral classes out of persons who go to church on Saturday, persons who speak Spanish, or persons who walk with crutches. The question is, what causes the behavior? Does it arise from the kind of a characteristic that belongs peculiarly to a group that the equal protection clause should specially protect?

Homosexuals are physically attracted to members of their own sex. That is the source of the behavior that we notice about them. Did they choose to be attracted by members of their own sex, rather than by members of the opposite sex? The answer, by the overwhelming weight of respectable authority, is "no." Sexual identity is established at a very early age; it is not a matter of conscious or controllable choice. Can homosexuals change their orientation? Again, from everything we now know, the answer is "no." At least they cannot change it without immense difficulty. . . . What would it take to get any one of us to change his or her sexual orientation?

For practical and constitutional purposes, then, homosexuality is an immutable characteristic, and the panel's opinion offers nothing to the contrary except its bare conclusion. When the government discriminates against homosexuals, it is discriminating against persons because of what they are, through no choice of their own, and what they are unable to change. Preventing such unfair discrimination is what the equal protection clause is all about.

The panel's opinion also concludes that homosexuals are not politically powerless. Its support for this proposition is that one state broadly bars employment discrimination against homosexuals, two other states more narrowly bar discrimination against homosexuals, and a few cities bar some types of discrimination. That showing is clearly insufficient to deprive homosexuals of the status of a suspect classification. Compare the situation with that of blacks, who clearly constitute a suspect category for equal protection purposes. Blacks are protected by three federal constitutional amendments, major federal Civil Rights Acts of 1866, 1870, 1871, 1875 (**ill-fated though it was**), 1957, 1960, 1964, 1965, and 1968, as well as by antidiscrimination laws in 48 of the states. By that comparison, and by absolute standards as well, homosexuals are politically powerless. They are so because of their numbers, which most estimates put at around 10 percent of the population, and by the fact that many of them keep their status secret to avoid discrimination. That secrecy inhibits organization of homosexuals as a pressure group. Certainly homosexuals as a class wield less political power than blacks, a suspect classification, or women, a quasi-suspect one. One can easily find examples of major political parties' openly tailoring their positions to appeal to black voters, and to female voters. One cannot find comparable examples of appeals to homosexual voters; homosexuals are regarded by the national parties as political pariahs.

■ HISTORY

ILL-FATED THOUGH IT WAS: Judge Canby alludes to the public accommodations law held unconstitutional in *The Civil Rights Cases* (1883).

Homosexuals, then, are exactly the kind of class that should trigger strict scrutiny when the government discriminates against them. The panel's opinion, by ruling that such discrimination may be justified merely by a rational basis, creates the opportunity for immense abuse. While one may hope that future courts faced with discrimination against homosexuals would apply the rather active rational basis review exemplified by *City of Cleburne v. Cleburne Living Center* (1985), there is no guarantee that this will happen. There is ample authority defining rational basis in such permissive terms that it really means no scrutiny at all. Thus the danger is great that an already much-vilified group will be subject to further governmental discrimination on the slightest of justifications. . . .

The panel's opinion seems to suggest that even if homosexuals otherwise qualify as a suspect class, they are precluded from being so because of *Bowers v. Hardwick* (1986). The suggestion is completely unfounded. In *Hardwick*, the Supreme Court held that the application of state sodomy laws to homosexuals did not violate any fundamental right of privacy protected by the due process clause. The *Hardwick* opinion pointed out, however, that no equal protection claim had been presented, and *Hardwick* is clearly not controlling on the suspect class issue. . . .

The final difficulty with the panel's proposition drawn from *Hardwick* is crucial. It assumes that the class of homosexuals is entirely defined by conduct that may be criminalized. The panel's error here is fundamental. In the first place, it is not proper to assume generally that "homosexual conduct" can be criminalized. There are many varieties of conduct that might be characterized as homosexual, from hand-holding to sodomy. *Hardwick* establishes only that the latter may be criminalized. Yet the Department of Defense invokes its expanded security clearance procedures when there is information indicating "deviant behavior," which it defines to include "homosexuality." If there is "homosexual activity" within the past 15 years, the expanded security procedure is followed. Nothing in the record suggests that the Department is confining its view of homosexual conduct to sodomy.

It is an error of massive proportions to define the entire class of homosexuals by sodomy. I will be the first to admit that homosexuals, in sexually expressing their affection for persons of their own sex, frequently engage in sodomy, as do heterosexuals sexually expressing their affection for persons of the opposite sex. Homosexuals and heterosexuals also engage in other affective conduct, criminalized nowhere. But homosexuality, like heterosexuality, is a status. As an amicus points out, one is a homosexual or a heterosexual while playing bridge just as much as while engaging in sexual activity. And the Department of Defense is discriminating against homosexuals for what they are, not what they do. The Department is not trying to send anyone to jail for sodomy. It is not asserting that acts of sodomy endanger national security. It is making the unsupported assumption that homosexuals are more likely to betray their country than other classes of persons, and it is discriminating against them because of that assumption. That is the key to this case.

flashforward

Executive Orders Involving Sexual Orientation. In 1995, President Clinton issued Executive Order 12968, revamping a number of executive branch procedures relating to security clearances. Within the order was a provision that ended the previous practice of automatically requiring intrusive background checks on gay applicants: "The United States Government does not discriminate on the basis of race, color, religion, sex, national origin, disability, or sexual orientation in granting access to classified information."

Currently, no federal statute expressly forbids private employers from discriminating on the basis of sexual orientation (although some states and local governments have such laws). However, President Clinton's Executive Order 13087 (1998) directed federal civilian agencies not to discriminate on the basis of sexual orientation in employment.

D. Equal Protection (1996): *Romer v. Evans*

Some Colorado cities (including Aspen, Boulder, and Denver) had enacted local ordinances forbidding discrimination on the basis of sexual orientation, similar to the Austin ordinance described in Ch. 21.A. In a statewide referendum held in 1992, Colorado voters enacted Amendment 2 to the state constitution, which read as follows:

> *No Protected Status Based on Homosexual, Lesbian or Bisexual Orientation.* Neither the State of Colorado, through any of its branches or departments, nor any of its agencies, political subdivisions, municipalities or school districts, shall enact, adopt or enforce any statute, regulation, ordinance or policy whereby homosexual, lesbian or bisexual orientation, conduct, practices or relationships shall constitute or otherwise be the basis of or entitle any person or class of persons to have or claim any minority status, quota preferences, protected status or claim of discrimination.

A Colorado state trial court ruled that Amendment 2 violated the Equal Protection Clause of the US Constitution. The Colorado Supreme Court agreed, in an opinion that applied strict scrutiny to laws that classified on the basis of sexual orientation. In *Romer v. Evans*, 517 U.S. 620 (1996), the US Supreme Court agreed (6–3) that Amendment 2 was unconstitutional, but in an opinion that did not expressly rely on strict scrutiny.

The majority first rejected the state's argument that Amendment 2 placed gay people on the same level as all others. To the contrary, the state had imposed a differential burden on them:

> Homosexuals, by state decree, are put in a solitary class with respect to transactions and relations in both the private and governmental spheres. The amendment withdraws from homosexuals, but no others, specific legal protection from the injuries caused by discrimination, and it forbids reinstatement of these laws and policies. . . . [As a result,] we cannot accept the view that Amendment 2's prohibition on specific legal protections does no more than deprive homosexuals of special rights. To the contrary, the amendment imposes a special disability upon those persons alone. Homosexuals are forbidden the safeguards that others enjoy or may seek without constraint.

Having identified a differential burden, the majority then scrutinized Amendment 2:

> The Fourteenth Amendment's promise that no person shall be denied the equal protection of the laws must coexist with the practical necessity that most legislation classifies for one purpose or another, with resulting disadvantage to various groups or persons. We have attempted to reconcile the principle with the reality by stating that, if a law neither burdens a fundamental right nor targets a suspect class, we will uphold the legislative classification so long as it bears a rational relation to some legitimate end.
>
> Amendment 2 fails, indeed defies, even this conventional inquiry. First, the amendment has the peculiar property of imposing a broad and undifferentiated disability on a single named group, an exceptional and, as we shall explain, invalid form of legislation. Second, its sheer breadth is so discontinuous with the reasons offered for it that the amendment seems inexplicable by anything but animus toward the class it affects; it lacks a rational relationship to legitimate state interests. . . . We must conclude that Amendment 2 classifies homosexuals not to further a proper legislative end but to make them unequal to everyone else.

Justice Scalia's furious dissent (joined by Chief Justice Rehnquist and Justice Thomas) said in part:

> Today's opinion has no foundation in American constitutional law, and barely pretends to. The people of Colorado have adopted an entirely reasonable provision which does not even disfavor homosexuals in any substantive sense, but merely denies them preferential treatment. Amendment 2 is designed to prevent piecemeal deterioration of the sexual morality favored by a majority of Coloradans, and is . . . an appropriate means to that legitimate end[.] Striking it down is an act, not of judicial judgment, but of political will.

E. Substantive Due Process (2003): *Lawrence v. Texas*

The Supreme Court revisited criminal sodomy statutes in *Lawrence v. Texas*. Unlike *Hardwick*, which was a civil suit seeking to invalidate a statute, *Lawrence* was an appeal of a criminal prosecution.

ITEMS TO CONSIDER WHILE READING
LAWRENCE V. TEXAS:

A. *Work through the items in the substantive due process Kickstarter.*

B. *The Texas law criminalized only same-sex sodomy. Why did the majority decide the case on freedom grounds, rather than equality grounds?*

C. *Justice Scalia's dissent claims the majority decision applied rational basis scrutiny. Is he correct? Should subsequent cases cite a dissent as a way to characterize a majority opinion?*

D. Does Lawrence *adequately justify overruling controlling precedent?*

E. Lawrence *cited* Planned Parenthood v. Casey *(1992) with approval, but that decision was overruled by* Dobbs v. Jackson Women's Health Organization *(2022). Does* Lawrence *survive* Dobbs?

Lawrence v. Texas,
539 U.S. 558 (2003)

Justice Kennedy delivered the opinion of the Court [joined by Justices Stevens, Souter, Breyer, and Ginsburg].

Liberty protects the person from unwarranted government intrusions into a dwelling or other private places. In our tradition the State is not omnipresent in the home. And there are other spheres of our lives and existence, outside the home, where the State should not be a dominant presence. Freedom extends beyond spatial bounds. Liberty presumes an autonomy of self that includes freedom of thought, belief, expression, and certain intimate conduct. The instant case involves liberty of the person both in its spatial and in its more transcendent dimensions.

I

The question before the Court is the validity of a Texas statute making it a crime for two persons of the same sex to engage in certain intimate sexual conduct.

In Houston, Texas, officers of the Harris County Police Department were dispatched to a private residence in response to a reported weapons disturbance. They entered an apartment where one of the petitioners, John Geddes Lawrence, resided. The right of the police to enter does not seem to have been questioned. The officers observed Lawrence and another man, Tyron Garner, engaging in a sexual act. The two petitioners were arrested, held in custody overnight, and charged and convicted before a Justice of the Peace.

Lawrence v. Texas

The complaints described their crime as "deviate sexual intercourse, namely anal sex, with a member of the same sex (man)." The applicable state law is Tex. Penal Code § 21.06(a). It provides: "A person commits an offense if he engages in deviate sexual intercourse with another individual of the same sex." The statute defines "deviate sexual intercourse" as follows:

John Lawrence and Tyron Garner

> (A) any contact between any part of the genitals of one person and the mouth or anus of another person; or
>
> (B) the penetration of the genitals or the anus of another person with an object.

The petitioners exercised their right to a trial *de novo* in Harris County Criminal Court. They challenged the statute as a violation of the Equal Protection Clause of the Fourteenth Amendment and of a like provision of the Texas Constitution. Those contentions were rejected. The petitioners, having entered a plea of *nolo contendere [no contest]*, were each fined $200 and assessed court costs of $141.25.

The Court of Appeals for the Texas Fourteenth District . . . rejected the constitutional arguments and affirmed the convictions. . . . We granted certiorari to consider three questions:

1. Whether petitioners' criminal convictions under the Texas Homosexual Conduct law—which criminalizes sexual intimacy by same-sex couples, but not identical behavior by different-sex couples—violate the Fourteenth Amendment guarantee of equal protection of the laws.
2. Whether petitioners' criminal convictions for adult consensual sexual intimacy in the home violate their vital interests in liberty and privacy protected by the Due Process Clause of the Fourteenth Amendment.
3. Whether *Bowers v. Hardwick* (1986) should be overruled.

The petitioners were adults at the time of the alleged offense. Their conduct was in private and consensual.

II

We conclude the case should be resolved by determining whether the petitioners were free as adults to engage in the private conduct in the exercise of their liberty under the Due Process Clause of the Fourteenth Amendment to the Constitution. For this inquiry we deem it necessary to reconsider the Court's holding in *Bowers*.

There are broad statements of the substantive reach of liberty under the Due Process Clause in earlier cases, including *Pierce v. Society of Sisters* (1925), and *Meyer v. Nebraska* (1923); but the most pertinent beginning point is our decision in *Griswold v. Connecticut* (1965).

In *Griswold* the Court invalidated a state law prohibiting the use of drugs or devices of contraception and counseling or aiding and abetting the use of contraceptives. The Court described the protected interest as a right to privacy and placed emphasis on the marriage relation and the protected space of the marital bedroom.

After *Griswold* it was established that the right to make certain decisions regarding sexual conduct extends beyond the marital relationship. In *Eisenstadt v. Baird* (1972), the Court invalidated a law prohibiting the distribution of contraceptives to unmarried persons. The case was decided under the Equal Protection Clause; but with respect to unmarried persons, the Court went on to state the fundamental proposition that the law impaired the exercise of their personal rights[.] . . .

The Court began its substantive discussion in *Bowers* as follows: "The issue presented is whether the Federal Constitution confers a fundamental right upon homosexuals to engage in sodomy and hence invalidates the laws of the many States that still make such conduct illegal and have done so for a very long time." That statement, we now conclude, discloses the Court's own failure to appreciate the extent of the liberty at stake. To say that the issue in *Bowers* was simply the right to engage in certain sexual conduct demeans the claim the individual put forward, just as it would demean a married couple were it to be said marriage is simply about the right to have sexual intercourse. The laws involved in *Bowers* and here are, to be sure, statutes that purport to do no more than prohibit a particular sexual act. Their penalties and purposes, though, have more far-reaching consequences, touching upon the most private human conduct, sexual behavior, and in the most private of places, the home. The statutes do seek to control a personal relationship that, whether or not entitled to formal recognition in the law, is within the liberty of persons to choose without being punished as criminals.

This, as a general rule, should counsel against attempts by the State, or a court, to define the meaning of the relationship or to set its boundaries absent injury to a person or abuse of an institution the law protects. It suffices for us to acknowledge that adults may choose to enter upon this relationship in the confines of their homes and their own private lives and still retain their dignity as free persons. When sexuality finds overt expression in intimate conduct with another person, the conduct can be but one element in a personal bond that is more enduring. The liberty protected by the Constitution allows homosexual persons the right to make this choice.

Lawrence v. Texas

Having misapprehended the claim of liberty there presented to it, and thus stating the claim to be whether there is a fundamental right to engage in consensual sodomy, the *Bowers* Court said: "Proscriptions against that conduct have ancient roots." In academic writings, and in many of the scholarly amicus briefs filed to assist the Court in this case, there are fundamental criticisms of the historical premises relied upon by the majority and concurring opinions in *Bowers*. We need not enter this debate in the attempt to reach a definitive historical judgment, but [we do not adopt] the definitive conclusions upon which *Bowers* placed such reliance. . . .

The policy of punishing consenting adults for private acts was not much discussed in the early legal literature. We can infer that one reason for this was the very private nature of the conduct. Despite the absence of prosecutions, there may have been periods in which there was public criticism of homosexuals as such and an insistence that the criminal laws be enforced to discourage their practices. But far from possessing "ancient roots," American laws targeting same-sex couples did not develop until the last third of the 20th century. The reported decisions concerning the prosecution of consensual, homosexual sodomy between adults for the years 1880–1995 are not always clear in the details, but a significant number involved conduct in a public place.

It was not until the 1970s that any State singled out same-sex relations for criminal prosecution, and only nine States have done so. Over the course of the last decades, States with same-sex prohibitions have moved toward abolishing them.

In summary, the historical grounds relied upon in *Bowers* are more complex than the majority opinion and the concurring opinion by Chief Justice Burger indicate. Their historical premises are not without doubt and, at the very least, are overstated.

It must be acknowledged, of course, that the Court in *Bowers* was making the broader point that for centuries there have been powerful voices to condemn homosexual conduct as immoral. The condemnation has been shaped by religious beliefs, conceptions of right and acceptable behavior, and respect for the traditional family. For many persons these are not trivial concerns but profound and deep convictions accepted as ethical and moral principles to which they aspire and which thus determine the course of their lives. These considerations do not answer the question before us, however. The issue is whether the majority may use the power of the State to enforce these views on the whole society through operation of the criminal law. "Our obligation is to define the liberty of all, not to mandate our own moral code." *Planned Parenthood v. Casey* (1992). . . .

In our own constitutional system the deficiencies in *Bowers* became even more apparent in the years following its announcement. The 25 States with laws prohibiting the relevant conduct referenced in the *Bowers* decision are reduced now to 13, of which 4 enforce their laws only against homosexual conduct. In those States where sodomy is still proscribed, whether for same-sex or heterosexual conduct, there is a pattern of nonenforcement with respect to consenting adults acting in private. The State of Texas admitted in 1994 that as of that date it had not prosecuted anyone under those circumstances.

Two principal cases decided after *Bowers* cast its holding into even more doubt. In *Planned Parenthood v. Casey* (1992), the Court reaffirmed the substantive force of the liberty protected by the Due Process Clause. The *Casey* decision again confirmed that our laws and tradition afford constitutional protection to personal decisions relating to marriage, procreation, contraception, family relationships, child rearing, and education. In explaining the respect the Constitution demands for the autonomy of the person in making these choices, we stated as follows:

> These matters, involving the most intimate and personal choices a person may make in a lifetime, choices central to personal dignity and autonomy, are central to the liberty protected by the Fourteenth Amendment. At the heart of liberty is the right to define one's own concept of existence, of meaning, of the universe, and of the mystery of human life. Beliefs about these matters could not define the attributes of personhood were they formed under compulsion of the State.

Persons in a homosexual relationship may seek autonomy for these purposes, just as heterosexual persons do. The decision in *Bowers* would deny them this right.

The second post-*Bowers* case of principal relevance is *Romer v. Evans* (1996). There the Court struck down class-based legislation directed at homosexuals as a violation of the Equal Protection Clause. *Romer* invalidated an amendment to Colorado's Constitution which named as a solitary class persons who were homosexuals, lesbians, or bisexual either by "orientation, conduct, practices or relationships," and deprived them of protection under state antidiscrimination laws. We concluded that the provision was "born of animosity toward the class of persons affected" and further that it had no rational relation to a legitimate governmental purpose.

As an alternative argument in this case, counsel for the petitioners and some amici contend that *Romer* provides the basis for declaring the Texas statute invalid under the Equal Protection Clause. That is a tenable argument, but we conclude the instant case requires us to address whether *Bowers* itself has continuing validity. Were we to hold the statute invalid under the Equal Protection Clause some might question whether a prohibition would be valid if drawn differently, say, to prohibit the conduct both between same-sex and different-sex participants.

Equality of treatment and the due process right to demand respect for conduct protected by the substantive guarantee of liberty are linked in important respects, and a decision on the latter point advances both interests. If protected conduct is made criminal and the law which does so remains unexamined for its substantive validity, its stigma might remain even if it were not enforceable as drawn for equal protection reasons. When homosexual conduct is made criminal by the law of the State, that declaration in and of itself is an invitation to subject homosexual persons to discrimination both in the public and in the private spheres. The central holding of *Bowers* has been brought in question by this case, and it should be addressed. Its continuance as precedent demeans the lives of homosexual persons.

Lawrence v. Texas

The stigma this criminal statute imposes, moreover, is not trivial. The offense, to be sure, is but a class C misdemeanor, a minor offense in the Texas legal system. Still, it remains a criminal offense with all that imports for the dignity of the persons charged. The petitioners will bear on their record the history of their criminal convictions. . . . We are advised that if Texas convicted an adult for private, consensual homosexual conduct under the statute here in question the convicted person would come within the [sex offender] registration laws of at least four States were he or she to be subject to their jurisdiction. This underscores the consequential nature of the punishment and the state-sponsored condemnation attendant to the criminal prohibition. Furthermore, the Texas criminal conviction carries with it the other collateral consequences always following a conviction, such as notations on job application forms, to mention but one example.

The foundations of *Bowers* have sustained serious erosion from our recent decisions in *Casey* and *Romer*. When our precedent has been thus weakened, criticism from other sources is of greater significance. In the United States criticism of *Bowers* has been substantial and continuing, disapproving of its reasoning in all respects, not just as to its historical assumptions. The courts of five different States have declined to follow it in interpreting provisions in their own state constitutions parallel to the Due Process Clause of the Fourteenth Amendment. [String cite including *Powell v. State*, 510 S.E.2d 18 (Ga. 1998), invalidating on state constitutional grounds the Georgia statute upheld in *Bowers*.]

To the extent *Bowers* relied on values we share with a wider civilization, it should be noted that the reasoning and holding in *Bowers* have been rejected elsewhere. The European Court of Human Rights has followed not *Bowers* but its own decision in *Dudgeon v. United Kingdom* [holding that a UK anti-sodomy law violated the European Convention on Human Rights]. Other nations, too, have taken action consistent with an affirmation of the protected right of homosexual adults to engage in intimate, consensual conduct. The right the petitioners seek in this case has been accepted as an integral part of human freedom in many other countries. There has been no showing that in this country the governmental interest in circumscribing personal choice is somehow more legitimate or urgent.

The doctrine of *stare decisis* is essential to the respect accorded to the judgments of the Court and to the stability of the law. It is not, however, an inexorable command. In *Casey* we noted that when a court is asked to overrule a precedent recognizing a constitutional liberty interest, individual or societal reliance on the existence of that liberty cautions with particular strength against reversing course. The holding in *Bowers*, however, has not induced detrimental reliance comparable to some instances where recognized individual rights are involved. Indeed, there has been no individual or societal reliance on *Bowers* of the sort that could counsel against overturning its holding once there are compelling reasons to do so. *Bowers* itself causes uncertainty, for the precedents before and after its issuance contradict its central holding.

The rationale of *Bowers* does not withstand careful analysis. In his dissenting opinion in *Bowers* Justice Stevens came to these conclusions:

> Our prior cases make two propositions abundantly clear. First, the fact that the governing majority in a State has traditionally viewed a particular practice as immoral is not a sufficient reason for upholding a law prohibiting the practice; neither history nor tradition could save a law prohibiting miscegenation from constitutional attack. Second, individual decisions by married persons, concerning the intimacies of their physical relationship, even when not intended to produce offspring, are a form of liberty protected by the Due Process Clause of the Fourteenth Amendment. Moreover, this protection extends to intimate choices by unmarried as well as married persons.

Justice Stevens' analysis, in our view, should have been controlling in *Bowers* and should control here.

Bowers was not correct when it was decided, and it is not correct today. It ought not to remain binding precedent. *Bowers v. Hardwick* should be and now is overruled.

The present case does not involve minors. It does not involve persons who might be injured or coerced or who are situated in relationships where consent might not easily be refused. It does not involve public conduct or prostitution. It does not involve whether the government must give formal recognition to any relationship that homosexual persons seek to enter. The case does involve two adults who, with full and mutual consent from each other, engaged in sexual practices common to a homosexual lifestyle. The petitioners are entitled to respect for their private lives. The State cannot demean their existence or control their destiny by making their private sexual conduct a crime. Their right to liberty under the Due Process Clause gives them the full right to engage in their conduct without intervention of the government. "It is a promise of the Constitution that there is a realm of personal liberty which the government may not enter." *Planned Parenthood v. Casey*. The Texas statute furthers no legitimate state interest which can justify its intrusion into the personal and private life of the individual.

Had those who drew and ratified the Due Process Clauses of the Fifth Amendment or the Fourteenth Amendment known the components of liberty in its manifold possibilities, they might have been more specific. They did not presume to have this insight. They knew times can blind us to certain truths and later generations can see that laws once thought necessary and proper in fact serve only to oppress. As the Constitution endures, persons in every generation can invoke its principles in their own search for greater freedom.

Lawrence v. Texas

Justice O'Connor, concurring in the judgment.

The Court today overrules *Bowers v. Hardwick* (1986). I joined *Bowers*, and do not join the Court in overruling it. Nevertheless, I agree with the Court that Texas' statute banning same-sex sodomy is unconstitutional. Rather than relying on the substantive component of the Fourteenth Amendment's Due Process Clause, as the Court does, I base my conclusion on the Fourteenth Amendment's Equal Protection Clause. . . .

This case raises a different issue than *Bowers*: whether, under the Equal Protection Clause, moral disapproval is a legitimate state interest to justify by itself a statute that bans homosexual sodomy, but not heterosexual sodomy. It is not. Moral disapproval of this group, like a bare desire to harm the group, is an interest that is insufficient to satisfy rational basis review under the Equal Protection Clause. *Department of Agriculture v. Moreno* (1973). Indeed, we have never held that moral disapproval, without any other asserted state interest, is a sufficient rationale under the Equal Protection Clause to justify a law that discriminates among groups of persons.

Moral disapproval of a group cannot be a legitimate governmental interest under the Equal Protection Clause because legal classifications must not be drawn for the purpose of disadvantaging the group burdened by the law. Texas' invocation of moral disapproval as a legitimate state interest proves nothing more than Texas' desire to criminalize homosexual sodomy. But the Equal Protection Clause prevents a State from creating a classification of persons undertaken for its own sake. And because Texas so rarely enforces its sodomy law as applied to private, consensual acts, the law serves more as a statement of dislike and disapproval against homosexuals than as a tool to stop criminal behavior. The Texas sodomy law raises the inevitable inference that the disadvantage imposed is born of animosity toward the class of persons affected. . . .

Justice Scalia, with whom Chief Justice Rehnquist and Justice Thomas join, dissenting.

"Liberty finds no refuge in a jurisprudence of doubt." *Planned Parenthood v. Casey* (1992). That was the Court's sententious response, barely more than a decade ago, to those seeking to overrule *Roe v. Wade*. The Court's response today, to those who have engaged in a 17-year crusade to overrule *Bowers v. Hardwick* is very different. The need for stability and certainty presents no barrier.

Most of the rest of today's opinion has no relevance to its actual holding—that the Texas statute "furthers no legitimate state interest which can justify" its application to petitioners under rational-basis review. Though there is discussion of "fundamental propositions" and "fundamental decisions," nowhere does the Court's opinion declare that homosexual sodomy is a "fundamental right" under the Due Process Clause; nor does it subject the Texas law to the standard of review that would be appropriate (strict scrutiny) if homosexual sodomy were a "fundamental right." Thus, while overruling the outcome of *Bowers*, the Court leaves strangely untouched its central legal conclusion: "Respondent would have us announce a fundamental right to engage in homosexual sodomy. This we are quite unwilling to do." Instead the Court simply describes petitioners' conduct as "an exercise of their liberty"—which it undoubtedly is—and proceeds to apply an unheard-of form of rational-basis review that will have far-reaching implications beyond this case.

I

I begin with the Court's surprising readiness to reconsider a decision rendered a mere 17 years ago in *Bowers v. Hardwick*. I do not myself believe in rigid adherence to *stare decisis* in constitutional cases; but I do believe that we should be consistent rather than manipulative in invoking the doctrine. . . .

It seems to me that the "societal reliance" on the principles confirmed in *Bowers* and discarded today has been overwhelming. Countless judicial decisions and legislative enactments have relied on the ancient proposition that a governing majority's belief that certain sexual behavior is immoral and unacceptable constitutes a rational basis for regulation. We ourselves relied extensively on *Bowers* when we concluded, in *Barnes v. Glen Theatre, Inc.*, 501 U.S. 560 (1991), that Indiana's public indecency statute furthered "a substantial government interest in protecting order and morality." State laws against bigamy, same-sex marriage, adult incest, prostitution, masturbation, adultery, fornication, bestiality, and obscenity are likewise sustainable only in light of *Bowers'* validation of laws based on moral choices. Every single one of these laws is called into question by today's decision; the Court makes no effort to cabin the scope of its decision to exclude them from its holding. The impossibility of distinguishing homosexuality from other traditional "morals" offenses is precisely why *Bowers* rejected the rational-basis challenge. "The law," it said, "is constantly based on notions of morality, and if all laws representing essentially moral choices are to be invalidated under the Due Process Clause, the courts will be very busy indeed." . . .

II

Having decided that it need not adhere to *stare decisis*, the Court still must establish that *Bowers* was wrongly decided and that the Texas statute, as applied to petitioners, is unconstitutional. . . .

Our opinions applying the doctrine known as "substantive due process" hold that the Due Process Clause prohibits States from infringing fundamental liberty interests, unless the infringement is narrowly tailored to serve a compelling state interest. We have held repeatedly, in cases the Court today does not overrule, that only fundamental rights qualify for this so-called "heightened scrutiny" protection—that is, rights which are "deeply rooted in this Nation's history and tradition." All other liberty interests may be abridged or abrogated pursuant to a validly enacted state law if that law is rationally related to a legitimate state interest.

Lawrence v. Texas

Bowers held, first, that criminal prohibitions of homosexual sodomy are not subject to heightened scrutiny because they do not implicate a "fundamental right" under the Due Process Clause. . . . The Court today does not overrule this holding. Not once does it describe homosexual sodomy as a "fundamental right" or a "fundamental liberty interest," nor does it subject the Texas statute to strict scrutiny. Instead, having failed to establish that the right to homosexual sodomy is "deeply rooted in this Nation's history and tradition," the Court concludes that the application of Texas's statute to petitioners' conduct fails the rational-basis test, and overrules *Bowers'* holding to the contrary. "The Texas statute furthers no legitimate state interest which can justify its intrusion into the personal and private life of the individual." . . .

III–V [Omitted.]

[CONCLUSION]

Today's opinion is the product of a Court, which is the product of a law-profession culture, that has largely signed on to the so-called homosexual agenda, by which I mean the agenda promoted by some homosexual activists directed at eliminating the moral opprobrium that has traditionally attached to homosexual conduct. . . .

Let me be clear that I have nothing against homosexuals, or any other group, promoting their agenda through normal democratic means. Social perceptions of sexual and other morality change over time, and every group has the right to persuade its fellow citizens that its view of such matters is the best. That homosexuals have achieved some success in that enterprise is attested to by the fact that Texas is one of the few remaining States that criminalize private, consensual homosexual acts. But persuading one's fellow citizens is one thing, and imposing one's views in absence of democratic majority will is something else. I would no more require a State to criminalize homosexual acts—or, for that matter, display any moral disapprobation of them—than I would forbid it to do so. What Texas has chosen to do is well within the range of traditional democratic action, and its hand should not be stayed through the invention of a brand-new constitutional right by a Court that is impatient of democratic change. It is indeed true that "later generations can see that laws once thought necessary and proper in fact serve only to oppress," and when that happens, later generations can repeal those laws. But it is the premise of our system that those judgments are to be made by the people, and not imposed by a governing caste that knows best.

One of the benefits of leaving regulation of this matter to the people rather than to the courts is that the people, unlike judges, need not carry things to their logical conclusion. . . . At the end of its opinion—after having laid waste the foundations of our rational-basis jurisprudence—the Court says that the present case "does not involve whether the government must give formal recognition to any relationship that homosexual persons seek to enter." Do not believe it. More illuminating than this bald, unreasoned disclaimer is the progression of thought displayed by an earlier passage in the Court's opinion, which notes the constitutional protections afforded to "personal decisions relating to marriage, procreation, contraception, family relationships, child rearing, and education," and then declares that "persons in a homosexual relationship may seek autonomy for these purposes, just as heterosexual persons do." . . . This case "does not involve" the issue of homosexual marriage only if one entertains the belief that principle and logic have nothing to do with the decisions of this Court. . . .

The matters appropriate for this Court's resolution are only three: Texas's prohibition of sodomy neither infringes a "fundamental right" (which the Court does not dispute), nor is unsupported by a rational relation to what the Constitution considers a legitimate state interest, nor denies the equal protection of the laws. I dissent.

Justice Thomas, dissenting.

I join Justice Scalia's dissenting opinion. I write separately to note that the law before the Court today is "uncommonly silly." *Griswold v. Connecticut* (1965) (Stewart, J., dissenting). If I were a member of the Texas Legislature, I would vote to repeal it. Punishing someone for expressing his sexual preference through noncommercial consensual conduct with another adult does not appear to be a worthy way to expend valuable law enforcement resources.

Notwithstanding this, I recognize that as a Member of this Court I am not empowered to help petitioners and others similarly situated. My duty, rather, is to decide cases agreeably to the Constitution and laws of the United States. And, just like Justice Stewart, I can find neither in the Bill of Rights nor any other part of the Constitution a general right of privacy, or as the Court terms it today, the "liberty of the person both in its spatial and more transcendent dimensions."

F. Substantive Due Process After *Lawrence*

In subsequent cases, lower courts disagreed over how to interpret *Lawrence*.

ITEMS TO CONSIDER WHILE READING EXCERPTS FROM *LOFTON* AND *WITT*:

A. *Which decision gives the most accurate reading of* Lawrence?

B. *After* Lofton *and* Witt *were decided, governmental actors other than federal judges (state courts and Congress, respectively) instituted significant legal changes. How might the federal litigation have affected these other actors, and vice versa?*

1. Eleventh Circuit (2004): *Lofton v. Secretary*

The plaintiffs in *Lofton v. Secretary of Dept. of Children & Family Services*, 358 F.3d 804 (11th Cir. 2004), were an unmarried gay male couple in Florida who were foster parents of several special needs children. They wished to become full legal parents through adoption, but a Florida statute barred adoption by any "homosexual person." The foster parents argued, among other things, that the law unconstitutionally burdened their rights under *Lawrence*. The Eleventh Circuit concluded that *Lawrence* stood for rational basis review.

> *Lawrence*'s holding was that substantive due process does not permit a state to impose a criminal prohibition on private consensual homosexual conduct. The effect of this holding was to establish a greater respect than previously existed in the law for the right of consenting adults to engage in private sexual conduct. Nowhere, however, did the Court characterize this right as "fundamental." Cf. *id.* (Scalia, J., dissenting) (observing that "nowhere does the Court's opinion declare that homosexual sodomy is a 'fundamental right' under the Due Process Clause"). Nor did the Court locate this right directly in the Constitution, but instead treated it as the by-product of several different constitutional principles and liberty interests.
>
> We are particularly hesitant to infer a new fundamental liberty interest from an opinion whose language and reasoning are inconsistent with standard fundamental-rights analysis. The Court has noted that it must "exercise the utmost care whenever it is asked to break new ground" in the field of fundamental rights, *Washington v. Glucksberg* (1997), which is precisely what the *Lawrence* petitioners and their amici curiae had asked the Court to do. That the Court declined the invitation is apparent from the absence of the two primary features of fundamental-rights analysis in its opinion. First, the *Lawrence* opinion contains virtually no inquiry into the question of whether the petitioners' asserted right is one of "those fundamental rights and liberties which are, objectively, deeply rooted in this Nation's history and tradition and implicit in the concept of ordered liberty, such that neither liberty nor justice would exist if they were sacrificed." Second, the opinion notably never provides the "careful description of the asserted fundamental liberty interest" that is to accompany fundamental-rights analysis. Rather, the constitutional liberty interests on which the Court relied were invoked, not with "careful description," but with sweeping generality. Most significant, however, is the fact that the *Lawrence* Court never applied strict scrutiny, the proper standard when fundamental rights are implicated, but instead invalidated the Texas statute on rational-basis grounds, holding that it "furthers no legitimate state interest which can justify its intrusion into the personal and private life of the individual." See also *id.* (Scalia, J., dissenting) (observing that the majority opinion did not

> "subject the Texas law to the standard of review that would be appropriate (strict scrutiny) if homosexual sodomy were a fundamental right").
>
> We conclude that it is a strained and ultimately incorrect reading of *Lawrence* to interpret it to announce a new fundamental right.

Having decided that *Lawrence* required only rational basis review, the 11th Circuit concluded that Florida's law allowing same-sex couples to be foster parents but not adoptive parents was rational.

flashforward

***Change in Florida Law After* Lofton.** Six years after *Lofton,* Florida state courts found that the statute barring adoption by gay people lacked a rational basis sufficient to satisfy the state constitution's version of equal protection. See *Florida Dep't of Children & Families v. Adoption of X.X.G.*, 45 So. 3d 79 (Fla. App. 2010).

2. Ninth Circuit (2008): *Witt v. Air Force*

The so-called "Don't Ask, Don't Tell" (DADT) statute of 1993 codified a longstanding US military policy requiring discharge of service members who engaged in "homosexual conduct" (which the statute defined to include statements that a person is gay, lesbian, or bisexual). Before *Lawrence,* several US Courts of Appeal had upheld the statute against challenges that it violated substantive due process and equal protection. The plaintiff in *Witt v. Air Force,* 527 F.3d 806 (9th Cir. 2008), was a Major in the Air Force who had been discharged on the basis of homosexual conduct. She challenged the statute on a due process theory, since the Equal Protection Clause was at that time foreclosed in the Ninth Circuit by *High Tech Gays.* In her case, the Ninth Circuit concluded that *Lawrence* required a form of heightened scrutiny.

> Major Witt argues that *Lawrence* recognized a fundamental right to engage in private, consensual, homosexual conduct and therefore requires us to subject DADT to heightened scrutiny. The Air Force argues that *Lawrence* applied only rational basis review[.] Because *Lawrence* is, perhaps intentionally so, silent as to the level of scrutiny that it applied, both parties draw upon language from *Lawrence* that supports their views. . . . In these ambiguous circumstances, we analyze *Lawrence* by considering what the Court actually did, rather than by dissecting isolated pieces of text. In so doing, we conclude that the Supreme

Court applied a heightened level of scrutiny in *Lawrence*.

Margaret Witt in 2006

We cannot reconcile what the Supreme Court did in *Lawrence* with the minimal protections afforded by traditional rational basis review. First, the Court overruled *Bowers*, an earlier case in which the Court had upheld a Georgia sodomy law under rational basis review. . . . But the Court's criticism of *Bowers* had nothing to do with the basis for the law; instead, the Court rejected *Bowers* because of the "Court's own failure to appreciate the extent of the liberty at stake." . . . This is inconsistent with rational basis review.

Second, the cases on which the Supreme Court explicitly based its decision in *Lawrence* are based on heightened scrutiny. As Major Witt pointed out, those cases include *Griswold, Roe,* and *Casey.* Moreover, the Court [in *Lawrence*] stated that *Casey*, a post-*Bowers* decision, cast its holding in *Bowers* into doubt. Notably, the Court did not . . . apply the post-*Bowers* case of *Romer v. Evans* (1996), in which the Court applied rational basis review to a law concerning homosexuals. Instead, the Court overturned *Bowers* because "its continuance as precedent demeans the lives of homosexual persons."

Third, the *Lawrence* Court's rationale for its holding—the analysis that it was applying—is inconsistent with rational basis review. The Court declared: "The Texas statute furthers no legitimate state interest which can justify its intrusion into the personal and private life of the individual." Were the Court applying rational basis review, it would not identify a legitimate state interest to "justify" the particular intrusion of liberty at issue in *Lawrence*; regardless of the liberty involved, any hypothetical rationale for the law would do.

We therefore conclude that *Lawrence* applied something more than traditional rational basis review. This leaves open the question whether the Court applied strict scrutiny, intermediate scrutiny, or another heightened level of scrutiny. . . . We hesitate to apply strict scrutiny when the Supreme Court did not discuss narrow tailoring or a compelling state interest in *Lawrence*, and we do not address the issue here.

Instead, we look to another recent Supreme Court case that applied a heightened level of scrutiny to a substantive due process claim—a scrutiny that resembles and expands upon the analysis performed in *Lawrence*. In *Sell v. United States*, 539 U.S. 166 (2003), the Court considered whether the Constitution permits the government to forcibly administer antipsychotic drugs to a mentally-ill defendant in order to render that defendant competent to stand trial. The Court held that the defendant has a significant constitutionally protected liberty interest at stake, so the drugs could be administered forcibly only if the treatment is medically appropriate, is substantially unlikely to have side effects that may undermine the fairness of the trial, and, taking account of less intrusive alternatives, is necessary significantly to further important governmental trial-related interests. . . .

We thus take our direction from the Supreme Court and . . . hold that when the government attempts to intrude upon the personal and private lives of homosexuals, in a manner that implicates the rights identified in *Lawrence*, the government must advance an important governmental interest, the intrusion must significantly further that interest, and the intrusion must be necessary to further that interest. In other words, for the third factor, a less intrusive means must be unlikely to achieve substantially the government's interest.

flashforward

***Change in Federal Law After* Witt.** On remand, a bench trial culminated in a ruling that Major Witt's discharge was unconstitutional. *Witt v. U.S. Dep't of Air Force*, 739 F. Supp. 2d 1308 (W.D. Wash. 2010). The government appealed, but before briefs were written, Congress repealed the Don't Ask, Don't Tell statute in December 2010.

G. Multiple Theories (1990s–2010s): Marriage Equality

From the 1990s through the 2010s (and with roots stretching back to the 1970s), a wave of legislation and litigation surrounded the question of marriage equality: whether the government could limit civil marriage only to different-sex couples. As you read the following cases, notice the range of legal theories offered in support of, or in opposition to, the challenged marriage laws—and consider why a lawyer (in writing a brief) or a judge (in writing an opinion) might choose to emphasize one theory over another.

1. Sex Equality Theories (1970s)

In the early 1970s, after several states passed Equal Rights Amendments forbidding sex discrimination, a handful of same-sex couples brought suits claiming a state constitutional right to marry. Their theory was that the laws discriminated on the basis of sex: a male plaintiff would have been allowed to marry a man if he had been female. All of the sex-based suits failed, with courts reasoning that the laws prohibited all persons, male and female, from marrying a person of the same sex. *Baker v. Nelson*, 191 N.W.2d 185 (Minn. 1971); *Singer v. Hara*, 522 P.2d 1187 (Wash. App. 1974). See also *Jones v. Hallahan*, 501 S.W.2d 588 (Ky. App. 1973).

flashforward

Sexual Orientation Discrimination as Sex Discrimination. Although the early marriage cases did not accept that sexual orientation discrimination was a form of sex discrimination, that view was adopted—at least under one federal statute—in *Bostock v. Clayton County*, 140 S. Ct. 1731 (2020). Gerald Bostock worked as a child welfare advocate for the government of Clayton County, Georgia. After a decade of service, he was fired when it became known that he was gay. He sued, alleging that the County had discriminated against him "because of sex" in violation of Title VII of the Civil Rights Act of 1964. 42 U.S.C. § 2000e–2(a)(1). A majority of the US Supreme Court held that "it is impossible to discriminate against a person for being homosexual or transgender without discriminating against that individual based on sex." This result was compelled by the logic and plain meaning of the text, said the majority, even though it was concededly not the result that legislators or the public would have predicted in 1964.

2. State Constitutions and the Defense of Marriage Act (1990s)

Litigation in the 1990s pursued two different theories. One was an equality theory on the basis of sexual orientation (rather than sex). Another was a freedom theory, arguing that the right to marry a consenting, competent, non-related adult of one's choice was a constitutionally protected liberty. Most of these cases proceeded under state constitutions, because litigants feared that an adverse result under the US Constitution would have far-reaching ill effects.

In *Baehr v. Lewin*, 852 P.2d 44 (Haw. 1993), the Hawaii Supreme Court allowed plaintiffs to proceed with their lawsuit asserting that the state marriage law violated the Equal Protection Clause of the state constitution. *Baehr* did not ultimately change the marriage law in Hawaii, because the state constitution was amended in 1998 to grant the state legislature power to limit marriage to different-sex couples (which it promptly did).

Baehr and the prospect of other cases like it prompted the US Congress in 1996 to pass the Defense of Marriage Act (DOMA). The statute decreed that same-sex couples could not be married for purposes of federal law, even if they were legally married under a state's laws. Many states followed with their own state-level DOMA laws (either as statutes or amendments to state constitutions), recognizing only different-sex marriages.

Notwithstanding DOMA, some states allowed same-sex couples to form legal relationships similar to marriage, under names like "civil union" or "domestic partnership." These began with judicial decisions interpreting state constitutions—the first being *Baker v. Vermont,* 744 A.2d 864 (Vt. 1999)—and then through legislation. In 2003, Massachusetts became the first state to hold that its state constitution protected the right of same sex couples to marry. *Goodridge v. Dep't of Public Health,* 798 N.E.2d 941 (Mass. 2003). By 2013, eight states had laws allowing same-sex civil unions or domestic partnerships, and twelve states and the District of Columbia had laws allowing same-sex marriages. This meant that numerous couples were married under state law, but not federal law.

3. Multiple Theories: *US v. Windsor* (2013)

■ WEBSITE

A fuller version of *US v. Windsor* is available for download from this casebook's companion website, www.CaplanIntegratedConLaw.com.

Edith Windsor and Thea Spyer of New York City had lived together as an unmarried couple for decades. In 2007, they married in Canada, taking advantage of its 2005 marriage equality law. At that time, New York recognized all lawful out-of-state marriages, regardless of the sex of the spouses—but under DOMA the federal government did not. Spyer died in 2009. If the couple were married for purposes of federal tax law, Windsor would inherit Spyer's assets tax-free. But since DOMA declared them federally unmarried, the IRS assessed an estate tax of over $360,000. Windsor sued for a refund.

The trial court ruled in favor of Windsor, relying on the "rational basis with bite" theory most often associated with *City of Cleburne v. Cleburne Living Center* (Ch. 18.E.1). 833 F.Supp.2d 394 (S.D.N.Y. 2012). The Second Circuit affirmed on a 2–1 vote. 699 F.3d 169 (2nd Cir. 2012). The majority declined to decide whether the *Cleburne* line of cases represented "rational basis plus or intermediate scrutiny minus" because "we think it is safe to say that there is some doctrinal instability in this area." Instead, the Court concluded that laws classifying on the basis of sexual orientation were "quasi-suspect" and hence subject to intermediate

Thea Spyer and Edith Windsor in 2007

scrutiny, just like laws that classify on the basis of sex or birth outside marriage. Under intermediate scrutiny, DOMA failed.

In the Supreme Court, a 5–4 majority held that it was unconstitutional for the United States to deny legal recognition for state-authorized marriages of same sex couples. *United States v. Windsor*, 570 U.S. 744 (2013). The majority opinion contained no express statements about the correct standard of review for laws that classify on the basis of sexual orientation. Instead, the opinion resembled *Lawrence* in avoiding orthodox labels.

The majority's objections to DOMA included some concerns about federalism. A federal statute imposing a blanket definition of marriage was atypical, because almost all federal laws treat couples as married for federal purposes whenever they were married for state purposes. "By history and tradition the definition and regulation of marriage . . . has been treated as being within the authority and realm of the separate States." The opinion's lengthy discussion of federalism was identified as dicta, with the majority concluding that "it is unnecessary to decide whether this federal intrusion on state power is a violation of the Constitution because it disrupts the federal balance."

Instead, the majority based its decision on individual rights. Its discussion spoke most often of "liberty" under the Due Process Clause of the Fifth Amendment, but this had long been understood to incorporate the Equal Protection Clause, see *Bolling v. Sharpe* (1954), Ch. 11.B.2. The majority observed that DOMA imposed "injury and indignity" on couples like Windsor and Spyer. "DOMA's principal effect is to identify a subset of state-sanctioned marriages and make them unequal. The principal purpose is to impose inequality." Pointing to statements in the legislative history that DOMA was declared to convey "moral disapproval of homosexuality," the majority concluded that the statute was "motivated by an improper animus."

Justice Scalia's dissent accused the majority of "nonspecific hand-waving" that relied "maybe on equal-protection grounds, maybe on substantive-due-process grounds, and perhaps with some amorphous federalism component playing a role."

flashforward

***Equal Protection After* Windsor.** As with *Lawrence*, the deliberately ambiguous wording in Justice Kennedy's *Windsor* opinion led to different interpretations in lower courts. All agreed that the opinion was rooted in Equal Protection, but its level of scrutiny was unclear.

In the Ninth Circuit, *SmithKline Beecham Corp. v. Abbot Laboratories*, 740 F.3d 471 (9th Cir. 2014), involved a civil suit between manufacturers of HIV drugs, where the defendant was accused of using its peremptory challenges to strike gay men off the jury. The Ninth Circuit concluded: "*Windsor* requires that when state action discriminates on the basis of sexual orientation, we must examine its actual purposes and carefully consider the resulting inequality to ensure that our most fundamental institutions neither send nor reinforce messages of stigma or second-class status. In short, *Windsor* requires heightened scrutiny." In so ruling, the Ninth Circuit overruled its earlier decision in *High Tech Gays v. DISCO* (1990), Ch. 22.C.

By contrast, *Robichaux v. Caldwell*, 2 F.Supp.3d 910 (E.D. La. 2014)—a challenge to Louisiana's refusal to allow same-sex marriages—read *Windsor* as a rational basis case. "As to standard of review, *Windsor* starkly avoids mention of heightened scrutiny," said the court. Moreover, any effort to portray *Windsor*'s "elusive" language as a declaration of heightened scrutiny "seems like intellectual anarchy." Until clearly notified otherwise, the court would apply laws that classify on the basis of sexual orientation for rational basis.

4. Multiple Theories (2015): *Obergefell v. Hodges*

After *Windsor*, same-sex couples initiated a fast-moving wave of litigation in federal courts, but this time relying on the US Constitution. The laws were found unconstitutional in 33 out of 36 trial courts, and four out of five Courts of Appeal.

The post-*Windsor* federal actions challenged statutes under equal protection (both its fundamental rights and suspect classification prongs) and substantive due process. To prevail under any of these theories, the states needed to persuade courts that good enough reasons existed to deny civil marriage to same-sex couples. The arguments most often raised in defense of the laws were these:

- Most sexually active different-sex couples will procreate, whether intentionally or unintentionally. The government has an interest in encouraging them to stay together for the sake of the children, and it may do so by offering the procreating couple legal benefits that would be available only if they marry. Since same-sex couples do not procreate on their own, there is no need to include them in the system of civil marriage.

- Children thrive better in households with two different-sex parents. Hence the government has an interest in favoring different-sex households over same-sex households.
- Changing the definition of who may marry will harm the public consensus that marriage is a valuable institution, with adverse (or at least unknown) results.
- The government has an interest in continuing to enforce long-held socio-legal traditions that continue to enjoy significant public support.

Most of the Courts of Appeal were not persuaded by these arguments and found the laws unconstitutional. As summarized in the following chart, the courts varied considerably in their reasoning. Some applied heightened scrutiny, while others applied rational basis review. Of the equal protection decisions, some relied on the fundamental rights prong and some on the suspect classifications prong—and within the suspect classifications opinions, most viewed the law as classifying on the basis of sexual orientation, while a concurrence in the Ninth Circuit opinion argued that the laws impermissibly classified on the basis of sex.

Reasoning in Post-Windsor Federal Court Marriage Equality Litigation

	Equal Protection: Fundamental Rights	Equal Protection: Suspect Classifications	Substantive Due Process
Kitchen v. Herbert, 755 F.3d 1193 (10th Cir. Jun. 25, 2014)	Law Fails: Strict Scrutiny		
Bostic v. Schaefer, 760 F.3d 352 (4th Cir. July 28, 2014)	Law Fails: Strict Scrutiny		
Baskin v. Bogan, 766 F.3d 648 (7th Cir. Sept. 4, 2014)		Law Fails: More Than Rational Basis	
Latta v. Otter, 771 F.3d 456 (9th Cir. Oct. 7, 2014)		Law Fails: Heightened Scrutiny	
DeBoer v. Snyder, 772 F.3d 388 (6th Cir. Nov. 6, 2014)	Law Upheld: Rational Basis	Law Upheld: Rational Basis	Law Upheld: Rational Basis

On October 6, 2014 the Supreme Court denied certiorari in *Kitchen*, *Bostic*, and *Baskin*. But after the Sixth Circuit ruled 2–1 in *DeBoer* that the challenged statutes survived rational basis review under all theories—creating an unavoidable circuit split—the Supreme Court granted certiorari in that case on January 6, 2015 under the name *Obergefell v. Hodges*.

ITEMS TO CONSIDER WHILE READING *OBERGEFELL V. HODGES*:

A. *Work through the items from the relevant Kickstarters. In what ways do the opinions of the Justices follow or not follow them? What are the benefits and drawbacks of the majority's approach?*

B. *After* Obergefell, *what allows a state to deny marriage licenses to siblings or first cousins? To deny marriage licenses to groups of more than two persons? To require a marriage license at all?*

C. *Would it have been preferable for the legality of same-sex civil marriage be decided through the political process? If so, how could the Court achieve that result?*

D. *Does* Obergefell *survive* Dobbs v. Jackson Women's Health Organization *(2022)?*

Obergefell v. Hodges,

576 U.S. 644 (2015)

Justice Kennedy delivered the opinion of the Court [joined by Justices Ginsburg, Breyer, Sotomayor, and Kagan].

The Constitution promises liberty to all within its reach, a liberty that includes certain specific rights that allow persons, within a lawful realm, to define and express their identity. The petitioners in these cases seek to find that liberty by marrying someone of the same sex and having their marriages deemed lawful on the same terms and conditions as marriages between persons of the opposite sex.

I

These cases come from Michigan, Kentucky, Ohio, and Tennessee, States that define marriage as a union between one man and one woman. The petitioners are 14 same-sex couples and two men [including James Obergefell] whose same-sex partners are deceased. The respondents are state officials responsible for enforcing the laws in question [including Richard Hodges, director of the Ohio Department of Health]. The petitioners claim the respondents violate the Fourteenth Amendment by denying them the right to marry or to have their marriages, lawfully performed in another State, given full recognition.

Petitioners filed these suits in United States District Courts in their home States. Each District Court ruled in their favor. . . . The respondents appealed the decisions against them to the United States Court of Appeals for the Sixth Circuit. It consolidated the cases and reversed the judgments of the District Courts. The Court of Appeals held [on a divided vote] that a State has no constitutional obligation to license same-sex marriages or to recognize same-sex marriages performed out of State.

The petitioners sought certiorari. This Court granted review, limited to two questions. The first, presented by the cases from Michigan and Kentucky, is whether the Fourteenth Amendment requires a State to license a marriage between two people of the same sex. The second, presented by the cases from Ohio, Tennessee, and, again, Kentucky, is whether the Fourteenth Amendment requires a State to recognize a same-sex marriage licensed and performed in a State which does grant that right.

II

Before addressing the principles and precedents that govern these cases, it is appropriate to note the history of the subject now before the Court.

A

From their beginning to their most recent page, the annals of human history reveal the transcendent importance of marriage. The lifelong union of a man and a woman always has promised nobility and dignity to all persons, without regard to their station in life. Marriage is sacred to those who live by their religions and offers unique fulfillment to those who find meaning in the secular realm. Its dynamic allows two people to find a life that could not be found alone, for a marriage becomes greater than just the two persons. Rising from the most basic human needs, marriage is essential to our most profound hopes and aspirations. . . .

There are untold references to the beauty of marriage in religious and philosophical texts spanning time, cultures, and faiths, as well as in art and literature in all their forms. It is fair and necessary to say these references were based on the understanding that marriage is a union between two persons of the opposite sex.

That history is the beginning of these cases. The respondents say it should be the end as well. To them, it would demean a timeless institution if the concept and lawful status of marriage were extended to two persons of the same sex. Marriage, in their view, is by its nature a gender-differentiated union of man and woman. This view long has been held—and continues to be held—in good faith by reasonable and sincere people here and throughout the world.

The petitioners acknowledge this history but contend that these cases cannot end there. Were their intent to demean the revered idea and reality of marriage, the petitioners' claims would be of a different order. But that is neither their purpose nor their submission. To the contrary, it is the enduring importance of marriage that underlies the petitioners' contentions. This, they say, is their whole point. Far from seeking to devalue marriage, the petitioners seek it for themselves because of their respect—and need—for its privileges and responsibilities. And their immutable nature dictates that same-sex marriage is their only real path to this profound commitment.

James Obergefell and John Arthur in 2013

Recounting the circumstances of three of these cases illustrates the urgency of the petitioners' cause from their perspective. Petitioner James Obergefell, a plaintiff in the Ohio case, met John Arthur over two decades ago. They fell in love and started a life together, establishing a lasting, committed relation. In 2011, however, Arthur was diagnosed with amyotrophic lateral sclerosis, or ALS. This debilitating disease is progressive, with no known cure. Two years ago, Obergefell and Arthur decided to commit to one another, resolving to marry before Arthur died. To fulfill their mutual promise, they traveled from Ohio to Maryland, where same-sex marriage was legal. It was difficult for Arthur to move, and so the couple were wed inside a medical transport plane as it remained on the tarmac in Baltimore. Three months later, Arthur died. Ohio law does not permit Obergefell to be listed as the surviving spouse on Arthur's death certificate. By statute, they must remain strangers even in death, a state-imposed separation Obergefell deems "hurtful for the rest of time." He brought suit to be shown as the surviving spouse on Arthur's death certificate.

[Other plaintiffs include April DeBoer and Jayne Rowse, a Michigan couple unable to adopt each other's children, and Ijpe DeKoe and Thomas Kostura, a military couple deemed married in New York but not in their Tennessee home.]

The cases now before the Court involve other petitioners as well, each with their own experiences. Their stories reveal that they seek not to denigrate marriage but rather to live their lives, or honor their spouses' memory, joined by its bond.

B

The ancient origins of marriage confirm its centrality, but it has not stood in isolation from developments in law and society. The history of marriage is one of both continuity and change. That institution—even as confined to opposite-sex relations—has evolved over time.

Obergefell v. Hodges

For example, marriage was once viewed as an arrangement by the couple's parents based on political, religious, and financial concerns; but by the time of the Nation's founding it was understood to be a voluntary contract between a man and a woman. As the role and status of women changed, the institution further evolved. Under the centuries-old doctrine of coverture, a married man and woman were treated by the State as a single, male-dominated legal entity. As women gained legal, political, and property rights, and as society began to understand that women have their own equal dignity, the law of coverture was abandoned. These and other developments in the institution of marriage over the past centuries were not mere superficial changes. Rather, they worked deep transformations in its structure, affecting aspects of marriage long viewed by many as essential.

These new insights have strengthened, not weakened, the institution of marriage. Indeed, changed understandings of marriage are characteristic of a Nation where new dimensions of freedom become apparent to new generations, often through perspectives that begin in pleas or protests and then are considered in the political sphere and the judicial process.

This dynamic can be seen in the Nation's experiences with the rights of gays and lesbians. Until the mid-20th century, same-sex intimacy long had been condemned as immoral by the state itself in most Western nations, a belief often embodied in the criminal law. . . . In the late 20th century, following substantial cultural and political developments, same-sex couples began to lead more open and public lives and to establish families. This development was followed by a quite extensive discussion of the issue in both governmental and private sectors and by a shift in public attitudes toward greater tolerance. As a result, questions about the rights of gays and lesbians soon reached the courts, where the issue could be discussed in the formal discourse of the law.

[The opinion here summarized *Bowers v. Hardwick* (1986), *Romer v. Evans* (1996), *Lawrence v. Texas* (2003), and the wave of marriage litigation before and after *US v. Windsor* (2013).]

After years of litigation, legislation, referenda, and the discussions that attended these public acts, the States are now divided on the issue of same-sex marriage.

III

Under the Due Process Clause of the Fourteenth Amendment, no State shall "deprive any person of life, liberty, or property, without due process of law." The fundamental liberties protected by this Clause include most of the rights enumerated in the Bill of Rights. In addition these liberties extend to certain personal choices central to individual dignity and autonomy, including intimate choices that define personal identity and beliefs. *See, e.g., Eisenstadt v. Baird* (1972); *Griswold v. Connecticut* (1965).

The identification and protection of fundamental rights is an enduring part of the judicial duty to interpret the Constitution. That responsibility, however, has not been reduced to any formula. Rather, it requires courts to exercise reasoned judgment in identifying interests of the person so fundamental that the State must accord them its respect. That process is guided by many of the same considerations relevant to analysis of other constitutional provisions that set forth broad principles rather than specific requirements. History and tradition guide and discipline this inquiry but do not set its outer boundaries. That method respects our history and learns from it without allowing the past alone to rule the present.

The nature of injustice is that we may not always see it in our own times. The generations that wrote and ratified the Bill of Rights and the Fourteenth Amendment did not presume to know the extent of freedom in all of its dimensions, and so they entrusted to future generations a charter protecting the right of all persons to enjoy liberty as we learn its meaning. When new insight reveals discord between the Constitution's central protections and a received legal stricture, a claim to liberty must be addressed.

Applying these established tenets, the Court has long held the right to marry is protected by the Constitution. In *Loving v. Virginia* (1967), which invalidated bans on interracial unions, a unanimous Court held marriage is "one of the vital personal rights essential to the orderly pursuit of happiness by free men." The Court reaffirmed that holding in *Zablocki v. Redhail*, 434 U.S. 374 (1978), which held the right to marry was burdened by a law prohibiting fathers who were behind on child support from marrying. The Court again applied this principle in *Turner v. Safley*, 482 U.S. 78 (1987), which held the right to marry was abridged by regulations limiting the privilege of prison inmates to marry. Over time and in other contexts, the Court has reiterated that the right to marry is fundamental under the Due Process Clause. See, e.g., *Griswold*, *Skinner v. Oklahoma* (1942); *Meyer v. Nebraska* (1923).

It cannot be denied that this Court's cases describing the right to marry presumed a relationship involving opposite-sex partners. The Court, like many institutions, has made assumptions defined by the world and time of which it is a part. . . . Still . . . this Court's cases have expressed constitutional principles of broader reach. In defining the right to marry these cases have identified essential attributes of that right based in history, tradition, and other constitutional liberties inherent in this intimate bond. And in assessing whether the force and rationale of its cases apply to same-sex couples, the Court must respect the basic reasons why the right to marry has been long protected.

This analysis compels the conclusion that same-sex couples may exercise the right to marry. The four principles and traditions to be discussed demonstrate that the reasons marriage is fundamental under the Constitution apply with equal force to same-sex couples.

Obergefell v. Hodges

A first premise of the Court's relevant precedents is that the right to personal choice regarding marriage is inherent in the concept of individual autonomy. This abiding connection between marriage and liberty is why *Loving* invalidated interracial marriage bans under the Due Process Clause. Like choices concerning contraception, family relationships, procreation, and childrearing, all of which are protected by the Constitution, decisions concerning marriage are among the most intimate that an individual can make. . . . The nature of marriage is that, through its enduring bond, two persons together can find other freedoms, such as expression, intimacy, and spirituality. This is true for all persons, whatever their sexual orientation. There is dignity in the bond between two men or two women who seek to marry and in their autonomy to make such profound choices.

A second principle in this Court's jurisprudence is that the right to marry is fundamental because it supports a two-person union unlike any other in its importance to the committed individuals. This point was central to *Griswold*, which held the Constitution protects the right of married couples to use contraception. . . . And in *Turner*, the Court again acknowledged the intimate association protected by this right, holding prisoners could not be denied the right to marry because their committed relationships satisfied the basic reasons why marriage is a fundamental right. The right to marry thus dignifies couples who wish to define themselves by their commitment to each other. Marriage responds to the universal fear that a lonely person might call out only to find no one there. It offers the hope of companionship and understanding and assurance that while both still live there will be someone to care for the other.

As this Court held in *Lawrence*, same-sex couples have the same right as opposite-sex couples to enjoy intimate association. . . . *Lawrence* confirmed a dimension of freedom that allows individuals to engage in intimate association without criminal liability, [and] it does not follow that freedom stops there. Outlaw to outcast may be a step forward, but it does not achieve the full promise of liberty.

A third basis for protecting the right to marry is that it safeguards children and families and thus draws meaning from related rights of childrearing, procreation, and education. The Court has recognized these connections by describing the varied rights as a unified whole: The right to "marry, establish a home and bring up children" is a central part of the liberty protected by the Due Process Clause. *Meyer v. Nebraska* (1923). . . . Marriage also affords the permanency and stability important to children's best interests.

As all parties agree, many same-sex couples provide loving and nurturing homes to their children, whether biological or adopted. And hundreds of thousands of children are presently being raised by such couples. . . . Excluding same-sex couples from marriage thus conflicts with a central premise of the right to marry. Without the recognition, stability, and predictability marriage offers, their children suffer the stigma of knowing their families are somehow lesser. They also suffer the significant material costs of being raised by unmarried parents, relegated through no fault of their own to a more difficult and uncertain family life. The marriage laws at issue here thus harm and humiliate the children of same-sex couples.

That is not to say the right to marry is less meaningful for those who do not or cannot have children. An ability, desire, or promise to procreate is not and has not been a prerequisite for a valid marriage in any State. In light of precedent protecting the right of a married couple not to procreate, it cannot be said the Court or the States have conditioned the right to marry on the capacity or commitment to procreate. The constitutional marriage right has many aspects, of which childbearing is only one.

Fourth and finally, this Court's cases and the Nation's traditions make clear that marriage is a keystone of our social order. Alexis de Tocqueville recognized this truth on his travels through the United States almost two centuries ago:

> There is certainly no country in the world where the tie of marriage is so much respected as in America . . . When the American retires from the turmoil of public life to the bosom of his family, he finds in it the image of order and of peace. . . . He afterwards carries that image with him into public affairs.

. . . Marriage remains a building block of our national community. For that reason, just as a couple vows to support each other, so does society pledge to support the couple, offering symbolic recognition and material benefits to protect and nourish the union. Indeed, while the States are in general free to vary the benefits they confer on all married couples, they have throughout our history made marriage the basis for an expanding list of governmental rights, benefits, and responsibilities. Indeed, while the States are in general free to vary the benefits they confer on all married couples, they have throughout our history made marriage the basis for an expanding list of governmental rights, benefits, and responsibilities. These aspects of marital status include: taxation; inheritance and property rights; rules of intestate succession; spousal privilege in the law of evidence; hospital access; medical decision-making authority; adoption rights; the rights and benefits of survivors; birth and death certificates; professional ethics rules; campaign finance restrictions; workers' compensation benefits; health insurance; and child custody, support, and visitation rules. Valid marriage under state law is also a significant status for over a thousand provisions of federal law. The States have contributed to the fundamental character of the marriage right by placing that institution at the center of so many facets of the legal and social order.

There is no difference between same- and opposite-sex couples with respect to this principle. . . . As the State itself makes marriage all the more precious by the significance it attaches to it, exclusion from that status has the effect of teaching that gays and lesbians are unequal in important respects. It demeans gays and lesbians for the State to lock them out of a central institution of the Nation's society.

Same-sex couples, too, may aspire to the transcendent purposes of marriage and seek fulfillment in its highest meaning.

Obergefell v. Hodges

The limitation of marriage to opposite-sex couples may long have seemed natural and just, but its inconsistency with the central meaning of the fundamental right to marry is now manifest. With that knowledge must come the recognition that laws excluding same-sex couples from the marriage right impose stigma and injury of the kind prohibited by our basic charter.

Objecting that this does not reflect an appropriate framing of the issue, the respondents refer to *Washington v. Glucksberg* (1997), which called for a "careful description" of fundamental rights. They assert the petitioners do not seek to exercise the right to marry but rather a new and nonexistent "right to same-sex marriage." *Glucksberg* did insist that liberty under the Due Process Clause must be defined in a most circumscribed manner, with central reference to specific historical practices. Yet while that approach may have been appropriate for the asserted right there involved (physician-assisted suicide), it is inconsistent with the approach this Court has used in discussing other fundamental rights, including marriage and intimacy. *Loving* did not ask about a "right to interracial marriage"; *Turner* did not ask about a "right of inmates to marry"; and *Zablocki* did not ask about a "right of fathers with unpaid child support duties to marry." Rather, each case inquired about the right to marry in its comprehensive sense, asking if there was a sufficient justification for excluding the relevant class from the right.

That principle applies here. If rights were defined by who exercised them in the past, then received practices could serve as their own continued justification and new groups could not invoke rights once denied. This Court has rejected that approach, both with respect to the right to marry and the rights of gays and lesbians. See *Loving*, *Lawrence*.

The right to marry is fundamental as a matter of history and tradition, but rights come not from ancient sources alone. They rise, too, from a better informed understanding of how constitutional imperatives define a liberty that remains urgent in our own era. Many who deem same-sex marriage to be wrong reach that conclusion based on decent and honorable religious or philosophical premises, and neither they nor their beliefs are disparaged here. But when that sincere, personal opposition becomes enacted law and public policy, the necessary consequence is to put the imprimatur of the State itself on an exclusion that soon demeans or stigmatizes those whose own liberty is then denied. Under the Constitution, same-sex couples seek in marriage the same legal treatment as opposite-sex couples, and it would disparage their choices and diminish their personhood to deny them this right.

The right of same-sex couples to marry that is part of the liberty promised by the Fourteenth Amendment is derived, too, from that Amendment's guarantee of the equal protection of the laws. The Due Process Clause and the Equal Protection Clause are connected in a profound way, though they set forth independent principles. Rights implicit in liberty and rights secured by equal protection may rest on different precepts and are not always co-extensive, yet in some instances each may be instructive as to the meaning and reach of the other. In any particular case one Clause may be thought to capture the essence of the right in a more accurate and comprehensive way, even as the two Clauses may converge in the identification and definition of the right. This interrelation of the two principles furthers our understanding of what freedom is and must become.

The Court's cases touching upon the right to marry reflect this dynamic. In *Loving* the Court invalidated a prohibition on interracial marriage under both the Equal Protection Clause and the Due Process Clause. . . .

The synergy between the two protections is illustrated further in *Zablocki*. There the Court invoked the Equal Protection Clause as its basis for invalidating the challenged law, which, as already noted, barred fathers who were behind on child-support payments from marrying without judicial approval. The equal protection analysis depended in central part on the Court's holding that the law burdened a right "of fundamental importance." It was the essential nature of the marriage right, discussed at length in *Zablocki*, that made apparent the law's incompatibility with requirements of equality. Each concept—liberty and equal protection—leads to a stronger understanding of the other.

Indeed, in interpreting the Equal Protection Clause, the Court has recognized that new insights and societal understandings can reveal unjustified inequality within our most fundamental institutions that once passed unnoticed and unchallenged. To take but one period, this occurred with respect to marriage in the 1970s and 1980s. Notwithstanding the gradual erosion of the doctrine of coverture, invidious sex-based classifications in marriage remained common through the mid-20th century. These classifications denied the equal dignity of men and women. . . . Responding to a new awareness, the Court invoked equal protection principles to invalidate laws imposing sex-based inequality on marriage. See, e.g., [citations including *Frontiero v. Richardson* (1973)]. Like *Loving* and *Zablocki*, these precedents show the Equal Protection Clause can help to identify and correct inequalities in the institution of marriage, vindicating precepts of liberty and equality under the Constitution. . . .

In *Lawrence* the Court acknowledged the interlocking nature of these constitutional safeguards in the context of the legal treatment of gays and lesbians. Although *Lawrence* elaborated its holding under the Due Process Clause, it acknowledged, and sought to remedy, the continuing inequality that resulted from laws making intimacy in the lives of gays and lesbians a crime against the State. . . .

These considerations lead to the conclusion that the right to marry is a fundamental right inherent in the liberty of the person, and under the Due Process and Equal Protection Clauses of the Fourteenth Amendment couples of the same-sex may not be deprived of that right and that liberty. The Court now holds that same-sex couples may exercise the fundamental right to marry. No longer may this liberty be denied to them. . . . The State laws challenged by Petitioners in these cases are now held invalid to the extent they exclude same-sex couples from civil marriage on the same terms and conditions as opposite-sex couples.

IV

There may be an initial inclination in these cases to proceed with caution—to await further legislation, litigation, and debate. The respondents warn there has been insufficient democratic discourse before deciding an issue so basic as the definition of marriage. . . .

Yet there has been far more deliberation than this argument acknowledges. There have been referenda, legislative debates, and grassroots campaigns, as well as countless studies, papers, books, and other popular and scholarly writings. There has been extensive litigation in state and federal courts. Judicial opinions addressing the issue have been informed by the contentions of parties and counsel, which, in turn, reflect the more general, societal discussion of same-sex marriage and its meaning that has occurred over the past decades. As more than 100 amici make clear in their filings, many of the central institutions in American life—state and local governments, the military, large and small businesses, labor unions, religious organizations, law enforcement, civic groups, professional organizations, and universities—have devoted substantial attention to the question. This has led to an enhanced understanding of the issue—an understanding reflected in the arguments now presented for resolution as a matter of constitutional law.

Of course, the Constitution contemplates that democracy is the appropriate process for change, so long as that process does not abridge fundamental rights. . . . Indeed, it is most often through democracy that liberty is preserved and protected in our lives. But . . . the dynamic of our constitutional system is that individuals need not await legislative action before asserting a fundamental right. . . . An individual can invoke a right to constitutional protection when he or she is harmed, even if the broader public disagrees and even if the legislature refuses to act. The idea of the Constitution "was to withdraw certain subjects from the vicissitudes of political controversy, to place them beyond the reach of majorities and officials and to establish them as legal principles to be applied by the courts." *West Virginia Bd. of Ed. v. Barnette* (1943). This is why "fundamental rights may not be submitted to a vote; they depend on the outcome of no elections." *Id.* It is of no moment whether advocates of same-sex marriage now enjoy or lack momentum in the democratic process. . . . Properly presented with the petitioners' cases, the Court has a duty to address these claims and answer these questions. . . .

The respondents also argue allowing same-sex couples to wed will harm marriage as an institution by leading to fewer opposite-sex marriages. This may occur, the respondents contend, because licensing same-sex marriage severs the connection between natural procreation and marriage. That argument, however, rests on a counterintuitive view of opposite-sex couple's decisionmaking processes regarding marriage and parenthood. Decisions about whether to marry and raise children are based on many personal, romantic, and practical considerations; and it is unrealistic to conclude that an opposite-sex couple would choose not to marry simply because same-sex couples may do so. . . .

V

These cases also present the question whether the Constitution requires States to recognize same-sex marriages validly performed out of State. . . . Leaving the current state of affairs in place would maintain and promote instability and uncertainty. For some couples, even an ordinary drive into a neighboring State to visit family or friends risks causing severe hardship in the event of a spouse's hospitalization while across state lines. In light of the fact that many States already allow same-sex marriage—and hundreds of thousands of these marriages already have occurred—the disruption caused by the recognition bans is significant and ever-growing. . . .

The Court, in this decision, holds same-sex couples may exercise the fundamental right to marry in all States. It follows that the Court also must hold—and it now does hold—that there is no lawful basis for a State to refuse to recognize a lawful same-sex marriage performed in another State on the ground of its same-sex character.

[CONCLUSION]

No union is more profound than marriage, for it embodies the highest ideals of love, fidelity, devotion, sacrifice, and family. In forming a marital union, two people become something greater than once they were. As some of the petitioners in these cases demonstrate, marriage embodies a love that may endure even past death. It would misunderstand these men and women to say they disrespect the idea of marriage. Their plea is that they do respect it, respect it so deeply that they seek to find its fulfillment for themselves. Their hope is not to be condemned to live in loneliness, excluded from one of civilization's oldest institutions. They ask for equal dignity in the eyes of the law. The Constitution grants them that right.

Chief Justice Roberts, with whom Justices Scalia and Thomas join, dissenting.

Petitioners make strong arguments rooted in social policy and considerations of fairness. They contend that same-sex couples should be allowed to affirm their love and commitment through marriage, just like opposite-sex couples. That position has undeniable appeal; over the past six years, voters and legislators in eleven States and the District of Columbia have revised their laws to allow marriage between two people of the same sex.

Obergefell v. Hodges

But this Court is not a legislature. Whether same-sex marriage is a good idea should be of no concern to us. Under the Constitution, judges have power to say what the law is, not what it should be. The people who ratified the Constitution authorized courts to exercise "neither force nor will but merely judgment." The Federalist #78. . . .

The majority's decision is an act of will, not legal judgment. The right it announces has no basis in the Constitution or this Court's precedent. The majority expressly disclaims judicial "caution" and omits even a pretense of humility, openly relying on its desire to remake society according to its own "new insight" into the "nature of injustice." As a result, the Court invalidates the marriage laws of more than half the States and orders the transformation of a social institution that has formed the basis of human society for millennia, for the Kalahari Bushmen and the Han Chinese, the Carthaginians and the Aztecs. Just who do we think we are?

It can be tempting for judges to confuse our own preferences with the requirements of the law. But as this Court has been reminded throughout our history, the Constitution "is made for people of fundamentally differing views." *Lochner v. New York* (1905) (Holmes, J., dissenting). Accordingly, "courts are not concerned with the wisdom or policy of legislation." *Id.* (Harlan, J., dissenting). The majority today neglects that restrained conception of the judicial role. It seizes for itself a question the Constitution leaves to the people, at a time when the people are engaged in a vibrant debate on that question. And it answers that question based not on neutral principles of constitutional law, but on its own "understanding of what freedom is and must become." I have no choice but to dissent.

Understand well what this dissent is about: It is not about whether, in my judgment, the institution of marriage should be changed to include same-sex couples. It is instead about whether, in our democratic republic, that decision should rest with the people acting through their elected representatives, or with five lawyers who happen to hold commissions authorizing them to resolve legal disputes according to law. The Constitution leaves no doubt about the answer.

I

Petitioners and their amici base their arguments on the "right to marry" and the imperative of "marriage equality." There is no serious dispute that, under our precedents, the Constitution protects a right to marry and requires States to apply their marriage laws equally. The real question in these cases is what constitutes "marriage," or—more precisely—who decides what constitutes "marriage"? . . .

A

As the majority acknowledges, marriage has existed for millennia and across civilizations. For all those millennia, across all those civilizations, "marriage" referred to only one relationship: the union of a man and a woman. . . . This universal definition of marriage as the union of a man and a woman is no historical coincidence. . . . It arose in the nature of things to meet a vital need: ensuring that children are conceived by a mother and father committed to raising them in the stable conditions of a lifelong relationship.

The premises supporting this concept of marriage are so fundamental that they rarely require articulation. The human race must procreate to survive. Procreation occurs through sexual relations between a man and a woman. When sexual relations result in the conception of a child, that child's prospects are generally better if the mother and father stay together rather than going their separate ways. Therefore, for the good of children and society, sexual relations that can lead to procreation should occur only between a man and a woman committed to a lasting bond.

Society has recognized that bond as marriage. And by bestowing a respected status and material benefits on married couples, society encourages men and women to conduct sexual relations within marriage rather than without. . . . To those who drafted and ratified the Constitution, this conception of marriage and family was a given: its structure, its stability, roles, and values accepted by all.

The Constitution itself says nothing about marriage, and the Framers thereby entrusted the States with the whole subject of the domestic relations of husband and wife. There is no dispute that every State at the founding—and every State throughout our history until a dozen years ago—defined marriage in the traditional, biologically rooted way . . . as the union of a man and a woman. . . .

As the majority notes, some aspects of marriage have changed over time. Arranged marriages have largely given way to pairings based on romantic love. States have replaced coverture, the doctrine by which a married man and woman became a single legal entity, with laws that respect each participant's separate status. Racial restrictions on marriage, which "arose as an incident to slavery" to promote "White Supremacy," were repealed by many States and ultimately struck down by this Court. *Loving*.

The majority observes that these developments "were not mere superficial changes" in marriage, but rather "worked deep transformations in its structure." They did not, however, work any transformation in the core structure of marriage as the union between a man and a woman. If you had asked a person on the street how marriage was defined, no one would ever have said, "Marriage is the union of a man and a woman, where the woman is subject to coverture." The majority may be right that the "history of marriage is one of both continuity and change," but the core meaning of marriage has endured.

B [Omitted]

Obergefell v. Hodges

II

Petitioners first contend that the marriage laws of their States violate the Due Process Clause. . . . The majority purports to identify four "principles and traditions" in this Court's due process precedents that support a fundamental right for same-sex couples to marry. In reality, however, the majority's approach has no basis in principle or tradition, except for the unprincipled tradition of judicial policymaking that characterized discredited decisions such as *Lochner v. New York*. . . .

A

Petitioners' "fundamental right" claim falls into the most sensitive category of constitutional adjudication. . . . Allowing unelected federal judges to select which unenumerated rights rank as "fundamental"—and to strike down state laws on the basis of that determination—raises obvious concerns about the judicial role. Our precedents have accordingly insisted that judges exercise the utmost care in identifying implied fundamental rights, lest the liberty protected by the Due Process Clause be subtly transformed into the policy preferences of the Members of this Court. *Washington v. Glucksberg* (1997).

The need for restraint in administering the strong medicine of substantive due process is a lesson this Court has learned the hard way. The Court first applied substantive due process to strike down a statute in *Dred Scott v. Sandford* (1857). There the Court invalidated the Missouri Compromise on the ground that legislation restricting the institution of slavery violated the implied rights of slaveholders. . . . *Dred Scott*'s holding was overruled on the battlefields of the Civil War and by constitutional amendment after Appomattox, but its approach to the Due Process Clause reappeared. In a series of early 20th-century cases, most prominently *Lochner v. New York*, this Court invalidated state statutes that presented "meddlesome interferences with the rights of the individual," and "undue interference with liberty of person and freedom of contract." . . . Eventually, the Court recognized its error and vowed not to repeat it. . . .

Rejecting *Lochner* does not require disavowing the doctrine of implied fundamental rights, and this Court has not done so. But to avoid repeating *Lochner*'s error of converting personal preferences into constitutional mandates, our modern substantive due process cases have stressed the need for judicial self-restraint. Our precedents have required that implied fundamental rights be "objectively, deeply rooted in this Nation's history and tradition," and "implicit in the concept of ordered liberty, such that neither liberty nor justice would exist if they were sacrificed." *Glucksberg* (internal citations omitted). . . . Many other cases both before and after have adopted the same approach.

Proper reliance on history and tradition of course requires looking beyond the individual law being challenged, so that every restriction on liberty does not supply its own constitutional justification. The Court is right about that. But given the few guideposts for responsible decisionmaking in this unchartered area, "an approach grounded in history imposes limits on the judiciary that are more meaningful than any based on [an] abstract formula," *Moore v. East Cleveland* (1977) (plurality opinion). Expanding a right suddenly and dramatically is likely to require tearing it up from its roots. Even a sincere profession of discipline in identifying fundamental rights does not provide a meaningful constraint on a judge, for "what he is really likely to be 'discovering,' whether or not he is fully aware of it, are his own values," John Hart Ely, Democracy and Distrust 44 (1980). The only way to ensure restraint in this delicate enterprise is "continual insistence upon respect for the teachings of history, solid recognition of the basic values that underlie our society, and wise appreciation of the great roles of the doctrines of federalism and separation of powers." *Griswold* (1965) (Harlan, J., concurring in judgment).

B

The majority acknowledges none of this doctrinal background, and it is easy to see why: Its aggressive application of substantive due process breaks sharply with decades of precedent and returns the Court to the unprincipled approach of *Lochner*.

1

. . . When the majority turns to the law, it relies primarily on precedents discussing the fundamental "right to marry." These cases do not hold, of course, that anyone who wants to get married has a constitutional right to do so. They instead require a State to justify barriers to marriage as that institution has always been understood. In *Loving*, the Court held that racial restrictions on the right to marry lacked a compelling justification. In *Zablocki*, restrictions based on child support debts did not suffice. In *Turner*, restrictions based on status as a prisoner were deemed impermissible.

None of the laws at issue in those cases purported to change the core definition of marriage as the union of a man and a woman. The laws challenged in *Zablocki* and *Turner* did not define marriage as "the union of a man and a woman, where neither party owes child support or is in prison." Nor did the interracial marriage ban at issue in *Loving* define marriage as "the union of a man and a woman of the same race." Removing racial barriers to marriage therefore did not change what a marriage was any more than integrating schools changed what a school was. . . .

In short, the "right to marry" cases stand for the important but limited proposition that particular restrictions on access to marriage as traditionally defined violate due process. These precedents say nothing at all about a right to make a State change its definition of marriage, which is the right petitioners actually seek here. Neither petitioners nor the majority cites a single case or other legal source providing any basis for such a constitutional right. None exists, and that is enough to foreclose their claim.

2 [Omitted]

3

. . . One immediate question invited by the majority's position is whether States may retain the definition of marriage as a union of two people. Although the majority randomly inserts the adjective "two" in various places, it offers no reason at all why the two-person element of the core definition of marriage may be preserved while the man-woman element may not. Indeed, from the standpoint of history and tradition, a leap from opposite-sex marriage to same-sex marriage is much greater than one from a two-person union to plural unions, which have deep roots in some cultures around the world. If the majority is willing to take the big leap, it is hard to see how it can say no to the shorter one. . . .

I do not mean to equate marriage between same-sex couples with plural marriages in all respects. There may well be relevant differences that compel different legal analysis. But if there are, petitioners have not pointed to any. When asked about a plural marital union at oral argument, petitioners asserted that a State "doesn't have such an institution." But that is exactly the point: the States at issue here do not have an institution of same-sex marriage, either.

4

. . . A Justice's commission does not confer any special moral, philosophical, or social insight sufficient to justify imposing those perceptions on fellow citizens under the pretense of "due process." There is indeed a process due the people on issues of this sort—the democratic process. Respecting that understanding requires the Court to be guided by law, not any particular school of social thought. As Judge Henry Friendly once put it, echoing Justice Holmes's dissent in *Lochner*, the Fourteenth Amendment does not enact John Stuart Mill's *On Liberty* any more than it enacts Herbert Spencer's *Social Statics*. And it certainly does not enact any one concept of marriage. . . .

III

In addition to their due process argument, petitioners contend that the Equal Protection Clause requires their States to license and recognize same-sex marriages. The majority does not seriously engage with this claim. Its discussion is, quite frankly, difficult to follow. The central point seems to be that there is a "synergy between" the Equal Protection Clause and the Due Process Clause, and that some precedents relying on one Clause have also relied on the other. Absent from this portion of the opinion, however, is anything resembling our usual framework for deciding equal protection cases. . . .

In any event, the marriage laws at issue here do not violate the Equal Protection Clause, because distinguishing between opposite-sex and same-sex couples is rationally related to the States' legitimate state interest in preserving the traditional institution of marriage. . . .

IV

. . . Nowhere is the majority's extravagant conception of judicial supremacy more evident than in its description—and dismissal—of the public debate regarding same-sex marriage. Yes, the majority concedes, on one side are thousands of years of human history in every society known to have populated the planet. But on the other side, there has been "extensive litigation," "many thoughtful District Court decisions," "countless studies, papers, books, and other popular and scholarly writings," and "more than 100" amicus briefs in these cases alone. What would be the point of allowing the democratic process to go on? It is high time for the Court to decide the meaning of marriage, based on five lawyers' "better informed understanding" of "a liberty that remains urgent in our own era." The answer is surely there in one of those amicus briefs or studies. . . .

By deciding this question under the Constitution, the Court removes it from the realm of democratic decision. There will be consequences to shutting down the political process on an issue of such profound public significance. Closing debate tends to close minds. People denied a voice are less likely to accept the ruling of a court on an issue that does not seem to be the sort of thing courts usually decide. . . . Indeed, however heartened the proponents of same-sex marriage might be on this day, it is worth acknowledging what they have lost, and lost forever: the opportunity to win the true acceptance that comes from persuading their fellow citizens of the justice of their cause. And they lose this just when the winds of change were freshening at their backs. . . .

Perhaps the most discouraging aspect of today's decision is the extent to which the majority feels compelled to sully those on the other side of the debate. The majority offers a cursory assurance that it does not intend to disparage people who, as a matter of conscience, cannot accept same-sex marriage. That disclaimer is hard to square with the very next sentence, in which the majority explains that "the necessary consequence" of laws codifying the traditional definition of marriage is to "demean or stigmatize" same-sex couples. The majority reiterates such characterizations over and over. By the majority's account, Americans who did nothing more than follow the understanding of marriage that has existed for our entire history—in particular, the tens of millions of people who voted to reaffirm their States' enduring definition of marriage—have acted to "lock out," "disparage," "disrespect and subordinate," and inflict "dignitary wounds" upon their gay and lesbian neighbors. These apparent assaults on the character of fairminded people will have an effect, in society and in court. Moreover, they are entirely gratuitous. It is one thing for the majority to conclude that the Constitution protects a right to same-sex marriage;

it is something else to portray everyone who does not share the majority's "better informed understanding" as bigoted. . . .

[CONCLUSION]

If you are among the many Americans—of whatever sexual orientation—who favor expanding same-sex marriage, by all means celebrate today's decision. Celebrate the achievement of a desired goal. Celebrate the opportunity for a new expression of commitment to a partner. Celebrate the availability of new benefits. But do not celebrate the Constitution. It had nothing to do with it.

I respectfully dissent.

Justice Scalia, with whom Justice Thomas joins, dissenting. [Omitted.]

Justice Thomas, with whom Justice Scalia joins, dissenting. [Omitted.]

Justice Alito, with whom Justices Scalia and Thomas join, dissenting. [Omitted.]

flashforward

1. ***Equality or Freedom?*** The *Obergefell* majority traced its holding to both Due Process and Equal Protection, but it admittedly gave more emphasis to marriage as an important "liberty" (freedom) that ought not be denied to anyone. The next Supreme Court decision to consider the rights of same-sex couples emphasized equality. The Arkansas statute in *Pavan v. Smith*, 582 U.S. 563 (2017), involved the presumption that a married woman's spouse is the child's parent (a topic explored in *Michael H. v. Gerald D.* (1988), Ch. 20.D.2). Existing law in Arkansas, like most states, provided that the husband of a married woman would be listed on birth certificates as the father for any child born during the marriage—regardless of his biological relationship to the child. But the state refused to do the same for a birth mother's wife. The Supreme Court emphasized language from *Obergefell* that a State may not "exclude same-sex couples from civil marriage on the same terms and conditions as opposite-sex couples." It remains to be seen whether other cases will similarly emphasize *Obergefell*'s equality aspect.

WEBSITE

A fuller version of *Pavan v. Smith* is available for download from this casebook's companion website, www.CaplanIntegratedConLaw.com.

2. *The Respect for Marriage Act.* In early 2022, *Dobbs v. Jackson Womens' Health Organization* overruled *Roe v. Wade* (1973) and its progeny. The majority in *Dobbs* said that its ruling did not mean the end of *Obergefell's* right to same-sex marriage; Justice Thomas's concurring opinion argued that it should; and the dissent feared that the court would take up Justice Thomas's suggestion. In December 2022 Congress enacted the Respect for Marriage Act (ROMA), 28 U.S.C. § 1738C, which was designed to protect same-sex couples like those in *Obergefell* and interracial couples like the one in *Loving* in the event of a future change in constitutional law.

ROMA began by repealing the 1996 Defense of Marriage Act (DOMA), the law denying federal recognition to same-sex marriages. (DOMA was found unconstitutional in *US v. Windsor* (2013), but it technically remained on the books.) Second, ROMA declared that states may not deny full faith and credit to out-of-state marriages "on the basis of the sex, race, ethnicity, or national origin" of the spouses. Third, it said that the federal government would treat as married any couple married under state law. ROMA's effect is largely symbolic, since it amounts to a partial codification of *Obergefell*. But if the decision is overruled, and if any state opts not to allow same-sex marriages, that state (and the federal government) must still treat as married any same-sex couples who married in jurisdictions allowing it.

APPENDIX A

Constitution of the United States

Passed by Constitutional Convention
September 17, 1787
Ratified June 21, 1788

We the People of the United States, in Order to form a more perfect Union, establish Justice, insure domestic Tranquility, provide for the common defence, promote the general Welfare, and secure the Blessings of Liberty to ourselves and our Posterity, do ordain and establish this Constitution for the United States of America.

Article I

Section 1. All legislative Powers herein granted shall be vested in a Congress of the United States, which shall consist of a Senate and House of Representatives.

Section 2. [Clause 1] The House of Representatives shall be composed of Members chosen every second Year by the People of the several States, and the Electors in each State shall have the Qualifications requisite for Electors of the most numerous Branch of the State Legislature.

[Clause 2] No Person shall be a Representative who shall not have attained to the age of twenty five Years, and been seven Years a Citizen of the United States, and who shall not, when elected, be an Inhabitant of that State in which he shall be chosen.

[Clause 3] Representatives and direct Taxes shall be apportioned among the several States which may be included within this Union, according to their respective Numbers, which shall be determined by adding to the whole Number of free Persons, including those bound to Service for a Term of Years, and excluding Indians not taxed, three fifths of all other Persons. The actual Enumeration shall be made within three Years after the first Meeting of the Congress of the United States, and within every subsequent Term of ten Years, in such Manner as they shall by Law direct. The Number of Representatives shall not exceed one for every thirty Thousand, but each State shall have at Least one Representative; and until

◄ AFFECTED BY 13TH AND 14TH AMENDMENTS

such enumeration shall be made, the State of New Hampshire shall be entitled to chuse three, Massachusetts eight, Rhode-Island and Providence Plantations one, Connecticut five, New-York six, New Jersey four, Pennsylvania eight, Delaware one, Maryland six, Virginia ten, North Carolina five, South Carolina five, and Georgia three.

[Clause 4] When vacancies happen in the Representation from any State, the Executive Authority thereof shall issue Writs of Election to fill such Vacancies.

[Clause 5] The House of Representatives shall chuse their Speaker and other Officers; and shall have the sole Power of Impeachment.

▸ AFFECTED BY 17TH AMENDMENT

SECTION 3. [Clause 1] The Senate of the United States shall be composed of two Senators from each State, chosen by the Legislature thereof, for six Years; and each Senator shall have one Vote.

[Clause 2] Immediately after they shall be assembled in Consequence of the first Election, they shall be divided as equally as may be into three Classes. The Seats of the Senators of the first Class shall be vacated at the Expiration of the second Year, of the second Class at the Expiration of the fourth Year, and the third Class at the Expiration of the sixth Year, so that one third may be chosen every second Year; and if Vacancies happen by Resignation, or otherwise, during the Recess of the Legislature of any State, the Executive thereof may make temporary Appointments until the next Meeting of the Legislature, which shall then fill such Vacancies.

▸ AFFECTED BY 17TH AMENDMENT

[Clause 3] No Person shall be a Senator who shall not have attained to the Age of thirty Years, and been nine Years a Citizen of the United States and who shall not, when elected, be an Inhabitant of that State for which he shall be chosen.

[Clause 4] The Vice President of the United States shall be President of the Senate, but shall have no Vote, unless they be equally divided.

[Clause 5] The Senate shall chuse their other Officers, and also a President pro tempore, in the Absence of the Vice President, or when he shall exercise the Office of President of the United States.

[Clause 6] The Senate shall have the sole Power to try all Impeachments. When sitting for that Purpose, they shall be on Oath or Affirmation. When the President of the United States is tried, the Chief Justice shall preside: And no Person shall be convicted without the Concurrence of two thirds of the Members present.

[Clause 7] Judgment in Cases of Impeachment shall not extend further than to removal from Office, and disqualification to hold and enjoy any Office of Honor, Trust or Profit under the United States: but the Party convicted shall nevertheless be liable and subject to Indictment, Trial, Judgment and Punishment, according to Law.

Section 4. [Clause 1] The Times, Places and Manner of holding Elections for Senators and Representatives, shall be prescribed in each State by the Legislature thereof; but the Congress may at any time by Law make or alter such Regulations, except as to the Places of chusing Senators. ◄ AFFECTED BY 17TH AMENDMENT

[Clause 2] The Congress shall assemble at least once in every Year, and such Meeting shall be on the first Monday in December, unless they shall by Law appoint a different Day. ◄ AFFECTED BY 20TH AMENDMENT

Section 5. [Clause 1] Each House shall be the Judge of the Elections, Returns and Qualifications of its own Members, and a Majority of each shall constitute a Quorum to do Business; but a smaller Number may adjourn from day to day, and may be authorized to compel the Attendance of absent Members, in such Manner, and under such Penalties as each House may provide.

[Clause 2] Each House may determine the Rules of its Proceedings, punish its Members for disorderly Behaviour, and, with the Concurrence of two thirds, expel a Member.

[Clause 3] Each House shall keep a Journal of its Proceedings, and from time to time publish the same, excepting such Parts as may in their Judgment require Secrecy; and the Yeas and Nays of the Members of either House on any question shall, at the Desire of one fifth of those Present, be entered on the Journal.

[Clause 4] Neither House, during the Session of Congress, shall, without the Consent of the other, adjourn for more than three days, nor to any other Place than that in which the two Houses shall be sitting.

Section 6. [Clause 1] The Senators and Representatives shall receive a Compensation for their Services, to be ascertained by Law, and paid out of the Treasury of the United States. ◄ AFFECTED BY 27TH AMENDMENT They shall in all Cases, except Treason, Felony and Breach of the Peace, be privileged from Arrest during their Attendance at the Session of their respective Houses, and in going to and returning from the same; and for any Speech or Debate in either House, they shall not be questioned in any other Place.

[Clause 2] No Senator or Representative shall, during the Time for which he was elected, be appointed to any civil Office under the Authority of the United States, which shall have been created, or the Emoluments whereof shall have been encreased during such time: and no Person holding any Office under the United States, shall be a Member of either House during his Continuance in Office.

Section 7. [Clause 1] All Bills for raising Revenue shall originate in the House of Representatives; but the Senate may propose or concur with Amendments as on other Bills.

[Clause 2] Every Bill which shall have passed the House of Representatives and the Senate, shall, before it become a Law, be presented to the President of the United States; if he approve he shall sign it, but if not he shall return it, with his Objections to that House in which it shall have originated, who shall enter the Objections at large on their Journal, and proceed to reconsider it. If after such Reconsideration two thirds of that House shall agree to pass the Bill, it shall be sent, together with the Objections, to the other House, by which it shall likewise be reconsidered, and if approved by two thirds of that House, it shall become a Law. But in all such Cases the Votes of both Houses shall be determined by Yeas and Nays, and the Names of the Persons voting for and against the Bill shall be entered on the Journal of each House respectively. If any Bill shall not be returned by the President within ten Days (Sundays excepted) after it shall have been presented to him, the Same shall be a Law, in like Manner as if he had signed it, unless the Congress by their Adjournment prevent its Return, in which Case it shall not be a Law.

[Clause 3] Every Order, Resolution, or Vote to which the Concurrence of the Senate and House of Representatives may be necessary (except on a question of Adjournment) shall be presented to the President of the United States; and before the Same shall take Effect, shall be approved by him, or being disapproved by him, shall be repassed by two thirds of the Senate and House of Representatives, according to the Rules and Limitations prescribed in the Case of a Bill.

Section 8. [Clause 1] Congress shall have the power to lay and collect Taxes, Duties, Imposts and Excises, to pay the Debts and provide for the common Defence and general Welfare of the United States; but all Duties, Imposts and Excises shall be uniform throughout the United States;

[Clause 2] To borrow Money on the credit of the United States;

[Clause 3] To regulate Commerce with foreign Nations, and among the several States, and with the Indian Tribes;

[Clause 4] To establish an uniform Rule of Naturalization, and uniform Laws on the subject of Bankruptcies throughout the United States;

[Clause 5] To coin Money, regulate the Value thereof, and of foreign Coin, and fix the Standard of Weights and Measures;

[Clause 6] To provide for the Punishment of counterfeiting the Securities and current Coin of the United States;

[Clause 7] To establish Post Offices and post Roads;

[Clause 8] To promote the Progress of Science and useful Arts, by securing for limited Times to Authors and Inventors the exclusive Right to their respective Writings and Discoveries;

[Clause 9] To constitute Tribunals inferior to the supreme Court;

[Clause 10] To define and punish Piracies and Felonies committed on the high Seas, and Offences against the Law of Nations;

[Clause 11] To declare War, grant Letters of Marque and Reprisal, and make Rules concerning Captures on Land and Water;

[Clause 12] To raise and support Armies, but no Appropriation of Money to that Use shall be for a longer Term than two Years;

[Clause 13] To provide and maintain a Navy;

[Clause 14] To make Rules for the Government and Regulation of the land and naval Forces;

[Clause 15] To provide for calling forth the Militia to execute the Laws of the Union, suppress Insurrections and repel Invasions;

[Clause 16] To provide for organizing, arming, and disciplining, the Militia, and for governing such Part of them as may be employed in the Service of the United States, reserving to the States respectively, the Appointment of the Officers, and the Authority of training the Militia according to the discipline prescribed by Congress;

[Clause 17] To exercise exclusive Legislation in all Cases whatsoever, over such District (not exceeding ten Miles square) as may, by Cession of particular States, and the Acceptance of Congress, become the Seat of the Government of the United States, and to exercise like Authority over all Places purchased by the Consent of the Legislature of the State in which the Same shall be, for the Erection of Forts, Magazines, Arsenals, dock-Yards, and other needful Buildings; —And

[Clause 18] To make all Laws which shall be necessary and proper for carrying into Execution the foregoing Powers, and all other Powers vested by this Constitution in the Government of the United States, or in any Department or Officer thereof.

SECTION 9. [Clause 1] The Migration or Importation of such Persons as any of the States now existing shall think proper to admit, shall not be prohibited by the Congress prior to the Year one thousand eight hundred and eight, but a Tax or duty may be imposed on such Importation, not exceeding ten dollars for each Person.

◄ AFFECTED BY 13TH AMENDMENT

[Clause 2] The Privilege of the Writ of Habeas Corpus shall not be suspended, unless when in Cases of Rebellion or Invasion the public Safety may require it.

[Clause 3]No Bill of Attainder or ex post facto Law shall be passed.

▸ AFFECTED BY 16TH AMENDMENT

[Clause 4] No Capitation, or other direct, Tax shall be laid, unless in Proportion to the Census or Enumeration herein before directed to be taken.

[Clause 5] No Tax or Duty shall be laid on Articles exported from any State.

[Clause 6] No Preference shall be given by any Regulation of Commerce or Revenue to the Ports of one State over those of another: nor shall Vessels bound to, or from, one State, be obliged to enter, clear or pay Duties in another.

[Clause 7] No Money shall be drawn from the Treasury, but in Consequence of Appropriations made by Law; and a regular Statement and Account of Receipts and Expenditures of all public Money shall be published from time to time.

[Clause 8] No Title of Nobility shall be granted by the United States: And no Person holding any Office of Profit or Trust under them, shall, without the Consent of the Congress, accept of any present, Emolument, Office, or Title, of any kind whatever, from any King, Prince, or foreign State.

Section 10. [Clause 1] No State shall enter into any Treaty, Alliance, or Confederation; grant Letters of Marque and Reprisal; coin Money; emit Bills of Credit; make any Thing but gold and silver Coin a Tender in Payment of Debts; pass any Bill of Attainder, ex post facto Law, or Law impairing the Obligation of Contracts, or grant any Title of Nobility.

[Clause 2] No State shall, without the Consent of the Congress, lay any Imposts or Duties on Imports or Exports, except what may be absolutely necessary for executing it's inspection Laws: and the net Produce of all Duties and Imposts, laid by any State on Imports or Exports, shall be for the Use of the Treasury of the United States; and all such Laws shall be subject to the Revision and Controul of the Congress.

[Clause 3] No State shall, without the Consent of Congress, lay any Duty of Tonnage, keep Troops, or Ships of War in time of Peace, enter into any Agreement or Compact with another State, or with a foreign Power, or engage in War, unless actually invaded, or in such imminent Danger as will not admit of delay.

Article II

Section 1. [Clause 1] The executive Power shall be vested in a President of the United States of America. He shall hold his Office during the Term of four

Years, and, together with the Vice President, chosen for the same Term, be elected, as follows:

[Clause 2] Each State shall appoint, in such Manner as the Legislature thereof may direct, a Number of Electors, equal to the whole Number of Senators and Representatives to which the State may be entitled in the Congress: but no Senator or Representative, or Person holding an Office of Trust or Profit under the United States, shall be appointed an Elector.

[Clause 3] The Electors shall meet in their respective States, and vote by Ballot for two Persons, of whom one at least shall not be an Inhabitant of the same State with themselves. And they shall make a List of all the Persons voted for, and of the Number of Votes for each; which List they shall sign and certify, and transmit sealed to the Seat of the Government of the United States, directed to the President of the Senate. The President of the Senate shall, in the Presence of the Senate and House of Representatives, open all the Certificates, and the Votes shall then be counted. The Person having the greatest Number of Votes shall be the President, if such Number be a Majority of the whole Number of Electors appointed; and if there be more than one who have such Majority, and have an equal Number of Votes, then the House of Representatives shall immediately chuse by Ballot one of them for President; and if no Person have a Majority, then from the five highest on the List the said House shall in like Manner chuse the President. But in chusing the President, the Votes shall be taken by States, the Representation from each State having one Vote; A quorum for this Purpose shall consist of a Member or Members from two thirds of the States, and a Majority of all the States shall be necessary to a Choice. In every Case, after the Choice of the President, the Person having the greatest Number of Votes of the Electors shall be the Vice President. But if there should remain two or more who have equal Votes, the Senate shall chuse from them by Ballot the Vice President.

◄ AFFECTED BY 12TH, 20TH, & 23RD AMENDMENTS

[Clause 4] The Congress may determine the Time of chusing the Electors, and the Day on which they shall give their Votes; which Day shall be the same throughout the United States.

[Clause 5] No Person except a natural born Citizen, or a Citizen of the United States, at the time of the Adoption of this Constitution, shall be eligible to the Office of President; neither shall any Person be eligible to that Office who shall not have attained to the Age of thirty five Years, and been fourteen Years a Resident within the United States.

[Clause 6] In Case of the Removal of the President from Office, or of his Death, Resignation, or Inability to discharge the Powers and Duties of the said Office, the Same shall devolve on the Vice President, and the Congress may by

◄ AFFECTED BY 25TH AMENDMENT

Law provide for the Case of Removal, Death, Resignation or Inability, both of the President and Vice President, declaring what Officer shall then act as President, and such Officer shall act accordingly, until the Disability be removed, or a President shall be elected.

[Clause 7] The President shall, at stated Times, receive for his Services, a Compensation, which shall neither be encreased nor diminished during the Period for which he shall have been elected, and he shall not receive within that Period any other Emolument from the United States, or any of them.

[Clause 8] Before he enter on the Execution of his Office, he shall take the following Oath or Affirmation:—"I do solemnly swear (or affirm) that I will faithfully execute the Office of President of the United States, and will to the best of my Ability, preserve, protect and defend the Constitution of the United States."

Section 2. [Clause 1] The President shall be Commander in Chief of the Army and Navy of the United States, and of the Militia of the several States, when called into the actual Service of the United States; he may require the Opinion, in writing, of the principal Officer in each of the executive Departments, upon any Subject relating to the Duties of their respective Offices, and he shall have Power to grant Reprieves and Pardons for Offences against the United States, except in Cases of Impeachment.

[Clause 2] He shall have Power, by and with the Advice and Consent of the Senate, to make Treaties, provided two thirds of the Senators present concur; and he shall nominate, and by and with the Advice and Consent of the Senate, shall appoint Ambassadors, other public Ministers and Consuls, Judges of the supreme Court, and all other Officers of the United States, whose Appointments are not herein otherwise provided for, and which shall be established by Law: but the Congress may by Law vest the Appointment of such inferior Officers, as they think proper, in the President alone, in the Courts of Law, or in the Heads of Departments.

[Clause 3] The President shall have Power to fill up all Vacancies that may happen during the Recess of the Senate, by granting Commissions which shall expire at the End of their next Session.

Section 3. He shall from time to time give to the Congress Information of the State of the Union, and recommend to their Consideration such Measures as he shall judge necessary and expedient; he may, on extraordinary Occasions, convene both Houses, or either of them, and in Case of Disagreement between them, with Respect to the Time of Adjournment, he may adjourn them to such Time as he shall think proper; he shall receive Ambassadors and other public Ministers; he shall take Care that the Laws be faithfully executed, and shall Commission all the Officers of the United States.

Section 4. The President, Vice President and all civil Officers of the United States, shall be removed from Office on Impeachment for, and Conviction of, Treason, Bribery, or other high Crimes and Misdemeanors.

Article III

Section 1. The judicial Power of the United States, shall be vested in one supreme Court, and in such inferior Courts as the Congress may from time to time ordain and establish. The Judges, both of the supreme and inferior Courts, shall hold their Offices during good Behaviour, and shall, at stated Times, receive for their Services, a Compensation, which shall not be diminished during their Continuance in Office.

Section 2. [Clause 1] The judicial Power shall extend to all Cases, in Law and Equity, arising under this Constitution, the Laws of the United States, and Treaties made, or which shall be made, under their Authority; —to all Cases affecting Ambassadors, other public Ministers and Consuls; —to all Cases of admiralty and maritime Jurisdiction; —to Controversies to which the United States shall be a Party; —to Controversies between two or more States; —between a State and Citizens of another State; —between Citizens of different States; —between Citizens of the same State claiming Lands under Grants of different States, and between a State, or the Citizens thereof, and foreign States, Citizens or Subjects.

◂ AFFECTED BY 11TH AMENDMENT

[Clause 2] In all Cases affecting Ambassadors, other public Ministers and Consuls, and those in which a State shall be Party, the supreme Court shall have original Jurisdiction. In all the other Cases before mentioned, the supreme Court shall have appellate Jurisdiction, both as to Law and Fact, with such Exceptions, and under such Regulations as the Congress shall make.

◂ AFFECTED BY 7TH AMENDMENT

[Clause 3]The Trial of all Crimes, except in Cases of Impeachment, shall be by Jury; and such Trial shall be held in the State where the said Crimes shall have been committed; but when not committed within any State, the Trial shall be at such Place or Places as the Congress may by Law have directed.

Section 3. [Clause 1] Treason against the United States, shall consist only in levying War against them, or in adhering to their Enemies, giving them Aid and Comfort. No Person shall be convicted of Treason unless on the Testimony of two Witnesses to the same overt Act, or on Confession in open Court.

[Clause 2] The Congress shall have Power to declare the Punishment of Treason, but no Attainder of Treason shall work Corruption of Blood, or Forfeiture except during the Life of the Person attainted.

Article IV

Section 1. Full Faith and Credit shall be given in each State to the public Acts, Records, and judicial Proceedings of every other State. And the Congress may by general Laws prescribe the Manner in which such Acts, Records, and Proceedings shall be proved, and the Effect thereof.

Section 2. [Clause 1] The Citizens of each State shall be entitled to all Privileges and Immunities of Citizens in the several States.

[Clause 2] A Person charged in any State with Treason, Felony, or other Crime, who shall flee from Justice, and be found in another State, shall on Demand of the executive Authority of the State from which he fled, be delivered up, to be removed to the State having Jurisdiction of the Crime.

▸ AFFECTED BY 13TH AMENDMENT

[Clause 3]No Person held to Service or Labour in one State, under the Laws thereof, escaping into another, shall, in Consequence of any Law or Regulation therein, be discharged from such Service or Labour, but shall be delivered up on Claim of the Party to whom such Service or Labour may be due.

Section 3. [Clause 1] New States may be admitted by the Congress into this Union; but no new States shall be formed or erected within the Jurisdiction of any other State; nor any State be formed by the Junction of two or more States, or Parts of States, without the Consent of the Legislatures of the States concerned as well as of the Congress.

[Clause 2] The Congress shall have Power to dispose of and make all needful Rules and Regulations respecting the Territory or other Property belonging to the United States; and nothing in this Constitution shall be so construed as to Prejudice any Claims of the United States, or of any particular State.

Section 4. The United States shall guarantee to every State in this Union a Republican Form of Government, and shall protect each of them against Invasion; and on Application of the Legislature, or of the Executive (when the Legislature cannot be convened) against domestic Violence.

Article V

The Congress, whenever two thirds of both Houses shall deem it necessary, shall propose Amendments to this Constitution, or, on the Application of the Legislatures of two thirds of the several States, shall call a Convention for proposing Amendments, which, in either Case, shall be valid to all Intents and Purposes, as Part of this Constitution, when ratified by the Legislatures of three fourths of the several States, or by Conventions in three fourths thereof, as the one or the other Mode of Ratification may be proposed by the Congress; Provided that no

Amendment which may be made prior to the Year One thousand eight hundred and eight shall in any Manner affect the first and fourth Clauses in the Ninth Section of the first Article; and that no State, without its Consent, shall be deprived of its equal Suffrage in the Senate.

Article VI

[Section 1] All Debts contracted and Engagements entered into, before the Adoption of this Constitution, shall be as valid against the United States under this Constitution, as under the Confederation.

[Section 2] This Constitution, and the Laws of the United States which shall be made in Pursuance thereof; and all Treaties made, or which shall be made, under the Authority of the United States, shall be the supreme Law of the Land; and the Judges in every State shall be bound thereby, any Thing in the Constitution or Laws of any State to the Contrary notwithstanding.

[Section 3] The Senators and Representatives before mentioned, and the Members of the several State Legislatures, and all executive and judicial Officers, both of the United States and of the several States, shall be bound by Oath or Affirmation, to support this Constitution; but no religious Test shall ever be required as a Qualification to any Office or public Trust under the United States.

Article VII

The Ratification of the Conventions of nine States, shall be sufficient for the Establishment of this Constitution between the States so ratifying the Same.

AMENDMENTS

I

Passed by Congress September 25, 1789
Ratified December 15, 1791

Congress shall make no law respecting an establishment of religion, or prohibiting the free exercise thereof; or abridging the freedom of speech, or of the press; or the right of the people peaceably to assemble, and to petition the Government for a redress of grievances.

II

Passed by Congress September 25, 1789
Ratified December 15, 1791

A well regulated Militia, being necessary to the security of a free State, the right of the people to keep and bear Arms, shall not be infringed.

III

Passed by Congress September 25, 1789
Ratified December 15, 1791

No Soldier shall, in time of peace be quartered in any house, without the consent of the Owner, nor in time of war, but in a manner to be prescribed by law.

IV

Passed by Congress September 25, 1789
Ratified December 15, 1791

The right of the people to be secure in their persons, houses, papers, and effects, against unreasonable searches and seizures, shall not be violated, and no Warrants shall issue, but upon probable cause, supported by Oath or affirmation, and particularly describing the place to be searched, and the persons or things to be seized.

V

Passed by Congress September 25, 1789
Ratified December 15, 1791

No person shall be held to answer for a capital, or otherwise infamous crime, unless on a presentment or indictment of a Grand Jury, except in cases arising in the land or naval forces, or in the Militia, when in actual service in time of War or public danger; nor shall any person be subject for the same offense to be twice put in jeopardy of life or limb; nor shall be compelled in any criminal case to be a witness against himself, nor be deprived of life, liberty, or property, without due process of law; nor shall private property be taken for public use, without just compensation.

VI

Passed by Congress September 25, 1789
Ratified December 15, 1791

In all criminal prosecutions, the accused shall enjoy the right to a speedy and public trial, by an impartial jury of the State and district wherein the crime shall have been committed, which district shall have been previously ascertained by law, and to be informed of the nature and cause of the accusation; to be confronted with the witnesses against him; to have compulsory process for obtaining witnesses in his favor, and to have the Assistance of Counsel for his defence.

VII

Passed by Congress September 25, 1789
Ratified December 15, 1791

In Suits at common law, where the value in controversy shall exceed twenty dollars, the right of trial by jury shall be preserved, and no fact tried by a jury, shall be otherwise re-examined in any Court of the United States, than according to the rules of the common law.

VIII

Passed by Congress September 25, 1789
Ratified December 15, 1791

Excessive bail shall not be required, nor excessive fines imposed, nor cruel and unusual punishments inflicted.

IX

Passed by Congress September 25, 1789
Ratified December 15, 1791

The enumeration in the Constitution, of certain rights, shall not be construed to deny or disparage others retained by the people.

X

Passed by Congress September 25, 1789
Ratified December 15, 1791

The powers not delegated to the United States by the Constitution, nor prohibited by it to the States, are reserved to the States respectively, or to the people.

XI

Passed by Congress March 4, 1794
Ratified December 7, 1795

The Judicial power of the United States shall not be construed to extend to any suit in law or equity, commenced or prosecuted against one of the United States by Citizens of another State, or by Citizens or Subjects of any Foreign State.

XII

Passed by Congress December 9, 1803
Ratified June 15, 1804

[NOTE: *As drafted, the Twelfth Amendment took the form of a single long paragraph with dashes separating portions of text. Here, paragraph breaks are added after the dashes for ease of reading.*]

The Electors shall meet in their respective states, and vote by ballot for President and Vice-President, one of whom, at least, shall not be an inhabitant of the same state with themselves; they shall name in their ballots the person voted for as President, and in distinct ballots the person voted for as Vice-President, and they shall make distinct lists of all persons voted for as President, and of all persons voted for as Vice-President and of the number of votes for each, which lists they shall sign and certify, and transmit sealed to the seat of the government of the United States, directed to the President of the Senate;—

The President of the Senate shall, in the presence of the Senate and House of Representatives, open all the certificates and the votes shall then be counted;—

▸ AFFECTED BY 20TH AND 25TH AMENDMENTS

The person having the greatest Number of votes for President, shall be the President, if such number be a majority of the whole number of Electors appointed; and if no person have such majority, then from the persons having the highest numbers not exceeding three on the list of those voted for as President, the House of Representatives shall choose immediately, by ballot, the President. But in choosing the President, the votes shall be taken by states, the representation from each state having one vote; a quorum for this purpose shall consist of a member or members from two-thirds of the states, and a majority of all the states shall be necessary to a choice. And if the House of Representatives shall not choose a President whenever the right of choice shall devolve upon them, before the fourth day of March next following, then the Vice-President shall act as President, as in the case of the death or other constitutional disability of the President.—

The person having the greatest number of votes as Vice-President, shall be the Vice-President, if such number be a majority of the whole number of Electors appointed, and if no person have a majority, then from the two highest numbers on the list, the Senate shall choose the Vice-President; a quorum for the purpose shall consist of two-thirds of the whole number of Senators, and a majority of the whole number shall be necessary to a choice. But no person constitutionally ineligible to the office of President shall be eligible to that of Vice-President of the United States.

XIII

Passed by Congress January 31, 1865
Ratified December 6, 1865

Section 1. Neither slavery nor involuntary servitude, except as a punishment for crime whereof the party shall have been duly convicted, shall exist within the United States, or any place subject to their jurisdiction.

Section 2. Congress shall have power to enforce this article by appropriate legislation.

XIV

Passed by Congress June 13, 1866
Ratified July 9, 1868

Section 1. All persons born or naturalized in the United States, and subject to the jurisdiction thereof, are citizens of the United States and of the State wherein they reside. No State shall make or enforce any law which shall abridge the privileges or immunities of citizens of the United States; nor shall any State deprive any person of life, liberty, or property, without due process of law; nor deny to any person within its jurisdiction the equal protection of the laws.

Section 2. Representatives shall be apportioned among the several States according to their respective numbers, counting the whole number of persons in each State, excluding Indians not taxed. But when the right to vote at any election for the choice of electors for President and Vice-President of the United States, Representatives in Congress, the Executive and Judicial officers of a State, or the members of the Legislature thereof, is denied to any of the male inhabitants of such State, being twenty-one years of age, and citizens of the United States, or in any way abridged, except for participation in rebellion, or other crime, the basis of representation therein shall be reduced in the proportion which the number of such male citizens shall bear to the whole number of male citizens twenty-one years of age in such State.

◄ AFFECTED BY 19TH AND 26TH AMENDMENTS

Section 3. No person shall be a Senator or Representative in Congress, or elector of President and Vice-President, or hold any office, civil or military, under the United States, or under any State, who, having previously taken an oath, as a member of Congress, or as an officer of the United States, or as a member of any State legislature, or as an executive or judicial officer of any State, to support the Constitution of the United States, shall have engaged in insurrection or rebellion against the same, or given aid or comfort to the enemies thereof. But Congress may by a vote of two-thirds of each House, remove such disability.

Section 4. The validity of the public debt of the United States, authorized by law, including debts incurred for payment of pensions and bounties for services in suppressing insurrection or rebellion, shall not be questioned. But neither the United States nor any State shall assume or pay any debt or obligation incurred in aid of insurrection or rebellion against the United States, or any claim for the loss or emancipation of any slave; but all such debts, obligations and claims shall be held illegal and void.

Section 5. The Congress shall have power to enforce, by appropriate legislation, the provisions of this article.

XV

Passed by Congress February 26, 1869
Ratified February 3, 1870

Section 1. The right of citizens of the United States to vote shall not be denied or abridged by the United States or by any State on account of race, color, or previous condition of servitude.

Section 2. The Congress shall have power to enforce this article by appropriate legislation.

XVI

Passed by Congress July 12, 1909
Ratified February 3, 1913

The Congress shall have power to lay and collect taxes on incomes, from whatever source derived, without apportionment among the several States, and without regard to any census or enumeration.

XVII

Passed by Congress May 13, 1912
Ratified April 8, 1913

[Section 1] The Senate of the United States shall be composed of two Senators from each State, elected by the people thereof, for six years; and each Senator shall have one vote. The electors in each State shall have the qualifications requisite for electors of the most numerous branch of the State legislatures.

[Section 2] When vacancies happen in the representation of any State in the Senate, the executive authority of such State shall issue writs of election to fill such vacancies: Provided, That the legislature of any State may empower the executive thereof to make temporary appointments until the people fill the vacancies by election as the legislature may direct.

[Section 3] This amendment shall not be so construed as to affect the election or term of any Senator chosen before it becomes valid as part of the Constitution.

XVIII

Passed by Congress December 18, 1917
Ratified January 16, 1919

▸ AFFECTED BY 21ST AMENDMENT

Section 1. After one year from the ratification of this article the manufacture, sale, or transportation of intoxicating liquors within, the importation thereof into, or the exportation thereof from the United States and all territory subject to the jurisdiction thereof for beverage purposes is hereby prohibited.

Section 2. The Congress and the several States shall have concurrent power to enforce this article by appropriate legislation.

Section 3. This article shall be inoperative unless it shall have been ratified as an amendment to the Constitution by the legislatures of the several States, as provided in the Constitution, within seven years from the date of the submission hereof to the States by the Congress.

◄ AFFECTED BY 21ST AMENDMENT

XIX

Passed by Congress June 4, 1919
Ratified August 8, 1920

[Section 1] The right of citizens of the United States to vote shall not be denied or abridged by the United States or by any State on account of sex.

[Section 2] Congress shall have power to enforce this article by appropriate legislation.

XX

Passed by Congress March 2, 1932
Ratified January 23, 1933

[Section 1] The terms of the President and Vice President shall end at noon on the 20th day of January, and the terms of Senators and Representatives at noon on the 3d day of January, of the years in which such terms would have ended if this article had not been ratified; and the terms of their successors shall then begin.

Section 2. The Congress shall assemble at least once in every year, and such meeting shall begin at noon on the 3d day of January, unless they shall by law appoint a different day.

Section 3. If, at the time fixed for the beginning of the term of the President, the President elect shall have died, the Vice President elect shall become President. If a President shall not have been chosen before the time fixed for the beginning of his term, or if the President elect shall have failed to qualify, then the Vice President elect shall act as President until a President shall have qualified; and the Congress may by law provide for the case wherein neither a President elect nor a Vice President elect shall have qualified, declaring who shall then act as President, or the manner in which one who is to act shall be selected, and such person shall act accordingly until a President or Vice President shall have qualified.

Section 4. The Congress may by law provide for the case of the death of any of the persons from whom the House of Representatives may choose a President whenever the right of choice shall have devolved upon them, and for the case of the death of any of the persons from whom the Senate may choose a Vice President whenever the right of choice shall have devolved upon them.

Section 5. Sections 1 and 2 shall take effect on the 15th day of October following the ratification of this article.

Section 6. This article shall be inoperative unless it shall have been ratified as an amendment to the Constitution by the legislatures of three-fourths of the several States within seven years from the date of its submission.

XXI

Passed by Congress February 20, 1933
Ratified December 5, 1933

Section 1. The eighteenth article of amendment to the Constitution of the United States is hereby repealed.

Section 2. The transportation or importation into any State, Territory, or possession of the United States for delivery or use therein of intoxicating liquors, in violation of the laws thereof, is hereby prohibited.

Section 3. The article shall be inoperative unless it shall have been ratified as an amendment to the Constitution by conventions in the several States, as provided in the Constitution, within seven years from the date of the submission hereof to the States by the Congress.

XXII

Passed by Congress March 24, 1947
Ratified February 27, 1951

Section 1. No person shall be elected to the office of the President more than twice, and no person who has held the office of President, or acted as President, for more than two years of a term to which some other person was elected President shall be elected to the office of the President more than once. But this Article shall not apply to any person holding the office of President, when this Article was proposed by the Congress, and shall not prevent any person who may be holding the office of President, or acting as President, during the term within which this Article becomes operative from holding the office of President or acting as President during the remainder of such term.

Section 2. This article shall be inoperative unless it shall have been ratified as an amendment to the Constitution by the legislatures of three-fourths of the several States within seven years from the date of its submission to the States by the Congress.

XXIII

Passed by Congress June 16, 1960
Ratified March 29, 1961

Section 1. The District constituting the seat of Government of the United States shall appoint in such manner as the Congress may direct: A number of electors of President and Vice President equal to the whole number of Senators and Representatives in Congress to which the District would be entitled if it were a State, but in no event more than the least populous State; they shall be in addition to those appointed by the States, but they shall be considered, for the purposes of the election of President and Vice President, to be electors appointed by a State; and they shall meet in the District and perform such duties as provided by the twelfth article of amendment.

Section 2. The Congress shall have power to enforce this article by appropriate legislation.

XXIV

Passed by Congress September 14, 1962
Ratified January 23, 1964

Section 1. The right of citizens of the United States to vote in any primary or other election for President or Vice President, for electors for President or Vice President, or for Senator or Representative in Congress, shall not be denied or abridged by the United States or any State by reason of failure to pay any poll tax or other tax.

Section 2. The Congress shall have power to enforce this article by appropriate legislation.

XXV

Passed by Congress July 6, 1965
Ratified February 10, 1967

Section 1. In case of the removal of the President from office or of his death or resignation, the Vice President shall become President.

Section 2. Whenever there is a vacancy in the office of the Vice President, the President shall nominate a Vice President who shall take office upon confirmation by a majority vote of both Houses of Congress.

Section 3. Whenever the President transmits to the President pro tempore of the Senate and the Speaker of the House of Representatives his written declaration that he is unable to discharge the powers and duties of his office, and until he transmits to them a written declaration to the contrary, such powers and duties shall be discharged by the Vice President as Acting President.

Section 4. [Clause 1] Whenever the Vice President and a majority of either the principal officers of the executive departments or of such other body as Congress may by law provide, transmit to the President pro tempore of the Senate and the Speaker of the House of Representatives their written declaration that the President is unable to discharge the powers and duties of his office, the Vice President shall immediately assume the powers and duties of the office as Acting President.

[Clause 2] Thereafter, when the President transmits to the President pro tempore of the Senate and the Speaker of the House of Representatives his written declaration that no inability exists, he shall resume the powers and duties of his office unless the Vice President and a majority of either the principal officers of the executive department or of such other body as Congress may by law provide, transmit within four days to the President pro tempore of the Senate and the Speaker of the House of Representatives their written declaration that the President is unable to discharge the powers and duties of his office. Thereupon Congress shall decide the issue, assembling within forty eight hours for that purpose if not in session. If the Congress, within twenty one days after receipt of the latter written declaration, or, if Congress is not in session, within twenty one days after Congress is required to assemble, determines by two thirds vote of both Houses that the President is unable to discharge the powers and duties of his office, the Vice President shall continue to discharge the same as Acting President; otherwise, the President shall resume the powers and duties of his office.

XXVI

Passed by Congress March 23, 1971
Ratified July 1, 1971

Section 1. The right of citizens of the United States, who are eighteen years of age or older, to vote shall not be denied or abridged by the United States or by any State on account of age.

Section 2. The Congress shall have power to enforce this article by appropriate legislation.

XXVII

Passed by Congress September 25, 1789
Ratified May 7, 1992

No law, varying the compensation for the services of the Senators and Representatives, shall take effect, until an election of Representatives shall have intervened.

APPENDIX B

Amendments Not Ratified

Congress passed several proposed amendments by the necessary two-thirds majority, but they were not ratified by the necessary three-fourths of the States.

The Congressional Apportionment Amendment

Passed by Congress September 25, 1789

After the first enumeration required by the first article of the Constitution, there shall be one Representative for every thirty thousand, until the number shall amount to one hundred, after which the proportion shall be so regulated by Congress, that there shall be not less than one hundred Representatives, nor less than one Representative for every forty thousand persons, until the number of Representatives shall amount to two hundred; after which the proportion shall be so regulated by Congress, that there shall not be less than two hundred Representatives, nor more than one Representative for every fifty thousand persons.

[*NOTE: This amendment was approved by Congress as part of the same package that resulted in Amendments 1–10 (the Bill of Rights) and 27. Unlike them, it has never been ratified.*]

The Titles of Nobility Amendment

Passed by Congress May 1, 1810

If any citizen of the United States shall accept, claim, receive or retain, any title of nobility or honour, or shall, without the consent of Congress, accept and retain any present, pension, office or emolument of any kind whatever, from any emperor, king, prince or foreign power, such person shall cease to be a citizen of the United States, and shall be incapable of holding any office of trust or profit under them, or either of them.

The Corwin Amendment

Passed by Congress March 2, 1861

No amendment shall be made to the Constitution which will authorize or give to Congress the power to abolish or interfere, within any State, with the domestic institutions thereof, including that of persons held to labor or service by the laws of said State.

[NOTE: Sponsored in the House of Representatives by Thomas Corwin of Ohio, this amendment passed Congress just days before the scheduled March 4 inauguration of Abraham Lincoln and a new Congress. The amendment was proposed in hopes of averting secession and civil war, but it did not lead to reconciliation.]

The Child Labor Amendment

Passed by Congress June 2, 1924

Section 1. The Congress shall have power to limit, regulate, and prohibit the labor of persons under eighteen years of age.

Section 2. The power of the several States is unimpaired by this article except that the operation of State laws shall be suspended to the extent necessary to give effect to legislation enacted by the Congress.

[NOTE: This amendment was passed by Congress as a response to Hammer v. Dagenhart, *247 U.S. 251 (1918) and* Bailey v. Drexel Furniture, *259 U.S. 20 (1922). Because Congress did not propose a deadline for states to act, the Amendment may be ratified at any time.* Coleman v. Miller, *307 U.S. 433 (1939).]*

The Equal Rights Amendment

Passed by Congress March 22, 1972

Section 1. Equality of rights under the law shall not be denied or abridged by the United States or by any State on account of sex.

Section 2. The Congress shall have the power to enforce, by appropriate legislation, the provisions of this article.

Section 3. This amendment shall take effect two years after the date of ratification.

[NOTE: The text of the ERA was first drafted in 1923, and it was proposed in every session of Congress until it finally passed both houses in 1972. The legislation sending the amendment to the states originally set a seven-year ratification deadline (1979) that was later extended another three years (1982). By any count, not enough states had ratified by 1979 or 1982; complicating matters further, six states purported to rescind previous ratifications. Decades later, three states purported to ratify: Nevada (2017), Illinois (2018), and Virginia (2020). The three states did not obtain the desired writ of mandamus ordering the US Archivist to add the ERA to the certified text of the US Constitution. Illinois v. Ferriero, *60 F.4th 704 (D.C. Cir. 2023).]*

District of Columbia Voting Rights Amendment

Passed by Congress August 22, 1978

Section 1. For purposes of representation in the Congress, election of the President and Vice President, and article V of this Constitution, the District constituting the seat of government of the United States shall be treated as though it were a State.

Section 2. The exercise of the rights and powers conferred under this article shall be by the people of the District constituting the seat of government, and as shall be provided by the Congress.

Section 3. The twenty-third article of amendment to the Constitution of the United States is hereby repealed.

Section 4. This article shall be inoperative, unless it shall have been ratified as an amendment to the Constitution by the legislatures of three-fourths of the several States within seven years from the date of its submission.

APPENDIX C

kickstarter

Master Kickstarter

The Master Kickstarter suggests an overall structure for organizing the most important doctrinal material into a topical outline. Within each topic, the principal cases are listed in chronological order. Cases with asterisks (*) have been wholly or partially overruled.

I. SOURCES OF GOV'T POWER

A. States: Sovereign Powers (Including Police Power)

B. Federal: Enumerated Powers

1. Commerce Clause

See Ch. 15.C.1 for Topical Kickstarter.

Gibbons v. Ogden (1824); *NLRB v. Jones & Laughlin Steel* (1937); *U.S. v. Carolene Products* (1938); *U.S. v. Darby* (1941); *Wickard v. Filburn* (1942); *Heart of Atlanta Motel v. U.S.* (1964); *Katzenbach v. McClung* (1964); *U.S. v. Lopez* (1995); *U.S. v. Morrison* (2000); *Reno v. Condon* (2000); *Gonzales v. Raich* (2005); *NFIB v. Sebelius* (2012)

Also: U.S. v. EC Knight (1895)*; *Hammer v. Dagenhart* (1918)*; *Schechter Poultry v. U.S.* (1935)*; *Carter v. Carter Coal* (1936) (overruled in part)*

2. Taxing Clause

See Ch. 15.A.1 for Topical Kickstarter.

Bailey v. Drexel Furniture (1922); *Carter v. Carter Coal* (1936) (overruled in part on other grounds); *Sonzinsky v. U.S.* (1937); *U.S. v. Kahriger* (1953); *NFIB v. Sebelius* (2012)

Also: Pollock v. Farmers' Loan and Trust Co. (1895)*

3. Spending Clause

See Ch. 15.B.1 for Topical Kickstarter.

South Dakota v. Dole (1987); *NFIB v. Sebelius* (2012)

Also: U.S. v. Butler (1935)*

4. Necessary & Proper Clause

See Ch. 15.D.1 for Topical Kickstarter.

McCulloch v. Maryland (1819); *Printz v. U.S.* (1997); *U.S. v. Comstock* (2010); *NFIB v. Sebelius* (2012); *Zivotofsky v. Kerry* (2015)

5. Civil Rights Enforcement Clauses

See Ch. 15.E.1 for Topical Kickstarter.

Strauder v. West Virginia (1879); *The Civil Rights Cases* (1883); *Heart of Atlanta Motel v. U.S.* (1964); *City of Boerne v. Flores* (1997); *U.S. v. Morrison* (2000); *Shelby County v. Holder* (2013)

6. Fugitive Slave Clause

Prigg v. Pennsylvania (1842)*

II. LIMITS ON GOV'T POWER: STRUCTURAL LIMITATIONS

A. Limits on States: Supremacy Clause

1. Preemption

See Ch. 13.A.1 for Topical Kickstarter.

McCulloch v. Maryland (1819); *Gibbons v. Ogden* (1824); *Kansas v. Garcia* (2020)

Also: Prigg v. Pennsylvania (1842)*

2. Dormant Commerce Clause Doctrine

See Ch. 13.B.1 for Topical Kickstarter.

Hunt v. Washington State Apple Advertising Commission (1977); *City of Philadelphia v. New Jersey* (1978); *Camps Newfound/Owatonna v. Town of Harrison* (1997)

B. Limits on Federal Government: Federalism

1. Commandeering

See 14.B.1 for Topical Kickstarter.

New York v. U.S. (1992); *Printz v. U.S.* (1997); *Reno v. Condon* (2000); *NFIB v. Sebelius* (2012); *Murphy v. NCAA* (2018)

2. Tenth Amendment

U.S. v. Darby (1941)

Also: U.S. v. E.C. Knight (1895)*; *Hammer v. Dagenhart* (1918)*

C. Limits on Federal Government: Separation of Powers

See Ch. 16.A for Topical Kickstarter.

1. Judicial & Legislative

Marbury v. Madison (1803); *Cooper v. Aaron* (1958); *City of Boerne v. Flores* (1997)

2. Legislative & Executive

Youngstown Sheet & Tube v. Sawyer (1952); *Zivotofsky v. Kerry (2015)*

3. Executive & Judicial

U.S. v. Nixon (1974); *Nixon v. Fitzgerald* (1982); *Clinton v. Jones* (1997); *Trump v. Vance* (2020); *Trump v. Mazars USA* (2020)

III. LIMITS ON GOV'T POWER: INDIVIDUAL RIGHTS

A. Equality Rights: Equal Protection Clause

See Ch. 18.A for Topical Kickstarter.

Strauder v. West Virginia (1879); *Yick Wo v. Hopkins* (1886); *Buck v. Bell* (1927); *U.S. v. Carolene Products* (1938); *Skinner v. Oklahoma* (1942); *Hirabayashi v. U.S.* (1943); *Korematsu v. U.S.* (1944); *Shelley v. Kraemer* (1948); *Railway Express Agency v. New York* (1949); *Brown v. Board of Education I* (1954); *Bolling v. Sharp* (1954); *Brown v. Board of Education II* (1955); *Williamson v. Lee Optical* (1955); *Cooper v. Aaron* (1958); *Harper v. Virginia State Board of Elections* (1966); *Loving v. Virginia* (1967); *Reed v. Reed* (1971); *Palmer v. Thompson* (1971); *Eisenstadt v. Baird* (1972); *San Antonio School District v. Rodriguez* (1973); *Frontiero v. Richardson* (1973); *U.S. Department of*

Agriculture v. Moreno (1973); *Geduldig v. Aiello* (1974); *Craig v. Boren* (1976); *Washington v. Davis* (1976); *City of New Orleans v. Dukes* (1976); *Village of Arlington Heights v. MHDC* (1977); *Regents of the University of California v. Bakke* (1978); *Personnel Administrator v. Feeney* (1979); *Palmore v. Sidoti* (1984); *City of Cleburne v. Cleburne Living Center* (1985); *City of Richmond v. J.A. Croson Co.* (1989); *City of Dallas v. Stanglin* (1989); *Edmonson v. Leesville Concrete Co.* (1991); *U.S. v. Virginia* (1996); *Romer v. Evans* (1996); *Vacco v. Quill* (1997); *Nguyen v. INS* (2001); *Johnson v. California* (2005); *Parents Involved in Community Schools v. Seattle School District* (2007); *U.S. v. Windsor* (2013); *Obergefell v. Hodges* (2015); *Fisher v. Univ. of Texas at Austin* (2016); *Sessions v. Morales-Santana* (2017); *Trump v. Hawaii* (2018).

Also: Scott v. Sandford (1857)*; *Pace v. Alabama* (1883)*; *Plessy v. Ferguson* (1896)*; *Hoyt v. Florida* (1961)*; *High Tech Gays v. DISCO* (1990)*

B. Fairness Rights: Procedural Due Process

See Ch. 19.B for Topical Kickstarter.

Moore v. Dempsey (1923); *Goldberg v. Kelly* (1970); *Board of Regents v. Roth* (1972); *Mathews v. Eldridge* (1976); *Cleveland Board of Education v. Loudermill* (1985); *Daniels v. Williams* (1986); *DeShaney v. Winnebago County* (1989); *Caperton v. Massey Coal Co.* (2009)

C. Freedom Rights: Substantive Due Process

See Ch. 20.A for Topical Kickstarter.

Buchanan v. Warley (1917); *Meyer v. Nebraska* (1923); *Pierce v. Society of Sisters* (1925); *Buck v. Bell* (1927); *West Coast Hotel v. Parrish* (1937); *U.S. v. Carolene Products* (1938); *Railway Express Agency v. New York* (1949); *Williamson v. Lee Optical* (1955); *Griswold v. Connecticut* (1965); *Loving v. Virginia* (1967); *Moore v. City of East Cleveland* (1977); *Michael H. v. Gerald D.* (1989); *Cruzan v. Director* (1990); *Washington v. Glucksberg* (1997); *Lawrence v. Texas* (2003); *U.S. v. Windsor* (2013); *Obergefell v. Hodges* (2015); *Dobbs v. Jackson Women's Health Organization* (2022).

Also: Allgeyer v. Louisiana (1897)*; *Lochner v. New York* (1905)*; *Adkins v. Children's Hospital* (1923)*; *Bowers v. Hardwick* (1986)*; *Roe v. Wade* (1973)*; *Planned Parenthood v. Casey* (1992)*.

D. Other Individual Rights Topics

1. Incorporation

Barron v. Baltimore (1833); *Bolling v. Sharpe* (1954)

2. Exceptions to the State Action Doctrine

See Ch. 21.A for Topical Kickstarter.

Shelley v. Kraemer (1948); *San Francisco Arts & Athletics v. U.S. Olympic Committee* (1987); *Edmonson v. Leesville Concrete Co.* (1991); *Brentwood Academy v. TSSAA* (2001)

3. Fourteenth Amendment Privileges or Immunities Clause

The Slaughterhouse Cases (1872); *Bradwell v. Illinois* (1872); *Minor v. Happersett* (1872); *U.S. v. Cruikshank* (1876)

4. Various Enumerated Rights

Calder v. Bull (1798) (Ex Post Facto Clause); *West Virginia State Board of Education v. Barnette* (1943) (1st Amendment); *Ingraham v. Wright* (1977) (8th Amendment); *Employment Division v. Smith* (1990) (First Amendment)

Also: Prigg v. Pennsylvania (1842)* (slave owner rights); *Dred Scott* (1857)* (slave owner rights); *Minersville School District v. Gobitis* (1940)* (First Amendment)

INDEX

E

Education

Employment Discrimination

End-of-Life Decisions

Equal Protection

Executive Branch

F

Federalism

W

Women's Rights

Workplace Regulations